The Total Spectrum of Technology

Personal Trainer® 3.0

Specially designed to enhance *Cost Management: Accounting & Control,* Personal Trainer 3.0 is an ideal teaching and learning companion! Interactive and powerful, Personal Trainer 3.0 features all of the end-of-chapter problems and exercises. This makes it easy for students to complete their assigned homework online—or even to sharpen their skills on unassigned homework. With Microsoft® Excel spreadsheets and full-featured gradebook functionality, Personal Trainer 3.0 provides an unprecedented real-time, guided, self-correcting, learning reinforcement system outside of the classroom—making it ideal for either a distance learning or traditional course. For instructors, this powerful technology program eases the time consuming task of grading homework.

Highlights of Personal Trainer 3.0

▶ **Enhanced Questions**

Personal Trainer 3.0 includes all exercises and problems from the text. Students can get help entering their answers in the proper format and run a spell check on their answers. On selected questions, students can call up additional, similar questions for extra practice.

▶ **Enhanced Instructor Capabilities**

The flexible gradebook can display and download any combination of student work, chapters, or activities. Capture grades on demand or set a particular time for grades to be automatically captured. Tag questions as "required" or "excluded," so students only access the questions instructors want them to complete.

▶ **Enhanced Hints**

Students can receive up to three hints per activity. These hints can be Microsoft® PowerPoint® slides, video clips, or images from the text. And instructors have the option of adding a hint of their own!

▶ **Enhanced Look and Feel**

Fast, reliable, dependable, and even easy to use, Personal Trainer 3.0 features an inviting graphic design.

▶ **Personal Trainer** is included in **WebTutor™ Advantage** or can be purchased separately online. Visit http://personaltrainer.swlearning.com for more information and a comprehensive tour of Personal Trainer 3.0, or contact your sales representative to order.

Xtra!

xtra!

Available to be packaged FREE with new copies of this text, Xtra! gives students an array of learning tools—including chapter reviews, interactive quizzes, crossword puzzles, and enhanced spreadsheet templates. To order, visit http://hansenxtra.swlearning.com, or contact your South-Western representative.

The Business & Company Resource Center

The *Business & Company Resource Center* (BCRC) provides online access to a wide variety of global business information, including current articles and business journals, detailed company and industry information, investment reports, stock quotes, and much more.

- ❱ **Conveniently accessible from anywhere with an Internet connection!** Students can access information at school, at home, or on the go.
- ❱ **A powerful and time-saving research tool for students –** whether they are completing a case analysis, preparing for a presentation, creating a business plan, or writing a reaction paper.
- ❱ **Instructors can use the BCRC like an online coursepack,** assigning readings and research-based assignments or projects without the inconvenience of library reserves, permissions, and printed materials.
- ❱ **BCRC filters out the "junk" information often found when searching the Internet,** providing only the high quality, safe, and reliable news and information sources.
- ❱ **Easily assign homework, share articles, create journal lists,** and save searches using BCRC *Infomarks.*

Instructors can combine the **BCRC** with their favorite **Harvard Business School Publishing** cases to provide students with a case analysis research tool at no additional cost.

Contact your local Thomson South-Western representative to learn how to include *Business & Company Resource Center* with your text.

Harvard Business Case Studies

The combination of preeminent cases and articles from **Harvard Business School Publishing** with the unparalleled scope and depth of customizable content from South-Western provides instructors and students with a wide array of learning materials. You can draw from multiple resources and disciplines to match the unique needs of your course.

- ❱ **Convenience for Instructors –** Instructors can work with one source instead of multiple vendors, allowing the local Thomson representative to manage the prompt delivery of teaching resources and students materials.
- ❱ **Convenience for Students –** Pricing for cases is very affordable, and when packaged with the textbook, students receive a significant discount on the text and coursepak.
- ❱ **Convenient Ordering –** Once you have identified the cases and articles you want to use, simply use an ordering form provided by your Thomson South-Western representative to indicate your selections and packaging preferences. A representative will call you within 48 hours to confirm your order and walk you through the rest of the process.

INSTRUCTORS: Contact your Thomson South-Western representative to learn how to package these resources with Hansen and Mowen's text!

To order call 1.800.423.0563
or visit http://hansen.swlearning.com

Cost Management

Accounting and Control

Fifth Edition

Don R. Hansen
Oklahoma State University

Maryanne M. Mowen
Oklahoma State University

Australia · Canada · Mexico · Singapore · Spain · United Kingdom · United States

THOMSON
SOUTH-WESTERN

Cost Management: Accounting and Control, Fifth Edition
Don R. Hansen and Maryanne M. Mowen

VP/Editorial Director:
Jack W. Calhoun

Publisher:
Rob Dewey

Aquisitions Editor:
Keith Chasse

Associate Developmental Editor:
Allison Rolfes

Marketing Manager:
Chris McNamee

Senior Production Editor:
Kara ZumBahlen

Manager of Technology, Editorial:
Vicky True

Technology Project Editor:
Sally Nieman

Web Coordinator:
Kelly Reid

Sr. Manufacturing Coordinator:
Doug Wilke

Production House:
LEAP Publishing Services, Inc.

Compositor:
GGS Information Services, Inc.

Printer:
CTPS

Art Director:
Chris A. Miller

Cover and Internal Designer:
Bethany Casey

Cover Image:
GettyImages

Photography Manager:
Deanna Ettinger

Photo Researcher:
Terri Miller

For permission to use material from this text or product, submit a request online at http://www.thomsonrights.com.

For more information about our product, contact us at: Thomson Learning, Academic Resource Center, 1-800-423-0563

Thomson Higher Education
5191 Natorp Boulevard
Mason, Ohio, 45040
USA

ASIA (including India)

Thomson Learning
5 Shenton Way
#01-01 UIC Building
Singapore 068808

CANADA
Thomson Nelson
1120 Birchmount Road
Toronto, Ontario
Canada M1K 5G4

AUSTRALIA/NEW ZEALAND
Thomson Learning Australia
102 Dodds Street
Southbank, Victoria 3006
Australia

UK/EUROPE/MIDDLE
EAST/AFRICA
Thomson Learning
High Holborn House
50-51 Bedford Row
London WC1R 4LR
United Kingdom

LATIN AMERICA
Thomson Learning
Seneca, 53
Colonia Polanco
11560 Mexico
D.F.Mexico

SPAIN (includes Portugal)
Thomson Paraninfo
Calle Magallanes, 25
28015 Madrid, Spain

To Our Parents
Lindell and Leola Wise and
John L. Myers and Marjorie H. Myers

Over the past twenty years, changes in the business environment have profoundly affected cost accounting and cost management. A few examples of these changes are an increased emphasis on providing value to customers, total quality management, time as a competitive element, advances in information and manufacturing technology, globalization of markets, service industry growth, deregulation, and heightened awareness of ethical and environmental business practices. These changes are driven by the need to create and sustain a competitive advantage. For many firms, the information required to realize a competitive advantage can no longer be derived from a traditional cost management information system. The traditional system relies on functional-based costing and control. In a functional-based system, costing and control are centered on organizational functions. Unfortunately, this functional-based approach often fails to provide information that is detailed, accurate, and timely enough to support the requirements of this new environment. This has resulted in the emergence of an activity-based cost management system. Typically, an activity-based cost management system is more detailed and more accurate than a functional-based cost management system and, thus, more costly to operate. Furthermore, the need to add a formal guidance mechanism to the new activity-based system has created a demand for strategic-based cost management. Thus, the new cost management system might be more accurately referred to as an activity- and strategic-based cost management system. The emergence and acceptance of activity- and strategic-based cost management therefore suggests that in many cases the benefits of this more sophisticated system outweigh its costs. On the other hand, the continued existence and reliance on functional-based systems suggests the opposite for other firms.

The coexistence of functional-based systems with activity- and strategic-based cost management systems necessitates the study of both systems, thus providing flexibility and depth of understanding. In creating a text on cost management, we had to decide how to design its structure. We believe that a systems approach provides a convenient and logical framework. Using a systems framework allows us to easily integrate the functional- and activity-based approaches in a way that students can easily grasp. Integration is achieved by developing a common terminology—a terminology that allows us to define each system and discuss how they differ. Then the functional and activity-based approaches can be compared and contrasted as they are applied to costing, control, and decision making. We believe this integration will allow students to appreciate the differences that exist between functional and activity-based approaches. This integration is especially useful in the decision-making chapters, as it allows students to see how decisions change as the information sets change. For example, how does a make-or-buy decision change as we move from a functional-based, traditional cost management system to the richer, activity-based cost management system?

This text has been streamlined by combining and eliminating some material. The number of chapters totals 21, as opposed to 24. Notably, international cost management has been eliminated as a separate chapter. Instead, important material has been reorganized into decision-making chapters. More specific international cost topics are left for international finance classes. Activity-based budgeting is now located in the budgeting chapter, where it can be compared and contrasted with traditional budgeting topics. Activity-based costing is now located early in the text, in Chapter 4, where it can include traditional plantwide overhead rates and applications.

Audience

This text is written primarily for students at the undergraduate level. The text presents a thorough treatment of traditional and contemporary approaches to cost management, accounting, and control and can be used for a one- or two-semester course. In our opinion, the text also has sufficient depth for graduate-level courses. In fact, we have successfully used the text at the graduate level.

Key Features

We feel that the text offers a number of distinctive and appealing features—features that should make it much easier to teach students about the emerging themes in today's business world. One of our objectives was to reduce the time and resources expended by instructors so that students can be more readily exposed to today's topics and practices. To help you understand the text's innovative approach, we have provided a detailed description of its key features.

Structure

The text's organization follows a systems framework and is divided into four parts:

1. *Part 1: Foundation Concepts.* Chapters 1 through 4 introduce the basic concepts and tools associated with cost management information systems.
2. *Part 2: Fundamental Costing and Control.* Chapters 5 through 10 provide thorough coverage of product costing, planning, and control in both functional-based and activity-based costing systems.
3. *Part 3: Advanced Costing and Control.* Chapters 11 through 16 present the key elements of the new cost management approaches. Examples of the topics covered in this section include activity-based customer and supplier costing, strategic cost management, activity-based budgeting, activity-based management, process value analysis, target costing, kaizen costing, quality costing, productivity, environmental cost management, and the Balanced Scorecard.
4. *Part 4: Decision Making.* Chapters 17 through 21 bring the costing and control tools together in the discussion of decision making.

This edition's structure permits integrated coverage of both the traditional and activity-based costing systems. In this way, students can see how each system can be used for costing, control, and decision making and can evaluate the advantages and disadvantages of each system. This approach helps students to see how cost management is applied to problems in today's world and to understand the richness of the approaches to business problems.

Contemporary Topics

The emerging themes of cost management are covered in depth. We have provided a framework for comprehensively treating both functional-based and activity-based topics. A common terminology links the two approaches; however, the functional- and activity-based approaches differ enough to warrant separate and comprehensive treatments. The nature and extent of the coverage of contemporary topics is described below. As this summary reveals, there is sufficient coverage of activity- and strategic-based topics to provide a course that strongly emphasizes these themes.

Historical Perspective

Chapter 1 provides a brief history of cost accounting. The historical perspective allows students to see why functional-based cost management systems work well in some settings but no longer work for other settings. The forces that are changing cost management practices are described. The changing role of the management accountant is also covered with particular emphasis on why the development of a cross-functional expertise is so critical in today's environment.

Value Chain Analysis

The provision of value to customers is illustrated by the internal value chain, which is first introduced in Chapter 1 and defined and illustrated more completely in Chapter 2. Chapter 11 provides a detailed discussion of value chain analysis and introduces the industrial value chain. Value chain analysis means that managers must understand and exploit internal and external linkages so that a sustainable competitive advantage can be achieved. Exploitation of these linkages requires a detailed understanding of the costs associated with both internal and external factors. This edition expands the treatment of value chain analysis by introducing, defining, and illustrating activity-based supplier costing and activity-based customer costing. The costing examples developed show how the value chain concepts can be operationalized—a characteristic not clearly described by other treatments. Thus, we believe that the operational examples are a significant feature of the text.

Accounting and Cost Management Systems

In Chapter 2, the accounting information system and its different subsystems are defined. Distinctions are made between the financial accounting and the cost management information systems and the differing purposes they serve. The cost management information system is broken down into the cost accounting information system and the operational control system. The differences between functional-based and activity-based cost management systems are defined and illustrated. The criteria for choosing an activity-based system over a functional-based system are also discussed.

In Chapter 2, three methods of cost assignment are delineated: direct tracing, driver tracing, and allocation. Activity drivers are also defined. Once the general cost assignment model is established, the model is used to help students understand the differences between functional-based and activity-based cost management systems. A clear understanding of how the two systems differ is fundamental to the organizational structure that the text follows.

Activity Costs Change as Activity Usage Changes

Chapter 3 is a comprehensive treatment of cost behavior. First, we define variable, fixed, and mixed activity cost behavior. Then, we discuss the activity resource usage model and detail the impact of flexible and committed resources on cost. Finally, we describe the methods of breaking out fixed and variable activity costs. This text goes beyond the typical text in explaining to students how to use the computer spreadsheet programs to perform regression analysis. The chapter on cost behavior analysis is more general than usual chapters that treat the subject. Traditional treatment usually focuses on cost as a function of production volume. We break away from this pattern and focus on cost as a function of changes in activity usage with changes in production activity as a special case. The activity resource usage model is used to define activity cost behavior (in terms of when resources are acquired) and is defined and discussed in Chapter 3. This resource usage model plays an important role in numerous contemporary applications. It is used in value chain analysis (Chapter 11), activity-based management (Chapter 12), and tactical decision and relevant costing analysis (Chapter 18). The extensive applications of the activity resource usage model represent a unique feature of the text.

Activity-Based Costing

Much has been written on the uses and applications of ABC. This text presents a comprehensive approach to activity-based costing and management. The activity-based product costing model is introduced in Chapter 2 and described in detail in Chapter 4. In this chapter, the advantages of ABC over functional-based costing are related. A completed discussion of how to design an ABC system is given. This includes identifying activities, creating an activity dictionary, assigning costs to activities, classifying activities as primary and secondary, and assigning costs to products. We have added new material that explores methods on simplifying a complex ABC system. The objectives of these methods are to reduce the number of drivers and activities used without significant reductions in product-costing accuracy. To fully understand how an ABC system works, students must understand the data needed to support the system. Thus, we show how the general ledger system must be unbundled to provide activity information. We also define and illustrate an ABC relational database. This unique feature of the text helps the student understand the very practical requirements of an ABC system.

Activity-Based Budgeting

Activity-based budgeting is now combined with traditional budgeting concepts in Chapter 8. This integrated treatment helps students to see how budgets can be extended with the power of activity-based cost concepts. This chapter introduces the basics of activity-based budgeting and gives an expanded example in a service setting. Flexible budgeting and the behavioral impact of budgets are also included in this chapter.

Just-in-Time Effects

JIT manufacturing and purchasing are defined and their own cost management practices discussed in Chapters 11 and 21. JIT is compared and contrasted with traditional manufacturing practices. The effects on areas such as cost traceability, inventory management, product costing, and responsibility accounting are carefully delineated.

Life Cycle Cost Management

In Chapter 11, we define and contrast three different life cycle viewpoints: production life cycle, marketing life cycle, and consumable life cycle. We then show how these concepts can be used for strategic planning and analysis. In later chapters, we show how life cycle concepts are useful for pricing and profitability analysis (Chapter 19). The use of life cycle costing for environmental cost management is also discussed (Chapter 16). The breadth, depth, and numerous examples illustrating life cycle cost applications allow the student to see the power and scope of this methodology.

Activity-Based Management and the Balanced Scorecard

There are three types of responsibility accounting systems: functional-based, activity-based, and strategic-based. These three systems are compared and contrasted, and the activity- and strategic-based responsibility accounting systems are discussed in detail. Activity-based responsibility accounting focuses on controlling and managing processes. The mechanism for doing this process value analysis is defined and thoroughly discussed in Chapter 12. Numerous examples are given to facilitate understanding. Value-added and non-value-added cost reports are described. Activity-based responsibility accounting also covers activity measures of performance, which are thoroughly covered in Chapter 13. The Balanced Scorecard is equivalent to what we are calling strategic-based responsibility accounting. The basic concepts and methods of the Balanced Scorecard are presented in Chapter 13.

Costs of Quality: Measurement and Control

Often, textual treatments simply define quality costs and present cost of quality reports. We go beyond this simple presentation (in Chapter 14) and discuss cost of quality performance reporting. We also describe quality activities in terms of their value-added content. Finally, we introduce and describe ISO 9000, an important quality assurance and reporting system that many firms must now follow.

Productivity: Measurement and Control

The new manufacturing environment demands innovative approaches to performance measurement. Productivity is one of these approaches; yet it is either only superficially discussed in most cost and management accounting texts or not treated at all. In Chapter 15, we offer a thorough treatment of the topic, including some new material on how to measure activity and process productivity.

Strategic Cost Management

A detailed introduction to strategic cost management is provided in Chapter 11. Understanding strategic cost analysis is a vital part of the new manufacturing environment. Strategic cost management is defined and illustrated. Strategic positioning is discussed. Structural and executional cost drivers are introduced. Value chain analysis is described with the focus on activity-based supplier and customer costing. The role of target costing in strategic cost management is also emphasized.

Environmental Costs: Measurement and Control

Chapter 16 reflects the growing strategic importance of environmental cost management. This chapter introduces and discusses the concept of ecoefficiency. It also defines, classifies, and illustrates the reporting of environmental costs and how to assign those costs to products and processes. The role of life-cycle costing in environmental cost management is detailed. Finally, we describe ways the Balanced Scorecard can be extended to include an environmental perspective.

Theory of Constraints

We introduce the theory of constraints (TOC) in Chapter 21. A linear programming framework is used to facilitate the description of TOC and provide a setting where students can see the value of linear programming. In fact, our treatment of linear programming is motivated by the need to develop the underlying concepts so that TOC can be presented and discussed. This edition expands the coverage of TOC by adding a discussion of constraint accounting.

Service Sector Focus

The significance of the service sector is recognized in this text through the extensive application of cost management principles to services. The text explains that services are not simply less complicated manufacturing settings but instead have their own characteristics. These characteristics require modification of cost management accounting principles. Sections addressing services appear in a number of chapters, including product costing, pricing, and quality and productivity measurement.

Professional Ethics

Strong professional ethics need to be part of every accountant's personal foundation. We are convinced that students are interested in ethical dimensions of business and can be taught areas in which ethical conflicts occur. Chapter 1 introduces the role of ethics and reprints the ethical standards developed by the Institute of Management Accountants. To reinforce coverage of ethics, every chapter includes an ethics case for discussion. In addition, many chapters include sections on ethics. For example, Chapter 19, on pricing and revenue analysis, includes material on the ethical dimensions of pricing.

Behavioral Issues

Ethical behavior is just one aspect of human behavior that is affected by cost management systems. The systems used for planning, control, and decision making can affect the way in which people act. Insights from behavioral decision theory are presented in appropriate sections of the text. For example, a discussion of the ways profit measurement can affect people's behavior is included in Chapter 19. Chapter 8, on activity-based budgeting, includes a section on the behavioral impact of budgets. We believe that an integration of behavioral issues with accounting issues leads to a more complete understanding of the role of the accountant today.

Real World Examples

Our years of experience in teaching cost and management accounting have convinced us that students like and understand real world applications of accounting concepts. These real world examples make the abstract accounting ideas concrete and provide meaning and color. Besides, they're interesting and fun. Therefore, real world examples are integrated throughout every chapter. Use of color for company names that appear in the chapters and the company index at the end of the text will help you locate these examples.

Outstanding Pedagogy

We think of this text as a tool that can help students learn cost accounting and cost management concepts. Of paramount importance is text readability. We have tried to write a very readable text and to provide numerous examples, real world applications, and illustrations of important cost accounting and cost management concepts. Specific "student-friendly" features of the pedagogy include the following:

- Whenever possible, graphical exhibits are provided to illustrate concepts. In our experience, some students need to "see" the concept; thus, we have attempted to portray key concepts to enhance understanding. Of course, many numerical examples are also provided.
- All chapters (except Chapter 1) include at least one review problem and solution. These problems demonstrate the computational aspects of chapter materials and reinforce the students' understanding of chapter concepts before they undertake end-of-chapter materials.
- A glossary of key terms is included at the end of the text. Key terms lists at the end of each chapter identify text pages for fuller explanation.
- All chapters include comprehensive end-of-chapter materials. These are divided into "Questions for Writing and Discussion," "Exercises," and "Problems." The Questions for Writing and Discussion emphasize communication skill development. Exercises and Problems to support every learning objective are included, and the relevant topics and learning objectives are noted in the text margins. The exercises and problems are graduated in difficulty from easy to challenging. CMA exam problems are included to enable the student to practice relevant problem material. Each chapter includes at least one ethics case. All chapters also include a cyber research case to give students practice in doing research on the Internet.

  CMA

  - This edition continues to offer cooperative learning exercises in the end-of-chapter materials in each chapter. These exercises encourage students to work in groups to solve cost management problems.
  - Spreadsheet template problems are identified in the end-of-chapter materials with an appropriate icon. These problems are designed to help students use spreadsheet applications to solve cost accounting problems.

Comprehensive Supplements Package

Check Figures. Key figures for solutions to selected problems and cases are provided in the solutions manual as an aid to students as they prepare their answers. Instructors may copy and distribute these as they see fit.

Study Guide, 0-324-23311-6 (Prepared by Al Chen, North Carolina State University). The study guide provides a detailed review of each chapter and allows students to check their understanding of the material through review questions and exercises. Specifically, students are provided with learning objectives, a chapter summary, a chapter review correlated to the learning objectives, self-test questions and exercises, and a "Can You?" Checklist that helps test their knowledge of key concepts in the chapter. Answers are provided for all assignment material.

Instructor's Manual, 0-324-23321-3 (Prepared by Kim Foreman, James Madison University). The instructor's manual contains a complete set of lecture notes for each chapter, a listing of all exercises and problems with estimated difficulty and time required for solution, and a set of transparency masters.

Solutions Manual, 0-324-23313-2 (Prepared by Don Hansen and Maryanne Mowen). The solutions manual contains the solutions for all end-of-chapter questions, exercises, and problems. Solutions have been error-checked to ensure their accuracy and reliability.

Solutions Transparencies, 0-324-23314-0. Acetate transparencies for selected solutions are available to adopters of the fifth edition.

Test Bank, 0-324-23315-9 (Prepared by Jane Stoneback, Central Connecticut State University). Extensively revised for the fifth edition, the test bank offers multiple-choice problems, short problems, and essay problems. Designed to make exam preparation as convenient as possible for the instructor, each test bank chapter contains enough questions and problems to permit the preparation of several exams without repetition of material.

ExamView Testing Software. This supplement contains all of the questions in the printed test bank. This program is an easy-to-use test creation software compatible with Microsoft Windows. Instructors can add or edit questions, instructions, and answers, and select questions (randomly or numerically) by previewing them on the screen. Instructors can also create and administer quizzes online, whether over the Internet, a local area network (LAN), or a wide area network (WAN).

Spreadsheet

Spreadsheet Templates (Prepared by Michael Blue, Bloomsburg University). Spreadsheet templates using Microsoft Excel® provide outlined formats of solutions for selected end-of-chapter exercises and problems. These exercises and problems are identified with a margin symbol. The templates allow students to develop spreadsheet and "what-if" analysis skills.

PowerPoint Slides (Prepared by Peggy Hussey). Selected transparencies of key concepts and exhibits from the text are available in PowerPoint presentation software. These slides provide a comprehensive outline of each chapter.

Instructor's Resource CD-ROM, 0-324-23317-5. Key instructor ancillaries (solutions manual, instructor's manual, test bank, and PowerPoint slides) are provided on CD-ROM, giving instructors the ultimate tool for customizing lectures and presentations.

Web Site (http://hansen.swlearning.com). A Web site designed specifically for *Cost Management,* fifth edition, provides online and downloadable resources for both instructors and students. The Web site features an interactive study center organized by chapter, with learning objectives, Web links, glossaries, and online quizzes with automatic feedback.

Personal Trainer® 3.0, 0-324-31164-8. Instructors consistently cite reading the text and completing graded homework assignments as a key to student success in managerial accounting; however, finding time to grade homework is difficult. Personal Trainer solves this problem by allowing professors to assign textbook exercises and problems. Personal Trainer will grade the homework and then post the grade into a full-blown gradebook, all in real time! Personal Trainer is an Internet-based homework tutor where students can complete the textbook homework assignments, receive hints, submit their answers and then receive immediate feedback on their answers.

WebTutor™ Advantage with Personal Trainer®. WebTutor Advantage complements *Cost Management*, fifth edition, by providing interactive reinforcement. WebTutor's online teaching and learning environment brings together content management, assessment, communication, and collaboration capabilities for enhancing in-class instruction or for delivering distance learning. For more information, including a demo, visit http://webtutor.swlearning.com/.

The Business & Company Resource Center. An easy way to give students access to a dynamic database of business information and resources is offered by way of the Business & Company Resource Center (BCRC). The BCRC provides online access to a wide variety of global business information including current articles and business journals, detailed company and industry information, investment reports, stock quotes, and much more. The BCRC saves valuable time and provides students a safe resource in which to hone their research skills and develop their analytical abilities. Other benefits of the BCRC include:

- Convenient access from anywhere with an Internet connection, allowing students to access information at school, at home, or on the go.
- A powerful and time-saving research tool for students—whether they are completing a case analysis, preparing for a presentation, creating a business plan, or writing a reaction paper.
- Serving as an online coursepack, allowing instructors to assign readings and research-based assignments or projects without the inconvenience of library reserves, permissions, and printed materials.
- Acts as a filter, eliminating the "junk" information often found when searching the Internet, providing only high-quality, safe, and reliable news and information sources.
- Infomarks that make it easy to assign homework, share articles, create journal lists, and save searches. Instructors can combine the BCRC with their favorite Harvard Business School Publishing cases to provide students a case analysis research tool at no additional cost. Contact your local Thomson South-Western representative to learn how to include Business & Company Resource Center with your text.

Harvard Business Case Studies. The leader in business education publishing partners with the leader in business cases to offer Harvard Business Case Studies. As part of Thomson South-Western's commitment to giving customers the greatest choice of teaching and learning solutions possible, we are proud to be an official distributor of Harvard Business School Publishing case collections and article reprints. The combination of preeminent cases and articles from Harvard Business School Publishing with the unparalleled scope and depth of customizable content from Thomson Business & Professional Publishing provides instructors and students with a wide array of learning materials. You can draw from multiple resources and disciplines to match the unique needs of your course. This bundling offers the following conveniences:

- *For Instructors:* Instructors can work with one source instead of multiple vendors, allowing the local Thomson representative to manage the prompt delivery of teaching resources and students materials.
- *For Students:* Pricing for cases is very affordable—and when packaged with the textbook, students receive a significant discount on the text and coursepak.
- *Ordering:* Once you have identified the cases and articles you want to use, simply use an order form provided by your Thomson representative to indicate your selections and packaging preferences. Once you return your form, you will be contacted within 48 hours by a Thomson Custom representative to confirm your order and walk you through the rest of the process.

Combine Harvard Business School cases and articles with the BCRC and take your coursepak to the next level. Contact your sales representative for details.

Many people have helped us to write this text. We appreciate the comments of reviewers and others who have helped make this a more readable text.

Jack Bailes, *Oregon State University*
Frank Collins, *Schreiner College*
Michael Cornick, *University of North Carolina—Charlotte*
Alan B. Czyzewski, *Indiana State University*
John B. Duncan, *University of Louisiana at Monroe*
Fara Elikai, *University of North Carolina at Wilmington*
Alan H. Friedberg, *Florida Atlantic University*
Donald W. Gribben, *Southern Illinois University*
Jeri W. Griego, *Laramie County Community College*
Jan Richard Heier, *Auburn University at Montgomery*
Eleanor G. Henry, *State University of New York at Oswego*
James Holmes, *University of Kentucky*
David R. Honodel, *University of Denver*
Dick Houser, *Northern Arizona University*
K. E. Hughes II, *Louisiana State University*
Bill Joyce, *Eastern Illinois University*
Leslie Kren, *University of Wisconsin—Milwaukee*
Ron Kucic, *University of Denver*
Amy Hing-Ling Lau, *The Hong Kong Polytechnic University*
Otto Martinson, *Old Dominion University*
William Ortega, *Western Washington University*
Joseph Weintrop, *Baruch College*

Special thanks are due to our verifiers, Judy Beebe of Western Oregon University, James Emig of Villanova University, and Kim Richardson of James Madison University. They error-checked the study guide, solutions manual, and test bank. Their efforts helped us to produce a higher-quality text and supplement package.

To the many students at Oklahoma State University who have reacted to the material in *Cost Management: Accounting and Control,* we owe special thanks. Students represent our true constituency. The common sense and good humor of our student reviewers have resulted in a clearer, more readable text.

We also want to express our gratitude to the Institute of Management Accountants for its permission to use adapted problems from past CMA examinations and to reprint the ethical standards of conduct for management accountants. We are also grateful to the American Institute of Certified Public Accountants for allowing us to adapt selected questions from past CPA examinations.

Finally, we wish to acknowledge the exceptional efforts of our project team at South-Western Publishing and Litten Editing and Production (LEAP). Allison Rolfes, developmental editor extraordinaire, consistently provided outstanding support. Her organizational and creative skills, not to mention flexibility and unflagging good humor, made this book a reality. Kara ZumBahlen, production editor, with Malvine Litten and Denise Morton of LEAP, took manuscript and transformed it into a text suited for the 21st century. Bethany Casey, designer, and Deanna Ettinger, photo manager, helped us transform abstract accounting concepts into state-of-the-art graphics and photos. The support and creative efforts of Keith Chasse, acquisitions editor, and Chris McNamee, marketing manager, are much appreciated.

Don R. Hansen and Maryanne M. Mowen

Don R. Hansen

Dr. Don R. Hansen is Head of the School of Accounting at Oklahoma State University. He received his Ph.D. from the University of Arizona in 1977. He has an undergraduate degree in mathematics from Brigham Young University. His research interests include activity-based costing and mathematical modeling. He has published articles in both accounting and engineering journals including *The Accounting Review, The Journal of Management Accounting Research, Accounting Horizons,* and *IIE Transactions.* He has served on the editorial board of *The Accounting Review.* His outside interests include family, church activities, reading, movies, watching sports, and studying Spanish.

Maryanne M. Mowen

Dr. Maryanne M. Mowen is Associate Professor of Accounting at Oklahoma State University. She received her Ph.D. from Arizona State University in 1979. Dr. Mowen brings an interdisciplinary perspective to teaching and writing in cost and management accounting, with degrees in history and economics. In addition, she does research in areas of behavioral decision making, activity-based costing, and the impact of the Sarbanes-Oxley Act. She has published articles in journals such as *Decision Science, The Journal of Economics and Psychology,* and *The Journal of Management Accounting Research.* Dr. Mowen's interests outside the classroom include reading mysteries, traveling, and working crossword puzzles.

Part 1: Foundation Concepts 1

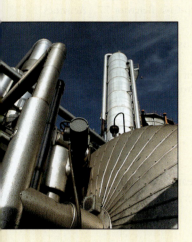

Contents

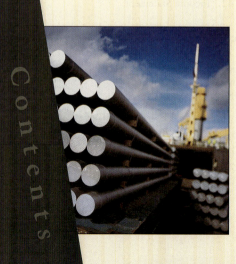

Contents

Part 3: Advanced Costing and Control 484

Contents

Cost Management

Accounting and Control

FOUNDATION CONCEPTS

PART 1

http://hansen.swlearning.com

CHAPTER

© RUBBERBALL PRODUCTIONS/GETTY IMAGES

1

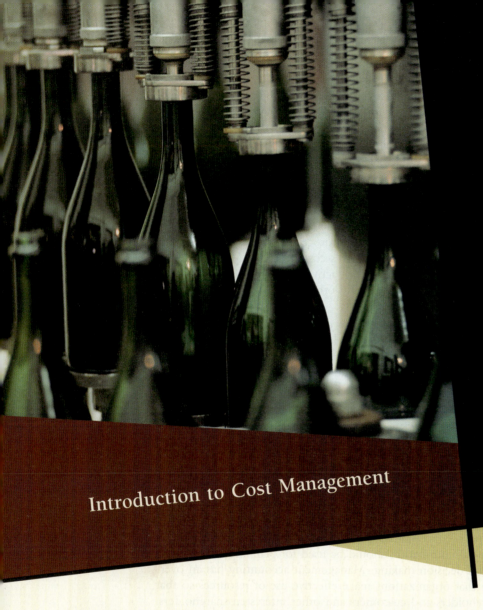

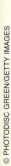
© PHOTODISC GREEN/GETTY IMAGES

Introduction to Cost Management

1

AFTER STUDYING THIS CHAPTER, YOU SHOULD BE ABLE TO:

1. List the similarities and differences between financial accounting and cost management.

2. Identify the current factors affecting cost management.

3. Discuss the importance of the accounting system for internal and external reporting.

4. Discuss the need for today's cost accountant to acquire cross-functional expertise.

5. Describe how management accountants function within an organization.

6. Understand the importance of ethical behavior for management accountants.

7. Identify the three forms of certification available to internal accountants.

Financial Accounting versus Cost Management

The accounting information system within an organization has two major subsystems: a financial accounting system and a cost management accounting system. One of the major differences between the two systems is the targeted user. Financial accounting is devoted to providing information for external users, including investors, creditors (e.g., banks and suppliers), and government agencies. These external users find the information helpful in making decisions to buy or sell shares of stock, buy bonds, issue loans and regulatory acts, and in making other financial decisions. Because the information needs of this group of external users are so diverse and the information must be so highly reliable, the financial accounting system is designed in accordance with clearly defined accounting rules and formats, or generally accepted accounting principles (GAAP). **Cost management** produces information for internal users. Specifically, cost management identifies, collects, measures, classifies, and reports information that is useful to managers for determining the cost of products, customers, and suppliers, and other relevant objects and for planning, controlling, making continuous improvements, and decision making.

Cost management has a much broader focus than that found in traditional costing systems. It is not only concerned with how much something costs but also with the factors that drive costs, such as cycle time, quality, and process productivity. Thus, cost management requires a deep understanding of a firm's cost structure. Managers must be able to determine the long- and short-run costs of activities and processes as well as the costs of goods, services, customers, suppliers, and other objects of interest. Causes of these costs are also carefully studied.

The costs of activities and processes do not appear on the financial statements. Yet, knowing these costs and their underlying causes is critical for companies engaging in such tasks as continuous improvement, total quality management, environmental cost management, productivity enhancement, and strategic cost management.

Cost management encompasses both the cost accounting and the management accounting information systems. Cost accounting attempts to satisfy costing objectives for both financial and management accounting. When **cost accounting** is used to comply with a financial accounting objective, it measures and assigns costs in accordance with GAAP. When used for internal purposes, cost accounting provides cost information about products, customers, services, projects, activities, processes, and other details that may be of interest to management. The cost information provided plays an important support role for planning, controlling, and decision making. This information need not, and often should not, follow GAAP.

Management accounting is concerned specifically with how cost information and other financial and nonfinancial information should be used for planning, controlling, continuous improvement, and decision making. Management accounting has an overall objective of making sure that organizations make effective use of resources so that value is maximized for shareholders and customers and other interested shareholders. **Porsche**, **Stihl**, **DaimlerChrysler,** and other German companies view management accounting as a distinct discipline and typically employ as many or more staff in management accounting as in financial accounting.[1]

It should be emphasized that both the cost management information system and the financial accounting information system are part of the total accounting information system. Unfortunately, the content of the cost management accounting system is all too often driven by the needs of the financial accounting system. The reports of both cost management and financial accounting are frequently derived from the same database, which was originally established to support the reporting requirements of financial accounting. Many organizations need to expand this database, or create additional databases, in order to satisfy more fully the needs of internal users. For example, a firm's profitability is of interest to investors, but managers need to know the profitability of individual products. The accounting system should be designed to provide both total profits and profits for individual products. The key point here is flexibility—the accounting system should be able to supply different data for different purposes.

Factors Affecting Cost Management

Over the last 25 years, worldwide competitive pressures, deregulation, growth in the service industry, and advances in information and manufacturing technology have

1. Paul A. Sharman, "German Cost Accounting," *Strategic Finance* (December 2003): 30–38.

OBJECTIVE *1*

List the similarities and differences between financial accounting and cost management.

OBJECTIVE 2

Identify the current factors affecting cost management.

changed the nature of our economy and caused many manufacturing and service industries to dramatically change the way in which they operate. These changes, in turn, have prompted the development of innovative and relevant cost management practices. For example, activity-based accounting systems have been developed and implemented in many organizations. Additionally, the focus of cost management accounting systems has been broadened to enable managers to better serve the needs of customers and manage the firm's business processes that are used to create customer value. A firm can establish a competitive advantage by providing more customer value for less cost than its competitors. To secure and maintain a competitive advantage, managers seek to improve time-based performance, quality, and efficiency. Accounting information must be produced to support these three fundamental organizational goals.

Global Competition

Vastly improved transportation and communication systems have led to a global market for many manufacturing and service firms. Several decades ago, firms neither knew nor cared what similar firms in Japan, France, Germany, and Singapore were producing. These foreign firms were not competitors since their markets were separated by geographical distance. Now, both small and large firms are affected by the opportunities offered by global competition. **Stillwater Designs**, a small firm that designs and markets Kicker speakers, has significant markets in Europe. The manufacture of the Kicker speakers is mostly outsourced to Asian producers. At the other end of the size scale, **Procter & Gamble**, **The Coca-Cola Company,** and **Mars, Inc.**, are developing sizable markets in China. Automobiles, currently being made in Japan, can be in the United States in two weeks. Investment bankers and management consultants can communicate with foreign offices instantly. Improved transportation and communication in conjunction with higher quality products that carry lower prices have upped the ante for all firms. This new competitive environment has increased the demand not only for more cost information but also for more accurate cost information. Cost information plays a vital role in reducing costs, improving productivity, and assessing product-line profitability.

Growth of the Service Industry

As traditional industries have declined in importance, the service sector of the economy has increased in importance. The service sector now comprises approximately three-quarters of the U.S. economy and employment. Many services—among them accounting services, transportation, and medical services—are exported. Experts predict that this sector will continue to expand in size and importance as service productivity grows. Deregulation of many services (e.g., airlines and telecommunications in the past and utilities in the present) has increased competition in the service industry. Many service organizations are scrambling to survive. The increased competition has made managers in this industry more conscious of the need to have accurate cost information for planning, controlling, continuous improvement, and decision making. Thus, the changes in the service sector add to the demand for innovative and relevant cost management information.

Advances in Information Technology

Three significant advances relate to information technology. One is intimately connected with computer-integrated applications. With automated manufacturing, computers are used to monitor and control operations. Because a computer is being used, a considerable amount of useful information can be collected, and managers can be informed about what is happening within an organization almost as it happens. It is now possible to track products continuously as they move through the factory and to report (on a real-time basis) such information as units produced, material used, scrap generated, and product cost. The outcome is an operational information system that fully integrates manufacturing with marketing and accounting data.

Enterprise resource planning (ERP) software has the objective of providing an integrated system capability—a system that can run all the operations of a company and provide access to real-time data from the various functional areas of a company. Using this real-time data enables managers to continuously improve the efficiency of organizational units and processes. To support continuous improvement, information that is timely, accurate, and detailed is needed.

Automation and integration increase both the quantity (detail) and the timeliness of information. For managers to fully exploit the value of the more complex information system, they must have access to the data of the system—they must be able to extract and analyze the data from the information system quickly and efficiently. This, in turn, implies that the tools for analysis must be powerful.

The second major advance supplies the required tools: the availability of personal computers (PCs), online analytic programs (OLAP), and decision-support systems (DSS). The PC serves as a communications link to the company's information system, and OLAP and DSS supply managers with the capability to use that information. PCs and software aids are available to managers in all types of organizations. Often, a PC acts as a networking terminal and is connected to an organization's database, allowing managers to access information more quickly, do their own analyses, and prepare many of their own reports. The ability to enhance the accuracy of product costing is now available. Because of advances in information technology, cost accountants have the flexibility to respond to the managerial need for more complex product costing methods such as activity-based costing (ABC).

ABC software is classified as online analytic software. Online analytic applications function independently of an organization's core transactions but at the same time are dependent on the data resident in an ERP system.[2] ABC software typically interfaces with DSS software and other online analytic software to facilitate applications such as cost estimating, product pricing, and planning and budgeting. This vast computing capability now makes it possible for accountants to generate individualized reports on an as-needed basis. Many firms have found that the increased responsiveness of a contemporary cost management system has allowed them to realize significant cost savings by eliminating the huge volume of internally generated monthly financial reports.

The third major advance is the emergence of electronic commerce. Electronic commerce (e-commerce) is any form of business that is executed using information and communications technology. Internet trading, electronic data interchange, and bar coding are examples of e-commerce. Internet trading allows buyers and sellers to come together and execute transactions from diverse locations and circumstances. Internet trading allows a company to act as a virtual organization, thus reducing overhead. Electronic data interchange (EDI) involves the exchange of documents between computers using telephone lines and is widely used for purchasing and distribution. The sharing of information among trading partners reduces costs and improves customer relations, thus leading to a stronger competitive position. EDI is an integral part of supply chain management (value-chain management). Supply chain management is the management of products and services from the acquisition of raw materials through manufacturing, warehousing, distribution, wholesaling, and retailing. The emergence of EDI and supply chain management has increased the importance of costing out activities in the value chain and determining the cost to the company of different suppliers and customers.

Advances in the Manufacturing Environment

Manufacturing management approaches such as the theory of constraints and just-in-time have allowed firms to increase quality, reduce inventories, eliminate waste, and re-

---

2. R. Shaw, "ABC and ERP: Partners at Last?" *Management Accounting* (November 1998): 56–58.

duce costs. Automated manufacturing has produced similar outcomes. The impact of improved manufacturing technology and practices on cost management is significant. Product costing systems, control systems, allocation, inventory management, cost structure, capital budgeting, variable costing, and many other accounting practices are being affected.

Theory of Constraints

The theory of constraints is a method used to continuously improve manufacturing and nonmanufacturing activities. It is characterized as a "thinking process" that begins by recognizing that all resources are finite. Some resources, however, are more critical than others. The most critical limiting factor, called a constraint, becomes the focus of attention. By managing this constraint, performance can be improved. To manage the constraint, it must be identified and exploited (i.e., performance must be maximized subject to the constraint). All other actions are subordinate to the exploitation decision. Finally, to improve performance, the constraint must be elevated. The process is repeated until the constraint is eliminated (i.e., it is no longer the critical performance limiting factor). The process then begins anew with the resource that has now become the critical limiting factor. Using this method, lead times and, thus, inventories can be reduced.

Just-in-Time Manufacturing

A demand-pull system, just-in-time (JIT) manufacturing strives to produce a product only when it is needed and only in the quantities demanded by customers. Demand, measured by customer orders, pulls products through the manufacturing process. Each operation produces only what is necessary to satisfy the demand of the succeeding operation. No production takes place until a signal from a succeeding process indicates the need to produce. Parts and materials arrive just in time to be used in production.

JIT manufacturing typically reduces inventories to much lower levels (theoretically to insignificant levels) than those found in conventional systems, increases the emphasis on quality control, and produces fundamental changes in the way production is organized and carried out. Basically, JIT manufacturing focuses on continual improvement by reducing inventory costs and dealing with other economic problems. Reducing inventories frees up capital that can be used for more productive investments. Increasing quality enhances the competitive ability of the firm. Finally, changing from a traditional manufacturing setup to JIT manufacturing allows the firm to focus more on quality and productivity and, at the same time, allows a more accurate assessment of what it costs to produce products.

Computer-Integrated Manufacturing

Automation of the manufacturing environment allows firms to reduce inventory, increase productive capacity, improve quality and service, decrease processing time, and increase output. Automation can produce a competitive advantage for a firm. The implementation of an automated manufacturing facility typically follows JIT and is a response to the increased needs for quality and shorter response times. As more firms automate, competitive pressures will force other firms to do likewise. For many manufacturing firms, automation may be equivalent to survival.

The three possible levels of automation are (1) the stand-alone piece of equipment, (2) the cell, and (3) the completely integrated factory. Before a firm attempts any level of automation, it should first do all it can to produce a more focused, simplified manufacturing process. For example, most of the benefits of going to a completely integrated factory can often be achieved simply by implementing JIT manufacturing.

If automation is justified, it may mean installation of a computer-integrated manufacturing (CIM) system. CIM implies the following capabilities: (1) the products are designed through the use of a computer-assisted design (CAD) system; (2) a computer-assisted engineering (CAE) system is used to test the design; (3) the product is manufactured using a computer-assisted manufacturing (CAM) system (CAMs use computer-controlled machines and robots); and (4) an information system connects the various automated components.

A particular type of CAM is the flexible manufacturing system. Flexible manufacturing systems are capable of producing a family of products from start to finish using robots and other automated equipment under the control of a mainframe computer. This ability to produce a variety of products with the same set of equipment is clearly advantageous.

Customer Orientation

Firms are concentrating on the delivery of value to the customer with the objective of establishing a competitive advantage. Accountants and managers refer to a firm's **value chain** as the set of activities required to design, develop, produce, market, and deliver products and services to customers. As a result, a key question to be asked about any process or activity is whether it is important to the customer. The cost management system must track information relating to a wide variety of activities important to customers (e.g., product quality, environmental performance, new product development, and delivery performance). Customers now count the delivery of the product or service as part of the product. Companies must compete not only in technological and manufacturing terms but also in terms of the speed of delivery and response. Firms like **Federal Express** have exploited this desire by identifying and developing a market the **U.S. Post Office** could not serve.

Companies have internal customers as well. The staff functions of a company exist to serve the line functions. The accounting department creates cost reports for production managers. Accounting departments that are "customer driven" assess the value of the reports to be sure that they communicate significant information in a timely and readable fashion. Reports that do not measure up are dropped.

New Product Development

A high proportion of production costs are committed during the development and design stage of new products. The effects of product development decisions on other parts of the firm's value chain are now widely acknowledged. This recognition has produced a demand for more sophisticated cost management procedures relating to new product development—procedures such as target costing and activity-based management. **Target costing** encourages managers to assess the overall cost impact of product designs over the product's life cycle and simultaneously provides incentives to make design changes to reduce costs. **Activity-based management** identifies the activities produced at each stage of the development process and assesses their costs. Activity-based management is complimentary to target costing because it enables managers to identify the activities that do not add value and then eliminate them so that overall life cycle costs can be reduced.

Total Quality Management

Continuous improvement and elimination of waste are the two foundation principles that govern a state of manufacturing excellence. Manufacturing excellence is the key to survival in today's world-class competitive environment. Producing products and services that actually perform according to specifications and with little waste are the twin objectives of world-class firms. A philosophy of **total quality management,** in which managers strive to create an environment that will enable organizations to produce defect-free products and services, has replaced the acceptable quality attitudes of the past.

The emphasis on quality applies to services as well as products. **Boeing Aerospace Support (AS)** provides maintenance and training support for Boeing aircraft. From 1999 to 2003, AS significantly improved the quality of its services. From 1998 to 2003, the "exceptional" and "very good" responses on customer satisfaction surveys increased by more than 23 percent. On-time delivery of maintenance services was about 95 percent. For one program, the turn-around time was about three days for AS, while its competitors were taking up to 40 days for the same services. As a consequence of the improved quality, AS more than doubled its revenues from 1999 to 2003 (especially impressive given that the market growth was flat during this period). The company also received the 2003 Malcolm Baldrige National Quality Award in the service category.[3]

The message is clear. Pursuing an objective of improving quality promises major benefits. Cost management supports this objective by providing crucial information concerning quality-related activities and quality costs. Managers need to know which quality-related activities add value and which ones do not. They also need to know what quality costs are and how they change over time.

Time as a Competitive Element

Time is a crucial element in all phases of the value chain. Firms can reduce time to market by redesigning products and processes, by eliminating waste, and by eliminating non-value-added activities. Firms can reduce the time spent on delivery of products or services, reworking a product, and unnecessary movements of materials and subassemblies.

Decreasing non-value-added time appears to go hand-in-hand with increasing quality. With quality improvements, the need for rework decreases, and the time to produce a good product decreases. The overall objective is to increase customer responsiveness.

Time and product life cycles are related. The rate of technological innovation has increased for many industries, and the life of a particular product can be quite short. Managers must be able to respond quickly and decisively to changing market conditions. Information to allow them to accomplish this goal must be available. **Hewlett-Packard** has found that it is better to be 50 percent over budget in new product development than to be six months late. This correlation between cost and time is a part of the cost management system.

Efficiency

While quality and time are important, improving these dimensions without corresponding improvements in financial performance may be futile, if not fatal. Improving efficiency is also a vital concern. Both financial and nonfinancial measures of efficiency are needed. Cost is a critical measure of efficiency. Trends in costs over time and measures of productivity changes can provide important measures of the efficacy of continuous improvement decisions. For these efficiency measures to be of value, costs must be properly defined, measured, and accurately assigned.

Production of output must be related to the inputs required, and the overall financial effect of productivity changes should be calculated. Activity-based costing and profit-linked productivity measurement are responses to these demands. Activity-based costing is a relatively new approach to cost accounting that provides more accurate and meaningful cost assignments. By analyzing underlying activities and processes, eliminating those that do not add value, and enhancing those that do add value, dramatic increases in efficiency can be realized.

---

3. As reported at http://www.nist.gov/public_affairs/releases/2003baldrigewinners.htm on May 5, 2004.

A Systems Approach

OBJECTIVE 3

Discuss the importance of the accounting system for internal and external reporting.

The accounting system can be viewed as an approach to record transactions. A firm may develop a system that ranges from simple to complex, depending on the underlying processes it describes. The financial system of a typical college student is quite simple. It may consist of a checkbook and a wallet. Cash on hand may be counted when necessary to see if a purchase is possible. Similarly, from time to time, the checkbook is balanced to see if the bank's view is similar to the checkbook holder's view. There probably is not much paperwork and no need for a journal and chart of accounts. One individual is responsible for purchases and payments. However, as the entity grows, say as a small business with several employees, the simple system does not work. One person cannot keep track of all the detail; several people may be responsible for payments and purchases as well as sales. Certain standardized techniques are required.

The systems approach for the modern company is a data-based, relationship accounting approach. Exhibit 1-1 shows the traditional accounting system as a funnel. Transactions occur, and supporting documents are accumulated. These documents contain a wealth of data. For example, a purchase order may show the type, amount, and cost of the materials to be purchased, as well as the date and the individual who requested the materials. This purchase is then entered into the journal, yet only the date, account name, and dollar amount are retained. In other words, much potentially useful information is eliminated.

Next, the amounts in the journal are aggregated in the general ledger; thus, more information is lost at this stage. Finally, the ledger amounts are summarized in financial reports—and still more information is deleted.

The data-based, or relationship, accounting system preserves information. The rectangle in Exhibit 1-1 represents the new accounting system. All information pertinent to a transaction is entered into a database. Various users of information can extract what they need from the database and create custom accounting reports. Information is not

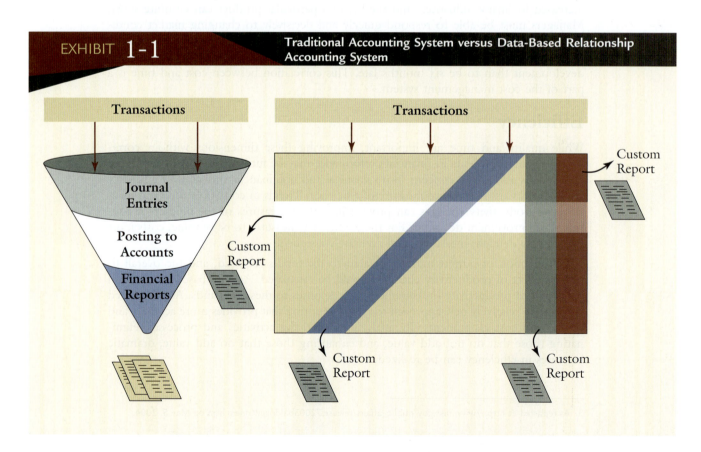

EXHIBIT 1-1   Traditional Accounting System versus Data-Based Relationship Accounting System

Transactions

Transactions

Journal Entries

Posting to Accounts

Financial Reports

Custom Report

Custom Report

Custom Report

Custom Report

lost; it is still available for other users with different needs. If a salesperson writes up an order, data on the customer's name and address, product ordered, quantity, price, and date to be delivered are entered into the database. The marketing manager may use information on the price and quantity ordered to determine the sales commission. The production manager may need information on product type, quantity, and delivery date to schedule production.

The moving force behind this shift from an external report-based accounting system to a relationship-based accounting system is the widespread availability of technology. Powerful personal computers and networked systems make the accounting system available to a wide variety of users within the company.

The development and adoption of powerful ERP programs (e.g., **SAP**, **Oracle**, **PeopleSoft**, and **JD Edwards**) have moved the concept of an integrated database from the realm of theory to reality. This has forced a shift in perspective. An ERP system integrates many information systems into one enterprise-wide system. This directly impacts costing systems such as activity-based costing (ABC). An ERP system provides access to timely information—both financial and nonfinancial—about many organizational units and processes. This facilitates the adoption and implementation of an ABC system.

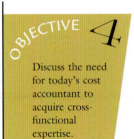

OBJECTIVE 4

Discuss the need for today's cost accountant to acquire cross-functional expertise.

Cost Management: A Cross-Functional Perspective

Today's cost accountant must understand many functions of a business's value chain, from manufacturing to marketing to distribution to customer service. This need is particularly important when the company is involved in international trade. Definitions of product cost vary. The company's internal accountants have moved beyond the traditional manufacturing cost approach to a more inclusive approach. This newer approach to product costing may take into account the costs of the value-chain activities defined by initial design and engineering, manufacturing, distribution, sales, and service. An individual who is well schooled in the various definitions of cost and who understands the shifting definitions of cost from the short run to the long run can be invaluable in determining what information is relevant in decision making.

Individuals with the ability to think cross-functionally can shift perspectives, expanding their understanding of problems and their solutions. Japanese automakers got their idea for JIT manufacturing from Taiichi Ohno's (the creator of **Toyota**'s JIT production system) 1956 trip to the United States. He toured American automobile factories and American supermarkets. The impressive array of goods in the supermarkets and their constant turnover led to Ohno's comprehension of the way that grocery customers "pulled" products through the stores. That understanding led to Toyota's attempt to "pull" parts through production precisely when and where needed.[4]

Why try to relate cost management to marketing, management, and logistics? On-time delivery affects costs. Cycle time affects costs. The way orders are received and processed from customers affects costs. The way goods are purchased and delivered affects costs—as do the quality of the components purchased and the reliability of suppliers. It is clearly difficult—if not impossible—to manage costs unless there is interaction and cooperation among all parts of a company.

The Need for Flexibility

No one cost management system exists. Costs important to one firm may be irrelevant to another. Similarly, costs that are important in one context to a firm are unimportant in other contexts.

---

4. Jeremy Main, "How to Steal the Best Ideas Around," *Fortune* (October 19, 1992): 102–106.

A member of the board of directors for **Stillwater's Mission of Hope**, a nonprofit shelter for the homeless, asked his accountant how to value the building used as the shelter. In other words, what did it cost? The accountant's answer was: "Why do you want to know? If you need to know the value for insurance purposes—to determine how much insurance to buy—then perhaps replacement cost would be the answer. If you are trying to set a price to sell the building (and build another one elsewhere), then current market value of the real estate would be the answer. If you need the cost for the balance sheet, then historical cost is required by GAAP." Different costs are needed for different purposes. The intelligent cost accountant must find the reason for the question in order to suggest an appropriate answer. A good cost management system facilitates these answers.

An understanding of the structure of the business environment in which the company operates is an important input in designing a cost management system. A primary distinction is made between manufacturing and service firms. However, overlap occurs because some manufacturing firms emphasize service to customers while some service firms emphasize the quality of their "product." Retailing is another classification, and its needs would require still another system.

Behavioral Impact of Cost Information

Cost information is not neutral; it does not stand in the background, merely reflecting what has happened in an unbiased way. Instead, the cost management information system also shapes business. By keeping track of certain information, business owners are saying that these things are important. The ignoring of other information implies that it is not important. An old joke states that an accountant is someone who knows the cost of everything and the value of nothing.

Today's accountant must be an expert at valuing things. This includes methods (1) of costing and achieving quality, (2) of differentiating between value-added and non-value-added activities, and (3) of measuring and accounting for productivity. Thus, it is crucial that owners, managers, and accountants be aware of the signals that are being sent out by the accounting information system and ensure that correct signals are being sent.

The Role of Today's Cost and Management Accountant

OBJECTIVE 5

Describe how management accountants funtion within an organization.

World-class firms are those that are at the cutting edge of customer support. They know their market and their product. They strive continually to improve product design, manufacture, and delivery. These companies can compete with the best of the best in a global environment. Accountants, too, can be termed world class. Those who merit this designation are intelligent and well prepared. They not only have the education and training to accumulate and provide financial information, but they stay up to date in their field and in business. In addition, world-class accountants must be familiar with the customs and financial accounting rules of the countries in which their firm operates.

Line and Staff Positions

The role of cost and management accountants in an organization is one of support and teamwork. They assist those who are responsible for carrying out an organization's basic objectives. Positions that have direct responsibility for the basic objectives of an organization are referred to as line positions. In general, individuals in line positions participate in activities that produce and sell their company's product or service. Positions that are supportive in nature and have only indirect responsibility for an organization's basic objectives are called staff positions.

In an organization whose basic mission is to produce and sell laser printers, the vice presidents of manufacturing and marketing, the factory manager, and the assemblers are all line positions. The vice presidents of finance and human resources, the cost accountant, and the purchasing manager are all staff positions.

The partial organization chart, shown in Exhibit 1-2, illustrates the organizational positions for production and finance. Because one of the basic objectives of the organization is to produce, those directly involved in production hold line positions. Although management accountants such as controllers and cost accounting managers may exercise considerable influence in the organization, they have no authority over the managers in the production area. The managers in line positions are the ones who set policy and make the decisions that impact production. However, by supplying and interpreting accounting information, accountants can have significant input into policies and decisions. Accountants also participate in project teams that are involved in decision making.

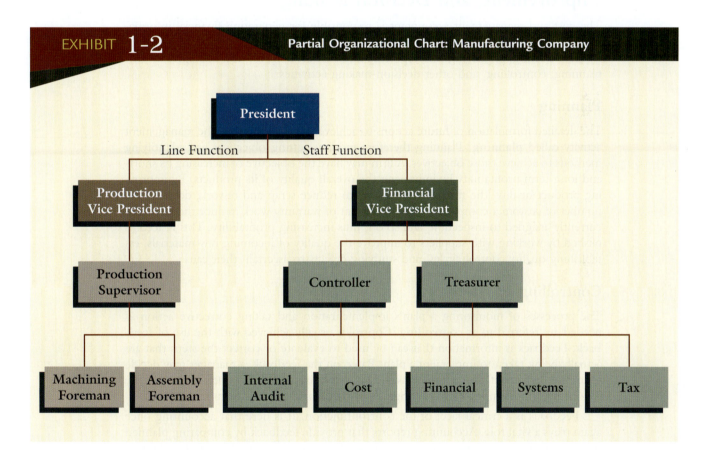

EXHIBIT 1-2   Partial Organizational Chart: Manufacturing Company

The Controller

The **controller**, the chief accounting officer, supervises all accounting departments. Because of the critical role that management accounting plays in the operation of an organization, the controller is often viewed as a member of the top management team and encouraged to participate in planning, controlling, and decision-making activities. As the chief accounting officer, the controller has responsibility for both internal and external accounting requirements. This charge may include direct responsibility for internal auditing, cost accounting, financial accounting [including Securities Exchange Commission (SEC) reports and financial statements], systems accounting (including analysis, design, and internal controls), budgeting support, economic analysis, and taxes.

The duties and organization of the controller's office vary from firm to firm. In some companies, the internal audit department may report directly to the financial vice president; similarly, the systems department may report directly to the financial vice president or even to another staff vice president. A possible organization of a controller's office is also shown in Exhibit 1-2.

The Treasurer

The **treasurer** is responsible for the finance function. Specifically, the treasurer raises capital and manages cash (banking and custody), investments, and investor relations. The treasurer may also be in charge of credit and collections as well as insurance. As shown in Exhibit 1-2, the treasurer reports to the financial vice president.

Information for Planning, Controlling, Continuous Improvement, and Decision Making

The cost and management accountant is responsible for generating financial information required by the firm for internal and external reporting. This involves responsibility for collecting, processing, and reporting information that will help managers in their planning, controlling, and other decision-making activities.

Planning

The detailed formulation of future actions to achieve a particular end is the management activity called **planning**. Planning therefore requires setting objectives and identifying methods to achieve those objectives. A firm may have the objective of increasing its short- and long-term profitability by improving the overall quality of its products. By improving product quality, the firm should be able to reduce scrap and rework, decrease the number of customer complaints and the amount of warranty work, reduce the resources currently assigned to inspection, and so on, thus increasing profitability. This is accomplished by working with suppliers to improve the quality of incoming raw materials, establishing quality control circles, and studying defects to ascertain their cause.

Controlling

The processes of monitoring a plan's implementation and taking corrective action as needed are referred to as **controlling**. Control is usually achieved with the use of **feedback**. Feedback is information that can be used to evaluate or correct the steps that are actually being taken to implement a plan. Based on the feedback, a manager may decide to let the implementation continue as is, take corrective action of some type to put the actions back in harmony with the original plan, or do some midstream replanning.

Feedback is a critical facet of the control function. It is here that accounting once again plays a vital role. Accounting reports that provide feedback by comparing planned (budgeted) data with actual data are called **performance reports**. Exhibit 1-3 shows a performance report that compares budgeted sales and cost of goods sold with the actual amounts for the month of August. Deviations from the planned amounts that increase profits are labeled "favorable," while those that decrease profits are called "unfavorable." These performance reports can have a dramatic impact on managerial actions—but they must be realistic and supportive of management plans. Revenue and spending targets must be based (as closely as possible) on actual operating conditions.

Continuous Improvement

In a dynamic environment, firms must continually improve their performance to remain competitive or to establish a competitive advantage. Continuous improvement has the goals to do better than before and to do better than competitors. **Continuous im-**

EXHIBIT 1-3	Performance Report Illustrated

Golding Foods, Inc.
Performance Report
For the Month Ended August 31, 2007

Budget Item	Actual	Budgeted	Variance
Sales	$800,000	$900,000	$100,000 U
Cost of goods sold	600,000	650,000	50,000 F

Note: U = Unfavorable; F = Favorable.

provement has been defined as "the relentless pursuit of improvement in the delivery of value to customers."[5] In practical terms, continuous improvement means searching for ways to increase overall efficiency by reducing waste, improving quality, and reducing costs. Cost management supports continuous improvement by providing information that helps identify ways to improve and then reports on the progress of the methods that have been implemented. It also plays a critical role by developing a control system that locks in and maintains any improvements realized.

Decision Making

The process of choosing among competing alternatives is **decision making**. Decisions can be improved if information about the alternatives is gathered and made available to managers. One of the major roles of the accounting information system is to supply information that facilitates decision making. This pervasive managerial function is an important part of both planning and control. A manager cannot plan without making decisions. Managers must choose among competing objectives and methods to carry out the chosen objectives. Only one of numerous mutually exclusive plans can be chosen. Similar comments can be made concerning the control function.

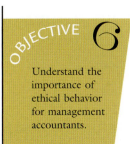

OBJECTIVE 6

Understand the importance of ethical behavior for management accountants.

Accounting and Ethical Conduct

Business ethics is learning what is right or wrong in the work environment and choosing what is right. Business ethics could also be described as the science of conduct for the work environment.[6] Principles of personal ethical behavior include concern for the well-being of others, respect for others, trustworthiness and honesty, fairness, doing good, and preventing harm to others. For professionals such as accountants, managers, engineers, and physicians, ethical behavior principles can be expanded to include concepts such as objectivity, full disclosure, confidentiality, due diligence, and avoiding conflicts of interest.

Benefits of Ethical Behavior

Attention to business ethics can bring significant benefits to a company. Companies with a strong code of ethics can create strong customer and employee loyalty. Observing

---

5. As defined in P. B. B. Turney and B. Anderson, "Accounting for Continuous Improvement," *Sloan Management Review* (Winter 1989): 37–47.

6. For a brief but thorough introduction to business ethics, see Carter McNamara, "Complete Guide to Ethics Management: An Ethics Toolkit for Managers," http://www.mapnp.org/library/ethics/ethxgde.htm as of May 10, 2004.

ethical practices now can avoid later litigation costs. Companies in business for the long term find that it pays to treat all of their constituents honestly and fairly. Furthermore, a company that values people more than profit and is viewed as operating with integrity and honor is more likely to be a commercially successful and responsible business. These observations are supported by a 1997 U.S. study and a more recent 2002 U.K. study concerning ethics and financial performance. Both studies find that publicly held firms with an emphasis on ethics outperform firms without any such emphasis (emphasis is measured by a management report mentioning ethics for the U.S. study and by the presence of an ethics code for the U.K. study).[7]

Standards of Ethical Conduct for Management Accountants

Organizations and professional associations often establish a code of ethics or standards of conduct for their managers and employees. All firms subject to the Sarbanes-Oxley Act of 2002 must establish a code of ethics. A survey taken by **Deloitte & Touche LLP** and the *Corporate Board Member* magazine in 2003 revealed that 83 percent of the corporations surveyed had established formal codes of ethics, 98 percent agreed that an ethics and compliance program is an essential part of corporate governance, and 75 percent of those with codes of ethics were actively monitoring compliance.[8] The Institute of Management Accountants (IMA) has established ethical standards for management accountants. Management accountants are subject to this professional code and have been advised that, "they shall not commit acts contrary to these standards nor shall they condone the commission of such acts by others in their organizations."[9] The standards and the recommended resolution of ethical conflict are presented in Exhibit 1-4. The code has five major divisions: competence, confidentiality, integrity, objectivity, and resolution of ethical conflict.

To illustrate an application of the code, suppose that the vice president of finance has informed Bill Johnson, a divisional controller, that the division's accounting staff will be reduced by 20 percent within the next four weeks. Furthermore, Bill Johnson is instructed to refrain from mentioning the layoffs because of the potential uproar that would be caused. One of the targeted layoffs is a cost accounting manager who happens to be a good friend. Bill Johnson also knows that his good friend is planning to buy a new sports utility vehicle within the next week. Bill is strongly tempted to inform his friend so that he can avoid tying up cash that he may need until a new position is found. Would it be unethical for Bill to share his confidential information with his friend? This situation is an example of an ethical dilemma. Informing the friend would violate II-1, the requirement that confidential information must not be disclosed unless authorized. Resolution of the conflict may be as simple as chatting with the vice president, explaining the difficulty, and obtaining permission to disclose the layoff.

Certification

A variety of certifications are available to management accountants. Three of the major certifications available are a Certificate in Management Accounting, a Certificate in

OBJECTIVE 7

Identify the three forms of certification available to internal accountants.

---

7. Curtis C. Verschoor, "Principles Build Profits," *Management Accounting* (October 1997): 42–46; Simon Webley and Elise Moore, "Does Business Ethics Pay?" *Executive Summary, Institute of Business Ethics*, http://www.ibe.org.uk as of May 11, 2004.

8. Deloitte & Touche LLP and *Corporate Board Member* magazine, "Business Ethics and Compliance in the Sarbanes-Oxley Era: A Survey," http://www.deloitte.com/US/corpgov as of May 11, 2004.

9. Statement on Management Accounting No. 1C, "Standards of Ethical Conduct for Management Accountants" (Montvale, NJ: Institute of Management Accountants, 1983). The Standards of Ethical Conduct are reprinted with permission from the Institute of Management Accountants.

EXHIBIT 1-4	Standards of Ethical Conduct for Management Accountants

I. Competence

Management accountants have a responsibility to:

1. Maintain an appropriate level of professional competence by ongoing development of their knowledge and skills.
2. Perform their professional duties in accordance with relevant laws, regulations, and technical standards.
3. Prepare complete and clear reports and recommendations after appropriate analyses of relevant and reliable information.

II. Confidentiality

Management accountants have a responsibility to:

1. Refrain from disclosing confidential information acquired in the course of their work except when authorized, unless legally obligated to do so.
2. Inform subordinates as appropriate regarding the confidentiality of information acquired in the course of their work and monitor their activities to ensure the maintenance of that confidentiality.
3. Refrain from using or appearing to use confidential information acquired in the course of their work for unethical or illegal advantage either personally or through a third party.

III. Integrity

Management accountants have a responsibility to:

1. Avoid actual or apparent conflicts of interest and advise all appropriate parties of any potential conflict.
2. Refrain from engaging in any activity that would prejudice their abilities to carry out their duties ethically.
3. Refuse any gift, favor, or hospitality that would influence their actions.
4. Refrain from either actively or passively subverting the attainment of the organization's legitimate and ethical objectives.
5. Recognize and communicate professional limitations or other constraints that would preclude responsible judgment or successful performance of an activity.
6. Communicate unfavorable as well as favorable information and professional judgments or opinions.
7. Refrain from engaging in or supporting any activity that would discredit the profession.

IV. Objectivity

Management accountants have a responsibility to:

1. Communicate information fairly and objectively.
2. Disclose fully all relevant information that could reasonably be expected to influence an intended user's understanding of the reports, comments, and recommendations presented.

Resolution of Ethical Conflict

In applying the standards of ethical conduct, management accountants may encounter problems in identifying unethical behavior or in resolving ethical conflict. When faced with significant ethical issues, management accountants should follow the established policies of the organization bearing on the resolution of such conflict. If these policies do not resolve the ethical conflict, management accountants should consider the following courses of action:

1. Discuss such problems with the immediate supervisor except when it appears that the superior is involved, in which case the problem should be presented initially to the next higher management level. If satisfactory resolution cannot be achieved when the problem is initially presented, submit the issues to the next higher management level.
2. If the immediate superior is the chief executive officer, or equivalent, the acceptable reviewing authority may be a group such as the audit committee, executive committee, board of directors, board of trustees, or owners. Contact with levels above the immediate superior should be initiated only with the superior's knowledge, assuming the superior is not involved.
3. Clarify relevant concepts by confidential discussion with an objective advisor to obtain an understanding of possible courses of action.
4. If the ethical conflict still exists after exhausting all levels of internal review, the management accountant may have no other recourse on significant matters than to resign from the organization and to submit an informative memorandum to an appropriate representative of the organization.
5. Except where legally prescribed, communication of such problems to authorities or individuals not employed or engaged by the organization is not considered appropriate.

Public Accounting, and a Certificate in Internal Auditing. Each certification offers particular advantages to a cost or management accountant. In each case, an applicant must meet specific educational and experience requirements and pass a qualifying examination to become certified. Thus, all three certifications offer evidence that the holder has achieved a minimum level of professional competence. Furthermore, all three certifications require the holder to engage in continuing professional education in order to maintain certification. Because certification reveals a commitment to professional competency, most organizations encourage their management accountants to be certified.

The Certificate in Management Accounting

In 1974, the Institute of Management Accountants (IMA) developed the Certificate in Management Accounting to meet the specific needs of management accountants. A **Certified Management Accountant (CMA)** has passed a rigorous qualifying examination, has met an experience requirement, and participates in continuing education.

One of the key requirements for obtaining the CMA certificate or designation is passing a qualifying examination. Four areas are emphasized: (1) economics, finance, and management; (2) financial accounting and reporting; (3) management reporting, analysis, and behavioral issues; and (4) decision analysis and information systems. The parts to the examination reflect the needs of management accounting and underscore the earlier observation that management accounting has more of an interdisciplinary flavor than other areas of accounting.

One of the main purposes of creating the CMA program was to establish management accounting as a recognized, professional discipline, separate from the profession of public accounting. Since its inception, the CMA program has been very successful. Many firms now sponsor and pay for classes that prepare their management accountants for the qualifying examination, as well as provide other financial incentives to encourage acquisition of the CMA certificate.

The Certificate in Public Accounting

The Certificate in Public Accounting is the oldest certification in accounting. Unlike the CMA designation, the purpose of the Certificate in Public Accounting is to provide evidence of a minimal professional qualification for external auditors. The responsibility of external auditors is to provide assurance concerning the reliability of the information contained in a firm's financial statements. Only **Certified Public Accountants (CPAs)** are permitted (by law) to serve as external auditors. CPAs must pass a national examination and be licensed by the state in which they practice. Although the Certificate in Public Accounting does not have a management accounting orientation, many management accountants hold it.

The Certificate in Internal Auditing

Another certification available to internal accountants is the Certificate in Internal Auditing. The forces that led to the creation of this certification in 1974 are similar to those that resulted in the CMA program. As an important part of the company's control environment, internal auditors evaluate and appraise various activities within the company. While internal auditors are independent of the departments being audited, they do report to the top management of the company. Since internal auditing differs from both external auditing and management accounting, many internal auditors felt a need for a specialized certification. To attain the status of a **Certified Internal Auditor (CIA)**, an individual must pass a comprehensive examination designed to ensure technical competence and have two years' work experience.

SUMMARY

Managers use accounting information to identify problems, solve problems, and evaluate performance. Essentially, accounting information helps managers carry out their roles of planning, controlling, and decision making. Planning is the detailed formulation of action to achieve a particular end. Controlling is the monitoring of a plan's implementation. Decision making is choosing among competing alternatives.

Management accounting differs from financial accounting primarily in its targeted users. Management accounting information is intended for internal users, whereas financial accounting information is directed toward external users. Management accounting is not bound by the externally imposed rules of financial reporting. It provides more detail than financial accounting, and it tends to be broader and multidisciplinary.

Management accountants are responsible for identifying, collecting, measuring, analyzing, preparing, interpreting, and communicating information used by management to achieve the basic objectives of the organization. Management accountants need to be sensitive to the information needs of managers. Management accountants serve as staff members of the organization and are responsible for providing information; they are usually intimately involved in the management process as valued members of the management team.

Changes in the manufacturing environment brought about by global competition, the advanced manufacturing environment, customer focus, total quality management, time as a competitive factor, and efficiency are having a significant effect on the management accounting environment. Many traditional management accounting practices will be altered because of the revolution taking place among many manufacturing firms. Deregulation and growth in the service sector of our economy are also increasing the demand for management accounting practices.

Management accounting aids managers in their efforts to improve the economic performance of the firm. Unfortunately, some managers have overemphasized the economic dimension and have engaged in unethical and illegal actions. Many of these actions have relied on the management accounting system to bring about and even support that unethical behavior. To emphasize the importance of the ever-present constraint of ethical behavior on profit-maximizing behavior, this text presents ethical issues in many of the problems appearing at the end of each chapter.

Three certifications are available to internal accountants: the CMA, the CPA, and the CIA certificates. The CMA certificate is designed especially for management accountants. The prestige of the CMA certificate or designation has increased significantly over the years and is now well regarded by the industrial world. The CPA certificate is primarily intended for those practicing public accounting; however, this certification is also highly regarded and is held by many management accountants. The CIA certificate serves internal auditors and is also well respected.

KEY TERMS

Activity-based management 8

Business ethics 15

Certified Internal Auditor (CIA) 18

Certified Management Accountant (CMA) 18

Certified Public Accountant (CPA) 18

Continuous improvement 14

Controller 13

Controlling 14

Cost accounting 4

QUESTIONS FOR WRITING AND DISCUSSION

1. What is cost management, and how does it differ from management accounting and cost accounting?
2. How do cost management and financial accounting differ?
3. Identify and discuss the factors that are affecting the focus and practice of cost management.
4. What is a flexible manufacturing system?
5. What is the role of the controller in an organization? Describe some of the activities over which he or she has control.
6. What is the difference between a line position and a staff position?
7. The controller should be a member of the top management staff. Do you agree or disagree with this statement? Explain.
8. Describe the connection among planning, controlling, and feedback.
9. What is the role of cost management with respect to the objective of continuous improvement?
10. What role do performance reports play with respect to the control function?
11. What is business ethics? Is it possible to teach ethical behavior in a management accounting course?
12. Firms with higher ethical standards will experience a higher level of economic performance than firms with lower or poor ethical standards. Do you agree? Why or why not?
13. Review the code of ethical conduct for management accountants. Do you believe that the code will have an effect on the ethical behavior of management accountants? Explain.
14. Identify the three forms of accounting certification. Which form of certification do you believe is best for a management accountant? Why?
15. What are the four parts to the CMA examination? What do they indicate about cost and management accounting versus financial accounting?

EXERCISES

1-1   FINANCIAL ACCOUNTING AND COST MANAGEMENT

LO1   Classify each of the following actions as either being associated with the financial accounting information system (FS) or the cost management information system (CMS):

a. Determining the future cash flows of a proposed flexible manufacturing system
b. Filing reports with the SEC
c. Determining the cost of a customer
d. Issuing a voluntary annual report on environmental costs and issues
e. Reducing costs by eliminating activities that do not add value
f. Preparing a performance report that compares actual costs with budgeted costs
g. Preparing financial statements that conform to GAAP
h. Determining the cost of a supplier
i. Using cost information to decide whether to accept or reject a special order
j. Reporting a large contingent liability to current and potential shareholders
k. Using future expected earnings to estimate the risk of investing in a public company
l. Preparing a performance report that compares budgeted costs with actual costs

1-2 CUSTOMER ORIENTATION, QUALITY, TIME-BASED COMPETITION

LO2 Byers Electronics produces hand-held calculators. Three of the major electronic components are produced internally (components 2X334K, 5Y227M, and 8Z555L). There is a separate department in the plant for each component. The three manufactured components and other parts are assembled (by the assembly department) and then tested (by the testing department). Any units that fail the test are sent to the rework department where the unit is taken apart and the failed component is replaced. Data from the testing department reveal that component 2X334K is the most frequent cause of calculator failure. One out of every 100 calculators fails because of a faulty 2X334K component.

Recently, Milton Lawson was hired to manage the 2X334K department. The plant manager told Milton that he needed to be more sensitive to the needs of the department's customers. This charge puzzled Milton somewhat—after all, the component is not sold to anyone but is used in producing the plant's calculators.

Required:
1. Explain to Milton who his "customers" are.
2. Discuss how Milton can be sensitive to his customers. Explain also how this increased sensitivity could improve the company's time-based competitive ability.
3. What role would cost management play in helping Milton be more sensitive to his customers?

1-3 CUSTOMER ORIENTATION

LO2 A number of mail-order computer and software companies have set up customer service telephone lines. Some are toll-free. Some are not. A customer can wait on hold anywhere from three seconds to 20 minutes.

Required:

Evaluate all of the costs that these companies might consider when setting up the customer service lines. (*Hint:* Should you consider costs to the customer?)

1-4 ETHICAL BEHAVIOR

LO3, LO4, LO6 Consider the following thoughts of a manager at the end of the company's third quarter:

If I can increase my reported profit by $2 million, the actual earnings per share will exceed analysts' expectations, and stock prices will increase, and the stock options that I am holding will become more valuable. The extra income will also make me eligible to receive a significant bonus. With a son headed to college, it would be good if I could cash in some of these options to help pay his expenses. However, my vice president of finance indicates that such an increase is unlikely. The projected profit for the fourth quarter will just about meet the expected earnings per share. There may be ways, though, that I can achieve the desired outcome. First, I can instruct all divisional managers that their preventive maintenance budgets are reduced by 25 percent for the fourth quarter. That should reduce maintenance expenses by approximately $1 million. Second, I can increase the estimated life of the existing equipment, producing a reduction of depreciation by another $500,000. Third, I can reduce the salary increases for those being promoted by 50 percent. And that should easily put us over the needed increase of $2 million.

Required:

Comment on the ethical content of the earnings management being considered by the manager. Is there an ethical dilemma? What is the right choice for the manager to make? Is there any way to redesign the accounting reporting system to discourage the type of behavior the manager is contemplating?

1-5 BEHAVIORAL IMPACT OF COST INFORMATION

LO4 Bill Christensen, the production manager, was grumbling about the new quality cost system the plant controller wanted to put into place. "If we start trying to track every bit of spoiled material, we'll never get any work done. Everybody knows when they ruin something. Why bother to keep track? This is a waste of time. Besides, this isn't the first time scrap reduction has been emphasized. You tell my workers to reduce scrap, and I'll guarantee it will go away, but not in the way you would like."

Required:

1. Why do you suppose that the controller wants a written record of spoiled material? If "everybody knows" what the spoilage rate is, what benefits can come from keeping a written record?
2. Now consider Bill Christensen's position. In what way(s) could he be correct? What did he mean by his remark concerning scrap reduction? Can this be avoided? Explain.

1-6 MANAGERIAL USES OF ACCOUNTING INFORMATION

LO5 Each of the following scenarios requires the use of accounting information to carry out one or more of the following managerial activities: (1) planning, (2) control and evaluation, (3) continuous improvement, or (4) decision making.

a. **MANAGER:** At the last board meeting, we established an objective of earning a 25 percent return on sales. I need to know how many units of our product we need to sell to meet this objective. Once I have estimated sales in units, we then need to outline a promotional campaign that will take us where we want to be. However, to compute the targeted sales in units, I need to know the unit sales price and the associated production and support costs.

b. **MANAGER:** We have a number of errors in our order entry process. Incorrect serial number of the system on the order entry, duplicate orders, and incorrect sales representative codes are examples. To improve the order entry process and reduce errors, we can improve communication, provide better training for sales representatives, and develop a computer program to check for prices and duplication of orders. Reducing errors will not only decrease costs, but will also increase sales as customer satisfaction increases.

c. **MANAGER:** This report indicates that we have spent 35 percent more on rework than originally planned. An investigation into the cause has revealed the problem. We have a large number of new employees who lack proper training on our production techniques. Thus, more defects were produced than expected, causing a higher than normal rework requirement. By providing the required training, we can eliminate the excess usage.

d. **MANAGER:** Our bank must decide whether the addition of fee-based products is in our best interest or not. We must determine the expected revenues and costs of producing the new products. We also need to know how much it will cost us to upgrade our information system and train our new employees in cross-selling tactics.

e. **MANAGER:** This cruise needs to make more money. I would like to know how much our profits would be if we reduce our variable costs by $10 per passenger while maintaining our current passenger volume. Also marketing claims that if we increase advertising expenditures by $500,000 and cut fares by 20 percent, we can increase the number of passengers by 30 percent. I would like to know which approach offers the most profit, or if a combination of the approaches may be best.

f. **MANAGER:** We are forming manufacturing cells for each major product, and we are automating our die-making process. I would like to know if the number of defects drops and if cycle time actually decreases as a result. Furthermore, do these changes reduce our production costs? I also want to know the cost of resources before and after the proposed changes to see if cost improvement is taking place.

g. **MANAGER:** We are considering the possibility of outsourcing our legal services. I need to know the types of services provided by our internal staff for the past five years. I want an accurate assessment of the cost per hour for each type of service that has been performed. Once I have an idea of the internal cost then I can compare our cost with the hourly billing rates of external law firms.

h. **MANAGER:** My engineers have said that by redesigning our two main production processes, we can reduce setup time by 90 percent. This would produce savings of nearly $200,000 per setup. They have also indicated that some additional minor modifications in the designs of our three main products would reduce our materials waste by 12 percent, saving nearly $70,000 per month.

Required:
1. Describe each of the four managerial responsibilities.
2. Identify the managerial activity or activities applicable for each scenario, and indicate the role of accounting information in the activity.

1-7 LINE VERSUS STAFF

LO5 The job responsibilities of three employees of Ruido Speakers, Inc., are described as follows:

Kaylin Hepworth, production manager, is responsible for production of the plastic casing in which the speaker components are placed. She supervises the line workers, helps develop the production schedule, and is responsible for meeting the production budget. She also takes an active role in reducing production costs.

Joseph Henson, plant manager, supervises all personnel in the plant. Kaylin and other production managers report directly to Joseph. Joseph is in charge of all that takes place in the plant, including production, logistics, personnel, and accounting. He helps develop the plant's production budgets and is responsible for controlling plant costs.

Leo Tidwell, plant controller, is responsible for all of the accounting functions within the plant. He supervises three cost accounting managers and four staff accountants. He is responsible for preparing all cost of production reports. For example, he prepares periodic performance reports that compare actual costs with budgeted costs. He helps explain and interpret the reports and provides advice to the plant manager on how to control costs.

Required:

Identify Kaylin, Joseph, and Leo as line or staff, and explain your reasons.

PROBLEMS

1-8   FINANCIAL ACCOUNTING VERSUS COST MANAGEMENT

LO1   Lily Shultz is a junior majoring in hotel and restaurant management. She wants to work for a large hotel chain with the goal of eventually managing a hotel. She is considering the possibility of taking a course in either financial accounting or cost management. Before choosing, however, she has asked you to provide her with some information about the advantages that each course offers.

Required:

Prepare a letter advising Lily about the differences and similarities between financial accounting and cost management. Describe the advantages each might offer the manager of a hotel.

1-9   ETHICAL ISSUES

LO6   John Biggs and Patty Jorgenson are both cost accounting managers for a manufacturing division. During lunch yesterday, Patty told John that she was planning on quitting her job in three months because she had accepted a position as controller of a small company in a neighboring state. The starting date was timed to coincide with the retirement of the current controller. Patty was excited because it allowed her to live near her family. Today, the divisional controller took John to lunch and informed him that he was taking a position at headquarters and that he had recommended that Patty be promoted to his position. He indicated to John that it was a close call between him and Patty and that he wanted to let John know personally about the decision before it was announced officially.

Required:

What should John do? Describe how you would deal with his ethical dilemma (considering the IMA code of ethics in your response).

1-10   ETHICAL ISSUES

LO6   Emily Henson, controller of an oil exploration division, has just been approached by Tim Wilson, the divisional manager. Tim told Emily that the projected quarterly profits were unacceptable and that expenses need to be reduced. He suggested that a clean and easy way to reduce expenses is to assign the exploration and drilling costs of four dry holes to those of two successful holes. By doing so, the costs could be capitalized and not expensed, reducing the costs that need to be recognized for the quarter. He further argued that the treatment is reasonable because the exploration and drilling all occurred in the same field; thus, the unsuccessful efforts really were the costs of identifying the successful holes. "Besides," he argued, "even if the treatment is wrong, it can be corrected in the annual financial statements. Next quarter's revenues will be more and can absorb any reversal without causing any severe damage to that quarter's profits. It's this quarter's profits that need some help."

Emily was uncomfortable with the request because generally accepted accounting principles do not sanction the type of accounting measures proposed by Tim.

Required:

1. Using the code of ethics for management accountants, recommend the approach that Emily should take.
2. Suppose Tim insists that his suggested accounting treatment be implemented. What should Emily do?

1-11   ETHICAL ISSUES

LO6

CMA

Silverado, Inc., is a closely held brokerage firm that has been very successful over the past five years, consistently providing most members of the top management group with 50 percent bonuses. In addition, both the chief financial officer and the chief executive officer have received 100 percent bonuses. Silverado expects this trend to continue.

Recently, the top management group of Silverado, which holds 40 percent of the outstanding shares of common stock, has learned that a major corporation is interested in acquiring Silverado. Silverado's management is concerned that this corporation may make an attractive offer to the other shareholders and that management would be unable to prevent the takeover. If the acquisition occurs, this executive group is uncertain about continued employment in the new corporate structure. As a consequence, the management group is considering changes to several accounting policies and practices that, although not in accordance with generally accepted accounting principles, would make the company a less attractive acquisition. Management has told Larry Stewart, Silverado's controller, to implement some of these changes. Stewart has also been informed that Silverado's management does not intend to disclose these changes at once to anyone outside the immediate top management group.

Required:

Using the code of ethics for management accountants, evaluate the changes that Silverado's management is considering, and discuss the specific steps that Larry Stewart should take to resolve the situation. *(CMA adapted)*

1-12   ETHICAL ISSUES

LO6

CMA

Emery Manufacturing Company produces component parts for the farm equipment industry and has recently undergone a major computer system conversion. Jake Murray, the controller, has established a trouble-shooting team to alleviate accounting problems that have occurred since the conversion. Jake has chosen Gus Swanson, assistant controller, to head the team that will include Linda Wheeler, cost accountant; Cindy Madsen, financial analyst; Randy Lewis, general accounting supervisor; and Max Crandall, financial accountant.

The team has been meeting weekly for the last month. Gus insists on being part of all the team conversations in order to gather information, to make the final decision on any ideas or actions that the team develops, and to prepare a weekly report for Jake. He has also used this team as a forum to discuss issues and disputes about him and other members of Emery's top management team. At last week's meeting, Gus told the team that he thought a competitor might purchase the common stock of Emery, because he had overheard Jake talking about this on the telephone. As a result, most of Emery's employees now informally discuss the sale of Emery's common stock and how it will affect their jobs.

Required:

Is Gus Swanson's discussion with the team about the prospective sale of Emery unethical? Discuss, citing specific standards from the code of ethical conduct to support your position. *(CMA adapted)*

1-13   ETHICAL ISSUES

LO6

CMA

The external auditors for Heart Health Procedures (HHP) are currently performing the annual audit of HHP's financial statements. As part of the audit, the external auditors have prepared a representation letter to be signed by HHP's chief executive officer (CEO) and chief financial officer (CFO). The letter provides, among other items, a representation that appropriate provisions have been made for:

> *Reductions of any excess or obsolete inventories to net realizable values, and Losses from any purchase commitments for inventory quantities in excess of requirements or at prices in excess of market.*

HHP began operations by developing a unique balloon process to open obstructed arteries to the heart. In the last several years, HHP's market share has grown significantly because its major competitor was forced by the Food and Drug Administration (FDA) to cease its balloon operations. HHP purchases the balloon's primary and most expensive component from a sole supplier. Two years ago, HHP entered into a 5-year contract with this supplier at the then current price, with inflation escalators built into each of the five years. The long-term contract was deemed necessary to ensure adequate supplies and discourage new competition. However, during the past year, HHP's major competitor developed a technically superior product, which utilizes an innovative, less costly component. This new product was recently approved by the FDA and has been introduced to the medical community, receiving high acceptance. It is expected that HHP's market share, which has already seen softness, will experience a large decline and that the primary component used in the HHP balloon will decrease in price as a result of the competitor's use of its recently developed superior, cheaper component. The new component has been licensed by the major competitor to several outside supply sources to maintain available quantity and price competitiveness. At this time, HHP is investigating the purchase of this new component.

HHP's officers are on a bonus plan that is tied to overall corporate profits. Jim Honig, vice president of manufacturing, is responsible for both manufacturing and warehousing. During the course of the audit, he advised the CEO and CFO that he was not aware of any obsolete inventory nor any inventory or purchase commitments where current or expected prices were significantly below acquisition or commitment prices. Jim took this position even though Marian Nevins, assistant controller, had apprised him of both the existing excess inventory attributable to the declining market share and the significant loss associated with the remaining years of the 5-year purchase commitment.

Marian has brought this situation to the attention of her superior, the controller, who also participates in the bonus plan and reports directly to the CFO. Marian worked closely with the external audit staff and subsequently ascertained that the external audit manager was unaware of the inventory and purchase commitment problems. Marian is concerned about the situation and is not sure how to handle the matter.

Required:

1. Assuming that the controller did not apprise the CEO and CFO of the situation, explain the ethical considerations of the controller's apparent lack of action by discussing specific provisions of the Standards of Ethical Conduct for Management Accountants.
2. Assuming Marian Nevins believes the controller has acted unethically and not apprised the CEO and CFO of the findings, describe the steps that she should take to resolve the situation. Refer to the Standards of Ethical Conduct for Management Accountants in your answer.
3. Describe actions that HHP can take to improve the ethical situation within the company. *(CMA adapted)*

1-14 COLLABORATIVE LEARNING EXERCISE

LO6 In the 1400s, Europeans valued the gold, gems, drugs, and spices that came from the Orient. However, these goods were very costly, since they could be transported to Europe only via long overland caravans. Portuguese sailors tried to reach the Orient by sea—around Africa. Christopher Columbus felt that a shorter, easier route lay to the west. He offered Queen Isabella of Spain a business proposition: financing for three completely outfitted ships, honors, titles, and a percentage of the trade in exchange for opening up a direct route to the Indies and establishing a city devoted to trade. King John II of Portugal had previously turned down his offer, but Queen Isabella accepted. On August 3, 1492, the Nina, Pinta, and Santa Maria set sail from Palos, Spain.

Required:

Form a cooperative learning group (typically a group of four or five). Using a single piece of paper and a pen, record the ideas/responses of each member of the group to the following two items:

1. Suppose a communication device had existed in 1492 that permitted Isabella to talk with Columbus for 15 minutes once each month during the 8-month voyage. What types of accounting information would she have wanted to obtain regarding the success of the enterprise? Write down a list of the questions she might have asked (each group member in turn should come up with a question).
2. Classify each question as a financial accounting (F) or cost management (CM) type of question. Do the questions change as the months progress? (*Hint:* A little reading up on Columbus in an encyclopedia will make the role playing in this problem easier.)

1-15 CYBER RESEARCH CASE

LO7 ### Research Assignment

Many other certifications are available to accountants other than the three described in the chapter. Using Internet resources, select three of these additional certifications and write a memo for each describing them. In describing the certifications, answer the following questions: What are the relative advantages of each certification for the internal accountant? What are the stated purposes for certification? Indicate when an accountant might wish to obtain each one. (*Hint:* Try http://www.taxsites.com/certification.html.)

CHAPTER 2

Basic Cost Management Concepts

AFTER STUDYING THIS CHAPTER, YOU SHOULD BE ABLE TO:

1. Describe a cost management information system, its objectives, and its major subsystems, and indicate how it relates to other operating and information systems.

2. Explain the cost assignment process.

3. Define tangible and intangible products, and explain why there are different product cost definitions.

4. Prepare income statements for manufacturing and service organizations.

5. Explain the differences between traditional and contemporary cost management systems.

The study of cost accounting and cost management requires an understanding of fundamental cost concepts, terms, and the associated information systems that produce them. We need a basic framework to help us make sense of the variety of topics that appear in the field of cost accounting and cost management. A systems perspective provides a useful framework for achieving this objective. But what is an *information system*? Are there different systems for different purposes? Similarly, what is meant by *cost*? Are there different costs for different purposes? This chapter addresses these basic questions and provides the necessary foundation for the study of the rest of the text. In providing this foundation, we make no attempt to be exhaustive in our coverage of different systems and costs. Other system and cost concepts will be discussed in later chapters. However, a thorough understanding of the concepts presented in this chapter is essential for success with later chapters.

A Systems Framework

A **system** is a set of interrelated parts that performs one or more processes to accomplish specific objectives. Consider a home air-conditioning system. This system has a number of interrelated parts such as the compressor, the fan, the thermostat, and the duct work. The most obvious process (or series of actions designed to accomplish an objective) is the cooling of air; another is the delivery of cooled air to various rooms in the house. The primary objective of the system is to provide a comfortable, cool environment for people in the house. Notice that each part of the system is critical for achievement of the overall objective. For example, if the duct system were missing, the air conditioner would not be able to cool the house even if the other parts were present and functional.

But how does a system work? A system uses processes to transform inputs into outputs that satisfy the system's objectives. Consider the cooling process. This process requires inputs such as warm air, freon, and electricity. The inputs are transformed into cooled air, an output of the cooling process. The output of the process, cooled air, is obviously critical to achieving the overall objective of the system. The cooled air and energy become inputs to the delivery process. This process transforms the inputs so that a portion of the total cooled air is delivered to each room of the house (the output is delivered air). In this way, all rooms are cooled to the desired temperature, thereby achieving the system's objective. The operational model for the air-conditioning system is shown in Exhibit 2-1.

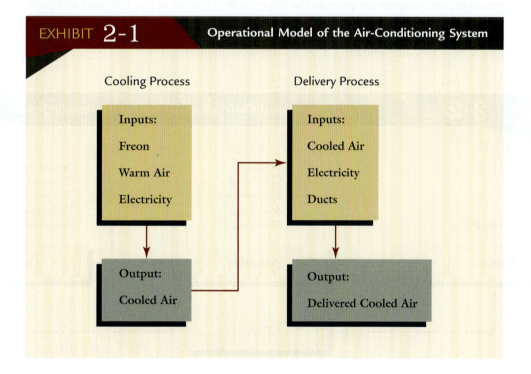

EXHIBIT 2-1   Operational Model of the Air-Conditioning System

Accounting Information Systems

An information system is designed to provide information to people in the company who might need it. For example, the human resource (HR) information system and materials requirements planning (MRP) system are both information systems. The HR system tracks people as they are hired. It includes data on date of hire, entry-level title and salary/wages, and any information needed for determining employee benefits. The MRP is a computerized system that keeps track of all raw materials used in manufacturing.

An **accounting information system** is one that consists of interrelated manual and computer parts and uses processes such as collecting, recording, summarizing, analyzing, and managing data to provide information to users. Like any system, an accounting information system has objectives, interrelated parts, processes, and outputs. The overall objective of an accounting information system is to provide information to users. The interrelated parts include order entry and sales, billing accounts receivable and cash receipts, inventory, general ledger, and cost accounting. Each of these interrelated parts is itself a system and is therefore referred to as a *subsystem* of the accounting information system. Processes include such things as collecting, recording, summarizing, and managing data. Some processes may also be formal decision models—models that use inputs and provide recommended decisions as the information output. The outputs are data and reports that provide needed information for users.

Two key features of the accounting information system distinguish it from other information systems. First, inputs for an accounting information system are usually economic events. Second, the operational model of an accounting information system is critically involved with the user of information, since the output of the information system produces user actions. In some cases, the output may serve as the basis for action. This is particularly true for tactical and strategic decisions but less true for day-to-day decisions. In other cases, the output may serve to confirm that the actions taken had the intended effects.[1] Another possible user action is feedback, which becomes an input for subsequent operational system performance. The operational model for an accounting information system is illustrated in Exhibit 2-2. Examples of the inputs, processes, and outputs are provided in the exhibit. (The list is not intended to be exhaustive.) Notice that personal communication is an information output. Often, users may not wish to wait for formal reports and can obtain needed information on a more timely basis by communicating directly with accountants.

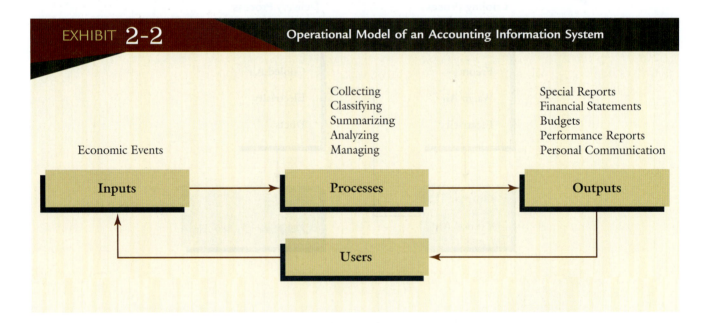

EXHIBIT 2-2   Operational Model of an Accounting Information System

Economic Events | Collecting / Classifying / Summarizing / Analyzing / Managing | Special Reports / Financial Statements / Budgets / Performance Reports / Personal Communication

Inputs → Processes → Outputs → Users → (feedback to Inputs)

---

1. This role of information is described in William J. Bruns, Jr., and Sharon M. McKinnon, "Information and Managers: A Field Study," *Journal of Management Accounting Research* 5 (Fall 1993): 86–108. The paper reports on a field study of how managers use accounting information. The authors point out that formal information output does not seem to be used for day-to-day decisions. Managers often use interpersonal relationships to acquire information for daily use. Apparently, accessing information through informal channels provides more timely information than the formal information system.

The accounting information system can be divided into two major subsystems: (1) the *financial accounting information system* and (2) the *cost management information system*. We will emphasize the second, although it should be noted that the two systems need not be independent.[2] Ideally, the two systems should be integrated and have linked databases. Output of each of the two systems can be used as input for the other system.

Financial Accounting Information System

The financial accounting information system is primarily concerned with producing outputs for *external* users. It uses well-specified economic events as inputs, and its processes follow certain rules and conventions. For financial accounting, the nature of the inputs and the rules and conventions governing processes are defined by the Securities and Exchange Commission (SEC) and the Financial Accounting Standards Board (FASB). Among its outputs are financial statements such as the balance sheet, income statement, and statement of cash flows for external users (investors, creditors, government agencies, and other outside users). Financial accounting information is used for investment decisions, stewardship evaluation, activity monitoring, and regulatory measures.

The Cost Management Information System

The cost management information system is primarily concerned with producing outputs for *internal* users using inputs and processes needed to satisfy management objectives. The cost management information system is not bound by externally imposed criteria that define inputs and processes. Instead, the criteria that govern the inputs and processes are set by people in the company. The cost management information system has three broad objectives that provide information for:

1. Costing out services, products, and other objects of interest to management
2. Planning and control
3. Decision making

The information requirements for satisfying the first objective depend on the nature of the object being costed and the reason management wants to know the cost. For example, product costs calculated in accordance with GAAP are needed to value inventories for the balance sheet and to calculate the cost of goods sold expense on the income statement. These product costs include the cost of materials, labor, and overhead. In other cases, managers may want to know all costs that are associated with a product for purposes of tactical and strategic profitability analysis. If so, then additional cost information may be needed concerning product design, development, marketing, and distribution. For example, pharmaceutical companies may want to associate research and development costs with individual drugs or drug families.

Cost information is also used for planning and control. It should help managers decide what should be done, why it should be done, how it should be done, and how well it is being done. For example, information about the *expected* revenues and costs for a new product could be used as an input for target costing. At this stage, the expected revenues and costs may cover the entire life of the new product. Thus, projected costs of design, development, testing, production, marketing, distribution, and servicing would be essential information.

Finally, cost information is a critical input for many managerial decisions. For example, a manager may need to decide whether to continue making a component internally

---

2. Much of the material from this point on in this section relies on information found in the following articles: Robert S. Kaplan, "The Four-Stage Model of Cost Systems Design," *Management Accounting* (February 1990): 22–26; Steven C. Schnoebelen, "Integrating an Advanced Cost Management System into Operating Systems (Part 1)," *Journal of Cost Management* (Winter 1993): 50–54; and Steven C. Schnoebelen, "Integrating an Advanced Cost Management System into Operating Systems (Part 2)," *Journal of Cost Management* (Spring 1993): 60–67.

or to buy it from an external supplier. In this case, the manager would need to know the cost of materials, labor, and other productive inputs associated with the manufacture of the component and which of these costs would vanish if the product were no longer produced. Also needed is information concerning the cost of purchasing the component, including any increase in cost for internal activities such as receiving and storing goods.

Relationship to Other Operational Systems and Functions

The cost information produced by the cost management information system must benefit the organization as a whole. Thus, a high-quality cost management system should have an organization-wide perspective. Managers in many different areas of a business require cost information. For example, an engineering manager must make strategic decisions concerning product design. Costs of production, marketing, and servicing can vary widely, depending on the design. Having reliable and accurate cost information about different designs is clearly critical for sound decision making. To provide this cost information, the cost management system must not only interact with the design and development system but also with the production, marketing, and customer service systems. Cost information for tactical decision making is also important. For example, a sales manager needs reliable and accurate cost information when faced with a decision concerning an order that may be sold for less than the normal selling price. Such a sale may only be feasible if the production system is reporting idle capacity. In this case, a sound decision mandates interaction among the cost management system, the marketing and distribution system, and the production system. These two examples illustrate that the cost management system should have an organization-wide perspective and that it must be properly integrated with the nonfinancial functions and systems within an organization. In the past, little effort was made to integrate the cost management system with other operational systems. However, the current competitive environment dictates that companies pay much greater attention to cost management in all functional areas. Exhibit 2-3 illustrates the expected interactive relationships.

Exhibit 2-3 implies that the cost management system receives information from all operational systems and also supplies information to these systems. To the extent possible, the cost management system should be integrated with the organization's operational systems. Integration reduces redundant storage and use of data, improves the timeliness of information, and increases the efficiency of producing reliable and accurate information. One way of accomplishing this is to implement an enterprise resource planning (ERP) system. ERP systems strive to input data once and make it available to people across the company for whatever purpose it may serve. For example, a sales order entered into an ERP system is used by marketing to update customer records, by production to schedule the manufacture of the goods ordered, and by accounting to record the sale.

Different Systems for Different Purposes

The financial accounting and cost management systems show us that different systems exist to satisfy different purposes. As indicated, these two systems are subsystems of the accounting information system. The cost management information system also has two major subsystems: the *cost accounting information system* and the *operational control information system*. The objectives of these two subsystems correspond to the first and second objectives mentioned earlier for the cost management information system (the costing and control objectives). The output of these two cost systems satisfies the third objective (the decision-making objective).

The cost accounting information system is a cost management subsystem designed to assign costs to individual products and services and other objects as specified by management. For external financial reporting, the cost accounting system must as-

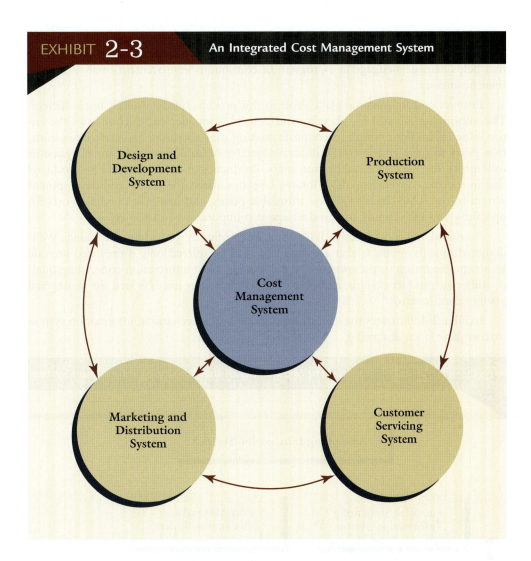

EXHIBIT 2-3   An Integrated Cost Management System

sign costs to products in order to value inventories and determine cost of sales. Furthermore, these assignments must conform to the rules and conventions set by the SEC and the FASB. These rules and conventions do not require that all costs assigned to individual products be causally related to the demands of individual products. Thus, using financial accounting principles to define product costs may lead to under- and overstatements of individual product costs. For reporting inventory values and cost of sales, this may not matter. Inventory values and cost of sales are reported in the aggregate, and the under- and overstatements may wash out to the extent that the values reported on the financial statements are reasonably accurate.

However, at the individual product level, distorted product costs can cause managers to make significant decision errors. For example, a manager might erroneously deemphasize and overprice a product that is, in reality, highly profitable. For decision making, accurate product costs are needed. If possible, the cost accounting system should produce product costs that simultaneously are accurate and satisfy financial reporting conventions. If not, then the cost system must produce two sets of product costs: one that satisfies financial reporting criteria and one that satisfies management decision-making needs.

The **operational control information system** is a cost management subsystem designed to provide accurate and timely feedback concerning the performance of managers and others relative to their planning and control of activities. Operational control is concerned with what activities should be performed and assessing how well they are performed. It focuses on identifying opportunities for improvement and helping to find ways to improve. A good operational control information system provides information that helps managers engage in a program of continuous improvement of all aspects of their businesses.

Product cost information plays a role in this process, but by itself, is not sufficient. The information needed for planning and control is broader and encompasses the entire value chain. For example, every profit making manufacturing and service organization exists to serve customers. Thus, one objective of an operational control system is to improve the value received by customers. Products and services should be produced that fit specific customer needs. (Observe how this affects the design and development system in the value chain.) Quality, affordable prices, and low post-purchase costs for operating and maintaining the product are also important to customers.

A second, related objective is to improve profits by providing this value. Well-designed, quality products that are affordable can be offered only if they also provide an acceptable return to the owners of the company. Cost information concerning quality, different product designs, and post-purchase customer needs is vital for managerial planning and control.[3]

Exhibit 2-4 illustrates the various subsystems of the accounting information system that we have been discussing.

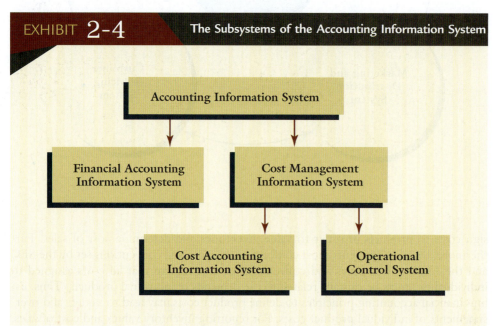

EXHIBIT 2-4 **The Subsystems of the Accounting Information System**

Accounting Information System

Financial Accounting Information System

Cost Management Information System

Cost Accounting Information System

Operational Control System

Cost Assignment: Direct Tracing, Driver Tracing, and Allocation

OBJECTIVE 2

Explain the cost assignment process.

To study cost accounting and operational control systems, it is necessary to understand the meaning of cost and to become familiar with the cost terminology associated with the two systems. One must also understand the process used to assign costs. Cost assignment is one of the key processes of the cost accounting system. Improving the cost

---

3. The two objectives—improving customer value and improving profits by providing this value—are discussed in more detail in the following article: Peter B. B. Turney, "Activity-Based Management," *Management Accounting* (January 1992): 20–25.

assignment process has been one of the major developments in the cost management field in recent years. Before discussing the cost assignment process, we first need to define what we mean by cost.

Cost is the cash or cash equivalent value sacrificed for goods and services that are expected to bring a current or future benefit to the organization. We say *cash equivalent* because noncash assets can be exchanged for the desired goods or services. For example, it may be possible to exchange equipment for materials used in production.

Costs are incurred to produce future benefits. In a profit making firm, future benefits usually mean revenues. As costs are used up in the production of revenues, they are said to expire. Expired costs are called expenses. In each period, expenses are deducted from revenues on the income statement to determine the period's profit. A loss is a cost that expires without producing any revenue benefit. For example, the cost of uninsured inventory destroyed by a flood would be classified as a loss on the income statement.

Many costs do not expire in a given period. These unexpired costs are classified as assets and appear on the balance sheet. Computers and factory buildings are examples of assets lasting more than one period. Note that the main difference between a cost being classified as an expense or as an asset is timing. This distinction is important and will be referred to in the development of other cost concepts later in the text.

Cost Objects

Management accounting systems are structured to measure and assign costs to cost objects. A cost object is any item, such as products, customers, departments, projects, activities, and so on, for which costs are measured and assigned. For example, if we want to determine what it costs to produce a bicycle, then the cost object is the bicycle. If we want to determine the cost of operating a maintenance department within a plant, then the cost object is the maintenance department. If we want to determine the cost of developing a new toy, then the cost object is the new toy development project. As a final example, activities should be mentioned. An activity is a basic unit of work performed within an organization. An activity can also be defined as an aggregation of actions within an organization useful to managers for purposes of planning, controlling, and decision making. In recent years, activities have emerged as important cost objects. Activities play a prominent role in assigning costs to other cost objects and are essential elements of an activity-based management accounting system. Examples of activities include setting up equipment for production, moving materials and goods, purchasing parts, billing customers, paying bills, maintaining equipment, expediting orders, designing products, and inspecting products. Notice that an activity is described by an action verb (e.g., paying and designing) and an object (e.g., bills and products) that receives the action. Notice also that the action verb and the object reveal very specific goals.

Accuracy of Assignments

Assigning costs *accurately* to cost objects is crucial. Our notion of accuracy is not evaluated based on knowledge of some underlying "true" cost. Rather, it is a relative concept and has to do with the reasonableness and logic of the cost assignment methods that are being used. The objective is to measure and assign as accurately as possible the cost of the resources used by a cost object. Some cost assignment methods are clearly more accurate than others. For example, suppose you want to determine the cost of lunch for Elaine Day, a student who frequents Hideaway, an off-campus pizza parlor. One cost assignment approach is to count the number of customers Hideaway has between 12:00 P.M. and 1:00 P.M. and then divide the total receipts earned by Hideaway during this period. Suppose that this divides out to $4.50 per lunchtime customer. Thus, based on this approach we would conclude that Elaine spends $4.50 per day for lunch. Another approach is to go with Elaine and observe how much she spends. Suppose that she has a slice of pizza and a medium drink each day, costing $2.50. It is not difficult to see which cost assignment is more accurate. The $4.50 cost assignment is distorted by the consumption patterns of other customers (cost objects). As it turns out, most lunchtime clients order the luncheon special for $4.99 (a mini-pizza, salad, and medium drink).

Distorted cost assignments can produce erroneous decisions and poor evaluations. For example, if a plant manager is trying to decide whether to continue producing power internally or to buy it from a local utility company, then an accurate assessment of how much it is costing to produce the power internally is fundamental to the analysis. If the cost of internal power production is overstated, the manager might decide to shut down the internal power department in favor of buying power from an outside company, whereas a more accurate cost assignment might suggest the opposite. It is easy to see that poor cost assignments can prove to be costly.

Traceability

The relationship of costs to cost objects can be exploited to help increase the accuracy of cost assignments. Costs are directly or indirectly associated with cost objects. **Indirect costs** are costs that cannot be traced easily and accurately to a cost object. **Direct costs** are those costs that can be traced easily and accurately to a cost object.[4] For costs to be traced easily means that the costs can be assigned in an economically feasible way. For costs to be traced accurately means that the costs are assigned using a *causal relationship*. Thus, **traceability** is simply the ability to assign a cost directly to a cost object in an economically feasible way by means of a causal relationship. The more costs that can be traced to the object, the greater the accuracy of the cost assignments. Establishing traceability is a key element in building accurate cost assignments. One additional point needs to be emphasized. Cost management systems typically deal with many cost objects. Thus, it is possible for a particular cost item to be classified as both a direct cost and an indirect cost. It all depends on *which* cost object is the point of reference. For example, if the plant is the cost object, then the cost of heating and cooling the plant is a direct cost; however, if the cost objects are products produced in the plant, then this utility cost is an indirect cost.

Methods of Tracing

Traceability means that costs can be assigned easily and accurately, using a causal relationship. Tracing costs to cost objects can occur in one of two ways: (1) *direct tracing* and (2) *driver tracing*. **Direct tracing** is the process of identifying and assigning costs to a cost object that are specifically or physically associated with the cost object. Identifying costs that are specifically associated with a cost object is most often accomplished by *physical observation*. For example, assume that the power department is the cost object. The salary of the power department's supervisor and the fuel used to produce power are examples of costs that can be specifically identified (by physical observation) with the cost object (the power department). As a second example, consider a pair of blue jeans. The materials (denim, zipper, buttons, and thread) and labor (to cut the denim according to the pattern and sew the pieces together) are physically observable; therefore, the costs of materials and labor can be directly charged to a pair of jeans. Ideally, all costs should be charged to cost objects using direct tracing.

Unfortunately, it is often not possible to physically observe the exact amount of resources being consumed by a cost object. The next best approach is to use cause-and-effect reasoning to identify factors—called *drivers*—that can be observed and which measure a cost object's resource consumption. **Drivers** are factors that *cause* changes in

---

4. This definition of direct costs is based on the glossary prepared by Computer Aided Manufacturing-International, Inc. (CAM-I). See Norm Raffish and Peter B. B. Turney, "Glossary of Activity-Based Management," *Journal of Cost Management* (Fall 1991): 53–63. Other terms defined in this chapter and in the text also follow the CAM-I glossary.

resource usage, activity usage, costs, and revenues. **Driver tracing** is the use of *drivers* to assign costs to cost objects. Although less precise than direct tracing, driver tracing is very accurate if the cause-and-effect relationship is sound. Consider the cost of electricity for the jeans manufacturing plant. The factory manager might want to know how much electricity is used to run the sewing machines. Physically observing how much electricity is used would require a meter to measure the power consumption of the sewing machines, which may not be practical. Thus, a driver such as "machine hours" could be used to assign the cost of electricity. If the electrical cost per machine hour is $0.50 and the sewing machines use 20,000 machine hours in a year, then $10,000 of the electricity cost ($0.50 $\times$ 20,000) would be assigned to the sewing activity. The use of drivers to assign costs to activities will be explained in more detail in Chapter 4.

Assigning Indirect Costs

Indirect costs cannot be traced to cost objects. This means that there is no causal relationship between the cost and the cost object, or that tracing is not economically feasible. Assignment of indirect costs to cost objects is called **allocation**. Since no causal relationship exists, allocating indirect costs is based on *convenience* or some *assumed* linkage. For example, consider the cost of heating and lighting a plant that manufactures five products. Suppose that this utility cost is to be assigned to the five products. Clearly, it is difficult to see any causal relationship. A convenient way to allocate this cost is simply to assign it in proportion to the direct labor hours used by each product. Arbitrarily allocating indirect costs to cost objects reduces the overall accuracy of the cost assignments. Accordingly, the best costing policy may be that of assigning only traceable direct costs to cost objects. However, it must be admitted that allocations of indirect costs may serve other purposes besides accuracy. For example, allocating indirect costs to products may be required for external reporting. Nonetheless, most managerial uses of cost assignments are better served by accuracy. At the very least, direct and indirect cost assignments should be reported separately.

Cost Assignment Summarized

The foregoing discussion reveals three methods of assigning costs to cost objects: direct tracing, driver tracing, and allocation. These methods are illustrated in Exhibit 2-5. Of the three methods, direct tracing is the most precise since it relies on physically observable causal relationships. Direct tracing is followed by driver tracing in terms of cost assignment accuracy. Driver tracing relies on causal factors called drivers to assign costs to cost objects. The precision of driver tracing depends on the strength of the causal relationship described by the driver. Identifying drivers and assessing the quality of the causal relationship is much more costly than either direct tracing or allocation. In fact, one advantage of allocation is that it is simple and inexpensive to implement. However, allocation is the least accurate cost assignment method, and its use should be avoided where possible. In many cases, the benefits of increased accuracy by driver tracing outweigh its additional measurement cost. This cost-benefit issue is discussed more fully later in the chapter. What the process really entails is choosing among competing cost management systems.

OBJECTIVE 3

Define tangible and intangible products, and explain why there are different product cost definitions.

Product and Service Costs

One of the most important cost objects is the output of organizations. The two types of output are tangible products and services. **Tangible products** are goods produced by converting raw materials through the use of labor and capital inputs such as plant, land, and machinery. Televisions, hamburgers, automobiles, computers, clothes, and furniture are examples of tangible products. **Services** are tasks or activities performed for a customer or an activity performed by a customer using an organization's products or facilities. Services are also produced using materials, labor, and capital inputs. Insurance coverage, medical care, dental care, funeral care, and accounting are examples of service

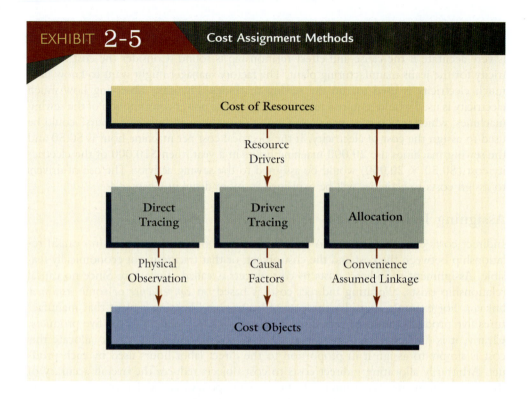

EXHIBIT 2-5   Cost Assignment Methods

activities performed for customers. Car rental, video rental, and skiing are examples of services where the customer uses an organization's products or facilities.

Services differ from tangible products on three important dimensions: intangibility, perishability, and inseparability. **Intangibility** means that buyers of services cannot see, feel, hear, or taste a service before it is bought. Thus, services are *intangible products.* **Perishability** means that services cannot be stored (there are a few unusual cases where tangible goods cannot be stored). Finally, **inseparability** means that producers of services and buyers of services must usually be in direct contact for an exchange to take place. In effect, services are often inseparable from their producers. For example, an eye examination requires both the patient and the optometrist to be present. However, producers of tangible products need not have direct contact with the buyers of their goods. Buyers of automobiles, for instance, never need to have contact with the engineers and assembly line workers who produce automobiles.

Organizations that produce tangible products are called *manufacturing* organizations. Those that produce intangible products are called *service* organizations. Managers of organizations that produce goods or services need to know how much individual products cost for a number of reasons, including profitability analysis and strategic decisions concerning product design, pricing, and product mix. For example, **Fleming Co.,** an Oklahoma City-based food distributor, notes that separating the cost of products from the cost of servicing the retail customer is a key part of its flexible marketing plan.[5] Individual product cost can refer to either a tangible or an intangible product. Thus, when we discuss product costs, we are referring to both intangible and tangible products.

Different Costs for Different Purposes

A fundamental cost management principle is "Different costs for different purposes." Thus, what a particular cost means depends on the managerial objective being served.

5. Glen A. Beres, "Fleming CEO Details Progress in Retooling," *Supermarket News* (September 18, 1995): 6, 62.

This principle should not be used as a justification for proliferation of product costing methods. Using more product costing methods than necessary can be confusing and could undermine the credibility of the cost management information system.[6]

Product cost definitions can differ according to the objective being served. Exhibit 2-6 provides three examples of product cost definitions and some of the objectives they satisfy. For pricing decisions, product mix decisions, and strategic profitability analysis, all traceable costs along the value chain need to be assigned to the product. (The value chain is discussed in detail in Chapter 11.) For strategic product design decisions and tactical profitability analysis, costs for production, marketing, and customer service (including customer post-purchase costs) are needed. For external financial reporting, FASB rules and conventions mandate that only production costs be used in calculating product costs. Other objectives may use still other product cost definitions.

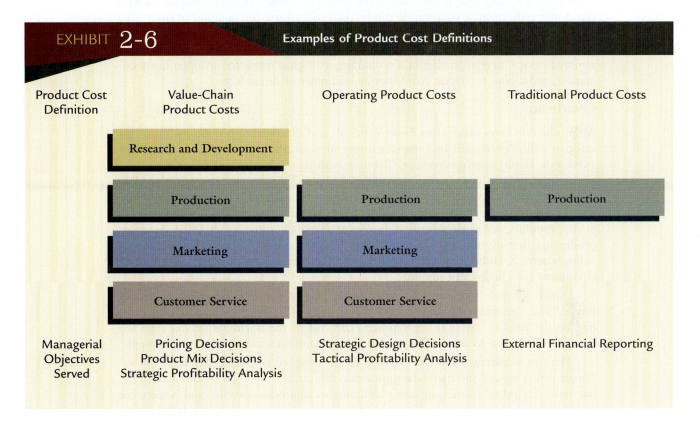

EXHIBIT 2-6   Examples of Product Cost Definitions

Product Cost Definition	Value-Chain Product Costs	Operating Product Costs	Traditional Product Costs
	Research and Development		
	Production	Production	Production
	Marketing	Marketing	
	Customer Service	Customer Service	
Managerial Objectives Served	Pricing Decisions Product Mix Decisions Strategic Profitability Analysis	Strategic Design Decisions Tactical Profitability Analysis	External Financial Reporting

Product Costs and External Financial Reporting

An important objective of a cost management system is the calculation of product costs for external financial reporting. For product costing purposes, externally imposed conventions require costs to be classified in terms of the special purposes, or functions, they serve. Costs are subdivided into two major functional categories: production and nonproduction. **Production (or product) costs** are those costs associated with the manufacture of goods or the provision of services. **Nonproduction costs** are those costs associated with the functions of selling and administration. For tangible goods, production and nonproduction costs are often referred to as *manufacturing costs* and *nonmanufacturing costs*, respectively. Production costs can be further classified as *direct materials*, *direct labor*, and *overhead*. Only these three cost elements can be assigned to products for external financial reporting.

6. For further discussion of this point, see Steven C. Schnoebelen, "Integrating an Advanced Cost Management System into Operating Systems (Part 2)," *Journal of Cost Management* (Spring 1993): 60–67.

Direct Materials

Direct materials are those materials traceable to the good or service being produced. The cost of these materials can be directly charged to products because physical observation can be used to measure the quantity consumed by each product. Materials that become part of a tangible product or those materials that are used in providing a service are usually classified as direct materials. For example, steel in an automobile, wood in furniture, alcohol in cologne, denim in jeans, braces for correcting teeth, surgical gauze and anesthesia for an operation, ribbon in a corsage, and food on an airline are all direct materials.

Direct Labor

Direct labor is labor that is traceable to the goods or services being produced. As with direct materials, physical observation can be used to measure the quantity of labor used to produce a product or service. Employees who convert raw materials into a product or who provide a service to customers are classified as direct labor. Workers on an assembly line at **Chrysler**, a chef in a restaurant, a surgical nurse for an open-heart operation, and a pilot for **Delta Air Lines** are examples of direct labor.

Overhead

All production costs other than direct materials and direct labor are lumped into one category called overhead. In a manufacturing firm, overhead is also known as *factory burden* or *manufacturing overhead*. The overhead cost category contains a wide variety of items. Many inputs other than direct labor and direct materials are needed to produce products. Examples include depreciation on buildings and equipment, maintenance, supplies, supervision, materials handling, power, property taxes, landscaping of factory grounds, and plant security. Supplies are generally those materials necessary for production that do not become part of the finished product or are not used in providing a service. Dishwasher detergent in a fast-food restaurant and oil for production equipment are examples of supplies.

Direct materials that form an insignificant part of the final product are usually lumped into the overhead category as a special kind of indirect material. This is justified on the basis of cost and convenience. The cost of the tracing is greater than the benefit of increased accuracy. The glue used in making furniture or toys is an example.

The cost of overtime for direct labor is usually assigned to overhead as well. The rationale is that typically no particular production run can be identified as the cause of the overtime. Accordingly, overtime cost is common to all production runs and is therefore an indirect manufacturing cost. Note that *only* the overtime cost itself is treated this way. If workers are paid an $8 regular rate and a $4 overtime premium, then only the $4 overtime premium is assigned to overhead. The $8 regular rate is still regarded as a direct labor cost. In certain cases, however, overtime is associated with a particular production run, such as a special order taken when production is at 100 percent capacity. In these special cases, it is appropriate to treat overtime premiums as a direct labor cost.

Nonproduction Costs

Nonproduction costs are divided into two categories: marketing (selling) costs and administrative costs. For external financial reporting, marketing and administrative costs are not inventoried and are called *period* costs. Period costs are expensed in the period in which they are incurred. Thus, none of these costs can be assigned to products or appear as part of the reported values of inventories on the balance sheet. In a manufacturing organization, the level of these costs can be significant (often greater than 25 percent of sales revenue), and controlling them may bring greater cost savings than the same control exercised in the area of production costs. For example, **General Motors** offers employee wellness and fitness classes to help lower its staggering $60 billion health care costs.[7] **Procter & Gamble**, on the other hand, spends enormous amounts on advertising in order to develop and dominate the market for shampoo and detergent in China. P&G buys more air time each month than even the most media-conscious Chinese companies spend in a year. Couple that with the cost of free samples and salaries for the thousands of Chinese who distribute them, we see that marketing expense in China is a significant portion of P&G's budget.[8] For service organizations, the relative importance of selling and administrative costs depends on the nature of the service being produced. Physicians and dentists, for example, generally do very little marketing and thus have very low selling costs. An airline, on the other hand, may incur substantial marketing costs.

Those costs necessary to market and distribute a product or service are **marketing (selling) costs**. They are often referred to as *order-getting* and *order-filling* costs. Examples of marketing costs include the following: salaries and commissions of sales personnel, advertising, warehousing, shipping, and customer service. The first two items are examples of order-getting costs; the last three are order-filling costs.

All costs associated with the general administration of the organization that cannot be reasonably assigned to either marketing or production are **administrative costs**. General administration has the responsibility of ensuring that the various activities of the organization are properly integrated so the overall mission of the firm is realized. The president of the firm, for example, is concerned with the efficiency of *both* marketing and production as they carry out their respective roles. Proper integration of these two functions is essential for maximizing the overall profits of a firm. Examples, then, of administrative costs are top-executive salaries, legal fees, the annual report printing, and general accounting. An important subset of administrative costs is research and development. These costs are also expensed in the period in which they are incurred.

Prime and Conversion Costs

The manufacturing and nonmanufacturing classifications give rise to some related cost concepts. The functional delineation between nonmanufacturing and manufacturing costs is essentially the basis for the concepts of noninventoriable costs and inventoriable costs—at least for purposes of external reporting. Combinations of different production costs also produce the concepts of conversion costs and prime costs.

Prime cost is the sum of direct materials cost and direct labor cost. **Conversion cost** is the sum of direct labor cost and overhead cost. For a manufacturing firm, conversion cost can be interpreted as the cost of converting raw materials into a final product.

Exhibit 2-7 illustrates the various types of production and nonproduction costs.

External Financial Statements

OBJECTIVE 4

Prepare income statements for manufacturing and service organizations.

The functional classification is the cost classification required for external reporting. In preparing an income statement, production and nonproduction costs are separated. The reason for the separation is that production costs are product costs—costs that are inventoried until the units are sold—and the nonproduction costs of marketing and administration are viewed as period costs. Thus, production costs attached to the units sold are recognized as an expense (cost of goods sold) on the income statement. Production costs attached to units that are not sold are reported as inventory on the balance sheet. Marketing and administrative expenses are viewed as costs of the period and must be deducted each and every period as expenses on the income statement. Nonproduction costs never appear on the balance sheet.

7. Ed Garston, "GM Health Care Bill Tops $60 Billion," *The Detroit News* (March 11, 2004), http://www.detnews.com/2004/autoinsider/0403/11/a01-88813.htm.
8. Joseph Kahn, "P&G Viewed China as a National Market and Is Conquering It," *The Wall Street Journal* (September 12, 1995): A1, A6.

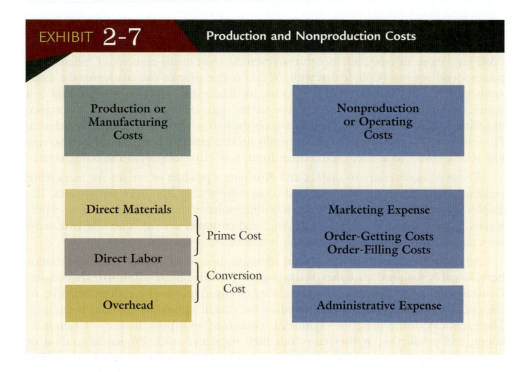

EXHIBIT **2-7** — Production and Nonproduction Costs

Income Statement: Manufacturing Firm

The income statement based on a functional classification for a manufacturing firm is displayed in Exhibit 2-8. This income statement follows the standard format taught in an introductory financial accounting course. Income computed by following a functional classification is frequently referred to as **absorption-costing income** or **full-costing income** because *all* manufacturing costs are fully assigned to the product.

EXHIBIT **2-8** — Income Statement: Manufacturing Organization

Manufacturing Organization
Income Statement
For the Year Ended December 31, 2007

Sales		$2,000,000
Less: Cost of goods sold		1,300,000
Gross margin		$ 700,000
Less operating expenses:		
Selling expenses	$300,000	
Administrative expenses	150,000	450,000
Operating income		$ 250,000

Under the absorption-costing approach, expenses are separated according to function and then deducted from revenues to arrive at operating income. As can be seen in Exhibit 2-9, the two major functional categories of expense are cost of goods sold and operating expenses. These categories correspond, respectively, to a firm's manufacturing and nonmanufacturing expenses. **Cost of goods sold** is the cost of direct materi-

---

EXHIBIT 2-9   Statement of Cost of Goods Manufactured

Statement of Cost of Goods Manufactured
For the Year Ended December 31, 2007

Direct materials:		
Beginning inventory	$200,000	
Add: Purchases	450,000	
Materials available	$650,000	
Less: Ending inventory	50,000	
Direct materials used in production		$ 600,000
Direct labor		350,000
Manufacturing overhead:		
Indirect labor	$122,500	
Depreciation on building	177,500	
Rental of equipment	50,000	
Utilities	37,500	
Property taxes	12,500	
Maintenance	50,000	450,000
Total manufacturing costs added		$1,400,000
Add: Beginning work in process		200,000
Less: Ending work in process		400,000
Cost of goods manufactured		$1,200,000

als, direct labor, and overhead attached to the units sold. To compute the cost of goods sold, it is first necessary to determine the cost of goods manufactured. We will next look at two supporting schedules for the income statement: the cost of goods manufactured and the cost of goods sold schedule.

Cost of Goods Manufactured

The **cost of goods manufactured** represents the total manufacturing cost of goods completed during the current period. The only costs assigned to goods completed are the manufacturing costs of direct materials, direct labor, and overhead. The details of this cost assignment are given in a supporting schedule, called the *statement of cost of goods manufactured*. An example of this supporting schedule for the cost of goods sold schedule in Exhibit 2-10 is shown in Exhibit 2-9.

EXHIBIT 2-10   Cost of Goods Sold Schedule

Cost of Goods Sold Schedule
For the Year Ended December 31, 2007

Cost of goods manufactured	$1,200,000
Add: Beginning inventory finished goods	250,000
Cost of goods available for sale	$1,450,000
Less: Ending inventory finished goods	150,000
Cost of goods sold	$1,300,000

Notice in Exhibit 2-9 that the *total manufacturing costs* of the period are added to the manufacturing costs found in beginning work in process. The costs found in ending work in process are then subtracted to arrive at the cost of goods manufactured. If the cost of goods manufactured is for a single product, then the average unit cost can be computed by dividing the cost of goods manufactured by the number of units produced. For example, assume that the statement in Exhibit 2-9 was prepared for the production of bottles of perfume and that 240,000 bottles were completed during the period. The average unit cost is $5 per bottle ($1,200,000/240,000).

Work in process consists of all partially completed units found in production at a given point in time. Beginning work in process consists of the partially completed units on hand at the beginning of a period. Ending work in process consists of those on hand at the period's end. In the statement of cost of goods manufactured, the cost of these partially completed units is reported as the cost of beginning work in process and the cost of ending work in process. The cost of beginning work in process represents the manufacturing costs carried over from the prior period; the cost of ending work in process represents the manufacturing costs that will be carried over to the next period. In both cases, additional manufacturing costs must be incurred to complete the units in work in process.

COST MANAGEMENT   Technology in Action

Some dot coms are changing the way they structure their income statements. The differences are disclosed in the notes to the financial statements and don't affect the bottom line, but they do impact heavily the computation of sales and gross margin.

CDNow sends customers e-coupons for $10 off their next purchase. Sounds like a purchase discount, doesn't it? Not at CDNow—instead the full purchase price is counted as sales and the $10 discount as marketing expense. **Priceline.com** reported as revenue the full value of the airline tickets it sold, rather than the commission it collected on those sales.

Many catalog companies treat fulfillment costs as part of cost of goods sold. However, a recent **Amazon.com** 10-K filing noted, "Fulfillment costs included in marketing and sales expenses represent those costs incurred in operating and staffing distribution and customer service centers, including costs attributable to receiving, inspecting, and warehousing inventories; picking, packaging, and preparing customers' orders for shipment; and responding to inquiries from customers." If Amazon.com had accounted for those costs as cost of goods sold, its gross profit for the first quarter of 2000 would have fallen from $128.1 million to $28.6 million. Gross margin would have been 5 percent of sales, not the reported 22.3 percent. (Amazon.com's 2002 annual report shows that fulfillments costs continue to be treated as operating expenses rather than cost of goods sold. In 2001, fulfillment costs represented nearly 47 percent of Amazon.com's gross profit; in 2002, these costs represented nearly 40 percent of gross profit.)

Why do dot coms play these games? Because they divert investors' attention from the net loss shown on the bottom line and focus it on other parts of the financial statements. Thus, gross margin becomes important, as do revenues and growth in revenues.

Source: Taken from Andy Kessler, "CreativeAccounting.com," *The Wall Street Journal* (July 24, 2000), http://interactive.swj.com/archive/retrieve .cgi?id=SB964396093512820667.djm. Information on fulfillment costs and gross profit for the years 2001 and 2002 can be found in the 2002 annual report for Amazon.com at http://media.corporate-ir.net/media_files/irol/97/97664/reports/2002_Annual_Report_FINAL.pdf.

Cost of Goods Sold

Once the cost of goods manufactured statement is prepared, the cost of goods sold can be computed. The cost of goods sold is the manufacturing cost of the units that were sold during the period. It is important to remember that the cost of goods sold may or may not equal the cost of goods manufactured. In addition, we must remember that the cost of goods sold is an expense, and it belongs on the income statement. The cost of goods sold schedule for a manufacturing company is shown in Exhibit 2-10.

Income Statement: Service Organization

The income statement for a service organization looks very similar to the one shown in Exhibit 2-8 for a manufacturing organization. However, the cost of goods sold does differ in some key ways. For one thing, the service firm has no finished goods inventories since services cannot be stored, although it is possible to have work in process for services. For example, an architect may have drawings in process and an orthodontist may have numerous patients in various stages of processing for braces. Additionally, some service firms add order fulfillment costs to the cost of goods sold. For example, a catalog company such as **Lands' End** does not manufacture the items it sells. Instead, it adds value by purchasing products, arranging for the manufacture of particular designs, and providing catalogs and convenient 1–800–numbers. The cost of storing goods, picking and packing them, and shipping them to customers is shown as part of cost of goods sold.

Functional-Based and Activity-Based Cost Management Systems

OBJECTIVE 5

Explain the differences between traditional and contemporary cost management systems.

Cost management systems can be broadly classified as *functional-based* or *activity-based*.[9] Both of these systems are found in practice. Currently, the functional-based cost management systems are more widely used than the activity-based systems. This is changing, however, as the need for highly accurate cost information increases. This is particularly true for organizations faced with increased product diversity, more product complexity, shorter product life cycles, increased quality requirements, and intense competitive pressures. These organizations often adopt a just-in-time manufacturing approach and implement advanced manufacturing technology (discussed in detail in Chapter 13). For firms operating in this advanced manufacturing environment, the functional-based cost management system may not work well. More relevant and timely cost information is needed for these organizations to build a sustainable long-term competitive advantage. Organizations must improve the value received by their customers while increasing their own profits at the same time. Better assessment of cost behavior, increased accuracy in product costing, and an attempt to achieve continuous cost improvement are all critical for the advanced manufacturing environment.

Functional-Based Cost Management Systems: A Brief Overview

Recall that cost management systems are made up of two subsystems: the cost accounting system and the operational control system. Thus, when discussing cost management systems, it is logical and convenient to discuss each subsystem separately. Of course, what is true for a subsystem is true for the overall cost management system.

Functional-Based Cost Accounting

A functional-based cost accounting system assumes that all costs can be classified as fixed or variable with respect to changes in the *units* or *volume* of product produced. Thus, units of product or other drivers highly correlated with units produced, such as direct labor hours and machine hours, are the only drivers *assumed* to be of importance. These unit- or volume-based drivers are used to assign production costs to products. A cost accounting system that uses only unit-based activity drivers to assign costs to

9. Both the functional-based costing system and the activity-based costing system are widely used in practice; sometimes they are used in the same company. As a result, this text integrates the treatment of the two types of costing systems.

cost objects is called a **functional-based cost system**. Since unit-based activity drivers usually are not the only drivers that explain causal relationships, much of the product cost assignment activity must be classified as allocation (recall that allocation is cost assignment based on *assumed* linkages or convenience). We can say, therefore, that functional-based cost accounting systems tend to be allocation-intensive.

The product costing objective of a functional-based cost accounting system is typically satisfied by assigning production costs to inventories and cost of goods sold for purposes of financial reporting. More comprehensive product cost definitions, such as the value-chain and operating cost definitions illustrated in Exhibit 2-6, are not available for management use. However, functional-based cost accounting systems often furnish useful variants of the traditional product cost definitions. For example, prime costs and variable manufacturing costs per unit may be reported. (Variable manufacturing costs are direct materials, direct labor, and variable overhead, where variable overhead is based on the number of units produced.)

Functional-Based Cost Control

A **functional-based operation control system** assigns costs to organizational units and then holds the organizational unit manager responsible for controlling the assigned costs. Performance is measured by comparing actual outcomes with standard or budgeted outcomes. The emphasis is on financial measures of performance (nonfinancial measures are usually ignored). Managers are rewarded based on their ability to control costs. This approach traces costs to individuals who are responsible for incurrence of costs. The reward system is used to motivate these individuals to manage costs. The approach assumes that maximizing the performance of the overall organization is achieved by maximizing the performance of individual organizational subunits (referred to as responsibility centers).

Activity-Based Cost Management Systems: A Brief Overview

Activity-based cost management systems have evolved in response to significant changes in the competitive business environment faced by both service and manufacturing firms. The overall objective of an activity-based cost management system is to improve the quality, content, relevance, and timing of cost information.[10] Generally, more managerial objectives can be met with an activity-based system than with a functional-based system.

Activity-Based Cost Accounting

An activity-based cost accounting system emphasizes tracing over allocation. The role of driver tracing is significantly expanded by identifying drivers unrelated to the volume of product produced (called *non-unit-based activity drivers*). The use of both unit- and non-unit-based activity drivers increases the accuracy of cost assignments and the overall quality and relevance of cost information. A cost accounting system that uses both unit- and non-unit-based activity drivers to assign costs to cost objects is called an **activity-based cost (ABC) system**. For example, consider the activity of "moving raw materials and partially finished goods from one point to another within a factory." The number of moves required for a product is a much better measure of the product's demand for the materials handling activity than the number of units produced. In fact, the number of units produced may have nothing to do whatsoever with measuring products' demands for materials handling. (A batch of 10 units of one product could require as much materials handling activity as a batch of 100 units of another

---

10. Steven C. Schnoebelen, "Integrating an Advanced Cost Management System into Operating Systems (Part 1)," *Journal of Cost Management* (Winter 1993): 50–54.

product.) Thus, we can say that an activity-based cost accounting system tends to be tracing-intensive.

Product costing in an activity-based system tends to be flexible. The activity-based cost management system is capable of producing cost information for a variety of managerial objectives, including the financial reporting objective. More comprehensive product costing definitions are emphasized for better planning, control, and decision making. Therefore, the maxim of "different costs for different purposes" takes on real meaning.

Activity-Based Cost Control

The activity-based operational control subsystem also differs significantly from that of a functional-based system. The emphasis of the traditional cost management accounting system is on managing costs. The emerging consensus, however, is that management of activities—not costs—is the key to successful control in the advanced manufacturing environment. Hence, *activity-based management* is the heart and soul of a contemporary operational control system. **Activity-based management (ABM)** focuses on the management of activities with the objective of improving the value received by the customer and the profit received by the company in providing this value. It includes driver analysis, activity analysis, and performance evaluation and draws on ABC as a major source of information.[11] In Exhibit 2-11, the vertical dimension traces the

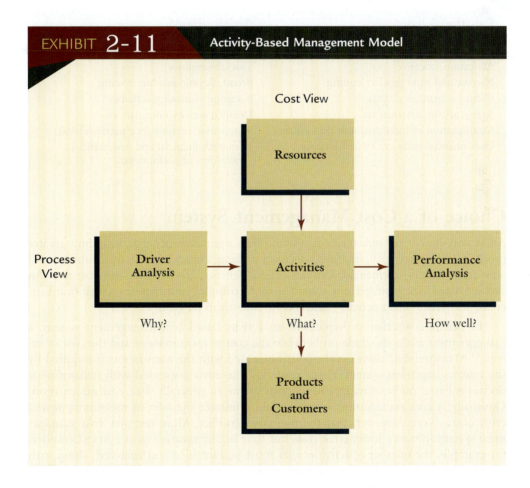

EXHIBIT 2-11   Activity-Based Management Model

Cost View

Resources

Process View

Driver Analysis → Activities → Performance Analysis

Why?   What?   How well?

Products and Customers

---

11. This definition of activity-based management and the illustrative model in Exhibit 2-11 are based on the following source: Norm Raffish and Peter B. B. Turney, "Glossary of Activity-Based Management," *Journal of Cost Management* (Fall 1991): 53–63. Other terms throughout the text relating to activity-based management are also drawn from this source.

cost of resources to activities and then to the cost objects. This is the activity-based costing dimension (referred to as the *cost view*). It serves as an important input to the control dimension, which is called the *process view*. The process view identifies factors that cause an activity's cost (explains why costs are incurred), assesses what work is done (identifies activities), and evaluates the work performed and the results achieved (how well the activity is performed). Thus, an activity-based control system requires detailed information on activities.

This new approach focuses on accountability for activities rather than costs and emphasizes the maximization of systemwide performance instead of individual performance. Activities cut across functional and departmental lines, are systemwide in focus, and require a global approach to control. Essentially, this form of control admits that maximizing the efficiency of individual subunits does not necessarily lead to maximum efficiency for the system as a whole. Another significant difference also should be mentioned. In the ABM operational control information system, both financial and nonfinancial measures of performance are important. Exhibit 2-12 compares the characteristics of the functional-based and activity-based cost management systems.

EXHIBIT 2-12	Comparison of Functional-Based and Activity-Based Cost Management Systems

Functional-Based	Activity-Based
Unit-based drivers	Unit- and non-unit-based drivers
Allocation-intensive	Tracing-intensive
Narrow and rigid product costing	Broad, flexible product costing
Focus on managing costs	Focus on managing activities
Sparse activity information	Detailed activity information
Maximization of individual unit performance	Systemwide performance maximization
Uses financial measures of performance	Uses both financial and nonfinancial measures of performance

Choice of a Cost Management System

An activity-based cost management system offers significant benefits, including greater product costing accuracy, improved decision making, enhanced strategic planning, and an increased ability to manage activities. These benefits, however, are not cost-free. An activity-based cost management system is more complex and requires a significant increase in measurement activity—and measurement can be costly.

In deciding whether to implement an activity-based cost management system, a manager must assess the trade-off between the cost of measurement and the cost of errors.[12] **Measurement costs** are the costs associated with the measurements required by the cost management system. **Error costs** are the costs associated with making poor decisions based on inaccurate product costs or, more generally, bad cost information. Optimally, a cost management system would minimize the sum of measurement and error costs. Note, however, that the two costs conflict. More complex cost management systems produce lower error costs but have higher measurement costs. (Consider, for example, the number of activities that must be identified and analyzed, along with the number of drivers that must be used to assign costs to products.) The trade-off be-

---

12. The discussion of these issues is based on the following article: Robin Cooper, "The Rise of Activity-Based Costing—Part Two: When Do I Need an Activity-Based Cost System?" *Journal of Cost Management* (Summer 1988): 45–54.

tween error and measurement costs is illustrated in Exhibit 2-13. The message is clear. For some organizations, the optimal cost system may not be an ABM system even though it is a more accurate system. Depending on the trade-offs, the optimal cost management system may very well be a simpler, functional-based system. This could explain, in part, why most firms still maintain this type of system.

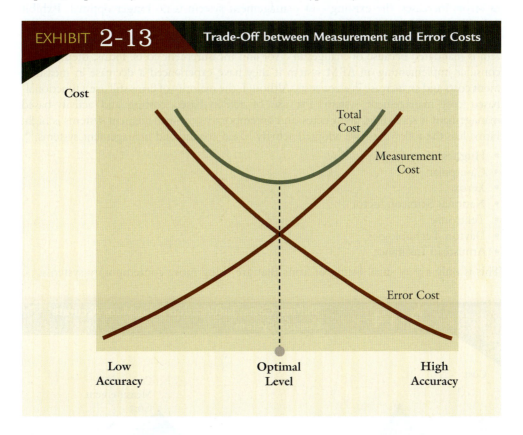

EXHIBIT **2-13**   **Trade-Off between Measurement and Error Costs**

Recent changes in the manufacturing environment, however, are increasing the attractiveness of more accurate, yet complex, cost management systems. New information technology decreases measurement costs; computerized production planning systems and more powerful, less expensive computers make it easier to collect data and perform calculations. As measurement costs decrease, the measurement cost curve shown in Exhibit 2-13 shifts downward and to the right, causing the total cost curve to shift to the right. The optimal cost management system is now one that allows more accuracy.

As the cost of measurement has decreased, the cost of errors has increased. Basically, errors consist of over- or undercosting products. If competition heats up for an overcosted product, the firm may drop what now *appears* to be an unprofitable product. If the nature of the competition changes, error costs can increase as well. For example, if single-product-focused competitors emerge, then their pricing and marketing strategies will be based on more accurate cost information (since all costs are known to belong to the single product). Because of better cost information, the more focused firms may gain market share at the expense of multiple-product producers (whose cost systems may be allocating rather than tracing costs to individual products). Other factors such as deregulation and JIT manufacturing (which leads to a more focused production environment) can also increase the cost of errors. As the cost of errors increases, the error-cost curve in Exhibit 2-13 shifts upward and to the right, causing the total cost curve to shift to the right, making a more accurate cost system the better choice.

Another cost, which is increasing for some firms, is the cost of unethical conduct. For example, **Metropolitan Life Insurance Company** paid over $20 million in fines and must refund more than $50 million to policyholders because some of its agents illegally sold policies as retirement plans.[13] An ABM system which tracks policy sales by type, age of policyholder, agent, and policyholder's objective could give an early warning signal of problems. A key point is that companies are expected to exercise control over their operations. If there is room for ethical misconduct, the company must develop the means to identify and correct abuses. As the cost of measurement decreases and the cost of errors increases, the existing cost management system is no longer optimal. Exhibit 2-14 illustrates how changing error and measurement costs can make an existing cost management system obsolete. As the exhibit illustrates, a more accurate cost management system is mandated because of changes in error and measurement costs. Firms, then, should consider implementing an ABM system if they have experienced a decrease in measurement costs and an increase in error costs. Although the majority of firms still use a functional-based cost management system, the use of activity-based costing and activity-based management is spreading, and interest in contemporary cost management systems is high. Firms like the following have adopted activity-based costing and management systems:[14]

- Hughes Aircraft
- Caterpillar
- Xerox
- National Semiconductor
- Tektronix
- Dayton Technologies
- Armistead Insurance

This is only a very small listing of firms that are using more contemporary systems.

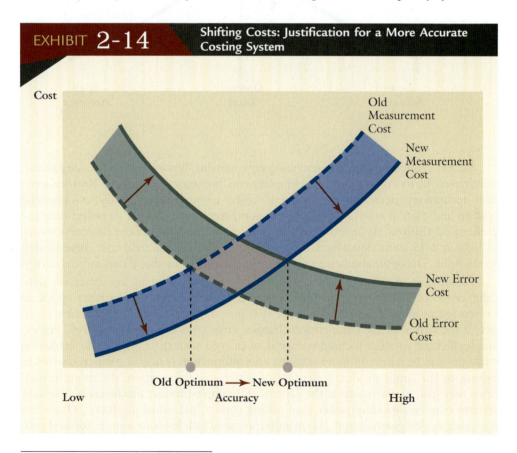

EXHIBIT 2-14　**Shifting Costs: Justification for a More Accurate Costing System**

13. Chris Roush, "Fields of Green—And Disaster Areas," *Business Week* (January 9, 1995): 94.

14. Peter B. B. Turney, "Activity-Based Management," *Management Accounting* (January 1992): 20–25; Jack Hedicke and David Feil, "Hughes Aircraft," *Management Accounting* (February 1991): 29–33; and Lou F. Jones, "Product Costing at Caterpillar," *Management Accounting* (February 1991): 34–42.

SUMMARY

A systems framework affords a logical basis for the study of cost management. The cost management system is a subsystem of the accounting information system and must be designed to satisfy costing, controlling, and decision-making objectives. The costing and controlling objectives serve to define two major subsystems: the cost accounting system and the operational control system.

A major feature of the operational model of the cost accounting system is the cost assignment process. The major objective of the cost accounting system is the assignment of costs to cost objects. This assignment process is achieved by three subprocesses: direct tracing, driver tracing, and allocation. Allocation is the least accurate and least desirable approach, and generally, a cost accounting system should be designed to minimize allocations. Understanding the assignment process is fundamental to understanding cost management systems. In this chapter, you need to grasp the broad, conceptual framework for cost assignment. Subsequent chapters will explore the mechanics of cost assignment in greater detail.

Product and service costs were also introduced. Several product cost definitions were provided. The product cost definition for external financial reporting is of particular importance and was discussed in detail. The format for external income statements was presented and discussed for both manufacturing and service firms. Given the increasing magnitude of the service sector, you should pay particular attention to what services are and how they differ from tangible products. Cost management for service organizations will receive more emphasis in this text than is traditionally available.

Finally, we discussed the difference between functional-based and activity-based cost management systems. Exhibit 2-12 lists some of the major differences between the two systems and should be studied carefully. Again, the objective is simply to provide a broad, conceptual understanding of the differences. An in-depth, detailed understanding of the differences will come only after studying the chapters that focus on the different types of systems.

REVIEW PROBLEMS AND SOLUTIONS

1 TYPES OF COSTS, COST OF GOODS MANUFACTURED, ABSORPTION-COSTING INCOME STATEMENT

Palmer Manufacturing produces weather vanes. For the year just ended, Palmer produced 10,000 weather vanes with the following total costs:

Direct materials	$20,000
Direct labor	35,000
Overhead	10,000
Selling expenses	6,250
Administrative expenses	14,400

During the year, Palmer sold 9,800 units for $12 each. Beginning finished goods inventory consisted of 630 units with a total cost of $4,095. There were no beginning or ending inventories of work in process.

Required:

1. Calculate the unit costs for the following: direct materials, direct labor, overhead, prime cost, and conversion cost.
2. Prepare schedules for cost of goods manufactured and cost of goods sold.
3. Prepare an absorption-costing income statement for Palmer Manufacturing.

SOLUTION

1. Unit direct materials = $20,000/10,000 = $2.00
   Unit direct labor = $35,000/10,000 = $3.50
   Unit overhead = $10,000/10,000 = $1.00
   Unit prime cost = $2.00 + $3.50 = $5.50
   Unit conversion cost = $3.50 + $1.00 = $4.50

2. Statement of cost of goods manufactured:

Direct materials used	$20,000
Direct labor	35,000
Overhead	10,000
Total manufacturing costs added	$65,000
Add: Beginning work in process	0
Less: Ending work in process	(0)
Cost of goods manufactured	$65,000

Cost of goods sold schedule:

Cost of goods manufactured	$65,000
Add: Beginning finished goods inventory	4,095
Less: Ending finished goods inventory*	(5,395)
Cost of goods sold	$63,700

*Units in ending finished goods inventory = 10,000 + 630 – 9,800 = 830;
830 × ($2.00 + $3.50 + $1.00) = $5,395.

3. Income statement:

Sales (9,800 × $12)		$117,600
Less: Cost of goods sold		63,700
Gross margin		$ 53,900
Less: Operating expenses:		
Selling expenses	$ 6,250	
Administrative expenses	14,400	20,650
Operating income		$ 33,250

2 SYSTEMS CONCEPTS

Kate Myers is a student at Midwestern University. Her system for tracking finances includes the following. Kate has two credit cards; each day she places the receipts for any items purchased on credit in a manila envelope on her desk. She checks these receipts against the credit card bills at the end of the month. Any other financial item that Kate thinks might be useful later is also placed into the envelope. (An example would be a payroll stub from her job as a worker in the dormitory cafeteria.) Kate records any check written in her checkbook register at the time she writes it. Shortly after her bank statement arrives, she enters any checks written and deposits made into Quicken® (the software program she uses to balance her checkbook). She then reconciles her bank statement against the Quicken account and prints a reconciliation report. From time to time, Kate phones home to ask her mother to add more money to her bank account. Her mother, who has copies of the deposit slips for Kate's account, mails a check (from her own account) with a deposit slip to Kate's account. Whenever this occurs, Kate logs on to Bluemountain.com and e-mails her mother an electronic thank-you card.

The following items are associated with this financial system:

a. Manila envelope
b. Checkbook
c. Checks and deposit slips
d. Computer and printer
e. Quicken program
f. Credit cards
g. Credit card receipts
h. Payroll stubs, etc.
i. Monthly bank statements
j. Reconciliation report
k. Phone

Required:

1. What are the objectives of Kate's financial system? What processes can you identify?
2. Classify the items into one of the following categories:
    a. Interrelated parts
    b. Inputs
    c. Outputs
3. Draw an operational model for the financial system.

SOLUTION

1. The objectives of Kate's financial system are to keep Kate financially solvent and to provide a clear and accurate picture of her checking account balance and bills incurred at any point in time. Processes include filing the credit card receipts, entering checks written and deposits made into both the manual and computerized systems, reconciling the bank statement with the computerized system, phoning home for additional funds, and e-mailing a thank-you card.

2. The items are classified as follows:
    a. Manila envelope—interrelated part
    b. Checkbook—interrelated part
    c. Checks and deposit slips—input
    d. Computer and printer—interrelated part
    e. Quicken program—interrelated part
    f. Credit cards—interrelated part
    g. Credit card receipts—input
    h. Payroll stubs, etc.—input
    i. Monthly bank statements—interrelated part
    j. Reconciliation report—output
    k. Phone—interrelated part

3. Operational model of Kate's financial system:

Inputs	*Processes*	*Objectives*
Checks	Filing credit card receipts	Stay financially solvent
Deposit slips	Entering checks/deposits	Be aware of bills incurred
Credit card receipts	Reconciling statements	Know account balance
Payroll stubs, etc.	Phoning for additional funds	
	E-mailing thank-you card	

KEY TERMS

Absorption-costing income 42

Accounting information system 30

Activity 35

Activity-based cost (ABC) system 46

Activity-based management (ABM) 47

Administrative costs 41

Allocation 37

Assets 35

Conversion cost 41

Cost 35

Cost accounting information system 32

Cost management information system 31

Cost object 35

Cost of goods manufactured 43

Cost of goods sold 42

Direct costs 36

Direct labor 40

Direct materials 40

Direct tracing 36

Driver tracing 37

Drivers 36

Error costs 48

Expenses 35

Financial accounting information system 31

Full-costing income 42

Functional-based cost system 46

Functional-based operation control system 46

Indirect costs 36

Inseparability 38

Intangibility 38

Loss 35

Marketing (selling) costs 41

Measurement costs 48

Nonproduction costs 39

Operational control information system 33

Overhead 40

Period costs 40

Perishability 38

Prime cost 41

Production (or product) costs 39

Services 37

Supplies 40

System 29

Tangible products 37

Traceability 36

Work in process 44

QUESTIONS FOR WRITING AND DISCUSSION

1. What is an accounting information system?
2. What is the difference between a financial accounting information system and a cost management information system?
3. What are the objectives of a cost management information system?
4. Define and explain the two major subsystems of the cost management information system.
5. What is a cost object? Give some examples.
6. What is an activity? Give some examples of activities within a manufacturing firm.
7. What is a direct cost? An indirect cost?
8. What does traceability mean?
9. What is allocation?
10. Explain how driver tracing works.
11. What is a tangible product?
12. What is a service? Explain how services differ from tangible products.
13. Give three examples of product cost definitions. Why do we need different product cost definitions?

14. Identify the three cost elements that determine the cost of making a product (for external reporting).
15. How do the income statements of a manufacturing firm and a service firm differ?

EXERCISES

2-1 SYSTEMS CONCEPTS

LO1 In general, systems are described by the following pattern: (1) interrelated parts, (2) processes, and (3) objectives. Operational models of systems also identify inputs and outputs.

The dishwashing system of a college cafeteria consists of the following steps. First, students dispose of any waste paper (e.g., napkins) in a trash can, then they file by an opening to the dishwashing area and drop off their trays. Persons 1 and 2 take the trays; rinse the extra food down the disposal; and stack the dishes, glasses, and silverware in heavy-duty plastic racks. These racks slide along a conveyor into the automatic dishwasher. When the racks emerge from the other end of the dishwasher, they contain clean, germ-free items. Person 3 removes the racks and, with Person 4, empties them of clean items; stacking the dishes, silverware, glasses, and trays for future use. The empty racks are returned to the starting position in front of Persons 1 and 2. The following items are associated with this dishwashing system:

a. Automatic dishwasher
b. Racks to hold the dirty glasses, silverware, and dishes
c. Electricity
d. Water
e. Waste disposal
f. Sinks and sprayers
g. Dish detergent
h. Gas heater to heat water to 180 degrees Fahrenheit
i. Conveyor belt
j. Persons 1, 2, 3, and 4
k. Clean, germ-free dishes
l. Dirty dishes
m. Half-eaten dinner
n. Aprons

Required:
1. What is the objective of the dishwashing system? What processes can you identify?
2. Classify the items into one of the following categories:
   a. Interrelated parts
   b. Inputs
   c. Outputs
3. Draw an operational model for the dishwashing system.
4. Discuss how a cost management information system is similar to and different from the dishwashing system.

2-2 COST ACCOUNTING INFORMATION SYSTEM

LO1 The following items are associated with a cost accounting information system:
a. Usage of direct materials
b. Assignment of direct materials cost to each product

c. Direct labor cost incurrence
d. Depreciation on production equipment
e. Cost accounting personnel
f. Submission of a bid, using product cost plus 25 percent
g. Power cost incurrence
h. Materials handling cost incurrence
i. Computer
j. Assignment of direct labor costs to products
k. Costing out of products
l. Decision to continue making a part rather than buying it
m. Printer
n. Report detailing individual product costs
o. Assignment of overhead costs to individual products

Required:

1. Classify the preceding items into one of the following categories:
    a. Interrelated parts
    b. Processes
    c. Objectives
    d. Inputs
    e. Outputs
    f. User actions
2. Draw an operational model that illustrates the cost accounting information system—with the preceding items used as examples for each component of the model.
3. Based on your operational model, identify which product cost definition is being used: value-chain, operating, or functional-based manufacturing.

2-3   COST ASSIGNMENT METHODS

LO2 Tasman Company produces electric tools including drills, nail guns, circular saws, and routers. Recently, Tasman switched from a traditional departmental assembly line system to a manufacturing cell in order to produce a specialized jig saw. Suppose that the jig saw manufacturing cell is the cost object. Assume that all or a portion of the following costs must be assigned to the cell:

a. Depreciation on the plant
b. Salary of cell supervisor
c. Power to heat and cool the plant in which the cell is located
d. Heavy duty steel used to produce the jig saw housings
e. Maintenance for the cell's equipment (provided by the maintenance department)
f. Labor used to align the steel in the stamping machine to produce the halves of the jig saw housing
g. Cost of janitorial services for the plant
h. Depreciation on stamping machines and automatic continuous welders used to produce the jig saws
i. Ordering costs for materials used in production
j. The salary of the industrial engineer (half of whose time is dedicated to the cell)
k. Cost of maintaining plant and grounds
l. Cost of plant's personnel office
m. Oil to lubricate the stamping machines
n. Plant receptionist's salary and benefits

Required:

Identify which cost assignment method would likely be used to assign the costs of each of the preceding activities to the jig saw manufacturing cell: direct tracing, driver tracing, or allocation. When driver tracing is selected, identify a potential activity driver that could be used for the tracing.

2-4 PRODUCT COST DEFINITIONS

LO3 Three possible product cost definitions were introduced: (1) value-chain, (2) operating, and (3) manufacturing. Identify which of the three product cost definitions best fits the following situations (justify your choice):

a. Setting the price for a new product
b. Valuation of finished goods inventories for external reporting
c. Determining whether to add a complementary product to the product line
d. Choosing among competing product designs
e. Calculating cost of goods sold for external reporting
f. Deciding whether to increase the price of an existing product
g. Deciding whether to accept or reject a special order, where the price offered is lower than the normal selling price
h. Determining which of several potential new products should be developed, produced, and sold
i. Deciding whether to produce and sell a product whose design and development costs were higher than budgeted

2-5 COST DEFINITIONS

LO4 Cardinal Company's southeastern factory provided the following information for the last calendar year:

Beginning inventory:
  Direct materials $49,300
  Work in process   55,400

Ending inventories:
  Direct materials $20,000
  Work in process   20,400

During the year, direct materials purchases amounted to $150,000, direct labor cost was $200,000, and overhead cost was $324,700. There were 100,000 units produced.

Required:

1. Calculate the total cost of direct materials used in production.
2. Calculate the cost of goods manufactured. Calculate the unit manufacturing cost.
3. Of the unit manufacturing cost calculated in Requirement 2, $1.70 is direct materials and $3.24 is overhead. What is the prime cost per unit? Conversion cost per unit?

2-6 COST DEFINITIONS AND CALCULATIONS

LO4 For each of the following independent situations, calculate the missing values:

1. The Chico plant purchased $275,000 of direct materials during May. Beginning direct materials inventory was $16,000, and direct materials used in production were $200,000. What is ending direct materials inventory?
2. Landsman Company produced 10,000 units at an average cost of $6 each. The beginning inventory of finished goods was $3,510. (The average unit cost was $5.85.) Landsman sold 8,900 units. How many units remain in ending finished goods inventory?

3. Beginning WIP was $50,000, and ending WIP was $18,750. If total manufacturing costs were $93,000, what was the cost of goods manufactured?
4. If the conversion cost is $32 per unit, the prime cost is $19.50, and the manufacturing cost per unit is $39.50, what is the direct materials cost per unit?
5. Total manufacturing costs for April were $156,900. Prime cost was $90,000, and beginning WIP was $60,000. The cost of goods manufactured was $125,000. Calculate the cost of overhead for April and the cost of ending WIP.

2-7 COST OF GOODS MANUFACTURED AND SOLD

LO4

Cimino Company manufactures staplers. At the beginning of June, the following information was supplied by its accountant:

Direct materials inventory	$51,200
Work-in-process inventory	10,000
Finished goods inventory	10,075

During June, direct labor cost was $22,000, direct materials purchases were $70,000, and the total overhead cost was $216,850. The inventories at the end of June were:

Direct materials inventory	$18,600
Work-in-process inventory	6,050
Finished goods inventory	8,475

Required:

1. Prepare a cost of goods manufactured statement for June.
2. Prepare a cost of goods sold schedule for June.

2-8 PRIME COST, CONVERSION COST, PREPARATION OF INCOME STATEMENT: MANUFACTURING FIRM

LO3, LO4

Photo-Dive, Inc., manufactures disposable underwater cameras. During the last calendar year, a total of 150,000 cameras were made, and 154,000 were sold for $8.00 each. The actual unit cost per camera is as follows:

Direct materials	$2.25
Direct labor	1.50
Variable overhead	0.65
Fixed overhead	0.70
Total unit cost	$5.10

The selling expenses consisted of a commission of $0.25 per unit sold and advertising co-payments totaling $36,000. Administrative expenses, all fixed, equaled $83,000. There were no beginning and ending work-in-process inventories. Beginning finished goods inventory was $30,600 for 6,000 cameras.

Required:

1. Calculate the number of cameras and the value of ending finished goods inventory.
2. Prepare a cost of goods sold statement.
3. Prepare an absorption-costing income statement.

2-9   COST OF GOODS MANUFACTURED AND SOLD

LO4

Spreadsheet

Araj Company, a manufacturing firm, has supplied the following information from its accounting records for the last calendar year:

Direct labor cost	$371,500
Purchases of direct materials	160,400
Freight-in on materials	1,000
Factory supplies used	37,800
Factory utilities	46,000
Commissions paid	80,000
Factory supervision and indirect labor	190,000
Advertising	23,900
Materials handling	26,750
Work-in-process inventory, January 1	201,000
Work-in-process inventory, December 31	98,000
Direct materials inventory, January 1	47,000
Direct materials inventory, December 31	17,000
Finished goods inventory, January 1	8,000
Finished goods inventory, December 31	62,700

Required:

1. Prepare a cost of goods manufactured statement.
2. Prepare a cost of goods sold statement.

2-10   INCOME STATEMENT, COST CONCEPTS, SERVICE COMPANY

LO3, LO4

Marcus Washington owns and operates three Compufix shops in the Chicago area. Compufix repairs and upgrades computers on site. In May, purchases of materials equaled $9,350, the beginning inventory of materials was $1,050, and the ending inventory of materials was $750. Payments for direct labor during the month totaled $18,570. Overhead incurred was $15,000. The Chicago shops also spent $5,000 on advertising during the month. Administrative costs (primarily accounting and legal services) amounted to $3,000 for the month. Revenues for May were $60,400.

Required:

1. What was the cost of materials used for repair and upgrade services during May?
2. What was the prime cost for May?
3. What was the conversion cost for May?
4. What was the total cost of services for May?
5. Prepare an income statement for May.

2-11   PRODUCT COST DEFINITIONS, VALUE CHAIN

LO1

Millennium Pharmaceuticals, Inc. (MPI), designs and manufactures a variety of drugs. One new drug, glaxane, has been in development for seven years. FDA approval has just been received, and MPI is ready to begin production and sales.

Required:

Refer to Exhibit 2-6. Which costs in the value chain would be considered by each of the following managers in their decision regarding glaxane?

1. Shelly Roberts is plant manager of the New Bern, North Carolina, plant where glaxane will be produced. Shelly has been assured that glaxane capsules will use

well-understood processes and not require additional training or capital investment.

2. Leslie Bothan is vice president of marketing. Leslie's job involves pricing and selling glaxane. Because glaxane is the first drug in its "drug family" to be commercially produced, there is no experience with potential side effects. Extensive testing did not expose any real problems (aside from occasional heartburn and insomnia), but the company could not be sure that such side effects did not exist.

3. Dante Fiorello is chief of research and development. His charge is to ensure that all reasearch projects, taken as a whole, eventually produce drugs that can support the R&D labs. He is assessing the potential for further work on drugs in the glaxane family.

2-12 FUNCTIONAL-BASED VERSUS ACTIVITY-BASED COST MANAGEMENT SYSTEMS

LO5 Jazon Manufacturing produces two different models of cameras. One model has an automatic focus, whereas the other requires the user to determine the focus. The two products are produced in batches. Each time a batch is produced, the equipment must be configured (set up) for the specifications of the camera model being produced. The manual-focus camera requires more parts than the automatic-focus model. The manual-focus model is also more labor-intensive, requiring much more assembly time but less machine time. Although the manual model is more labor-intensive, the machine configuration required for this product is more complex, causing the manual model to consume more of the setup activity resources than the automatic camera. Many, but not all, of the parts for the two cameras are purchased from external suppliers. Because it has more parts, the manual model makes more demands on the purchasing and receiving activities than does the automatic camera. Jazon currently assigns only manufacturing costs to the two products. Overhead costs are collected in one plantwide pool and are assigned to the two products in proportion to the direct labor hours used by each product. All other costs are viewed as period costs.

Jazon budgets costs for all departments within the plant—both support departments like maintenance and purchasing and production departments like machining and assembly. Departmental managers are evaluated and rewarded on their ability to control costs. Individual managerial performance is assessed by comparing actual costs with budgeted costs.

Required:

1. Is Jazon using a functional-based or an activity-based cost management system? Explain.

2. Assume that you want to design a more accurate cost accounting system. What changes would you need to make? Be specific. Explain why the changes you make will improve the accuracy of cost assignments.

3. What changes would need to be made to implement an activity-based operational control system? Explain why you believe the changes will offer improved control.

2-13 DIRECT MATERIALS COST, PRIME COST, CONVERSION COST, COST OF GOODS MANUFACTURED

LO3 Shellenberger Company provided the following information for last year:

Beginning inventory:
Direct materials	$41,600
Work in process	26,000
Finished goods	75,000

Ending inventories:
  Direct materials $ 31,600
  Work in process   51,000

  Finished goods   140,000

During the year, direct materials purchases amounted to $270,000, direct labor cost was $320,000, and overhead cost was $490,000. During the year, 25,000 units were completed.

Required:

1. Calculate the total cost of direct materials used in production.
2. Calculate the cost of goods manufactured. Calculate the unit manufacturing cost.
3. Of the unit manufacturing cost calculated in Requirement 2, $11 is direct materials and $12 is overhead. What is the prime cost per unit? Conversion cost per unit?

2-14 COST OF GOOD SOLD, INCOME STATEMENT

LO3, LO4   Refer to **Exercise 2-13**. Last year, Shellenberger recognized revenue of $1,380,000 and had selling and administrative expense of $216,300.

Required:

1. What is the cost of goods sold for last year?
2. Prepare an income statement for Shellenberger for last year.

PROBLEMS

2-15 COST INFORMATION AND DECISION MAKING, RESOURCE AND ACTIVITY DRIVERS, ACTIVITY-BASED VERSUS FUNCTIONAL-BASED SYSTEMS

LO5   Wright Plastic Products is a small company that specialized in the production of plastic dinner plates until several years ago. Although profits for the company had been good, they have been declining in recent years because of increased competition. Many competitors offer a full range of plastic products, and management felt that this created a competitive disadvantage. The output of the company's plants was exclusively devoted to plastic dinner plates. Three years ago, management made a decision to add additional product lines. They determined that existing idle capacity in each plant could easily be adapted to produce other plastic products. Each plant would produce one additional product line. For example, the Atlanta plant would add a line of plastic cups. Moreover, the variable cost of producing a package of cups (one dozen) was virtually identical to that of a package of plastic plates. (Variable costs referred to here are those that change in total as the units produced change. The costs include direct materials, direct labor, and unit-based variable overhead such as power and other machine costs.) Since the fixed expenses would not change, the new product was forecast to increase profits significantly (for the Atlanta plant).

Two years after the addition of the new product line, the profits of the Atlanta plant (as well as other plants) had not improved—in fact, they had dropped. Upon investigation, the president of the company discovered that profits had not increased as expected because the so-called fixed cost pool had increased dramatically. The president interviewed the manager of each support department at the Atlanta plant. Typical responses from four of those managers are given next.

Materials Handling: The additional batches caused by the cups increased the demand for materials handling. We had to add one forklift and hire additional materials handling labor.

Inspection: Inspecting cups is more complicated than plastic plates. We only inspect a sample drawn from every batch, but you need to understand that the number of batches has increased with this new product line. We had to hire more inspection labor.

Purchasing: The new line increased the number of purchase orders. We had to use more resources to handle this increased volume.

Accounting: There were more transactions to process than before. We had to increase our staff.

Required:

1. Explain why the results of adding the new product line were not accurately projected.
2. Could this problem have been avoided with an activity-based cost management system? If so, would you recommend that the company adopt this type of system? Explain and discuss the differences between an activity-based cost management system and a functional-based cost management system.

2-16 SYSTEMS CONCEPTS, FUNCTIONAL-BASED VERSUS ACTIVITY-BASED COST ACCOUNTING SYSTEMS

LO1, LO5 The following items are associated with a functional-based cost accounting information system, an activity-based cost accounting information system, or both (that is, some elements are common to the two systems):

a. Usage of direct materials
b. Direct materials cost assigned to products using direct tracing
c. Direct labor cost incurrence
d. Direct labor cost assigned to products using direct tracing
e. Setup cost incurrence
f. Setup cost assigned using number of setups as the activity driver
g. Setup cost assigned using direct labor hours as the activity driver
h. Cost accounting personnel
i. Submission of a bid, using product cost plus 25 percent
j. Purchasing cost incurrence
k. Purchasing cost assigned to products using direct labor hours as the activity driver
l. Purchasing cost assigned to products using number of orders as the activity driver
m. Materials handling cost incurrence
n. Materials handling cost assigned using the number of moves as the activity driver
o. Materials handling cost assigned using direct labor hours as the activity driver
p. Computer
q. Costing out of products
r. Decision to continue making a part rather than buying it
s. Printer
t. Customer service cost incurred
u. Customer service cost assigned to products using number of complaints as the activity driver
v. Report detailing individual product costs
w. Commission cost

x. Commission cost assigned to products using units sold as the activity driver
y. Plant depreciation
z. Plant depreciation assigned to products using direct labor hours

Required:

1. For each cost system, classify the items into one of the following categories:
    a. Interrelated parts
    b. Processes
    c. Objectives
    d. Inputs
    e. Outputs
    f. User actions

2. Explain the choices that differ between the two systems. Which system will provide the best support for the user actions? Explain.
3. Draw an operational model that illustrates each cost accounting system—with the items that belong to the system used as examples for each component of the model.
4. Based on the operational models, comment on the relative costs and benefits of the two systems. Which system should be chosen?

2-17 ACTIVITY-BASED VERSUS FUNCTIONAL-BASED OPERATIONAL CONTROL SYSTEMS

LO1, LO5 The actions listed next are associated with either an activity-based operational control system or a functional-based operational control system:

a. Budgeted costs for the maintenance department are compared with the actual costs of the maintenance department.
b. The maintenance department manager receives a bonus for "beating" budget.
c. The costs of resources are traced to activities and then to products.
d. The purchasing department is set up as a responsibility center.
e. Activities are identified and listed.
f. Activities are categorized as adding or not adding value to the organization.
g. A standard for a product's material usage cost is set and compared against the product's actual materials usage cost.
h. The cost of performing an activity is tracked over time.
i. The distance between moves is identified as the cause of materials handling cost.
j. A purchasing agent is rewarded for buying parts below the standard price set by the company.
k. The cost of the materials handling activity is reduced dramatically by redesigning the plant layout.
l. An investigation is undertaken to find out why the actual labor cost for the production of 1,000 units is greater than the labor standard allowed.
m. The percentage of defective units is calculated and tracked over time.
n. Engineering has been given the charge to find a way to reduce setup time by 75 percent.
o. The manager of the receiving department lays off two receiving clerks so that the fourth-quarter budget can be met.

Required:

Classify the preceding actions as belonging to either an activity-based operational control system or a functional-based control system. Explain why you classified each action as you did.

2-18 INCOME STATEMENT, COST OF GOODS MANUFACTURED

LO3, LO4

Spreadsheet

Dalal Company produced 150,000 floor lamps during the past calendar year. These lamps sell for $50 each. Dalal had 2,500 floor lamps in finished goods inventory at the beginning of the year. At the end of the year, there were 11,500 floor lamps in finished goods inventory. Dalal's accounting records provide the following information:

Purchases of direct materials	$1,550,000
Direct materials inventory, January 1	290,000
Direct materials inventory, December 31	112,000
Direct labor	2,000,000
Indirect labor	790,000
Depreciation, factory building	1,100,000
Depreciation, factory equipment	630,000
Property taxes on the factory	65,000
Utilities, factory	150,000
Insurance on the factory	200,000
Salary, sales supervisor	85,000
Commissions, salespersons	490,000
General administration	390,000
Work-in-process inventory, January 1	450,000
Work-in-process inventory, December 31	750,000
Finished goods inventory, January 1	107,500
Finished goods inventory, December 31	489,000

Required:

1. Prepare a cost of goods manufactured statement.
2. Compute the cost of producing one floor lamp last year.
3. Prepare an income statement on an absorption-costing basis.

2-19 COST OF GOODS MANUFACTURED, COST IDENTIFICATION, SOLVING FOR UNKNOWNS

LO2, LO4

CPA-Skilz Company creates, produces, and sells CD-ROM-based CPA review courses for individual use. Susan Wayans, head of human resources, is convinced that question development employees must have strong analytical and problem-solving skills. She asked Jeremy Slater, controller for CPA-Skilz, to help develop problems to help screen applicants before they are interviewed. One of the problems Jeremy developed is based on the following data for a mythical company for the previous year:

a. Conversion cost was $360,000 and was four times the prime cost.
b. Direct materials used in production equaled $75,000.
c. Cost of goods manufactured was $415,000.
d. Beginning work in process is one-half the cost of ending work in process.
e. There are no beginning or ending inventories for direct materials.
f. Cost of goods sold was 80 percent of cost of goods manufactured.
g. Beginning finished goods inventory was $14,400.

Required:

1. Calculate the cost of goods manufactured for the previous year.
2. Calculate the cost of goods sold for the previous year.

2-20   INCOME STATEMENT, COST OF SERVICES PROVIDED, SERVICE ATTRIBUTES

LO3, LO4   Young, Andersen, and Touche (YAT) is a tax services firm. The firm is located in San Diego and employs 10 professionals and eight staff. The firm does tax work for small businesses and well-to-do individuals. The following data are provided for the last fiscal year. (The Young, Andersen, and Touche fiscal year runs from July 1 through June 30.)

Returns processed	2,000
Returns in process, beginning of year	$ 78,000
Returns in process, end of year	134,000
Cost of services sold	890,000
Beginning direct materials inventory	20,000
Purchases, direct materials	40,000
Direct labor	800,000
Overhead	100,000
Administrative	57,000
Selling	65,000

Required:

1. Prepare a statement of cost of services sold.
2. Refer to the statement prepared in Requirement 1. What is the dominant cost? Will this always be true of service organizations? If not, provide an example of an exception.
3. Assuming that the average fee for processing a return is $700, prepare an income statement for Young, Andersen, and Touche.
4. Discuss three differences between services and tangible products. Calculate the average cost of preparing a tax return for last year. How do the differences between services and tangible products affect the ability of YAT to use the last year's average cost of preparing a tax return in budgeting the cost of tax return services to be offered next year?

2-21   COST OF GOODS MANUFACTURED, INCOME STATEMENT

LO3, LO4   Jordan Company produces a chemical reagent used by medical laboratories. For 2007, Jordan reported the following:

Work-in-process inventory, January 1	$ 13,250
Work-in-process inventory, December 31	13,250
Finished goods inventory, January 1 (24,000 units)	170,000
Finished goods inventory, December 31 (12,000 units)	85,000
Direct materials inventory, January 1	15,600
Direct materials inventory, December 31	14,000
Direct materials used	120,000
Direct labor	72,000
Plant depreciation	9,500
Salary, production supervisor	45,000
Indirect labor	36,000
Utilities, factory	5,700
Sales commissions	66,000
Salary, sales supervisor	40,000

(continued)

Depreciation, factory equipment	$25,000
Administrative expenses	52,000
Supplies (half used in the factory, half used in the sales office)	4,000

Jordan produced 100,000 units during 2007 and sold 127,000 units at $6 per unit.

Required:

1. Prepare a statement of cost of goods manufactured.
2. Prepare an absorption-costing income statement.

2-22   COLLABORATIVE LEARNING EXERCISE

LO2, LO4, LO5   Divide the class into groups of four or five students. Each group should have one piece of paper and a pen or pencil. The paper and pencil pass clockwise around the group, giving each student a chance to write down his/her response to the following exercise. As the student writes the response, he/she should say the response aloud to the group. (This both involves the group and alerts the remaining members that the response has already been considered.) After five to 10 minutes, have a representative from each group read their group's responses aloud to the class.

List as many interrelated parts, processes, and objectives of an accounting information system as possible.

2-23   CYBER RESEARCH CASE

LO2   On the Internet, access the homepages of several enterprise resource planning (ERP) vendors (e.g., http://www.baan.com; http://www.cai.com; http://www.jdedwards.com; http://www.oracle.com; http://www.peoplesoft.com; http://www.sap.com). What are the advantages touted by each? Does there appear to be any difference between the companies? Write a memo from the CFO (chief financial officer) of a medium-sized manufacturing company to the CEO (chief executive officer) recommending the installation of an ERP system, discussing the differences and similarities among the ERP vendors.

Cost Behavior

AFTER STUDYING THIS CHAPTER, YOU SHOULD BE ABLE TO:

1. Define and describe fixed, variable, and mixed costs.
2. Explain the use of resources and activities and their relationship to cost behavior.
3. Separate mixed costs into their fixed and variable components using the high-low method, the scatterplot method, and the method of least squares.
4. Evaluate the reliability of the cost formula.
5. Explain how multiple regression can be used to assess cost behavior.
6. Define the learning curve, and discuss its impact on cost behavior.
7. Discuss the use of managerial judgment in determining cost behavior.

Costs can display variable, fixed, or mixed behavior. Knowing how costs change as activity output changes is an essential part of planning, controlling, and decision making. For example, budgeting, deciding to keep or drop a product line, and evaluating the performance of a segment all benefit from knowledge of cost behavior. In fact, not knowing and understanding cost behavior can lead to poor—and even disastrous—decisions. This chapter discusses cost behavior in depth so that a proper foundation is laid for its use in studying other cost management topics. A variable-costing system, for example, requires that all costs be classified as fixed or variable. But can all costs realistically be classified into one of these two categories? What are the assumptions and limitations associated with classifying costs in this way? Furthermore, just how good are our definitions of variable and fixed costs? Finally, what procedures can we use to break out the fixed and variable components of mixed costs? How do we assess the reliability of these procedures?

Basics of Cost Behavior

OBJECTIVE **1**

Define and describe fixed, variable, and mixed costs.

Cost behavior is the general term for describing whether a cost changes when the level of output changes. A cost that does not change as activity output changes is a *fixed cost*. A *variable cost*, on the other hand, increases in total with an increase in activity output and decreases in total with a decrease in activity output. In economics, it is usually *assumed* that fixed and variable costs are known. Management accountants must deal with the requirements to assess fixed and variable costs. Let's first review the basics of cost and output measures. Then, we will look at fixed, variable, and mixed costs. Finally, we will assess the impact of time horizon on cost behavior.

Measures of Activity Output

In order to determine the behavior of a cost, we need to have a good grasp of the cost under consideration and a measure of the output associated with the cost object. The terms *fixed cost* and *variable cost* do not exist in a vacuum; they only have meaning when related to some output measure or driver. Therefore, in order to understand the behavior of costs, we must first determine the underlying activities and the associated drivers that measure the capacity of an activity and its output. For example, materials handling output may be measured by the number of moves, shipping goods output may be measured by the units sold, and laundering hospital bedding output may be measured by the pounds of laundry. The choice of driver is tailored not only to the particular firm but also to the particular activity or cost being measured.

Activity drivers explain changes in activity costs by measuring changes in activity output (usage). The two general categories of activity drivers are *unit-level drivers* and *non-unit-level drivers*. **Unit-level drivers** explain changes in cost as units produced change. Pounds of direct materials, kilowatt-hours used to run production machinery, and direct labor hours are examples of unit-based activity drivers. Notice that while none of these drivers is equal to the number of units produced, each one does vary proportionately with the number of units produced. **Non-unit-level drivers** explain changes in costs as factors other than changes in units produced. Examples of non-unit-based activity output measures include setups, work orders, engineering change orders, inspection hours, and material moves.

In a functional-based cost management system, cost behavior is assumed to be described by unit-based drivers only. In an activity-based cost management system, both unit- and non-unit-based drivers are used. Thus, the ABC system tends to produce a much richer view of cost behavior than would a functional-based system. A need exists, however, to identify cost behavior patterns for a much broader set of activities.

We now take a closer look at fixed, variable, and mixed costs. In each case, the cost is related to only one measure of output.

Fixed Costs

Fixed costs are costs that *in total* are constant within the relevant range as the level of the activity driver varies. To illustrate fixed cost behavior, consider a plant operated by Days Computers, Inc., that produces personal computers. One of the departments of the plant inserts a 3½-inch disk drive into each computer passing through the department. The activity is drive insertion, and the activity driver is the number of computers processed. The department operates two production lines. Each line can process up to 10,000 computers per year. The production workers of each line are supervised by a production-line manager who is paid $24,000 per year. For production up to 10,000 units, only one manager is needed; for production between 10,001 and 20,000 units, two managers are needed. The cost of supervision for several levels of production for the plant is given as follows:

Days Computers, Inc.

Supervision	Computers Processed	Unit Cost
$24,000	4,000	$6.00
24,000	8,000	3.00
24,000	10,000	2.40
48,000	12,000	4.00
48,000	16,000	3.00
48,000	20,000	2.40

The first step in assessing cost behavior is defining an appropriate activity driver. In this case, the activity driver is the number of computers processed. The second step is defining what is meant by **relevant range**, the range over which the assumed cost relationship is valid for the normal operations of a firm. Assume that the relevant range is 12,000 to 20,000 computers processed. Notice that the *total* cost of supervision remains constant within this range as more computers are processed. Days Computers pays $48,000 for supervision regardless of whether it processes 12,000, 16,000, or 20,000 computers.

Pay particular attention to the words *in total* in the definition of fixed costs. While the total cost of supervision remains unchanged as more computers are processed, the unit cost does change as the level of the activity driver changes. As the example in the table shows, within the relevant range, the unit cost of supervision decreases from $4.00 to $2.40. Because of the behavior of per-unit fixed costs, it is easy to get the impression that fixed costs are affected by changes in the level of the activity driver, when in reality they are not. Unit fixed costs can often be misleading and may adversely affect some decisions. It is often safer to work with total fixed costs.

Let's take a look at the graph of fixed cost behavior given in Exhibit 3-1. We see that, for the relevant range, fixed cost behavior is described by a horizontal line. Notice

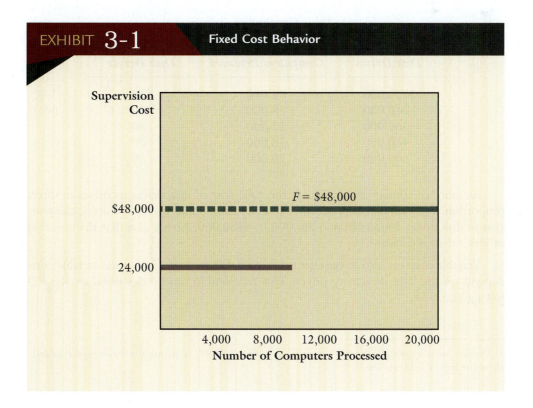

EXHIBIT 3-1   Fixed Cost Behavior

that at 12,000 computers processed, supervision cost is $48,000; at 16,000 computers processed, supervision is also $48,000. This line visually demonstrates that cost remains unchanged as the level of the activity driver varies. For the relevant range, total fixed costs can be represented by the following simple linear equation:

$$F = \text{Total fixed costs}$$

In our example for Days Computers, supervision cost amounted to $48,000 for any level of output between 10,001 and 20,000 computers processed. Thus, supervision is a fixed cost, and the fixed cost equation in this case is $F = \$48,000$. Strictly speaking, this equation assumes that the fixed costs are $48,000 for all levels (as if the line extends to the vertical axis as indicated by the dashed portion in Exhibit 3-1). Although this assumption is not true, it is harmless if the operating decisions are confined to the relevant range.

Can fixed costs change? Of course they can, but this does not make them variable. They are fixed at a new higher (or lower) rate. Going back to the example of Days Computers, suppose that the company gives a raise to the drive insertion line supervisors. Instead of being paid $24,000 per year, they are paid $26,000 per year. Now the cost of supervision is $52,000 per year (2 × $26,000). However, supervisory costs are still fixed with respect to the number of computers produced. Can you draw in the new fixed cost line on Exhibit 3-1?[1]

Variable Costs

Variable costs are defined as costs that in total vary in direct proportion to changes in an activity driver. To illustrate, let's expand the Days Computers example to include the cost of the 3½-inch disk drives. Here, the cost is the cost of direct materials—the disk drive—and the activity driver is the number of computers processed. Each computer requires one 3½-inch disk drive costing $30. The total cost of disk drives for various levels of production is given as follows:

Days Computers, Inc.

Total Cost of Disk Drives	Number of Computers Produced	Unit Cost of Disk Drives
$120,000	4,000	$30
240,000	8,000	30
360,000	12,000	30
480,000	16,000	30
600,000	20,000	30

As more computers are produced, the total cost of disk drives increases in direct proportion. For example, as production doubles from 8,000 to 16,000 units, the *total* cost of disk drives doubles from $240,000 to $480,000. Notice also that the unit cost of disk drives is constant.

Variable costs can also be represented by a linear equation. Here, total variable costs depend on the level of activity driver. This relationship can be described by the following equation:

---

1. The new line is a horizontal line that intersects the y-axis at $52,000. Note that it is drawn parallel to and above the original fixed cost line.

$$Y_v = VX$$

where

Y_v = Total variable costs
V = Variable cost per unit
X = Number of units of the driver

The relationship that describes the cost of disk drives is $Y_v = \$30X$, where X = the number of computers processed. Exhibit 3-2 shows graphically that variable cost behavior is represented by a straight line coming out of the origin. Notice that at zero units processed, total variable cost is zero. However, as units produced increase, the total variable cost also increases. Note that total variable cost increases in direct proportion to increases in the number of computers processed (the activity driver); the rate of increase is measured by the slope of the line. At 12,000 computers processed, the total variable cost of disk drives is $360,000 (or $30 × 12,000 computers processed); at 16,000 computers processed, the total variable cost is $480,000.

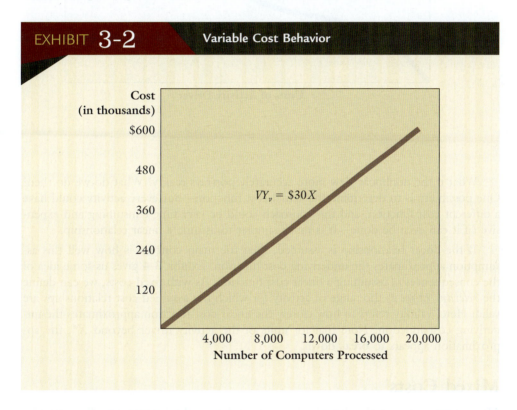

EXHIBIT 3-2   **Variable Cost Behavior**

Linearity Assumption

The definition of variable costs just given and the graph in Exhibit 3-2 imply a linear relationship between the cost of disk drives and the number of computers processed. How reasonable is the assumption that costs are linear? Do costs really increase in direct proportion to increases in the level of the activity driver? If not, then how well does this assumed linear cost function approximate the underlying cost function?

Economists usually assume that variable costs increase at a decreasing rate up to a certain volume, at which point they increase at an increasing rate. This type of *non-linear behavior* is displayed in Exhibit 3-3. Here, variable costs increase as the number of units increases, but not in direct proportion.

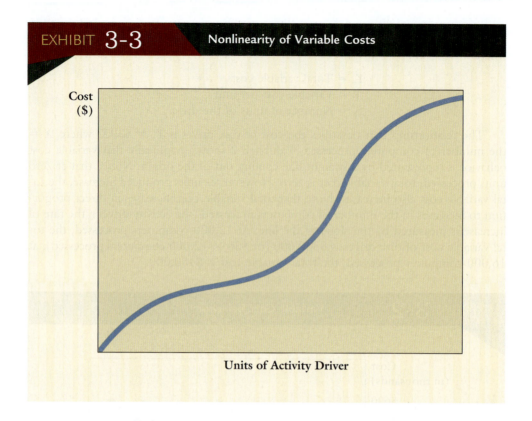

EXHIBIT **3-3**   Nonlinearity of Variable Costs

Cost ($)

Units of Activity Driver

What if the nonlinear view more accurately portrays reality? What do we do then? One possibility is to determine the actual cost function—but every activity could have a different cost function, and this approach could be very time consuming and expensive (if it can even be done). It is much simpler to assume a linear relationship.

If the linear relationship is assumed, then the main concern is how well this assumption approximates the underlying cost function. Exhibit 3-4 gives us some idea of the consequences of assuming a linear cost function. As with fixed costs, we can define the *relevant range* as the range of activity for which the assumed cost relationships are valid. Here, validity refers to how closely the linear cost function approximates the underlying cost function. Note that for units of the activity driver beyond X^*, the approximation appears to break down.

Mixed Costs

Mixed costs are costs that have both a fixed and a variable component. For example, sales representatives are often paid a salary plus a commission on sales. Suppose that Days Computers has 10 sales representatives, each earning a salary of $30,000 per year plus a commission of $50 per computer sold. The activity is selling, and the activity driver is units sold. If 10,000 computers are sold, then the total selling cost (associated with the sales representatives) is $800,000—the sum of the fixed salary cost of $300,000 (10 × $30,000) and the variable cost of $500,000 ($50 × 10,000).

The linear equation for a mixed cost is given by:

$$Y = \text{Fixed cost} + \text{Total variable cost}$$
$$Y = F + VX$$

where

$$Y = \text{Total cost}$$

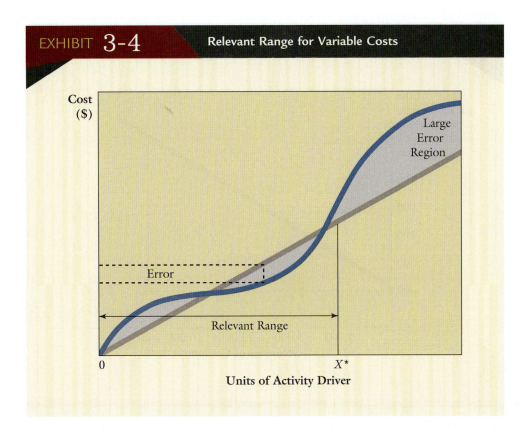

EXHIBIT 3-4   Relevant Range for Variable Costs

For Days Computers, the selling cost is represented by the following equation:

$$Y = \$300,000 + \$50X$$

The following table shows the selling cost for different levels of sales activity:

Days Computers, Inc.

Total Fixed Cost of Selling	Total Variable Cost of Selling	Total Cost	Computers Sold	Selling Cost per Unit
$300,000	$ 200,000	$ 500,000	4,000	$125.00
300,000	400,000	700,000	8,000	87.50
300,000	600,000	900,000	12,000	75.00
300,000	800,000	1,100,000	16,000	68.75
300,000	1,000,000	1,300,000	20,000	65.00

The graph for our mixed cost example is given in Exhibit 3-5. (The graph assumes that the relevant range is 0 to 20,000 units.) Mixed costs are represented by a line that intercepts the vertical axis (at $300,000, for this example). The intercept corresponds to the fixed cost component, and the slope of the line gives the variable cost per unit of activity driver (slope is $50 for the example portrayed).

Time Horizon

Determining whether a cost is fixed or variable depends on the time horizon. According-ing to economics, in the **long run**, all costs are variable; in the **short run**, at least one cost is fixed. But how long is the short run? Different costs have short runs of different

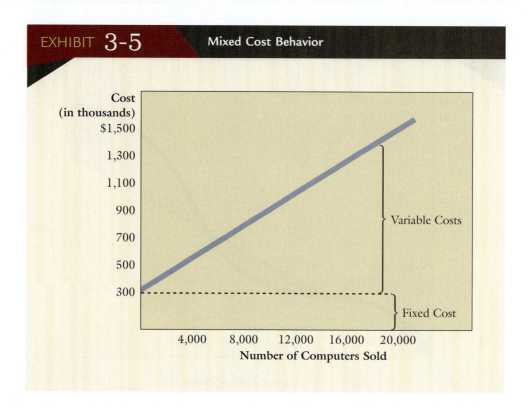

EXHIBIT 3-5   **Mixed Cost Behavior**

lengths. Direct materials, for example, are relatively easy to adjust. **Starbucks Coffee** may treat coffee beans (a direct material) as strictly variable, even though for the next few hours the amount already on hand is fixed. The lease of space for its coffee shop in Denver's Cherry Creek area, however, is more difficult to adjust; it may run for one or more years. Thus, this cost is typically seen as fixed. The length of the short-run period depends to some extent on management judgment and the purpose for which cost behavior is being estimated. For example, submitting a bid on a 1-time, special order may span only a month—long enough to create a bid and produce the order. Other types of decisions, such as product discontinuance or product mix decisions, will affect a much longer period of time. In this case, the costs that must be considered are long-run variable costs, including product design, product development, market development, and market penetration. Short-run costs often do not adequately reflect all the costs necessary to design, produce, market, distribute, and support a product. Recently, there have been some new insights that help shed light on the nature of long- and short-run cost behaviors.[2] These insights relate to activities and the resources needed to enable an activity to be performed.

Resources, Activities, and Cost Behavior

Resources are simply economic elements that enable one to perform activities. Common resources of a manufacturing plant include direct materials, direct labor, electricity, equipment, and so on. When a company spends money on resources, it is *acquiring* the ability or capacity to perform an activity. Recall from Chapter 2, that an activity is simply a task, such as setting up equipment, purchasing materials, assembling materi-

OBJECTIVE 2

Explain the use of resources and activities and their relationship to cost behavior.

---

2. The concepts presented in the remainder of this section are based on Alfred M. King, "The Current Status of Activity-Based Costing: An Interview with Robin Cooper and Robert S. Kaplan," *Management Accounting* (September 1991): 22–26; and Robin Cooper and Robert S. Kaplan, "Activity-Based Systems: Measuring the Costs of Resource Usage," *Accounting Horizons* (September 1992): 1–13.

als, and packing completed units in boxes. When a firm acquires the resources needed to perform an activity, it is obtaining **activity capacity**. Usually, we can assume that the amount of activity capacity needed corresponds to the level where the activity is performed efficiently. This efficient level of activity performance is called **practical capacity**.

If all of the activity capacity acquired is not used, then we have **unused capacity**, which is the difference between the acquired capacity and the actual activity output. The relationship between resource spending and resource usage can be used to define variable and fixed cost behavior.

Flexible Resources

Resources can be categorized as (1) flexible and (2) committed. **Flexible resources** are supplied as used and needed; they are acquired from outside sources, where the terms of acquisition do not require any long-term commitment for any given amount of the resource. Thus, the organization is free to buy what it needs, when it needs it. As a result, the quantity of the resource supplied equals the quantity demanded. There is no unused capacity for this category of resources (resource usage = resources supplied).

Since the cost of flexible resources equals the cost of resources used, the total cost of the resource increases as demand for the resource increases. Therefore, we generally can treat the cost of flexible resources as a variable cost. For example, in a just-in-time manufacturing environment, materials are purchased when needed. Using units produced as the output measure, or driver, it is clear that as the units produced increase, the usage (and cost) of direct materials would increase proportionately. Similarly, power is a flexible resource. Using kilowatt-hours as the activity output measure (activity driver), as the demand for power increases, the cost of power increases. Note that in both examples, resource supply and usage is measured by an output measure, or driver.

Committed Resources

Committed resources are supplied in advance of usage. They are acquired by the use of either an explicit or implicit contract to obtain a given quantity of resource, regardless of whether the quantity of the resource available is fully used or not. Committed resources may exceed the demand for their usage; thus, unused capacity is possible.

Many resources are acquired before the actual demands for the resource are realized. There are two examples of this category of resource acquisition. First, organizations acquire many *multiperiod service capacities* by paying cash up front or by entering into an explicit contract that requires periodic cash payments. Buying or leasing buildings and equipment are examples of this form of advance resource acquisition. The annual expense associated with the multiperiod category is independent of actual usage of the resource. Often, these expenses are referred to as **committed fixed expenses**. They essentially correspond to committed resources—costs incurred that provide long-term activity capacity.

A second and more important example concerns organizations that acquire resources in advance through implicit contracts—usually with their employees. These implicit contracts require an ethical focus, since they imply that the organization will maintain employment levels even though there may be temporary downturns in the quantity of activity used. Companies may manage the difficulties associated with maintaining this fixed level of expense by using contingent, or temporary, workers when needed. Many companies have indicated that the key reason for the use of contingent workers is flexibility—in meeting demand fluctuations, in controlling downsizing, and in buffering core workers against job loss.[3]

---

3. "Contingent Employment on the Rise," *Deloitte & Touche Review* (September 4, 1995): 1–2.

COST MANAGEMENT   Technology in Action

Cost behavior is important to companies. First, of course, the company must determine appropriate cost objects. This is relatively easy in a manufacturing firm; the cost object is typically the tangible product. In service firms, the logical cost object is the service. For example, hospitals may view particular services such as blood tests or radiology services as primary cost objects.

The Internet, however, has fundamentally changed the way companies do business with their suppliers and customers. Price competition is severe so firms cannot, typically, succeed using a low-price strategy. Instead, they use a customer-service strategy. Internet-based companies strive to provide a shopping experience that is user friendly, with an abundance of information tailored to customer needs, and a secure payment system. Ideally, the company provides a seamless interface for customers, taking them from information search, through product/service choice, payment, and post-sale follow up. Software that tracks ongoing customer preferences is a large part of the enhanced customer shopping experience. (**Amazon.com** is an excellent example of this, as it welcomes new and returning customers and makes the shopping experience fun and easy.) As a result, "Internet-based firms rely much less on traditional infrastructure assets, such as buildings, and more on computers, specialized software, and intellectual capital that cater to customers in cyberspace." This means that the customer is the appropriate cost object, and activities and drivers that are tied to customer service are important data to Internet-based firms.

Source: Taken from Lawrence A. Gordon and Martin P. Loeb, "Distinguishing Between Direct and Indirect Costs Is Crucial for Internet Companies," *Management Accounting Quarterly*, Summer 2001, Vol. II, No. 4, pp. 12–17.

Resource spending for this category essentially corresponds to **discretionary fixed expenses**—costs incurred for the acquisition of short-term activity capacity. Hiring three sustaining engineers for $150,000 who can supply the capacity of processing 7,500 change orders is an example of implicit contracting (change orders is the driver used to measure resource capacity and usage).[4] Certainly, none of the three engineers would expect to be laid off if only 5,000 change orders were actually processed—unless, of course, the downturn in demand is viewed as being permanent.

Implications for Control and Decision Making

The activity-based resource usage model just described can improve both managerial control and decision making. Operational control information systems encourage managers to pay more attention to controlling resource usage and spending. A well-designed operational system would allow managers to assess the changes in resource demands that will occur from new product mix decisions. Adding new, customized products may increase the demand for various overhead activities; if sufficient unused activity capacity does not exist, then resource spending must increase.

Similarly, if activity management brings about excess activity capacity (by finding ways to reduce resource usage), managers must carefully consider what to do with the excess capacity. Eliminating the excess capacity may decrease resource spending and thus improve overall profits. Alternatively, using the excess capacity to increase output could increase revenues without a corresponding increase in resource spending.

The activity-based resource usage model also allows managers to calculate the changes in resource supply and demand resulting from implementing such decisions as to make or buy, accept or reject special orders, and keep or drop product lines. Additionally, the model increases the power of a number of traditional management accounting decision-making models. The impact on decision making is explored in the decision-making chapters found in Part 4 (Chapters 17–21). Most of the decision-making models in those chapters depend heavily on knowledge of cost behavior.

---

4. Often, in response to customer feedback and competitive pressures, products need to be redesigned or modified. An engineering change order is the document that initiates this process.

Step-Cost Behavior

In our discussion of cost behavior, we have assumed that the cost function (either linear or nonlinear) is continuous. In reality, some cost functions may be discontinuous, as shown in Exhibit 3-6. This type of cost function is known as a *step function*. A **step-cost function** displays a constant level of cost for a range of activity output and then jumps to a higher level of cost at some point, where it remains for a similar range of activity. In Exhibit 3-6, the cost is $100, as long as activity output is between 0 and 20 units. If the volume is between 20 and 40 units, the cost jumps to $200.

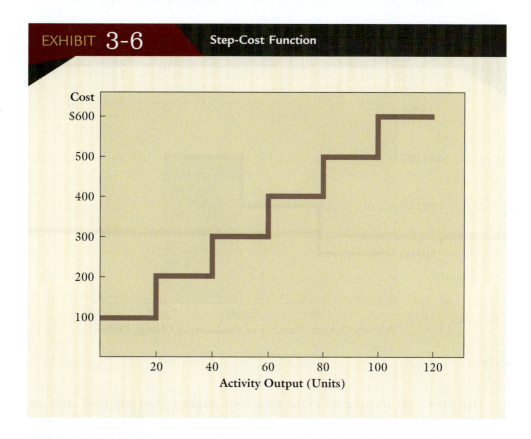

EXHIBIT 3-6   Step-Cost Function

Step-Variable Costs

Items that display a step-cost behavior must be purchased in chunks. The width of the step defines the range of activity output for which a quantity of the resource must be acquired. The width of the step in Exhibit 3-6 is 20 units of activity. If the width of the step is narrow, as in Exhibit 3-6, the cost of the resource changes in response to fairly small changes in resource usage (as measured by activity output). Costs that follow a step-cost behavior with narrow steps are defined as **step-variable costs**. If the width of the step is narrow, we usually approximate step-variable costs with a strictly variable cost assumption.

Step-Fixed Costs

In reality, many so-called fixed costs probably are best described by a step-cost function. Many committed resources—particularly those that involve implicit contracting—follow a step-cost function. Suppose, for example, that a company hires three sustaining engineers—engineers who are responsible for redesigning existing products to meet customer requirements. By hiring the engineers, the company has acquired the ability to perform an activity: engineering redesign. The salaries paid to the engineers represent the cost of acquiring the engineering redesign capacity. The number of engineering changes that can be *efficiently* processed by the three engineers is a quantitative measure of that capacity. The number of change orders processed, on the other hand, is a measure of the actual usage. Assume the engineers are each paid an annual salary of $50,000 and that each engineer can process 2,500 engineering change orders per year. The company has acquired the capacity to process 7,500 (3 × 2,500) change orders per year at a total cost of $150,000 (3 × $50,000). The nature of the resource requires that the capacity be acquired in chunks (one engineer hired at a time). The cost function for this example is displayed in Exhibit 3-7. Notice that the width of the steps is 2,500 units—a much wider step than the cost function displayed in Exhibit 3-6. Costs that follow a step-cost behavior with wide steps are defined as **step-fixed costs**.

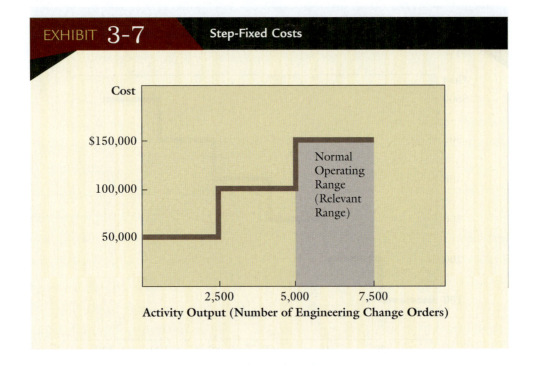

EXHIBIT 3-7   Step-Fixed Costs

Step-fixed costs are assigned to the fixed cost category. Most step-fixed costs are fixed over the normal operating range of a firm. If that range is 5,000 to 7,500 change orders (as shown in Exhibit 3-7), then the firm will spend $150,000 on engineering resources. This is equivalent to spending $20 per change order ($150,000/7,500). The average unit cost, obtained by dividing the resource expenditure by the activity's practical capacity, is the **activity rate**. The activity rate is used to calculate the cost of resource usage and the cost of unused activity.

For example, the company may not actually process 7,500 orders during the year—that is, all of the available order-processing capacity may not be used. Resource usage is the number of change orders *actually* processed. Assume that 6,000 change orders were processed during the year. The cost of resource usage is the activity rate times the actual activity output: $20 × 6,000 = $120,000. Further, the cost of unused activity is the activity rate times the unused activity: $20 × 1,500 = $30,000. Note that the cost of unused capacity occurs because the resource (engineering redesign) must be acquired in lumpy (whole) amounts. Even if the company had anticipated the need for only 6,000 change orders, it would have been difficult to hire the equivalent of 2.4 engineers (6,000/2,500).

This example illustrates that when resources are acquired in advance, there may be a difference between the *resources supplied* and the *resources used (demanded)* to perform activities. This can only occur for activity costs that display a fixed cost behavior (resources acquired in advance of usage). Typically, the traditional cost management system provides information only about the cost of the resources supplied. A contemporary cost management system, on the other hand, tells us how much of the activity is used and the cost of its usage. Furthermore, the relationship between resources supplied and resources used is expressed by either of the following two equations:

$$\text{Activity availability} = \text{Activity output} + \text{Unused capacity} \qquad (3.1)$$

$$\text{Cost of activity supplied} = \text{Cost of activity used} + \text{Cost of unused activity} \qquad (3.2)$$

Equation 3.1 expresses the relationship between supply and demand in physical units, while Equation 3.2 expresses it in financial terms.

For the engineering order example, the relationships appear as follows:

Physical units (Equation 3.1):

$$\text{Available orders} = \text{Orders used} + \text{Orders unused}$$
$$7,500 \text{ orders} = 6,000 \text{ orders} + 1,500 \text{ orders}$$

Financial terms (Equation 3.2):

$$\text{Cost of orders supplied} = \text{Cost of orders used} + \text{Cost of unused orders}$$
$$7,500(\$20) = 6,000(\$20) + 1,500(\$20)$$
$$\$150,000 = \$120,000 + \$30,000$$

Activities and Mixed Cost Behavior

It is possible for activities to have resources associated with them that are acquired in advance and resources that are acquired as needed. Thus, activity costs can display a mixed cost behavior. Assume that a plant has its own power department. The plant has acquired long-term capacity for supplying power by investing in a building and equipment (resources acquired in advance). The plant also acquires fuel to produce power as needed (resources acquired as needed). The cost of the building and equipment is independent of the kilowatt-hours produced, but the cost of fuel increases as the demand for kilowatt-hours increases. The activity of supplying power has both a fixed cost component and a variable cost component, using kilowatt-hours as the activity output measure.

What the Accounting Records Reveal

Sometimes it is easy to identify the variable and fixed components of a mixed cost, as in the example given earlier for the sales representatives. Many times, however, the only information available is the total cost of an activity and a measure of activity output (the variables Y and X). For example, the accounting system will usually record both the total cost of the maintenance activity for a given period and the number of maintenance hours provided during that period. The accounting records do not reveal the amount of the total maintenance cost representing a fixed charge and the amount representing a variable charge. (In fact, the accounting records may not even reveal the breakdown of costs in the sales representative example.) Often, the total cost is simply recorded with no attempt to segregate the fixed and variable costs.

Need for Cost Separation

Since accounting records typically reveal only the total cost and the associated activity output of a mixed cost item, it is necessary to separate the total cost into its fixed and variable components. Only through a formal effort to separate costs can they all be classified into the appropriate cost behavior categories.

If mixed costs are a very small percentage of total costs, however, formal cost separation may be more trouble than it's worth. In this case, mixed costs could be assigned to either the fixed or variable cost category without much concern for the classification error or its effect on decision making. Alternatively, the total mixed cost could be arbitrarily divided between the two cost categories. This option is seldom available, though. Mixed costs for many firms are large enough to warrant separation. Given the need for separating costs, how is this done?

Methods for Separating Mixed Costs into Fixed and Variable Components

OBJECTIVE 3

Separate mixed costs into their fixed and variable components using the high-low method, the scatterplot method, and the method of least squares.

The three widely used methods of separating a mixed cost into its fixed and variable components are the high-low method, the scatterplot method, and the method of least squares. Each method requires us to make the simplifying assumption of a linear cost relationship. Therefore, before we examine each of these methods more closely, let's review the expression of cost as an equation for a straight line.

$$Y = F + VX$$

where

Y = Total activity cost (the dependent variable)
F = Fixed cost component (the intercept parameter)
V = Variable cost per unit of activity (the slope parameter)
X = Measure of activity output (the independent variable)

The **dependent variable** is a variable whose value depends on the value of another variable. In the preceding equation, total activity cost is the dependent variable; it is the cost we are trying to predict. The **independent variable** is a variable that measures activity output and explains changes in the activity cost. It is an activity driver. The choice of an independent variable is related to its economic plausibility. That is, the manager will attempt to find an independent variable that causes or is closely associated with the dependent variable. The **intercept parameter** corresponds to fixed activity cost. Graphically, the intercept parameter is the point at which the mixed cost line intercepts the cost (vertical) axis. The **slope parameter** corresponds to the variable cost per unit of activity. Graphically, this represents the slope of the mixed cost line.

Since the accounting records reveal only X and Y, those values must be used to estimate the parameters F and V. With estimates of F and V, the fixed and variable components can be estimated, and the behavior of the mixed cost can be predicted as activity output changes. As mentioned at the beginning of this section, three methods will be described for estimating F and V: the high-low method, the scatterplot method, and the method of least squares.

The same data will be used with each method so that comparisons among them can be made. As an example, the data have been accumulated for a materials handling activity. The plant manager believes that the number of material moves is a good activity driver for the activity. Assume that the accounting records of Anderson Company disclose the following materials handling costs and number of material moves for the past 10 months:

Month	Materials Handling Cost	Number of Moves
January	$2,000	100
February	3,090	125
March	2,780	175
April	1,990	200
May	7,500	500
June	5,300	300
July	4,300	250
August	6,300	400
September	5,600	475
October	6,240	425

The High-Low Method

From basic geometry, we know that two points are needed to determine a line. If we know two points on a line, then its equation can be determined. Recall that F, the fixed cost component, is the intercept of the total cost line, and V, the variable cost per unit, is the slope of the line. Given two points, the slope and the intercept can be determined. The **high-low method** preselects the two points that will be used to compute the parameters F and V. Specifically, the high-low method uses the high and low points. The *high point* is defined as the point with the *highest activity level*. The *low point* is defined as the point with the *lowest activity level*.

Letting (X_1, Y_1) be the low point and (X_2, Y_2) be the high point, the equations for determining the slope and intercept are, respectively:

$$V = \text{Change in cost/Change in activity}$$
$$= (Y_2 - Y_1)/(X_2 - X_1)$$

$$F = \text{Total mixed cost} - \text{Variable cost}$$
$$= Y_2 - VX_2$$

or

$$F = Y_1 - VX_1$$

Notice that the fixed cost component is computed using the total cost at either (X_1, Y_1) or (X_2, Y_2).

For Anderson, the high point is 500 moves with an associated cost of $7,500, or (500, $7,500). The low point is 100 moves with an associated cost of $2,000, or (100, $2,000). Once the high and low points are defined, the values of F and V can be computed.

$$V = (Y_2 - Y_1)/(X_2 - X_1)$$
$$= (\$7,500 - \$2,000)/(500 - 100)$$
$$= \$5,500/400$$
$$= \$13.75$$

$$F = Y_2 - VX_2$$
$$= \$7,500 - (\$13.75 \times 500)$$
$$= \$625$$

The cost formula using the high-low method is:

$$Y = \$625 + \$13.75X$$

If the number of moves for November is expected to be 350, this cost formula will predict a total cost of $5,437.50, with fixed costs of $625 and variable costs of $4,812.50.

The high-low method has two advantages. First, it is objective. That is, any two people using the high-low method on a particular data set will arrive at the same answer. Second, it is simple to calculate. The high-low method allows a manager to get a quick fix on a cost relationship using only two data points. For example, a manager may have only two months of data. Sometimes, this will be enough to get a crude approximation of the cost relationship.

The high-low method is usually not as good as the other methods. Why? First, the high and low points often can be what are known as outliers. They may represent atypical cost-activity relationships. If so, the cost formula computed using these two points will not represent what usually takes place. The **scatterplot method** can help a manager avoid this trap by selecting two points that appear to be representative of the general cost-activity pattern. Second, even if these points are not outliers, other pairs of points may clearly be more representative. Again, the scatterplot method allows the choice of the more representative points.

Scatterplot Method

The first step in applying the scatterplot method is to plot the data points so that the relationship between materials handling costs and activity output can be seen. This plot is referred to as a **scattergraph** and is shown in Exhibit 3-8, Graph A. The vertical axis is total activity cost (materials handling cost), and the horizontal axis is the driver or output measure (number of moves). Looking at Exhibit 3-8, Graph A, we see that the relationship between materials handling costs and number of moves is reasonably linear; cost goes up as the number of moves goes up, and vice versa.

Now let's examine Exhibit 3-8, Graph B, to see if the line determined by the high and low points is representative of the overall relationship. It does look relatively representative. Does that mean that the high-low line should be chosen? Not necessarily. Suppose that management believes the variable costs of materials handling will go down in the near future. In that case, the high-low line gives a somewhat higher variable cost (slope) than desired. The scatterplot line will be chosen with a shallower slope.

Thus, one purpose of a scattergraph is to assess the validity of the assumed linear relationship. Additionally, inspecting the scattergraph may reveal several points that do not seem to fit the general pattern of behavior. Upon investigation, it may be discovered that these points (the outliers) were due to some irregular occurrences. This knowledge can provide justification for their elimination and perhaps lead to a better estimate of the underlying cost function.

A scattergraph can help provide insight concerning the relationship between cost and activity output. In fact, a scattergraph allows one to visually fit a line to the points on the scattergraph. In doing so, the line chosen should appear to best fit the points. In making that choice, a manager or cost analyst is free to use past experience with the behavior of the cost item. Experience may provide a manager/analyst with a good intuitive sense of how materials handling costs behave; the scattergraph then becomes a useful tool to quantify this intuition. Fitting a line to the points in this way is how the scatterplot method works. Keep in mind that the scattergraph and the other statistical aids are tools that can help managers improve their judgment. Using the tools does not restrict the manager from using his or her own judgment to alter any of the estimates produced by formal methods.

Examine Exhibit 3-8, Graph A, carefully. Based only on the information contained in the graph, how would you fit a line to the points in it? Of course, there are an infinite number of lines that might go through the data, but let's choose one that goes through the point for January (100, $2,000) and intersects the y-axis at $800. Now, we have the straight line shown in Exhibit 3-8, Graph C. The fixed cost, of course, is $800, the intercept. We can use the high-low method to determine the variable rate.

First, remember that our two points are (100, $2,000) and (0, $800). Next, use these two points to compute the slope:

$$V = (Y_2 - Y_1)/(X_2 - X_1)$$
$$= (\$2,000 - \$800)/(100 - 0)$$
$$= \$1,200/100$$
$$= \$12$$

Thus, the variable cost per material move is $12.

The fixed and varia ble components of the materials handling cost have now been identified. The cost formula for the materials handling activity can be expressed as:

$$Y = \$800 + \$12X$$

Using this formula, the total cost of materials handling for activity output between 100 and 500 can be predicted and then broken down into fixed and variable components. For example, assume that 350 moves are planned for November. Using the cost for-

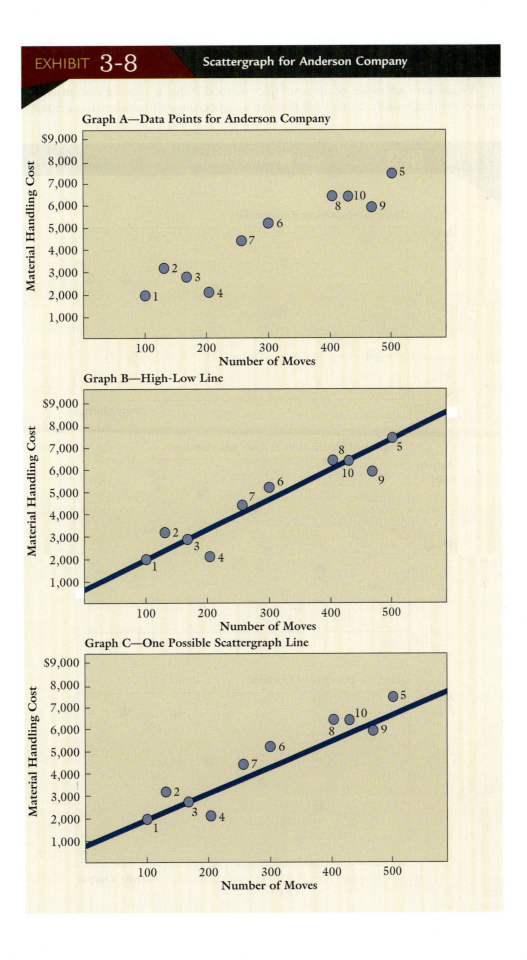

EXHIBIT 3-8   Scattergraph for Anderson Company

Graph A—Data Points for Anderson Company

Graph B—High-Low Line

Graph C—One Possible Scattergraph Line

mula, the predicted cost is $5,000 [$800 + ($12 × 350)]. Of this total cost, $800 is fixed, and $4,200 is variable.

A significant advantage of the scatterplot method is that it allows a cost analyst to inspect the data visually. Exhibit 3-9 illustrates cost behavior situations that are not ap-

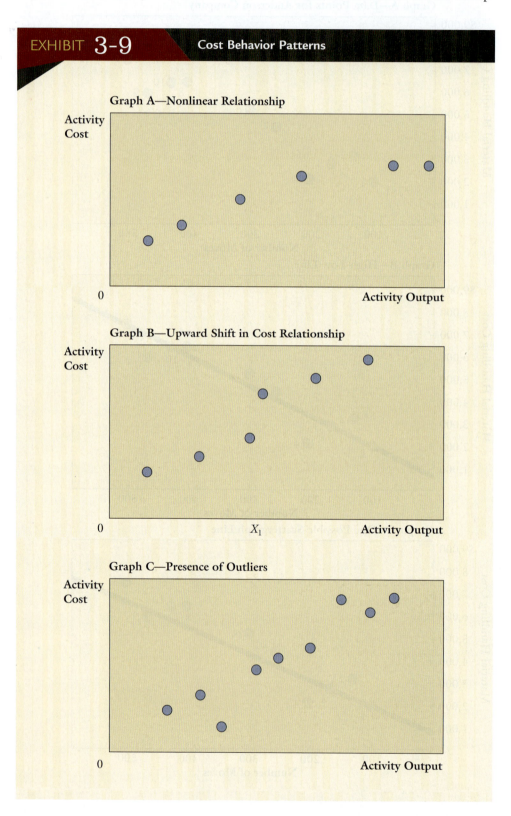

EXHIBIT 3-9   Cost Behavior Patterns

Graph A—Nonlinear Relationship

Graph B—Upward Shift in Cost Relationship

Graph C—Presence of Outliers

propriate for the simple application of the high-low method. Graph A shows a non-linear relationship between cost and output. An example of this is a volume discount given on direct materials or evidence of learning by workers (e.g., as more hours are worked, the total cost increases at a decreasing rate due to the increased efficiency of the workers). Graph B shows an upward shift in cost if more than X_1 units are made—perhaps due to the costs of paying an additional supervisor or running a second shift. Graph C shows outliers that do not represent the overall cost relationship.

The cost formula for materials handling was obtained by fitting a line to two points [(0, $800) and (100, $2,000)] in Exhibit 3-8, Graph C. We used our judgment to select the line. Whereas one person may decide that the best-fitting line is the one passing through those two points, others, using their own judgment, may decide that the best line passes through other pairs of points.

The scatterplot method suffers from the lack of any objective criterion for choosing the best-fitting line. The quality of the cost formula depends on the quality of the subjective judgment of the analyst. The high-low method removes the subjectivity in the choice of the line. Regardless of who uses the method, the same line will result.

Looking again at Exhibit 3-8, Graphs B and C, we can compare the results of the scatterplot method with those of the high-low method. There is a difference between the fixed cost components and the variable rates. The predicted materials handling cost for 350 moves is $5,000 according to the scatterplot method and $5,437.50 according to the high-low method. Which is "correct"? Since the two methods can produce significantly different cost formulas, the question of which method is the best naturally arises. Ideally, a method that is objective and, at the same time, produces the best-fitting line is needed. The **method of least squares** defines *best-fitting* and is objective in the sense that using the method for a given set of data will produce the same cost formula.

The Method of Least Squares

Up to this point, we have alluded to the concept of a line that best fits the points shown on a scattergraph. What is meant by a best-fitting line? Intuitively, it is the line to which the data points are closest. But what is meant by closest?

Consider Exhibit 3-10. Here, an arbitrary line ($Y = F + VX$) has been drawn. The closeness of each point to the line can be measured by the vertical distance of the point from the line. This vertical distance is the difference between the actual cost and the cost predicted by the line. For point 8, this is $E_8 = Y_8 - F + VX_8$, where Y_8 is the actual cost, $F + VX_8$ is the predicted cost, and the deviation is represented by E_8. The **deviation** is the difference between the predicted and actual costs, which is shown by the distance from the point to the line.

The vertical distance measures the closeness of a single point to the line, but we really need a measure of closeness of *all* points to the line. One possibility is to add all the single measures to obtain an overall measure. However, since the single measures can have positive or negative signs, this overall measure may not be very meaningful. For example, the sum of small positive deviations could result in an overall measure greater in magnitude than the sum of large positive deviations and large negative deviations because of the cancelling effect of positive and negative numbers. To correct this problem, we could first square each single measure of closeness and then sum these squared deviations as the overall measure of closeness. Squaring the deviations avoids the cancellation problem caused by a mix of positive and negative numbers.

To illustrate this concept, a measure of closeness will be calculated for the cost formula produced by the scatterplot method.

EXHIBIT 3-10   Line Deviations

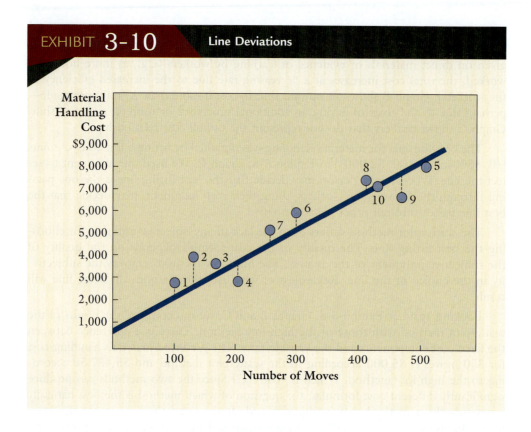

Actual Cost	Predicted Cost[a]	Deviation[b]	Deviation Squared
$2,000	$2,000	0	0
3,090	2,300	790	624,100
2,780	2,900	−120	14,400
1,990	3,200	−1,210	1,464,100
7,500	6,800	700	490,000
5,300	4,400	900	810,000
4,300	3,800	500	250,000
6,300	5,600	700	490,000
5,600	6,500	−900	810,000
6,240	5,900	340	115,600
Total measure of closeness			5,068,200

[a]Predicted cost = $800 + $12X, where X is the actual measure of activity output associated with the actual activity cost and cost is rounded to the nearest dollar.
[b]Deviation = Actual cost − Predicted cost.

Since the measure of closeness is the sum of the squared deviations of the points from the line, the smaller the measure, the better the line fits the points. For example, the scatterplot method line has a closeness measure of 5,068,200. A similar calculation produces a closeness measure of 5,402,013 for the high-low line. Thus, the scatterplot line fits the points better than the high-low line. This outcome supports the earlier claim that the use of judgment in the scatterplot method is superior to the high-low method.

In principle, comparing closeness measures can produce a ranking of all lines from best to worst. The line that fits the points better than any other line is called the *best-fitting line*. It is the line with the smallest (least) sum of squared deviations. The method of least squares identifies the best-fitting line. We rely on statistical theory to obtain the formulas that produce the best-fitting line.

Using Regression Programs

Computing the regression formula manually is tedious, even with only a few data points. As the number of data points increases, manual computation becomes impractical. (When multiple regression is used, manual computation is virtually impossible.) Fortunately, spreadsheet packages such as Microsoft Excel[5] have regression routines that will perform the computations. All that you need to do is input the data. The spreadsheet regression program supplies more than the estimates of the coefficients. It also provides information that can be used to see how reliable the cost equation is, a feature that is not available for the scatterplot and high-low methods.

The first step in using the computer to calculate regression coefficients is to enter the data. Exhibit 3-11 shows the computer screen you would see if you entered the Anderson Company data on materials handling cost and moves into a spreadsheet. It is a good idea to label your variables as is done in the exhibit: the months are labeled, column B is labeled for materials handling costs, and column C is labeled for the number of moves. The next step is to run the regression. In Excel and Quattro Pro, the regression routine is located under the "tools" menu (toward the top right of the screen). When you pull down the "tools" menu, you will see other menu possibilities. In Quattro Pro, choose "numeric tools" and then "regression." In Excel, choose "add in" and then add the "data analysis tools." When the data analysis tools have been added, "data analysis" will appear at the bottom of the "tools" menu; click on "data analysis," and then "regression."

EXHIBIT 3-11   Spreadsheet Data for Anderson Company

Speadsheet Data for Anderson Company.xls

	A	B	C	D	E	F	G	H	I
1	Month	Cost	# Moves						
2	January	$2,000	100						
3	February	3,090	125						
4	March	2,780	175						
5	April	1,990	200						
6	May	7,500	500						
7	June	5,300	300						
8	July	4,300	250						
9	August	6,300	400						
10	September	5,600	475						
11	October	6,240	425						
12									
13									
14									
15									
16									
17									
18									
19									
20									

Sheet1 / Sheet2 / Sheet3 /

---

5. Lotus 1-2-3 are registered trademarks of the Lotus Development Corporation. Quattro Pro is a registered trademark of Novell, Inc. Excel is a registered trademark of Microsoft Corporation. Any further reference to Lotus 1-2-3, Quattro Pro, or Excel refers to this footnote.

When the "regression" screen pops up, you can tell the program where the dependent and independent variables are located. Simply place the cursor at the beginning of the "independent" rectangle and then (again using the cursor) block the values under the independent variable column, in this case, cells c2 through c11. Then, move the cursor to the beginning of the "dependent" rectangle, and block the values in cells b2 through b11. Finally, you need to tell the computer where to place the output. Block a nice-sized rectangle—for example, cells a13 through f20—and click on "OK." In less than the blink of an eye, the regression output is complete. The regression output is shown in Exhibit 3-12.

EXHIBIT 3-12 Regression Output for Anderson Company

Regression Output for Anderson Company.xls

	A	B	C	D	E	F
1	SUMMARY OUTPUT					
2	*Regression Statistics*					
3	Multiple R	0.928949080				
4	R Square	0.862946394				
5	Adjusted R	0.845814693				
6						
7	Square					
8	Standard Error	770.4987038				
9	Observations	10				
10						
11	ANOVA					
12		*df*	*SS*	*MS*	*F*	*Significance F*
13	Regression	1	29903853.98	29903853.98	50.37132077	0.000102268
14	Residual	8	4749346.021	593668.2526		
15	Total	9	34653200			
16						
17						
18		*Coefficients*	*Standard Error*	*t Stat*	*P-value*	
19	Intercept	854.4993582	569.7810263	1.499697811	0.172079925	
20	X Variable 1	12.3915276	1.745955536	7.097275588	0.000102268	
21						

Sheet1 / Sheet2 / Sheet3

Now, let's take a look at the output in Exhibit 3-12. First, locate the fixed cost and variable rate coefficients. At the bottom of the exhibit, the intercept and *X* Variable 1 are shown, and the next column gives their coefficients. Rounding, the fixed cost is $854.50, and the variable rate is $12.39. Now, we can construct the following cost formula for materials handling cost:

Materials handling cost = $854.50 + ($12.39 × Number of moves)

We can use this formula to predict materials handling cost for future months as we did with the formulas for the high-low and scatterplot methods.

Since the regression cost formula is the best-fitting line, it should produce better predictions of materials handling costs. For 350 moves, the estimate predicted by the least-squares line is $5,191 [$854.50 + ($12.39 × 350)], with a fixed component of $854.50 plus a variable component of $4,336.50. Using this prediction as a standard, the scatterplot line most closely approximates the least-squares line.

While the computer output in Exhibit 3-12 can give us the fixed and variable cost coefficients, its major usefulness lies in its ability to provide information about how reliable the estimated cost formula is. The scatterplot or high-low methods do not provide this feature.

Reliability of Cost Formulas

Regression routines provide information that can be used to assess how reliable the estimated cost formula is. This is a feature not provided by either the scatterplot or high-low methods. Exhibit 3-12 will serve as the point of reference for discussing three statistical assessments concerning the cost formula's reliability: *hypothesis test of cost parameters*, *goodness of fit*, and *confidence intervals*. The hypothesis test of cost parameters indicates whether the parameters are different from zero. For our setting, goodness of fit measures the degree of association between cost and activity output. This measure is important because the method of least squares identifies the best-fitting line, but it does not reveal how good the fit is. The best-fitting line may not be a good-fitting line. It may perform miserably when it comes to predicting costs. A confidence interval provides a range of values for the actual cost with a prespecified degree of confidence. Confidence intervals allow managers to predict a range of values instead of a single prediction. Of course, if the degree of association is perfect, then the confidence interval will consist of a single point and the actual cost will always coincide with the predicted cost. Thus, goodness of fit and confidence intervals are related, and they provide cost analysts some idea of how reliable the resulting cost equation is.

Hypothesis Test of Parameters

Refer once again to Exhibit 3-12. The fourth column of the bottom table, labeled "*t* Stat," presents the *t* statistics for each parameter. These *t* statistics are used to test the hypothesis that the parameters are different from zero. The fifth column, labeled "*P*-value," is the level of significance achieved. The fixed cost parameter, *F*, is significant at the 0.172 level. This is NOT significant at the 0.05 or even the 0.10 levels. The variable cost parameter is significant at the 0.0001 level. Thus, the number of moves appears to be a highly significant explanatory variable—a driver for materials handling costs. However, the presence of fixed materials handling costs is questionable. The third column presents the standard error for each parameter. This value is used to compute the *t* statistic in column 4: the coefficient in column 2 is divided by the corresponding standard error.

Goodness of Fit Measures

Initially, we assume that a single activity driver (activity output variable) explains changes (variability) in activity cost. Our experience with the Anderson Company example suggests that the number of moves can explain changes in materials handling costs. The scattergraph shown back in Exhibit 3-8 confirms this belief because it reveals that materials handling cost and activity output (as measured by the number of moves) seem to move together. It is quite likely that a significant percentage of the total variability in cost is explained by our activity output variable.

We can determine statistically just how much variability is explained by looking at the coefficient of determination. The percentage of variability in the dependent variable explained by an independent variable (in this case, a measure of activity output) is called the coefficient of determination. This percentage is a goodness of fit measure. The higher the percentage of cost variability explained, the better the fit. Since the coefficient is the percentage of variability explained, it always has a value between 0 and 1.00.

In Exhibit 3-12, the coefficient of determination is labeled "R Square" (R^2). The value given is 0.86, which means that 86 percent of the variability in materials handling cost is explained by the number of moves. How good are these results? There is no cut-off point for a good versus a bad coefficient of determination. Clearly, the closer R^2 is to 1.00, the better. However, is 86 percent good enough? How about 73 percent?

Or even 46 percent? The answer is that it depends. If your cost equation yields a co-efficient of determination of 75 percent, you know that your independent variable explains three-fourths of the variability in cost. You also know that some other factor or combination of factors explains the remaining one-fourth. Depending on your tolerance for error, you may want to improve the equation by trying different independent variables (for example, materials handling hours worked rather than number of moves) or by trying multiple independent variables (or multiple regression, which is explained in a succeeding section of this chapter).

We note from the computer output in Exhibit 3-12, that the R^2 for materials handling cost is 0.86. In other words, material moves explain about 86 percent of the variability in the materials handling cost. This is not bad; however, something else explains the remaining 14 percent. In addition, the fixed cost coefficient is not significant. Anderson Company may want to consider other variables and perhaps use multiple regression.

Coefficient of Correlation

An alternative measure of goodness of fit is the **coefficient of correlation**, which is the square root of the coefficient of determination. Since square roots can be negative, the value of the coefficient of correlation can range between -1 and $+1$. If the coefficient of correlation is positive, then the two variables (in this example, cost and activity) move together in the same direction and positive correlation exists. Perfect positive correlation would yield a value of 1.00 for the coefficient of correlation. If, on the other hand, the coefficient of correlation is negative, then the two variables move in a predictable fashion but in opposite directions. Perfect negative correlation would yield a coefficient of correlation of -1.00. A coefficient of correlation value close to zero indicates no correlation. That is, knowledge of the movement of one variable gives us no clue as to the movement of the other variable. Exhibit 3-13 illustrates the concept of correlation.

For the Anderson Company example, the coefficient of correlation (r) is 0.929. Notice that r is the positive square root of R^2, computed previously. The square root is positive because the correlation between X and Y is positive. In other words, as the number of moves increases, the materials handling cost increases. This positive correlation is reflected by a positive value for V, the variable rate. If cost decreases as activity output increases, then the coefficient of correlation (and the value of V) is negative. The sign of V reveals the sign of the coefficient of correlation. The very high positive correlation between materials handling cost and the number of moves indicates that the number of moves represents a good choice for an activity driver.

Confidence Intervals

The least-squares cost equation can be used to predict cost for different levels of activity output. For example, if the number of moves is 200, then the materials handling cost predicted by the least-squares equation is $3,332.50 [$854.50 + $12.39(200)]. Usually, we can expect the predicted value to be different from the actual cost, and there are two reasons. First, in building the cost equation, only one activity driver (independent variable) has been used. It is possible that the cost equation has omitted other important factors, such as outlier activity output that affects cost (the dependent variable). These omitted factors are assumed to randomly affect the cost variable. The consequence of omission is to produce a distribution of cost values for every value of X (the measure of activity output appearing in the cost equation). This distribution is assumed to be normal. Second, the cost equation is based on estimated values using a sample of observed outcomes. Errors in estimating the slope, V, and the intercept, F, of the cost equation can also cause a discrepancy between the actual cost and the predicted cost.

The dispersion caused by these two effects can be measured, and the resulting measure can be used to help build a confidence interval around a predicted cost. If the

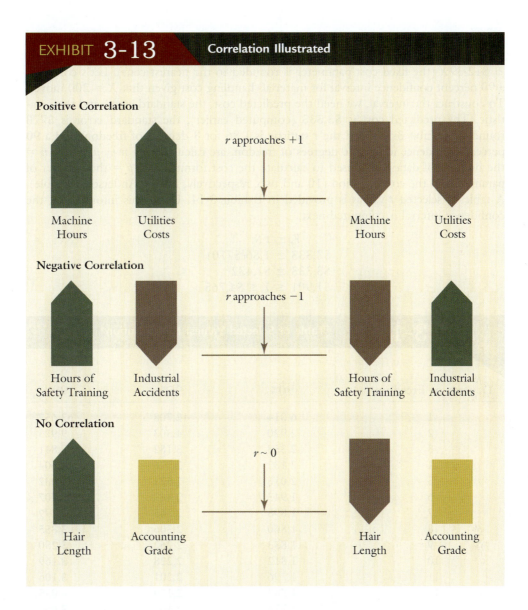

EXHIBIT 3-13   **Correlation Illustrated**

number of data points is large enough, the measure of dispersion can be approximated by the standard error, S_e. For example, in Exhibit 3-12, the standard error is $770.50.[6]

Given S_e, a confidence interval for the predicted value of Y can be constructed by using a t statistic for the desired level of confidence:

$$Y_f \pm t\, S_e$$

where

$$Y_f = \text{The predicted cost for a given level of activity}$$

By adding and subtracting a multiple of the standard error to the predicted cost, a range of possible values is created. Using the t statistic, a degree of confidence can be specified. The degree of confidence is a measure of the likelihood that the prediction interval will contain the actual cost. Thus, a 95 percent confidence interval means that if repeated samples were taken and 100 confidence intervals were constructed, we would expect 95 of the 100 to contain the actual cost.

6. For simplicity, we will always use the standard error even when the sample size is small.

The construction of a confidence interval can be illustrated using the Anderson Company example. From Exhibit 3-12, the least-squares cost equation is $Y = \$854.50 + \$12.39X$ (the fixed cost parameter is rounded to the nearest cent). Let's construct a 90 percent confidence interval for materials handling cost given that $X = 200$ moves. To construct the interval, we need the predicted cost, the standard error, and the t statistic. The predicted cost is \$3,333 (computed earlier), the standard error is \$770 rounded (Exhibit 3-12), and the t statistic is 1.86 for 8 degrees of freedom and a 90 percent confidence level. The degrees of freedom are calculated by $n - p$, where $n =$ the number of data points used to calculate the cost formula and $p =$ the number of parameters in the cost equation (10 and two, respectively, for the Anderson example). A table of selected t values is provided in Exhibit 3-14. Using this information, the confidence interval is computed next:

$$Y_f \pm t\, S_e$$
$$\$3{,}333 \pm 1.86(\$770)$$
$$\$3{,}333 \pm \$1{,}432$$
$$\$1{,}901 \leq Y \leq \$4{,}765$$

EXHIBIT 3-14	Table of Selected Values: t Distribution*		
Degrees of Freedom	**90%**	**95%**	**99%**
1	6.314	12.708	63.657
2	2.920	4.303	9.925
3	2.353	3.182	5.841
4	2.132	2.776	4.604
5	2.015	2.571	4.032
6	1.943	2.447	3.707
7	1.895	2.365	3.499
8	1.860	2.306	3.355
9	1.833	2.262	3.250
10	1.812	2.228	3.169
11	1.796	2.201	3.106
12	1.782	2.179	3.055
13	1.771	2.160	3.055
14	1.761	2.145	3.012
15	1.753	2.131	2.947
16	1.746	2.120	2.921
17	1.740	2.110	2.898
18	1.734	2.101	2.878
19	1.729	2.093	2.861
20	1.725	2.086	2.845
30	1.697	2.042	2.750
00	1.645	1.960	2.576

*Values are based on the assumption that two tails are important—as they would be with confidence intervals and hypothesis tests of regression coefficients. For values above 30, simply use the last row.

Thus, we can say with 90 percent confidence that the actual cost, Y, associated with 200 moves will be between \$1,901 and \$4,765. This outcome produces a very large range of possible values, revealing very quickly that the cost equation is not as useful for prediction as it might first appear based only on the coefficient of determination. The width of the interval diminishes the attractiveness of the cost equation. However, the width of this interval often can be reduced by using a larger sample (more data points) to calculate the cost equation. With a larger sample, the standard error may decrease, and the t statistic will decrease. If a company has a limited history for the activity being evaluated (sample size must be small), it may have to rely more on the detection of association than cost prediction. Finding a strong statistical association between an activity cost and an activity driver, however, can provide evidence to a manager about the correctness of the driver selection—an important issue when searching for causal factors to assign costs to cost objects.

Multiple Regression

OBJECTIVE 5

Explain how multiple regression can be used to assess cost behavior.

In the Anderson Company example, 86 percent of the variability in materials handling cost was explained by changes in activity output (number of moves). As a result, the company may want to search for additional explanatory variables. For example, total distance moved might be useful—particularly if the plant layout is such that significant time is consumed moving parts and products from one location to another.

In the case of two explanatory variables (activity drivers), the linear equation is expanded to include the additional variable:

$$Y = F + V_1X_1 + V_2X_2$$

where

$$X_1 = \text{Number of moves}$$
$$X_2 = \text{The total distance}$$

With three variables (Y, X_1, X_2), a minimum of three points is needed to compute the parameters F, V_1, and V_2. Seeing the points becomes difficult because they must be plotted in three dimensions. Using the scatterplot method or the high-low method is not practical.

However, the extension of the method of least squares is straightforward. It is relatively simple to develop a set of equations that provides values for F, V_1, and V_2 that yields the best-fitting equation. Whenever least squares is used to fit an equation involving two or more explanatory variables, the method is called **multiple regression**. The computational complexity of multiple regression, which increases significantly, is facilitated by the computer. In fact, any practical application of multiple regression requires use of a computer.

Let's return to the Anderson Company example. Recall that the R^2 is just 86 percent and that the fixed cost coefficient was not significant. Perhaps there is another variable that could help to explain materials handling costs. Suppose that the controller for Anderson Company investigates and finds that in some months many more pounds of materials were moved than in other months. When the heavier materials were moved, additional equipment was used to handle the increased load.

The controller adds the variable "pounds moved" and gathers information on the 10 months.

Month	Materials Handling Cost	Number of Moves	Pounds Moved
January	$2,000	100	6,000
February	3,090	125	15,000
March	2,780	175	7,800
April	1,990	200	600
May	7,500	500	29,000
June	5,300	300	23,000
July	4,300	250	17,000
August	6,300	400	25,000
September	5,600	475	12,000
October	6,240	425	22,400

Now let's run a multiple regression using the number of moves and the number of pounds moved as the independent variables. A computer screen for the regression is shown in Exhibit 3-15.

EXHIBIT 3-15   **Multiple Regression for Anderson Company**

Multiple Regression for Anderson Company.xls

	A	B	C	D	E	F
1	SUMMARY OUTPUT					
2	*Regression Statistics*					
3	Multiple R	0.999420				
4	R Square	0.998841				
5	Adjusted R	0.998509				
6						
7	Square					
8	Standard Error	75.76272				
9	Observations	10				
10						
11	ANOVA					
12		*df*	*SS*	*MS*	*F*	*Significance F*
13	Regression	2	34613020	17306510	3015.076722	5.30799E-11
14	Residual	7	40179.93	5739.99		
15	Total	9	34653200			
16						
17						
18		*Coefficients*	*Standard Error*	*t Stat*	*P-value*	
19	Intercept	507.3097	57.3225	8.850098	4.7575E-05	
20	X Variable 1	7.835162	0.234048	33.47672	5.49745E-09	
21	X Variable 2	0.107181	0.003742	28.64286	1.62622E-08	
22						

Sheet1 / Sheet2 / Sheet3

The computer screen conveys some very interesting and useful information. The cost equation is defined by the first two columns of the lowest table. The first column identifies the individual cost components. The intercept is the fixed activity cost, the first X variable is the number of moves, and the second X variable is the number of pounds moved. The column labeled "Coefficients" identifies the estimated fixed cost and the variable cost per unit for each activity driver. Thus, the cost equation can be written as follows:

$$Y = \$507 + \$7.84X_1 + \$0.11X_2$$

As with the cost equation involving a single activity driver, the preceding equation can be used to predict activity cost. Suppose that in November the company is expected to have 350 moves with 17,000 pounds of material moved. The predicted materials handling cost is as follows:

$$
\begin{aligned}
Y &= \$507 + \$7.84(350) + \$0.11(17,000) \\
&= \$507 + \$2,744 + \$1,870 \\
&= \$5,121
\end{aligned}
$$

Notice in Exhibit 3-15 that the coefficient of determination is 99 percent—a significant improvement in explanatory power is achieved by adding the pounds moved variable. In addition, all three coefficients are highly significant.

For multiple regression, R^2 is usually referred to as the multiple coefficient of determination. Notice also that the standard error of estimate, S_e, is available in a multiple regression setting. As indicated earlier, the standard error of estimate can be used to build confidence intervals around cost predictions. To illustrate, consider the 95 percent confidence interval for the predicted materials handling cost when $X_1 = 350$ moves and X_2 = 17,000 pounds moved (t = 2.365 for 95 percent confidence and 7 degrees of freedom):[7]

$$\$5,121 - 2.365(\$76) \leq Y \leq q\$5,121 + 2.365(\$76)$$
$$\$4,941 \leq Y \leq \$5,301$$

Refer once again to Exhibit 3-15. Columns four and five of the lowest table present some statistical data concerning the three parameters. The fourth column presents t statistics for each of these parameters. These t statistics are used to test the hypothesis that the parameters are different from zero. The fifth column presents the level of significance achieved. All parameters are significant at the 0.0001 level. Thus, we can have some confidence that the two drivers are useful and that the materials handling activity has a fixed cost component. This example illustrates very clearly that multiple regression can be a useful tool for identifying the behavior of activity costs.

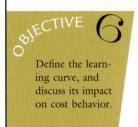

OBJECTIVE 6

Define the learning curve, and discuss its impact on cost behavior.

The Learning Curve and Nonlinear Cost Behavior

An important type of nonlinear cost curve is the learning curve. The **learning curve** shows how the labor hours worked per unit decrease as the volume produced increases. The basis of the learning curve is almost intuitive—as we perform an action over and over, we improve, and each additional performance takes less time than the preceding ones. We are learning how to do the task, becoming more efficient, and smoothing out the rough spots. In a manufacturing firm, learning takes place throughout the process: workers learn their tasks and managers learn to schedule production more efficiently and to arrange the flow of work. This effect was first documented in the aircraft industry.

Managers can now see that the ideas behind the learning curve can extend to the service industry as well as to manufacturing firms. Costs in marketing, distribution, and service after the sale also decrease as the number of units produced and sold increases.

The learning curve model takes two common forms: the cumulative average-time learning curve model and the incremental unit-time learning curve model.

Cumulative Average-Time Learning Curve

The **cumulative average-time learning curve model** states that the cumulative average time per unit decreases by a constant percentage, or learning rate, each time the cumulative quantity of units produced doubles. The **learning rate** is expressed as a percent, and it gives the percentage of time needed to make the next unit, based on the time it took to make the previous unit. The learning rate is determined through experience and must be between 50 and 100 percent. A 50 percent learning rate would eventually result in no labor time per unit—an absurd result. A 100 percent learning rate implies no learning (since the amount of decrease is zero). An 80 percent learning curve is often used to illustrate this model (possibly because the original learning curve work with the aircraft industry found an 80 percent learning curve). Exhibit 3-16 gives data for a cumulative average-time learning curve with an 80 percent learning rate and 100 direct labor hours for the first unit.

We see in Exhibit 3-16 that the bold rows give us the cumulative average time and cumulative total time according to the doubling formula. How do we obtain

---

7. Degrees of freedom is computed as $n - p$, where p is the number of parameters being estimated. For this example, there are 10 data points and three parameters. The three parameters are F, X_1, and X_2. The t statistics come from Exhibit 3-14.

EXHIBIT 3-16	Data for Cumulative Average-Time Learning Curve with 80 Percent Learning Rate		
Cumulative Number of Units (1)	Cumulative Average Time per Unit in Hours (2)	Cumulative Total Time: Labor Hours (3) = (1) × (2)	Individual Unit Time for *n*th Unit: Labor Hours (4)
1	100	100	100
2	80 (0.8 × 100)	160	60
3	70.21	210.63	50.63
4	64 (0.8 × 80)	256	45.37
5	59.57	297.85	41.85
6	56.17	337.02	39.17
7	53.45	374.15	37.13
8	51.20 (0.8 × 64)	409.60	35.45
16	40.96	655.36	28.06
32	32.77	1,048.64	

Note: The rows in bold give the traditional doubling of output.

these amounts for units that are not doubles of the original amount? This is done by realizing that the cumulative average-time learning model takes a logarithmic relationship.

$$Y = pX^q$$

where

Y = Cumulative average time per unit
X = Cumulative number of units produced
p = Time in labor hours required to produce the first unit
q = Rate of learning

Therefore:

$$q = \ln (\text{percent learning})/\ln 2$$

For an 80 percent learning curve:

$$q = -0.2231/0.6931 = -0.3219$$

So, when $X = 3$, $p = 100$, and $q = -0.3219$,

$$Y = 100 \times 3^{-0.3219} = 70.21 \text{ labor hours}$$

It is easy to see, then, that the number of hours required for the third unit is 50.63 (or 210.63 − 160.0). Had we estimated the number of hours required for the third unit by the doubling calculations, we would have taken 256 − 160 = 96 and then divided that result by 2 (the number of units between 2 and 4) and estimated the marginal time for the third unit as 48 hours. Notice that the more accurate result recognizes that the third unit really required 50.63 hours and the fourth unit 45.37 hours.

Exhibit 3-17 shows the graph of both the cumulative average time per unit (the bottom line) and the cumulative total hours required (top line). We can see that the time per unit decreases as output increases, but that it decreases at a decreasing rate. We also see that the total labor hours increase as output increases, but they increase at a decreasing rate.

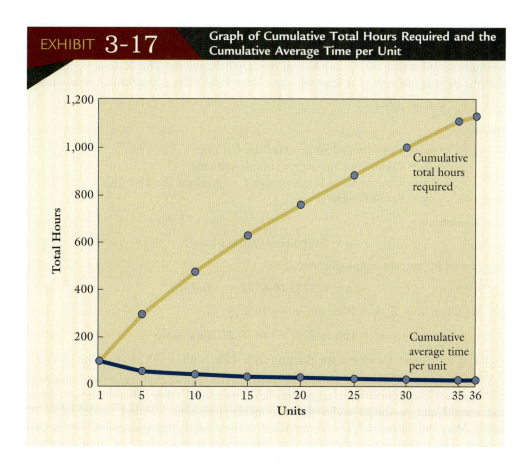

EXHIBIT 3-17 Graph of Cumulative Total Hours Required and the Cumulative Average Time per Unit

Incremental Unit-Time Learning Curve

The **incremental unit-time learning curve model** decreases by a constant percentage each time the cumulative quantity of units produced doubles. Exhibit 3-18 gives data for an incremental unit-time learning curve with an 80 percent learning rate and 100 direct labor hours for the first unit.

EXHIBIT 3-18 Data for an Incremental Unit-Time Learning Curve with an 80 Percent Learning Rate

Cumulative Number of Units (1)	Individual Unit Time for nth Unit in Labor Hours (2)	Cumulative Total Time: Labor Hours (3)	Cumulative Average Time per Unit: Labor Hours (4) = (3)/(1)
1	100	100	100
2	80 (0.8 × 100)	180	90
3	70.21	250.21	83.40
4	64 (0.8 × 80)	314.21	78.55
5	59.57	373.78	74.76
6	56.17	429.95	71.66
7	53.45	483.40	69.06
8	51.20 (0.8 × 64)	534.60	66.83
16	40.96	892.00	55.75

We see in Exhibit 3-18 that the bold rows give us the cumulative average time and cumulative total time according to the doubling formula. How do we obtain these amounts for units that are not doubles of the original amount? This is done by realizing that the incremental unit-time learning curve model also takes a logarithmic relationship.

$$m = pX^q$$

where

m = Time needed to produce the last unit
X = Cumulative number of units produced
p = Time in labor hours required to produce the first unit
q = Rate of learning

Therefore:

$$q = \ln \text{ (percent learning)}/\ln 2$$

For an 80 percent learning curve:

$$q = -0.2231/0.6931 = -0.3219$$

So, when $X = 3$, $p = 100$, and $q = -0.3219$,

$$m = 100 \times 3^{-0.3219} = 70.21 \text{ labor hours}$$

The cumulative total time for three units is $100 + 80 + 70.21 = 250.21$.

Let's look more closely at Exhibits 3-16 and 3-18. Notice that the second unit produced under the cumulative average-time learning model takes 60 labor hours, while the second unit produced under the incremental unit-time learning model takes 80 hours. Why the difference? The difference is in the underlying assumptions of the two models. The cumulative average-time learning model assumes that the cumulative *average* time for every unit produced is just 80 percent of the amount for the previous output level. Thus, when we look at the time to produce two units, the average time for each of the units is assumed to be 80 percent of the time for the first unit. However, the incremental unit-time learning model assumes that only the *last* (incremental) unit experiences the decrease in time, so the second unit takes 80 hours, but the first still takes 100 hours. Thus, the total time is 180 (100 + 80) hours.

The use of the learning curve concepts permits management to be more accurate in budgeting and performance evaluation for processes in which learning occurs. While the learning curve was originally developed for manufacturing processes, it can also apply in service industries. For example, insurance companies develop new policies and new methods of selling policies. There is a learning component to each new policy as employees discover glitches that were unexpected in the development process and then learn how to fix those glitches and become more efficient.

Of course, it is important to note that the learning rate can differ for each process. Management must estimate the rate, usually on the basis of past experience.

Managerial Judgment

OBJECTIVE 7

Discuss the use of managerial judgment in determining cost behavior.

Managerial judgment is critically important in determining cost behavior and is by far the most widely used method in practice. Many managers simply use their experience and past observation of cost relationships to determine fixed and variable costs. This method, however, may take a number of forms. Some managers simply assign particular activity costs to the fixed category and others to the variable category. They ignore the possibility of mixed costs. Thus, a chemical firm may regard materials and utilities as strictly variable, with respect to pounds of chemical produced, and all other costs as fixed. Even labor, the textbook example of a unit-based variable cost, may be fixed for this firm. The appeal of this method is simplicity. Before opting for this course of action, management would do well to make sure that each cost is predominantly fixed or variable and that the decisions being made are not highly sensitive to errors in classifying costs as fixed or variable.

To illustrate the use of judgment in assessing cost behavior, consider **Elgin Sweeper Company**, a leading manufacturer of motorized street sweepers. Using production volume as the measure of activity output, Elgin revised its chart of accounts to organize costs into fixed and variable components. Elgin's accountants used their knowledge of the company to assign expenses to either a fixed or variable category, using a decision rule that categorized an expense as fixed if it were fixed 75 percent of the time and as variable if it were variable 75 percent of the time.[8]

Management may instead identify mixed costs and divide these costs into fixed and variable components by deciding just what the fixed and variable parts are—that is, using experience to say that a certain amount of a cost is fixed and therefore that the rest must be variable. Then, the variable component can be computed using one or more cost/volume data points. This use of judgment has the advantage of accounting for mixed costs but is subject to a similar type of error as the strict fixed/variable dichotomy. That is, management may be wrong in its assessment.

Finally, management may use experience and judgment to refine statistical estimation results. Perhaps the experienced manager might "eyeball" the data and throw out several points as being highly unusual, or the manager might revise results of estimation to take into account projected changes in cost structure or technology. For example, **Tecnol Medical Products, Inc.**, radically changed its method of manufacturing medical face masks. Traditionally, face-mask production was very labor intensive, requiring hand stitching. Tecnol developed its own highly automated equipment and became the industry's low-cost supplier—besting both **Johnson & Johnson** and **3M**. Tecnol's rapid expansion into new product lines and European markets means that historical data on costs and revenues are, for the most part, irrelevant.[9] Tecnol's management must look forward, not back, to predict the impact of changes on profit. Statistical techniques are highly accurate in depicting the past, but they cannot foresee the future, which of course is what management really wants.

The advantage of using managerial judgment to separate fixed and variable costs is its simplicity. In situations in which the manager has a deep understanding of the firm and its cost patterns, this method can give good results. However, if the manager does not have good judgment, errors will occur. Therefore, it is important to consider the experience of the manager, the potential for error, and the effect that error could have on related decisions.

---

8. John P. Callan, Wesley N. Tredup, and Randy S. Wissinger, "Elgin Sweeper Company's Journey Toward Cost Management," *Management Accounting* (July 1991): 24–27.
9. Stephanie Anderson Forest, "Who's Afraid of J&J and 3M?" *Business Week* (December 5, 1994): 66, 68.

SUMMARY

Cost behavior is the way in which a cost changes in relation to changes in activity output. The time horizon is important in determining cost behavior because costs can change from fixed to variable, depending on whether the decision takes place over the short run or the long run. Variable costs are those which change in total as activity usage changes. Usually, we assume that variable costs increase in direct proportion to increases in activity output. Fixed costs are those which do not change in total as activity output changes. Mixed costs have both a variable and a fixed component. The resource usage model adds additional understanding of cost behavior.

Resources can be classified as either flexible or committed. Flexible resources are acquired as used and needed. There is no excess capacity for these resources, and they are usually considered variable costs. Committed resources, on the other hand, are acquired in advance of usage. These resources may have excess capacity, and frequently they are fixed. Some costs—especially discretionary fixed costs—tend to follow a step-cost function. These resources are acquired in lumpy amounts. If the width of the step is sufficiently large, then the costs are viewed as fixed; otherwise, they are approximated by a variable cost function.

The three formal mathematical methods of separating mixed costs are the high-low method, the scatterplot method, and the method of least squares. In the high-low method, the two points chosen from the scattergraph are the high and the low points with respect to activity level. These two points are then used to compute the intercept and the slope of the line on which they lie. The high-low method is objective and easy. However, if either the high or low point is not representative of the true cost relationship, the relationship will be misestimated.

The scatterplot method involves inspecting a scattergraph (a plot showing total mixed cost at various activity levels) and selecting two points that seem to best represent the relationship between cost and activity. Since two points determine a line, the two selected points can be used to determine the intercept and the slope of the line on which they lie. The intercept gives an estimate of the fixed cost component, and the slope gives an estimate of the variable cost per unit of activity. The scatterplot method is a good way to identify nonlinearity, the presence of outliers, and the presence of a shift in the cost relationship. Its disadvantage is that it is subjective.

The method of least squares uses all of the data points (except outliers) on the scattergraph and produces a line that best fits all of the points. The line is best-fitting in the sense that it is closest to all the points as measured by the sum of the squared deviations of the points from the line. The method of least squares produces the line that best fits the data points and is therefore recommended over the high-low and scatterplot methods.

The least-squares method has the advantage of offering methods to assess the reliability of cost equations. The coefficient of determination allows an analyst to compute the amount of cost variability explained by a particular activity driver. The standard error of estimate can be used to build a prediction interval for cost. If the interval is too wide, it may suggest that the equation is not very useful for prediction, even if the driver explains a high percentage of the cost variability. The least-squares method can also be used to build a cost equation using more than one activity output. Equations built using multiple regression can be evaluated for their reliability as well.

The learning curve describes a nonlinear relationship between labor hours and output. The two formulations of the learning curve are the cumulative average-time curve model and the incremental unit-time learning curve model. Both show that a doubling of output requires less than a doubling of labor time.

Managerial judgment can be used alone or in conjunction with the high-low, scatterplot, or least-squares methods. Managers use their experience and knowledge of cost and activity-level relationships to identify outliers, understand structural shifts, and adjust parameters due to anticipated changing conditions.

REVIEW PROBLEMS AND SOLUTIONS

1 RESOURCE USAGE AND COST BEHAVIOR

Thompson Manufacturing Company has three salaried clerks to process purchase orders. Each clerk is paid a salary of $28,000 and is capable of processing 5,000 purchase orders per year (working efficiently). In addition to the salaries, Thompson spends $7,500 per year for forms, postage, etc. Thompson assumes 15,000 purchase orders will be processed. During the year, 12,500 orders were processed.

Required:

1. Calculate the activity rate for the purchase order activity. Break the activity into fixed and variable components.
2. Compute the total activity availability, and break this into activity output and unused activity.
3. Calculate the total cost of the resource supplied, and break this into the cost of activity output and the cost of unused activity.

1. Activity rate = [(3 × $28,000) + $7,500]/15,000
                 = $6.10/order
   Fixed rate = $84,000/15,000
              = $5.60/order
   Variable rate = $7,500/15,000
                 = $0.50/order

2. Activity availability = Activity output + Unused activity
       15,000 orders = 12,500 orders + 2,500 orders

3.   Cost of activity supplied = Cost of activity output + Cost of unused activity
   $84,000 + ($0.50 × 12,500) = ($6.10 × 12,500) + ($5.60 × 2,500)
                 $90,250 = $76,250 + $14,000

2 HIGH-LOW METHOD AND METHOD OF LEAST SQUARES

Linda Jones, an accountant for Golding, Inc., has decided to estimate the fixed and variable components associated with the company's repair activity. She has collected the following data for the past six months:

Repair Hours	Total Repair Costs
10	$ 800
20	1,100
15	900
12	900
18	1,050
25	1,250

Required:

1. Estimate the fixed and variable components for the repair costs using the high-low method. Using the cost formula, predict the total cost of repair if 14 hours are used.

2. Estimate the fixed and variable components using the method of least squares. Translate your results into the form of a cost formula, and using that formula, predict the total cost of repairs if 14 hours are used.

3. Using the method of least squares, what are the coefficient of determination and the coefficient of correlation?

SOLUTION

1. The estimate of fixed and variable costs using the high-low method, where $Y =$ total cost and $X =$ number of hours, is as follows:

$$V = (Y_2 - Y_1)/(X_2 - X_1)$$
$$= (\$1{,}250 - \$800)/(25 - 10)$$
$$= \$450/15$$
$$= \$30 \text{ per hour}$$

$$F = Y_2 - VX_2$$
$$= \$1{,}250 - \$30(25)$$
$$= \$500$$

$$Y = \$500 + \$30X$$
$$= \$500 + \$30(14)$$
$$= \$920$$

2. Regression is performed using Excel, with the results as follows:

Summary Output

Regression Statistics

Multiple R	0.984523
R Square	0.969285
Adjusted R Square	0.961607
Standard Error	32.19657
Observations	6

ANOVA

	df	SS	MS	F	Significance F
Regression	1	130853.5	130853.5	126.2311	0.000357
Residual	4	4146.476	1036.619		
Total	5	135000			

	Coefficients	Standard Error	t Stat	P-value	Lower 95%	Upper 95%	Lower 95.0%	Upper 95.0%
Intercept	509.9119	45.55789	11.19261	0.000363	383.4227	636.4011	383.4227	636.4011
X Variable 1	29.40529	2.617232	11.23526	0.000357	22.13867	36.6719	22.13867	36.6719

The calculation using the method of least squares is as follows:

$$Y = \$509.91 + \$29.41X$$
$$= \$509.91 + \$29.41(14)$$
$$= \$921.65$$

3. The coefficient of determination (R^2) is 0.969, and the correlation coefficient (r) is 0.985 (the square root of 0.969).

KEY TERMS

Activity capacity 75

Activity rate 78

Coefficient of correlation 90

Coefficient of determination 89

Committed fixed expenses 75

Committed resources 75

Confidence interval 89

Cost behavior 68

Cumulative average-time learning curve model 95

Dependent variable 80

Deviation 85

Discretionary fixed expenses 76

Fixed costs 68

Flexible resources 75

Goodness of fit 89

High-low method 81

Hypothesis test of cost parameters 89

Incremental unit-time learning curve model 97

Independent variable 80

Intercept parameter 80

Learning curve 95

Learning rate 95

Long run 73

Method of least squares 85

Mixed costs 72

Multiple regression 93

Non-unit-level drivers 68

Practical capacity 75

Relevant range 69

Scattergraph 82

Scatterplot method 81

Short run 73

Slope parameter 80

Step-cost function 77

Step-fixed costs 78

Step-variable costs 77

Unit-level drivers 68

Unused capacity 75

Variable costs 70

QUESTIONS FOR WRITING AND DISCUSSION

1. Why is knowledge of cost behavior important for managerial decision making? Give an example to illustrate your answer.
2. How does the length of the time horizon affect the classification of a cost as fixed or variable? What is the meaning of short run? Long run?
3. Explain the difference between resource spending and resource usage.
4. What is the relationship between flexible resources and cost behavior?
5. What is the relationship between committed resources and cost behavior?
6. Describe the difference between a variable cost and a step-variable cost. When is it reasonable to treat step-variable costs as if they were variable costs?
7. Why do mixed costs pose a problem when it comes to classifying costs into fixed and variable categories?
8. Why is a scattergraph a good first step in separating mixed costs into their fixed and variable components?
9. What are the advantages of the scatterplot method over the high-low method? The high-low method over the scatterplot method?

10. Describe the method of least squares. Why is this method better than either the high-low method or the scatterplot method?
11. What is meant by the best-fitting line? Is the best-fitting line necessarily a good-fitting line? Explain.
12. When is multiple regression required to explain cost behavior?
13. Explain the meaning of the learning curve. How do managers determine the appropriate learning curve percentage to use?
14. Assume you are the manager responsible for implementing a new service. The time to perform the service is subject to the learning curve. Would you prefer that the new service follow the cumulative average-time learning curve model or the incremental unit-time learning curve model? Why?
15. Some firms assign mixed costs to either the fixed or variable cost categories without using any formal methodology to separate them. Explain how this practice can be defended.

EXERCISES

3-1 VARIABLE, FIXED, AND MIXED COSTS

LO1 Classify the following costs of activity inputs as variable, fixed, or mixed. Identify the activity and the associated activity driver that allow you to define the cost behavior. For example, assume that the resource input is "cloth in a shirt." The activity would be "sewing shirts," the cost behavior "variable," and the activity driver "units produced." Prepare your answers in the following format:

Activity	*Cost Behavior*	*Activity Driver*
Sewing shirts	Variable	Units produced

    a. Power to operate a drill
    b. Engine in a lawn mower
    c. Advertising
    d. Sales commissions
    e. Fuel for a forklift
    f. Depreciation on a warehouse
    g. Depreciation on a forklift used to move partially completed goods
    h. X-ray film used in the radiology department of a hospital
    i. Rental car provided for a client
    j. Amalgam used by a dentist
    k. Salaries, equipment, and materials used for setting up production equipment
    l. Forms used to file insurance claims
    m. Equipment, labor, and parts used to repair and maintain production equipment
    n. Printing and postage for advertising circulars
    o. Salaries, forms, and postage associated with purchasing

3-2 COST BEHAVIOR

LO1 Gupta Company manufactures miniature speakers that are built into the headrests of high-end lounge chairs. Based on past experience, Gupta has found that its total annual overhead costs can be represented by the following formula: Overhead cost = $175,000 + $1.10X$, where X = number of speakers. Last year, Gupta produced 70,000 speakers. Actual overhead costs for the year were as expected.

Required:

1. What is the driver for the overhead activity?
2. What is the total overhead cost incurred by Gupta last year?
3. What is the total fixed overhead cost incurred by Gupta last year?
4. What is the total variable overhead cost incurred by Gupta last year?
5. What is the overhead cost per unit produced?
6. What is the fixed overhead cost per unit?
7. What is the variable overhead cost per unit?
8. Recalculate Requirements 5, 6, and 7 for the following levels of production: (a) 50,000 units and (b) 100,000 units. Explain this outcome.

3-3   COST BEHAVIOR CLASSIFICATION

LO1   Mazlow Company produces specialty tubing for large-scale construction applications. Its factory has six extruding lines that form tubing of different diameters. Each line can produce up to 5,000 feet of tubing per year. Each line has one supervisor who is paid $25,000 per year. Depreciation on equipment averages $12,000 per year. Direct materials and power cost about $2.50 per foot of tubing.

Required:

1. Prepare a graph for each of these three costs: equipment depreciation, supervisors' wages, and direct materials and power. Use the vertical axis for cost and the horizontal axis for feet of tubing. Assume that tubing sales range from 0 to 30,000 feet of tubing.
2. Assume that the normal operating range for the company is 26,000 to 29,000 feet of tubing per year. How would you classify each of the three types of cost?

3-4   RESOURCE USAGE MODEL AND COST BEHAVIOR

LO2   For the following activities and their associated resources, identify the following: (1) a cost driver, (2) flexible resources, and (3) committed resources. Also, label each resource as one of the following with respect to the cost driver: (a) variable and (b) fixed.

Activity	*Resource Description*
Maintenance	Equipment, labor, and parts
Inspection	Test equipment, inspectors (each inspector can inspect five batches per day), and units inspected (process requires destructive sampling*)
Packing	Materials, labor (each packer places five units in a box), and conveyor belt
Payable processing	Clerks, materials, equipment, and facility
Assembly	Conveyor belt, supervision (one supervisor for every three assembly lines), direct labor, and materials

*Destructive sampling occurs whenever it is necessary to destroy a unit as inspection occurs.

3-5   RESOURCE USAGE AND SUPPLY, ACTIVITY RATES, SERVICE ORGANIZATION

LO2   PhotoQuik is a film developing company. Customers mail their undeveloped rolls of film to the company and receive the completed photographs in return mail. The

PhotoQuik facility is built and staffed to handle the processing of 100,000 rolls of film per year. The lab facility cost $330,000 to build and is expected to last 20 years. Processing equipment cost $592,500 and has a life expectancy of five years. Both facility and equipment are depreciated on a straight-line basis. PhotoQuik has five salaried processing technicians, each of whom is paid $15,000. In addition to the salaries, facility, and equipment, PhotoQuik expects to spend $400,000 for chemicals, photo paper, envelopes, and other supplies (assuming 100,000 rolls of film are processed). Last year, 96,000 rolls of film were processed.

Required:

1. Classify the resources associated with the film-processing activity into one of the following types: (1) committed resources and (2) flexible resources.
2. Calculate the total activity rate for the film-processing activity. Break the activity rate into fixed and variable components.
3. Compute the total activity availability, and break this into activity output and unused activity.
4. Calculate the total cost of resources supplied, and break this into the cost of activity used and the cost of unused activity.

3-6 STEP COSTS, RELEVANT RANGE

LO2 Vargas, Inc., produces industrial machinery. Vargas has a machining department and a group of direct laborers called machinists. Each machinist is paid $30,000 and can machine up to 500 units per year. Vargas also hires supervisors to develop machine specification plans and to oversee production within the machining department. Given the planning and supervisory work, a supervisor can oversee three machinists, at most. Vargas's accounting and production history reveal the following relationships between units produced and the costs of direct labor and supervision (measured on an annual basis):

Units Produced	Direct Labor	Supervision
0–500	$ 30,000	$ 45,000
501–1,000	60,000	45,000
1,001–1,500	90,000	45,000
1,501–2,000	120,000	90,000
2,001–2,500	150,000	90,000
2,501–3,000	180,000	90,000
3,001–3,500	210,000	135,000
3,501–4,000	240,000	135,000

Required:

1. Prepare two graphs: one that illustrates the relationship between direct labor cost and units produced and one that illustrates the relationship between the cost of supervision and units produced. Let cost be the vertical axis and units produced the horizontal axis.
2. How would you classify each cost? Why?
3. Suppose that the normal range of activity is between 1,300 and 1,450 units and that the exact number of machinists is currently hired to support this level of activity. Further suppose that production for the next year is expected to increase by an additional 400 units. How much will the cost of direct labor increase (and how will this increase be realized)? Cost of supervision?

3-7 SCATTERGRAPH METHOD, HIGH-LOW METHOD

LO3

Spreadsheet

Tad Jennings opened a tanning salon in a new shopping center. He had anticipated that the costs for the tanning service would be primarily fixed, but he found that tanning salon costs increased with the number of visits. Costs for this service over the past nine months are as follows:

Month	Tanning Visits	Total Cost
January	700	$2,628
February	1,500	4,000
March	3,100	6,564
April	1,700	4,205
May	2,300	5,350
June	1,800	4,000
July	1,400	3,775
August	1,200	2,800
September	2,000	4,765

Required:

1. Prepare a scattergraph based on the preceding data. Use cost for the vertical axis and number of tanning visits for the horizontal axis. Based on an examination of the scattergraph, does there appear to be a linear relationship between the cost of tanning services and the number of visits?
2. Compute the cost formula for tanning services using the high-low method.
3. Calculate the predicted cost of tanning services for October for 2,200 visits using the formula found in Requirement 2.

3-8 METHOD OF LEAST SQUARES, GOODNESS OF FIT

LO3, LO4 Refer to the data in **Exercise 3-7**.

Required:

1. Compute the cost formula for tanning services using the method of least squares.
2. Using the formula computed in Requirement 1, what is the predicted cost of tanning services for October for 2,200 appointments?
3. What does the coefficient of determination tell you about the cost formula computed in Requirement 1? What are the t statistics for the number of appointments and the intercept term? What do these statistics tell you about the choice of number of appointments as the independent variable and the probability that there are fixed costs?

3-9 HIGH-LOW METHOD, COST FORMULAS

LO3 The controller of the Beresford plant of Gamerco, Inc., monitored activities associated with purchasing and receiving raw materials. The high and low levels of resource usage occurred in October and March for three different resources associated with purchasing and receiving. The number of purchase orders is the driver. The total costs of the three resources and the activity output, as measured by purchase orders, for the two different levels are presented as follows:

Resource	Purchase Orders	Total Cost
Supplier verification:		
Low	12,000	$ 43,000
High	30,000	43,000
Receiving:		
Low	12,000	$ 81,600
High	30,000	204,000
Processing purchase orders:		
Low	12,000	$ 43,200
High	30,000	97,200

Required:

1. Determine the cost behavior formula of each resource. Use the high-low method to assess the fixed and variable components.
2. Using your knowledge of cost behavior, predict the cost of each item for an activity output level of 25,000 purchase orders.
3. Construct a cost formula that can be used to predict the total cost of the three resources combined. Using this formula, predict the total purchasing and receiving cost if activity output is 22,000 purchase orders. In general, when can cost formulas be combined to form a single cost formula?

3-10   METHOD OF LEAST SQUARES, EVALUATION OF COST EQUATION

LO3, LO4

A company used the method of least squares to develop a cost equation to predict the cost of receiving. There were 80 data points for the regression, and the following computer output was generated:

Intercept	$17,350
Slope	12
Coefficient of correlation	0.92
Standard error	$220

The activity driver used was the number of receiving orders.

Required:

1. What is the cost formula?
2. Using the cost formula, predict the cost of receiving if 10,000 orders are processed. Now prepare a 95 percent confidence interval for this prediction.
3. What percentage of the variability in receiving cost is explained by the number of receiving orders? Do you think the equation will predict well? Why or why not?

3-11   MULTIPLE REGRESSION

LO5

Kidstuff, Inc., was started 10 years ago by selling children's clothing through catalogs. Jan Switzer, Kidstuff's controller, had determined that the cost of filling and shipping orders was fairly consistently related to the number of orders. She had been using the following formula to describe monthly order filling costs:

$$\text{Order filling cost} = \$7,800 + \$7.50 \times \text{orders}$$

Lately, however, Jan noticed that order filling costs varied widely and did not seem to follow the above relationship. After a number of discussions with order pickers and

fillers, Jan determined that Kidstuff's expansion into children's toys had made order filling a more complex operation. Number of orders was still an important variable, but
so were the number of categories included in an order (an order for just clothing was
quicker to pick, fill, and pack than an order with both clothing and toys) and whether
or not any items needed to be gift wrapped. Jan ran a multiple regression on the past
24 months of data for Kidstuff for three variables: the cost of filling orders (picking and
packing the order for shipment), the number of orders, and the number of complex
orders (orders with both clothing and toys) and gifts (the number of gift-wrapped
items). The following printout was obtained:

Parameter	Estimate	t for H_o Parameter = 0	Pr > t	Standard Error of Parameter
Intercept	9,320	93.00	0.0001	479.00
Number of orders	5.14	3.60	0.0050	1.56
Number of complex orders	2.06	5.58	0.0050	2.00
Number of gifts	1.30	2.96	0.0250	0.75

$R^2 = 0.92$
$S_e = 150$
Observations: 24

Required:

1. Write out the cost equation for Kidstuff's monthly order filling cost.
2. If Kidstuff expects to have 300 orders next month (65 with both clothing and
   toys) and expects that 100 items must be gift wrapped, what are the anticipated
   order filling costs?
3. Calculate a 99 percent confidence interval for the prediction made in Requirement 2.
4. What does R^2 mean in this equation? Overall, what is your evaluation of the cost
   equation that was developed for the cost of order filling? Suppose that Kidstuff
   charges an extra $2.50 to gift wrap an item. How might Jan use the results of
   the regression equation to see whether or not the $2.50 charge is appropriate?

3-12 MULTIPLE REGRESSION

LO5 Allmen, Inc., a manufacturer of heavy machinery, is interested in improving its factory
safety record. Jennifer Cybert, Allmen's controller, has investigated the past four years
of industrial accidents, both at Allmen and at other similar factories. She has found that
more accidents seem to happen during months with greater hours of overtime worked.
In addition, she thinks that employee safety could be enhanced by a vigorous safety
program. To test her hypotheses, she ran a multiple regression on 48 months of data
for Allmen for three variables: the cost of industrial accidents, the number of hours of
safety training, and the number of hours of overtime worked by production workers.
The following printout was obtained:

Parameter	Estimate	t for H_o Parameter = 0	Pr > t	Standard Error of Parameter
Intercept	2,150	70.00	0.0001	150.00
Number of overtime hours	17	3.60	0.0050	23.45
Hours of safety training	−8.50	−1.96	0.0250	5.13

$R^2 = 0.89$
$S_e = 250$
Observations: 48

Required:

1.   Write out the cost equation for Allmen's industrial accident cost.
2.   If Allmen expects to have 280 overtime hours worked next month and expects to spend 200 hours on safety training, what are the anticipated accident costs?
3.   Calculate a 99 percent confidence interval for the prediction made in Requirement 2.
4.   Is number of overtime hours positively or negatively correlated with accident costs? Are hours of safety training positively or negatively correlated with accident costs?
5.   What does R^2 mean in this equation? Overall, what is your evaluation of the cost equation that was developed for the cost of industrial accidents?

3-13   COST BEHAVIOR PATTERNS

LO1, LO2   The graphs below represent cost behavior patterns that might occur in a company's cost structure. The vertical axis represents total cost, and the horizontal axis represents activity output.

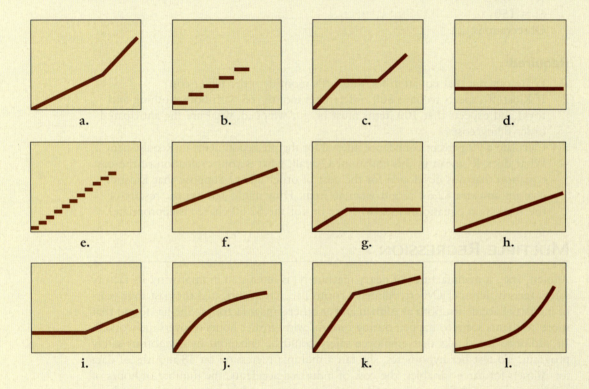

a.   b.   c.   d.

e.   f.   g.   h.

i.   j.   k.   l.

Required:

For each of the following situations, choose the graph from the group a–l that best illustrates the cost pattern involved. Also, for each situation, identify the driver that measures activity output.

1.   The cost of power when a fixed fee of $500 per month is charged plus an additional charge of $0.12 per kilowatt-hour used.
2.   Commissions paid to sales representatives. Commissions are paid at the rate of 5 percent of sales made up to total annual sales of $500,000, and 7 percent of sales above $500,000.
3.   A part purchased from an outside supplier costs $12 per part for the first 3,000 parts and $10 per part for all parts purchased in excess of 3,000 units.

4. The cost of surgical gloves, which are purchased in increments of 100 units (gloves come in boxes of 100 pairs).
5. The cost of tuition at a local college that charges $250 per credit hour up to 15 credit hours. Hours taken in excess of 15 are free.
6. The cost of tuition at another college that charges $4,500 per semester for any course load ranging from 12 to 16 credit hours. Students taking fewer than 12 credit hours are charged $375 per credit hour. Students taking more than 16 credit hours are charged $4,500 plus $300 per credit hour in excess of 16.
7. A beauty shop's purchase of soaking solution to remove artificial nails. Each jar of solution can soak off approximately 50 nails before losing its effectiveness.
8. Purchase of diagnostics equipment by a company for inspection of incoming orders.
9. Use of disposable gowns by patients in a hospital.
10. Cost of labor at a local fast-food restaurant. Three employees are always on duty during working hours; more employees can be called in during periods of heavy demand to work on an "as-needed" basis.
11. A manufacturer found that the maintenance cost of its heavy machinery was tied to the age of the equipment. Experience indicated that the maintenance cost increased at an increasing rate as the equipment aged.

PROBLEMS

3-14 COST BEHAVIOR, RESOURCE USAGE, EXCESS CAPACITY

LO1, LO2   Rolertyme Company manufactures roller skates. With the exception of the rollers, all parts of the skates are produced internally. Neeta Booth, president of Rolertyme, has decided to make the rollers instead of buying them from external suppliers. The company needs 100,000 sets per year (currently it pays $1.90 per set of rollers).

The rollers can be produced using an available area within the plant. However, equipment for production of the rollers would need to be leased ($30,000 per year lease payment). Additionally, it would cost $0.50 per machine hour for power, oil, and other operating expenses. The equipment will provide 60,000 machine hours per year. Direct material costs will average $0.75 per set, and direct labor will average $0.25 per set. Since only one type of roller would be produced, no additional demands would be made on the setup activity. Other overhead activities (besides machining and setups), however, would be affected. The company's cost management system provides the following information about the current status of the overhead activities that would be affected. (The supply and demand figures do not include the effect of roller production on these activities.) The lumpy quantity indicates how much capacity must be purchased should any expansion of activity supply be needed. The purchase price is the cost of acquiring the capacity represented by the lumpy quantity. This price also represents the cost of current spending on existing activity supply (for each block of activity).

Activity Price	Cost Driver	Supply	Usage	Lumpy Quantity	Purchase
Purchasing	Orders	25,000	23,000	5,000	$25,000
Inspection	Hours	10,000	9,000	2,000	30,000
Materials handling	Moves	4,500	4,300	500	15,000

Production of rollers would place the following demands on the overhead activities:

Activity	Resource Demands
Machining	50,000 machine hours
Purchasing	2,000 purchase orders (associated with raw materials used to make the rollers)
Inspection	750 inspection hours
Materials handling	500 moves

Producing the rollers also means that the purchase of outside rollers will cease. Thus, purchase orders associated with the outside acquisition of rollers will drop by 5,000. Similarly, the moves for the handling of incoming orders will decrease by 200. The company has not inspected the rollers purchased from outside suppliers.

Required:

1. Classify all resources associated with the production of rollers as flexible resources and committed resources. Label each committed resource as a short- or long-term commitment. How should we describe the cost behavior of these short- and long-term resource commitments? Explain.
2. Calculate the total annual resource spending (for all activities except for setups) that the company will incur after production of the rollers begins. Break this cost into fixed and variable activity costs. In calculating these figures, assume that the company will spend no more than necessary. What is the effect on resource spending caused by production of the rollers?
3. Refer to Requirement 2. For each activity, break down the cost of activity supplied into the cost of activity output and the cost of unused activity.

3-15 COST BEHAVIOR, HIGH-LOW METHOD, PRICING DECISION

LO1, LO3   St. Luke's Medical Center (SLMC) offers a number of specialized medical services, including neuroscience, cardiology, and oncology. SLMC's strong reputation for quality medical care allowed it to branch out into other services. It is now ready to expand its orthopedic services and has just added a free-standing orthopedic clinic offering a full range of outpatient, surgical, and physical therapy services. The cost of the orthopedic facility is depreciated on a straight-line basis. All equipment within the facility is leased.

Since the clinic had no experience with in-patient orthopedic services (for patients recovering for hip and knee replacements, for example), it decided to operate the orthopedic center for two months before determining how much to charge per patient day on an ongoing basis. As a temporary measure, the clinic adopted a patient-day charge of $190, an amount equal to the fees charged by a hospital specializing in orthopedic care in a nearby city.

This initial per-day charge was quoted to patients entering the orthopedic center during the first two months with assurances that if the actual operating costs of the new center justified it, the charge could be less. In no case would the charges be more. A temporary policy of billing after 60 days was adopted so that any adjustments could be made.

The orthopedic center opened on January 1. During January, the center had 2,100 patient days of activity. During February, the activity was 2,250 patient days. Costs for these two levels of activity output are as follows:

	2,100 Patient Days	2,250 Patient Days
Salaries, nurses	$ 15,000	$ 15,000
Aides	2,000	2,000
Pharmacy	217,300	232,300
Laboratory	55,700	58,700
Depreciation	12,000	12,000
Laundry	16,800	18,000
Administration	17,000	17,000
Lease (equipment)	30,000	30,000

Required:

1. Classify each cost as fixed, variable, or mixed, using patient days as the activity driver.
2. Use the high-low method to separate the mixed costs into fixed and variable.
3. Lynley Jackson, the administrator of the orthopedic center, has estimated that the center will average 2,000 patient days per month. If the center is to be operated as a nonprofit organization, how much will it need to charge per patient day? How much of this charge is variable? How much is fixed?
4. Suppose the orthopedic center averages 2,500 patient days per month. How much would need to be charged per patient day for the center to cover its costs? Explain why the charge per patient day decreased as the activity output increased.

3-16 HIGH-LOW METHOD, METHOD OF LEAST SQUARES, CORRELATION, CONFIDENCE INTERVAL

LO2, LO3, LO4 PriceCut, a discount store, has gathered data on its overhead activities and associated costs for the past 10 months. Adrienne Sanjay, a member of the controller's department, believes that overhead activities and costs should be classified into groups that have the same driver. She has decided that unloading incoming goods, counting goods, and inspecting goods can be grouped together as a more general receiving activity, since these three activities are all driven by the number of purchase orders. The following 10 months of data have been gathered for the receiving activity:

Month	Purchase Orders	Receiving Cost
1	1,000	$18,600
2	700	14,000
3	1,500	28,000
4	1,200	17,500
5	1,300	25,000
6	1,100	21,000
7	1,600	28,000
8	1,400	24,000
9	1,700	26,000
10	900	16,000

Required:

1. Prepare a scattergraph, plotting the receiving costs against the number of purchase orders. Use the vertical axis for costs and the horizontal axis for orders.
2. Select two points that make the best fit, and compute a cost formula for receiving costs.
3. Using the high-low method, prepare a cost formula for the receiving activity.

4. Using the method of least squares, prepare a cost formula for the receiving activity. What is the coefficient of determination?
5. Prepare a 95 percent confidence interval for receiving costs when 1,200 purchase orders are expected.

3-17 COST FORMULAS, SINGLE AND MULTIPLE ACTIVITY DRIVERS, COEFFICIENT OF CORRELATION

LO1, LO3, LO4, LO5

Kimball Company has developed the following cost formulas:

$$\text{Material usage: } Y_m = \$80X; \ r = 0.95$$
$$\text{Labor usage (direct): } Y_l = \$20X; \ r = 0.96$$
$$\text{Overhead activity: } Y_o = \$350,000 + \$100X; \ r = 0.75$$
$$\text{Selling activity: } Y_s = \$50,000 + \$10X; \ r = 0.93$$

where

$$X = \text{Direct labor hours}$$

The company has a policy of producing on demand and keeps very little, if any, finished goods inventory (thus, units produced = units sold). Each unit uses one direct labor hour for production.

The president of Kimball Company has recently implemented a policy that any special orders will be accepted if they cover the costs that the orders cause. This policy was implemented because Kimball's industry is in a recession and the company is producing well below capacity (and expects to continue doing so for the coming year). The president is willing to accept orders that minimally cover their variable costs so that the company can keep its employees and avoid layoffs. Also, any orders above variable costs will increase overall profitability of the company.

Required:

1. Compute the total unit variable cost. Suppose that Kimball has an opportunity to accept an order for 20,000 units at $220 per unit. Should Kimball accept the order? (The order would not displace any of Kimball's regular orders.)
2. Explain the significance of the coefficient of correlation measures for the cost formulas. Did these measures have a bearing on your answer in Requirement 1? Should they have a bearing? Why or why not?
3. Suppose that a multiple regression equation is developed for overhead costs: $Y = \$100,000 + \$100X_1 + \$5,000X_2 + \$300X_3$, where $X_1 =$ direct labor hours, $X_2 =$ number of setups, and $X_3 =$ engineering hours. The coefficient of determination for the equation is 0.94. Assume that the order of 20,000 units requires 12 setups and 600 engineering hours. Given this new information, should the company accept the special order referred to in Requirement 1? Is there any other information about cost behavior that you would like to have? Explain.

3-18 SCATTERGRAPH, HIGH-LOW METHOD, METHOD OF LEAST SQUARES, USE OF JUDGMENT

LO3, LO4, LO5

The management of Wheeler Company has decided to develop cost formulas for its major overhead activities. Wheeler uses a highly automated manufacturing process, and power costs are a significant manufacturing cost. Cost analysts have decided that power costs are mixed; thus, they must be broken into their fixed and variable elements so that the cost behavior of the power usage activity can be properly described. Machine hours have been selected as the activity driver for power costs. The following data for the past eight quarters have been collected:

Quarter	Machine Hours	Power Cost
1	20,000	$26,000
2	25,000	38,000
3	30,000	42,500
4	22,000	35,000
5	21,000	34,000
6	18,000	31,400
7	24,000	36,000
8	28,000	42,000

Required:

1. Prepare a scattergraph by plotting power costs against machine hours. Does the scattergraph show a linear relationship between machine hours and power cost?
2. Using the high and low points, compute a power cost formula.
3. Use the method of least squares to compute a power cost formula. Evaluate the coefficient of determination.
4. Rerun the regression and drop the point (20,000; $26,000) as an outlier. Compare the results from this regression to those for the regression in Requirement 3. Which is better?

3-19 METHOD OF LEAST SQUARES

LO1, LO3, LO4, LO5 DeMarco Company is developing a cost formula for its packing activity. Discussion with the workers in the packing department has revealed that packing costs are associated with the number of customer orders, the size of the orders, and the relative fragility of the items (more fragile items must be specially wrapped in bubble wrap and Styrofoam). Data for the past 20 months have been gathered:

Month	Packing Cost	Number of Orders	Weight of Orders	Number of Fragile Items
1	$ 45,000	11,200	24,640	1,120
2	58,000	14,000	31,220	1,400
3	39,000	10,500	18,000	1,000
4	35,600	9,000	19,350	850
5	90,000	21,000	46,200	4,000
6	126,000	31,000	64,000	5,500
7	90,600	20,000	60,000	1,800
8	63,000	15,000	40,000	750
9	79,000	16,000	59,000	1,500
10	155,000	40,000	88,000	2,500
11	450,000	113,500	249,700	11,800
12	640,000	150,000	390,000	14,000
13	41,000	10,000	23,000	900
14	54,000	14,000	29,400	890
15	58,000	15,000	30,000	1,500
16	58,090	14,500	31,900	1,340
17	80,110	18,000	50,000	3,000
18	123,000	30,000	75,000	2,000
19	108,000	27,000	63,450	1,900
20	76,000	18,000	41,400	1,430

Required:

1. Using the method of least squares, run a regression using the number of orders as the independent variable.
2. Run a multiple regression using three independent variables: the number of orders, the weight of orders, and the number of fragile items. Which regression equation is better? Why?
3. Predict the total packing cost for 25,000 orders, weighing 40,000 pounds, with 4,000 fragile items. Prepare a 99 percent confidence interval for this estimate of total packing cost.
4. How much would the cost estimated for Requirement 3 change if the 25,000 orders weighed 40,000 pounds, but only 2,000 were fragile items?

3-20   HIGH-LOW METHOD, SCATTERPLOT, REGRESSION

LO2, LO3,   Weber Valley Regional Hospital has collected data on all of its activities for the past 16
LO4, LO5   months. Data for cardiac nursing care follow:

	Y Cost	X Hours of Nursing Care
May 2006	$59,600	1,400
June 2006	57,150	1,350
July 2006	61,110	1,460
August 2006	65,800	1,600
September 2006	69,500	1,700
October 2006	64,250	1,550
November 2006	52,000	1,200
December 2006	66,000	1,600
January 2007	83,000	1,800
February 2007	66,550	1,330
March 2007	79,500	1,700
April 2007	76,000	1,600
May 2007	68,500	1,400
June 2007	73,150	1,550
July 2007	73,175	1,505
August 2007	66,150	1,290

Required:

1. Using the high-low method, calculate the variable rate per hour and the fixed cost for the nursing care activity.
2. Run a regression on the data, using hours of nursing care as the independent variable. Predict cost for the cardiac nursing care for September 2007 if 1,400 hours of nursing care are forecast. Evaluate the regression equation. How comfortable are you with the predicted cost for September 2007?
3. Upon looking into the events that happened at the end of 2006, you find that the cardiology ward bought a cardiac-monitoring machine for the nursing station. Administrators also decided to add a new supervisory position for the evening shift. Monthly depreciation on the monitor and the salary of the new supervisor together total $10,000. Now, run two regression equations, one for the observations from 2006 and the second using only the observations for the eight months in 2007. Discuss your findings. What is your predicted cost of the cardiac nursing care activity for September 2007?

3-21   COMPARISON OF REGRESSION EQUATIONS

LO1, LO3, LO4, LO5

Friendly Bank is attempting to determine the cost behavior of its small business lending operations. One of the major activities is the application activity. Two possible activity drivers have been mentioned: application hours (number of hours to complete the application) and number of applications. The bank controller has accumulated the following data for the setup activity:

Month	Application Costs	Application Hours	Number of Applications
February	$ 7,700	2,000	70
March	7,650	2,100	50
April	10,052	3,000	50
May	9,400	2,700	60
June	9,584	3,000	20
July	8,480	2,500	40
August	8,550	2,400	60
September	9,735	2,900	50
October	10,500	3,000	90

Required:

1. Estimate a regression equation with application hours as the activity driver and the only independent variable. If the bank forecasts 2,600 application hours for the next month, what will be the budgeted application cost?
2. Estimate a regression equation with number of applications as the activity driver and the only independent variable. If the bank forecasts 80 applications for the next month, what will be the budgeted application cost?
3. Which of the two regression equations do you think does a better job of predicting application costs? Explain.
4. Run a multiple regression to determine the cost equation using both activity drivers. What are the budgeted application costs for 2,600 application hours and 80 applications?

3-22   MULTIPLE REGRESSION, CONFIDENCE INTERVALS, RELIABILITY OF COST FORMULAS

LO2, LO4, LO5

Randy Harris, controller, has been given the charge to implement an advanced cost management system. As part of this process, he needs to identify activity drivers for the activities of the firm. During the past four months, Randy has spent considerable effort identifying activities, their associated costs, and possible drivers for the activities' costs.

Initially, Randy made his selections based on his own judgment using his experience and input from employees who perform the activities. Later, he used regression analysis to confirm his judgment. Randy prefers to use one driver per activity, provided that an R^2 of at least 80 percent can be produced. Otherwise, multiple drivers will be used, based on evidence provided by multiple regression analysis. For example, the activity of inspecting finished goods produced an R^2 of less than 80 percent for any single activity driver. Randy believes, however, that a satisfactory cost formula can be developed using two activity drivers: the number of batches and the number of inspection hours. Data collected for a 14-month period are as follows:

Inspection Costs	Hours of Inspection	Number of Batches
$17,689	100	10
18,350	120	20
13,125	60	15
28,000	320	30
30,560	240	25
31,755	200	40
40,750	280	35
29,500	230	22
47,570	350	50
36,740	270	45
43,500	350	38
26,780	200	18
28,500	140	28
17,000	160	14

Required:

1. Calculate the cost formula for inspection costs using the two drivers, inspection hours and number of batches. Are both activity drivers useful? What does the R^2 indicate about the formula?
2. Using the formula developed in Requirement 1, calculate the inspection cost when 300 inspection hours are used and 30 batches are produced. Prepare a 90 percent confidence interval for this prediction.

3-23 SIMPLE AND MULTIPLE REGRESSION, EVALUATING RELIABILITY OF AN EQUATION

LO2, LO3, LO4

CMA

The Lockit Company manufactures door knobs for residential homes and apartments. Lockit is considering the use of simple (single-driver) and multiple regression analyses to forecast annual sales because previous forecasts have been inaccurate. The new sales forecast will be used to initiate the budgeting process and to identify more completely the underlying process that generates sales.

Larry Husky, the controller of Lockit, has considered many possible independent variables and equations to predict sales and has narrowed his choices to four equations. Husky used annual observations from 20 prior years to estimate each of the four equations.

Following are a definition of the variables used in the four equations and a statistical summary of these equations:

$$S_t = \text{Forecasted sales in dollars for Lockit in period } t$$
$$S_{t-1} = \text{Actual sales in dollars for Lockit in period } t - 1$$
$$G_t = \text{Forecasted U.S. gross domestic product in period } t$$
$$G_{t-1} = \text{Actual U.S. gross domestic product in period } t - 1$$
$$N_{t-1} = \text{Lockit's net income in period } t - 1$$

Required:

1. Write Equations 2 and 4 in the form $Y = a + bx$.
2. If actual sales are $1,500,000 in 2006, what would be the forecasted sales for Lockit in 2007?
3. Explain why Larry Husky might prefer Equation 3 to Equation 2.
4. Explain the advantages and disadvantages of using Equation 4 to forecast sales.

Statistical Summary of Four Equations

Equation	Dependent Variable	Independent Variable(s)	Intercept	Independent Variable (Rate)	Standard Error	R Square	t Value
1	S_t	S_{t-1}	$ 500,000	$ 1.10	$500,000	0.94	5.50
2	S_t	G_t	1,000,000	0.00001	510,000	0.90	10.00
3	S_t	G_{t-1}	900,000	0.000012	520,000	0.81	5.00
4	S_t		600,000		490,000	0.96	
		N_{t-1}		10.00			4.00
		G_t		0.000002			1.50
		G_{t-1}		0.000003			3.00

(CMA adapted)

3-24 LEARNING CURVE

LO6 Harriman Industries manufactures engines for the aerospace industry. It has completed manufacturing the first unit of the new ZX-9 engine design. Management believes that the 1,000 labor hours required to complete this unit are reasonable and is prepared to go forward with the manufacture of additional units. An 80 percent cumulative average-time learning curve model for direct labor hours is assumed to be valid. Data on costs are as follows:

Direct materials	$10,500
Direct labor	$30 per direct labor hour
Variable manufacturing overhead	$40 per direct labor hour

Required:

1. Set up a table with columns for cumulative number of units, cumulative average time per unit in hours, cumulative total time in hours, and individual unit time for the nth unit in hours. Complete the table for 1, 2, 4, 8, 16, and 32 units.
2. What are the total variable costs of producing 1, 2, 4, 8, 16, and 32 units? What is the variable cost per unit for 1, 2, 4, 8, 16, and 32 units?

3-25 LEARNING CURVE

LO6 Refer to **Problem 3-24**. Now assume that an 80 percent incremental unit-time learning curve model is applicable.

Required:

1. Set up a table with columns for cumulative number of units, individual unit time for the nth unit in hours, cumulative total time in hours, and cumulative average time per unit in hours. Complete the table for 1, 2, 4, 8, 16, and 32 units.
2. What are the total variable costs of producing 1, 2, 4, 8, 16, and 32 units?
3. Why do the results for this problem vary from those for **Problem 3-24**?

3-26 LEARNING CURVE

LO6 Thames Assurance Company sells a variety of life and health insurance products. Recently, Thames developed a long-term care policy for sale to members of university and college alumni associations. Thames estimated that the sale and service of this type of policy would be subject to a 90 percent incremental unit-time learning curve model.

Each unit consists of 350 policies sold. The first unit is estimated to take 1,000 hours to sell and service.

Required:

1. Set up a table with columns for cumulative number of units, individual unit time for the *n*th unit in hours, cumulative total time in hours, and cumulative average time per unit in hours. Complete the table for 1, 2, 4, 8, 16, and 32 units.
2. Suppose that Thames revises its assumption to an 80 percent learning curve. How will this affect the amount of time needed to sell and service eight units? How do you suppose that Thames estimates the percent learning rate?

3-27   LEARNING CURVE

LO6   Using the same data from **Problem 3-26**, apply a cumulative average-time learning curve model with a 90 percent learning rate.

Required:

1. Set up a table with columns for cumulative number of units, cumulative average time per unit in hours, cumulative total time in hours, and individual unit time for the *n*th unit in hours. Complete the table for 1, 2, 4, 8, 16, and 32 units.
2. Why do the results from this table differ from those in Requirement 1 of **Problem 3-26**?

3-28   COLLABORATIVE LEARNING EXERCISE

LO1, LO2   Divide students into groups of four or five. Have each group choose a business that is familiar to them (e.g., pizza parlor) and list as many flexible and committed resources as possible. One group member, the reporter, should write down the group's responses and then share them with the rest of the class.

3-29   CYBER RESEARCH CASE

LO6   Check the Boeing Web site at http://www.boeing.com, and go to commercial aircraft orders. Boeing gives the number of orders per type of plane (e.g., 767). For which type of plane would you expect Boeing to gain the most from learning effects? Why? What impact will this have on costs? Prices? Time to delivery?

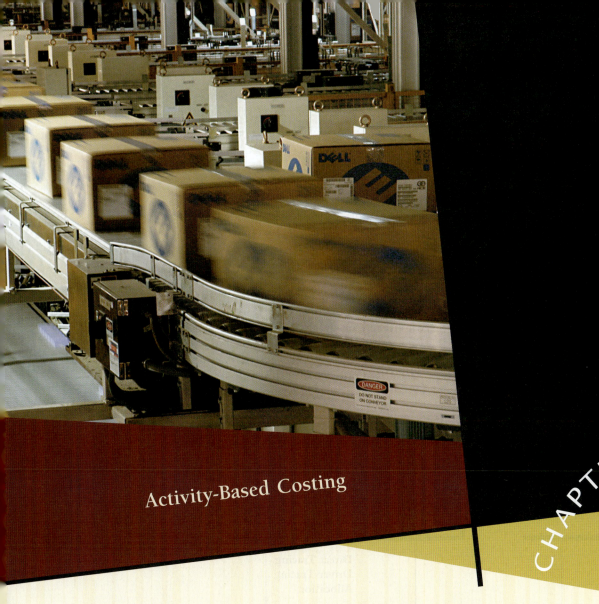

Activity-Based Costing

CHAPTER

4

AFTER STUDYING THIS CHAPTER, YOU SHOULD BE ABLE TO:

1. Describe the basics of plantwide and departmental overhead costing.

2. Explain why plantwide and departmental overhead costing may not be accurate.

3. Provide a detailed description of activity-based product costing.

4. Explain how the number of activity rates can be reduced.

5. Describe activity-based system concepts including an ABC relational database and ABC software.

In Chapter 2, we mentioned that cost management information systems can be divided into two types: functional-based and activity-based. The functional-based costing systems use traditional product cost definitions and use only unit-based activity drivers to assign overhead to products. This chapter begins by describing how functional-based costing is used for computing traditional product costs. This enables us to compare and contrast functional-based and activity-based costing approaches. An activity-based cost accounting system offers greater product costing accuracy but at an increased cost. The justification for adopting an activity-based costing approach must rely on the benefits of improved decisions resulting from materially different product costs. It is important to understand that a necessary condition for improved decisions is that the accounting numbers produced by an activity-based costing system must be significantly different from those produced by a functional-based costing system. When will this be the case? Are there any signals that management might receive which would indicate that functional-based costing is no

© BLOOMBERG NEWS/LANDOV

longer working? Finally, assuming that an activity-based cost accounting system is called for, how does it work? What are its basic features? Detailed features? What steps must be followed for successful implementation of an ABC system? This chapter addresses these questions and other related issues.

Unit-Level Product Costing

OBJECTIVE *1*

Describe the basics of plantwide and departmental overhead costing.

Functional-based product costing assigns only manufacturing costs to products. Exhibit 4-1 shows the general functional-based product costing model. Assigning the cost of direct materials and direct labor to products poses no particular challenge. These costs can be assigned to products using direct tracing, and most functional-based costing systems are designed to ensure that this tracing takes place. Overhead costs, on the other hand, pose a different problem. The physically observable input-output relationship that exists between direct labor, direct materials, and products is simply not available for overhead. Thus, assignment of overhead must rely on driver tracing and perhaps allocation. Functional-based costing first assigns overhead costs to a functional unit, creating either plant or departmental cost pools. Next, these pooled costs are assigned to products using *predetermined overhead rates* based on unit-level drivers.

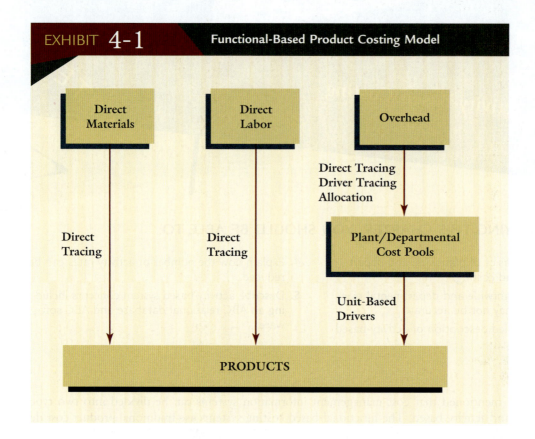

EXHIBIT 4-1   **Functional-Based Product Costing Model**

A **predetermined overhead rate** is calculated at the beginning of the year using the following formula:

Overhead rate = Budgeted annual overhead/Budgeted annual driver level

Predetermined rates are used because overhead and production often are incurred nonuniformly throughout the year, and it is not possible to wait until the end of the year to calculate the actual overhead cost assignments (managers need unit product cost information throughout the year). A cost system that uses predetermined overhead rates and actual costs for direct materials and direct labor is referred to as a **normal cost system**. Budgeted overhead is simply the firm's best estimate of the amount of overhead (utilities, indirect labor, depreciation, etc.) to be incurred in the coming year. The estimate is often based on last year's figures, adjusted for anticipated changes in the coming year. The second input requires that the predicted level for an activity driver be specified. Assignment of overhead costs should follow, as nearly as possible, a cause-and-effect relationship. Drivers are simply causal factors that measure the consumption of overhead by products. In functional-based costing, only *unit-level drivers* are used to calculate overhead rates.

Unit-level drivers are factors that measure the demands placed on unit-level activities by products. Unit-level activities are activities performed each and every time a unit of a product is produced. The five most commonly used unit-level drivers are:

1. Units produced
2. Direct labor hours
3. Direct labor dollars
4. Machine hours
5. Direct material dollars

Unit-level drivers increase as units produced increase. Thus, the use of only unit-based drivers to assign overhead costs to products assumes that all overhead consumed by products is highly correlated with the number of units produced. To the extent that this assumption is true, functional-based costing can produce accurate cost assignments.

Plantwide or departmental predetermined overhead rates are used to assign or apply overhead costs to production as the actual production activity unfolds. The total overhead assigned to actual production at any point in time is called **applied overhead**. Applied overhead is computed using the following formula:

$$\text{Applied overhead} = \text{Overhead rate} \times \text{Actual driver usage}$$

Overhead Assignment: Plantwide Rates

For plantwide rates, all budgeted overhead costs are assigned to a plantwide pool (first-stage cost assignment). Next, a plantwide rate is computed using a single unit-level driver, which is usually direct labor hours. Finally, overhead costs are assigned to products by multiplying the rate by the actual total direct labor hours used by each product (second-stage assignment).

These points are best illustrated with an example. Suncalc, Inc., produces two unique, solar-powered products: a pocket calculator and a currency translator used to convert foreign currency into dollars and vice versa. Suncalc uses a plantwide rate based on direct labor hours to assign its overhead costs. The company has the following estimated and actual data for the coming year:

Budgeted overhead		$360,000
Expected activity (in direct labor hours)		120,000
Actual activity (in direct labor hours):		
Pocket calculator	40,000	
Currency translator	60,000	
		100,000
Actual overhead		$320,000
Units produced:		
Pocket calculator		80,000
Currency translator		90,000

The overhead rate to be used is calculated as follows:

$$\text{Predetermined overhead rate} = \text{Budgeted overhead/Normal activity}$$
$$= \$360,000/120,000 \text{ direct labor hours}$$
$$= \$3 \text{ per DLH}$$

Using the overhead rate, applied overhead for the year is:

$$\text{Applied overhead} = \text{Overhead rate} \times \text{Actual activity usage}$$
$$= \$3 \text{ per DLH} \times 100,000 \text{ DLH}$$
$$= \$300,000$$

Per-Unit Overhead Cost

The predetermined overhead rate is the basis for per-unit overhead cost calculation:

	Pocket Calculator	Currency Translator
Units produced	80,000	90,000
Direct labor hours	40,000	60,000
Overhead applied to production ($3 × DLH)	$120,000	$180,000
Overhead per unit*	$1.50	$2.00

*Overapplied/Units produced.

Under- and Overapplied Overhead

Notice that the amount of overhead applied to production ($300,000) differs from the actual overhead ($320,000). Since the predetermined overhead rate is based on estimated data, applied overhead will rarely equal actual overhead. Since only $300,000 was applied in our example, the firm has underapplied overhead by $20,000. If applied overhead had been $330,000, too much overhead would have been applied to production. The firm would have overapplied overhead by $10,000. The difference between actual overhead and applied overhead is an **overhead variance**. If actual overhead is greater than applied overhead, then the variance is called **underapplied overhead**. If applied overhead is greater than actual overhead, then the variance is called **overapplied overhead**.

Overhead variances occur because it is impossible to perfectly estimate future overhead costs and production activity. Costs reported on the financial statements must be actual—not estimated—amounts. Accordingly, at the end of a reporting period, procedures must exist to dispose of any overhead variance.

Disposition of Overhead Variances

An overhead variance is disposed of in one of two ways:

1. If immaterial, it is assigned to cost of goods sold.
2. If material, it is allocated among work-in-process inventory, finished goods inventory, and cost of goods sold.

Assigned to Cost of Goods Sold

The most common practice is simply to assign the entire overhead variance to cost of goods sold. This practice is justified on the basis of materiality, the same principle used to justify expensing the entire cost of a pencil sharpener in the period acquired rather than allocating (through depreciation) its cost over the life of the sharpener. Thus, the overhead variance is added to cost of goods sold if underapplied and subtracted from cost of goods sold if overapplied. For example, assume that Suncalc has an ending balance in its cost of goods sold account equal to $500,000. The underapplied variance of $20,000 would be added to produce a new, adjusted balance of $520,000. Assuming that both actual and applied overhead are accumulated in the overhead control account, the journal entry associated with this adjustment would be:

Cost of Goods Sold	20,000	
Overhead Control		20,000

Allocation to Production Accounts

If the overhead variance is material, it should be allocated to the period's production. Conceptually, the overhead costs of a period belong to goods started but not completed (work-in-process inventory), goods finished but not sold (finished goods inventory), and goods finished and sold (cost of goods sold). The recommended way to achieve this allocation is to prorate the overhead variance based on the ending applied overhead balances in each account. Using applied overhead captures the original cause-and-effect relationships used to assign overhead. Using another balance, such as total manufacturing costs, may result in an unfair assignment of the additional overhead. For example, two products identical on all dimensions except for the cost of direct material inputs should receive the same overhead assignment. Yet, if total manufacturing costs were used to allocate an overhead variance, then the product with the more expensive direct materials would receive a higher overhead assignment.

To illustrate the disposition of the overhead variance using the recommended approach, assume that Suncalc's accounts had the following applied overhead balances at the end of the year:

Work-in-Process Inventory	$ 60,000
Finished Goods Inventory	90,000
Cost of Goods Sold	150,000
Total	$300,000

Given the preceding data, the percentage allocation of any overhead variance to the three accounts is:

Work-in-Process Inventory	20% ($60,000/$300,000)
Finished Goods Inventory	30% ($90,000/$300,000)
Cost of Goods Sold	50% ($150,000/$300,000)

Recall that Suncalc had a $20,000 underapplied overhead variance. Thus, Work-in-Process Inventory would receive 20 percent of $20,000 (or $4,000), Finished Goods Inventory would receive 30 percent of $20,000 (or $6,000), and Cost of Goods Sold would receive 50 percent of $20,000 (or $10,000). The associated journal entries for this adjustment would be:

Work-in-Process Inventory	4,000	
Finished Goods Inventory	6,000	
Cost of Goods Sold	10,000	
Overhead Control		20,000

Since underapplied means that too little overhead was assigned, these individual prorated amounts would be added to the ending account balances. Adding these amounts produces the following new adjusted balances of the three accounts:

	Unadjusted Balance	Prorated Underapplied Overhead	Adjusted Balance
Work-in-Process Inventory	$ 60,000	$ 4,000	$ 64,000
Finished Goods Inventory	90,000	6,000	96,000
Cost of Goods Sold	150,000	10,000	160,000

Of course, if too much overhead is assigned to production, the overapplied amount is subtracted from the account balances.

Overhead Application: Departmental Rates

For departmental rates, overhead costs are assigned to individual production departments, creating departmental overhead cost pools. In the first stage, producing departments are cost objects, and budgeted overhead costs are assigned using direct tracing, driver tracing, and allocation. Once costs are assigned to individual production departments, then unit-level drivers such as direct labor hours (for labor-intensive departments) and machine hours (for machine-intensive departments) are used to compute predetermined overhead rates for each department. Products passing through the departments are assumed to consume overhead resources in proportion to the departments' unit-based drivers (machine hours or direct labor hours used). Thus, in the second stage, overhead is assigned to products by multiplying the departmental rates by the amount of the driver used in the respective departments. The total overhead assigned to products is simply the sum of the amounts received in each department. Increased accuracy is the usual justification offered for the use of departmental rates.

The Suncalc example will again be used to illustrate departmental rates. Assume that Suncalc has two producing departments: fabrication and assembly. Machine hours are used to assign the overhead of fabrication, and direct labor hours are used to assign the overhead of assembly. The following data are provided:

	Fabrication	Assembly	Total
Overhead	$280,000	$80,000	$360,000
Direct labor hours:			
Pocket calculator	10,000	30,000	40,000
Currency translator	10,000	50,000	60,000
Total	20,000	80,000	100,000
Machine hours:			
Pocket calculator	5,000	1,000	6,000
Currency translator	15,000	2,000	17,000
Total	20,000	3,000	23,000

There is a predetermined rate calculated for each department:

Fabrication (based on machine hours):   Rate = $280,000/20,000
                                                = $14 per machine hour
Assembly (based on direct labor hours):   Rate = $80,000/80,000
                                                = $1 per direct labor hour

The per-unit overhead cost for each product can now be calculated:

	Pocket Calculator	Currency Translator
Units produced	80,000	90,000
Overhead applied to production:		
Fabrication:		
$14 × 5,000	$ 70,000	
$14 × 15,000		$210,000
Assembly:		
$1 × 30,000	30,000	
$1 × 50,000		50,000
Total	$100,000	$260,000
Overhead per unit*	$1.25	$2.89

*Overapplied/Units produced.

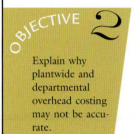

OBJECTIVE 2

Explain why plantwide and departmental overhead costing may not be accurate.

Limitations of Plantwide and Departmental Rates

Plantwide and departmental rates have been used for decades and continue to be used successfully by many organizations. In some settings, however, they do not work well and may actually cause severe product cost distortions. Of course, to cause a significant cost distortion, overhead costs must be a significant percentage of total manufacturing costs. For some manufacturers, overhead costs are a small percentage (e.g., 5 percent or less), and the system in which these costs are assigned is not a major issue. In this case, using a very simple, uncomplicated approach such as plantwide rates is appropriate. Assuming, however, that the overhead costs are a significant percentage of total manufacturing costs, at least two major factors can impair the ability of the unit-based plantwide and departmental rates to assign overhead costs accurately: (1) the proportion of non-unit-related overhead costs to total overhead costs is large, and (2) the degree of product diversity is great.

Non-Unit-Related Overhead Costs

The use of either plantwide rates or departmental rates assumes that a product's consumption of overhead resources is related strictly to the units produced. But what if there are overhead activities that are unrelated to the number of units produced? Setup costs, for example, are incurred each time a batch of products is produced. A batch may consist of 1,000 or 10,000 units, and the cost of setup is the same. Yet, as more setups are done, setup costs increase. The number of setups, not the number of units produced, is the cause of setup costs. Furthermore, product engineering costs may depend on the number of different engineering work orders rather than the units produced of any given product. Both these examples illustrate the existence of non-unit-based drivers. **Non-unit-based drivers** are factors, other than the number of units produced, that measure the demands that cost objects place on activities. Thus, unit-level drivers cannot assign these costs accurately to products. In fact, using only unit-level drivers to assign non-unit-related overhead costs can create distorted product costs. The severity of this distortion depends on what proportion of total overhead costs these non-unit-based costs represent. For many companies, this percentage can be significant—reaching more than 40 or 50 percent of the total. Clearly, as this percentage decreases, the acceptability of using unit-based drivers for assigning costs increases.

Product Diversity

Significant nonunit overhead costs will not cause product cost distortions provided products consume the nonunit overhead activities in the same proportion as the unit-level overhead activities. Product diversity, on the other hand, can cause product cost distortion. **Product diversity** simply means that products consume overhead activities in different proportions. Product diversity is caused by such things as differences in product size, product complexity, setup time, and size of batches. The proportion of each activity consumed by a product is defined as the **consumption ratio**. The way that nonunit overhead costs and product diversity can produce distorted product costs (when only unit-level drivers are used to assign overhead costs) is best illustrated with an example.

An Example Illustrating the Failure of Unit-Based Overhead Rates

To illustrate the failure of plantwide and departmental rates, consider Goodmark Company, a company with a plant that produces two products: scented and regular birthday cards. Scented cards emit a pleasant fragrance when opened. The two producing departments are cutting and printing. Cutting is responsible for shaping the cards, and printing is responsible for design and wording (including the insertion of the fragrance for the scented cards). Expected product costing data are given in Exhibit 4-2. The units are boxes of one dozen cards. Because the quantity of regular cards produced is 10 times greater than that of scented cards, we can label the regular cards a high-volume product and scented cards a low-volume product. The cards are produced in batches.

For ease of presentation, only four types of overhead activities, performed by four distinct support departments, are assumed: setting up the equipment for each batch, machining, inspecting, and moving a batch. Each box of 12 cards is inspected after each department's operations. After cutting, the cards are inspected individually to ensure correct shape. After printing, the boxes of cards are also inspected individually to ensure correct wording, absence of smudges, insertion of fragrance, etc. Overhead costs are assigned to the two production departments using the direct method (described in Chapter 7). Setup costs are assigned based on the number of setups handled by each department. Since the number is identical, each department receives 50 percent of the total setup costs. Machining costs are assigned in proportion to the number of machine hours used by each department. Finally, inspection costs are assigned in proportion to the number of inspection hours used. The costs of moving materials are assigned by the number of moves used by each department (which is the same for each department).

Plantwide Overhead Rate

The total overhead for the plant is $720,000, the sum of the overhead for each department ($216,000 + $504,000). Assume that direct labor hours are used as the unit-based activity driver. Dividing the total overhead by the total direct labor hours yields the following overhead rate:

$$\text{Plantwide rate} = \$720,000/180,000 \text{ direct labor hours}$$
$$= \$4.00 \text{ per direct labor hour}$$

Using this plantwide rate and other information from Exhibit 4-2, the unit costs for each product are calculated and shown in Exhibit 4-3. Prime costs are assigned using direct tracing.

Departmental Rates

Based on the distribution of labor hours and machine hours in Exhibit 4-2, the cutting department is labor intensive, and the printing department is machine intensive. Moreover, the overhead costs of the cutting department are almost 43 percent of those

EXHIBIT 4-2 — Product Costing Data

	Scented Cards	Regular Cards	Total
Units produced per year	20,000	200,000	—
Prime costs	$160,000	$1,500,000	$1,660,000
Direct labor hours	20,000	160,000	180,000
Number of setups	60	40	100
Machine hours	10,000	80,000	90,000
Inspection hours	2,000	16,000	18,000
Number of moves	180	120	300

Departmental Data

	Cutting Dept.	Printing Dept.	Total
Direct labor hours:			
Scented cards	10,000	10,000	20,000
Regular cards	150,000	10,000	160,000
Total	160,000	20,000	180,000
Machine hours:			
Scented cards	2,000	8,000	10,000
Regular cards	8,000	72,000	80,000
Total	10,000	80,000	90,000
Overhead costs:			
Setting up equipment	$120,000	$120,000	$240,000
Moving materials	60,000	60,000	120,000
Machining	20,000	180,000	200,000
Inspecting products	16,000	144,000	160,000
Total	$216,000	$504,000	$720,000

EXHIBIT 4-3 — Unit Cost Computation: Plantwide Rates

	Scented	Regular
Prime costs	$160,000	$1,500,000
Overhead costs:		
$4.00 × 20,000	80,000	
$4.00 × 160,000		640,000
Total manufacturing costs	$240,000	$2,140,000
Units of production	÷ 20,000	÷ 200,000
Unit cost	$ 12.00	$ 10.70

of the printing department. Based on these observations, it could be argued that departmental overhead rates would reflect the consumption of overhead better than would a plantwide rate. If true, product costs would be more accurate. This approach would yield the following departmental rates, using direct labor hours for the cutting department and machine hours for the printing department.

$$\text{Cutting department rate} = \$216{,}000/160{,}000 \text{ direct labor hours}$$
$$= \$1.35 \text{ per direct labor hour}$$

$$\text{Printing department rate} = \$504{,}000/80{,}000 \text{ machine hours}$$
$$= \$6.30 \text{ per machine hour}$$

Using these departmental rates and the data from Exhibit 4-2, the computations of the unit costs for each product are shown in Exhibit 4-4. (Prime costs are assigned using direct tracing.)

EXHIBIT 4-4   Unit Cost Computation: Departmental Rates

	Scented	Regular
Prime costs	$160,000	$1,500,000
Overhead costs:		
[($1.35 × 10,000) + ($6.30 × 8,000)].	63,900	
[($1.35 × 150,000) + ($6.30 × 72,000)]		656,100
Total manufacturing costs	$223,900	$2,156,100
Units of production	÷ 20,000	÷ 200,000
Unit cost.	$ 11.20*	$ 10.78*

*Rounded to the nearest cent.

Problems with Costing Accuracy

The accuracy of the overhead cost assignment can be challenged regardless of whether plantwide or departmental rates are used. The main problem with either procedure is the assumption that machine hours or direct labor hours drive or cause all overhead costs.

From Exhibit 4-2, we know that regular cards, the high-volume product, use eight times the direct labor hours used by the scented cards, the low-volume product (160,000 hours versus 20,000 hours). Thus, if a plantwide rate is used, the regular cards will receive eight times more overhead cost than will the scented cards. But is this reasonable? Do unit-based activity drivers explain the consumption of all overhead activities? In particular, can we reasonably assume that each product's consumption of overhead increases in direct proportion to the direct labor hours used? Let's look at the four overhead activities and see if unit-based drivers accurately reflect the demands of the regular and scented cards for overhead resources.

Machining and inspection appear to be unit-level costs, since they represent resources consumed each time a unit (card) is produced (recall that inspection is 100 percent). Thus, using direct labor hours to assign these costs appears reasonable. However, the data in Exhibit 4-2 suggest that a significant portion of overhead costs is not driven or caused by the units produced (measured by direct labor hours). For example, each product's demands for the setup and material-moving activities are more logically related to the number of production runs and the number of moves, respectively. These nonunit activities represent 50 percent ($360,000/$720,000) of the total overhead costs—a significant percentage. Notice that the low-volume product, scented cards, uses one and one-half times as many runs as do the regular cards (60/40) and one and one-half as many moves (180/120). However, use of direct labor hours, a unit-based activity driver, and a plantwide rate assigns eight times more setup and materials handling costs to the regular cards than to the scented. Thus, we have product diversity, and we should expect product cost distortion because the quantity of unit-based overhead that each product consumes does not vary in direct proportion to the quantity consumed of non-unit-based overhead. The consumption ratios for the two products are illustrated in Exhibit 4-5. Consumption ratios are simply the proportion of each activity consumed by a product. The consumption ratios suggest that a plantwide rate based on direct labor hours will overcost the regular cards and undercost the scented cards.

EXHIBIT 4-5	Product Diversity: Consumption Ratios		
	Consumption Ratios		
Overhead Activity	**Scented**	**Regular**	**Activity Driver**
Setups	0.60[a]	0.40[a]	Production runs
Moving materials	0.60[b]	0.40[b]	Number of moves
Machining	0.11[c]*	0.89[c]*	Machine hours
Inspection	0.11[d]*	0.89[d]*	Inspection hours

[a]60/100 (scented) and 40/100 (regular).
[b]180/300 (scented) and 120/300 (regular).
[c]10,000/90,000 (scented) and 80,000/90,000 (regular).
[d]2,000/18,000 (scented) and 16,000/18,000 (regular).
*Rounded.

The problem is only aggravated when departmental rates are used. In the cutting department, regular cards consume 15 times as many direct labor hours as do the scented cards (150,000/10,000). In the printing department, regular cards consume nine times as many machine hours as the scented cards (72,000/8,000). Thus, the regular cards receive about 15 times more overhead than do the scented cards in the cutting department, and in the printing department, they receive nine times more overhead. As Exhibit 4-4 shows, with departmental rates, the unit cost of the scented cards decreases by $0.80 to $11.20, and the unit cost of the regular cards increases by $0.08 to $10.78. This change is in the wrong direction, which emphasizes the failure of unit-based activity drivers to reflect accurately each product's demands for the setup and material-moving costs.

Activity Rates: A Possible Solution

The most direct method of overcoming the distortions caused by the unit-level rates is to expand the number of rates used so that the rates reflect the actual consumption of overhead costs by the various products. Thus, instead of pooling the overhead costs in plant or departmental pools, rates are calculated for each individual overhead activity. The rates are based on causal factors that measure consumption (unit- and non-unit-level activity drivers). Using this approach and the data from Exhibit 4-2, the following activity rates are computed for each activity:

Setting up equipment: $240,000/100 setups = $2,400 per setup
Machining: $200,000/90,000 machine hours = $2.22* per machine hour
Inspecting: $160,000/18,000 inspection hours = $8.89* per inspection hour
Moving materials: $120,000/300 moves = $400 per move

*Rounded.

Costs are assigned to each product by multiplying the activity rates by the amount consumed by each activity (as measured by the activity driver). The unit costs using activity rates are shown in Exhibit 4-6.

EXHIBIT **4-6**	Unit Cost Computation: Activity Rates	
	Scented	**Regular**
Prime costs	$160,000	$1,500,000
Overhead costs:		
Setting up:		
$2,400 × 60	144,000	
$2,400 × 40		96,000
Machining:		
$2.22 × 10,000	22,200	
$2.22 × 80,000		177,600
Inspecting:		
$8.89 × 2,000	17,780	
$8.89 × 16,000		142,240
Moving materials:		
$400 × 180	72,000	
$400 × 120		48,000
Total manufacturing costs	$415,980	$1,963,840
Units of production	÷ 20,000	÷ 200,000
Unit cost	$ 20.80*	$ 9.82*

*Rounded to the nearest cent.

Comparison of Different Product Costing Methods

In Exhibit 4-7, the unit costs from activity-based costing are compared with the unit costs produced by functional-based costing using either a plantwide or departmental rate. This comparison clearly illustrates the effects of using only unit-based activity drivers to assign overhead costs. The activity-based cost assignment duplicates the pattern of overhead consumption and is therefore the most accurate of the three costs shown in Exhibit 4-7. Functional-based costing undercosts the scented cards and overcosts the regular cards. In fact, the ABC assignment increases the cost of the scented cards by at least $8.80 per box and decreases the cost of the regular cards by at least $0.88. Thus, in the presence of significant nonunit overhead costs and product diversity, using only unit-based activity drivers can lead to one product subsidizing another (as the regular cards are subsidizing the scented cards). This subsidy could create the appearance that one group of products is highly profitable and can adversely impact the pricing and competitiveness of another group of products. In a highly competitive environment, the more accurate the cost information, the better the planning and decision making.

EXHIBIT 4-7   **Comparison of Unit Costs**

	Scented Cards	Regular Cards	Source
Activity-based cost	$20.80	$ 9.82	Exhibit 4-6
Functional-based cost:			
Plantwide rate.	12.00	10.70	Exhibit 4-3
Departmental rates	11.20	10.78	Exhibit 4-4

ABC Users

The Goodmark Company example also helps us understand when ABC may be useful for a firm. First, multiple products are needed. ABC offers no increase in product costing accuracy for a single-product setting. Second, there must be product diversity. If products consume non-unit-level activities in the same proportion as unit-level activities, then ABC assignments will be the same as functional-based assignments. Third, non-unit-level overhead must be a significant percentage of production cost. If it is not, then it hardly matters how it is assigned. Thus, firms that have plants with multiple products, high product diversity, and significant non-unit-level overhead are candidates for an ABC system.

One survey studied this concept.[1] Of those firms surveyed, 49 percent had adopted ABC. When compared with nonadopting firms, it was found that adopting firms reported a higher potential for distorted costs and a higher level of overhead when expressed as a percentage of total production costs. Adopting firms also reported a greater need or utility for accurate cost information for decision making.

OBJECTIVE 3

Provide a detailed description of activity-based product costing.

Activity-Based Costing System

The Goodmark Company example shows quite clearly that prime costs are assigned in the same way for functional- or activity-based costing. The example also demonstrates that the total amount of overhead costs is assigned under either approach. The amount assigned to each product, though, can differ significantly, depending on which method is used. The theoretical premise of activity-based costing is that it assigns costs according to the resource consumption pattern of products. If this is true, then activity-based costing should produce more accurate product costs if there is product diversity simply because unit-based drivers cannot capture the full consumption pattern of products. The Goodmark example suggests that we simply need to choose among a plantwide cost pool, departmental cost pools, or activity cost pools. While this is true, it is also true that we are talking about different levels of aggregation. In reality, if there is no product diversity and a plantwide cost pool is chosen, all we need is the cost of overhead resources taken from the general ledger accounts: depreciation, salaries, utilities, rent, etc. On the other hand, departmental cost pools require more detail and less aggregation because costs must be assigned to every producing department. Finally, activity-based costing requires the most detail and the least aggregation because each activity performed and its associated costs must be identified.

As Exhibit 4-8 illustrates, an **activity-based costing (ABC) system** first traces costs to activities and then to products and other cost objects. The underlying assumption is

---

1. Kip Krumwiede, "ABC: Why It's Tried and How It Succeeds," *Management Accounting* (April 1998): 32–38.

that activities consume resources, and products and other cost objects consume activities. In designing an ABC system, there are six essential steps, as listed in Exhibit 4-9.

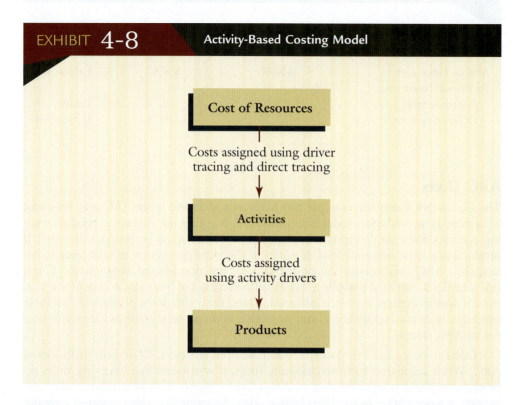

EXHIBIT **4-8**   Activity-Based Costing Model

Cost of Resources

Costs assigned using driver tracing and direct tracing

Activities

Costs assigned using activity drivers

Products

EXHIBIT **4-9**   Design Steps for an ABC System

1. Identify, define, and classify activities and key attributes.
2. Assign the cost of resources to activities.
3. Assign the cost of *secondary* activities to *primary* activities.
4. Identify cost objects and specify the amount of each activity consumed by specific cost objects.
5. Calculate primary activity rates.
6. Assign activity costs to cost objects.

Activity Identification, Definition, and Classification

Identifying activities is a logical first step in designing an activity-based costing system. Activities represent actions taken or work performed by equipment or people for other people. Identifying an activity is equivalent to describing action taken—usually by using an action verb and an object that receives the action. A simple list of the activities identified is called an **activity inventory**. A sample activity inventory for an electronics manufacturer is listed in Exhibit 4-10. Of course, the actual inventory of activities for most organizations would list many more than 12 activities (200 to 300 are not uncommon).

Activity Definition

Once an inventory of activities exists, then activity attributes are used to define activities. **Activity attributes** are nonfinancial and financial information items that describe

EXHIBIT **4-10**   **Sample Activity Inventory**

1. Developing test programs
2. Making probe cards
3. Testing products
4. Setting up lots
5. Collecting engineering data
6. Handling wafer lots
7. Inserting dies
8. Providing utilities
9. Providing space
10. Purchasing materials
11. Receiving materials
12. Paying for materials

individual activities. An **activity dictionary** lists the activities in an organization along with desired attributes. The attributes selected depend on the purpose being served. Examples of activity attributes with a product costing objective include tasks that describe the activity, types of resources consumed by the activity, amount (percentage) of time spent on an activity by workers, cost objects that consume the activity, and a measure of activity consumption (activity driver). Activities are the building blocks for both product costing and continuous improvement. An activity dictionary provides crucial information for activity-based costing as well as activity management. It is a key source of information for building an activity-based database that is discussed later in the chapter.

Activity Classification

Attributes define and describe activities and, at the same time, become the basis for activity classification. Activity classification facilitates the achievement of key managerial objectives such as product or customer costing, continuous improvement, total quality management, and environmental cost management. For example, for costing purposes, activities can be classified as primary or secondary. A **primary activity** is an activity that is consumed by a final cost object such as a product or customer. A **secondary activity** is one that is consumed by intermediate cost objects such as primary activities, materials, or other secondary activities. Recognizing the difference between the two types of activities facilitates product costing. Exhibit 4-8 indicates that activities consume resources. Thus, in the first stage of activity-based costing, the cost of resources is assigned to activities. Exhibit 4-8 also reveals that products consume activities—but only primary activities. Thus, before assigning the costs of primary activities to products, the costs of the secondary activities consumed by primary activities must be assigned to the primary activities. Many other useful activity classifications exist. For example, activities can be classified as *value-added* or *non-value-added* (defined and discussed in detail in Chapter 12), as *quality-related* (discussed in Chapter 14), or as *environmental* (discussed in Chapter 16). In designing an activity costing system, the desired attributes and essential classifications need to be characterized up front so that the necessary data can be collected for the activity dictionary.

Gathering the Necessary Data

Interviews, questionnaires, surveys, and observation are means of gathering data for an ABC system. Interviews with managers or other knowledgeable representatives of functional departments are perhaps the most common approach for gathering the needed information. Interview questions can be used to identify activities and activity attributes needed for costing or other managerial purposes. The information derived from interview questions serves as the basis for constructing an activity dictionary and provides data helpful for assigning resource costs to individual activities. In structuring an interview, the questions should reveal certain key attributes. Interview questions should be structured to provide answers that allow the desired attributes to be identified and measured. An example is perhaps the best way to show how an interview can be used to collect the data for an activity dictionary.

Illustrative Example

Suppose that a hospital is carrying out an ABC pilot study to determine the nursing cost for different types of cardiology patients. The cardiology unit is located on one floor of the hospital. The interview with the unit's nursing supervisor is provided below. Questions are given along with their intended purposes and the supervisor's responses. The interview is not intended to be viewed as an exhaustive analysis but rather represents a sample of what could occur.

Question 1 (Activity Identification): Can you describe what your nurses do for patients in the cardiology unit? (Activities are people doing things for other people.)

Response: There are four major activities: treating patients (administering medicine and changing dressings), monitoring patients (checking vital signs and posting patient information), providing hygienic and physical care for patients (bathing, changing bedding and clothes, walking the patient, etc.), and responding to patient requests (counseling, providing snacks, and answering calls).

Question 2 (Activity Identification): Do any patients use any equipment? (Activities also can be equipment doing work for other people.)

Response: Yes. In the cardiology unit, monitors are used extensively. Monitoring is an important activity for this type of patient.

Question 3 (Activity Identification): What role do you have in the cardiology unit? (Activities are people doing things for other people.)

Response: I have no direct contact with the patients. I am responsible for scheduling, evaluations, and resolving problems with the ward's nurses.

Question 4 (Resource Identification): What resources are used by your nursing care activities (equipment, materials, energy)? (Activities consume resources in addition to labor.)

Response: Uniforms (which are paid for by the hospital), computers, nursing supplies such as scissors and instruments (supplies traceable to a patient are charged to the patient), and monitoring equipment at the nursing station.

Question 5 (Resource Driver Identification): How much time do nurses spend on each activity? How much equipment time is spent on each activity? (Information is needed to assign the cost of labor and equipment to activities.)

Response: We recently completed a work survey. About 25 percent of a nurse's time is spent treating patients, 20 percent providing hygienic care, 40 percent responding to patient requests, and 15 percent on monitoring patients. My time is 100 percent supervision. The monitoring equipment is used 100 percent for monitoring activity. Use of the computer is divided between 40 percent for supervisory work and 60 percent for monitoring. (Posting readings to patient records is viewed as a monitoring task.)

Question 6 (Potential Activity Drivers): What are the outputs of each activity? That is, how would you measure the demands for each activity? (This question helps identify activity drivers.)

Response: Treating patients: number of treatments; providing hygienic care: hours of care; responding to patient requests: number of requests; and monitoring patients: monitoring hours.

Question 7 (Potential Cost Objects Identified): Who or what uses the activity output? (Identifies the cost object: products, other activities, customers, etc.)

Response: Well, for supervising, I schedule, evaluate performance, and try to ensure that the nurses carry out their activities efficiently. Nurses benefit from what I do. Patients receive the benefits of the nursing care activities. We have three types of cardiology patients: intensive care, intermediate care, and normal care. These patients make quite different demands on the nursing activities. For example, intensive care patients rarely have walking time but use a lot of treatments and need more monitoring time.

Activity Dictionary

Based on the answers to the interview, an activity dictionary can now be prepared. Exhibit 4-11 illustrates the dictionary for the cardiology unit. The activity dictionary names the activity (typically by using an action verb and an object that receives the action), describes the tasks that make up the activity, classifies the activity as primary or secondary, lists the users (cost objects), and identifies a measure of activity output (activity driver). For example, the supervising activity is consumed by the following primary activities: treating patients, providing hygienic care, responding to patient requests, and monitoring patients. The three products—intensive care patients, intermediate care patients, and normal care patients—in turn, consume the primary activities.

EXHIBIT 4-11 — Activity Dictionary: Cardiology Unit

Activity Name	Activity Description	Activity Type	Cost Object(s)	Activity Driver
Supervising nurses	Scheduling, coordinating, and performance evaluation	Secondary	Activities within department	Percentage of time nurses spend on each activity
Treating patients	Administering medicine and changing dressings	Primary	Patient types	Number of treatments
Providing hygienic care	Bathing, changing bedding and clothes, walking patients	Primary	Patient types	Labor hours
Responding to patient requests	Answering calls, counseling, providing snacks, etc.	Primary	Patient types	Number of requests
Monitoring patients	Checking vital signs and posting patient information	Primary	Patient types	Monitoring hours

Assigning Costs to Activities

After identifying and describing activities, the next task is determining how much it costs to perform each activity. The cost of an activity is simply the cost of the resources consumed by each activity. Activities consume resources such as labor, materials, energy, and capital. The cost of these resources is found in the general ledger, but how much is spent on each activity is not revealed. Resource costs must be assigned to activities using direct and driver tracing. For labor resources, a *work distribution matrix* is often used. A work distribution matrix simply identifies the amount of labor consumed by each activity and is derived from the interview process (or a written survey). For example, the nursing supervisor of the cardiology unit disclosed the following information about labor usage by the individual activities (see Question 5):

Percentage of Time on Each Activity

Activity	Supervisor	Nurses
Supervising nurses	100%	0%
Treating patients	0	25
Providing hygienic care	0	20
Responding to requests	0	40
Monitoring patients	0	15

The time spent on each activity is the driver used to assign the labor costs to the activity. If the time spent is 100 percent, then labor is exclusive to the activity, and direct tracing is the cost assignment method (such as the labor cost of supervision). On the other hand, the nursing resource is shared by several activities, and driver tracing is used for the cost assignment. These drivers are called resource drivers. **Resource drivers** are factors that measure the consumption of resources by activities. To illustrate, assume the general ledger reveals that the supervisor's salary is $50,000 and that the salaries of the nurses total $300,000. The amount of nursing cost assigned to each activity is as follows:

Supervising nurses	$50,000 (by direct tracing)
Treating patients	$75,000 (0.25 × $300,000)
Providing hygienic care	$60,000 (0.20 × $300,000)
Responding to requests	$120,000 (0.40 × $300,000)
Monitoring patients	$45,000 (0.15 × $300,000)

Interviews, survey forms, questionnaires, and timekeeping systems are examples of tools that can be used to collect data on resource drivers. Notice that tracking the effort spent on different activities is similar to tracking the time that laborers spend on different jobs. However, there is one critical difference. The percent of effort spent on various activities is usually fairly constant and may only need to be measured periodically (perhaps annually). The same constancy property also exists for other types of resource drivers. In effect, the labor time is a standard used to assign the cost of resources. Actual times need not be constantly measured and used to achieve the desired cost assignment.

Labor is only one of many resources consumed by activities. Activities also consume materials, capital, and energy. The interview, for example, reveals that cardiology care activities also include the use of monitors (capital), a computer (capital), uniforms (materials), and supplies (materials). The cost of these other resources is also assigned to activities using direct tracing and resource drivers. The cost of monitors, for example, is assigned using direct tracing. If the general ledger cost of the monitors were $80,000, then this additional amount would be assigned directly to the monitoring activity. On the other hand, the cost of the computer is a resource shared by supervisory work (40 percent) and monitoring (60 percent) and is assigned using hours of usage, a time-based resource driver. Thus, if the cost of the computer were $1,200 per year, then an additional $480 would be assigned to the supervising activity and $720 to the monitoring activity. Up to this point, the cost of the monitoring activity is $125,720 ($45,000 + $80,000 + $720), and the cost of the supervising activity is $50,480 ($50,000 + $480). Repeating this process for all resources, the total cost of each activity can be calculated (e.g., assigning in the cost of uniforms and supplies, the monitoring activity is assumed to end up with a cost of $127,920 and supervising with a cost of $52,280—see Exhibit 4-12).

The assignment of resource costs to activities requires that the resource costs described in the general ledger be unbundled and reassigned. In a traditional accounting system, the general ledger reports costs by department and by spending account (based on a chart of accounts). The $300,000 of nursing salaries, for example, would be recorded as part of the total salaries of the cardiology unit. The general ledger indicates what is spent, but it does not reveal how the resources are spent. Of course, the resources are spent on the basic work (activities) performed in the department. In an activity-based cost system, costs must be reported by activity. Thus, an ABC system must restate the general ledger costs so that the new system reveals how the resources are being consumed. Exhibit 4-12 illustrates the unbundling concept for nursing care activities in the cardiology unit. As the exhibit indicates, the reassignment of resource costs to individual activities contributes to the creation of an ABC database for the organization.

EXHIBIT 4-12	Unbundling of General Ledger Costs

General Ledger ➞ ABC Database

Cardiology Unit

Chart of Accounts View		ABC View	
Supervision	$ 50,000	Supervising nurses	$ 52,280
Supplies	40,600	Treating patients	90,000
Uniforms	8,200	Providing hygienic care	76,600
Salaries	300,000	Responding to requests	133,200
Computer	1,200	Monitoring patients	127,920
Monitor	80,000	Total	$480,000
Total	$480,000		

Assigning Secondary Activity Costs to Primary Activities

Assigning costs to activities completes the first stage of activity-based costing. In this first stage, activities are classified as primary and secondary. If there are secondary activities, then intermediate stages exist. In an intermediate stage, the cost of secondary activities is assigned to those activities (or other intermediate cost objects) that consume their output. For example, supervising nurses is a secondary activity. The output measure is the percentage of nursing time spent on each activity (see the sample activity dictionary in Exhibit 4-11). From the work distribution matrix prepared earlier, we know that the four primary activities use nursing resources in these proportions: 25

percent, 20 percent, 40 percent, and 15 percent. Assuming that supervising is consumed in proportion to the labor content of the four primary activities, the cost of supervising would be assigned using the four ratios just listed. The new costs using this secondary activity driver and the activity costs from Exhibit 4-12 are calculated and presented in Exhibit 4-13.

EXHIBIT **4-13**	Assignment of Secondary Activity Costs to Primary Activities

Treating patients	$103,070[a]
Providing hygienic care	87,056[b]
Responding to requests	154,112[c]
Monitoring patients	135,762[d]

[a]$90,000 + (0.25 \times $52,280)$.
[b]$76,600 + (0.20 \times $52,280)$.
[c]$133,200 + (0.40 \times $52,280)$.
[d]$127,920 + (0.15 \times $52,280)$.

Cost Objects and Bills of Activities

Once the costs of primary activities are determined, these costs can then be assigned to products or other cost objects in proportion to their usage of the activity, as measured by activity drivers. However, before any assignment is made, the cost objects must be identified and the demands these objects place on the activities must be measured. Many different cost objects are possible: products, materials, customers, distribution channels, suppliers, and geographical regions are some examples. For our example, the cost objects are products (services): intensive cardiology care, intermediate cardiology care, and normal cardiology care. How to deal with cost assignment for other cost objects is discussed in a later section. **Activity drivers** measure the demands that cost objects place on activities. Most ABC system designs choose between one of two types of activity drivers: transaction drivers and duration drivers. **Transaction drivers** measure the number of times an activity is performed, such as the number of treatments and the number of requests. **Duration drivers** measure the demands in terms of the time it takes to perform an activity, such as hours of hygienic care and monitoring hours. Duration drivers should be used when the time required to perform an activity varies from transaction to transaction. If, for example, treatments for normal care patients average 10 minutes but for intensive care patients average 45 minutes, then treatment hours may be a much better measure of the demands placed on the activity of treating patients than the number of treatments.

With the drivers defined, a bill of activities can be created. A **bill of activities** specifies the product, expected product quantity, activities, and amount of each activity expected to be consumed by each product. Exhibit 4-14 presents a bill of activities for the cardiology care example.

Activity Rates and Product Costing

Primary activity rates are computed by dividing the budgeted activity costs by practical activity capacity, where activity capacity is the amount of activity output (as measured by the activity driver). Practical capacity is the activity output that can be produced if the activity is performed efficiently. Using data from Exhibits 4-13 and 4-14, the activity rates for the cardiology unit nursing care example can now be calculated:

EXHIBIT 4-14	Bill of Activities: Cardiology Unit				
Activity	**Activity Driver**	**Normal**	**Intermediate**	**Intensive**	**Total**
Production (output)	Patient days....................	10,000	5,000	3,000	
Treating patients	Treatments	5,000	10,000	15,000	30,000
Providing hygienic care	Hygienic hours................	5,000	2,500	8,500	16,000
Responding to requests	Requests	30,000	40,000	10,000	80,000
Monitoring patients	Monitoring hours..............	20,000	60,000	120,000	200,000

Rate Calculations:

Treating patients: $103,070/30,000 = $3.44 per treatment
Providing hygienic care: $87,056/16,000 = $5.44 per hour of care
Responding to requests: $154,112/80,000 = $1.93 per request
Monitoring patients: $135,762/200,000 = $0.68 per monitoring hour

Note: Rates are rounded to the nearest cent.

These rates provide the price charged for activity usage. Using these rates, costs are assigned as shown in Exhibit 4-15. As should be evident, the assignment process is the

EXHIBIT 4-15	Assigning Costs: Final Cost Objects		
	Patient Type		
	Normal	**Intermediate**	**Intensive**
Treating patients:			
$3.44 × 5,000	$ 17,200		
$3.44 × 10,000		$ 34,400	
$3.44 × 15,000			$ 51,600
Providing hygienic care:			
$5.44 × 5,000	27,200		
$5.44 × 2,500		13,600	
$5.44 × 8,500			46,240
Responding to requests:			
$1.93 × 30,000	57,900		
$1.93 × 40,000		77,200	
$1.93 × 10,000			19,300
Monitoring patients:			
$0.68 × 20,000	13,600		
$0.68 × 60,000		40,800	
$0.68 × 120,000..............			81,600
Total costs.................	$115,900	$166,000	$198,740
Units.......................	÷ 10,000	÷ 5,000	÷ 3,000
Nursing cost per patient day........	$ 11.59	$ 33.20	$ 66.25

same as that for the Goodmark example illustrated earlier in Exhibit 4-6 (see p. 132). However, we now know the details behind the development of the activity rates and usage measures. Furthermore, the hospital setting emphasizes the utility of activity-based costing in service organizations.

Classifying Activities

To help identify activity drivers and enhance the management of activities, activities are often classified into one of the following four general activity categories: (1) unit-level, (2) batch-level, (3) product-level, and (4) facility-level. **Unit-level activities** are those that are performed each time a unit is produced. Grinding, polishing, and assembly are examples of unit-level activities. **Batch-level activities** are those that are performed each time a batch is produced. The costs of batch-level activities vary with the number of batches but are fixed (and, therefore, independent) with respect to the number of units in each batch. Setups, inspections (if done by sampling units from a batch), purchasing, and materials handling are examples of batch-level activities. **Product-level activities** are those activities performed that enable the various products of a company to be produced. These activities and their costs tend to increase as the number of different products increases. Engineering changes (to products), developing product-testing procedures, introducing new products, and expediting goods are examples of product-level activities. **Facility-level activities** are those that sustain a factory's general manufacturing processes. Providing facilities, maintaining grounds, and providing plant security are examples.

Classifying activities into these general categories facilitates product costing because the costs of activities associated with the different levels respond to different types of activity drivers. (Cost behavior differs by level.) Knowing the activity level is important because it helps management identify the activity drivers that measure the amount of each activity output being consumed by individual products. Activity-based costing systems improve product costing accuracy by recognizing that many of the so-called fixed overhead costs vary in proportion to changes other than production volume. Level classification also provides insights concerning the root causes of activities and thus can help managers in their efforts to improve activity performance.

By understanding what causes these costs to increase or decrease, they can be traced to individual products. This cause-and-effect relationship allows managers to improve product costing accuracy, which can significantly improve decision making. Additionally, this large pool of fixed overhead costs is no longer so mysterious. Knowing the underlying behavior of many of these costs allows managers to exert more control over the activities that cause the costs. It also allows managers to identify which of the activities add value and which do not. Value analysis is the heart of activity-based management and is the basis for continuous improvement. Activity-based management and continuous improvement are explored in later chapters.

Reducing the Size and Complexity of an ABC System

OBJECTIVE 4

Explain how the number of activity rates can be reduced.

In principle, ABC requires an activity rate for each activity. An organization may have hundreds of different activities and, thus, hundreds of activity rates. Although information technology certainly is capable of handling this volume, there is merit to reducing the number of rates if it can be done without suffering a significant decrease in the accuracy of the cost assignments. After all, increased accuracy of cost assignments is the source of the decision benefits and the justification for using ABC. Fewer rates may produce more readable and manageable product cost reports, reducing the perceived complexity of an activity-based costing system and increasing its likelihood of managerial acceptance. For example, if there are a large number of activities on a bill of activities, managers are likely to find it too complex to read, interpret, and use. In this case, the more complex ABC system will not likely be sustained. One of the oft-cited reasons for refusing to implement an ABC system or for abandoning it, once implemented, is the perceived complexity of the system. Fewer rates may also reduce the ongoing cost of operating an ABC system. Predetermined rates require that actual activity data be collected so that overhead can be applied. Fewer rates thus reduce the ongoing data collection activity required. In practical terms, a complex ABC system may not be sustainable simply because there is too much actual driver data to collect effectively.

Approximately Relevant ABC Systems

It is possible that an organization is better off having an approximately relevant ABC system rather than a precisely useless one.[2] One intriguing suggestion for obtaining an approximately relevant ABC system is to do an analysis of the activity accounting system and to use only the most expensive activities for ABC assignment.[3] The costs of all other activities can be added to the cost pools of the expensive activities. For example, the costs of the less expensive activities could be allocated in proportion to the costs in each of the expensive activities. In this way, most costs are assigned to the products accurately. The costs of the most expensive activities are still assigned using appropriate cause-and-effect drivers, while the added costs are assigned somewhat arbitrarily. The advantages of this approach are that it is simple, easy to understand, and easy to implement. It also often provides a good approximation of the ABC costs.

To illustrate the approximately relevant ABC concept, consider the data for Sencillo Electronics presented in Exhibit 4-16 on page 144. Sencillo produces two types of wafers: Wafer A and Wafer B. A wafer is a thin slice of silicon used as a base for integrated circuits or other electronic components. The dies on each wafer represent a particular configuration—a configuration designed for use by a particular end product. Sencillo produces wafers in batches, where each batch corresponds to a particular type of wafer (A or B). In the wafer inserting and sorting process, dies are inserted, and the wafers are tested to ensure that the dies are not defective. From Exhibit 4-16, we see that the activity-based costs for Wafer A and Wafer B are $800,000 and $1,200,000, respectively. These activity-based costs are calculated using the 12 drivers. We also see that four activities (developing test programs, testing products, inserting dies, and purchasing materials) account for 75 percent of the total costs. The cost assignments using the cost pools and the associated drivers of these four activities are shown in Exhibit 4-17 on page 145. The costs of the inexpensive activities are allocated to the four expensive activities in proportion to their original cost.

Exhibit 4-17 illustrates that the ABC costs are approximated quite well by the reduced system of four drivers. For Wafer A, the error is about 2.5 percent [($820,000 − $800,000)/$800,000], using the larger 12-driver system in Exhibit 4-16 as the benchmark. If activity costs roughly follow the Pareto principle or 80/20 rule (80 percent of the overhead costs are caused by 20 percent of the activities), then this approach for reducing the size of the system has some promise. For example, if a system has 100 activities, then the top 20 activities (as measured by their cost) need to account for a very high percentage of the total costs. In those cases where this holds, a reduced system may work reasonably well because *most* of the costs are assigned using cause-and-effect relationships. Even so, there may be some who would balk at the notion of using 15–20 drivers. The approach also loses its usefulness for those companies where a small number of activities do not account for a large share of the overhead costs.

---

2. Tom Pryor, "Simplify Your ABC," *Cost Management Newsletter* (June 2004), Issue No. 152.
3. Ibid.

EXHIBIT 4-16		Data for Sencillo Electronics			

Activity	Budgeted Activity Cost	Driver	Expected Consumption Ratios		
			Quantity[a]	Wafer A	Wafer B
Inserting and sorting process					
1. Developing test programs	$ 400,000	Engineering hours	10,000	0.25	0.75
2. Making probe cards	58,750	Development hours	4,000	0.10	0.90
3. Testing products	300,000	Test hours	20,000	0.60	0.40
4. Setting up batches	40,000	Number of batches	100	0.55	0.45
5. Engineering design	80,000	Number of change orders	50	0.15	0.85
6. Handling wafer lots	90,000	Number of moves	200	0.45	0.55
7. Inserting dies	350,000	Number of dies	2,000,000	0.70	0.30
Procurement process:					
8. Purchasing materials	450,000	Number of purchase orders	2,500	0.20	0.80
9. Unloading materials	60,000	Number of receiving orders	3,000	0.35	0.65
10. Inspecting materials	75,000	Inspection hours	5,000	0.65	0.35
11. Moving materials	30,000	Distance moved	3,000	0.50	0.50
12. Paying suppliers	66,250	Number of invoices	3,500	0.30	0.70
Total activity cost	$2,000,000				
Unit-level (plantwide) cost assignment[b]				$1,400,000	$600,000
Activity cost assignment[c]				$800,000	$1,200,000

[a]Total amount of the activity expected to be used by both products.
[b]Calculated using *number of dies* as the single unit-level driver: Wafer A = 0.7 × $2,000,000; Wafer B = 0.3 × $2,000,000.
[c]Calculated using *each* activity cost and either the associated consumption ratios or activity rates. For example, the cost assigned to Wafer A using the consumption ratio for *developing test programs* is 0.25 × $400,000 = $100,000. Repeating this for each activity and summing yields a total of $800,000 assigned to Wafer A.

Equally Accurate Reduced ABC Systems

Another approach is to use expected consumption ratios to reduce the number of drivers.[4] Consider again the 12 activities of Exhibit 4-16. The product costs assigned to Wafer A and Wafer B were $800,000 and $1,200,000, respectively. Thus, Wafer A is expected to consume 40 percent ($800,000/$2,000,000) of the total cost being assigned, and Wafer B is expected to consume 60 percent ($1,200,000/$2,000,000) of the total costs being assigned. Thus, Wafer A has an *expected global consumption ratio* of 0.40, and Wafer B has an *expected global consumption ratio* of 0.60. The **expected global consumption ratio** is the proportion of the total activity costs consumed by a given product (cost object). The expected global consumption ratio pattern for Sencillo Electronics is (0.40, 0.60). Each activity also has a consumption ratio pattern. For example, the consumption ratio pattern for the activity, *testing products*, is (0.60, 0.40). For a 2-product example, the activity consumption ratio patterns are always described by an array of two components. For the Sencillo Electronics example, the first ratio in the array is the proportion of the activity consumed by Wafer A, and the second ratio is the proportion consumed by Wafer B. As the number of products increases, the number of consumption ratio components also increases. The dimension of the consump-

---

4. Don R. Hansen and Shannon Leikam, "Reducing Complexity While Preserving Accuracy in Product Cost Systems," *Working Paper* (July 2004).

EXHIBIT 4-17   A Reduced System with Approximate ABC Assignments

Activity	Budgeted Activity Cost[a]	Driver	Expected Consumption Ratios		
			Quantity	Wafer A	Wafer B
1. Developing test programs	$ 533,333	Engineering hours	10,000	0.25	0.75
3. Testing products	400,000	Test hours	20,000	0.60	0.40
7. Inserting dies	466,667	Number of dies	2,000,000	0.70	0.30
8. Purchasing materials	600,000	Number of purchase orders	2,500	0.20	0.80
Total activity cost	$2,000,000				
Reduced system ABC assignment[b]				$820,000	$1,180,000

[a]Original activity cost plus share of the costs of the remaining "inexpensive" activities. The costs of the inexpensive activities are allocated in proportion to the original costs of the expensive activities (as shown in Exhibit 4-16). For example, the cost pool for purchasing materials is $450,000 + [($450,000/$1,500,000) \times $500,000] = $600,000.

[b]Costs are assigned to each product using the consumption ratios of the drivers of the respective cost pools. For example, the cost assigned to Wafer A for purchasing materials is 0.25 \times $600,000 = $150,000. Repeating this calculation for the other three activities and summing yields a total of $820,000 assigned to Wafer A.

tion ratio pattern array corresponds to the number of products. When the number of activities is more than the number of products, it is always possible to find a reduced system that *duplicates* the cost assignments of the larger system. To achieve this duplication, the number of drivers needed is *at most* equal to the number of products.

For example, with the 2-product, 12-activity example of Exhibit 4-16, a reduced system of two drivers can always be identified that will achieve the *same* cost assignment as the larger 12-driver system.[5] Thus, once a larger system has been identified, a smaller system with the same accuracy can be created. To illustrate, consider two activities from Exhibit 4-16, testing products and purchasing materials. The consumption ratio vectors for the two activities are (0.6, 0.4) and (0.2, 0.8), respectively. For each product, the global consumption ratio can be expressed as a weighted combination of the consumption ratios for the two activities:

$$0.60w_1 + 0.20w_2 = 0.40 \text{ (Wafer A)} \tag{1}$$
$$0.40w_1 + 0.80w_2 = 0.60 \text{ (Wafer B)} \tag{2}$$

This gives two equations in two unknowns, w_1 and w_2 (there would be three equations for a 3-product setting, four for a 4-product setting, etc.). The weights are associated with the consumption ratios for each activity and product. These weights are used as *allocation rates* to create a cost pool for each activity. Solving Equations 1 and 2 yields $w_1 = 1/2$ and $w_2 = 1/2$. Multiplying 1/2 by the total cost of $2,000,000 yields a cost pool of $1,000,000 for testing products and a similar calculation produces a cost pool of $1,000,000 for purchasing materials. Exhibit 4-18 summarizes this analysis. Notice that when the resulting weights are 1/2, this corresponds to the average of the two sets of consumption ratios: [(0.6, 0.4) + (0.2, 0.8)]/2 = (*1/2*) (0.6, 0.4) + (*1/2*) (0.2, 0.8) = (0.4, 0.6).

The steps that should be followed to achieve the desired simplification are: (1) Calculate the expected global consumption ratio (ABC product cost/total overhead cost); (2) Select the needed number of activities (equal to the number of products); (3) Form

---

5. Ibid.

EXHIBIT 4-18   Reduced, Equally Accurate ABC System

Activity	Budgeted Activity Cost[a]	Driver	Expected Consumption Ratios		
			Quantity	Wafer A	Wafer B
3. Testing products	$1,000,000	Test hours	20,000	0.60	0.40
8. Purchasing materials	1,000,000	Purchase orders	2,500	0.20	0.80
Total activity cost	$2,000,000				
Reduced system ABC assignment[b]				$800,000	$1,200,000

[a]1/2 × $2,000,000 for each product, where the allocation ratio to detemine the cost pool is obtained by solving Equations 1 and 2.
[b]Costs are assigned to each product using the consumption ratios of the drivers of the respective cost pools. For example, the cost assigned to Wafer A is (0.60 × $1,000,000) + (0.20 × $1,000,000) = $800,000. If activity rates are used, then the rates would be $1,000,000/20,000 = $50 per test hour and $1,000,000/2,500 = $400 per purchase order. Wafer A is expected to use 12,000 (0.60 × 20,000) test hours and 500 (0.20 × 2,500) purchase orders. Using the rates and the expected usage produces the same expected product cost of $800,000.

equations by multiplying the consumption ratios of each product by the allocation weights and set this equal to the product's consumption ratio; (4) Solve the simultaneous set of equations; and (5) Use the weights to form the cost pools that will duplicate the larger ABC system cost assignments.

Exhibit 4-18 shows that an equally accurate simplified system can be derived from the more complex ABC system. Instead of using 12 drivers, it is possible to use only two drivers and achieve the same cost assignment of the more complex system. This reduced system represents an *after-the-fact* simplification. The reduced system is derived from an *existing* complex ABC data set. Of course, the same is true for the approximately relevant reduced system that uses the Pareto principle to achieve the reduction. The value of after-the-fact simplification is based on two key justifications. First, the reduced system eliminates the perceived complexity of the system. For example, it is much easier for nonfinancial users to read, interpret, and use a 2-driver system compared to a 12-driver system. Second, the reduced ABC system needs to collect actual driver data only for the drivers being used to assign the costs to products. For example, in the case of Sencillo Electronics, only actual data for testing hours and number of purchase orders need to be collected so that overhead costs can be assigned (applied) to the two products. This is much less costly than collecting actual data for 12 drivers. Finally, it should also be pointed out that the two drivers in Exhibit 4-18 are only one of many 2-driver combinations that can be used to reduce the ABC system without sacrificing the assignment accuracy of the more complex system.

ABC System Concepts

OBJECTIVE 5

Describe activity-based system concepts including an ABC relational database and ABC software.

One thing that should be immediately evident is that ABC is a much more detailed system than the more traditional functional-based system. This is also true for simplified ABC systems because they are after-the-fact simplifications. Although some firms use before-the-fact simplifications, such as simply selecting 10–15 drivers, there is no guarantee that they are achieving more accurate cost assignments (than their prior functional-based system) because they do not know the detailed ABC, cause-and-effect relationships. The emergence of ABC as a viable alternative to existing cost management systems is largely due to significant advances in information technology. Computations that once required the use of cumbersome mainframe computers can now be carried out with efficient, flexible ABC software using network PCs or even laptop computers. Furthermore, integrated database systems, known as enterprise resource planning (ERP) systems, are being widely adopted with the potential promise of integrating the activity-based costing system with that of a firmwide operational control costing system. ABC software requires the development of an activity-based costing (ABC) database, and an ERP system may facilitate its development.

ABC Database

An **ABC database** is the collected data sets that are organized and interrelated for use by an organization's activity-based costing information system. A **data set** is a grouping of logically related data. Creating an ABC database requires three steps. First, we must define and model the entities (objects) that are involved in the operation of an activity-based costing system. **Entities** are objects about which data are produced and gathered. The two most fundamental entities are activities and products. Other entities such as customers and distribution channels can also be defined. Second, a conceptual view must be developed that portrays the entities and the logical relationships that exist among the entities. Most of the chapter has been devoted to developing a conceptual understanding of the logical relationships that exist among activities and products. Third, the attributes that should be associated with each entity must be identified. These attributes are determined by the objectives of the information system being supported and by the needs of the users. For example, the objective of building homogeneous cost pools requires the following activity attributes: process membership, activity-level membership, activity driver, and budgeted activity costs. To complete the first stage, pool rates must be calculated. An additional activity attribute is needed for this purpose: activity capacity (measured in terms of the activity driver associated with the activity's homogeneous pool). Recall that pool rates are computed by dividing the budgeted pool costs by activity capacity.

Once the attributes and the entities are defined and identified, then a model must be selected that reflects the data structure implied by the entities and attributes. There are numerous ways of representing data structure. We will illustrate only one: relational structure. A **relational structure** uses a table to represent the overall logical view within a database. The table is made up of rows and columns, where the entity defines the rows, and the attributes define the columns. The tables needed for a relational database are defined by the relationships that exist among the entities. Each table should satisfy the following three properties: (1) the rows are fixed in length (each row has the same number of attributes), (2) each row is unique, and (3) the attributes for each row are directly related to a single entity.

To illustrate a relational table, consider once again the Sencillo Electronics example. Exhibit 4-19, on the following page, presents Sencillo's activity relational table. Notice that each row of the table is the same length (has the same number of attributes). Also, each row is unique, since each row corresponds to a different activity. Each activity is identified by an activity number, which acts as the unique primary key. A **primary key** is the attribute that uniquely identifies each row of data in a table (often referred to as a record). The activity number is the number associated with each activity in the activity inventory. For this example, the activity name is unique and could also serve as the primary key. Finally, notice that all nonkey attributes are fully dependent upon the primary key.

Once a database has been created, then data can be retrieved as needed. For example, the relational table in Exhibit 4-19 provides all the information needed to calculate individual activity rates. For example, the rate for activity 1 (developing test programs) is $40 per engineering hour ($400,000/10,000). Similar computations can be made for each activity. With the computation of the activity rates, the first stage of activity-based costing is completed.

The second stage assigns the pooled activity costs to individual products. Assigning costs to products necessitates the specification of activity demands, as measured by the drivers associated with each pool. Thus, a second relational table is needed: a

EXHIBIT 4-19   Activity Relational Table Illustrated

Activity Relational Table: Sencillo Electronics

Activity	Activity Name	Process	Activity Driver	Capacity	Cost
1	Developing test programs	Sorting	Engineering hours	10,000	$400,000
2	Making probe cards	Sorting	Development hours	4,000	58,750
3	Testing products	Sorting	Test hours	20,000	300,000
4	Setting up batches	Sorting	No. of batches	100	40,000
5	Engineering design	Sorting	No. of change orders	50	80,000
6	Handling wafer lots	Sorting	No. of moves	200	90,000
7	Inserting dies	Sorting	No. of dies	2,000,000	350,000
8	Purchasing materials	Procurement	No. of purchase orders	2,500	450,000
9	Unloading materials	Procurement	No. of receiving orders	3,000	60,000
10	Inspecting materials	Procurement	Inspection hours	5,000	75,000
11	Moving materials	Procurement	Distance moved	3,000	30,000
12	Paying suppliers	Procurement	No. of invoices	3,500	66,250

product relational table. This table is centered on the "product" entity and must have attributes that identify how costs are to be assigned. A product number or name that uniquely identifies each product can be used as the primary key. The attributes for carrying out the second stage of activity-based costing are the product's demands for each pool's activity driver and the units produced of each. The product relational table for Sencillo Electronics is shown in Exhibit 4-20. The table is structured to facilitate the addition or deletion of drivers as circumstances change. The product relational table illustrates the use of concatenated keys. **Concatenated keys** are two or more keys that uniquely identify a record. (Notice that one key, such as product name, is not sufficient.)

For example, in the product relational table, a row is uniquely identified by product number and driver number (or by product name and driver name). The information in this second table is vital for the second stage of ABC: assigning costs to individual products. To illustrate, consider how the costs of activity 1 (developing test programs) are assigned to Wafer A. The rate is $40 per engineering hour. From the product relational table in Exhibit 4-20, Wafer A is expected to use 2,500 engineering hours. Thus, the amount of activity 1's costs assigned to Wafer A is $100,000 ($40 × 2,500). This type of calculation would be repeated for every activity until the total cost assigned to Wafer A is determined. The same process is applied to every product.

ABC and ERP Systems

Activity-based software typically uses a relational structure for data. ABC software is an integral part of any successful ABC model design. Poor model design and architecture can lead to project failure. Choosing the correct ABC software is absolutely essential. The chosen software should have features that correlate with the functional capabilities of a firm's ABC system design. For example, every ABC system design identifies activities, assigns the cost of resources to the activities, and then assigns the cost of activities to products, customers, and other important cost objects. Thus, ABC software should have at least three distinct modules: resources, activities, and cost objects. Modules are structures that allow data to be entered, manipulated, and viewed. How the data can be manipulated is critical and reveals the functional flexibility of different software packages.

EXHIBIT 4-20   Product Relational Table Illustrated

Product Relational Table: Sencillo Electronics

Product Number	Product Name	Activity Driver Number	Activity Driver Name	Activity Usage
1	Wafer A	1	Engineering hours	2,500
1	Wafer A	2	Development hours	400
1	Wafer A	3	Test hours	12,000
1	Wafer A	4	No. of batches	55
1	Wafer A	5	No. of change orders	8
1	Wafer A	6	No. of moves	90
1	Wafer A	7	No. of dies	1,400,000
1	Wafer A	8	No. of purchase orders	500
1	Wafer A	9	No. of receiving orders	1,050
1	Wafer A	10	Inspection hours	3,250
1	Wafer A	11	Distance moved	1,500
1	Wafer A	12	No. of invoices	1,050
2	Wafer B	1	Engineering hours	7,500
2	Wafer B	2	Development hours	3,600
2	Wafer B	3	Test hours	8,000
2	Wafer B	4	No. of batches	45
2	Wafer B	5	No. of change orders	33
2	Wafer B	6	No. of moves	110
2	Wafer B	7	No. of dies	600,000
2	Wafer B	8	No. of purchase orders	2,000
2	Wafer B	9	No. of receiving orders	1,950
2	Wafer B	10	Inspection hours	1,750
2	Wafer B	11	Distance moved	1,500
2	Wafer B	12	No. of invoices	2,450

To illustrate, consider an activity module. ABC software should allow costs to be assigned both within the activity module and between the activity module and the other modules. The ability to assign costs within the activity module allows a firm to distribute costs from secondary activities to primary activities. Transferring costs across modules allows costs to be assigned from primary activities (activity module) to products (cost object module). Thus, the cost assignment paths allowed by a software package are important features to consider. The more cost assignment paths allowed, the more flexible is the ABC system design allowed (by the particular software).

In addition to identifying functional requirements and matching these requirements with software capabilities, a manager should identify the information required by key users of an ABC system and then specify the output needed. The information needs define the output. For example, suppose that the environmental manager wants to know the environmental costs associated with the company's products and processes. In this case, the ABC system would need to identify all environmental activities and assign the costs of these activities to the products and processes. The output needed would then include environmental cost reports.

COST MANAGEMENT
Technology in Action

Activity-based costing is useful for all types of organizations and businesses. For example, the Small Business Administration (SBA) uses Oros®, activity-based costing software, to determine the costs of its activities and cost objects. The SBA adopted an ABC system because it provides a more accurate revelation of the costs of programs and services. This enables the SBA to engage in improvements that produce a more efficient delivery of its programs and services. ABC is used to prepare the SBA's annual statement of net costs. It is also used to prepare other unit cost reports. To maintain the accuracy of the assignment of resources costs to the various activities, the SBA conducts a survey (at least annually) of its employees to assess the amount of time spent on activities. Thus, the SBA's ABC work distribution matrix is frequently updated to ensure accurate activity cost determination.

Source: Taken from the Web site, http://www.sba.gov/cfo/abc, accessed July 16, 2004.

Implementation of ABC systems and the selection of ABC software are being affected by the desire to also utilize enterprise resource planning (ERP) systems. ERP software has the objective of using real-time data to improve the efficiency of organizational units and processes. Therefore, ERP applications are primarily concerned with a company's operational control information system. ERP applications require the use of actual costs measured with a high degree of precision and focus on supporting the objective of continuous improvement. To support continuous improvement, timely, accurate, and detailed information is needed. ABC systems, on the other hand, focus on customer and product profitability and seek to identify opportunities for process improvement. ABC assigns costs using predetermined activity rates; thus, the costs assigned do not necessarily correspond to actual costs. ABC also provides cost information about the entire value chain: suppliers, products, and customers. It is much broader in scope than the organizational-unit perspective of ERP applications. Because the two systems have different purposes, scopes, and cost definitions, it may not be possible to fully integrate them. It is important to recognize that there are different systems for different purposes.

However, even though ABC and ERP systems have different purposes, the two systems need to be integrated so that they can exchange vital information. As Exhibit 4-21 illustrates, ERP systems are a major source of data for the ABC model. ERP systems simplify and improve the data collection requirements of an ABC system. In principle, ERP systems integrate all the information systems of an organization into one enterprise-wide system. Thus, an ERP system can provide data from such diverse sources as human resources, inventory, financial accounting, production, and sales; consequently, much of the input data needed by the ABC model, such as resource drivers, activity drivers, and resource costs, can be provided efficiently and economically. In effect, the ABC software that supports the ABC system is analytic application software and functions independently of an organization's core transactions while simultaneously being dependent on the data found within an ERP system.[6] ERP systems, for example, can provide data for transactional activity drivers such as the number of purchase orders processed in the purchasing department or the number of purchase orders processed from the receiving department.

Exhibit 4-21 also illustrates that the relationship between the two systems is not one way. ABC sends results back to the operational control system. For example, ABC provides accurate costs for products, customers, activities, and processes. ABC can also signal where attention should be directed for continuous improvement efforts by calculating the potential savings from eliminating unnecessary activities or improving the

---

6. This point is emphasized by R. Shaw, "ABC and ERP: Partners at Last?" *Management Accounting* (November 1998): 56–58.

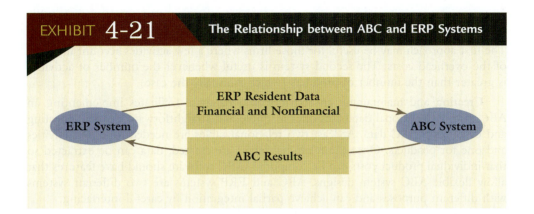

EXHIBIT 4-21   The Relationship between ABC and ERP Systems

efficiency of processes. Moreover, ABC supplies key information to support tactical and strategic decisions. For instance, ABC could provide the costs of purchasing activities as input to a make-or-buy decision being examined by the operational control system. This complimentary relationship coupled with the independent value of ABC and ERP applications suggests an attractive partnership. Indeed, this appears to be the case as many ERP companies such as **SAP**, **Oracle**, **JD Edwards**, and **PeopleSoft** have acquired or developed ABC modules for their ERP products.[7] The market for analytic applications is expected to grow, and ABC is supposedly the analytic application that is expected to receive the most attention for the next several years.[8] The bottom line is that ERP systems are increasing the likelihood that ABC systems will be implemented and used by forward-thinking organizations.

---

7. Ibid., 56–58.
8. Ibid., 57.

SUMMARY

Overhead costs have increased in significance over time and, in many firms, represent a much higher percentage of product costs than does direct labor. At the same time, many overhead activities are unrelated to the units produced. Functional-based costing systems are unable to properly assign the costs of these non-unit-related overhead activities. These overhead activities are consumed by products in different proportions than are unit-based overhead activities. Because of this, assigning overhead using only unit-based drivers can distort product costs. This can be a serious matter if the non-unit-based overhead costs are a significant proportion of total overhead costs.

Overhead assignments should reflect the amount of overhead demanded (consumed) by each product. Activity-based costing recognizes that not all overhead varies with the number of units produced. By using both unit- and non-unit-based activity drivers, overhead can be more accurately traced to individual products. This tracing is achieved by implementing the following steps: (1) identify, define, and classify activities and key attributes; (2) assign the cost of resources to activities; (3) assign the cost of secondary activities to primary activities; (4) identify cost objects and specify the amount of each activity consumed by specific cost objects; (5) calculate primary activity rates; and (6) assign activity costs to cost objects.

Simplified ABC systems can be derived from complex ABC systems. These simplified systems facilitate the presentation and use of ABC information. They also reduce the cost of collecting actual driver data. Two approaches were discussed: the approximately relevant reduced ABC system and the equally accurate reduced ABC system. The first approach may be useful for those firms where a few activities account for most of the overhead costs. The second system is useful whenever the number of activities is greater than the number of products (which is usually the case).

Creating and maintaining an activity-based database facilitates implementing an ABC system. Relational databases offer a simple and straightforward way of collecting and organizing ABC data. At least two relational tables are needed: one for activities and one for products. Once the relational tables are created, data can be extracted so that individual product costs can be computed. ABC software should have features that allow flexible ABC system designs. ABC and ERP systems are two different systems with different purposes and can achieve partial integration by careful interfacing.

REVIEW PROBLEM AND SOLUTION

FUNCTIONAL VERSUS ACTIVITY-BASED COSTING

Tyson Lamp Company is noted for its full line of quality lamps. The company operates one of its plants in Green Bay, Wisconsin. That plant produces two types of lamps: classical and modern. Jane Martinez, president of the company, recently decided to change from a unit-based, traditional costing system to an activity-based costing system. Before making the change companywide, she wanted to assess the effect on the product costs of the Green Bay plant. This plant was chosen because it produces only two types of lamps; most other plants produce at least a dozen.

To assess the effect of the change, the following data have been gathered (for simplicity, assume one process):

Lamp	Quantity	Prime Costs	Machine Hours	Material Moves	Setups
Classical	400,000	$800,000	81,250	300,000	100
Modern	100,000	$150,000	43,750	100,000	50
Dollar amount	—	$950,000	$500,000*	$900,000	$600,000

*The cost of operating the production equipment.

Under the current system, the costs of operating equipment, materials handling, and setups are assigned to the lamps on the basis of machine hours. Lamps are produced and moved in batches.

Required:

1. Compute the unit cost of each lamp using the current unit-based approach.
2. Compute the unit cost of each lamp using an activity-based costing approach.
3. Show how a reduced system using two cost pools and two drivers, moves and setups, can be used to achieve the same cost assignments obtained in Requirement 2.

1. Total overhead is $2,000,000. The plantwide rate is $16 per machine hour ($2,000,000/125,000). Overhead is assigned as follows:

Classical lamps: $16 × 100,000 = $1,600,000
Modern lamps: $16 × 25,000 = $400,000

The unit costs for the two products are as follows:

Classical lamps: ($800,000 + $1,600,000)/400,000 = $6.00
Modern lamps: ($150,000 + $400,000)/100,000 = $5.50

2. In the activity-based approach, a rate is calculated for each activity:

Machining: $500,000/125,000 = $4.00 per machine hour
Moving materials: $900,000/400,000 = $2.25 per move
Setting up: $600,000/150 = $4,000 per setup

Overhead is assigned as follows:

Classical lamps:

$4.00 × 81,250	$ 325,000
$2.25 × 300,000	675,000
$4,000 × 100	400,000
Total	$1,400,000

Modern lamps:

$4.00 × 43,750	$ 175,000
$2.25 × 100,000	225,000
$4,000 × 50	200,000
Total	$ 600,000

This produces the following unit costs:

Classical lamps:

Prime costs	$ 800,000
Overhead costs	1,400,000
Total costs	$2,200,000
Units produced	÷ 400,000
Unit cost	$ 5.50

Modern lamps:

Prime costs	$ 150,000
Overhead costs	600,000
Total costs	$ 750,000
Units produced	÷ 100,000
Unit cost	$ 7.50

3. First, calculate the activity consumption ratios:

	Moving	*Setups*
Classical	300,000/400,000 = 3/4	100/150 = 2/3
Modern	100,000/400,000 = 3/4	50/150 = 1/3

Second, calculate the global consumption ratios (information from Requirement 2 is needed):

	ABC Assignments	*Global Ratios*
Overhead assigned to classical	$1,400,000	$1,400,000/$2,000,000 = 0.70
Overhead assigned to modern	600,000	$600,000/$2,000,000 = 0.30
Total	$2,000,000	

Third, set up and solve the consumption ratio equations:

$$(3/4)w_1 + (2/3)w_2 = 0.70$$
$$(1/4)w_1 + (1/3)w_2 = 0.30$$

Solving, we have the allocation ratios: $w_1 = 0.40$ and $w_2 = 0.60$. Thus, the cost pools for the two activities are:

$$\text{Moving: } 0.40 \times \$2,000,000 = \$800,000$$
$$\text{Setups: } 0.60 \times \$2,000,000 = \$1,200,000$$

The activity rates for the reduced system would be:

$$\text{Moving: } \$800,000/400,000 = \$2.00 \text{ per move}$$
$$\text{Setups: } \quad \$1,200,000/150 = \$8,000 \text{ per setup}$$

Overhead cost assignments:

Classical lamps:

$2.00 × 300,000	$ 600,000
$8,000 × 100	800,000
Total	$1,400,000

Modern lamps:

$2.00 × 100,000	$ 200,000
$8,000 × 50	400,000
Total	$ 600,000

KEY TERMS

QUESTIONS FOR

QUESTIONS FOR WRITING AND DISCUSSION

1. What is a predetermined overhead rate? Explain why it is used.
2. Describe what is meant by under-and overapplied overhead.
3. Explain how a plantwide overhead rate, using a unit-based driver, can produce distorted product costs. In your answer, identify two major factors that impair the ability of plantwide rates to assign cost accurately.
4. What are non-unit-related overhead activities? Non-unit-based cost drivers? Give some examples.
5. What is an overhead consumption ratio?
6. Overhead costs are the source of product cost distortions. Do you agree or disagree? Explain.
7. What is activity-based product costing?
8. What are the six steps that define the design of an activity-based costing system?
9. Explain how the cost of resources is assigned to activities. What is meant by the phrase "unbundling the general ledger accounts"?
10. What is a bill of activities?
11. Identify and define two types of activity drivers.
12. What are unit-level activities? Batch-level activities? Product-level activities? Facility-level activities?
13. Describe two ways to reduce a complex ABC system. Of the two ways, which has the most merit?
14. How is an activity relational table constructed? A product relational table? In providing your answer, explain how attributes are selected.
15. Explain why ABC and ERP systems cannot be fully integrated. Now discuss how partial integration can be achieved.

EXERCISES

4-1 PREDETERMINED OVERHEAD RATE, APPLIED OVERHEAD, UNIT COST

LO1 Morrison, Inc., costs products using a normal costing system. The following data are available for last year:

Budgeted:	
Overhead	$952,000
Machine hours	140,000
Direct labor hours	34,000
Actual:	
Overhead	$950,000
Machine hours	137,000
Direct labor hours	33,100
Prime cost	$3,500,000
Number of units	500,000

Overhead is applied on the basis of direct labor hours.

Required:

1. What was the predetermined overhead rate?
2. What was the applied overhead for last year?
3. Was overhead over- or underapplied, and by how much?
4. What was the total cost per unit produced (carry your answer to four decimal places)?

4-2 PREDETERMINED OVERHEAD RATE, APPLICATION OF OVERHEAD

LO1   Bill Company and Ted Company both use predetermined overhead rates to apply manufacturing overhead to production. Bill's is based on machine hours, and Ted's is based on materials cost. Budgeted production and cost data for Bill and Ted are as follows:

	Bill	Ted
Manufacturing overhead	$304,000	$220,000
Units	10,000	20,000
Machine hours	16,000	7,500
Materials cost	$150,000	$400,000

At the end of the year, Bill Company had incurred overhead of $305,000 and had produced 9,800 units using 15,990 machine hours and materials costing $147,000. Ted Company had incurred overhead of $216,000 and had produced 20,500 units using 7,550 machine hours and materials costing $395,000.

Required:

1. Compute the predetermined overhead rates for Bill and Ted.
2. Was overhead over- or underapplied for each company, and by how much?

4-3 PREDETERMINED OVERHEAD RATE, OVERHEAD VARIANCES, JOURNAL ENTRIES

LO1   Menotti Company uses a predetermined overhead rate to assign overhead to jobs. Because Menotti's production is machine intensive, overhead is applied on the basis of machine hours. The expected overhead for the year was $3.8 million, and the practical level of activity is 250,000 machine hours.

During the year, Menotti used 255,000 machine hours and incurred actual overhead costs of $3.82 million. Menotti also had the following balances of applied overhead in its accounts:

Work-in-Process Inventory	$ 384,000
Finished Goods Inventory	416,000
Cost of Goods Sold	1,200,000

Required:

1. Compute a predetermined overhead rate for Menotti.
2. Compute the overhead variance, and label it as under- or overapplied.
3. Assuming the overhead variance is immaterial, prepare the journal entry to dispose of the variance at the end of the year.
4. Assuming the overhead variance is material, prepare the journal entry that appropriately disposes of the overhead variance at the end of the year.

4-4   DEPARTMENTAL OVERHEAD RATES

LO1   Mondragon Company produces machine tools and currently uses a plantwide overhead rate, based on machine hours. Alfred Cimino, the plant manager, has heard that departmental overhead rates can offer significantly better cost assignments than can a plantwide rate. Mondragon has the following data for its two departments for the coming year:

	Department A	*Department B*
Overhead costs (expected)	$60,000	$15,000
Normal activity (machine hours)	10,000	5,000

Required:

1. Compute a predetermined overhead rate for the plant as a whole based on machine hours.
2. Compute predetermined overhead rates for each department using machine hours.
3. Suppose that a machine tool (Product 12X75) used 20 machine hours from department A and 50 machine hours from department B. A second machine tool (Product 32Y15) used 50 machine hours from department A and 20 machine hours from department B. Compute the overhead cost assigned to each product using the plantwide rate computed in Requirement 1. Repeat the computation using the departmental rates found in Requirement 2. Which of the two approaches gives the fairest assignment? Why?
4. Repeat Requirement 3 assuming the expected overhead cost for department B is $30,000. Now would you recommend departmental rates over a plantwide rate?

4-5   DRIVERS AND PRODUCT COSTING ACCURACY

LO2, LO3   Larsen Company produces two types of leather purses: standard and handcrafted. Both purses use equipment for cutting and stitching. The equipment also has the capability of creating standard designs. The standard purses use only these standard designs. They are all of the same size to accommodate the design features of the equipment. The handcrafted purses can be cut to any size because the designs are created manually. Many of the manually produced designs are in response to specific requests of retailers. The equipment must be specially configured to accommodate the production of a batch of purses that will receive a handcrafted design. Larsen Company assigns overhead using direct labor dollars. Merle Jones, sales manager, is convinced that the purses are not being costed correctly.

To illustrate his point, he decided to focus on the expected annual setup and machine-related costs, which are as follows:

Setup equipment	$18,000
Depreciation	20,000*
Operating costs	22,000

*Computed on a straight-line basis, book value at the beginning of the year was $100,000.

The machine has the capability of supplying 100,000 machine hours over its remaining life.

Merle also collected the expected annual prime costs for each purse, the machine hours, and the expected production (which is the normal output for the company).

	Standard Purse	Handcrafted Purse
Direct labor	$12,000	$36,000
Direct materials	$12,000	$12,000
Units	3,000	3,000
Machine hours	18,000	2,000
Number of setups	40	40
Setup time	400 hrs.	200 hrs.

Required:

1. Do you think that the direct labor costs and direct materials costs are accurately traced to each type of purse? Explain.
2. The controller has suggested that overhead costs be assigned to each product using a plantwide rate based on direct labor dollars. Machine costs and setup costs are overhead costs. Assume that these are the only overhead costs. For each type of purse, calculate the overhead per unit that would be assigned using a direct labor dollars overhead rate. Do you think that these costs are traced accurately to each purse? Explain.
3. Now calculate the overhead cost per unit per purse using two overhead rates: one for the setup activity and one for the machining activity. In choosing a driver to assign the setup costs, did you use number of setups or setup hours? Why? As part of your explanation, define transaction and duration drivers. Do you think machine costs are traced accurately to each type of purse? Explain.

4-6 MULTIPLE VERSUS SINGLE OVERHEAD RATES, ACTIVITY DRIVERS

LO3, LO4   Plata Company has identified the following overhead activities, costs, and activity drivers for the coming year:

Activity	Expected Cost	Activity Driver	Activity Capacity
Setting up equipment	$120,000	Number of setups	300
Ordering costs	90,000	Number of orders	9,000
Machine costs	210,000	Machine hours	21,000
Receiving	100,000	Receiving hours	5,000

Plata produces two models of dishwashers with the following expected prime costs and activity demands:

	Model A	Model B
Direct materials	$150,000	$200,000
Direct labor	$120,000	$120,000
Units completed	8,000	4,000
Direct labor hours	3,000	1,000
Number of setups	200	100
Number of orders	3,000	6,000
Machine hours	12,000	9,000
Receiving hours	1,500	3,500

The company's normal activity is 4,000 direct labor hours.

Required:

1. Determine the unit cost for each model using direct labor hours to apply overhead.
2. Determine the unit cost for each model using the four activity drivers.
3. Which method produces the more accurate cost assignment? Why?

4-7 ACTIVITY-BASED COSTING; ACTIVITY IDENTIFICATION, ACTIVITY DICTIONARY

LO3 Golding Bank is in the process of implementing an activity-based costing system. A copy of an interview with the manager of Golding's credit card department follows:.

Question 1: How many employees are in your department?

Response: There are eight employees, including me.

Question 2: What do they do (please describe)?

Response: There are four major activities: supervising employees, processing credit card transactions, issuing customer statements, and answering customer questions.

Question 3: Do customers outside your department use any equipment?

Response: Yes. Automatic bank tellers service customers who require cash advances.

Question 4: What resources are used by each activity (equipment, materials, energy)?

Response: We each have our own computer, printer, and desk. Paper and other supplies are needed to operate the printers. Of course, we each have a telephone as well.

Question 5: What are the outputs of each activity?

Response: Well, for supervising, I manage employees' needs and try to ensure that they carry out their activities efficiently. Processing transactions produces a posting for each transaction in our computer system and serves as a source for preparing the monthly statements. The number of monthly customer statements has to be the product for the issuing activity, and I suppose that the number of customers served is the output for the answering activity. And I guess that the number of cash advances would measure the product of the automatic teller activity, although the teller really generates more transactions for other products such as checking and savings accounts. So, perhaps the number of teller transactions is the real output.

Question 6: Who or what uses the activity output?

Response: We have three products: classic, gold, and platinum credit cards. Transactions are processed for these three types of cards, and statements are sent to clients holding these cards. Similarly, answers to questions are all directed to clients who hold these cards. As far as supervising, I spend time ensuring the proper coordination and execution of all activities except for the automatic teller. I really have no role in managing that particular activity.

Question 7: How much time do workers spend on each activity? By equipment?

Response: I just completed a work survey and have the percentage of time calculated for each worker. All seven clerks work on each of the three departmental activities. About 40 percent of their time is spent processing transactions, with the rest of their time split evenly between issuing statements and answering questions. Phone time for all seven workers is used only for answering client questions. Computer time is 70 percent transaction processing, 20 percent statement preparation, and 10 percent question answering. Furthermore, my own time and that of my computer and telephone are 100 percent administrative. Credit card transactions represent about 20 percent of the total automatic teller transactions.

Required:

Prepare an activity dictionary using five columns: activity name, activity description, activity type (primary or secondary), cost object(s), and activity driver.

4-8 ASSIGNING RESOURCE COSTS TO ACTIVITIES, RESOURCE DRIVERS, PRIMARY AND SECONDARY ACTIVITIES

LO3   Refer to the interview in **Exercise 4-7** (especially to Questions 4 and 7). The general ledger reveals the following annual costs:

Supervisor's salary	$ 64,600
Clerical salaries	210,000
Computers, desks, and printers	32,000
Computer supplies	7,200
Telephone expenses	4,000
ATM	1,250,000

All nonlabor resources, other than the ATM, are spread evenly among the eight credit department employees (in terms of assignment and usage). Credit department employees have no contact with ATMs. Printers and desks are used in the same ratio as computers by the various activities.

Required:

1. Determine the cost of all primary and secondary activities.
2. Assign the cost of secondary activities to the primary activities.

4-9 ASSIGNING RESOURCE COSTS TO ACTIVITIES, RESOURCE DRIVERS, PRIMARY AND SECONDARY ACTIVITIES

LO3   Bob Randall, cost accounting manager for Hemple Products, was asked to determine the costs of the activities performed within the company's manufacturing engineering department. The department has the following activities: creating bills of materials (BOMs), studying manufacturing capabilities, improving manufacturing processes, training employees, and designing tools. The general ledger accounts reveal the following expenditures for manufacturing engineering:

Salaries	$500,000
Equipment	100,000
Supplies	30,000
Total	$630,000

The equipment is used for two activities: improving processes and designing tools. The equipment's time is divided by two activities: 40 percent for improving processes and 60 percent for designing tools. The salaries are for nine engineers, one who earns $100,000 and eight who earn $50,000 each. The $100,000 engineer spends 40 percent of her time training employees in new processes and 60 percent of her time on improving processes. One engineer spends 100 percent of her time on designing tools, and another engineer spends 100 percent of his time on improving processes. The remaining six engineers spend equal time on all activities. Supplies are consumed in the following proportions:

Creating BOMs	10%
Studying capabilities	5
Improving processes	35
Training employees	20
Designing tools	30

After determining the costs of the engineering activities, Bob was then asked to describe how these costs would be assigned to jobs produced within the factory. (The company manufactures machine parts on a job-order basis.) Bob responded by indicating that creating BOMs and designing tools were the only primary activities. The remaining were secondary activities. After some analysis, Bob concluded that studying manufacturing capabilities was an activity that enabled the other four activities to be realized. He also noted that all of the employees being trained are manufacturing workers—employees who work directly on the products. The major manufacturing activities are cutting, drilling, lathing, welding, and assembly. The costs of these activities are assigned to the various products using hours of usage (grinding hours, drilling hours, etc.). Furthermore, tools were designed to enable the production of specific jobs. Finally, the process improvement activity focused only on the five major manufacturing activities.

Required:

1. What is meant by unbundling general ledger costs? Why is it necessary?
2. What is the difference between a general ledger database system and an activity-based database system?
3. Using the resource drivers and direct tracing, calculate the costs of each manufacturing engineering activity. What are the resource drivers?
4. Describe in detail how the costs of the engineering activities would be assigned to jobs using activity-based costing. Include a description of the activity drivers that might be used. Where appropriate, identify both a possible transaction driver and a possible duration driver.

4-10   PROCESS IDENTIFICATION AND ACTIVITY CLASSIFICATION

LO3   Calzado Company produces leather shoes in batches. The shoes are produced in one plant located on 20 acres. The plant operates two shifts, five days per week. Each time a batch is produced, just-in-time suppliers deliver materials to the plant. When the materials arrive, a worker checks the quantity and type of materials with the bill of materials for the batch. The worker then makes an entry at a PC terminal near the point of delivery acknowledging receipt of the material. An accounts payable clerk reviews all deliveries at the end of each day and then prints and mails checks the same day materials are received. Prior to producing a batch, the equipment must be configured to reflect style and size features. Once configured, the batch is produced passing through three operations: cutting, sewing, and attaching buckles and other related parts such as heels. At the end of the production process, a sample of shoes is inspected to ensure the right level of quality.

After inspection, the batch is divided into lots based on the customer orders for the shoes. The lots are packaged in boxes and then transferred to a staging area to await shipment. After a short wait (usually within two hours), the lots are loaded onto trucks and delivered to customers (retailers).

Within the same plant, the company also has a team of design engineers who respond to customer feedback on style and comfort issues. This department modifies existing designs, develops new shoe designs, builds prototypes, and test markets the prototypes before releasing the designs for full-scale production.

Required:

1. Identify Calzado's processes and their associated activities.
2. Classify each activity within each process as unit-level, batch-level, product-level, or facility-level.

4-11 APPROXIMATELY RELEVANT ABC

LO4   Golder Company has identified the following overhead activities, costs, and activity drivers for the coming year:

Activity	Expected Cost	Activity Driver	Activity Capacity
Setting up equipment	$252,000	Number of setups	300
Ordering materials	36,000	Number of orders	1,800
Machining	252,000	Machine hours	21,000
Receiving	60,000	Receiving hours	2,500

Golder produces two models of cell phones with the following expected activity demands:

	Model A	Model B
Units completed	10,000	20,000
Number of setups	200	100
Number of orders	600	1,200
Machine hours	12,000	9,000
Receiving hours	750	1,750

Required:

1. Determine the total overhead assigned to each product using the four activity drivers.
2. Determine the total overhead assigned to each model using the two most expensive activities. The costs of the two relatively inexpensive activities are allocated to the two expensive activities in proportion to their costs.
3. Using ABC as the benchmark, calculate the percentage error and comment on the accuracy of the reduced system. Explain why this approach may be desirable.

4-12 EQUALLY ACCURATE REDUCED ABC SYSTEM

LO4   Refer to **Exercise 4-11**.

Required:

1. Calculate the global consumption ratios for the two products.
2. Using the activity consumption ratios for number of orders and number of setups, show that the same cost assignment can be achieved using these two drivers as that of the complete, 4-driver ABC system.

4-13 ACTIVITY RELATIONAL TABLE

LO5   Riobamba Manufacturing produces specially machined parts. The parts are produced in batches in one continuous manufacturing process. Each part is custom produced and requires special engineering design activity (based on customer specifications). Once the design is completed, the equipment can be set up for batch production. Once the batch is completed, a sample is taken and inspected to see if the parts are within the tolerances allowed. Thus, the manufacturing process has four activities: engineering, setups, machining, and inspecting. In addition, there is a sustaining process with two activities: providing utilities (plantwide) and providing space. Costs have been assigned to each activity using direct tracing and resource drivers as follows:

Engineering	$100,000
Setups	90,000
Machining	200,000
Inspecting	80,000
Providing space	25,000
Providing utilities	18,000

Activity drivers for each activity have been identified and their expected usage listed as follows:

Machine Hours	Number of Setups	Engineering Hours	Inspection Hours
20,000	150	4,000	2,000

The costs of facility-level activities are assigned using machine hours.

Required:

1. Identify the activities within each process as unit-level, batch-level, product-level, or facility-level.
2. Create an activity relational table that can be used to calculate activity rates.
3. Using the information in the activity relational table, calculate activity rates.

4-14   PRODUCT RELATIONAL TABLE, ABC

LO5

Maxwell Company recently installed an activity-based relational database. Using the information contained in the activity relational table, the following activity rates have been computed:

$200 per purchase order
$12 per machine hour, Process R
$15 per machine hour, Process D
$40 per engineering hour
$2 per packing order
$100 per square foot

Two products are produced by Maxwell: a deluxe disk player and a regular disk player. Each product has an area in the plant that is dedicated to its production. The plant has two manufacturing processes: the regular process (Process R) and the deluxe process (Process D). Other processes include engineering, product handling, and procurement. The product relational table for Maxwell is shown at the top of the following page.

Required:

1. Identify two different concatenated keys. What is the purpose of concatenated keys?
2. Using the activity rates and the information from the product relational table, calculate the unit overhead cost for each product.

Product Name	Activity Driver Number	Activity Driver Name	Activity Usage
Regular	1	Units	800,000
Regular	2	Purchase orders	1,000
Regular	3	Machine hours	320,000
Regular	4	Engineering hours	5,000
Regular	5	Packing orders	400,000
Regular	6	Square footage	6,000
Deluxe	1	Units	100,000
Deluxe	2	Purchase orders	500
Deluxe	3	Machine hours	40,000
Deluxe	4	Engineering hours	6,000
Deluxe	5	Packing orders	100,000
Deluxe	6	Square footage	4,000

PROBLEMS

4-15 PREDETERMINED OVERHEAD RATES, OVERHEAD VARIANCES, UNIT COSTS

LO1 Maricopa Company produces two products and uses a predetermined overhead rate to apply overhead. Maricopa currently applies overhead using a plantwide rate based on direct labor hours. Consideration is being given to the use of departmental overhead rates where overhead would be applied on the basis of direct labor hours in department 1 and on the basis of machine hours in department 2. At the beginning of the year, the following estimates are provided:

	Department 1	Department 2
Direct labor hours	200,000	40,000
Machine hours	20,000	60,000
Overhead cost	$120,000	$360,000

Actual results reported by department and product during the year are as follows:

	Department 1	Department 2
Direct labor hours	196,000	42,000
Machine hours	22,000	64,000
Overhead cost	$125,000	$385,000

	Product 1	Product 2
Direct labor hours:		
Department 1	150,000	46,000
Department 2	30,000	12,000
Machine hours:		
Department 1	13,000	10,000
Department 2	13,000	50,000

Required:

1. Compute the plantwide predetermined overhead rate, and calculate the overhead assigned to each product.
2. Calculate the predetermined departmental overhead rates, and calculate the overhead assigned to each product.
3. Using departmental rates, compute the applied overhead for the year. What is the under- or overapplied overhead for the firm?
4. Prepare the journal entry that disposes of the overhead variance calculated in Requirement 3, assuming it is not material in amount. What additional information would you need if the variance is material to make the appropriate journal entry?

4-16   FUNCTIONAL-BASED VERSUS ACTIVITY-BASED COSTING

LO2

Bienstar Company produces treadmills. One of its plants produces two versions: a standard model and a deluxe model. The deluxe model has a wider and sturdier base and a variety of electronic gadgets to help the exerciser monitor heartbeat, calories burned, distance traveled, etc. At the beginning of the year, the following data were prepared for this plant:

	Standard Model	*Deluxe Model*
Expected quantity	20,000	10,000
Selling price	$280	$575
Prime costs	$3 million	$3.5 million
Machine hours	25,000	25,000
Direct labor hours	50,000	50,000
Engineering support (hours)	9,000	21,000
Receiving (orders processed)	2,000	3,000
Materials handling (number of moves)	10,000	30,000
Purchasing (number of requisitions)	500	1,000
Maintenance (hours used)	4,000	16,000
Paying suppliers (invoices processed)	2,500	2,500
Setting up batches (number of setups)	40	360

Additionally, the following overhead activity costs are reported:

Maintenance	$ 400,000
Engineering support	600,000
Materials handling	800,000
Setups	500,000
Purchasing	300,000
Receiving	200,000
Paying suppliers	200,000
	$3,000,000

Required:

1. Calculate the cost per unit for each product using direct labor hours to assign all overhead costs.
2. Calculate activity rates and determine the overhead cost per unit. Compare these costs with those calculated using the functional-based method. Which cost is the most accurate? Explain.

4-17   ABC, RESOURCE DRIVERS, SERVICE INDUSTRY

LO2, LO3   Cushing Medical Clinic operates a cardiology care unit and a maternity care unit. Ned Carson, the clinic's administrator, is investigating the charges assigned to cardiology patients. Currently, all cardiology patients are charged the same rate per patient day for daily care services. Daily care services are broadly defined as occupancy, feeding, and nursing care. A recent study, however, revealed several interesting outcomes. First, the demands patients place on daily care services vary with the severity of the case being treated. Second, the occupancy activity is a combination of two activities: lodging and use of monitoring equipment. Since some patients require more monitoring than others, these activities should be separated. Third, the daily rate should reflect the difference in demands resulting from differences in patient type. Separating the occupancy activity into two separate activities also required the determination of the cost of each activity. Determining the costs of the monitoring activity was fairly easy because its costs were directly traceable. Lodging costs, however, are shared by two activities: lodging cardiology patients and lodging maternity care patients. The total lodging costs for the two activities were $3,800,000 per year and consisted of such items as building depreciation, building maintenance, and building utilities. The cardiology floor and the maternity floor each occupy 20,000 square feet. Carson determined that lodging costs would be assigned to each unit based on square feet.

To compute a daily rate that reflected the difference in demands, patients were placed in three categories according to illness severity, and the following annual data were collected:

Activity	Cost of Activity	Activity Driver	Quantity
Lodging	$1,900,000	Patient days	15,000
Monitoring	1,400,000	Monitoring hours used	20,000
Feeding	300,000	Patient days	15,000
Nursing care	3,000,000	Nursing hours	150,000
Total	$6,600,000		

The demands associated with patient severity are also provided:

Severity	Patient Days	Monitoring Hours	Nursing Hours
High	5,000	10,000	90,000
Medium	7,500	8,000	50,000
Low	2,500	2,000	10,000

Required:

1. Suppose that the costs of daily care are assigned using only patient days as the activity driver (which is also the measure of output). Compute the daily rate using this functional-based approach of cost assignment.
2. Compute activity rates using the given activity drivers (combine activities with the same driver).
3. Compute the charge per patient day for each patient type using the activity rates from Requirement 2 and the demands on each activity.
4. Suppose that the product is defined as "stay and treatment" where the treatment is bypass surgery. What additional information would you need to cost out this newly defined product?
5. Comment on the value of activity-based costing in service industries.

4-18 ACTIVITY-BASED COSTING, SERVICE FIRM

LO2, LO3   Glencoe First National Bank operated for years under the assumption that profitability can be increased by increasing dollar volumes. Historically, First National's efforts were directed toward increasing total dollars of sales and total dollars of account balances. In recent years, however, First National's profits have been eroding. Increased competition, particularly from savings and loan institutions, was the cause of the difficulties. As key managers discussed the bank's problems, it became apparent that they had no idea what their products were costing. Upon reflection, they realized that they had often made decisions to offer a new product, which promised to increase dollar balances without any consideration of what it cost to provide the service.

After some discussion, the bank decided to hire a consultant to compute the costs of three products: checking accounts, personal loans, and the gold VISA. The consultant identified the following activities, costs, and activity drivers (annual data):

Activity	Activity Cost	Activity Driver	Activity Capacity
Providing ATM service	$ 100,000	No. of transactions	200,000
Computer processing	1,000,000	No. of transactions	2,500,000
Issuing statements	88,000	No. of statements	55,000
Customer inquiries	360,000	Telephone minutes	600,000

The following annual information on the three products was also made available:

	Checking Accounts	Personal Loans	Gold VISA
Units of product	30,000	5,000	10,000
ATM transactions	180,000	0	20,000
Computer transactions	2,000,000	200,000	300,000
Number of statements	350,000	50,000	150,000
Telephone minutes	350,000	90,000	160,000

In light of the new cost information, Larry Roberts, the bank president, wanted to know whether a decision made two years ago to modify the bank's checking account product was sound. At that time, the service charge was eliminated on accounts with an average annual balance greater than $1,000. Based on increases in the total dollars in checking, Larry was pleased with the new product. The checking account product is described as follows: (1) Checking account balances greater than $500 earn interest of 2 percent per year, and (2) A service charge of $5 per month is charged for balances less than $1,000. The bank earns 4 percent on checking account deposits. Fifty percent of the accounts are less than $500 and have an average balance of $400 per account. Ten percent of the accounts are between $500 and $1,000 and average $750 per account. Twenty-five percent of the accounts are between $1,000 and $2,767; the average balance is $2,000. The remaining accounts carry a balance greater than $2,767. The average balance for these accounts is $5,000. Research indicates that the $2,000 category was by far the greatest contributor to the increase in dollar volume when the checking account product was modified two years ago.

Required:

1. Calculate rates for each activity.
2. Using the rates computed in Requirement 1, calculate the cost of each product.
3. Evaluate the checking account product. Are all accounts profitable? Compute the average annual profitability per account for the four categories of accounts

described in the problem. What recommendations would you make to increase the profitability of the checking account product?

4-19   PRODUCT COSTING ACCURACY, CORPORATE STRATEGY, ABC

LO2, LO3

Autotech Manufacturing is engaged in the production of replacement parts for automobiles. One plant specializes in the production of two parts: Part 127 and Part 234. Part 127 produced the highest volume of activity, and for many years it was the only part produced by the plant. Five years ago, Part 234 was added. Part 234 was more difficult to manufacture and required special tooling and setups. Profits increased for the first three years after the addition of the new product. In the last two years, however, the plant faced intense competition, and its sales of Part 127 dropped. In fact, the plant showed a small loss in the most recent reporting period. Much of the competition was from foreign sources, and the plant manager was convinced that the foreign producers were guilty of selling the part below the cost of producing it. The following conversation between Patty Goodson, plant manager, and Joseph Fielding, divisional marketing manager, reflects the concerns of the division about the future of the plant and its products.

JOSEPH: You know, Patty, the divisional manager is really concerned about the plant's trend. He indicated that in this budgetary environment, we can't afford to carry plants that don't show a profit. We shut one down just last month because it couldn't handle the competition.

PATTY: Joe, you and I both know that Part 127 has a reputation for quality and value. It has been a mainstay for years. I don't understand what's happening.

JOSEPH: I just received a call from one of our major customers concerning Part 127. He said that a sales representative from another firm offered the part at $20 per unit—$11 less than what we charge. It's hard to compete with a price like that. Perhaps the plant is simply obsolete.

PATTY: No. I don't buy that. From my sources, I know we have good technology. We are efficient. And it's costing a little more than $21 to produce that part. I don't see how these companies can afford to sell it so cheaply. I'm not convinced that we should meet the price. Perhaps a better strategy is to emphasize producing and selling more of Part 234. Our margin is high on this product, and we have virtually no competition for it.

JOSEPH: You may be right. I think we can increase the price significantly and not lose business. I called a few customers to see how they would react to a 25 percent increase in price, and they all said that they would still purchase the same quantity as before.

PATTY: It sounds promising. However, before we make a major commitment to Part 234, I think we had better explore other possible explanations. I want to know how our production costs compare to those of our competitors. Perhaps we could be more efficient and find a way to earn our normal return on Part 127. The market is so much bigger for this part. I'm not sure we can survive with only Part 234. Besides, my production people hate that part. It's very difficult to produce.

After her meeting with Joseph, Patty requested an investigation of the production costs and comparative efficiency. She received approval to hire a consulting group to make an independent investigation. After a 3-month assessment, the consulting group provided the following information on the plant's production activities and costs associated with the two products:

	Part 127	Part 234
Production	500,000	100,000
Selling price	$31.86	$24.00
Overhead per unit*	$12.83	$5.77
Prime cost per unit	$8.53	$6.26
Number of production runs	100	200
Receiving orders	400	1,000
Machine hours	125,000	60,000
Direct labor hours	250,000	22,500
Engineering hours	5,000	5,000
Material moves	500	400

*Calculated using a plantwide rate based on direct labor hours. This is the
current way of assigning the plant's overhead to its products.

The consulting group recommended switching the overhead assignment to an
activity-based approach. It maintained that activity-based cost assignment is more accurate and will provide better information for decision making. To facilitate this recommendation, it grouped the plant's activities into homogeneous sets with the following
costs:

Setup costs	$ 240,000
Machine costs	1,750,000
Receiving costs	2,100,000
Engineering costs	2,000,000
Materials handling costs	900,000
Total	$6,990,000

Required:

1. Verify the overhead cost per unit reported by the consulting group using direct
   labor hours to assign overhead. Compute the per-unit gross margin for each
   product.
2. After learning of activity-based costing, Patty asked the controller to compute
   the product cost using this approach. Recompute the unit cost of each product using activity-based costing. Compute the per-unit gross margin for each
   product.
3. Should the company switch its emphasis from the high-volume product to the
   low-volume product? Comment on the validity of the plant manager's concern
   that competitors are selling below the cost of making Part 127.
4. Explain the apparent lack of competition for Part 234. Comment also on the
   willingness of customers to accept a 25 percent increase in price for Part 234.
5. Assume that you are the manager of the plant. Describe what actions you would
   take based on the information provided by the activity-based unit costs.

4-20   ACTIVITY-BASED COSTING, REDUCING THE NUMBER OF DRIVERS AND EQUAL ACCURACY

LO2, LO4   Reducir, Inc., produces two different types of hydraulic cylinders. Reducir produces a
major subassembly for the cylinders in the cutting and welding department. Other
parts and the subassembly are then assembled in the assembly department. The activities, expected costs, and drivers associated with these two manufacturing processes are
as follows:

Process	Activity	Cost	Activity Driver	Expected Quantity
Cutting and welding	Welding	$ 776,000	Welding hours	4,000
	Machining	450,000	Machine hours	10,000
	Inspecting	448,250	No. of inspections	1,000
	Materials handling	300,000	No. of batches	12,000
	Setups	240,000	No. of setups	100
		$2,214,250		
Assembly	Changeover	$ 180,000	Changeover hours	1,000
	Rework	61,750	Rework orders	50
	Testing	300,000	No. of tests	750
	Materials handling	380,000	No. of parts	50,000
	Engineering support	130,000	Engineering hours	2,000
		$1,051,750		

Note: In the assembly process, the materials handling activity is a function of product characteristics rather than batch activity.

Other overhead activities, their costs, and drivers are as follows:

Activity	Cost	Activity Driver	Quantity
Purchasing	$135,000	Purchase requisitions	500
Receiving	274,000	Receiving orders	2,000
Paying suppliers	225,000	No. of invoices	1,000
Providing space and utilities	100,000	Machine hours	10,000
	$734,000		

Other production information concerning the two hydraulic cylinders is also provided as follows:

	Cylinder A	Cylinder B
Units produced	1,500	3,000
Welding hours	1,600	2,400
Machine hours	3,000	7,000
Inspections	500	500
Moves	7,200	4,800
Batches	45	55
Changeover hours	540	460
Rework orders	5	45
Tests	500	250
Parts	40,000	10,000
Engineering hours	1,500	500
Requisitions	425	75
Receiving orders	1,800	200
Invoices	650	350

Required:

1. Using a plantwide rate based on machine hours, calculate the total overhead cost assigned to each product and the unit overhead cost.
2. Using activity rates, calculate the total overhead cost assigned to each product and the unit overhead cost. Comment on the accuracy of the plantwide rate.

3. Calculate the global consumption ratios.
4. Calculate the consumption ratios for welding and materials handling (assembly) and show that two drivers, welding hours and number of parts, can be used to achieve the same ABC product costs calculated in Requirement 2. Explain the value of this simplification.
5. Calculate the consumption ratios for inspection and engineering and show that the drivers for these two activities also duplicate the ABC product costs calculated in Requirement 2.

4-21   APPROXIMATELY RELEVANT ABC

LO4   Refer to the data given in **Problem 4-20** and suppose that the expected activity costs are reported as follows (all other data remain the same):

Process	Activity	Cost
Cutting and welding	Welding	$2,000,000
	Machining	1,000,000
	Inspecting	50,000
	Materials handling	72,000
	Setups	400,000
		$3,522,000
Assembly	Changeover	$ 28,000
	Rework	50,000
	Testing	40,000
	Materials handling	60,000
	Engineering support	70,000
		$ 248,000

Other overhead activities:

Activity	Cost
Purchasing	$ 50,000
Receiving	70,000
Paying suppliers	80,000
Providing space and utilities	30,000
	$230,000

The per-unit overhead costs using the 14 activity-based drivers are $1,108 and $779 for Cylinder A and Cylinder B, respectively.

Required:

1. Determine the percentage of total costs represented by the three most expensive activities.
2. Allocate the costs of all other activities to the three activities identified in Requirement 1. Allocate the other activity costs to the three activities in proportion to their individual activity costs. Now assign these total costs to the products using the drivers of the three chosen activities.
3. Using the costs assigned in Requirement 1, calculate the percentage error using the ABC costs as a benchmark. Comment on the value and advantages of this ABC simplification.

4-22   ABC AND RELATIONAL TABLES

LO5   BKM Foundry manufactures different kinds of equipment used by the aerospace, commercial aircraft, and electronic industries. Twenty different products are created using two major manufacturing processes: molding and assembly. The procurement and sustaining processes are also used in the plant. The activity and product relational tables follow (for simplicity, only two products of the 20 produced are shown in the product relational table):

Activity Relational Table: BKM Foundry

Activity Number	Activity Name	Process	Level	Activity Driver	Activity Capacity	Cost
1	Designing molds	Molding	Product	No. of products	20	$600,000
2	Making molds	Molding	Product	No. of products	20	320,000
3	Inspecting molds	Molding	Batch	No. of setups	400	120,000
4	Setting up batches	Molding	Batch	No. of setups	400	120,000
5	Engineering design	Assembly	Product	Change orders	40	130,000
6	Materials handling	Assembly	Batch	No. of subassemblies	400	90,000
7	Machining	Assembly	Unit	Machine hours	200,000	225,000
8	Purchasing materials	Procurement	Batch	Purchase orders	1,000	200,000
9	Receiving materials	Procurement	Batch	Purchase orders	1,000	320,000
10	Paying suppliers	Procurement	Product	No. of molds	20,000	180,000
11	Providing utilities	Sustaining	Facility	Machine hours	20,000	20,000
12	Providing space	Sustaining	Facility	Machine hours	20,000	50,000

Product Relational Table: BKM Foundry

Product Number	Product Name	Activity Driver Number	Activity Driver Name	Activity Usage
1	Component A	1	Units	1,000
1	Component A	2	No. of molds	2,000
1	Component A	3	No. of setups	10
1	Component A	4	Change orders	4
1	Component A	5	No. of products	1
1	Component A	6	Purchase orders	50
1	Component A	7	No. of subassemblies	2
1	Component A	8	Machine hours	800
2	Component B	1	Units	2,000
2	Component B	2	No. of molds	6,000
2	Component B	3	No. of setups	20
2	Component B	4	Change orders	3
2	Component B	5	No. of products	1
2	Component B	6	Purchase orders	60
2	Component B	7	No. of subassemblies	3
2	Component B	8	Machine hours	1,000

Required:

1. Describe how activity and product relational tables are created.
2. Using the preceding tables, provide examples of the following:
   a. Primary key
   b. Concatenated key

    c. Record
    d. Activity attribute
    e. Product attribute
    f. Entity
3. Using the information from the relational tables, calculate activity rates for the molding process. Combine activities with the same driver into one cost pool.
4. Using the activity rates computed in Requirement 3, assign molding process costs to Component A. What is the molding overhead cost per unit?

4-23 PRODUCT COSTING ACCURACY, PLANTWIDE AND DEPARTMENTAL RATES, ABC

LO1, LO2, LO3

Springs Company produces two type of calculators: scientific and business. Both products pass through two producing departments. The business calculator is by far the most popular. The following data have been gathered for these two products:

Product-Related Data

	Scientific	Business
Units produced per year	30,000	300,000
Prime costs	$100,000	$1,000,000
Direct labor hours	40,000	400,000
Machine hours	20,000	200,000
Production runs	40	60
Inspection hours	800	1,200
Maintenance hours	900	3,600

Department Data

	Department 1	Department 2
Direct labor hours:		
Scientific calculator	30,000	10,000
Business calculator	45,000	355,000
Total	75,000	365,000
Machine hours:		
Scientific calculator	10,000	10,000
Business calculator	160,000	40,000
Total	170,000	50,000
Overhead costs:		
Setup costs	$ 90,000	$ 90,000
Inspection costs	70,000	70,000
Power	100,000	60,000
Maintenance	80,000	100,000
Total	$340,000	$320,000

Required:

1. Compute the overhead cost per unit for each product using a plantwide, unit-based rate.

2. Compute the overhead cost per unit for each product using departmental rates. In calculating departmental rates, use machine hours for department 1 and direct labor hours for department 2. Repeat using direct labor hours for department 1 and machine hours for department 2.
3. Compute the overhead cost per unit for each product using activity-based costing.
4. Comment on the ability of departmental rates to improve the accuracy of product costing.

4-24   COLLABORATIVE LEARNING EXERCISE

LO2, LO3   Primo Paper, Inc., has three paper mills, one of which is located in Seattle, Washington. The Seattle mill produces 200 different types of coated and uncoated specialty printing papers. This large variety of products was the result of a full-line marketing strategy adopted by Primo's management. Management was convinced that the value of variety more than offset the extra costs of the increased complexity.

During 2007, the Seattle mill produced 240,000 tons of coated paper and 160,000 tons of uncoated stock. Of the 400,000 tons produced, 360,000 were sold. Thirty different products account for 80 percent of the tons sold. Thus, 170 products are classified as low-volume products.

Lightweight lime hopsack in cartons (LLHC) is one of the low-volume products. LLHC is produced in rolls, converted into sheets of paper, and then sold in cartons. In 2007, the cost to produce and sell one ton of LLHC was as follows:

Direct materials:		
Pulps	2,225 pounds	$ 540
Additives (11 different items)	200 pounds	600
Tub size	75 pounds	12
Recycled scrap paper	296 pounds	(24)
Total direct materials		$1,128
Direct labor		$ 540
Overhead:		
Paper machine (1.25 tons @ $120 per ton)		$ 150
Finishing machine (1.25 tons @ $144 per ton)		180
Total overhead		$ 330
Shipping and warehousing		$ 36
Total manufacturing and selling cost		$2,034

Overhead is applied using a 2-stage process. First, overhead is allocated to the paper and finishing machines using the direct method of allocation with carefully selected activity drivers. Second, the overhead assigned to each machine is divided by the budgeted tons of output. These rates are then multiplied by the number of tons required to produce one good ton.

In 2007, LLHC sold for $2,500 per ton, making it one of the most profitable products. A similar examination of some of the other low-volume products revealed that they also had very respectable profit margins. Unfortunately, the performance of the high-volume products was less impressive, with many showing losses or very low profit margins. This situation led Emily Hansen to call a meeting with her marketing vice president, Natalie Nabors, and her controller, Carson Chesser. Their conversation follows.

EMILY: The above-average profitability of our low-volume specialty products and the poor profit performance of our high-volume products make me believe that we should switch our marketing emphasis to the low-volume line. Perhaps we should drop some of our high-volume products, particularly those showing a loss.

NATALIE: I'm not convinced that the solution you are proposing is the right one. I know our high-volume products are of high quality, and I am convinced that we are as efficient in our production as other firms. I think that somehow our costs are not being assigned correctly. For example, the shipping and warehousing costs are assigned by dividing these costs by the total tons of paper sold. Yet . . .

CARSON: Natalie, I hate to disagree, but the $36 per ton charge for shipping and warehousing seems reasonable. I know that our method to assign these costs is identical to a number of other paper companies.

NATALIE: Well, that may be true, but do these other companies have the variety of products that we have? Our low-volume products require special handling and processing, but when we assign shipping and warehousing costs, we average these special costs across our entire product line. Every ton produced in our mill passes through our mill shipping department and is either sent directly to the customer or to our distribution center and then eventually to customers. My records indicate quite clearly that virtually all the high-volume products are sent directly to customers, whereas most of the low-volume products are sent to the distribution center. Now all the products passing through the mill shipping department should receive a share of the $4,000,000 annual shipping costs. Yet, as currently practiced, all products receive a share of the receiving and shipping costs of the distribution center.

EMILY: Carson, is this true? Does our system allocate our shipping and warehousing costs in this way?

CARSON: Yes, I'm afraid it does. Natalie may have a point. Perhaps we need to reevaluate our method to assign these costs to the product lines.

EMILY: Natalie, do you have any suggestions concerning how the shipping and warehousing costs ought to be assigned?

NATALIE: It seems reasonable to make a distinction between products that spend time in the distribution center and those that do not. We should also distinguish between the receiving and shipping activities at the distribution center. All incoming shipments are packed on pallets and weigh one ton each. (There are 14 cartons of paper per pallet.) In 2007, receiving processed 112,000 tons of paper. Receiving employs 50 people at an annual cost of $2,400,000. Other receiving costs total about $2,000,000. I would recommend that these costs be assigned using tons processed. Shipping, however, is different. There are two activities associated with shipping: picking the order from inventory and loading the paper. We employ 60 people for picking and 35 for loading at an annual cost of $4,800,000. Other shipping costs total $4,400,000. Picking and loading are more concerned with the number of shipping items rather than tonnage. That is, a shipping item may consist of two or three cartons instead of pallets. Accordingly, the shipping costs of the distribution center should be assigned using the number of items shipped. In 2007, for example, we handled 380,000 shipping items.

EMILY: These suggestions have merit. Carson, I would like to see what effect Natalie's suggestions have on the per-unit assignment of shipping and warehousing for LLHC. If the effect is significant, then we will expand the analysis to include all products.

CARSON: I'm willing to compute the effect, but I'd like to suggest one additional feature. Currently, we have a policy to carry about three tons of LLHC in inventory. Our current costing system totally ignores the cost of carrying this inventory. Since it costs us $1,998 to produce each ton of this product, we are tying up a lot of money in inventory—money that could be invested in other productive opportunities. In fact, the return lost is about 14 percent per year. This cost should also be assigned to the units sold.

EMILY: Carson, this also sounds good to me. Go ahead and include the carrying cost in your computation.

To help in the analysis, Carson gathered the following data for LLHC for 2007:

Tons sold	10
Average cartons per shipment	2
Average shipments per ton	7

Required:

Work through the requirements below before coming to class. Next, form groups of three to four students, and compare and contrast the answers within the group. Finally, form modified groups by exchanging one member of your group with a member of another group. The modified groups will compare and contrast each group's answers to the requirements.

1. Identify the flaws associated with the current method to assign shipping and warehousing costs to Primo's products.
2. Compute the shipping and warehousing costs per ton of LLHC sold using the new method suggested.
3. Using the new costs computed in Requirement 2, compute the profit per ton of LLHC. Compare this with the profit per ton computed using the old method. Do you think that this same effect would be realized for other low-volume products? Explain.
4. Comment on Emily's proposal to drop some high-volume products and place more emphasis on low-volume products. Discuss the role of the accounting system in supporting this type of decision making.
5. After receiving the analysis of LLHC, Emily decided to expand the analysis to all products. She also asked Carson to reevaluate the way in which mill overhead was assigned to products. After the restructuring was completed, Emily took the following actions: (a) the prices of most low-volume products were increased, (b) the prices of several high-volume products were decreased, and (c) some low-volume products were dropped. Explain why Emily's strategy changed so dramatically.

4-25   CYBER RESEARCH CASE

LO5   ABC software is a critical component of an ABC system implementation. ABC software produces the results that will be used by decision makers. Thus, the capabilities of ABC software are extremely important. The choice of ABC software can have a dramatic effect on the success or failure of an organization's ABC initiative. Non-ERP companies may choose stand-alone ABC software packages. Depending on the size of the application, PC software may be adequate.

The emergence of ERP systems (and, of course, ERP software) is also having an effect on ABC software selection. ERP companies will not usually choose stand-alone ABC software. Essentially, ERP systems demand some form of integration. Two choices are available for achieving this integration:

a. An ERP system that has an add-on module.
b. ABC software that has linking and importing capabilities to establish a bridge between the two systems.

Required:

1. Using an Internet search, identify three stand-alone software packages that have the following features:
   a. Windows 98 or higher platform or Windows NT platform
   b. ABC budgeting

     c.   Excel interface

     d.   Data export

     e.   Profit analysis

     f.   Resource, activity, and cost object modules and possibly more

     After identifying software with the above features, which would you select? Why? Are there other important features that you read about that you would like to include as part of the selection criteria?

2. ERP and ABC vendors have joined forces in creating an ABC-ERP partnership. Examples include the following:

     a.   SAP's acquistion of ABC Technologies

     b.   Armstrong-Laing and JD Edwards

     Search the Internet for two online articles that discuss ABC and ERP software issues. Write a brief summary of each article.

FUNDAMENTAL COSTING AND CONTROL

PART 2

http://hansen.swlearning.com

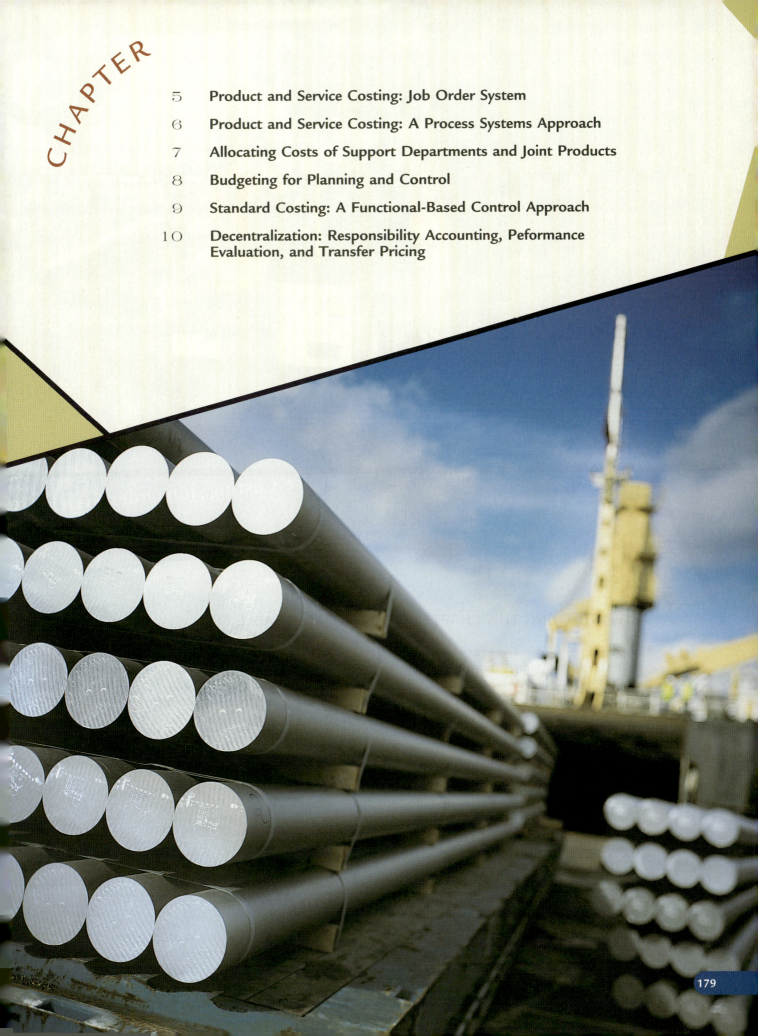

CHAPTER

5

Product and Service Costing: Job-Order System

AFTER STUDYING THIS CHAPTER, YOU SHOULD BE ABLE TO:

1. Differentiate the cost accounting systems of service and manufacturing firms and of unique and standardized products.

2. Discuss the interrelationship of cost accumulation, cost measurement, and cost assignment.

3. Explain the difference between job-order and process costing, and identify the source documents used in job-order costing.

4. Describe the cost flows associated with job-order costing, and prepare the journal entries.

5. Explain why multiple overhead rates may be preferred to a single, plantwide rate.

6. Explain how spoilage is treated in a job order costing stystem.

Now that we have an understanding of basic cost terminology and the ways of applying overhead to production, we need to look more closely at the system that the firm sets up to account for costs. In other words, we need to determine how we accumulate costs and associate them with different cost objects.

Characteristics of the Production Process

In general, a firm's cost management system mirrors the production process. A cost management system modeled after the production process allows managers to better monitor the economic performance of the firm. A production process may yield a tangible product or a service. Those products or services may be similar in nature or unique. These characteristics of the production process determine the best approach for developing a cost management system.

Manufacturing Firms versus Service Firms

Manufacturing involves joining together direct materials, direct labor, and overhead to produce a new product. The good produced is tangible and can be inventoried and transported from the plant to the customer. A service is characterized by its intangible nature. It is not separable from the customer and cannot be inventoried. Traditional cost accounting has emphasized manufacturing and virtually ignored services. Now, more than ever, that approach will not do. Our economy has become increasingly service oriented. Managers must be able to track the costs of services rendered just as precisely as they must track the costs of goods manufactured. In fact, a company's controller may find it necessary to cost both goods and services as managers take an internal customer approach.

The range of manufacturing and service firms can be represented by a continuum as shown in Exhibit 5-1. The pure service is shown at the left. The pure service involves no raw materials and no tangible item for the customer. There are few pure services. Perhaps an example would be an Internet cafe. In the middle of the continuum and still very much a service is a beauty salon, which uses direct materials on customers when performing the service, e.g., hair spray and styling gel. At the other end of the continuum is the manufactured product. Examples include automobiles, cereals, cosmetics, and drugs. Even these, however, often have a service component. For example, a prescription drug must be prescribed by a physician and dispensed by a licensed pharmacist. Automobile dealers stress the continuing service associated with their cars. And how would we categorize food services? Does **Taco Bell** provide a product or a service? There are elements of both.

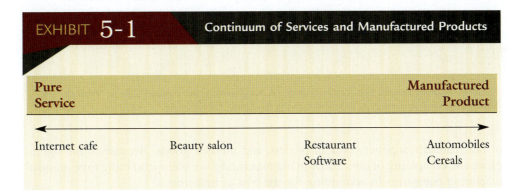

EXHIBIT 5-1   **Continuum of Services and Manufactured Products**

Pure Service			Manufactured Product
Internet cafe	Beauty salon	Restaurant Software	Automobiles Cereals

Four areas in which services differ from products are intangibility, inseparability, heterogeneity, and perishability. **Intangibility** refers to the nonphysical nature of services as opposed to products. **Inseparability** means that production and consumption are inseparable for services. **Heterogeneity** refers to the greater chances for variation in the performance of services than in the production of products. **Perishability** means that services cannot be inventoried but must be consumed when performed. These differences affect the types of information needed for planning, control, and decision making in the production of services. Exhibit 5-2 illustrates the features associated with the production of services and their interface with the cost management system.

Intangibility of services leads to a major difference in the accounting for services as opposed to products. A service company cannot inventory the service and therefore has a minimal to moderate inventory of supplies. A manufacturing company has inventories

EXHIBIT 5-2	Features of Service Firms and Their Interface with the Cost Management System

Feature*	Relationship to Business*	Impact on Cost Management System
Intangibility	Services cannot be stored.	There are no inventory accounts.
	Services cannot be protected through patents.	There is a strong ethical code.
	Services cannot readily be displayed or communicated.	
	Prices are difficult to set.	Costs must be related to entire organization.
Inseparability	Consumer is involved in production.	Costs are accounted for by customer type.
	Other consumers are involved in production.	
	Centralized mass production of services is difficult.	System must be generated to encourage consistent quality.
Heterogeneity	Standardization and quality control are difficult.	A strong systems approach is needed.
		Productivity measurement is ongoing.
		TQM is critical.
Perishability	Service benefits expire quickly.	There are no inventories.
	Service may be repeated often for one customer.	There needs to be a standardized system to handle repeat customers.

*First two columns adapted from Valarie Zeithaml, A. Parasuraman, and Leonard L. Berry, "Problems and Strategies in Services Marketing," *Journal of Marketing* 49 (Spring 1985): 34–46.

of raw materials, supplies, work in process, and finished goods. Because of the significance and complexity of inventories in manufacturing, we will spend more time on manufacturing companies in accounting for the cost of inventories.

Service companies typically rank lower than manufacturing companies in ratings of customer satisfaction.[1] An important reason for this is that service firms have a greater degree of heterogeneity of labor. Service firms are keenly aware of the importance of human resources; the service is provided by people. A key assumption of microeconomics is the homogeneity of labor. That is, one direct laborer is assumed to be identical to another. This assumption is the basis of labor standards in standard costing. Service companies know that one worker is not identical to another. For example, **Walt Disney World** hires "backstage employees" and "on-stage employees." The backstage employees may do maintenance, sew costumes, and work in personnel (called "central casting"), but they do not work with the paying public (called guests). On-stage employees, hired both for their particular skills and their ability to interact well with peo-

---

1. Jaclyn Fierman, "Americans Can't Get No Satisfaction," *Fortune* (December 11, 1995): 186–194.

ple, work directly with the guests. A further aspect of labor heterogeneity is that a worker is not the same from one day to the next. Workers can be affected by the job undertaken, the mix of other individuals with whom they work, their education and experience, and personal factors such as health and home life. These factors make the provision of a consistent level of service difficult. The measurement of productivity and quality in a service company must be ongoing and sensitive to these factors.

Inseparability means that differences in customers affect the service firm more than the manufacturing firm. When **Proctor-Silex** sells a toaster, the mood and personal qualities of the customer are irrelevant. When **Memorial Sloan-Kettering Hospital** sells a service to a customer, however, the disposition of the customer may affect the amount of service required as well as the quality of the service rendered. Inseparability also means that customers evaluate services differently from products. As a result, service companies may need to spend more money on some resources and less on others than would be necessary in a manufacturing plant. For example, consumers may use price and physical facilities as the major cues to service quality. Service firms, then, tend to incur higher costs for attractive places of business than do manufacturing firms. Your initial impression of a manufacturing plant may be how large, noisy, and dingy it is. Floors are concrete; the ceiling is typically unfinished. In short, it is not a pretty sight. However, as long as a high-quality product is made, the consumer does not care. This is very different from most consumers' attitudes toward the service environment. Banks, doctors' offices, and restaurants are pleasant places, tastefully decorated, and filled with plants. This is cost effective to the extent that customers are drawn to such an environment to conduct business. In addition, the environment may allow the service firm to charge a higher price—signaling its higher quality.

Perishability of services is very similar to intangibility. For example, there are no work-in-process or finished goods inventories of services. However, there is a subtle distinction between intangibility and perishability that merits discussion. A service is perishable if the effects are short term. Not all services fall into this category. Plastic surgery is not perishable, but haircuts are. The impact on cost management is that perishable services require systems to easily handle repeat customers. The repetitive nature of the service also leads us to the use of standardized processes and costing. Examples are financial services (e.g., check clearing by banks), janitorial services, and beauty and barber shops.

Customers may perceive greater risk when buying services than when buying products. Ethics are important here. The internal accountant who is responsible for gathering data on service quality must accurately report the bad news as well as the good. A customer who has been stung once by misleading advertising or a firm's failure to deliver the promised performance will be loathe to try that firm again. A manufacturer can offer a warranty or product replacement. But the service firm must consider the customer's wasted time. Therefore, the service firm must be especially careful to avoid promising more than can or will be delivered. Consider the example of **Lexus,** which discovered a defect shortly after introducing the car into the United States. Lexus dealers contacted each buyer personally and arranged for loaner cars while the defect was being fixed. In the case of buyers who lived far from a dealership, Lexus brought the repair people to the buyers. Contrast this experience with service experiences undergone by many **GM** buyers who must go through several layers of automotive hierarchy in order to get a defect repaired. Clearly, Lexus understood the value of customers' time in arranging the service.

Service companies are particularly interested in planning and control techniques that apply to their special types of firms. Productivity measurement and quality control are very important. Pricing may involve different considerations for the service firm.

The important point is that service and manufacturing companies may have different needs for accounting data and techniques. It is important for the accountant to be aware of relevant differences in order to provide appropriate support. It is critical that the accountant be cross-functionally trained. Take **McDonald's** as an example. Is this a manufacturing or service entity? In the kitchen, McDonald's runs a production line. The product is rigidly consistent. Each hamburger contains the same amount of meat, mustard, ketchup, and pickles. The buns are identical. The burgers are cooked the prescribed amount of time to the right temperature. They are wrapped in a methodical manner and join other burgers in the warming bin. Standard cost accounting techniques work well for this phase, and McDonald's uses them. At the counter, however, the company becomes a service organization. Customers want their orders taken and filled quickly and correctly. In addition, they want pleasant service and maybe some help finding certain items on the menu. Clean restrooms are critical. McDonald's emphasizes nonfinancial measures of performance for service areas: counter customers are to be served within 60 seconds; drive-through customers are to be served within 90 seconds; restrooms are to be checked and cleaned at least once an hour.

Unique versus Standardized Products and Services

A second way of characterizing products and services is according to the degree of uniqueness. If a firm produces unique products in small batches, and if those products incur different costs, then the firm must keep track of the costs of each product or batch. This is referred to as a job-order costing system, the focus of this chapter. At the other extreme, the company may make many identical units of the same product. Since the units are the same, the costs of each unit are also the same. Accounting for the costs of the identical units is relatively easy and is referred to as a process-costing system, examined in Chapter 6.

It is important to note that the uniqueness of the products (or units) for cost accounting purposes relates to unique costs. Consider a large construction company that builds houses in developments across the Midwest. While the houses are based on several standard models, buyers can customize their houses by selecting different types of brick, tile, carpet, and so on. However, these selections are taken from a set menu of choices. Therefore, while one house is painted white and its neighbor house is painted green, the cost is the same. However, if different selections have different costs, then those costs must be accounted for separately. Thus, if one home buyer selects a whirlpool tub while another selects a standard model, the different cost of the two tubs must be tracked to the correct house. As one builder said, "All we can do is offer choices and keep close track of our costs."[2] Therefore, a production process that appears to produce similar products may incur different costs for each product. In this type of situation, the firm should track costs using a job-order costing system.

Both service and manufacturing firms use the job-order costing approach. Custom-cabinet makers and home builders manufacture unique products, which must be accounted for using a job-order costing approach. Dental and medical services also use job-order costing. The costs associated with a simple dental filling clearly differ from those associated with a root canal. Printing, automotive repair, and appliance repair are also services using job-order costing.

Firms in process industries mass-produce large quantities of similar, or homogeneous, products. Each product is essentially indistinguishable from its companion product. Examples of process manufacturers include food, cement, petroleum, and chemical firms. The important point here is that the cost of one product is identical to the cost of another. Therefore, service firms can also use a process-costing ap-

---

2. June Fletcher, "New Developments: Same Frames, One-of-a-Kind Frills," *The Wall Street Journal* (September 8, 1995): B1, B8.

proach. Discount stockbrokers, for example, incur much the same cost to execute a customer order for one stock as for another; check-clearing departments of banks incur a uniform cost to clear a check, no matter the value of the check or to whom it is written.

Interestingly, companies are gravitating toward job-order costing because of the increased variety of products. Improved technology is making customization possible. For example, Israel's **Indigo, Ltd.**, a new Omnium One-Shot Color printing system, makes it possible to print cans, bottles, labels, etc., in smaller lots than ever before. The Omnium machine could be used to print soft drink cans customized for weekend tailgate parties ("Ride 'em, Cowboys!"), or to print coordinated kitchen curtains and tiles.[3] Thus, a combination of customer demand for specialized products, flexible manufacturing, and improved information technology has led world-class manufacturers to approximate a job-order environment.

Setting Up the Cost Accounting System

OBJECTIVE 2

Discuss the interrelationship of cost accumulation, cost measurement, and cost assignment.

Given the characteristics of a firm's production process, it is time to set up the system to be used in generating appropriate cost information. A good cost accounting information system is flexible and reliable. It provides information for a variety of purposes and can be used to answer different types of questions. In general, the system is used to satisfy the needs for cost accumulation, cost measurement, and cost assignment. **Cost accumulation** is the recognition and recording of costs. **Cost measurement** involves determining the dollar amounts of direct materials, direct labor, and overhead used in production. **Cost assignment** is the association of production costs with the units produced. Exhibit 5-3 illustrates the relationship of cost accumulation, cost measurement, and cost assignment.

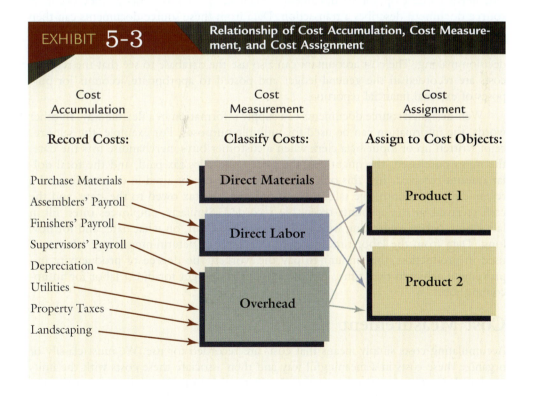

EXHIBIT 5-3   Relationship of Cost Accumulation, Cost Measurement, and Cost Assignment

3. Peter Coy and Neal Sandler, "A Package for Every Person," *Business Week* (February 6, 1995): 44.

Enterprise resource planning (ERP) systems are very useful in job-order firms. These programs, used to manage people and materials, can track the availability of various materials and are used to input new orders into the system and arrange them so as to get the fastest delivery. The furniture manufacturing industry is one that has taken to ERP to coordinate and speed up its job-order manufacturing systems.

Previously, ordering furniture was a lengthy and frustrating experience. Typically, a customer browsed in a furniture store and selected a sofa or dining room set. Then, various options were considered and entered into the order (for example, the fabric and frame style of the sofa). The order was submitted to the manufacturer, and the customer was told that the order would be ready in three months or so. Four or five months later, the order was often still not in—and information on its progress was difficult, if not impossible, to come by.

Let's fast-forward to today's furniture-buying experience. Consider **Bassett Furniture Industries, Inc.**, a leading manufacturer of a wide variety of home furnishings—including bedroom and dining room suites, tables, entertainment units, upholstered furniture, and mattress sets. Bassett operates in 11 states and 33 foreign countries; it coordinates its manufacturing and selling processes with **JD Edwards**' ERP system. A Bassett sales representative, working directly with a customer, can access real time data to find out if a desired frame or fabric is in stock. The order can be placed, and the representative can see immediately when the piece will be manufactured and delivered. At any point in time, the progress of the order can be tracked and the customer kept up to date. Dave Bilyeu, CIO for Bassett Furniture, says, "With JD Edwards' software, we can provide our customers with a new level of service, which translates into a competitive advantage."

Source: Taken from JD Edwards' Customer Profile on Bassett Furniture Industries, Inc.

Cost Accumulation

Cost accumulation refers to the recognition and recording of costs. The cost accountant needs to develop source documents which keep track of costs as they occur. A source document describes a transaction. Data from these source documents can then be recorded in a database. The recording of data in a database allows accountants and managers the flexibility to analyze subsets of the data as needed to aid in management decision making. The cost accountant can also use the database to see that the relevant costs are recorded in the general ledger and posted to appropriate accounts for purposes of external financial reporting.

Well-designed source documents can supply information in a flexible way. In other words, the information can be used for multiple purposes. For example, the sales receipt written up or input by a clerk when a customer buys merchandise lists the date, the items purchased, the quantities, the prices, the sales tax paid, and the total dollar amount received. Just this one source document can be used in determining sales revenue for the month, the sales by each product, the tax owed to the state, and the cash received or the accounts receivable recorded. Similarly, employees often fill in labor time tickets, indicating which jobs they worked on, on what date, and for how long. Data from the labor time ticket can be used in determining direct labor cost used in production, the amount to pay the worker, the degree of productivity improvement achieved over time, and the amount to budget for direct labor for an upcoming job.

Cost Measurement

Accumulating costs simply means that costs are recorded for use. We must classify or organize these costs in a meaningful way and then associate these costs with the units produced. Cost measurement refers to classifying the costs; it consists of determining the dollar amounts of direct materials, direct labor, and overhead used in production. The dollar amounts may be the actual amounts expended for the manufacturing inputs or they may be estimated amounts. Often, bills for overhead items arrive after the unit cost must be calculated; therefore, estimated amounts are used to ensure timeliness of cost information and to control costs.

The two commonly used ways to *measure* the costs associated with production are actual costing and normal costing. Actual costing requires the firm to use the actual cost of all resources used in production to determine unit cost. While intuitively reasonable, this method has drawbacks, as we shall see. The second method, normal costing, requires the firm to apply actual costs of direct materials and direct labor to units produced. However, overhead is applied based on a predetermined estimate. Normal costing, introduced in Chapter 4, is more widely used in practice; it will be further discussed in this chapter.

Actual versus Normal Costing

An actual cost system uses actual costs for direct materials, direct labor, and overhead to determine unit cost. In practice, strict actual cost systems are rarely used because they cannot provide accurate unit cost information on a timely basis. Per-unit computation of the direct materials and direct labor costs is not the source of the difficulty. Direct materials and direct labor can be traced to units produced. The main problem with using actual costs for calculation of unit cost is with manufacturing overhead. There are three reasons why this is so.

First, a traditional system applies overhead using unit-level drivers. However, many overhead items cannot be traced to units of production. Depreciation on plant and equipment, purchasing, and receiving are costs that are not associated with unit-level drivers. Activity-based costing is a way of overcoming this difficulty by using multiple drivers—both unit-level and non-unit-level.

Second, many overhead costs are not incurred uniformly throughout the year. Thus, they can differ significantly from one period to the next. For example, a factory located in the Northeast may incur higher utilities costs in the winter as it heats the factory. Even if the factory always produced 10,000 units a month, the per-unit overhead cost in December would be higher than the per-unit overhead cost in June. As a result, one unit of product costs more in one month than another, even though the units are identical, and the production process is the same. The difference in the per-unit overhead cost is due to overhead costs that were incurred nonuniformly.

The third reason is that per-unit overhead costs fluctuate dramatically because of nonuniform production levels. For example, suppose a factory has seasonal production. Perhaps it produces 10,000 units in March, but 30,000 units in September as it gears up for the Christmas buying season. Then, if all other costs remain the same, month to month, the per-unit overhead of the product would be approximately three times as high in March as in September. Again, the units are identical; the production process is the same.

The problem of fluctuating per-unit overhead costs can be avoided if the firm waits until the end of the year to assign the overhead costs. Unfortunately, waiting until the end of the year to compute an overhead rate is unacceptable. A company needs unit cost information throughout the year. This information is needed on a timely basis both for interim financial statements and to help managers make decisions such as pricing. Most decisions requiring unit cost information simply cannot wait until the end of the year. Managers must react to day-to-day conditions in the marketplace in order to maintain a sound competitive position.

Normal costing solves these problems associated with actual costing. A cost system that measures overhead costs on a predetermined basis and uses actual costs for direct materials and direct labor is called a normal costing system. Predetermined overhead or activity rates are calculated at the beginning of the year and are used to apply overhead to production as the year goes on. Any difference between actual and applied overhead is handled as an overhead variance. Chapter 4 explained the treatment of overhead variances.

Virtually all firms assign overhead to production on a predetermined basis. This fact seems to suggest that most firms successfully approximate the end-of-the-year overhead rate. Thus, the measurement problems associated with the use of actual overhead costs are solved by the use of estimated overhead costs. A job-order costing system that uses actual costs for direct materials and direct labor and estimated costs for overhead is called a *normal job-order costing system.*

Cost Assignment

Once costs have been accumulated and measured, they are assigned to units of product manufactured or units of service delivered. Unit costs are important for a wide variety of purposes. For example, bidding is a common requirement in markets for custom homes and industrial buildings. It is virtually impossible to submit a meaningful bid without knowing the costs associated with the units to be produced. Product cost information is vital in a number of other areas as well. Decisions concerning product design and introduction of new products are affected by expected unit costs. Decisions to make or buy a product, to accept or reject a special order, or to keep or drop a product line require unit cost information.

In its simplest form, computing the unit manufacturing or service cost is easy. The unit cost is the total product cost associated with the units produced divided by the number of units produced. For example, if a toy company manufactures 100,000 tricycles and the total cost of direct materials, direct labor, and overhead for these tricycles is $1,500,000, then the cost per tricycle is $15 ($1,500,000/100,000). Although the concept is simple, the practical reality of the computation is more complex and breaks down when there are products that differ from one another or when the company needs to know the cost of the product before all of the actual costs associated with its production are known.

Importance of Unit Costs to Manufacturing Firms

Unit cost is a critical piece of information for a manufacturer. Unit costs are essential for valuing inventory, determining income, and making a number of important decisions.

Disclosing the cost of inventories and determining income are financial reporting requirements that a firm faces at the end of each period. In order to report the cost of its inventories, a firm must know the number of units on hand and the unit cost. The cost of goods sold, used to determine income, also requires knowledge of the units sold and their unit cost.

Whether or not the unit cost information should include all manufacturing costs depends on the purpose for which the information is going to be used. For financial reporting, full or absorption unit cost information is required. If a firm is operating below its production capacity, however, variable cost information may be much more useful in a decision to accept or reject a special order. Simply put, unit cost information needed for external reporting may not supply the information necessary for a number of internal decisions, especially those decisions that are short run in nature. Different costs are needed for different purposes.

It should be pointed out that full cost information is useful as an input for a number of important internal decisions as well as for financial reporting. In the long run, for any product to be viable, its price must cover its full cost. Decisions to introduce a new product, to continue a current product, and to analyze long-run prices are examples of important internal decisions that rely on full unit cost information.

Importance of Unit Costs to Nonmanufacturing Firms

Service and nonprofit firms also require unit cost information. Conceptually, the way companies accumulate and assign costs is the same whether or not the firm is a manufacturing firm. The service firm must first identify the service "unit" being provided. In an auto repair shop, the service unit would be the work performed on an individual customer's car. Because each car is different in terms of the work required (an oil change versus a transmission overhaul, for example), the costs must be assigned individually to each job. A hospital would accumulate costs by patient, patient day, and type of procedure (e.g., X-ray, complete blood count test). A governmental agency must also identify the service provided. For example, city government might provide household trash collection and calculate the cost by truck run or by collection per house.

Service firms use cost data in much the same way that manufacturing firms do. They use costs to determine profitability, the feasibility of introducing new services, and so on. However, because service firms do not produce physical products, they do not need to value work-in-process and finished goods inventories. Of course, they may have supplies, and the inventory of supplies is simply valued at historical cost.

Nonprofit firms must track costs to be sure that they provide their services in a cost-efficient way. Governmental agencies have a fiduciary responsibility to taxpayers to use funds wisely. This requires accurate accounting for costs.

Production of Unit Cost Information

To produce unit cost information, both cost measurement and cost assignment are required. We have already considered two types of cost measurement systems, actual costing and normal costing. We have seen that normal costing is preferred because it provides information on a more timely basis. Shortly, we will address the cost assignment method of job-order costing. First, however, it is necessary to take a closer look at determining costs per unit.

Direct materials and direct labor costs are simply traced to units of production. There is a clear relationship between the amount of materials and labor used and the level of production. Actual costs can be used because the actual cost of materials and labor are known reasonably well at any point in time.

Overhead is applied using a predetermined rate based on budgeted overhead costs and budgeted amount of driver. Two considerations arise. One is the choice of the activity base or driver. The other is the activity level.

There are many different measures of production activity. In assigning overhead costs, it is important to select an activity base that is correlated with overhead consumption. This will ensure that individual products receive an accurate assignment of overhead costs. In a traditional costing system, a unit-level driver is used. Five commonly used unit-level drivers are:

1. Units produced
2. Direct labor hours
3. Direct labor dollars
4. Machine hours
5. Direct materials dollars or cost

The most obvious measure of production activity is output. If there is only one product, then overhead costs are clearly incurred to produce that product. In a single-product setting, the overhead costs of the period are directly traceable to the period's output. Clearly, for this case, units produced satisfies the cause-and-effect criterion. Most firms, however, produce more than one product. Since different products typically consume different amounts of overhead, this assignment method is inaccurate. At **Kraft**, for example, one plant produces salad dressing, ketchup, and marshmallow creme—each in a range of sizes from personal application packs to 32-ounce jars. In a multiple-product setting like this, overhead costs are common to more than one product, and different products may consume overhead at different rates.

The position taken in this text is that the assignment of overhead costs should follow, as nearly as possible, a cause-and-effect relationship. Efforts should be made to identify those factors that cause the consumption of overhead. Once identified, these causal factors, or *activity drivers*, should be used to assign overhead to products. It seems reasonable to argue that for products using the lathe, machine hours reflect differential machine time and consequently the consumption of machine cost. Units produced does not necessarily reflect machine time or consumption of the machine cost; therefore, it can be argued that machine hours is a better activity driver and should be used to assign this overhead cost.

As this example illustrates, activity measures other than units of product are needed when a firm has multiple products. The last four measures listed earlier (direct labor hours, direct labor dollars, machine hours, and direct materials dollars or cost) are all useful for multiple-product settings. Some may be more useful than others, depending on how well they correlate with the actual overhead consumption. As we will discuss later, it may even be appropriate to use multiple rates.

Choosing the Activity Level

Now that we have determined which measure of activity to use, we still need to predict the level of activity usage that applies to the coming year. Although any reasonable level of activity could be chosen, the two leading candidates are expected actual activity and normal activity. **Expected activity level** is simply the production level the firm expects to attain for the coming year. **Normal activity level** is the average activity usage that a firm experiences in the long term (normal volume is computed over more than one year).

For example, assume that Paulos Manufacturing expects to produce 18,000 units next year and has budgeted overhead for the year at $216,000. Exhibit 5-4 gives the data on units produced by Paulos Manufacturing for the past four years, as well as the expected production for next year. If expected actual capacity is used, Paulos Manufacturing will apply overhead using a predetermined rate of $12 ($216,000/18,000). However, if normal capacity is used, then the denominator of the equation for predetermined overhead is the average of the past four years of activity, or 20,000 units [(22,000 + 17,000 + 21,000 + 20,000)/4]. Then the predetermined overhead rate to be used for the coming year is $10.80 ($216,000/20,000).

EXHIBIT 5-4	Paulos Manufacturing Data
Year	**Units Produced**
Year 1	22,000
Year 2	17,000
Year 3	21,000
Year 4	20,000
Expected for next year	18,000

Which choice is better? Of the two, normal activity has the advantage of using much the same activity level year after year. As a result, it produces less fluctuation from year to year in the assignment of per-unit overhead cost. Of course, if activity stays fairly stable, then the normal capacity level is roughly equal to the expected actual capacity level.

Other activity levels used for computing predetermined overhead rates are those corresponding to the theoretical and practical levels. **Theoretical activity level** is the absolute maximum production activity of a manufacturing firm. It is the output that can be realized if everything operates perfectly. **Practical activity level** is the maximum output that can be realized if everything operates efficiently. Efficient operation allows for some imperfections such as normal equipment breakdowns, some shortages, and workers operating at less than peak capability. Normal and expected actual activities tend to reflect consumer demand, while theoretical and practical activities reflect a firm's production capabilities. Exhibit 5-5 illustrates these four measures of activity level.

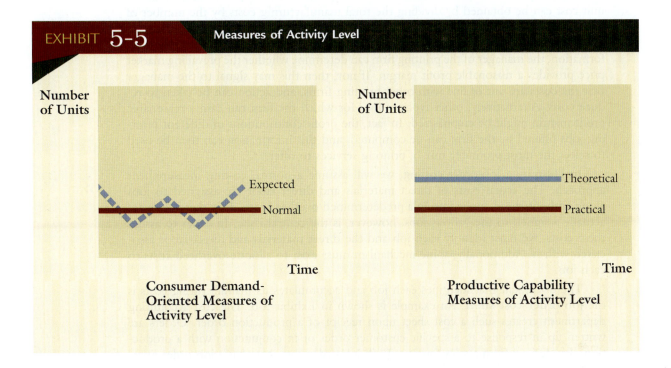

EXHIBIT 5-5   Measures of Activity Level

Given budgeted overhead, an activity driver, and an activity level, a predetermined overhead rate can be computed and applied to production. Understanding exactly how overhead is applied is critical to understanding normal costing.

OBJECTIVE 3

Explain the difference between job-order and process costing, and identify the source documents used in job-order costing.

The Job-Order Costing System: General Description

As we have seen, manufacturing and service firms can be divided into two major industrial types based on the uniqueness of their product. The degree of product or service heterogeneity affects the way in which we track costs. As a result, two different cost assignment systems have been developed: job-order costing and process costing. Job-order costing systems will be described in this chapter.

Overview of the Job-Order Costing System

Firms operating in job-order industries produce a wide variety of products or jobs that are usually quite distinct from each other. Customized or built-to-order products fit into this category, as do services that vary from customer to customer. Examples of job-order processes include printing, construction, furniture making, automobile repair, and beautician services. In manufacturing, a job may be a single unit such as a house, or it may be a batch of units such as eight tables. Job-order systems may be used to produce goods for inventory that are subsequently sold in the general market. Often, however, a job is associated with a particular customer order. The key feature of job-order costing is that the cost of one job differs from that of another job and must be monitored separately.

For job-order production systems, costs are accumulated by *job*. This approach to assigning costs is called a **job-order costing system**. In a job-order firm, collecting costs by job provides vital information for management. Once a job is completed, the unit cost can be obtained by dividing the total manufacturing costs by the number of units produced. For example, if the production costs for printing 100 wedding announcements total $300, then the unit cost for this job is $3. Given the unit cost information, the manager of the printing firm can determine whether the prevailing market price provides a reasonable profit margin. If not, then this may signal to the manager that the costs are out of line with other printing firms, and action can be taken to reduce costs. Alternatively, other types of jobs for which the firm can earn a reasonable profit margin might be emphasized. In fact, the profit contributions of different printing jobs offered by the firm can be computed, and this information can then be used to select the most profitable mix of printing services to offer.

In illustrating job-order costing, we will assume a normal costing measurement approach. The actual costs of direct materials and direct labor are assigned to jobs along with overhead applied using a predetermined overhead rate. *How* these costs are actually assigned to the various jobs, however, is the central issue. In order to assign these costs, we must identify each job and the direct materials and direct labor associated with it. Additionally, some mechanism must exist to allocate overhead costs to each job.

The document that identifies each job and accumulates its manufacturing costs is the **job-order cost sheet**. An example is shown in Exhibit 5-6. The cost accounting department creates such a cost sheet upon receipt of a production order. Orders are written up in response to a specific customer order or in conjunction with a production plan derived from a sales forecast. Each job-order cost sheet has a job-order number that identifies the new job.

In a manual accounting system, the job-order cost sheet is a document. In today's world, however, most accounting systems are automated. The cost sheet usually corresponds to a record in a work-in-process inventory master file. The collection of all job cost sheets defines a **work-in-process inventory file**. In a manual system, the file would be located in a filing cabinet, whereas in an automated system, it is stored electronically on magnetic tape or disk. In either system, the file of job-order cost sheets serves as a subsidiary work-in-process inventory ledger.

Both manual and automated systems require the same kind of data in order to accumulate costs and track the progress of a job. A job-order costing system must have the capability to identify the quantity of direct materials, direct labor, and overhead consumed by each job. In other words, documentation and procedures are needed to associate the manufacturing inputs used by a job with the job itself. This need is satisfied through the use of materials requisitions for direct material, time tickets for direct labor, and predetermined rates for overhead.

Materials Requisitions

The cost of direct materials is assigned to a job by the use of a source document known as a **materials requisition form**, illustrated in Exhibit 5-7 on page 194. Notice that the form asks for the description, quantity, and unit cost of the direct materials issued and, most importantly, for the job number. Using this form, the cost accounting de-

EXHIBIT 5-6	The Job-Order Cost Sheet

Job Number _____ 16 _____

For _____ Benson Company _____   Date Ordered _____ April 2, 2007 _____

Item Description _____ Valves _____   Date Completed __ April 24, 2007 __

Quantity Completed _____ 100 _____   Date Shipped _____ April 25, 2007 _____

Direct Materials		Direct Labor				Overhead		
Requisition Number	Amount	Ticket Number	Hours	Rate	Amount	Hours	Rate	Amount
12	$300	68	8	$6	$ 48	8	$10	$ 80
18	450	72	10	7	70	10	10	100
	$750				$118			$180

Cost Summary

Direct materials ___ $750 ___

Direct labor _____ 118 _____

Overhead _____ 180 _____

Total cost _____ $1,048 _____

Unit cost _____ $10.48 _____

partment can enter the total cost of direct materials directly onto the job-order cost sheet. If the accounting system is automated, the data are entered directly at a computer terminal, using the materials requisition forms as source documents. A program then enters the cost of direct materials onto the record for each job.

In addition to providing essential information for assigning direct materials costs to jobs, the materials requisition form may also have other data items such as requisition number, date, and signature. These data items are useful for maintaining proper control over a firm's inventory of direct materials. The signature, for example, transfers responsibility for the materials from the storage area to the person receiving the materials, usually a production supervisor.

No attempt is made to trace the cost of other materials, such as supplies, lubricants, and so on, to a particular job. You will recall that these indirect materials are assigned to jobs through the predetermined overhead rate.

Job Time Tickets

Direct labor also must be associated with each particular job. The means by which direct labor costs are assigned to individual jobs is the source document known as a **time ticket** (see Exhibit 5-8 on page 195). When an employee works on a particular job, she fills out a time ticket that identifies her name, wage rate, hours worked, and job number. These time tickets are collected daily and transferred to the cost

---

EXHIBIT 5-7   **Materials Requisition Form**

Date _____ April 8, 2007 _____

Materials Requisition
Number 678

Department_____ Grinding_____

Job Number _____ 62 _____

Description	Quantity	Cost/Unit	Total Cost
Casing	100	$3	$300

Authorized Signature ____ *Jim Lawson* _____

---

accounting department, where the information is used to post the cost of direct labor to individual jobs. Again, in an automated system, posting involves entering the data onto the computer.

Time tickets are used only for direct laborers. Since indirect labor is common to all jobs, these costs belong to overhead and are allocated using the predetermined overhead rate.

Overhead Application

Jobs are assigned overhead costs with the predetermined overhead rate. Typically, direct labor hours is the measure used to calculate overhead. For example, assume a firm has estimated overhead costs for the coming year of $900,000 and expected activity is 90,000 direct labor hours. The predetermined overhead rate is $900,000/90,000 direct labor hours = $10 per direct labor hour.

Since the number of direct labor hours charged to a job is known from time tickets, the assignment of overhead costs to jobs is simple once the predetermined rate has been computed. For instance, Exhibit 5-8 reveals that Ann Wilson worked a total of eight hours on Job 16. From this time ticket, overhead totaling $80 ($10 × 8 hours) would be assigned to Job 16.

What if overhead is assigned to jobs based on something other than direct labor hours? Then the other driver must be accounted for as well. That is, the actual amount used of the other driver (for example, machine hours) must be collected and posted to the job cost sheets. Employees must create a source document that will track the machine hours used by each job. A machine time ticket could easily accommodate this need.

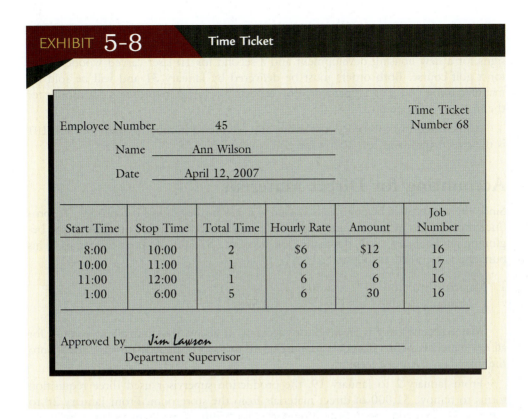

EXHIBIT 5-8   Time Ticket

					Time Ticket Number 68

Employee Number _____45_____

Name _____Ann Wilson_____

Date _____April 12, 2007_____

Start Time	Stop Time	Total Time	Hourly Rate	Amount	Job Number
8:00	10:00	2	$6	$12	16
10:00	11:00	1	6	6	17
11:00	12:00	1	6	6	16
1:00	6:00	5	6	30	16

Approved by _____*Jim Lawson*_____
        Department Supervisor

Unit Cost Calculation

Once a job is completed, its total manufacturing cost is computed by first totaling the costs of direct materials, direct labor, and overhead, and then summing these individual totals. The grand total is divided by the number of units produced to obtain the unit cost. (Exhibit 5-6 illustrates these computations.)

All completed job-order cost sheets of a firm can serve as a subsidiary ledger for the finished goods inventory. In a manual accounting system, the completed sheets would be transferred from the work-in-process inventory files to the finished goods inventory file. In an automated accounting system, an updating run would delete the finished job from the work-in-process inventory master file and add this record to the finished goods inventory master file. In either case, adding the totals of all completed job-order cost sheets gives the cost of finished goods inventory at any point in time.

As finished goods are sold and shipped, the cost records would be pulled (or deleted) from the finished goods inventory file. These records then form the basis for calculating a period's cost of goods sold.

OBJECTIVE 4

Describe the cost flows associated with job-order costing, and prepare the journal entries.

Job-Order Costing: Specific Cost Flow Description

Recall that cost flow is how we account for costs from the point at which they are incurred to the point at which they are recognized as an expense on the income statement. Of principal interest in a job-order costing system is the flow of manufacturing costs. Accordingly, we begin with a description of exactly how we account for the three manufacturing cost elements (direct materials, direct labor, and overhead).

A simplified job shop environment is used as the framework for this description. All Signs Company, recently formed by Bob Fredericks, produces a wide variety of customized signs. Bob leased a small building and bought the necessary production equipment. For the first month of operation (January), Bob has finalized two orders: one for 20 street signs for a new housing development and a second for 10 laser-carved wooden signs for a golf course. Both orders must be delivered by January 31 and will be sold for manufacturing cost plus 50 percent. Bob expects to average two orders per month for the first year of operation.

Bob created two job-order cost sheets and assigned a number to each job. Job 101 is the street signs, and Job 102 is the golf course signs.

Accounting for Direct Materials

Since the company is beginning its business, it has no beginning inventories. To produce the 30 signs in January and retain a supply of direct materials on hand at the beginning of February, Bob purchases, on account, $2,500 of direct materials. This purchase is recorded as follows:

1. Materials Inventory   2,500
       Accounts Payable   2,500

Materials Inventory is an inventory account. It also is the controlling account for all raw materials. When materials are purchased, the cost of these materials "flows" into the materials inventory account.

From January 2 to January 19, the production supervisor used three requisition forms to remove $1,000 of direct materials from the storeroom. From January 20 to January 31, two additional requisition forms for $500 of direct materials were used. The first three forms revealed that the direct materials were used for Job 101; the last two requisitions were for Job 102. Thus, for January, the cost sheet for Job 101 would have a total of $1,000 in direct materials posted, and the cost sheet for Job 102 would have a total of $500 in direct materials posted. In addition, the following entry would be made:

2. Work-in-Process Inventory   1,500
       Materials Inventory   1,500

This second entry captures the notion of direct materials flowing from the storeroom to work in process. All such flows are summarized in the work-in-process inventory account as well as being posted individually to the respective jobs. Work-in-Process Inventory is a controlling account, and the job cost sheets are the subsidiary accounts. Exhibit 5-9 summarizes the direct materials cost flows. Notice that the source document that drives the direct materials cost flows is the materials requisition form.

Accounting for Direct Labor Cost

Since two jobs were in progress during January, time tickets filled out by direct laborers must be sorted by each job. Once the sorting is completed, the hours worked and the wage rate of each employee are used to assign the direct labor cost to each job. For Job 101, the time tickets showed 60 hours at an average wage rate of $10 per hour, for a total direct labor cost of $600. For Job 102, the total was $250, based on 25 hours at an average hourly wage of $10. In addition to the postings to each job's cost sheet, the following summary entry would be made:

3. Work-in-Process Inventory   850
       Wages Payable   850

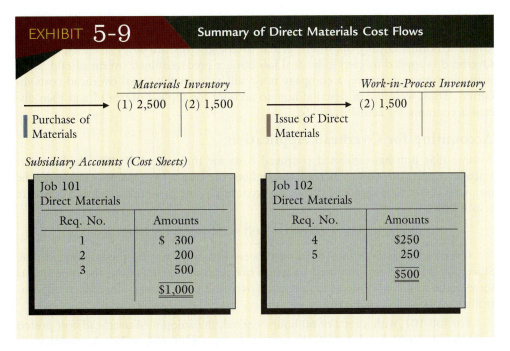

EXHIBIT 5-9   **Summary of Direct Materials Cost Flows**

Source Documents: Materials Requisition Forms

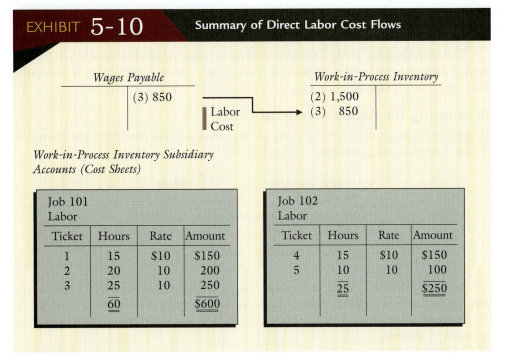

EXHIBIT 5-10   **Summary of Direct Labor Cost Flows**

Source Documents: Time Tickets

The summary of the direct labor cost flows is given in Exhibit 5-10. Notice that the direct labor costs assigned to the two jobs exactly equal the total assigned to Work-in-Process Inventory. Note also that the time tickets filled out by the individual laborers are the source of information for posting the labor cost flows. Remember that the labor cost flows reflect only direct labor cost. Indirect labor is assigned as part of overhead.

Accounting for Overhead

Under a normal costing approach, actual overhead costs are *never* assigned to jobs. Overhead is applied to each individual job using a predetermined overhead rate. Even with this system, however, a company must still account for actual overhead costs incurred. Thus, we will first describe how to account for applied overhead and then discuss accounting for actual overhead.

Accounting for Overhead Application

Assume that Bob has estimated overhead costs for the year at $9,600. Additionally, since he expects business to increase throughout the year as he becomes established, he estimates 2,400 total direct labor hours. Accordingly, the predetermined overhead rate is as follows:

$$\text{Overhead rate} = \$9,600/2,400 = \$4 \text{ per direct labor hour}$$

Overhead costs flow into Work-in-Process Inventory via the predetermined rate. Since direct labor hours are used to assign overhead into production, the time tickets serve as the source documents for assigning overhead to individual jobs and to the controlling work-in-process inventory account.

For Job 101, with a total of 60 hours worked, the amount of overhead cost posted is $240 ($4 × 60). For Job 102, the overhead cost is $100 ($4 × 25). A summary entry reflects a total of $340 (i.e., all overhead applied to jobs worked on during January) in applied overhead.

4. Work-in-Process Inventory	340	
Overhead Control		340

The credit balance in the overhead control account equals the total applied overhead at a given point in time. In normal costing, only applied overhead ever enters the work-in-process inventory account.

Accounting for Actual Overhead Costs

To illustrate how actual overhead costs are recorded, assume that All Signs Company incurred the following indirect costs for January:

Lease payment	$200
Utilities	50
Equipment depreciation	100
Indirect labor	65
Total overhead costs	$415

As indicated earlier, actual overhead costs never enter the work-in-process inventory account. The usual procedure is to record actual overhead costs on the debit side of the overhead control account. For example, the actual overhead costs would be recorded as follows:

5. Overhead Control	415	
Lease Payable		200
Utilities Payable		50
Accumulated Depreciation—Equipment		100
Wages Payable		65

Thus, the debit balance in Overhead Control gives the total actual overhead costs at a given point in time. Since actual overhead costs are on the debit side of this account and applied overhead costs are on the credit side, the balance in Overhead Control is the overhead variance at a given point in time. For All Signs Company at the end of January, the actual overhead of $415 and applied overhead of $340 produce underapplied overhead of $75 ($415 − $340).

The flow of overhead costs is summarized in Exhibit 5-11. To apply overhead to work-in-process inventory, a company needs information from the time tickets and a predetermined overhead rate based on direct labor hours.

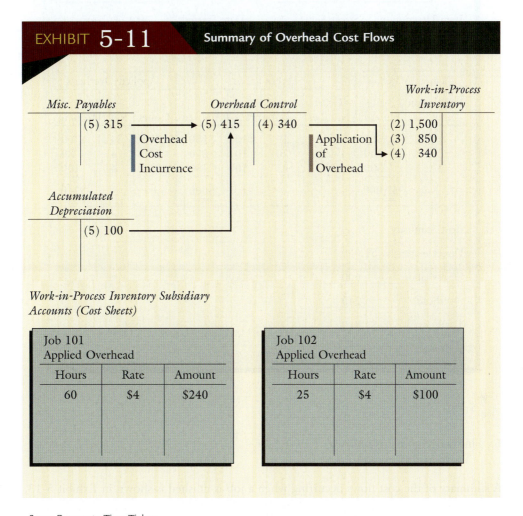

EXHIBIT 5-11   Summary of Overhead Cost Flows

Source Documents: Time Ticket
Other Source: Predetermined Rate

Accounting for Finished Goods Inventory

We have already seen what takes place when a job is completed. The columns for direct materials, direct labor, and applied overhead are totaled. These totals are then transferred to another section of the cost sheet where they are summed to yield the manufacturing cost of the job. This job cost sheet is then transferred to a finished goods inventory file. Simultaneously, the costs of the completed job are transferred from the work-in-process inventory account to the finished goods inventory account.

For example, assume that Job 101 was completed in January with the completed job-order cost sheet shown in Exhibit 5-12. Since Job 101 is completed, the total manufacturing costs of $1,840 must be transferred from the work-in-process inventory account to the finished goods inventory account. This transfer is described by the following entry:

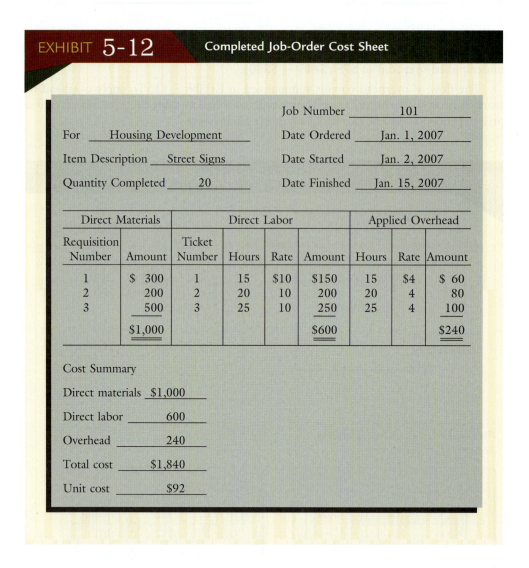

EXHIBIT 5-12   Completed Job-Order Cost Sheet

Job Number _____ 101 _____

For ____ Housing Development ____   Date Ordered ____ Jan. 1, 2007 ____

Item Description ____ Street Signs ____   Date Started ____ Jan. 2, 2007 ____

Quantity Completed ____ 20 ____   Date Finished ____ Jan. 15, 2007 ____

Direct Materials		Direct Labor				Applied Overhead		
Requisition Number	Amount	Ticket Number	Hours	Rate	Amount	Hours	Rate	Amount
1	$ 300	1	15	$10	$150	15	$4	$ 60
2	200	2	20	10	200	20	4	80
3	500	3	25	10	250	25	4	100
	$1,000				$600			$240

Cost Summary

Direct materials ____ $1,000 ____

Direct labor _____ 600 _____

Overhead _____ 240 _____

Total cost _____ $1,840 _____

Unit cost _____ $92 _____

6. Finished Goods Inventory   1,840
      Work-in-Process Inventory   1,840

A summary of the cost flows occurring when a job is finished is shown in Exhibit 5-13.

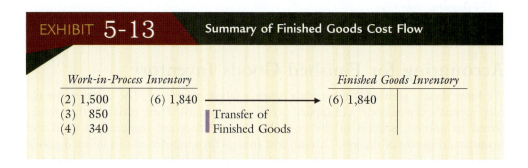

EXHIBIT 5-13   Summary of Finished Goods Cost Flow

Work-in-Process Inventory		Finished Goods Inventory	
(2) 1,500	(6) 1,840	(6) 1,840	
(3) 850			
(4) 340			

Transfer of Finished Goods

Completion of goods in a manufacturing process represents an important step in the flow of manufacturing costs. Because of the importance of this stage in a manufacturing operation, a schedule of the cost of goods manufactured is prepared periodically to summarize the cost flows of all production activity. This report is an important input for a firm's income statement and can be used to evaluate a firm's manufacturing effort. The statement of cost of goods manufactured was first introduced in Chapter 2. However, in a normal costing system, the report is somewhat different from the actual cost report presented in that chapter.

The statement of cost of goods manufactured presented in Exhibit 5-14 summarizes the production activity of All Signs Company for January. The key difference between this report and the one appearing in Chapter 2 is the use of applied overhead to arrive at the cost of goods manufactured. Finished goods inventories are carried at normal cost rather than the actual cost.

EXHIBIT 5-14	Statement of Cost of Goods Manufactured

All Signs Company
Statement of Cost of Goods Manufactured
For the Month Ended January 31, 2007

Direct materials:		
Beginning direct materials inventory	$ 0	
Add: Purchases of direct materials	2,500	
Total direct materials available	$2,500	
Less: Ending direct materials	1,000	
Direct materials used		$1,500
Direct labor		850
Manufacturing overhead:		
Lease	$ 200	
Utilities	50	
Depreciation	100	
Indirect labor	65	
	$ 415	
Less: Underapplied overhead	75	
Overhead applied		340
Current manufacturing costs		$2,690
Add: Beginning work-in-process inventory		0
Less: Ending work-in-process inventory		(850)
Cost of goods manufactured		$1,840

Notice that ending work-in-process inventory is $850. Where did we obtain this figure? Of the two jobs, Job 101 was finished and transferred to Finished Goods Inventory at a cost of $1,840. This amount is credited to Work-in-Process Inventory, leaving an ending balance of $850. Alternatively, we can add up the amounts debited to Work-in-Process Inventory for all remaining unfinished jobs. Job 102 is the only job still in process. The manufacturing costs assigned thus far are direct materials, $500; direct labor, $250; and overhead applied, $100. The total of these costs gives the cost of ending work-in-process inventory.

Accounting for Cost of Goods Sold

In a job-order firm, units can be produced for a particular customer or they can be produced with the expectation of selling the units as market conditions warrant. When the job is shipped to the customer, the cost of the finished job becomes the cost of the goods sold. When Job 101 is shipped, the following entries would be made. (Recall that the selling price is 150 percent of manufacturing cost.)

7a.	Cost of Goods Sold	1,840	
	Finished Goods Inventory		1,840
7b.	Accounts Receivable	2,760	
	Sales Revenue		2,760

In addition to these entries, a statement of cost of goods sold usually is prepared at the end of each reporting period (e.g., monthly and quarterly). Exhibit 5-15 presents such a statement for All Signs Company for January. Typically, the overhead variance is not material and is therefore closed to the cost of goods sold account. Cost of goods sold *before* adjustment for an overhead variance is called **normal cost of goods sold**. After adjustment for the period's overhead variance takes place, the result is called the **adjusted cost of goods sold**. It is this latter figure that appears as an expense on the income statement.

EXHIBIT 5-15   Statement of Cost of Goods Sold

All Signs Company
Statement of Cost of Goods Sold
For the Month Ended January 31, 2007

Beginning finished goods inventory	$ 0
Cost of goods manufactured	1,840
Goods available for sale	$1,840
Less: Ending finished goods inventory	0
Normal cost of goods sold	$1,840
Add: Underapplied overhead	75
Adjusted cost of goods sold	$1,915

However, closing the overhead variance to the cost of goods sold account is not done until the end of the year. Variances are expected each month because of nonuniform production and nonuniform actual overhead costs. As the year unfolds, these monthly variances should, by and large, offset each other so that the year-end variance is small. Nonetheless, to illustrate how the year-end overhead variance would be treated, we will close out the overhead variance experienced by All Signs Company in January.

Closing the underapplied overhead to cost of goods sold requires the following entry:

8.	Cost of Goods Sold	75	
	Overhead Control		75

Notice that debiting Cost of Goods Sold is equivalent to adding the underapplied amount to the normal cost of goods sold figure. If the overhead variance had been overapplied, then the entry would reverse, and Cost of Goods Sold would be credited.

If Job 101 had not been ordered by a customer but had been produced with the expectation that the signs could be sold to various other developers, then all 20 units may not be sold at the same time. Assume that on January 31, fifteen signs were sold. In this case, the cost of goods sold figure is the unit cost times the number of units sold ($92 × 15, or $1,380). The unit cost figure is found on the job-order cost sheet in Exhibit 5-12 (page 200).

Closing out the overhead variance to Cost of Goods Sold completes the description of manufacturing cost flows. To facilitate a review of these important concepts, Exhibit 5-16 shows a complete summary of the manufacturing cost flows for All Signs Company. Notice that these entries summarize information from the underlying job-order cost sheets. Although the description in this exhibit is specific to the example, the pattern of cost flows shown would be found in any manufacturing firm that uses a normal job-order costing system.

EXHIBIT 5-16   **All Signs Company Summary of Manufacturing Cost Flows**

Materials Inventory				Wages Payable				Overhead Control		
(1)	2,500	(2)	1,500			(3)	850	(5)	415	(4)	340
										(8)	75

Work-in-Process Inventory				Finished Goods Inventory				Cost of Goods Sold		
(2)	1,500	(6)	1,840	(6)	1,840	(7a)	1,840	(7a)	1,840	
(3)	850							(8)	75	
(4)	340									

(1) Purchase of direct materials	$2,500	
(2) Issue of direct materials	1,500	
(3) Incurrence of direct labor cost	850	
(4) Application of overhead	340	
(5) Incurrence of actual overhead cost	415	
(6) Transfer of Job 101 to finished goods	1,840	
(7a) Cost of goods sold of Job 101	1,840	
(8) Closing out underapplied overhead	75	

Manufacturing cost flows, however, are not the only cost flows experienced by a firm. Nonmanufacturing costs are also incurred. A description of how we account for these costs follows.

Accounting for Nonmanufacturing Costs

Recall that costs associated with selling and general administrative activities are classified as nonmanufacturing costs. These costs are period costs and are never assigned to the product in a traditional costing system. They are not part of the manufacturing cost flows. They do not belong to the overhead category and are treated as a totally separate category.

To illustrate how these costs are accounted for, assume All Signs Company had the following additional transactions in January:

Advertising circulars	$ 75
Sales commission	125
Office salaries	500
Depreciation, office equipment	50

The following compound entry could be used to record the preceding costs:

Selling Expense Control	200	
Administrative Expense Control	550	
Accounts Payable		75
Wages Payable		625
Accumulated Depreciation—Office Equipment		50

Controlling accounts accumulate all of the selling and administrative expenses for a period. At the end of the period, all of these costs flow to the period's income statement. An income statement for All Signs Company is shown in Exhibit 5-17.

EXHIBIT 5-17   Income Statement

All Signs Company
Income Statement
For the Month Ended January 31, 2007

Sales		$2,760
Less: Cost of goods sold		1,915
Gross margin		$ 845
Less selling and administrative expenses:		
Selling expenses.	$200	
Administrative expenses	550	750
Operating income		$ 95

With the description of the accounting procedures for selling and administrative expenses completed, the basic essentials of a normal job-order costing system are also complete. This description has assumed that a single plantwide overhead rate was being used.

Single versus Multiple Overhead Rates

OBJECTIVE 5

Explain why multiple overhead rates may be preferred to a single, plantwide rate.

Using a single rate based on direct labor hours to assign overhead to jobs may result in unfair cost assignments (unfair in the sense that too much or too little overhead is assigned to a job). This can occur if direct labor hours do not correlate well with the consumption of overhead resources.

To illustrate, consider a company with two departments, one that is labor-intensive (department A) and another that is machine-intensive (department B). The expected annual overhead costs and the expected annual usage of direct labor hours and machine hours for each department are shown in Exhibit 5-18.

Currently, the company uses a plantwide overhead rate based on direct labor hours. Thus, the overhead rate used for product costing is $12 per direct labor hour ($240,000/20,000).

Now consider two recently completed jobs, Job 23 and Job 24. Exhibit 5-19 provides production-related data concerning each job. The data reveal that Job 23 spent all of its time in department A, while Job 24 spent all of its time in department B. Using the plantwide overhead rate, Job 23 would receive a $6,000 overhead assignment ($12 × 500 direct labor hours), and Job 24 would receive a $12 overhead assignment

EXHIBIT 5-18	Departmental Overhead Costs and Activity		
	Department A	**Department B**	**Total**
Overhead costs	$60,000	$180,000	$240,000
Direct labor hours	15,000	5,000	20,000
Machine hours	5,000	15,000	20,000

($12 × 1 direct labor hour). Thus, the total manufacturing cost of Job 23 is $11,000 ($5,000 + $6,000), yielding a unit cost of $11. The total manufacturing cost of Job 24 is $5,012 ($5,000 + $12), yielding a unit cost of $5.012. Clearly, something is wrong. Using a plantwide rate, Job 23 received 500 times the overhead cost assignment that Job 24 received. Yet, as Exhibit 5-18 shows, Job 24 was produced in a department that is responsible for producing 75 percent of the plant's total overhead. Imagine the difficulties that this type of costing distortion can cause for a company. Some products would be overcosted, while others would be undercosted; the result could be incorrect pricing decisions that adversely affect the firm's competitive position.

EXHIBIT 5-19	Production Data for Jobs 23 and 24		
	Job 23		
	Department A	**Department B**	**Total**
Prime costs	$5,000	$0	$5,000
Direct labor hours	500	0	500
Machine hours	1	0	1
Units produced	1,000	0	1,000
	Job 24		
	Department A	**Department B**	**Total**
Prime costs	$0	$5,000	$5,000
Direct labor hours	0	1	1
Machine hours	0	500	500
Units produced	0	1,000	1,000

This distortion in product costs is caused by the assumption that direct labor hours properly reflect the overhead consumed by the individual jobs. One driver for the firm as a whole does not seem to work. This type of problem can be resolved by using multiple overhead rates, where each rate uses a different activity driver. For this example, a satisfactory solution might be to develop an overhead rate for each department. In the case of the machine-intensive department B, the rate could be based on machine hours instead of direct labor hours. It seems reasonable to believe that machine hours relate better to machine-related overhead than direct labor hours do and that direct labor hours would be a good driver for a labor-intensive department. If so, more accurate product costing can be achieved by computing two departmental rates instead of one plantwide rate. Therefore, in this example, we are making two improvements: using departmental overhead rates and basing the rates on different drivers.

Using data from Exhibit 5-18, the overhead rate for department A is $4 per direct labor hour ($60,000/15,000), and the overhead rate for department B is $12 per machine hour ($180,000/15,000). Using these rates, Job 23 would be assigned $2,000 of overhead ($4 × 500 direct labor hours) and Job 24 $6,000 of overhead ($12 × 500 machine hours). Job 24 now receives three times as much overhead cost as Job 23, which seems more sensible, since department B incurs three times as much overhead cost as does department A.

	Department A	*Department B*
Overhead cost	$60,000	$180,000
Cost driver	15,000 DLH	15,000 MHr
Department overhead rate	$4/DLH	$12/MHr
Overhead applied to Job 23	$2,000	—
Overhead applied to Job 24	—	$6,000

Moving to departmental rates may be considered a step toward activity-based costing, especially in the example just used where different activity drivers were chosen based on the types of overhead incurred in each department. While departmental rates may provide sufficient product costing accuracy for some firms, even more attention to how overhead is assigned may be necessary for other firms. This chapter has focused on activity drivers that are correlated with production volume (e.g., direct labor hours and machine hours). Greater product costing accuracy may be possible through the use of non-volume-related activity drivers. However, this discussion is left to a later chapter.

SUMMARY

In this chapter, we have examined the cost accounting system and its relationship to the production process. Two characteristics of the production process were shown to have an impact on cost accounting. These characteristics are the tangible product versus service nature of the firm and the degree of uniqueness of the product or service.

The cost accounting system is set up to serve the company's needs for cost accumulation, cost measurement, and cost assignment. In general, normal costing is preferred to actual costing in determining unit production costs. In normal costing, actual prime costs are assigned to units, but overhead is applied based on a predetermined rate.

Job-order costing is used for both manufacturing and service firms that produce unique or heterogeneous products. Cost is accounted for by the individual job using a subsidiary account called the job-order cost sheet.

Sometimes, a single overhead rate may not adequately capture the cause-and-effect relationship between overhead cost and production. In such cases, multiple overhead rates may be required.

Appendix: Accounting for Spoilage in a Traditional Job-Order System

OBJECTIVE **6**

Explain how spoilage is treated in a job-order costing system.

Throughout this chapter, we have assumed that the units produced are good units. In this case, all manufacturing costs are associated with good units and flow into cost of goods sold. However, on occasion, mistakes are made; defective units are produced and are either thrown away or reworked and sold. How do we account for those costs?

Traditional job-order costing makes a distinction between normal and abnormal spoilage. To understand this distinction, let's look at an example. Petris, Inc., manufactures cabinets on a job-order basis. Job 98-12 calls for 100 units with the following costs.

Direct materials	$2,000
Direct labor (100 hours)	1,000

Overhead is applied at the rate of 150 percent of direct labor dollars. At the end of the job, 100 units are produced. However, three of the cabinets required rework due to improper installation of shelving. The rework involved six extra direct labor hours and an additional $50 of material. How is the rework accounted for? It depends on the reason for the defective work.

If the defective work was a consequence of the demanding nature of this particular job, then rework is assigned to the job as follows.

Direct materials	$2,050
Direct labor	1,060
Overhead	1,590
Total job cost	$4,700
Unit job cost	$ 47

On the other hand, suppose that the defective work was a consequence of assigning new, untrained labor to the job. Defects are expected in that case, and the rework is not assigned to the job but instead to overhead control. The costs are assigned as follows.

Job 98-12		*Debited to Overhead Control*	
Direct materials	$2,000	Direct materials	$ 50
Direct labor	1,000	Direct labor	60
Overhead	1,500	Overhead	90
Total job cost	$4,500	Total	$200
Unit job cost	$ 45		

The cost of spoiled units that cannot be reworked are similarly charged to the job if caused by the demands of the job, and to overhead control if not.

REVIEW PROBLEM AND SOLUTION

JOB COST, APPLIED OVERHEAD, UNIT COST

Bostian Company uses a normal job-order costing system. It processes most jobs through two departments. Selected budgeted and actual data for the past year follow. Data for one of several jobs completed during the year also follow.

	Department A	Department B
Budgeted overhead	$100,000	$500,000
Actual overhead	$110,000	$520,000
Expected activity (direct labor hours)	50,000	10,000
Expected machine hours	10,000	50,000

(continued)

	Job 10
Direct materials	$20,000
Direct labor cost:	
Department A (5,000 hrs. @ $6 per hr.)	$30,000
Department B (1,000 hrs. @ $6 per hr.)	$6,000
Machine hours used:	
Department A	100
Department B	1,200
Units produced	10,000

Bostian Company uses a plantwide, predetermined overhead rate to assign overhead (OH) to jobs. Direct labor hours (DLH) is used to compute the predetermined overhead rate. Bostian prices its jobs at cost plus 30 percent.

Required:

1. Compute the predetermined overhead rate.
2. Using the predetermined rate, compute the per-unit manufacturing cost for Job 10.
3. Assume that Job 10 was completed in May and sold in September. Prepare journal entries for the completion and sale of Job 10.
4. Recalculate the unit manufacturing cost for Job 10 using departmental overhead rates. Use direct labor hours for department A and machine hours for department B. Does this approach provide a more accurate unit cost? Explain.
5. Assume that Job 10 was completed in May and sold in September. Using your work from Requirement 4, prepare journal entries for the completion and sale of Job 10.

SOLUTION

1. Predetermined overhead rate = $600,000/60,000 = $10 per DLH. Add the budgeted overhead for the two departments, and divide by the total expected direct labor hours (DLH = 50,000 + 10,000).

2.

Direct materials	$ 20,000
Direct labor	36,000
Overhead ($10 × 6,000 DLH)	60,000
Total manufacturing costs	$116,000
Unit cost ($116,000/10,000)	$ 11.60

3.

Finished Goods	116,000	
Work in Process		116,000
Cost of Goods Sold	116,000	
Finished Goods		116,000
Sales*	150,800	
Accounts Receivable		150,800

*Sales = $116,000 + (0.3)($116,000) = $150,800.

4. Predetermined rate for department A: $100,000/50,000 = $2 per DLH. Predetermined rate for department B: $500,000/50,000 = $10 per machine hour.

Direct materials	$20,000
Direct labor	36,000
Overhead:	
Department A: $2 \times 5,000	10,000
Department B: $10 \times 1,200	12,000
Total manufacturing costs	$78,000
Unit cost ($78,000/10,000)	$ 7.80

Overhead assignment using departmental rates is more accurate because there is a higher correlation with the overhead assigned and the overhead consumed. Notice that Job 10 spends most of its time in department A, the least overhead intensive of the two departments. Departmental rates reflect this differential time and consumption better than plantwide rates do.

5.	Finished Goods	78,000	
	Work in Process		78,000
	Cost of Goods Sold	78,000	
	Finished Goods		78,000
	Sales*	101,400	
	Accounts Receivable		101,400

*Sales = $78,000 + (0.3)($78,000) = $101,400.

KEY TERMS

Actual cost system 187	Materials requisition form 192
Adjusted cost of goods sold 202	Normal activity level 190
Cost accumulation 185	Normal cost of goods sold 202
Cost assignment 185	Normal costing system 187
Cost measurement 185	Perishability 181
Expected activity level 190	Practical activity level 191
Heterogeneity 181	Source document 186
Inseparability 181	Theoretical activity level 191
Intangibility 181	Time ticket 193
Job-order cost sheet 192	Work-in-process inventory file 192
Job-order costing system 192	

QUESTIONS FOR WRITING AND DISCUSSION

1. What is cost measurement? Cost accumulation? What is the difference between the two?
2. Why is actual costing rarely used for product costing?
3. Explain the differences between job-order costing and process costing.
4. What are some differences between a manual job-order costing system and an automated job-order costing system?
5. What is the role of materials requisition forms in a job-order costing system? Time tickets? Predetermined overhead rates?

6. Explain why multiple overhead rates are often preferred to a plantwide overhead rate.

7. Explain the role of activity drivers in assigning costs to products.

8. Define the following terms: *expected actual activity*, *normal activity*, *practical activity*, and *theoretical activity*.

9. Why would some prefer normal activity to expected actual activity to compute a predetermined overhead rate?

10. When computing a predetermined overhead rate, why are units of output not commonly used as a measure of production?

11. Wilson Company has a predetermined overhead rate of $5 per direct labor hour. The job-order cost sheet for Job 145 shows 1,000 direct labor hours costing $10,000 and materials requisitions totaling $7,500. Job 145 had 500 units completed and transferred to finished goods inventory. What is the cost per unit for Job 145?

12. Why are the accounting requirements for job-order costing more demanding than those for process costing?

13. Explain the difference between normal cost of goods sold and adjusted cost of goods sold.

14. (Appendix) Amber Company produces custom framing. For one job, the trainee assigned to cut the mat entered the mat dimensions incorrectly into the computer. The mat was unusable and had to be discarded; another mat was cut to the correct dimensions. How is the cost of the spoiled mat handled?

15. (Appendix) Amber Company produces custom framing. For one job, the dimensions of the picture were such that the computer-controlled, mat-cutting device could not be used. Amber warned the customer that this was a particularly difficult job, and her normal price would be increased to reflect its difficulty. Amber cut the mat by hand, but the cut was not as straight as she would have liked. So, she threw out the first mat and cut another one. How is the cost of the spoiled mat handled?

EXERCISES

5-1 CLASSIFYING FIRMS AS EITHER MANUFACTURING OR SERVICE

LO1   Classify the following types of firms as either manufacturing or service. Explain the reasons for your choice in terms of the four features of service firms (heterogeneity, inseparability, intangibility, and perishability).

a. Bicycle production
b. Pharmaceuticals
c. Income tax preparation
d. Application of artificial nails
e. Glue production
f. Child care

5-2 CHARACTERISTICS OF PRODUCTION PROCESS, COST MEASUREMENT

LO1, LO2   Tony Jefferson, of Rainking Company, designs and installs custom lawn and garden irrigation systems for homes and businesses throughout the state. Each job is different, requiring different materials and labor for installing the systems. Rainking estimated the following for the year:

Number of installations	250
Number of direct labor hours	5,000
Direct material cost	$60,000
Direct labor cost	$75,000
Overhead cost	$65,000

During the year, the following actual amounts were experienced:

Number of installations	245
Number of direct labor hours	5,040
Direct materials used	$59,350
Direct labor incurred	$75,600
Overhead incurred	$64,150

Required:

1. Should Rainking use process costing or job-order costing? Explain.
2. If Rainking uses a normal costing system and overhead is applied on the basis of direct labor hours, what is the cost of an installation that takes $3,500 of direct materials and 50 direct labor hours?
3. Explain why Rainking would have difficulty using an actual costing system.

5-3 CHARACTERISTICS OF PRODUCTION PROCESS, COST MEASUREMENT

LO1, LO2   Tony Jefferson, owner of Rainking of **Exercise 5-2**, noticed that the watering systems for many houses in a local subdivision had the same layout and required virtually identical amounts of prime cost. Tony met with the subdivision builders and offered to install a basic watering system in each house. The idea was accepted enthusiastically, so Tony created a new company, Waterpro, to handle the subdivision business. In its first three months in business, Waterpro experienced the following:

	June	July	August
Number of systems installed	25	50	100
Direct materials used	$5,000	$10,000	$20,000
Direct labor incurred	$5,250	$10,500	$21,000
Overhead	$15,000	$6,000	$8,400

Required:

1. Should Waterpro use process costing or job-order costing? Explain.
2. If Waterpro uses an actual costing system, what is the cost of a single system installed in June? In July? In August?
3. Now assume that Waterpro uses a normal costing system. Estimated overhead for the year is $60,000, and estimated production is 600 watering systems. What is the predetermined overhead rate per system? What is the cost of a single system installed in June? In July? In August?

5-4 ACTIVITY LEVELS USED TO COMPUTE OVERHEAD RATES

LO2   Landon Poteet has just started a new business—building and installing custom garage organization systems. Landon builds the cabinets and work benches in his workshop and then installs them in clients' garages. Landon figures his overhead for the coming year will be $9,000. Since his business is labor intensive, he plans to use direct labor hours as his overhead driver. For the coming year, he expects to complete 75 jobs, averaging 20 direct labor hours each. However, he has the capacity to complete 125 jobs averaging 20 direct labor hours each.

Required:

1. Four measures of activity level were mentioned in the text. Which two measures is Landon considering in computing a predetermined overhead rate?
2. Compute the predetermined overhead rates using each of the measures in your answer to Requirement 1.
3. Which one should Landon use? Why?

5-5   SOURCE DOCUMENTS, JOB COST FLOWS

LO3, LO4   Refer to **Exercise 5-4**.

Required:

1. What source documents will Landon need to account for costs in his new business?
2. Suppose Landon's business grows, and he expands his workshop and hires three additional carpenters to help him. What source documents will he need now?

5-6   JOB COSTS, ENDING WORK IN PROCESS

LO4   During March, Molson Company worked on three jobs. Data relating to these three jobs follow:

	Job 62	*Job 63*	*Job 64*
Units in each order	110	200	165
Units sold	—	200	—
Materials requisitioned	$560	$740	$1,600
Direct labor hours	260	300	500
Direct labor cost	$3,120	$3,600	$6,000

Overhead is assigned on the basis of direct labor hours at a rate of $7 per direct labor hour. During March, Jobs 62 and 63 were completed and transferred to finished goods inventory. Job 63 was sold by the end of the month. Job 64 was the only unfinished job at the end of the month.

Required:

1. Calculate the per-unit cost of Jobs 62 and 63.
2. Compute the ending balance in the work-in-process inventory account.
3. Prepare the journal entries reflecting the completion of Jobs 62 and 63 and the sale of Job 63. The selling price is 140 percent of cost.

5-7   PREDETERMINED OVERHEAD RATE, APPLICATION OF OVERHEAD TO JOBS, JOB COST

LO3 LO4   On April 1, Kurena Company had the following balances in its inventory accounts:

Materials Inventory	$16,350
Work-in-Process Inventory	21,232
Finished Goods Inventory	15,200

Work-in-process inventory is made up of three jobs with the following costs:

	Job 30	Job 31	Job 32
Direct materials	$2,650	$1,900	$3,650
Direct labor	1,900	1,340	4,000
Applied overhead	1,520	1,072	3,200

During April, Kurena experienced the following transactions:

a. Purchases materials on account for $21,000.
b. Requisitioned materials: Job 30, $12,500; Job 31, $11,200; and Job 32, $5,500.
c. Collected and summarized job tickets: Job 30, 250 hours at $12 per hour; Job 31, 275 hours at $15 per hour; and Job 32, 140 hours at $20 per hour.
d. Applied overhead on the basis of direct labor cost.
e. Actual overhead was $8,718.
f. Completed and transferred Job 31 to the finished goods warehouse.
g. Shipped Job 31 and billed the customer for 130 percent of the cost.

Required:

1. Calculate the predetermined overhead rate based on direct labor cost.
2. Calculate the ending balance for each job as of April 30.
3. Calculate the ending balance of Work in Process as of April 30.
4. Calculate the cost of goods sold for April.
5. Assuming that Kurena prices its jobs at cost plus 30 percent, calculate the price of the one job that was sold during April. (Round to the nearest dollar.)

5-8   JOB COST FLOWS, JOURNAL ENTRIES

LO4   Refer to **Exercise 5-7**.

Required:

1. Prepare journal entries for the April transactions.
2. Calculate the ending balances of each of the inventory accounts as of April 30.

5-9   PREDETERMINED OVERHEAD RATE, APPLICATION OF OVERHEAD TO JOBS, JOB COST, UNIT COST

LO2, LO4   On June 1, Dabo Company's work-in-process inventory consisted of three jobs with the following costs:

	Job 70	Job 71	Job 72
Direct materials	$1,600	$2,000	$850
Direct labor	1,900	1,300	900
Applied overhead	1,425	975	675

During June, four more jobs were started. Information on costs added to the seven jobs during June is as follows:

	Job 70	Job 71	Job 72	Job 73	Job 74	Job 75	Job 76
Direct materials	$ 800	$1,235	$3,550	$5,000	$300	$560	$ 80
Direct labor	1,000	1,400	2,200	1,800	600	860	172

Before the end of June, Jobs 70, 72, 73, and 75 were completed. On June 30, Jobs 72 and 75 were sold.

Required:

1. Calculate the predetermined overhead rate based on direct labor cost.
2. Calculate the ending balance for each job as of June 30.
3. Calculate the ending balance in Work-in-Process Inventory as of June 30.
4. Calculate the cost of goods sold for June.
5. Assuming that Dabo prices its jobs at cost plus 20 percent, calculate Dabo's sales revenue for June.

5-10 INCOME STATEMENT

LO4   Refer to **Exercise 5-9**. Dabo's marketing and administrative expense for June was $1,200.

Required:

Prepare an income statement for Dabo Company for June.

5-11 JOURNAL ENTRIES, T-ACCOUNTS

LO4   Kaycee, Inc., manufactures brown paper grocery bags. During the month of May, the following occurred:

a. Purchased materials on account for $23,175.
b. Requisitioned materials totaling $19,000 for use in production.
c. Incurred direct labor payroll for the month of $17,850, with an average wage of $8.50 per hour.
d. Incurred and paid actual overhead of $15,500.
e. Charged manufacturing overhead to production at the rate of $7 per direct labor hour.
f. Transferred completed units costing $36,085 to finished goods.
g. Sold bags costing $30,000 on account for $36,000.

Beginning balances as of May 1 were:

Materials	$ 5,170
Work-in-Process Inventory	11,200
Finished Goods Inventory	2,630

Required:

1. Prepare the journal entries for the preceding events.
2. Calculate the ending balances of:
   a. Materials Inventory
   b. Work-in-Process Inventory
   c. Overhead Control
   d. Finished Goods Inventory

5-12 UNIT COST, ENDING WORK-IN-PROCESS INVENTORY, JOURNAL ENTRIES

LO4, LO5   During October, Molson Company worked on three jobs. Data relating to these three jobs follow:

	Job 43	Job 44	Job 45
Units in each order	120	200	165
Units sold	—	200	—
Materials requisitioned	$744	$640	$600
Direct labor hours	360	400	200
Direct labor cost	$1,980	$2,480	$1,240

Overhead is assigned on the basis of direct labor hours at a rate of $5.30 per direct labor hour. During October, Jobs 43 and 44 were completed and transferred to finished goods inventory. Job 44 was sold by the end of the month. Job 45 was the only unfinished job at the end of the month.

Required:

1. Calculate the per-unit cost of Jobs 43 and 44.
2. Compute the ending balance in the work-in-process inventory account.
3. Prepare the journal entries reflecting the completion of Jobs 43 and 44 and the sale of Job 44. The selling price is 140 percent of cost.

5-13   ACTIVITY-BASED COSTING, UNIT COST, ENDING WORK-IN-PROCESS INVENTORY, JOURNAL ENTRIES

LO4, LO5   Smeyak Company uses an ABC system to apply overhead. There are three activity rates:

Purchasing	$30 per purchase order
Machining	$5 per machine hour
Other overhead	60% of direct labor cost

During August, Smeyak worked on three jobs. Data relating to these jobs follow:

	Job 80	Job 81	Job 82
Units in each order	110	400	100
Units sold	—	200	—
Materials requisitioned	$1,730	$3,000	$1,200
Direct labor cost	$2,000	$4,600	$800
Machine hours	60	40	20
Purchase orders	20	16	25

During August, Jobs 80 and 82 were completed and transferred to finished goods inventory. Job 80 was sold by the end of the month. Job 81 was the only unfinished job at the end of the month.

Required:

1. Calculate the per-unit cost of Jobs 80 and 82.
2. Compute the ending balance in the work-in-process inventory account.
3. Prepare the journal entries reflecting the completion of Jobs 80 and 82 and the sale of Job 80. The selling price is 140 percent of cost.

5-14   JOURNAL ENTRIES, T-ACCOUNTS

LO4   Porter Company uses job-order costing. During January, the following data were reported:

a. Purchased materials on account: direct materials, $82,000; indirect materials, $10,500.
b. Issued materials: direct materials, $72,500; indirect materials, $7,000.
c. Incurred labor cost: direct labor, $52,000; indirect labor, $15,750.
d. Incurred other manufacturing costs (all payables) of $49,000.
e. Applied overhead on the basis of 125 percent of direct labor cost.
f. Finished and transferred work to Finished Goods Inventory costing $160,000.
g. Sold finished goods costing $140,000 on account for 150 percent of cost.
h. Closed any over- or underapplied overhead to Cost of Goods Sold.

Required:

1. Prepare journal entries to record these transactions.
2. Prepare a T-account for Overhead Control. Post all relevant information to this account. What is the ending balance in this account?
3. Prepare a T-account for Work-in-Process Inventory. Assume a beginning balance of $10,000, and post all relevant information to this account. Did you assign any actual overhead costs to Work-in-Process Inventory? Why or why not?

5-15 ACTIVITY-BASED COSTING, UNIT COST, ENDING WORK-IN-PROCESS INVENTORY

LO4, LO5

Zavner Company is a job-order costing firm that uses activity-based costing to apply overhead to jobs. Zavner identified three overhead activities and related drivers. Budgeted information for the year is as follows:

Activity	Cost	Driver	Amount of Driver
Engineering design	$120,000	Engineering hours	3,000
Purchasing	80,000	Number of parts	10,000
Other overhead	250,000	Direct labor hours	40,000

Zavner worked on five jobs in July. Data are as follows:

	Job 60	Job 61	Job 62	Job 63	Job 64
Balance, July 1	$32,450	$40,770	$29,090	$0	$0
Direct materials	$26,000	$37,900	$25,350	$11,000	$13,560
Direct labor	$40,000	$38,500	$43,000	$20,900	$18,000
Engineering hours	20	10	15	100	200
Number of parts	150	180	200	500	300
Direct labor hours	2,500	2,400	2,600	1,200	1,100

By July 31, Jobs 60 and 62 were completed and sold. The remaining jobs were in process.

Required:

1. Calculate the activity rates for each of the three overhead activities.
2. Prepare job-order cost sheets for each job showing all costs through July 31.
3. Calculate the balance in Work in Process on July 31.
4. Calculate cost of goods sold for July.

PROBLEMS

5-16 JOURNAL ENTRIES, T-ACCOUNTS, COST OF GOODS MANUFACTURED AND SOLD

LO4, LO5   During May, the following transactions were completed and reported by Perlmutter Products, Inc.:

Spreadsheet

a. Purchased materials on account for $50,100.
b. Issued materials to production to fill job-order requisitions: direct materials, $30,000; indirect materials, $15,000.
c. Accumulated payroll for the month: direct labor, $70,000; indirect labor, $32,000; administrative, $18,000; sales, $9,900.
d. Accrued depreciation on factory plant and equipment of $13,400.
e. Accrued property taxes during the month for $1,450 (on factory).
f. Recorded expired insurance with a credit to the prepaid insurance account of $6,200.
g. Incurred factory utilities costs of $6,000.
h. Paid advertising costs of $7,200.
i. Accrued depreciation: office equipment, $1,500; sales vehicles, $650.
j. Paid legal fees for preparation of lease agreements of $750.
k. Charged overhead to production at a rate of $9 per direct labor hour. Recorded 8,000 direct labor hours during the month.
l. Incurred cost of jobs completed during the month of $158,000.

The company also reported the following beginning balances in its inventory accounts:

Materials Inventory	$ 5,000
Work-in-Process Inventory	30,000
Finished Goods Inventory	60,000

Required:

1. Prepare journal entries to record the transactions occurring in May.
2. Prepare T-accounts for Materials Inventory, Overhead Control, Work-in-Process Inventory, and Finished Goods Inventory. Post all relevant entries to these accounts.
3. Prepare a schedule of cost of goods manufactured.
4. If the overhead variance is all allocated to Cost of Goods Sold, by how much will Cost of Goods Sold decrease or increase?

5-17 OVERHEAD APPLICATION, ACTIVITY-BASED COSTING, BID PRICES

LO4, LO5   Karanth Company manufactures specialty tools to customer order. Budgeted overhead for the coming year is as follows:

Purchasing	$30,000
Setups	35,000
Engineering	15,000
Other	10,000

Previously, Sharon Benetton, Karanth Company's controller, had applied overhead on the basis of machine hours. Expected machine hours for the coming year are 10,000. Sharon has been reading about activity-based costing, and she wonders whether or not it might offer some advantages to her company. She decided that appropriate drivers for overhead activities are purchase orders for purchasing, number of setups for setup cost, engineering hours for engineering cost, and machine hours for other. Budgeted amounts for these drivers are 5,000 purchase orders, 500 setups, and 500 engineering hours.

Sharon has been asked to prepare bids for two jobs with the following information:

	Job 1	*Job 2*
Direct materials	$3,700	$8,900
Direct labor	$1,000	$2,000
Number of setups	2	3
Number of purchase orders	15	20
Number of engineering hours	25	10
Number of machine hours	200	200

The typical bid price includes a 30 percent markup over full manufacturing cost.

Required:

1. Calculate a plantwide rate for Karanth Company based on machine hours. What is the bid price of each job using this rate?
2. Calculate activity rates for the four overhead activities. What is the bid price of each job using these rates?
3. Which bids are more accurate? Why?

5-18 PLANTWIDE OVERHEAD RATE, ACTIVITY-BASED COSTING, JOB COSTS

LO5 Anselmo's Kwik Print provides a variety of photocopying and printing services. On June 5, Anselmo invested in some computer-aided photography equipment that enables customers to reproduce a picture or illustration, input it digitally into the computer, enter text into the computer, and then print out a 4-color professional quality brochure. Prior to the purchase of this equipment, Kwik Print's overhead averaged $35,000 per year. After the installation of the new equipment, the total overhead increased to $85,000 per year. Kwik Print has always costed jobs on the basis of actual materials and labor plus overhead assigned using a predetermined overhead rate based on direct labor hours. Budgeted direct labor hours for the year are 5,000, and the wage rate is $6 per hour.

Required:

1. What was the predetermined overhead rate prior to the purchase of the new equipment?
2. What was the predetermined overhead rate after the new equipment was purchased?
3. Suppose Jim Hargrove brought in several items he wanted photocopied. The job required 100 sheets of paper at $0.015 each and 12 minutes of direct labor time. What would have been the cost of Jim's job on May 20? On June 20?
4. Suppose that Anselmo decides to calculate two overhead rates, one for the photocopying area based on direct labor hours as before, and one for the computer-aided printing area based on machine time. Estimated overhead applicable to the computer-aided printing area is $50,000, and forecasted usage of the machines is

2,000 hours. What are the two overhead rates? Which overhead rate system is better—one rate or two?

5-19 PLANTWIDE OVERHEAD RATE VERSUS DEPARTMENTAL RATES, EFFECTS ON PRICING DECISIONS

LO5 Cherise Ortega, marketing manager for Romer Company, was puzzled by the outcome of two recent bids. The company's policy was to bid 150 percent of the full manufacturing cost. One job (labeled Job 97-28) had been turned down by a prospective customer, who had indicated that the proposed price was $3 per unit higher than the winning bid. A second job (Job 97-35) had been accepted by a customer, who was amazed that Romer could offer such favorable terms. This customer revealed that Romer's price was $43 per unit lower than the next lowest bid.

Cherise has been informed that the company was more than competitive in terms of cost control. Accordingly, she began to suspect that the problem was related to cost assignment procedures. Upon investigating, Cherise was told that the company uses a plantwide overhead rate based on direct labor hours. The rate is computed at the beginning of the year using budgeted data. Selected budgeted data are as follows:

	Department A	Department B	Total
Overhead	$500,000	$2,000,000	$2,500,000
Direct labor hours	200,000	50,000	250,000
Machine hours	20,000	120,000	140,000

Cherise also discovered that the overhead costs in department B were higher than those in department A because B has more equipment, higher maintenance, higher power consumption, higher depreciation, and higher setup costs. In addition to the general procedures for assigning overhead costs, Cherise was supplied with the following specific manufacturing data on Jobs 97-28 and 97-35:

Job 97-28

	Department A	Department B	Total
Direct labor hours	5,000	1,000	6,000
Machine hours	200	500	700
Prime costs	$100,000	$20,000	$120,000
Units produced	14,400	14,400	14,400

Job 97-35

	Department A	Department B	Total
Direct labor hours	400	600	1,000
Machine hours	200	3,000	3,200
Prime costs	$10,000	$40,000	$50,000
Units produced	1,500	1,500	1,500

Required:

1. Using a plantwide overhead rate based on direct labor hours, develop the bid prices for Jobs 97-28 and 97-35 (express the bid prices on a per-unit basis).
2. Using departmental overhead rates (use direct labor hours for department A and machine hours for department B), develop per-unit bid prices for Jobs 97-28 and 97-35.

3. Compute the difference in gross profit that would have been earned had the company used departmental rates in its bids instead of the plantwide rate.
4. Explain why the use of departmental rates in this case provides a more accurate product cost.

5-20   APPENDIX: COST OF SPOILED UNITS

LO6   Garvey Company is a specialty print shop. Usually, printing jobs are priced at standard cost plus 50 percent. Job 95-301 involved printing 500 wedding invitations with the following standard costs:

Direct materials	$200
Direct labor	20
Overhead	30
Total	$250

Normally, the invitations would be taken from the machine, the top one inspected for correct wording, spelling, and quality of print, and all of the invitations wrapped in plastic and stored on shelves designated for completed jobs. In this case, however, the technician decided to go to lunch before inspecting and wrapping the job. He stacked the unwrapped invitations beside the printing press and left. One hour later, he returned and found the invitations had fallen on the floor and been stepped on. It turned out that about 100 invitations were ruined and had to be discarded. An additional 100 invitations were then printed to complete the job.

Required:

1. Calculate the cost of the spoiled invitations. How should the spoilage cost be accounted for?
2. What is the price of Job 95-301?
3. Suppose that another job, 95-442, also required 500 wedding invitations. The standard costs are identical to those of Job 95-301. However, Job 95-442 required an unusual color of ink which could only be obtained in a formula which was difficult to use. Garvey printers know from experience that getting this ink color to print correctly requires trial and error. In the case of Job 95-442, the first 100 invitations had to be discarded due to inconsistencies in the color of ink. What is the cost of the spoilage, and how would it be treated?
4. What is the price of Job 95-442?

5-21   APPENDIX: COST OF REWORKED UNITS

LO6   Jackson's Sporting Goods Store sells a variety of sporting goods and clothing. In a back room, Jackson's has set up heat-transfer equipment to personalize T-shirts for Little League teams. Typically, each team has the name of the individual player put on the back of the T-shirt. Last week, Taffy Barnhart, coach of the Stingers, brought in a list of names for her team. Her team consisted of 12 players with the following names: Freda, Cara, Katie, Tara, Heather, Sarah, Kim, Jennifer, Mary Beth, Elizabeth, Kyle, and Wendy. Taffy was quoted a price of $0.50 per letter.

Chip Russell, Jackson's newest employee, was assigned to Taffy's job. He selected the appropriate letters, arranged the letters in each name carefully on a shirt, and heat-pressed them on. When Taffy returned, she was appalled to see that the names were on the front of the shirts. Jim Jackson, owner of the sporting goods store, assured Taffy that the letters could easily be removed by applying more heat and lifting them off. This process ruins the old letters, so new letters must then be placed correctly on the shirt backs. He promised to correct the job immediately and have it ready in an hour and a half.

Costs for heat-transferring are as follows:

Letters (each)	$0.15
Direct labor (per hour)	8.00
Overhead (per direct labor hour)	4.00

Taffy's job originally took one hour of direct labor time. The removal process goes more quickly and should take only 15 minutes.

Required:

1. What was the original cost of Taffy's job?
2. What is the cost of rework on Taffy's job? How should the rework cost be treated?
3. How much did Jim Jackson charge Taffy?

5-22   JOB-ORDER COSTING, HOUSING

LO3, LO4   Sutton Construction, Inc., is a privately held, family-founded corporation that builds single- and multiple-unit housing. Most projects Sutton Construction undertakes involve the construction of multiple units. Sutton Construction has adopted a job-order costing system for determining the cost of each unit. The costing system is fully computerized. Each project's costs are divided into the following five categories:

1. *General conditions*, including construction site utilities, project insurance permits and licenses, architect's fees, decorating, field office salaries, and cleanup costs.
2. *Hard costs*, such as subcontractors, direct materials, and direct labor.
3. *Finance costs*, including title and recording fees, inspection fees, and taxes and discounts on mortgages.
4. *Land costs*, which refer to the purchase price of the construction site.
5. *Marketing costs*, such as advertising, sales commissions, and appraisal fees.

Recently, Sutton Construction purchased land for the purpose of developing 20 new single-family houses. The cost of the land was $250,000. Lot sizes vary from 1/4 to 1/2 acre. The 20 lots occupy a total of eight acres.

General conditions costs for the project totaled $120,000. This $120,000 is common to all 20 units that were constructed on the building site.

Job 3, the third house built in the project, occupied a 1/4-acre lot and had the following hard costs:

Direct materials	$ 8,000
Direct labor	6,000
Subcontractor	14,000

For Job 3, finance costs totaled $4,765 and marketing costs, $800. General conditions costs are allocated on the basis of units produced. Each unit's selling price is determined by adding 40 percent to the total of all costs.

Required:

1. Identify all production costs that are directly traceable to Job 3. Are all remaining production costs equivalent to overhead found in a manufacturing firm? Are there nonproduction costs that are directly traceable to the housing unit? Which ones?

2. Develop a job-order cost sheet for Job 3. What is the cost of building this house? Did you include finance and marketing costs in computing the unit cost? Why or why not? How did you determine the cost of land for Job 3?
3. Which of the five cost categories corresponds to overhead? Do you agree with the way in which this cost is allocated to individual housing units? Can you suggest a different allocation method?
4. Calculate the selling price of Job 3. Calculate the profit made on the sale of this unit.

5-23 CASE ON JOB-ORDER COSTING: DENTAL PRACTICE

LO3, LO4 Dr. Sherry Bird is employed by Dental Associates. Dental Associates recently installed a computerized job-order costing system to help monitor the cost of its services. Each patient is treated as a job and assigned a job number when he or she checks in with the receptionist. The receptionist-bookkeeper notes the time the patient enters the treatment area and when the patient leaves the area. This difference between the entry and exit times is the number of patient hours used and the direct labor time assigned to the dental assistant. (A dental assistant is constantly with the patient.) The direct labor time assigned to the dentist is 50 percent of the patient hours. (The dentist typically splits her time between two patients.)

The chart filled out by the dental assistant provides additional data that are entered into the computer. For example, the chart contains service codes that identify the nature of the treatment, such as whether the patient received a crown, a filling, or a root canal. The chart not only identifies the type of service but its level as well. For example, if a patient receives a filling, the dental assistant indicates (by a service-level code) whether the filling was one, two, three, or four surfaces. The service and service-level codes are used to determine the rate to be charged to the patient. The costs of providing different services and their levels also vary.

Costs assignable to a patient consist of materials, labor, and overhead. The types of materials used—and the quantity—are identified by the assistant and entered into the computer by the bookkeeper. Material prices are kept on file and accessed to provide the necessary cost information. Overhead is applied on the basis of patient hours. The rate used by Dental Associates is $20 per patient hour. Direct labor cost is also computed using patient hours and the wage rates of the direct laborers. Dr. Bird is paid an average of $36 per hour for her services. Dental assistants are paid an average of $6 per hour. Given the treatment time, the software program calculates and assigns the labor cost for the dentist and her assistant; overhead cost is also assigned using the treatment time and the overhead rate.

The overhead rate does not include a charge for any X-rays. The X-ray department is separate from dental services; X-rays are billed and costed separately. The cost of an X-ray is $3.50 per film; the patient is charged $5 per film. If cleaning services are required, cleaning labor costs $9 per patient hour.

Glen Johnson, a patient (Job 267), spent 30 minutes in the treatment area and had a 2-surface filling. He received two Novocain shots and used three ampules of amalgam. The cost of the shots was $1. The cost of the amalgam was $3. Other direct materials used are insignificant in amount and are included in the overhead rate. The rate charged to the patient for a 2-surface filling is $45. One X-ray was taken.

Required:

1. Prepare a job-order cost sheet for Glen Johnson. What is the cost for providing a 2-surface filling? What is the gross profit earned? Is the X-ray a direct cost of the service? Why are the X-rays costed separately from the overhead cost assignment?
2. Suppose that the patient time and associated patient charges are given for the following fillings:

	1-Surface	2-Surface	3-Surface	4-Surface
Time	20 minutes	30 minutes	40 minutes	50 minutes
Charge	$35	$45	$55	$65

Compute the cost for each filling and the gross profit for each type of filling. Assume that the cost of Novocain is $1 for all fillings. Ampules of amalgam start at two and increase by one for each additional surface. Assume also that only one X-ray film is needed for all four cases. Does the increase in billing rate appear to be fair to the patient? Is it fair to the dental corporation?

5-24 CASE ON JOB-ORDER COSTING AND PRICING DECISIONS

LO3, LO4 Nutratask, Inc., is a pharmaceutical manufacturer of amino-acid-chelated minerals and vitamin supplements. The company was founded in 1974 and is capable of performing all manufacturing functions, including packaging and laboratory functions. Currently, the company markets its products in the United States, Canada, Australia, Japan, and Belgium.

Mineral chelation enhances the mineral's availability to the body, making the mineral a more effective supplement. Most of the chelates supplied by Nutratask are in powder form, but the company has the capability to make tablets or capsules.

The production of all chelates follows a similar pattern. Upon receiving an order, the company's chemist prepares a load sheet (a bill of materials that specifies the product, the theoretical yield, and the quantities of materials that should be used). Once the load sheet is received by production, the materials are requisitioned and sent to the blending room. The chemicals and minerals are added in the order specified and blended together for two to eight hours, depending on the product. After blending, the mix is put on long trays and sent to the drying room, where it is allowed to dry until the moisture content is 7 to 9 percent. Drying time for most products is from one to three days.

After the product is dry, several small samples are taken and sent to a laboratory to be checked for bacterial level and to determine whether the product meets customer specifications. If the product is not fit for human consumption or if it fails to meet customer specifications, additional materials are added under the direction of the chemist to bring the product up to standard. Once the product passes inspection, it is ground into a powder of different meshes (particle sizes) according to customer specifications. The powder is then placed in heavy cardboard drums and shipped to the customer (or, if requested, put in tablet or capsule form and then shipped).

Since each order is customized to meet the special needs of its customers, Nutratask uses a job-order costing system. Recently, Nutratask received a request for a 300-kilogram order of potassium aspartate. The customer offered to pay $8.80 per kilogram. Upon receiving the request and the customer's specifications, Lanny Smith, the marketing manager, requested a load sheet from the company's chemist. The load sheet prepared showed the following material requirements:

Material	Amount Required
Aspartic acid	195.00 kg
Citric acid	15.00
K_2CO_3 (50%)	121.50
Rice	30.00

The theoretical yield is 300 kg.

Lanny also reviewed past jobs that were similar to the requested order and discovered that the expected direct labor time was 16 hours. The production workers at Nutratask earn an average of $6.50 per hour plus $6 per hour for taxes, insurance, and additional benefits.

Purchasing sent Lanny a list of prices for the materials needed for the job.

	Material Price per Kilogram
Aspartic acid	$5.75
Citric acid	2.02
K_2CO_3	4.64
Rice	0.43

Overhead is applied using a companywide rate based on direct labor dollars. The rate for the current period is 110 percent of direct labor dollars.

Whenever a customer requests a bid, Nutratask usually estimates the manufacturing costs of the job and then adds a markup of 30 percent. This markup varies depending on the competition and general economic conditions. Currently, the industry is thriving, and Nutratask is operating at capacity.

Required:

1. Prepare a job-order cost sheet for the proposed job. What is the expected per-unit cost? Should Nutratask accept the price offered by the prospective customer? Why or why not?
2. Suppose Nutratask and the prospective customer agree on a price of cost plus 30 percent. What is the gross profit that Nutratask expects to earn on the job?
3. Suppose that the actual costs of producing 300 kg of potassium aspartate were as follows:

Direct materials:	
Aspartic acid	$1,170.00
Citric acid	30.00
K_2CO_3	577.00
Rice	13.00
Total materials cost	$1,790.00
Direct labor	$ 225.00
Overhead	247.50

What is the actual per-unit cost? The bid price is based on expected costs. How much did Nutratask gain (or lose) because of the actual costs differing from the expected costs? Suggest some possible reasons why the actual costs differed from the projected costs.

4. Assume that the customer had agreed to pay *actual* manufacturing costs plus 30 percent. Suppose the actual costs are as described in Requirement 3 with one addition: an underapplied overhead variance is allocated to Cost of Goods Sold and spread across all jobs sold in proportion to their total cost (unadjusted cost of goods sold). Assume that the underapplied overhead cost added to the job in question is $30. Upon seeing the addition of the underapplied overhead in the itemized bill, the customer calls and complains about having to pay for Nutratask's inefficient use of overhead costs. If you were assigned to deal with this customer, what kind of response would you prepare? How would you explain and justify the addition of the underapplied overhead cost to the customer's bill?

5-25 RESEARCH ASSIGNMENT

LO1, LO2, LO3   Interview an accountant who works for a service organization that uses job-order costing. For a small firm, you may need to talk to an owner/manager. Examples are a funeral home, insurance firm, repair shop, medical clinic, and dental clinic. Write a paper that describes the job-order costing system used by the firm. Some of the questions that the paper should address are:

a. What service(s) does the firm offer?
b. What document or procedure do you use to collect the costs of the services performed for each customer?
c. How do you assign the cost of direct labor to each job?
d. How do you assign overhead to individual jobs?
e. How do you assign the cost of direct materials to each job?
f. How do you determine what to charge each customer?
g. How do you account for a completed job?

As you write the paper, state how the service firm you investigated adapted the job-order accounting procedures described in this chapter to its particular circumstances. Were the differences justified? If so, explain why. Also, offer any suggestions you might have for improving the approach that you observed.

5-26   COLLABORATIVE LEARNING EXERCISE

**LO1, LO2,
LO3**

Use "think-pair-share" to work on this exercise. First, read the following exercise. Then, take one to two minutes to think of your answers. Pair with another student to discuss your answers. Finally, be prepared to share your responses with the rest of the class.

Name a product and a service you have purchased that you believe was accounted for using job-order costing. Explain why you think so. Then, think how that product and service can be transformed such that process costing would be appropriate.

5-27   CYBER RESEARCH CASE

Hospitals, clinics, and doctors' offices use a job-order costing system. This has led to extensive paperwork involving patients' records, billings, and insurance company reimbursements. A number of medical offices are exploring the possibility of paperless offices. For example, Kaiser Permanente, Hawaii's largest HMO, began its move to paperless records in 2004. (See Kristen Sawada, "Kaiser Prepares Switch to Paperless Medical Records," *Pacific Business News*, March 19, 2004, http://www.bizjournals.com/pacific/stories/2004/03/22/focus3.html?jst=s_rs_hl.) Discuss the problems that are driving medical offices to electronic record keeping, and the systems that have been developed to serve this field. Use the Internet to find firms that have developed software to improve productivity and efficiency in medical environments. What problems remain to be solved?

CHAPTER 6

Product and Service Costing: A Process Systems Approach

AFTER STUDYING THIS CHAPTER, YOU SHOULD BE ABLE TO:

1. Describe the basic characteristics of process costing, including cost flows, journal entries, and the cost of production report.

2. Describe process costing for settings without work-in-process inventories.

3. Define *equivalent units*, and explain their role in process costing.

4. Prepare a departmental production report using the FIFO method.

5. Prepare a departmental production report using the weighted average method.

6. Prepare a departmental production report with transferred-in goods and changes in output measures.

7. Describe the basic features of operation costing.

8. Explain how spoilage is treated in a process-costing system.

Process-Costing Systems: Basic Operational and Cost Concepts

To understand a process-costing system, it is necessary to understand the underlying operational system. An operational process system is characterized by a large number of homogeneous products passing through a series of *processes*, where each process is responsible for one or more operations that bring a product one step closer to completion. Thus, a **process** is a series of activities (operations) that are linked to perform

OBJECTIVE 1

Describe the basic characteristics of process costing, including cost flows, journal entries, and the cost of production report.

a specific objective. For example, Estrella Company, a manufacturer of a widely used pain medication has three processes: mixing, tableting, and bottling. Consider the mixing process. The mixing process consists of four linked activities: selecting, sifting, measuring, and blending. Direct laborers select the appropriate chemicals (active and inert ingredients), sift the materials to remove any foreign substances, and then the materials are *measured* and *combined* in a mixer to blend them thoroughly in the prescribed proportions.

In each process, materials, labor, and overhead inputs may be needed (typically in equal amounts for each unit of product). Upon completion of a particular process, the partially completed goods are transferred to another process. For example, when the mix prepared by the mixing department is finished, the resulting mixture is sent to the tableting process. The tableting process consists of three linked activities: loading, pressing, and coating. Initially, the blend is loaded into a machine and a binding agent is added, next the mixture is pressed into a tablet shape, and finally each tablet is coated to make swallowing easier. The final process is bottling. It has four linked activities: loading, counting, capping, and packing. Tablets are transferred to this department, loaded into a hopper, and automatically counted into bottles. Filled bottles are mechanically capped, and direct labor then manually packs the correct number of bottles into boxes that are transferred to the warehouse. Exhibit 6-1 summarizes the operational process system for the pain medication manufacturer.

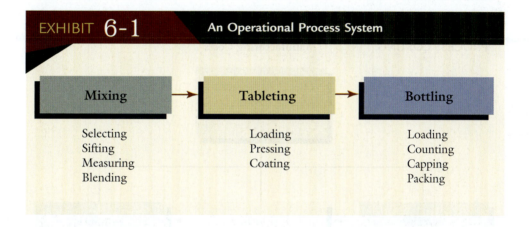

EXHIBIT 6-1   An Operational Process System

Mixing	Tableting	Bottling
Selecting	Loading	Loading
Sifting	Pressing	Counting
Measuring	Coating	Capping
Blending		Packing

Cost Flows

The cost flows for a process-costing system are basically similar to those of a job-order costing system. There are two key differences. First, a job-order costing system accumulates production costs by job, and a process-costing system accumulates production costs by process. Second, for manufacturing firms, the job-order costing system uses a single work-in-process account, while the process-costing system has a work-in-process account for every process. Exhibit 6-2, on the following page, illustrates the first key difference: the different approaches to cost accumulation. Notice that job systems assign manufacturing costs to jobs (which act as subsidiary work-in-process accounts) and transfer these costs directly to the finished goods account when the job is completed. When units are finished for a process, manufacturing costs are transferred from one process department's account to the next. The last process transfers the costs to Finished Goods. Exhibit 6-3, on page 229, highlights the cost flow differences involving work-in-process accounts.

Exhibit 6-3 not only illustrates the use of multiple work-in-process accounts, but it also reveals some important concepts concerning the nature of process costing. Consider, for example, the journal entries for the tableting department.

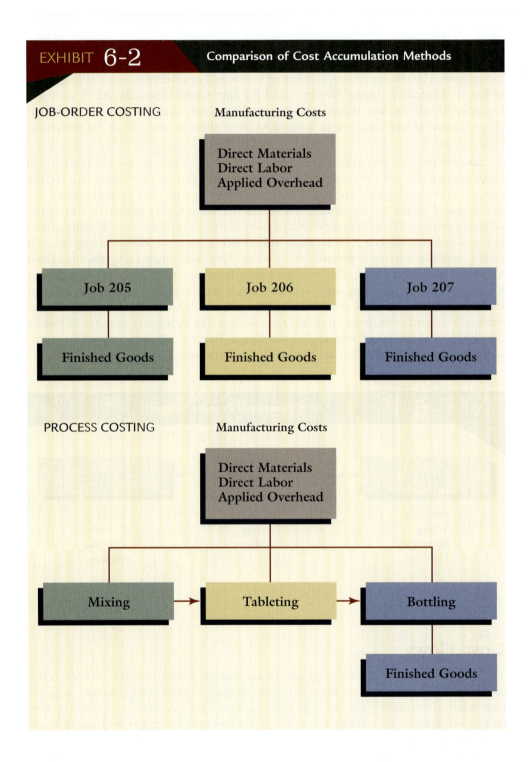

EXHIBIT **6-2**   **Comparison of Cost Accumulation Methods**

1. Work in Process—Tableting	600	
Work in Process—Mixing		600
To transfer goods to tableting.		

2. Work in Process—Tableting	400	
Materials		100
Payroll		125
Overhead Control		175
To record additional manufacturing costs.		

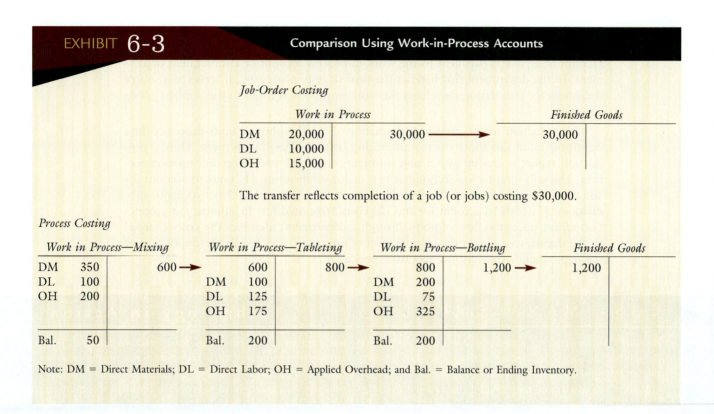

EXHIBIT 6-3   Comparison Using Work-in-Process Accounts

Job-Order Costing

Work in Process				Finished Goods	
DM	20,000	30,000 →		30,000	
DL	10,000				
OH	15,000				

The transfer reflects completion of a job (or jobs) costing $30,000.

Process Costing

Work in Process—Mixing			Work in Process—Tableting			Work in Process—Bottling			Finished Goods	
DM	350	600 →		600	800 →		800	1,200 →	1,200	
DL	100		DM	100		DM	200			
OH	200		DL	125		DL	75			
			OH	175		OH	325			
Bal.	50		Bal.	200		Bal.	200			

Note: DM = Direct Materials; DL = Direct Labor; OH = Applied Overhead; and Bal. = Balance or Ending Inventory.

3. Work in Process—Bottling	800	
Work in Process—Tableting		800
To transfer goods to bottling.		

When goods are completed in one process, they are transferred with their costs to the subsequent process. For example, mixing transferred $600 of its costs to tableting, and tableting (after further processing) transferred $800 of costs to bottling. A cost transferred from a prior process to a subsequent process is referred to as a **transferred-in cost**. These transferred-in costs are (from the viewpoint of the process receiving them) a type of direct materials cost. This is true because the subsequent process receives a partially completed unit that must be subjected to additional manufacturing activity, which includes more direct labor, more overhead, and, in some cases, additional direct materials. For example, the second journal entry for the tableting department reveals that $400 of additional manufacturing costs were added after receiving the transferred-in goods from mixing. Thus, while mixing sees the active and inert powders as a combination of direct materials, direct labor, and overhead costs, tableting sees only the powder—a direct material, costing $600.

Although a process-costing system has more work-in-process accounts than a job-order costing system, it is a simpler and less expensive system to operate. In a process-costing system, there are no individual jobs, no job-order cost sheets, and no need to track materials to individual jobs. Materials are tracked to processes, but there are far fewer processes than jobs. Further, there is no need to use time tickets for assigning labor costs to processes. Since laborers typically work their entire shift within a particular process, no detailed tracking of labor is needed. In fact, in many firms, labor costs are such a small percentage of total process costs that they are simply combined with overhead costs, creating a conversion cost category.

The Production Report

In process-costing systems, costs are accumulated by department for a period of time. The **production report** is the document that summarizes the manufacturing activity that takes place in a process department for a given period of time. The production report also serves as a source document for transferring costs from the work-in-process account of a prior department to the work-in-process account of a subsequent department. In the department that handles the final stage of processing, it serves as a source document for transferring costs from the work-in-process account to the finished goods account.

A production report provides information about the physical units processed in a department and also about the manufacturing costs associated with them. Thus, a production report is divided into a unit information section and a cost information section. The unit information section has two major subdivisions: (1) units to account for and (2) units accounted for. Similarly, the cost information section has two major subdivisions: (1) costs to account for and (2) costs accounted for. In summary, a production report traces the flow of units through a department, identifies the costs charged to the department, shows the computation of unit costs, and reveals the disposition of the department's costs for the reporting period.

COST MANAGEMENT   Technology in Action

Although process-costing systems have less data collection demands than job-order costing systems, they can be very demanding in terms of the calculations required. These calculations, the associated reports, and the detailed tracking of costs from process to process are facilitated by enterprise resource planning (ERP) software. **Fiat Auto Argentina** invested in ERP software to standardize its business processes and to allow access to integrated business information. Fiat implemented **Oracle** ERP software and experienced a 20 percent reduction in internal costs; productivity has improved, and processes have been modernized. Fiat reports that using an Oracle ERP system has produced a reduction in paper flow. Furthermore, an integrated database provides quick access to up-to-date business information critical for decision making.

ERP systems have the capability of linking processes, people, suppliers, and customers. The Oracle sytem has created a single point of contact for servicing its customers, improved relationships with suppliers, and has allowed Fiat to track distributor activities throughout Argentina.

Source: http://success.oracle.com/customers/profiles/PROFILE9033.HTM, accessed August 20, 2004.

Unit Costs

A key input to the cost of production report is unit costs. In principle, calculating unit costs in a process-costing system is very simple. First, measure the manufacturing costs for a process department for a given period of time. Second, measure the output of the process department for the same period of time. Finally, the unit cost for a process is computed by dividing the costs of the period by the output of the period. With the exception of the final process, the unit cost calculated is for a *partially completed unit*. The unit cost for the final process is the cost of the fully completed product. Exhibit 6-4 summarizes the basic features of a process-costing system.

While the basic features seem relatively simple, the actual details of process-costing systems are somewhat more complicated. A major source of difficulty is dealing with how costs and output of the period are defined when calculating the unit cost of each process. The presence of significant work-in-process inventories complicates the cost and output definitions needed for the unit cost calculation. For example, partially finished units in the beginning work-in-process inventory carry with them work and costs associated with a prior period. Yet, these units must be finished this period, and they will also have current-period costs and work associated with them. A fundamental question is how to deal with the prior-period costs and work. Another important and

> **EXHIBIT 6-4**   Basic Features of a Process-Costing System
>
> 1. Homogeneous units pass through a series of similar processes.
> 2. Each unit in each process receives a similar dose of manufacturing costs.
> 3. Manufacturing costs are accumulated by a process for a given period of time.
> 4. There is a work-in-process account for each process.
> 5. Manufacturing cost flows and the associated journal entries are generally similar to job-order costing.
> 6. The departmental production report is the key document for tracking manufacturing activity and costs.
> 7. Unit costs are computed by dividing the departmental costs of the period by the output of the period.

related complicating factor is nonuniform application of production costs, i.e., units half completed may not have half of each input needed. Much of our discussion of process-costing systems will deal with the approaches taken to deal with these complicating factors.

OBJECTIVE 2

Describe process costing for settings without work-in-process inventories.

Process Costing with No Work-in-Process Inventories

Perhaps it is best to begin with a discussion of process costing in settings where there are no work-in-process inventories. Seeing how process costing works without work-in-process inventories makes it easier to understand the procedures that are needed to deal with work-in-process inventories. Study of the no-inventory setting is also justified because many firms operate in such a setting.

Service Organizations

Services that are basically homogeneous and repetitively produced can take advantage of a process-costing approach. Processing tax returns, sorting mail by zip code, check processing in a bank, changing oil, air travel between Dallas and New York City, checking baggage, and laundering and pressing shirts are all examples of homogeneous services that are repetitively produced. Although many services consist of a single process, some services require a sequence of processes. Air travel between Dallas and New York City, for example, involves the following sequence of services: reservation, ticketing, baggage checking and seat confirmation, flight, and baggage delivery and pickup. Although services cannot be stored, it is possible for firms engaged in service production to have work-in-process inventories. For example, a batch of tax returns can be partially completed at the end of a period. However, many services are provided in such a way that there are no work-in-process inventories. Teeth cleaning, funerals, surgical operations, sonograms, and carpet cleaning are a few examples where work-in-process inventories would be virtually nonexistent.

To illustrate how services without work-in-process inventories are costed using a process-costing approach, consider the teeth-cleaning process offered by most dentists. This is a single process usually carried out in a room dedicated to the service, with a hygienist (direct labor), materials, and equipment. In this case, the service is labor and overhead intensive. The direct materials used in the process are a small percentage of the total service cost. The production costs and the number of cleanings (patients served) for the month of March are as follows:

Direct materials	$ 400
Hygienist's salary	3,500
Overhead	2,100
Total production cost	$6,000
Number of cleanings	300

Given the preceding data, the unit cost of the service can be computed as follows:

$$\text{Unit cost} = \text{Costs of the period/Output of the period}$$
$$= \$6{,}000/300 \text{ cleanings}$$
$$= \$20 \text{ per cleaning}$$

This calculation illustrates the **process-costing principle**: *To calculate the period's unit cost, divide the costs of the period by the output of the period.* Theoretically, the current-period unit cost should use only costs and output that belong to the period. This principle is a theoretical concept and applies in settings that are more complicated.

JIT Manufacturing Firms

Many firms have adopted a just-in-time (JIT) manufacturing approach.[1] The overall thrust of JIT manufacturing is supplying a product that is needed, when it is needed, and in the quantity that is needed. JIT manufacturing emphasizes continuous improvement and the elimination of waste. Since carrying unnecessary inventory is viewed as wasteful, JIT firms strive to minimize inventories. *Successful* implementation of JIT policies tends to reduce work-in-process inventories to insignificant levels. Furthermore, the way manufacturing is carried out in a JIT firm usually is structured so that process costing can be used to determine product costs. Essentially, work cells are created that produce a product or subassembly from start to finish.

Costs are collected by cell for a period of time, and output for the cell is measured for the same period. Unit costs are computed by dividing the costs of the period by output of the period (following the process-costing principle). The computation is identical to that used by service organizations, as illustrated by the teeth-cleaning example. Why? Because there is no ambiguity concerning what costs belong to the period and how output is measured. One of the objectives of JIT manufacturing is simplification. Keep this in mind as you study the process-costing requirements of manufacturing firms that carry work-in-process inventories. The difference between the two settings is impressive and demonstrates one of the significant benefits of JIT.

The Role of Activity-Based Costing

Activity-based costing can have a role in process settings provided multiple products are being produced. The role of ABC for both cellular and independent process manufacturing is to assign overhead shared by processes or cells to the individual processes and cells. Since each process (cell) is dedicated to the production of a single product, the overhead located within the cell belongs exclusively to the product. However, activities may be shared by processes (cells) such as moving materials, inspecting output, ordering materials, etc. Activity rates are used to assign overhead to individual processes, and this overhead is assigned to process ouput using the usual approaches.

---

1. JIT manufacturing and its implications for cost accounting and control are discussed in detail in Chapters 11 and 21.

Define *equivalent units*, and explain their role in process costing.

Process Costing with Ending Work-in-Process Inventories

The unit cost is needed both to compute the cost of goods transferred out of a process department and to value ending work-in-process inventories. Work-in-process inventories affect the unit cost computation by affecting the way output of the period is measured. For example, consider a medical laboratory (a service organization) that serves a metropolitan area and several of its outlying communities. The laboratory has several departments, one of which specializes in PSA tests for urologists. Urologists in the region send blood samples to the laboratory. The PSA department runs the test and inputs the resulting data into the computer so that a statistical analysis of the PSA level can be conducted. The PSA levels are also tracked over time for patients who follow a regimen of annual examinations. Printouts are sent to urologists so that they can be placed in the patients' records. During the month of January, 20,000 tests were run and analyzed, and printouts were sent to the referring urologists. These "units" were finished and transferred out by mailing the results of the tests to the urologists. Because of the holiday season, the PSA department rarely has any work in process at the beginning of January. However, at the end of January, there were units (blood samples) that were worked on but not finished, producing an ending work-in-process inventory. By definition, ending work in process is not complete. Thus, a unit completed and transferred out during the period is not identical (or equivalent) to one in ending work-in-process inventory, and the cost attached to the two units should not be the same. In computing the unit cost, the output of the period must be defined. A major problem of process costing is determining this definition.

Equivalent Units as Output Measures

To illustrate the output problem created by work-in-process inventories, assume that the PSA department had the following data for January (output is measured in number of tests):

Units, beginning work in process	—
Units started	24,000
Units completed	20,000
Units, ending work in process (25% complete)	4,000
Total production costs	$168,000

What is the output in January for this department? 20,000 units? 24,000 units? If we say 20,000 units, then we ignore the effort expended on the units in ending work in process. Furthermore, the production costs incurred in January belong to both the units completed and to the partially completed units in ending work in process. On the other hand, if we say 24,000 units, we ignore the fact that the 4,000 units in ending work in process are only partially completed. Somehow, output must be measured so that it reflects the effort expended on both completed and partially completed units.

The solution is to calculate equivalent units of output. **Equivalent units of output** are the complete units that could have been produced given the total amount of productive effort expended for the period under consideration. Determining equivalent units of output for transferred-out units is easy; a unit would not be transferred out unless it were complete. Thus, every transferred-out unit is an equivalent unit. Units remaining in ending work-in-process inventory, however, are not complete. Someone in production must "eyeball" ending work in process to estimate its degree of completion. In the example, the 4,000 units in ending work in process are 25 percent complete with respect to all production costs; this is equivalent to 1,000 fully completed units (4,000 × 25%). Therefore, the equivalent units for January would be the 20,000 completed units plus 1,000 equivalent units in ending work in process, a total of 21,000 units of output.

Cost of Production Report Illustrated

Recall that the cost of production report has a unit information section and a cost information section. The unit information section is concerned with output measurement, and the cost information section is concerned with unit cost computation and cost assignment and reconciliation. The unit information section has two major subdivisions: (1) units to account for and (2) units accounted for. Similarly, the cost information section has two major subdivisions: (1) costs to account for and (2) costs accounted for. A cost of production report for the PSA department example is illustrated in Exhibit 6-5.

EXHIBIT 6-5 **PSA Department Production Report for January**

Unit Information

Units to account for:

Units in beginning work in process	0
Units started	24,000
Total units to account for	24,000

	Physical Flow	Equivalent Units
Units accounted for:		
Units completed	20,000	20,000
Units in ending work in process		
(25% complete)	4,000	1,000
Units accounted for	24,000	
Work completed		21,000

Cost Information

Costs to account for:	
Beginning work in process	$ 0
Incurred during the period	168,000
Total costs to account for	$168,000
Divided by equivalent units	÷ 21,000
Cost per equivalent unit	$ 8
Costs accounted for:	
Goods transferred out ($8 × 20,000)	$160,000
Ending work in process ($8 × 1,000)	8,000
Total costs accounted for	$168,000

The computations in Exhibit 6-5 illustrate several important points. Knowing the output for a period (equivalent work completed of 21,000 units) and the production costs for the department for that period ($168,000 in this example), we can calculate a unit cost, which in this case is $8 per unit ($168,000/21,000). The unit cost is used to assign a cost of $160,000 ($8 × 20,000) to the 20,000 units transferred out and a cost of $8,000 ($8 × 1,000) to the 4,000 units in ending work in process. This unit cost is $8 per *equivalent* unit. Thus, when valuing ending work in process, the $8 unit cost is multiplied by the equivalent units, not the actual number of physical units in process.

Five steps must be followed in preparing a cost of production report:
1. Analysis of the flow of physical units
2. Calculation of equivalent units
3. Computation of unit cost
4. Valuation of inventories (goods transferred out and ending work in process)
5. Cost reconciliation

Knowing the physical units in beginning and ending work in process, their stage of completion, and the units completed and transferred out (step 1) provides essential information for the computation of equivalent units (step 2). This computation, in turn, is a prerequisite to computing the unit cost (step 3). Unit cost information and information from the equivalent units schedule are both needed to value goods transferred out and goods in ending work in process (step 4). Finally, the costs in beginning work in process and the costs incurred during the current period should equal the total costs assigned to goods transferred out and to goods in ending work in process (step 5). Step 5 (**cost reconciliation**), of course, is simply a check on the accuracy of the report itself.

Nonuniform Application of Productive Inputs

Up to this point, we have assumed that work in process being 25 percent complete meant that 25 percent of direct materials, direct labor, and overhead needed to complete the process have been used and that another 75 percent are needed to finish the units. In other words, we have assumed that the productive inputs are applied uniformly as the manufacturing process unfolds.

Assuming uniform application of conversion costs (direct labor and overhead) is not unreasonable. Direct labor input is usually needed throughout the process, and overhead is normally assigned on the basis of direct labor hours. Direct materials, on the other hand, are not as likely to be applied uniformly. In many instances, direct materials are added at either the beginning or the end of the process.

For example, consider the PSA department in Exhibit 6-5. It is more likely that materials (e.g., special chemicals) would be added at the beginning of the process rather than uniformly throughout the process. If so, then ending work in process that is 25 percent complete with respect to conversion inputs would be 100 percent complete with respect to material inputs.

Different percentage completion figures for productive inputs at the same stage of completion pose a problem for the calculation of equivalent units. Fortunately, the solution is relatively simple. Equivalent units calculations are done for each category of input. Thus, there are equivalent units calculated for *each* category of direct materials and for conversion costs. For the PSA department, if direct materials are added at the beginning of the process, equivalent units of work for each category would be calculated as follows:

	Direct Materials	Conversion Costs
Units completed	20,000	20,000
Units, ending work in process:		
4,000 × 100%	4,000	
4,000 × 25%		1,000
Equivalent units of output	24,000	21,000

Of course, having separate categories of equivalent units requires that the costs of each category be measured separately. Unit costs are then calculated for each input category, and the total unit cost is the sum of the individual category unit costs. For example, the following cost breakdown would produce the indicated unit costs:

	Direct Materials	*Conversion*	*Total*
Total cost	$126,000	$42,000	$168,000
Equivalent units	24,000	21,000	—
Unit cost	$5.25	$2.00	$7.25

Beginning Work-in-Process Inventories

The PSA department example only showed the effect of ending work-in-process inventories on output measurement. The presence of beginning work-in-process inventories also complicates output measurement. Since many firms have partially completed units in process at the beginning of a period, there is a clear need to address the issue. The work done on these partially completed units represents prior-period work, and the costs assigned to them are prior-period costs. In computing a *current-period* unit cost for a department, two approaches have evolved for dealing with the prior-period output and prior-period costs found in beginning work in process: the *first-in, first-out (FIFO) costing method* and the *weighted average method*. Both methods follow the same five steps described for preparing a cost of production report. However, the two methods usually only produce the same result for step 1. The two methods are best illustrated by example. The FIFO method is discussed first, followed by a discussion of the weighted average method.

FIFO Costing Method

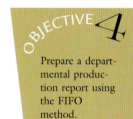

The process-costing principle requires that the costs of the period be divided by the output of the period. Thus, theoretically, only *current*-period costs and *current*-period output should be used to compute *current*-period unit costs. The FIFO method attempts to follow this theoretical guideline. Under the **FIFO costing method**, the equivalent units and manufacturing costs in beginning work in process are *excluded* from the current-period unit cost calculation. Thus, the FIFO method recognizes that the work and costs carried over from the prior period legitimately belong to that period.

Since FIFO excludes prior-period work and costs, we need to create two categories of completed units. FIFO assumes that units in beginning work in process are completed first, before any new units are started. Thus, one category of completed units is that of beginning work-in-process units. The second category is for those units started *and* completed during the current period.

These two categories of completed units are needed in the FIFO method so that each category can be costed correctly. For the units started and completed, the unit cost is obtained by dividing total current manufacturing costs by the current-period equivalent output. However, for the beginning work-in-process units, the total associated manufacturing costs are the sum of the prior-period costs plus the costs incurred in the current period to finish the units. Thus, the unit cost is this total cost divided by the units in beginning work in process.

To illustrate the FIFO method, let's return to Estrella Company, a company that mass produces a widely used pain medication (see discussion on pp. 227–229). Recall that this company uses three processes: mixing, tableting, and bottling. October's cost and production data for the mixing department are given in Exhibit 6-6. All materials are added at the beginning of the mixing process. Output is measured in ounces. Given the October data for Estrella, the five steps of the FIFO method can be illustrated.

EXHIBIT 6-6

EXHIBIT **6-6**	Estrella Company Mixing Department Production and Cost Data: October

Production:

Units in process, October 1, 70% complete*	10,000
Units completed and transferred out	60,000
Units in process, October 31, 40% complete*	20,000

Costs:

Work in process, October 1:

Direct materials	$ 1,000
Conversion costs	350
Total work in process	$ 1,350

Current costs:

Direct materials	$12,600
Conversion costs	3,050
Total current costs	$15,650

*With respect to conversion cost. Direct materials are 100 percent complete because they are added at the beginning of the process.

Step 1: Physical Flow Analysis

The purpose of step 1 is to trace the physical units of production. Physical units are *not* equivalent units; they are units that may be in any stage of completion. The data reveal that there are 80,000 physical units (ounces) to account for. In this example, 10,000 units are from beginning inventory. Another 70,000 units were started in October. Finally, 20,000 units remain in ending inventory, 40 percent complete. The analysis of physical flow of units is usually accomplished by preparing a **physical flow schedule** similar to the one shown in Exhibit 6-7.

To construct the schedule from the information given in the example, two calculations are needed. First, units started and completed in this period are obtained by subtracting the units in beginning work in process from the total units completed. Next,

EXHIBIT **6-7**	Physical Flow Schedule: Mixing Department

Units to account for:

Units, beginning work in process		10,000
Units started during October		70,000
Total units to account for		80,000

Units accounted for:

Units completed and transferred out:

Started and completed	50,000	
From beginning work in process	10,000	60,000
Units in ending work in process (40% complete)		20,000
Total units accounted for		80,000

the units started are obtained by adding the units started and completed to the units in ending work in process. Notice that the "total units to account for" must equal the "total units accounted for." The physical flow schedule in Exhibit 6-7 is important because it contains the information needed to calculate equivalent units (step 2).

Step 2: Calculation of Equivalent Units

Exhibit 6-8 illustrates the calculation of equivalent units under the FIFO method. Notice that the equivalent units in beginning work in process—work done in the prior period—are not counted as part of the total equivalent work (work means either adding direct materials or conversion activity). Only the equivalent work to be completed this period is counted. The equivalent work to be completed for the units from the prior period is computed by multiplying the number of units in beginning work in process by the percentage of work remaining. Since in this example the direct materials are added at the beginning of the process, no additional direct materials are needed. However, the units are only 70 percent complete with respect to conversion activity. Thus, 30 percent additional conversion activity is needed, which converts to 3,000 additional equivalent units of work (30% × 10,000).

EXHIBIT 6-8   **Equivalent Units of Production: FIFO Method**

	Direct Materials	Conversion Costs
Units started and completed.	50,000	50,000
Add: Units in beginning work in process × Percentage to complete:		
10,000 × 0% direct materials	—	
10,000 × 30% conversion costs.		3,000
Add: Units in ending work in process × Percentage complete:		
20,000 × 100% direct materials.	20,000	—
20,000 × 40% conversion costs.	—	8,000
Equivalent units of output	70,000	61,000

Step 3: Computation of Unit Cost

The computation of the unit cost relies only on current costs and current output. The calculation is as follows:

$$\text{Unit direct materials cost} = \$12,600/70,000 = \$0.18$$
$$\text{Unit conversion costs} = \$3,050/61,000 = \$0.05$$
$$\text{Unit cost} = \text{Unit direct materials cost} + \text{Unit conversion costs}$$
$$= \$0.18 + \$0.05$$
$$= \$0.23 \text{ per ounce}$$

Step 4: Valuation of Inventories

The FIFO method unit costs are used to value output that is related to the *current period*. There are three categories of current-period output: equivalent units in ending work in process, units started and completed, and the equivalent units of work necessary to *finish* the units in beginning work in process.

Since all equivalent units in ending work in process are current-period units (see Exhibit 6-8), the cost of ending work in process is computed as follows:

Cost of ending work in process:	
Direct materials ($0.18 × 20,000)	$3,600
Conversion costs ($0.05 × 8,000)	400
Total	$4,000

When it comes to valuing goods transferred out, two categories of completed units must be considered: those that were started and completed and those that were completed from beginning work in process. Of the 60,000 completed units, 50,000 are units started and completed in the current period, and 10,000 are units completed from beginning work in process (see Exhibit 6-7). The 50,000 units that were started and completed in the current period represent current output and are valued at $0.23 per unit. For these units, the use of the current-period unit cost is entirely appropriate. However, the cost of the 10,000 beginning work-in-process units that were transferred out is another matter. These units started the period with $1,350 of manufacturing costs already incurred (cost taken from Exhibit 6-6), 10,000 equivalent units of direct materials already added, and 7,000 equivalent units of conversion activity already completed. To these beginning costs, additional costs were needed to finish the units. As we saw in step 2, the effort expended to complete these units required an additional 3,000 equivalent units of conversion activity. These 3,000 equivalent units of conversion activity were produced this period at a cost of $0.05 per equivalent unit. Thus, the total cost of finishing the units in beginning work in process is $150 ($0.05 × 3,000). Adding this $150 to the $1,350 in cost carried over from the prior period gives a total manufacturing cost for these units of $1,500. The total cost of goods transferred out can be summarized as follows:

Units started and completed ($0.23 × 50,000)		$11,500
Units, beginning work in process:		
Prior-period costs	$1,350	
Costs to finish ($0.05 × 3,000)	150	1,500
Total		$13,000

Step 5: Cost Reconciliation

Manufacturing costs are reconciled as follows:

Costs to account for:		
Beginning work in process		$ 1,350
Incurred during the period:		
Direct materials	$12,600	
Conversion costs	3,050	15,650
Total costs to account for		$17,000
Costs accounted for:		
Goods transferred out:		
Units, beginning work in process		$ 1,500
Units started and completed		11,500
Goods in ending work in process		4,000
Total costs accounted for		$17,000

The cost of production report for the FIFO method is given in Exhibit 6-9.

EXHIBIT 6-9   Production Report: Mixing Department

Estrella Company
Mixing Department
Production Report for October
(FIFO Method)

Unit Information

Units to account for:		Units accounted for:	
Units, beginning work in process	10,000	Units completed	60,000
Units started	70,000	Units, ending work in process	20,000
Total units to account for	80,000	Total units accounted for	80,000

	Equivalent Units	
	Direct Materials	Conversion Costs
Units started and completed	50,000	50,000
Units, beginning work in process	—	3,000
Units, ending work in process	20,000	8,000
Equivalent units of output	70,000	61,000

Cost Information

Costs to account for:

	Direct Materials	Conversion Costs	Total
Beginning work in process	$ 1,000	$ 350	$ 1,350
Incurred during the period	12,600	3,050	15,650
Total costs to account for	$13,600	$ 3,400	$17,000

Cost per equivalent unit:

	Direct Materials	Conversion Costs	Total
Current costs	$12,600	$ 3,050	
Divided by equivalent units	÷70,000	÷61,000	
Cost per equivalent unit	$ 0.18	$ 0.05	$ 0.23

Costs accounted for:
Units transferred out:
Units, beginning work in process:

From prior period	$ 1,350	
From current period ($0.05 × 3,000)	150	
Units started and completed ($0.23 × 50,000)	11,500	$13,000

Ending work in process:

Direct materials (20,000 × $0.18)	$ 3,600	
Conversion costs (8,000 × $0.05)	400	4,000
Total costs accounted for		$17,000

Journal Entries

The journal entries associated with the mixing department's activities for October are as follows:

1. Work in Process—Mixing	12,600	
Materials		12,600
To record requisitions of materials for October.		
2. Work in Process—Mixing	3,050	
Conversion Cost Control		3,050
To record the application of overhead and the *incurrence of direct labor.*		
3. Work in Process—Tableting	13,000	
Work in Process—Mixing		13,000
To record the transfer of cost of goods completed *from mixing to tableting.*		

OBJECTIVE 5

Prepare a departmental production report using the weighted average method.

Weighted Average Costing Method

Excluding prior-period work and costs creates some bookkeeping and computational complexity that can be avoided if certain conditions are satisfied. Specifically, if the costs of production remain very stable from one period to the next, then it may be possible to use the weighted average method. This method does not track prior-period output and costs separately from current-period output and costs. The **weighted average costing method** picks up beginning inventory costs and the accompanying equivalent output and treats them as if they belong to the current period. Prior-period output and manufacturing costs found in beginning work in process are merged with the current-period output and manufacturing costs.

The merging of beginning inventory output and current-period output is accomplished by the way in which equivalent units are calculated. Under the weighted average method, equivalent units of output are computed by adding units completed to equivalent units in ending work in process. The equivalent units in beginning work in process are included in the computation. Thus, these units are counted as part of the current period's equivalent units of output.

The weighted average method merges prior-period costs with current-period costs by simply adding the manufacturing costs in beginning work in process to the manufacturing costs incurred during the current period. The total cost is treated as if it were the current period's total manufacturing cost.

The illustration of the weighted average method is based on the Estrella Company data found in Exhibit 6-6 on page 237. Using the same data highlights the differences between the two methods. The five steps for costing out production follow.

Step 1: Physical Flow Analysis

The purpose of step 1 is to trace the physical units of production. This is accomplished by preparing a physical flow schedule. This schedule, shown in Exhibit 6-10, is identical for both methods.

Step 2: Calculation of Equivalent Units

Given the information in the physical flow schedule, the weighted average equivalent units for October can be calculated. This calculation is shown in Exhibit 6-11.

Notice that October's output is measured as 80,000 units for direct materials and 68,000 units for conversion activity. The 10,000 equivalent units of direct materials (10,000 × 100%) found in beginning work in process are included in the 60,000 units

EXHIBIT 6-10	Physical Flow Schedule: Mixing Department

Units to account for:
Units, beginning work in process.		10,000
Units started during October		70,000
Total units to account for.		80,000

Units accounted for:
Units completed and transferred out:		
Started and completed	50,000	
From beginning work in process	10,000	60,000
Units, ending work in process (40% complete)		20,000
Total units accounted for		80,000

EXHIBIT 6-11	Equivalent Units of Production: Weighted Average Method

	Direct Materials	Conversion Costs
Units completed	60,000	60,000
Add: Units in ending work in process × Percentage complete:		
20,000 × 100%	20,000	—
20,000 × 40%	—	8,000
Equivalent units of output	80,000	68,000

completed. Similarly, the 7,000 equivalent units of conversion costs (70% × 10,000) found in beginning work in process are also included in the 60,000 units completed for the conversion category.[2] Thus, beginning inventory units are treated as if they were started and completed during the current period.

Step 3: Computation of Unit Cost

In addition to the period's equivalent units, the period's direct materials cost and conversion costs are needed to compute a unit cost. The weighted average method merges current manufacturing costs and the manufacturing costs associated with the units in beginning work in process. Thus, the total direct materials cost for October is defined as $13,600 ($1,000 + $12,600), and the total conversion costs are defined as $3,400 ($350 + $3,050).

When different categories of equivalent units exist, a unit cost for each category must be computed. The cost per completed unit is the sum of these individual unit costs. The computations are as follows:

---

2. You should note that if we subtract the 10,000 equivalent units of direct material from the 80,000 units computed by the weighted average method, we arrive at the 70,000 units computed by the FIFO method; similarly, if we subtract out the 7,000 equivalent units from the 68,000 conversion costs equivalent units computed by the weighted average method, we obtain the 61,000 units computed by the FIFO method. This illustrates the point that the weighted average method counts prior-period output in the measurement of output for the current period.

$$\text{Unit direct materials cost} = (\$1{,}000 + \$12{,}600)/80{,}000$$
$$= \$0.17$$
$$\text{Unit conversion costs} = (\$350 + \$3{,}050)/68{,}000$$
$$= \$0.05$$
$$\text{Total unit cost} = \text{Unit direct materials cost} + \text{Unit conversion costs}$$
$$= \$0.17 + \$0.05$$
$$= \$0.22 \text{ per completed unit}$$

Step 4: Valuation of Inventories

Valuation of goods transferred out (step 4) is accomplished by multiplying the unit cost by the goods completed.

$$\text{Cost of goods transferred out} = \$0.22 \times 60{,}000$$
$$= \$13{,}200$$

Costing out ending work in process is done by obtaining the cost of each manufacturing input and then adding these individual input costs. For our example, this requires adding the cost of the direct materials in ending work in process to the conversion costs in ending work in process.

The cost of direct materials is the unit direct materials costs multiplied by the direct materials equivalent units in ending work in process. Similarly, the total conversion costs in ending work in process is the unit conversion costs times the conversion costs equivalent units. Thus, the cost of ending work in process is calculated as follows:

Direct materials: $0.17 × 20,000	$3,400	
Conversion costs: $0.05 × 8,000	400	
Total cost	$3,800	

Step 5: Cost Reconciliation

The total manufacturing costs are accounted for as follows:

Costs to account for:	
Beginning work in process	$ 1,350
Incurred during the period	15,650
Total costs to account for	$17,000
Costs accounted for:	
Goods transferred out	$13,200
Ending work in process	3,800
Total costs accounted for	$17,000

Production Report

Steps 1 through 5 provide all of the information needed to prepare a production report for the mixing department for October. This report is given in Exhibit 6-12 on page 244. The journal entries for the weighted average method follow the same pattern shown for the FIFO method. Thus, there is no reason to repeat the entries.

FIFO Compared with Weighted Average

The FIFO and weighted average methods differ on two key dimensions: (1) how output is computed and (2) what costs are used for calculating the period's unit cost. The unit cost computation for the mixing department is as follows:

EXHIBIT 6-12   **Production Report: Mixing Department**

Estrella Company
Mixing Department
Production Report for October
(Weighted Average Method)

Unit Information

Units to account for:		Units accounted for:	
Units, beginning work in process	10,000	Units completed	60,000
Units started	70,000	Units, ending work in process	20,000
Total units to account for	80,000	Total units accounted for	80,000

	Equivalent Units	
	Direct Materials	*Conversion Costs*
Units completed	60,000	60,000
Units, ending work in process	20,000	8,000
Equivalent units of output	80,000	68,000

Cost Information

Costs to account for:

	Direct Materials	*Conversion Costs*	*Total*
Beginning work in process	$ 1,000	$ 350	$ 1,350
Incurred during the period	12,600	3,050	15,650
Total costs to account for	$13,600	$ 3,400	$17,000
Divided by equivalent units	÷80,000	÷68,000	
Cost per equivalent unit	$ 0.17	$ 0.05	$ 0.22

Costs accounted for:			
Units transferred out (60,000 × $0.22)			$13,200
Ending work in process:			
Direct materials (20,000 × $0.17)		$ 3,400	
Conversion costs (8,000 × $0.05)		400	3,800
Total costs accounted for			$17,000

	FIFO		Weighted Average	
	Direct Materials	*Conversion Costs*	*Direct Materials*	*Conversion Costs*
Costs	$12,600	$3,050	$13,600	$3,400
Output (units)	70,000	61,000	80,000	68,000
Unit cost	$0.18	$0.05	$0.17	$0.05

The two methods use different total costs and different measures of output. The FIFO method is the more theoretically appealing because it divides the cost of the period by the output of the period. The weighted average method, however, merges costs in beginning work in process with current-period costs and merges the output found in beginning work in process with current-period output. This creates the possibility for errors—particularly if the weighted average method is used for settings where input costs are changing significantly from one period to the next.

In the mixing department example, the FIFO method unit cost and the weighted average method unit cost for conversion costs are the same; evidently, the cost of this input remained the same for the two periods being considered. The unit direct materials cost for the FIFO method, however, is $0.18 versus $0.17 for the weighted average method. Apparently, the cost of direct materials has increased, and merging the lower direct materials cost of the prior period with that of the current period creates a weighted average direct materials cost that underestimates the current-period direct materials cost. The resulting difference in the cost of a fully completed unit is only $0.01 ($0.23 − $0.22). On the surface, this seems harmless.

The difference in the costs reported under each method for goods transferred out and the ending work-in-process inventories is only $200 (see Exhibits 6-9 and 6-12). This is less than a 2 percent difference for goods transferred out and only about a 5 percent difference for ending work in process. The $0.01 unit cost difference does not appear to be material. Yet, if the final product is considered, even a $0.01 difference may be significant. Recall that Estrella passes the powder from the mixing department to the tableting department, where the powder is converted to caplets. Next, the caplets are sent to the bottling department where eight tablets are placed in small metal boxes. The output of the mixing department is measured in ounces. Suppose that four ounces of powder convert to eight tablets. The difference in the cost of the final product would be understated by $0.04—not $0.01. Using this unit cost information may produce erroneous decisions such as under- or overpricing. Furthermore, if the other two departments also use the weighted average method, the costs in those departments could also be understated. The cumulative effect could produce a significant distortion in cost for the final product—magnifying the effect.

A second disadvantage of weighted average costing should be mentioned as well. The weighted average method also combines the performance of the current period with that of a prior period. Often, it is desirable to exercise control by comparing the actual costs of the current period with the budgeted or standard costs for the period. The weighted average method makes this comparison suspect because the performance of the current period is not independent of the prior period.

The major benefit of the weighted average method is simplicity. By treating units in beginning work in process as belonging to the current period, all equivalent units belong to the same time period when it comes to calculating unit costs. As a consequence, the requirements for computing unit cost are greatly simplified. Yet, as has been discussed, accuracy and performance measurement are impaired. The FIFO method overcomes both of these disadvantages. It should be mentioned, however, that both methods are widely used. Perhaps we can conclude that there are many settings in which the distortions caused by the weighted average method are not serious enough to be of concern.

OBJECTIVE 6

Prepare a departmental production report with transferred-in goods and changes in output measures.

Treatment of Transferred-In Goods

In process manufacturing, some departments invariably receive partially completed goods from prior departments. For example, under the FIFO method, the transfer of goods from mixing to tableting is valued at $13,000. These transferred-in goods are a type of direct material for the subsequent process—materials that are added at the beginning of the subsequent process. The usual approach is to treat transferred-in goods as a separate material category when calculating equivalent units. Thus, we now have three categories of manufacturing inputs: transferred-in materials, direct materials added, and conversion costs. For the Estrella Company example, tableting receives transferred-in materials, a powdered mixture, from mixing; adds a binder and coating (direct materials); and uses labor and overhead to convert the powder into tablets.

In dealing with transferred-in goods, three important points should be remembered. First, the cost of this material is the cost of the goods transferred out computed in the prior department. Second, the units started in the subsequent department correspond to the units transferred out from the prior department, assuming that there is a one-to-one relationship between the output measures of both departments. Third, the units of the transferring department may be measured differently than the units of the receiving department. If this is the case, then the goods transferred in must be converted to the units of measure used by the second department.

To illustrate how process costing works for a department that receives transferred-in work, we will use the tableting department of the Estrella Company. The tableting department receives a powder from mixing, adds a binder, presses the powder into caplet shapes, and then coats the tablets. The units of the mixing department are measured in ounces, and the units of the tableting department are measured in tablets. To convert ounces to tablets, we need to know the relationship between ounces and tablets. The binding agent is added at the beginning of the process and increases the ounces of material by 10 percent. Every ounce of this new mix then converts to four tablets. Thus, to convert the transferred-in material to the new output measure, we must first multiply by 1.1 and then multiply by four, or equivalently, we must multiply the transferred-in units by 4.4.

Now let's consider the month of October for Estrella Company and focus our attention on the tableting department. We will assume that Estrella Company uses the weighted average method. October's cost and production data for the tableting department are given in Exhibit 6-13. Notice that the transferred-in cost for October is the mixing department's transferred-out cost. (Exhibit 6-12 shows that the mixing department transferred out 60,000 ounces of powder, costing $13,200.) Also notice that output for the tableting department is measured in tablets. Given the data in Exhibit 6-13, the five steps of process costing can be illustrated for the tableting department.

EXHIBIT 6-13	Estrella Company Tableting Department Production and Cost Data: October

Production:	
Units in process, October 1, 80% complete[a]	16,000 (tablets)
Units completed and transferred out	250,000
Units in process, October 31, 30% complete[a]	30,000

Costs:	
Work in process, October 1:	
Transferred-in cost	$ 800
Direct materials (binding agent)[b]	300
Conversion costs	180
Total work in process	$ 1,280
Current costs:	
Transferred-in costs	$13,200
Direct materials (binding agent)[b]	2,500
Conversion costs	5,000
Total current costs	$20,700

[a]With respect to conversion costs. Direct materials are 100 percent complete because they are added at the beginning of the process.

[b]The cost of tablet coating materials is insignificant and therefore added to the conversion costs category.

Step 1: Physical Flow Schedule

In constructing a physical flow schedule for the tableting department, its dependence on the mixing department must be considered:

Units to account for:		
Units, beginning work in process		16,000
Units transferred in during October		264,000*
Total units to account for		280,000
Units accounted for:		
Units completed and transferred out:		
Started and completed	234,000	
From beginning work in process	16,000	250,000
Units, ending work in process		30,000
Total units accounted for		280,000

*60,000 × 4.4 (converts transferred-in units from ounces to tablets)

Step 2: Calculation of Equivalent Units

The calculation of equivalent units of production using the weighted average method is shown in Exhibit 6-14. Notice that the transferred-in goods from mixing are treated as materials added at the beginning of the process. Transferred-in materials are always 100 percent complete, since they are added at the beginning of the process.

EXHIBIT 6-14	Equivalent Units of Production: Weighted Average Method

	Transferred-In Materials	Direct Materials Added	Conversion Costs
Units completed	250,000	250,000	250,000
Add: Units in ending work in process × Percentage complete:			
30,000 × 100%	30,000	—	—
30,000 × 100%	—	30,000	—
30,000 × 30%	—	—	9,000
Equivalent units of output	280,000	280,000	259,000

Step 3: Computation of Unit Costs

The unit cost is computed by calculating the unit cost for each input category:

$$\text{Unit transferred-in cost} = (\$800 + \$13{,}200)/280{,}000 = \$0.05$$
$$\text{Unit direct materials cost} = (\$300 + \$2{,}500)/280{,}000 = \$0.01$$
$$\text{Unit conversion costs} = (\$180 + \$5{,}000)/259{,}000 = \$0.02$$
$$\text{Total unit cost} = \$0.05 + \$0.01 + \$0.02$$
$$= \$0.08$$

Step 4: Valuation of Inventories

The cost of goods transferred out is simply the unit cost multiplied by the goods completed:

$$\text{Cost of goods transferred out} = \$0.08 \times 250{,}000 = \$20{,}000$$

Costing out ending work in process is done by computing the cost of each input and then adding to obtain the total:

Transferred-in materials: $0.05 \times 30,000$	$1,500
Direct materials added: $0.01 \times 30,000$	300
Conversion costs: $0.02 \times 9,000$	180
Total	$1,980

The cost of production report for Estrella Company for the month of October, including Step 5 (which was skipped), is shown in Exhibit 6-15.

EXHIBIT 6-15   **Production Report: Tableting Department**

Estrella Company
Tableting Department
Production Report for October
(Weighted Average Method)

Unit Information

Units to account for:		Units accounted for:	
Units, beginning work in process	16,000	Units completed	250,000
Units started	264,000	Units, ending work in process	30,000
Total units to account for	280,000	Total units accounted for	280,000

Equivalent Units	Transferred-In Materials	Direct Materials	Conversion Costs
Units completed	250,000	250,000	250,000
Units, ending work in process	30,000	30,000	9,000
Total equivalent units	280,000	280,000	259,000

Cost Information

Costs to account for:	Transferred-In Materials	Direct Materials	Conversion Costs	Total
Beginning work in process	$ 800	$ 300	$ 180	$ 1,280
Incurred during the period	13,200	2,500	5,000	20,700
Total costs to account for	$ 14,000	$ 2,800	$ 5,180	$21,980
Divided by equivalent units	÷280,000	÷280,000	÷259,000	
Cost per equivalent unit	$ 0.05	$ 0.01	$ 0.02	$ 0.08

Costs accounted for:		
Units transferred out (250,000 × $0.08)		$20,000
Ending work in process:		
Transferred-in materials ($0.05 × 30,000)	$1,500	
Direct materials (30,000 × $0.01)	300	
Conversion costs (9,000 × $0.02)	180	1,980
Total costs accounted for		$21,980

The only additional complication introduced in the analysis for a subsequent department is the presence of the transferred-in category. As we have just shown, dealing with this category is similar to handling any other category. However, remember that the current cost of this special type of material is the cost of the units transferred in from the prior process and that the units transferred in are the units started (adjusted for any differences in output measurement).

Operation Costing

Not all manufacturing firms have a pure job production environment or a pure process production environment. Some manufacturing firms have characteristics of both job and process environments. Firms in these *hybrid* settings often use *batch production processes*. **Batch production processes** produce batches of different products which are identical in many ways but differ in others. In particular, many firms produce products that make virtually the same demands on conversion inputs but different demands on direct materials inputs. Thus, the conversion activities are similar or identical, but the direct materials used are significantly different. For example, the conversion activities required to produce cans of pie filling are essentially identical for apple or cherry pie filling, but the cost of the direct materials can differ significantly. Similarly, the conversion activities for women's skirts may be identical, but the cost of direct materials can differ dramatically, depending on the nature of the fabric used (wool versus polyester, for example). Clothes, textiles, shoes, and food industries are examples where batch production may take place. For these firms, a costing system known as *operation costing* is often adopted.

Basics of Operation Costing

Operation costing is a blend of job-order and process-costing procedures applied to batches of homogeneous products. This costing system uses *job-order procedures* to assign direct materials costs to batches and *process procedures* to assign conversion costs. A hybrid costing approach is used because each batch uses different doses of direct materials but makes the same demands on the conversion resources of individual processes (usually called operations). Although different batches may pass through different operations, the demands for conversion activities for the *same* process do not differ among batches.

Work orders are used to collect production costs for each batch. Work orders also are used to initiate production. Using work orders to initiate and track costs to each batch is a job-costing characteristic. However, since individual products of different batches consume the same conversion resources as they pass through the same operation, then each product (regardless of batch membership) can be treated as a single homogeneous unit. This last trait is a process-costing characteristic and can be exploited to simplify the assignment of conversion costs.

Materials requisition forms are used to identify the direct materials, quantity and prices, and work order number. Using the materials requisition form as the source document, the cost of direct materials is posted to the work order sheet. Conversion costs are collected by *process* and assigned to products using a *predetermined conversion rate* (identical in concept to predetermined overhead rates). Conversion costs are budgeted for each department, and a single conversion rate is computed for each department (process) using a unit-based activity driver such as direct labor hours or machine hours. For example, assume that the budgeted conversion costs for a sewing operation are $100,000 (consisting of items such as direct labor, depreciation, supplies, and power), and the practical capacity of the operation is 10,000 machine hours. The conversion rate is computed as follows:

$$\text{Conversion rate} = \$100,000/10,000 \text{ machine hours}$$
$$= \$10 \text{ per machine hour}$$

Now consider two batches of shoes that pass through the sewing operation: one batch consists of 50 pairs of men's leather boots, and the second batch consists of 50 pairs of women's leather sandals. First, it should be clear that the batches have different direct material requirements so the cost of direct materials should be tracked separately (job-costing feature). Second, it should also be obvious that the sewing activity is the same for each in the sense that one hour of sewing time should consume the same resources regardless of whether the product is boots or sandals (the process-costing feature). If the batch of boots takes 25 machine hours, the batch will be assigned $250 of conversion costs ($10 × 25 hours). If the batch of sandals takes 12 machine hours, it will be assigned $120 of conversion costs ($10 × 12). Again, even though the products consume the same resources per machine hour, the batches can differ in total amount of resources consumed in an operation. So it is necessary to use a work order for each batch to collect costs.

Exhibit 6-16 illustrates the physical flow and cost flow features of operation costing. The illustration is for two batches and three processes. Panel A illustrates the physical flows, and Panel B shows the cost flows. The letters *a* and *f* represent the assignment of direct materials cost to the two batches. This example assumes that all direct materials are issued at the very beginning. Thus, direct materials cost would be assigned to the work-in-process account for the beginning process for each batch. The example also illustrates that batches do not have to participate in every process. Batch A uses Processes 2 and 3, while Batch B uses Processes 1 and 2. The letters immediately following the process represent the application of conversion costs to the respective batches.

Operation Costing Example

To illustrate operation costing, consider a company that produces a variety of vitamin and mineral products. The company produces a multivitamin and mineral product as well as single vitamin and mineral products, e.g., bottles of vitamins C and E, calcium, etc. Assume that the company also produces different strengths of vitamins (for example, 200 mg and 1,000 mg doses of vitamin C). The company also uses different sizes of bottles (for example, 60 and 120 capsules). There are four operations: picking, encapsulating, tableting, and bottling. Consider the following two work orders:

	Work Order 100	*Work Order 101*
Direct materials	Ascorbic acid	Vitamin E
	Capsules	Vitamin C
	Bottle (100 capsules)	Vitamin B-1
	Cap and labels	Vitamin B-2
		Vitamin B-4
		Vitamin B-12
		Biotin
		Zinc
		Bottle (60 tablets)
		Cap and labels
Operations	Picking	Picking
	Encapsulating	Tableting
	Bottling	Bottling
Number in batch	5,000 bottles	10,000 bottles

Notice how the work order specifies the direct materials needed, the operation required, and the size of the batch. Assume the following costs are collected by work order:

EXHIBIT 6-16   Basic Features of Operation Costing

Panel A: Physical Flows

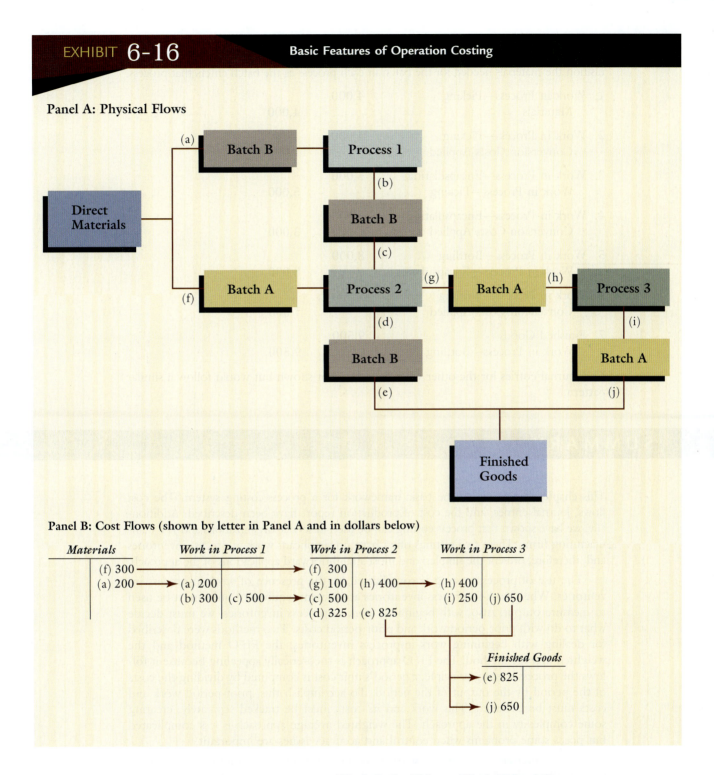

Panel B: Cost Flows (shown by letter in Panel A and in dollars below)

Materials	Work in Process 1	Work in Process 2	Work in Process 3
(f) 300		(f) 300	
(a) 200 → (a) 200		(g) 100	(h) 400 → (h) 400
	(b) 300	(c) 500 → (c) 500	(i) 250	(j) 650
		(d) 325	(e) 825	

Finished Goods

(e) 825

(j) 650

	Work Order 100	Work Order 101
Direct materials	$4,000	$15,000
Conversion costs:		
Picking	1,000	3,000
Encapsulating	3,000	—
Tableting	—	4,000
Bottling	1,500	2,000
Total production costs	$9,500	$24,000

The journal entries associated with Work Order 100 follow. The first entry assumes that all materials needed for the batch are requisitioned at the start. Another possibility is to requisition the materials needed for the batch in each process as the batch enters that process.

1. Work in Process—Picking	4,000	
Materials		4,000
2. Work in Process—Picking	1,000	
Conversion Costs Applied		1,000
3. Work in Process—Encapsulating	5,000	
Work in Process—Picking		5,000
4. Work in Process—Encapsulating	3,000	
Conversion Costs Applied		3,000
5. Work in Process—Bottling	8,000	
Work in Process—Encapsulating		8,000
6. Work in Process—Bottling	1,500	
Conversion Costs Applied		1,500
7. Finished Goods	9,500	
Work in Process—Bottling		9,500

The journal entries for the other work order are not shown but would follow a similar pattern.

SUMMARY

This chapter has presented the basic framework for a process-costing system. The cost flows, journal entries, and the cost of production report have been described. Additionally, we have shown that process costing can be used in service organizations and JIT manufacturing firms. These two settings often have no significant work-in-process inventories and, therefore, present the simplest and most straightforward applications of the approach.

The use of process costing is complicated by the presence of work-in-process inventories. When work-in-process inventories are present, equivalent units must be used to measure output. Also, with beginning work-in-process inventories, we must decide what to do with prior-period work and prior-period costs. Two methods were described for dealing with beginning work-in-process inventories: the FIFO method and the weighted average method. The FIFO approach is theoretically appealing because it follows the process-costing principle: a period's unit cost is computed by dividing the costs of the period by the output of the period. To accomplish this, prior-period work and costs must be excluded. This work and its costs must be tracked separately, creating some complexity in the approach. The weighted average approach is less complicated but poses some problems when control and accuracy issues are important.

The chapter also illustrates how to apply process costing to a multiple department setting. We explored the effect of transferred-in goods and possible changes in the way output is measured. Finally, we introduced a hybrid costing approach called operation costing. This approach is useful for manufacturing settings where batches of homogeneous products are produced.

Appendix: Spoiled Units

When spoilage takes place in a process-costing situation, its effects ripple through the cost of production report. Let's take Payson Company as an example. Payson Com-

OBJECTIVE 8

Explain how spoilage is treated in a process-costing system.

pany produces a product that passes through two departments: mixing and cooking. In the mixing department, all direct materials are added at the beginning of the process. All other manufacturing inputs are added uniformly. The following information pertains to the mixing department for February:

a. Beginning work in process (BWIP), February 1: 100,000 pounds, 40 percent complete with respect to conversion costs. The costs assigned to this work are as follows:

Direct materials	$20,000
Direct labor	10,000
Overhead	30,000

b. Ending work in process (EWIP), February 28: 50,000 pounds, 60 percent complete with respect to conversion costs.

c. Units completed and transferred out: 360,000 pounds. The following costs were added during the month:

Direct materials	$211,000
Direct labor	100,000
Overhead	270,000

d. All units are inspected at the 80 percent point of completion, and any spoiled units identified are discarded. During February, 10,000 pounds were spoiled. We can look at the five steps of the cost of production report. First, we must create a physical flow schedule.

Units to account for:	
Units, beginning work in process	100,000
Units started	320,000
Total units to account for	420,000
Units accounted for:	
Units transferred out	360,000
Units spoiled	10,000
Units, ending work in process	50,000
Total units accounted for	420,000

The second step is the creation of a schedule of equivalent units, shown below.

	Direct Materials	Conversion Costs
Units completed	360,000	360,000
Units spoiled × Percentage complete:		
Direct materials (10,000 × 100%)	10,000	
Conversion costs (10,000 × 80%)		8,000
Units in ending work in process × Percentage complete:		
Direct materials (50,000 × 100%)	50,000	—
Conversion costs (50,000 × 60%)	—	30,000
Equivalent units of output	420,000	398,000

The cost per equivalent unit is as follows:

DM unit cost ($20,000 + $211,000)/420,000	$0.55
CC unit cost ($40,000 + $370,000)/398,000	1.03*
Total cost per equivalent unit	$1.58

*Rounded.

Now we must calculate the cost of goods transferred out and the cost of ending work in process. If the spoilage is normal (expected), the cost of spoiled units is added to the cost of the good units. In this case, the inspection occurred at the 80 percent point of completion. Therefore, none of the spoiled units are from ending work in process (as these units are only 60 percent complete and have not yet been inspected). Thus, all spoilage cost is assigned to the good units transferred out.

Cost of goods transferred out:

Good units $1.58 × 360,000		$568,800
Spoiled units ($0.55 × 10,000) + ($1.03 × 8,000)		13,740
		$582,540

Cost of ending work in process = ($0.55 × 50,000) + ($1.03 × 30,000) = $58,400

Costs are reconciled as follows:

Costs to account for:	
Beginning work in process	$ 60,000
Costs added	581,000
Total costs to account for	$641,000
Costs accounted for:	
Goods transferred out	$582,540
Ending work in process	58,400
Total costs accounted for	$640,940*

*$60 difference is due to rounding.

Suppose that the spoilage was abnormal. Then the spoilage cost is assigned to a spoilage loss account. The costs are accounted for as follows:

Cost of good units transferred out = $1.58 × 360,000 = $568,800
Spoiled units = ($0.55 × 10,000) + ($1.03 × 8,000) = $13,740
Cost of ending work in process = ($0.55 × 50,000) + ($1.03 × 30,000) = $58,400

Costs are reconciled as follows:

Costs to account for:	
Beginning work in process	$ 60,000
Costs added	581,000
Total costs to account for	$641,000
Costs accounted for:	
Goods transferred out	$568,800
Loss from abnormal spoilage	13,740
Ending work in process	58,400
Total costs accounted for	$640,940*

*$60 difference is due to rounding.

Notice the difference between the treatment of normal and abnormal spoilage. When spoilage is assumed to be normal, it is not tracked separately but is embedded in the total cost of good units. As a result, no one knows precisely how much spoilage adds to total manufacturing costs and whether or not an effort should be made to reduce it. The treatment of spoilage as abnormal is more in keeping with an emphasis on total quality management where there is no tolerance allowed for waste. At least the product cost of spoiled goods is tracked in a separate account. Of course, a factory engaged in total quality management would not stop at classifying spoilage as abnormal.

It would also identify the activities that are associated with these spoiled goods in an effort to discover the root causes of poor quality.

REVIEW PROBLEM AND SOLUTION

PHYSICAL FLOW, EQUIVALENT UNITS

Payson Company produces a product that passes through two departments: mixing and cooking. Both departments use the weighted average method. In the mixing department, all direct materials are added at the beginning of the process. All other manufacturing inputs are added uniformly. The following information pertains to the mixing department for February:

a. Beginning work in process (BWIP), February 1: 100,000 pounds, 100 percent complete with respect to direct materials and 40 percent complete with respect to conversion costs. The costs assigned to this work are as follows:

Direct materials	$20,000
Direct labor	10,000
Overhead	30,000

b. Ending work in process (EWIP), February 28: 50,000 pounds, 100 percent complete with respect to direct materials and 60 percent complete with respect to conversion costs.

c. Units completed and transferred out: 370,000 pounds. The following costs were added during the month:

Direct materials	$211,000
Direct labor	100,000
Overhead	270,000

Required:

1. Prepare a physical flow schedule.
2. Prepare a schedule of equivalent units.
3. Compute the cost per equivalent unit.
4. Compute the cost of goods transferred out and the cost of ending work in process.
5. Prepare a cost reconciliation.
6. Repeat Requirements 2–4 using the FIFO method.

SOLUTION   1. Physical flow schedule:

Units to account for:		
Units, BWIP		100,000
Units started		320,000
Total units to account for		420,000
Units accounted for:		
Units completed and transferred out:		
Started and completed	270,000	
From BWIP	100,000	370,000
Units, EWIP		50,000
Total units accounted for		420,000

2. Schedule of equivalent units:

	Direct Materials	Conversion Costs
Units completed	370,000	370,000
Units, EWIP × Percentage complete:		
Direct materials (50,000 × 100%)	50,000	—
Conversion costs (50,000 × 60%)	—	30,000
Equivalent units of output	420,000	400,000

3. Cost per equivalent unit:

DM unit cost ($20,000 + $211,000)/420,000	$0.550
CC unit cost ($40,000 + $370,000)/400,000	1.025
Total cost per equivalent unit	$1.575

4. Cost of goods transferred out and cost of ending work in process:

Cost of goods transferred out = $1.575 × 370,000 = $582,750
Cost of EWIP = ($0.55 × 50,000) + ($1.025 × 30,000) = $58,250

5. Cost reconciliation:

Costs to account for:	
BWIP	$ 60,000
Costs added	581,000
Total costs to account for	$641,000

Costs accounted for:	
Goods transferred out	$582,750
EWIP	58,250
Total costs accounted for	$641,000

6. FIFO results:

Schedule of equivalent units:

	Direct Materials	Conversion Costs
Units started and completed	270,000	270,000
Units, BWIP × Percentage complete:	—	60,000
Units, EWIP × Percentage complete:		
Direct materials (50,000 × 100%)	50,000	—
Conversion costs (50,000 × 60%)	—	30,000
Equivalent units of output	320,000	360,000

Cost per equivalent unit:

DM unit cost $211,000/320,000	$0.659*
CC unit cost $370,000/360,000	1.028*
Total cost per equivalent unit	$1.687

*Rounded.

Cost of goods transferred out and cost of ending work in process:

$$\text{Cost of goods transferred out} = (\$1.687 \times 270,000) + (\$1.028 \times 60,000)$$
$$+ \$60,000 = \$577,170$$
$$\text{Cost of EWIP} = (\$0.659 \times 50,000) + (\$1.028 \times 30,000) = \$63,790$$

KEY TERMS

Batch production processes 249	Process 226
Cost reconciliation 235	Process-costing principle 232
Equivalent units of output 233	Production report 229
FIFO costing method 236	Transferred-in cost 229
Operation costing 249	Weighted average costing method 241
Physical flow schedule 237	Work orders 249

QUESTIONS FOR WRITING AND DISCUSSION

1. What is a process? Provide an example that illustrates the definition.
2. Describe the differences between process costing and job-order costing.
3. What journal entry would be made as goods are transferred out from one department to another department? From the final department to the warehouse?
4. What are transferred-in costs?
5. Explain why transferred-in costs are a special type of material for the receiving department.
6. What is a production report? What purpose does this report serve?
7. Can process costing be used for a service organization? Explain.
   Explain how process costing can be used for JIT manufacturing firms.
8. What are equivalent units? Why are they needed in a process-costing system?
9. How is the equivalent unit calculation affected when direct materials are added at the beginning or end of the process rather than uniformly throughout the process?
10. Describe the five steps in accounting for the manufacturing activity of a processing department, and indicate how they interrelate.
11. Under the weighted average method, how are prior-period costs and output treated? How are they treated under the FIFO method?
12. Under what conditions will the weighted average and FIFO methods give essentially the same results?
13. In assigning costs to goods transferred out, how do the weighted average and FIFO methods differ?
14. How are transferred-in costs treated in the calculation of equivalent units?
15. What is operation costing? When is it used?

EXERCISES

6-1   JOURNAL ENTRIES

LO1, LO2 Lawson Company has three process departments: mixing, encapsulating, and bottling. At the beginning of the fiscal year (July 1), there were no work-in-process or finished goods inventories. The following data are available for the month of July:

Spreadsheet

Department	Manufacturing Costs Added*	Ending Work in Process
Mixing	$540,000	$135,000
Encapsulating	495,000	112,500
Bottling	450,000	22,500

*Includes only the direct materials, direct labor, and the overhead used to process the partially finished goods received from the prior department. The transferred-in cost is not included.

Required:

1. Prepare journal entries that show the transfer of costs from one department to the next (including the entry to transfer the costs of the final department).
2. Prepare T-accounts for the entries made in Requirement 1. Use arrows to show the flow of costs.

6-2 PROCESS COSTING, SERVICE ORGANIZATION

LO2 A local barbershop cuts the hair of 1,000 customers per month. The clients are men, and the barbers offer no special styling. During the month of March, 1,000 customers were serviced. The cost of haircuts includes the following:

Direct labor	$ 7,000
Direct materials	1,000
Overhead	2,000
Total	$10,000

Required:

1. Explain why process costing is appropriate for this haircutting operation.
2. Calculate the cost per haircut.
3. Can you identify some possible direct materials used for this haircutting service? Is the usage of direct materials typical of services? If so, provide examples of services that use direct materials. Can you think of some services that would not use direct materials?

6-3 JIT MANUFACTURING AND PROCESS COSTING, ABC

LO1, LO2 Manzer Company uses JIT manufacturing. Several manufacturing cells are set up within one of its factories. One of the cells makes speakers for computers. The cost of production for the month of April is as follows:

Cell labor	$ 80,000
Direct materials	200,000
Overhead	160,000
Total	$440,000

During April, 10,000 sets of speakers were produced and sold.

Required:

1. Explain why process costing can be used for computing the cost of production for the speakers.
2. Calculate the cost per unit for a speaker.
3. Explain how activity-based costing can be used to determine the overhead assigned to the cell.

6-4 PHYSICAL FLOW, EQUIVALENT UNITS, UNIT COSTS, NO BEGINNING WIP INVENTORY, ACTIVITY-BASED COSTING

LO2, LO3 Mizukawa, Inc., produces a subassembly used in the production of hydraulic cylinders. The subassemblies are produced in three departments: plate cutting, rod cutting, and welding. Overhead is applied using the following drivers and activity rates:

Driver	Rate	Actual Usage (by Plate Cutting)
Direct labor cost	150% of direct labor cost	$366,000
Inspection hours	$20 per hour	3,725 hours
Purchase orders	$500 per order	400 orders

Other data for the plate cutting department are as follows:

Beginning work in process	—
Units started	370,000
Direct materials cost	$1,850,000
Units, ending work in process	
(100% materials; 80% conversion)	20,000

Required:

1. Prepare a physical flow schedule.
2. Calculate equivalent units of production for:
   a. Direct materials
   b. Conversion costs
3. Calculate unit costs for:
   a. Direct materials
   b. Conversion costs
   c. Total manufacturing
4. Provide the following information:
   a. The total cost of units transferred out
   b. The journal entry for transferring costs from plate cutting to welding
   c. The cost assigned to units in ending inventory

6-5 PRODUCTION REPORT, NO BEGINNING INVENTORY

LO1, LO3 Deercreek Company manufactures insect repellant. The mixing department, the first process department, mixes the chemicals required for the repellant. The following data are for 2007:

Work in process, January 1, 2007	—
Gallons started	300,000
Gallons transferred out	25,000
Direct materials cost	$300,000
Direct labor cost	$595,200
Overhead applied	$892,800

Direct materials are added at the beginning of the process. Ending inventory is 95 percent complete with respect to direct labor and overhead.

Required:

Prepare a production report for the mixing department for 2007.

6-6 WEIGHTED AVERAGE METHOD, FIFO METHOD, PHYSICAL FLOW, EQUIVALENT UNITS

LO3, LO4, LO5

Darim Company manufactures a product that passes through two processes: fabrication and assembly. The following information was obtained for the fabrication department for June:

a. All materials are added at the beginning of the process.
b. Beginning work in process had 60,000 units, 30 percent complete with respect to conversion costs.
c. Ending work in process had 12,000 units, 25 percent complete with respect to conversion costs.
d. Started in process, 75,000 units.

Required:

1. Prepare a physical flow schedule.
2. Compute equivalent units using the weighted average method.
3. Compute equivalent units using the FIFO method.

6-7 FIFO METHOD, VALUATION OF GOODS TRANSFERRED OUT AND ENDING WORK IN PROCESS

LO4

Alden Company uses the FIFO method to account for the costs of production. For crushing, the first processing department, the following equivalent units schedule has been prepared:

	Direct Materials	Conversion Costs
Units started and completed	22,000	22,000
Units, beginning work in process:		
10,000 × 0%	—	—
10,000 × 40%	—	4,000
Units, ending work in process:		
6,000 × 100%	6,000	—
6,000 × 75%	—	4,500
Equivalent units of output	28,000	30,500

The cost per equivalent unit for the period was as follows:

Direct materials	$3.00
Conversion costs	5.00
Total	$8.00

The cost of beginning work in process was direct materials, $30,000; conversion costs, $25,000.

Required:

1. Determine the cost of ending work in process and the cost of goods transferred out.
2. Prepare a physical flow schedule.

6-8   EQUIVALENT UNITS—WEIGHTED AVERAGE METHOD

LO5   The following data are for four independent process-costing departments. Inputs are added continuously.

	A	B	C	D
Beginning inventory	3,000	2,000	—	25,000
Percent completion	30%	75%	—	60%
Units started	19,000	20,000	48,000	35,000
Ending inventory	4,000	—	8,000	10,000
Percent completion	20%	—	25%	10%

Required:

Compute the equivalent units of production for each of the preceding departments using the weighted average method.

6-9   EQUIVALENT UNITS, FIFO METHOD

LO4   Using the data from **Exercise 6-8**, compute the equivalent units of production for each of the four departments using the FIFO method.

6-10   WEIGHTED AVERAGE METHOD, UNIT COST, VALUATION OF GOODS TRANSFERRED OUT AND ENDING WORK IN PROCESS

LO5   Watson Products, Inc., produces plastic cases used for video cameras. The product passes through three departments. For May, the following equivalent units schedule was prepared for the first department:

	Direct Materials	Conversion Costs
Units completed	5,000	5,000
Units, ending work in process × Percentage complete:		
6,000 × 100%	6,000	—
6,000 × 50%	—	3,000
Equivalent units of output	11,000	8,000

Costs assigned to beginning work in process: direct materials, $30,000; conversion costs, $5,000. Manufacturing costs incurred during May: direct materials, $25,000; conversion costs, $65,000. Watson uses the weighted average method.

Required:

1. Compute the unit cost for May.
2. Determine the cost of ending work in process and the cost of goods transferred out.

6-11   FIFO METHOD, UNIT COST, VALUATION OF GOODS TRANSFERRED OUT AND ENDING WORK IN PROCESS

LO4   Dama Company produces women's blouses and uses the FIFO method to account for its manufacturing costs. The product Dama makes passes through two processes:

cutting and sewing. During April, Dama's controller prepared the following equivalent units schedule for the cutting department:

	Direct Materials	Conversion Costs
Units started and completed	40,000	40,000
Units, beginning work in process:		
10,000 × 0%	—	—
10,000 × 50%	—	5,000
Units, ending work in process:		
20,000 × 100%	20,000	—
20,000 × 25%	—	5,000
Equivalent units of output	60,000	50,000

Costs in beginning work in process were direct materials, $20,000; conversion costs, $80,000. Manufacturing costs incurred during April were direct materials, $240,000; conversion costs, $320,000.

Required:

1. Prepare a physical flow schedule for April.
2. Compute the cost per equivalent unit for April.
3. Determine the cost of ending work in process and the cost of goods transferred out.
4. Prepare the journal entry that transfers the costs from cutting to sewing.

6-12   WEIGHTED AVERAGE METHOD, EQUIVALENT UNITS, UNIT COST, MULTIPLE DEPARTMENTS

LO5, LO6   Fordman Company has a product that passes through two processes: grinding and polishing. During December, the grinding department transferred 20,000 units to the polishing department. The cost of the units transferred into the second department was $40,000. Direct materials are added uniformly in the second process. Units are measured the same way in both departments.

The second department (polishing) had the following physical flow schedule for December:

Units to account for:	
Units, beginning work in process	4,000 (40% complete)
Units started	?
Total units to account for	?
Units accounted for:	
Units, ending work in process	8,000 (50% complete)
Units completed	?
Units accounted for	?

Costs in beginning work in process for the polishing department were direct materials, $5,000; conversion costs, $6,000; and transferred in, $8,000. Costs added during the month: materials, $32,000; conversion costs, $50,000; and transferred in, $40,000.

Required:

1. Assuming the use of the weighted average method, prepare a schedule of equivalent units.
2. Compute the unit cost for the month.

6-13 FIFO METHOD, EQUIVALENT UNITS, UNIT COST, MULTIPLE DEPARTMENTS

LO4, LO6 Using the same data found in **Exercise 6-12**, assume the company uses the FIFO method.

Required:

Prepare a schedule of equivalent units, and compute the unit cost for the month of December.

6-14 JOURNAL ENTRIES, COST OF ENDING INVENTORIES

LO1, LO3 Baxter Company has two processing departments: assembly and finishing. A predetermined overhead rate of $10 per direct labor hour is used to assign overhead to production. The company experienced the following operating activity for April:
a. Issued materials to assembly, $24,000.
b. Incurred direct labor cost: assembly, 500 hours at $9.20 per hour; finishing, 400 hours at $8 per hour.
c. Applied overhead to production.
d. Transferred goods to finishing, $32,500.
e. Transferred goods to finished goods warehouse, $20,500.
f. Incurred actual overhead, $10,000.

Required:

1. Prepare the required journal entries for the preceding transactions.
2. Assuming assembly and finishing have no beginning work-in-process inventories, determine the cost of each department's ending work-in-process inventories.

6-15 OPERATION COSTING: BREAD MANUFACTURING

LO7 Tasty Bread makes and supplies bread throughout the state of Kansas. Three types of bread are produced: loaves, rolls, and buns. Seven operations describe the production process.

a. Mixing: Flour, milk, yeast, salt, butter, and so on, are mixed in a large vat.
b. Shaping: A conveyor belt transfers the dough to a machine that weighs it and shapes it into loaves, rolls, or buns, depending on the type being produced.
c. Rising: The individually shaped dough is allowed to sit and rise.
d. Baking: The dough is moved to a 100-foot-long funnel oven. (The dough enters the oven on racks and spends 20 minutes moving slowly through the oven.)
e. Cooling: The bread is removed from the oven and allowed to cool.
f. Slicing: For loaves and buns (hamburger and hot dog), the bread is sliced.
g. Packaging: The bread is wrapped (packaged).

Tasty produces its products in batches. The size of the batch depends on the individual orders that must be filled (orders come from retail grocers throughout the state). Usually, as soon as one batch is mixed, a second batch begins the mixing operation.

Required:

1. Identify the conditions that must be present for operation costing to be used in this setting. If these conditions are not met, explain how process costing would be used. If process costing is used, would you recommend the weighted average method or the FIFO method? Explain.
2. Assume that operation costing is the best approach for this bread manufacturer. Describe in detail how you would use operation costing. Use a batch of dinner rolls (consisting of 1,000 packages of 12 rolls) and a batch of whole wheat loaves (consisting of 5,000, 24-oz. sliced loaves) as examples.

PROBLEMS

6-16 WEIGHTED AVERAGE METHOD, PHYSICAL FLOW, EQUIVALENT UNITS, UNIT COSTS, COST ASSIGNMENT, ABC

LO2, LO3, LO5

Norton Parts, Inc., manufactures bumpers (plastic or metal, depending on the plant) for automobiles. Each bumper passes through three processes: molding, drilling, and painting. In August, the molding department of the Oklahoma City plant reported the following data:

a. In molding, all direct materials are added at the beginning of the process.
b. Beginning work in process consisted of 27,000 units, 20 percent complete with respect to direct labor and overhead. Costs in beginning inventory included direct materials, $810,000; direct labor, $148,400; and applied overhead, $100,000.
c. Costs added to production during the month were direct materials, $1,710,000 and direct labor, $2,314,100. Overhead was assigned using the following activity information:

Activity	Rate	Actual Driver Usage
Inspection	$100 per inspection hour	4,000 inspection hours
Maintenance	$500 per maintenance hour	1,600 maintenance hours
Receiving	$200 per receiving order	2,000 receiving orders

d. At the end of the month, 81,000 units were transferred out to drilling, leaving 9,000 units in ending work in process, 25 percent complete.

Required:

1. Prepare a physical flow schedule.
2. Calculate equivalent units of production for direct materials and conversion costs.
3. Compute unit cost.
4. Calculate the cost of goods transferred to drilling at the end of the month. Calculate the cost of ending inventory.
5. Prepare the journal entry that transfers the goods from molding to drilling.

6-17 FIFO METHOD, PHYSICAL FLOW, EQUIVALENT UNITS, UNIT COSTS, COST ASSIGNMENT

LO3, LO4   Refer to the data in **Problem 6-16**. Assume that the FIFO method is used.

Required:

1. Prepare a physical flow schedule.
2. Calculate equivalent units of production for direct materials and conversion costs.
3. Compute unit cost.
4. Calculate the cost of goods transferred to drilling at the end of the month. Calculate the cost of ending inventory.

6-18 WEIGHTED AVERAGE METHOD, SINGLE DEPARTMENT ANALYSIS, UNIFORM COSTS

LO5   Stewart Company produces a product that passes through three processes: fabrication, assembly, and finishing. All manufacturing costs are added uniformly for both processes. The following information was obtained for the assembly department for May 2007:

a. Work in process, May 1, had 10,000 units (40 percent completed) and the following costs:

Direct materials $12,000
Direct labor   18,000
Overhead   6,000

b. During the month of May, 30,000 units were completed and transferred to the finishing department, and the following costs were added to production:

Direct materials $36,000
Direct labor   24,000
Overhead   18,000

c. On May 30, there were 7,500 partially completed units in process. These units were 80 percent complete.

Required:

Prepare a cost of production report for the assembly department for May using the weighted average method of costing. The report should disclose the physical flow of units, equivalent units, and unit costs and should track the disposition of manufacturing costs.

6-19   FIFO METHOD, SINGLE DEPARTMENT ANALYSIS, ONE COST CATEGORY

LO4   Refer to the data in **Problem 6-18**.

Required:

Prepare a cost of production report for the assembly department for May using the FIFO method of costing.

6-20   SERVICE ORGANIZATION WITH WORK-IN-PROCESS INVENTORIES, MULTIPLE DEPARTMENTS, FIFO METHOD, UNIT COST

LO3, LO4, LO6   Granger Credit Corporation is a wholly owned subsidiary of a large manufacturer of computers. Granger is in the business of financing computers, software, and other services that the parent corporation sells. Granger has two departments that are involved in financing services: the credit department and the business practices department. The credit department receives requests for financing from field sales representatives, records customer information on a preprinted form, and then enters the information into the computer system to check the creditworthiness of the customer. (Other actions may be taken if the customer is not in the database.) Once creditworthiness information is known, a printout is produced with this information plus other customer specific information. The completed form is transferred to the business practices department.

The business practices department modifies the standard loan covenant as needed (in response to customer request or customer risk profile). When this activity is completed, the loan is priced. This is done by keying information from the partially processed form into a personal computer spreadsheet program. The program provides a recommended interest rate for the loan. Finally, a form specifying the loan terms is attached to the transferred-in document. A copy of the loan-term form is sent to the sales representative and serves as the quote letter.

The following cost and service activity data for the business practices department are provided for the month of May:

Transferred-in applications	2,800
Applications in process, May 1, 40% complete*	500
Applications in process, May 31, 25% complete*	800

*All materials and supplies are used at the end of the process.

	Transferred In	Direct Materials	Conversion Costs
Costs:			
Beginning work in process	$ 4,500	—	$ 2,800
Costs added	28,000	$1,250	37,500

Required:

1. How would you define the output of the business practices department?
2. Using the FIFO method, prepare the following for the business practices department:
   a. A physical flow schedule
   b. An equivalent units schedule
   c. Calculation of unit costs
   d. Cost of ending work in process and cost of units transferred out
   e. A cost reconciliation

6-21 WEIGHTED AVERAGE METHOD, JOURNAL ENTRIES

LO1, LO5, LO6

Muskoge Company uses a process-costing system. The company manufactures a product that is processed in two departments: molding and assembly. In the molding department, direct materials are added at the beginning of the process; in the assembly department, additional direct materials are added at the end of the process. In both departments, conversion costs are incurred uniformly throughout the process. As work is completed, it is transferred out. The following table summarizes the production activity and costs for February:

	Molding	Assembly
Beginning inventories:		
Physical units	10,000	8,000
Costs:		
Transferred in	—	$45,200
Direct materials	$22,000	—
Conversion costs	$13,800	$16,800
Current production:		
Units started	25,000	?
Units transferred out	30,000	35,000
Costs:		
Transferred in	—	?
Direct materials	$56,250	$39,550
Conversion costs	$103,500	$136,500
Percentage of completion:		
Beginning inventory	40%	50%
Ending inventory	80%	50%

Required:

1. Using the weighted average method, prepare the following for the molding department:
   a. A physical flow schedule
   b. An equivalent units calculation
   c. Calculation of unit costs
   d. Cost of ending work in process and cost of goods transferred out
   e. A cost reconciliation
2. Prepare journal entries that show the flow of manufacturing costs for the molding department.
3. Repeat Requirements 1 and 2 for the assembly department.

6-22   FIFO METHOD, TWO-DEPARTMENT ANALYSIS

LO2, LO4, LO6   Refer to the data in **Problem 6-21**.

Required:

Repeat the requirements in **Problem 6-21** using the FIFO method.

6-23   WEIGHTED AVERAGE METHOD, TWO-DEPARTMENT ANALYSIS, CHANGE IN OUTPUT MEASURE

LO5, LO6   Healthway uses a process-costing system to compute the unit costs of the minerals that it produces. It has three departments: mixing, tableting, and bottling. In mixing, the ingredients for the minerals are measured, sifted, and blended together. The mix is transferred out in gallon containers. The tableting department takes the powdered mix and places it in capsules. One gallon of powdered mix converts to 1,600 capsules. After the capsules are filled and polished, they are transferred to bottling where they are placed in bottles, which are then affixed with a safety seal and a lid and labeled. Each bottle receives 50 capsules.

During July, the following results are available for the first two departments (direct materials are added at the beginning in both departments):

	Mixing	*Tableting*
Beginning inventories:		
Physical units	5 gallons	4,000 capsules
Costs:		
Direct materials	$120	$32
Direct labor	$128	$20
Overhead	?	?
Transferred in	—	$140
Current production:		
Transferred out	125 gallons	198,000 capsules
Ending inventory	6 gallons	6,000 capsules
Costs:		
Direct materials	$3,144	$1,584
Transferred in	—	?
Direct labor	$4,096	$1,944
Overhead	?	?
Percentage of completion:		
Beginning inventory	40%	50%
Ending inventory	50%	40%

Overhead in both departments is applied as a percentage of direct labor costs. In the mixing department, overhead is 200 percent of direct labor. In the tableting department, the overhead rate is 150 percent of direct labor.

Required:

1. Prepare a production report for the mixing department using the weighted average method. Follow the five steps outlined in the chapter.
2. Prepare a production report for the tableting department. Follow the five steps outlined in the chapter.

6-24 FIFO METHOD, TWO-DEPARTMENT ANALYSIS

LO4, LO6 Refer to the data in **Problem 6-23**.

Required:

Prepare a production report for each department using the FIFO method.

6-25 OPERATION COSTING: UNIT COSTS AND JOURNAL ENTRIES

LO7 Jacson Company produces two brands of a popular pain medication: regular strength and extra strength. Regular strength is produced in tablet form, and extra strength is produced in capsule form. All direct materials needed for each batch are requisitioned at the start. The work orders for two batches of the products follow, along with some associated cost information:

	Work Order 121 (Regular Strength)	Work Order 122 (Extra Strength)
Direct materials (actual costs):	$9,000	$15,000
Applied conversion costs:		
Mixing	?	?
Tableting	$5,000	—
Encapsulating	—	$6,000
Bottling	?	?
Batch size (bottles of 100 units)	12,000	18,000

In the mixing department, conversion costs are applied on the basis of direct labor hours. Budgeted conversion costs for the department for the year were $60,000 for direct labor and $190,000 for overhead. Budgeted direct labor hours were 5,000. It takes one minute of labor time to mix the ingredients needed for a 100-unit bottle (for either product).

In the bottling department, conversion costs are applied on the basis of machine hours. Budgeted conversion costs for the department for the year were $400,000. Budgeted machine hours were 20,000. It takes one-half minute of machine time to fill a bottle of 100 units.

Required:

1. What are the conversion costs applied in the mixing department for each batch? The bottling department?
2. Calculate the cost per bottle for the regular and extra strength pain medications.
3. Prepare the journal entries that record the costs of the 12,000 regular strength batch as it moves through the various operations.

4. Suppose that the direct materials are requisitioned by each department as needed for a batch. For the 12,000 regular strength batch, direct materials are requisitioned for the mixing and bottling departments. Assume that the amount of cost is split evenly between the two departments. How will this change the journal entries made in Requirement 3?

6-26   CASE ON PROCESS COSTING, OPERATION COSTING, IMPACT ON RESOURCE ALLOCATION DECISION

LO3, LO5, LO7   Golding Manufacturing, a division of Farnsworth Sporting, Inc., produces two different models of bows and eight models of knives. The bow-manufacturing process involves the production of two major subassemblies: the limbs and the handle. The limbs pass through four sequential processes before reaching final assembly: lay-up, molding, fabricating, and finishing. In the lay-up department, limbs are created by laminating layers of wood. In molding, the limbs are heat treated, under pressure, to form a strong resilient limb. In the fabricating department, any protruding glue or other processing residue is removed. Finally, in finishing, the limbs are cleaned with acetone, dried, and sprayed with the final finishes.

The handles pass through two processes before reaching final assembly: pattern and finishing. In the pattern department, blocks of wood are fed into a machine that is set to shape the handles. Different patterns are possible, depending on the machine's setting. After coming out of the machine, the handles are cleaned and smoothed. They then pass to the finishing department where they are sprayed with the final finishes. In final assembly, the limbs and handles are assembled into different models using purchased parts such as pulley assemblies, weight adjustment bolts, side plates, and string.

Golding, since its inception, has been using process costing to assign product costs. A predetermined overhead rate is used based on direct labor dollars (80 percent of direct labor dollars). Recently, Golding has hired a new controller, Karen Jenkins. After reviewing the product costing procedures, Karen requested a meeting with the divisional manager, Aaron Suhr. The following is a transcript of their conversation:

KAREN: Aaron, I have some concerns about our cost accounting system. We make two different models of bows and are treating them as if they were the same product. Now I know that the only real difference between the models is the handle. The processing of the handles is the same, but the handles differ significantly in the amount and quality of wood used. Our current costing does not reflect this difference in direct materials input.

AARON: Your predecessor is responsible. He believed that tracking the difference in direct materials cost wasn't worth the effort. He simply didn't believe that it would make much difference in the unit cost of either model.

KAREN: Well, he may have been right, but I have my doubts. If there is a significant difference, it could affect our views of which model is more important to the company. The additional bookkeeping isn't very stringent. All we have to worry about is the pattern department. The other departments fit what I view as a process-costing pattern.

AARON: Why don't you look into it? If there is a significant difference, go ahead and adjust the costing system.

After the meeting, Karen decided to collect cost data on the two models: the Deluxe model and the Econo model. She decided to track the costs for one week. At the end of the week, she had collected the following data from the pattern department:

a. There were a total of 2,500 bows completed: 1,000 Deluxe models and 1,500 Econo models.

b. There was no beginning work in process; however, there were 300 units in ending work in process: 200 Deluxe and 100 Econo models. Both models were 80 percent complete with respect to conversion costs and 100 percent complete with respect to direct materials.

c. The pattern department experienced the following costs:

Direct materials $114,000
Direct labor 45,667

d. On an experimental basis, the requisition forms for direct materials were modified to identify the dollar value of the direct materials used by the Econo and Deluxe models:

Econo model $30,000
Deluxe model 84,000

Required:

1. Compute the unit cost for the handles produced by the pattern department assuming that process costing is totally appropriate.
2. Compute the unit cost of each handle using the separate cost information provided on materials.
3. Compare the unit costs computed in Requirements 1 and 2. Is Karen justified in her belief that a pure process-costing relationship is not appropriate? Describe the costing system that you would recommend.
4. In the past, the marketing manager has requested more money for advertising the Econo line. Aaron has repeatedly refused to grant any increase in this product's advertising budget because its per-unit profit (selling price less manufacturing cost) is so low. Given the results in Requirements 1 through 3, was Aaron justified in his position?

6-27 APPENDIX: NORMAL AND ABNORMAL SPOILAGE

LO5, LO8 Larkin Company produces leather strips for western belts using three processes: cutting, design and coloring, and punching. The weighted average method is used for all three departments. The following information pertains to the design and coloring department for the month of June.

a. There was no beginning work in process.
b. There were 400,000 units transferred in from cutting.
c. Ending work in process, June 30: 50,000 strips, 80 percent complete with respect to conversion costs.
d. Units completed and transferred out: 330,000 strips. The following costs were added during the month:

Transferred in $2,000,000
Direct materials 600,000
Conversion costs 780,000

e. Direct materials are added at the beginning of the process.
f. Inspection takes place at the end of the process. All spoilage is considered normal.

Required:

1. Calculate equivalent units of production for transferred-in materials, direct materials added, and conversion costs.
2. Calculate unit costs for the three categories of Requirement 1.
3. What is the total cost of units transferred out? What is the cost of ending work-in-process inventory? How is the cost of spoilage treated?
4. Assume that all spoilage is considered abnormal. Now, how is spoilage treated? Give the journal entry to account for the cost of the spoiled units. Some companies view all spoilage as abnormal. Explain why.

5. Assume that 80 percent of the units spoiled are abnormal and 20 percent are normal spoilage. Show the spoilage treatment for this scenario.

6-28   APPENDIX: NORMAL AND ABNORMAL SPOILAGE IN PROCESS COSTING

LO8   Novel Toys, Inc., manufactures plastic water guns. Each gun's left and right frames are produced in the molding department. The left and right frames are then transferred to the assembly department where the trigger mechanism is inserted and the halves are glued together. (The left and right halves together define the unit of output for the molding department.) In June, the molding department reported the following data:

a. In the molding department, all direct materials are added at the beginning of the process.

b. Beginning work in process consisted of 3,000 units, 20 percent complete with respect to direct labor and overhead. Costs in beginning inventory included direct materials, $450; and conversion costs, $138.

c. Costs added to production during the month were direct materials, $950; and conversion costs, $2,174.50.

d. Inspection takes place at the end of the process. Malformed units are discarded. All spoilage is considered abnormal.

e. During the month, 7,000 units were started, and 8,000 good units were transferred out to finishing. All other units finished were malformed and discarded. There were 1,000 units that remained in ending work in process, 25 percent complete.

Required:

1. Prepare a physical flow schedule.
2. Calculate equivalent units of production using the weighted average method.
3. Calculate the unit cost.
4. What is the cost of goods transferred out? Ending work in process? Loss due to spoilage?
5. Prepare the journal entry to remove spoilage from the molding department.

6-29   APPENDIX: NORMAL AND ABNORMAL SPOILAGE IN PROCESS COSTING, CHANGES IN OUTPUT MEASURES, MULTIPLE DEPARTMENTS

LO6, LO8   Grayson Company produces an industrial chemical used for cleaning and lubricating machinery. In the mixing department, liquid and dry chemicals are blended to form slurry. Output is measured in gallons. In the baking department, the slurry is subjected to high heat, and the residue appears in irregular lumps. Output is measured in pounds. In the grinding department, the irregular lumps are ground into a powder, and this powder is placed in 50-pound bags. Output is measured in bags produced. In April, the company reported the following data:

a. The mixing department transferred 50,000 gallons to the baking department, costing $250,000. Each gallon of slurry weighs two pounds.

b. The baking department transferred 100,000 pounds (irregular lumps) to the grinding department. At the beginning of the month, there were 5,000 gallons of slurry in process, 25 percent complete, costing $35,000 (transferred-in cost of $25,000 plus conversion cost of $10,000). No additional direct materials are added in the baking department. At the end of April, there was no ending work in process. Conversion costs for the month totaled $205,000. Normal loss during baking is 5 percent of good output. All transferred-in materials are lost, but since loss occurs uniformly throughout the process, only 50 percent of the conversion units are assumed to be lost.

c. The grinding department transferred 2,500 bags of chemicals to its finished goods warehouse. Beginning work in process for this department was 25,000 pounds, 40 percent complete with the following costs: transferred-in cost, $132,500 and conversion cost, $15,000. Bags are used at the end of the process and cost $1.50 each. During bagging, normally one out of every 11 bags is torn and must be discarded. No powder is lost (the tearing occurs when the bag is being attached to a funnel). Conversion costs for the month's production are $172,500. There is no ending work in process.

Required:

1. Calculate the cost per bag of chemicals transferred to the finished goods warehouse. Show all work necessary for the calculation.
2. Prepare the journal entries needed to remove spoilage from the baking and grinding departments.

6-30   COLLABORATIVE LEARNING EXERCISE: STRUCTURED PROBLEM SOLVING (CASE ON EQUIVALENT UNITS, VALUATION OF WORK-IN-PROCESS INVENTORIES, FIFO VERSUS WEIGHTED AVERAGE)

LO1, LO3, LO4, LO5, LO6   AKL Foundry manufactures metal components for different kinds of equipment used by the aerospace, commercial aircraft, medical equipment, and electronics industries. The company uses investment casting to produce the required components. Investment casting consists of creating, in wax, a replica of the final product and pouring a hard shell around it. After removing the wax, molten metal is poured into the resulting cavity. What remains after the shell is broken is the desired metal object ready to be put to its designated use.

Metal components pass through eight processes: gating, shell creating, foundry work, cut-off, grinding, finishing, welding, and strengthening. Gating creates the wax mold and clusters the wax pattern around a sprue (a hole through which the molten metal will be poured through the gates into the mold in the foundry process), which is joined and supported by gates (flow channels) to form a tree of patterns. In the shell creating process, the wax molds are alternately dipped in a ceramic slurry and a fluidized bed of progressively coarser refractory grain until a sufficiently thick shell (or mold) completely encases the wax pattern. After drying, the mold is sent to the foundry process. Here, the wax is melted out of the mold, and the shell is fired, strengthened, and brought to the proper temperature. Molten metal is then poured into the dewaxed shell. Finally, the ceramic shell is removed, and the finished product is sent to the cut-off process, where the parts are separated from the tree by the use of a band saw. The parts are then sent to grinding, where the gates that allowed the molten metal to flow into the ceramic cavities are ground off using large abrasive grinders. In finishing, rough edges caused by the grinders are removed by small hand-held pneumatic tools. Parts that are flawed at this point are sent to welding for corrective treatment. The last process uses heat to treat the parts to bring them to the desired strength.

In 2007, the two partners who owned AKL Foundry decided to split up and divide the business. In dissolving their business relationship, they were faced with the problem of dividing the business assets equitably. Since the company had two plants—one in Arizona and one in New Mexico—a suggestion was made to split the business on the basis of geographic location—one partner would assume ownership of the plant in New Mexico and the other would assume ownership of the plant in Arizona. However, this arrangement had one major complication: the amount of work-in-process inventory located in the Arizona plant.

The Arizona facilities had been in operation for more than a decade and were full of work in process. The New Mexico facility had been operational for only two years and had much smaller work-in-process inventories. The partner located in New Mexico argued that to disregard the unequal value of the work-in-process inventories would be grossly unfair.

Unfortunately, during the entire business history of AKL Foundry, work-in-process inventories had never been assigned any value. In computing the cost of goods sold each year, the company had followed the policy of adding depreciation to the out-of-pocket costs of direct labor, direct materials, and overhead. Accruals for the company are nearly nonexistent, and there are hardly ever any ending inventories of materials.

During 2007, the Arizona plant had sales of $2,028,670. The cost of goods sold is itemized as follows:

Direct materials	$378,000
Direct labor	530,300
Overhead	643,518

Upon request, the owners of AKL provided the following supplementary information (percentages are cumulative):

	Costs Used by Each Process as a Percentage of Total Cost	
	Direct Materials	*Direct Total Labor Cost*
Gating	23%	35%
Shell creating	70	50
Foundry work	100	70
Cut-off	100	72
Grinding	100	80
Finishing	100	90
Welding	100	93
Strengthening	100	100

The gating department had 10,000 units in beginning work in process, 60 percent complete. Assume that all materials are added at the beginning of each process. During the year, 50,000 units were completed and transferred out. The ending inventory had 11,000 unfinished units, 60 percent complete.

Required:

Form groups of three to five students. Each group will act as a consulting team to solve the valuation problem for AKL Foundry (for a time specified by the instructor within class). At the end of the indicated time, one person from each group will be chosen by the instructor to act as the spokesperson for the group. Thus, every member of the group should be prepared to provide their group's solution. Each group should answer the following questions:

1. The partners of AKL want a reasonable estimate of the cost of work-in-process inventories. Using the gating department's inventory as an example, prepare an estimate of the cost of the ending work in process. What assumptions did you make? Did you use the FIFO or weighted average method? Why?
2. Assume that the shell creating process has 8,000 units in beginning work in process, 20 percent complete. During the year, 50,000 units were completed and

transferred out. (All 50,000 units were sold; no other units were sold.) The ending work-in-process inventory had 8,000 units, 30 percent complete. Compute the value of the shell creating department's ending work in process. What additional assumptions had to be made?

6-31 COLLABORATIVE LEARNING EXERCISE: JIGSAW METHOD FOR COLLABORATIVE LEARNING, COST OF PRODUCTION REPORT, ETHICAL BEHAVIOR

LO3 Consider the following conversation between Keri Swasey, manager of a division that produces riding lawn mowers, and her controller, Stoney Lawson, a CMA and CPA:

KERI: Stoney, we have a real problem. Our operating cash is too low, and we are in desperate need of a loan. As you know, our financial position is marginal, and we need to show as much income as possible—and our assets need bolstering as well.

STONEY: I understand the problem, but I don't see what can be done at this point. This is the last week of the fiscal year, and it looks as if we'll report income just slightly above break even.

KERI: I know all this. What we need is some creative accounting. I have an idea that might help us, and I wanted to see if you would go along with it. We have 600 partially finished mowers in process, about 20 percent complete. That compares with the 3,000 units that we completed and sold during the year. When you computed the per-unit cost, you used 3,120 equivalent units, giving us a manufacturing cost of $1,500 per unit. That per-unit cost gives us cost of goods sold equal to $4.5 million and ending work in process worth $180,000. The presence of the work in process gives us a chance to improve our financial position. If we report the units in work in process as 80 percent complete, this will increase our equivalent units to 3,480. This, in turn, will decrease our unit cost to about $1,345 and cost of goods sold to $4.035 million. The value of our work in process will increase to $645,600. With those financial stats, the loan would be a cinch.

STONEY: Keri, I don't know. What you're suggesting is risky. It wouldn't take much auditing skill to catch this one.

KERI: You don't have to worry about that. The auditors won't be here for at least six to eight more weeks. By that time, we can have those partially completed units completed and sold. I can bury the labor cost by having some of our more loyal workers work overtime for some bonuses. The overtime will never be reported. And, as you know, bonuses come out of the corporate budget and are assigned to overhead—next year's overhead. Stoney, this will work. If we look good and get the loan to boot, corporate headquarters will treat us well. If we don't do this, we could lose our jobs.

Required:

Form groups of three to five students, where the total number of groups is divisible by four. The numbers 1, 2, 3, or 4 will be assigned to each group. Groups with number 1 will solve Requirement 1, groups with number 2 will solve Requirement 2, etc. Each group will share their answers with the other groups.

1. Should Stoney agree to Keri's proposal? Why or why not? To assist in deciding, review the standards of ethical conduct for management accountants described in Chapter 1. Do any apply?
2. Assume that Stoney refuses to cooperate and that Keri accepts this decision and drops the matter. Does Stoney have any obligation to report the divisional manager's behavior to a superior? Explain.

3. Assume that Stoney refuses to cooperate. However, Keri insists that the changes be made. Now what should Stoney do? What would you do?
4. Suppose that Stoney is 63 years old and that his prospects for employment elsewhere are bleak. Assume again that Keri insists that the changes should be made. Stoney also knows that Keri's superior, the owner of the company, is her father-in-law. Under these circumstances, would your recommendations for Stoney differ? If you were Stoney, what would you do?

6-32 CYBER RESEARCH CASE

LO1, LO3, LO8
Understanding the nature of process manufacturing helps to understand the nature of process costing. Using an Internet search, find the home pages of one or more cement companies where the processes used to manufacture portland cement are described. Other Internet resources such as an online encyclopedia might also prove to be useful.

Required:

1. Describe in detail each process in the manufacture of portland cement. Now provide a flow diagram that describes the entire manufacturing process from start to finish.
2. Identify the inputs and output(s) of each process.
3. How would you measure the output of each process? Do any of your units of measure change as you go from one process to the next? How would you deal with this change in units when calculating the cost of a unit transferred out to a subsequent process?
4. Do you think that the amount of direct materials that enter the kiln will be the same as the amount that leave it? Explain. How would you deal with the possibility that output is less than the total units of input?
5. Suppose that the output is a 50-pound bag of cement. List all the resources that you can identify that made the manufacture of this product possible.

CHAPTER 7

Allocating Costs of Support Departments and Joint Products

AFTER STUDYING THIS CHAPTER, YOU SHOULD BE ABLE TO:

1. Describe the difference between support departments and producing departments.
2. Calculate charging rates, and distinguish between single and dual charging rates.
3. Allocate support center costs to producing departments using the direct method, the sequential method, and the reciprocal method.
4. Calculate departmental overhead rates.
5. Identify the characteristics of the joint production process, and allocate joint costs to products.

Mutually beneficial costs, which occur when the same resource is used in the output of two or more services or products, are known as common costs. These common costs may pertain to periods of time, individual responsibilities, sales territories, and classes of customers. A special case of common costs is that of the joint production process. This chapter will first focus on the costs common to departments and to products, and then on the common costs of the joint production process.

An Overview of Cost Allocation

The complexity of many modern firms leads the accountant to allocate costs of support departments to producing departments and individual product lines. Allocation is simply a means of dividing a pool of costs and assigning those costs to various subunits. It is important to realize that allocation does not affect the total cost. Total cost is neither reduced nor increased by allocation. However, the amounts of cost assigned to the subunits can be affected by the allocation procedure chosen. Because cost allocation can affect bid prices, the profitability of individual products, and the behavior of managers, it is an important topic. For example, the wages paid to security guards at a factory are a common cost of all of the different products manufactured there. The benefits of security are applicable to each product, yet the assignment of security cost to the individual products is an arbitrary process. In other words, while it is clear that the products (or services) require the common resource and that the resource cost should be assigned to these cost objects, it is often not clear how best to go about assigning the cost. Usually, common cost assignment is made through a series of consistent allocation procedures.

Types of Departments

The first step in cost allocation is to determine just what the cost objects are. Usually, they are departments. There are two categories of departments: producing departments and support departments. **Producing departments** are directly responsible for creating the products or services sold to customers. In a large public accounting firm, examples of producing departments are auditing, tax, and management advisory services (computer systems services). In a manufacturing setting such as **Volkswagen (VW)**, producing departments are those that work directly on the products being manufactured (e.g., assembly and painting). **Support departments** provide essential services for producing departments. These departments are indirectly connected with an organization's services or products. At VW, those departments might include engineering, maintenance, personnel, and building and grounds.

Once the producing and support departments have been identified, the overhead costs incurred by each department can be determined. Note that this involves tracing costs to the departments, not allocating costs, because the costs are directly associated with the individual department. A factory cafeteria, for example, would have food costs, wages of cooks and servers, depreciation on dishwashers and stoves, and supplies (e.g., napkins and plastic forks). Overhead directly associated with a producing department such as assembly in a furniture-making plant would include utilities (if measured in that department), supervisory salaries, and depreciation on equipment used in that department. Overhead that cannot be easily assigned to a producing or support department is assigned to a catchall department such as general factory. General factory might include depreciation on the factory building, rental of a Santa Claus suit for the factory Christmas party, the cost of restriping the parking lot, the plant manager's salary, and telephone service. In this way, all costs are assigned to a department.

Exhibit 7-1, on the following page, shows how a manufacturing firm and a service firm can be divided into producing and support departments. The manufacturing plant, which makes furniture, may be departmentalized into two producing departments (assembly and finishing) and four support departments (materials storeroom, cafeteria, maintenance, and general factory). The service firm, a bank, might be departmentalized into three producing departments (auto loans, commercial lending, and personal banking) and three support departments (drive through, data processing, and bank administration). Overhead costs are traced to each department. Note that each factory or service company overhead cost must be assigned to one, and only one, department.

Once the company has been departmentalized and all overhead costs have been traced to the individual departments, support department costs are assigned to producing departments, and overhead rates are developed to cost products. Although support departments do not work directly on the products or services that are sold, the costs of providing these support services are part of the total product cost and must be assigned to the products. This assignment of costs consists of a two-stage allocation: (1) allocation of support department costs to producing departments and (2) assignment

EXHIBIT 7-1	Examples of Departmentalization for a Manufacturing Firm and a Service Firm

Manufacturing Firm: Furniture Maker

Producing Departments	Support Departments

Assembly:
  Supervisors' salaries
  Small tools
  Indirect materials
  Depreciation on machinery
Finishing:
  Sandpaper
  Depreciation on sanders and buffers
	Materials Storeroom:
	  Clerk's salary
	  Depreciation on forklift
	Cafeteria:
	  Food
	  Cooks' salaries
	  Depreciation on stoves
	Maintenance:
	  Janitors' salaries
	  Cleaning supplies
	  Machine oil and lubricants
	General Factory:
	  Depreciation on building
	  Security
	  Utilities

Service Firm: Bank

Producing Departments	Support Departments

Auto Loans:
  Loan processors' salaries
  Forms and supplies
Commercial Lending:
  Lending officers' salaries
  Depreciation on office equipment
  Bankruptcy prediction software
Personal Banking:
  Supplies and postage for statements
	Drive Through:
	  Tellers' salaries
	  Depreciation on equipment
	Data Processing:
	  Personnel salaries
	  Software
	  Depreciation on hardware
	Bank Administration:
	  Salary of CEO
	  Receptionist's salary
	  Telephone costs
	  Depreciation on bank and vault

of these allocated costs to individual products. The second-stage allocation, achieved through the use of departmental overhead rates, is necessary because there are multiple products being worked on in each producing department. If there were only one product within a producing department, all the support costs allocated to that department would belong to that product. Recall that a predetermined overhead rate is computed by taking total estimated overhead for a department and dividing it by an estimate of an appropriate base. Now we see that a producing department's overhead consists of two parts: overhead directly associated with a producing department and overhead allocated to the producing department from the support departments. A support department cannot have an overhead rate that assigns overhead costs to units produced, because it does not make a salable product. That is, products do not pass through support departments. The nature of support departments is to service producing departments, not the products that pass through the producing departments. For example, maintenance personnel repair and maintain the equipment in the assembly department, not the furniture that is assembled in that department. Exhibit 7-2 summarizes the steps involved.

EXHIBIT 7-2   **Steps in Allocating Support Department Costs to Producing Departments**

1. Departmentalize the firm.
2. Classify each department as a support department or a producing department.
3. Trace all overhead costs in the firm to a support or producing department.
4. Allocate support department costs to the producing departments.
5. Calculate predetermined overhead rates for producing departments.
6. Allocate overhead costs to the units of individual product through the predetermined overhead rates.

Types of Allocation Bases

In effect, producing departments *cause* support activities; therefore, the costs of support departments are also caused by the activities of the producing departments. **Causal factors** are variables or activities within a producing department that provoke the incurrence of support costs. In choosing a basis for allocating support department costs, every effort should be made to identify appropriate causal factors (activity drivers). Using causal factors results in product costs being more accurate. Furthermore, if the causal factors are known, managers are more able to control the consumption of services.

COST MANAGEMENT — Technology in Action

Did you get my order? Did you ship it? If not, when are you going to? These are the three big questions that **Mott's** North America customers want answered—and they want them answered in real time. Mott's, which sells juices and processed fruit products (including applesauce, Clamato, Mr. and Mrs. T drink mixer, and Rose's Holland House) to food brokers, uses SAP R/3 integrated applications to provide customer service and support. While many companies assign customer service to a support department, Mott's believes that customer service is the most critical issue in their business. The company wants to provide more timely information about order status, the availability of products, and production schedules and delivery. This requires integration across order taking, billing, accounts receivable, production, and shipping.

"Orders come in through EDI, telephone, or fax," says Jeff Morgan, vice president of information technology. "Cus-tomer service takes the order and checks availability to confirm delivery date. If there is insufficient product in inventory, the service representative checks the production plan. This automatically calculates lead times to determine delivery of the entire order or partial shipment and balance delivery date. The order is launched, financials are updated as it works its way through the system, and an invoice is generated. As soon as any data are entered into the system, they are immediately available for access by other users throughout the system."

Further benefits are gained through the elimination of duplicate data entry and the need to reconcile transactions between the formerly "siloed" support departments. The end results are a reduction in cost, improvement in customer service, and better understanding of the relationship between production and support costs.

Source: Taken from SAP materials and the Web site: http://www.sap.com/usa.

To illustrate the types of causal factors, or activity drivers, that can be used, consider the following three support departments: power, personnel, and materials handling. For power costs, a logical allocation base is kilowatt-hours, which can be measured by separate meters for each department. If separate meters do not exist, perhaps machine hours used by each department would provide a good proxy, or a means of approximating power usage. For personnel costs, both the number of producing department employees and the labor turnover (e.g., number of new hires) are possible activity drivers. For materials handling, the number of material moves, the hours of materials handling used, and the quantity of material moved are all possible activity drivers. Exhibit 7-3 lists some possible activity drivers that can be used to allocate support department costs. When competing activity drivers exist, managers need to assess which factor provides the most convincing relationship.

EXHIBIT 7-3	Examples of Possible Activity Drivers for Support Departments

Accounting:
  Number of transactions
Cafeteria:
  Number of employees
Data Processing:
  Number of lines entered
  Number of hours of service
Engineering:
  Number of change orders
  Number of hours
Maintenance:
  Machine hours
  Maintenance hours
Materials Storeroom:
  Number of material moves
  Pounds of material moved
  Number of different parts
	Payroll:
	  Number of employees
	Personnel:
	  Number of employees
	  Number of firings or layoffs
	  Number of new hires
	  Direct labor cost
	Power:
	  Kilowatt-hours
	  Machine hours
	Purchasing:
	  Number of orders
	  Cost of orders
	Shipping:
	  Number of orders

While the use of a causal factor to allocate common cost is the best solution, sometimes an easily measured causal factor cannot be found. In that case, the accountant looks for a good proxy. For example, the common cost of plant depreciation may be allocated to producing departments on the basis of square footage. Though square footage does not cause depreciation, it can be argued that the number of square feet a department occupies is a good proxy for the services provided to it by the factory building. The choice of a good proxy to guide allocation is dependent upon the company's objectives for allocation.

Objectives of Allocation

A number of important objectives are associated with the allocation of support department costs to producing departments and ultimately to specific products. The following major objectives have been identified by the IMA:[1]

1. To obtain a mutually agreeable price
2. To compute product-line profitability
3. To predict the economic effects of planning and control
4. To value inventory
5. To motivate managers

---

1. *Statements of Management Accounting (Statement 4B)*, "Allocation of Service and Administrative Costs" (Montvale, NJ: NAA, 1985). The NAA is now known as the Institute of Management Accountants (IMA).

Competitive pricing requires an understanding of costs. Only by knowing the costs of each service or product can the firm create meaningful bids. If costs are not accurately allocated, some costs could be overstated, resulting in bids that are too high and a loss of potential business. Alternatively, if the costs are understated, bids could be too low, producing losses on these products.

Good estimates of individual product costs also allow a manager to assess the profitability of individual products and services. Multiproduct companies need to be sure that all products are profitable and that the overall profitability of the firm is not disguising the poor performance of individual products. This meets the profitability objective identified by the IMA.

By assessing the profitability of various support services, a manager may evaluate the mix of support services offered by the firm. From this evaluation, executives may decide to drop some support services, reallocate resources from one to another, reprice certain support services, or exercise greater cost control in some areas. These steps would meet the IMA's planning and control objective. The validity of any evaluation, however, depends to a great extent on the accuracy of the cost assignments made to individual products.

For a service organization such as a hospital, the IMA objective of inventory valuation is not relevant. For manufacturing organizations, however, this objective must be given special attention. Rules of financial reporting (GAAP) require that all direct and indirect manufacturing costs be assigned to the products produced. Since support department costs are indirect manufacturing costs, they must be assigned to products. This is accomplished through support department cost allocation. Inventories and cost of goods sold, then, include direct materials, direct labor, and all manufacturing overhead, including the cost of support departments.

Allocations also can be used to motivate managers. If the costs of support departments are not allocated to producing departments, managers may tend to overconsume these services. Consumption of a support service may continue until the marginal benefit of the service equals zero. In reality, the marginal cost of a service is, of course, greater than zero. By allocating the costs and holding managers of producing departments responsible for the economic performance of their units, the organization ensures that managers will use a support service until the marginal benefit of the service equals its marginal cost. Thus, allocation of support department costs helps each producing department select the correct level of support service consumption.

There are other behavioral benefits. Allocation of support department costs to producing departments encourages managers of those departments to monitor the performance of support departments. Since the costs of the support departments affect the economic performance of their own departments, those managers have an incentive to control these costs through means other than simple usage of the support service. For instance, the managers can compare the internal costs of the support service with the costs of acquiring it externally. If a support department is not as cost effective as an outside source, perhaps the company should not continue to supply the service internally. Many university libraries, for example, are moving toward the use of outside contractors for photocopying services. They have found that these contractors are more cost efficient and provide a higher level of service to library users than did the previous method of using professional librarians to make change, keep the copy machines supplied with paper, fix paper jams, etc. This possibility of comparison should result in a more efficient internal support department. Monitoring by managers of producing departments will also encourage managers of support departments to be more sensitive to the needs of the producing departments.

Clearly, then, there are good reasons for allocating support department costs. The validity of these reasons depends, however, on the accuracy and fairness of the cost assignments made. Although it may not be possible to identify a single method of allocation that simultaneously satisfies all of these objectives, several guidelines have been developed to assist in determining the best allocation method. These guidelines are cause and effect, benefits received, fairness, and ability to bear. Another guideline to be used in conjunction with any of the others is cost-benefit. That is, the method used must provide sufficient benefits to justify any effort involved.

Cause and effect requires the determination of causal factors to guide allocation. For example, a corporate legal department may track the number of hours spent on legal work for its various divisions (e.g., handling patent applications, lawsuits, etc.). The number of hours worked by lawyers and paralegals has a clear cause-and-effect relationship with the overall cost of the legal department and may be used to allocate the cost of the corporate legal department to the various company divisions.

The benefits-received guideline associates the cost with perceived benefits. Research and development (R&D) costs, for example, may be allocated on the basis of the sales of each division. Although some R&D efforts may be unsuccessful and while the successful efforts may happen to benefit one division in one year, all divisions have a stake in corporate R&D and will at some point have increased sales because of it.

Fairness or equity is a guideline often mentioned in government contracting. In the case of cost allocation methods, fairness usually means that the government contract should be costed in a method similar to nongovernmental contracts. For example, an airplane engine manufacturer may allocate a portion of corporate legal department costs to the government contract if these costs are usually allocated to private contracts.

Ability to bear is the least desirable guideline. It tends to "penalize" the most profitable division by allocating to it the largest proportion of a support department cost—regardless of whether the profitable division receives any services from the allocated department. As a result, no motivational benefits of allocation are realized.

In determining how to allocate support department costs, the guideline of cost-benefit must be considered. In other words, the costs of implementing a particular allocation scheme must be compared to the benefits expected to be derived. As a result, companies try to use easily measured and understood bases for allocation.

Allocating One Department's Costs to Another Department

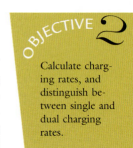

OBJECTIVE 2

Calculate charging rates, and distinguish between single and dual charging rates.

Frequently, the costs of a support department are allocated to another department through the use of a charging rate. In this case, we focus on the allocation of one department's costs to other departments. For example, a company's data processing department may serve various other departments. The cost of operating the data processing department is then allocated to the user departments. While this seems simple and straightforward, a number of considerations go into determining an appropriate charging rate. The two major factors are (1) the choice of a single or a dual charging rate and (2) the use of budgeted versus actual support department costs.

A Single Charging Rate

Some companies prefer to develop a single charging rate. Suppose, for example, that Hamish and Barton, a large regional public accounting firm, develops an in-house photocopying department to serve its three producing departments (audit, tax, and management advisory systems, or MAS). The costs of the photocopying department include fixed costs of $26,190 per year (salaries and machine rental) and variable costs of $0.023 per page copied (paper and toner). Estimated usage (in pages) by the three producing departments is as follows:

Audit department	94,500
Tax department	67,500
MAS department	108,000
Total	270,000

If a single charging rate is used, the fixed costs of $26,190 will be combined with estimated variable costs of $6,210 (270,000 × $0.023). Total costs of $32,400 are divided by the estimated 270,000 pages to be copied to yield a rate of $0.12 per page.

The amount charged to the producing departments is solely a function of the number of pages copied. Suppose that the actual usage for audit is 92,000 pages, 65,000 pages for tax, and 115,000 pages for MAS. The total photocopying department charges would be as shown:

Number of Pages × *Charge per Page* = *Total Charges*

	Number of Pages	Charge per Page	Total Charges
Audit	92,000	$0.12	$11,040
Tax	65,000	0.12	7,800
MAS	115,000	0.12	13,800
Total	272,000		$32,640

Notice that the use of a single rate treats the fixed cost as if it were variable. In fact, to the producing departments, photocopying is strictly variable. Did the photocopying department need $32,640 to copy 272,000 pages? No, it needed only $32,446 [$26,190 + (272,000 × $0.023)]. The extra amount charged is due to the treatment of a fixed cost in a variable manner.[2]

Dual Charging Rates

While the use of a single rate is simple, it ignores the differential impact of changes in usage on costs. The variable costs of a support department increase as the level of service increases. For example, the costs of paper and toner for the photocopying department increase as the number of pages copied increases. Fixed costs, on the other hand, do not vary with the level of service. For example, the rental payment for photocopying machines does not change as the number of pages increases or decreases. We can avoid the treatment of fixed costs as variable by developing two rates: one for fixed costs and one for variable costs. The development of dual charging rates (which are used as the basis for pricing) is particularly important in companies such as public utilities.

Developing a Fixed Rate

Fixed service costs can be considered capacity costs; they are incurred to provide the capacity necessary to deliver the service units required by the producing departments. When the support department was established, its delivery capability was designed to serve the long-term needs of the producing departments. Since the original support needs caused the creation of the support service capacity, it seems reasonable to allocate fixed costs based on those needs.

Either the normal or peak activity of the producing departments provides a reasonable measure of original support service needs. Normal capacity is the average capacity achieved over more than one fiscal period. If service is required uniformly over the time period, normal capacity is a good measure of activity. Peak capacity allows for variation in the need for the support department, and the size of the department is structured to allow for maximum need. In our example, the tax department may need much more photocopying during the first four months of the year, and its usage may be based on that need. The choice of normal or peak capacity in allocating budgeted fixed service costs depends on the needs of the individual firm. Budgeted fixed costs are allocated in this way regardless of whether the purpose is product costing or performance evaluation.

---

2. Note that the photocopying department would have charged out less than the cost needed if the number of pages copied had been less than the budgeted number of pages. You might calculate the total cost charged for a total of 268,000 pages ($0.12 × 268,000 = $32,160) and compare it with the cost incurred of $32,354 [$26,190 + (268,000 × $0.023)].

The allocation of fixed costs follows a 3-step procedure:

1. *Determination of budgeted fixed support service costs.* The fixed support service costs that should be incurred for a period need to be identified.
2. *Computation of the allocation ratio.* Using the practical or normal capacity of each producing department, it is necessary to compute an allocation ratio. The allocation ratio simply gives a producing department's share or percentage of the total capacity of all producing departments.

    Allocation ratio = Producing department capacity/Total capacity

3. *Allocation.* The fixed support service costs are then allocated in proportion to each producing department's original support service needs.

    Allocation = Allocation ratio × Budgeted fixed support service costs

Let's assume that the three departments in our example originally decided that they would need the number of photocopies equal to the budgeted number given earlier:

	Original Number of Copies	Percent	Budgeted Fixed Cost	Allocated Fixed Cost
Audit	94,500	35%	$26,190	$ 9,166.50
Tax	67,500	25	26,190	6,547.50
MAS	108,000	40	26,190	10,476.00
Total	270,000	100%		$26,190.00

The fixed costs allocated, then, are the relevant percentages for each department multiplied by the support department's budgeted fixed costs.

Developing a Variable Rate

The variable rate depends on the costs that change as the activity driver changes. In the photocopying department, the activity driver is the number of pages copied. As the number of pages increases, more paper and toner are used. Since these materials average $0.023 per page, the variable rate is $0.023. This variable rate is used in conjunction with the fixed amount allocated to determine total charges. In our example, the audit department would be allocated 35 percent of fixed cost plus $0.023 per page copied. The tax department would be allocated 25 percent of fixed cost plus $0.023 per page copied. MAS would be allocated 40 percent of fixed cost plus $0.023 per page copied. Let's see how variable photocopying costs are allocated under the dual-rate method.

	Actual Number of Copies	×	Variable Rate	=	Variable Amount	+	Fixed Amount	=	Total Charge
Audit	92,000		$0.023		$2,116		$ 9,167		$11,283
Tax	65,000		0.023		1,495		6,548		8,043
MAS	115,000		0.023		2,645		10,476		13,121
Total	272,000				$6,256		$26,191		$32,447

Total Allocation

Under the dual charging rates, the fixed photocopying rates are charged to the departments in accordance with their original capacity needs. Especially in a case like this one, in which fixed costs are such a high proportion of total costs, the additional effort needed to develop the dual rates may be worthwhile.

The dual-rate method has the benefit of sending the correct signal regarding increased usage of the support department. Suppose that the tax department wants to have several research articles on tax law changes photocopied for clients. Should this be done "in house" by the photocopying department or sent to a private photocopying firm that charges $0.06 per page? Under the single-rate method, the in-house cost charged would be too high because it wrongly assumes that fixed cost will increase as pages copied increase. However, under the dual-rate method, the additional cost would be only $0.023 per page, which correctly approximates the additional cost of the job.

COST MANAGEMENT

Technology in Action

Over the past 10 to 15 years, companies such as **Hewlett-Packard**, **IBM**, and **Dow Chemical**, have taken certain support departments and formed shared services centers (SSCs). The SSC performs activities that are used across a wide array of the company's divisions and departments. For example, payroll, receiving, and customer billing and accounts receivable processing have each formed the basis of an SSC. The company reaps the savings that accrue to economies of scale and standardized process design. Tools to measure performance are also incorporated into the SSC design. The SSC is faced with three important cost questions:

1. What causes costs in our operation?

2. How much should be charged back to the customers/producing departments?

3. How do our costs compare with those of outsourcing firms that perform the same service?

Activity-based costing and activity-based management are a natural fit for the SSCs. The drivers used to develop charging rates are seldom unit-based drivers (based on production). Instead, they might include the number of transactions processed and the percentage of errors in customer-provided information. Because ABC provides a better understanding of costs and their related drivers, it provides a better framework for managing SSC costs than traditional cost accounting systems.

Source: Taken from Ann Triplett and Jon Scheumann, "Managing Shared Services with ABM," *Strategic Finance* (February 2000): 40–45.

Budgeted versus Actual Usage

The second factor to be considered in charging costs from a single service department to other departments is whether actual usage or budgeted usage should be the basis for allocating costs. In truth, this factor only has an impact on allocated costs when fixed costs are involved. As a result, we need to consider it in the case of a single charging rate (which combines fixed with variable costs to generate a rate) and of the fixed portion of the dual charging rate.

When we allocate support department costs to the producing departments, should we allocate actual or budgeted costs? The answer is budgeted costs. There are two basic reasons for allocating support department costs. One reason is to cost the units produced. In this case, the budgeted support department costs are allocated to producing departments as a preliminary step in forming the overhead rate. Recall that the overhead rate is calculated at the beginning of the period, when actual costs are unknown. Thus, budgeted costs must be used. The second usage of allocated support department costs is for performance evaluation. In this case, too, budgeted support department costs are allocated to producing departments.

Managers of support and producing departments usually are held accountable for the performance of their departments. Their ability to control costs is an important factor in their performance evaluations. This ability is usually measured by comparing actual costs with planned or budgeted costs. If actual costs exceed budgeted costs, the department may be operating inefficiently, with the difference between the two costs serving as the measure of that inefficiency. Similarly, if actual costs are less than budgeted costs, the department may be operating efficiently.

A general principle of performance evaluation is that managers should not be held responsible for costs or activities over which they have no control. Since managers of producing departments have significant input regarding the level of support service consumed, they should be held responsible for their share of support service costs. This statement, however, has an important qualification: A department's evaluation should not be affected by the degree of efficiency achieved by another department.

This qualifying statement has an important implication for the allocation of support department costs. *Actual* costs of a support department should not be allocated to producing departments because they include efficiencies or inefficiencies achieved by the support department. Managers of producing departments have no control over the degree of efficiency achieved by a support department manager. By allocating *budgeted* costs instead of actual costs, no inefficiencies or efficiencies are transferred from one department to another.

Whether budgeted usage or actual usage is used depends on the purpose of the allocation. For *product costing*, the allocation is done at the beginning of the year on the basis of budgeted usage so that a predetermined overhead rate can be computed. If the purpose is *performance evaluation*, however, the allocation is done at the end of the period and is based on actual usage. The use of cost information for performance evaluation is covered in more detail in Chapter 9.

Let's return to our photocopying example. Recall that annual budgeted fixed costs were $26,190 and the budgeted variable cost per page was $0.023. The three producing departments—audit, tax, and MAS—estimated usage at 94,500 copies, 67,500 copies, and 108,000 copies, respectively. Given these data, the costs allocated to each department at the *beginning* of the year are shown in Exhibit 7-4.

EXHIBIT 7-4 — Use of Budgeted Data for Product Costing: Comparison of Single- and Dual-Rate Methods

Single-Rate Method

	Number of Copies	×	Total Rate	=	Allocated Cost
Audit	94,500		$0.12		$11,340
Tax	67,500		0.12		8,100
MAS	108,000		0.12		12,960
Total	270,000				$32,400

Dual-Rate Method

	Number of Copies	×	Variable Rate	+	Fixed Allocation	=	Allocated Cost
Audit	94,500		$0.023		$ 9,167		$11,340*
Tax	67,500		0.023		6,548		8,100*
MAS	108,000		0.023		10,476		12,960
Total	270,000						$32,400

*Rounded down.

Note that the single-rate method produces the same allocation as does the dual-rate method when budgeted figures are used. This is because budgeted fixed cost is just absorbed by the number of budgeted pages.

When the allocation is done for the purpose of budgeting the producing departments' costs, then, of course, the budgeted support department costs are used. The photocopying costs allocated to each department would be added to other producing department costs—including those directly traceable to each department plus other support department allocations—to compute each department's anticipated spending. In a manufacturing plant, the allocation of budgeted support department costs to the producing departments would precede the calculation of the predetermined overhead rate.

During the year, each producing department would also be responsible for actual charges incurred based on the actual number of pages copied. Going back to the actual usage assumed previously, a second allocation is now made to measure the actual performance of each department against its budget. The actual photocopying costs allocated to each department for performance evaluation purposes are shown in Exhibit 7-5.

EXHIBIT 7-5 — Use of Actual Data for Performance Evaluation Purposes: Comparison of Single- and Dual-Rate Methods

Single-Rate Method

	Number of Copies	×	Total Rate	=	Allocated Cost
Audit	92,000		$0.12		$11,040
Tax	65,000		0.12		7,800
MAS	115,000		0.12		13,800
Total	272,000				$32,640

Dual-Rate Method

	Number of Copies	×	Variable Rate	+	Fixed Allocation	=	Allocated Cost
Audit	92,000		$0.023		$ 9,167		$11,283
Tax	65,000		0.023		6,548		8,043
MAS	115,000		0.023		10,476		13,121
Total	272,000						$32,447

Fixed versus Variable Bases: A Note of Caution

Using normal or practical capacity to allocate fixed support service costs provides a *fixed* base. As long as the capacities of the producing departments remain at the level originally anticipated, there is no reason to change the allocation ratios. Thus, each year, the audit department receives 35 percent of the budgeted fixed photocopying costs, the tax department 25 percent, and the MAS department 40 percent, no matter what their actual usage is. If the capacities of the departments change, the ratios should be recalculated.

In practice, some companies choose to allocate fixed costs in proportion to actual usage or expected actual usage. Since usage may vary from year to year, allocation of fixed costs would then use a variable base. Variable bases, however, have a significant drawback: they allow the actions of one department to affect the amount of cost allocated to another department.

To see how this is demonstrated, let's return to Hamish and Barton's photocopying department and assume that fixed costs are allocated on the basis of anticipated usage for the coming year. The audit and tax departments budget the same number of copies as before. However, the MAS department anticipates much less activity due to a regional recession, which will cut down the number of new clients served; the anticipated number of photocopies for this department falls to 68,000. The adjusted fixed cost allocation ratios and allocated fixed cost based on the newly budgeted usage are as follows.

	Number of Copies	Percent	Allocated Fixed Cost
Audit	94,500	41.1%	$10,764
Tax	67,500	29.3	7,674
MAS	68,000	29.6	7,752
Total	230,000	100.0%	$26,190

Notice that both the audit and tax departments' allocation of fixed costs increased even though the fixed costs of the photocopying department remained unchanged. This increase is caused by a decrease in the MAS department's use of photocopying. In effect, the audit and tax departments are being penalized because of MAS's decision to reduce the number of pages copied for the MAS department. Imagine the feelings of the first two managers when they realize that their copying charges have increased due to the increase in allocated fixed costs! The penalty occurs because a variable base is used to allocate fixed support service costs; it can be avoided by using a fixed base.

Choosing a Support Department Cost Allocation Method

OBJECTIVE 3

Allocate support center costs to producing departments using the direct method, the sequential method, and the reciprocal method.

So far, we have considered cost allocation from a single support department to several producing departments. We used the direct method of support department cost allocation, in which support department costs are allocated only to producing departments. This was appropriate in the earlier example because no other support departments existed. This would also be appropriate when there is no possibility of interaction among support departments. Many companies do have multiple support departments, and they frequently interact. For example, in a factory, personnel and cafeteria serve each other, other support departments, and the producing departments.

Ignoring these interactions and allocating support costs directly to producing departments may produce unfair and inaccurate cost assignments. For example, power, although a support department, may use 30 percent of the services of the maintenance department. The maintenance costs caused by the power department belong to the power department. By not assigning these costs to the power department, its costs are understated. In effect, some of the costs caused by power are "hidden" in the maintenance department because maintenance costs would be lower if the power department did not exist. As a result, a producing department that is a heavy user of power and an average or below-average user of maintenance may then receive, under the direct method, a cost allocation that is understated.

In determining which support department cost allocation method to use, companies must determine the extent of support department interaction. In addition, they must weigh the costs and benefits associated with the three methods described and illustrated in the following sections: the direct, sequential, and reciprocal methods.

Direct Method of Allocation

When companies allocate support department costs only to the producing departments, they are using the **direct method** of allocation. The direct method is the simplest and most straightforward way to allocate support department costs. Variable service costs are allocated directly to producing departments in proportion to each department's usage of the service. Fixed costs are also allocated directly to the producing department, but in proportion to the producing department's normal or practical capacity.

Exhibit 7-6 illustrates the lack of support department reciprocity on cost allocation in using the direct method. In Exhibit 7-6, we see that by using the direct method, support department cost is allocated to producing departments only. No cost from one support department is allocated to another support department. Thus, no support department interaction is recognized.

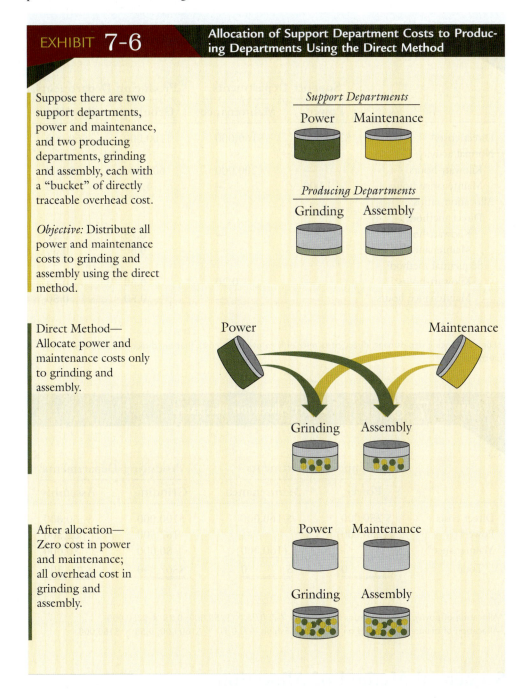

EXHIBIT 7-6   Allocation of Support Department Costs to Producing Departments Using the Direct Method

Suppose there are two support departments, power and maintenance, and two producing departments, grinding and assembly, each with a "bucket" of directly traceable overhead cost.

Objective: Distribute all power and maintenance costs to grinding and assembly using the direct method.

Support Departments
Power   Maintenance

Producing Departments
Grinding   Assembly

Direct Method— Allocate power and maintenance costs only to grinding and assembly.

Power   Maintenance

Grinding   Assembly

After allocation— Zero cost in power and maintenance; all overhead cost in grinding and assembly.

Power   Maintenance

Grinding   Assembly

To illustrate the direct method, consider the data in Exhibit 7-7 on the following page. The data show the budgeted activity and budgeted costs of two support departments and two producing departments. (Note that the same data are used to illustrate the sequential method; for the time being, ignore the allocation ratios at the bottom of Exhibit 7-7 that correspond to the sequential method.) Assume that the causal factor for power costs is kilowatt-hours, and the causal factor for maintenance costs is maintenance hours. These causal factors are used as the bases for allocation. In the direct method, only the kilowatt-hours and the maintenance hours in the producing departments are used to compute the allocation ratios. The direct allocations based on the data given in Exhibit 7-7 are shown in Exhibit 7-8. (To simplify the illustration, no distinction is made between fixed and variable costs.)

EXHIBIT 7-7　　Data for Illustrating Allocation Methods

	Support Departments		Producing Departments	
	Power	**Maintenance**	**Grinding**	**Assembly**
Direct costs*	$250,000	$160,000	$100,000	$60,000
Normal activity:				
Kilowatt-hours	—	200,000	600,000	200,000
Maintenance hours	1,000	—	4,500	4,500
Allocation ratios:				
Direct method:				
Kilowatt-hours	—	—	0.75	0.25
Maintenance hours	—	—	0.50	0.50
Sequential method:				
Kilowatt-hours	—	0.20	0.60	0.20
Maintenance hours	—	—	0.50	0.50

*For a producing department, direct costs refer only to overhead costs that are directly traceable to the department.

EXHIBIT 7-8　　Direct Allocation Illustrated

	Support Departments		Producing Departments	
	Power	**Maintenance**	**Grinding**	**Assembly**
Direct costs	$ 250,000	$ 160,000	$100,000	$ 60,000
Power[a]	(250,000)	—	187,500	62,500
Maintenance[b]	—	(160,000)	80,000	80,000
Total	$　　0	$　　0	$367,500	$202,500

[a]Allocation of power based on ratios from Exhibit 7-7: 0.75 × $250,000; 0.25 × $250,000.
[b]Allocation of maintenance based on ratios from Exhibit 7-7: 0.50 × $160,000; 0.50 × $160,000.

Sequential Method of Allocation

The **sequential (or step) method** of allocation recognizes that interactions among the support departments do occur. However, the sequential method does not fully recognize support department interaction. Cost allocations are performed in step-down fashion, following a predetermined ranking procedure. This ranking can be performed in various ways. For example, a company could rank the support departments in order of the percentage of service they render to other support departments. Usually, however, the sequence is defined by ranking the support departments in order of the amount of service rendered, from the greatest to the least. Degree of support service is usually measured by the direct costs of each support department; the department with the highest cost is seen as rendering the greatest service.

Exhibit 7-9, on the following page, illustrates the sequential method. First, the support departments are ranked, usually in accordance with direct costs; here power is first, then maintenance. Next, power costs are allocated to maintenance and the two producing departments. Then, the costs of maintenance are allocated only to producing departments.

The costs of the support department rendering the greatest support service are allocated first. They are distributed to all support departments below it in the sequence and to all producing departments. Then, the costs of the support department next in sequence are similarly allocated, and so on. In the sequential method, once a support department's costs are allocated, it never receives a subsequent allocation from another support department. In other words, costs of a support department are never allocated to support departments *above* it in the sequence. Also note that the costs allocated from a support department are its direct costs *plus* any costs it receives in allocations from other support departments. The direct costs of a department are those that are directly traceable to the department.

To illustrate the sequential method, consider the data provided in Exhibit 7-7. Using cost as a measure of service, the support department rendering more service is power. Thus, its costs will be allocated first, followed by those for maintenance. The allocation ratios shown in Exhibit 7-7 will be used to execute the allocation. Note that the allocation ratios for the maintenance department ignore the usage by the power department, since its costs cannot be allocated to a support department above it in the allocation sequence.

The allocations obtained with the sequential method are shown in Exhibit 7-10 on page 293. Notice that $50,000 of the power department's costs are allocated to the maintenance department. This reflects the fact that the maintenance department uses 20 percent of the power department's output. As a result, the cost of operating the maintenance department increases from $160,000 to $210,000. Also notice that when the costs of the maintenance department are allocated, no costs are allocated back to the power department, even though it uses 1,000 hours of the output of the maintenance department.

The sequential method may be more accurate than the direct method because it recognizes some interactions among the support departments. It does not recognize all interactions, however; no maintenance costs were assigned to the power department even though it used 10 percent of the maintenance department's output. The reciprocal method corrects this deficiency.

Reciprocal Method of Allocation

The **reciprocal method** of allocation recognizes all interactions of support departments. Under the reciprocal method, the usage of one support department by another is used to determine the total cost of each support department, where the total cost reflects interactions among the support departments. Then, the new total of support department costs is allocated to the producing departments. This method fully accounts for support department interaction.

Total Cost of Support Departments

To determine the total cost of a support department so that this total cost reflects interactions with other support departments, a system of simultaneous linear equations must be solved. Each equation, which is a cost equation for a support department, is the sum of the department's direct costs plus the proportion of service received from other support departments.

$$\text{Total cost} = \text{Direct costs} + \text{Allocated costs}$$

The method is best described using an example. The same data used to illustrate the direct and sequential methods will be used to illustrate the reciprocal method in

Suppose there are two support departments, power and maintenance, and two producing departments, grinding and assembly, each with a "bucket" of directly traceable overhead cost.

Objective: Distribute all power and maintenance costs to grinding and assembly using the sequential method.

Support Departments

Power   Maintenance

Producing Departments

Grinding   Assembly

Step 1: Rank support departments— #1 power, #2 maintenance.

Step 2: Distribute power to maintenance, grinding, and assembly.

Power

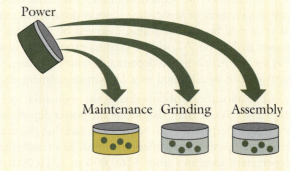

Maintenance   Grinding   Assembly

Then, distribute maintenance to grinding and assembly.

Maintenance

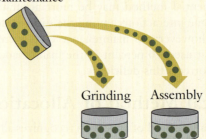

Grinding   Assembly

After allocation— Zero cost in power and maintenance; all overhead cost in grinding and assembly.

Power   Maintenance

Grinding   Assembly

EXHIBIT 7-10	Sequential Allocation Illustrated			

	Support Departments		Producing Departments	
	Power	**Maintenance**	**Grinding**	**Assembly**
Direct costs	$ 250,000	$ 160,000	$100,000	$ 60,000
Power[a]	(250,000)	50,000	150,000	50,000
Maintenance[b]	—	(210,000)	105,000	105,000
Total	$ 0	$ 0	$355,000	$215,000

[a]Allocation of power based on ratios from Exhibit 7-7: 0.20 × $250,000; 0.60 × $250,000; 0.20 × $250,000.
[b]Allocation of maintenance costs based on ratios from Exhibit 7-7: 0.50 × $210,000; 0.50 × $210,000.

EXHIBIT 7-11	Data for Illustrating Reciprocal Method			

	Support Departments		Producing Departments	
	Power	**Maintenance**	**Grinding**	**Assembly**
Direct costs:*				
Fixed	$200,000	$100,000	$ 80,000	$50,000
Variable	50,000	60,000	20,000	10,000
Total	$250,000	$160,000	$100,000	$60,000
Normal activity:				
Kilowatt-hours	—	200,000	600,000	200,000
Maintenance hours	1,000	—	4,500	4,500
Proportion of Output Used by				
	Power	**Maintenance**	**Grinding**	**Assembly**
Allocation ratios:				
Power	—	0.20	0.60	0.20
Maintenance	0.10	—	0.45	0.45

*For a producing department, direct costs are defined as overhead costs that are directly traceable to the department.

Exhibit 7-11. The allocation ratios needed for the simultaneous equations are interpreted as follows: maintenance receives 20 percent of power's output, and power receives 10 percent of maintenance's output.

Now let P equal the total cost of the power department and M equal the total cost of the maintenance department. As indicated previously, the total cost of a support department is the sum of its direct costs plus the proportion of service received from other support departments. Using the data and allocation ratios from Exhibit 7-11, the cost equation for each support department can be expressed as follows:

$$P = \text{Direct costs} + \text{Share of maintenance's cost} \qquad (7.1)$$
$$= \$250{,}000 + 0.1M \text{ (maintenance's cost equation)}$$

$$M = \text{Direct costs} + \text{Share of power's costs} \qquad (7.2)$$
$$= \$160{,}000 + 0.2P \text{ (power's cost equation)}$$

The direct-cost components of each equation are taken from Exhibit 7-11, as are the allocation ratios.

The power cost equation (Equation 7.1) and the maintenance cost equation (Equation 7.2) can be solved simultaneously to yield the total cost for each support department. Substituting Equation 7.1 into Equation 7.2 gives the following:

$$M = \$160{,}000 + 0.2(\$250{,}000 + 0.1M)$$
$$M = \$160{,}000 + \$50{,}000 + 0.02M$$
$$0.98M = \$210{,}000$$
$$M = \$214{,}286$$

Substituting this value for M into Equation 7.1 yields the total cost for power:

$$P = \$250{,}000 + 0.1(\$214{,}286)$$
$$= \$250{,}000 + \$21{,}429$$
$$= \$271{,}429$$

After the equations are solved, the total costs of each support department are known. These total costs, unlike the direct or sequential methods, reflect all interactions between support departments.

Allocation to Producing Departments

Once the total costs of each support department are known, the allocations to the producing departments can be made. These allocations, based on the proportion of output used by each producing department, are shown in Exhibit 7-12. Notice that the total costs allocated to the producing departments equal $410,000, the total direct costs of the two support departments ($250,000 + $160,000).

EXHIBIT 7-12 Reciprocal Allocation Illustrated

		Allocated to	
	Total Cost	**Grinding**[a]	**Assembly**[b]
Power	$271,429	$162,857	$ 54,285*
Maintenance	214,286	96,429	96,429
Total		$259,286	$150,714

[a]Power: 0.60 × $271,429; Maintenance: 0.45 × $214,286.
[b]Power: 0.20 × $271,429; Maintenance: 0.45 × $214,286.
*Rounded down.

Comparison of the Three Methods

Exhibit 7-13 gives the cost allocations from the power and maintenance departments to the grinding and assembly departments using the three support department cost allocation methods. How different are the results? Does it really matter which method is used? Depending on the degree of interaction of the support departments, the three allocation methods can give radically different results. In this particular example, the di-

EXHIBIT 7-13	Comparison of Support Department Cost Allocations Using the Direct, Sequential, and Reciprocal Methods					
	Direct Method		**Sequential Method**		**Reciprocal Method**	
	Grinding	Assembly	Grinding	Assembly	Grinding	Assembly
Direct costs	$100,000	$ 60,000	$100,000	$ 60,000	$100,000	$ 60,000
Allocated from power	187,500	62,500	150,000	50,000	162,857	54,285
Allocated from maintenance	80,000	80,000	105,000	105,000	96,429	96,429
Total cost	$367,500	$202,500	$355,000	$215,000	$359,286	$210,714

rect method (as compared to the sequential method) allocated $12,500 more to the grinding department (and $12,500 less to the assembly department). Surely, the manager of the assembly department would prefer the direct method and the manager of the grinding department would prefer the sequential method. Because allocation methods do affect the cost responsibilities of managers, it is important for the accountant to understand the consequences of the different methods and to have good reasons for the eventual choice.

It is important to keep a cost-benefit perspective in choosing an allocation method. The accountant must weigh the advantages of better allocation against the increased cost using a more theoretically preferred method, such as the reciprocal method. For example, about 20 years ago, the controller for the IBM Poughkeepsie plant decided that the reciprocal method of cost allocation would do a better job of allocating support department costs. He identified over 700 support departments and solved the system of equations using a computer. Computationally, he had no problems. However, the producing department managers did not understand the reciprocal method. They were sure that extra cost was being allocated to their departments, but they were not sure just how. After months of meetings with the line managers, the controller threw in the towel and returned to the sequential method—which everyone did understand.

Another factor to be considered in allocating support department cost is the rapid change in technology. Many firms currently find that support department cost allocation is useful for them. However, the move toward activity-based costing and just-in-time manufacturing can virtually eliminate the need for support department cost allocation. In the case of the JIT factory with manufacturing cells, much of the service (e.g., maintenance, materials handling, and setups) is performed by cell workers. Allocation is not necessary.

OBJECTIVE 4

Calculate departmental overhead rates.

Departmental Overhead Rates and Product Costing

Upon allocating all support service costs to producing departments, an overhead rate can be computed for each department. This rate is computed by adding the allocated service costs to the overhead costs that are directly traceable to the producing department and dividing this total by some measure of activity, such as direct labor hours or machine hours.

For example, from Exhibit 7-10, the total overhead costs for the grinding department after allocation of support service costs are $355,000. Assume that machine hours are the base for assigning overhead costs to products passing through the grinding department and that the normal level of activity is 71,000 machine hours. The overhead rate for the grinding department is computed as follows:

Overhead rate = $355,000/71,000 machine hours
= $5 per machine hour

Similarly, assume that the assembly department uses direct labor hours to assign its overhead. With a normal level of activity of 107,500 direct labor hours, the overhead rate for the assembly department is as follows:

Overhead rate = $215,000/107,500 direct labor hours
= $2 per direct labor hour

Using these rates, the product's unit cost can be determined. To illustrate, suppose a product requires two machine hours of grinding per unit produced and one hour of assembly. The overhead cost assigned to one unit of this product would be $12 [(2 × $5) + (1 × $2)]. If the same product uses $15 of materials and $6 of labor (totalled from grinding and assembly), then its unit cost is $33 ($12 + $15 + $6).

One might wonder, however, just how accurate this $33 cost is. Is this amount really what it costs to produce the product in question? Since materials and labor are directly traceable to products, the accuracy of product costs depends largely on the accuracy of the assignment of overhead costs. This in turn depends on the degree of correlation between the factors used to allocate support service costs to departments and the factors used to allocate the department's overhead costs to the products. For example, if power costs are highly correlated with kilowatt-hours and machine hours are highly correlated with a product's consumption of the grinding department's overhead costs, then we can have some confidence that the $5 overhead rate accurately assigns costs to individual products. However, if the allocation of support service costs to the grinding department or the use of machine hours is faulty—or both—then product costs will be distorted. The same reasoning can be applied to the assembly department. To ensure accurate product costs, great care should be used in identifying and using causal factors for both stages of overhead assignment. More will be said about this in a later chapter.

Accounting for Joint Production Processes

OBJECTIVE 5

Identify the characteristics of the joint production process, and allocate joint costs to products.

Joint products are two or more products produced simultaneously by the same process up to a "split-off" point. The **split-off point** is the point at which the joint products become separate and identifiable. For example, oil and natural gas are joint products. When a company drills for oil, it gets natural gas as well. As a result, the costs of exploration, acquisition of mineral rights, and drilling are incurred to the initial split-off point. Such costs are necessary to bring crude oil and natural gas out of the ground, and they are common costs to both products. Of course, some joint products may require processing beyond the split-off point. For example, crude oil can be processed further into aviation fuel, gasoline, kerosine, naptha, and other petrochemicals. The key point, however, is that the direct materials, direct labor, and overhead costs incurred up to the initial split-off point are joint costs that can be allocated to the final product only in some arbitrary manner. Joint products are so enmeshed that once the decision to produce has been made, management decision has little effect on the output, at least to the initial split-off point. Exhibit 7-14 depicts the joint production process. Exhibit 7-15 depicts the usual production process in which two products are manufactured independently from a common material. For example, a Taurus and a Mustang require steel, but the purchase of steel by **Ford Motor Company** does not require the manufacture of either model of car.

Joint products are related to each other such that an increase in the output of one increases the output of the others, although not necessarily in the same ratio. Up to the split-off point, you cannot get more of one product without getting more of the other(s). Whether considering the direct materials and conversion costs incurred prior to the initial split-off point as depicted in Exhibit 7-14, or the costs of heat, fuel, and

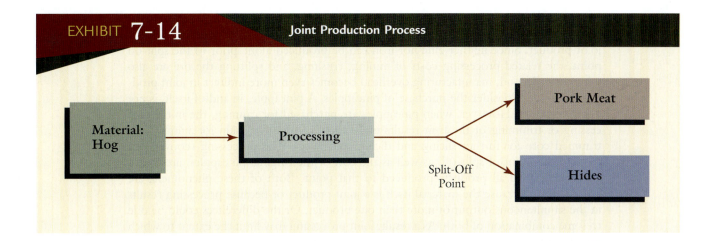

EXHIBIT 7-14   Joint Production Process

depreciation incurred in the type of multiple-product production depicted in Exhibit 7-15, one characteristic stands out. They are all indirect costs in the sense that allocation among the various products is necessary: that is, such costs cannot be traced directly to the ultimate products they benefit.

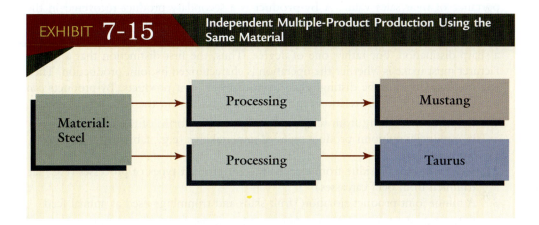

EXHIBIT 7-15   Independent Multiple-Product Production Using the Same Material

Cost Separability and the Need for Allocation

Costs are either separable or not. **Separable costs** are easily traced to individual products and offer no particular problem. If not separable, they must be allocated to various products for various reasons. Cost allocations are arbitrary. That is, there is no well-accepted theoretical way to determine which product incurs what part of the joint cost. In reality, all joint products benefit from the entire joint cost. The objective in joint cost allocation is to determine the most appropriate way to allocate a cost that is not really separable. The primary reason for joint cost allocation is that financial reporting (GAAP) and federal income tax law require it. In addition, these product costs are somewhat useful in calculating the cost of special lots or orders including government cost-type contracts and in justifying prices for legislative or administrative regulations. It is important to note that the allocation of joint costs is not appropriate for certain types of management decisions. The impact of joint costs on decision making is reserved for Chapter 18.

There are two important differences between costs incurred up to the split-off point in joint product situations and those indirect costs incurred for products that are produced independently. First, certain costs such as direct materials and direct labor, which are directly traceable to products when two or more products are separately produced, become indirect and indivisible when used prior to the split-off point to produce joint products. For example, if ore contains both iron and zinc, the direct material itself is a joint product. Since neither zinc nor iron can be produced alone prior to the split-off point, the related processing costs of mining, crushing, and splitting the ore are also joint costs. Second, manufacturing overhead becomes even more indirect in joint product situations. Consider the purchase of pineapples. A pineapple, in and of itself, is not a joint product. However, when pineapples are purchased for canning, the initial processing or trimming of the fruit results in a variety of products (skin for animal feed, trimmed core for further slicing and dicing, and juice). The processing (conversion) costs to the point of split-off, as well as the cost of the original pineapples, are mutually beneficial to all products produced to that point. Both of these phenomena are caused either because the material itself is a joint product or because processing results in the simultaneous output of more than one product. Or the differences could be due to some combination of both. As a result, joint processing may limit the extent to which activity drivers in an activity-based costing system can effectively indicate a cause-and-effect relationship between overhead costs and joint products.

Distinction and Similarity between Joint Products and By-Products

The distinction between joint products and by-products rests solely on the relative importance of their sales value. A **by-product** is a secondary product recovered in the course of manufacturing a primary product. It is a product whose total sales value is relatively minor in comparison with the sales value of the main product(s). This is not a sharp distinction, but rather one of degree. Thus, the first distinction that a manufacturer must make is whether the operation is characterized by joint production. Then any by-products must be distinguished from main or joint products. By-products can be characterized by their relationship to the main products in the following manner:

1. By-product resulting from scrap, trimmings, and so forth, of the main products in essentially nonjoint product types of undertakings (e.g., fabric trimmings from clothing pieces)
2. Scrap and other residue from essentially joint product types of processes (e.g., fat trimmed from beef carcasses)
3. A minor joint product situation (fruit skins and trimmings used as animal feed)

Relationships between joint products and by-products change, as do the classes of products within each of these classifications. When the relative importance of the individual products changes, the products need to be reclassified and the costing procedures changed. In fact, many by-products began as waste materials, became economically significant (and thus become by-products), and grow in importance to finally become full-fledged joint products. For example, sawdust and chips in sawmill operations were originally waste, but over the years, they have gained value as a major component of particle board. The various methods of accounting for by-products reflect this development. Generally, accounting for by-products began as an extension of accounting for waste material. Revenue from the sale of the by-products is recorded as separate income, when the amount of income is so small that it has little impact on either overall cost or sales. As the value of by-product revenues becomes more significant, the cost of the main product is reduced by recoveries, and finally the by-products achieve near main product status and are allocated a share of the joint cost incurred prior to split-off.

There are a number of ways to account for by-products. Typically, joint costs are not allocated to by-products because the products themselves are considered to be immaterial. Instead, revenue for the sale of the by-product is accounted for as "revenue from by-products" or as "other income." Any further processing costs needed (beyond the split-off point) are deducted from revenue. On occasion, net revenue from the sale of the by-product is accounted for as a deduction from the cost of goods sold of the joint products.

Accounting for Joint Product Costs

The accounting for overall joint costs of production (direct materials, direct labor, and overhead) is no different from the accounting for product costs in general. It is the *allocation* of joint costs to the individual products that is the source of difficulty. Still, the allocation must be done for financial reporting purposes—to value inventory carried on the balance sheet and to determine income. Thus, an allocation method must be found that, though arbitrary, allocates the costs on as reasonable a basis as possible. Because judgment is involved, equally competent accountants can arrive at different costs for the same product. There are a variety of methods for allocating joint costs. These methods include the physical units method, the weighted average method, the sales-value-at-split-off method, the net realizable value method, and the constant gross margin percentage method. These are covered in the following sections.

Physical Units Method

Under the **physical units method**, joint costs are distributed to products on the basis of some physical measure. These physical measures may be expressed in units such as pounds, tons, gallons, board feet, atomic weight, or heat units. If the joint products do not share the same physical measure (e.g., one product is measured in gallons, another in pounds), some common denominator may be used. For example, a producer of fuels may take gallons, barrels, and tons and convert each one into BTUs (British thermal units) of energy.

Computationally, the physical units method allocates to each joint product the same proportion of joint cost as the underlying proportion of units. So, if a joint process yields 300 pounds of Product A and 700 pounds of Product B, Product A receives 30 percent of the joint cost and Product B receives 70 percent. An alternative computation is to divide total joint costs by total output to find an average unit cost. The average unit cost is then multiplied by the number of units of each product. Although the method is not wholly satisfactory, it has a measure of logic behind it. Since all products are manufactured by the same process, it is impossible to say that one costs more per unit to produce than the other.

For example, suppose that a sawmill processes logs into four grades of lumber totaling 3,000,000 board feet as follows.

Grades	Board Feet
First and second	450,000
No. 1 common	1,200,000
No. 2 common	600,000
No. 3 common	750,000
Total	3,000,000

Total joint cost is $186,000. Using the physical units method, how much joint cost is allocated to each grade of lumber? First, we find the proportion of the total units for each grade; then, we assign each grade its proportion of joint cost.

Grades	Board Feet	Percent of Units	Joint Cost Allocation
First and second	450,000	0.15	$ 27,900
No. 1 common	1,200,000	0.40	74,400
No. 2 common	600,000	0.20	37,200
No. 3 common	750,000	0.25	46,500
Totals	3,000,000		$186,000

We could also calculate the average unit cost of $0.062 ($186,000/3,000,000) and multiply it by the board feet for each grade.

For example, manufacturers of forest products may add the average cost of logs entering the mill to the average conversion cost to arrive at an average finished product cost. This cost is applied to all finished products, no matter their type, grade, or market value. This method serves the purpose of product costing.

The physical units method may be used in any industry that processes joint products of differing grades (e.g., flour milling, tobacco, and lumber). However, a disadvantage of the physical units method is that high profits may be reflected from the sale of the high grades, with low profits or losses reflected on the sale of lower grades. This may result in incorrect managerial decisions if the data are not properly interpreted.

The physical units method presumes that each unit of material in the final product costs just as much to produce as any other. This is especially true where the dominant element can be traced to the product. Many feel this method often is unsatisfactory because it ignores the fact that not all costs are directly related to physical quantities. Also, the product might not have been handled at all if it had been physically separable before the split-off point from the part desired.

Weighted Average Method

In an attempt to overcome the difficulties encountered under the physical units method, weight factors can be assigned. These weight factors may include such diverse elements as amount of material used, difficulty to manufacture, time consumed, difference in type of labor used, and size of unit. These factors and their relative weights are usually combined in a single value, which we might call the **weight factor**. In the canning industry, the weight factor is used in the calculation of a basic case.

An example of the use of weight factors is found in the canning industry.[3] One type of weight factor is used to convert different-size cases of peaches into a uniform size for purposes of allocating joint costs to each case. Thus, if a basic case contains 24 cans of peaches in size 2½ cans, that case is assigned a weight factor of 1.0. A case with 24 cans in size 303 (a can roughly half the size 2½ can) receives a weight of 0.57, and so on. Once all types of cases have been converted into basic cases using the weight factors, joint costs can be allocated according to the physical units method. Peaches can also be assigned weight factors according to grade (e.g., fancy, choice, standard, and pie). If the standard grade is weighted at 1.00, then the better grades are weighted more heavily and the pie grade less heavily.

For example, suppose that a peach-canning factory purchases $5,000 of peaches; grades them into fancy, choice, standard, and pie quality; and then cans each grade. The following data on grade, number of cases, and weight factor apply.

Grades	Number of Cases	Weight Factor	Weighted Number of Cases	Percent	Allocated Joint Cost
Fancy	100	1.30	130	0.21667	$1,083
Choice	120	1.10	132	0.22000	1,100
Standard	303	1.00	303	0.50500	2,525
Pie	70	0.50	35	0.05833	292
			600		$5,000

By multiplying the number of cases by the weight factor, we obtain the weighted number of cases. Then, the physical units method can be applied as the percentage of weighted

3. The peach-canning example is adapted from K. E. Jankowski, "Cost and Sales Control in the Canning Industry," *N.A.C.A. Bulletin* 36 (November 1954): 376.

cases for each grade is obtained and multiplied by the joint cost to yield the allocated joint cost. The effect is to allocate relatively more of the joint cost to the fancy and choice grades because they represent more desirable peaches. The pie grade peaches, the good bits and pieces from bruised peaches, are relatively less desirable and are assigned a lower weight.

Frequently, weight factors are predetermined and set up as part of either an estimated cost or a standard cost system. The use of carefully constructed weight factors enables the cost accountant to give more attention to several influences and, therefore, results in more reasonable allocations. The real danger, of course, is that weights may be used that are either inappropriate in the first place or become so through the passage of time. Obviously, if arbitrary rates are used, the resulting costs of individual products will be arbitrary.

Allocation Based on Relative Market Value

Many accountants believe that joint costs should be allocated to individual products according to their ability to absorb joint costs. The advantage of this approach is that joint cost allocation will not produce consistently profitable or unprofitable items. The rationale for using ability to bear is the assumption that costs would not be incurred unless the jointly produced products together would yield enough revenue to cover all costs plus a reasonable return. The reverse also would be consistent with this theory; that is, a derived cost that the purchaser of materials and other joint costs is willing to incur for any individual product could be obtained by relating costs to sales values. On the other hand, fluctuations in the market value of any one or more of the end products automatically change the apportionment of the joint costs, though actually it costs no more or no less to produce than before.

The relative market value approach to joint cost allocation is better than the physical units approach if two conditions hold: (1) the physical mix of output can be altered by incurring more (less) total joint costs and (2) this alteration produces more (less) total market value.[4] Several variants of the relative market value method are found in practice.

Sales-Value-at-Split-Off Method

The sales-value-at-split-off method allocates joint cost based on each product's proportionate share of market or sales value at the split-off point. Under this method, the higher the market value, the greater the share of joint cost charged against the product. As long as the prices at split-off are stable, or the fluctuations in prices of the various products are synchronized (not necessarily in amount, but in the rate of change), their respective allocated costs remain constant.

Using the same example of lumber mill costs given in the preceding discussion of the physical units method, the joint cost of $186,000 is distributed to the various grades on the basis of their market value at split-off.

Grades	Quantity Produced (board ft.)	Price at Split-Off (per 1,000 board ft.)	Sales Value at Split-Off	Percent of Total Market Value	Allocated Joint Cost
First and second	450,000	$300	$135,000	0.2699	$ 50,201
No. 1 common	1,200,000	200	240,000	0.4799	89,261
No. 2 common	600,000	121	72,600	0.1452	27,007
No. 3 common	750,000	70	52,500	0.1050	19,530
Totals	3,000,000		$500,100		$185,999*

*Does not sum to $186,000 due to rounding.

4. William Cats-Baril, James F. Gatti, and D. Jacque Grinnell, "Joint Product Costing in the Semiconductor Industry," *Management Accounting* (February 1986): 29.

Note that the joint cost is allocated in proportion to sales value at the split-off point. No. 1 common, for example, is valued at $240,000 at split-off, and that amount is 47.99 percent of the total sales value. Therefore, 47.99 percent of total joint cost is assigned to the No. 1 common grade.

The sales-value-at-split-off method can be approximated through the use of weighting factors based on price. The advantage is that the price-based weights do not change as market prices do. An example of this method is found in the glue industry. Material is put into process in the cooking department. The products resulting from the cooking operations are the several "runs of glue." The first run is of the highest grade, has the highest market value, and costs the least. Successive runs require higher temperatures, cost more, and produce lower grades of products. Glue factories do not attempt to determine the actual cost of each skimming because the effect would be to show the lowest cost on the first grade of product and the highest cost on the lowest grade. Instead, the cost of all glue produced is determined, and this total cost is spread over the various grades on the basis of their respective tests of purity. The relative degree of purity is an indicator of the quality and, therefore, of the market value of each run or grade produced. Hence, multiplying the yield for each run by its relative purity is equivalent to multiplying it by the market value. The amounts weighted by purity are used to allocate the joint costs to each run. Additional runs would be undertaken, of course, only as long as the incremental revenue of the additional run is equal to or exceeds the incremental costs incurred.

The weighting factor based on market value at split-off is conceptually the same as the weighting factor method under physical units. However, in this case, the weighting factor is based on sales value, while the weighting factor described in the physical units section could be based on various other considerations such as processing difficulty, size, and so on. These other considerations may or may not be related to market value.

Net Realizable Value Method

When market value is used to allocate joint costs, we are talking about market value *at the split-off point*. However, on occasion, there is no ready market price for the individual products at the split-off point. In this case, the net realizable value method can be used. First, we obtain a **hypothetical sales value** for each joint product by subtracting all separable (or further) processing costs from the eventual market value. This approximates the sales value at split-off. Then, the **net realizable value method** can be used to prorate the joint costs based on each product's share of hypothetical sales value.

Suppose that a company manufactures two products, Alpha and Beta, from a joint process. One production run costs $5,750 and results in 1,000 gallons of Alpha and 3,000 gallons of Beta. Neither product is salable at split-off, but must be further processed such that the separable cost for Alpha is $1 per gallon and for Beta is $2 per gallon. The eventual market price for Alpha is $5 and for Beta, $4. Joint cost allocation using the net realizable value method is as follows:

	Market Price	Further Processing Cost	Hypothetical Market Price	Number of Units	Hypothetical Market Value	Allocated Joint Cost
Alpha	$5	$1	$4	1,000	$ 4,000	$2,300
Beta	4	2	2	3,000	6,000	3,450
					$10,000	$5,750

Note that joint cost is allocated on the basis of each product's share of hypothetical market value. Thus, Alpha receives 40 percent of the joint cost ($2,300) because it accounts for 40 percent of the hypothetical market value. The net realizable value method is particularly useful when one or more products cannot be sold at the split-off point but must be processed further.

Constant Gross Margin Percentage Method

The net realizable value method is easy to apply. However, it assigns all profit to the hypothetical market value. In other words, the further processing costs are assumed to have no profit value even though they are critical to selling the products. The **constant gross margin percentage method** corrects for this by recognizing that costs incurred after the split-off point are part of the cost total on which profit is expected to be earned, and it allocates joint cost such that the gross margin percentage is the same for each product.

Using the data for Alpha and Beta, we can allocate the $5,750 joint cost using the constant gross margin percentage method. First, total revenues and costs are calculated to determine overall gross margin and the gross margin percentage. Then, revenues for the individual products are adjusted for gross margin, separable costs are deducted, and the resulting figure is the allocated joint cost.

		Percent
Revenue [($5 × 1,000) + ($4 × 3,000)]	$17,000	100%
Costs [$5,750 + ($1 × 1,000) + ($2 × 3,000)]	12,750	75
Gross margin	$ 4,250	25%

	Alpha	*Beta*
Eventual market value	$5,000	$12,000
Less: Gross margin at 25% of market value	1,250	3,000
Cost of goods sold	$3,750	$ 9,000
Less: Separable costs	1,000	6,000
Allocated joint costs	$2,750	$ 3,000

The constant gross margin percentage method allocates more joint cost to Alpha than did the net realizable value method. This is due to the assumption of a relationship between cost and the cost-created value. That is, the net realizable value assumed no gross margin attributable to further processing costs, while the constant gross margin percentage method assumed not only that further processing yields profit but also that it yields an identical profit percentage across products. Which assumption is correct? There are two important questions: first, whether there is a "direct relationship" between cost and value and, second, whether the relationship is necessarily the same for all products jointly produced before and after the split-off point. The practice of product-line pricing to meet competition tends to make such assumptions invalid. Although exceptions exist, many companies do not try to maintain more-or-less equal margins between prices and full costs on their various products.

SUMMARY

Producing departments create the products or services that the firm is in business to manufacture and sell. Support departments serve producing departments but do not themselves create a salable product. Because support departments exist to support a variety of producing departments, the costs of the support departments are common to all producing departments and must be allocated to them to satisfy a number of important objectives. These objectives include inventory valuation, product-line profitability, pricing, and planning and control. Allocation can also be used to encourage favorable managerial behavior.

When the costs of one support department are allocated to other departments, a charging rate must be developed. A single rate combines variable and fixed costs of the support department to generate a charging rate. A dual rate separates the fixed and variable costs. Fixed support department costs are allocated on the basis of original capacity, and a variable rate is developed on the basis of budgeted usage.

Budgeted costs, not actual costs, should be allocated so that the efficiencies or inefficiencies of the support departments themselves are not passed on to the producing departments. Because the causal factors can differ for fixed and variable costs, these types of cost should be allocated separately.

Three methods can be used to allocate support service costs to producing departments: the direct method, the sequential method, and the reciprocal method. These methods differ in the degree of support department interaction considered. By noting support department interactions, more accurate product costing is achieved. The result can be improved planning, control, and decision making. Two methods of allocation recognize interactions among support departments: the sequential (or step) method and the reciprocal method. These methods allocate support service costs among some (or all) interacting support departments before allocating costs to the producing departments.

Departmental overhead rates are calculated by adding direct departmental overhead costs to those costs allocated from the support departments and dividing the sum by the budgeted departmental base.

Joint production processes result in the output of two or more products which are produced simultaneously. Joint or main products have relatively significant sales value. By-products have relatively less significant sales value. Joint costs must be allocated to the individual products for purposes of financial reporting. Several methods have been developed to allocate joint costs. These include the physical units method, the weighted average method, the sales-value-at-split-off method, the net realizable value method, and the constant gross margin method.

Typically, by-products are not allocated any of the joint product costs. Instead, by-product sales are listed as "Other income" on the income statement, or they are treated as a credit to Work In Process of the main product(s).

Joint cost allocation may interfere with management decision making because the joint costs must be incurred to produce all of the products. Thus, allocated costs are not useful for output and pricing decisions. Further processing costs, or separable costs, are used in management decision making.

The arbitrary nature of joint cost allocation has led to a dizzying array of accounting methods. These methods are meant to respond to each company's individual circumstances. A few of the more widely used methods have been covered in this chapter.

REVIEW PROBLEMS AND SOLUTIONS

1 ALLOCATION: DIRECT, SEQUENTIAL, AND RECIPROCAL METHODS

Antioch Manufacturing produces machine parts on a job-order basis. Most business is obtained through bidding. Most firms competing with Antioch bid full cost plus a 20 percent markup. Recently, with the expectation of gaining more sales, Antioch reduced its markup from 25 percent to 20 percent. The company operates two service departments and two producing departments. The budgeted costs and the normal activity levels for each department are as follows:

	Service Departments		Producing Departments	
	A	B	C	D
Overhead costs	$100,000	$200,000	$100,000	$50,000
Number of employees	8	7	30	30
Maintenance hours	2,000	200	6,400	1,600
Machine hours	—	—	10,000	1,000
Labor hours	—	—	1,000	10,000

The direct costs of department A are allocated on the basis of employees; those of department B are allocated on the basis of maintenance hours. Departmental overhead rates are used to assign costs to products. Department C uses machine hours, and department D uses labor hours.

The firm is preparing to bid on a job (Job K) that requires three machine hours per unit produced in department C and no time in department D. The expected prime costs per unit are $67.

Required:

1. Allocate the service costs to the producing departments using the direct method.
2. What will the bid be for Job K if the direct method of allocation is used?
3. Allocate the service costs to the producing departments using the sequential method.
4. What will the bid be for Job K if the sequential method is used?
5. Allocate the service costs to the producing departments using the reciprocal method.
6. What will the bid be for Job K if the reciprocal method is used?

SOLUTION 1.

	Service Departments		Producing Departments	
	A	B	C	D
Direct costs	$ 100,000	$ 200,000	$100,000	$ 50,000
Department A[a]	(100,000)	—	50,000	50,000
Department B[b]	—	(200,000)	160,000	40,000
Total	$ 0	$ 0	$310,000	$140,000

[a]Department A costs are allocated on the basis of the number of employees in the producing departments, departments C and D. The percentage of department A cost allocated to department C = 30/(30 + 30) = 0.50. Cost of department A allocated to department C = 0.50 × $100,000 = $50,000. The percentage of department A cost allocated to department D = 30/(30 + 30) = 0.50. Cost of department A allocated to department D = 0.50 × $100,000 = $50,000.

[b]Department B costs are allocated on the basis of maintenance hours used in the producing departments, departments C and D. The percentage of department B cost allocated to department C = 6,400/(6,400 + 1,600) = 0.80. Cost of department B allocated to department C = 0.80 × $200,000 = $160,000. The percentage of department B cost allocated to department D = 1,600/(6,400 + 1,600) = 0.20. Cost of department B allocated to department D = 0.20 × $200,000 = $40,000.

2. Department C: Overhead rate = $310,000/10,000 = $31 per machine hour.
   Product cost and bid price:

Prime cost	$ 67
Overhead (3 × $31)	93
Total unit cost	$160
Bid price ($160 × 1.2)	$192

3.

	Service Departments		Producing Departments	
	A	B	C	D
Direct costs	$ 100,000	$ 200,000	$100,000	$ 50,000
Department B[a]	40,000	(200,000)	128,000	32,000
Department A[b]	(140,000)	—	70,000	70,000
Total	$ 0	$ 0	$298,000	$152,000

[a]Department B is ranked first because its direct costs are higher than those of department A. Department B costs are allocated on the basis of maintenance hours used in the lower ranking support department, department A, and the producing departments, departments C and D. The percentage of department B cost allocated to department A = 2,000/(2,000 + 6,400 + 1,600) = 0.20. Cost of department B allocated to department A = 0.20 × $200,000 = $40,000. The percentage of department B cost allocated to department C = 6,400/(2,000 + 6,400 + 1,600) = 0.64. Cost of department B allocated to department C = 0.64 × $200,000 = $128,000. The percentage of department B cost allocated to department D = 1,600/(2,000 + 6,400 + 1,600) = 0.16. Cost of department B allocated to department D = 0.16 × $200,000 = $32,000.

[b]Department A costs are allocated on the basis of number of employees in the producing departments, departments C and D. The percentage of department A cost allocated to department C = 30/(30 + 30) = 0.50. Cost of department A allocated to department C = 0.50 × $140,000 = $70,000. The percentage of department A cost allocated to department D = 30/(30 + 30) = 0.50. Cost of department A allocated to department D = 0.50 × $140,000 = $70,000. (*Note:* Department A cost is no longer $100,000. It is $140,000 due to the $40,000 that was allocated from department B.)

4.   Department C: Overhead rate = $298,000/10,000 = $29.80 per machine hour. Product cost and bid price:

Prime cost	$ 67.00
Overhead (3 × $29.80)	89.40
Total unit cost	$156.40
Bid price ($156.40 × 1.2)	$187.68

5.   Allocation ratios:

	Proportion of Output Used by			
	A	B	C	D
A	—	0.1045	0.44775	0.44775
B	0.2000	—	0.6400	0.1600

$$A = \$100{,}000 + 0.2000B$$
$$B = \$200{,}000 + 0.1045A$$
$$A = \$100{,}000 + 0.2(\$200{,}000 + 0.1045A)$$
$$A = \$100{,}000 + \$40{,}000 + 0.0209A$$
$$0.9791A = \$140{,}000$$
$$A = \$142{,}988$$
$$B = \$200{,}000 + 0.1045(\$142{,}988)$$
$$B = \$214{,}942$$

	Service Departments		Producing Departments	
	A	B	C	D
Direct costs	$ 100,000	$ 200,000	$100,000	$ 50,000
Department B	42,988	(214,942)	137,563	34,391
Department A	(142,988)	14,942	64,023	64,023
Total	$ (0)	$ 0	$301,586	$148,414

6. Department C: Overhead rate = $301,586/10,000 = $30.16 per machine hour.
    Product cost and bid price:

Prime cost	$ 67.00
Overhead (3 × $30.16)	90.48
Total unit cost	$157.48
Bid price ($157.48 × 1.2)	$188.98

2 JOINT COST ALLOCATION, FURTHER PROCESSING

Sanders Pharmaceutical Company purchases a material which is then processed to yield three chemicals: anarol, estyl, and betryl. In June, Sanders purchased 10,000 gallons of the material at a cost of $250,000, and the company incurred joint conversion costs of $70,000. June sales and production information are as follows:

	Gallons Produced	Price at Split-Off	Further Processing Cost per Gallon	Eventual Sales Price
Anarol	2,000	$55	—	—
Estyl	3,000	40	—	—
Betryl	5,000	30	$5	$60

Anarol and estyl are sold to other pharmaceutical companies at the split-off point. Betryl can be sold at the split-off point or processed further and packaged for sale as an asthma medication.

Required:

1. Allocate the joint costs to the three products using the physical units method, the sales-value-at-split-off method, the net realizable value method, and the constant gross margin percentage method.
2. Suppose that half of June's production of estyl could be purified and mixed with all of the anarol to produce a veterinary grade anesthetic. All further processing costs amount to $35,000. The selling price for the veterinary grade anarol is $112 per gallon. Should Sanders further process the estyl into the anarol anesthetic?

1. Total joint cost to be allocated = $250,000 + $70,000 = $320,000

    Physical Units Method:

	Gallons Produced	Percent of Gallons Produced	×	Joint Cost	Joint Cost Allocation
Anarol	2,000	(2,000/10,000) = 0.20		$320,000	$ 64,000
Estyl	3,000	(3,000/10,000) = 0.30		320,000	96,000
Betryl	5,000	(5,000/10,000) = 0.50		320,000	160,000
Total	10,000				$320,000

    Sales-Value-at-Split-Off Method:

	Gallons Produced	Price at Split-Off	Revenue at Split-Off	Percent of Revenue	×	Joint Cost	Joint Cost Allocation
Anarol	2,000	$55	$110,000	0.28947		$320,000	$ 92,630
Estyl	3,000	40	120,000	0.31579		320,000	101,053
Betryl	5,000	30	150,000	0.39474		320,000	126,317
Total			$380,000				$320,000

Net Realizable Value Method:

Step 1: Determine hypothetical sales revenue.

	Eventual Price	−	Further Processing Cost per Gallon	=	Hypothetical Sales Price	×	Gallons	=	Hypothetical Revenue
Anarol	$55		—		$55		2,000		$110,000
Estyl	40		—		40		3,000		120,000
Betryl	60		$5		55		5,000		275,000
Total									$505,000

Step 2: Allocate joint cost as a proportion of hypothetical sales revenue.

	Hypothetical Sales Revenue	Percent	×	Joint Cost	=	Joint Cost Allocation
Anarol	$110,000	0.21782		$320,000		$ 69,702
Estyl	120,000	0.23762		320,000		76,039*
Betryl	275,000	0.54456*		320,000		174,259
Total margin	$505,000					$320,000

*Rounded up.

Constant Gross Margin Percentage Method:

	Dollars	Percent
Revenue		
[($55 × 2,000) + ($40 × 3,000) + ($60 × 5,000)]	$530,000	100.00%
Costs [$320,000 + ($5 × 5,000)]	345,000	65.09
Gross margin	$185,000	34.91%

	Anarol	Estyl	Betryl
Eventual market value	$110,000	$120,000	$300,000
Less: Gross margin at 34.91%	38,401	41,892	104,730
Cost of goods sold	$ 71,599	$ 78,108	$195,270
Less: Separable costs	—	—	(25,000)
Joint cost allocation	$ 71,599	$ 78,108	$170,270

Note: $71,599 + $78,108 + $170,270 = $319,977; there is a rounding error of $23.

2. Joint costs are irrelevant to this decision. Instead, further processing costs and the opportunity cost of lost contribution margin on the estyl diverted to anarol purification must be considered.

Added revenue ($112 − $55)(2,000)	$114,000
Less: Further processing of anarol mixture	(35,000)
Less: Lost contribution margin on estyl (1,500 × $40)	(60,000)
Increased operating income	$ 19,000

KEY TERMS

By-product 298

Causal factors 279

Common costs 276

Constant gross margin percentage method 303

Direct method 288

Hypothetical sales value 302

Joint products 296

Net realizable value method 302

Physical units method 299

Producing departments 277

Reciprocal method 291

Sales-value-at-split-off method 301

Separable costs 297

Sequential (or step) method 290

Split-off point 296

Support departments 277

Weight factor 300

QUESTIONS FOR WRITING AND DISCUSSION

1. Describe the two-stage allocation process for assigning support service costs to products in a traditional manufacturing environment.
2. Why must support service costs be assigned to products for purposes of inventory valuation?
3. Explain how allocation of support service costs is useful for planning and control and in making pricing decisions.
4. Assume that a company has decided not to allocate any support service costs to producing departments. Describe the likely behavior of the managers of the producing departments. Would this be good or bad? Explain why allocation would correct this type of behavior.
5. Explain how allocating support service costs will encourage service departments to operate more efficiently.
6. Why is it important to identify and use causal factors to allocate support service costs?
7. Explain why it is better to allocate budgeted support service costs rather than actual support service costs.
8. Why is it desirable to allocate variable costs and fixed costs separately?
9. Explain why either normal or peak capacity of the producing (or user) departments should be used to allocate the fixed costs of support departments.
10. Explain why variable bases should not be used to allocate fixed costs.
11. Why is the dual-rate charging method better than the single-rate method? In what circumstances would it not matter whether dual or single rates were used?
12. Explain the difference between the direct method and the sequential method.
13. The reciprocal method of allocation is more accurate than either the direct or sequential methods. Do you agree or disagree? Explain.
14. What is a joint cost? How does it relate to by-products?
15. How do joint costs differ from other common costs?

EXERCISES

7-1 CLASSIFYING DEPARTMENTS AS PRODUCING OR SUPPORT—MANUFACTURING FIRM

LO1   Classify each of the following departments in a factory that produces crème-filled snack cakes as a producing department or a support department.

a. Janitorial
b. Baking
c. Inspection
d. Mixing
e. Engineering
f. Grounds
g. Purchasing
h. Packaging
i. Icing (frosts top of snack cakes and adds decorative squiggle)
j. Filling (injects crème mixture into baked snack cakes)
k. Personnel
l. Cafeteria
m. General factory
n. Machine maintenance
o. Bookkeeping

7-2 CLASSIFYING DEPARTMENTS AS PRODUCING OR SUPPORT—SERVICE FIRM

LO1 Classify each of the following departments in a large metropolitan law firm as a producing department or a support department.
a. Copying
b. WESTLAW computer research
c. Tax planning
d. Environmental law
e. Oil and gas law
f. Custodians
g. Word processing
h. Corporate law
i. Small business law
j. Personnel

7-3 IDENTIFYING CAUSAL FACTORS FOR SUPPORT DEPARTMENT COST ALLOCATION

LO1 Identify some possible causal factors for the following support departments:
a. Cafeteria
b. Custodial services
c. Laundry
d. Receiving, shipping, and stores
e. Maintenance
f. Personnel
g. Accounting
h. Power
i. Building and grounds

7-4 OBJECTIVES OF COST ALLOCATION

LO1 Dr. Fred Poston, "Dermatologist to the Stars," has a practice in southern California. The practice includes three dermatologists, three medical assistants, an office manager, and a receptionist. The office space, which is rented for $5,000 per month, is large enough to accommodate four dermatologists, but Dr. Poston has not yet found the right physician to fill the fourth spot. Dr. Poston developed a skin cleanser for his patients that is nongreasy and does not irritate skin that is still recovering from the effects of chemical peels and dermabrasion. The cleanser requires $0.50 worth of ingredients per 8-ounce bottle. A medical assistant mixes up several bottles at a time during lulls in her schedule. She waits until she has about 15 minutes free and then mixes 10 bottles of cleanser. She is paid $2,250 per month. Dr. Poston charges $5.00 per bottle and sells approximately 5,000 bottles annually. His accountant is considering various ways of costing the skin cleanser.

Required:

1. Give two reasons for allocating overhead cost to the cleanser. How should the cost of the office space and the medical assistant's salary be allocated to the cleanser? Explain.
2. Suppose that *Healthy You* magazine runs an article on Dr. Poston and his skin cleanser, which causes demand to skyrocket. Consumers across the country buy the cleanser via phone or mail order. Now, Dr. Poston believes that he can sell about 40,000 bottles annually. He can hire someone part time, for $1,000 per month, to mix and bottle the cleanser and to handle the financial business of the cleanser. An unused office and examining room can be dedicated to the production of the cleanser. Would your allocation choice for Requirement 1 change in this case? Explain.

7-5   OBJECTIVES OF ALLOCATION

LO1 Leanne and Janine are planning a trip to Padre Island, Texas, during spring break. Members of the varsity volleyball team, they are looking forward to five days of beach volleyball and parasailing. They will drive Leanne's car and estimate that they will pay the following costs during the trip:

Motel	$625
Food (each)	75
Gas (total)	50
Parasailing & equipment rental	125

They have reservations at the Beach-Vue Motel, which charges $95 per night for a single, $125 per night for a double, and an additional $20 per night if a rollaway bed is added to a double room.

Leanne's little sister, Cher, wants to go along. She isn't into sports but thinks that five days of partying and relaxing on the beach would be a great way to unwind from the rigors of school. She figures that she could ride with Leanne and Janine and share their room.

Required:

1. Using incremental costs only, what would it cost Cher to accompany Leanne and Janine?
2. Using the benefits-received method, what would it cost Cher to go on the trip?

7-6   SINGLE AND DUAL CHARGING RATES

LO2 Barry Alexander owns a block of shops on a street just off Rodeo Drive. Of the 10 store spaces in the building, seven are rented by boutique owners, and three are vacant. Barry has decided that offering more services to stores in the mall would enable him to increase occupancy. He has decided to use one of the vacant spaces to provide, at cost, a gift-wrapping service to shops in the mall. The boutiques are enthusiastic about the new service. Most of them are staffed minimally, which means that every time they have to wrap a gift, phones go unanswered and other customers in line grow impatient. Barry figured that the gift-wrapping service would incur the following costs: The store space would normally rent for $2,000 per month; part-time gift wrappers could be hired for

$1,000 per month; and wrapping paper and ribbon would average $1.50 per gift. The boutique owners estimated the following number of gifts to be wrapped per month.

Store	Number of Gifts Wrapped per Month
The Paper Chase	175
Reservation Art	400
Kid-Sports	100
Sugar Shack	75
Designer Shoes	20
Boutique de Donatessa	130
Alan's Drug and Sundries	100

After the service had been in effect for six months, Barry calculated the following actual average monthly number of gifts wrapped for each of the stores.

Store	Actual Average Number of Gifts Wrapped per Month
The Paper Chase	170
Reservation Art	310
Kid-Sports	240
Sugar Shack	10
Designer Shoes	50
Boutique de Donatessa	200
Alan's Drug and Sundries	450

Required:

1. Calculate a single charging rate, on a per-gift basis, to be charged to the shops. Based on the shops' actual number of gifts wrapped, how much would be charged to each shop using the single charging rate?
2. Based on the shops' actual number of gifts wrapped, how much would be charged to each shop using the dual charging rate?
3. Which shops would prefer the single charging rate? Why? Which would prefer the dual charging rate, and why?
4. Several of the shop owners were angry about their bill for the gift-wrapping service. They pointed out that they were to be charged only for the cost of the service. How could you make a case for them?

7-7 ACTUAL VERSUS BUDGETED COSTS

LO2

Spreadsheet

Kumar, Inc., evaluates managers of producing departments on their ability to control costs. In addition to the costs directly traceable to their departments, each production manager is held responsible for a share of the costs of a support center, the human resources (HR) department. The total costs of HR are allocated on the basis of actual direct labor hours used. The total costs of HR and the actual direct labor hours worked by each producing department are as follows:

	Year 1	Year 2
Direct labor hours worked:		
Department A	24,000	25,000
Department B	36,000	25,000
Total hours	60,000	50,000
Actual HR cost	$120,000	$120,000
Budgeted HR cost	115,000*	112,500*

*$0.25 per direct labor hour plus $100,000.

Required:

1. Allocate the HR costs to each producing department for Year 1 and Year 2 using the direct method with actual direct labor hours and actual HR costs.
2. Discuss the following statement: "The costs of human resource-related matters increased by 25 percent for department A and decreased by over 16 percent for department B. Thus, the manager of department B must be controlling HR costs better than the manager of department A."
3. Can you think of a way to allocate HR costs so that a more reasonable and fair assessment of cost control can be made? Explain.

7-8 FIXED AND VARIABLE COST ALLOCATION

LO2

Refer to the data in **Exercise 7-7**. When the capacity of the HR department was originally established, the normal usage expected for each department was 20,000 direct labor hours. This usage is also the amount of activity planned for the two departments in Year 1 and Year 2.

Required:

1. Allocate the costs of the HR department using the direct method and assuming that the purpose is product costing.
2. Allocate the costs of the HR department using the direct method and assuming that the purpose is to evaluate performance.

7-9 DIRECT METHOD AND OVERHEAD RATES

LO3

Pagilla Company manufactures both sunscreen and tubes of lip balm, with each product manufactured in separate departments. Three support departments support the production departments: power, general factory, and purchasing. Budgeted data on the five departments are as follows:

| | Support Departments | | | Producing Departments | |
	Power	General Factory	Purchasing	Sunscreen	Lip Balm
Overhead	$120,000	$540,000	$220,000	$137,500	$222,500
Square feet	3,000	—	3,000	9,600	8,400
Machine hours	—	1,403	1,345	8,000	24,000
Purchase orders	20	40	7	60	120

The company does not break overhead into fixed and variable components. The bases for allocation are: power—machine hours, general factory—square feet, and purchasing—purchase orders.

Required:

1. Allocate the overhead costs to the producing departments using the direct method. (Take allocation ratios out to four significant digits.)
2. Using machine hours, compute departmental overhead rates. (Round the overhead rates to the nearest cent.)

7-10 SEQUENTIAL METHOD

LO3 Refer to the data in **Exercise 7-9**. The company has decided to use the sequential method of allocation instead of the direct method.

Spreadsheet

Required:

1. Allocate the overhead costs to the producing departments using the sequential method. (Take allocation ratios out to four significant digits.)
2. Using machine hours, compute departmental overhead rates. (Round the overhead rates to the nearest cent.)

7-11 RECIPROCAL METHOD

LO3   Stubing Company has two producing departments and two support centers. The following budgeted data pertain to these four departments:

| | Support Departments | | Producing Departments | |
	Maintenance	Personnel	Assembly	Painting
Overhead	$200,000	$60,000	$43,000	$74,000
Square footage	—	2,700	5,400	5,400
Number of employees	30	—	72	198
Direct labor hours	—	—	25,000	40,000

Required:

1. Allocate the overhead costs of the support departments to the producing departments using the reciprocal method.
2. Using direct labor hours, compute departmental overhead rates.

7-12 DIRECT METHOD

LO3   Refer to the data in **Exercise 7-11**. The company has decided to simplify its method of allocating support service costs by switching to the direct method.

Required:

1. Allocate the costs of the support departments to the producing departments using the direct method.
2. Using direct labor hours, compute departmental overhead rates.

7-13 SEQUENTIAL METHOD

LO3   Refer to the data in **Exercise 7-11**.

Required:

1. Allocate the costs of the support departments using the sequential method.
2. Using direct labor hours, compute departmental overhead rates.

7-14 PHYSICAL UNITS METHOD

LO5   Alomar Company manufactures four products from a joint production process: andol, incol, ordol, and exsol. The joint costs for one batch are as follows:

Direct materials	$56,300
Direct labor	28,000
Overhead	15,700

At the split-off point, a batch yields 1,000 andol, 1,500 incol, 2,500 ordol, and 3,000 exsol. All products are sold at the split-off point: andol sells for $20 per unit; incol sells for $75 per unit; ordol sells for $64 per unit, and exsol sells for $22.50 per unit.

Required:

1. Allocate the joint costs using the physical units method.
2. Suppose that the products are weighted as follows:

Andol	3.0
Incol	2.0
Ordol	0.4
Exsol	1.0

   Allocate the joint costs using the weighted average method.

7-15 SALES-VALUE-AT-SPLIT-OFF METHOD

LO5 Refer to **Exercise 7-14** and allocate the joint costs using the sales-value-at-split-off method.

7-16 NET REALIZABLE VALUE METHOD, DECISION TO SELL AT SPLIT-OFF OR PROCESS FURTHER

LO5 Presley, Inc., produces two products, ups and downs, in a single process. The joint costs of this process were $42,000, and 39,000 units of ups and 21,000 units of downs were produced. Separable processing costs beyond the split-off point were as follows: ups, $18,000; downs, $5,780. Ups sell for $2.00 per unit; downs sell for $2.18 per unit.

Required:

1. Allocate the $42,000 joint costs using the estimated net realizable value method.
2. Suppose that ups could be sold at the split-off point for $1.80 per unit. Should Presley sell ups at split-off or process them further? Show supporting computations.

PROBLEMS

7-17 ALLOCATION: FIXED AND VARIABLE COSTS, BUDGETED FIXED AND VARIABLE COSTS

LO2 Biotechtron, Inc., has two research laboratories in the Midwest, one in Tulsa, Oklahoma, and one in Ames, Iowa. The owner of Biotechtron centralized the legal services function in the Tulsa office and had both laboratories send any legal questions or issues to the Tulsa office. The legal services support center has budgeted fixed costs of $60,000 per year and a budgeted variable rate of $40 per hour of professional time. The normal usage of the legal services center is 1,625 hours per year for the Tulsa office and 875 hours per year for the Ames office. This corresponds to the expected usage for the coming year.

Required:

1. Determine the amount of legal services support center costs that should be assigned to each office.
2. Since the offices produce services, not tangible products, what purpose is served by allocating the budgeted costs?
3. Now, assume that during the year, the legal services center incurred actual fixed costs of $59,000 and actual variable costs of $91,500. It delivered 2,300 hours of professional time—1,200 hours to Tulsa and 1,100 hours to Ames. Determine the amount of the legal services center's costs that should be allocated to each office. Explain the purposes of this allocation.

4. Did the costs allocated differ from the costs incurred by the legal services center? If so, why?

7-18   DIRECT METHOD, VARIABLE VERSUS FIXED, COSTING AND PERFORMANCE EVALUATION

LO2, LO3

Spreadsheet

AirBorne is a small airline operating out of Boise, Idaho. Its three flights travel to Salt Lake City, Reno, and Portland. The owner of the airline wants to assess the full cost of operating each flight. As part of this assessment, the costs of two support departments (maintenance and baggage) must be allocated to the three flights. The two support departments that support all three flights are located in Boise (any maintenance or baggage costs at the destination airports are directly traceable to the individual flights). Budgeted and actual data for the year are as follows for the support departments and the three flights:

| | Support Centers | | Flights | | |
	Maintenance	Baggage	Salt Lake City	Reno	Portland
Budgeted data:					
Fixed overhead	$240,000	$150,000	$20,000	$18,000	$30,000
Variable overhead	$30,000	$64,000	$5,000	$10,000	$6,000
Hours of flight time*	—	—	2,000	4,000	2,000
Number of passengers*	—	—	10,000	15,000	5,000
Actual data:					
Fixed overhead	$235,000	$156,000	$22,000	$17,000	$29,500
Variable overhead	$80,000	$33,000	$6,200	$11,000	$5,800
Hours of flight time	—	—	1,800	4,200	2,500
Number of passengers	—	—	8,000	16,000	6,000

*Normal activity levels.

Required:

1. Using the direct method, allocate the support service costs to each flight, assuming that the objective is to determine the cost of operating each flight.
2. Using the direct method, allocate the support service costs to each flight, assuming that the objective is to evaluate performance. Do any costs remain in the two support departments after the allocation? If so, how much? Explain.

7-19   COMPARISON OF METHODS OF ALLOCATION

LO3

Homestead Pottery, Inc., is divided into two operating divisions: pottery and retail. The company allocates power and human resources department costs to each operating division. Power costs are allocated on the basis of the number of machine hours and human resources costs on the basis of the number of employees. No effort is made to separate fixed and variable costs; however, only budgeted costs are allocated. Allocations for the coming year are based on the following data:

| | Support Departments | | Operating Divisions | |
	Power	Human Resources	Pottery	Retail
Overhead costs	$100,000	$205,000	$80,000	$50,000
Machine hours	2,000	2,000	3,000	5,000
Number of employees	20	60	60	80

Required:

1. Allocate the support service costs using the direct method.
2. Allocate the support service costs using the sequential method.
3. Allocate the support service costs using the reciprocal method.

7-20 DIRECT METHOD, RECIPROCAL METHOD, OVERHEAD RATES

LO3, LO4

CMA

Barrylou Corporation is developing departmental overhead rates based on direct labor hours for its two production departments—molding and assembly. The molding department employs 20 people, and the assembly department employs 80 people. Each person in these two departments works 2,000 hours per year. The production-related overhead costs for the molding department are budgeted at $200,000, and the assembly department costs are budgeted at $320,000. Two support departments—repair and power—directly support the two production departments and have budgeted costs of $48,000 and $250,000, respectively. The production departments' overhead rates cannot be determined until the support departments' costs are properly allocated. The following schedule reflects the use of the repair department's and power department's output by the various departments.

	Repair	*Power*	*Molding*	*Assembly*
Repair hours	—	1,000	1,000	8,000
Kilowatt-hours	240,000	—	840,000	120,000

Required:

1. Calculate the overhead rates per direct labor hour for the molding department and the assembly department using the direct allocation method to charge the production departments for support department costs.
2. Calculate the overhead rates per direct labor hour for the molding department and the assembly department using the reciprocal method to charge support department costs to each other and to the production departments.
3. Explain the difference between the methods, and indicate the arguments generally presented to support the reciprocal method over the direct allocation method. *(CMA adapted)*

7-21 PHYSICAL UNITS METHOD, RELATIVE SALES VALUE METHOD

LO5

Petro-Chem, Inc., is a small company that acquires high-grade crude oil from low-volume production wells owned by individuals and small partnerships. The crude oil is processed in a single refinery into Two Oil, Six Oil, and impure distillates. Petro-Chem does not have the technology or capacity to process these products further and sells most of its output each month to major refineries. There were no beginning finished goods or work-in-process inventories on November 1. The production costs and output of Petro-Chem for November are as follows:

Crude oil acquired and placed into production	$5,000,000
Direct labor and related costs	2,000,000
Manufacturing overhead	3,000,000

Production and sales:
Two Oil, 300,000 barrels produced; 80,000 barrels sold at $20 each.
Six Oil, 240,000 barrels produced; 120,000 barrels sold at $30 each.
Distillates, 120,000 barrels produced and sold at $15 per barrel.

Required:

1. Calculate the amount of joint production cost that Petro-Chem would allocate to each of the three joint products by using the physical units method. (Carry out the ratio calculation to four decimal places.)
2. Calculate the amount of joint production cost that Petro-Chem would allocate to each of the three joint products by using the relative sales value method.

7-22 FIXED AND VARIABLE COST ALLOCATION

LO2 Welcome Inns is a chain of motels serving business travelers in Arizona and southern Nevada. The chain has grown from one motel in 2004 to five motels. In 2007, the owner of the company decided to set up an internal accounting department to centralize control of financial information. (Previously, local CPAs handled each motel's bookkeeping and financial reporting.) The accounting office was opened in January 2007 by renting space adjacent to corporate headquarters in Glendale, Arizona. All motels have been supplied with personal computers and modems by which to transfer information to central accounting on a weekly basis.

The accounting department has budgeted fixed costs of $85,000 per year. Variable costs are budgeted at $26 per hour. In 2007, actual cost for the accounting department was $182,500. Further information is as follows:

	Actual Revenues		Actual Hours of Accounting
	2006	2007	2007
Henderson	$337,500	$431,800	1,475
Boulder City	450,000	508,000	400
Kingman	360,000	381,000	938
Flagstaff	540,000	635,000	562
Glendale	562,500	584,200	375

Required:

1. Suppose the total costs of the accounting department are allocated on the basis of 2007 sales revenue. How much will be allocated to each motel?
2. Suppose that Welcome Inns views 2006 sales figures as a proxy for budgeted capacity of the motels. Thus, fixed accounting department costs are allocated on the basis of 2006 sales, and variable costs are allocated according to 2007 usage multiplied by the variable rate. How much accounting department cost will be allocated to each motel?
3. Comment on the two allocation schemes. Which motels would prefer the method in Requirement 1? The method in Requirement 2? Explain.

7-23 PHYSICAL UNITS METHOD, RELATIVE SALES-VALUE-AT-SPLIT-OFF METHOD, NET REALIZABLE VALUE METHOD, DECISION MAKING

LO5 Sonimad Sawmill, Inc., (SSI) purchases logs from independent timber contractors and processes them into the following three types of lumber products.

CMA
1. Studs for residential construction (e.g., walls and ceilings)
2. Decorative pieces (e.g., fireplace mantels and beams for cathedral ceilings)
3. Posts used as support braces (e.g., mine support braces and braces for exterior fences around ranch properties)

These products are the result of a joint sawmill process that involves removing bark from the logs, cutting the logs into a workable size (ranging from 8 to 16 feet in length), and then cutting the individual products from the logs, depending upon the type of wood (pine, oak, walnut, or maple) and the size (diameter) of the log.

The joint process results in the following costs and output of products during a typical month:

Joint production costs	
Materials (rough timber logs)	$ 500,000
Debarking (labor and overhead)	50,000
Sizing (labor and overhead)	200,000
Product cutting (labor and overhead)	250,000
Total joint costs	$1,000,000

Product yield and average sales value on a per-unit basis from the joint process are as follows:

Product	Monthly Output	Fully Processed Sales Price
Studs	75,000	$ 8
Decorative pieces	5,000	100
Posts	20,000	20

The studs are sold as rough-cut lumber after emerging from the sawmill operation without further processing by SSI. Also, the posts require no further processing. The decorative pieces must be planed and further sized after emerging from the SSI sawmill. This additional processing costs SSI $100,000 per month and normally results in a loss of 10 percent of the units entering the process. Without this planing and sizing process, there is still an active intermediate market for the unfinished decorative pieces where the sales price averages $60 per unit.

Required:

1. Based on the information given for Sonimad Sawmill, Inc., allocate the joint processing costs of $1,000,000 to each of the three product lines using the:
   a. Relative sales-value-at-split-off method
   b. Physical units method at split-off
   c. Estimated net realizable value method
2. Prepare an analysis for Sonimad Sawmill, Inc., to compare processing the decorative pieces further as it presently does, with selling the rough-cut product immediately at split-off. Be sure to provide all calculations.
3. Assume Sonimad Sawmill, Inc., announced that in six months it will sell the rough-cut product at split-off due to increasing competitive pressure. Identify at least three types of likely behavior that will be demonstrated by the skilled labor in the planing and sizing process as a result of this announcement. Explain how this behavior could be improved by management. *(CMA adapted)*

7-24   SINGLE CHARGING RATES

LO2   House Corporation Board (HCB) of Tri-Gamma Sorority is responsible for the operation of a two-story sorority house on the State University campus. HCB has set a normal capacity of 60 women. At any given point in time, there are 100 members of the chapter: 60 living in the house and 40 living elsewhere (e.g., in the freshman dorms on campus). HCB needs to set rates for the use of the house for the coming year. The following costs are budgeted: $240,000 fixed and $34,800 variable. The fixed costs are fairly insensitive to the number of women living in the house. Food is budgeted at $40,000 and is included in the fixed costs; food does not seem to vary greatly given the stated capacity. The variable expenses consist of telephone bills and some of the utilities. HCB is not responsible for chapter dues, party fees, pledging and initiation fees, and other social expenditures. Women living in the house eat 20 meals per week there and live in a 2-person room. (All in-house members' rooms, bathroom facilities, etc., are on the second floor.) All members eat Monday dinner at the house and have full use of house facilities (e.g., the two TV lounges, kitchens, access to milk and cereal at any time, study facilities, and so on).

HCB has traditionally set two rates: one for in-house members and one for out-of-house members. There are 32 weeks in a school year.

Required:

1. Discuss the factors that might go into determining the charging rate for the two types of sorority members.
2. Set charging rates for the in-house and out-of-house members.

7-25   CASE USING A HOSPITAL SETTING, ALLOCATION METHODS, UNIT-COST DETERMINATION AND PRICING DECISIONS

LO2, LO3   Paula Barneck, the newly appointed director of the Lambert Medical Center (LMC), a large metropolitan hospital, was reviewing the financial report for the most recent quarter. The hospital had again shown a loss. For the past several years, it had been struggling financially. The financial problems had begun with the introduction of the federal government's new diagnostic-related group (DRG) reimbursement system. Under this system, the government mandated fixed fees for specific treatments or illnesses. The fixed fees were supposed to represent what the procedures should cost and differed from the traditional cost objective of the patient day of prior years. Although no formal assessment had been made, the general feeling of hospital management was that the DRG reimbursement was hurting LMC's financial state.

The increasing popularity of health maintenance organizations (HMOs) and physician provider organizations (PPOs) was also harming the hospital's financial well-being. In HMOs, physicians, who are employed full time, are usually located in a clinic owned by the HMO, and subscribers must use these physicians. In PPOs, hospitals provide contracts with a group of physicians in private practice. These physicians usually serve non-PPO patients as well as PPO patients. The PPO patient can select any physician from the list of physicians under contract with the particular PPO. The PPO approach usually offers a greater selection of physicians and tends to preserve the patient's traditional freedom of choice. More and more of the hospital's potential patients were joining HMOs and PPOs, and, unfortunately, LMC was not capturing its fair share of the HMO and PPO business. HMOs and PPOs routinely asked for bids on hospital services and provided their business to the lowest bidder. In too many cases, LMC had not won that work.

Paula had accepted the position of hospital administrator knowing that she was expected to produce dramatic improvements in LMC's financial state. She was convinced that she needed more information about the hospital's product costing methods. Only by having accurate cost information for the various procedures offered by the hospital could she evaluate the effects of DRG reimbursement and the hospital's bidding strategy.

Paula requested a meeting with Eric Rose, the hospital's controller. Their conversation follows:

PAULA: Eric, as you know, we recently lost a bid on some laboratory tests that would be performed on a regular basis for a local HMO. In fact, I was told by the director of the HMO that we had the highest bid of the three submitted. I know the identity of the other two hospitals that submitted bids, and I have a hard time believing that their costs for these tests are any lower than ours. Describe exactly how we determine the cost of these lab procedures.

ERIC: First, we classify all departments as either revenue-producing centers or service centers. Next, the costs of the service centers are allocated to the revenue-producing centers. The costs directly traceable to the revenue-producing centers are then added to the allocated costs to obtain the total cost of operating the revenue-producing center. This total cost is divided by the total revenues of the revenue-producing center to obtain a cost-to-charges ratio. Finally, the cost of a particular procedure is computed by multiplying the charge for that procedure by the cost-to-charges ratio.

PAULA: Let me see if I understand. The costs of laundry, housekeeping, maintenance, and other service departments are allocated to all of the revenue-producing departments. Let's assume that the lab receives $100,000 as its share of these allocated costs. The $100,000 is then added to the direct costs—let's assume these are also $100,000—to obtain total operating costs of $200,000. If the laboratory earns revenues of $250,000, the cost-to-charges ratio is 0.80 ($200,000/$250,000). Finally, if I want to know the cost of a particular lab procedure, say a blood test for which we normally charge $20, then all I do is multiply the cost-to-charges ratio of 0.8 by $20 to obtain the cost of $16. Am I right?

ERIC: Absolutely. In the laboratory testing bid that we just lost, our bid was at cost, as computed using our cost-to-charges formula. Perhaps the other hospitals are bidding below their cost to capture the business.

PAULA: Eric, I don't agree. The cost-to-charges ratio is a traditional approach for costing hospital products, but I'm afraid that it is no longer useful. Given the new environment in which we're operating, we need more accurate product costing information. We need accuracy to improve our bidding, to help us assess and deal with the new DRG reimbursement system, and to evaluate the mix of services we offer. The cost-to-charges ratio approach backs into the product cost. It is indirect and inaccurate. Some procedures require more labor, more materials, and more expensive equipment than others. The cost-to-charges approach doesn't reflect these potential differences.

ERIC: Well, I'm willing to change the cost accounting system so that it meets our needs. Do you have any suggestions?

PAULA: Yes. I'm in favor of a more direct computation of product costs. Allocating support service costs to the revenue-producing departments is only the first stage in product costing. We do need to allocate these support service costs to the producing departments—but we need to be certain that we are allocating them in the right way. We also need to go a step further and assign the costs accumulated in the revenue-producing departments to individual products. The costs directly traceable to each product should be identified and assigned directly to those products; indirect costs can be assigned through one or more overhead rates. The base for assigning the overhead costs should be associated with their incurrence. If at all possible, allocations should reflect the usage of support services by the revenue-producing departments; moreover, the same criterion should govern the assignment of overhead costs to the products within the department.

ERIC: Sounds like an interesting challenge. With over 30,000 products, a job-order costing system would be too burdensome and costly. I think some system can be developed, however, that will do essentially what you want.

PAULA: Good. Listen, for our next meeting, come prepared to brief me on why and how you allocate these service department costs to the revenue-producing departments. I think this is a critical step in accurate product costing. I also want to know how you propose to assign the costs accumulated in each revenue-producing department to that department's products.

As Eric mentally reviewed his meeting with Paula, he realized that the failure of bids could be attributable to inaccurate cost assignments. Because of this possibility, Eric decided to do some additional investigation to see if the cost-to-charges ratio method of costing services was responsible.

Eric pulled the current year's budgeted data from his files. He found the following data. The number of departments and the budget have been reduced for purposes of simplification.

	Support Departments			**Revenue Departments**	
	Administrative	*Laundry*	*Janitorial*	*Laboratory*	*Nursing*
Overhead	$20,000	$75,000	$50,000	$43,000	$150,000
Employees	1	4	7	8	20
Pounds of laundry	50	200	400	1,000	4,000
Square feet	1,000	1,200	500	5,000	20,000

Support department costs are allocated using the direct method.

Eric decided to compute the costs of three different lab tests using the cost-to-charges ratio and then recompute them using a more direct method, as suggested by Paula. By comparing the unit costs under each approach, he could evaluate the cost-estimating ability of the cost-to-charges ratio. The three tests selected for study were the blood count test (Test B), cholesterol test (Test C), and a chemical blood analysis (Test CB).

After careful observation of the three tests, Eric concluded that the consumption of the resources of the laboratory could be associated with the relative amount of time taken by each test. Based on the amount of time needed to perform each test, Eric developed relative value units (RVUs) and associated the consumption of materials and labor with these units. The RVUs for each test and the cost per RVU for materials and labor are as follows:

Test	RVUs	Material per RVU	Labor per RVU
B	1	$2.00	$2.00
C	2	2.50	2.00
CB	3	1.00	2.00

Eric also concluded that the pool of overhead costs collected within the laboratory should be applied using RVUs. (He was convinced that RVU was a good activity driver for overhead.) The laboratory's expected RVUs for the year were 22,500. The laboratory usually performs an equal number of the three tests over a year. This year was no exception.

Eric also noted that the hospital usually priced its services so that revenues exceeded costs by a specified percentage. Based on the past total costs of the laboratory, this pricing strategy had led to the following fees for the three blood tests:

	Test B	Test C	Test CB
Fees charged	$5.00	$19.33	$22.00

Required:

1. Allocate the costs of the support departments to the two revenue-producing departments using the direct method.
2. Assuming that the three blood tests are the only tests performed in the laboratory, compute the cost-to-charges ratio (total costs of the laboratory divided by the laboratory's total revenues).

3. Using the cost-to-charges ratio computed in Requirement 2, estimate the cost per test for each blood test.
4. Compute the cost per test for each test using RVUs.
5. Which unit cost—the one using the cost-to-charges ratio or the one using RVUs—do you think is the most accurate? Explain.
6. Assume that Lambert Medical Center has been requested by an HMO to bid on Test CB. Using a 5 percent markup, prepare the bid using the cost computed in Requirement 3. Repeat, using the cost prepared in Requirement 4. Suppose that anyone who bids $20 or less will win the bid. Discuss the implications of costing accuracy on the hospital's problems with its bidding practices.

7-26   COLLABORATIVE LEARNING EXERCISE: COMPARISON OF METHODS OF ALLOCATION

LO3, LO4   Divide the class into groups of six. Within each group, form pairs. One pair works Requirement 1(a); another pair works Requirement 1(b); and the remaining pair works Requirement 1(c). When the pairs have completed their work, they reform their group, and each pair teaches the other how to complete Requirement 1. Then, the groups discuss Requirement 2.

Kare Foods Company specializes in the production of frozen dinners. The first of the two operating departments cooks the food. The second is responsible for packaging and freezing the dinners. The dinners are sold by the case, each case containing 25 dinners.

Two support departments provide support for Kare's operating units: maintenance and power. Budgeted data for the coming quarter follow. The company does not separate fixed and variable costs.

	Support Departments		Producing Departments	
	Maintenance	Power	Cooking	Packaging and Freezing
Overhead costs	$340,000	$200,000	$ 75,000	$55,000
Machine hours	—	40,000	40,000	20,000
Kilowatt-hours	20,000	—	100,000	80,000
Direct labor hours	—	—	5,000	30,000

The predetermined overhead rate for cooking is computed on the basis of machine hours; direct labor hours are used for packaging and freezing. The prime costs for one case of standard dinners total $16. It takes two machine hours to produce a case of dinners in the cooking department and 0.5 direct labor hour to process a case of standard dinners in the packaging and freezing department.

Recently, the Air Force has requested a bid on a 3-year contract that would supply standard frozen dinners to Minuteman missile officers and staff on duty in the field. The locations of the missile sites were remote, and the Air Force had decided that frozen dinners were the most economical means of supplying food to personnel on duty.

The bidding policy of Kare Foods is full manufacturing cost plus 20 percent. Assume that the lowest bid of other competitors is $48.80 per case.

Required:

1. Prepare bids for Kare Foods using each of the following allocation methods:
    a. Direct method
    b. Sequential method
    c. Reciprocal method

2. Refer to Requirement 1. Did all three methods produce winning bids? If not, explain why. Which method most accurately reflects the cost of producing the cases of dinners? Why?

7-27 CYBER RESEARCH CASE

Have each student find the Web sites of four companies—two service companies and two manufacturing companies. By reviewing the description of each company's operations, determine what types of support departments are needed. Do the Web sites refer to these support departments?

Budgeting for Planning and Control

AFTER STUDYING THIS CHAPTER, YOU SHOULD BE ABLE TO:

1. Define budgeting, and discuss its role in planning, controlling, and decision making.

2. Prepare the operating budget, identify its major components, and explain the interrelationships of the various components.

3. Identify the components of the financial budget, and prepare a cash budget.

4. Define flexible budgeting, and discuss its role in planning, control, and decision making.

5. Define activity-based budgeting, and discuss its role in planning, control, and decision making.

6. Identify and discuss the key features that a budgetary system should have to encourage managers to engage in goal-congruent behavior.

. . . .

Careful planning is vital to the health of any organization. Failure to plan, either formally or informally, can lead to financial disaster. Managers of businesses, whether small or large, must know their resource capabilities and have a plan that details the use of these resources. In this chapter, the basics of budgeting are discussed, and traditional master budgets using functional-based accounting data are developed. Flexible and activity-based budgeting are also presented, along with extensive discussion of the behavioral aspects of budgeting and its use in control.

The Role of Budgeting in Planning and Control

OBJECTIVE *1*

Define budgeting, and discuss its role in planning, controlling, and decision making.

Budgeting plays a crucial role in planning and control. Plans identify objectives and the actions needed to achieve them. **Budgets** are the quantitative expressions of these plans, stated in either physical or financial terms or both. When used for planning, a budget is a method for translating the goals and strategies of an organization into operational terms. Budgets can also be used in control. **Control** is the process of setting standards, receiving feedback on actual performance, and taking corrective action whenever actual performance deviates significantly from planned performance. Thus, budgets can be used to compare actual outcomes with planned outcomes, and they can steer operations back on course, if necessary.

Exhibit 8-1 illustrates the relationship of budgets to planning, operating, and control. Budgets evolve from the long-run objectives of the firm; they form the basis for operations. Actual results are compared with budgeted amounts through control. This comparison provides feedback both for operations and for future budgets.

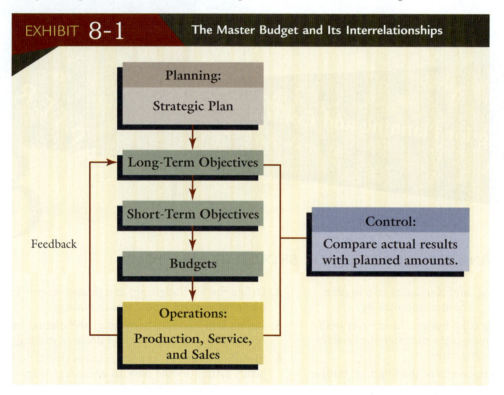

EXHIBIT 8-1   The Master Budget and Its Interrelationships

Purposes of Budgeting

Budgets are usually prepared for areas within an organization (departments, plants, divisions, and so on) and for activities (sales, production, research, and so on). This system of budgets serves as the comprehensive financial plan for the organization as a whole and gives an organization several advantages.

1. It forces managers to plan.
2. It provides resource information that can be used to improve decision making.
3. It aids in the use of resources and employees by setting a benchmark that can be used for the subsequent evaluation of performance.
4. It improves communication and coordination.

Budgeting forces management to plan for the future—to develop an overall direction for the organization, foresee problems, and develop future policies. When managers plan, they grow to understand the capabilities of their businesses and where the resources of the business should be used. All businesses and not-for-profit entities should budget. All large businesses do budget. In fact, the budgeting activity of a company such as **Conoco** or **IBM** consumes significant amounts of time and involves many managers at a variety of levels. Some small businesses do not budget, and many of those go out of business in short order.

Budgets enable managers to make better decisions. For example, a cash budget points out potential shortfalls. If a company foresees a cash deficiency, it may want to improve accounts receivable collection or postpone plans to purchase new assets.

Budgets set standards that can control the use of a company's resources and control and motivate employees. Fundamental to the overall success of a budgetary system, control ensures that steps are being taken to achieve the objectives outlined in an organization's master plan.

Budgets also serve to communicate the plans of the organization to each employee and to coordinate their efforts. Accordingly, all employees can be aware of their role in achieving those objectives. This is why explicitly linking the budget to the long-run plans of the organization is so important. The budget is not a series of vague, rosy scenarios, but a set of specific plans to achieve those objectives. Budgets encourage coordination because the various areas and activities of the organization must all work together to achieve the stated objectives. The role of communication and coordination becomes more important as an organization increases in size.

The Budgeting Process

The budgeting process can range from the fairly informal process undergone by a small firm, to an elaborately detailed, several-month procedure employed by large firms. Key features of the process include directing and coordinating the compilation of the budget.

Directing and Coordinating

Every organization must have someone responsible for directing and coordinating the overall budgeting process. This **budget director** is usually the controller or someone who reports to the controller. The budget director works under the direction of the budget committee. The **budget committee** has the responsibility to review the budget, provide policy guidelines and budgetary goals, resolve differences that may arise as the budget is prepared, approve the final budget, and monitor the actual performance of the organization as the year unfolds. The budget committee is also responsible for ensuring that the budget is linked to the strategic plan of the organization. The president of the organization appoints the members of the committee, who are usually the president, vice presidents, and the controller.

Types of Budgets

The **master budget** is a comprehensive financial plan for the year made up of various individual departmental and activity budgets. A master budget can be divided into *operating* and *financial* budgets. **Operating budgets** are concerned with the income-generating activities of a firm: sales, production, and finished goods inventories. The ultimate outcome of the operating budgets is a pro forma or budgeted income statement. Note that "pro forma" is synonymous with "budgeted" and "estimated." In effect, the pro forma income statement is done "according to form" but with estimated, not historical, data. **Financial budgets** are concerned with the inflows and outflows of cash and with financial position. Planned cash inflows and outflows are detailed in a cash budget, and expected financial position at the end of the budget period is shown in a budgeted, or pro forma, balance sheet. Exhibit 8-2 illustrates the components of the master budget.

The master budget is usually prepared for a 1-year period corresponding to the company's fiscal year. The yearly budgets are broken down into quarterly and monthly

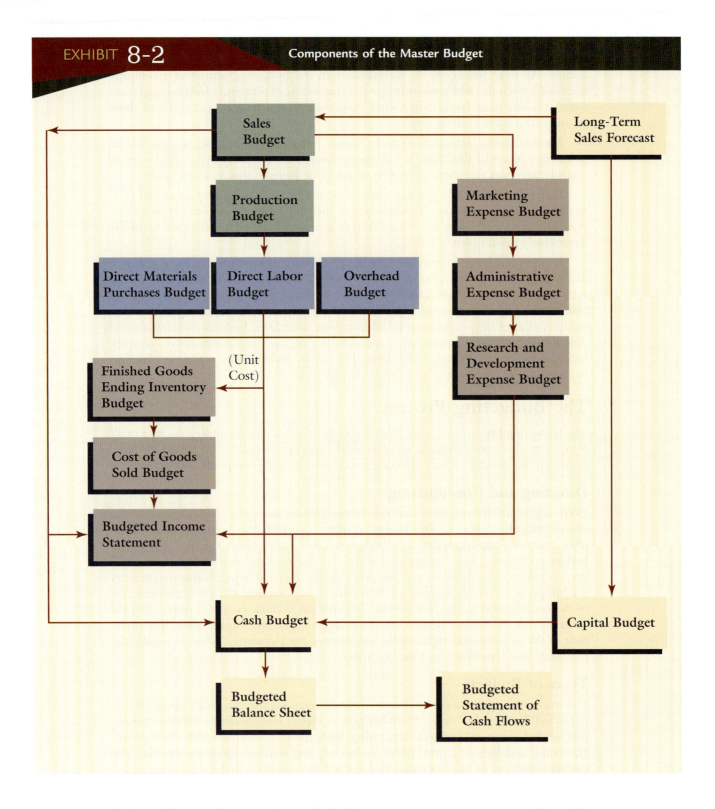

EXHIBIT 8-2   **Components of the Master Budget**

budgets. The use of shorter time periods allows managers to compare actual data with budgeted data as the year unfolds and to make timely corrections. Because progress can be checked more frequently with monthly budgets, problems are less likely to become too serious.

Most organizations prepare the budget for the coming year during the last four or five months of the current year. However, some organizations have developed a continuous budgeting philosophy. A **continuous (or rolling) budget** is a moving 12-month budget. As a month expires in the budget, an additional month in the future is added so that the company always has a 12-month plan on hand. Proponents of continuous budgeting maintain that it forces managers to plan ahead constantly. The majority of CFOs believe that rolling forecasts are very valuable, and companies that do use them typically roll the forecasts out for five or six quarters rather than four.[1]

Similar to a continuous budget is a continuously updated budget. The objective of this budget is not to have 12 months of budgeted information at all times, but instead to update the master budget each month as new information becomes available. For example, every autumn, **Chandler Engineering** prepares a budget for the coming year. Then at the end of each month of the year, the budget is transformed into a rolling forecast by recording year-to-date results and the forecast for the remainder of the year. In essence, the budget is continually updated throughout the year.

Gathering Information for Budgeting

At the beginning of the master budgeting process, the budget director alerts all segments of the company to the need for gathering budget information. The data used to create the budget come from many sources. Historical data are one possibility. For example, last year's direct materials costs may give the production manager a good feel for potential materials costs for next year. Still, historical data alone cannot tell a company what to expect in the future.

Forecasting Sales

The sales forecast is the basis for the sales budget, which, in turn, is the basis for all of the other operating budgets and most of the financial budgets. Accordingly, the accuracy of the sales forecast strongly affects the soundness of the entire master budget.

Creating the sales forecast is usually the responsibility of the marketing department. One approach is for the chief sales executive to have individual salespeople submit sales predictions, which are aggregated to form a total sales forecast. The accuracy of this sales forecast may be improved by considering other factors such as the general economic climate, competition, advertising, pricing policies, and so on. Some companies supplement the marketing department forecast with more formal approaches, such as time-series analysis, correlation analysis, econometric modeling, and industry analysis.

To illustrate an actual sales forecasting approach, consider the practices of a company that manufactures oil field equipment on a job-order basis. Each month, the finance and sales departments' heads meet to construct a sales forecast based on bookings. A booking is a probable sales order submitted by sales personnel in the field; it is meant to alert the engineering and manufacturing departments to a potential job. Past experience has shown that bookings are generally followed by sales/shipments within 30 to 45 days. Exhibit 8-3, on the following page, shows the short-term bookings forecast for the company. Notice that the dollar amount of each booking is multiplied by its probability of occurrence to obtain a weighted dollar amount. The sum of weighted amounts is the forecast for sales for the month. The probability estimate requires additional explanation. The probability is determined jointly by the salesperson and the controller. Each probability is initially set at 50 percent. Then, it is adjusted upward or downward based on any additional information about the sale. The probability is really a prediction of a compound event, the prediction of both getting the order and determining the month in which it will happen. The sales department tends toward overconfidence—both in terms of getting the order

---

1. Omar Aguilar, "How Strategic Performance Management Is Helping Companies Create Business Value," *Strategic Finance* (January 2003): 44–49.

EXHIBIT 8-3				**Short-Term Bookings Forecast for Oil Field Equipment Company**		

Quote #	Region/ Country	Customer	Product	Dollar Amount	Probability	Weighted Month Total
March 2007						
1194-17	Spain	Valencia	repair 3224	$ 37,500	100%	$ 37,500
1294-03	Bulgaria	Luecim	1256, 7188	74,145	80	59,316
0195-55	USA	Exxon	4498	25,000	95	23,750
0295-19	USA	BP/TX	6766, 1267	150,442	100	150,442
0295-23	China	China Res	7541, 8875	55,900	75	41,925
0295-45	China	China Res	8879, 0944	34,500	80	27,600
0395-36	Abu Dhabi	ADES	7400, 6751, 5669 & spares	30,000	50	15,000
March Total						$355,533
April 2007						
1294-14	China	Jiang Han	6524, 5523, 0412, 4578, 3340	$234,000	80%	$187,200
0295-43	Russia	Geoserv	3356	76,800	60	46,080
0295-10	Venezuela	Petrolina	4450, 6713, 7122	112,500	90	101,250
0395-37	Indonesia	Chevron	8890, 0933	98,000	65	63,700
0395-71	Italy	CV International	7815	16,000	70	11,200
April Total						$409,430
May 2007						
0295-21	Mexico	Instituto Mexicana	8900 & spares	$ 34,000	40%	$ 13,600
0395-29	Venezuela	Petrolina	8416, 8832	165,000	50	82,500
0495-11	USA	Branchwater, Inc.	9043, 8891	335,000	60	201,000
0495-68	Saudi Arabia	Aramco	0453	3,500	50	1,750
May Total						$298,850

and in landing it sooner rather than later. As a result, the controller takes a more pessimistic view and modifies the forecast. The end result is the form shown in the exhibit.

Forecasting Other Variables

Of course, sales are not the only concern in budgeting. Costs and cash-related items are critical. Many of the same factors considered in sales forecasting apply to cost forecasting. Here, historical amounts can be of real value. Managers can adjust past figures based on their knowledge of coming events. For example, a 3-year union contract takes much of the uncertainty out of wage prediction. (Of course, if the contract is expiring, the uncertainty returns.) Alert purchasing agents will have an idea of changing materials prices. In fact, large companies such as **Nestlé** and **The Coca-Cola Company** have entire departments devoted to the forecasting of commodity prices and supplies. They invest in commodity futures to smooth out price fluctuations, an action that facilitates budgeting. Overhead is broken down into its component costs; these can be predicted using past data and relevant inflation figures.

The cash budget is a critically important part of the master budget, and some of its components, especially payment of accounts receivable, also require forecasting. This is discussed in more detail in the section on cash budgeting.

OBJECTIVE 2

Prepare the operating budget, identify its major components, and explain the interrelationships of the various components.

Preparing the Operating Budget

The first section of the master budget is the operating budget. It consists of a series of schedules for all phases of operations, culminating in a budgeted income statement. The following are the components of the operating budget.

1. Sales budget
2. Production budget
3. Direct materials purchases budget
4. Direct labor budget
5. Overhead budget
6. Ending finished goods inventory budget
7. Cost of goods sold budget
8. Marketing expense budget
9. Research and development expense budget
10. Administrative expense budget
11. Budgeted income statement

You may want to refer back to Exhibit 8-2 to see how these components of the operating budget fit into the master budget.

The example used to illustrate the components of the operating budget is based on ABT, Inc., a manufacturer of concrete block and pipe for the construction industry. For simplicity, we will prepare the operating budget for ABT's concrete block line. (The budget for the pipe product line is prepared in the same way and merged into the overall company budget.)

Sales Budget

The **sales budget** is the projection approved by the budget committee that describes expected sales for each product in units and dollars.

Schedule 1 illustrates the sales budget for ABT's concrete block line. (For a multiple-product firm, the sales budget reflects sales for each product in units and sales dollars.) Notice that the sales budget reveals that ABT's sales fluctuate seasonally. Most sales (75 percent) take place in the spring and summer. Also, note that ABT expects

Schedule 1
(in thousands)

Sales Budget
For the Year Ended December 31, 2007

	Quarter				
	1	*2*	*3*	*4*	*Year*
Units	2,000	6,000	6,000	2,000	16,000
Unit selling price	×$0.70	×$0.70	×$0.80	×$0.80	× $0.75
Sales	$ 1,400	$ 4,200	$ 4,800	$ 1,600	$12,000

price to increase from $0.70 to $0.80 in the summer quarter. Because of the price change within the year, an average price must be used for the column that describes the total year's activities ($0.75 = $12,000/16,000 units).

Production Budget

The production budget describes how many units must be produced in order to meet sales needs and satisfy ending inventory requirements. From Schedule 1, we know how many concrete blocks are needed to satisfy sales demand for each quarter and for the year. If there were no inventories, the concrete blocks to be produced would just equal the units to be sold. In the JIT firm, for example, units sold equal units produced, since a customer order triggers production.

Usually, however, the production budget must consider the existence of beginning and ending inventories. Assume that ABT company policy sets desired ending inventory of concrete blocks for each quarter as follows.

Quarter	Ending Inventory
1	500,000
2	500,000
3	100,000
4	100,000

To compute the units to be produced, we must know both unit sales and units in desired finished goods inventory.

$$\text{Units to be produced} = \text{Units, ending inventory} + \text{Unit sales} - \text{Units, beginning inventory}$$

The formula is the basis for the production budget in Schedule 2. Notice that the production budget is expressed in terms of units; we do not yet know how much they will cost.

Schedule 2
(in thousands)

Production Budget
For the Year Ended December 31, 2007

	Quarter				
	1	*2*	*3*	*4*	*Year*
Sales (Schedule 1)	2,000	6,000	6,000	2,000	16,000
Desired ending inventory	500	500	100	100	100
Total needs	2,500	6,500	6,100	2,100	16,100
Less: Beginning inventory	100	500	500	100	100
Units to be produced	2,400	6,000	5,600	2,000	16,000

Direct Materials Purchases Budget

After the production schedule is completed, budgets for direct materials, direct labor, and overhead can be prepared. The **direct materials purchases budget** is similar in format to the production budget; it is based on the amount of materials needed for production and the inventories of direct materials.

Expected direct materials usage is determined by the input-output relationship (the technical relationship existing between direct materials and output). This relationship is often determined by the engineering department or the industrial designer. For example, one lightweight concrete block requires approximately 26 pounds of materials (cement, sand, gravel, shale, pumice, and water). The relative mix of these ingredients is fixed for a specific kind of concrete block. Thus, it is fairly easy to determine expected usage for each material from the production budget by multiplying the amount of material needed per unit of output times the number of units of output.

Once expected usage is computed, the purchases (in units) are computed as follows:

Purchases = Desired ending inventory of direct materials + Expected usage
         − Beginning inventory of direct materials

The quantity of direct materials in inventory is determined by the firm's inventory policy. ABT's policy is to have 2,500 tons of materials (5 million pounds) in ending inventory for the third and fourth quarters and 4,000 tons of materials (8 million pounds) in ending inventory for the first and second quarters. The direct materials purchases budget for ABT is presented in Schedule 3. For simplicity, all materials are treated jointly (as if there were only one material input). In reality, a separate schedule would be needed for each kind of material.

Schedule 3 (in thousands)

Direct Materials Purchases Budget **For the Year Ended December 31, 2007**					
	Quarter				
	1	*2*	*3*	*4*	*Year*
Units to be produced (Schedule 2)	2,400	6,000	5,600	2,000	16,000
Direct materials per unit (lbs.)	× 26	× 26	× 26	× 26	× 26
Production needs (lbs.)	62,400	156,000	145,600	52,000	416,000
Desired ending inventory (lbs.)	8,000	8,000	5,000	5,000	5,000
Total needs	70,400	164,000	150,600	57,000	421,000
Less: Beginning inventory*	5,000	8,000	8,000	5,000	5,000
Direct materials to be purchased (lbs.)	65,400	156,000	142,600	52,000	416,000
Cost per pound	× $0.01	× $0.01	× $0.01	× $0.01	× $0.01
Total purchase cost	$ 654	$ 1,560	$ 1,426	$ 520	$ 4,160

*Follows the inventory policy of having 8 million pounds of materials on hand at the end of the first and second quarters and 5 million pounds on hand at the end of the third and fourth quarters.

Direct Labor Budget

The **direct labor budget** shows the total direct labor hours needed and the associated cost for the number of units in the production budget. As with direct materials, the usage of direct labor is determined by the technological relationship between labor and output. For example, if a batch of 100 concrete blocks requires 1.5 direct labor hours, then the direct labor time per block is 0.015 hour. Assuming that the labor is used efficiently, this rate is fixed for the existing technology. The relationship will change only if a new approach to manufacturing is introduced.

Given the direct labor used per unit of output and the units to be produced from the production budget, the direct labor budget is computed as shown in Schedule 4. In the direct labor budget, the wage rate used ($8 per hour in this example) is the *average* wage paid the direct laborers associated with the production of the concrete blocks. Since it is an average, it allows for the possibility of differing wage rates paid to individual laborers.

Schedule 4
(in thousands)

	Direct Labor Budget **For the Year Ended December 31, 2007**				
	Quarter				
	1	2	3	4	Year
Units to be produced (Schedule 2)	2,400	6,000	5,600	2,000	16,000
Direct labor time per unit (hrs.)	×0.015	×0.015	×0.015	×0.015	×0.015
Total hours needed	36	90	84	30	240
Wage per hour	× $8	× $8	× $8	× $8	× $8
Total direct labor cost	$ 288	$ 720	$ 672	$ 240	$1,920

Overhead Budget

The **overhead budget** shows the expected cost of all indirect manufacturing items. Unlike direct materials and direct labor, there is no readily identifiable input-output relationship for overhead items. Recall, however, that overhead consists of two types of costs: variable and fixed. Past experience can be used as a guide to determine how overhead varies with activity level. Items that vary with activity level are identified (e.g., supplies and utilities), and the amount that is expected to be spent for each item per unit of activity is estimated. Individual rates are then totaled to obtain a variable overhead rate. For ABT, assume that the variable overhead rate is $8 per direct labor hour.

Since fixed overhead does not vary with the activity level, total fixed overhead is simply the sum of all amounts budgeted. Assume that fixed overhead is budgeted at $1.28 million ($320,000 per quarter). Using this information and the budgeted direct labor hours from the direct labor budget, the overhead budget in Schedule 5 is prepared.

Schedule 5 (in thousands)

	Overhead Budget **For the Year Ended December 31, 2007**				
	Quarter				
	1	2	3	4	Year
Budgeted direct labor hours (Schedule 4)	36	90	84	30	240
Variable overhead rate	× $8	× $8	× $8	× $8	× $8
Budgeted variable overhead	$288	$ 720	$672	$240	$1,920
Budgeted fixed overhead*	320	320	320	320	1,280
Total overhead	$608	$1,040	$992	$560	$3,200

*Includes $200,000 of depreciation in each quarter.

Ending Finished Goods Inventory Budget

The **ending finished goods inventory budget** supplies information needed for the balance sheet and also serves as an important input for the preparation of the cost of goods sold budget. To prepare this budget, the unit cost of producing each concrete block must be calculated using information from Schedules 3, 4, and 5. The unit cost of a concrete block and the cost of the planned ending inventory are shown in Schedule 6.

Schedule 6
(in thousands)

Ending Finished Goods Inventory Budget
For the Year Ended December 31, 2007

Unit cost computation:
Direct materials (26 lbs. @ $0.01)[a]	$0.26
Direct labor (0.015 hr. @ $8)[b]	0.12
Overhead:	
Variable (0.015 hr. @ $8)[c]	0.12
Fixed (0.015 hr. @ $5.33)[d]	0.08
Total unit cost	$0.58

	Units	Unit Cost	Total
Finished goods: Concrete blocks	100	$0.58	$58

[a]Amounts taken from Schedule 3.
[b]Amounts taken from Schedule 4.
[c]Amounts taken from Schedule 5.
[d]Budgeted fixed overhead (Schedule 5)/Budgeted direct labor hours (Schedule 4) = $1,280/240 = $5.33.

Cost of Goods Sold Budget

Assuming that the beginning finished goods inventory is valued at $55,000, the budgeted cost of goods sold schedule can be prepared using Schedules 3, 4, 5, and 6. The cost of goods sold schedule (Schedule 7) will be used as an input for the budgeted income statement.

Schedule 7
(in thousands)

Cost of Goods Sold Budget
For the Year Ended December 31, 2007

Direct materials used (Schedule 3)*	$4,160
Direct labor used (Schedule 4)	1,920
Overhead (Schedule 5)	3,200
Budgeted manufacturing costs	$9,280
Beginning finished goods	55
Goods available for sale	$9,335
Less: Ending finished goods (Schedule 6)	58
Budgeted cost of goods sold	$9,277

*Production needs × $0.01 = 416,000 × $0.01.

Marketing Expense Budget

The next budget to be prepared—the **marketing expense budget**—outlines planned expenditures for selling and distribution activities. As with overhead, marketing expenses can be broken into fixed and variable components. Such items as sales commissions, freight, and supplies vary with sales activity. Salaries of the marketing staff, depreciation on office equipment, and advertising are fixed expenses. The marketing expense budget is illustrated in Schedule 8.

Schedule 8 (in thousands)

Marketing Expense Budget For the Year Ended December 31, 2007					
	Quarter				
	1	*2*	*3*	*4*	*Year*
Planned sales in units (Schedule 1)	2,000	6,000	6,000	2,000	16,000
Variable marketing expense per unit	×$0.05	×$0.05	×$0.05	×$0.05	×$0.05
Total variable expenses	$ 100	$ 300	$ 300	$ 100	$ 800
Fixed marketing expense:					
Salaries	$ 10	$ 10	$ 10	$ 10	$ 40
Advertising	10	10	10	10	40
Depreciation	5	5	5	5	20
Travel	3	3	3	3	12
Total fixed expenses	$ 28	$ 28	$ 28	$ 28	$ 112
Total marketing expenses	$ 128	$ 328	$ 328	$ 128	$ 912

Research and Development Expense Budget

ABT, Inc., has a small research and development group that works on product line extensions, for example, brick and paving tile. The expenditures by this group are estimated for the coming year and presented in the **research and development expense budget**. This budget is illustrated, by quarter, in Schedule 9.

Research and Development Expense Budget For the Year Ended December 31, 2007					
	Quarter				
	1	*2*	*3*	*4*	*Year*
Salaries	$18	$18	$18	$18	$ 72
Prototype design and development	10	10	10	10	40
Total R&D expenses	$28	$28	$28	$28	$112

Schedule 9 (in thousands)

Administrative Expense Budget

The final budget to be developed for operations is the administrative expense budget. Like the research and development or marketing expense budgets, the **administrative expense budget** consists of estimated expenditures for the overall organization and operation of the company. Most administrative expenses are fixed with respect to sales. They include salaries, depreciation on the headquarters building and equipment, legal and auditing fees, and so on. The administrative expense budget is shown in Schedule 10.

Schedule 10
(in thousands)

Administrative Expense Budget For the Year Ended December 31, 2007					
	Quarter				
	1	*2*	*3*	*4*	*Year*
Salaries	$25	$25	$25	$25	$100
Insurance	—	—	15	—	15
Depreciation	10	10	10	10	40
Travel	2	2	2	2	8
Total administrative expenses	$37	$37	$52	$37	$163

Budgeted Income Statement

With the completion of the administrative expense schedule, ABT has all the operating budgets needed to prepare an estimate of operating income. This budgeted income statement is shown in Schedule 11. The 10 schedules already prepared, along with the budgeted income statement, define the operating budget for ABT.

Schedule 11
(in thousands)

Budgeted Income Statement For the Year Ended December 31, 2007	
Sales (Schedule 1)	$12,000
Less: Cost of goods sold (Schedule 7)	9,277
Gross margin	$ 2,723
Less: Marketing expenses (Schedule 8)	912
Research and development expenses (Schedule 9)	112
Administrative expenses (Schedule 10)	163
Operating income	$ 1,536
Less: Interest expense (Schedule 12)	42
Income before income taxes	$ 1,494
Less: Income taxes	600
Net income	$ 894

Operating income is *not* equivalent to the net income of a firm. To yield net income, interest expense and taxes must be subtracted from operating income. The interest expense deduction is taken from the cash budget (shown in Schedule 12 on page 341). The taxes owed depend on the current tax laws.

Operating Budgets for Merchandising and Service Firms

While the budgets in the master budget described previously are widely used in manufacturing firms, the special needs of service and merchandising firms deserve mention.

In a merchandising firm, the production budget is replaced with a merchandise purchases budget. This budget identifies the quantity of each item that must be purchased for resale, the unit cost of the item, and the total purchase cost. The format is identical to that of the direct materials purchases budget in a manufacturing firm. The only other difference between the operating budgets of manufacturing and merchandising firms is the absence of direct materials purchases and direct labor budgets in a merchandising firm.

In a for-profit service firm, the sales budget is also the production budget. The sales budget identifies each service and the quantity of it that will be sold. Since finished goods inventories are nonexistent, the services produced will be identical to the services sold. For example, the **Colorado Rockies** baseball team budgets the number of seats it expects to fill at each game and the price per ticket. Other revenues (such as television royalties and concession sales) are also budgeted.

In a not-for-profit service firm, the sales budget is replaced by a budget that identifies the levels of the various services that will be offered for the coming year and the associated funds that will be assigned to the services. The source of the funds may be tax revenues, contributions, payments by users of the services, or some combination. For example, a local **United Way**'s board of directors will budget the campaign target (dollars of contributions) for the coming year and then distribute the total funds among the qualifying agencies according to three possible levels of contribution—pessimistic, expected, and optimistic.

Both for-profit and not-for-profit service organizations lack finished goods inventory budgets. However, all the remaining operating budgets found in a manufacturing organization have counterparts in service organizations. A not-for-profit service organization's income statement is replaced by a statement of sources and uses of funds.

We saw how the firm developed a master budget and used it to plan for the coming year. Once the plan is developed, however, the budget can be used for control and decision making. For this to occur, it may be necessary to adjust the level of production or other measures of output. Flexible budgeting can be used to create plans for various levels of activity. Furthermore, the company that uses activity-based costing may find activity-based budgeting (ABB) to be more valuable than traditional budgeting. Activity-based budgets can be more accurate in planning and are more useful for control. Finally, we consider the impact of budgets on behavior.

Preparing the Financial Budget

OBJECTIVE 3

Identify the components of the financial budget, and prepare a cash budget.

The remaining budgets found in the master budget are the financial budgets. The typical financial budgets prepared are the cash budget, the budgeted balance sheet, the budgeted statement of cash flows, and the budget for capital expenditures.

While the master budget is a plan for one year, the capital expenditures budget is a financial plan outlining the expected acquisition of long-term assets and typically covers a number of years. Decision making in regard to capital expenditures is considered in Chapter 20. Details on the budgeted statement of cash flows are appropriately reserved for another course. Accordingly, only the cash budget and the budgeted balance sheet will be illustrated here.

The Cash Budget

Knowledge of cash flows is critical to managing a business. Often, a business is successful in producing and selling a product but fails because of timing problems associated with cash inflows and outflows. By knowing when cash deficiencies and surpluses are likely to occur, a manager can plan to borrow cash when needed and to repay the loans during periods of excess cash. Bank loan officers use a company's cash budget to document the need for cash, as well as the company's ability to repay. Because cash flow is the lifeblood of an organization, the cash budget is one of the most important budgets in the master budget.

Components of the Cash Budget

The cash budget is the detailed plan that shows all expected sources and uses of cash. The cash budget, illustrated in Exhibit 8-4, has the following five main sections:

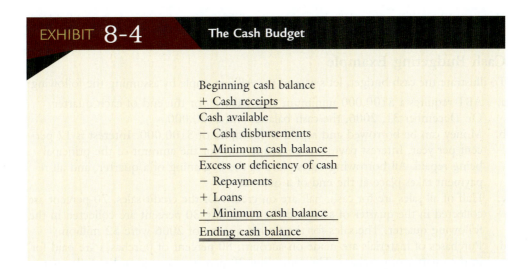

EXHIBIT 8-4   The Cash Budget

Beginning cash balance
+ Cash receipts
Cash available
− Cash disbursements
− Minimum cash balance
Excess or deficiency of cash
− Repayments
+ Loans
+ Minimum cash balance
Ending cash balance

1. Total cash available
2. Cash disbursements
3. Cash excess or deficiency
4. Financing
5. Cash balance

The cash available section consists of the beginning cash balance and the expected cash receipts. Expected cash receipts include all sources of cash for the period being considered. The principal source of cash is from sales. Because a significant proportion of sales is usually on account, a major task of an organization is to determine the pattern of collection for its accounts receivable. If a company has been in business for a while, it can use past experience to create an accounts receivable aging schedule. In other words, the company can determine, on average, what percentages of its accounts receivable are paid in the months following the sales.

The cash disbursements section lists all planned cash outlays for the period except for interest payments on short-term loans (these payments appear in the financing section). All expenses not resulting in a cash outlay are excluded from the list. (Depreciation, for example, is never included in the disbursements section.)

The cash excess or deficiency section compares the cash available with the cash needed. Cash needed includes the total cash disbursements plus the minimum cash balance required by company policy. The minimum cash balance is simply the lowest amount of cash on hand that the firm finds acceptable. Consider your own checking account. You probably try to keep at least some cash in the account, perhaps because a minimum balance avoids service charges or because it allows you to make an unplanned purchase. Similarly, companies also require minimum cash balances. The amount varies from firm to firm and is determined by each company's particular needs and policies. If the total cash available is less than the cash needs, a deficiency exists. In such a case, a short-term loan will be needed. On the other hand, with a cash excess (cash available is greater than the firm's cash needs), the firm has the ability to repay loans and perhaps make some temporary investments.

The financing section of the cash budget consists of borrowings and repayments. If there is a deficiency, the financing section shows the necessary amount to be borrowed. When excess cash is available, the financing section shows planned repayments, including interest.

The final section of the cash budget is the planned ending cash balance. Remember that the minimum cash balance was subtracted to find the cash excess or deficiency.

However, the minimum cash balance is not a disbursement, so it must be added back to yield the planned ending balance.

Cash Budgeting Example

To illustrate the cash budget, let's extend the ABT example by assuming the following:

a. ABT requires a $100,000 minimum cash balance for the end of each quarter. On December 31, 2006, the cash balance was $120,000.

b. Money can be borrowed and repaid in multiples of $100,000. Interest is 12 percent per year. Interest payments are made only for the amount of the principal being repaid. All borrowing takes place at the beginning of a quarter, and all repayment takes place at the end of a quarter.

c. Half of all sales are for cash; half are on credit. Of the credit sales, 70 percent are collected in the quarter of sale, and the remaining 30 percent are collected in the following quarter. The sales for the fourth quarter of 2006 were $2 million.

d. Purchases of materials are made on account; 80 percent of purchases are paid for in the quarter of purchase. The remaining 20 percent are paid in the following quarter. The purchases for the fourth quarter of 2006 were $500,000.

e. Budgeted depreciation is $200,000 per quarter for overhead.

f. The capital budget for 2007 revealed plans to purchase additional equipment to handle increased demand at a small plant in Nevada. The cash outlay for the equipment, $600,000, will take place in the first quarter. The company plans to finance the acquisition of the equipment with operating cash, supplementing it with short-term loans as necessary.

g. Corporate income taxes are approximately $600,000 and will be paid at the end of the fourth quarter (refer to Schedule 11).

Given the preceding information, the cash budget for ABT is shown in Schedule 12 (all figures are rounded to the nearest thousand).

Much of the information needed to prepare the cash budget comes from the operating budgets. In fact, Schedules 1, 3, 4, 5, 8, 9, and 10 all supply essential input. However, these schedules by themselves do not supply all of the needed information. The collection pattern for revenues and the payment pattern for materials must be known before the cash flow for sales and purchases on credit can be found.

Exhibit 8-5, on page 342, displays the pattern of cash inflows from both cash and credit sales. Of course, the credit sales must be adjusted to show how much will be paid in cash during a particular quarter. Let's look at the cash receipts for the first quarter of 2007. Cash sales during the quarter are budgeted for $700,000 (0.5 × $1,400,000). Collections on account for the first quarter relate to credit sales made during the last quarter of the previous year and the first quarter of 2007. Quarter 4, 2006, credit sales equaled $1,000,000 (0.5 × $2,000,000), and $300,000 of those sales (0.3 × $1,000,000) remain to be collected in Quarter 1, 2007. Quarter 1, 2007, credit sales are budgeted at $700,000, and 70 percent will be collected in that quarter. Therefore, a total of $490,000 will be collected on account for credit sales made in that quarter. Similar computations are made for the remaining quarters.

Cash is disbursed for purchases of materials, payment of wages, and payment of other expenses. This information comes from Schedules 3, 4, 5, 8, 9, and 10. However, all noncash expenses, such as depreciation, need to be removed from the total amounts reported in the expense budgets. Thus, the budgeted expenses in Schedules 5, 8, and 10 were reduced by the budgeted depreciation for each quarter. Overhead expenses in Schedule 5 were reduced by depreciation of $200,000 per quarter. Marketing expenses and administrative expenses were reduced by $5,000 per quarter and $10,000 per quarter, respectively. The net amounts are what appear in the cash budget.

The cash budget shown in Schedule 12 underscores the importance of breaking down the annual budget into smaller time periods. The cash budget for the year gives the impression that sufficient operating cash will be available to finance the acquisition of the

Schedule 12 (in thousands)

Cash Budget **For the Year Ended December 31, 2007**						
	Quarter					
	1	*2*	*3*	*4*	*Year*	*Source[a]*
Beginning cash balance	$ 120	$ 113	$ 152	$1,334	$ 120	a
Collections:						
Cash sales	700	2,100	2,400	800	6,000	c, 1
Credit sales:						
Current quarter	490	1,470	1,680	560	4,200	c, 1
Prior quarter	300	210	630	720	1,860	c, 1
Total cash available	$1,610	$3,893	$4,862	$3,414	$12,180	
Less disbursements:						
Materials:						
Current quarter	$ 523	$1,248	$1,141	$ 416	$ 3,328	d, 3
Prior quarter	100	131	312	285	828	d, 3
Direct labor	288	720	672	240	1,920	4
Overhead	408	840	792	360	2,400	e, 5
Marketing expense	123	323	323	123	892	8
R&D expense	28	28	28	28	112	9
Administrative	27	27	42	27	123	10
Income taxes	—	—	—	600	600	g, 11
Equipment	600	—	—	—	600	f
Total disbursements	$2,097	$3,317	$3,310	$2,079	$10,803	
Minimum cash balance	100	100	100	100	100	a
Total cash needs	$2,197	$3,417	$3,410	$2,179	$10,903	
Excess (deficiency) of cash available over needs	$ (587)	$ 476	$1,452	$1,235	$ 1,277	
Financing:						
Borrowings	600	—	—	—	600	
Repayments (outflows)	—	(400)	(200)	—	(600)	b
Interest[b] (outflows)	—	(24)	(18)	—	(42)	b
Total financing	$ 600	$ (424)	$ (218)	$ —	$ (42)	
Plus: Minimum cash balance	100	100	100	100	100	
Ending cash balance[c]	$ 113	$ 152	$1,334	$1,335	$ 1,335	

[a]Letters refer to the information on page 340. Numbers refer to schedules already developed.
[b]Interest payments are $6/12 \times 0.12 \times \$400$ and $9/12 \times 0.12 \times \$200$, respectively. Since borrowings occur at the beginning of the quarter and repayments at the end of the quarter, the first principal repayment takes place after six months, and the second principal repayment takes place after nine months.
[c]Total cash available minus total disbursements plus (or minus) total financing.

new equipment. Quarterly information, however, shows the need for short-term borrowing because of both the acquisition of the new equipment and the timing of the firm's cash flows. Breaking down the annual cash budget into quarterly time periods conveys more information. Even smaller time periods often prove to be useful. Most firms prepare monthly cash budgets, and some even prepare weekly and daily cash budgets.

Another significant piece of information emerges from ABT's cash budget. By the end of the third quarter, the firm holds a considerable amount of cash ($1,334,000). ABT should consider investing this cash in short-term marketable securities rather than

EXHIBIT 8-5 Schedule of Cash Receipts for ABT, Inc.

Source	Quarter 1	Quarter 2	Quarter 3	Quarter 4
Cash sales	$ 700,000	$2,100,000	$2,400,000	$ 800,000
Received on account from sales in:				
Quarter 4, 2006	300,000			
Quarter 1, 2007	490,000	210,000		
Quarter 2, 2007		1,470,000	630,000	
Quarter 3, 2007			1,680,000	720,000
Quarter 4, 2007				560,000
Total cash receipts	$1,490,000	$3,780,000	$4,710,000	$2,080,000

allowing it to sit idly in a bank account. The management of ABT should consider paying dividends and making long-term investments. At the very least, the excess cash should be invested in short-term marketable securities. Once plans are finalized for use of the excess cash, the cash budget should be revised to reflect those plans. Budgeting is a dynamic process. As the budget is developed, new information becomes available and better plans can be formulated.

Budgeted Balance Sheet

The budgeted balance sheet depends on information contained in the current balance sheet and in the other budgets in the master budget. The balance sheet for the beginning of the year is given in Exhibit 8-6. The budgeted balance sheet for December 31, 2007, is given in Schedule 13 on page 344. Explanations for the budgeted figures follow the schedule.

As we have described the individual budgets that make up the master budget, the interdependencies of the component budgets have become apparent. You may want to refer back to Exhibit 8-2 to review these interrelationships.

Shortcomings of the Traditional Master Budget Process

Criticisms of the master budget can be classified into several categories. The traditional master budget is:

1. Department oriented and does not recognize the interdependencies among departments
2. Static, not dynamic
3. Results, not process, oriented

Let's look more closely at each of these.

Departmental Orientation

In traditional budgeting, each department develops its own budget. These budgets are then aggregated to form the overall company budget. The focus on planning department by department results in planning forward from resources to outputs. That is, a department may start by determining what resources (i.e., labor, supplies, etc.) it currently has and then adjust those levels for the potential level of output. The activity-based budgeting approach is the opposite. ABB starts by asking what level of output is desired and then works backward to see what resources are necessary to achieve that level of output. We might ask, what difference does it make? Couldn't you achieve the

EXHIBIT 8-6	Balance Sheet for ABT, Inc.

ABT, Inc.
Balance Sheet
December 31, 2006
(in thousands)

Assets

Current assets:

Cash.	$ 120	
Accounts receivable	300	
Materials inventory.	50	
Finished goods inventory.	55	
Total current assets		$ 525
Property, plant, and equipment (PP&E):		
Land	$ 2,500	
Buildings and equipment.	9,000	
Accumulated depreciation	(4,500)	
Total PP&E.		7,000
Total assets.		$7,525

Liabilities and Stockholders' Equity

Current liabilities:

Accounts payable		$ 100
Stockholders' equity:		
Common stock, no par	$ 600	
Retained earnings.	6,825	
Total stockholders' equity		7,425
Total liabilities and stockholders' equity		$7,525

same effect whether you go backward or forward? The answer, rooted in human behavior, is no. By concentrating on last year's costs and going forward, a department locks in past ways of doing things. Companies that use ABB, however, start first with the desired output and then figure out what resources are needed. That level of resources may or may not be the same as last year's level.

As a result, traditional budgeting may have managers feeling embattled. There is a sense of "every department for itself." Managers feel encouraged to use every cent of budgeted resources, whether or not those resources are needed. Indeed, if the department did not use the full level of budgeted resources, it would have a hard time making a case for increased—or even the same level of—resources in the coming year.

Static Budgets

A static budget is one developed for a single level of activity. Recall that the master budget is on budgeted sales for the coming year. Once that amount is determined, production, marketing, and administrative budgets are built around it. An adjunct to the static nature of the budget is the use of last year's budget to create this year's budget. Often, the current budget is based on last year's amounts as adjusted for inflation. This approach to budgeting, called the incremental approach, has the effect of incorporating last year's inefficiencies into the current budget. Under the incremental approach, heads of budgeting units often strive to spend all of the year's budget so that no surplus exists at the end of the year. (This is particularly true for government agencies.) This action is taken to maintain the current level of the budget and enable

ABT, Inc.
Budgeted Balance Sheet
December 31, 2007

Assets

Current assets:

Cash..	$ 1,335[a]	
Accounts receivable	240[b]	
Materials inventory...............................	50[c]	
Finished goods inventory..........................	58[d]	
Total current assets		$1,683

Property, plant, and equipment (PP&E):

Land	$ 2,500[e]	
Buildings and equipment.........................	9,600[f]	
Accumulated depreciation	(5,360)[g]	
Total PP&E.....................................		6,740
Total assets....................................		$8,423

Liabilities and Stockholders' Equity

Current liabilities:

Accounts payable		$ 104[h]

Stockholders' equity:

Common stock, no par...........................	$ 600[i]	
Retained earnings...............................	7,719[j]	
Total stockholders' equity		8,319
Total liabilities and stockholders' equity		$8,423

[a]Ending balance from Schedule 12.
[b]30 percent of fourth-quarter credit sales (0.30 × $800,000)—see Schedules 1 and 12.
[c]From Schedule 3 (5,000,000 lbs. × $0.01).
[d]From Schedule 6.
[e]From the December 31, 2006, balance sheet.
[f]December 31, 2006, balance ($9,000,000) plus new equipment acquisition of $600,000 (see the 2006 ending balance sheet and Schedule 12).
[g]From the December 31, 2006, balance sheet and Schedules 5, 8, and 10 ($4,500,000 + $800,000 + $20,000 + $40,000).
[h]20 percent of fourth-quarter purchases (0.20 × $520,000)—see Schedules 3 and 12.
[i]From the December 31, 2006, balance sheet.
[j]$6,825,000 + $894,000 (December 31, 2006, balance plus net income from Schedule 11).

the head of the unit to request additional funds. For example, at an Air Force base, a bomber wing was faced with the possibility of a surplus at the end of the fiscal year. The base commander, however, found ways to spend the extra money before the year ended. Missile officers, who normally drove to the missile command site, were flown to the sites in helicopters; several bags of lawn fertilizer were given away to all personnel with houses on base; and new furniture was acquired for the bachelor officer quarters. The waste and inefficiency portrayed in this example are often perpetuated and encouraged by incremental budgeting.

Zero-base budgeting is an alternative approach.[2] Unlike incremental budgeting, the prior year's budgeted level is not taken for granted. Existing operations are analyzed, and continuance of the activity or operation must be justified on the basis of its

---

2. Zero-base budgeting was developed by Peter Pyhrr of Texas Instruments. For a detailed discussion of the approach, see Peter Pyhrr, *Zero-Base Budgeting* (New York: Wiley, 1973).

need or usefulness to the organization. The burden of proof is on each manager to justify why any money should be spent at all. Zero-base budgeting requires extensive, indepth analysis. Although this approach has been used successfully in industry and government (e.g., **Texas Instruments** and the state of Georgia), it is time consuming and costly. Advocates of the incremental approach argue that incremental budgeting also uses extensive, in-depth reviews but not as frequently because they are not justified on a cost-benefit basis. A reasonable compromise may be to use zero-base budgeting every three to five years in order to weed out waste and inefficiency. Especially in a period of intense competition and reengineering, zero-base budgeting can force managers to "break set" and see their units in a different perspective.

Results Orientation

Closely allied to the static nature of the master budget is a results orientation. By focusing on results instead of process, managers, in effect, disconnect the process from its output. When budgets are resource driven rather than output driven, then managers concentrate on resources and may fail to see the link between resources and output. Then, when the need for cost cutting arises, they make across-the-board cuts, slicing every department's budget by the same percentage. This has the superficial appearance of fairness—in that every department "shares the pain." Unfortunately, some departments have more fat than others, and some may be downright unneeded. Across-the-board cuts do not cut true waste and inefficiency; that is not their point.

Why, if it has all of these problems, has the traditional approach to budgeting been used for so long? It is important to realize that the master budget is not inherently flawed. In fact, it has been very useful over the decades. However, the past 30 or so years have been characterized by rapid change. In a period of change, managers may not realize that previously acceptable ways of doing things no longer work. This is the case for the master budget. For example, consider its static nature. If sales are much the same from year to year, if the production process does not change, and if the firm's product mix is fairly simple and stable, then a static budget based in large part on last year's numbers makes sense. However, this is not the situation for the vast majority of businesses today. Flexible budgets can give managers some feel for the impact of fixed and variable costs. Activity-based budgets go further, by recognizing the numerous drivers for variable costs and by starting with outputs and working backwards to resources.

Flexible Budgets for Planning and Control

OBJECTIVE 4
Define flexible budgeting, and discuss its role in planning, control, and decision making.

Budgets are useful control measures. To be used in performance evaluation, however, two major considerations must be addressed. The first is to determine how budgeted amounts should be compared with actual results. The second consideration involves the impact of budgets on human behavior.

Static Budgets versus Flexible Budgets

Master budget amounts, while vital for planning, are less useful for control. The reason for this is because the anticipated level of activity rarely equals the actual level of activity. Therefore, the costs and revenues associated with the anticipated level of activity cannot be readily compared with actual costs and revenues for a different level of activity.

Static Budgets

Master budgets are developed around a particular level of activity; they are static budgets. Because the revenues and costs prepared for static budgets depend on a level of activity that rarely equals actual activity, they are not very useful when it comes to preparing performance reports.

To illustrate, let's return to the ABT, Inc., example used in developing the master budget. Suppose that ABT provides quarterly performance reports. Recall that ABT anticipated sales of 2 million in the first quarter and had budgeted production of 2.4 million units to support that level of sales. Now, let's suppose that sales activity was greater than expected in the first quarter; 2.6 million concrete blocks were sold instead of the 2 million budgeted in the sales budget; and, because of increased sales activity, production was increased over the planned level. Instead of producing 2.4 million units, ABT produced 3 million units. A performance report comparing the actual production costs for the first quarter with the original planned production costs is given in Exhibit 8-7.

	Actual	Budgeted	Variance
EXHIBIT 8-7 Performance Report: Quarterly Production Costs (in thousands)			
Units produced	3,000	2,400	600 F[a]
Direct materials cost	$ 927.3	$ 624.0[b]	$303.3 U[c]
Direct labor cost	360.0	288.0[d]	72.0 U
Overhead:[e]			
Variable:			
Supplies	80.0	72.0	8.0 U
Indirect labor	220.0	168.0	52.0 U
Power	40.0	48.0	(8.0)F
Fixed:			
Supervision	90.0	100.0	(10.0)F
Depreciation	200.0	200.0	0.0
Rent	30.0	20.0	10.0 U
Total	$1,947.3	$1,520.0	$427.3 U

[a]F means the variance is favorable.
[b]2,400,000 units × $0.26.
[c]U means the variance is unfavorable.
[d]2,400,000 units × $0.12.
[e]Variable overhead equals 2,400,000 units times the unit amounts from Schedule 6. Budgeted fixed overhead per quarter is given in Schedule 5.

According to the report, unfavorable variances occur for direct materials, direct labor, supplies, indirect labor, and rent. However, there is something fundamentally wrong with the report. Actual costs for production of *3 million concrete blocks* are being compared with planned costs for production of *2.4 million*. Because direct materials, direct labor, and variable overhead are variable costs, we would expect them to be greater at a higher activity level. Thus, even if cost control were perfect for the production of 3 million units, unfavorable variances would be produced for all variable costs.

To create a meaningful performance report, actual costs and expected costs must be compared at the *same* level of activity. Since actual output often differs from planned output, some method is needed to compute what the costs should have been for the actual output level.

Flexible Budgets

The budget that (1) provides expected costs for a range of activity or (2) provides budgeted costs for the actual level of activity is called a **flexible budget**. Flexible budgeting can be used in planning by showing what costs will be at various levels of activity. When used this way, managers can deal with uncertainty by examining the expected financial results for a number of plausible scenarios. Spreadsheets are particularly useful in developing this type of flexible budget.

The flexible budget can be used after the fact, for control, to compute what costs should have been for the actual level of activity. Once expected costs are known for the actual level of activity, a performance report that compares those expected costs to actual costs can be prepared. When used for control, flexible budgets help managers compare "apples to apples" in assessing performance.

To illustrate the power of flexible budgeting, let's prepare a budget for ABT for three different activity levels (the number of concrete blocks produced). Since the flexible budget gives the expected cost at various levels of activity, we must know the cost behavior patterns of each budget item. Recall that the cost behavior pattern can be expressed as the sum of the fixed cost and a variable rate multiplied by activity level. The variable rates for direct materials ($0.26 per unit), direct labor ($0.12 per unit), supplies ($0.03), indirect labor ($0.07), and power ($0.02) are given in Schedule 6. Finally, we know from Schedule 5 that fixed overhead is budgeted at $320,000 per quarter. Exhibit 8-8 displays a flexible budget for production costs when 2.4, 3, and 3.6 million concrete blocks are produced.

EXHIBIT 8-8 — Flexible Production Budget (in thousands)

	Variable Cost per Unit	Range of Production (units)		
		2,400	3,000	3,600
Production costs:				
Variable:				
Direct materials	$0.26	$ 624	$ 780	$ 936
Direct labor	0.12	288	360	432
Variable overhead:				
Supplies	0.03	72	90	108
Indirect labor	0.07	168	210	252
Power	0.02	48	60	72
Total variable costs	$0.50	$1,200	$1,500	$1,800
Fixed overhead:				
Supervision		$ 100	$ 100	$ 100
Depreciation		200	200	200
Rent		20	20	20
Total fixed costs		$ 320	$ 320	$ 320
Total production costs		$1,520	$1,820	$2,120

Notice in Exhibit 8-8 that total budgeted production costs increase as the activity level increases. Budgeted costs change because of variable costs. Because of this, a flexible budget is sometimes referred to as a **variable budget**.

Exhibit 8-8 reveals what the costs should have been for the actual level of activity (3 million blocks). A revised performance report that compares actual and budgeted costs for the actual level of activity is given in Exhibit 8-9 on the following page.

The revised performance report in Exhibit 8-9 paints a much different picture than the one in Exhibit 8-7. By comparing budgeted costs for the actual level of activity with actual costs for the same level, **flexible budget variances** are generated. Managers can locate possible problem areas by examining these variances. According to the ABT flexible budget variances, expenditures for direct materials are excessive. (The other unfavorable variances seem relatively small.) With this knowledge, management can search for the causes of the excess expenditures and prevent the same problems from occurring in the future.

| EXHIBIT 8-9 | Actual versus Flexible Performance Report: Quarterly Production Costs (in thousands) | | |

	Actual	**Budgeted***	**Variance**
Units produced	3,000	3,000	—
Production costs:			
Direct materials	$ 927.3	$ 780.0	$147.3 U
Direct labor	360.0	360.0	0.0
Variable overhead:			
Supplies	80.0	90.0	(10.0) F
Indirect labor	220.0	210.0	10.0 U
Power	40.0	60.0	(20.0) F
Total variable costs	$1,627.3	$1,500.0	$127.3 U
Fixed overhead:			
Supervision	$ 90.0	$ 100.0	$ (10.0) F
Depreciation	200.0	200.0	0.0
Rent	30.0	20.0	10.0 U
Total fixed costs	$ 320.0	$ 320.0	$ 0.0
Total production costs	$1,947.3	$1,820.0	$127.3 U

*From Exhibit 8-8.

Budgets can be used to examine the efficiency and effectiveness of a company. **Efficiency** is achieved when the business process is performed in the best possible way, with little or no waste. The flexible budget provides an assessment of the efficiency of a manager. This is so because the flexible budget compares the actual costs for a given level of output with the budgeted costs for the same level. **Effectiveness** means that a manager achieves or exceeds the goals described by the static budget. Thus, efficiency examines how well the work is done, and effectiveness examines whether or not the right work is being accomplished. Any differences between the flexible budget and the static budget are attributable to differences in volume. They are called *volume variances.* A 5-column performance report that reveals both the flexible budget variances and the volume variances can be used. Exhibit 8-10 provides an example of this report using the ABT data.

As the report in Exhibit 8-10 reveals, production volume was 600,000 units greater than the original budgeted amount. Thus, the manager exceeded the output goal. This volume variance is labeled *favorable* because it exceeds the original production goal. (Recall that the *reason* for the extra production was because the demand for the product was greater than expected. Thus, the increase in production over the original amount was truly favorable.) On the other hand, the budgeted variable costs are greater than expected because of the increased production. This difference is labeled unfavorable because the costs are greater than expected; however, the increase in costs is because of an increase in production. Thus, it is totally reasonable. For this particular example, the effectiveness of the manager is not in question; thus, the main issue is how well the manager controlled costs as revealed by the flexible budget variances.

Flexible budgeting may also be accomplished using data from an activity-based costing system. In this case, a variety of drivers would be used rather than the single unit-based driver in the previous example. We can think of flexible budgeting using ABC costs and drivers as a simplified sort of activity-based budgeting. The ABC flexible budget is a more accurate tool for planning and does give an indication of more costly ver-

	Actual Results (1)	Flexible Budget (2)	Flexible Budget Variances (3) = (1) − (2)	Static Budget (4)	Volume Variances (5) = (2) − (4)
Units produced	3,000	3,000	—	2,400	600 F
Production costs:					
Direct materials	$ 927.3	$ 780.0	$147.3 U	$ 624.0	$156.0 U
Direct labor	360.0	360.0	0.0	288.0	72.0 U
Supplies	80.0	90.0	(10.0) F	72.0	18.0 U
Indirect labor	220.0	210.0	10.0 U	168.0	42.0 U
Power	40.0	60.0	(20.0) F	48.0	12.0 U
Supervision	90.0	100.0	(10.0) F	100.0	0.0
Depreciation	200.0	200.0	0.0	200.0	0.0
Rent	30.0	20.0	10.0 U	20.0	0.0
Total costs	$1,947.3	$1,820.0	$127.3 U	$1,520.0	$300.0 U

EXHIBIT 8-10 — Managerial Performance Report: Quarterly Production (in thousands)

sus less costly activities. Thus, an ABC flexible budget can support continuous improvement and process management.

Let's use the experience of a factory in costing overhead to see how an ABC flexible budget is developed. Suppose the factory has identified five overhead activities: maintenance, machining, inspection, setups, and purchasing. Then, an appropriate driver must be identified for each of the activities, and cost behavior concepts can be used to develop cost formulas. This has been done for the factory as follows:

Activity	Cost Formula
Maintenance	$20,000 + $5.50 per machine hour
Machining	$15,000 + $2 per machine hour
Inspection	$80,000 + $2,100 per batch
Setups	$1,800 per batch
Purchasing	$211,000 + $1 per purchase order

In principle, the fixed cost component for each activity should correspond to committed resources, and the variable–cost component for each activity should correspond to flexible resources (those acquired as needed). This is how an ABC flexible budget is developed. This multiple formula approach allows managers to predict more accurately what costs ought to be for different levels of activity, as measured by driver usage. These costs can then be compared with the actual costs to assess budgetary performance. Exhibit 8-11, on the following page, illustrates the activity flexible budget at two levels of activity. The first one supports output requiring 8,000 machine hours, 25 batches, and 15,000 purchase orders. The second one supports output requiring 16,000 machine hours, 30 batches, and 25,000 purchase orders.

In Exhibit 8-11, we have an ABC flexible budget for two levels of activity. This is a flexible budget according to our first definition of flexible budgeting and can be used for planning. If we want to use the ABC flexible budget for control, we will need to know the actual cost of each activity and compare that to the flexible budget amount for actual activity. Let's assume that the first activity level for each driver in Exhibit 8-11

EXHIBIT 8-11   Activity Flexible Budget

	Driver: Machine Hours			
	Formula		**Level of Activity**	
	Fixed	**Variable**	**8,000**	**16,000**
Maintenance	$ 20,000	$ 5.50	$ 64,000	$108,000
Machining	15,000	2.00	31,000	47,000
Subtotal	$ 35,000	$ 7.50	$ 95,000	$155,000
	Driver: Number of Batches			
	Fixed	**Variable**	**25**	**30**
Inspection	$ 80,000	$2,100	$132,500	$143,000
Setups	0	1,800	45,000	54,000
Subtotal	$ 80,000	$3,900	$177,500	$197,000
	Driver: Number of Orders			
	Fixed	**Variable**	**15,000**	**25,000**
Purchasing	$211,000	$ 1	$226,000	$236,000

corresponds to the actual activity usage levels. Then, Exhibit 8-12 compares these budgeted costs for actual activity usage with the actual costs. We can see that variances exist for all activities, with an overall variance of $22,500. As is always true of variance analysis, we cannot tell why variances occur until we investigate. Managers may want to determine which of the variances appear out of line and then investigate. In addition, the ABC flexible budget spotlights the most costly activities, and this may trigger an investigation of purchasing, for example, even if its variance is not considered significant.

EXHIBIT 8-12   Activity-Based Performance Report

	Actual Costs	**Budgeted Costs**	**Budget Variance**
Maintenance	$ 55,000	$ 64,000	$ 9,000 F
Machining	29,000	31,000	2,000 F
Inspection	125,500	132,500	7,000 F
Setups	46,500	45,000	1,500 U
Purchases	220,000	226,000	6,000 F
Total	$476,000	$498,500	$25,500 F

We can see that flexible budgeting is a powerful tool for planning and control. The ability to determine costs at varying levels of activity helps managers to overcome the drawback of the static nature of the master budget. Activity-based budgeting adds still more power to the manager's budgeting toolkit.

OBJECTIVE 5

Define activity-based budgeting, and discuss its role in planning, control, and decision making.

Activity-Based Budgets

We just saw that flexible budgeting can solve some of the problems that arise from using static budgets for performance evaluation. Flexible budgeting allows the firm to create a budget for varying levels of activity. However, just as the static master budget was useful for firms that faced relatively constant sales and production from year to year, the flexible budget is useful for a particular set of circumstances as well. The ABT situation is tailor made for flexible budgeting. The output is homogeneous, and the production process is fairly simple. Basing variable costs on a volume-based driver works well. However, many firms have found that product diversity means that the richer set of drivers of activity-based costing are necessary to describe their cost structure. These firms will find that activity-based budgeting (ABB) is more useful for their needs.[3]

The activity-based budget begins with output and then determines the resources necessary to create that output. Ideally, the organization translates its vision into a strategy with definable objectives in order to create value. Ways of creating value include growing market share, improving sales rates, reducing expenses, increasing profit margins, increasing productivity, and reducing the cost of capital. We can see how clearly ABB is related to performance evaluation and, in particular, to economic value added (as discussed in Chapter 10).

We can look at a department's budget from three perspectives: a traditional functional-based approach, a flexible budgeting approach, and an activity-based approach. Traditional budgeting relies on the use of functional-based line items, such as salaries, supplies, depreciation on equipment, and so on. The flexible budget uses knowledge of cost behavior to split the functional-based line items into fixed and variable components. The activity-based budget works backward from activities and their drivers to the underlying costs.

Let's use the new secure-care department of a large regional public accounting firm to illustrate the differences among traditional, flexible, and activity-based budgeting. First, let's review the history of the secure-care department. A couple of years ago, Brad Covington, one of the firm's younger partners, persuaded his other partners to put an eldercare program into effect. Eldercare is a multifaceted program of personal financial and assurance services. The typical client is the elderly parent(s) of a grown child who lives outside the parents' city. The parents may need help paying monthly bills, balancing their checking account, and finding and paying for in-home health and personal care. Brad felt that there was a need for eldercare services in the metropolitan area and that his accounting firm was ideally suited to provide these services. Not only were the financial services a natural for a public accounting firm, but the high confidence the public placed in accountants made it likely that clients would feel comfortable relying on their expertise in finding appropriate caretakers. The main problem, in Brad's mind, was the term "eldercare." After some discussion among firm members, the name secure-care was chosen. The secure-care department was established two years ago.

During the 2-year period, Brad developed a client base of 60. A variety of services were offered. For all clients, all business mail was rerouted to the accounting firm. The clients' checking, savings, and money market accounts were kept up to date and reconciled each month by the firm. All bills were paid from the appropriate accounts. In addition, personal and household services were contracted out. The secure-care department advertised for, interviewed, and investigated the backgrounds of all individuals hired to provide personal and household services to clients. Monthly personal visits were made to each client to ensure that their needs were being met. Finally, a monthly

---

3. Much of this section relies on ideas expressed in James A. Brimson and John Antos, *Driving Value Using Activity-Based Budgeting* (New York, NY: John Wiley & Sons, 1999). This book is a thorough approach to the subject.

report on the financial and personal status of each client was prepared and delivered to the clients and any concerned adult children.

The secure-care department consisted of a receptionist, two administrative assistants, and Brad—the managing partner for the department. Because there was insufficient room in the main offices of the accounting firm, Brad rented office space across the street. All investigative services (for background checks) were contracted out to a local private investigator with extensive experience in this area.

Exhibit 8-13 depicts the traditional budget for the coming year for the secure-care department. Notice that the expense categories are listed along with a dollar amount for each one. How would a typical company using functional budgeting arrive at these figures? It would be a safe bet to assume that they would be based to a large extent on the level of those same expenses for the previous year. Maybe there would be some adjustment of certain figures (e.g., if salaries were expected to rise by 3 percent due to anticipated raises).

EXHIBIT 8-13	Traditional Budget for the Secure-Care Department	
Expense Category		**Budgeted Amounts**
Salaries and benefits:		
Brad	$110,000	
Administrative assistants	70,000	
Receptionist	30,000	$210,000
Rent		36,000
Supplies		10,000
PCs and Internet		4,000
Travel		3,000
Investigative services		6,000
Telephone		4,800
Total		$273,800

Now, suppose that Brad thinks the costs of the secure-care department might vary according to the number of clients. Cost behavior concepts can be used to break the expense categories into fixed and variable components. Assume that supplies are strictly variable, at $166.67 per client. Telephone is a mixed cost, with a fixed component of $1,200 and a variable rate of $60 per client. The remaining expenses appear to be predominantly fixed. Then, a flexible budget for the following year's 60 estimated clients would appear as the one shown in Exhibit 8-14. Notice that the total amount is still $273,800. The flexible budget shown here does not look like a great step forward. Its power lies in its ability to show changes in total cost as activity level changes. For example, the budget could be extended to show total costs at 50 and 70 clients as well. The key requirement is that the product is much the same from unit to unit. In the case of the secure-care department, that would mean the needs of each client are very similar.

Brad was not satisfied with the results of the flexible budget. He knew that many of the expense categories were variable but that they did not necessarily vary with the number of clients. For example, one important and time-consuming activity was paying monthly bills. However, the number of bills varied greatly from client to client. Similarly, some clients had just a couple of checking and savings accounts while others had five or six checking, money market, and savings accounts. Each of these had to be

---

EXHIBIT 8-14   Flexible Budget for the Secure-Care Department

Expense Category		Budgeted Amounts for 60 Clients
Variable expenses:		
Supplies	$ 10,000	
Telephone	3,600	
Total variable expenses		$ 13,600
Fixed expenses:		
Salaries and benefits	$210,000	
Rent	36,000	
PCs and Internet	4,000	
Travel	3,000	
Investigative services	6,000	
Telephone	1,200	
Total fixed expenses		260,200
Total expenses		$273,800

---

monitored and reconciled at the end of the month. In summary, there was considerable diversity among the clients. Therefore, Brad decided to build an activity-based budget.

To build an activity-based budget for the secure-care department, four steps are needed: (1) the output of the department must be determined; (2) the activities needed to deliver the output, along with their related drivers, must be identified; (3) the demand for each activity must be estimated; and (4) the cost of resources required to produce the relevant activities must be determined. It is critically important to see that ABB is based on expected output. The traditional budget often plans forward from last year's experience, while the ABB plans backward from next year's output. The differences between the two approaches are more than semantic. While it may appear that the same results would hold in both cases, in practice, that is not so. In addition, the ABB approach, using resources and activities to create output, gives the manager much more information as well as ability to consider eliminating nonvalue-added activities.

The following information about the secure-care department was developed:

- All clients received varying levels of the department's activities.
- The first activity is "processing mail." Brad decided that number of clients was a reasonable driver for this activity. All clients had mail, and the amount varied from week to week. The receptionist opened all the mail and sorted it into folders by client. It took approximately two hours a day to perform this task.
- The second activity is "paying bills." There were approximately 1,000 bills per month, or 12,000 per year. The number of bills varied widely from client to client. The administrative assistants performed this activity, using computer software to enter and pay bills. Based on the amount of time this took and the cost of supplies, software, and postage, the average cost of paying one bill was $1.75.
- The third activity is "reconciling accounts." The administrative assistants performed this activity, and it took about 30 minutes per account each month. There were 350 accounts. This averaged out to one administrative assistant working full time on reconciling accounts. Related supplies and the use of a computer and software added another $4,900 to the total.
- The firm advertised for and interviewed caregivers for their clients as needed. The driver for this activity is number of new hires. The yearly cost, including newspaper

advertising and the time of the administrative assistants, totaled $7,200 per year. On average, there were estimated to be 60 new hires in a year.

- A private investigator was retained to perform thorough background checks of prospective caregivers. Each background check cost $25, and an average of four prospective caregivers was checked for every successful new hire.
- Every month, the administrative assistants made personal visits to each client. The number of clients was a good driver for this activity, and the total cost was about $650 per client, per year.
- Each month, Brad or one of the administrative assistants prepared a monthly report for every client. The report detailed the financial activity and included the notes taken from the home visits. Prospective issues and problems were raised. These reports were sent to the clients as well as to interested adult children. The cost of time, supplies, and postage averaged $175 per client, per year.
- The final activity is managing the department and signing up new clients. Brad is responsible for the bulk of this activity. The activity does not have a driver, but instead, consists of the remaining costs of the department.

The secure-care department's activity-based budget is shown in Exhibit 8-15. Notice that the department has identified eight activities and four drivers. This level of detail is much richer than that for the flexible budget presented in Exhibit 8-14, where there was only one driver, the number of clients. With an activity-based budget, we get a feel for the diversity among the clients. Some have more accounts, and some more bills to pay. In other words, "clients" are not all the same. There is considerable product diversity, and this diversity is not captured in either the traditional or the simple flexible budget.

EXHIBIT 8-15	Activity-Based Budget for the Secure-Care Department			
Activity Description	**Activity Driver**	**Cost per Unit of Driver**	**Amount of Driver**	**Activity Cost**
Processing mail	Number of clients	$125.00	60	$ 7,500
Paying bills	Number of bills	1.75	12,000	21,000
Reconciling accounts	Number of accounts	114.00	350	39,900
Advertising/interviewing	Number of new hires	120.00	60	7,200
Investigating	Number of new hires	100.00	60	6,000
Visiting homes	Number of clients	650.00	60	39,000
Writing reports	Number of clients	175.00	60	10,500
Managing department				142,700
Total				$273,800

The traditional, flexible, and activity-based budgets for the secure-care department all total $273,800. But notice the richness of detail in the activity-based budget. Here, we can see the relationship between output and resource usage. The manager's attention is also focused on the most costly activities: paying bills, reconciling accounts, and visiting homes. Brad may want to use this information in pricing the various parts of the secure-care service.

Earlier in this chapter, we noted that both the traditional and flexible budgeting approaches worked well for particular sets of circumstances. Recall that a key feature is that the environment of the company remains stable. When that is the case, one year is much like the next. The technology is the same, and there is little product diversity. A single volume-based driver works well to account for any changes. However, many companies now face an environment that is changing rapidly in many ways. These companies are ill served by budgets that are founded on the notion that everything remains

COST MANAGEMENT   Technology in Action

The series of layoffs that occurred in the 2001 recession differed from those in the recession of 1990–1991 in an important way. In the earlier recession, cost cutting meant downsizing, and the resultant layoffs relied on across-the-board cuts. In July 2000, **Tenneco Automotive Inc.**, a manufacturer of mufflers and shock absorbers, started to adjust to the economic downturn by instituting a 4-for-1 attrition program. In other words, for every four employees who left, only one would be replaced. The remaining employees were expected to pick up the slack. Unfortunately, not all units had slack. Some had been operating at capacity. For example, many engineers felt stretched and unable to fully compensate for those engineers who had left. During the time period, the company's stock price tumbled 58 percent.

By early 2001, Tenneco changed its focus. The company still wanted to trim costs. However, it put the spotlight on underperforming units and employees. This approach is the one dictated by activity-based budgeting. Resources necessary to support the production of products and services are maintained; non-value-added activities and their resources are trimmed. ABB allows managers to better understand the relationships among resources, costs, and output. Instead of relying on a single driver, labor hours, managers using ABB know that a variety of drivers must be assessed to correctly budget for changes in product mix and volume.

Source: Jon E. Hilsenrath, "Experts Say Corporate Layoffs Often Hurt More than Help," *The Wall Street Journal* (February 21, 2001): A2.

the same. Companies in a changing environment, whether it relates to changing technology, competition, or customer base, need a much more flexible technique for planning and control. The activity-based budget can be extended to include feature costing. This provides an even more powerful tool for planning and control.

Feature costing assigns costs to activities and products or services based on the product's or service's features.[4] In the secure-care department, we could see that one client was not necessarily the same as another. In other words, different clients had different features that required the department to use different sets of activities to handle them. A client with only one checking account and a few repetitive bills took little time. Other clients had numerous accounts and bills. Some clients may be difficult to get along with, leading to rapid turnover of their caregivers and necessitating additional interviewing and background investigation. If the company wanted to extend the ABB process, it could add feature costing. That is, it could determine what features of clients differentiate them into groups that require different sets of activities. We can easily imagine that the company might delve further into the various features, asking what leads (root cause analysis) to the different features and what could be done to remove the more costly features. For example, perhaps the monthly reports could be posted, using appropriate security, on the Internet. The reports could be updated relatively easily, and postage and printing costs could be minimized.

OBJECTIVE 6

Identify and discuss the key features that a budgetary system should have to encourage managers to engage in goal-congruent behavior.

The Behavioral Dimension of Budgeting

Budgets are often used to judge the actual performance of managers. Bonuses, salary increases, and promotions are all affected by a manager's ability to achieve or beat budgeted goals. Since a manager's financial status and career can be affected, budgets can have a significant behavioral effect. Whether that effect is positive or negative depends to a large extent on how budgets are used.

Positive behavior occurs when the goals of individual managers are aligned with the goals of the organization and the manager has the drive to achieve them. The alignment of managerial and organizational goals is often referred to as **goal congruence**. In addition to goal congruence, however, a manager must also exert effort to achieve the goals of the organization.

---

4. Ibid., 87.

If the budget is improperly administered, the reaction of subordinate managers may be negative. This negative behavior can be manifested in numerous ways, but the overall effect is subversion of the organization's goals. **Dysfunctional behavior** involves individual behavior that is in basic conflict with the goals of the organization.

A theme underlying the behavioral dimension of budgeting is ethics. The importance of budgets in performance evaluation and managers' pay raises and promotions leads to the possibility of unethical action. All of the dysfunctional actions regarding budgets that a manager may choose to take can have an unethical aspect. For example, a manager who deliberately underestimates sales and overestimates costs for the purpose of making the budget easier to achieve is engaging in unethical behavior. It is the responsibility of the company to create budgetary incentives that do not encourage unethical behavior. It is the responsibility of the manager to avoid engaging in such behavior.

Characteristics of a Good Budgetary System

An ideal budgetary system is one that achieves complete goal congruence and simultaneously creates a drive in managers to achieve the organization's goals in an ethical manner. While an ideal budgetary system probably does not exist, research and practice have identified some key features that promote a reasonable degree of positive behavior. These features include frequent feedback on performance, monetary and nonmonetary incentives, participation, realistic standards, controllability of costs, and multiple measures of performance.

Frequent Feedback on Performance

Managers need to know how they are doing as the year unfolds. Providing them with frequent, timely performance reports allows them to know how successful their efforts have been and gives them time to take corrective actions and change plans as necessary. Frequent performance reports can reinforce positive behavior and give managers the time and opportunity to adapt to changing conditions.

The use of flexible budgets allows management to see if actual costs and revenues are in accord with budgeted amounts. Selective investigation of significant variances allows managers to focus only on areas that need attention. This process is called *management by exception*.

Monetary and Nonmonetary Incentives

A sound budgetary system encourages goal-congruent behavior. **Incentives** are the means that are used to encourage managers to work toward achieving the organization's goals. Incentives can be either negative or positive. Negative incentives use fear of punishment to motivate; positive incentives use rewards. What incentives should be tied to an organization's budgetary system?

The most successful companies view people as their most important asset. Their budgets reflect their underlying philosophy by including significant expenditures on recruiting and career development. **Intel**, for example, spends 6 percent of its total payroll on an in-house university. In addition, it rewards performance with monetary incentives. At **Federal Express** and Intel, all employees qualify for variable pay, which may include stock ownership, options, and bonuses.[5]

Of course, negative incentives can be used as well. The most serious negative incentive is the threat of dismissal. Jack Welch, former CEO of **GE**, notes that "making your numbers but not demonstrating our values is grounds for dismissal."[6] Interestingly, the Welch quotation points out that budgets are important for control (making your numbers), but that budget numbers are not the most important factor in a successful company.

---

5. Anne Fisher, "The World's Most Admired Companies," *Fortune* (October 27, 1997): 220–240.
6. Ibid., 232.

Participative Budgeting

Rather than imposing budgets on subordinate managers, **participative budgeting** allows subordinate managers considerable say in how the budgets are established. Typically, overall objectives are communicated to the manager, who helps develop a budget that will accomplish these objectives. In participative budgeting, the emphasis is on the accomplishment of the broad objectives, not on individual budget items.

The budget process described earlier for ABT uses participative budgeting. The company provides the sales forecast to its profit centers and requests a budget that shows planned expenditures and expected profits given that specific level of sales. The managers of the profit centers are fully responsible for preparing the budgets by which they will later be evaluated. Although the budgets must be approved by the president, disapproval is uncommon; the budgets are usually in line with the sales forecast and last year's operating results adjusted for expected changes in revenues and costs.

Participative budgeting communicates a sense of responsibility to subordinate managers and fosters creativity. Since the subordinate manager creates the budget, it is more likely that the budget's goals will become the manager's personal goals, resulting in greater goal congruence. Advocates of participative budgeting claim that the increased responsibility and challenge inherent in the process provide nonmonetary incentives that lead to a higher level of performance. They argue that individuals involved in setting their own standards will work harder to achieve them. In addition to the behavioral benefits, participative budgeting has the advantage of involving individuals whose knowledge of local conditions may enhance the entire planning process.

Participative budgeting has three potential problems that should be mentioned:

1. Setting standards that are either too high or too low
2. Building slack into the budget (often referred to as *padding the budget*)
3. Pseudoparticipation

Some managers may tend to set the budget either too loose or too tight. Since budgeted goals tend to become the manager's goals when participation is allowed, making this mistake in setting the budget can result in decreased performance levels. If goals are too easily achieved, a manager may lose interest, and performance may actually drop. Challenge is important to aggressive and creative individuals. Similarly, setting the budget too tight ensures failure to achieve the standards and frustrates the manager. This frustration, too, can lead to poor performance. The trick is to get managers in a participative organization to set high but achievable goals.

The second problem with participative budgeting is the opportunity for managers to build slack into the budget. **Budgetary slack** exists when a manager deliberately underestimates revenues or overestimates costs. Either approach increases the likelihood that the manager will achieve the budget and consequently reduces the risk that the manager faces. Padding the budget also unnecessarily ties up resources that might be used more productively elsewhere.

Slack in budgets can be virtually eliminated if top management dictates lower expense budgets. However, the benefits to be gained from participation may far exceed the costs associated with padding the budget. Even so, top management should carefully review budgets proposed by subordinate managers and provide input, where needed, in order to decrease the effects of building slack into the budget.

The third problem with participation occurs when top management assumes total control of the budgeting process, seeking only superficial participation from lower-level managers. This practice is termed **pseudoparticipation**. Top management is simply obtaining formal acceptance of the budget from subordinate managers, not seeking real input. Accordingly, none of the behavioral benefits of participation will be realized.

Realistic Standards

Budgeted objectives are used to gauge performance; accordingly, they should be based on realistic conditions and expectations. Budgets should reflect operating realities such as actual levels of activity, seasonal variations, efficiencies, and general economic trends. Flexible budgets, for example, are used to ensure that the budgeted costs provide standards that are compatible with the actual activity level. Another factor to consider is that of seasonality. Some businesses receive revenues and incur costs uniformly throughout the year; thus, spreading the annual revenues and costs evenly over quarters and months is reasonable for interim performance reports. However, for businesses with seasonal variations, this practice would result in distorted performance reports.

Factors such as efficiency and general economic conditions are also important. Occasionally, top management makes arbitrary cuts in prior-year budgets with the belief that the cuts will reduce fat or inefficiencies that allegedly exist. In reality, some units may be operating efficiently and others inefficiently. An across-the-board cut without any formal evaluation may impair the ability of some units to carry out their missions. General economic conditions also need to be considered. Budgeting for a significant increase in sales when a recession is projected is not only foolish but potentially harmful. For example, for years, **Kodak** confidently predicted that their film business would grow by 8 percent when the industry was growing by only 4 percent.[7] The predicted growth did not occur. This type of unfounded optimism did nothing to improve sales and only hurt stock analysts' perception of the company.

Controllability of Costs

Conventional thought maintains that managers should be held accountable only for costs over which they have control. **Controllable costs** are costs whose level a manager can influence. In this view, a manager who has no responsibility for a cost should not be held accountable for it. For example, divisional managers have no power to authorize such corporate-level costs as research and development and salaries of top managers. Therefore, they should not be held accountable for the incurrence of those costs.

Many firms, however, do put noncontrollable costs in the budgets of subordinate managers. Making managers aware of the need to cover all costs is one rationale for this practice. If noncontrollable costs are included in a budget, they should be separated from controllable costs and labeled as *noncontrollable*.

Multiple Measures of Performance

Often, organizations make the mistake of using budgets as their only measure of managerial performance. Overemphasis on this measure can lead to a form of dysfunctional behavior called *milking the firm* or *myopia*. **Myopic behavior** occurs when a manager takes actions that improve budgetary performance in the short run but bring long-run harm to the firm.

There are numerous examples of myopic behavior. To meet budgeted cost objectives or profits, managers can reduce expenditures for preventive maintenance, advertising, and new product development. Managers can also fail to promote deserving employees to keep the cost of labor low and can choose to use lower-quality materials to reduce the cost of materials. In the short run, these actions will lead to improved budgetary performance, but in the long run, productivity will fall, market share will decline, and capable employees will leave for more attractive opportunities.

Managers who engage in this kind of behavior often have a short tenure. In these cases, managers spend three to five years before being promoted or moving to a new area of responsibility. Their successors are the ones who pay the price for their myopic behavior. The best way to prevent myopic behavior is to measure the performance of managers on several dimensions, including some long-run attributes. Productivity, quality, and personnel development are examples of other areas of performance that could be evaluated. Financial measures of performance are important, but overemphasis on them can be counterproductive.

---

7. Peter Nulty, "Digital Imaging Had Better Boom Before Kodak Film Busts," *Fortune* (May 1, 1995): 80–83.

SUMMARY

Budgeting is the creation of a plan of action expressed in financial terms. Budgeting plays a key role in planning, controlling, and decision making. Budgets also serve to improve communication and coordination, a role that becomes increasingly important as organizations grow in size.

The master budget, the comprehensive financial plan of an organization, is made up of the operating and financial budgets. The operating budget is the budgeted income statement and all supporting schedules. These schedules include the sales budget, the production budget, the direct materials purchases budget, the direct labor budget, the overhead budget, the ending finished goods inventory budget, the cost of goods sold budget, the marketing expense budget, the research and development expense budget, and the administrative expense budget. The budgeted income statement outlines the net income to be realized if budgeted plans come to fruition.

The financial budget includes the cash budget, the capital expenditures budget, and the budgeted balance sheet. The cash budget is simply the beginning balance in the cash account, plus anticipated receipts, minus anticipated disbursements, plus or minus any necessary borrowing. The budgeted (or pro forma) balance sheet gives the anticipated ending balances of the asset, liability, and equity accounts if budgeted plans hold.

Traditional budgeting has problems that make it less useful in the current business environment. In particular, the traditional master budget (1) does not recognize the interdependencies among departments, (2) is static, and (3) is results, not process, oriented. Flexible budgets, which use cost behavior concepts to split costs into fixed and variable components, can be used to address the problem of static budgets. Activity-based budgeting, however, is needed to recognize the interdependencies among departments and to focus on business processes.

The success of a budgetary system depends on how seriously human factors are considered. To discourage dysfunctional behavior, organizations should avoid overemphasizing budgets as a control mechanism. Other areas of performance should be evaluated in addition to budget adherence. Budgets can be improved as performance measures by the use of participative budgeting and other nonmonetary incentives, by providing frequent feedback on performance, by the use of flexible budgeting, by ensuring that the budgetary objectives reflect reality, and by holding managers accountable for only controllable costs.

REVIEW PROBLEMS AND SOLUTIONS

1   SALES, PRODUCTION, DIRECT MATERIALS, AND DIRECT LABOR BUDGETS

Young Products produces coat racks. The projected sales for the first quarter of the coming year and the beginning and ending inventory data are as follows:

Sales	100,000 units
Unit price	$15
Beginning inventory	8,000 units
Targeted ending inventory	12,000 units

The coat racks are molded and then painted. Each rack requires four pounds of metal, which cost $2.50 per pound. The beginning inventory of materials is 4,000 pounds.

Young Products wants to have 6,000 pounds of metal in inventory at the end of the quarter. Each rack produced requires 30 minutes of direct labor time, which is billed at $9 per hour.

Required:

1. Prepare a sales budget for the first quarter.
2. Prepare a production budget for the first quarter.
3. Prepare a direct materials purchases budget for the first quarter.
4. Prepare a direct labor budget for the first quarter.

SOLUTION

1.

Young Products
Sales Budget
For the First Quarter

Units	100,000
Unit selling price	× $15
Sales	$1,500,000

2.

Young Products
Production Budget
For the First Quarter

Sales (in units)	100,000
Desired ending inventory	12,000
Total needs	112,000
Less: Beginning inventory	8,000
Units to be produced	104,000

3.

Young Products
Direct Materials Purchases Budget
For the First Quarter

Units to be produced	104,000
Direct materials per unit (lbs.)	× 4
Production needs (lbs.)	416,000
Desired ending inventory (lbs.)	6,000
Total needs (lbs.)	422,000
Less: Beginning inventory (lbs.)	4,000
Materials to be purchased (lbs.)	418,000
Cost per pound	× $2.50
Total purchase cost	$1,045,000

4.

Young Products
Direct Labor Budget
For the First Quarter

Units to be produced	104,000
Labor time per unit	× 0.5
Total hours needed	52,000
Wage per hour	× $9
Total direct labor cost	$468,000

2 FLEXIBLE BUDGETING

Archer Company manufactures backpacks, messenger bags, and rolling duffel bags. Archer's accountant has estimated the following cost formulas for overhead:

Indirect labor cost = $90,000 + $0.50 per direct labor hour
Maintenance = $45,000 + $0.40 per machine hour
Power = $0.15 per machine hour
Depreciation = $150,000
Other = $63,000 + $1.30 per direct labor hour

In the coming year, Archer is considering three budgeting scenarios: conservative (assumes increased competition from other companies), expected, and optimistic (assumes a particularly robust economy). Anticipated quantities sold of each type of product appear in the following table:

Product	Conservative	Expected	Optimistic
Backpacks	50,000	100,000	150,000
Messenger bags	20,000	40,000	80,000
Rolling duffel bags	15,000	25,000	50,000

The standard amounts for one unit of each type of product are as follows:

	Backpacks	Messenger Bags	Rolling Duffel Bags
Direct materials	$5.00	$4.00	$8.00
Direct labor hours	1.2 hours	1.0 hour	2.5 hours
Machine hours	1.0 hour	0.75 hour	2.0 hours

Direct labor costs $8 per hour.

Required:

1. Prepare an overhead budget for the three potential scenarios.
2. Now, suppose that the actual level of activity for the year was 120,000 backpacks, 45,000 messenger bags, and 40,000 rolling duffel bags. Actual overhead costs were as follows:

Indirect labor	$230,400
Maintenance	145,500
Power	38,000
Depreciation	150,000
Other	435,350

Prepare a performance report for overhead costs.

SOLUTION

1.

Direct Labor Hours	Conservative	Expected	Optimistic
Backpacks (@ 1.2 DLH)	60,000	120,000	180,000
Messenger bags (@ 1.0 DLH)	20,000	40,000	80,000
Rolling duffel bags (@ 2.5 DLH)	37,500	62,500	125,000
Total direct labor hours	117,500	222,500	385,000

Machine Hours	Conservative	Expected	Optimistic
Backpacks (@ 1.0 MHr)	50,000	100,000	150,000
Messenger bags (@ 0.75 MHr)	15,000	30,000	60,000
Rolling duffel bags (@ 2.0 MHr)	30,000	50,000	100,000
Total machine hours	95,000	180,000	310,000

Flexible Overhead Budget	Conservative	Expected	Optimistic
Variable overhead:			
Indirect labor ($0.50 × DLH)	$ 58,750	$111,250	$ 192,500
Maintenance ($0.40 × MHr)	38,000	72,000	124,000
Power ($0.15 × MHr)	14,250	27,000	46,500
Other ($1.30 × DLH)	152,750	289,250	500,500
Total variable overhead	$263,750	$499,500	$ 863,500
Fixed overhead:			
Indirect labor	$ 90,000	$ 90,000	$ 90,000
Maintenance	45,000	45,000	45,000
Depreciation	150,000	150,000	150,000
Other	63,000	63,000	63,000
Total fixed overhead	$348,000	$348,000	$ 348,000
Total overhead	$611,750	$847,500	$1,211,500

2. Flexible budget based on actual output:

	Direct Labor Hours	Machine Hours
Backpacks:		
(1.2 × 120,000)	144,000	
(1.0 × 120,000)		120,000
Messenger bags:		
(1.0 × 45,000)	45,000	
(0.75 × 45,000)		33,750
Rolling duffel bags:		
(2.5 × 40,000)	100,000	
(2.0 × 40,000)		80,000
Total	289,000	233,750

	Flexible Budget Amount*	Actual	Variance
Indirect labor	$234,500	$230,400	$4,100 F
Maintenance	138,500	145,500	7,000 U
Power	35,063	38,000	2,937 U
Depreciation	150,000	150,000	—
Other	438,700	435,350	3,350 F
Total overhead	$996,763	$999,250	$2,487 U

*Indirect labor = $90,000 + ($0.50 × 289,000)
Maintenance = $45,000 + ($0.40 × 233,750)
Power = $0.15 × 233,750
Other = $63,000 + ($1.30 × 289,000)

KEY TERMS

QUESTIONS FOR WRITING AND DISCUSSION

1. Define *budget*. How are budgets used in planning?
2. Define *control*. How are budgets used to control?
3. Discuss some of the reasons for budgeting.
4. What is the master budget? An operating budget? A financial budget?
5. Explain the role of a sales forecast in budgeting. What is the difference between a sales forecast and a sales budget?
6. All budgets depend on the sales budget. Is this true? Explain.
7. What is an accounts receivable aging schedule? Why is it important?
8. Suppose that the vice president of sales is a particularly pessimistic individual. If you were in charge of developing the master budget, how, if at all, would you be influenced by this knowledge?
9. Suppose that the controller of your company's largest factory is a particularly optimistic individual. If you were in charge of developing the master budget, how, if at all, would you be influenced by this knowledge?
10. What impact does the learning curve have on budgeting? What specific budgets might be affected? (*Hint:* Refer to Chapter 3 for material on the learning curve.)
11. While many small firms do not put together a complete master budget, nearly every firm creates a cash budget. Why do you think that is so?
12. Discuss the shortcomings of the traditional master budget. In what situations would the master budget perform well?
13. Define *static budget*. Give an example that shows how reliance on a static budget could mislead management.

14. What are the two meanings of a flexible budget? How is the first type of flexible budget used? The second type?
15. What are the steps involved in building an activity-based budget? How do these steps differentiate the ABB from the master budget?

EXERCISES

8-1   PRODUCTION BUDGET

LO2   Caddo Company produces floor mats used in gyms and dojos. The sales budget for four months of the year is as follows:

	Unit Sales	Dollar Sales
July	12,000	$ 240,000
August	50,000	1,000,000
September	30,000	600,000
October	28,000	560,000

Company policy requires that ending inventories for each month be 15 percent of next month's sales. At the beginning of July, the beginning inventory of mats met that policy.

Required:

Prepare a production budget for the third quarter of the year. Show the number of units that should be produced each month as well as for the quarter in total.

8-2   SALES AND PRODUCTION BUDGETS

LO2   Galvin Company produces a variety of rolling briefcases. Two popular types are the road warrior and the prepster. The road warrior, meant for business people who travel frequently, sells for $50, and the prepster, a new model designed for school children, sells for $30. Projected sales of the two types of brief cases for the coming four quarters are as follows:

Spreadsheet

	Road Warrior	Prepster
First quarter	15,000	84,000
Second quarter	16,500	24,500
Third quarter	20,000	98,000
Fourth quarter	25,500	35,000

The president of the company believes that the projected sales are realistic and can be achieved by the company.

In the factory, the production supervisor has received the projected sales figures and gathered information needed to compile production budgets. He found that 1,300 road warriors and 1,170 prepsters were in inventory on January 1. Company policy dictates that ending inventory should equal 20 percent of the next quarter's sales for road warriors and 10 percent of next quarter's sales for prepsters.

Required:

1. Prepare a sales budget for each quarter and for the year in total. Show sales by product and in total for each time period.

2. What factors might Galvin Company have considered in preparing the sales budget?
3. Prepare a separate production budget for each product for each of the first three quarters of the year.

8-3 DIRECT MATERIALS PURCHASES BUDGET, DIRECT LABOR BUDGET

LO2

Spreadsheet

APO Company produces stuffed toy animals; one of these is "Elliebelle the Cow." Each elliebelle takes 0.20 yard of fabric (white with irregular black splotches) and eight ounces of polyfiberfill. Material costs $3.50 per yard, and polyfiberfill is $0.05 per ounce. APO has budgeted production of elliebelles for the next four months as follows:

	Units
October	42,000
November	90,000
December	50,000
January	40,000

Inventory policy requires that sufficient fabric be in ending monthly inventory to satisfy 20 percent of the following month's production needs and sufficient polyfiberfill be in inventory to satisfy 40 percent of the following month's production needs. Inventory of fabric and polyfiberfill at the beginning of October equals exactly the amount needed to satisfy the inventory policy.

Each elliebelle produced requires (on average) 0.1 direct labor hour. The average cost of direct labor is $15 per hour.

Required:

1. Prepare a direct materials purchases budget of material for the last quarter of the year showing purchases in units and in dollars for each month and for the quarter in total.
2. Prepare a direct materials purchases budget of polyfiberfill for the last quarter of the year showing purchases in units and in dollars for each month and for the quarter in total.
3. Prepare a direct labor budget for the last quarter of the year showing the hours needed and the direct labor cost for each month and for the quarter in total.

8-4 SALES FORECAST AND BUDGET

LO2

Audio-2-Go, Inc., manufactures MP3 players. Models A-1, A-2, and A-3 are small and light. They are attached to arm bands and use flash memory. Models A-4 and A-5 are somewhat larger and use a built-in hard drive; they can be put into fanny packs for use while working out. It is now early 2007, and Audio-2-Go's budgeting team is finalizing the sales budget for 2007. Sales in units and dollars for 2006 were as follows:

Model	*Number Sold*	*Price*	*Revenue*
A-1	20,000	$ 50	$1,000,000
A-2	30,000	75	2,250,000
A-3	50,000	90	4,500,000
A-4	15,000	120	1,800,000
A-5	2,000	200	400,000
			$9,950,000

In looking over the 2006 sales figures, Audio-2-Go's sales budgeting team recalled the following:

a. Model A-1 costs were rising faster than the price could rise. Preparatory to phasing out this model, Audio-2-Go, Inc., planned to slash advertising for this model and raise its price by 30 percent. The number of units of Model A-1 to be sold was forecast to be 50 percent of 2006 units.

b. Model A-5 was introduced on November 1, 2006. It contains a built-in 20 GB hard drive and can be synchronized with several popular music software programs. Audio-2-Go brought out this model to match competitors' audio players, but the price is so much higher than other Audio-2-Go products that sales have been disappointing. The company plans to discontinue this model on June 30, 2007, and thinks that 2007 monthly sales will remain at the 2006 level if the sales price remains at the 2006 level.

c. Audio-2-Go plans to introduce Model A-6 on July 1, 2007. It will be a high-end player that will be lighter and more versatile than Model A-5 (which it will replace). The target price for this model is $180; unit sales are estimated to equal 2,500 per month.

d. A competitor has announced plans to introduce an improved version of Model A-3. Audio-2-Go believes that the Model A-3 price must be cut 20 percent to maintain unit sales at the 2006 level.

e. It was assumed that unit sales of all other models would increase by 10 percent, prices remaining constant.

Required:

Prepare a sales forecast by product and in total for Audio-2-Go, Inc., for 2007.

8-5   PURCHASES BUDGET

LO2   Central Drug Store carries a variety of health and beauty aids, including elastic ankle braces. The sales budget for ankle braces for the first six months of the year is as follows:

	Unit Sales	*Dollar Sales*
January	150	$1,200
February	140	1,120
March	145	1,160
April	160	1,280
May	200	1,600
June	260	2,080

The owner of Central Drug believes that ending inventories should be sufficient to cover 20 percent of the next month's projected sales. On January 1, there were 84 ankle braces in inventory.

Required:

1. Prepare a merchandise purchases budget in units of ankle braces for as many months as you can.
2. If ankle braces are priced at cost plus 60 percent, what is the dollar cost of purchases for each month of your purchases budget?

8-6   SCHEDULE OF CASH RECEIPTS

LO3   Rick Moreno owns The Steak Place in Orlando, Florida. The Steak Place is an affordable restaurant near International Drive—a tourist mecca. Rick accepts cash and checks. Checks are deposited immediately. The bank charges $0.50 per check; the amount per check averages $75. "Bad" checks that Rick cannot collect make up 2 percent of check revenue.

During a typical month, The Steak Place has sales of $75,000. About 75 percent are cash sales. Estimated sales for the next three months are as follows:

April	$60,000
May	75,000
June	80,000

Required:

Prepare a schedule of cash receipts for May and June.

8-7 SCHEDULE OF CASH RECEIPTS

LO3   Refer to **Exercise 8-6**. Rick thinks that it may be time to refuse to accept checks and to start accepting credit cards. He is negotiating with VISA/MasterCard and American Express, and he would start the new policy on April 1. Rick estimates that with the drop in sales from the "no checks" policy and the increase in sales from the acceptance of credit cards, the net increase in sales will be 20 percent. The credit cards do involve added costs as follows:

VISA/MasterCard: Rick will accumulate these credit card receipts throughout the month and submit them in one bundle for payment on the last day of the month. The money will be credited to his account by the fifth day of the following month. A fee of 3.5 percent is charged by the credit card company.

American Express: Rick will accumulate these receipts throughout the month and mail them to American Express for payment on the last day of the month. American Express will credit his account by the sixth day of the following month. A fee of 5.5 percent is charged by American Express.

Rick estimates the following breakdown of revenues among the various payment methods.

Cash	5%
VISA/Mastercard	75
American Express	20

Required:

Prepare a schedule of cash receipts for May and June that incorporates the changes in policy.

8-8 CASH BUDGET

LO3   Crash Dobson, former all-state high school football player, owns a retail store that sells new and used sporting equipment. Crash has requested a cash budget for October. After examining the records of the company, you find the following:

Spreadsheet

a.   Cash balance on October 1 is $1,980.
b.   Actual sales for August and September are as follows:

	August	September
Cash sales	$15,000	$ 20,000
Credit sales	80,000	90,000
Total sales	$95,000	$110,000

c. Credit sales are collected over a 3-month period: 50 percent in the month of sale, 30 percent in the second month, and 15 percent in the third month. The remaining sales are uncollectible.

d. Inventory purchases average 70 percent of a month's total sales. Of those purchases, 40 percent are paid for in the month of purchase. The remaining 60 percent are paid for in the following month.

e. Salaries and wages total $2,000 per month.

f. Rent is $2,700 per month.

g. Taxes to be paid in October are $5,000.

h. Crash usually withdraws $4,000 each month as his salary.

i. Advertising is $500 per month.

j. Other operating expenses total $800 per month.

Crash tells you that he expects cash sales of $10,000 and credit sales of $65,000 for October. He likes to have $2,000 on hand at the end of the month and is concerned about the potential October ending balance.

Required:

1. Prepare a cash budget for October. Include supporting schedules for cash collections and cash payments.

2. Did the business meet Crash's desired ending cash balance for October? Assuming that the owner has no hope of establishing a line of credit for the business, what recommendations would you give the owner for meeting the desired cash balance?

8-9 BUDGETED CASH COLLECTIONS, BUDGETED CASH PAYMENTS

LO3

CMA

Historically, Pine Hill Wood Products has had no significant bad debt experience with its customers. There are no cash sales, all sales are made on credit. Payments for credit sales have been received as follows:

40 percent of credit sales in the month of the sale.
30 percent of credit sales in the first subsequent month.
25 percent of credit sales in the second subsequent month.
5 percent of credit sales in the third subsequent month.

The forecast for both cash and credit sales is as follows.

January	$95,000
February	65,000
March	70,000
April	80,000
May	85,000

Required:

1. What is the forecasted cash inflow for Pine Hill Wood Products for May?

2. Due to deteriorating economic conditions, Pine Hill Wood Products has now decided that its cash forecast should include a bad debt adjustment of 2 percent of credit sales, beginning with sales for the month of April. Because of this policy change, what will happen to the total expected cash inflow related to sales made in April? (*CMA adapted*)

8-10 SCHEDULE OF CASH RECEIPTS

LO3   David Campbell's is a men's clothing store in Mesa, Arizona. David Campbell's has its own house charge accounts and has found from past experience that 20 percent of its sales are for cash. The remaining 80 percent are on credit. An aging schedule for accounts receivable reveals the following pattern:

15 percent of credit sales are paid in the month of sale.
65 percent of credit sales are paid in the first month following the sale.
18 percent of credit sales are paid in the second month following the sale.
2 percent of credit sales are never collected.

Credit sales that have not been paid until the second month following the sale are considered overdue and are subject to a 2 percent late charge.

David Campbell's has developed the following sales forecast:

May	$66,000
June	85,000
July	55,000
August	75,000
September	80,000

Required:

Prepare a schedule of cash receipts for August and September.

8-11   CASH DISBURSEMENTS SCHEDULE

LO3 Refer to **Exercise 8-10**. David Campbell's purchases clothing evenly throughout the month. All purchases are on account. On the first of every month, Moira Campbell, David's wife, pays for all of the previous month's purchases. Terms are 2/10, n/30 (i.e., a 2 percent discount can be taken if the bill is paid within 10 days; otherwise, the entire amount is due within 30 days).

The forecast purchases for the months of May through September are as follows:

May	$48,000
June	25,000
July	35,000
August	40,000
September	50,000

Required:

1. Prepare a cash disbursements schedule for the months of August and September.
2. Now, suppose that David wants to see what difference it would make to have someone pay for any purchases that have been made three times per month, on the 1st, the 11th, and the 21st. Prepare a cash disbursements schedule for the months of July and August assuming this new payment schedule.
3. Suppose that Moira (who works full time as a school teacher and is the mother of two small children) does not have time to make payments on two extra days per month and that a temporary employee is hired on the 11th and 21st at $22 per hour, for four hours each of those two days. Is this a good decision? Explain.

8-12   PRODUCTION, PURCHASES, AND DIRECT LABOR BUDGETS

LO2 Rokat Corporation is a manufacturer of tables sold to schools, restaurants, hotels, and other institutions. The table tops are manufactured by Rokat, but the table legs are purchased from an outside supplier. The assembly department takes a manufactured table top and attaches the four purchased table legs. It takes 18 minutes of labor to assemble a table. The company follows a policy of producing enough tables to ensure that 40 percent of next month's sales are in the finished goods inventory. Rokat also purchases sufficient materials to ensure that materials inventory is 60 percent of the following month's scheduled production. Rokat's sales budget in units for the next quarter is as follows:

July	2,300
August	2,500
September	2,100

Rokat's ending inventories in units for June 30, 2007, are as follows:

Finished goods	1,900
Materials (legs)	4,000

Required:

1. Calculate the number of tables to be produced during August 2007.
2. Disregarding your response to Requirement 1, assume the required production units for August and September are 1,600 and 1,800, respectively, and the July 31, 2007, materials inventory is 4,200 units. Compute the number of table legs to be purchased in August.
3. Assume that Rokat Corporation will produce 1,800 units in September 2007. How many employees will be required for the assembly department in September? (Fractional employees are acceptable since employees can be hired on a part-time basis. Assume a 40-hour week and a 4-week month.) *(CMA adapted)*

8-13 FLEXIBLE BUDGET

LO4 In an attempt to improve budgeting, the controller for Zebro Products has developed a flexible budget for overhead costs. Zebro Products makes two types of paper-based cloths: counter wipes and floor wipes. Zebro expects to produce 500,000 rolls of each product during the coming year. Counter wipes require 0.01 direct labor hour per roll, and floor wipes require 0.05. The controller has developed the following cost formulas for each of the four overhead items:

	Cost Formula
Maintenance	$10,000 + $0.20 *DLH*
Power	$0.50 *DLH*
Indirect labor	$43,600 + $1.50 *DLH*
Rent	$24,000

Required:

1. Prepare an overhead budget for the expected activity level for the coming year.
2. Prepare an overhead budget that reflects production that is 10 percent higher than expected (for both products) and a budget for production that is 20 percent lower than expected.

8-14 FLEXIBLE BUDGET

LO4 Refer to **Exercise 8-13**. At the end of the year, Zebro Products actually produced 550,000 rolls of counter wipes and 500,000 of floor wipes. The actual overhead costs incurred were:

Maintenance	$15,600
Power	17,250
Indirect labor	89,000
Rent	24,000

Required:

Prepare a performance report for the period.

8-15 SALES FORECAST AND FLEXIBLE BUDGET

LO2, LO4   Sandman, Inc., manufactures three models of mattresses: the sleepeze, the plushette, and the ultima. Forecast sales for 2007 are 15,000 for the sleepeze, 12,000 for the plushette, and 5,000 for the ultima. Gene Dixon, vice president of sales, has provided the following information:

a.   Salaries for his office (including himself at $65,000, a marketing research assistant at $40,000, and an administrative assistant at $25,000) are budgeted for $130,000 next year.

b.   Depreciation on the offices and equipment is $20,000 per year.

c.   Office supplies and other expenses total $21,000 per year.

d.   Advertising has been steady at $20,000 per year. However, the ultima is a new product and will require extensive advertising to educate consumers on the unique features of this high-end mattress. Gene believes the company should spend 15 percent of first-year ultima sales for a print and television campaign.

e.   Commissions on the sleepeze and plushette lines are 5 percent of sales. These commissions are paid to independent jobbers who sell the mattresses to retail stores.

f.   Last year, shipping for the sleepeze and plushette lines averaged $50 per unit sold. Gene expects the ultima line to ship for $75 per unit sold since this model features a larger mattress.

Required:

1.   Suppose that Gene is considering three sales scenarios as follows:

| | Pessimistic | | Expected | | Optimistic | |
	Price	Quantity	Price	Quantity	Price	Quantity
Sleepeze	$180	12,500	$ 200	15,000	$ 200	18,000
Plushette	300	10,000	350	12,000	360	14,000
Ultima	900	2,000	1,000	5,000	1,200	5,000

Prepare a revenue budget for the sales division for the coming year for each scenario.

2.   Prepare a flexible expense budget for the sales division for the three scenarios above.

8-16 ACTIVITY-BASED BUDGET

LO5   Refer to **Exercise 8-15**. Suppose Gene determines that next year's sales division activities include the following:

Research—researching current and future conditions in the industry

Shipping—arranging for shipping of mattresses and handling calls from purchasing agents at retail stores to trace shipments and correct errors

Jobbers—coordinating the efforts of the independent jobbers who sell the mattresses

Basic ads—placing print and television ads for the sleepeze and plushette lines

Ultima ads—choosing and working with the advertising agency on the ultima account

Office management—operating the sales division office

The percentage of time spent by each employee of the sales division on each of the above activities is given in the following table:

	Gene	Research Assistant	Administrative Assistant
Research	—	75%	—
Shipping	30%	—	20%
Jobbers	15	10	20
Basic ads	—	15	40
Ultima ads	30	—	5
Office management	25	—	15

Additional information is as follows:

a. Depreciation on the office equipment belongs to the office management activity.
b. Of the $21,000 for office supplies and other, $5,000 can be assigned to telephone costs, which can be split evenly between the shipping and jobbers' activities. An additional $2,400 per year is attributable to Internet connections and fees, and the bulk of these costs (80 percent) are assignable to research. The remainder is a cost of office management. All other office supplies and costs are assigned to the office management activity.

Required:

1. Prepare an activity-based budget for next year by activity. Use the expected level of sales activity.
2. On the basis of the budget prepared in Requirement 1, advise Gene regarding actions that might be taken to reduce expenses.

PROBLEMS

8-17 OPERATING BUDGET, COMPREHENSIVE ANALYSIS

LO2, LO3 Leitner Manufacturing, Inc., produces control valves used in the production of oil field equipment. The control valves are sold to various gas and oil engineering companies throughout the United States. Projected sales in units for the coming four months are as follows:

January	20,000
February	25,000
March	30,000
April	30,000

The following data pertain to production policies and manufacturing specifications followed by Leitner:

a. Finished goods inventory on January 1 is 13,000 units. The desired ending inventory for each month is 70 percent of the next month's sales.
b. The data on materials used are as follows:

Direct Material	Per-Unit Usage	Unit Cost
Part 714	5	$4
Part 502	3	3

Inventory policy dictates that sufficient materials be on hand at the beginning of the month to produce 50 percent of that month's estimated sales. This is exactly the amount of material on hand on January 1.

c. The direct labor used per unit of output is two hours. The average direct labor cost per hour is $15.

d. Overhead each month is estimated using a flexible budget formula. (Activity is measured in direct labor hours.)

	Fixed Cost Component	Variable Cost Component
Supplies	$ —	$1.00
Power	—	0.20
Maintenance	28,000	1.10
Supervision	14,000	—
Depreciation	100,000	—
Taxes	7,000	—
Other	56,000	1.60

e. Monthly selling and administrative expenses are also estimated using a flexible budgeting formula. (Activity is measured in units sold.)

	Fixed Costs	Variable Costs
Salaries	$30,000	—
Commissions	—	$0.75
Depreciation	5,000	—
Shipping	—	2.60
Other	10,000	0.40

f. The unit selling price of the control valve is $90.

g. In February, the company plans to purchase land for future expansion. The land costs $90,000.

h. All sales and purchases are for cash. Cash balance on January 1 equals $162,900. If the firm develops a cash shortage by the end of the month, sufficient cash is borrowed to cover the shortage. Any cash borrowed is repaid one month later, as is the interest due. The interest rate is 12 percent per annum.

Required:

Prepare a monthly operating budget for the first quarter with the following schedules:
1. Sales budget
2. Production budget
3. Direct materials purchases budget
4. Direct labor budget
5. Overhead budget
6. Selling and administrative expense budget
7. Ending finished goods inventory budget
8. Cost of goods sold budget
9. Budgeted income statement (ignore income taxes)
10. Cash budget

8-18 CASH BUDGET, PRO FORMA BALANCE SHEET

LO3 Bernard Creighton is the controller for Creighton Hardware Store. In putting together the cash budget for the fourth quarter of the year, he has assembled the following data:

a. Sales

July (actual)	$100,000
August (actual)	120,000
September (estimated)	90,000
October (estimated)	100,000
November (estimated)	135,000
December (estimated)	150,000

b. Each month, 20 percent of sales are for cash, and 80 percent are on credit. The collection pattern for credit sales is 20 percent in the month of sale, 50 percent in the following month, and 30 percent in the second month following the sale.

c. Each month, the ending inventory exactly equals 40 percent of the cost of next month's sales. The markup on goods is 33.33 percent of cost.

d. Inventory purchases are paid for in the month following purchase.

e. Recurring monthly expenses are as follows:

Salaries and wages	$10,000
Depreciation on plant and equipment	4,000
Utilities	1,000
Other	1,700

f. Property taxes of $15,000 are due and payable on September 15.

g. Advertising fees of $6,000 must be paid on October 20.

h. A lease on a new storage facility is scheduled to begin on November 2. Monthly payments are $5,000.

i. The company has a policy to maintain a minimum cash balance of $10,000. If necessary, it will borrow to meet its short-term needs. All borrowing is done at the beginning of the month. All payments on principal and interest are made at the end of the month. The annual interest rate is 9 percent. The company must borrow in multiples of $1,000.

j. A partially completed balance sheet as of August 31 follows. (Accounts payable is for inventory purchases only.)

	Assets	Liabilities & Owners' Equity
Cash	$?	
Accounts receivable	?	
Inventory	?	
Plant and equipment	431,750	
Accounts payable		$?
Common stock		220,000
Retained earnings		268,750
Total	$?	$?

Required:

1. Complete the balance sheet given in part (j).

2. Bernard wants to see how the company is doing prior to starting the month of December. Prepare a cash budget for the months of September, October, and November and for the 3-month period in total (the period begins on September 1). Provide a supporting schedule of cash collections.

3. Prepare a pro forma balance sheet as of November 30.

8-19 PRODUCTION, DIRECT LABOR, DIRECT MATERIALS, SALES BUDGETS, BUDGETED CONTRIBUTION MARGIN

LO2

Bullen & Company makes and sells high-quality glare filters for microcomputer monitors. John Crave, controller, is responsible for preparing Bullen's master budget and has assembled the following data for 2007.

The direct labor rate includes wages, all employee-related benefits, and the employer's share of FICA. Labor saving machinery will be fully operational by March. Also, as of March 1, the company's union contract calls for an increase in direct labor wages that is included in the direct labor rate. Bullen expects to have 10,000 glare filters in inventory at December 31, 2006, and has a policy of carrying 50 percent of the following month's projected sales in inventory.

	2007			
	January	*February*	*March*	*April*
Estimated unit sales	20,000	24,000	16,000	18,000
Sales price per unit	$80	$80	$75	$75
Direct labor hours per unit	4.0	4.0	3.5	3.5
Direct labor hourly rate	$15	$15	$16	$16
Direct materials cost per unit	$10	$10	$10	$10

Required:

1. Prepare the following monthly budgets for Bullen & Company for the first quarter of 2007. Be sure to show supporting calculations.
   a. Production budget in units
   b. Direct labor budget in hours
   c. Direct materials cost budget
   d. Sales budget
2. Calculate the total budgeted contributions margin for Bullen & Company for the first quarter of 2007. Be sure to show supporting calculations. (*CMA adapted*)

8-20 CASH BUDGET

LO3

Friendly Freddie's is an independently owned major appliance and electronics discount chain with seven stores located in a Midwest metropolitan area. Rapid expansion has created the need for careful planning of cash requirements to ensure that the chain is able to replenish stock adequately and meet payment schedules to creditors. Fred Ferguson, founder of the chain, has established a banking relationship that provides a $200,000 line of credit to Friendly Freddie's. The bank requires that a minimum balance of $8,200 be kept in the chain's checking account at the end of each month. When the balance goes below $8,200, the bank automatically extends the line of credit in multiples of $1,000 so that the checking account balance is at least $8,200 at month-end.

Friendly Freddie's attempts to borrow as little as possible and repays the loans quickly in multiples of $1,000 plus 2 percent monthly interest on the entire loan balance. Interest payments and any principal payments are paid at the end of the month following the loan. The chain currently has no outstanding loans.

The following cash receipts and disbursements data apply to the fourth quarter of the current calendar year:

Estimated beginning cash balance	$ 8,800
Estimated cash sales:	
October	$ 14,000
November	29,000
December	44,000
Sales on account:	
July (actual)	$130,000
August (actual)	104,000
September (actual)	128,000
October (estimated)	135,000
November (estimated)	142,000
December (estimated)	188,000

Projected cash collection of sales on account is estimated to be 70 percent in the month following the sale, 20 percent in the second month following the sale, and 6 percent in the third month following the sale. The 4 percent beyond the third month following the sale is determined to be uncollectible. In addition, the chain is scheduled to receive $13,000 cash on a note receivable in October.

All inventory purchases are made on account as the chain has excellent credit with all vendors because of a strong payment history. The following information regarding inventory purchases is available:

Inventory Purchases

September (actual)	$120,000
October (estimated)	112,000
November (estimated)	128,000
December (estimated)	95,000

Cash disbursements for inventory are made in the month following purchase using an average cash discount of 3 percent for timely payment. Monthly cash disbursements for operating expenses during October, November, and December are estimated to be $38,000, $41,000, and $46,000, respectively.

Required:

Prepare Friendly Freddie's cash budget for the months of October, November, and December showing all receipts, disbursements, and credit line activity, where applicable. *(CMA adapted)*

8-21   FLEXIBLE BUDGET

LO4   The controller for Muir Company's Salem plant is analyzing overhead in order to determine appropriate drivers for use in flexible budgeting. She decided to concentrate on the past 12 months since that time period was one in which there was little important change in technology, product lines, and so on. Data on overhead costs, number of machine hours, number of setups, and number of purchase orders are given in the following table:

Month	Overhead Costs	Number of Machine Hours	Number of Setups	Number of Purchase Orders
January	$ 32,296	1,000	20	216
February	31,550	930	18	250
March	36,280	1,100	21	300
April	36,867	1,050	23	270
May	36,790	1,170	22	285
June	37,800	1,200	25	240
July	40,024	1,235	27	237
August	39,256	1,190	24	303
September	33,800	1,070	20	255
October	33,779	1,210	22	195
November	37,225	1,207	23	270
December	27,500	1,084	15	150
Total	$423,167	13,446	260	2,971

Required:

1. Calculate an overhead rate based on machine hours using the total overhead cost and total machine hours. (Round the overhead rate to the nearest cent and predicted overhead to the nearest dollar.) Use this rate to predict overhead for each of the 12 months.
2. Run a regression equation using only machine hours as the independent variable. Prepare a flexible budget for overhead for the 12 months using the results of this regression equation. (Round the intercept and x coefficient to the nearest cent and predicted overhead to the nearest dollar.) Is this flexible budget better than the budget in Requirement 1? Why or why not?

8-22 FLEXIBLE BUDGET, MULTIPLE REGRESSION

LO4   Refer to **Problem 8-21** for data.

Required:

1. Run a multiple regression equation using machine hours, number of setups, and number of purchase orders as independent variables. Prepare a flexible budget for overhead for the 12 months using the results of this regression equation. (Round the regression coefficients to the nearest cent and predicted overhead to the nearest dollar.) Which flexible budget is better—the one based on simple regression (with machine hours as the only independent variable) or the one based on multiple regression? Why?
2. Now, suppose that the controller remembers that the factory throws two big parties each year, one for the 4th of July and the other for Christmas. Rerun the multiple regression with machine hours, number of setups, and number of purchase orders, and add a dummy variable called "Party." (This variable takes the value 1 for months with a factory-sponsored party, and 0 otherwise.) Prepare a flexible budget for the 12 months using the results of this regression. Discuss the implications of using this new regression for decision making.

8-23 FLEXIBLE BUDGET FOR A SERVICE FIRM

LO2, LO4   Dorian Dermatology Associates consists of a medical suite of offices with two MDs, one office manager, two medical assistants, and one receptionist. The office manager provided the following information on Dorian's operations:

a.   Rent for the office suite is $1,200 per month.

b. Depreciation on furnishings and equipment is $1,000 per month.

c. When a patient calls for an appointment, the receptionist determines how long the appointment should take and allots one, two, three, or four 15-minute time slots. (For example, an initial visit is allotted 30 minutes, or two 15-minute time slots, but a followup visit might take only one 15-minute time slot.)

d. The office manager estimates that each patient seen during the month costs about $10 for office supplies. The estimate for medical supplies is a bit more complex. One of the medical assistants feels that patients with longer appointments use more medical supplies than patients who need only a shorter appointment. After much discussion, she thinks that each patient uses about $5 of medical supplies for every 15-minute time slot. (That is, a patient who requires only a brief visit of 15 minutes would use about $5 in supplies, and one who requires a 1-hour visit would average $20 of medical supplies.)

e. The office manager earns a yearly salary of $25,000, each medical assistant earns $18,000, and the receptionist's salary is $15,000.

f. Utilities run about $500 per month.

g. A janitorial service cleans the offices twice a week for $250 per month.

h. Accounting and financial services cost $28,800 on average for the year.

i. Insurance runs about $36,000 per year.

j. Other expenses (magazine subscriptions, plants, and the like) are about $700 per month.

For the coming month, it is estimated that the doctors will see 800 patients, who will use a total of 1,200 15-minute time slots.

Required:

1. Categorize each cost as fixed or variable, and give its driver.

2. Prepare an overhead budget for May. Since the doctors split the profit from the practice, do not worry about the doctors' salaries and consider all other expenses of the practice as overhead.

8-24   ACTIVITY-BASED BUDGET FOR A SERVICE FIRM

LO5   Refer to **Problem 8-23**. Suppose that the accountant for the practice, Sally Bains, decides to prepare an activity-based budget for Dorian Dermatology Associates. Her interviews with the office manager, receptionist, and medical assistants provided the following information:

a. There are essentially six activities for the medical practice: scheduling appointments, initial patient screening, assisting the doctors, filing insurance, handling disputed insurance claims, and providing facilities.

b. Scheduling appointments is done by the receptionist. It takes about half of her time and requires a special software package. The number of phone calls to the office is the driver for this activity. The cost per unit of driver is $1 per call.

c. The initial screening requires the medical assistant to call each patient from the waiting room to an examining room. The assistant then takes a brief medical history and determines the nature of the complaint. If it is a repeat appointment, the assistant can occasionally handle it. The driver is the number of patients seen, and the cost per unit of driver is $7.25.

d. The activity of assisting doctors is performed by the medical assistants. After the initial screening, the doctor examines the patient and determines the diagnosis and course of treatment. Occasionally, the treatment requires assistance with a procedure (e.g., minor surgery). The driver for the activity is the number of procedures, and the cost per unit of driver is $7.25.

e. Filing insurance claims is handled by the office manager and receptionist. This takes about 60 percent of the office manager's time and the remaining half of the receptionist's time. Office supplies and computer programs are also required. The driver is the number of claims filed, and the cost is $9.27 per claim filed.

f. Sometimes, insurance claims are disputed by the insurance companies. When this occurs, considerable more time and effort are required by the office manager. She also needs help from the medical assistants to check for errors in charts and clarify diagnoses. Supplies and office machinery (fax machine and long distance calls) are also required. The driver is the number of disputed claims, and the cost is $123.50 per disputed claim.

g. The final activity is providing facilities. These costs total $8,550 per month and include rent, noncomputer depreciation, utilities, janitorial services, accounting and financial services, insurance, and other expenses.

For the month of May, the following amounts of each driver are estimated: 875 phone calls for appointments, 800 patients to be seen, 400 procedures to be performed, 650 insurance claims to be filed, and 40 disputed claims.

Required:

1. Prepare an activity-based overhead budget for the month of May.
2. Based on the given information, what managerial advice would you give to Dorian Dermatology Associates?

8-25   PARTICIPATIVE VERSUS IMPOSED BUDGETING

LO6

CMA

An effective budget converts the goals and objectives of an organization into data. The budget serves as a blueprint for management's plans. The budget is also the basis for control. Management performance can be evaluated by comparing actual results with the budget.

Thus, creating the budget is essential for the successful operation of an organization. Finding the resources to implement the budget—that is, moving from a starting point to the ultimate goal—requires the extensive use of human resources. How managers perceive their roles in the process of budgeting is important to the successful use of the budget as an effective tool for planning, communicating, and controlling.

Required:

1. Discuss the behavioral implications of planning and control when a company's management employs:
    a. An imposed budgetary approach
    b. A participative budgetary approach
2. Communications plays an important role in the budgetary process whether a participative or an imposed budgetary approach is used.
    a. Discuss the differences between communication flows in these two budgetary approaches.
    b. Discuss the behavioral implications associated with the communication process for each of the budgetary approaches. *(CMA adapted)*

8-26   INFORMATION FOR BUDGETING, ETHICS

LO1, LO6

CMA

Norton Company, a manufacturer of infant furniture and carriages, is in the initial stages of preparing the annual budget for 2007. Scott Ford has recently joined Norton's accounting staff and is interested in learning as much as possible about the company's budgeting process. During a recent lunch with Marge Atkins, sales manager, and Pete Granger, production manager, Scott initiated the following conversation.

SCOTT: Since I'm new around here and am going to be involved with the preparation of the annual budget, I'd be interested in learning how the two of you estimate sales and production numbers.

MARGE: We start out very methodically by looking at recent history, discussing what we know about current accounts, potential customers, and the general state of consumer spending. Then, we add that usual dose of intuition to come up with the best forecast we can.

PETE: I usually take the sales projections as the basis for my projections. Of course, we have to make an estimate of what this year's closing inventories will be, which is sometimes difficult.

SCOTT: Why does that present a problem? There must have been an estimate of closing inventories in the budget for the current year.

PETE: Those numbers aren't always reliable since Marge makes some adjustments to the sales numbers before passing them on to me.

SCOTT: What kind of adjustments?

MARGE: Well, we don't want to fall short of the sales projections so we generally give ourselves a little breathing room by lowering the initial sales projection anywhere from 5 to 10 percent.

PETE: So, you can see why this year's budget is not a very reliable starting point. We always have to adjust the projected production rates as the year progresses, and of course, this changes the ending inventory estimates. By the way, we make similar adjustments to expenses by adding at least 10 percent to the estimates; I think everyone around here does the same thing.

Required:

1. Marge Atkins and Pete Granger have described the use of budgetary slack.
   a. Explain why Marge and Pete behave in this manner, and describe the benefits they expect to realize from the use of budgetary slack.
   b. Explain how the use of budgetary slack can adversely affect Marge and Pete.
2. As a management accountant, Scott Ford believes that the behavior described by Marge and Pete may be unethical and that he may have an obligation not to support this behavior. By citing the specific standards of competence, confidentiality, integrity, and/or objectivity from the "Standards of Ethical Conduct for Management Accountants" (in Chapter 1), explain why the use of budgetary slack may be unethical. *(CMA adapted)*

8-27   COLLABORATIVE LEARNING EXERCISE

LO1

Karmee Company has been accumulating operating data in order to prepare an annual profit plan. Details regarding Karmee's sales for the first six months of the coming year are as follows:

Estimated Monthly Sales		*Type of Monthly Sale*	
January	$600,000	Cash sales	20%
February	650,000	Credit sales	80
March	700,000		
April	625,000		
May	720,000		
June	800,000		

Collection Pattern for Credit Sales	
Month of sale	30%
First month following sale	40
Second month following sale	25

Karmee's cost of goods sold averages 40 percent of the sales value. Karmee's objective is to maintain a target inventory equal to 30 percent of the next month's sales. Purchases of merchandise for resale are paid for in the month following the sale.

The variable operating expenses (other than cost of goods sold) for Karmee are 10 percent of sales and are paid for in the month following the sale. The annual fixed operating expenses follow. All of these are incurred uniformly throughout the year and paid monthly except for insurance and property taxes. Insurance is paid quarterly in January, April, July, and October. Property taxes are paid twice a year in April and October.

Annual Fixed Operating Costs

Advertising	$ 720,000
Salaries	1,080,000
Depreciation	420,000
Property taxes	240,000
Insurance	180,000

Required:

Form groups of two or three. Within each group, calculate the following:

1. The amount of cash collected in March for Karmee Company from the sales made during March.
2. Karmee Company's total cash receipts for the month of April.
3. The purchases of merchandise that Karmee Company will need to make during February.
4. The amount of cost of goods sold that will appear on Karmee Company's pro forma income statement for the month of February.
5. The total cash disbursements that Karmee Company will make for the operating expenses (expenses other than the cost of goods sold) during the month of April. (*CMA adapted*)

8-28 CYBER RESEARCH CASE

LO1, LO2 Search the Internet for five companies in different industries. Then, see what clues are given on the Web sites as to factors affecting sales budgeting for each company. Write a brief, 1-page description of the factors affecting sales budgeting for each of your companies.

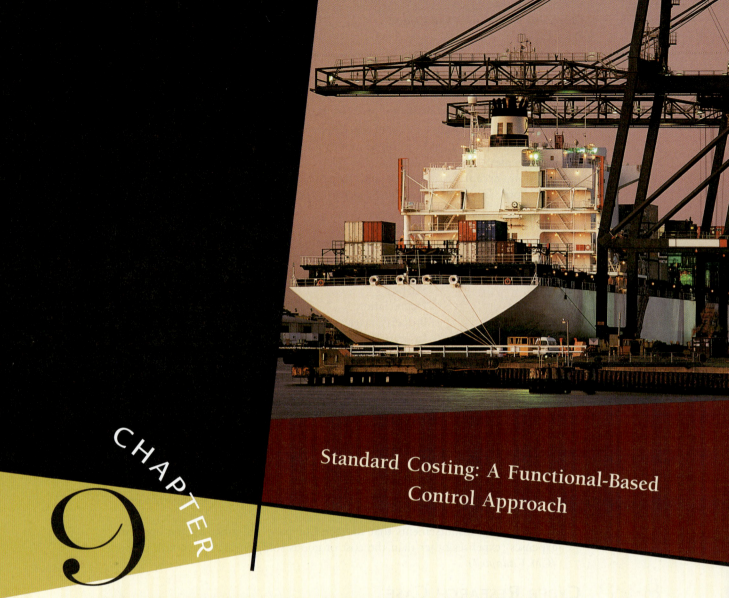

CHAPTER

9

Standard Costing: A Functional-Based Control Approach

AFTER STUDYING THIS CHAPTER, YOU SHOULD BE ABLE TO:

1. Describe how unit input standards are developed, and explain why standard costing systems are adopted.
2. Explain the purpose of a standard cost sheet.
3. Compute and journalize the direct materials and direct labor variances, and explain how they are used for control.
4. Compute overhead variances three different ways, and explain overhead accounting.
5. Calculate mix and yield variances for direct materials and direct labor.

Budgets help managers in planning and, at the same time, set standards that are used to control and evaluate managerial performance. In Chapter 8, we saw how budgets can be classified as static or flexible. Static budgets are not very useful for assessing efficiency; their main value is to assess whether or not the targeted level of activity is achieved and, thus, provide some insight concerning managerial effectiveness. On the other hand, flexible budgets evaluate efficiency by comparing the actual costs and actual revenues with the corresponding budgeted amounts for the *same* level of activity. These flexible budget variances generate important feedback for managers but fail to reveal whether the sources of the variances are attributable to input prices, input quantities, or both.

Developing Unit Input Standards

OBJECTIVE 1

Describe how unit input standards are developed, and explain why standard costing systems are adopted.

Although flexible budget variances provide significant information for control, developing standards for input prices and input quantities allows a more detailed understanding of the sources of these variances. **Price standards** specify how much should be paid for the quantity of the input to be used. **Quantity standards** specify how much of the input should be used per unit of output. The **unit standard cost** is defined as the product of these two standards: Standard price $\times$ Standard quantity ($SP \times SQ$).

For example, an ice cream company may decide that 25 ounces of yogurt should be used for every quart of frozen yogurt produced (the quantity standard) and that the price of the yogurt should be \$0.02 per ounce (the price standard). The standard cost of the yogurt per quart of frozen yogurt is then \$0.50 (\$0.02 $\times$ 25). The standard cost of yogurt per quart can be used to predict what the total cost of yogurt should be as the activity level varies; it thus becomes a flexible budget formula. If 20,000 quarts of frozen yogurt are produced, the total expected cost of yogurt is \$10,000 (\$0.50 $\times$ 20,000); if 30,000 quarts are produced, the total expected cost of yogurt is \$15,000 (\$0.50 $\times$ 30,000). Standard costs, therefore, facilitate budgeting, but the input price and quantity standards will also allow us to obtain a more detailed analysis of the flexible budget variance.

Establishing Standards

Developing standards requires significant input from a variety of sources. Historical experience, engineering studies, and input from operating personnel are three potential sources of quantitative standards. Historical experience should be used with caution because relying on input-output relationships from the past may perpetuate operating inefficiencies. Engineers and operating personnel can provide valuable insights concerning efficient levels of input quantities. Similar comments can be made about input price standards. Price standards are the joint responsibility of operations, purchasing, personnel, and accounting. Operations determines the quality of the inputs required; personnel and purchasing have the responsibility to acquire the input quality requested at the lowest price. Market forces, trade unions, and other external forces limit the range of choices for price standards. In setting price standards, purchasing must consider discounts, freight, and quality; personnel, on the other hand, must consider payroll taxes, fringe benefits, and qualifications. Accounting is responsible for recording price standards and for preparing reports that compare actual performance to the standard.

Standards are often classified as either *ideal* or *currently attainable*. **Ideal standards** are standards that demand maximum efficiency and can be achieved only if everything operates perfectly. No machine breakdowns, slack, or lack of skill (even momentarily) are allowed. **Currently attainable standards** can be achieved under efficient operating conditions. Allowance is made for normal breakdowns, interruptions, less than perfect skill, and so on. These standards are demanding but achievable. One cautionary observation about standards should be made. If standards are too tight and never achievable, workers become frustrated, and performance levels decline. However, challenging but achievable standards can lead to higher performance levels—particularly when the individuals subject to the standards have participated in their creation.

Kaizen Standards

Another type of standard known as a *kaizen* standard is also possible. **Kaizen standards** are continuous improvement standards. Kaizen standards reflect a planned improvement and are a type of currently attainable standard. Kaizen standards by their very nature have a cost reduction focus and because of their emphasis on continuous improvement are constantly changing. (They are dynamic standards.) Kaizen standards are discussed in detail in Chapter 12. This chapter focuses on the more traditional standard cost system.

Standards and Activity-Based Costing

Standards also play an important role in activity-based systems. An activity's cost is determined by the amount of resources consumed by each activity. To avoid measuring the amount of resource consumption on an ongoing basis for literally hundreds of activities, standard consumption patterns are identified based on historical experience. The purpose of standards in this case is to facilitate cost assignments. Control is not an issue. Standards used in this sense were discussed in Chapter 4. Activity-based systems also use standards for control, where control is specifically defined as cost reduction. Activities are classified as either those that add value or those that do not. For each activity, the ideal output is identified and then efforts are made to reduce activity production to this ideal level. This activity-based approach to control is described in Chapter 12.

Usage of Standard Costing Systems

Standard costing systems are widely used. For example, according to one survey, 74 percent of the respondents were using a standard costing system, with the usage emphasis being placed on planning and control.[1] Several reasons for adopting a standard costing system can be mentioned: managing costs, improving planning and control, facilitating decision making, and facilitating product costing.

Cost Management

Standard costing allows managers to manage costs by establishing standards that reflect efficient operating conditions. Standards also help managers understand what needs to be done to improve current and future performance. Furthermore, for firms concerned with continuous improvement, kaizen standards are useful aids in achieving significant cost reductions.

Planning and Control

Standard costing systems enhance planning and control and improve performance measurement. Unit standards are a fundamental requirement for a flexible budgeting system, which is a key feature of a meaningful planning and control system. Budgetary control systems compare actual costs with budgeted costs by computing variances, the difference between the actual and planned costs for the actual level of activity. By developing unit price and quantity standards, an overall variance can be decomposed into a *price variance* and a *usage* or *efficiency variance*. By performing this decomposition, a manager has more information. For example, a manager can tell whether the variance is attributable to discrepancies between planned prices and actual prices, to discrepancies between planned usage and actual usage, or to both. Thus, in principle, the use of efficiency variances enhances operational control. Additionally, by breaking out the price variance, over which managers have little control, the system provides an improved measure of managerial efficiency.

Decision Making and Product Costing

Standard costing systems also facilitate decision making and product costing. For example, standard costing systems provide readily available unit cost information that can be used for pricing decisions. This is particularly useful for companies that engage in extensive bidding and for companies that are paid on a cost-plus basis. Standard product costs are determined using quantity and price standards for direct materials, direct labor, and overhead. In contrast, a normal costing system predetermines overhead costs for the purpose of product costing but assigns direct materials and direct labor to products by using actual costs. An actual costing system assigns the actual costs of all three manufacturing inputs to products. Exhibit 9-1 summarizes these three cost assignment approaches.

---

1. Norwood Whittle, "Older and Wiser," *Management Accounting* (July/August 2000): 34–36.

EXHIBIT 9-1   Cost Assignment Approaches

	Manufacturing Costs		
	Direct Materials	**Direct Labor**	**Overhead**
Actual costing system	Actual	Actual	Actual
Normal costing system	Actual	Actual	Budgeted
Standard costing system	Standard	Standard	Standard

Standard costing also simplifies product costing for firms in process industries. For example, if a process-costing system uses standard costing to assign product costs, there is no need to compute a unit cost for each equivalent unit-cost category. A standard unit cost would exist for direct materials, transferred-in materials, and conversion costs categories.[2] Usually, a standard process-costing system will follow the equivalent-unit calculation of the FIFO approach. That is, *current* equivalent units of work are calculated. By calculating current equivalent units of work, current actual production costs can be compared with standard costs (costs allowed for current production) for control purposes.

OBJECTIVE 2

Explain the purpose of a standard cost sheet.

Standard Cost Sheets

Standard costing systems can be used in both manufacturing and service organizations. Both products and services use inputs such as direct materials, direct labor, and overhead. Standard costing simply establishes price and quantity standards for these inputs and is oblivious as to whether the inputs are associated with tangible or intangible products. To illustrate standard costing for a service setting, consider standard costing in a hospital. Hospital costing systems often use a homogeneous work unit called a **relative value unit (RVU)**. An RVU measures the relative amount of time required to perform

---

2. If you have not read the chapter on process costing (Chapter 6), the discussion on the merits of standard costing will not be as meaningful. However, the point being made is still relevant. Standard costing can produce useful computational savings.

a procedure. Although the exact time to perform a particular test is not revealed, the relative time for performing two or more distinct tests has been computed. Thus, a test with an RVU of three will take three times as long to perform as a test with an RVU of one. Historical standards can be computed by dividing the variable direct labor costs of a hospital department by the number of RVUs performed by that department. This standard direct labor cost per RVU can then be multiplied by the RVUs of a given procedure to obtain the standard direct labor cost for that procedure.[3]

As indicated, standard costs are developed for direct materials, direct labor, and overhead used in producing a product or service. Using these costs, the **standard cost per unit** is computed. The **standard cost sheet** provides the detail underlying the standard unit cost. To illustrate, let us develop a standard cost sheet for a quart of deluxe strawberry frozen yogurt, produced by Helado Company. (Helado sells its frozen yogurt only at specialty shops.) The production of the strawberry frozen yogurt begins by creating two different mixtures. The first mixture consists of milk and gelatin. These two ingredients are mixed, heated, and then cooled. The second mixture consists of yogurt, whipped cream, and crushed strawberries. The two mixtures are blended and mixed well. This final mixture is then poured into a one-quart container and frozen. The process is automated. Direct labor is used to operate the equipment and inspect the product for consistency and flavor. The standard cost sheet is given in Exhibit 9-2.

EXHIBIT **9-2**	Standard Cost Sheet for Deluxe Strawberry Frozen Yogurt			
Description	**Standard Price**	**Standard Usage**	**Standard Cost**	**Subtotal**
Direct materials:				
Yogurt	$0.020	× 25 oz. =	$0.50	
Strawberries	0.010	× 10 oz. =	0.10	
Milk	0.015	× 8 oz. =	0.12	
Whipped cream	0.025	× 4 oz. =	0.10	
Gelatin	0.010	× 1 oz. =	0.01	
Container	0.030	× 1 =	0.03	
Total direct materials				$0.86
Direct labor:				
Machine operators	8.00	× 0.01 hr. =	$0.08	
Total direct labor				0.08
Overhead:				
Variable overhead	6.00	× 0.01 hr. =	$0.06	
Fixed overhead	20.00	× 0.01 hr. =	0.20	
Total overhead				0.26
Total standard unit cost				$1.20

Five materials are used to produce the deluxe strawberry frozen yogurt: yogurt, strawberries, milk, whipped cream, and gelatin. The container in which the yogurt is placed is also classified as a direct material. Direct labor consists of machine operators (who also inspect). Variable overhead is made up of three costs: gas (used in cooking),

3. For an entertaining and interesting description of how historical labor standards can be developed in a hospital setting, see Richard D. McDermott, Kevin D. Stocks, and Joan Ogden, *Code Blue* (Syracuse, Utah: Traemus Books, 2000), pp. 212–221.

electricity (used to operate the equipment), and water (used for cleaning); it is applied using direct labor hours. Fixed overhead is also applied using direct labor hours and consists of salaries, depreciation, taxes, and insurance. Notice that 37 ounces of liquids (yogurt, milk, and whipped cream) are used to produce a quart of frozen yogurt. This extra input is needed for two reasons. First, some liquid is lost through evaporation. Second, Helado wants slightly more than 32 ounces of frozen yogurt placed in each container to ensure customer satisfaction.

Exhibit 9-2 also reveals other important insights. The standard usage for variable and fixed overhead is tied to the direct labor standards. For variable overhead, the rate is $6.00 per direct labor hour. Since one quart of frozen yogurt uses 0.01 direct labor hour, the variable overhead cost assigned to a quart is $0.06 ($6.00 × 0.01). For fixed overhead, the rate is $20 per direct labor hour, making the fixed overhead cost per quart $0.20 ($20 × 0.01). Using direct labor hours as the only driver to assign overhead reveals that Helado uses a functional-based cost accounting system.

The standard cost sheet also reveals the quantity of each input that should be used to produce one unit of output. The unit quantity standards can be used to compute the total amount of inputs allowed for the actual output. This computation is an essential component in computing efficiency variances. A manager should be able to compute the **standard quantity of materials allowed** (SQ) and the **standard hours allowed** (SH) for the actual output. This computation must be done for every class of direct material and for every class of direct labor. Assume, for example, that 20,000 quarts of deluxe strawberry frozen yogurt are produced during the first week of April. How much yogurt should have been used for the actual output of 20,000 quarts? The unit quantity standard is 25 ounces of yogurt per quart (see Exhibit 9-2). For 20,000 quarts, the standard quantity of yogurt allowed is computed as follows:

$$SQ = \text{Unit quantity standard} \times \text{Actual output}$$
$$= 25 \times 20,000$$
$$= 500,000 \text{ ounces}$$

The computation of standard direct labor hours allowed can also be illustrated. From Exhibit 9-2, we see that the unit quantity standard is 0.01 hour per quart produced. Thus, if 20,000 quarts are produced, the standard hours allowed are computed as follows:

$$SH = \text{Unit quantity standard} \times \text{Actual output}$$
$$= 0.01 \times 20,000$$
$$= 200 \text{ direct labor hours}$$

OBJECTIVE 3

Compute and journalize the direct materials and direct labor variances, and explain how they are used for control.

Variance Analysis and Accounting: Direct Materials and Direct Labor

A flexible budget can be used to identify the direct material or direct labor input costs that should have been incurred for the actual level of activity. This planned cost is obtained by multiplying the amount of input allowed for the actual output by the standard unit price. Letting SP be the standard unit price of an input and SQ the standard quantity of inputs allowed for the actual output, the planned or budgeted input cost is $SP \times SQ$. The actual input cost is $AP \times AQ$, where AP is the actual price per unit of the input, and AQ is the actual quantity of input used. The **total budget variance** is simply the difference between the actual cost of the input and its planned cost:

$$\text{Total budget variance} = (AP \times AQ) - (SP \times SQ)$$

The total budget variance measures the difference between the actual cost of direct materials and direct labor and their budgeted costs for the actual level of activity. To illustrate, consider these selected data for Helado Company for the first week of May.

To keep the example simple, only one direct material (yogurt) is used. A complete analysis for the company would include all categories of direct materials.

> Actual production: 30,000 quarts
> Actual yogurt usage: 780,000 ounces (no beginning or ending yogurt inventory)
> Actual price paid per ounce of yogurt: $0.025
> Actual direct labor hours: 325 hours
> Actual wage rate: $8.20 per hour

Using the above actual data and the unit standards from Exhibit 9-2, a performance report for the first week of May is developed and illustrated in Exhibit 9-3. The report provides total budget variances for yogurt and direct labor. The total input variances can be divided into price and usage variances, providing more control information to the manager. We will first look at the price and usage variances for direct materials and then we will examine them for direct labor.

EXHIBIT 9-3	Performance Report: Total Budget Variances		
	Actual Costs	Budgeted Costs*	Total Budget Variance**
Yogurt	$19,500	$15,000	$4,500 U
Direct labor	2,665	2,400	265 U

*The standard quantities for direct materials and direct labor are computed as follows, using unit quantity standards from Exhibit 9-2: Yogurt: 25 × 30,000 = 750,000 ounces; Direct labor: 0.01 × 30,000 = 300 hours. Multiplying these standard quantities by the unit standard prices given in Exhibit 9-2 produces the budgeted amounts appearing in this column.

**U signifies an unfavorable variance (the actual costs are greater than the planned costs).

Calculating Direct Materials Price and Usage Variances

The total budget variance can be broken down into price and usage variances. **Price (rate) variance** is the difference between the actual and standard unit prices of an input multiplied by the actual quantity of inputs. **Usage (efficiency) variance** is the difference between the actual and standard quantity of inputs multiplied by the standard unit price of the input. An **unfavorable (U) variance** occurs whenever actual prices or usage of inputs are greater than standard prices or usage. When the opposite occurs, a **favorable (F) variance** is obtained. A graphical, 3-pronged approach illustrating how the direct materials price and usage variances are calculated is shown in Exhibit 9-4 (for the Helado Company example). Only the price and usage variances for yogurt are shown.

Using Formulas to Compute Direct Materials Price and Usage Variances

The direct materials price and usage variances can be calculated using variance formulas. Some find this approach easier. The **direct materials price variance (MPV)** measures the difference between what should have been paid for direct materials and what was actually paid. A simple formula for computing this variance is:

$$MPV = (AP \times AQ) - (SP \times AQ)$$

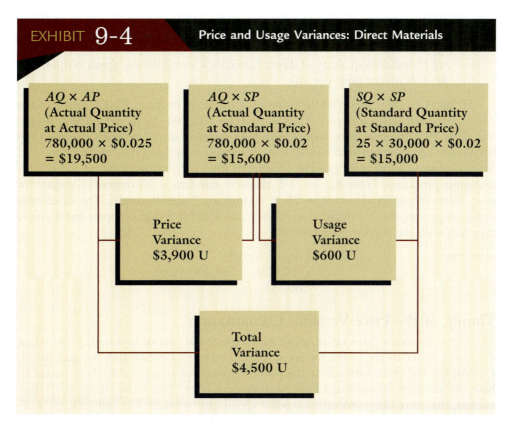

EXHIBIT 9-4   Price and Usage Variances: Direct Materials

$AQ \times AP$
(Actual Quantity at Actual Price)
$780,000 \times \$0.025$
$= \$19,500$

$AQ \times SP$
(Actual Quantity at Standard Price)
$780,000 \times \$0.02$
$= \$15,600$

$SQ \times SP$
(Standard Quantity at Standard Price)
$25 \times 30,000 \times \$0.02$
$= \$15,000$

Price Variance $3,900 U

Usage Variance $600 U

Total Variance $4,500 U

Notice that the right side of the three-pronged diagram is simply the amount of direct materials allowed per unit × the units produced × the standard price.

or, factoring, we have:

$$MPV = (AP - SP)AQ$$

where

AP = Actual price per unit
SP = Standard price per unit
AQ = Actual quantity of direct material used

Helado Company purchased and used 780,000 ounces of yogurt for the first week of May. The purchase price was $0.025 per ounce. Thus, AP is $0.025, AQ is 780,000 ounces, and SP (from Exhibit 9-2) is $0.02. Using this information, the direct materials price variance is computed as follows (see Exhibit 9-4 to compare the graphical, 3-pronged approach with the formula approach):

$$
\begin{aligned}
MPV &= (AP - SP)AQ \\
&= (\$0.025 - \$0.020)780,000 \\
&= \$0.005 \times 780,000 \\
&= \$3,900 \text{ U}
\end{aligned}
$$

The **direct materials usage variance (MUV)** measures the difference between the direct materials actually used and the direct materials that should have been used for the actual output. The formula for computing this variance is:

$$MUV = (SP \times AQ) - (SP \times SQ)$$

or, factoring, we have:

$$MUV = (AQ - SQ)SP$$

where

AQ = Actual quantity of direct materials used
SQ = Standard quantity of direct materials allowed for the actual output
SP = Standard price per unit

Helado Company used 780,000 ounces of yogurt to produce 30,000 quarts of the deluxe strawberry frozen yogurt. Therefore, AQ is 780,000. From Exhibit 9-2, we see that SP is $0.02 per ounce of yogurt. Although standard direct materials allowed (SQ) has already been computed in Exhibit 9-3, the details underlying the computation need to be reviewed. Recall that SQ is the product of the unit quantity standard and the actual units produced. From Exhibit 9-2, the unit standard is 25 ounces of yogurt for every quart of yogurt. Thus, SQ is $25 \times 30,000$, or 750,000 ounces. The direct materials usage variance is computed as follows (see Exhibit 9-4 to compare the formula approach with the 3-pronged approach):

$$MUV = (AQ - SQ)SP$$
$$= (780,000 - 750,000)\$0.02$$
$$= \$600 \ U$$

Timing of the Price Variance Computation

The direct materials price variance can be computed at one of two points: (1) when the direct materials are issued for use in production or (2) when they are purchased. Computing the price variance at the point of purchase is preferable. It is better to have information on variances earlier rather than later. The more timely the information, the more likely proper managerial action can be taken. Old information is often useless information. Direct materials may sit in inventory for weeks or months before they are needed in production. By the time the direct materials price variance is computed, signaling a problem, it may be too late to take corrective action. Or, even if corrective action is still possible, the delay may cost the company thousands of dollars.

If the direct materials price variance is computed at the point of purchase, then AQ needs to be redefined as the actual quantity of direct materials *purchased*, rather than actual direct materials used. Since the direct materials purchased may differ from the direct materials used, the overall direct materials budget variance is not necessarily the sum of the direct materials price variance and the direct materials usage variance. When the direct materials purchased are all used in production for the period in which the variances are calculated, the two variances will equal the total budget variance. If this is not the case, then the only way to compute each direct materials variance is by using the formula approach. The 3-pronged approach will not work.

Timing of the Computation of the Direct Materials Usage Variance

The direct materials usage variance should be computed as direct materials are issued for production. To facilitate this process, many companies use three forms: a standard bill of materials, color-coded excessive usage forms, and color-coded returned-materials forms. The **standard bill of materials** identifies the quantity of direct materials that should be used to produce a predetermined quantity of output. A standard bill of materials for Helado Company is illustrated in Exhibit 9-5.

The standard bill of materials acts as a materials requisition form. The production manager presents this form to the materials manager and receives the standard quantity allowed for the indicated output. If the production manager has to requisition more direct materials later, the excessive usage form is used. This form, different in color from the standard bill of materials, provides immediate feedback to the production manager that excess direct materials are being used. If, on the other hand, fewer direct materials are used than the standard requires, the production manager can return the leftover direct materials, along with the returned-materials form. This form also provides immediate feedback.

EXHIBIT 9-5	Standard Bill of Materials

Product: Quarts of Deluxe Strawberry Frozen Yogurt		Output: 30,000 Quarts
Direct Material	**Unit Standard**	**Total Requirements**
Yogurt	25 oz.	750,000 oz.
Strawberries	10 oz.	300,000 oz.
Milk	8 oz.	240,000 oz.
Whipped cream	4 oz.	120,000 oz.
Gelatin	1 oz.	30,000 oz.
Containers	1 container	30,000 containers

Accounting for Direct Materials Price and Usage Variances

As a general rule, in a *standard costing system, all inventories are carried at standard.* Actual costs are never entered into an inventory account. Following this general rule means that the direct materials price variance is computed at the point of purchase. In recording variances, unfavorable variances are always debits, and favorable variances are always credits. The general form of the journal entry associated with the purchase of direct materials for a standard costing system follows. This entry assumes an unfavorable *MPV* and that *AQ* is defined as direct materials purchased.

Materials	$(SP \times AQ)$	
Direct Materials Price Variance	$(AP - SP)AQ$	
Accounts Payable		$AP \times AQ$

For the Helado Company example, the entry pertaining to the acquisition of yogurt would be:

Materials	15,600	
Direct Materials Price Variance	3,900	
Accounts Payable		19,500

   The direct materials usage variance is recognized when direct materials are issued. The standard cost of the direct materials issued is assigned to Work in Process. The general form for the entry to record the issuance and usage of direct materials, assuming an unfavorable *MUV*, is as follows:

Work in Process	$SQ \times SP$	
Direct Materials Usage Variance	$(AQ - SQ)SP$	
Materials		$AQ \times SP$

The entry to record Helado's usage of yogurt during the first week of May is as follows:

Work in Process	15,000	
Direct Materials Usage Variance	600	
Materials		15,600

Calculating Direct Labor Variances

The rate (price) and efficiency (usage) variances for direct labor can be calculated using either the graphical, 3-pronged approach or a formula approach. The 3-pronged calculation is illustrated in Exhibit 9-6 for direct labor at the Helado Company plant. The calculation using formulas is discussed next.

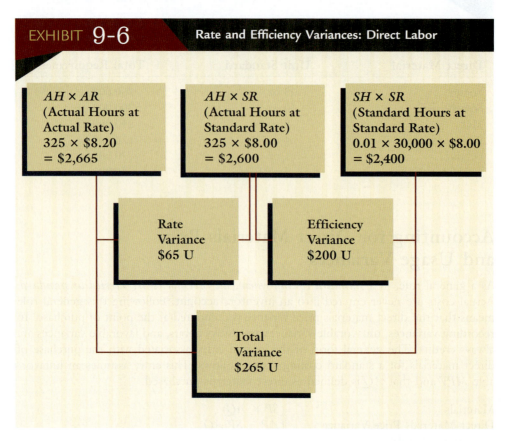

EXHIBIT 9-6   Rate and Efficiency Variances: Direct Labor

$AH \times AR$
(Actual Hours at Actual Rate)
$325 \times \$8.20$
$= \$2,665$

$AH \times SR$
(Actual Hours at Standard Rate)
$325 \times \$8.00$
$= \$2,600$

$SH \times SR$
(Standard Hours at Standard Rate)
$0.01 \times 30,000 \times \$8.00$
$= \$2,400$

Rate Variance
$65 U

Efficiency Variance
$200 U

Total Variance
$265 U

Note: As shown in the third prong, the standard hours allowed are computed by multiplying the unit standard by the units produced.

Direct Labor Rate and Efficiency Variances: Formula Approach

The **direct labor rate variance (LRV)** computes the difference between what was paid to direct laborers and what should have been paid:

$$LRV = (AR \times AH) - (SR \times AH)$$

or, factoring, we have:

$$LRV = (AR - SR)AH$$

where

$$AR = \text{Actual hourly wage rate}$$
$$SR = \text{Standard hourly wage rate}$$
$$AH = \text{Actual direct labor hours used}$$

Direct labor activity for Helado Company's machine operators will be used to illustrate the computation of the direct labor rate variance. We know that 325 hours were used during the first week in May. The actual hourly wage paid for machine operation was $8.20. From Exhibit 9-2, the standard wage rate is $8.00. Thus, AH is 325, AR is $8.20, and SR is $8.00. The direct labor rate variance is computed as follows:

$$
\begin{aligned}
LRV &= (AR - SR)AH \\
&= (\$8.20 - \$8.00)325 \\
&= \$0.20 \times 325 \\
&= \$65 \ U
\end{aligned}
$$

The **direct labor efficiency variance (LEV)** measures the difference between the direct labor hours that were actually used and the direct labor hours that should have been used:

$$LEV = (AH \times SR) - (SH \times SR)$$

or, factoring, we have:

$$LEV = (AH - SH)SR$$

where

AH = Actual direct labor hours used
SH = Standard direct labor hours that should have been used
SR = Standard hourly wage rate

Helado Company used 325 direct labor hours while producing 30,000 quarts of yogurt. From Exhibit 9-2, 0.01 hour per quart at a cost of $8.00 per hour should have been used. The standard hours allowed are 300 (0.01 × 30,000). Thus, AH is 325, SH is 300, and SR is $8.00. The direct labor efficiency variance is computed as follows:

$$
\begin{aligned}
LEV &= (AH - SH)SR \\
&= (325 - 300)\$8.00 \\
&= 25 \times \$8.00 \\
&= \$200 \text{ U}
\end{aligned}
$$

Accounting for the Direct Labor Rate and Efficiency Variances

The journal entry to record the direct labor rate and efficiency variance is made simultaneously. The general form of this journal entry follows. (It assumes a favorable direct labor rate variance and an unfavorable direct labor efficiency variance.)

Work in Process	$SH \times SR$	
Direct Labor Efficiency Variance	$(AH - SH)SR$	
Direct Labor Rate Variance		$(AR - SR)AH$
Wages Payable		$AH \times AR$

Notice that only standard hours and standard rates are used to assign direct labor costs to Work in Process. Actual prices and quantities are not used. This emphasizes the principle that all inventories are carried at standard.

The journal entry for Helado's use of direct labor during the first week of May follows. Since both variances are unfavorable, the variance accounts are debited:

Work in Process	2,400	
Direct Labor Rate Variance	65	
Direct Labor Efficiency Variance	200	
Wages Payable		2,665

Investigating Direct Materials and Labor Variances

Rarely will actual performance exactly meet the established standards, nor does management expect it to do so. Random variations around the standard are expected. Because of this, management should have in mind an acceptable range of performance. When variances are within this range, they are assumed to be caused by random factors. When a variance falls outside this range, the deviation is likely to be caused by nonrandom factors, either factors that managers can control or factors they cannot control. In the noncontrollable case, managers need to revise the standard. For the controllable case, an investigation should be undertaken only if the anticipated benefits are greater than the expected costs. In making this assessment, a manager must consider whether a variance will recur. If so, the process may be permanently out of control, meaning that periodic savings may be achieved if corrective action is taken. For example, consider Helado's unfavorable materials usage variance. Assume that investigation reveals that the unfavorable direct variance was the result of rejecting a 1,200-quart batch because of poor consistency and flavor. Some settings in the mixing process had been mistakenly altered, resulting in a faulty mix of ingredients. The setting was corrected, and no further problems were noticed.

Because it is difficult to assess the costs and benefits of variance analysis on a case-by-case basis, many firms adopt the general guideline of investigating variances only if they fall outside an acceptable range. The acceptable range is the standard, plus or minus an allowable deviation. The top and bottom measures of the allowable range are called the **control limits**. The *upper control limit* is the standard plus the allowable deviation, and the *lower control limit* is the standard minus the allowable deviation. Current practice sets the control limits subjectively: based on past experience, intuition, and judgment, management determines the allowable deviation from standard.[4]

The control limits are usually expressed both as a percentage of the standard and as an absolute dollar amount. For example, the allowable deviation may be expressed as the lesser of 10 percent of the standard amount or $10,000. In other words, management will not accept a deviation of more than $10,000 even if that deviation is less than 10 percent of the standard. Alternatively, even if the dollar amount is less than $10,000, an investigation is required if the deviation is more than 10 percent of the standard amount. Formal statistical procedures can also be used to set the control limits. In this way, less subjectivity is involved and a manager can assess the likelihood of the variance being caused by random factors. The use of such formal procedures has gained little acceptance.

Responsibility for the Direct Materials Variances

The responsibility for controlling the direct materials price variance is usually the purchasing agent's. Admittedly, the price of direct materials is largely beyond his or her control; however, the price variance can be influenced by such factors as quality, quantity discounts, distance of the source from the plant, and so on. These factors are often under the control of the agent. The production manager is generally responsible for direct materials usage. Minimizing scrap, waste, and rework are all ways in which the manager can ensure that the standard is met. However, at times, the cause of the variance is attributable to others outside the production area. For example, the purchase of lower-quality direct materials may produce bad output. In this case, responsibility would be assigned to purchasing rather than production.

Using the price variance to evaluate the performance of purchasing has some limitations. Emphasis on meeting or beating the standard can produce some undesirable outcomes. For example, if the purchasing agent feels pressured to produce favorable variances, he or she may purchase direct materials of a lower quality than desired or acquire too much inventory in order to take advantage of quantity discounts. As with the price variance, applying the usage variance to evaluate performance can lead to undesirable behavior. For example, a production manager feeling pressure to produce a favorable variance might allow a defective unit to be transferred to finished goods. While this avoids the problem of wasted direct materials, it may create customer-relations problems once a customer gets stuck with the bad product.

Responsibility for the Direct Labor Variances

Direct labor rates are largely determined by such external forces as labor markets and union contracts. When direct labor rate variances occur, they often do so because an av-

---

4. Bruce R. Gaumnitz and Felix P. Kollaritsch, "Manufacturing Variances: Current Practices and Trends," *Journal of Cost Management* (Spring 1991): 58–64. In this article, the authors report that about 45–47 percent of firms use dollar or percentage control limits. Most of the remaining use judgment rather than any formal identification of limits.

erage wage rate is used for the rate standard or because more skilled and more highly paid laborers are used for less skilled tasks. Wage rates for a particular direct labor activity often differ among workers because of differing levels of seniority. Rather than selecting direct labor rate standards reflecting those different levels, an average wage rate is often chosen. As the seniority mix changes, the average rate changes. This will give rise to a direct labor rate variance; it also calls for a new standard to reflect the new seniority mix. Controllability is not assignable for this cause of a direct labor rate variance.

However, the *use* of direct labor is controllable by the production manager. The use of more skilled workers to perform less skilled tasks (or vice versa) is a decision that a production manager consciously makes. For this reason, responsibility for the direct labor rate variance is generally assigned to the individuals who decide how direct labor will be used. The same is true of the direct labor efficiency variance. However, as is true of all variances, once the cause is discovered, responsibility may be assigned elsewhere. For example, frequent breakdowns of machinery may cause interruptions and nonproductive use of direct labor. But the responsibility for these breakdowns may be faulty maintenance. If so, the maintenance manager should be charged with the unfavorable direct labor efficiency variance.

Production managers may be tempted to engage in dysfunctional behavior if too much emphasis is placed on the direct labor variances. For example, to avoid losing hours and using additional hours because of possible rework, a production manager could deliberately transfer defective units to finished goods.

Disposition of Direct Materials and Direct Labor Variances

Most companies dispose of variances at the end of the year by either closing them to Cost of Goods Sold or prorating them among Work in Process, Cost of Goods Sold, and Finished Goods. If the variances are immaterial, then the most expedient disposition is simply to assign them to Cost of Goods Sold. To illustrate, assume that the variances we have computed for the first week in May are the year-end variances (for Helado Company). Assuming the variances are immaterial, the following entry would be made to dispose of them:

Cost of Goods Sold	4,765	
Direct Materials Price Variance		3,900
Direct Materials Usage Variance		600
Direct Labor Rate Variance		65
Direct Labor Efficiency Variance		200

If the variances are judged to be material, then the proration option is usually exercised. This option is driven by GAAP requirements that inventories and cost of goods sold be reported at actual costs. Yet, if variances are measures of inefficiency, it seems difficult to justify carrying costs of inefficiency as assets. It seems more logical to write off the costs of inefficiency as a cost of the period. With this conceptual qualification, we will illustrate one method of proration, using Helado's May variances as year-end variances. We will assume that direct materials and direct labor are added uniformly throughout the process; thus, the direct materials and direct labor variances can be assigned in proportion to the total prime costs in each of the three inventory accounts. Assume that the standard prime costs (before allocation of the direct materials and direct labor variances) are as follows (these are assumed values):

	Prime Costs	*Percentage of Total*
Work in Process	$ 0	0%
Finished Goods	3,480	20
Cost of Goods Sold	13,920	80
Total	$17,400	100%

Using these percentages, the materials and labor variances would be assigned as follows:

Finished Goods: 0.2 × $4,765 = $953
Cost of Goods Sold: 0.8 × $4,765 = $3,812

The journal entry to close out the variance accounts is as follows:

Finished Goods	953	
Cost of Goods Sold	3,812	
Direct Materials Price Variance		3,900
Direct Materials Usage Variance		600
Direct Labor Rate Variance		65
Direct Labor Efficiency Variance		200

Other proration variations are possible. For example, direct materials variances could be assigned in proportion to the total direct materials cost in each account, and the direct labor variances could be assigned in proportion to the total direct labor costs. Some even argue that finer assignments of the variances may be needed. The direct materials price variance, for example, could be assigned to the MUV account, the materials inventory account, work in process, finished goods, and the cost of goods sold account (with the other variances assigned only to the usual three inventory accounts).

Variance Analysis: Overhead Costs

OBJECTIVE 4

Compute overhead variances three different ways, and explain overhead accounting.

For direct materials and direct labor, total variances are broken down into price and efficiency variances. The total overhead variance—the difference between applied and actual overhead—is also broken down into component variances. The number of component variances computed depends on the method of variance analysis used. We will emphasize the 4-variance method: two variances for variable overhead and two variances for fixed overhead. We first divide overhead into categories: variable and fixed. Next, we look at component variances for each category. The total variable overhead variance is divided into two components: the variable overhead spending variance and the variable overhead efficiency variance. Similarly, the total fixed overhead variance is divided into two components: the fixed overhead spending variance and the fixed overhead volume variance. Although the 4-variance method provides the most detail, it also requires a company to identify the actual variable and fixed costs as well as budgeted rates and costs. For companies that wish to avoid the need to track actual variable and fixed costs, the 2-variance and 3-variance methods can be used. These methods also will be briefly reviewed.

In analyzing overhead variances, a traditional approach is assumed. Standard overhead rates are computed in basically the same way that was described in Chapter 4. Traditional overhead rate computations rely on unit-level drivers such as direct labor hours and machine hours. The overhead analysis in this chapter assumes that direct labor hours is the only driver used to assign overhead costs to products. Thus, when we speak of variable and fixed overhead, we are assuming that it is fixed or variable with respect to direct labor hours, a unit-level driver. In Chapter 12, variance analysis is extended to a more general setting where both unit- and nonunit-level drivers are allowed.

Four-Variance Method: The Two Variable Overhead Variances

To illustrate the variable overhead variances, we will examine activity for Helado Company during the month of May. The following data were gathered for this time period:

Variable overhead rate (standard)	$6.00 per direct labor hour[a]
Actual variable overhead costs	$7,540
Actual hours worked	1,300
Quarts of deluxe strawberry frozen yogurt produced	120,000
Hours allowed for production	1,200[b]
Applied variable overhead	$7,200[c]

[a]Budgeted variable overhead/Standard hours allowed for practical volume.
[b]0.01 × 120,000 (See Exhibit 9-2 for unit standards and prices.)
[c]$6.00 × 1,200 (Overhead is applied using standard hours allowed.)

The total variable overhead variance is the difference between the actual and the applied variable overhead. For our example, the total variable overhead variance is computed as follows:

$$\text{Total variance} = \$7,540 - \$7,200$$
$$= \$340 \text{ U}$$

A graphical, 3-pronged approach for dividing this total variance into spending and efficiency variances is illustrated in Exhibit 9-7.

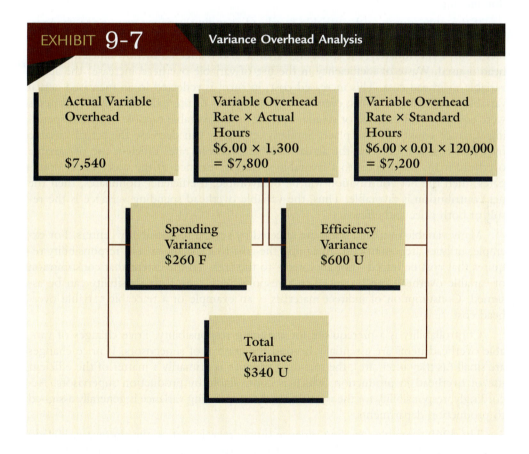

EXHIBIT 9-7   Variance Overhead Analysis

Variable Overhead Spending Variance

The **variable overhead spending variance** measures the aggregate effect of differences in the actual variable overhead rate (*AVOR*) and the standard variable overhead rate (*SVOR*). The actual variable overhead rate is simply actual variable overhead divided by actual hours. For our example, this rate is $5.80 ($7,540/1,300 hrs.). The formula for computing the variable overhead spending variance is as follows:

$$
\begin{aligned}
\text{Variable overhead spending variance} &= (AVOR \times AH) - (SVOR \times AH) \\
&= (AVOR - SVOR)AH \\
&= (\$5.80 - \$6.00)1,300 \\
&= \$260 \text{ F}
\end{aligned}
$$

The variable overhead spending variance is similar to the price variances of direct materials and direct labor, although there are some conceptual differences. Variable overhead is not a homogeneous input—it is made up of a large number of individual items such as indirect materials, indirect labor, electricity, maintenance, and so on. The standard variable overhead rate represents the weighted cost per direct labor hour that should be incurred for all variable overhead items. The difference between what should have been spent per hour and what actually was spent per hour is a type of price variance.

A variable overhead spending variance can arise because prices for individual variable overhead items have increased or decreased. Assume, for the moment, that the price changes of individual overhead items are the only cause of the spending variance. If the spending variance is unfavorable, then price increases for individual variable overhead items are the cause; if the spending variance is favorable, then price decreases are dominating.

If the only source of the variable overhead spending variance were price changes, then it would be completely analogous to the price variances of direct materials and direct labor. Unfortunately, the spending variance also is affected by how efficiently overhead is used. Waste or inefficiency in the use of variable overhead increases the actual variable overhead cost. This increased cost, in turn, is reflected in an increased actual variable overhead rate. Thus, even if the actual prices of the individual overhead items were equal to the budgeted or standard prices, an unfavorable variable overhead spending variance could still take place. Similarly, efficiency can decrease the actual variable overhead cost and decrease the actual variable overhead rate. Efficient use of variable overhead items contributes to a favorable spending variance. If the waste effect dominates, then the net contribution will be unfavorable; if efficiency dominates, then the net contribution is favorable. Thus, the variable overhead spending variance is the result of both price and efficiency.

Many variable overhead items are affected by several responsibility centers. For example, utilities are a joint cost. Assigning the cost to a specific area of responsibility requires that cost be traced—not allocated—to the area. To the extent that consumption of variable overhead can be traced to a responsibility center, responsibility can be assigned. Consumption of indirect materials is an example of a traceable variable overhead cost.

Controllability is a prerequisite for assigning responsibility. Price changes of variable overhead items are essentially beyond the control of supervisors. If price changes are small (as they often are), the spending variance is primarily a matter of the efficient use of overhead in production, which is controllable by production supervisors. Accordingly, responsibility for the variable overhead spending variance is generally assigned to production departments.

The $260 favorable spending variance simply reveals that, in the aggregate, Helado Company spent less on variable overhead than expected. Even if the variance was insignificant, it reveals nothing about how well costs of individual variable overhead items were controlled. Control of variable overhead requires line-by-line analysis for each individual item. Exhibit 9-8 presents a performance report that supplies the line-by-line information essential for proper control of variable overhead. Assuming that Helado investigates any item that deviates more than 10 percent from budget, the cost of gas would be the only item that would be investigated. The investigation reveals that the utility company lowered the price of natural gas as a result of a state regulatory hear-

| EXHIBIT 9-8 | Variable Overhead Spending Variance by Item |

Helado Company
Performance Report
For the Month Ended May 31, 2007

	Cost Formula[a]	Actual Costs	Budget[b]	Spending Variance
Natural gas	$3.80	$4,400	$4,940	$540 F
Electricity	2.00	2,840	2,600	240 U
Water	0.20	300	260	40 U
Total	$6.00	$7,540	$7,800	$260 F

[a]Per direct labor hour.
[b]The budget allowance is computed using the cost formula and an activity level of 1,300 actual direct labor hours.

ing. The reduction is expected to be permanent. In this case, the cause of the favorable variance is beyond the control of the company. The correct response is to revise the budget formula to reflect the decreased cost of natural gas.

Variable Overhead Efficiency Variance

Variable overhead is assumed to vary as the production volume changes. Thus, variable overhead changes in proportion to changes in the direct labor hours used. The **variable overhead efficiency variance** measures the change in variable overhead consumption that occurs because of efficient (or inefficient) use of direct labor. The efficiency variance is computed using the following formula:

$$\text{Variable overhead efficiency variance} = (AH - SH)SVOR$$
$$= (1,300 - 1,200)\$6.00$$
$$= \$600 \text{ U}$$

The variable overhead efficiency variance is directly related to the direct labor efficiency or usage variance. If variable overhead is truly driven by direct labor hours, then like the direct labor usage variance, the variable overhead efficiency variance is caused by efficient or inefficient use of direct labor. If more (or fewer) direct labor hours are used than the standard calls for, then the total variable overhead cost will increase (or decrease). The validity of the measure depends on the validity of the relationship between variable overhead costs and direct labor hours. In other words, do variable overhead costs *really* change in proportion to changes in direct labor hours? If so, responsibility for the variable overhead efficiency variance should be assigned to the individual who has responsibility for the use of direct labor: the production manager.

The reasons for the unfavorable variable overhead efficiency variance are generally the same as those offered for the unfavorable labor usage variance. For example, some of the variance can be explained by the fact that overtime hours were used during the first week to make up for a bad batch of yogurt. The remaining deficiency was caused by the use of new employees who took longer to carry out tasks because of their lack of experience.

More information concerning the effect of direct labor usage on variable overhead is available in a line-by-line analysis of individual variable overhead items. This can be accomplished by comparing the budget allowance for the actual hours used with the budget allowance for the standard hours allowed for each item. A performance report that makes this comparison for all variable overhead costs is shown in Exhibit 9-9. From Exhibit 9-9, we can see that the cost of natural gas is affected most by inefficient use of direct labor. For example, the extra time required to make up for a bad batch would increase gas consumption. Similarly, inexperienced laborers may heat the mix of gelatin and milk longer than is really needed, thus using more gas.

| EXHIBIT **9-9** | | | Variable Overhead Spending and Efficiency Variances by Item | | | |

Helado Company Performance Report For the Month Ended May 31, 2007						
Cost	Cost Formula[a]	Actual Costs	Budget for Actual Hours	Spending Variance[b]	Budget for Standard Hours	Efficiency Variance[c]
Natural gas	$3.80	$4,400	$4,940	$540 F	$4,560	$380 U
Electricity	2.00	2,840	2,600	240 U	2,400	200 U
Water	0.20	300	260	40 U	240	20 U
Total	$6.00	$7,540	$7,800	$260 F	$7,200	$600 U

[a]Per direct labor hour.
[b]Spending variance = Actual costs − Budget for actual hours.
[c]Efficiency variance = Budget for actual hours − Budget for standard hours.

The column labeled *Budget for Standard Hours* gives the amount that should have been spent on variable overhead for the actual output. The total of all items in this column is the applied variable overhead, the amount assigned to production in a standard costing system. Note that in a standard costing system, variable overhead is applied using the hours allowed for the actual output (SH), while in normal costing, variable overhead is applied using actual hours. Although not shown in Exhibit 9-9, the difference between actual costs and this column is the total variable overhead variance (underapplied by $340). Thus, the underapplied variable overhead variance is the sum of the spending and efficiency variances.

Four-Variance Analysis: The Two Fixed Overhead Variances

We will again use the Helado Company example to illustrate the computation of the fixed overhead variances. The data needed for the calculation are as follows:

Budgeted/Planned Items (May)

Budgeted fixed overhead	$20,000
Expected activity	1,000 direct labor hours[a]
Standard fixed overhead rate	$20[b]

[a]Hours allowed to produce 100,000 quarts of frozen yogurt (0.01 × 100,000).
[b]$20,000/1,000.

	Actual Results
Actual production	120,000 quarts
Actual fixed overhead cost	$20,500
Standard hours allowed for actual production	1,200[a]

[a] 0.01 × 120,000.

The total fixed overhead variance is the difference between actual fixed overhead and applied fixed overhead, when applied fixed overhead is obtained by multiplying the standard fixed overhead rate by the standard hours allowed for the actual output. Thus, the applied fixed overhead is calculated as follows:

$$\text{Applied fixed overhead} = \text{Standard fixed overhead rate} \times \text{Standard hours}$$
$$= \$20 \times 1,200$$
$$= \$24,000$$

The total fixed overhead variance is the difference between the actual fixed overhead and the applied fixed overhead:

$$\text{Total fixed overhead variance} = \$20,500 - \$24,000$$
$$= \$3,500 \text{ Overapplied}$$

To help managers understand why fixed overhead was overapplied by $3,500, the total variance can be broken down into two variances: the fixed overhead spending variance and the fixed overhead volume variance. The calculations of the two variances are illustrated graphically in Exhibit 9-10.

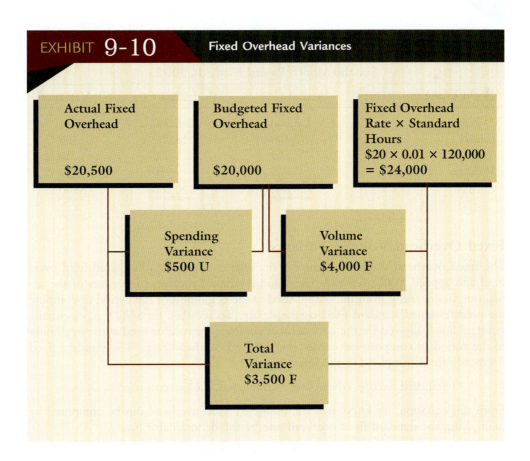

EXHIBIT 9-10   Fixed Overhead Variances

Actual Fixed Overhead	Budgeted Fixed Overhead	Fixed Overhead Rate × Standard Hours $20 × 0.01 × 120,000 = $24,000
$20,500	$20,000	

Spending Variance $500 U

Volume Variance $4,000 F

Total Variance $3,500 F

The Fixed Overhead Spending Variance

The **fixed overhead spending variance** is defined as the difference between the actual fixed overhead and the budgeted fixed overhead. The spending variance is favorable because less was spent on fixed overhead items than was budgeted. The formula for computing the fixed overhead variance follows (*AFOH* = Actual fixed overhead and *BFOH* = Budgeted fixed overhead):

$$\text{Fixed overhead spending variance} = AFOH - BFOH$$
$$= \$20,500 - \$20,000$$
$$= \$500 \text{ U}$$

Fixed overhead is made up of a number of individual items such as salaries, depreciation, taxes, and insurance. Many fixed overhead items—long-run investments, for instance—are not subject to change in the short run; consequently, fixed overhead costs are often beyond the immediate control of management. Since many fixed overhead costs are affected primarily by long-run decisions, not by changes in production levels, the budget variance is usually small. For example, depreciation, salaries, taxes, and insurance costs are not likely to be much different than planned.

Because fixed overhead is made up of many individual items, a line-by-line comparison of budgeted costs with actual costs provides more information concerning the causes of the spending variance. Exhibit 9-11 provides such a report. The report reveals that the fixed overhead spending variance is essentially in line with expectations. The fixed overhead spending variances, both on a line-item basis and in the aggregate, are relatively small (all less than 10 percent of the budgeted costs).

EXHIBIT 9-11

Helado Company
Performance Report
For the Month Ended May 31, 2007

Fixed Overhead Items	Actual Cost	Budgeted Cost	Variance
Depreciation	$ 5,000	$ 5,000	$ —
Salaries	13,400	13,000	400 U
Taxes	1,100	1,050	50 U
Insurance	1,000	950	50 U
Total	$20,500	$20,000	$500 U

Fixed Overhead Volume Variance

The **fixed overhead volume variance** is the difference between budgeted fixed overhead and applied fixed overhead. The volume variance measures the effect of the actual output departing from the output used at the beginning of the period to compute the predetermined standard fixed overhead rate. To see this, let $SH(D)$ represent the standard hours allowed for the denominator volume (the volume used at the beginning of the period to compute the predetermined fixed overhead rate). The standard fixed overhead rate is computed in the following way:

$$\text{Standard fixed overhead rate} = \text{Budgeted fixed overhead}/SH(D)$$

From this equation, we know that the budgeted fixed overhead can be computed by multiplying the standard fixed overhead rate by the denominator hours.

$$\text{Budgeted fixed overhead} = \text{Standard fixed overhead rate} \times SH(D)$$

From Exhibit 9-10, we know that the volume variance can be computed as follows:

$$
\begin{aligned}
\text{Volume variance} &= \text{Budgeted fixed overhead} - \text{Applied fixed overhead} \\
&= [\text{Standard fixed overhead rate} \times SH(D)] - (\text{Standard fixed} \\
&\quad\ \text{overhead rate} \times SH) \\
&= \text{Standard fixed overhead rate} \times [SH(D) - SH] \\
&= \$20(1{,}000 - 1{,}200) \\
&= \$4{,}000 \text{ F}
\end{aligned}
$$

Thus, for a volume variance to occur, the denominator hours, $SH(D)$, must differ from the standard hours allowed for the actual volume, SH. Assume Helado expected to produce 100,000 quarts of frozen yogurt in May, using 1,000 direct labor hours. The actual outcome was 120,000 quarts produced, using 1,200 standard hours. Therefore, more was produced than expected, and a favorable volume variance arises.

But what is the meaning of this variance? The variance occurs because the actual output differs from the denominator output volume. At the beginning of the month, if management had expected 120,000 quarts with 1,200 standard hours as the denominator volume, the volume variance would not have existed. In this view, the volume variance is seen as prediction error—a measure of the inability of management to select the correct volume over which to spread fixed overhead.

If, however, the denominator volume represented the amount that management believed *could* be produced and sold, the volume variance conveys more significant information. If the actual volume is more than the denominator volume, the volume variance signals that a gain has occurred (relative to expectations). That gain is not equivalent, however, to the dollar value of the volume variance. The gain is equal to the increase in contribution margin on the extra units produced and sold. However, the volume variance is positively correlated with the gain. Suppose that the contribution margin per standard direct labor hour is $50. By producing 120,000 quarts of frozen yogurt instead of 100,000 quarts, the company gained sales of 20,000 quarts. This is equivalent to 200 hours ($0.01 \times 20{,}000$). At $50 per hour, the gain is $10,000 ($50 \times 200$). The favorable volume variance of $4,000 signals this gain but understates it. In this sense, the volume variance is a measure of this year's *planned* utilization of capacity.

On the other hand, if *practical capacity* is used as the denominator volume, then the volume variance is a direct measure of capacity utilization. Practical capacity measures the most that can be produced under efficient operating conditions (and, thus, represents the productive capacity the firm has acquired). The difference between available hours of production and actual hours is a measure of underutilization, and when multiplied by the standard fixed overhead rate, the volume variance becomes a measure of the cost of underutilization of capacity. This is similar in concept to the activity capacity utilization measure described in Chapter 3. The principal difference is that the fixed overhead rate used to measure the cost of unused capacity contains more than the cost of acquiring the productive capacity. Fixed overhead is made up of many costs incurred for reasons other than obtaining productive capacity (e.g., the salaries of the plant supervisor, janitors, and industrial engineers).

Assuming that volume variance measures capacity utilization implies that the general responsibility for this variance should be assigned to the production department. At times, however, investigation into the reasons for a significant volume variance may reveal the cause to be factors beyond the control of production. In this instance, specific responsibility may be assigned elsewhere. For example, if purchasing acquires a direct material of lower quality than usual, significant rework time may result, causing lower production and an unfavorable volume variance. In this case, responsibility for the variance rests with purchasing, not production.

Graphical Representation of Fixed Overhead Variances

Exhibit 9-12, on the following page, provides a graph that illustrates the fixed overhead variances. The graph is structured so that the actual fixed overhead is greater than

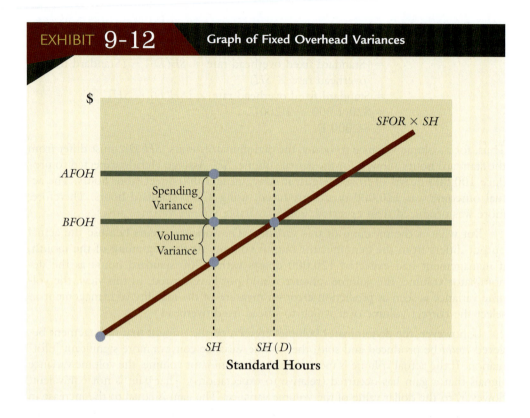

EXHIBIT 9-12   Graph of Fixed Overhead Variances

the budgeted fixed overhead. Notice that applying fixed overhead by multiplying the fixed overhead rate by the standard hours allowed for production has the effect of converting fixed overhead into a unit-level variable cost ($SFOR \times SH$ is represented by a line coming out of the origin, with slope $SFOR$, where $SFOR$ is the standard fixed overhead rate). Converting a fixed cost into a variable cost contributes significantly to the creation of the volume variance (as well as to the total fixed overhead variance). Notice also that the volume variance has a lot to do with how well we estimate SH (the hours allowed for actual production). If $SH = SH(D)$, there is no volume variance. (This is where the applied line intersects with the $BFOH$ line.) Notice also how the total variance breaks down into the spending and volume variances.

Accounting for Overhead Variances

Overhead is applied to production by debiting Work in Process and crediting variable and fixed overhead control accounts. The amount assigned is simply the respective overhead rates multiplied by the standard hours allowed for actual production. The actual overhead is accumulated on the debit side of the overhead control accounts. Periodically (e.g., monthly), overhead variance reports are prepared. At the end of the year, the applied variable and fixed overhead costs and the actual fixed overhead costs are closed out and the variances isolated. The overhead variances are then disposed of by closing them to Cost of Goods Sold if they are not material or by prorating them among Work in Process, Finished Goods, and Cost of Goods Sold if they are material. We will use the May transactions for Helado Company to illustrate the process that would occur at the end of the year. Essentially, we are assuming that the May transactions reflect an entire year for illustrative purposes.

To assign overhead to production, we have the following entry:

Work in Process	31,200	
Variable Overhead Control		7,200
Fixed Overhead Control		24,000

To recognize the incurrence of actual overhead, the following entry is needed:

Variable Overhead Control	7,540	
Fixed Overhead Control	20,500	
Miscellaneous Accounts		28,040

To recognize the variances, the following entry is needed:

Fixed Overhead Control	3,500	
Variable Overhead Efficiency Variance	600	
Fixed Overhead Spending Variance	500	
Variable Overhead Control		340
Variable Overhead Spending Variance		260
Fixed Overhead Volume Variance		4,000

Finally, to close out the variances to Cost of Goods Sold, we would have the following entries. (Entries assume that variances are immaterial.)

Fixed Overhead Volume Variance	4,000	
Variable Overhead Spending Variance	260	
Cost of Goods Sold		4,260
Cost of Goods Sold	1,100	
Variable Overhead Efficiency Variance		600
Fixed Overhead Spending Variance		500

Two- and Three-Variance Analyses

The 2- and 3-variance analyses do not require knowledge of actual variable and actual fixed overhead. These methods provide less detail and, thus, less information. We will simply present the method of computation for the two forms of analysis. The 4-variance method is recommended over these two approaches. The May data for Helado Company will be used to illustrate the two methods with the assumption that only the total actual overhead is known: $28,040.

Two-Variance Analysis

The 2-variance analysis is shown in Exhibit 9-13 on the following page. (*SVOR* designates the standard variable overhead rate.) Several points should be made relative to the 4-variance analysis appearing in Exhibits 9-7 and 9-10. First, the total variance is the sum of the total fixed and variable overhead variances. Second, the volume variance is the same as that of the 4-variance method. Notice that in the computation of the volume variance, the applied variable overhead term, $SVOR \times SH$, is common to the middle and right prongs of the diagram. Thus, when the right number is subtracted from the left number, we are left with the $BFOH - SFOR \times SH$ term, which is the fixed overhead volume variance. Third, the budget variance is the sum of the spending and efficiency variances of the 4-variance method ($260 F + $500 U + $600 U = $840 U). As indicated, the 2-variance method sacrifices a lot of information.

Three-Variance Analysis

The 3-variance analysis is shown in Exhibit 9-14 on the following page. Again, some observations can be made about this method relative to the 4-variance method. First, the total variance is again the sum of the total variable and fixed overhead variances. Second, the spending variance is the sum of the variable and fixed overhead spending variances. The variable overhead efficiency and the fixed overhead volume variances are the same. The 3-variance method also illustrates that the budget variance of the 2-variance method breaks down into spending and efficiency variances.

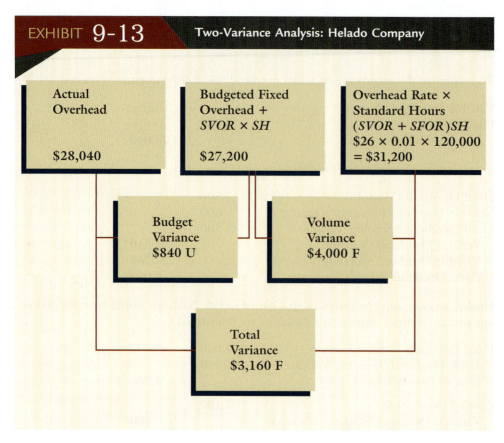

EXHIBIT 9-13 Two-Variance Analysis: Helado Company

Actual Overhead

$28,040

Budgeted Fixed Overhead + *SVOR* × *SH*

$27,200

Overhead Rate × Standard Hours ($SVOR + SFOR$)SH $26 × 0.01 × 120,000 = $31,200

Budget Variance $840 U

Volume Variance $4,000 F

Total Variance $3,160 F

Note: SFOR = Standard fixed overhead rate
SVOR = Standard variable overhead rate

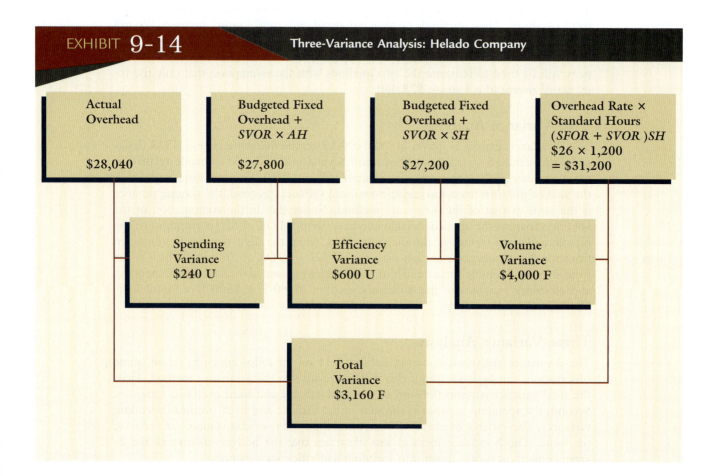

EXHIBIT 9-14 Three-Variance Analysis: Helado Company

Actual Overhead

$28,040

Budgeted Fixed Overhead + *SVOR* × *AH*

$27,800

Budgeted Fixed Overhead + *SVOR* × *SH*

$27,200

Overhead Rate × Standard Hours ($SFOR + SVOR$)SH $26 × 1,200 = $31,200

Spending Variance $240 U

Efficiency Variance $600 U

Volume Variance $4,000 F

Total Variance $3,160 F

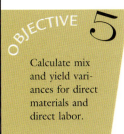

OBJECTIVE 5

Calculate mix and yield variances for direct materials and direct labor.

Mix and Yield Variances: Materials and Labor

For some production processes, it may be possible to substitute one direct material input for another or one type of direct labor for another. Usually, a standard mix specification identifies the proportion of each direct material and the proportion of each type of direct labor that should be used for producing the product. For example, in producing an orange-pineapple fruit drink, the standard direct materials mix may call for 30 percent pineapple and 70 percent orange, and the standard direct labor mix may call for 33 percent of fruit preparation labor and 67 percent of fruit processing labor. Clearly, within reason, it is possible to make input substitutions. Substituting direct materials or direct labor, however, may produce *mix* and *yield* variances. A **mix variance** is created whenever the actual mix of inputs differs from the standard mix. A **yield variance** occurs whenever the actual yield (output) differs from the standard yield. For direct materials, the sum of the mix and yield variances equals the direct materials usage variance; for direct labor, the sum is the direct labor efficiency variance.

Direct Materials Mix and Yield Variances

To illustrate direct materials mix and yield variances, let us look at Malcom Nut Company. Malcom produces a variety of mixed nuts. One type of mixed nuts uses peanuts and almonds. Malcom developed the following standard mix for producing 120 pounds of mixed nuts. (Almonds and peanuts are purchased in the shell and processed.)

Standard Mix Information: Direct Materials

Direct Material	Mix	Mix Proportion	SP	Standard Cost
Peanuts	128 lbs.	0.80	$0.50	$64
Almonds	32	0.20	1.00	32
Total	160 lbs.			$96

Yield   120 lbs.
Yield ratio: 0.75 (120/160)
Standard cost of yield (*SPy*): $0.80 per pound ($96/120 pounds of yield)

Now suppose that Malcom processes a batch of 1,600 pounds and produces the following actual results:

Direct Material	Actual Mix	Percentages*
Peanuts	1,120 lbs.	70%
Almonds	480	30
Total	1,600 lbs.	100%
Yield	1,300 lbs.	81.3%

*Uses 1,600 lbs. as the base.

Direct Materials Mix Variance

The mix variance is the difference in the standard cost of the actual mix of inputs used and the standard cost of the mix of inputs that should have been used. Let *SM* be the quantity of each input that should have been used given the total actual input quantity. This quantity is computed as follows for each direct material input:

$$SM = \text{Standard mix proportion} \times \text{Total actual input quantity}$$

For example, the standard mix proportion for peanuts is 0.80. Thus, if 1,600 pounds of actual input were used, then the mix standard calls for the following amount of peanuts:[5]

$$SM(\text{peanuts}) = 0.80 \times 1,600 = 1,280 \text{ pounds}$$

A similar computation produces $SM = 320$ pounds for almonds ($0.20 \times 1,600$).

Given SM, the mix variance is computed as follows:

$$\text{Mix variance} = \sum (AQi - SMi)SPi \qquad (9.1)$$

The formula can be applied most easily using the following approach:

Direct Material	AQ	SM	AQ − SM	SP	(AQ − SM)SP
Peanuts	1,120	1,280	(160)	$0.50	$ (80)
Almonds	480	320	160	1.00	160
Mix variance					$ 80 U

Notice that the mix variance is unfavorable. This occurs because more almonds are used than are called for in the standard mix, and almonds are a more expensive input. If the mix variance is material, then an investigation should be undertaken to determine the cause of the variance so that corrective action can be taken.

Direct Materials Yield Variance

Using the standard mix information and the actual results, the yield variance is computed by the following formula:

$$\text{Yield variance} = (\text{Standard yield} - \text{Actual yield})SPy \qquad (9.2)$$

where

$$\text{Standard yield} = \text{Yield ratio} \times \text{Total actual inputs}$$

Thus, for the actual input of 1,600 pounds, the standard yield is 1,200 pounds ($0.75 \times 1,600$). The yield variance is computed as follows:

$$\begin{aligned} \text{Yield variance} &= (1,200 - 1,300)\$0.80 \\ &= \$80 \text{ F} \end{aligned}$$

The yield variance is favorable because the actual yield is greater than the standard yield. Direct material yield variance should be investigated to find the root causes. Corrective action to restore the process to the standards may be required or it may lead to a change in standards if the joint effect of the mix and yield variances is favorable.

Direct Labor Mix and Yield Variances

The direct labor mix and yield variances are computed in the same way as the direct materials mix and yield variances. Specifically, Equations 9.1 and 9.2 apply to direct labor in the same way with the notation defined appropriately for direct labor. For example, AQ, in Equation 9.1, is interpreted as AH, the actual hours used, and SP as the stan-

---

5. The standard mix amounts are not the standard quantities allowed for actual output. The total standard quantity allowed is computed by dividing the actual yield by the standard yield ratio. The total standard input allowed is then multiplied by the standard mix ratios to compute the quantity of each direct material input that should have been used of the actual output. Alternatively, the unit direct material standards can be developed by dividing the standard input mix quantity by the standard yield. Multiplying the unit standards by the actual yield will also produce SQ for each input.

dard price of labor. With this understanding, the computation of mix and yield variances will be illustrated using the Malcom Nut Company example. Suppose that Malcom has two types of direct labor, shelling labor and mixing labor. Malcom has developed the following standard mix for direct labor. (Yield, of course, is measured in pounds of output and corresponds to the same batch size used for the direct materials standards.)

Standard Mix Information: Direct Labor

Direct Labor Type	Mix	Mix Proportion	SP	Standard Cost
Shelling	3 hrs.	0.60	$ 8.00	$24
Mixing	2	0.40	15.00	30
Total	5 hrs.			$54

Yield   120 lbs.
Yield ratio: 24 = (120/5), or 2,400%
Standard cost of yield (SPy): $0.45 per pound ($54/120 pounds of yield)

As discussed earlier, suppose that Malcom processes 1,600 pounds of nuts and produces the following actual results:

Direct Labor Type	Actual	Mix Percentages*
Shelling	20 hrs.	40%
Mixing	30	60
Total	50 hrs.	100%
Yield	1,300 lbs.	2,600%

*Uses 50 hours as the base.

Direct Labor Mix Variance

The standard mix proportion for shelling labor is 0.60. Thus, if 50 hours of actual input were used, then the mix standard calls for the following amount of shelling labor:

$$SM(\text{shelling}) = 0.60 \times 50$$
$$= 30 \text{ hours}$$

A similar computation produces SM = 20 hours for mixing labor (0.40 × 50).

Given SM, the direct labor mix variance is computed as follows (using Equation 9.1):

Direct Labor Type	AH	SM	AH − SM	SP	(AH − SM)SP
Shelling	20	30	(10)	$ 8.00	$ (80)
Mixing	30	20	10	15.00	150
Direct labor mix variance					$ 70 U

Notice that the direct labor mix variance is unfavorable. This occurs because more mixing labor was used than was called for in the standard mix, and mixing labor is more expensive than shelling labor.

Direct Labor Yield Variance

Using the standard mix information and the actual results, the direct labor yield variance is computed as follows:

$$\text{Direct labor yield variance} = (\text{Standard yield} - \text{Actual yield})SPy$$
$$= [(24 \times 50) - 1,300]\$0.45$$
$$= (1,200 - 1,300)\$0.45$$
$$= \$45 \text{ F}$$

The direct labor yield variance is favorable because the actual yield is greater than the standard yield.

SUMMARY

A standard costing system budgets quantities and costs on a unit basis. These unit budgets are for direct labor, direct materials, and overhead. Standard costs, therefore, are the amount that should be expended to produce a product or service. Standards are set using historical experience, engineering studies, and input from operating personnel, marketing, and accounting. Currently attainable standards are those that can be achieved under efficient operating conditions. Ideal standards are those achievable under maximum efficiency—under ideal operating conditions. Standard costing systems are adopted to improve planning and control and to facilitate product costing. By comparing actual outcomes with standards and breaking the variance into price and quantity components, detailed feedback is provided to managers. This information allows managers to exercise a greater degree of cost control than is typically found in a normal or actual costing system. Decisions such as bidding are also made easier when a standard costing system is in place.

The standard cost sheet provides the detail for the computation of the standard cost per unit. It shows the standard costs for direct materials, direct labor, variable overhead, and fixed overhead. It also reveals the quantity of each input that should be used to produce one unit of output. Using these unit quantity standards, the standard quantity of direct materials allowed and the standard hours allowed can be computed for the actual output. These computations play an important role in variance analysis.

REVIEW PROBLEM AND SOLUTION

MATERIALS, LABOR, AND OVERHEAD VARIANCES

Bertgon Manufacturing has the following standard cost sheet for one of its products:

Direct materials (6 ft. @ $5)	$30
Direct labor (1.5 hrs. @ $10)	15
Fixed overhead (1.5 hrs. @ $2*)	3
Variable overhead (1.5 hrs. @ $4*)	6
Standard unit cost	$54

*Rate based on expected activity of 17,000 hours.

During the most recent year, the following actual results were recorded:

Production	12,000 units
Fixed overhead	$33,000
Variable overhead	$69,000
Direct materials (71,750 ft. purchased)	$361,620
Direct labor (17,900 hrs.)	$182,580

Required:

Compute the following variances:
1. Direct materials price and usage variances.
2. Direct labor rate and efficiency variances.

3. Variable overhead spending and efficiency variances.
4. Fixed overhead spending and volume variances.

SOLUTION 1. Direct materials variances:

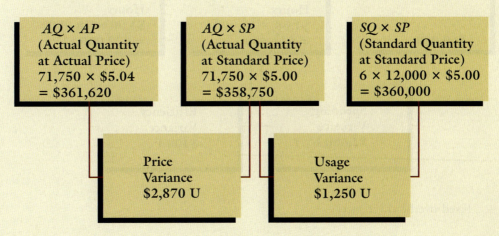

| $AQ \times AP$ (Actual Quantity at Actual Price) 71,750 × $5.04 = $361,620 | $AQ \times SP$ (Actual Quantity at Standard Price) 71,750 × $5.00 = $358,750 | $SQ \times SP$ (Standard Quantity at Standard Price) 6 × 12,000 × $5.00 = $360,000 |

| Price Variance $2,870 U | Usage Variance $1,250 U |

Or, using formulas:

$$MPV = (AP - SP)AQ$$
$$= (\$5.04 - \$5.00)71{,}750$$
$$= \$2{,}870 \text{ U}$$

$$MUV = (AQ - SQ)SP$$
$$= (71{,}750 - 72{,}000)\$5.00$$
$$= \$1{,}250 \text{ F}$$

2. Direct labor variances:

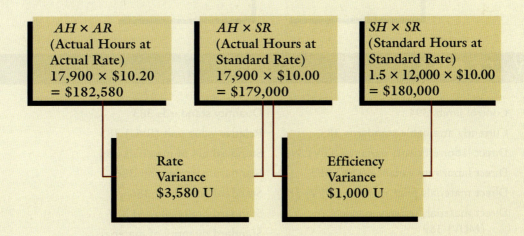

| $AH \times AR$ (Actual Hours at Actual Rate) 17,900 × $10.20 = $182,580 | $AH \times SR$ (Actual Hours at Standard Rate) 17,900 × $10.00 = $179,000 | $SH \times SR$ (Standard Hours at Standard Rate) 1.5 × 12,000 × $10.00 = $180,000 |

| Rate Variance $3,580 U | Efficiency Variance $1,000 U |

Or, using formulas:

$$LRV = (AR - SR)AH$$
$$= (\$10.20 - \$10.00)17{,}900$$
$$= \$3{,}580 \text{ U}$$

$$LEV = (AH - SH)SR$$
$$= (17{,}900 - 18{,}000)\$10.00$$
$$= \$1{,}000 \text{ F}$$

3. Variable overhead variances:

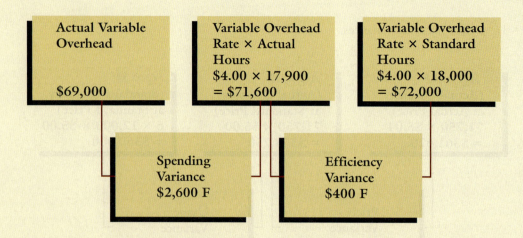

4. Fixed overhead variances:

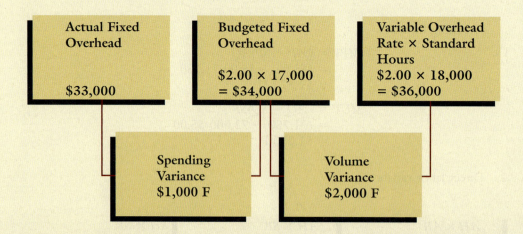

KEY TERMS

QUESTIONS FOR WRITING AND DISCUSSION

1. Discuss the difference between budgets and standard costs.
2. What is the quantity decision? The pricing decision?
3. Why is historical experience often a poor basis for establishing standards?
4. What are ideal standards? Currently attainable standards? Of the two, which is usually adopted? Why?
5. How does standard costing improve the control function?
6. The budget variance for variable production costs is broken down into quantity and price variances. Explain why the quantity variance is more useful for control purposes than the price variance.
7. Explain why the direct materials price variance is often computed at the point of purchase rather than at the point of issuance.
8. The direct materials usage variance is always the responsibility of the production supervisor. Do you agree or disagree? Why?
9. The direct labor rate variance is never controllable. Do you agree or disagree? Why?
10. Suggest some possible causes of an unfavorable direct labor efficiency variance.
11. Explain why the variable overhead spending variance is not a pure price variance.
12. What is the cause of an unfavorable volume variance? Does the volume variance convey any meaningful information to managers?
13. What are control limits, and how are they set?
14. Explain how the 2-, 3-, and 4-variance overhead analyses are related.
15. Explain what mix and yield variances are.

EXERCISES

9-1   SETTING STANDARDS, ETHICAL BEHAVIOR

LO1, LO2

Quincy Farms is a producer of items made from farm products that are distributed to supermarkets. For many years, Quincy's products have had strong regional sales on the basis of brand recognition. However, other companies have been marketing similar products in the area, and price competition has become increasingly important. Doug Gilbert, the company's controller, is planning to implement a standard costing system for Quincy and has gathered considerable information from his coworkers on production and direct materials requirements for Quincy's products. Doug believes that the use of standard costing will allow Quincy to improve cost control and make better operating decisions.

Quincy's most popular product is strawberry jam. The jam is produced in 10-gallon batches, and each batch requires six quarts of good strawberries. The fresh strawberries are sorted by hand before entering the production process. Because of imperfections in the strawberries and spoilage, one quart of strawberries is discarded for every four quarts of acceptable berries. Three minutes is the standard direct labor time required for sorting strawberries in order to obtain one quart of strawberries. The acceptable strawberries are then processed with the other ingredients: processing requires 12 minutes of direct labor time per batch. After processing, the jam is packaged in quart containers. Doug has gathered the following information from Joe Adams, Quincy's cost accountant, relative to processing the strawberry jam.

a. Quincy purchases strawberries at a cost of $0.80 per quart. All other ingredients cost a total of $0.45 per gallon.
b. Direct labor is paid at the rate of $9.00 per hour.

c. The total cost of direct material and direct labor required to package the jam is $0.38 per quart.

Joe has a friend who owns a strawberry farm that has been losing money in recent years. Because of good crops, there has been an oversupply of strawberries, and prices have dropped to $0.50 per quart. Joe has arranged for Quincy to purchase strawberries from his friend's farm in hopes that the $0.80 per quart will put his friend's farm in the black.

Required:

1. Discuss which coworkers Doug probably consulted to set standards. What factors should Doug consider in establishing the standards for direct materials and direct labor?
2. Develop the standard cost sheet for the prime costs of a 10-gallon batch of strawberry jam.
3. Citing the specific standards of the IMA code of ethics described in Chapter 1, explain why Joe's behavior regarding the cost information provided to Doug is unethical. *(CMA adapted)*

9-2   COMPUTATION OF INPUTS ALLOWED, DIRECT MATERIALS AND DIRECT LABOR

LO2   During the year, Vandy Company produced 300,000 drilling components for oil and gas rigs. Vandy's direct materials and direct labor standards are as follows:

Direct materials (6.25 lbs. @ $4)	$25.00
Direct labor (1.5 hrs. @ $13)	19.50

Required:

1. Compute the standard pounds of direct materials allowed for the production of 300,000 units.
2. Compute the standard direct labor hours allowed for the production of 300,000 units.

9-3   DIRECT MATERIALS AND DIRECT LABOR VARIANCES

LO3   Choco Company produces a popular candy bar called Megusta. The candy is produced in Cost Rica and exported to the United States. Recently, the company adopted the following standards for one 5-ounce bar of the candy:

Spreadsheet

Direct materials (5.5 oz. @ $0.06)	$0.33
Direct labor (0.05 hr. @ $2.00)	0.10
Standard prime cost	$0.43

During the first week of operation, the company experienced the following actual results:
a. Bars produced: 150,000.
b. Ounces of direct materials purchased: 855,000 ounces at $0.055.
c. There are no beginning or ending inventories of direct materials.
d. Direct labor: 7,800 hours at $2.25.

Required:

1. Compute price and usage variances for direct materials.
2. Compute the rate variance and the efficiency variance for direct labor.
3. Prepare the journal entries associated with direct materials and direct labor.

9-4 OVERHEAD VARIANCES, FOUR-VARIANCE ANALYSIS

LO4

Spreadsheet

Young, Inc., uses a standard costing system and develops its overhead rates from the current annual budget. The budget is based on an expected annual output of 220,000 units requiring 1,100,000 direct labor hours. (Practical capacity is 1,210,000 hours.) Annual budgeted overhead costs total $962,500, of which $412,500 is fixed overhead. A total of 228,800 units using 1,188,000 direct labor hours was produced during the year. Actual variable overhead costs for the year were $572,000, and actual fixed overhead costs were $440,000.

Required:

1. Compute the fixed overhead spending and volume variances. How would you interpret the spending variance? Discuss the possible interpretations of the volume variance. Which is most appropriate for this example?
2. Compute the variable overhead spending and efficiency variances. How is the variable overhead spending variance like the price variances of direct labor and direct materials? How is it different? How is the variable overhead efficiency variance related to the direct labor efficiency variance?

9-5 OVERHEAD VARIANCES, TWO- AND THREE-VARIANCE ANALYSES

LO4   Refer to the data in **Exercise 9-4**.

Required:

1. Compute overhead variances using a 2-variance analysis.
2. Compute overhead variances using a 3-variance analysis.
3. Illustrate how the 2- and 3-variance analyses are related to the 4-variance analysis.

9-6 DIRECT MATERIALS MIX AND YIELD VARIANCES

LO5   Verde Sabor produces a green enchilada sauce using tomatoes and green chili peppers. Verde developed the following standard cost sheet:

Direct Material	Mix	Mix Proportion	SP	Standard Cost
Tomatoes	630 ounces	0.90	$0.020	$12.60
Chili peppers	70	0.10	0.026	1.82
Total	700 ounces			$14.42
Yield	577.5 ounces			

On March 2, Verde produced a batch of 112,000 ounces with the following actual results:

Direct Material	Actual Mix
Tomatoes	89,600 ounces
Chili peppers	22,400
Total	112,000 ounces
Yield	88,900 ounces

Required:

1. Calculate the yield ratio.
2. Calculate the standard cost per unit of yield.
3. Calculate the direct materials yield variance.
4. Calculate the direct materials mix variance.

9-7   DIRECT MATERIALS VARIANCES, JOURNAL ENTRIES

LO3, LO5   Refer to **Exercise 9-6**. Verde Sabor purchased the amount used of each direct material input on March 2 for the following actual prices, tomatoes, $0.025 per ounce and chili peppers, $0.024 per ounce.

Required:

1. Compute and journalize the direct materials price variances.
2. Compute and journalize the direct materials usage variances.
3. Offer some possible reasons for why the variances occurred.

9-8   DIRECT LABOR MIX AND YIELD VARIANCES

LO5   Sanderson Company uses two types of direct labor for the manufacturing of its integrated electronic components: soldering and testing. Sanderson has developed the following standard mix for direct labor, where output is measured in number of circuit boards.

Direct Labor Type	Mix	SP	Standard Cost
Soldering	4 hrs.	$16	$64
Testing	1	11	11
Total	5 hrs.		$75
Yield	25 hours		

During the second week in April, Sanderson produced the following results:

Labor Type	Actual Mix
Soldering	30,000 hrs.
Testing	4,000
Total	34,000 hrs.
Yield	150,000 hours

Required:

1. Calculate the yield ratio.
2. Calculate the standard cost per unit of yield.
3. Calculate the direct labor yield variance.
4. Calculate the direct labor mix variance.

9-9   DIRECT LABOR AND DIRECT MATERIALS VARIANCES, JOURNAL ENTRIES

LO3   Molano Company produces ponchos. The company has established the following direct materials and direct labor standards for one poncho:

Wool (3 yds. @ $3)	$ 9.00
Labor (3.5 hrs. @ $5)	17.50
Total prime cost	$26.50

During the first quarter of the year, Molano produced 25,000 ponchos. The company purchased and used 78,200 yards of wool at $2.90 per yard. Actual direct labor used was 90,000 hours at $5.20 per hour.

Required:

1. Calculate the direct materials price and usage variances.
2. Calculate the direct labor rate and efficiency variances.
3. Prepare the journal entries for the direct materials and direct labor variances.
4. Describe how flexible budgeting variances relate to the direct materials and direct labor variances computed in Requirements 1 and 2.

9-10 INVESTIGATION OF VARIANCES

LO3 Franklin Company uses the following rule to determine whether direct labor efficiency variances ought to be investigated. A direct labor efficiency variance will be investigated anytime the amount exceeds the lesser of $16,000 or 10 percent of the standard labor cost. Reports for the past five weeks provided the following information:

Week	LEV	Standard Labor Cost
1	$14,000 F	$160,000
2	15,600 U	150,000
3	12,000 F	160,000
4	18,000 U	170,000
5	14,000 U	138,000

Required:

1. Using the rule provided, identify the cases that will be investigated.
2. Suppose that investigation reveals that the cause of an unfavorable direct labor efficiency variance is the use of lower-quality direct materials than are usually used. Who is responsible? What corrective action would likely be taken?
3. Suppose that investigation reveals that the cause of a significant favorable direct labor efficiency variance is attributable to a new approach to manufacturing that takes less labor time but causes more direct materials waste. Upon examining the direct materials usage variance, it is discovered to be unfavorable, and it is larger than the favorable direct labor efficiency variance. Who is responsible? What action should be taken? How would your answer change if the unfavorable variance were smaller than the favorable?

9-11 OVERHEAD VARIANCES, FOUR-VARIANCE ANALYSIS, JOURNAL ENTRIES

LO4 Jackman, Inc., uses a standard costing system. The predetermined overhead rates are calculated using practical capacity. Practical capacity for a year is defined as 1,000,000 units requiring 250,000 standard direct labor hours. Budgeted overhead for the year is $750,000, of which $300,000 is fixed overhead. During the year, 900,000 units were produced using 230,000 direct labor hours. Actual annual overhead costs totaled $800,000, of which $300,000 is fixed overhead.

Required:

1. Calculate the fixed overhead spending and volume variances. Explain the meaning of the volume variance to the manager of Jackman.
2. Calculate the variable overhead spending and efficiency variances. Is the spending variance the same as the direct materials price variance? If not, explain how it differs.
3. Prepare the journal entries that reflect the following:
   a. Assignment of overhead to production.
   b. Recognition of the incurrence of actual overhead.
   c. Recognition of overhead variances.
   d. Closing out overhead variances, assuming they are not material.

PROBLEMS

9-12   STANDARD COSTS, DECOMPOSITION OF BUDGET VARIANCES, DIRECT MATERIALS AND DIRECT LABOR

LO2, LO3   Vaquero Corporation produces cowboy boots. The company uses a standard costing system and has set the following standards for direct materials and direct labor (for one pair of boots):

Leather (6 strips @ $10)	$60
Direct labor (2 hrs. @ $12)	24
Total prime cost	$84

During the year, Vaquero produced 8,000 pairs of boots. The actual leather purchased was 49,600 strips at $9.98 per strip. There were no beginning or ending inventories of leather. Actual direct labor was 16,800 hours at $12.25 per hour.

Required:

1. Compute the costs of leather and direct labor that should have been incurred for the production of 8,000 pairs of boots.
2. Compute the total budget variances for direct materials and direct labor.
3. Break down the total budget variance for direct materials into a price variance and a usage variance. Prepare the journal entries associated with these variances.
4. Break down the total budget variance for direct labor into a rate variance and an efficiency variance. Prepare the journal entries associated with these variances.

9-13   OVERHEAD APPLICATION, OVERHEAD VARIANCES, JOURNAL ENTRIES

Spreadsheet

LO4   Iverson Company produces microwave ovens. Iverson's plant in Buffalo uses a standard costing system. The standard costing system relies on direct labor hours to assign overhead costs to production. The direct labor standard indicates that four direct labor hours should be used for every microwave unit produced. (The Buffalo plant produces only one model.) The normal production volume is 120,000 units. The budgeted overhead for the coming year is as follows:

Fixed overhead	$1,286,400
Variable overhead	888,000*

*At normal volume.

Iverson applies overhead on the basis of direct labor hours.

During the year, Iverson produced 119,000 units, worked 487,900 direct labor hours, and incurred actual fixed overhead costs of $1.3 million and actual variable overhead costs of $927,010.

Required:

1. Calculate the standard fixed overhead rate and the standard variable overhead rate.
2. Compute the applied fixed overhead and the applied variable overhead. What is the total fixed overhead variance? Total variable overhead variance?
3. Break down the total fixed overhead variance into a spending variance and a volume variance. Discuss the significance of each.
4. Compute the variable overhead spending and efficiency variances. Discuss the significance of each.
5. Now assume that Iverson's cost accounting system reveals only the total actual overhead. In this case, a 3-variance analysis can be performed. Using the relationships between a 3- and 4-variance analysis, indicate the values for the three overhead variances.
6. Prepare the journal entries that would be related to fixed and variable overhead during the year and at the end of the year. Assume variances are closed to Cost of Goods Sold.

9-14 DIRECT MATERIALS, DIRECT LABOR, AND OVERHEAD VARIANCES, JOURNAL ENTRIES

LO3, LO4   The Bartlesville plant of Harmon Company produces an industrial chemical. At the beginning of the year, the Bartlesville plant had the following standard cost sheet:

Direct materials (10 lbs. @ $1.60)	$16.00
Direct labor (0.75 hr. @ $18.00)	13.50
Fixed overhead (0.75 hr. @ $4.00)	3.00
Variable overhead (0.75 hr. @ $3.00)	2.25
Standard cost per unit	$34.75

The Bartlesville plant computes its overhead rates using practical volume, which is 72,000 units. The actual results for the year are as follows:

a. Units produced: 70,000.
b. Direct materials purchased: 744,000 pounds at $1.50 per pound.
c. Direct materials used: 736,000 pounds.
d. Direct labor: 56,000 hours at $17.90 per hour.
e. Fixed overhead: $214,000.
f. Variable overhead: $175,400.

Required:

1. Compute price and usage variances for direct materials.
2. Compute the direct labor rate and labor efficiency variances.
3. Compute the fixed overhead spending and volume variances. Interpret the volume variance.
4. Compute the variable overhead spending and efficiency variances.
5. Prepare journal entries for the following:
    a. The purchase of direct materials.
    b. The issuance of direct materials to production (Work in Process).
    c. The addition of direct labor to Work in Process.
    d. The addition of overhead to Work in Process.   *(continued)*

e. The incurrence of actual overhead costs.

f. Closing out of variances to Cost of Goods Sold.

9-15   SOLVING FOR UNKNOWNS

LO2, LO3, LO4   Misterio Company uses a standard costing system. During the past quarter, the following variances were computed:

Variable overhead efficiency variance	$ 24,000 U
Direct labor efficiency variance	120,000 U
Direct labor rate variance	10,400 U

Misterio applies variable overhead using a standard rate of $2 per direct labor hour allowed. Two direct labor hours are allowed per unit produced. (Only one type of product is manufactured.) During the quarter, Misterio used 30 percent more direct labor hours than should have been used.

Required:

1. What were the actual direct labor hours worked? The total hours allowed?
2. What is the standard hourly rate for direct labor? The actual hourly rate?
3. How many actual units were produced?

9-16   BASIC VARIANCE ANALYSIS, REVISION OF STANDARDS, JOURNAL ENTRIES

LO1, LO2, LO3, LO4   Nosemer Company produces engine parts for large motors. The company uses a standard cost system for production costing and control. The standard cost sheet for one of its higher volume products (a valve), is as follows:

Direct materials (5 lbs. @ $4.00)	$20.00
Direct labor (1.4 hrs. @ $10.50)	14.70
Variable overhead (1.4 hrs. @ $6.00)	8.40
Fixed overhead (1.4 hrs. @ $3.00)	4.20
Standard unit cost	$47.30

During the year, Nosemer experienced the following activity relative to the production of valves:

a. Production of valves totaled 25,000 units.

b. A total of 130,000 pounds of direct materials was purchased at $3.70 per pound.

c. There were 10,000 pounds of direct materials in beginning inventory (carried at $4 per pound). There was no ending inventory.

d. The company used 36,500 direct labor hours at a total cost of $392,375.

e. Actual fixed overhead totaled $95,000.

f. Actual variable overhead totaled $210,000.

Nosemer produces all of its valves in a single plant. Normal activity is 22,500 units per year. Standard overhead rates are computed based on normal activity measured in standard direct labor hours.

Required:

1. Compute the direct materials price and usage variances.
2. Compute the direct labor rate and efficiency variances.
3. Compute overhead variances using a 2-variance analysis.
4. Compute overhead variances using a 4-variance analysis.
5. Assume that the purchasing agent for the valve plant purchased a lower-quality direct material from a new supplier. Would you recommend that the company

continue to use this cheaper direct material? If so, what standards would likely need revision to reflect this decision? Assume that the end product's quality is not significantly affected.

6. Prepare all possible journal entries (assuming a 4-variance analysis of overhead variances).

9-17   UNIT COSTS, MULTIPLE PRODUCTS, VARIANCE ANALYSIS, JOURNAL ENTRIES

LO1, LO2, LO3, LO4   Business Specialty, Inc., manufactures two staplers: small and regular. The standard quantities of direct labor and direct materials per unit for the year are as follows:

	Small	Regular
Direct materials (oz.)	6.0	10.00
Direct labor (hrs.)	0.1	0.15

The standard price paid per pound of direct materials is $1.60. The standard rate for labor is $8.00. Overhead is applied on the basis of direct labor hours. A plantwide rate is used. Budgeted overhead for the year is as follows:

Budgeted fixed overhead	$360,000
Budgeted variable overhead	480,000

The company expects to work 12,000 direct labor hours during the year; standard overhead rates are computed using this activity level. For every small stapler produced, the company produces two regular staplers.

Actual operating data for the year are as follows:

a. Units produced: small staplers, 35,000; regular staplers, 70,000.
b. Direct materials purchased and used: 56,000 pounds at $1.55—13,000 for the small stapler and 43,000 for the regular stapler. There were no beginning or ending direct materials inventories.
c. Direct labor: 14,800 hours—3,600 hours for the small stapler; 11,200 hours for the regular stapler. Total cost of direct labor: $114,700.
d. Variable overhead: $607,500.
e. Fixed overhead: $350,000.

Required:

1. Prepare a standard cost sheet showing the unit cost for each product.
2. Compute the direct materials price and usage variances for each product. Prepare journal entries to record direct materials activity.
3. Compute the direct labor rate and efficiency variances. Prepare journal entries to record direct labor activity.
4. Compute the variances for fixed and variable overhead. Prepare journal entries to record overhead activity. All variances are closed to Cost of Goods Sold.
5. Assume that you know only the total direct materials used for both products and the total direct labor hours used for both products. Can you compute the total direct materials and direct labor usage variances? Explain.

9-18   DIRECT MATERIALS USAGE VARIANCE, DIRECT MATERIALS MIX AND YIELD VARIANCES

LO3, LO5   Limpio, Inc., produces a key ingredient for liquid laundry detergents. Two chemical solutions, Chem A and Chem B, are mixed and heated to produce a cleansing chemical that is sold to companies that produce liquid detergents. The cleansing ingredient is produced in batches and has the following standards:

Direct Material	Standard Mix	Standard Unit Price	Standard Cost
Chem A	15,000 gallons	$2.00 per gallon	$30,000
Chem B	5,000	3.00	15,000
Total	20,000 gallons		$45,000
Yield	15,000 gallons		

During March, the following actual production information was provided:

Direct Material	Actual Mix
Chem A	140,000 gallons
Chem B	60,000
Total	200,000 gallons
Yield	158,400 gallons

Required:

1. Compute the direct materials mix and yield variances.
2. Compute the total direct materials usage variance for Chem A and Chem B. Show that the total direct materials usage variance is equal to the sum of the direct materials mix and yield variances.

9-19   DIRECT LABOR EFFICIENCY VARIANCE, DIRECT LABOR MIX AND YIELD VARIANCES

LO3, LO5   Refer to the data in **Problem 9-18**. Limpio, Inc., also uses two different types of direct labor in producing the cleansing chemical: mixing and drum-filling labor (the completed product is placed into 50-gallon drums). For each batch of 20,000 gallons of direct materials input, the following standards have been developed for direct labor:

Direct Labor Type	Mix	SP	Standard Cost
Mixing	2,000 hrs.	$11.00	$22,000
Drum-filling	1,000	8.00	8,000
Total	3,000 hrs.		$30,000
Yield	15,000 gallons		

The actual direct labor hours used for the output produced in March are also provided:

Labor Type	Mix
Mixing	18,000 hrs.
Drum-filling	12,000
Total	30,000 hrs.
Yield	158,400 gallons

Required:

1. Compute the direct labor mix and yield variances.
2. Compute the total direct labor efficiency variance. Show that the total direct labor efficiency variance is equal to the sum of the direct labor mix and yield variances.

9-20 DIRECT MATERIALS USAGE VARIANCES, DIRECT MATERIALS MIX AND YIELD VARIANCES

LO3, LO5

CMA

Energy Products Company produces a gasoline additive, Gas Gain. This product increases engine efficiency and improves gasoline mileage by creating a more complete burn in the combustion process.

Careful controls are required during the production process to ensure that the proper mix of input chemicals is achieved and that evaporation is controlled. If the controls are not effective, there can be a loss of output and efficiency.

The standard cost of producing a 500-liter batch of Gas Gain is $135. The standard direct materials mix and related standard cost of each chemical used in a 500-liter batch are as follows:

Chemical	Mix	SP	Standard Cost
Echol	200 liters	$0.200	$ 40.00
Protex	100	0.425	42.50
Benz	250	0.150	37.50
CT-40	50	0.300	15.00
Total	600 liters		$135.00

The quantities of chemicals purchased and used during the current production period are shown in the following schedule. A total of 140 batches of Gas Gain were manufactured during the current production period. Energy Products determines its cost and chemical usage variations at the end of each production period.

Chemical	Quantity Used
Echol	26,600 liters
Protex	12,880
Benz	37,800
CT-40	7,140
Total	84,420 liters

Required:

Compute the total direct materials usage variance, and then break down this variance into its mix and yield components. *(CMA adapted)*

9-21 SOLVING FOR UNKNOWNS, OVERHEAD ANALYSIS

LO3, LO4

Nuevo Company produces a single product. Nuevo employs a standard cost system and uses a flexible budget to predict overhead costs at various levels of activity. For the most recent year, Nuevo used a standard overhead rate equal to $6.25 per direct labor hour. The rate was computed using expected activity. Budgeted overhead costs are $80,000 for 10,000 direct labor hours and $120,000 for 20,000 direct labor hours. During the past year, Nuevo generated the following data:

a. Actual production: 4,000 units.
b. Fixed overhead volume variance: $1,750 U.

c. Variable overhead efficiency variance: $3,200 F.
d. Actual fixed overhead costs: $41,335.
e. Actual variable overhead costs: $70,000.

Required:

1. Determine the fixed overhead spending variance.
2. Determine the variable overhead spending variance.
3. Determine the standard hours allowed per unit of product.
4. Assuming the standard labor rate is $9.50 per hour, compute the direct labor efficiency variance.

9-22   FLEXIBLE BUDGET, STANDARD COST VARIANCES, T-ACCOUNTS

LO1, LO3, LO4   Correr Company manufactures a line of running shoes. At the beginning of the period, the following plans for production and costs were revealed:

Units to be produced and sold	25,000
Standard cost per unit:	
Direct materials	$10
Direct labor	8
Variable overhead	4
Fixed overhead	3
Total unit cost	$25

During the year, 30,000 units were produced and sold. The following actual costs were incurred:

Direct materials	$320,000
Direct labor	220,000
Variable overhead	125,000
Fixed overhead	89,000

There were no beginning or ending inventories of direct materials. The direct materials price variance was $5,000 unfavorable. In producing the 30,000 units, a total of 39,000 hours were worked, 4 percent more hours than the standard allowed for the actual output. Overhead costs are applied to production using direct labor hours.

Required:

1. Prepare a performance report comparing expected costs to actual costs.
2. Determine the following:
   a. Direct materials usage variance.
   b. Direct labor rate variance.
   c. Direct labor usage variance.
   d. Fixed overhead spending and volume variances.
   e. Variable overhead spending and efficiency variances.
3. Use T-accounts to show the flow of costs through the system. In showing the flow, you do not need to show detailed overhead variances. Show only the over- and underapplied variances for fixed and variable overhead.

9-23   STANDARD COSTING: PLANNED VARIANCES

LO2, LO3   As part of its cost control program, Tracer Company uses a standard costing system for all manufactured items. The standard cost for each item is established at the be-

CMA ginning of the fiscal year, and the standards are not revised until the beginning of the next fiscal year. Changes in costs, caused during the year by changes in direct materials or direct labor inputs or by changes in the manufacturing process, are recognized as they occur by the inclusion of planned variances in Tracer's monthly operating budgets.

The following direct labor standard was established for one of Tracer's products, effective June 1, 2007, the beginning of the fiscal year:

Assembler A labor (5 hrs. @ $10)	$ 50
Assembler B labor (3 hrs. @ $11)	33
Machinist labor (2 hrs. @ $15)	30
Standard cost per 100 units	$113

The standard was based on the direct labor being performed by a team consisting of five persons with Assembler A skills, three persons with Assembler B skills, and two persons with machinist skills; this team represents the most efficient use of the company's skilled employees. The standard also assumed that the quality of direct materials that had been used in prior years would be available for the coming year.

For the first seven months of the fiscal year, actual manufacturing costs at Tracer have been within the standards established. However, the company has received a significant increase in orders, and there is an insufficient number of skilled workers to meet the increased production. Therefore, beginning in January, the production teams will consist of eight persons with Assembler A skills, one person with Assembler B skills, and one person with machinist skills. The reorganized teams will work more slowly than the normal teams, and as a result, only 80 units will be produced in the same time period in which 100 units would normally be produced. Faulty work has never been a cause for units to be rejected in the final inspection process, and it is not expected to be a cause for rejection with the reorganized teams.

Furthermore, Tracer has been notified by its direct materials supplier that lower-quality direct materials will be supplied beginning January 1. Normally, one unit of direct materials is required for each good unit produced, and no units are lost due to defective direct materials. Tracer estimates that 6 percent of the units manufactured after January 1 will be rejected in the final inspection process due to defective direct materials.

Required:

1. Determine the number of units of lower-quality direct materials that Tracer Company must enter into production in order to produce 47,000 good finished units.
2. How many hours of each class of direct labor must be used to manufacture 47,000 good finished units?
3. Determine the amount that should be included in Tracer's January operating budget for the planned direct labor variance caused by the reorganization of the direct labor teams and the lower-quality direct materials. (*CMA adapted*)

9-24 VARIANCE ANALYSIS IN A PROCESS-COSTING SETTING (CHAPTER 6 REQUIRED), SERVICE FIRM

LO2, LO3   Aspen Medical Laboratory performs comprehensive blood tests for physicians and clinics throughout the Southwest. Aspen uses a standard process-costing system for its comprehensive blood work. Skilled technicians perform the blood tests. Because Aspen uses a standard costing system, equivalent units are calculated using the FIFO method. The standard cost sheet for the blood test follows (these standards were used throughout the calendar year):

Direct materials (4 oz. @ $4.50)	$18
Direct labor (2 hrs. @ $18.00)	36
Variable overhead (2 hrs. @ $5.00)	10
Fixed overhead (2 hrs. @ $10.00)	20
Standard cost per test	$84

For the month of November, Aspen reported the following actual results:

a. Beginning work in process: 1,250 tests, 60 percent complete.
b. Tests started: 25,000.
c. Ending work in process: 2,500 tests, 40 percent complete.
d. Direct labor: 47,000 hours at $19 per hour.
e. Direct materials purchased and used: 102,000 at $4.25 per ounce.
f. Variable overhead: $144,000.
g. Fixed overhead: $300,000.
h. Direct materials are added at the beginning of the process.

Required:

1. Explain why the FIFO method is used for process costing when a standard costing system has been adopted.
2. Calculate the cost of goods transferred out (tests completed and transferred out) for the month of November. Does standard costing simplify process costing? Explain.
3. Calculate price and quantity variances for direct materials and direct labor.

9-25   SETTING STANDARDS, CALCULATING AND USING VARIANCES

LO1, LO3

CMA

Leather Works is a family-owned maker of leather travel bags and briefcases located in the northeastern part of the United States. Foreign competition has forced its owner, Heather Gray, to explore new ways to meet the competition. One of her cousins, Walace Hayes, who recently graduated from college with a major in accounting, told her about the use of cost variance analysis to learn about efficiencies of production.

In May 2006, Heather asked Matt Jones, chief accountant, and Alfred Prudest, production manager, to implement a standard costing system. Matt and Alfred, in turn, retained Shannon Leikam, an accounting professor at Harding's College, to set up a standard costing system by using information supplied to her by Matt's and Alfred's staff. To verify that the information was accurate, Shannon visited the plant and measured workers' output using time and motion studies. During those visits, she was not accompanied by either Matt or Alfred, and the workers knew about Shannon's schedule in advance. The cost system was implemented in June 2006.

Recently, the following dialogue took place among Heather, Matt, and Alfred:

HEATHER: How is the business performing?

ALFRED: You know, we are producing a lot more than we used to, thanks to the contract that you helped obtain from Lean, Inc., for laptop covers. (Lean is a national supplier of computer accessories.)

MATT: Thank goodness for that new product. It has kept us from sinking even more due to the inroads into our business made by those foreign suppliers of leather goods.

HEATHER: What about the standard costing system?

MATT: The variances are mostly favorable, except for the first few months when the supplier of leather started charging more.

HEATHER: How did the union members take to the standards?

ALFRED: Not bad. They grumbled a bit at first, but they have taken it in stride. We've consistently shown favorable direct labor efficiency variances and direct materials usage variances. The direct labor rate variance has been flat.

MATT: It should be since direct labor rates are negotiated by the union representative at the start of the year and remain the same for the entire year.

HEATHER: Matt, would you send me the variance report for laptop covers immediately?

The following chart summarizes the direct materials and direct labor variances from November 2006 through April 2007 (extracted form the report provided by Matt) Standards for each laptop cover are as follows:
a. Three feet of direct materials at $7.50 per foot.
b. Forty-five minutes of direct labor at $14 per hour.

Month	Actual Cost (Direct Materials + Direct Labor)	Direct Materials Price Variance	Direct Materials Efficiency Variance	Direct Labor Rate Variance	Direct Labor Efficiency Variance
November	$150,000	$10,000 U	$5,000 F	$100 U	$5,000 F
December	155,000	11,000 U	5,200 F	110 U	6,500 F
January	152,000	10,100 U	4,900 F	105 U	7,750 F
February	151,000	9,900 U	4,500 F	95 U	6,950 F
March	125,000	9,000 U	3,000 F	90 U	8,200 F
April	115,000	8,000 U	2,000 F	90 U	8,500 F

In addition, the data for May 2007, but not the variances for the month, are as follows:

Laptop covers made in May	2,900 units
Total actual direct materials costs incurred	$68,850
Actual quantity of direct materials purchased and used	8,500 feet
Total actual direct labor cost incurred	$25,910
Total actual direct labor hours	1,837.6 hours

Actual direct labor cost per hour exceeded the budgeted rate by $0.10 per hour.

Required:

1. For May 2007, calculate the price and quantity variances for direct labor and direct materials.
2. Discuss the trend of the direct materials and labor variances.
3. What type of actions must the workers have taken during the period they were being observed for the setting of standards?
4. What can be done to ensure that the standards are set correctly? *(CMA adapted)*

9-26   COLLABORATIVE LEARNING EXERCISE: STRUCTURED PROBLEM SOLVING; THREE STAY, ONE STRAY: ESTABLISHMENT OF STANDARDS, VARIANCE ANALYSIS

LO1, LO2, LO3   Tasty Apple, an apple chip manufacturer, was established in 1972 by Katherine English. In 2002, Katherine English died, and her son, Mark, took control of the business. By 2007, the company was facing stiff competition from national snack-food companies. Mark was advised that the company's plants needed to gain better control over production costs. To achieve this objective, he hired a consultant to install a standard costing system. To help the consultant in establishing the necessary standards, Mark sent her the following memo:

MEMO

To: Darlene Swasey, CMA

From: Mark English, President, Tasty Apple

Subject: Description and Data Relating to the Production of Our Cinnamon Apple Chips

Date: November 28, 2007

The manufacturing process for our chips begins when the apples are placed into a large vat in which they are automatically washed. After washing, the apples flow directly to equipment that automatically peels and removes the apple's core. The peeled and decored apples then pass by inspectors who manually cut out deep bruises or other blemishes. After inspection, the apples are automatically sliced and dropped into the cooking oil. The frying process is closely monitored by an employee. After they are cooked, the chips pass by more inspectors, who sort out the unacceptable finished chips (those that are discolored or too small). The chips then continue on the conveyor belt to a bagging machine that bags them in 1-pound bags. The bags are then placed in a box and shipped. Each box holds 16 bags.

The raw apple pieces (bruised and blemished), peelings, and rejected finished chips are sold to animal feed producers for $0.08 per pound. The cores are sold to a juice producer for $0.16 per pound. The company uses this revenue to reduce the cost of apples; we would like this fact reflected in the price standard relating to apples.

Tasty Apple purchases high-quality apples at a cost of $0.256 per pound. Each apple averages 4.25 ounces. Under efficient operating conditions, it takes four apples to produce one 16-ounce bag of chips. Although we label bags as containing 16 ounces, we actually place 16.2 ounces in each bag. We plan to continue this policy to ensure customer satisfaction. In addition to apples, other raw materials are the cooking oil, cinnamon, bags, and boxes. Cooking oil costs $0.04 per ounce, and we use 3.3 ounces of oil per bag of chips. The cost of cinnamon is so small that we add it to overhead. Bags cost $0.12 each and boxes $0.62.

Our plant produces 9.2 million bags of chips per year. A recent engineering study revealed that we would need the following direct labor hours to produce this quantity if our plant operates at peak efficiency:

Raw apple inspection	3,150
Finished chip inspection	12,000
Frying monitor	6,300
Machine operators	6,300
Boxing	16,250

I'm not sure that we can achieve the level of efficiency advocated by the study. In my opinion, the plant is operating efficiently for the level of output indicated if the hours allowed are about 10 percent higher.

The hourly labor rates agreed upon with the union are as follows:

Raw apple inspectors	$17.68
Finished chip inspectors	13.00
Frying monitor	16.00
Boxing	13.68
Machine operators	15.00

Overhead is applied on the basis of direct labor dollars. We have found that variable overhead averages about 112 percent of our direct labor cost. Our fixed overhead is budgeted at $2,419,026 for the coming year.

Required:

Form groups of three or four students. Each group should complete the following requirements. One member from each group will rotate to another group. The rotating member has the responsibility of comparing and contrasting the solution of his or her group with that of the group being visited.

1. Discuss the benefits of a standard costing system for Tasty Apple.
2. Discuss the president's concern about using the result of the engineering study to set the labor standards. What standard would you recommend?
3. Develop a standard cost sheet for Tasty Apple's cinnamon apple chips.
4. Suppose that the level of production was 9.2 million bags of apple chips for the year as planned. Assuming that 9.8 million pounds of apples were used, compute the direct materials usage variance for apples.

9-27   CYBER RESEARCH CASE

SETTING AND USING STANDARDS IN A SERVICE SETTING

LO1, LO3   Standard costing concepts can also be applied to services. Standard service costs are similar in concept to standard product costs. In the medical field, costs of caring for a patient have been increasing at a high rate for many years. Hospitals, for example, have often been paid on a retrospective basis. Essentially, they have been able to recover (from Medicare or their insurers) most of what they spent in treating a patient. Hospitals have thus had very little incentive to control costs. Some argue that retrospective payments encourage hospitals to acquire new and expensive technology and to offer more and more complex procedures. Prospective payments have emerged as an alternative to retrospective payments. Recently a new type of prospective payment has emerged known as "per-case payment."

Required:

Conduct an Internet search on per-case payments, and answer the following questions:
1. What is per-case payment?
2. Explain the following: "Per-case payment can become a viable payment scheme only if the hospital's case mix can be properly measured."
3. Discuss the merits of using diagnostic related groups (DRGs) to measure case mix.
4. Patient management categories (PMCs) have been suggested as an alternative approach to measuring case mix. Define PMCs, and discuss their merits.
5. Describe how the per-case payment approaches are forms of standard costing discussed in this chapter.

CHAPTER

10

Decentralization: Responsibility Accounting, Performance Evaluation, and Transfer Pricing

AFTER STUDYING THIS CHAPTER, YOU SHOULD BE ABLE TO:

1. Define responsibility accounting, and describe the four types of responsibility centers.

2. Explain why firms choose to decentralize.

3. Compute and explain return on investment (ROI), residual income (RI), and economic value added (EVA).

4. Discuss methods of evaluating and rewarding managerial performance.

5. Explain the role of transfer pricing in a decentralized firm.

6. Discuss the methods of setting transfer prices.

. . . .

As a firm grows, duties are divided, and spheres of responsibility are created that eventually become centers of responsibility. Closely allied to the subject of responsibility is decision-making authority. Most companies tend to be decentralized in decision-making authority. Issues related to decentralization include performance evaluation, management compensation, and transfer pricing.

Responsibility Accounting

OBJECTIVE *1*

Define responsibility accounting, and describe the four types of responsibility centers.

In general, a company is organized along the lines of responsibility. The traditional organizational chart, with its pyramid shape, illustrates the lines of responsibility flowing from the CEO through the vice presidents to middle- and lower-level managers. As organizations increase in size, these lines of responsibility become longer and more numerous. A strong link exists between the structure of an organization and its responsibility accounting system. Ideally, the responsibility accounting system mirrors and supports the structure of an organization.

Types of Responsibility Centers

As the firm grows, top management typically creates areas of responsibility, which are known as responsibility centers, and assigns subordinate managers to those areas. A **responsibility center** is a segment of the business whose manager is accountable for specified sets of activities. **Responsibility accounting** is a system that measures the results of each responsibility center and compares those results with some measure of expected or budgeted outcome. The four major types of responsibility centers are as follows:

1. **Cost center**: A responsibility center in which a manager is responsible only for costs.
2. **Revenue center**: A responsibility center in which a manager is responsible only for revenues.
3. **Profit center**: A responsibility center in which a manager is responsible for both revenues and costs.
4. **Investment center**: A responsibility center in which a manager is responsible for revenues, costs, and investments.

A production department within the factory, such as assembly or finishing, is an example of a cost center. The supervisor of a production department does not set price or make marketing decisions, but he or she can control manufacturing costs. Therefore, the production department supervisor is evaluated on the basis of how well costs are controlled.

The marketing department manager sets price and projected sales. Therefore, the marketing department may be evaluated as a revenue center. Direct costs of the marketing department and overall sales are the responsibility of the sales manager.

In some companies, plant managers are given the responsibility to price and market products they manufacture. These plant managers control both costs and revenues, putting them in control of a profit center. Operating income would be an important performance measure for profit center managers.

Finally, divisions are often cited as examples of investment centers. In addition to having control over cost and pricing decisions, divisional managers have the power to make investment decisions, such as plant closings and openings, and decisions to keep or drop a product line. As a result, both operating income and some type of return on investment are important performance measures for investment center managers.

It is important to realize that while the responsibility center manager has responsibility for only the activities of that center, decisions made by that manager can affect other responsibility centers. For example, the sales force at a floor care products firm routinely offers customers price discounts at the end of the month. Sales increase dramatically, and the factory is forced to institute overtime shifts to keep up with demand.

The Role of Information and Accountability

Information is the key to appropriately holding managers responsible for outcomes. For example, a production department manager is held responsible for departmental costs but not for sales. This is because the production department manager not only controls some of these costs but also is best informed regarding them. Any deviation between actual and expected costs can best be explained at this level. Sales are the responsibility of the sales manager, again because this manager can best explain what is happening regarding price and quantity sold.

The management accountant has an expanded role in the development of a responsibility accounting system in the global business environment. Business looks to the accountant for financial and business expertise. The accountant's job is not cut and dried. Knowledge, creativity, and flexibility are needed to help managers make decisions. Good training, education, and staying up to date with one's field are important to any accountant. However, the job of the accountant in the international firm is made more challenging by the ambiguous and ever-changing nature of global business. Since much of the accountant's job is to provide relevant information to management, staying up to date requires reading books and articles in a variety of business areas, including information systems, marketing, management, politics, and economics. In addition, the accountant must be familiar with the financial accounting rules of the countries in which the firm operates.

An example of the modern accountant is Nick, one of the authors' students who graduated from Oklahoma State University in the 1990s. Nick spent three years with a Big-6 (at the time) firm in Tulsa. He was drawn by opportunities in the international arena and joined *PricewaterhouseCoopers'* office in Vladivostok. Nick's focus in Russia was on business development and consulting. In essence, he was a management accountant working for a public accounting firm. Major hurdles Nick faced include language (he had to get up to speed on Russian quickly), legal differences (often, bodyguards armed with uzis accompanied him on trips to client firms), tax differences (Russia's ever-changing, and frequently retroactive, tax laws drove a number of foreign firms out of the country), and cultural differences.

Responsibility also entails accountability. Accountability implies performance measurement, which means that actual outcomes are compared with expected or budgeted outcomes. This system of responsibility, accountability, and performance evaluation is often referred to as *responsibility accounting* because of the key role that accounting measures and reports play in the process.

Decentralization

OBJECTIVE 2

Explain why firms choose to decentralize.

Firms with multiple responsibility centers usually choose one of two approaches to manage their diverse and complex activities: centralized decision making or decentralized decision making. In **centralized decision making**, decisions are made at the very top level, and lower-level managers are charged with implementing these decisions. On the other hand, **decentralized decision making** allows managers at lower levels to make and implement key decisions pertaining to their areas of responsibility. **Decentralization** is the practice of delegating or decentralizing decision-making authority to the lower levels.

Organizations range from highly centralized to strongly decentralized. Although some firms lie at either end of the continuum, most fall somewhere between the two extremes, with the majority of these tending toward a decentralized approach. A special case of the decentralized firm is the **multinational corporation (MNC)**. The MNC is a corporation that "does business in more than one country in such a volume that its well-being and growth rest in more than one country."[1]

Reasons for Decentralization

Seven reasons why firms may prefer the decentralized approach to management include better access to local information, cognitive limitations, more timely response, focusing

---

1. Yair Aharoni, "On the Definition of a Multinational Corporation," in A. Kapoor and Phillip D. Grub, eds., *The Multinational Enterprise in Transition* (Princeton, NJ: Darwin Press, 1972), 4.

of central management, training and evaluation of segment managers, motivation of segment managers, and enhanced competition. These reasons for delegating decision-making authority to lower levels of management are discussed in more detail in the following sections.

Better Access to Local Information

The quality of decisions is affected by the quality of information available. Lower-level managers who are in contact with immediate operating conditions (e.g., the strength and nature of local competition, the nature of the local labor force, and so on) have better access to local information. As a result, local managers are often in a position to make better decisions. This advantage of decentralization is particularly applicable to multinational corporations, where far-flung divisions may be operating in a number of different countries, subject to various legal systems and customs. This is particularly true in MNCs, where far-flung divisions may be operating in a number of different countries, subject to various legal systems and customs. As a result, local managers arc often in a position to make better decisions. Decentralization allows an organization to take advantage of this specialized knowledge. For example, **Loctite Corporation** has local managers run their own divisions. In particular, marketing and pricing are under local administration. Language is not a problem as local managers are in control. Similarly, local managers are conversant with their own laws and customs.

Cognitive Limitations

Even if local information somehow were made available to central management, those managers would face another problem. In a large, complex organization that operates in diverse markets with hundreds or thousands of different products, no one person has all of the expertise and training needed to process and use the information. Cognitive limitations means that individuals with specialized skills would still be needed. Rather than having different individuals at headquarters for every specialized area, why not let these individuals have direct responsibility in the field? In this way, the firm can avoid the cost and bother of collecting and transmitting local information to headquarters. The structure of American business is changing. No longer are middle managers individuals with "people skills" and organization skills only. They must have specific fields of expertise in addition to managerial talent. For example, a middle manager in a bank may refer to herself as a financial specialist even though she manages 20 people. The capability to add skilled expertise is seen as crucial in today's downsized environment.

More Timely Response

In a centralized setting, time is needed to transmit the local information to headquarters and to transmit the decision back to the local unit. These two transmissions cause delay and increase the potential for miscommunication, decreasing the effectiveness of the response. In a decentralized organization, where the local manager both makes and implements the decision, this problem does not arise.

Local managers in the MNC are capable of a more timely response in decision making. They are able to respond quickly to customer discount demands, local government demands, and changes in the political climate. The different languages native to managers of divisions in the MNC make miscommunication an even greater problem. MNCs address this problem in two ways. First, a decentralized structure pushes decision making down to the local manager level, eliminating the need to interpret instructions from above. Second, MNCs are learning to incorporate technology that overrides the language barrier and eases cross-border data transfer. Technology is of great help in smoothing communication difficulties between parent and subsidiary and between one subsidiary and another. Loctite's plant in Ireland uses computerized labeling on adhesives bound for Britain or Israel. Bar code technology "reads" the labels, eliminating the need for foreign language translation.

Focusing of Central Management

The nature of the hierarchical pyramid is that higher-level managers have broader responsibilities and powers. By decentralizing the operating decisions, central management is free to focus on strategic planning and decision making. The long-run survival of the organization should be of more importance to central management than day-to-day operations.

Training and Evaluation of Segment Managers

An organization always has a need for well-trained managers to replace higher-level managers who retire or move to take advantage of other opportunities. By decentralizing, lower-level managers are given the opportunity to make decisions as well as to implement them. What better way to prepare a future generation of higher-level managers than by providing them the opportunity to make significant decisions? These opportunities also enable top managers to evaluate the local manager's capabilities. Those who make the best decisions are the ones who can be selected for promotion to central management.

Just as decentralization gives the lower-level managers in the home country a chance to develop managerial skills, foreign subsidiary managers also gain valuable experience. Just as important, home country managers gain broader experience by interacting with managers of foreign divisions. The chance for learning from each other is much greater in a decentralized MNC. Off and on throughout the latter half of the twentieth century, a tour of duty at a foreign subsidiary has been a part of the manager's climb to the top. Now, foreign subsidiary managers may expect to spend some time at headquarters in the home office, as well. At **GE**, for example, senior executives are sent on 4-week tours of foreign markets and return to brief top management. Other senior executives are posted to Asian and Indian divisions. Similarly, foreign executives receive GE management training.

Motivation of Segment Managers

By giving local managers freedom to make decisions, some of their higher-level needs (self-esteem and self-actualization) are being met. Greater responsibility can produce more job satisfaction and motivate the local manager to exert greater effort. More initiative and more creativity can be expected. Of course, the extent to which the motivational benefits can be realized depends to a large degree on how managers are evaluated and rewarded for their performance.

Enhanced Competition

In a highly centralized company, large overall profit margins can mask inefficiencies within the various subdivisions. A decentralized approach allows the company to determine each division's contribution to profit and to expose each division to market forces.

The Units of Decentralization

Decentralization is usually achieved by segmenting the company into *divisions*. One way in which divisions are differentiated is by the types of goods or services produced. For example, **Armstrong World Industries, Inc.**, has four product divisions: floor coverings (resilient sheet and tile); building products (acoustical ceilings and wall panels); industry products (insulation for heating, cooling, plumbing, and refrigeration systems); and ceramic tile. **PepsiCo** divisions include the Snack Ventures Europe division (a joint venture with **General Mills**), **Frito-Lay, Inc.**, **Tropicana**, and **Tricon Global Restaurants**, as well as its flagship soft drink division. Some divisions depend on other divisions. At Tricon's **Pizza Hut** and **KFC**, for example, the cola you purchase will be Pepsi—not Coke. In a decentralized setting, some interdependencies usually exist; otherwise, a company would merely be a collection of totally separate entities. The presence of these interdependencies creates the need for transfer pricing, which is discussed later in this chapter.

In a similar vein, companies create divisions according to the type of customer served. **Wal-Mart** has four divisions. The Wal-Mart stores division targets discount store customers. **Sam's Club** focuses on buyers for small business. **McLane Company** is a distribution and food manufacturing operation that supplies convenience stores. Finally, the international division concentrates on global opportunities.

Organizing divisions as responsibility centers not only differentiates them on the degree of decentralization but also creates the opportunity for control of the divisions through the use of responsibility accounting. Control of cost centers is achieved by evaluating the efficiency and the effectiveness of divisional managers. **Efficiency** means how well activities are performed. Efficiency might be measured by the number of units produced per hour or by the cost of those units. **Effectiveness**, in this case, can be defined as whether the manager has performed the right activities. Measures of effectiveness might focus on value-added versus non-value-added activities.

Performance reports are the typical instruments used in evaluating efficiency and effectiveness. Profit centers are evaluated by assessing the unit's profit contribution, measured on income statements. Since performance reports and contribution income statements have been discussed previously, this chapter will focus on the evaluation of managers of investment centers.

OBJECTIVE 3

Compute and explain return on investment (ROI), residual income (RI), and economic value added (EVA).

Measuring the Performance of Investment Centers

When companies decentralize decision making, they maintain control by organizing responsibility centers, developing performance measures for each, and basing rewards on an individual's performance at controlling the responsibility center.

Performance measures are developed to provide some direction for managers of decentralized units and to evaluate their performance. The development of performance measures and the specification of a reward structure are major issues for a decentralized organization. Because performance measures can affect the behavior of managers, the measures chosen should encourage a high degree of goal congruence. In other words, they should influence managers to pursue the company's objectives. Three performance evaluation measures for investment centers are return on investment, residual income, and economic value added.

Return on Investment

Because each division of a company has an income statement, couldn't we simply rank the divisions on the basis of net income? Unfortunately, the use of income statements may provide misleading information regarding segment performance. For example, suppose that two divisions report profits of $100,000 and $200,000, respectively. Can we say that the second division is performing better than the first? What if the first division used an investment of $500,000 to produce the contribution of $100,000, while the second used an investment of $2 million to produce the $200,000 contribution? Does your response change? Clearly, relating the reported operating profits to the assets used to produce them is a more meaningful measure of performance.

One way to relate operating profits to assets employed is to compute the profit earned per dollar of investment. For example, the first division earned $0.20 per dollar invested ($100,000/$500,000); the second division earned only $0.10 per dollar invested ($200,000/$2,000,000). In percentage terms, the first division is providing a 20 percent rate of return and the second division, 10 percent. This method of computing the relative profitability of investments is known as the return on investment.

Return on investment (ROI) is the most common measure of performance for an investment center. It is of value both externally and internally. Externally, ROI is used by stockholders as an indicator of the health of a company. Internally, ROI is used to measure the relative performance of divisions.

ROI can be defined in the following three ways:

$$\text{ROI} = \text{Operating income/Average operating assets}$$
$$= (\text{Operating income/Sales}) \times (\text{Sales/Average operating assets})$$
$$= \text{Operating income margin} \times \text{Operating asset turnover}$$

Of course, **operating income** refers to earnings before interest and income taxes. Operating income is typically used for divisions, and net income is used in the calculation of ROI for the company as a whole. **Operating assets** are all assets acquired to generate operating income. They usually include cash, receivables, inventories, land, buildings, and equipment. The figure for average operating assets is computed as follows:

$$\text{Average operating assets} = (\text{Beginning net book value} + \text{Ending net book value})/2$$

Opinions vary regarding how long-term assets (plant and equipment) should be valued (e.g., gross book value versus net book value or historical cost versus current cost). Most firms use historical cost net book value.[2]

Margin and Turnover

The initial ROI formula is decomposed into two component ratios: *margin* and *turnover*. **Margin** is the ratio of operating income to sales. It expresses the portion of sales that is available for interest, income taxes, and profit. **Turnover** is a different measure; it is found by dividing sales by average operating assets. The result shows how productively assets are being used to generate sales.

Both measures can affect ROI. For example, **C&C Group** has three divisions; Alcohol, International Spirit & Liqueurs, and Soft Drinks and Snacks. C&C Group expected 2004 group turnover to have increased by approximately 4 percent in the period, while margins, on a constant currency basis, were broadly unchanged.[3] As a result, ROI was expected to increase. The company further noted that this represented reasonably good performance in light of the impact of the ban on smoking in the workplace and mixed summer weather.

Let's examine the relationship of margin, turnover, and ROI more closely by considering the data presented in Exhibit 10-1. The Snack Foods Division improved its ROI from 18 percent to 20 percent from Year 1 to Year 2. The Appliance Division's ROI, however, dropped from 18 percent to 15 percent. A better picture of what caused the change in rates is revealed by computing the margin and turnover ratios for each division. These ratios are also presented in Exhibit 10-1.

Notice that the margins for both divisions dropped from Year 1 to Year 2. In fact, the divisions experienced the *same* percentage of decline (16.67 percent). A declining margin could be explained by increasing expenses, by competitive pressures (forcing a decrease in selling prices), or both.

In spite of the declining margin, the Snack Foods Division was able to increase its rate of return. This increase resulted from an increase in the turnover rate that more than compensated for the decline in margin. The increase in turnover could be explained by a deliberate policy to reduce inventories. (Notice that the average assets employed remained the same for the Snack Foods Division even though sales increased by $10 million.)

2. For a discussion of the relative merits of gross book value, see James S. Reese and William R. Cool, "Measuring Investment Center Performance," *Harvard Business Review* (May–June 1978): 28–46, 174–176.

3. "C&C Group: 1H Grp Turnover Up 4%," *The Wall Street Journal*, http://online.wsj.com/article/0,,BT_CO_20040826_000549,00.html as of August 26, 2004.

EXHIBIT **10-1**	Comparison of Divisional Performance

Comparison of ROI

	Snack Foods Division	Appliance Division
Year 1:		
Sales	$30,000,000	$117,000,000
Operating income	1,800,000	3,510,000
Average operating assets	10,000,000	19,500,000
ROI[a]	18%	18%
Year 2:		
Sales	$40,000,000	$117,000,000
Operating income	2,000,000	2,925,000
Average operating assets	10,000,000	19,500,000
ROI[a]	20%	15%

Margin and Turnover Comparisons

	Snack Foods Division		Appliance Division	
	Year 1	Year 2	Year 1	Year 2
Margin[b]	6.0%	5.0%	3.0%	2.5%
Turnover[c]	× 3.0	× 4.0	× 6.0	× 6.0
ROI	18.0%	20.0%	18.0%	15.0%

[a]Operating income divided by average operating assets.
[b]Operating income divided by sales.
[c]Sales divided by average operating assets.

The Appliance Division, on the other hand, faced decreasing ROI because margin declined and the turnover rate remained unchanged. Although more information is needed before any definitive conclusion is reached, the different responses to similar difficulties may say something about the relative skills of the two managers.

Advantages of the ROI Measure

When ROI is used to evaluate division performance, division managers naturally try to increase it. This can be accomplished by increasing sales, decreasing costs, and decreasing investment. Three advantages of the use of ROI are as follows:

1. It encourages managers to pay careful attention to the relationships among sales, expenses, and investment, as should be the case for a manager of an investment center.
2. It encourages cost efficiency.
3. It discourages excessive investment in operating assets.

Each of these three advantages is discussed in turn.

The first advantage is that ROI encourages managers to consider the interrelationship of income and investment. Suppose that a division manager is faced with the suggestion from her marketing vice president that the advertising budget be increased by $100,000. The marketing vice president is confident that this increase will boost sales by $200,000 and raise the contribution margin by $110,000. If the division were evaluated on the basis of operating income, this information might be enough. However, if the division is evaluated on the basis of ROI, the manager will want to know how much additional investment, if any, is required to support the anticipated increase in production and sales. Suppose that an additional $50,000 of operating assets will be needed. Currently, the division has sales of $2 million, operating income of $150,000, and operating assets of $1 million.

If advertising increased by $100,000 and the contribution margin by $110,000, operating income would increase by $10,000 ($110,000 − $100,000). Investment in operating assets must also increase by $50,000. The ROI without the additional advertising is 15 percent ($150,000/$1,000,000). With the additional advertising, the ROI is 15.24 percent ($160,000/$1,050,000). Since the ROI is increased by the proposal, the divisional manager should increase advertising.

The second advantage is that ROI encourages cost efficiency. The manager of an investment center always has control over costs. Therefore, increasing efficiency through judicious cost reduction is a common method of increasing ROI. For example, **Tenneco, Inc.**, is focusing on cost reduction in its plants by reducing non-value-added activities. Materials handling costs are very high at some plants. Improving the layout of the plants to reduce the time and distance materials must travel is a way of reducing handling costs. Notice that encouraging cost efficiency means that non-value-added costs must be reduced or productivity must be improved. There are ways to decrease costs in the short run that have a harmful effect on the business. This possibility is discussed in the section on disadvantages of ROI.

The third advantage is that ROI encourages efficient investment. Divisions that have cut costs to the extent possible must focus on investment reduction. For example, operating assets can be trimmed through the reduction of materials inventory and work-in-process inventory, perhaps by installing just-in-time purchasing and manufacturing systems. New, more productive machinery can be installed, inefficient plants can be closed, and so on. Companies are taking a hard look at their level of investment and acting to reduce it. This is a positive result of ROI-based evaluation.

Disadvantages of the ROI Measure

The use of ROI to evaluate performance also has disadvantages. Two negative aspects associated with ROI are frequently mentioned.

1. It discourages managers from investing in projects that would decrease the divisional ROI but would increase the profitability of the company as a whole. (Generally, projects with an ROI less than a division's current ROI would be rejected.)
2. It can encourage myopic behavior, in that managers may focus on the short run at the expense of the long run.

The first disadvantage can be illustrated by an example. Consider a Cleaning Products Division that has the opportunity to invest in two projects for the coming year. The outlay required for each investment, the dollar returns, and the ROI are as follows:

	Project I	*Project II*
Investment	$10,000,000	$4,000,000
Operating income	1,300,000	640,000
ROI	13%	16%

The division is currently earning an ROI of 15 percent, using operating assets of $50 million to generate operating income of $7.5 million. The division has approval to request up to $15 million in new investment capital. Corporate headquarters requires that all investments earn at least 10 percent (this rate represents how much the corporation must earn to cover the cost of acquiring the capital). Any capital not used by a division is invested by headquarters so that it earns exactly 10 percent.

The divisional manager has four alternatives: (a) add Project I, (b) add Project II, (c) add both Projects I and II, and (d) maintain the status quo (invest in neither project). The divisional ROI was computed for each alternative.

	Add Project I	*Add Project II*	*Add Both Projects*	*Maintain Status Quo*
Operating income	$ 8,800,000	$ 8,140,000	$ 9,440,000	$ 7,500,000
Operating assets	60,000,000	54,000,000	64,000,000	50,000,000
ROI	14.67%	15.07%	14.75%	15.00%

The divisional manager chose to invest only in Project II, since it would have a favorable effect on the division's ROI (15.07 percent is greater than 15.00 percent).

Assuming that any capital not used by the division is invested at 10 percent, the manager's choice produced a lower profit for the company than could have been realized. If Project I had been selected, the company would have earned $1.3 million. By not selecting Project I, the $10 million in capital is invested at 10 percent, earning only $1 million (0.10 × $10,000,000). By maximizing the division's ROI, then, the divisional manager cost the company $300,000 in profits ($1,300,000 − $1,000,000).

The second disadvantage of evaluating performance using ROI is that it can encourage myopic behavior. We saw earlier that one of the advantages of ROI is that it encourages cost reduction. However, while cost reduction can result in more efficiency, it can also result in lower efficiency in the long run. The emphasis on short-run results at the expense of the long run is **myopic behavior**. Managers engaging in myopic behavior usually try to cut operating expenses by attacking discretionary costs. Examples are laying off more highly paid employees, cutting the advertising budget, delaying promotions and employee training, reducing preventive maintenance, and using cheaper materials.

Each of these steps reduces expenses, increases income, and raises ROI. While these actions increase the profits and ROI in the short run, they have some long-run negative consequences. Laying off more highly paid salespeople may adversely affect the division's future sales. For example, it has been estimated that the average monthly cost of replacing a sales representative with five to eight years' experience with a representative with less than one year of experience was $36,000 of lost sales. Low employee turnover has been linked to high customer satisfaction.[4] Future sales could also be harmed by cutting back on advertising and using cheaper materials. By delaying promotions, employee morale would be affected, which could, in turn, lower productivity and future sales. Finally, reducing preventive maintenance will likely cut into the productive capability of the division by increasing downtime and decreasing the life of the productive equipment. While these actions raise current ROI, they lead to lower future ROI.

Residual Income

In an effort to overcome the tendency to use ROI to turn down investments that are profitable for the company but that lower a division's ROI, some companies have adopted an alternative performance measure known as *residual income*. **Residual income** is the difference between operating income and the minimum dollar return required on a company's operating assets:

Residual income = Operating income − (Minimum rate of return × Operating assets)

---

4. James L. Heskett, Thomas O. Jones, Gary W. Loveman, W. Earl Sasser, Jr., and Leonard A. Schlesinger, "Putting the Service-Profit Chain to Work," *Harvard Business Review* 74, No. 2 (March/April 1994): 164–174.

Advantages of Residual Income

To illustrate the use of residual income, consider the Cleaning Products Division example again. Recall that the division manager rejected Project I because it would have reduced divisional ROI, which cost the company $300,000 in profits. The use of residual income as the performance measure would have prevented this loss. The residual income for each project is computed below.

Project I

$$
\begin{aligned}
\text{Residual income} &= \text{Operating income} - (\text{Minimum rate of return} \times \text{Operating assets}) \\
&= \$1,300,000 - (0.10 \times \$10,000,000) \\
&= \$1,300,000 - \$1,000,000 \\
&= \$300,000
\end{aligned}
$$

Project II

$$
\begin{aligned}
\text{Residual income} &= \$640,000 - (0.10 \times \$4,000,000) \\
&= \$640,000 - \$400,000 \\
&= \$240,000
\end{aligned}
$$

Notice that both projects increase residual income; in fact, Project I increases divisional residual income more than Project II does. Thus, both would be selected by the divisional manager. For comparative purposes, the divisional residual income for each of the four alternatives identified earlier follows:

	Add Project I	Add Project II	Add Both Projects	Maintain Status Quo
Operating assets	$60,000,000	$54,000,000	$64,000,000	$50,000,000
Operating income	$ 8,800,000	$ 8,140,000	$ 9,440,000	$ 7,500,000
Minimum return*	6,000,000	5,400,000	6,400,000	5,000,000
Residual income	$ 2,800,000	$ 2,740,000	$ 3,040,000	$ 2,500,000

*0.10 × Operating assets.

As indicated, selecting both projects produces the greatest increase in residual income. Adding both projects is now the preferred alternative. With this new measure employed, managers are encouraged to accept any project that earns above the minimum rate.

Disadvantages of Residual Income

Two disadvantages of residual income are that it is an absolute measure of return and that it does not discourage myopic behavior. Absolute measures of return make it difficult to directly compare the performance of divisions. For example, consider the residual income computations for Division A and Division B, where the minimum required rate of return is 8 percent.

	Division A	Division B
Average operating assets	$15,000,000	$2,500,000
Operating income	$ 1,500,000	$ 300,000
Minimum return[a]	1,200,000	200,000
Residual income	$ 300,000	$ 100,000
Residual return[b]	2%	4%

[a]0.08 × Operating assets.
[b]Residual income divided by operating assets.

At first glance, it is tempting to claim that Division A is outperforming Division B, since its residual income is three times higher. Notice, however, that Division A used six times as many assets to produce this difference. If anything, Division B is more efficient.

One possible way to correct this disadvantage is to compute a residual return on investment by dividing residual income by average operating assets. This measure indicates that Division B earned 4 percent while Division A earned only 2 percent. Another possibility is to compute both return on investment and residual income and use both measures for performance evaluation. ROI could then be used for interdivisional comparisons.[5]

The second disadvantage of residual income is that it, like ROI, can encourage a short-run orientation. Just as a manager can choose to cut maintenance, training, and sales force expenses when being evaluated under ROI, the manager being evaluated on the basis of residual income can take the same actions. The problem of myopic behavior is not solved by switching to this measure. A preferable method of reducing the myopic behavior problem of residual income is the economic value added method, discussed next.

Economic Value Added

Another measure of profitability for performance evaluation of investment centers is *economic value added*.[6] **Economic value added (EVA)** is after-tax operating income minus the total annual cost of capital. If EVA is positive, the company is creating wealth. If it is negative, then the company is destroying capital. Over the long term, only those companies creating capital, or wealth, can survive. Many companies today are passionate believers in the power of EVA. When EVA is used to adjust management compensation, it encourages managers to use existing and new capital for maximum gain. **The Coca-Cola Company**, **General Electric**, **Intel**, and **Merck** are a few of the companies that have seen increasing EVA during the past fifteen years.[7]

EVA is a dollar figure, not a percentage rate of return. However, it does bear a resemblance to rates of return such as ROI because it links net income (return) to capital employed. The key feature of EVA is its emphasis on *after-tax* operating income and the *actual* cost of capital. Other return measures may use accounting book value numbers which may or may not represent the true cost of capital. Residual income, for example, typically uses a minimum expected rate of return. Investors like EVA because it relates profit to the amount of resources needed to achieve it.

Calculating EVA

EVA is after-tax operating income minus the dollar cost of capital employed. The equation for EVA is expressed as follows:

$$EVA = \text{After-tax operating income} - (\text{Weighted average cost of capital} \times \text{Total capital employed})$$

The difficulty faced by most companies is computing the cost of capital employed. Two steps are involved: (1) determine the weighted average cost of capital (a percentage figure) and (2) determine the total dollar amount of capital employed.

5. In their study, Reese and Cool found that only 2 percent of the companies surveyed used residual income by itself, whereas 28 percent used both residual income and return on investment. See Reese and Cool, "Measuring Investment Center Performance."
6. EVA® is a registered trademark of Stern Stewart & Co.
7. Richard Teitelbaum, "America's Greatest Wealth Creators," *Fortune* (November 10, 1997): 265–276. and Tad Leahy, "Measures of the Future," *Business Finance*, February 1999. http://www.businessfinancemag.com/magazine/archives/article.html?articleID=5027&pg=2

To calculate the weighted average cost of capital, the company must identify all sources of invested funds. Typical sources are borrowing and equity (stock issued). Any borrowed money usually has an interest rate attached, and that rate can be adjusted for its tax deductibility. For example, if a company has issued 10-year bonds at an annual interest rate of 8 percent and the tax rate is 40 percent, then the after-tax cost of the bonds is 4.8 percent [0.08 − (0.4 × 0.08)]. Equity is handled differently. The cost of equity financing is the opportunity cost to investors. Over time, stockholders have received an average return that is six percentage points higher than the return on long-term government bonds. If these bond rates are about 6 percent, then the average cost of equity is 12 percent. Riskier stocks command a higher return; more stable and less risky stocks offer a somewhat lower return. Finally, the proportionate share of each method of financing is multiplied by its percentage cost and summed to yield a weighted average cost of capital.

Suppose that a company has two sources of financing: $2 million of long-term bonds paying 9 percent interest and $6 million of common stock, which is considered to be of average risk. If the company's tax rate is 40 percent and the rate of interest on long-term government bonds is 6 percent, the company's weighted average cost of capital is computed as follows:

	Amount	*Percent*	×	*After-Tax Cost*	=	*Weighted Cost*
Bonds	$2,000,000	0.25		0.09(1 − 0.4) = 0.054		0.0135
Equity	6,000,000	0.75		0.06 + 0.06 = 0.120		0.0900
Total	$8,000,000					0.1035

Thus, the company's weighted average cost of capital is 10.35 percent.

The second datum necessary to calculate the dollar cost of capital employed is the amount of capital employed. Clearly, the amount paid for buildings, land, and machinery must be included. However, other expenditures meant to have a long-term payoff, such as research and development, employee training, and so on, should also be included. Despite the fact that these latter are classified by GAAP as expenses, EVA is an internal management accounting measure, and therefore, they can be thought of as the investments that they truly are.

EVA Example

Suppose that Furman, Inc., had after-tax operating income last year of $1,583,000. Three sources of financing were used by the company: $2 million of mortgage bonds paying 8 percent interest, $3 million of unsecured bonds paying 10 percent interest, and $10 million in common stock, which was considered to be no more or less risky than other stocks. Furman, Inc., pays a marginal tax rate of 40 percent. The after-tax cost of the mortgage bonds is 0.048 [0.08 − (0.4 × 0.08)]. The after-tax cost of the unsecured bonds is 0.06 [0.10 − (0.4 × 0.10)]. There are no tax adjustments for equity, so the cost of the common stock is 12 percent (6 percent return on long-term Treasury bonds plus the 6 percent average premium). The **weighted average cost of capital** is computed by taking the proportion of capital from each source of financing and multiplying it by its cost. The weighted average cost of capital for Furman, Inc., is computed as follows:

	Amount	*Percent*	×	*After-Tax Cost*	=	*Weighted Cost*
Mortgage bonds	$ 2,000,000	0.133		0.048		0.006
Unsecured bonds	3,000,000	0.200		0.060		0.012
Common stock	10,000,000	0.667		0.120		0.080
Total	$15,000,000					
Weighted average cost of capital						0.098

When the weighted average cost of capital is multiplied by total capital employed, the dollar cost of capital is known. For Furman, Inc., the amount of capital employed is $15 million, so the cost of capital is $1,470,000 (0.098 × $15,000,000).

Furman, Inc.'s EVA is calculated as follows:

After-tax operating income	$1,583,000
Less: Weighted average cost of capital	1,470,000
EVA	$ 113,000

The positive EVA means that Furman, Inc., earned operating income over and above the cost of the capital used. It is creating wealth.

Behavioral Aspects of EVA

A number of companies have discovered that EVA helps to encourage the right kind of behavior from their divisions in a way that emphasis on operating income alone cannot. The underlying reason is EVA's reliance on the true cost of capital. In many companies, the responsibility for investment decisions rests with corporate management. As a result, the cost of capital is considered a corporate expense. If a division builds inventories and investment, the cost of financing that investment is passed along to the overall income statement. It does not show up as a reduction from the division's operating income; investment seems free to the divisions, and of course, they want more. As a result, EVA should be measured for subsets of the company. For example, **Briggs and Stratton**, manufacturer of engines, divided up the company into areas according to types of engine and critical function (e.g., manufacturing and distribution). It then calculates EVA for each area. The result is to make the performance of different areas of the company clearer.[8]

Suppose that Supertech, Inc., has two divisions, the Hardware Division and the Software Division. Operating income statements for the divisions are as follows:

	Hardware Division	Software Division
Sales	$5,000,000	$2,000,000
Cost of goods sold	2,000,000	1,100,000
Gross profit	$3,000,000	$ 900,000
Divisional selling and administrative expenses	2,000,000	400,000
Operating income	$1,000,000	$ 500,000

It looks as if the Hardware Division is doing a good job, and so is Software. Now, let's consider each division's use of capital. Suppose that Supertech's weighted average cost of capital is 11 percent. Hardware, through a buildup of inventories of components and finished goods, use of warehouses, and so on, uses capital amounting to $10 million, so its dollar cost of capital is $1,100,000 (0.11 × $10,000,000). Software does not need large materials inventories, but it does invest heavily in research and development and training. Its capital usage is $2 million, and its dollar cost of capital is $220,000 (0.11 × $2,000,000). The EVA for each division can be calculated as follows:

	Hardware Division	Software Division
Operating income	$1,000,000	$500,000
Less: Cost of capital	1,100,000	220,000
EVA	$ (100,000)	$280,000

---

8. G. Bennett Stewart III, "EVA Works—But Not If You Make These Common Mistakes," *Fortune* (May 1, 1995): 117–118.

Now, it is clear that the Hardware Division is actually losing money by using too much capital. The Software Division, on the other hand, has created wealth for Supertech. By using EVA, the Hardware Division's manager will no longer consider inventories and warehouses to be "free" goods. Instead, the manager will strive to reduce capital usage and increase EVA. A reduction of capital usage to $8 million, for example, would boost EVA to $120,000 [$1,000,000 − (0.11 × $8,000,000)].

Quaker Oats faced a similar situation. Prior to 1991, Quaker Oats evaluated its business segments on the basis of quarterly profits. In order to keep quarterly earnings on an upward march, segment managers offered sharp discounts on products at the end of each quarter. This resulted in huge orders from retailers and sharp surges in production at Quaker's plants at the end of each 3-month period. This practice is called trade loading because it "loads up the trade" (retail stores) with product. It can be expensive, however, because trade loading requires massive amounts of capital— e.g., working capital, inventories, and warehouses to store the quarterly spikes in output. Quaker's plant in Danville, Illinois, produces snack foods and breakfast cereals. Before EVA, the Danville plant ran well below capacity throughout the early part of the quarter. Purchasing, however, bought huge quantities of boxes, plastic wrappers, granola, and chocolate chips. The materials purchases buildup was in anticipation of the production surge of the last six weeks of the quarter. As the products were finished, Quaker packed 15 warehouses with finished goods. All costs associated with inventories were absorbed by corporate headquarters. As a result, they appeared to be free to the plant managers, who were encouraged to build ever higher inventories. The advent of EVA and the cancellation of trade loading led to a smoothing of production throughout the quarter, higher overall production (and sales), and lower inventories. Quaker's Danville plant reduced inventories from $15 million to $9 million. Quaker has closed one-third of its 15 warehouses, saving $6 million annually in salaries and capital costs.[9]

EVA can be used in the public sector, as well. The U.S. Postal Service (USPS) uses EVA to measure its performance. The cost of capital is 12 percent for the USPS, and senior staff bonuses are tied to their ability to create value (i.e., positive EVA).[10]

Multiple Measures of Performance

ROI, residual income, and EVA are important measures of managerial performance. However, they are financial measures. As such, the temptation exists for managers to focus only on dollar figures. This focus may not tell the whole story for the company. In addition, lower-level managers and employees may feel helpless to affect net income or investment. As a result, nonfinancial operating measures have been developed. For example, top management could look at such factors as market share, customer complaints, personnel turnover ratios, and personnel development. By letting lower-level managers know that attention to long-run factors is also vital, the tendency to overemphasize financial measures is reduced.

Modern managers are especially likely to use multiple measures of performance and to include nonfinancial as well as financial measures. For example, **Home Depot** surveys customers to get a measure of customer support and tracks the number of hours of training it offers employees each year (23 million hours of training in 2004).[11] The Balanced Scorecard (discussed in Chapter 13) was developed to measure a firm's performance in multiple areas.

---

9. Ibid.

10. Jaclyn Fierman, "Americans Can't Get No Satisfaction," *Fortune* (December 11, 1995): 186–194.

11. Julie Schlosser, "It's His Home Depot Now," *Fortune* (September 20, 2004): 115–119.

OBJECTIVE 4

Discuss methods of evaluating and rewarding managerial performance.

Measuring and Rewarding the Performance of Managers

While some companies consider the performance of the division to be equivalent to the performance of the manager, there is a compelling reason to separate the two. Often, the performance of the division is subject to factors beyond the manager's control. It is particularly important, then, to take a responsibility accounting approach. That is, managers should be evaluated on the basis of factors under their control. A serious concern is the creation of a compensation plan that is closely tied to the performance of the division. This is important in the determination of managerial compensation.

Incentive Pay for Managers— Encouraging Goal Congruence

The subjects of managerial evaluation and incentive pay would be of little concern if all managers were equally likely to perform up to the best of their abilities, and if those abilities were known in advance. In the case of a small company, owned and managed by the same person, there is no problem. The owner puts in as much effort as she or he wishes and receives all of the income from the firm as a reward for his or her performance. However, in most companies, the owner hires managers to operate the company on a day-to-day basis and delegates decision-making authority to them. For example, the stockholders of a company hire the CEO through the board of directors. Similarly, division managers are hired by the CEO to operate their divisions on behalf of the owners. Then, the owners must ensure that the managers are providing good service.

Why wouldn't managers provide good service? There are three reasons: (1) they may have an inadequate ability to perform the job, (2) they may prefer not to work hard, and (3) they may prefer to spend company resources on perquisites. The first reason requires owners to discover information about the manager before hiring him. Think back to the reasons for decentralization—one was that it provided training for future managers. This is true, and it also provides signals to higher management about the managerial ability of division managers. The second and third reasons require the owner to monitor the manager or to arrange an incentive scheme that will more closely ally the manager's goals with those of the owner. Some managers may not want to do hard or routine work. In addition, some may be risk-averse and not take actions which expose them, and the company, to risky situations. Thus, it is necessary to compensate them for undertaking risk and hard work. Closely related to the desire of some managers to shirk responsibility is the tendency of managers to overuse perquisites. Perquisites are a type of fringe benefit received over and above salary. Some examples are a nice office, use of a company car or jet, expense accounts, and company-paid country club memberships. While some perquisites are legitimate uses of company resources, they can be abused. A well-structured incentive pay plan can help to encourage goal congruence between managers and owners.

Managerial Rewards

Managerial rewards frequently include incentives tied to performance. The objective is to encourage goal congruence, so that managers will act in the best interests of the firm. Arranging managerial compensation to encourage managers to adopt the same goals as the overall firm is an important issue. Managerial rewards include salary increases, bonuses based on reported income, stock options, and noncash compensation.

Cash Compensation

Cash compensation includes salaries and bonuses. One way a company may reward good managerial performance is by granting periodic raises. However, once the raise takes effect, it is usually permanent. Bonuses give a company more flexibility. Many companies use a combination of salary and bonus to reward performance by keeping salaries fairly level and allowing bonuses to fluctuate with reported income. Managers may find their bonuses tied to divisional net income or to targeted increases in net income. For example, a division manager may receive an annual salary of $75,000 and a yearly bonus of 5 percent of the increase in reported net income. If net income does not rise, the manager's bonus is zero. This incentive pay scheme makes increasing net income, an objective of the owner, important to the manager as well.

Of course, income-based compensation can encourage dysfunctional behavior. The manager may engage in unethical practices, such as postponing needed maintenance. If the bonus is capped at a certain amount (say the bonus is equal to 1 percent of net income but cannot exceed $50,000), managers may postpone revenue recognition from the end of the year in which the maximum bonus has already been achieved to the next year. Those who structure the reward systems need to understand both the positive incentives built into the system as well as the potential for negative behavior.

Profit-sharing plans make employees partial owners in the sense that they receive a share of the profits. They are not owners in the sense of decision making or downside risk sharing. This is a form of risk sharing, in particular, sharing of upside risk. Typically, employees are paid a flat rate, and then, any profits to be shared are over and above wages. The objective is to provide an incentive for employees to work harder and smarter.

Stock-Based Compensation

Stock is a share in the company, and theoretically, it should increase in value as the company does well and decrease in value as the company does poorly. Thus, the issue of stock to managers makes them part owners of the company and should encourage goal congruence. Many companies encourage employees to purchase shares of stock, or they grant shares as a bonus. A disadvantage of stock as compensation is that share price can fall for reasons beyond the control of managers. For example, **Wal-Mart** stock rose and fell in value in the early 1990s. When the stock price fell, managers worried about employee morale. To keep morale high, the company created a cash bonus pool to be distributed for meeting sales and income targets.

Companies frequently offer stock options to managers. A **stock option** is the right to buy a certain number of shares of the company's stock, at a particular price and after a set length of time. The objective of awarding stock options is to encourage managers to focus on the longer term. The price of the option shares is usually set approximately at market price at the time of issue. Then, if the stock price rises in the future, the manager may exercise the option, thus purchasing stock at a below-market price and realizing an immediate gain.

For example, Lois Canfield, head of the Toiletries Division of Palgate, Inc., was granted an option to purchase 100,000 shares of Palgate stock at the current market price of $20 per share. The option was granted in August 2005 and could be exercised after two years. If, by August 2007, Palgate stock has risen to $23 per share, Lois can purchase all 100,000 shares for $2,000,000 (100,000 × $20 option price) and immediately sell them for $2,300,000 (100,000 × $23). She will realize a profit of $300,000. Of course, if Palgate stock drops below $20, Lois will not exercise the option. Typically, however, stock prices rise along with the market, and Lois can safely bet on a future profit as long as Palgate does not perform worse than the market.

Companies are becoming more aware of the impact on options of the overall movement of the stock market. If the market moves strongly higher, there is the potential for windfall profits. That is, any profit realized from selling stock based on low cost options may be more closely related to the overall rise in the stock market and less related to outstanding performance by top management. In addition, top executives with a number of options may focus on the short-term movements of the stock price rather than on the long-term indicators of company performance. In essence, they may trade long-term returns for short-term returns.

Typically, there are constraints on the exercise of the options. For example, the stock purchased with options may not be sold for a certain period of time. A disadvantage of stock options is that the price of the stock is based on many factors and is not completely within the manager's control.

Issues to Consider in Structuring Income-Based Compensation

The underlying objective of a company that uses income-based compensation is goal congruence between owner and manager. To the extent that the owners of the company want net income and stock price to rise, basing management compensation on such increases helps to encourage managerial efforts in that direction. However, single measures of performance, which are often the basis of bonuses, are frequently subject to gaming behavior. That is, managers may increase short-term measures at the expense of long-term measures. For example, a manager may keep net income high by refusing to invest in more modern and efficient equipment. Depreciation expense remains low, but so do productivity and quality. Clearly, the manager has an incentive to understand the computation of the accounting numbers used in performance evaluation. An accounting change from FIFO to LIFO or in the method of depreciation, for example, will change net income even though sales and costs remain unchanged. Frequently, we see that a new CEO of a troubled corporation will take a number of losses (e.g., inventory write-downs) all at once. This is referred to as the "big bath" and usually results in very low (or negative) net income in that year. Then, the books are cleared for a good increase in net income, and a correspondingly large bonus, for the next year.

Both cash bonuses and stock options can encourage a short-term orientation. To encourage a longer-term orientation, some companies are requiring top executives to purchase and hold a certain amount of company stock to retain employment. **Eastman Kodak**, **Xerox**, **CSX Corporation**, **Gerber Products**, **Union Carbide Corporation**, and **Hershey Foods** are all companies that have stock ownership guidelines for their top management.

Another issue to be considered in structuring management compensation plans is that frequently owners and managers are affected differently by risk. When managers have so much of their own capital—both financial and human—invested in the company, they may be less apt to take risks. Owners, because of their ability to diversify away some of the risk, may prefer a more risk-taking attitude. As a result, managers must be somewhat insulated from catastrophic downside risk in order to encourage them to make entrepreneurial decisions.

Noncash Compensation

Noncash compensation is an important part of the management reward structure. Autonomy in the conduct of their daily business is an important type of noncash compensation. At **Hewlett-Packard**, cross-functional teams "own" their business and have the authority to reinvest earnings to react quickly to changing markets.

Perquisites are also important. We often see managers who trade off increased salary for improvements in title, office location and trappings, use of expense accounts, and so on. Perquisites can be well used to make the manager more efficient. For example, a busy manager may be able to effectively employ several assistants and may find that use of a corporate jet allows him or her to more efficiently schedule travel in overseeing far-flung divisions. However, perquisites may be abused as well. For instance, one wonders how the shareholders of **Tyco** benefitted from their 50 percent share of the

$2 million party that former Tyco chief Dennis Kozlowski threw for his wife's birthday, or from Kozlowski's $6,000 shower curtain.[12]

Measuring Performance in the Multinational Firm

It is important for the MNC to separate the evaluation of the *manager* of a division from the evaluation of the *division*. The manager's evaluation should not include factors over which he exercises no control, such as currency fluctuations, income taxes, and so on. Instead, managers should be evaluated on the basis of revenues and costs incurred. It is particularly difficult to compare the performance of a manager of a division (or subsidiary) in one country with the performance of a manager of a division in another country. Even divisions that appear to be similar in terms of production may face very different economic, social, or political forces. The manager should be evaluated on the basis of the performance he or she can control. Once a manager is evaluated, then the subsidiary financial statements can be restated to the home currency and uncontrollable costs can be allocated.[13]

International environmental conditions may be very different from, and more complex than, domestic conditions. Environmental variables facing local managers of divisions include economic, legal, political, social, and educational factors.

Some important economic variables are inflation, foreign currency exchange rates, income taxes, and transfer prices. For example, MNCs have invested heavily in developing countries. The result is that those countries have built considerable manufacturing capacity and are now competing aggressively around the world. This has led to lower prices and deflation on a global basis. As a result, MNCs, used to dealing with the inflationary environment of the 1970s and 1980s, will have to shift gears to deal with deflation. In this case, cost control is essential.

Legal and political factors also have differing impacts. For example, a country may not allow cash outflows or may forbid the import of certain items. U.S. agricultural laws do not allow rooted plants to enter the country. This posed a problem for U.S. florists who sell poinsettias during the Christmas season. They need many poinsettias, but they do not have the greenhouse capacity to grow them throughout the rest of the year. Mexico provides an ideal growing environment for the plants. However, potted plants cannot enter the United States. Plant science advances solved the importation problem. The plants are imported as cuttings that have been quick cooled, bagged, and shipped in dry ice. They clear Customs in this form, arriving at their destination within the 72-hour window.[14] The result is a thriving poinsettia-growing industry in Mexico and many more of the colorful plants available for U.S. consumers.

Educational, infrastructure, and cultural variables affect how the multinational firm is treated by the subsidiary's country. For example, when **Wal-Mart** expanded into Brazil, its system of just-in-time restocking of shelves did not work. In Brazil, the company did not own its distribution system, meaning that stores in Brazil processed up to 300 deliveries daily, versus seven in the United States. On the cultural front, Wal-Mart had to change its credit policies by accepting postdated checks—the most common form of credit in Brazil.[15] Many clothing distributors in the United States depend on factories in developing countries to do the manufacturing. However, first, those companies had to develop the area, putting in roads and communication equipment and providing training for workers.

12. "Tyco Jurors View $2 Million Party Video," *CBSNews.com*, http://www.cbsnews.com/stories/2003/11/25/national/main585633.shtml as of October 28, 2003. (The trial ended in a mistrial, and the case is set to be retried in 2005.)

13. Helen Gernon and Gary Meek, *Accounting: An International Perspective* (Homewood, IL: Richard D. Irwin-McGraw-Hill, 2001).

14. Joel Millman, "For Holiday Poinsettias, Growers Go South of the Border," *The Wall Street Journal* (December 17, 1998): B1.

15. Jonathan Friedland and Louise Lee, "The Wal-Mart Way Sometimes Gets Lost in Translation Overseas," *The Wall Street Journal* (October 8, 1997): A1 and A12.

Comparison of Divisional ROI

The existence of differing environmental factors makes interdivisional comparison of ROI potentially misleading. For example, the lack of consistency in internal reporting may obscure interdivisional comparison. A minimum wage law in one country may restrict the manager's ability to affect labor costs. Another country may prevent the export of cash. Still others may have a well-educated workforce but poor infrastructure (transportation and communication facilities). Therefore, the corporation must be aware of and control these differing environmental factors when assessing managerial performance.

The accountant in the MNC must be aware of more than business and finance. Political and legal systems have important implications for the company. Sometimes, the political system changes quickly, throwing the company into crisis mode. Other times, the situation evolves more slowly. For example, **General Electric** has been affected by drug trafficking in Colombia as the Colombian drug lords turned to appliance exporting as a means of laundering their U.S. profits. Honest U.S. and Colombian retail appliance dealers have been hurt by the smugglers' low prices. GE was forced to institute tough audit procedures to ferret out the illegal activity. The result was a drop in GE's market share in the Miami area and an increase in accounting expense.[16]

On occasion, the political structure may mean that standard U.S.-based methods of control may not "work" in foreign countries. For example, under the communist regime in the former USSR, manufacturers received a budget, actual results were compared with the budget, and variances were computed. However, variance analysis did not have the same meaning that it has in the United States. If a company faced a variance, the solution was to send the plant's senior political operative to Central Planning Headquarters with a case of champagne or cognac. The hoped-for result was a change in the budget so that it matched actual results and the variance disappeared. The business objective was not efficiency or effectiveness, but a compliance with the central plan. While the Central Planning Headquarters no longer exists, this culture of altering the plan to match the actual results does continue to exist.

Multiple Measures of Performance

Rigid evaluation of the performance of foreign divisions of the MNC ignores the overarching strategic importance of developing a global presence. The interconnectedness of the global company weakens the independence or stand-alone nature of any one segment. As a result, residual income and ROI are less important measures of managerial performance for divisions of the MNC. MNCs must use additional measures of performance that relate more closely to the long-run health of the company. In addition to ROI and residual income, top management looks at such factors as market potential and market share. For example, **Gillette** began to sell Oral-B toothbrushes in China. The size of the Chinese market means that even if Gillette gets only 10 percent of the market, it will sell more toothbrushes in China than in the United States. **Procter & Gamble**, **Bausch & Lomb**, and **Citicorp** are expanding into Indian and Asian markets for the same reason.

Additionally, the use of ROI and RI in the evaluation of managerial performance in divisions of an MNC is subject to problems beyond those faced by a decentralized company that operates in only one country. It is particularly important, then, to take a responsibility accounting approach and evaluate managers on the basis of factors under their control. For example, the manager of the Moscow **McDonald's** cannot simply purchase food; it is not available for purchase locally, and imports from Denmark and Finland are very expensive. As a result, some food is grown locally. Similar difficulties are faced by companies in Eastern Europe. Multiple measures of performance, keyed to

16. Michael Allen, "A Tangled Tale of GE, Appliance Smuggling and Laundered Money," *The Wall Street Journal* (December 21, 1998): A1 and A6.

local operating conditions, can spotlight managers' responses to different and difficult operating conditions.

Transfer Pricing

OBJECTIVE 5

Explain the role of transfer pricing in a decentralized firm.

Often, the output of one division can be used as input for another division. For example, integrated circuits produced by one division can be used by a second division to make video recorders. Transfer prices are the prices charged for goods produced by one division and transferred to another. The price charged affects the revenues of the transferring division and the costs of the receiving division. As a result, the profitability, return on investment, and managerial performance evaluation of both divisions are affected.

The Impact of Transfer Pricing on Income

Exhibit 10-2 illustrates the effect of the transfer price on two divisions of ABC, Inc. Division A produces a component and sells it to another division of the same company, Division C. The $30 transfer price is revenue to Division A and increases division income; clearly, Division A wants the price to be as high as possible. Conversely, the $30 transfer price is cost to Division C and decreases division income, just like the cost of any materials. Division C prefers a lower transfer price. For the company as a whole, A's revenue minus C's cost equals zero.

EXHIBIT 10-2	Impact of Transfer Price on Transferring Divisions and the Company as a Whole

ABC, Inc.	
Division A	**Division C**
Produces component and transfers it to C for transfer price of $30 per unit	Purchases component from A at transfer price of $30 per unit and uses it in production of final product
Transfer price = $30 per unit	Transfer price = $30 per unit
Revenue to A	Cost to C
Increases net income	Decreases net income
Increases ROI	Decreases ROI

Transfer price revenue = Transfer price cost
Zero impact on ABC, Inc.

While the actual transfer price nets out for the company as a whole, transfer pricing can affect the level of profits earned by the company as a whole if it affects divisional behavior. Divisions, acting independently, may set transfer prices that maximize divisional profits but adversely affect firmwide profits. For example, suppose that Division A in Exhibit 10-2 sets a transfer price of $30 for a component that costs $24 to produce. If Division C can obtain the component from an outside supplier for $28, it will refuse to buy from Division A. Division C will realize a savings of $2 per component ($30 internal transfer price − $28 external price). However, assuming that Division A cannot replace the internal sales with external sales, the company as a whole will be worse off by $4 per component ($28 external cost − $24 internal cost). This outcome would increase the total cost to the firm as a whole. Thus, how transfer prices are set can be critical for profits of the business as a whole.

OBJECTIVE 6

Discuss the methods of setting transfer prices.

Setting Transfer Prices

A transfer pricing system should satisfy three objectives: accurate performance evaluation, goal congruence, and preservation of divisional autonomy.[17] Accurate performance evaluation means that no one divisional manager should benefit at the expense of another (in the sense that one division is made better off while the other is made worse off). Goal congruence means that divisional managers select actions that maximize firmwide profits. Autonomy means that central management should not interfere with the decision-making freedom of divisional managers. The transfer pricing problem concerns finding a system that simultaneously satisfies all three objectives.

We can evaluate the degree to which a transfer price satisfies the objectives of a transfer pricing system by considering the opportunity cost of the goods transferred. The *opportunity cost approach* can be used to describe a wide variety of transfer pricing practices. Under certain conditions, this approach is compatible with the objectives of performance evaluation, goal congruence, and autonomy.

The opportunity cost approach identifies the minimum price that a selling division would be willing to accept and the maximum price that the buying division would be willing to pay. These minimum and maximum prices correspond to the opportunity costs of transferring internally. They are defined for each division as follows:

1. The minimum transfer price, or floor, is the transfer price that would leave the selling division no worse off if the good is sold to an internal division.
2. The maximum transfer price, or ceiling, is the transfer price that would leave the buying division no worse off if an input is purchased from an internal division.

The opportunity cost rule signals when it is possible to increase firmwide profits through internal transfers. Specifically, a good should be transferred internally whenever the opportunity cost (minimum price) of the selling division is less than the opportunity cost (maximum price) of the buying division. By its very definition, this approach ensures that the divisional manager of either division is no worse off by transferring internally. This means that total divisional profits are not decreased by the internal transfer.

Rarely does central management set specific transfer prices. Instead, most companies develop some general policies that divisions must follow. Three commonly used policies are market-based transfer pricing, negotiated transfer pricing, and cost-based transfer pricing. Each of these can be evaluated according to the opportunity cost approach.

Market Price

If there is an outside market for the intermediate product (the good to be transferred) and that outside market is perfectly competitive, the correct transfer price is the market price.[18] In such a case, divisional managers' actions will simultaneously optimize divisional profits and firmwide profits. Furthermore, no division can benefit at the expense of another division. In this setting, central management will not be tempted to intervene.

The opportunity cost approach also signals that the correct transfer price is the market price. Since the selling division can sell all that it produces at the market price, transferring internally at a lower price would make that division worse off. Similarly, the

---

17. Joshua Ronen and George McKinney, "Transfer Pricing for Divisional Autonomy," *Journal of Accounting Research* (Spring 1970): 100–101.

18. A perfectly competitive market for the intermediate product requires four conditions: (1) the division producing the intermediate product is small relative to the market as a whole and cannot influence the price of the product; (2) the intermediate product is indistinguishable from the same product of other sellers; (3) firms can easily enter and exit the market; and (4) consumers, producers, and resource owners have perfect knowledge of the market.

buying division can always acquire the intermediate good at the market price, so it would be unwilling to pay more for an internally transferred good. Since the minimum transfer price for the selling division is the market price and since the maximum price for the buying division is also the market price, the only possible transfer price is the market price.

In fact, moving away from the market price will decrease the overall profitability of the firm. This principle can be used to resolve divisional conflicts that may occur, as the following example illustrates.

Yarrow Manufacturers is a large, privately held corporation that produces small appliances. The company has adopted a decentralized organizational structure. The Parts Division, which is at capacity, produces parts that are used by the Motor Division. The parts can also be sold to other manufacturers and to wholesalers at a market price of $8. For all practical purposes, the market for the parts is perfectly competitive.

Suppose that the Motor Division, operating at 70 percent capacity, receives a special order for 100,000 motors at a price of $30. Full manufacturing cost of the motors is $31, broken down as follows.

Direct materials	$10
Transferred-in part	8
Direct labor	2
Variable overhead	1
Fixed overhead	10
Total cost	$31

Notice that the motor includes a part transferred in from the Parts Division at a market-based transfer price of $8. Should the Parts Division lower the transfer price to allow the Motor Division to accept the special order? We can use the opportunity cost approach to answer this question.

Since the Parts Division can sell all that it produces, the minimum transfer price is the market price of $8. Any lower price would make the Parts Division worse off. For the Motor Division, identifying the maximum transfer price that can be paid so that it is no worse off is a bit more complex.

Since the Motor Division is under capacity, the fixed overhead portion of the motor's cost is not relevant. The relevant costs are those additional costs that will be incurred if the order is accepted. These costs, excluding for the moment the cost of the transferred-in component, equal $13 ($10 + $2 + $1). Thus, the contribution to profits before considering the cost of the transferred-in component is $17 ($30 − $13). The division could pay as much as $17 for the component and still break even on the special order. However, since the component can always be purchased from an outside supplier for $8, the maximum price that the division should pay internally is $8. As a result, the market price is the best transfer price.

Negotiated Transfer Prices

Perfectly competitive markets rarely exist. In most cases, producers *can* influence price (e.g., by being large enough to influence demand by dropping the price of the product or by selling closely related but differentiated products). When imperfections exist in the market for the intermediate product, market price may no longer be suitable. In this case, negotiated transfer prices may be a practical alternative. Opportunity costs can be used to define the boundaries of the negotiation set.

Negotiated outcomes should be guided by the opportunity costs facing each division. A negotiated price should be agreed to only if the opportunity cost of the selling division is less than the opportunity cost of the buying division.

Example 1: Avoidable Distribution Costs

To illustrate, assume that a division produces a circuit board that can be sold in the outside market for $22. The division can sell all that it produces to the outside market at $22. If it does so, however, it incurs a distribution cost of $2 per unit. Currently, the division sells 1,000 units per day, with a variable manufacturing cost of $12 per unit. Alternatively, the board can be sold internally to the company's recently acquired Electronic Games Division. The distribution cost is avoidable if the board is sold internally.

The Electronic Games Division is also at capacity, producing and selling 350 games per day. These games sell for $45 per unit and have a variable manufacturing cost of $32 per unit. Variable selling expenses of $3 per unit are also incurred. Sales and production data for each division are summarized in Exhibit 10-3.

EXHIBIT 10-3 — Summary of Sales and Production Data

	Circuit Board Division	Games Division
Units sold:		
Per day	1,000	350
Per year*	260,000	91,000
Unit data:		
Selling price	$22	$45
Variable costs:		
Manufacturing	$12	$32
Selling	$2	$3
Annual fixed costs	$1,480,000	$610,000

*There are 260 selling days in a year.

How could the Games Division and the Circuit Board Division set a transfer price? Let's assume that the Games Division currently pays $22 per circuit board. Clearly, the Games Division would refuse to pay more than $22; thus, the maximum transfer price is $22. The minimum transfer price is set by the Circuit Board Division. While this division prices its circuit boards at $22, it will avoid $2 of distribution cost if it sells internally. Therefore, the minimum transfer price is $20 ($22 − $2). If a bargaining range exists, the transfer price will fall somewhere between $22 and $20.

Suppose that the Game Division manager offered a transfer price of $20. That division would be better off by $2 per circuit board, since it had previously paid $22 per board. Its profits would increase by $700 per day ($2 × 350 units per day). The Circuit Board Division, on the other hand, would be no better, or worse, off than before and no incremental profit would accrue to the division. While a transfer price of $20 per circuit board is possible, it is unlikely that the Circuit Board manager would agree to it.

Now suppose that the Circuit Board Division counters with an offer of $21.10 per board. That transfer price allows the Circuit Board Division to increase its profits by $385 per day [($21.10 − $20.00) × 350 units]. The Games Division would increase its profits by $315 per day [($22 − $21.10) × 350 units].

While we cannot tell exactly where the Circuit Board Division and the Games Division would set a transfer price, we can see that it will be somewhere within the bargaining range. [The minimum transfer price ($20) and the maximum transfer price

($22) set the limits of the bargaining range.] Exhibit 10-4 provides income statements for each division before and after the agreement. Notice how the total profits of the firm increase by $182,000 as claimed; notice, too, how that profit increase is split between the two divisions.

EXHIBIT 10-4	Comparative Income Statements		
Before Negotiation: All Sales External			
	Circuit Board Division	**Games Division**	**Total**
Sales	$ 5,720,000	$ 4,095,000	$ 9,815,000
Less variable expenses:			
Cost of goods sold	(3,120,000)	(2,912,000)	(6,032,000)
Variable selling	(520,000)	(273,000)	(793,000)
Contribution margin	$ 2,080,000	$ 910,000	$ 2,990,000
Less: Fixed expenses	1,480,000	610,000	2,090,000
Operating income	$ 600,000	$ 300,000	$ 900,000
After Negotiation: Internal Transfers @ $21.10			
	Circuit Board Division	**Games Division**	**Total**
Sales	$ 5,638,100	$ 4,095,000	$ 9,733,100
Less variable expenses:			
Cost of goods sold	(3,120,000)	(2,830,100)	(5,950,100)
Variable selling	(338,000)	(273,000)	(611,000)
Contribution margin	$ 2,180,100	$ 991,900	$ 3,172,000
Less: Fixed expenses	1,480,000	610,000	2,090,000
Operating income	$ 700,100	$ 381,900	$ 1,082,000
Change in operating income	$ 100,100	$ 81,900	$ 182,000

Example 2: Excess Capacity

In perfectly competitive markets, the selling division can sell all that it wishes at the prevailing market price. In a less ideal setting, a selling division may be unable to sell all that it produces; accordingly, the division may reduce its output and, as a consequence, have excess capacity.[19]

To illustrate the role of transfer pricing and negotiation in this setting, consider the dialogue between Sharon Bunker, manager of a Plastics Division, and Carlos Rivera, manager of a Pharmaceutical Division:

CARLOS: Sharon, my division has shown a loss for the past three years. When I took over the division at the beginning of the year, I set a goal with headquarters to break even. At this point, projections show a loss of $5,000—but I think I have a way to reach my goal, if I can get your cooperation.

---

19. Output can be increased by decreasing selling price. Of course, decreasing selling price to increase sales volume may not increase profits—in fact, profits could easily decline. We assume in this example that the divisional manager has chosen the most advantageous selling price and that the division is still left with excess capacity.

SHARON: If I can help, I certainly will. What do you have in mind?

CARLOS: I need a special deal on your plastic bottle Model 3. I have the opportunity to place our aspirins with a large retail chain on the West Coast—a totally new market for our product. But we have to give them a real break on price. The chain has offered to pay $0.85 per bottle for an order of 250,000 bottles. My variable cost per unit is $0.60, not including the cost of the plastic bottle. I normally pay $0.40 for your bottle, but if I do that, the order will lose me $37,500. I cannot afford that kind of loss. I know that you have excess capacity. I'll place an order for 250,000 bottles, and I'll pay your variable cost per unit, provided it is no more than $0.25. Are you interested? Do you have sufficient excess capacity to handle a special order of 250,000 bottles?

SHARON: I have enough excess capacity to handle the order easily. The variable cost per bottle is $0.15. Transferring at that price would make me no worse off; my fixed costs will be there whether I make the bottles or not. However, I would like to have some contribution from an order like this. I'll tell you what I'll do. I'll let you have the order for $0.20. That way, we both make a $0.05 contribution per bottle, for a total contribution of $12,500. That'll put you in the black and help me get closer to my budgeted profit goal.

CARLOS: Great! This is better than I expected. If this West Coast chain provides more orders in the future—as I expect it will—and at better prices, I'll make sure you get our business.

Notice the role that opportunity costs play in the negotiation. In this case, the minimum transfer price is the Plastic Division's variable cost ($0.15), representing the incremental outlay if the order is accepted. Since the division has excess capacity, only variable costs are relevant to the decision. By covering the variable costs, the order does not affect the division's total profits. For the buying division, the maximum transfer price is the purchase price that would allow the division to cover its incremental costs on the special order ($0.25). Adding the $0.25 to the other costs of processing ($0.60), the total incremental costs incurred are $0.85 per unit. Since the selling price is also $0.85 per unit, the division is made no worse off. Both divisions, however, can be better off if the transfer price is between the minimum price of $0.15 and the maximum price of $0.25.

Comparative statements showing the contribution margin earned by each division and the firm as a whole are shown in Exhibit 10-5, on the following page, for each of the four transfer prices discussed. These statements show that the firm earns the same profit for all four transfer prices; however, different prices do affect the individual divisions' profits differently. Because of the autonomy of each division, there is no guarantee that the firm will earn the maximum profit. For example, if Sharon had insisted on maintaining the price of $0.40, no transfer would have taken place, and the overall $25,000 increase in profits would have been lost.

Disadvantages of Negotiated Transfer Prices

Negotiated transfer prices have three disadvantages that are commonly mentioned.

1. One divisional manager, possessing private information, may take advantage of another divisional manager.
2. Performance measures may be distorted by the negotiating skills of managers.
3. Negotiation can consume considerable time and resources.

It is interesting to observe that Carlos, the manager of the Pharmaceutical Division, did not know the variable cost of producing the plastic bottle. Yet, that cost was a key to the negotiation. This lack of knowledge gave Sharon, the other divisional manager, the opportunity to exploit the situation. For example, she could have claimed that the variable cost was $0.27 and offered to sell for $0.25 per unit as a favor to Carlos, saying that she would be willing to absorb a $5,000 loss in exchange for a promise of

EXHIBIT **10-5** **Comparative Statements**

Transfer Price of $0.40

	Pharmaceuticals	Plastics	Total
Sales	$212,500	$100,000	$312,500
Less: Variable expenses	250,000	37,500	287,500
Contribution margin	$ (37,500)	$ 62,500	$ 25,000

Transfer Price of $0.25

	Pharmaceuticals	Plastics	Total
Sales	$212,500	$ 62,500	$275,000
Less: Variable expenses	212,500	37,500	250,000
Contribution margin	$ 0	$ 25,000	$ 25,000

Transfer Price of $0.20

	Pharmaceuticals	Plastics	Total
Sales	$212,500	$ 50,000	$262,500
Less: Variable expenses	200,000	37,500	237,500
Contribution margin	$ 12,500	$ 12,500	$ 25,000

Transfer Price of $0.15

	Pharmaceuticals	Plastics	Total
Sales	$212,500	$ 37,500	$250,000
Less: Variable expenses	187,500	37,500	225,000
Contribution margin	$ 25,000	$ 0	$ 25,000

future business. In this case, she would capture the full $25,000 benefit of the transfer. Alternatively, she could have misrepresented the figure and used it to turn down the request, thus preventing Carlos from achieving his budgetary goal; after all, she may be competing with Carlos for promotions, bonuses, salary increases, and so on.

Fortunately, Sharon displayed sound judgment and acted with integrity. For negotiation to work, managers must be willing to share relevant information. How can this requirement be satisfied? The answer lies in the use of good internal control procedures.

Perhaps the best course of action is to hire managers with integrity—managers who have a commitment to ethical behavior. Additionally, top management can take other actions to discourage the use of private information for exploitive purposes. For example, corporate headquarters could base some part of the management reward structure on overall profitability to encourage actions that are in the best interests of the company as a whole.

The second disadvantage of negotiated transfer prices is that the practice distorts the measurement of managerial performance. According to this view, divisional profitability may be affected too strongly by the negotiating skills of managers, masking the actual management of resources entrusted to each manager. Although this argument may have some merit, it ignores the fact that negotiating skill is also a desirable managerial skill. Perhaps divisional profitability should reflect differences in negotiating skills.

The third criticism of this technique is that negotiating can be very time consuming. The time spent in negotiation by divisional managers could be spent managing other activities, which may have a bearing on the success of the division. Sometimes, negotiations may reach an impasse, forcing top management to spend time mediating the process.[20] Although the use of managerial time may be costly, a mutually satisfactory negotiated outcome can produce increased profits for the firm that easily exceed the cost of the managerial time involved. Furthermore, negotiation does not have to be repeated each time for similar transactions.

Advantages of Negotiated Transfer Prices

Although time consuming, negotiated transfer prices offer some hope of complying with the three criteria of goal congruence, autonomy, and accurate performance evaluation. As previously mentioned, decentralization offers important advantages for many firms. Just as important, however, is the process of making sure that actions of the different divisions mesh together so that the company's overall goals are attained. If negotiation helps ensure goal congruence, the temptation for central management to intervene is diminished considerably. There is, quite simply, no need to intervene. Finally, if negotiating skills of divisional managers are comparable or if the firm views these skills as an important managerial skill, concerns about motivation and accurate performance measures are avoided.

Cost-Based Transfer Prices

Three forms of cost-based transfer pricing will be considered: full cost, full cost plus markup, and variable cost plus fixed fee. In all three cases, to avoid passing on the inefficiencies of one division to another, standard costs should be used to determine the transfer price. For example, the Micro Products Division of **Tandem Computers, Inc.**, uses a corporate materials overhead rate, rather than the division-specific rate, to facilitate cost-based transfers between divisions.[21] A more important issue, however, is the propriety of cost-based transfer prices. Should they be used? If so, under what circumstances?

Full-Cost Transfer Pricing

Perhaps the least desirable type of transfer pricing approach is that of full cost. Its only real virtue is simplicity. Its disadvantages are considerable. Full-cost transfer pricing can provide perverse incentives and distort performance measures. As we have seen, the opportunity costs of both the buying and selling divisions are essential for determining the propriety of internal transfers. At the same time, they provide useful reference points for determining a mutually satisfactory transfer price. Only rarely will full cost provide accurate information about opportunity costs.

A full-cost transfer price would have shut down the negotiated prices described earlier. In the first example, the manager would never have considered transferring internally if the price had to be full cost. Yet, by transferring at selling price less some distribution expenses, both divisions—and the firm as a whole—were better off. In the second example, the manager of the Pharmaceutical Division could never have accepted the special order with the West Coast chain. Both divisions and the company would have been worse off, both in the short run and in the long run.

Full Cost Plus Markup

Full cost plus markup suffers from virtually the same problems as full cost. It is somewhat less perverse, however, if the markup can be negotiated. For example, a

---

20. The involvement of top management may be very cursory, however. In the case of a very large oil company that negotiates virtually all transfer prices, two divisional managers could not come to an agreement after several weeks of effort and appealed to their superior. His response: "Either come to an agreement within 24 hours, or you are both fired." Needless to say, an agreement was reached within the allotted time.

21. Earl D. Bennett, Sarah A. Reed, and Ted Simmonds, "Learning from a CIM Experience," *Management Accounting* (July 1991): 28–33.

full-cost-plus-markup formula could have been used to represent the negotiated transfer price of the first example. In some cases, a full-cost-plus-markup formula may be the outcome of negotiation; if so, it is simply another example of negotiated transfer pricing. In these cases, the use of this method is fully justified. Using full cost plus markup to represent all negotiated prices, however, is not possible (e.g., it could not be used to represent the negotiated price of the second example). The superior approach is negotiation, since more cases can be represented, and full consideration of opportunity costs is possible.

Variable Cost Plus Fixed Fee

Like full cost plus markup, variable cost plus fixed fee can be a useful transfer pricing approach provided that the fixed fee is negotiable. This method has one advantage over full cost plus markup: if the selling division is operating below capacity, variable cost is its opportunity cost. Assuming that the fixed fee is negotiable, the variable cost approach can be equivalent to negotiated transfer pricing. Negotiation with full consideration of opportunity costs is preferred.

Propriety of Use

In spite of the disadvantages of cost-based transfer prices, many companies use these methods, especially full cost and full cost plus markup. There must be some compelling reasons for their use—reasons that outweigh the benefits associated with negotiated transfer prices and the disadvantages of these methods. The methods do have the virtue of being simple and objective. These qualities, by themselves, cannot justify their use, however. Some possible explanations for the use of these methods can be given. In many cases, transfers between divisions have a small impact on the profitability of either division. For this situation, it may be cost beneficial to use an easy-to-identify, cost-based formula rather than spending valuable time and resources on negotiation.

In other cases, the use of full cost plus markup may simply be the formula agreed upon in negotiations. That is, the full-cost-plus-markup formula is the outcome of negotiation, but the transfer pricing method being used is reported as full cost plus markup. Once established, this formula could be used until the original conditions change to

---

COST MANAGEMENT   Technology in Action

Companies can use ERP packages or customized software to support their international marketing. **Cisco** is an example of a company applying ERP in the international arena. An important feature of Cisco's Oracle system has been its multicurrency functionality. Customers can be billed in their own currency, while Cisco itself uses U.S. currency. In addition, Pete Solvik, Cisco's chief information officer, points out that "we can also deal with the tax and regulatory issues in every country where we do business, without problems, because our system is based primarily in the United States. And we're also focusing on Euro support."

Cisco points out that **Oracle** supports its globalization initiatives. The company would not have been able to acquire close to 30 companies in five years if it had not had the ability to integrate companies into one Oracle-based, worldwide system. In addition, Cisco relies on Oracle's manufacturing applications to run its worldwide outsource factory across almost 50 outsource buyers and manufacturers of goods.

Twentieth Century Fox uses a customized Internet software package, Eight Ball, to speed the distribution of data and improve decision making. Eight Ball puts a massive, constantly updated database at the disposal of Fox executives around the world. If a movie or video is not "selling well in Paris, for example, executives will be able, in hours, to tweak the advertising budget to compensate." An executive in Hong Kong can communicate with other Fox executives around the world for ideas on how to spice up in-store displays.

Sources: Information on Cisco taken from Oracle's Web site, "Oracle at Work with Cisco Systems, Inc."; information on Fox taken from Ronald Grover, "Fox's New Star: The Internet," *Business Week E. Biz* (November 1, 1999): 42–46.

the point where renegotiation is necessary. In this way, the time and resources of negotiation can be minimized. For example, the goods transferred may be custom-made, and the managers may have little ability to identify an outside market price. In this case, reimbursement of full costs plus a reasonable rate of return may be a good surrogate for the transferring division's opportunity costs.

Transfer Pricing and the Multinational Firm

For the multinational firm, transfer pricing must accomplish two objectives, performance evaluation and optimal determination of income taxes. If all countries had the same tax structure, then transfer prices would be set independently of income taxes. However, there are high-tax countries (like the United States) and low-tax countries (such as the Cayman Islands). As a result, MNCs may use transfer pricing to shift costs to high-tax countries and shift revenues to low-tax countries.

Exhibit 10-6 illustrates this concept, as two transfer prices are set. The first transfer price is $100 as title for the goods passes from the Belgian subsidiary to the reinvoicing center in Puerto Rico. Because the first transfer price is equal to full cost, profit is zero, and income taxes on zero profit also equal zero. The second transfer price is set at $200 by the reinvoicing center in Puerto Rico. The transfer from Puerto Rico to the United States does result in profit, but this profit does not result in any income tax because Puerto Rico has no corporate income taxes. Finally, the U.S. subsidiary sells the product to an external party at the $200 transfer price. Again, price equals cost, so there is no profit on which to pay income taxes. Consider what would have happened without the reinvoicing center. The goods would have gone directly from Belgium to the United States. If the transfer price was set at $200, the profit in Belgium would have been $100, subject to the 42 percent tax rate. Alternatively, if the transfer price set was $100, no Belgian income tax would have been paid, but the U.S. subsidiary would have realized a profit of $100, and that would have been subject to the U.S. corporate income tax rate of 35 percent.

EXHIBIT 10-6	Use of Transfer Pricing to Affect Income Taxes Paid
Action	**Tax Impact**
Belgian subsidiary of Parent Company produces a component at a cost of $100 per unit. Title to the component is transferred to a Reinvoicing Center* in Puerto Rico at a transfer price of $100/unit.	42% tax rate $100 revenue − $100 cost = $0 Taxes paid = $0
Reinvoicing Center in Puerto Rico, also a subsidiary of Parent Company, transfers title of component to U.S. subsidiary of Parent Company at a transfer price of $200/unit.	0% tax rate $200 revenue − $100 cost = $100 Taxes paid = $0
U.S. subsidiary sells component to external company at $200 each.	35% tax rate $200 revenue − $200 cost = $0 Taxes paid = $0

*A reinvoicing center takes title to the goods but does not physically receive them. The primary objective of a reinvoicing center is to shift profits to divisions in low-tax countries.

U.S.-based multinationals are subject to Internal Revenue Code Section 482 on the pricing of intercompany transactions. This section gives the IRS the authority to reallocate income and deductions among divisions if it believes that such reallocation will reduce potential tax evasion. Basically, Section 482 requires that sales be made at "arm's length." That is, the transfer price set should match the price that would be set if the transfer were being made by unrelated parties, adjusted for differences that have a measurable effect on the price. Differences include landing costs and marketing costs. Landing costs (e.g., freight, insurance, customs duties, and special taxes) can increase the allowable transfer price. Marketing costs are usually avoided for internal transfers and reduce the transfer price. The IRS allows three pricing methods that approximate arm's-length pricing. In order of preference, these are the comparable uncontrolled price method, the resale price method, and the cost-plus method. The **comparable uncontrolled price method** is essentially market price. The **resale price method** is equal to the sales price received by the reseller less an appropriate markup. That is, the subsidiary purchasing a good for resale sets a transfer price equal to the resale price less a gross profit percentage. The **cost-plus method** is simply the cost-based transfer price.

Let's use ABC, Inc., as an example. Division B (in the United States) purchases a component from Division C (in Canada). The component can be purchased externally for $38 each. The freight and insurance on the item amount to $5; however, commissions of $3.80 need not be paid. In this case, the appropriate transfer pricing method is the comparable uncontrolled price method and is found as follows:

Market price	$38.00
Plus: Freight and insurance	5.00
Less: Commissions	(3.80)
Transfer price	$39.20

Suppose instead, that there is no outside market for the component that Division C transfers to Division B. Then, the comparable uncontrolled price method cannot be used. Let's try the resale price method. If Division B sells the component for $42 and normally receives a 40 percent markup on cost of goods sold, then the transfer price would be $30, computed as follows:

$$\text{Resale price} = \text{Transfer price} + 0.40 \text{ Transfer price}$$
$$\$42 = 1.40 \times \text{Transfer price}$$
$$\text{Transfer price} = \$42/1.40$$
$$= \$30$$

Finally, let's assume that there is no external market for the component transferred from Division C to Division B, and that the component is used in the manufacture of another product (i.e., it is not resold). Then, the cost-plus method is used, and we need to know Division C's manufacturing cost. Let's assume it is $20. Now, Division B can add the $5 cost of freight and insurance to the $20 manufacturing cost to arrive at a cost-based transfer price of $25.

The determination of an arm's-length price is a difficult one. Many times, the transfer pricing situation facing a company does not "fit" any of the three preferred methods just outlined. Then, the IRS will permit a fourth method—a transfer price negotiated between the company and the IRS. The IRS, taxpayers, and the Tax Court have struggled with negotiated transfer prices for years. However, this type of negotiation occurs after the fact—after income tax returns have been submitted and the company is being audited. Recently, the IRS has authorized the issuance of **advance pricing agreements (APAs)** to assist tax-paying firms to determine whether a proposed transfer price is acceptable to the IRS in advance of income tax filing. "An APA is an agreement between the IRS and a taxpayer on the pricing method to be applied in an international transaction. It can cover transfers of intangibles (such as royalties on licenses), sales of property, provision of services, and other items. An APA is binding on both the IRS and the taxpayer for the years specified in the APA and is not made public."[22] Since the APA procedure is so new, neither the IRS nor the firms are sure of the informational requirements. Currently, the IRS may limit its advance rulings on transactions between U.S.-based companies and divisions in treaty countries, such as Australia, Canada, Japan, and the United Kingdom. For example, **Apple Computer** obtained an advance pricing agreement from the IRS on transfers of Apple products to its Australian subsidiary.[23]

Transfer pricing abuses are illegal—if they can be proved to be abuses. Many examples exist of both foreign and U.S. firms charging unusual transfer prices. The IRS successfully showed that **Toyota** had been overcharging its U.S. subsidiary for cars, trucks, and parts sold in the United States. The effect was to lower Toyota's reported income substantially in the United States and increase income reported in Japan. The settlement reportedly approached $1 billion.[24]

The IRS also regulates the transfer pricing of foreign companies with U.S. subsidiaries. A U.S. company that is at least 25 percent foreign owned must keep extensive documentation of arm's-length transfer pricing.

Of course, MNCs are also subject to taxation by other countries as well as the United States. Since income taxes are virtually universal, consideration of income tax effects pervades management decision making. Canada, Japan, the European Union, and South Korea have all issued transfer pricing regulations within the past 12 years. This increased emphasis on transfer price justification may account for the increased use of market prices as the transfer price by MNCs. A survey of transfer pricing methods used by *Fortune 500* companies in 1977 and 1990 showed that MNCs reduced their reliance on cost-based transfer prices in favor of market-based transfer prices over the 13-year period.[25] Additionally, the most important environmental variable considered by MNCs in setting a transfer pricing policy is overall profit to the company—with overall profit including the income tax impact of intracompany transfers.

The Secretaria de Hacienda y Credito Publico (Hacienda), the income tax authority of Mexico, now requires maquiladoras to comply with both Mexican and U.S. transfer pricing rules. Because the United States sees maquiladoras as service providers, an appropriate transfer pricing approach is a markup on operating expenses. The amount of markup depends on the particular circumstances of each maquiladora. Hacienda has an additional enforcement tool, the 1.8 percent Mexican asset tax. Maquiladoras, out of compliance with transfer pricing rules, must pay the asset tax on all noninventory assets in Mexico. The tax implications for U.S. companies operating in Mexico include not only income taxes, but also the customs valuation of goods imported into Mexico and merchandise assembled by the maquiladora and returned to the United States, as well as the NAFTA Certificat of Origin computations. This is a case where the APA may be especially valuable.[26]

Managers may legally avoid income taxes; they may not evade them. The distinction is important. Unfortunately, the difference between avoidance and evasion is less a line than a blurry gray area. While the situation depicted in Exhibit 10-6 is clearly abusive, other tax-motivated actions are not. For example, an MNC may decide to establish a needed research and development center within an existing subsidiary in a high-tax country, since the costs are deductible. MNCs may have income tax-planning information systems that attempt to accomplish global income tax minimization. This is not an easy task.

22. "New Intercompany Pricing Rulings Create and Eliminate Tax Uncertainty," *Deloitte & Touche Review* (March 25, 1991): 6.

23. Roger Y. W. Tang, "Transfer Pricing in the 1990s," *Management Accounting* (February 1992): 22–26.

24. "The Corporate Shell Game," *Newsweek* (April 15, 1991): 48–49.

25. Tang, op. cit.

26. "Maquiladoras: Transfer Pricing and Customs Planning," *Deloitte & Touche Review* (February 6, 1995): 5–6; and "Mexico Sets Tight Deadline on Maquiladora Transfer Pricing," *Deloitte & Touche Review* (April 17, 1995): 5–6.

SUMMARY

Responsibility accounting is closely allied to the structure and decision-making authority of the firm. In order to increase overall efficiency, many companies choose to decentralize. The essence of decentralization is decision-making freedom. In a decentralized organization, lower-level managers make and implement decisions, whereas in a centralized organization, lower-level managers are responsible only for implementing decisions.

Reasons for decentralization are numerous. Companies decentralize because local managers can make better decisions using local information. Local managers can also provide a more timely response to changing conditions. Additionally, decentralization for large, diversified companies is necessary because of cognitive limitations—it is impossible for any one central manager to be fully knowledgable concerning all products and markets. Other reasons include training and motivating local managers and freeing top management from day-to-day operating conditions so that they can spend time on longer-range activities, such as strategic planning.

Three measures of divisional performance are return on investment (ROI), residual income, and economic value added (EVA). All three relate income to the operating assets used to achieve the income.

Decentralized firms may encourage goal congruence by constructing management compensation programs that reward managers for taking actions which benefit the firm. Possible reward systems include cash compensation, stock options, and noncash benefits.

When one division of a company produces a product that can be used in production by another division, transfer pricing exists. The transfer pricing problem involves finding a mutually satisfactory transfer price that is compatible with the company's goals of accurate performance evaluation, divisional autonomy, and goal congruence. Three methods are commonly used for setting transfer prices: market-based, cost-based, and negotiated. In general, the market price is best, followed by negotiated, and then cost-based transfer prices.

The accountant provides financial and business expertise. The job of the accountant in the international firm is made more challenging by the ambiguous and ever-changing nature of global business. He or she must stay up to date in a variety of business areas ranging from information systems to marketing, to management, to politics, and to economics. In addition, the accountant must be familiar with the financial accounting rules of the countries in which his or her firm operates.

Companies involved in international business may structure their activities in three major ways. They may engage in import/export activities; they may purchase wholly owned subsidiaries; or they may participate in joint ventures. Accountants must be aware of the potential exposure of their firms to transaction risk, economic risk, and translation risk. They may hedge to limit exposure to these risks.

MNCs choose to decentralize for much the same reasons domestic companies choose to decentralize. Reasons for decentralization are numerous. Companies decentralize because local managers can make better decisions using local information. Local managers can also provide a more timely response to changing conditions. Additionally, decentralization for large, diversified companies is necessary because of cognitive limitations—it is impossible for any one central manager to be fully knowledgeable of all products and markets. Other reasons include training and motivating local managers and freeing up top management from day-to-day operating conditions so that they can spend time on more long-range activities, such as strategic planning.

Environmental factors are those social, economic, political, legal, and cultural factors that differ from country to country and that managers cannot change. These factors, however, do affect profits and ROI. Therefore, evaluation of the divisional manager should be separated from evaluation of the subsidiary.

When one division of a company produces a product that can be used in production by another division, transfer pricing exists. The transfer price is revenue to the selling division and cost to the buying division. As is the case with domestic companies, MNCs may use transfer prices in performance evaluation. MNCs with subsidiaries in both high-tax and low-tax countries may use transfer pricing to shift costs to the high-tax countries (where their deductibility will lower income tax payments) and to shift revenues to low-tax countries.

MNCs face ethical issues different from those of domestic companies. Other countries have business customs and laws that differ from those of the home country. The firm must determine whether a particular custom is merely a different way of doing business or a violation of its own code of ethics.

REVIEW PROBLEMS AND SOLUTIONS

1   TRANSFER PRICING

The Components Division produces a part that is used by the Goods Division. The cost of manufacturing the part is as follows:

Direct materials	$10
Direct labor	2
Variable overhead	3
Fixed overhead*	5
Total cost	$20

*Based on a practical volume of 200,000 parts.

Other costs incurred by the Components Division are as follows:

Fixed selling and administrative	$500,000
Variable selling	$1 per unit

The part usually sells for between $28 and $30 in the external market. Currently, the Components Division is selling it to external customers for $29. The division is capable of producing 200,000 units of the part per year; however, because of a weak economy, only 150,000 parts are expected to be sold during the coming year. The variable selling expenses are avoidable if the part is sold internally.

The Goods Division has been buying the same part from an external supplier for $28. It expects to use 50,000 units of the part during the coming year. The manager of the Goods Division has offered to buy 50,000 units from the Components Division for $18 per unit.

Required:

1. Determine the minimum transfer price that the Components Division would accept.
2. Determine the maximum transfer price that the manager of the Goods Division would pay.
3. Should an internal transfer take place? Why or why not? If you were the manager of the Components Division, would you sell the 50,000 components for $18 each? Explain.

4. Suppose that the average operating assets of the Components Division total $10 million. Compute the ROI for the coming year, assuming that the 50,000 units are transferred to the Goods Division for $21 each.

SOLUTION

1. The minimum transfer price is $15. The Components Division has idle capacity and so must cover only its incremental costs, which are the variable manufacturing costs. (Fixed costs are the same whether or not the internal transfer occurs; the variable selling expenses are avoidable.)

2. The maximum transfer price is $28. The Goods Division would not pay more for the part than the price it would have to pay an external supplier.

3. Yes, an internal transfer ought to occur; the opportunity cost of the selling division is less than the opportunity cost of the buying division. The Components Division would earn an additional $150,000 profit ($3 × 50,000). The total joint benefit, however, is $650,000 ($13 × 50,000). The manager of the Components Division should attempt to negotiate a more favorable outcome for that division.

4. Income statement:

Sales [($29 × 150,000) + ($21 × 50,000)]	$ 5,400,000
Less: Variable cost of goods sold ($15 × 200,000)	(3,000,000)
Variable selling expenses ($1 × 150,000)	(150,000)
Contribution margin	$ 2,250,000
Less: Fixed overhead ($5 × 200,000)	(1,000,000)
Fixed selling and administrative	(500,000)
Operating income	$ 750,000

$$\text{ROI} = \text{Operating income/Average operating assets}$$
$$= \$750,000/\$10,000,000$$
$$= 0.075$$

2 EVA

Surfit Company, which manufactures surfboards, has been in business for six years. Sam Foster, owner of Surfit, is pleased with the firm's profit picture and is considering taking the company public (i.e., selling stock in Surfit on the NASDAQ exchange). Data for the past year are as follows:

After-tax operating income	$ 250,000
Total capital employed	1,060,000
Long-term debt (interest at 9%)	100,000
Owner's equity	900,000

Surfit Company pays taxes at the rate of 35 percent.

Required:

1. Calculate the weighted average cost of capital, assuming that owner's equity is valued at the average cost of common stock of 12 percent. Calculate the total cost of capital for Surfit Company last year.
2. Calculate EVA for Surfit Company.

SOLUTION 1.

	Amount	Percent	×	After-Tax Cost	=	Weighted Cost
Long-term debt	$ 100,000	0.10		0.0585		0.0059
Owner's equity	900,000	0.90		0.1200		0.1080
Total	$1,000,000					0.1139

The weighted average cost of capital is 11.39 percent.
The cost of capital last year = 0.1139 × $1,060,000 = $120,734.

2. EVA = $250,000 − $120,734 = $129,266

3 CURRENCY EXCHANGE, TRANSFER PRICING

Golo, Inc., has two manufacturing plants, one in Singapore and the other in San Antonio. The San Antonio plant is located in a foreign trade zone. On March 1, Golo received a large order from a Japanese customer. The order is for ¥10,000,000 to be paid on receipt of the goods, scheduled for June 1. The goods are to be delivered by Golo to the Japanese company's Los Angeles division. Golo assigned this order to the San Antonio plant; however, one necessary component for the order is to be manufactured by the Singapore plant. The component will be transferred to San Antonio on April 1 using a cost-plus transfer price of $10,000 (U.S. dollars). Typically, two percent of the Singapore parts are defective. U.S. tariff on the component parts is 30 percent. Carrying cost for Golo is 15 percent per year.

The spot rates for $1 U.S. are as follows:

	Exchange Rates of $1 for	
	Yen	Singapore Dollars
March 1	107.00	1.60
April 1	107.50	1.55
June 1	107.60	1.50

Required:

1. What is the total cost of the imported parts from Singapore to the San Antonio plant in U.S. dollars?
2. If the San Antonio plant was not located in a foreign trade zone, what would be the total cost of the imported parts from Singapore?
3. How much does Golo expect to receive from the Japanese customer in U.S. dollars using the spot rate at the time of the order?
4. How much does Golo expect to receive from the Japanese customer in U.S. dollars using the spot rate at the time of payment?
5. Suppose that on March 1, the forward rate for June 1 delivery of $1 for yen is 107.20. If Golo's policy is to hedge foreign currency transactions, what is the amount Golo expects to receive on June 1 in U.S. dollars?

SOLUTION 1.

Transfer price	$10,000
Tariff ($9,800 × 0.3)	2,940
Total cost	$12,940

The transfer price was set in U.S. dollars, so there is no currency exchange involved for the San Antonio plant. The San Antonio plant is in a foreign trade zone, so the 30 percent tariff is paid only on the good parts costing $9,800 ($10,000 × 0.98). (*Note:* If the delivery of goods was to Japan instead of Los Angeles, no tariff would be due since the imported parts would never enter the United States.)

2. If the San Antonio plant were located outside the foreign trade zone, the cost of the imported parts would be as follows:

Transfer price	$10,000
Tariff ($10,000 × 0.3)	3,000
Carrying cost of tariff*	75
Total cost	$13,075

*$3,000 × 2/12 × 0.15 = $75.

3. On March 1, Golo expects to receive $93,458 (¥10,000,000/107).

4. On June 1, Golo expects to receive $92,937 (¥10,000,000/107.60).

5. If Golo hedges, the forward rate is used, and the amount to be received on June 1 is $93,284 (¥10,000,000/107.20).

KEY TERMS

Advance pricing agreements (APAs) 460

Centralized decision making 432

Comparable uncontrolled price method 460

Cost center 431

Cost-plus method 460

Decentralization 432

Decentralized decision making 432

Economic value added (EVA) 441

Effectiveness 435

Efficiency 435

Investment center 431

Margin 436

Maximum transfer price 451

Minimum transfer price 451

Multinational corporation (MNC) 432

Myopic behavior 439

Operating assets 436

Operating income 436

Opportunity cost approach 451

Perquisites 445

Profit center 431

Resale price method 460

Residual income 439

Responsibility accounting 431

Responsibility center 431

Return on investment (ROI) 436

Revenue center 431

Stock option 446

Transfer prices 450

Transfer pricing problem 451

Turnover 436

Weighted average cost of capital 442

QUESTIONS FOR WRITING AND DISCUSSION

1. What is decentralization? Discuss the differences between centralized and decentralized decision making.
2. Explain why firms choose to decentralize.

3. Explain how access to local information can improve decision making.
4. What are margin and turnover? Explain how these concepts can improve the evaluation of an investment center.
5. What are the three benefits of ROI? Explain how each can lead to improved profitability.
6. What are two disadvantages of ROI? Explain how each can lead to decreased profitability.
7. What is residual income? Explain how residual income overcomes one of ROI's disadvantages.
8. What is EVA? How does it differ from ROI and residual income?
9. What is a stock option? How can it encourage goal congruence?
10. What is a transfer price?
11. What is the transfer pricing problem?
12. If the minimum transfer price of the selling division is less than the maximum transfer price of the buying division, the intermediate product should be transferred internally. Do you agree or disagree? Why?
13. If an outside, perfectly competitive market exists for the intermediate product, what should the transfer price be? Why?
14. Identify three cost-based transfer prices. What are the disadvantages of cost-based transfer prices? When might it be appropriate to use cost-based transfer prices?
15. What is the purpose of Internal Revenue Code Section 482? What four methods of transfer pricing are acceptable under this section?

EXERCISES

10-1   ROI, MARGIN, TURNOVER

LO3   Gilliam Corporation presented two years of data for its Sporting Goods Division and its Camping Division.

Sporting Goods Division:

	Year 1	Year 2
Sales	$70,000,000	$75,000,000
Operating income	2,800,000	3,000,000
Average operating assets	20,000,000	20,000,000

Camping Division:

	Year 1	Year 2
Sales	$24,000,000	$25,000,000
Operating income	1,200,000	1,000,000
Average operating assets	10,000,000	10,000,000

Required:

1. Compute the ROI and the margin and turnover ratios for each year for the Sporting Goods Division.
2. Compute the ROI and the margin and turnover ratios for each year for the Camping Division.
3. Explain the change in ROI from Year 1 to Year 2 for each division.

10-2 ROI and Investment Decisions

LO3 Refer to **Exercise 10-1** for data. At the end of Year 2, the manager of the Camping Division is concerned about the division's performance. As a result, he is considering the opportunity to invest in two independent projects. The first is called the "Ever-Tent"; it is a small 2-person tent capable of withstanding the high winds at the top of Mt. Everest. While the market for actual Everest climbers is small, the manager expects that well-to-do weekend campers will buy it due to the cachet of the name and its light weight. The second is a "KiddieKamp" kit which includes a child-sized sleeping bag and a colorful pup tent that can be set up easily in one's back yard. Without the investments, the division expects that Year 2 data will remain unchanged. The expected operating incomes and the outlay required for each investment are as follows:

	Ever-Tent	KiddieKamp
Operating income	$ 55,000	$ 38,000
Outlay	500,000	400,000

Gilliam's corporate headquarters has made available up to $1 million of capital for this division. Any funds not invested by the division will be retained by headquarters and invested to earn the company's minimum required rate of return, 9 percent.

Required:

1. Compute the ROI for each investment.
2. Compute the divisional ROI for each of the following four alternatives:
   a. The Ever-Tent is added.
   b. The KiddieKamp is added.
   c. Both investments are added.
   d. Neither investment is made; the status quo is maintained.
   Assuming that divisional managers are evaluated and rewarded on the basis of ROI performance, which alternative do you think the divisional manager will choose?

10-3 Residual Income and Investment Decisions

LO3 Refer to the data given in **Exercise 10-2**.

Required:

1. Compute the residual income for each of the opportunities.
2. Compute the divisional residual income for each of the following four alternatives:
   a. The Ever-Tent is added.
   b. The KiddieKamp is added.
   c. Both investments are added.
   d. Neither investment is made; the status quo is maintained.
   Assuming that divisional managers are evaluated and rewarded on the basis of residual income, which alternative do you think the divisional manager will choose?
3. Based on your answer in Requirement 2, compute the profit or loss from the divisional manager's investment decision. Was the correct decision made?

10-4 Calculating EVA

LO3 Brewster Company manufactures elderberry wine. Last year, Brewster earned operating income of $210,000 after income taxes. Capital employed equaled $2 million.

Brewster is 50 percent equity and 50 percent 10-year bonds paying 6 percent interest. Brewster's marginal tax rate is 35 percent. The company is considered a fairly risky investment and probably commands a 12-point premium above the 6 percent rate on long-term Treasury bonds.

Mortimer Brewster's aunts, Abby and Martha, have just retired, and Mortimer is the new CEO of Brewster Company. He would like to improve EVA for the company. Compute EVA under each of the following independent scenarios that Mortimer is considering. (Use a spreadsheet to perform your calculations.)

Required:

1. No changes are made; calculate EVA using the original data.
2. Sugar will be used to replace another natural ingredient (arsenic) in the elderberry wine. This should not affect costs but will begin to affect the market assessment of Brewster Company, bringing the premium above long-term Treasury bills to 9 percent the first year and 6 percent the second year. Calculate revised EVA for both years.
3. Brewster is considering expanding but needs additional capital. The company could borrow money, but it is considering selling more common stock, which would increase equity to 80 percent of total financing. Total capital employed would be $3,000,000. The new after-tax operating income would be $450,000. Using the original data, calculate EVA. Then, recalculate EVA assuming the materials substitution described in Requirement 2. New after-tax income will be $450,000, and in Year 1, the premium will be 9 percent above the long-term Treasury rate. In Year 2, it will be 6 percent above the long-term Treasury rate. (*Hint:* You will calculate three EVAs for this requirement.)

10-5 OPERATING INCOME FOR SEGMENTS

LO3

Whirlmore, Inc., manufactures and sells washers and dryers through three divisions: Home-Supreme, Apartment, and International. Each division is evaluated as a profit center. Data for each division for last year are as follows (numbers in thousands).

	Home-Supreme	*Apartment*	*International*
Sales	$2,700	$2,400	$1,300
Cost of goods sold	1,770	1,870	1,040
Selling and administrative expenses	640	180	100

The income tax rate for Whirlmore, Inc., is 30 percent. Whirlmore, Inc., has two sources of financing: bonds paying 8 percent interest, which account for 20 percent of total investment, and equity accounting for the remaining 80 percent of total investment. Whirlmore, Inc., has been in business for over 15 years and is considered a relatively stable stock, despite its link to the cyclical construction industry. As a result, Whirlmore stock has an opportunity cost of 5 percent over the 6 percent long-term government bond rate. Whirlmore's total capital employed is $3 million ($2,100,000 for the Home-Supreme Division, $500,000 for the Apartment Division, and the remainder for the International Division).

Required:

1. Prepare a segmented income statement for Whirlmore, Inc., for last year.
2. Calculate Whirlmore's weighted average cost of capital.
3. Calculate EVA for each division and for Whirlmore, Inc.
4. Comment on the performance of each of the divisions.

10-6   TRANSFER PRICING, IDLE CAPACITY

LO5, LO6   VSOP, Inc., has a number of divisions that produce liquors, malt beverages, and glass-ware. The Glassware Division manufactures a variety of bottles which can be sold externally (to soft-drink and juice bottlers) or internally to VSOP's Malt Beverage Division. Sales and cost data on a case of 24 basic 12-ounce bottles are as follows:

Unit selling price	$2.80
Unit variable cost	$1.15
Unit product fixed cost*	$0.70
Practical capacity in cases	500,000

*$350,000/500,000.

During the coming year, the Glassware Division expects to sell 390,000 cases of this bottle. The Malt Beverage Division currently plans to buy 100,000 cases on the outside market for $2.80 each. Jill Von Holstein, manager of the Glassware Division, approached Eric Alman, manager of the Malt Beverage Division, and offered to sell the 100,000 cases for $2.75 each. Jill explained to Eric that she can avoid selling costs of $0.10 per case by selling internally and that she would split the savings by offering a $0.05 discount on the usual price.

Required:

1. What is the minimum transfer price that the Glassware Division would be willing to accept? What is the maximum transfer price that the Malt Beverage Division would be willing to pay? Should an internal transfer take place? What would be the benefit (or loss) to the firm as a whole if the internal transfer takes place?
2. Suppose Eric knows that the Glassware Division has idle capacity. Do you think that he would agree to the transfer price of $2.75? Suppose he counters with an offer to pay $2.40. If you were Jill, would you be interested in this price? Explain with supporting computations.
3. Suppose that VSOP's policy is that all internal transfers take place at full manufacturing cost. What would the transfer price be? Would the transfer take place?

10-7   TRANSFER PRICING AND SECTION 482

LO6   Auto-Lite Manufacturing, Inc., has a division in the United States that produces a variety of headlamps and interior light packages for automobiles. One type of headlamp for compact cars is transferred to a Manufacturing Division in Italy. The headlamps can be (and are) sold externally in the United States for $25 each. It costs $0.75 per headlamp for shipping and $2.00 per headlamp for import duties. When the headlamps are sold externally, Auto-Lite Manufacturing spends $2.50 per headlamp for commissions and an average of $0.30 per headlamp for advertising.

Required:

1. Which Section 482 method should be used to calculate the allowable transfer price?
2. Using the appropriate Section 482 method, calculate the transfer price.

10-8   TRANSFER PRICING AND SECTION 482

LO6   Perrex, Inc., has a division in Honduras that makes a powder used to coat wire, and another division in the United States that manufactures wire. The Powder Division incurs manufacturing costs of $0.83 for one pound of powder.

The Wire Division currently buys its powder coating from an outside supplier for $0.95 per pound. If the Wire Division purchases the powder from the Honduran division, the shipping costs will be $0.05 per pound, but sales commissions of $0.06 per pound will be avoided with an internal transfer.

Required:

1. Which Section 482 method should be used to calculate the allowable transfer price? Calculate the appropriate transfer price per pound.
2. Assume that the Wire Division cannot buy this type of powder externally since it has an unusual formula that prevents electrical conductance. Which Section 482 method should be used to calculate the allowable transfer price? Calculate the appropriate transfer price per pound.

10-9   TRANSFER PRICING AND SECTION 482

LO6   Zetter, Inc., has a division in Canada that makes paint. Zetter has another U.S. division, the Retail Division, that operates a chain of home improvement stores. The Retail Division would like to buy the unique, long-lasting paint from the Canadian division, since this type of paint is not currently available. The Paint Division incurs manufacturing costs of $4.60 for one gallon of paint.

If the Retail Division purchases the paint from the Canadian division, the shipping costs will be $0.45 per gallon, but sales commissions of $1.30 per gallon will be avoided with an internal transfer. The Retail Division plans to sell the paint for $18 per gallon. Normally, the Retail Division earns a gross margin of 50 percent above cost of goods sold.

Required:

1. Which Section 482 method should be used to calculate the allowable transfer price?
2. Calculate the appropriate transfer price per gallon.

10-10   ROI AND RESIDUAL INCOME

LO3   A multinational corporation has a number of divisions, two of which are the Pacific-Rim Division and the European Division. Data on the two divisions are as follows:

	Pacific-Rim	*European*
Average operating assets	900,000	9,000,000
Operating income	126,000	1,350,000
Minimum required return	12%	12%

Required:

1. Compute residual income for each division. By comparing residual income, is it possible to make a useful comparison of divisional performance? Explain.
2. Compute the residual rate of return by dividing the residual income by the average operating assets. Is it possible now to say that one division outperformed the other? Explain.
3. Compute the return on investment for each division. Can we make meaningful comparisons of divisional performance? Explain.
4. Add the residual rate of return computed in Requirement 2 to the required rate of return. Compare these rates with the ROI computed in Requirement 3. Will this relationship always be the same?

10-11 MARGIN, TURNOVER, ROI

LO3 Consider the data for each of the following four independent companies:

	A	B	C	D
Revenue	$10,000	$48,000	$96,000	?
Expenses	$8,000	?	$90,000	?
Operating income	$2,000	$12,000	?	?
Assets	$40,000	?	$48,000	$9,600
Margin	?	25%	?	6.25%
Turnover	?	0.50	?	2.00
ROI	?	?	?	?

Required:

1. Calculate the missing values in the above table.
2. Assume that the cost of capital is 9 percent for each of the four firms. Compute the residual income for each of the four firms.

10-12 ROI, RESIDUAL INCOME

LO3 The following selected data pertain to the Silverthorne Division for last year:

Sales	$1,000,000
Variable costs	$600,000
Traceable fixed costs	$100,000
Average invested capital	$1,500,000
Imputed interest rate	15%

Required:

1. How much is the residual income?
2. How much is the return on investment?

10-13 STOCK OPTIONS

LO4 Roselle, Inc., has acquired two new companies, one in consumer products and the other in financial services. Roselle's top management believes that the executives of the two newly acquired companies can be most quickly assimilated into the parent company if they own shares of Roselle stock. Accordingly, on April 1, Roselle approved a stock option plan whereby each of the top four executives of the new companies could purchase up to 20,000 shares of Roselle stock at $15 per share. The option will expire in five years.

Required:

1. If Roselle stock rises to $34 per share by December 1, what is the value of the option to each executive?
2. Discuss some of the advantages and disadvantages of the Roselle stock option plan.

PROBLEMS

10-14 TRANSFER PRICING

LO5, LO6 Truman Industries is a vertically integrated firm with several divisions that operate as decentralized profit centers. Truman's Systems Division manufactures scientific in-

CMA

struments and uses the products of two of Truman's other divisions. The Board Division manufactures printed circuit boards (PCBs). One PCB model is made exclusively for the Systems Division using proprietary designs, while less complex models are sold in outside markets. The products of the Transistor Division are sold in a well-developed competitive market; however, one transistor model is also used by the Systems Division. The costs per unit of the products used by the Systems Division are as follows:

	PCB	Transistor
Direct materials	$2.00	$0.40
Direct labor	4.00	1.00
Variable overhead	2.35	0.50
Fixed overhead	0.80	0.75
Total cost	$9.15	$2.65

The Board Division sells its commercial product at full cost plus a 34 percent markup and believes the proprietary board made for the Systems Division would sell for $12.25 per unit on the open market. The market price of the transistor used by the Systems Division is $3.40 per unit.

Required:

1. What is the minimum transfer price for the Transistor Division? What is the maximum transfer price of the transistor for the Systems Division?
2. Assume the Systems Division is able to purchase a large quantity of transistors from an outside source at $2.90 per unit. Further assume that the Transistor Division has excess capacity. Can the Transistor Division meet this price?
3. The Board and Systems divisions have negotiated a transfer price of $11 per printed circuit board. Discuss the impact this transfer price will have on each division. *(CMA adapted)*

10-15   ROI, RESIDUAL INCOME

LO1, LO3, LO4

CMA

Raddington Industries produces tool and die machinery for manufacturers. The company expanded vertically in 2007 by acquiring one of its suppliers of alloy steel plates, Reigis Steel Company. To manage the two separate businesses, the operations of Reigis are reported separately as an investment center.

Raddington monitors its divisions on the basis of both unit contribution and return on average investment (ROI), with investment defined as average operating assets employed. Management bonuses are determined on ROI. All investments in operating assets are expected to earn a minimum return of 11 percent before income taxes.

Reigis's cost of goods sold is considered to be entirely variable, while the division's administrative expenses are not dependent on volume. Selling expenses are a mixed cost with 40 percent attributed to sales volume. Reigis contemplated a capital acquisition with an estimated ROI of 11.5 percent; however, division management decided against the investment because it believed that the investment would decrease Reigis's overall ROI.

The 2008 operating statement for Reigis follows. The division's operating assets employed were $15,750,000 at November 30, 2008, a 5 percent increase over the 2007 year-end balance.

Reigis Steel Company
Operating Statement
For the Year Ended November 30, 2008
($000 omitted)

Sales revenue		$25,000
Less expenses:		
Cost of goods sold	$16,500	
Administrative expenses	3,955	
Selling expenses	2,700	23,155
Operating income before income taxes		$ 1,845

Required:

1. Calculate the unit contribution for Reigis Steel Company if 1,484,000 units were produced and sold during the year ended November 30, 2008.
2. Calculate the following performance measures for 2008 for Reigis Steel Company:
   a. Pretax return on average investment in operating assets employed (ROI).
   b. Residual income calculated on the basis of average operating assets employed.
3. Explain why the management of Reigis Steel Company would have been more likely to accept the contemplated capital acquisition if residual income rather than ROI were used as a performance measure.
4. Reigis Steel Company is a separate investment center within Raddington Industries. Identify several items that Reigis should control if it is to be evaluated fairly by either the ROI or residual income performance measures. *(CMA adapted)*

10-16   BONUSES AND STOCK OPTIONS

LO4   Casey Bertholt graduated from State U with a major in accounting five years ago. She obtained a position with a well-known professional services firm upon graduation and has become one of their outstanding performers. In the course of her work, she has developed numerous contacts with business firms in the area. One of them, Litton, Inc., recently offered her a position as head of their Financial Services Division. The offer includes a salary of $40,000 per year, annual bonuses of 1 percent of divisional operating income, and a stock option for 10,000 shares of Litton stock to be exercised at $12 per share in two years. Last year, the Financial Services Division earned $1,110,000. This year, it is budgeted to earn $1,600,000. Litton stock has increased in value at the rate of 15 percent per year over the past five years. Casey currently earns $55,000.

Required:

Advise Casey on the relative merits of the Litton offer.

10-17   SETTING TRANSFER PRICES—MARKET PRICE VERSUS FULL COST

LO5, LO6   Macalester, Inc., manufactures heating and air conditioning units in its six divisions. One division, the Components Division, produces electronic components that can be used by the other five. All the components produced by this division can be sold to outside customers; however, from the beginning, about 70 percent of its output has been used internally. The current policy requires that all internal transfers of components be transferred at full cost.

Recently, Loren Ferguson, the new chief executive officer of Macalester, decided to investigate the transfer pricing policy. He was concerned that the current method of pricing internal transfers might force decisions by divisional managers that would be suboptimal for the firm. As part of his inquiry, he gathered some information concerning Part 4CM, used by the Small AC Division in its production of a window air conditioner, Model 7AC.

The Small AC Division sells 100,000 units of Model 7AC each year at a unit price of $55. Given current market conditions, this is the maximum price that the division can charge for Model 7AC. The cost of manufacturing the air conditioner is computed as follows:

Part 4CM	$ 7
Direct materials	20
Direct labor	16
Variable overhead	3
Fixed overhead	6
Total unit cost	$52

The window unit is produced efficiently, and no further reduction in manufacturing costs is possible.

The manager of the Components Division indicated that she could sell 10,000 units (the division's capacity for this part) of Part 4CM to outside buyers at $12 per unit. The Small AC Division could also buy the part for $12 from external suppliers. She supplied the following detail on the manufacturing cost of the component:

Direct materials	$3.00
Direct labor	0.50
Variable overhead	1.50
Fixed overhead	2.00
Total unit cost	$7.00

Required:

1. Compute the firmwide contribution margin associated with Part 4CM and Model 7AC. Also, compute the contribution margin earned by each division.
2. Suppose that Loren Ferguson abolishes the current transfer pricing policy and gives divisions autonomy in setting transfer prices. Can you predict what transfer price the manager of the Components Division will set? What should be the minimum transfer price for this part? The maximum transfer price?
3. Given the new transfer pricing policy, predict how this will affect the production decision for Model 7AC of the manager of the Small AC Division. How many units of Part 4CM will the manager of the Small AC Division purchase, either internally or externally?
4. Given the new transfer price set by the Components Division and your answer to Requirement 3, how many units of 4CM will be sold externally?
5. Given your answers to Requirements 3 and 4, compute the firmwide contribution margin. What has happened? Was Loren's decision to grant additional decentralization good or bad?

10-18 TRANSFER PRICING WITH IDLE CAPACITY

LO3, LO5, LO6   Chapin, Inc., owns a number of food service companies. Two divisions are the Coffee Division and the Donut Shop Division. The Coffee Division purchases and roasts coffee beans for sale to supermarkets and specialty shops. The Donut Shop Division operates a chain of donut shops where the donuts are made on the premises. Coffee is an important item for sale along with the donuts and, to date, has been purchased from the Coffee Division. Company policy permits each manager the freedom to decide whether or not to buy or sell internally. Each divisional manager is evaluated on the basis of return on investment and residual income.

Recently, an outside supplier has offered to sell coffee beans, roasted and ground, to the Donut Shop Division for $4.00 per pound. Since the current price paid to the Coffee Division is $4.50 per pound, Brandi Alzer, the manager of the Donut Shop Division, was interested in the offer. However, before making the decision to switch to the outside supplier, she decided to approach Raymond Jasson, manager of the Coffee Division, to see if he wanted to offer an even better price. If not, then Brandi would buy from the outside supplier.

Upon receiving the information from Brandi about the outside offer, Raymond gathered the following information about the coffee:

Direct materials	$0.90
Direct labor	0.40
Variable overhead	0.70
Fixed overhead*	1.50
Total unit cost	$3.50

*Fixed overhead is based on $1,500,000/1,000,000 pounds.

Selling price per pound	$4.50
Production capacity	1,000,000 pounds
Internal sales	100,000 pounds

Required:

1. Suppose that the Coffee Division is producing at capacity and can sell all that it produces to outside customers. How should Raymond respond to Brandi's request for a lower transfer price? What will be the effect on firmwide profits? Compute the effect of this response on each division's profits.
2. Now, assume that the Coffee Division is currently selling 950,000 pounds. If no units are sold internally, total coffee sales will drop to 850,000 pounds. Suppose that Raymond refuses to lower the transfer price from $4.50. Compute the effect on firmwide profits and on each division's profits.
3. Refer to Requirement 2. What are the minimum and maximum transfer prices? Suppose that the transfer price is the maximum price less $1. Compute the effect on the firm's profits and on each division's profits. Who has benefited from the outside bid?
4. Refer to Requirement 2. Suppose that the Coffee Division has operating assets of $2,000,000. What is divisional ROI based on the current situation? Now, refer to Requirement 3. What will divisional ROI be if the transfer price of the maximum price less $1 is implemented? How will the change in ROI affect Raymond? What information has he gained as a result of the transfer pricing negotiations?

10-19 TRANSFER PRICING: VARIOUS COMPUTATIONS

LO5, LO6   Owens Company has a decentralized organization with a divisional structure. Two of these divisions are the Appliance Division and the Manufactured Housing Division. Each divisional manager is evaluated on the basis of ROI.

The Appliance Division produces a small automatic dishwasher that the Manufactured Housing Division can use in one of its models. Appliance can produce up to 10,000 of these dishwashers per year. The variable costs of manufacturing the dishwashers are $44. The Manufactured Housing Division inserts the dishwasher into the model house and then sells the manufactured house to outside customers for $23,000 each. The division's capacity is 2,000 units. The variable costs of the manufactured house (in addition to the cost of the dishwasher itself) are $12,600.

Required:

Assume each part is independent, unless otherwise indicated.
1. Assume that all of the dishwashers produced can be sold to external customers for $120 each. The Manufactured Housing Division wants to buy 2,000 dishwashers per year. What should the transfer price be?
2. Refer to Requirement 1. Assume $12 of avoidable distribution costs. Identify the maximum and minimum transfer prices. Identify the actual transfer price, assuming that negotiation splits the difference.
3. Assume that the Appliance Division is operating at 75 percent capacity. The Manufactured Housing Division is currently buying 2,000 dishwashers from an outside supplier for $90 each. Assume that any joint benefit will be split evenly between the two divisions. What is the expected transfer price? How much will the profits of the firm increase under this arrangement? How much will the profits of the Appliance Division increase, assuming that it sells the extra 2,000 dishwashers internally?

10-20 MANAGERIAL PERFORMANCE EVALUATION

LO1, LO2, LO3

CMA

Greg Peterson has recently been appointed vice president of operations for Webster Corporation. Greg has a manufacturing background and previously served as operations manager of Webster's Tractor Division. The business segments of Webster include the manufacture of heavy equipment, food processing, and financial services.

In a recent conversation with Carol Andrews, Webster's chief financial officer, Greg suggested that segment managers be evaluated on the basis of the segment data appearing in Webster's annual financial report. This report presents revenues, earnings, identifiable assets, and depreciation for each segment for a 5-year period. Greg believes that evaluating segment managers by criteria similar to that used in evaluating the company's top management would be appropriate. Carol has expressed her reservations about using segment information from the annual financial report for this purpose and has suggested that Greg consider other ways to evaluate the performance of segment managers.

Required:

1. Explain why the segment information prepared for public reporting purposes may not be appropriate for the evaluation of segment management performance.
2. Describe the possible behavioral impact of Webster Corporation's segment managers if their performance is evaluated on the basis of the information in the annual financial report.
3. Identify and describe several types of financial information that would be more appropriate for Greg to review when evaluating the performance of segment managers. *(CMA adapted)*

10-21 MANAGEMENT COMPENSATION

LO4

Renslen, Inc., a truck manufacturing conglomerate, has recently purchased two divisions: Meyers Service Company and Wellington Products, Inc. Meyers provides maintenance service on large truck cabs for 10-wheeler trucks, and Wellington produces air brakes for the 10-wheeler trucks.

The employees at Meyers take pride in their work, as Meyers is proclaimed to offer the best maintenance service in the trucking industry. The management of Meyers, as a group, has received additional compensation from a 10 percent bonus pool based on income before income taxes and bonus. Renslen plans to continue to compensate the Meyers management team on this basis as it is the same incentive plan used for all other Renslen divisions, except for the Wellington division.

Wellington offers a high-quality product to the trucking industry and is the premium choice even when compared to foreign competition. The management team at Wellington strives for zero defects and minimal scrap costs; current scrap levels are at 2 percent. The incentive compensation plan for Wellington management has been a 1 percent bonus based on gross margin. Renslen plans to continue to compensate the Wellington management team on this basis.

The following condensed income statements are for both divisions for the fiscal year ended May 31, 2007:

Renslen, Inc.
Divisional Income Statements
For the Year Ended May 31, 2007

	Meyers Service Company	Wellington Products, Inc.
Revenues	$4,000,000	$10,000,000
Cost of product	$ 75,000	$ 4,950,000
Salaries*	2,200,000	2,150,000
Fixed selling expenses	1,000,000	2,500,000
Interest expense	30,000	65,000
Other operating expenses	278,000	134,000
Total expenses	$3,583,000	$ 9,799,000
Income before income taxes and bonus	$ 417,000	$ 201,000

*Each division has $1,000,000 of management salary expense that is eligible for the bonus pool.

Renslen has invited the management teams of all its divisions to an off-site management workshop in July where the bonus checks will be presented. Renslen is concerned that the different bonus plans at the two divisions may cause some heated discussion.

Required:

1. Determine the 2007 bonus pool available for the management team at:
    a. Meyers Service Company
    b. Wellington Products, Inc.
2. Identify at least two advantages and disadvantages to Renslen, Inc., of the bonus pool incentive plan at:
    a. Meyers Service Company
    b. Wellington Products, Inc.
3. Having two different types of incentive plans for two operating divisions of the same corporation can create problems.
    a. Discuss the behavioral problems that could arise within management for Meyers Service Company and Wellington Products, Inc., by having different types of incentive plans.
    b. Present arguments that Renslen, Inc., can give to the management teams of both Meyers and Wellington to justify having two different incentive plans.

10-22   ROI, RESIDUAL INCOME, BEHAVIORAL ISSUES

LO3

CMA

Jump Start Company (JSC), a subsidiary of Mason Industries, manufactures go-carts and other recreational vehicles. Family recreational centers that feature go-cart tracks along with miniature golf, batting cages, and arcade games have increased in popularity. As a result, JSC has been pressured by Mason management to diversify into some of these other recreational areas. Recreational Leasing, Inc. (RLI), one of the largest firms leasing arcade games to these family recreational centers, is looking for a friendly buyer. Mason's top management believes that RLI's assets could be acquired for an investment of $3.2 million and has strongly urged Bill Grieco, division manager of JSC, to consider acquiring RLI.

Bill has reviewed RLI's financial statements with his controller, Marie Donnelly, and they believe that the acquisition may not be in the best interest of JSC.

"If we decide not to do this, the Mason people are not going to be happy," said Bill. "If we could convince them to base our bonuses on something other than return on investment, maybe this acquisition would look more attractive. How would we do if the bonuses were based on residual income using the company's 15 percent cost of capital?"

Mason has traditionally evaluated all of its divisions on the basis of return on investment, which is defined as the ratio of operating income to total assets. The desired rate of return for each division is 20 percent. The management team of any division reporting an annual increase in the return on investment is automatically eligible for a bonus. The management of divisions reporting a decline in the return on investment must provide convincing explanations for the decline to be eligible for a bonus, and this bonus is limited to 50 percent of the bonus paid to divisions reporting an increase.

The following condensed financial statements are for both JSC and RLI for the fiscal year ended May 31, 2007:

	JSC	RLI
Sales revenue	$10,500,000	
Leasing revenue		$ 2,800,000
Variable expenses	(7,000,000)	(1,000,000)
Fixed expenses	(1,500,000)	(1,200,000)
Operating income	$ 2,000,000	$ 600,000
Current assets	$ 2,300,000	$ 1,900,000
Long-term assets	5,700,000	1,100,000
Total assets	$ 8,000,000	$ 3,000,000
Current liabilities	$ 1,400,000	$ 850,000
Long-term liabilities	3,800,000	1,200,000
Stockholders' equity	2,800,000	950,000
Total liabilities and stockholders' equity	$ 8,000,000	$ 3,000,000

Required:

1. If Mason Industries continues to use return on investment as the sole measure of division performance, explain why JSC would be reluctant to acquire RLI. Be sure to support your answer with appropriate calculations.
2. If Mason Industries could be persuaded to use residual income to measure the performance of JSC, explain why JSC would be more willing to acquire RLI. Be sure to support your answer with appropriate calculations.

3. Discuss how the behavior of division managers is likely to be affected by the use of:
   a. Return on investment as a performance measure
   b. Residual income as a performance measure *(CMA adapted)*

10-23   TRANSFER PRICING IN THE MNC

LO5   Carnover, Inc., manufactures a broad line of industrial and consumer products. One of its plants is located in Madrid, Spain, and another in Singapore. The Madrid plant is operating at 85 percent capacity. Its main product, electric motors, has experienced softness in the market, which has led to predictions of further softening of the market and predictions of a decline in production to 65 percent capacity. If that happens, workers will have to be laid off and one wing of the factory closed. The Singapore plant manufactures heavy-duty industrial mixers that use the motors manufactured by the Madrid plant as an integral component. Demand for the mixers is strong. Price and cost information for the mixers are as follows:

Price	$2,200
Direct materials	630
Direct labor	125
Variable overhead	250
Fixed overhead	100

Fixed overhead is based on an annual budgeted amount of $3,500,000 and budgeted production of 35,000 mixers. The direct materials cost includes the cost of the motor at $200 (market price).

The Madrid plant capacity is 20,000 motors per year. Cost data are as follows:

Direct materials	$ 75
Direct labor	60
Variable overhead	60
Fixed overhead	100

Fixed overhead is based on budgeted fixed overhead of $2,000,000.

Required:

1. What is the maximum transfer price the Singapore plant would accept?
2. What is the minimum transfer price the Madrid plant would accept?
3. Consider the following environmental factors:

Madrid Plant	*Singapore Plant*
Full employment is very important.	Cheap labor is plentiful.
Local government prohibits layoffs without permission (which is rarely granted).	Accounting is based on British-American model, oriented toward decision-making needs of creditors and investors.
Accounting is legalistic and conservative, designed to ensure compliance with government objectives.	

How might these environmental factors impact the transfer pricing decision?

10-24 CASE ON ROI AND RESIDUAL INCOME, ETHICAL CONSIDERATIONS

LO3 Grate Care Company specializes in producing products for personal grooming. The company operates six divisions, including the Hair Products Division. Each division is treated as an investment center. Managers are evaluated and rewarded on the basis of ROI performance. Only those managers who produce the best ROIs are selected to receive bonuses and to fill higher-level managerial positions. Fred Olsen, manager of the Hair Products Division, has always been one of the top performers. For the past two years, Fred's division has produced the largest ROI; last year, the division earned an operating income of $2.56 million and employed average operating assets valued at $16 million. Fred is pleased with his division's performance and has been told that if the division does well this year, he will be in line for a headquarters position.

For the coming year, Fred's division has been promised new capital totaling $1.5 million. Any of the capital not invested by the division will be invested to earn the company's required rate of return (9 percent). After some careful investigation, the marketing and engineering staff recommended that the division invest in equipment that could be used to produce a crimping and waving iron, a product currently not produced by the division. The cost of the equipment was estimated at $1.2 million. The division's marketing manager estimated operating earnings from the new line to be $156,000 per year.

After receiving the proposal and reviewing the potential effects, Fred turned it down. He then wrote a memo to corporate headquarters, indicating that his division would not be able to employ the capital in any new projects within the next eight to 10 months. He did note, however, that he was confident that his marketing and engineering staff would have a project ready by the end of the year. At that time, he would like to have access to the capital.

Required:

1. Explain why Fred Olsen turned down the proposal to add the capability of producing a crimping and waving iron. Provide computations to support your reasoning.
2. Compute the effect that the new product line would have on the profitability of the firm as a whole. Should the division have produced the crimping and waving iron?
3. Suppose that the firm used residual income as a measure of divisional performance. Do you think Fred's decision might have been different? Why?
4. Explain why a firm like Grate Care might decide to use both residual income and return on investment as measures of performance.
5. Did Fred display ethical behavior when he turned down the investment? In discussing this issue, consider why he refused to allow the investment.

10-25 COLLABORATIVE LEARNING EXERCISE

LO5, LO6

CMA Lynsar Corporation started as a single plant that produced the major components assembled into electric motors—the company's main product. Lynsar later expanded by developing outside markets for some of the components used in its motors. Eventually, Lynsar reorganized into four manufacturing divisions: Bearing, Casing, Switch, and Motor. Each of the four manufacturing divisions operates as an autonomous unit, and divisional performance is the basis for year-end bonuses.

Lynsar's transfer pricing policy permits the manufacturing divisions to sell externally to outside customers as well as internally to the other divisions. The price for goods transferred between divisions is to be negotiated between the buying and selling divisions without any interference from top management.

Lynsar's profits have dropped for the current year even though sales have increased, and the drop in profits can be traced almost entirely to the Motor Division. Jere Feldon, Lynsar's chief financial officer, has discovered that the Motor Division has purchased switches for its motors from an outside supplier during the current year rather than buying them from the Switch Division. The Switch Division is at capacity and has refused to sell the switches to the Motor Division because it can sell them to outside customers at a price higher than the actual full (absorption) manufacturing cost that has always been negotiated in the past with the Motor Division. When the Motor Division refused to meet the price the Switch Division was receiving from its outside buyer, the Motor Division had to purchase the switches from an outside supplier at an even higher price.

Jere is reviewing Lynsar's transfer pricing policy because he believes that suboptimization has occurred. While the Switch Division made the correct decision to maximize its divisional profit by not transferring the switches at actual full manufacturing cost, this decision was not necessarily in the best interest of Lynsar. The Motor Division paid more for the switches than the selling price the Switch Division charged its outside customers. The Motor Division has always been Lynsar's largest division and has tended to dominate the smaller divisions. Jere has learned that the Casing and Bearing divisions are also resisting the Motor Division's desires to continue using actual full manufacturing cost as the negotiated price.

Jere has requested that the corporate accounting department study alternative transfer pricing methods that would promote overall goal congruence, motivate divisional management performance, and optimize overall company performance. Three of the transfer pricing methods being considered are listed below. If one of these methods should be selected, it would be applied uniformly across all divisions.

a. Standard full manufacturing costs plus markup
b. Market selling price of the products being transferred
c. Outlay (out-of-pocket) costs incurred to the point of transfer plus opportunity cost per unit

Required:

Form a group of six students. First, brainstorm answers to the following three requirements. Then, split your group into three pairs; each pair is responsible for writing up the answer to one of the requirements and turning it in as part of a group assignment for the following class period.

1. a. Discuss both the positive and negative behavioral implications that can arise from employing a negotiated transfer pricing system for goods that are exchanged between divisions.
   b. Explain the behavioral problems that can arise from using actual full (absorption) manufacturing costs as a transfer price.
2. Discuss the behavioral problems that could arise if Lynsar Corporation decides to change from its current policy covering the transfer of goods between divisions to a revised transfer pricing policy that would apply uniformly to all divisions.
3. Discuss the likely behavior of both "buying" and "selling" divisional managers for each of the following transfer pricing methods being considered by Lynsar Corporation.
   a. Standard full manufacturing costs plus markup
   b. Market selling price of the products being transferred
   c. Outlay (out-of-pocket) costs incurred to the point of transfer plus opportunity cost per unit *(CMA adapted)*

10-26   CYBER RESEARCH CASE

LO3   Using an Internet search engine, find the home page for the firm that registered the EVA trademark. When did this happen? Write a 1- to 2-page paper giving your opinion of this action. What are the advantages and disadvantages of registering an acronym such as this one? Should Robert Kaplan have registered the term "Balanced Scorecard"? Should someone have registered "ROI"? Discuss this issue from the point of view of the registering firm as well as that of the accounting profession as a whole.

ADVANCED COSTING AND CONTROL

PART 3

http://hansen.swlearning.com

CHAPTER

CHAPTER

11

Strategic Cost Management

AFTER STUDYING THIS CHAPTER, YOU SHOULD BE ABLE TO:

1. Explain what strategic cost management is and how it can be used to help a firm create a competitive advantage.

2. Discuss value-chain analysis and the strategic role of activity-based customer and supplier costing.

3. Tell what life-cycle cost management is and how it can be used to maximize profits over a product's life cycle.

4. Identify the basic features of JIT purchasing and manufacturing.

5. Describe the effect JIT has on cost traceability and product costing.

Why is one brand of ice cream viewed as better than another brand? It may reflect a deliberate decision by an ice cream producer to design and make an ice cream product that uses special ingredients and flavors rather than simply the ordinary. It is a means of differentiating the product and making it unlike those of competitors. It also may mean a conscious decision has been made to target certain types of consumers—consumers who are willing to pay for a higher quality, specialized ice cream. Whether this is a good strategy or not depends on its profitability. Cost management plays a vital role in strategic decision making. Cost information is critical in formulating and choosing strategies as well as in evaluating the continued viability of existing strategic positions.

In Chapter 4, the basic concepts of activity-based costing were introduced. These concepts were illustrated using the traditional product cost definition. Activity-based product costing can significantly improve the accuracy of traditional product costs. Thus, inventory valuation is improved, and managers (and other information users) have better information concerning the costs of products leading to more informed decision making. Yet, the value of the traditional product cost definition is limited and may not be very useful in certain decision contexts. For example, corporations engage in decision making that affects their long-run competitive position and profitability. Strategic planning and decision making require a much broader set of cost information than that provided by product costs. Cost information about customers, suppliers, and different product designs is also needed to support strategic management objectives.

This broader set of information should satisfy two requirements. First, it should include information about the firm's environment and internal workings. Second, it must be prospective and thus should provide insight about future periods and activities. A value-chain framework with cost data to support a value-chain analysis satisfies the first requirement. Cost information to support product life-cycle analysis is needed to satisfy the second requirement. Value-chain analysis can produce organizational changes that fundamentally alter the nature and demand for cost information. Just-in-time (JIT) manufacturing is an example of a strategic approach that alters the nature of the cost accounting information system. In this chapter, we introduce strategic cost management, life-cycle cost management, and JIT manufacturing. The JIT approach is used to illustrate the value-chain concepts. However, given the breadth of its application and its effect on cost accounting, JIT is a topic that by itself merits study. Furthermore, JIT's linkages to strategic cost management justify this topic's inclusion in the same chapter with strategic cost management.

Strategic Cost Management: Basic Concepts

OBJECTIVE 1

Explain what strategic cost management is and how it can be used to help a firm create a competitive advantage.

Decision making that affects the long-term competitive position of a firm must explicitly consider the strategic elements of a decision. The most important strategic elements for a firm are its long-term growth and survival. Thus, strategic decision making is choosing among alternative strategies with the goal of selecting a strategy, or strategies, that provides a company with reasonable assurance of long-term growth and survival. The key to achieving this goal is to gain a *competitive advantage*. Strategic cost management is the use of cost data to develop and identify superior strategies that will produce a sustainable competitive advantage.

Strategic Positioning: The Key to Creating and Sustaining a Competitive Advantage

Competitive advantage is creating better customer value for the same or lower cost than offered by competitors or creating equivalent value for lower cost than offered by competitors. Customer value is the difference between what a customer receives (customer realization) and what the customer gives up (customer sacrifice). What a customer receives is more than simply the basic level of performance provided by a product.[1] What is received is called the *total product*. The total product is the complete range of tangible and intangible benefits that a customer receives from a purchased product. Thus, customer realization includes basic and special product features, service, quality, instructions for use, reputation, brand name, and any other factors deemed important by customers. Customer sacrifice includes the cost of purchasing the product, the time and effort spent acquiring and learning to use the product, and post-purchase costs, which are the costs of using, maintaining, and disposing of the product.

---

1. Keep in mind that our definition of *product* includes services. Services are intangible products.

Increasing customer value to achieve a competitive advantage is tied closely to judicious strategy selection. Three general strategies have been identified: *cost leadership*, *product differentiation*, and *focusing*.[2]

Cost Leadership

The objective of a cost leadership strategy is to provide the same or better value to customers at a *lower cost* than offered by competitors. Essentially, if customer value is defined as the difference between realization and sacrifice, a low-cost strategy increases customer value by minimizing customer sacrifice. In this case, cost leadership is the goal of the organization. For example, a company might redesign a product so that fewer parts are needed, lowering production costs and the costs of maintaining the product after purchase.

Differentiation

A differentiation strategy, on the other hand, strives to increase customer value by increasing what the customer receives (customer realization). A competitive advantage is created by providing something to customers that is not provided by competitors. Therefore, product characteristics must be created that set the product apart from its competitors. This differentiation can occur by adjusting the product so that it is different from the norm or by promoting some of the product's tangible or intangible attributes. Differences can be functional, aesthetic, or stylistic. For example, a retailer of computers might offer on-site repair service, a feature not offered by other rivals in the local market. Or a producer of crackers may offer animal-shaped crackers, as **Nabisco** did with Teddy Grahams®, to differentiate its product from other brands with more conventional shapes. To be of value, however, customers must see the variations as important. Furthermore, the value added to the customer by differentiation must exceed the firm's costs of providing the differentiation. If customers see the variations as important and if the value added to the customer exceeds the cost of providing the differentiation, then a competitive advantage has been established.

Focusing

A focusing strategy is selecting or emphasizing a market or customer segment in which to compete. One possibility is to select the markets and customers that appear attractive and then develop the capabilities to serve these targeted segments. Another possibility is to select specific segments where the firm's core competencies in the segments are superior to those of competitors. A focusing strategy recognizes that not all segments (e.g., customers and geographic regions) are the same. Given the capabilities and potential capabilities of the organization, some segments are more attractive than others.

Strategic Positioning

In reality, many firms will choose not just one general strategy, but a combination of the three general strategies. Strategic positioning is the process of selecting the optimal mix of these three general strategic approaches. The mix is selected with the objective of creating a sustainable competitive advantage. A strategy, reflecting combinations of the three general strategies, can be defined as:

> . . . choosing the market and customer segments the business unit intends to serve, identifying the critical internal business processes that the unit must excel at to deliver the value propositions to customers in the targeted market segments, and selecting the individual and organizational capabilities required for the internal, customer, and financial objectives.[3]

---

2. See M. E. Porter, *Competitive Advantage: Creating and Sustaining Superior Performance* (New York: Free Press, 1985) for a more complete discussion of the three strategic positions.
3. Robert S. Kaplan and David P. Norton, *The Balanced Scorecard* (Boston: Harvard Business School Press, 1996): 37.

As used in the definition, "choosing the market and customer segments" is actually focusing; "deliver[ing] the value propositions" is choosing to increase customer realization and/or decrease sacrifice and, therefore, entails cost leadership and/or differentiation strategies, or a combination of the two. Developing the necessary capabilities to serve the segments is related to all three general strategies.

What is the role of cost management in strategic positioning? The *objective* of strategic cost management is to *reduce* costs while simultaneously *strengthening* the chosen strategic position. Remember that a competitive advantage is tied to costs. For example, suppose that an organization is providing the same customer value at a higher cost than its competitors. By increasing customer value for specific customer segments (e.g., differentiation and focusing are used to strengthen the strategic position) and, at the same time, *decreasing* costs, the organization might reach a state where it is providing greater value at the same or less cost than its competitors, thus creating a competitive advantage.

Value-Chain Framework, Linkages, and Activities

Choosing an optimal (or most advantageous) strategic position requires managers to understand the activities that contribute to its achievement. Successful pursuit of a sound strategic position mandates an understanding of the *industrial value chain*. The **industrial value chain** is the linked set of value-creating activities from basic raw materials to the disposal of the finished product by end-use customers. Exhibit 11-1, on the following page, illustrates a possible industrial value chain for the petroleum industry. A given firm operating in the oil industry may not—and likely will not—span the entire value chain. The exhibit illustrates that different firms participate in different portions of the value chain. Most large oil firms such as **Exxon-Mobil** and **ConocoPhillips** are involved in the value chain from exploration to service stations (like Firm A in Exhibit 11-1). Yet, even these oil giants purchase oil from other producers and also supply gasoline to service station outlets that are owned by others. Furthermore, there are many oil firms that engage exclusively in smaller segments of the chain such as exploration and production or refining and distribution (like Firms B and C in Exhibit 11-1). Regardless of its position in the value chain, to create and sustain a competitive advantage, a firm must understand the entire value chain and not just the portion in which it operates.

Thus, breaking down the value chain into its strategically relevant activities is basic to successful implementation of cost leadership and differentiation strategies. A value-chain framework is a compelling approach to understanding a firm's strategically important activities. Fundamental to a value-chain framework is the recognition that there exist complex linkages and interrelationships among activities both within and beyond the firm. Two types of linkages must be analyzed and understood: *internal linkages* and *external linkages*. **Internal linkages** are relationships among activities that are performed within a firm's portion of the value chain. **External linkages**, on the other hand, describe the relationship of a firm's value-chain activities that are performed with its suppliers and customers. External linkages, therefore, are of two types: *supplier linkages* and *customer linkages*.

External linkages emphasize the fact that a company must understand the entire value chain and not just the portion of the chain in which it participates. An *external* focus is needed for effective strategic cost management. A company cannot ignore supplier and customer linkages and expect to establish a sustainable competitive advantage. A company needs to understand its relative position in the industrial value chain. An assessment of the economic strength and relationships of each stage in the entire value-chain system can provide a company with several significant strategic insights. For example, knowing the revenues and costs of the different stages may reveal the need to forward or backward integrate to increase overall economic performance. Alternatively, it may reveal that divestiture and a narrowing of participation in the industrial value chain is a good strategy. Finally, knowing the supplier power and buyer power can have

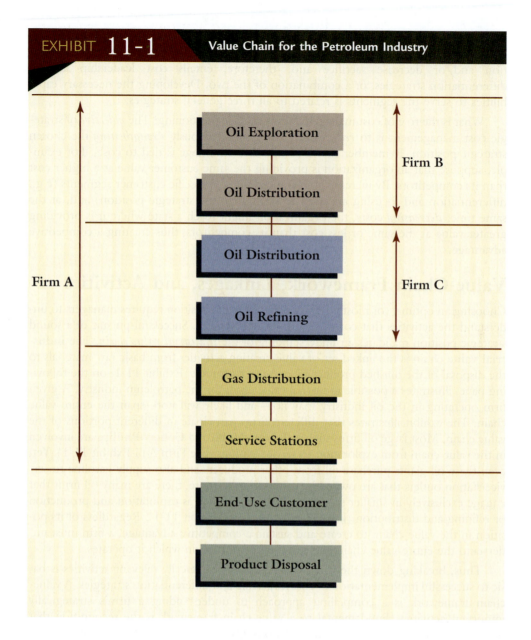

EXHIBIT 11-1   Value Chain for the Petroleum Industry

a significant effect on how external linkages are exploited. Supplier and buyer power can be assessed for a company by comparing the percentage of profits earned in the industrial value chain with the percentages earned by suppliers and by customers. For example, suppose that the profit earned per gallon of gasoline by an independent refiner and producer is $0.15 and the profit earned by a network of service stations that buy the gasoline (not owned by the independent) is $0.05 per gallon. The percentage of profit earned in this segment of the value chain by the downstream stage is 25 percent ($0.05/$0.20), while the independent earns 75 percent of the profit. Buyer power is weak relative to the refiner and producer. If, in addition, the return on assets being earned by the service station segment is high, this may reveal that integrating forward is both desirable and possible.

To exploit a firm's internal and external linkages, we must identify the firm's activities and select those that can be used to produce (or sustain) a competitive advantage. This selection process requires knowledge of the cost and value of each activity. For strategic analysis, activities are classified as *organizational activities* and *operational activities*; the costs of these activities, in turn, are determined by *organizational* and *operational cost drivers*.

Organizational Activities and Cost Drivers

Organizational activities are of two types: *structural* and *executional*. **Structural activities** are activities that determine the underlying economic structure of the organization. **Executional activities** are activities that define the processes and capabilities of an organization and thus are directly related to the ability of an organization to execute successfully. **Organizational cost drivers** are structural and executional factors that determine the long-term cost structure of an organization. Thus, there are two types of organizational drivers: *structural cost drivers* and *executional cost drivers*. Possible structural and executional activities with their cost drivers are listed by category in Exhibit 11-2.

EXHIBIT 11-2   Organizational Activities and Drivers

Structural Activities	Structural Cost Drivers
Building plants	Number of plants, scale, degree of centralization
Management structuring	Management style and philosophy
Grouping employees	Number and type of work units
Complexity	Number of product lines, number of unique processes, number of unique parts, degree of complexity
Vertically integrating	Scope, buying power, selling power
Selecting and using process technologies	Types of process technologies, experience

Executional Activities	Executional Cost Drivers
Using employees	Degree of involvement
Providing quality	Quality management approach
Providing plant layout	Plant layout efficiency
Designing and producing products	Product configuration
Providing capacity	Capacity utilization

As the exhibit shows, it is possible (and perhaps common) that a given organizational activity can be driven by more than one driver. For example, the cost of building plants is affected by number of plants, scale, and degree of centralization. Firms that have a commitment to a high degree of centralization may build larger plants so that there can be more geographic concentration and greater control. Similarly, complexity may be driven by number of different products, number of unique processes, and number of unique parts.

Organizational drivers are factors that affect an organization's long-term cost structure. This is readily understood by simply considering the various drivers shown in Exhibit 11-2. Among the structural drivers are the familiar drivers of scale, scope, experience, technology, and complexity. For example, economies and diseconomies of scale are well-known economic phenomena, and the learning curve effect (experience) is also well documented. An interesting property of structural cost drivers is that more is not always better. Moreover, the efficiency level of a structural driver can change. For example, changes in technology can affect the scale driver by changing the optimal size of a plant. In the steel industry, minimill technology has eliminated scale economies (in the form of megamills) as a competitive advantage. Plants of much smaller scale can now achieve the same level of efficiency once produced only by larger steel plants.

Of more recent interest and emphasis are executional drivers. Considerable managerial effort is being expended to improve how things are done in an organization. Continuous improvement and its many faces (employee empowerment, total quality management, process value analysis, life-cycle assessment, etc.) are what executional efficiency is all about. Consider employee involvement and empowerment. The cost of using employees decreases as the degree of involvement increases. Employee or worker involvement refers to the culture, degree of participation, and commitment to the objective of continuous improvement.

Operational Activities and Drivers

Operational activities are day-to-day activities performed as a result of the structure and processes selected by the organization. Examples include receiving and inspecting incoming parts, moving materials, shipping products, testing new products, servicing products, and setting up equipment. Operational cost drivers (activity drivers) are those factors that drive the cost of operational activities. They include such factors as number of parts, number of moves, number of products, number of customer orders, and number of returned products. As should be evident, operational activities and drivers are the focus of activity-based costing. Possible operational activities and their drivers are listed in Exhibit 11-3.

EXHIBIT 11-3   Operational Activities and Drivers

Unit-Level Activities	Unit-Level Drivers
Grinding parts	Grinding machine hours
Assembling parts	Assembly labor hours
Drilling holes	Drilling machine hours
Using materials	Pounds of material
Using power	Number of kilowatt-hours
Batch-Level Activities	**Batch-Level Drivers**
Setting up equipment	Number of setups
Moving batches	Number of moves
Inspecting batches	Inspection hours
Reworking products	Number of defective units
Product-Level Activities	**Product-Level Drivers**
Redesigning products	Number of change orders
Expediting	Number of late orders
Scheduling	Number of different products
Testing products	Number of procedures

The structural and executional activities define the number and nature of the day-to-day activities performed within the organization. For example, if an organization decides to produce more than one product at a facility, then this structural choice produces a need for scheduling, a product-level activity. Similarly, providing a plant layout defines the nature and extent of the materials handling activity (usually a batch-level activity). Furthermore, although organizational activities define operational activities, analysis of operational activities and drivers can be used to suggest strategic choices of organizational activities and drivers. For example, knowing that the number of moves is a measure of consumption of the materials handling activity by individual products may suggest that resource spending can be reduced if the plant layout is redesigned to reduce the number of moves needed. Operational and organizational activities and their associated drivers are strongly interrelated. Exhibit 11-4 illustrates the circular nature of these relationships.

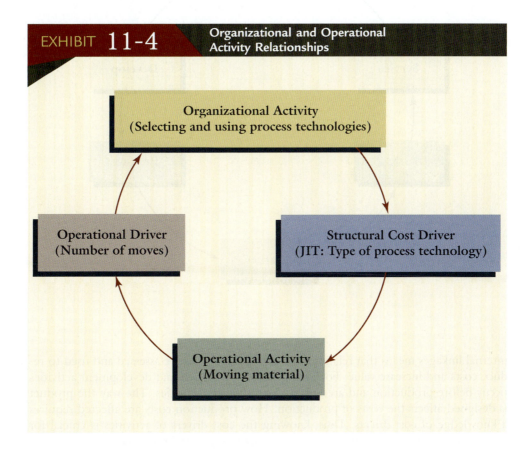

EXHIBIT 11-4   Organizational and Operational Activity Relationships

Value-Chain Analysis

OBJECTIVE 2

Discuss value-chain analysis and the strategic role of activity-based customer and supplier costing.

Value-chain analysis is identifying and exploiting internal and external linkages with the objective of strengthening a firm's strategic position. The exploitation of linkages relies on analyzing how costs and other nonfinancial factors vary as different bundles of activities are considered. For example, organizations change their structure and processes as needed to meet new challenges and take advantage of new opportunities. This may include new approaches to differentiation. Additionally, managing organizational and operational cost drivers to create long-term cost reduction outcomes is an important input in value-chain analysis when cost leadership is emphasized. The objective, of course, is to control cost drivers better than competitors can (thus creating a competitive advantage).

Exploiting Internal Linkages

Sound strategic cost management mandates the consideration of that portion of the value chain in which a firm participates (called the *internal value chain*). Exhibit 11-5 reviews the internal value-chain activities for an organization. Activities before and after production must be identified and their linkages recognized and exploited. Exploiting

EXHIBIT **11-5**   **Internal Value Chain**

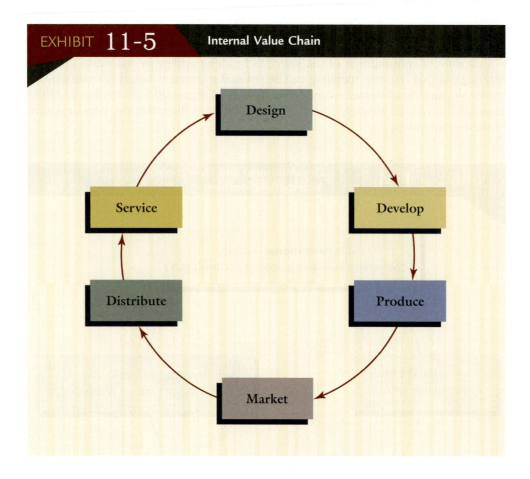

internal linkages means that relationships between activities are assessed and used to reduce costs and increase value. For example, product design and development activities occur before production and are linked to production activities. The way the product is designed affects the costs of production. How production costs are affected requires a knowledge of cost drivers. Thus, knowing the cost drivers of activities is crucial for understanding and exploiting linkages. If design engineers know that the number of parts is a cost driver for various production activities (material usage, direct labor usage, assembly, inspection, materials handling, and purchasing are examples of activities where costs could be affected by number of parts), then redesigning the product so that it has standard parts, multiple sources, short lead times, and high quality can significantly reduce the overall cost of the product.

The design activity is also linked to the service activity in the firm's value chain. By producing a product with fewer parts, there is less likelihood of product failure and, thus, less cost associated with warranty agreements (an important customer service). Furthermore, the cost of repairing products under warranty should also decrease because fewer parts usually means simpler repair procedures.

Internal Linkage Analysis: An Example

To provide a more concrete foundation for the internal linkage concepts, let's consider a specific numerical example. Assume that a firm produces a variety of high-tech medical products. One of the products has 20 parts. Design engineers have been told that the number of parts is a significant cost driver (operational cost driver) and that reducing the number of parts will reduce the demand for various activities downstream in the value chain. Based on this input, design engineering has produced a new configuration for the product that requires only eight parts. Management wants to know the cost reduction produced by the new design. They plan on reducing the price per unit by the per-unit savings. Currently, 10,000 units of the product are produced. The effect of the new design on the demand for four activities follows. Activity capacity, current activity demand (based on the 20-part configuration), and expected activity demand (based on the 8-part configuration) are provided.

Activities	Activity Driver	Activity Capacity	Current Activity Demand	Expected Activity Demand
Material usage	Number of parts	200,000	200,000	80,000
Assembling parts	Direct labor hours	10,000	10,000	5,000
Purchasing parts	Number of orders	15,000	12,500	6,500
Warranty repair	Number of defective products	1,000	800	500

Additionally, the following activity cost data are provided:

Material usage: $3 per part used; no fixed activity cost.

Assembling parts: $12 per direct labor hour; no fixed activity cost.

Purchasing parts: Three salaried clerks, each earning a $30,000 annual salary; each clerk is capable of processing 5,000 purchase orders. Variable activity costs: $0.50 per purchase order processed for forms, postage, etc.

Warranty repair: Two repair agents, each paid a salary of $28,000 per year; each repair agent is capable of repairing 500 units per year. Variable activity costs: $20 per product repaired.

Using the information in the table and the cost data, the potential savings produced by the new design are given in Exhibit 11-6. Cost behavior of individual activities is vital for assessing the impact of the new design. Knowing the cost of different design strategies is made possible by assessing the linkages of activities and the effects of changes in demand for the activities. Notice the key role that the resource usage model plays in this analysis.[4] The purchasing activity currently supplies 15,000 units of activity capacity, acquired in steps of 5,000 units. (Capacity is measured in the number of purchase orders—see Exhibit 11-7, on the following page, for a graphical illustration of the activity's step-cost behavior.) Unused activity for the current product configuration is 2,500

EXHIBIT 11-6   Cost Reduction from Exploiting Internal Linkages

Material usage	$360,000[a]
Labor usage	60,000[b]
Purchasing	33,000[c]
Warranty repair	34,000[d]
Total	$487,000
Units	10,000
Unit savings	$48.70

[a](200,000 − 80,000)$3.
[b](10,000 − 5,000)$12.
[c][$30,000 + $0.50(12,500 − 6,500)].
[d][$28,000 + $20(800 − 500)].

---

4. The resource usage model was introduced in Chapter 3.

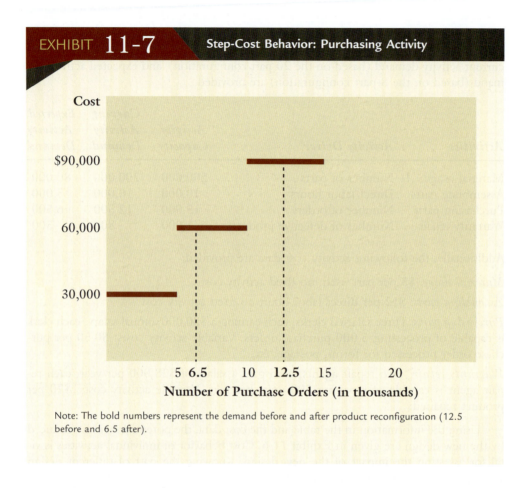

EXHIBIT 11-7   **Step-Cost Behavior: Purchasing Activity**

Note: The bold numbers represent the demand before and after product reconfiguration (12.5 before and 6.5 after).

units (15,000 − 12,500). Reconfiguring the product reduces the demand from 12,500 orders to 6,500 orders. This increases the unused activity capacity to 8,500 units (15,000 − 6,500). At this point, management has the capability of reducing resource spending on the resources acquired in advance of usage. Since activity capacity is acquired in chunks of 5,000 units, resource spending can be reduced by $30,000 (the price of one purchasing clerk). Furthermore, since demand decreases, resource spending for the resources acquired as needed is also reduced $3,000 by the variable component ($0.50 × 6,000). A similar analysis is carried out for the warranty activity. The activity-based costing model and knowledge of activity cost behavior are powerful and integral components of strategic cost management.

In the example, we implicitly assumed that resource spending on the engineering design activity would remain unchanged. Therefore, there was no cost to exploiting the linkage. Suppose, however, that an increase in resource spending of $50,000 is needed to exploit the linkages between engineering design and activities downstream in the firm's value chain. Spending $50,000 to save $487,000 is certainly sound. Spending on one activity to save on the cost of other activities is a fundamental principle of strategic cost analysis.

Exploiting Supplier Linkages

Although each firm has its own value chain, as was shown in Exhibit 11-1 on p. 490, each firm also belongs to a broader value chain—the *industrial value chain*. The value-chain system also includes value-chain activities that are performed by suppliers and buyers. A firm cannot ignore the interaction between its own value-chain activities and those of its suppliers and buyers. Linkages with activities external to the firm can also be exploited. Exploiting external linkages means managing these linkages so that both the company and the external parties receive an increase in benefits.

Suppliers provide inputs and, as a consequence, can have a significant effect on a user's strategic positioning. For example, assume that a company adopts a *total quality control* approach to differentiate and reduce overall quality costs. **Total quality control** is an approach to managing quality that demands the production of defect-free products. Reducing defects, in turn, reduces the total costs spent on quality activities. Yet, if the components are delivered late and are of low quality, then there is no way the buying company can produce high-quality products and deliver them on time to its customers. To achieve a defect-free state, a company is strongly dependent on its suppliers' ability to provide defect-free parts. Once this linkage is understood, then a company can work closely with its suppliers so that the product being purchased meets its needs. **Honeywell** understands this linkage and has established a supplier review board with the objective of improving business relationships and material quality. Its evaluation and selection of suppliers is based on factors such as product quality, delivery, reliability, continuous improvement, and overall relations. Suppliers are expected to meet certain quality and delivery standards such as 500 parts per million (defect rate), 99 percent on-time delivery, and a 99 percent lot acceptance rate.[5]

Managing Procurement Costs

Clearly, to avoid weakening its strategic position, a firm must carefully choose its suppliers. To encourage purchasing managers to choose suppliers whose quality, reliability, and delivery performance are acceptable, two essential requirements have been identified.[6] First, a broader view of component costs is needed. Functional-based costing systems typically reward purchasing managers solely on purchase price (e.g., materials price variances). A broader view means that the costs associated with quality, reliability, and late deliveries are added to the purchase costs. Purchasing managers are then required to evaluate suppliers based on total cost, not just purchase price. Second, supplier costs are assigned to products using causal relationships.

Activity-based costing is the key to satisfying both requirements. To satisfy the first requirement, suppliers are defined as a cost object and costs relating to purchase, quality, reliability, and delivery performance are traced to suppliers. In the second case, products are the cost objects, and supplier costs are traced to specific products. By tracing supplier costs to products—rather than averaging them over all products as functional-based costing does—managers can see the effect of large numbers of unique components requiring specialty suppliers versus products with only standard components. Knowing the costs of more complex products helps product designers better evaluate the tradeoffs between functionality and cost as they design new products. Additional functions should provide more benefits (by an increased selling price) than costs. By accurately tracing supplier costs to products, a better understanding of product profitability is produced, and product designers are more capable of choosing among competing product designs.

Activity-Based Supplier Costing

To illustrate activity-based supplier costing, assume that a purchasing manager uses two suppliers, Fielding Electronics and Oro Limited, as the source of two electronic components: Component X1Z and Component Y2Z. The purchasing manager prefers to use Fielding because it provides the components at a lower price; however, the second supplier is used as well to ensure a reliable supply of the components. Now consider two activities: *reworking products* and *expediting products*. Reworking products occurs because of component failure or process failure. Expediting products takes place due to late delivery of components or process failure. Component failure and late delivery are

---

5. As reported at http://www.honeywell.com on September 4, 2004.

6. These requirements are discussed in Robin Cooper and Regine Slagmulder, "The Scope of Strategic Cost Management," *Management Accounting* (February 1998): 16–18. Much of the discussion in this section is based on this article.

attributable to suppliers, and process failure costs are attributable to internal processes. Rework costs attributable to component failure are assigned to suppliers using the number of failed components as the driver. The costs of expediting attributable to late deliveries are assigned using the number of late shipments as the driver. Exhibit 11-8 provides the activity cost information and other data needed for supplier costing.

EXHIBIT 11-8	Data for Supplier Costing Example

I. Activity Costs

Activity	Component Failure/Late Delivery	Process Failure
Reworking products	$200,000	$40,000
Expediting products	50,000	10,000

II. Supplier Data

	Fielding Electronics		Oro Limited	
	X1Z	Y2Z	X1Z	Y2Z
Unit purchase price	$10	$26	$12	$28
Units purchased	40,000	20,000	5,000	5,000
Failed units	800	190	5	5
Late shipments	30	20	0	0

Using the data from Exhibit 11-8, the activity rates for assigning costs to suppliers are computed as follows:

$$\text{Reworking rate} = \$200,000/1,000^*$$
$$= \$200 \text{ per failed component}$$

*(800 + 190 + 5 + 5).

$$\text{Expediting rate} = \$50,000/50^*$$
$$= \$1,000 \text{ per late delivery}$$

*(30 + 20).

Using these rates and the activity data in Exhibit 11-8, the total purchasing cost per unit of each component is computed and shown in Exhibit 11-9. The results show that the "low-cost" supplier actually costs more when the linkages with the internal activities of reworking and expediting are considered. If the purchasing manager is provided all costs, then the choice becomes clear: Oro Limited is the better supplier. It provides a higher-quality product on a timely basis and at a lower overall cost per unit.

Exploiting Customer Linkages

Customers can also have a significant influence on a firm's strategic position. Choosing marketing segments, of course, is one of the principal elements that define strategic position. For example, selling a medium-level quality product to low-end dealers for a special, low price because of idle capacity could threaten the main channels of distribution for the product. This is true even if the dealers apply their own private labels to the product. Why? Because selling the product to low-end dealers creates a direct competitor for its regular, medium-level dealers. Potential customers of the regular retail outlets could switch to the lower-end outlets because they can buy the same qual-

EXHIBIT 11-9	Supplier Costing			
	Fielding Electronics		**Oro Limited**	
	X1Z	**Y2Z**	**X1Z**	**Y2Z**
Purchase cost:				
$10 × 40,000	$400,000			
$26 × 20,000		$520,000		
$12 × 5,000			$60,000	
$28 × 5,000				$140,000
Reworking products:				
$200 × 800	160,000			
$200 × 190		38,000		
$200 × 5			1,000	
$200 × 5				1,000
Expediting products:				
$1,000 × 30	30,000			
$1,000 × 20		20,000		
Total costs	$590,000	$578,000	$61,000	$141,000
Units	÷ 40,000	÷ 20,000	÷ 5,000	÷ 5,000
Total unit cost	$ 14.75	$ 28.90	$ 12.20	$ 28.20

ity for a lower price. And what if the regular outlets deduce what has happened? What effect would this have on the company's medium-level differentiation strategy? The long-term damage to the company's profitability may be much greater than any short-run benefit from selling the special order.

Managing Customer Service Costs

A key objective for strategic costing is the identification of a firm's sources of profitability. In a functional-based costing system, selling and general and administrative costs are usually treated as period costs and, if assigned to customers, are typically assigned in proportion to the revenues generated. Thus, the message of functional-based costing is that servicing customers either costs nothing or they all appear to cost the same percentage of their sales revenue. If customer-servicing costs are significant, then failure to assign them at all or to assign them accurately will prevent sales representatives from managing the customer mix effectively. Why? Because sales representatives will not be able to distinguish between customers who place significant demands on servicing resources and those who place virtually no demand on these resources. This lack of knowledge can lead to actions that will weaken a firm's strategic position. To avoid this outcome and encourage actions that strengthen strategic position, customer-related costs should be assigned to customers using activity-based costing. Accurate assignment of customer-related costs allows the firm to classify customers as profitable or unprofitable.

Once customers are identified as profitable or unprofitable, actions can be taken to strengthen the strategic position of the firm. For profitable customers, an organization can undertake efforts to increase satisfaction by offering higher levels of service, lower prices, new services, or some combination of the three. For unprofitable customers, an organization can attempt to deliver the customer services more efficiently (thus, decreasing service costs), increase prices to reflect the cost of the resources being consumed, encourage unprofitable customers to leave (by reducing selling efforts to this segment), or some combination of the three actions.

Activity-Based Customer Costing

An example may help illustrate the importance of customer costing. Suppose that Thompson Company produces precision parts for 11 major buyers. An activity-based costing system is used to assign manufacturing costs to products. The company prices each customer's order by adding order-filling costs to manufacturing costs and then adding a 20 percent markup (to cover any administrative costs plus profits). Order-filling costs total $606,000 and are currently assigned in proportion to sales volume (measured by number of parts sold). Of the 11 customers, one accounts for 50 percent of sales, with the other 10 accounting for the remainder of sales. The 10 smaller customers purchase parts in roughly equal quantities. Orders placed by the smaller customers are also about the same size. Data concerning Thompson's customer activity are as follows:

	One Large Customer	Ten Smaller Customers
Units purchased	500,000	500,000
Orders placed	2	200
Manufacturing cost	$3,000,000	$3,000,000
Order-filling cost allocated*	$303,000	$303,000
Order cost per unit	$0.606	$0.606

*Order-filling capacity is purchased in blocks of 45, each block costing $40,400; variable order-filling activity costs are $2,000 per order. The activity capacity is 225 orders; thus, the total order-filling cost is $606,000 [(5 × $40,400) + ($2,000 × 202)]. This total is allocated in proportion to the units purchased; therefore, the large customer receives half the total cost.

Now assume that this customer complains about the price being charged and threatens to take its business elsewhere. The customer reveals a bid from a Thompson competitor that is $0.50 per part less than what Thompson charges. Confident that the ABC costing system is assigning manufacturing costs accurately, Thompson investigates the assignment of order-filling cost and discovers that the number of sales orders processed is a much better cost driver than number of parts sold. Thus, activity demand is measured by the number of sales orders, and ordering costs should be assigned to customers using an activity rate of $3,000 per order ($606,000/202 orders). Using this rate, the large customer should be charged $6,000 for order-filling costs. The large customer is being overcharged $297,000 each year, or about $0.59 per part ($297,000/500,000 parts). Actually, the overcharging is compounded by the 20 percent markup, producing a price that is about $0.71 too high (1.2 × $0.59). Armed with this information, Thompson's management immediately offers to reduce the price charged to its large customer by at least $0.50.

Thus, one benefit to the large customer is a price correction. This also benefits Thompson, because the price correction is needed to maintain half of its current business. Thompson, unfortunately, is also facing the difficult task of announcing a price increase for its smaller customers. However, the analysis should go much deeper than accurate cost assignment and fair pricing. Identifying the right cost driver (number of orders processed) reveals a linkage between the order-filling activity and customer behavior. Smaller, frequent orders are imposing costs on Thompson, which are then passed on to all customers through the use of the sales volume allocation. Since the total cost is marked up 20 percent, the price charged is even higher. Decreasing the number of orders will decrease Thompson's order-filling costs. Knowing this, Thompson can offer price discounts for larger orders. For example, doubling the size of the orders of the small customers would cut the number of orders by 50 percent, saving $280,800 for Thompson [(2 × $40,400) + (100 × $2,000)], almost enough to make it unnecessary to increase the selling price to the smaller customers. But there are other possible linkages as well. Larger and less frequent orders will also decrease the demand on other internal activities, such as setting up equipment and materials handling. Reduc-

COST MANAGEMENT   Technology in Action

The modern cost management information system uses a much broader information set than has been traditionally used. It provides information about costs, quality, cycle time, drivers, and outputs. This integrated management accounting framework is built in what is referred to as a data warehousing/business intelligence environment (DW/BI). Using the DW/BI programs, companies can easily calculate supplier costs and customer profitability. A number of companies such as **Barclays Bank**, **Avnet, Inc.**, **BellSouth**, and **Ford** are using DW/BI programs. For example, Barclays Bank uses information from its DW/BI program to segment its customers on the basis of life-time value. This segmentation allows the bank to offer targeted, differentiated services and pricing. **First Union Corporation** (merged with Wachovia in 2001 and is now known as Wachovia Corporation. The post-merger Wachovia is the fourth-largest bank in the United States.) is a good example of how customer profitability information can be used for purposes of offering differentiated serv-ices and pricing. First Union used a computerized, color-coded information system that revealed information about customer profitability to bank employees who serviced customers. Customers asking for specific services received a yes, maybe, or no answer depending on their color-code ranking. A red code signaled that the customer was losing money for the bank; a green code meant the customer was a source of significant profits for the bank; and a yellow code was for in-between customers. Green-code customers who requested a lower credit card interest rate or a fee waved for a bounced check got a positive answer, customers with a red code almost always received a negative answer, while customers with a yellow code had a chance to negotiate. First Union estimated that this type of approach would increase its annual revenue by $100 million. About half of this $100 million was from extra fees and other funds collected from unprofitable customers and from the increased deposits gained by retaining preferred customers targeted to receive more services.

Sources: Steve Williams, "Delivering Strategic Business Value," *Strategic Finance* (August 2004) 40–49, and Rick Brooks, "Alienating Customers Isn't Always a Bad Idea, Many Firms Discover," *The Wall Street Journal* (January 7, 1999): A1 and A12.

tion in other activity demands could produce further cost reductions and additional price cuts, making Thompson more competitive. Ultimately, exploiting customer linkages can make both the seller and the buyer better off.

Life-Cycle Cost Management

Strategic cost management emphasizes the importance of an external focus and the need to recognize and exploit both internal and external linkages. Life-cycle cost management is a related approach that builds a conceptual framework which facilitates management's ability to exploit internal and external linkages. To understand what is meant by life-cycle cost management, we first need to understand basic product life-cycle concepts.

Product Life-Cycle Viewpoints

Product life cycle is simply the time a product exists—from conception to abandonment. Usually product life cycle refers to a product class as a whole—such as automobiles—but it can also refer to specific forms (such as station wagons) and to specific brands or models (such as a Toyota Camry). Also, by replacing "conception" with "purchase," we obtain a customer-oriented definition of product life cycle. The producer-oriented definition refers to the life of classes, forms, or brands, whereas the customer-oriented definition refers to the life of a specific unit of product. These producer and customer orientations can be refined by looking at the concepts of revenue-producing life and consumable life. Revenue-producing life is the time a product generates revenue for a company. A product begins its revenue-producing life with the sale of the first product. Consumable life, on the other hand, is the length of time that a product serves the needs of a customer. Revenue-producing life is clearly of most interest to the producer, while consumable life is of most interest to the customer. Consumable life, however, is also of interest to the producer because it can be used as a competitive tool.

Marketing Viewpoint

The producer of goods or services has two viewpoints concerning product life cycle: the marketing viewpoint and the production viewpoint. The marketing viewpoint describes the general sales pattern of a product as it passes through distinct life-cycle stages. Exhibit 11-10 illustrates the general pattern of the marketing view of product life cycle. The distinct stages identified by the exhibit are introduction, growth, maturity, and decline. The **introduction stage** is characterized by preproduction and startup activities, where the focus is on obtaining a foothold in the market. As the graph indicates, there are no sales for a period of time (the preproduction period) and then slow sales growth as the product is introduced. The **growth stage** is a period of time when sales increase more quickly. The **maturity stage** is a period of time when sales increase more slowly. Eventually, the slope (of the sales curve) in the maturity stage becomes neutral and then turns negative. This **decline stage** is when the product loses market acceptance and sales begin to decrease.

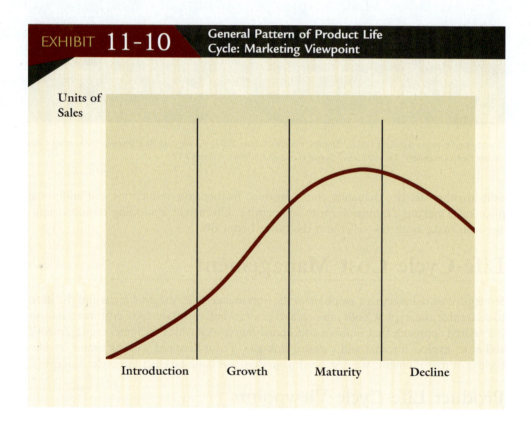

EXHIBIT 11-10   **General Pattern of Product Life Cycle: Marketing Viewpoint**

Production Viewpoint

The production viewpoint of the product life cycle defines stages of the life cycle by changes in the type of activities performed: research and development activities, production activities, and logistical activities. The production viewpoint emphasizes life-cycle costs, whereas the market viewpoint emphasizes sales revenue behavior. **Life-cycle costs** are all costs associated with the product for its entire life cycle. These costs include research (product conception), development (planning, design, and testing), production (conversion activities), and logistics support (advertising, distribution, warranty, customer service, product servicing, and so on). The product life cycle and the associated cost commitment curve are illustrated in Exhibit 11-11. Notice that 90 percent or more of the costs associated with a product are *committed* during the development stage of the product's life cycle. Committed means that most costing the costs that will be incurred are predetermined—set by the nature of the product design and the processes needed to produce the design.

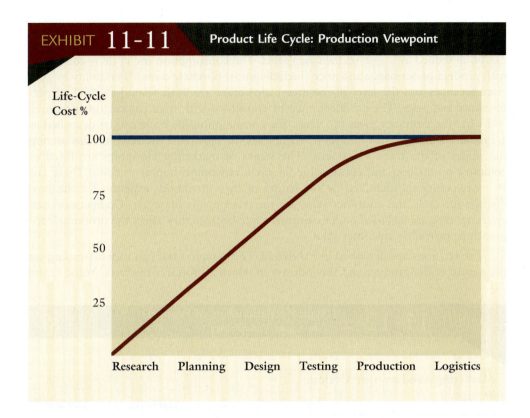

EXHIBIT 11-11 Product Life Cycle: Production Viewpoint

Consumable Life-Cycle Viewpoint

Like the production life cycle, the consumption life-cycle's stages are related to activities. These activities define four stages: purchasing, operating, maintaining, and disposal. The consumable life-cycle viewpoint emphasizes product performance for a given price. Price refers to the costs of ownership, which include the following elements: purchase cost, operating costs, maintenance costs, and disposal costs. Thus, total customer satisfaction is affected by both the purchase price and post-purchase costs. Because customer satisfaction is affected by post-purchase costs, producers also have a vital interest in managing the level of these costs. How producers can exploit the linkage of post-purchase activities with producer activities is a key element of product life-cycle cost management.

Interactive Viewpoint

All three life-cycle viewpoints offer insights that can be useful to producers of goods and services. In fact, producers cannot afford to ignore any of the three. A comprehensive life-cycle cost management program must pay attention to the variety of viewpoints that exist. This observation produces an integrated, comprehensive definition of life-cycle cost management. **Life-cycle cost management** consists of actions taken that cause a product to be designed, developed, produced, marketed, distributed, operated, maintained, serviced, and disposed of so that life-cycle profits are maximized. Maximizing life-cycle profits means producers must understand and capitalize on the relationships that exist among the three life-cycle viewpoints. Once these relationships are understood, then actions can be implemented that take advantage of revenue enhancement and cost reduction opportunities.

Relationships among Life-Cycle Viewpoints

The marketing viewpoint is concerned with the nature of the sales pattern over the life cycle of the product; it is a *revenue-oriented viewpoint*. The production viewpoint, however, emphasizes the internal activities needed to develop, produce, market, and service products. The production stages exist to support the sales objectives of the marketing stages. This sales support requires resource expenditure; thus, the production life cycle can be described as a *cost-oriented viewpoint*. The consumption life cycle is concerned with product performance and price (including post-purchase costs). The ability to generate revenues and the level of resource expenditure are both related to product performance and price. The producer must be concerned with what the customer receives and what the customer gives up. Thus, the consumption life cycle can be described as a *customer-value oriented viewpoint*. Exhibit 11-12 illustrates the relationships among the stages of the three viewpoints. The stages of marketing viewpoint are listed as columns; production and consumable life-cycle viewpoints appear as rows. These last two viewpoints are identified by the nature of their attributes: expenses for the production life cycle and customer value for the consumable life cycle. Competition and customer type are included under customer value because they affect the producer's approach to providing customer value.

The relationships described in Exhibit 11-12 are typical but can vary depending on the nature of the product and the industry in which a producer operates. Some expla-

---

EXHIBIT 11-12   **Typical Relationships of Product Life-Cycle Viewpoints**

Marketing Product Life Cycles:

Attributes	Introduction	Growth	Maturity	Decline
Sales	Low	Rapid growth	Slow growth, peak sales	Declining

Production Life Cycle:

Attributes	Introduction	Growth	Maturity	Decline
Expenses:				
Product R&D	High	Moderate	Moderate	Low
Product R&D	Moderate	High	Moderate	Low
Plant & equipment	Low to moderate	High	Moderate	Low
Advertising	Moderate to high	High	Moderate	Low
Service	Low	Moderate	High	Low

Consumable Life Cycle:

Attributes	Introduction	Growth	Maturity	Decline
Customer value:				
Customer type	Innovators	Mass market	Mass market, differentiated	Laggards
Performance sensitivity	High	High	High	Moderate
Price sensitivity	Low	Moderate	High	Moderate
Competition	None	Growing	High	Low

Attributes	Introduction	Growth	Maturity	Decline
Profits	Negligible to loss	Peak levels	Moderate to high	Low

nation of the relationships should reveal the potential for producers to exploit them. Relationships can be viewed vertically or horizontally. Consider, for example, the introduction stage, and examine the vertical relationships. In this stage, we would expect losses or negligible profits because of high levels of expenditure in research and development and marketing. Customers at this stage are described as innovators. These are simply the first customers to buy the product. Innovators are venturesome, willing to try something new. They are usually more concerned with the performance of the new product than with its price. This fact, coupled with the lack of competitors, may allow a high price to be charged for the new product. If the barriers to entry in the marketplace are high, then a high price may continue to be charged for some time. However, if competition grows as indicated by the horizontal dimension of the table, and if price sensitivity increases, then the producer will need to rely on further research and development and differentiation to maintain a competitive advantage.

Revenue Enhancement

Revenue-generating approaches depend on marketing life-cycle stages and on customer value effect. Pricing strategy, for example, varies with stages. In the introductory stage, as mentioned earlier, higher prices can be charged because customers are less price sensitive and more interested in performance.

In the maturity stage, customers are highly sensitive to both price and performance. This suggests that adding features, increasing durability, improving maintainability, and offering customized products may all be good strategies to follow. In this stage, differentiation is important. For revenue enhancement to be viable, however, the customer must be willing to pay a premium for any improvement in product performance. Furthermore, this premium must exceed the cost the producer incurs in providing the new product attribute. In the decline stage, revenues may be enhanced by finding new uses and new customers for the product. A good example is the use of **Arm & Hammer**'s baking soda to absorb refrigerator odors in addition to its normal role in baking goods.[7]

Cost Reduction

Cost reduction, not cost control, is the emphasis of life-cycle cost management. Cost reduction strategies should explicitly recognize that actions taken in the early stages of the production life cycle can lower costs for later production and consumption stages. Since 90 percent or more of a product's life-cycle costs are determined during the development stage, it makes sense to emphasize management of activities during this phase of a product's existence. Studies have shown that every dollar spent on preproduction activities saves $8–$10 on production and postproduction activities, including customer maintenance, repair, and disposal costs.[8] Apparently, many opportunities for cost reduction occur before production begins. Managers need to invest more in preproduction assets and dedicate more resources to activities in the early phases of the product life cycle to reduce production, marketing, and post-purchase costs.

Product design and process design afford multiple opportunities for cost reduction by designing to reduce: (1) manufacturing costs, (2) logistical support costs, and (3) post-purchase costs, which include customer time involved in maintenance, repair, and disposal. For these approaches to be successful, managers of producing companies must have a good understanding of activities and cost drivers and know how the activities interact. Manufacturing, logistical, and post-purchase activities are not independent. Some designs may reduce post-purchase costs and increase manufacturing costs. Others may simultaneously reduce production, logistical, and post-purchase costs.

---

7. Sak Onkvisit and John J. Shaw, "Competition and Product Management: Can the Product Life Cycle Help?" *Business Horizons* (July–August 1986): 51–52.
8. Mark D. Shields and S. Mark Young, "Managing Product Life Cycle Costs: An Organizational Model" and R. L. Engwall, "Cost Management for Defense Contractors," *Cost Accounting for the 90's, Responding to Technological Change* (Montvale, NJ: National Association of Accountants, 1988).

Cost Reduction: An Example

A functional-based costing system usually will not supply the information needed to support life-cycle cost management. Functional-based costing systems emphasize the use of unit-based cost drivers to describe cost behavior, focus on production activities, ignore logistical and post-purchase activities, and expense research and development and other nonmanufacturing costs as they are incurred. Functional-based costing systems never collect a complete history of a product's costs over its life cycle. Essentially, the GAAP-driven costing system does not support the demands of life-cycle costing. An activity-based costing system, however, produces information about activities, including both preproduction and postproduction activities, and cost drivers.

To illustrate the importance of knowing activity information, consider Gray Company, a company that produces industrial power tools. Gray currently uses a functional-based costing system, which assumes that all conversion costs are driven by direct labor hours. Because of competitive forces, management has instructed its design engineers to develop new product and process designs for existing products to reduce manufacturing costs. (The products targeted for design improvements are estimated to be entering the final growth stage of their marketing life cycle.) If, however, manufacturing costs are driven by factors other than direct labor hours, then design actions may produce costs much different than expected. For example, suppose that engineers are considering two new product designs for one of its power tools. Both designs reduce direct materials and direct labor content over the current model. The anticipated effects of the two designs on manufacturing, logistical, and post-purchase activities follow, for both the functional-based costing system and an ABC system.

Cost Behavior

Functional-based system:
Variable conversion activity rate: $40 per direct labor hour
Material usage rate: $8 per part

ABC system:
Labor usage: $10 per direct labor hour
Material usage (direct materials): $8 per part
Machining: $28 per machine hour
Purchasing activity: $60 per purchase order
Setup activity: $1,000 per setup hour
Warranty activity: $200 per returned unit (usually requires extensive rework)
Customer repair cost: $10 per repair hour

Activity and Resource Information (annual estimates)

	Design A	Design B
Units produced	10,000	10,000
Direct material usage	100,000 parts	60,000 parts
Labor usage	50,000 hours	80,000 hours
Machine hours	25,000	20,000
Purchase orders	300	200
Setup hours	200	100
Returned units	400	75
Repair time (customer)	800	150

The cost analysis for each design under both the functional-based costing and ABC systems is shown in Exhibit 11-13. The functional-based system computes the unit product cost using only manufacturing costs. The results of the functional-based

EXHIBIT 11-13	Cost Analysis: Competing Product Designs

A. Traditional Costing System

	Design A	Design B
Direct materials[a]	$ 800,000	$ 480,000
Conversion cost[b]	2,000,000	3,200,000
Total manufacturing costs	$2,800,000	$3,680,000
Units produced	÷ 10,000	÷ 10,000
Unit cost	$ 280	$ 368

[a]$8 × 100,000; $8 × 60,000.
[b]$40 × 50,000; $40 × 80,000.

B. ABC System

	Design A	Design B
Direct materials	$ 800,000	$ 480,000
Direct labor[a]	500,000	800,000
Machining[b]	700,000	560,000
Purchasing[c]	18,000	12,000
Setups[c]	200,000	100,000
Warranty[c]	80,000	15,000
Total product costs	$2,298,000	$1,967,000
Units produced	÷ 10,000	÷ 10,000
Unit cost	$ 230*	$ 197*
Postpurchase costs	$ 80,000	$ 15,000

[a]$10 × 50,000; $10 × 80,000.
[b]$28 × 25,000; $28 × 20,000.
[c]$60 × 300; $60 × 200; $1,000 × 200; $1,000 × 100; $200 × 400; $200 × 75.
*Rounded to the nearest dollar.

analysis favor Design A. Thus, Gray would choose Design A over Design B. The ABC analysis reveals a much different picture. Relative to Design A, Design B simultaneously reduces the costs of manufacturing, logistical, and post-purchase activities. Ignoring post-purchase costs, the cost advantage is $331,000 per year for Design B. With post-purchase costs included, the advantage jumps to $396,000. Notice that the customer repair hours per unit produced for Design A are 0.08 (800/10,000), but they are only 0.015 (150/10,000) for Design B. This indicates that Design B has a higher level of serviceability than does Design A and, thus, more customer value.

Role of Target Costing

Life-cycle cost management emphasizes cost reduction, not cost control. Target costing becomes a particularly useful tool for establishing cost reduction goals during the design stage. A **target cost** is the difference between the sales price needed to capture a predetermined market share and the desired per-unit profit. The sales price reflects the product specifications or functions valued by the customer (referred to as *product functionality*). If the target cost is less than what is currently achievable, then management must find cost reductions that move the actual cost toward the target cost. Finding those cost reductions is the principal challenge of target costing.

Three cost reduction methods are typically used: (1) reverse engineering, (2) value analysis, and (3) process improvement. In reverse engineering, the competitors' products are closely analyzed (a "tear down" analysis) in an attempt to discover more design features that create cost reductions. Value analysis attempts to assess the value placed on various product functions by customers. If the price customers are willing to pay for a particular function is less than its cost, the function is a candidate for elimination. Another possibility is to find ways to reduce the cost of providing the function, e.g., using common components. Both reverse engineering and value analysis focus on product design to achieve cost reductions. The processes used to produce and market the product are also sources of potential cost reductions. Thus, redesigning processes to improve their efficiency can also contribute to achieving the needed cost reductions. The target-costing model is summarized in Exhibit 11-14.

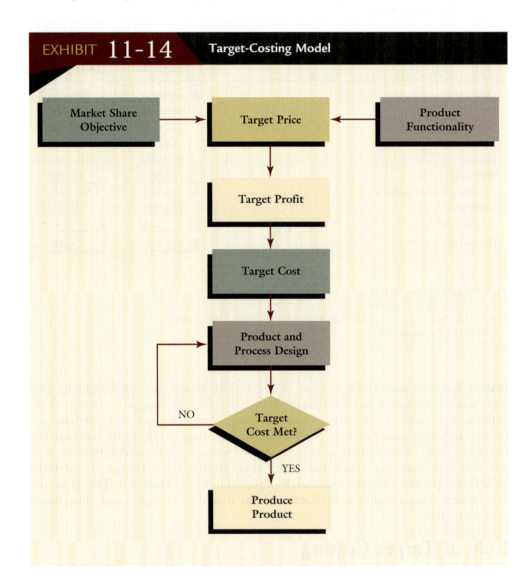

EXHIBIT 11-14   **Target-Costing Model**

A simple example can be used to illustrate the concepts described by Exhibit 11-14. Assume that a company is considering the production of a new trencher. Current product specifications and the targeted market share call for a sales price of $250,000. The required profit is $50,000 per unit. The target cost is computed as follows:

$$\text{Target cost} = \$250,000 - \$50,000$$
$$= \$200,000$$

It is estimated that the current product and process designs will produce a cost of $225,000 per unit. Thus, the cost reduction needed to achieve the target cost and desired profit is $25,000 ($225,000 − $200,000). A tear down analysis of a competitor's trencher revealed a design improvement that promised to save $5,000 per unit. When compared with the $25,000 reduction needed, additional effort was still necessary. A marketing study of customer reactions to product functions revealed that the extra trenching speed in the new design was relatively unimportant. Changing the design to reflect a lower trenching speed saved $10,000. The company's supplier also proposed the use of a standardized component, reducing costs by another $5,000. Finally, the design team was able to change the process design and reduce the test time by 50 percent. This saved $6,000 per unit. The last change reached the threshold value, and production for the new model was approved.

Target costs are a type of currently attainable standard. But they are conceptually different from traditional standards. What sets them apart is the motivating force. Traditional standards are internally motivated and set, based on concepts of efficiency developed by industrial engineers and production managers. Target costs, on the other hand, are externally driven, generated by an analysis of markets and competitors.

Supplier and Firm Interaction

The example just given indicated that one source of cost reduction came from a supplier suggestion. During the design stage, target costing requires a close interaction between the firm and its suppliers. This interaction should produce lower cost solutions than would be possible if the design teams acted in isolation.[9] Joint design efforts require cooperative relationships. Incentives for such relationships come from a willingness to search for mutually beneficial solutions.

Short Life Cycles

Although life-cycle cost management is important for all manufacturing firms, it is particularly important for firms that have products with short life cycles. Products must recover all life-cycle costs and provide an acceptable profit. If a firm's products have long life cycles, profit performance can be increased by such actions as redesigning, changing prices, reducing costs, and altering the product mix. In contrast, firms that have products with short life cycles usually do not have time to react in this way so their approach must be proactive. Thus, for short life cycles, good life-cycle planning is critical, and prices must be set properly to recover all the life-cycle costs and provide a good return. Activity-based costing can be used to encourage good life-cycle planning. By careful selection of cost drivers, design engineers can be motivated to choose cost-minimizing designs.

Identify the basic features of JIT purchasing and manufacturing.

Just-in-Time (JIT) Manufacturing and Purchasing

JIT manufacturing and purchasing systems offer a prominent example of how managers can use the strategic concepts discussed earlier in the chapter to bring about significant changes within an organization. Firms that implement JIT are pursuing a cost reduction strategy by redefining the structural and procedural activities performed within an organization. Cost reduction is supportive of either a cost leadership or differentiation strategy. Cost reduction is directly related to cost leadership. Successful differentiation depends on offering greater value; yet, this value added must be more than the cost of providing it. JIT can help add value by reducing waste. Successful implementation of

9. Robin Cooper and Regine Slagmulder, "Cost Management Beyond the Boundaries of the Firm," *Management Accounting* (March 1998): 18–20.

JIT has brought about significant improvements, such as better quality, increased productivity, reduced lead times, major reductions in inventories, reduced setup times, lower manufacturing costs, and increased production rates. For example, **Oregon Cutting Systems**, a manufacturer of cutting chain (for chain saws), timber-harvesting equipment, and sporting equipment—within a period of three to five years—reduced defects by 80 percent, waste by 50 percent, setup times from hours to minutes (one punch press had setup time reduced from three hours to 4.5 minutes), lead times from 21 days to three days, and manufacturing costs by 35 percent.[10] JIT techniques have also been implemented by the following companies with similar results:

Wal-Mart	**Chrysler**	**Intel**
General Motors	**Hewlett-Packard**	**Borg-Warner**
Toys "R" Us	**Harley-Davidson**	**Westinghouse**
Ford	**Motorola**	**John Deere**
General Electric	**AT&T**	**Mercury Marine**
Black & Decker	**Xerox**	

Adopting a JIT manufacturing system has a significant effect on the nature of the cost management accounting system. Installing a JIT system affects the traceability of costs, enhances product costing accuracy, diminishes the need for allocation of service-center costs, changes the behavior and relative importance of direct labor costs, impacts job-order and process-costing systems, decreases the reliance on standards and variance analysis, and decreases the importance of inventory tracking systems. To understand and appreciate these effects, we need a fundamental understanding of what JIT manufacturing is and how it differs from traditional manufacturing.

JIT manufacturing is a demand-pull system. The objective of **JIT manufacturing** is to eliminate waste by producing a product only when it is needed and only in the quantities demanded by customers. Demand pulls products through the manufacturing process. Each operation produces only what is necessary to satisfy the demand of the succeeding operation. No production takes place until a signal from a succeeding process indicates a need to produce. Parts and materials arrive just in time to be used in production. JIT assumes that all costs other than direct materials are driven by time and space drivers. JIT then focuses on eliminating waste by compressing time and space.

Inventory Effects

Usually, the push-through system produces significantly higher levels of finished goods inventory than does a JIT system. JIT manufacturing relies on the exploitation of a customer linkage. Specifically, production is tied to customer demand. This linkage extends back through the value chain and also affects how a manufacturer deals with suppliers. **JIT purchasing** requires suppliers to deliver parts and materials just in time to be used in production. Thus, supplier linkages are also vital. Supply of parts must be linked to production, which is linked to demand. One effect of successful exploitation of these linkages is to reduce all inventories to much lower levels. Since 1980, inventories in the United States have fallen from 26 to 15 percent of the gross domestic product; furthermore, JIT is saving U.S. automakers more than $1 billion annually in inventory carrying costs.[11]

Traditionally, inventories of raw materials and parts are carried so that a firm can take advantage of quantity discounts and hedge against future price increases of the items purchased. The objective is to lower the cost of inventory. JIT achieves the same objective without carrying inventories. The JIT solution is to exploit supplier linkages

---

10. Jack C. Bailes and Ilene K. Kleinsorge, "Cutting Waste with JIT," *Management Accounting* (May 1992): 28–32.
11. Art Raymond, "Is JIT Dead?" *FDM; Des Plaines* (January 2002): 30–32.

by negotiating long-term contracts with a few chosen suppliers located as close to the production facility as possible and by establishing more extensive supplier involvement. Suppliers are not selected on the basis of price alone.

Performance—the quality of the component and the ability to deliver as needed—and commitment to JIT purchasing are vital considerations. Every effort is made to establish a partners-in-profits relationship with suppliers. Suppliers need to be convinced that their well-being is intimately tied to the well-being of the buyer.

To help reduce the uncertainty in demand for the supplier and establish the mutual confidence and trust needed in such a relationship, JIT manufacturers emphasize long-term contracts. Other benefits of long-term contracts exist. They stipulate prices and acceptable quality levels. Long-term contracts also reduce dramatically the number of orders placed, which helps to drive down the ordering and receiving costs. Another effect of long-term contracting is a reduction in the cost of parts and materials—usually in the range of 5 percent to 20 percent less than what was paid in a traditional setting. The need to develop close supplier relationships often drives the supplier base down dramatically. For example, **Mercedes-Benz U.S. Internationalis** factory in Vance, Alabama, saved time and money by streamlining its supplier list from 1,000 to 100 primary suppliers. In exchange for annual 5 percent price cuts, the chosen suppliers have multiyear contracts (as opposed to the yearly bidding process practiced at other Mercedes' plants) and can adapt off-the-shelf parts to Mercedes' needs. The end result is lower costs for both Mercedes and its suppliers.[12] Suppliers also benefit. The long-term contract ensures a reasonably stable demand for their products. A smaller supplier base typically means increased sales for the selected suppliers. Thus, both buyers and suppliers benefit, a common outcome when external linkages are recognized and exploited.

By reducing the number of suppliers and working closely with those that remain, the quality of the incoming materials can be improved significantly—a crucial outcome for the success of JIT. As the quality of incoming materials increases, some quality-related costs can be avoided or reduced. For example, the need to inspect incoming materials disappears, and rework requirements decline.

Plant Layout

The type and efficiency of plant layout is another executional cost driver that is managed differently under JIT manufacturing. (See Exhibit 11-2 on p. 491 for a review of executional cost drivers.) In traditional job and batch manufacturing, products are moved from one group of identical machines to another. Typically, machines with identical functions are located together in an area referred to as a *department* or *process*. Workers who specialize in the operation of a specific machine are located in each department. Thus, the executional cost driver for a traditional setting is departmental structure. JIT replaces this traditional plant layout with a pattern of manufacturing cells. The executional cost driver for a JIT setting is cell structure. Cell structure is chosen over departmental structure because it increases the ability of the organization to "execute" successfully. Some of the efficiencies cited earlier for Oregon Cutting Systems (OCS), such as reduced lead times and lower manufacturing costs, are a direct result of the cellular structure. The cellular manufacturing design can also affect structural activities, such as plant size and number of plants, because it typically requires less space. OCS, for example, cut its space requirement by 40 percent. Space savings like this can reduce the demand to build new plants and will affect the size of new plants when they are needed.

Manufacturing cells contain machines that are grouped in families, usually in a semicircle. The machines are arranged so that they can be used to perform a variety of

12. David Woodruff and Karen Lowry Miller, "Mercedes' Maverick in Alabama," *Business Week* (September 11, 1995): 64–65.

operations in sequence. Each cell is set up to produce a particular product or product family. Products move from one machine to another from start to finish. Workers are assigned to cells and are trained to operate all machines within the cell. In other words, labor in a JIT environment is multiskilled, not specialized. Each manufacturing cell is essentially a minifactory; in fact, cells are often referred to as a *factory within a factory*. A comparison of the JIT's plant layout with the traditional pattern is shown in Exhibit 11-15.

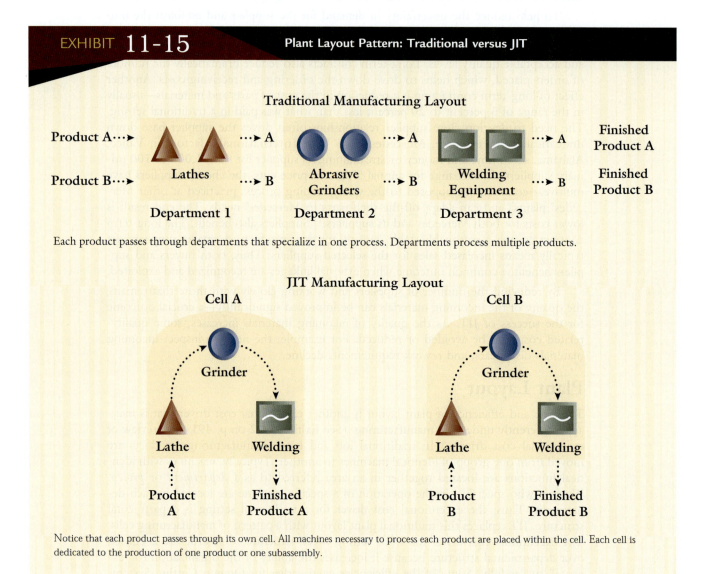

EXHIBIT 11-15 Plant Layout Pattern: Traditional versus JIT

Traditional Manufacturing Layout

Each product passes through departments that specialize in one process. Departments process multiple products.

JIT Manufacturing Layout

Notice that each product passes through its own cell. All machines necessary to process each product are placed within the cell. Each cell is dedicated to the production of one product or one subassembly.

Grouping of Employees

Another major structural difference between JIT and traditional organizations relates to how employees are grouped. As just indicated, each cell is viewed as a minifactory; thus, each cell requires easy and quick access to support services, which means that centralized service departments must be scaled down and their personnel reassigned to work directly with manufacturing cells. For example, with respect to raw materials, JIT calls for multiple stock points, each one located near where the material will be used. There is no need for a central store location—in fact, such an arrangement actually hinders efficient production. A purchasing agent can be assigned to each cell to handle material requirements. Similarly, other service personnel, such as manufacturing and quality engineers, can be assigned to cells.

Other support services may be relocated to the cell by training cell workers to perform the services. For example, in addition to direct production work, cell workers may perform setup duties, move partially completed goods from station to station within the cell, perform preventive maintenance and minor repairs, conduct quality inspections, and perform janitorial tasks. This multiple task capability is directly related to the pull-through production approach. Producing on demand means that production workers (formerly direct laborers) may often have "free" time. This nonproduction time can be used to perform some of the other support activities.

Employee Empowerment

A major procedural difference between traditional and JIT environments is the degree of participation allowed workers in the management of the organization. According to the JIT view, increasing the degree of participation (the executional cost driver) increases productivity and overall cost efficiency. Workers are allowed a say in how the plant operates. For example, workers are allowed to shut down production to identify and correct problems. Managers seek workers' input and use their suggestions to improve production processes. Workers are often involved in interviewing and hiring other employees, sometimes even prospective bosses. The reason? If the "chemistry is right," then the workforce will be more efficient, and they will work together better.

Employee empowerment, a procedural activity, also affects other structural and procedural activities. The management structure must change in response to greater employee involvement. Because workers assume greater responsibilities, fewer managers are needed, and the organizational structure becomes flatter. Flatter structures speed up and increase the quality of information exchange. The style of management needed in the JIT firm also changes. Managers in the JIT environment need to act as facilitators more than as supervisors. Their role is to develop people and their skills so that they can make value-adding contributions.

Total Quality Control

JIT necessarily carries with it a much stronger emphasis on managing quality. A defective part brings production to a grinding halt. Poor quality simply cannot be tolerated in a manufacturing environment that operates without inventories. Simply put, JIT cannot be implemented without a commitment to total quality control (TQC). TQC is essentially a never-ending quest for perfect quality: the striving for a defect-free product design and manufacturing process. This approach to managing quality is diametrically opposed to the traditional doctrine, called **acceptable quality level (AQL)**. AQL permits or allows defects to occur provided they do not exceed a predetermined level.

The major differences between JIT manufacturing and traditional manufacturing are summarized in Exhibit 11-16 on the following page. These differences will be referred to and discussed in greater detail as the implications of JIT manufacturing for cost management are examined.

OBJECTIVE **5**

Describe the effect JIT has on cost traceability and product costing.

JIT and Its Effect on the Cost Management System

The numerous changes in structural and procedural activities that we have described for a JIT system also change traditional cost management practices. Both the cost

| EXHIBIT 11-16 | Comparison of JIT Approaches with Traditional Manufacturing and Purchasing |

JIT	Traditional
1. Pull-through system	1. Push-through system
2. Insignificant inventories	2. Significant inventories
3. Small supplier base	3. Large supplier base
4. Long-term supplier contracts	4. Short-term supplier contracts
5. Cellular structure	5. Departmental structure
6. Multiskilled labor	6. Specialized labor
7. Decentralized services	7. Centralized services
8. High employee involvement	8. Low employee involvement
9. Facilitating management style	9. Supervisory management style
10. Total quality control	10. Acceptable quality level
11. Buyers' market	11. Sellers' market
12. Value-chain focus	12. Value-added focus

accounting and operational control systems are affected. In general, the organizational changes simplify the cost management accounting system and simultaneously increase the accuracy of the cost information being produced.

Traceability of Overhead Costs

Costing systems use three methods to assign costs to individual products: direct tracing, driver tracing, and allocation. Of the three methods, the most accurate is direct tracing; for this reason, it is preferred over the other two methods. In a JIT environment, many overhead costs assigned to products using either driver tracing or allocation are now directly attributable to products. Cellular manufacturing, multiskilled labor, and decentralized service activities are the major features of JIT responsible for this change in traceability.

In a departmental structure, many different products may be subjected to a process located in a single department (e.g., grinding). After completion of the process, the products are then transferred to other processes located in different departments (e.g., assembly, painting, and so on). Although a different set of processes is usually required for each product, most processes are applicable to more than one product. For example, 30 different products may need grinding. Because more than one product is processed in a department, the costs of that department are common to all products passing through it, and therefore the costs must be assigned to products using activity drivers or allocation. In a manufacturing-cell structure, however, all processes necessary for the production of each product or major subassembly are collected in one area called a cell. Thus, the costs of operating that cell can be assigned to the cell's product or subassembly using direct tracing. (However, if a family of products uses a cell, then we must resort to drivers and allocation to assign costs.)

Equipment formerly located in other departments, for example, is now reassigned to cells, where it may be dedicated to the production of a single product or subassembly. In this case, depreciation is now a directly attributable product cost. Multiskilled workers and decentralized services add to the effect. Workers in the cell are trained to set up the equipment in the cell, maintain it, and operate it. Additionally, cell workers may also be used to move a partially finished part from one machine to the next or to perform maintenance, setups, and materials handling. These support functions were previously done by a different set of laborers for all product lines. Additionally, people with specialized skills (e.g., industrial engineers and production schedulers) are assigned directly to manufacturing cells. Because of multitask assignments and redeployment of other support personnel, many support costs can now be assigned to a product using direct tracing. Exhibit 11-17 compares the traceability of some selected costs in a traditional manufacturing environment with their traceability in the JIT environment (assuming single-product cells). Comparisons are based on the three cost assignment methods.

EXHIBIT 11-17	Product Cost Assignment: Traditional versus JIT Manufacturing	
Manufacturing Cost	**Traditional Environment**	**JIT Environment**
Direct labor	Direct tracing	Direct tracing
Direct materials	Direct tracing	Direct tracing
Materials handling	Driver tracing	Direct tracing
Repairs and maintenance	Driver tracing	Direct tracing
Energy	Driver tracing	Direct tracing
Operating supplies	Driver tracing	Direct tracing
Supervision (department)	Allocation	Direct tracing
Insurance and taxes	Allocation	Allocation
Plant depreciation	Allocation	Allocation
Equipment depreciation	Driver tracing	Direct tracing
Custodial services	Allocation	Direct tracing
Cafeteria services	Driver tracing	Driver tracing

Product Costing

One consequence of increasing directly attributable costs is to increase the accuracy of product costing. Directly attributable costs are associated (usually by physical observation) with the product and can safely be said to belong to it. Other costs, however, are common to several products and must be assigned to these products using activity drivers and allocation. Because of cost and convenience, activity drivers that are less than perfectly correlated with the consumption of overhead activities may be chosen. JIT manufacturing reduces the need for this difficult assessment by converting many common costs to directly attributable costs. Note, however, that the driving force behind these changes is not the cost management system itself but the changes in the structural and procedural activities brought about by implementing a JIT system. While activity-based costing offers significant improvement in product costing accuracy, focusing offers even more potential improvement.

Exhibit 11-17 illustrates that JIT does not convert all costs into directly traceable costs. Even with JIT in place, some overhead activities remain common to the manufacturing cells. These remaining support activities are mostly facility-level activities. In a JIT system, the batch size is one unit of product. Thus, all batch-level activities convert into unit-level activities. Additionally, many of the batch-level activities are reduced or eliminated. For example, materials handling may be significantly reduced because of the reorganization from a departmental structure to a cellular structure. Similarly, for single-product cells, there is no setup activity. Even for cells that produce a family of products, setup times would be minimal. Furthermore, it is likely that the need to use activity drivers for the cost of product-level activities is significantly diminished because of decentralizing these support activities to the cell level. Is there, then, a role for ABC in a JIT firm?

Although JIT diminishes the value of ABC for tracing manufacturing costs to individual products, an activity-based costing system has much broader application than just tracing manufacturing costs to products. For many strategic and tactical decisions, the product cost definition needs to include nonmanufacturing costs. For example, value-line and operational product costing is an invaluable tool for strategic costing analysis and for life-cycle cost management. Also, including post-purchase costs as part of the product cost definition provides valuable insights. Thus, knowing and understanding general and administrative, research, development, marketing, customer service, and post-purchase activities and their cost drivers is essential for sound cost analysis. Furthermore, as we have already seen, using ABC to assign costs accurately to suppliers and customers is an essential part of strategic cost management.

JIT's Effect on Job-Order and Process-Costing Systems

In implementing JIT in a job-order setting, the firm should first separate its repetitive business from its unique orders. Manufacturing cells can then be established to deal with the repetitive business. For those products where demand is insufficient to justify its own manufacturing cell, groups of dissimilar machines can be set up in a cell to make families of products or parts that require the same manufacturing sequence.

With this reorganization of the manufacturing layout, job orders are no longer needed to accumulate product costs. Instead, costs can be accumulated at the cellular level. Additionally, because lot sizes are now too small (as a result of reducing work-in-process and finished goods inventories), it is impractical to have job orders for each job. Add to this the short lead time of products occurring because of the time and space compression features of JIT (virtually no setup time and cellular structures), and it becomes difficult to track each piece moving through the cell. In effect, the job environment has taken on the nature of a process-costing system.

JIT simplifies process costing. A key feature of JIT is lower inventories. Assuming that JIT is successful in reducing work in process (Oregon Cutting Systems, for example, reduced work in process by 85 percent), the need to compute equivalent units vanishes. Calculating product costs follows the simple pattern of collecting costs for a cell for a period of time and dividing the costs by the units produced for that period.

Backflush Costing

The JIT system also offers the opportunity to simplify the accounting for manufacturing cost flows. Given low inventories, it may not be desirable to spend resources tracking the cost flows through all the inventory accounts. In a traditional system, there was a work-in-process account for each department so that manufacturing costs could be traced as work proceeded through the factory. Under JIT, there are no departments, a 14-day lead time (for example) has been decreased to four hours, and it would be absurd to trace costs from station to station within a cell. After all, if production cycle time is in minutes or hours, and goods are shipped immediately upon completion, then all of each day's manufacturing costs flow to Cost of Goods Sold. Recognizing this outcome leads to a simplified approach of accounting for manufacturing cost flows. This simplified approach, called **backflush costing**, uses trigger points to determine when manufacturing costs are assigned to key inventory and temporary accounts.

Varying the number and location of trigger points creates several types of backflush costing. Trigger points are simply events that prompt ("trigger") the accounting recognition of certain manufacturing costs. There are four variations, depending on the definition of the trigger points (which, in turn, depends on how fully the firm has implemented JIT):

1. The purchase of raw materials (trigger point 1) and the completion of the goods (trigger point 2).

2. The purchase of raw materials (trigger point 1) and the sale of goods (trigger point 2).
3. The completion of goods (only trigger point).
4. The sale of goods (only trigger point).

Variations 1 and 2

For Variations 1 and 2, the first trigger point is the purchase of raw materials. When materials are purchased in a JIT system, they are immediately placed into process. Raw Materials and In Process Inventory (RIP) is debited, and Accounts Payable is credited. The RIP inventory account is used only for tracking the cost of raw materials. There is no separate materials inventory account and no work-in-process inventory account. Combining direct labor and overhead into one category is a second feature of backflush costing. As firms implement JIT and become automated, the traditional direct labor cost category disappears. Multiskilled workers perform setup activities, machine-loading activities, maintenance, and materials handling, etc. As labor becomes multifunctional, the ability to track and report direct labor separately becomes impossible. Consequently, backflush costing usually combines direct labor costs with overhead costs in a temporary account called *Conversion Cost Control*. This account accumulates the *actual* conversion costs on the debit side and the applied conversion costs on the credit side. Any difference between the actual conversion costs and the applied conversion costs is closed to Cost of Goods Sold.

In the first variant of backflush costing, the completion of goods triggers the recognition of the manufacturing costs used to produce the goods (the second trigger point). At this point, conversion cost application is recognized by debiting Finished Goods Inventory and crediting Conversion Cost Control; the cost of direct materials is recognized by debiting Finished Goods Inventory and crediting the RIP inventory account. Therefore, the costs of manufacturing are "flushed" out of the system after the goods are completed.

In the second variant of backflush costing, the second trigger point is defined by the point when goods are sold rather than when they are completed. For this variant, the costs of manufacturing are flushed out of the system *after* the goods are sold. Thus, the application of conversion cost and the transfer of direct materials cost are accomplished by debiting Cost of Goods Sold and crediting Conversion Cost Control and RIP Inventory, respectively. Other entries are the same as Variation 1.

Variations 3 and 4

Under Variations 3 and 4, there is only one trigger point. Both variations recognize actual conversion costs by debiting Conversion Cost Control and crediting various accounts (such as Accumulated Depreciation). Neither variation makes any entry for the purchase of raw materials. For Variation 3, when the goods are completed, all costs, including direct materials cost, are flushed out of the system. This is done by debiting Finished Goods Inventory for the cost of all manufacturing inputs and crediting Accounts Payable for the cost of direct materials and Conversion Cost Control for the application of conversion costs. For Variation 4, the costs are flushed out of the system when the goods are sold. Thus, Cost of Goods Sold is debited, and Accounts Payable and Conversion Cost Control are credited. Of the four variations, only Variation 4 avoids all inventory accounts and, thus, would be the approach used for a pure JIT firm.

Example: Backflush Variations Illustrated and Compared with Traditional Cost Flow Accounting

To illustrate backflush costing and compare it with the traditional approach, assume that a JIT company had the following transactions during June:

1. Purchased raw materials on account for $160,000.
2. Placed all materials received into production.
3. Incurred actual direct labor costs of $25,000.

4. Incurred actual overhead costs of $225,000.
5. Applied conversion costs of $235,000.
6. Completed all work for the month.
7. Sold all completed work.
8. Computed the difference between actual and applied costs.

The journal entries for Variation 1 of backflush costing and the traditional system are compared in Exhibit 11-18.

EXHIBIT 11-18   **Cost Flows: Traditional Compared with JIT**

Transaction	Traditional Journal Entries			Backflush Journal Entries: Variation One		

1. Purchase of raw materials.	Materials Inventory
	    Accounts Payable
		160,000	160,000	Raw Materials and
				in Process Inventory
				    Accounts Payable
					160,000	160,000

2. Materials issued to production.	Work-in-Process Inventory Materials Inventory	160,000	160,000	No entry		

3. Direct labor cost incurred.	Work-in-Process Inventory
	    Wages Payable
		25,000	25,000	Combined with overhead: See
				    next entry.		

4. Overhead cost incurred.	Overhead Control
	    Accounts Payable
		225,000	225,000	Conversion Cost Control
				    Wages Payable
				    Accounts Payable
					250,000	25,000
						225,000

5. Application of overhead.	Work-in-Process Inventory Overhead Control	210,000	210,000	No entry		

6. Completion of goods.	Finished Goods Inventory
	    Work-in-Process Inventory
		395,000	395,000	Finished Goods Inventory
				    Raw Materials and
				    in Process Inventory
				    Conversion Cost Control
					395,000	160,000
						235,000

7. Goods are sold.	Cost of Goods Sold
	    Finished Goods Inventory
		395,000	395,000	Cost of Goods Sold
				    Finished Goods Inventory
					395,000	395,000

8. Variance is recognized.	Cost of Goods Sold
	    Overhead Control
		15,000	15,000	Cost of Goods Sold
				    Conversion Cost Control
					15,000	15,000

Variation 2 replaces the entries of Variation 1 for Transactions 6 and 7 in Exhibit 11-18 with the following entry:

Cost of Goods Sold	395,000	
Conversion Cost Control		235,000
Raw Materials and In Process Inventory		160,000

All other entries follow those of Variation 1.

Variation 3 differs from the entries in Exhibit 11-18 for Transactions 1 and 6. There is no entry for Transaction 1 (there is no RIP inventory account). Additionally, Variation 3 replaces the entry for Transaction 6 with the following:

Finished Goods Inventory	395,000	
Accounts Payable		160,000
Conversion Cost Control		235,000

All other entries are the same as those shown for Variation 1.

Variation 4 also has no entry for Transaction 1 and replaces the entries for Transactions 6 and 7 in Exhibit 11-18 with the following:

Cost of Goods Sold	395,000	
Accounts Payable		160,000
Conversion Cost Control		235,000

All other entries are the same. Variation 4 has three entries compared with eight for the traditional, non-JIT firm.

SUMMARY

Obtaining a competitive advantage so that long-term survival is ensured is the goal of strategic cost management. Different strategies create different bundles of activities. By assigning costs to activities, the costs of different strategies can be assessed. There are three generic or general strategies: cost leadership, differentiation, and focusing. The particular mix and relative emphasis of these three strategies define a firm's strategic position. The objective of strategic cost management is to reduce costs while simultaneously strengthening a firm's strategic position. Knowledge of organizational and operational activities and their associated cost drivers is fundamental to strategic cost analysis. Knowledge of the firm's value chain and the industrial value chain is also critical. Value-chain analysis relies on identifying and exploiting internal and external linkages. Good cost management of supplier and customer linkages requires an understanding of what suppliers cost and how much it costs to service customers. Activity-based assignments to suppliers and customers provide the accurate cost information needed.

Life-cycle cost management is related to strategic cost analysis and, in fact, could be called a type of strategic cost analysis. Life-cycle cost management requires an understanding of the three types of life-cycle viewpoints: the marketing viewpoint, the production viewpoint, and the consumable life viewpoint. By considering the interrelationships among the three viewpoints, insights are developed that help managers maximize life-cycle profits. Target costing plays an essential role in life-cycle cost management by providing a methodology for reducing costs in the design stage by considering and exploiting both customer and supplier linkages.

JIT purchasing and manufacturing offer a totally different set of structural and procedural activities from those of the traditional organization. The differences between JIT and traditional organizational structures can be used to illustrate the types of organizational activities and cost drivers that can be managed so a competitive advantage can be created and sustained. JIT also impacts the cost management system by changing the traceability of costs, increasing product costing accuracy, and in general, offering a simpler cost accounting system.

REVIEW PROBLEMS AND SOLUTIONS

1 STRATEGIC COST MANAGEMENT, TARGET COSTING

Assume that a firm has the following activities and associated cost behaviors:

Activities	Cost Behavior
Assembling components	$10 per direct labor hour
Setting up equipment	Variable: $100 per setup
	Step-fixed: $30,000 per step, 1 step = 10 setups
Receiving goods	Step-fixed: $40,000 per step, 1 step = 2,000 hours

Activities with step-cost behavior are being fully utilized by existing products. Thus, any new product demands will increase resource spending on these activities.

Two designs are being considered for a new product: Design I and Design II. The following information is provided about each design (1,000 units of the product will be produced):

Activity Driver	Design I	Design II
Direct labor hours	3,000	2,000
Number of setups	10	20
Receiving hours	2,000	4,000

The company has recently developed a cost equation for manufacturing costs using direct labor hours as the driver. The equation has $R^2 = 0.60$ and is as follows:

$$Y = \$150{,}000 + \$20X$$

Required:

1. Suppose that Design Engineering is told that only direct labor hours drive manufacturing costs (based on the direct labor cost equation). Compute the cost of each design. Which design would be chosen based on this unit-based cost assumption?
2. Now compute the cost of each design using all driver and activity information. Which design will now be chosen? Are there any other implications associated with the use of the more complete activity information set?
3. Consider the following statement: "Strategic cost analysis should exploit internal linkages." What does this mean? Explain, using the results of Requirements 1 and 2.
4. An outside consultant indicated that target costing ought to be used in the design stage. Explain what target costing is, and describe how it requires an understanding of both supplier and customer linkages.
5. What other information would be useful to have concerning the two designs? Explain.

SOLUTION

1. Design I: $20 × 3,000 = $60,000 + $150,000 = $210,000
   Design II: $20 × 2,000 = $40,000 + $150,000 = $190,000
   The unit-based analysis would lead to the selection of Design II.

2. Design I:

Assembling components ($10 × 3,000)	$ 30,000
Setting up equipment [(10 × $100) + (1 × $30,000)]	31,000
Receiving goods (1 × $40,000)	40,000
Total	$101,000

Design II:

Assembling components ($10 × 2,000)	$ 20,000
Setting up equipment [(20 × $100) + (2 × $30,000)]	62,000
Receiving goods (2 × $40,000)	80,000
Total	$162,000

Design I has the lowest total cost. Notice also the difference in expected total manufacturing costs. The direct labor driver approach produces a much higher cost for both designs. This difference in cost could produce significant differences in pricing strategies.

3. Exploiting internal linkages means taking advantage of the relationships among the activities that exist within a firm's segment of the value chain. To do this, we must know what the activities are and how they are related. Activity costs and drivers are an essential part of this analysis. Using only unit-based drivers for design decisions, as in Requirement 1, ignores the effect that different designs have on non-unit-based activities. The results of Requirement 2 illustrate a significant difference between two designs—relative to the unit-based analysis. The traditional costing system simply is not rich enough to supply the information needed for a thorough analysis of linkages.

4. Target costing specifies the unit cost required to achieve a given share of the market for a product with certain functional specifications. This target cost is then compared with the expected unit cost. If the expected unit cost is greater than the target cost, then actions are taken to reduce the costs to the desired level. Three general methods of cost reduction are used: (1) tear down engineering, (2) value analysis, and (3) process improvement. Tear down engineering dismantles competitors' products to search for more efficient product designs. Value engineering evaluates customer reactions to proposed functions and determines whether or not they are worth the cost to produce. Process improvement seeks to improve the efficiency of the process that will be used to produce the new product. The first two methods are concerned with improving product design, while the third is concerned with improving process design. Involving both customers and suppliers in the process has the objective of producing lower costs than would be obtained if the design team worked in isolation. Suppliers, for example, may suggest alternative designs that will reduce the cost of the components that go into the product. Customers, of course, can indicate whether or not they value a particular design feature and, if so, how much they would be willing to pay for it.

5. Linkages also extend to the rest of the firm's internal value-chain activities. It would be useful to know how design choices affect, and are affected by, logistical activities. Furthermore, external linkages would also help. For example, it would be interesting to know how post-purchase activities and costs are affected by the two designs.

2 BACKFLUSH COSTING

Foster Company has implemented a JIT system and is considering the use of backflush costing. Foster had the following transactions for the first quarter of the current fiscal year. (Conversion cost variances are recognized quarterly.)
1. Purchased raw materials on account for $400,000.
2. Placed all materials received into production.
3. Incurred actual direct labor costs of $60,000.
4. Incurred actual overhead costs of $400,000.

5. Applied conversion costs of $470,000.
6. Completed all work for the month.
7. Sold all completed work.
8. Computed the difference between actual and applied costs.

Required:

Prepare journal entries for Variations 2 and 4 of backflush costing.

SOLUTION

Transaction	Backflush Journal Entries: Variation 2		
1. Purchase of raw materials.	Raw Materials and in Process Inventory	400,000	
	Accounts Payable		400,000
2. Overhead cost incurred.	Conversion Cost Control	460,000	
	Wages Payable		60,000
	Accounts Payable		400,000
3. Goods are sold.	Cost of Goods Sold	870,000	
	Raw Materials and in Process Inventory		400,000
	Conversion Cost Control		470,000
4. Variance is recognized.	Conversion Cost Control	10,000	
	Cost of Goods Sold		10,000

Transaction	Backflush Journal Entries: Variation 4		
1. Overhead cost incurred.	Conversion Cost Control	460,000	
	Wages Payable		60,000
	Accounts Payable		400,000
2. Goods are sold.	Cost of Goods Sold	870,000	
	Accounts Payable		400,000
	Conversion Cost Control		470,000
3. Variance is recognized.	Conversion Cost Control	10,000	
	Cost of Goods Sold		10,000

KEY TERMS

QUESTIONS FOR WRITING AND DISCUSSION

1. What does it mean to obtain a competitive advantage? What role does the cost management system play in helping to achieve this goal?
2. What is customer value? How is customer value related to a cost leadership strategy? To a differentiation strategy? To strategic positioning?
3. Explain what internal and external linkages are.
4. What are organizational and operational activities? Organizational cost drivers? Operational cost drivers?
5. What is the difference between a structural cost driver and an executional cost driver? Provide examples of each.
6. What is value-chain analysis? What role does it play in strategic cost analysis?
7. What is an industrial value chain? Explain why a firm's strategies are tied to what happens in the rest of the value chain. Using total quality control as an example, explain how the success of this quality management approach is dependent on supplier linkages.
8. What are the three viewpoints of product life cycle? How do they differ?
9. What are the four stages of the marketing life cycle?
10. What are life-cycle costs? How do these costs relate to the production life cycle?
11. What are the four stages of the consumption life cycle? What are post-purchase costs? Explain why a producer may want to know post-purchase costs.
12. "Life-cycle cost reduction is best achieved during the development stage of the production life cycle." Do you agree or disagree? Explain.
13. What is target costing? What role does it have in life-cycle cost management?
14. Explain why JIT with dedicated cellular manufacturing increases product costing accuracy.
15. Explain how backflush costing works.

EXERCISES

11-1 COMPETITIVE ADVANTAGE: BASIC CONCEPTS

LO1 Jason Iba has decided to purchase a personal computer. He has narrowed his choices to two: Brand A and Brand B. Both brands have the same processing speed, the same hard disk capacity, 3.5-inch disk and CD-ROM drives, and the same basic software support package. Both come from companies with good reputations. The selling price for each is identical. After some review, Jason discovers that the cost of operating and maintaining Brand A over a 3-year period is estimated to be $200. For Brand B, the operating and maintenance cost is $600. The sales agent for Brand A emphasized the lower operating and maintenance cost. She claimed that it was lower than any other PC brand. The sales agent for Brand B, however, emphasized the service reputation of the product. He provided Jason with a copy of an article appearing in a PC magazine that rated service performance of various PC brands. Brand B was rated number one. Based on all the information, Jason decided to buy Brand B.

Required:

1. What is the total product purchased by Jason?
2. Is the Brand A company pursuing a cost leadership or differentiation strategy? The Brand B company? Explain.
3. When asked why he purchased Brand B, Jason replied, "I think Brand B offered more value than Brand A." What are the possible sources of this greater value? If Jason's reaction represents the majority opinion, what suggestions could you offer to help improve the strategic position of Brand A?

11-2   STRATEGIC POSITIONING

LO1   San Jose Goodwill Bank has been experiencing significant competition from nonbanking financial service providers such as mutual funds. As a result, interest rates were lower, and the bank found it more difficult to maintain or increase deposits. Profits had declined for the past two years. Concerned about the situation, the bank's executive managers commissioned a consulting group to assess the profitability of the bank's products and customers. The consulting group implemented an ABC system that traced costs to both products and customers. An ABC customer profitability analysis rated the customers on a scale of one to five, with one being the most lucrative. Customers in the number one category earned an average profit of $1,500 per year for the bank, while customers in the fifth category were costing the bank an average of $500 per year. The consulting group also conducted a marketing survey and discovered that the higher-end customers were leaving for banks that offered a broader range of financial products. Armed with the financial and marketing information provided by the consulting group, the banking executives decided to implement the following:

1. Broaden the markets to include investment and insurance products. The goal was to become a complete financial services provider to stop the loss of the higher-end customers. The broadening would also reduce the dependence of the bank on interest-based revenue. (Investment and insurance products produce fee-based revenues.)
2. Alter the customer mix by targeting only the upper three customer segments.
3. Set the bank apart from competitors by offering special, high-quality services to targeted customers:[13]
   a. The upper segment of customers will be classfied as "Premier One" and will be issued a gold card. When presenting the card to a concierge at the door, the customer will be taken to a special teller window with no line, or to the desk of a specially trained bank officer.
   b. For the highest-end customers, no-questions asked refunds on fees that they think they shouldn't pay (categories one and two). Middle-end customers can negotiate. Low-end customers must pay the fees (categories four and five).
   c. Provide secret, toll-free "VIP" numbers to customers in the Premier One category. In this way, they will have immediate access to a bank official for any inquiry they may have.
   d. Impose a $4 teller fee for lower-end customers (categories four and five).
4. Improve operating efficiency by increasing productivity and eliminating costs that produce no revenues.

---

13. Many of these services are actually being offered by banks. See Rick Brooks, "Alienating Customers Isn't Always a Bad Idea, Many Firms Discover," *The Wall Street Journal* (January 7, 1999): A1 and A12.

Required:

1. Describe the strategic positioning of San Jose Goodwill Bank in terms of the three general strategies: cost leadership, differentiation, and focusing. Of the three, which one(s) are apparently receiving the most emphasis?
2. Describe the role of cost management in defining the strategic position of the bank. What role do you think cost management will play as the bank attempts to establish and enhance its strategic position?

11-3 DRIVER CLASSIFICATION

LO1 Classify the following cost drivers as structural, executional, or operational.

    a. Number of plants
    b. Number of moves
    c. Degree of employee involvement
    d. Capacity utilization
    e. Number of product lines
    f. Number of distribution channels
    g. Engineering hours
    h. Direct labor hours
    i. Scope
    j. Product configuration
    k. Quality management approach
    l. Number of receiving orders
    m. Number of defective units
    n. Employee experience
    o. Types of process technologies
    p. Number of purchase orders
    q. Type and efficiency of layout
    r. Scale
    s. Number of functional departments
    t. Number of planning meetings

11-4 OPERATIONAL AND ORGANIZATIONAL ACTIVITIES

LO1 McConkie Company has decided to pursue a cost leadership strategy. This decision is prompted, in part, by increased competition from foreign firms. McConkie's management is confident that costs can be reduced by more efficient management of the firm's operational activities. Improving operational activity efficiency, however, often requires some strategic changes in organizational activities. McConkie currently uses a very traditional manufacturing approach. Plants are organized along departmental lines. Management follows a typical pyramid structure. Labor is specialized and located in departments. Quality management follows a conventional acceptable quality level approach. (Batches of products are accepted if the number of defective units is below some predetermined level.) Materials are purchased from a large number of suppliers, and sizable inventories of materials, work in process, and finished goods are maintained. The company produces many different products that use a variety of different parts, many of which are purchased from suppliers.

Required:

Given this brief description of the firm and its setting, for each of the following operational activities and their associated drivers, suggest some strategic changes in organizational activities (and drivers) that might reduce the cost of performing the indicated operational activity. Explain your reasoning.

Operational Activity	Operational Cost Driver
Inspecting products	Number of inspection hours
Moving materials	Distance moved
Reworking products	Number of defective units
Setting up equipment	Setup time
Purchasing parts	Number of different parts
Storing goods and materials	Days in inventory
Expediting orders	Number of late orders
Warranty work	Number of bad units sold

11-5 EXTERNAL LINKAGES, ACTIVITY-BASED SUPPLIER COSTING

LO2

Aldredge Company manufactures dental equipment. Aldredge produces all the components necessary for the production of its product except for one. This component is purchased from two local suppliers: Grayson Machining and Lambert, Inc. Grayson sells the component for $144 per unit, while Lambert sells the same component for $129. Because of the lower price, Aldredge purchases 80 percent of its components from Lambert. Aldredge purchases the remaining 20 percent from Grayson to ensure an alternative source. The total annual demand is 1,000,000 components.

Grayson's sales manager is pushing Aldredge to purchase more of its units, arguing that its component is of much higher quality and so should prove to be less costly than Lambert's lower-quality component. Grayson has sufficient capacity to supply all the components needed and is asking for a long-term contract. With a 5-year contract for 800,000 or more units, Grayson will sell the component for $135 per unit with a contractual provision for an annual product-specific inflationary adjustment. Aldredge's purchasing manager is intrigued by the offer and wonders if the higher-quality component actually does cost less than the lower-quality Lambert component. To help assess the cost effect of the two components, the following data were collected for quality-related activities and suppliers:

I. Activity data:

Activity	Cost
Inspecting components (sampling only)	$ 1,200,000
Expediting work (due to late delivery)	960,000
Reworking products (due to failed component)	6,844,500
Warranty work (due to failed component)	21,600,000

II. Supplier data:

	Grayson	Lambert
Unit purchase price	$144	$129
Units purchased	200,000	800,000
Expediting orders	10	90
Sampling hours*	20	980
Rework hours	90	1,410
Warranty hours	200	3,800

*The quality control department indicates that sampling inspection for the Grayson component has been reduced because the reject rate is so low.

Required:

1. Calculate the cost per component for each supplier, taking into consideration the costs of the quality-related activities and using the current prices and sales volume. Given this information, what do you think the purchasing manager ought to do? Explain.
2. Suppose the quality control department estimates that the company loses $4,500,000 in sales per year because of the reputation effect of defective units attributable to failed components. What information would you like to have to assign this cost to each supplier? Suppose that you had to assign the cost of lost sales to each supplier using one of the drivers already listed. Which would you choose? Using this driver, calculate the change in the cost of the Lambert component attributable to lost sales.

11-6 EXTERNAL LINKAGES, CUSTOMER COSTING, CUSTOMER PROFITABILITY

LO2 Dino Company sells machine parts to industrial equipment manufacturers for an average price of $0.75 per part. There are two types of customers: those who place small, frequent orders and those who place larger, less frequent orders. Each time an order is placed and processed, a setup is required. Scheduling is also needed to coordinate the many different orders that come in and place demands on the plant's manufacturing resources. Dino also inspects a sample of the products each time a batch is produced to ensure that the customer's specifications have been met. Inspection takes essentially the same time regardless of the type of part being produced. Dino's cost accounting department has provided the following budgeted data for customer-related activities and costs (the amounts expected for the coming year):

	Frequently Ordering Customers	Less Frequently Ordering Customers
Sales orders	10,000	1,000
Average order size	1,000	10,000
Number of setups	12,500	2,500
Scheduling hours	17,500	2,500
Inspections	12,500	2,500
Average unit cost*	$0.40	$0.40

*This cost does not include the cost of the following "customer-related" activities:

Customer-related activity costs:	
Processing sales orders	$1,100,000
Scheduling production	600,000
Setting up equipment	1,800,000
Inspecting batches	2,400,000
Total	$5,900,000

Required:

1. Assign the customer-related activity costs to each category of customers in proportion to the sales revenue earned by each customer type. Calculate the profitability of each customer type. Discuss the problems with this measure of customer profitability.
2. Assign the customer-related activity costs to each customer type using activity rates. Now calculate the profitability of each customer category. As a manager, how would you use this information?

11-7   PRODUCT LIFE CYCLE

LO3   The following series of statements or phrases are associated with product life-cycle viewpoints. Identify whether each one is associated with the marketing, production, or customer viewpoint. Where possible, identify the particular characteristic being described. If the statement or phrase fits more than one viewpoint, label it as interactive. Explain the interaction.

a. Sales are increasing at an increasing rate.
b. The cost of maintaining the product after it is purchased.
c. The product is losing market acceptance and sales are beginning to decrease.
d. A design is chosen to minimize post-purchase costs.
e. Ninety percent or more of the costs are committed during the development stage.
f. The length of time that the product serves the needs of a customer.
g. All the costs associated with a product for its entire life cycle.
h. The time in which a product generates revenue for a company.
i. Profits tend to reach peak levels during this stage.
j. Customers have the lowest price sensitivity during this stage.
k. Describes the general sales pattern of a product as it passes through distinct life-cycle stages.
l. The concern is with product performance and price.
m. Actions taken so that life-cycle profits are maximized.
n. Emphasizes internal activities that are needed to develop, produce, market, and service products.

11-8   JIT AND TRACEABILITY OF COSTS

LO5   Assume that a company has recently switched to JIT manufacturing. Each manufacturing cell produces a single product or major subassembly. Cell workers have been trained to perform a variety of tasks. Additionally, many services have been decentralized. Costs are assigned to products using direct tracing, driver tracing, and allocation. For each cost listed, indicate the most likely product cost assignment method used *before* JIT and *after* JIT. Set up a table with three columns: Cost Item, Before JIT, and After JIT. You may assume that direct tracing is used whenever possible, followed by driver tracing, with allocation being the method of last resort.

a. Inspection costs
b. Power to heat, light, and cool plant
c. Minor repairs on production equipment
d. Salary of production supervisor (department/cell)
e. Oil to lubricate machinery
f. Salary of plant supervisor
g. Costs to set up machinery
h. Salaries of janitors
i. Power to operate production equipment
j. Taxes on plant and equipment
k. Depreciation on production equipment
l. Raw materials
m. Salary of industrial engineer
n. Parts for machinery
o. Pencils and paper clips for production supervisor (department/cell)
p. Insurance on plant and equipment
q. Overtime wages for cell workers
r. Plant depreciation
s. Materials handling
t. Preventive maintenance

11-9 JIT Features and Product Costing Accuracy

LO4, LO5

Spreadsheet

Prior to installing a JIT system, Pohlson Company, a producer of bicycle parts, used maintenance hours to assign maintenance costs to its three products (wheels, seats, and handle bars). The maintenance costs totaled $1,960,000 per year. The maintenance hours used by each product and the quantity of each product produced are as follows:

	Maintenance Hours	Quantity Produced
Wheels	60,000	52,500
Seats	60,000	52,500
Handle bars	80,000	70,000

After installing JIT, three manufacturing cells were created, and cell workers were trained to perform preventive maintenance and minor repairs. A full-time maintenance person was also assigned to each cell. Maintenance costs for the three cells still totaled $1,960,000; however, these costs are now traceable to each cell as follows:

Cell, wheels	$532,000
Cell, seats	588,000
Cell, handle bars	840,000

Required:

1. Compute the pre-JIT maintenance cost per unit for each product.
2. Compute the maintenance cost per unit for each product after installing JIT.
3. Explain why the JIT maintenance cost per unit is more accurate than the pre-JIT cost.

11-10 Backflush Costing versus Traditional: Variation 1

LO5

Spreadsheet

Kaylin Company has installed a JIT purchasing and manufacturing system and is using backflush accounting for its cost flows. It currently uses the purchase of materials as the first trigger point and the completion of goods as the second trigger point. During the month of May, Kaylin had the following transactions:

Raw materials purchased	$810,000
Direct labor cost	135,000
Overhead cost	675,000
Conversion cost applied	877,500*

*$135,000 labor plus $742,500 overhead.

There were no beginning or ending inventories. All goods produced were sold with a 60 percent markup. Any variance is closed to Cost of Goods Sold. (Variances are recognized monthly.)

Required:

1. Prepare the journal entries that would have been made using a traditional accounting approach for cost flows.
2. Prepare the journal entries for the month using backflush costing.

11-11 Backflush Costing: Variation 2

LO5   Refer to **Exercise 11-10**.

Required:

Prepare the journal entries for the month of May using backflush costing, assuming that Kaylin uses the sale of goods as the second trigger point instead of the completion of goods.

11-12   BACKFLUSH COSTING VERSUS TRADITIONAL: VARIATIONS 3 AND 4

LO5   Refer to Exercise 11-10.

Required:

1. Prepare the journal entries for the month of May using backflush costing, assuming that Kaylin uses the completion of goods as the only trigger point.
2. Prepare the journal entries for the month of May using backflush costing, assuming that Kaylin uses the sale of goods as the only trigger point.

11-13   COST ASSIGNMENT AND JIT

LO4, LO5   Caltor Company produces two types of space heaters (regular and super). Both pass through two producing departments: fabrication and assembly. It also has a materials handling department that is responsible for moving materials and goods to and between departments. Budgeted data for the three departments are as follows:

	Materials Handling	Fabrication	Assembly
Overhead	$160,000	$240,000	$68,000
Number of moves	—	30,000	10,000
Direct labor hours	—	24,000	12,000

In the fabrication department, the regular model requires one hour of direct labor and the super model, two hours. In the assembly department, the regular model requires 0.5 hour of direct labor and the super model, one hour. Expected production: regular model, 8,000 units; super model, 8,000 units.

Immediately after preparing the budgeted data, a consultant suggests that two manufacturing cells be created: one for the manufacture of the regular model and the other for the manufacture of the super model. Raw materials would be delivered to each cell, and goods would be shipped immediately to customers upon completion. The total direct overhead costs estimated for each cell would be $76,000 for the regular cell and $240,000 for the super cell.

Required:

1. Allocate the materials handling costs to each department, and compute the overhead cost per unit for each heater. (Overhead rates use direct labor hours.)
2. Compute the overhead cost per unit if manufacturing cells are created. Which unit overhead cost do you think is more accurate—the one computed with a departmental structure, or the one computed using a cell structure? Explain.
3. Note that the total overhead costs for the cell structure are lower. Explain why.

PROBLEMS

11-14   INTERNAL LINKAGES, COST MANAGEMENT, AND STRATEGIC DECISION MAKING

LO2   Evans, Inc., has a functional-based costing system. Evans's Miami plant produces 10 different electronic products. The demand for each product is about the same. Although they differ in complexity, each product uses about the same labor time and materials.

The plant has used direct labor hours for years to assign overhead to products. To help design engineers understand the assumed cost relationships, the cost accounting department developed the following cost equation. (The equation describes the relationship between total manufacturing costs and direct labor hours; the equation is supported by a coefficient of determination of 60 percent.)

$$Y = \$5,000,000 + \$30X, \text{ where } X = \text{direct labor hours}$$

The variable rate of $30 is broken down as follows:

Direct labor	$ 9
Variable overhead	5
Direct materials	16

Because of competitive pressures, product engineering was given the charge to redesign products to reduce the total cost of manufacturing. Using the above cost relationships, product engineering adopted the strategy of redesigning to reduce direct labor content. As each design was completed, an engineering change order was cut, triggering a series of events such as design approval, vendor selection, bill of materials update, redrawing of schematic, test runs, changes in setup procedures, development of new inspection procedures, and so on.

After one year of design changes, the normal volume of direct labor was reduced from 250,000 hours to 200,000 hours, with the same number of products being produced. Although each product differs in its labor content, the redesign efforts reduced the labor content for all products. On average, the labor content per unit of product dropped from 1.25 hours per unit to one hour per unit. Fixed overhead, however, increased from $5,000,000 to $6,600,000 per year.

Suppose that a consultant was hired to explain the increase in fixed overhead costs. The consultant's study revealed that the $30 per hour rate captured the unit-level variable costs; however, the cost behavior of other activities was quite different. For example, setting up equipment is a step-fixed cost, where each step is 2,000 setup hours, costing $90,000. The study also revealed that the cost of receiving goods is a function of the number of different components. This activity has a variable cost of $2,000 per component type and a fixed cost that follows a step-cost pattern. The step is defined by 20 components with a cost of $50,000 per step. Assume also that the consultant indicated that the design adopted by the engineers increased the demand for setups from 20,000 setup hours to 40,000 setup hours and the number of different components from 100 to 250. The demand for other non-unit-level activities remained unchanged. The consultant also recommended that management take a look at a rejected design for its products. This rejected design increased direct labor content from 250,000 hours to 260,000 hours, decreased the demand for setups from 20,000 hours to 10,000 hours, and decreased the demand for purchasing from 100 component types to 75 component types, while the demand for all other activities remained unchanged.

Required:

1. Using normal volume, compute the manufacturing cost per labor hour before the year of design changes. What is the cost per unit of an "average" product?
2. Using normal volume after the one year of design changes, compute the manufacturing cost per hour. What is the cost per unit of an "average" product?
3. Before considering the consultant's study, what do you think is the most likely explanation for the failure of the design changes to reduce manufacturing costs? Now use the information from the consultant's study to explain the increase in the average cost per unit of product. What changes would you suggest to improve Evans's efforts to reduce costs?
4. Explain why the consultant recommended a second look at a rejected design. Provide computational support. What does this tell you about the strategic importance of cost management?

11-15   EXTERNAL LINKAGES, ACTIVITY-BASED SUPPLIER COSTING

LO2   Amado, Inc., manfactures riding lawn mowers. Amado uses JIT manufacturing and carries insignificant levels of inventory. Amado manufactures everything needed for the riding lawn mowers except for the engines. Several sizes of mowers are produced. The most popular line is the small mower line. The engines for the small mower line are purchased from two sources: Rivera Engines and Bach Machining. The Rivera engine is the more expensive of the two sources and has a price of $300. The Bach engine is $270 per unit. Amado produces and sells 13,200 units of the small mower. Of the 13,200 engines purchased, 2,400 are purchased from Rivera Engines, and 10,800 are purchased from Bach Machining. Although Bill Jackson, production manager, prefers the Rivera engine, Carlos Lopez, purchasing manager, maintains that the price difference is too great to buy more than the 2,400 units currently purchased. Carlos, however, does want to maintain a significant connection with Rivera just in case the less expensive source cannot supply the needed quantities. Even though Bill understands the price argument, he has argued in many meetings that the quality of the Rivera engine is worth the price difference. Carlos remains unconvinced.

Sam Miller, controller, has recently overseen the implementation of an activity-based costing system. He has indicated that an ABC analysis would shed some light on the conflict between production and purchasing. To support this position, the following data have been collected:

I.   Activity cost data:

Testing engines[a]	$240,000
Reworking products[b]	400,000
Expediting orders[c]	300,000
Repairing engines[d]	540,000

[a]All units are tested after assembly, and a certain percentage are rejected because of engine failure.
[b]Defective engines are removed, replaced (supplier will replace any failed engine), and retested before being sold to customers. Engine failure often causes collateral damage, and other parts need to be remanufactured and replaced before the unit is again functional.
[c]Due to late or failed delivery of engines.
[d]Repair work is for units under warranty and almost invariably is due to engine failure. Repair usually means replacing the engine. This cost plus labor, transportation, and other costs make warranty work very expensive.

II. Supplier data:

	Bach	Rivera
Engines replaced by source	990	10
Rework hours	4,900	100
Late or failed shipments	99	1
Warranty repairs (by source)	1,220	30

Upon hearing of the proposed ABC analysis, Bill and Carlos were both supportive. Carlos, however, noted that even if the analysis revealed that the Rivera engine was actually less expensive, it would be unwise to completely abandon Bach. He argued that Rivera may be hard pressed to meet the entire demand. Its productive capacity was not sufficient to handle the kind of increased demand that would be imposed. Additionally, having only one supplier was simply too risky.

Required:

1. Calculate the total supplier cost (acquisition cost plus supplier-related activity costs). Convert this to a per-engine cost to find out how much the company is paying for the engines. Which of the two suppliers is the low-cost supplier? Explain why this is a better measure of engine cost than the usual purchase costs assigned to the engines.

2. Consider the supplier cost information obtained in Requirement 1. Suppose further that Rivera can supply only a total of 6,000 units. What actions would you advise Amado to undertake with its suppliers? Comment on the strategic value of activity-based supplier costing.

11-16   EXTERNAL LINKAGES, ACTIVITY-BASED CUSTOMER COSTING, AND STRATEGIC DECISION MAKING

LO2   Moss Manufacturing produces several types of bolts. The products are produced in batches according to customer order. Although there are a variety of bolts, they can be grouped into three product families. The number of units sold is the same for each family. The selling prices for the three families range from $0.50 to $0.80 per unit. Because the product families are used in different kinds of products, customers also can be grouped into three categories, corresponding to the product family they purchase. Historically, the costs of order entry, processing, and handling were expensed and not traced to individual products. These costs are not trivial and totaled $6,300,000 for the most recent year. Furthermore, these costs had been increasing over time. Recently, the company had begun to emphasize a cost reduction strategy; however, any cost reduction decisions had to contribute to the creation of a competitive advantage.

Because of the magnitude and growth of order-filling costs, management decided to explore the causes of these costs. They discovered that order-filling costs were driven by the number of customer orders processed. Further investigation revealed the following cost behavior:

Step-fixed cost component: $70,000 per step; 2,000 orders define a step*
Variable cost component: $28 per order

*Moss currently has sufficient steps to process 100,000 orders.

The expected customer orders for the year total 140,000. The expected usage of the order-filling activity and the average size of an order by product family are as follows:

	Family A	Family B	Family C
Number of orders	70,000	42,000	28,000
Average order size	600	1,000	1,500

As a result of the cost behavior analysis, the marketing manager recommended the imposition of a charge per customer order. The president of the company concurred. The charge was implemented by adding the cost per order to the price of each order (computed using the projected ordering costs and expected orders). This ordering cost was then reduced as the size of the order increased and eliminated as the order size reached 2,000 units. (The marketing manager indicated that any penalties imposed for orders greater than this size would lose sales from some of the smaller customers.) Within a short period of communicating this new price information to customers, the average order size for all three product families increased to 2,000 units.

Required:

1. Moss traditionally has expensed order-filling costs (following GAAP guidelines). Under this approach, how much cost is assigned to customers? Do you agree with this practice? Explain.

2. Consider the following claim: By expensing the order-filling costs, all products were undercosted; furthermore, products ordered in small batches are significantly undercosted. Explain, with supporting computations where possible. Explain how this analysis also reveals the costs of various customer categories.

3. Calculate the reduction in order-filling costs produced by the change in pricing strategy. (Assume that resource spending is reduced as much as possible and that the total units sold remain unchanged.) Explain how exploiting customer linkages produced this cost reduction. Moss also noticed that other activity costs, such as those for setups, scheduling, and materials handling costs, were reduced significantly as a result of this new policy. Explain this outcome, and discuss its implications.

4. Suppose that one of the customers complains about the new pricing policy. This buyer is a lean, JIT firm that relies on small frequent orders. In fact, this customer accounted for 30 percent of the Family A orders. How should Moss deal with this customer?

5. One of Moss's goals is to reduce costs so that a competitive advantage might be created. Describe how the management of Moss might use this outcome to help create a competitive advantage.

11-17   INTERNAL AND EXTERNAL LINKAGES, STRATEGIC COST MANAGEMENT

LO2   Maxwell Company produces a variety of kitchen appliances, including cooking ranges and dishwashers. Over the past several years, competition has intensified. In order to maintain—and perhaps increase—its market share, Maxwell's management decided that the overall quality of its products had to be increased. Furthermore, costs needed to be reduced so that the selling prices of its products could be reduced. After some investigation, Maxwell concluded that many of its problems could be traced to the unreliability of the parts that were purchased from outside suppliers. Many of these components failed to work as intended, causing performance problems. Over the years, the company had increased its inspection activity of the final products. If a problem could be detected internally, then it was usually possible to rework the appliance so that the desired performance was achieved. Management also had increased its warranty coverage; warranty work had been increasing over the years.

David Haight, president of Maxwell Company, called a meeting with his executive committee. Lee Linsenmeyer, chief engineer, Kit Applegate, controller, and Jeannie Mitchell, purchasing manager, were all in attendance. How to improve the company's competitive position was the meeting's topic. The conversation of the meeting was recorded as follows:

DAVID: We need to find a way to improve the quality of our products and at the same time reduce costs. Lee, you said that you have done some research in this area. Would you share your findings?

LEE: As you know, a major source of our quality problems relates to the poor quality of the parts we acquire from the outside. We have a lot of different parts, and this adds to the complexity of the problem. What I thought would be helpful would be to redesign our products so that they can use as many interchangeable parts as possible. This will cut down the number of different parts, make it easier to inspect, and cheaper to repair when it comes to warranty work. My engineering staff has already come up with some new designs that will do this for us.

JEANNIE: I like this idea. It will simplify the purchasing activity significantly. With fewer parts, I can envision some significant savings for my area. Lee has shown me the designs so I know exactly what parts would be needed. I also have a suggestion. We need to embark on a supplier evaluation program. We have too many suppliers. By reducing the number of different parts, we will need fewer suppliers. And we really don't need to use all the suppliers that produce the parts demanded by the new designs. We should pick suppliers that will work with us and provide the quality of parts that we need. I have done some preliminary research and have identified five suppliers that seem willing to work with us and assure us of the quality we need. Lee may need to send some of his engineers into their plants to make sure that they can do what they are claiming.

DAVID: This sounds promising. Kit, can you look over the proposals and their estimates and give us some idea if this approach will save us any money? And if so, how much can we expect to save?

KIT: Actually, I am ahead of the game here. Lee and Jeannie have both been in contact with me and have provided me with some estimates on how these actions would affect different activities. I have prepared a handout that includes an activity table revealing what I think are the key activities affected. I have also assembled some tentative information about activity costs. The table gives the current demand and the expected demand after the changes are implemented. With this information, we should be able to assess the expected cost savings.

Handout

Activities	Activity Driver	Capacity	Current Demand	Expected Demand
Purchasing parts	Number of different parts	2,000	2,000	500
Inspecting products	Inspection hours	50,000	50,000	25,000
Reworking products	Number reworked	As needed	62,500	25,000
Warranty repair	Number of defective products	10,000	9,000	3,500

Additionally, the following activity cost data are provided:

Purchasing parts: Variable activity cost: $30 per part number; 20 salaried clerks, each earning a $45,000 annual salary. Each clerk is capable of processing orders associated with 100 part numbers.

Inspecting parts: Twenty-five inspectors, each earning a salary of $40,000 per year. Each inspector is capable of 2,000 hours of inspection.

Reworking products: Variable activity cost: $25 per unit reworked (labor and parts).

Warranty: Twenty repair agents, each paid a salary of $35,000 per year. Each repair agent is capable of repairing 500 units per year. Variable activity costs: $15 per product repaired.

Required:

1. Compute the total savings possible as reflected by Kit's handout. Assume that resource spending is reduced where possible.
2. Explain how redesign and supplier evaluation are linked to the savings computed in Requirement 1. Discuss the importance of recognizing and exploiting internal and external linkages.
3. Identify the organizational and operational activities involved in the strategy being considered by Maxwell Company. What is the relationship between organizational and operational activities?

11-18 EXTERNAL LINKAGES AND STRATEGIC COST MANAGEMENT

LO1, LO2 Pawnee Works makes machine parts for manufacturers of industrial equipment. Over the years, Pawnee has been a steady and reliable supplier of quality parts to medium and small machine manufacturers. Michael Murray, owner of Pawnee Works, once again was disappointed in the year-end income statement. Profits had again failed to meet expectations. The performance was particularly puzzling given that the shop was operating at 100 percent capacity and had been for two years—ever since it had landed a *Fortune 500* firm as a regular customer. This firm currently supplies 40 percent of the business—a figure that had grown over the two years. Convinced that something was wrong, Michael called Brooke Harker, a partner in a large regional CPA firm. Brooke agreed to look into the matter.

A short time later, Brooke made an appointment to meet with Michael. Their conversation was recorded as follows:

BROOKE: Michael, I think I have pinpointed your problem. I think your main difficulty is poor pricing—you're undercharging your major customer. The firm is getting high-precision machined parts for much less than the cost to you. And I bet that you have been losing some of your smaller customers. You may want to rethink your strategic position. You are a small player in the industrial machine industry. This *Fortune 500* customer has 40 percent of the industrial machine market. Over the years, you have carved out a good reputation among small- and medium-size manufacturers. Right?

MICHAEL: Well, you're right. Over the years, our customers have not been giants. But we saw this business with the *Fortune 500* company as an opportunity to play in the big leagues. We thought it might mean the opportunity to expand the size of our operation. And we have expanded—at least we have added employees and some specialized engineering equipment. My engineering and programming costs have skyrocketed—resource increases we needed, though, to meet the specs of this larger customer. Profits have increased slightly, but nothing like I expected. You're also right about losing some of our smaller customers. Many have complained that the price of their jobs has increased. They have all indicated that they like the work we do and that we are conveniently located, but they argue that they simply cannot afford to keep paying the price we require. The small customers we have kept are also complaining and threatening to go elsewhere. I doubt we'll be able to hold onto their business for much longer—unless a change is made. So far, though, the business we have lost has been replaced with more orders from our large customer. I expect we could do even more business for the large customer. But how can the large buyer be getting the great deal you've described? It has the same markup as our regular jobs—full manufacturing cost plus 25 percent.

BROOKE: I have prepared a report illustrating the total overhead costs for a typical quarter. This report details your major activities and their associated costs. It also provides a comparison of a typical job for your small customers and the typical job for your large customer. Part of the problem is that your accounting system does not react to certain external events. It fails to show the effect of the large customer's activities on your activities and those that relate to your other customers. Given that you assign overhead costs using machine hours, I think you'll find it quite revealing.

MICHAEL: I'll have my controller examine the report for me. You know, if you are right about underpricing the large customer, I have a big problem. I'm not sure that I can increase the price of the parts without losing this big guy's business. After all, it can go to a dozen machine shops like mine and get the work done. A price increase may not work. Then I'd be faced with the loss of 40 percent of my jobs. I suppose, though, that I might be able to regain most of the business with the small customers. In fact, I am positive that we could get most of that business back. I wonder if that's what I ought to do.

Report Regional CPA Firm

I. Major Activities and Their Costs

Activity	Total Activity Costs	Cost Behavior*
Setups	$209,000	Variable
Engineering	151,200	Step-fixed, step = 105 hours
NC programming	130,400	Variable
Machining	100,000	Variable
Rework	101,400	Variable
Inspecting	23,000	Step-fixed, step = 230 hours
Sales support	80,000	Step-fixed, step = 23 orders
Total	$795,000	

*Behavior is defined with respect to individual cost drivers. The costs given are total costs for the quarter's activities. Thus, for step-fixed costs, the reported activity cost is for all steps being used by the activity; the cost per step is the total cost divided by the number of steps being used.

II. Job Profiles

Resources Used	Small Customer Job	Fortune 500 Job
Setup hours	3	10
Engineering hours	2	6
Programming hours	1	8
Defective units	20	10
Inspection hours	2	2
Machine hours	2,000	200
Prime costs	$14,000	$1,600
Other data:		
Job size	1,000 parts	100 parts
Quarterly jobs (orders)	15	100
Overhead rate	$14.30 per machine hour	$14.30 per machine hour

Note: All activities are being fully utilized each quarter. (There is no unused activity capacity.)

Required:

1. Without any calculation, explain why the machining company is losing money. Discuss the strategic insights provided by knowledge of activities, their costs, and customer linkages. Comment on the observation made by Brooke that the current accounting system fails to reflect external events. What changes would be needed to correct this deficiency (if true)?

2. Compute the unit price currently being charged each customer type (using machine hours to assign overhead costs).

3. Compute the unit price that would be charged each customer assuming that overhead is assigned using an ABC approach. Was the CPA right? Is the large customer paying less than the cost of producing the unit? How is this conclusion affected if the sales support activity is traced to jobs? (Use orders—jobs—as the cost driver.)

4. Compute the quarterly profit that is currently being earned and the amount that would be earned if Pawnee Works sold only to small customers (a small customer strategy). For the second income statement, use ABC for cost assignments. For the second income statement, the large customer is replaced with 10 smaller customers with the same characteristics as the 15 currently buying parts from Pawnee. Assume that any opportunities to reduce resource spending and usage will be reflected in the profit associated with a small customer strategy. Also,

only the cost of activity usage is assigned to jobs. Any cost of unused activity is reported as a separate item on the income statement. Report sales support as a period expense.

5. What change in strategy would you recommend? In making this recommendation, consider the firm's value-chain framework.

11-19   LIFE-CYCLE COST MANAGEMENT AND TARGET COSTING

LO3   Nico Parts, Inc., produces electronic products with short life cycles (of less than two years). Development has to be rapid, and the profitability of the products is tied strongly to the ability to find designs that will keep production and logistics costs low. Recently, management has also decided that post-purchase costs are important in design decisions. Last month, a proposal for a new product was presented to management. The total market was projected at 200,000 units (for the 2-year period). The proposed selling price was $130 per unit. At this price, market share was expected to be 25 percent. The manufacturing and logistics costs were estimated to be $120 per unit.

Upon reviewing the projected figures, Brian Metcalf, president of Nico, called in his chief design engineer, Mark Williams, and his marketing manager, Cathy McCourt. The following conversation was recorded.

BRIAN: Mark, as you know, we agreed that a profit of $15 per unit is needed for this new product. Also, as I look at the projected market share, 25 percent isn't acceptable. Total profits need to be increased. Cathy, what suggestions do you have?

CATHY: Simple. Decrease the selling price to $125 and we expand our market share to 35 percent. To increase total profits, however, we need some cost reductions as well.

BRIAN: You're right. However, keep in mind that I do not want to earn a profit that is less than $15 per unit.

MARK: Does that $15 per unit factor in preproduction costs? You know we have already spent $100,000 on developing this product. To lower costs will require more expenditure on development.

BRIAN: Good point. No, the projected cost of $120 does not include the $100,000 we have already spent. I do want a design that will provide a $15-per-unit profit, including consideration of preproduction costs.

CATHY: I might mention that post-purchase costs are important as well. The current design will impose about $10 per unit for using, maintaining, and disposing our product. That's about the same as our competitors. If we can reduce that cost to about $5 per unit by designing a better product, we could probably capture about 50 percent of the market. I have just completed a marketing survey at Mark's request and have found out that the current design has two features not valued by potential customers. These two features have a projected cost of $6 per unit. However, the price consumers are willing to pay for the product is the same with or without the features.

Required:

1. Calculate the target cost associated with the initial 25 percent market share. Does the initial design meet this target? Now calculate the *total* life-cycle profit that the current (initial) design offers (including preproduction costs).
2. Assume that the two features that are apparently not valued by consumers will be eliminated. Also assume that the selling price is lowered to $125.
   a. Calculate the target cost for the $125 price and 35 percent market share.
   b. How much more cost reduction is needed?
   c. What are the total life-cycle profits now projected for the new product?

      d.   Describe the three general approaches that Nico can take to reduce the projected cost to this new target. Of the three approaches, which is likely to produce the most reduction?

3.   Suppose that the engineering department has two new designs: Design A and Design B. Both designs eliminate the two nonvalued features. Both designs also reduce production and logistics costs by an *additional* $8 per unit. Design A, however, leaves post-purchase costs at $10 per unit, while Design B reduces post-purchase costs to $4 per unit. Developing and testing Design A costs an additional $150,000, while Design B costs an additional $300,000. Calculate the total life-cycle profits under each design. Which would you choose? Explain. What if the design you chose cost an additional $500,000 instead of $150,000 or $300,000? Would this have changed your decision?

4.   Refer to Requirement 3. For every extra dollar spent on preproduction activities, how much benefit was generated? What does this say about the importance of knowing the linkages between preproduction activities and later activities?

11-20   LIFE-CYCLE COST MANAGEMENT

LO3   Jolene Askew, manager of Feagan Company, has committed her company to a strategically sound cost reduction program. Emphasizing life-cycle cost management is a major part of this effort. Jolene is convinced that production costs can be reduced by paying more attention to the relationships between design and manufacturing. Design engineers need to know what causes manufacturing costs. She instructed her controller to develop a manufacturing cost formula for a newly proposed product. Marketing had already projected sales of 25,000 units for the new product. (The life cycle was estimated to be 18 months. The company expected to have 50 percent of the market and priced their product to achieve this goal.) The projected selling price was $20 per unit. The following cost formula was developed:

$$Y = \$200,000 + \$10X_1$$

where

X_1 = Machine hours (The product is expected to use one machine hour for every unit produced.)

    Upon seeing the cost formula, Jolene quickly calculated the projected gross profit to be $50,000. This produced a gross profit of $2 per unit, well below the targeted gross profit of $4 per unit. Jolene then sent a memo to the engineering department, instructing them to search for a new design that would lower the costs of production by at least $50,000 so that the target profit could be met.

    Within two days, the engineering department proposed a new design that would reduce unit-variable cost from $10 per machine hour to $8 per machine hour (Design Z). The chief engineer, upon reviewing the design, questioned the validity of the controller's cost formula. He suggested a more careful assessment of the proposed design's effect on activities other than machining. Based on this suggestion, the following revised cost formula was developed. This cost formula reflected the cost relationships of the most recent design (Design Z).

$$Y = \$140,000 + \$8X_1 + \$5,000X_2 + \$2,000X_3$$

where

X_1 = Units sold
X_2 = Number of batches
X_3 = Number of engineering change orders

Based on scheduling and inventory considerations, the product would be produced in batches of 1,000; thus, 25 batches would be needed over the product's life cycle.

Furthermore, based on past experience, the product would likely generate about 20 engineering change orders.

This new insight into the linkage of the product with its underlying activities led to a different design (Design W). This second design also lowered the unit-level cost by $2 per unit but decreased the number of design support requirements from 20 orders to 10 orders. Attention was also given to the setup activity, and the design engineer assigned to the product created a design that reduced setup time and lowered variable setup costs from $5,000 to $3,000 per setup. Furthermore, Design W also creates excess activity capacity for the setup activity, and resource spending for setup activity capacity can be decreased by $40,000, reducing the fixed cost component in the equation by this amount.

Design W was recommended and accepted. As prototypes of the design were tested, an additional benefit emerged. Based on test results, the post-purchase costs dropped from an estimated $0.70 per unit sold to $0.40 per unit sold. Using this information, the marketing department revised the projected market share upward from 50 percent to 60 percent (with no price decrease).

Required:

1. Calculate the expected gross profit per unit for Design Z using the controller's original cost formula. According to this outcome, does Design Z reach the targeted unit profit? Repeat, using the engineer's revised cost formula. Explain why Design Z failed to meet the targeted profit. What does this say about the use of functional-based costing for life-cycle cost management?
2. Calculate the expected profit per unit using Design W. Comment on the value of activity information for life-cycle cost management.
3. The benefit of the post-purchase cost reduction of Design W was discovered in testing. What direct benefit did it create for Feagan Company (in dollars)? Reducing post-purchase costs was not a specific design objective. Should it have been? Are there any other design objectives that should have been considered?

11-21   JIT, TRACEABILITY OF COSTS, PRODUCT COSTING ACCURACY, JIT EFFECTS ON COST ACCOUNTING SYSTEMS

LO4, LO5   Homer Manufacturing produces different models of 22-calibre rifles. The manufacturing costs assigned to its economy model rifle before and after installing JIT are given in the following table. Cell workers do all maintenance and are also responsible for moving materials, cell janitorial work, and inspecting products. Janitorial work outside the cells is still handled by the janitorial department.

In both the pre- and post-JIT setting, 10,000 units of the economy model are manufactured. In the JIT setting, manufacturing cells are used to produce each product. The management of Homer Manufacturing reported a significant decrease in manufacturing costs for all of its rifles after JIT was installed. It also reported less inventory-related costs and a significant decrease in lead times. Accounting costs also decreased because Homer switched from a job-order costing system to a process-costing system.

	Before	*After*
Direct materials	$ 60,000	$ 55,000
Direct labor	40,000	50,000
Maintenance	50,000	30,000
Inspection	30,000	10,000
Rework	60,000	9,000
Power	10,000	6,000

(continued)

	Before	After
Depreciation	12,500	10,000
Materials handling	8,000	2,000
Engineering	80,000	50,000*
Setups	15,000	0
Janitorial	40,000	20,000
Building and grounds	11,800	12,400
Supplies	4,000	3,000
Supervision (plant)	10,000	8,000
Cell supervision	—	35,000
Cost accounting	40,000	25,000
Departmental supervision	18,000	—
Total	$489,300	$325,400

*Salary of engineer assigned to the cell.

Required:

1. Compute the unit cost of the product before and after JIT.
2. Explain why the JIT unit cost is more accurate. Also explain what JIT features may have produced a decrease in production costs. Use as many specific cost items as possible to illustrate your explanation.
3. Explain why Homer Manufacturing switched from a job-order costing system to a process-costing system after JIT was implemented.
4. Classify the costs in the JIT environment according to how they are assigned to the cell: direct tracing, driver tracing, or allocation. Which cost assignment method is most common? What does this imply regarding product costing accuracy?

11-22   JIT AND PRODUCT COSTING

LO4, LO5

Spreadsheet

Mott Company recently implemented a JIT manufacturing system. After one year of operation, Heidi Burrows, president of the company, wanted to compare product cost under the JIT system with product cost under the old system. Mott's two products are weed eaters and lawn edgers. The unit prime costs under the old system are as follows:

	Eaters	Edgers
Direct materials	$12	$45
Direct labor	4	30

Under the old manufacturing system, the company operated three service centers and two production departments. Overhead was applied using departmental overhead rates. The direct overhead costs associated with each department for the year preceding the installation of JIT are as follows:

Maintenance	$110,000
Materials handling	90,000
Building and grounds	150,000
Machining	280,000
Assembly	175,000
Total	$805,000

Under the old system, the overhead costs of the service departments were allocated directly to the producing departments and then to the products passing through them. (Both products passed through each producing department.) The overhead rate for the machining department was based on machine hours, and the overhead rate for assembly was based on direct labor hours. During the last year of operations for the old system, the machining department used 80,000 machine hours, and the assembly department used 20,000 direct labor hours. Each weed eater required one machine hour in machining and 0.25 direct labor hour in assembly. Each lawn edger required two machine hours in machining and 0.5 hour in assembly. Bases for allocation of the service costs are as follows:

	Machine Hours	Number of Material Moves	Square Feet of Space
Machining	80,000	90,000	80,000
Assembly	20,000	60,000	40,000
Total	100,000	150,000	120,000

Upon implementing JIT, a manufacturing cell for each product was created to replace the departmental structure. Each cell occupied 40,000 square feet. Maintenance and materials handling were both decentralized to the cell level. Essentially, cell workers were trained to operate the machines in each cell, assemble the components, maintain the machines, and move the partially completed units from one point to the next within the cell. During the first year of the JIT system, the company produced and sold 20,000 weed eaters and 30,000 lawn edgers. This output was identical to that for the last year of operations under the old system. The following costs have been assigned to the manufacturing cells:

	Eater Cell	Edger Cell
Direct materials	$185,000	$1,140,000
Direct labor	66,000	660,000
Direct overhead	99,000	350,500
Allocated overhead*	75,000	75,000
Total	$425,000	$2,225,500

*Building and grounds are allocated on the basis of square footage.

Required:

1. Compute the unit cost for each product under the old manufacturing system.
2. Compute the unit cost for each product under the JIT system.
3. Which of the unit costs is more accurate? Explain. Include in your explanation a discussion of how the computational approaches differ.
4. Calculate the decrease in overhead costs under JIT, and provide some possible reasons that explain the decrease.

11-23   BACKFLUSH COSTING, CONVERSION RATE

LO4, LO5   Morgan Company has implemented a JIT flexible manufacturing system. Michael Anderson, controller of the company, has decided to reduce the accounting requirements given the expectation of lower inventories. For one thing, he has decided to treat direct labor cost as a part of overhead and to discontinue the detailed direct labor accounting of the past. The company has created two manufacturing cells, each capable of producing a family of products: the Small engine cell and the battery cell. The output of both cells is sold to a sister division and to customers who use the batteries and engines for repair activity. Product-level overhead costs outside the cells are assigned to each cell using appropriate drivers. Facility-level costs are allocated to each cell on the basis of square footage. The budgeted direct labor and overhead costs are as follows:

	Engine Cell	*Battery Cell*
Direct labor costs	$ 180,000	$ 90,000
Direct overhead	720,000	360,000
Product sustaining	270,000	108,000
Facility level	180,000	90,000
Total conversion cost	$1,350,000	$648,000

The predetermined conversion cost rate is based on available production hours in each cell. The engine cell has 45,000 hours available for production, and the battery cell has 27,000 hours. Conversion costs are applied to the units produced by multiplying the conversion rate by the actual time required to produce the units. The engine cell produced 81,000 units, taking 0.5 hour to produce one unit of product (on average). The battery cell produced 90,000 units, taking 0.25 hour to produce one unit of product (on average).

Other actual results for the year are as follows:

Direct materials purchased and issued	$1,530,000
Direct labor costs	270,000
Overhead	1,890,000

All units produced were sold. Any conversion cost variance is closed to Cost of Goods Sold.

Required:

1. Calculate the predetermined conversion cost rates for each cell.
2. Prepare journal entries using backflush accounting. Assume two trigger points, with completion of goods as the second trigger point.
3. Repeat Requirement 2, assuming that the second trigger point is the sale of the goods.
4. Explain why there is no need to have a work-in-process inventory account.
5. Two variants of backflush costing were presented in which each used two trigger points, with the second trigger point differing. Suppose that the only trigger point for recognizing manufacturing costs occurs when the goods are sold. How would the entries be listed here? When would this backflush variant be considered appropriate?

11-24 JIT, CREATION OF MANUFACTURING CELLS, BEHAVIORAL CONSIDERATIONS, IMPACT ON COSTING PRACTICES

LO4, LO5   Reddy Heaters, Inc., produces insert heaters that can be used for various applications, ranging from coffeepots to submarines. Because of the wide variety of insert heaters produced, Reddy uses a job-order costing system. Product lines are differentiated by the size of the heater. In the early stages of the company's history, sales were strong and profits steadily increased. In recent years, however, profits have been declining, and the company has been losing market share. Alarmed by the deteriorating financial position of the company, President Doug Young requested a special study to identify the problems. Sheri Butler, the head of the internal audit department, was put in charge of the study. After two months of investigation, Sheri was ready to report her findings.

SHERI: Doug, I think we have some real concerns that need to be addressed. Production is down, employee morale is low, and the number of defective units that we have to scrap is way up. In fact, over the past several years, our scrap rate has increased from 9 percent to 15 percent of total production. And scrap is expensive. We don't detect defective units until the end of the process. By that time, we lose everything. The nature of the product simply doesn't permit rework.

DOUG: I have a feeling that the increased scrap rate is related to the morale problem you've encountered. Do you have any feel for why morale is low?

SHERI: I get the feeling that boredom is a factor. Many employees don't feel challenged by their work. Also, with the decline in performance, they are receiving more pressure from their supervisors, which simply aggravates the problem.

DOUG: What other problems have you detected?

SHERI: Well, much of our market share has been lost to foreign competitors. The time it takes us to process an order, from time of receipt to delivery, has increased from 20 to 30 days. Some of the customers we have lost have switched to Japanese suppliers, from whom they receive heaters in less than 15 days. Added to this delay in our delivery is an increase in the number of complaints about poorly performing heaters. Our quality has definitely taken a nosedive over the past several years.

DOUG: It's amazing that it has taken us this long to spot these problems. It's incredible to me that the Japanese can deliver a part faster than we can, even in our more efficient days. I wonder what their secret is.

SHERI: I investigated that very issue. It appears that they can produce and deliver their heaters rapidly because they use a JIT purchasing and manufacturing system.

DOUG: Can we use this system to increase our competitive ability?

SHERI: I think so, but we'll need to hire a consultant to tell us how to do it. Also, it might be a good idea to try it out on only one of our major product lines. I suggest the small heater line. It is having the most problems and has been showing a loss for the past two years. If JIT can restore this line to a competitive mode, then it'll work for the other lines as well.

Within a week, Reddy Heaters hired the services of a large CPA firm. The firm sent Kim Burnham, one of its managers, to do the initial background work. After spending some time at the plant, Kim wrote up the following description of the small heater production process:

> *The various departments are scattered throughout the factory. Labor is specialized and trained to operate the machines in the respective departments. Additionally, the company has a centralized stores area that provides the raw materials for production, a centralized maintenance department that has responsibility for maintaining all production equipment, and a group of laborers responsible for moving the partially completed units from department to department.*
>
> *Under the current method of production, small heaters pass through several departments, where each department has a collection of similar machines. The first department cuts a metal pipe into one of three lengths: three, four, or five inches long. The cut pipe is then taken to the laser department, where the part number is printed on the pipe. In a second department, ceramic cylinders—cut to smaller lengths than the pipe—are wrapped with a fine wire (using a wrapping machine). The pipe and the wrapped ceramic cylinders are then taken to the welding department, where the wrapped ceramic cylinders are placed inside the pipe, centered, and filled with a substance that prevents electricity from reaching the metal pipe. Finally, the ends of the pipe are welded shut with two wire leads protruding from one end. This completed heater is then transferred to the testing department, which uses special equipment to see if the heater functions properly.*
>
> *The small heaters are produced in batches of 300. It takes 50 hours to cut 300 metal pipes and prepare 300 ceramic cylinders (1/6 hr. per unit, both processes occurring at the same time). After 50 hours of production time, the 300 metal pipes are transported to the laser department (20 minutes transport time), and the 300 ceramic cylinders are transported to the welding department (20 minutes trans-*

port time). In the laser department, it takes 50 hours to imprint the part number (1/6 hr. per pipe). The 300 metal pipes are then transported to the welding department. In the welding department, the ceramic and metal pipes are joined and welded. The welding process takes 50 hours (1/6 hr. per pipe). Finally, the 300 units are transported (20 minutes) to the testing department. Each unit requires 1/6 hour for testing, or a total of 50 hours for the 300 units. From start to finish, the total production time for the 300 units is as follows:

Cutting and ceramic	50 hrs.
Laser	50
Welding	50
Testing	50
Moving	1
Total time	201 hrs.

Notice that laser must wait 50 hours before it can begin imprinting. Similarly, welding must wait 100 hours before it can begin working on the batch, and finally, testing must wait 150 hours before it can begin working on the batch.

Based on the information gathered, Kim estimated that the production time for 300 units could be cut from 201 hours to about 50 hours by creating a small heater manufacturing cell.

Required:

1. One of the first actions taken by Reddy Heaters was to organize a manufacturing cell for the small heater line. Describe how you would organize the manufacturing cell. How does it differ from the traditional arrangement? Will any training costs be associated with the transition to JIT? Explain.
2. Explain, with computational support, how the production time for 300 units can be reduced to about 50 hours. If this is a true reduction in production time, what implications does it have for Reddy's competitive position?
3. Describe the organizational and operational activities that must be managed to bring about the reduction in production time. What are the cost drivers associated with these activities? For operational drivers, indicate the expected effect on activity costs.
4. Initially, the employees resented the change to JIT. After a small period of time, however, morale improved significantly. Explain why the change to JIT increased employee morale.
5. Within a few months, Reddy was able to offer a lower price for its small heaters. Additionally, the number of complaints about the performance of the small heaters declined sharply. By the end of the second year, the product line was reporting profits greater than had ever been achieved. Discuss the JIT features that may have made the lower price and higher profits possible.
6. Within a year of the JIT installation, Reddy's controller remarked, "We have a much better idea than ever before of what it is costing us to produce these small insert heaters." Offer some justification for the controller's statement.
7. Discuss the impact that JIT has on other management accounting practices.

11-25 COLLABORATIVE LEARNING EXERCISE

Don Homer, cost accounting manager for Tibbings, Inc., was having dinner with Spencer Gee, a friend since college days. The two had attended the same university and belonged to the same fraternity. Upon graduation, they had taken positions with two competitors whose headquarters were located in the same city. Two years ago, the top management of Tibbings had implemented a life-cycle cost management program. Since then, Don had worked closely with design engineering, providing information about activities and their costs. He, in turn, became very well informed about the new product development projects. Spencer was also an accountant and had recently been promoted to assistant controller. Eventually, the conversation turned to work topics.

SPENCER: How are things going at work?

DON: Very well. Our new life-cycle cost management approach has made a real difference in our profitability. The latest two products have each earned significantly more than in the past.

SPENCER: Interesting. How many new products are coming out this year?

DON: We have three new ones coming out—two of which should provide some significant challenges for your company.

SPENCER: The last two certainly did. Our competing products earned 30 percent less profit—all because of yours. I don't know how you did it, but the customers seemed to like yours better.

DON: We gathered information on the cost of maintaining and using the products and then made a real effort to design the new products so that they reduced these costs. We also looked at design so that production costs were lowered. This way, we could sell the products for less and still make the same per-unit profit. It worked. Our total profits went up by about $40,000 on each product.

SPENCER: What about these three new ones? Are they coming out soon? Are you planning on selling them for less than you usually do as well?

DON: As I understand it, they should all be on the market within two weeks. And yes, we will sell for less than normal. They cost less. Linking design to downstream activities has been a real benefit.

SPENCER: Well, maybe we need to do something similar. Our competing products will probably come out later than yours as well. That's not good for us. Oh well. Let's talk about something more pleasant. We get enough of work during the week.

Required:

Read the ethical problem, and decide on your evaluation of the ethical conduct of Don and Spencer. (This can be done as a homework assignment or as an in-class assignment.) Form groups of three of four students. Each group member should write on a slip of paper the word TALK. This piece of paper is the Talking Chip. The Talking Chip is the ticket that allows a group member to speak. Group discussion begins with a volunteer. After making his/her contribution, this person places the Talking Chip down in full view of the other members. Another person of the group then contributes and subsequently places the Talking Chip down in full view. This continues until all members have contributed. Once all members have contributed, the talking chips can be retrieved, and a second round of discussion can begin.

11-26   CYBER RESEARCH CASE

LO2   Supply chain management can be a major source of cost savings for manufacturing and service firms. A firm can reduce its costs by understanding the linkages it has with its suppliers and customers. A major factor in assessing and understanding these linkages is the measurement of costs across the supply chain. Activity-based costing is now assuming a major role in this measurement requirement. The role of ABC in supply chain management needs to be explored carefully.

Required:

Using Internet resources, answer the following questions. (In addition to a general search, you might try http://www.bettermanagement.com, and check out its library resources.)

1. What is supply chain management?
2. Why has supply chain management become such an important topic?
3. Are businesses actually measuring and using supply chain costs?
4. Why is ABC considered important in supply chain management?

12

Activity-Based Management

AFTER STUDYING THIS CHAPTER, YOU SHOULD BE ABLE TO:

1. Describe how activity-based management and activity-based costing differ.
2. Define process value analysis.
3. Describe activity-based financial performance measurement.

4. Discuss the implementation issues associated with an activity-based management system.
5. Explain how activity-based management is a form of responsibility accounting, and tell how it differs from financial-based responsibility accounting.

Many firms operate in rapidly changing environments. Typically, these firms face stiff national and international competition. This stringent competitive environment demands that firms offer customized products and services to diverse customer segments. This, in turn, means that firms must find cost efficient ways of producing high-variety, low-volume products. To find ways to improve performance, firms operating in this kind of environment not only must know what it currently *costs* to do things, but they must also evaluate *why* and *how* they do things. Improving performance translates into constantly searching for ways to eliminate waste—a process known as **continuous improvement**. Activity-based costing and activity-based management are important tools in this ongoing improvement effort.

© PHOTODISC RED/GETTY IMAGES

OBJECTIVE *1*

Describe how
activity-based
management and
activity-based
costing differ.

The Relationship of Activity-Based Costing and Activity-Based Management

Activity accounting is an essential factor for operationalizing continuous improvement. Processes are the source of many of the improvement opportunities that exist within an organization. Processes are made up of activities that are linked to perform a specific objective. Improving processes means improving the way activities are performed. Thus, management of activities, not costs, is the key to successful control for firms operating in continuous improvement environments. The realization that activities are crucial to both improved product costing and effective control has led to a new view of business processes called activity-based management.

Activity-based management (ABM) is a systemwide, integrated approach that focuses management's attention on activities with the objectives of improving customer value and the profit achieved by providing this value. ABC is the major source of information for activity-based management. Thus, the activity-based management model has two dimensions: a cost dimension and a process dimension. This two-dimensional model is presented in Exhibit 12-1. The cost dimension provides cost information about resources, activities, and cost objects of interests such as products, customers, suppliers, and distribution channels. The objective of the cost dimension is improving the accuracy of cost assignments. As the model suggests, the cost of resources is traced to activities, and then the cost of activities is assigned to cost objects. This activity-based costing dimension is useful for product costing, strategic cost management, and tactical analysis. The second dimension, the process dimension, provides information about what activities are performed, why they are performed, and how well they are performed. This dimension's

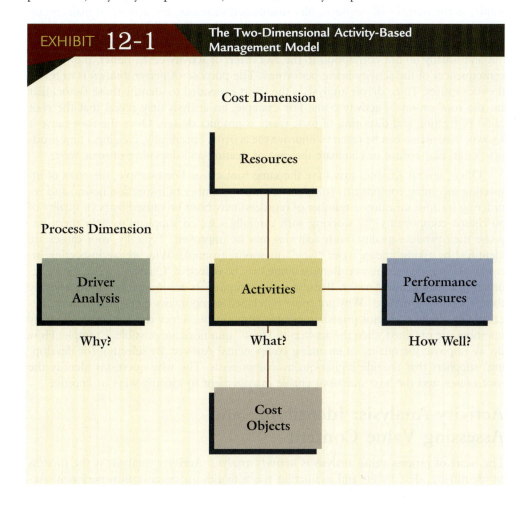

EXHIBIT 12-1 **The Two-Dimensional Activity-Based Management Model**

Cost Dimension

Resources

Process Dimension

Driver Analysis	Activities	Performance Measures
Why?	What?	How Well?

Cost Objects

objective is cost reduction. It is this dimension that provides the ability to engage in and measure continuous improvement. To understand how the process view connects with continuous improvement, a more explicit understanding of process value analysis is needed.

Process Value Analysis

OBJECTIVE 2

Define process value analysis.

Process value analysis (PVA) is fundamental to activity-based responsibility accounting, focuses on accountability for activities rather than costs, and emphasizes the maximization of systemwide performance instead of individual performance. Process value analysis moves activity management from a conceptual basis to an operational basis. As the model in Exhibit 12-1 illustrates, process value analysis is concerned with (1) *driver analysis*, (2) *activity analysis*, and (3) *performance measurement*.

Driver Analysis: Defining Root Causes

Managing activities requires an understanding of what factors cause activities to be performed and what causes activity costs to change. Activities consume inputs (resources) and produce outputs. For example, if the activity is maintaining the payroll master file, the resources used would be such things as a payroll clerk, a computer, a printer, computer paper, and disks. The output would be an updated employee file. An **activity output measure** is the number of times the activity is performed. It is the quantifiable measure of the output. For example, the number of employee files maintained is a possible output measure for maintaining the payroll master file.

The output measure calculates the demands placed on an activity and is an *activity driver*. As the demands for an activity change, the cost of the activity can change. For example, as the number of employee files maintained increases, the activity of maintaining the master payroll may need to consume more inputs (labor, disks, paper, and so on). However, output measures (activity drivers), such as the number of files maintained, may not and usually do not correspond to the *root causes* of activity costs; rather, they are the consequences of the activity being performed. The purpose of *driver analysis* is to reveal the root causes. Thus, **driver analysis** is the effort expended to identify those factors that are the root causes of activity costs. For example, an analysis may reveal that the root cause of treating and disposing of toxic waste is product design. Once the root cause is known, then action can be taken to improve the activity. Specifically, creating a new product design may reduce or eliminate the cost of treating and disposing of toxic waste.

Often, several activities may have the same root cause. For example, the costs of inspecting incoming components (output measure = number of inspection hours) and reordering (output measure = number of reorders) may both be caused by poor quality of purchased components. By working with carefully selected suppliers to help them improve their product quality, both activities may be improved. Typically, root causes are identified by asking one or more "why" questions. Example: Why are we inspecting incoming components? Answer: Because some may be defective. Question: Why are we reordering components? Answer: Because some components are judged to be defective by the inspection. Question: Why are some purchased components defective? Answer: Because our suppliers are not providing reliable components. Once the answers to the why questions are obtained, then the answers to "how" questions are possible. Example: How do we improve the quality of incoming components? Answer: By selecting (or developing) suppliers that provide higher-quality components. The why questions identify the root causes, and the how questions enable management to identify ways to improve.

Activity Analysis: Identifying and Assessing Value Content

The heart of process value analysis is *activity analysis*. **Activity analysis** is the process of identifying, describing, and evaluating the activities an organization performs. Activity analysis should produce four outcomes: (1) what activities are performed, (2) how many people perform the activities, (3) the time and resources required to perform the activities, and (4) an assessment of the value of the activities to the organization, including a recommendation to select and keep only those that add value. Steps 1–3 have been described in Chapter 4. Those steps were critical for assigning costs. Step 4, determining the value-added content of activities, is concerned with cost reduction rather than cost assignment. Thus, this may be considered the most important part of activity analysis. Activities can be classified as *value-added* or *non-value-added*.

Value-Added Activities

Value-added activities are those activities necessary to remain in business. Value-added activities contribute to customer value and/or help meet an organization's needs. Activities that comply with legal mandates are value-added because they exist to meet organizational needs. Moreover, they add to customer value by allowing the business to continue operating so that the products and services desired by the customer can be obtained. Even though mandated activities are necessary, customers should insist that they be performed as efficiently as possible to reduce the cost impact on goods and services. Examples of mandated activities include those needed to comply with the reporting requirements of the SEC and the filing requirements of the IRS. The remaining activities in the firm are *discretionary*. Classifying discretionary activities as value-added is more of an art than a science and depends heavily on subjective judgment. However, it is possible to identify three conditions, which if simultaneously met, are sufficient to classify a discretionary activity as value-added. These conditions are as follows: (1) the activity produces a change of state, (2) the change of state was not achievable by preceding activities, and (3) the activity enables other activities to be performed.

For example, consider the production of metal components used in medical equipment. The first activity, gating, creates a wax mold replica of the final product. The next activity, shelling, creates a ceramic shell around the wax mold. After removing the wax, molten metal is poured into the resulting cavity. The shell is then broken to reveal the desired metal component. The gating activity is value-added because (1) it causes a change of state—unformed wax is transformed into a wax mold, (2) no prior activity was supposed to create this change of state, and (3) it enables the shelling activity to be performed. Similar comments hold for the shelling and pouring activities. The value-added properties are easy to see for operational activities like gating and shelling, but what about a more general activity like supervising production workers? A managerial activity is specifically designed to manage other value-added activities— to ensure that they are performed in an efficient and timely manner. Supervision certainly satisfies the enabling condition. Is there a change in state? There are two ways of answering in the affirmative. First, supervising can be viewed as an enabling resource that is consumed by the operational activities that do produce a change of state. Thus, supervising is a secondary activity that serves as an input needed to help bring about the change of state expected for value-added primary activities. Second, it could be argued that the supervision brings order by changing the state from uncoordinated activities to coordinated activities.

Once value-added activities are identified, we can define value-added costs. Value-added costs are the costs to perform value-added activities with perfect efficiency. Implicit in this definition is the notion that value-added activities may contain nonessential actions that create unnecessary cost.

Non-Value-Added Activities

Non-value-added activities are unnecessary and are not valued by internal or external customers. Non-value-added activities often are those that fail to produce a change in state or those that replicate work because it wasn't done correctly the first time. Inspecting wax molds, for example, is a non-value-added activity. Inspection is a state-detection activity, not a state-changing activity. (It tells us the state of the mold—whether or not it is of the right shape.) As a general rule, state-detection activities are not value-added. Now, consider the activity of recasting molds that fail inspection. This recasting is designed to bring the mold from a nonconforming state to a conforming state. Thus, a change of state occurs. Yet, the activity is non-value-added because it *repeats* work; it is doing something that should have been done by preceding activities (the first time the wax mold was cast). Non-value-added costs are costs that are caused either by non-value-added activities or the inefficient performance of value-added activities. Because of increased competition, many firms are attempting to eliminate non-value-added activities and nonessential portions of value-added activities because they add unnecessary cost and impede performance. Therefore, activity analysis attempts to identify and eventually eliminate all unnecessary activities and, simultaneously, increase the efficiency of necessary activities.

COST MANAGEMENT   Technology in Action

US Airways implemented an activity-based cost management (ABCM) system to manage its in-house engine maintenance business unit. First, ABCM helped determine the cost of engine maintenance with increased accuracy. Second, ABCM provided operational and financial information that allowed work teams to identify opportunities for improvement. Thus, ABCM provided accurate cost information and simultaneously revealed opportunities for improvement. ABCM identified 410 activities—activities such as tear down, welding, waiting for tooling, and rework.

Of the 410 activities, 47 were identified as non-value-added. The non-value-added activities were rank-ordered on the basis of activity cost, providing information about where the most significant process improvement opportunities were located. Root cause analysis was undertaken by the various work teams to determine the causes for the efforts being expended on the non-value-added activities. Once the root causes were identified, the teams took action to reduce or eliminate the non-value-added activities. The net effect was to produce $4.3 million in process savings per year.

Source: Taken from Joe Donnelly and Dave Buchanan, "Implementation Lands $4.3 Million in Process Improvement Savings," an online article at http://www.bettermanagement.com as of September 7, 2004.

Assessing the value content of activities enables managers to eliminate waste. As waste is eliminated, costs are reduced. Cost reduction *follows* the elimination of waste. Note the value of managing the *causes* of the costs rather than the costs themselves. Increasing the efficiency of a non-value-added activity is not a good long-term strategy. For example, training inspectors in sampling procedures may increase the efficiency of the activity of inspecting incoming components, but it is better to implement a supplier evaluation program that leads to suppliers that provide defect-free components, thus eliminating the need for inspection.

Examples of Non-Value-Added Activities

Reordering parts, expediting production, and rework due to defective parts are examples of non-value-added activities. Other examples include warranty work, handling customer complaints, and reporting defects. Non-value-added activities can exist anywhere in the organization. In the manufacturing operation, five major activities are often cited as wasteful and unnecessary:

1. *Scheduling.* An activity that uses time and resources to determine when different products have access to processes (or when and how many setups must be done) and how much will be produced.
2. *Moving.* An activity that uses time and resources to move materials, work in process, and finished goods from one department to another.
3. *Waiting.* An activity in which materials or work in process use time and resources by waiting on the next process.
4. *Inspecting.* An activity in which time and resources are spent ensuring that the product meets specifications.

5. *Storing.* An activity that uses time and resources while a good or material is held in inventory.

None of these activities adds any value for the customer. Scheduling, for example, is not necessary if the company has learned how to produce on demand. Similarly, inspecting would not be necessary if the product is produced correctly the first time. The challenge of activity analysis is to find ways to produce the good without using any of these activities.

Cost Reduction through Activity Management

Competitive conditions dictate that companies must deliver products the customers want, on time, and at the lowest possible cost. This means that an organization must continually strive for cost improvement. Kaizen costing is characterized by constant, incremental improvements to existing processes and products. Activity management is a fundamental part of kaizen costing. Activity management can reduce costs in four ways:[1]

1. Activity elimination
2. Activity selection
3. Activity reduction
4. Activity sharing

Activity elimination focuses on eliminating non-value-added activities. For example, the activity of expediting production seems necessary at times to ensure that customers' needs are met. Yet, this activity is necessary only because of the company's failure to produce efficiently. By improving cycle time, a company may eventually eliminate the need for expediting. Cost reduction then follows.

Activity selection involves choosing among various sets of activities that are caused by competing strategies. Different strategies cause different activities. Different product design strategies, for example, can require significantly different activities. Activities, in turn, cause costs. Each product design strategy has its own set of activities and associated costs. All other things being equal, the lowest cost design strategy should be chosen. In a kaizen cost framework, *redesign* of existing products and processes can lead to a different, lower cost set of activities. Thus, activity selection can have a significant effect on cost reduction.

Activity reduction decreases the time and resources required by an activity. This approach to cost reduction should be aimed primarily at improving the efficiency of necessary activities or act as a short-term strategy for moving non-value-added activities toward the point of elimination. For example, by improving product quality, customer complaints should decrease and, consequently, the demand for handling customer complaints should decrease.

Activity sharing increases the efficiency of necessary activities by using economies of scale. Specifically, the quantity of the cost driver is increased without increasing the total cost of the activity itself. This lowers the per-unit cost of the cost driver and the amount of cost traceable to the products that consume the activity. For example, a new product can be designed to use components already being used by other products. By using existing components, the activities associated with these components already exist, and the company avoids the creation of a whole new set of activities.

Assessing Activity Performance

Activity performance measurement is designed to assess how well an activity was performed and the results achieved. Measures of activity performance are both financial and nonfinancial and center on three major dimensions: (1) efficiency, (2) quality, and (3) time. *Efficiency* is concerned with the relationship of activity outputs to activity inputs. For example, activity efficiency is improved by producing the same activity output with

---

1. Peter B. B. Turney, "How Activity-Based Costing Helps Reduce Cost," *Journal of Cost Management* (Winter 1991): 29–35.

less inputs. Costs trending downward is evidence that activity efficiency is improving. *Quality* is concerned with doing the activity right the first time it is performed. If the activity output is defective, then the activity may need to be repeated, causing unnecessary cost and reduction in efficiency. The *time* required to perform an activity is also critical. Longer times usually mean more resource consumption and less ability to respond to customer demands. Time measures of performance tend to be nonfinancial, whereas efficiency and quality measures are both financial and nonfinancial.

Financial Measures of Activity Efficiency

OBJECTIVE 3

Describe activity-based financial performance measurement.

Assessing activity performance should reveal the current level of efficiency and the potential for increased efficiency. Both financial and nonfinancial measures are used to reveal past performance and signal future potential gains in efficiency. Financial measures of activity performance are emphasized in this chapter, and nonfinancial measures are discussed in Chapter 13. Financial measures of performance should provide specific information about the dollar effects of activity performance changes. Thus, financial measures should indicate both potential and actual savings. Financial measures of activity efficiency include (1) value- and non-value-added activity costs, (2) trends in activity costs, (3) kaizen standard setting, (4) benchmarking, (5) activity flexible budgeting, and (6) activity capacity management.

Reporting Value- and Non-Value-Added Costs

Reducing non-value-added costs is one way to increase activity efficiency. A company's accounting system should distinguish between value-added costs and non-value-added costs because improving activity performance requires eliminating non-value-added activities and optimizing value-added activities. A firm should identify and formally report the value- and non-value-added costs of each activity. Highlighting non-value-added costs reveals the magnitude of the waste the company is currently experiencing, thus providing some information about the potential for improvement. This encourages managers to place more emphasis on controlling non-value-added activities. Progress can then be assessed by preparing trend and cost reduction reports. Tracking these costs over time permits managers to assess the effectiveness of their activity management programs.

Knowing the amount of costs saved is important for strategic purposes. For example, if an activity is eliminated, then the costs saved should be traceable to individual products. These savings can produce price reductions for customers, making the firm more competitive. Changing the pricing strategy, however, requires knowledge of the cost reductions realized by activity analysis. A cost-reporting system, therefore, is an important ingredient in an activity-based responsibility accounting system.

Value-added costs are the only costs that an organization should incur. The *value-added standard* calls for the complete elimination of non-value-added activities; for these activities, the optimal output is zero, with zero cost. The value-added standard also calls for the complete elimination of the inefficiency of activities that are necessary but inefficiently carried out. Hence, value-added activities also have an optimal output level. A value-added standard, therefore, identifies the optimal activity output. Identifying the optimal activity output requires activity output measurement.

Setting value-added standards does not mean that they will be (or should be) achieved immediately. The idea of continuous improvement is to move toward the ideal. Workers (teams) can be rewarded for improvement. Moreover, nonfinancial activity performance measures can be used to supplement and support the goal of eliminating non-value-added costs (these are discussed later in the chapter). Finally, measuring the efficiency of individual workers and supervisors is not the way to eliminate non-value-added activities. Remember, activities cut across departmental boundaries and are part of processes. Focusing on activities and providing incentives to improve processes is a more productive approach. Improving the process should lead to improved results.

By comparing actual activity costs with value-added activity costs, management can assess the level of activity inefficiency and the potential for improvement. To identify and calculate value- and non-value-added costs, output measures for each activity must be defined. Once output measures are defined, then value-added standard quantities (SQ) for each activity can be defined. Value-added costs can be computed by multiplying the value-added standard quantities by the price standard (SP). Non-value-added costs can be calculated as the difference between the actual level of the activity's output (AQ) and the value-added level (SQ), multiplied by the standard price. These formulas are presented in Exhibit 12-2. Some further explanation is needed.

EXHIBIT 12-2   Formulas for Value- and Non-Value-Added Costs

$$\text{Value-added costs} = SQ \times SP$$
$$\text{Non-value-added costs} = (AQ - SQ)SP$$

Where

SQ = The value-added output level for an activity
SP = The standard price per unit of activity output measure
AQ = The actual quantity used of flexible resources or the practical activity capacity acquired for committed resources

---

For flexible resources (resources acquired as needed), AQ is the actual quantity of activity used. For committed resources (resources acquired in advance of usage), AQ represents the actual quantity of activity capacity acquired, as measured by the activity's practical capacity. This definition of AQ allows the computation of non-value-added costs for both variable and fixed activity costs. For fixed activity costs, SP is the budgeted activity costs divided by AQ, where AQ is practical activity capacity.

To illustrate the power of these concepts, consider the following four production activities for a manufacturing firm: purchasing materials, molding, inspecting molds, and grinding imperfect molds. Purchasing and molding are necessary activities; inspection and grinding are unnecessary. The following data pertain to the four activities:

Activity	Activity Driver	SQ	AQ	SP
Purchasing	Purchasing hours	20,000	23,000	$20
Molding	Molding hours	30,000	34,000	12
Inspecting	Inspection hours	0	6,000	15
Grinding	Number of units	0	5,000	6

Notice that the value-added standards (SQ) for inspection and grinding call for their elimination. Ideally, there should be no defective molds; by improving quality, changing production processes, and so on, inspection and grinding can eventually be eliminated. Exhibit 12-3 classifies the costs for the four activities as value-added or non-value-added. For simplicity and to show the relationship to actual costs, the actual price per unit of the activity driver is assumed to be equal to the standard price. In this case, the value-added cost plus the non-value-added cost equals actual cost.

The cost report in Exhibit 12-3 allows managers to see the non-value-added costs; as a consequence, it emphasizes the opportunity for improvement. By redesigning the products and reducing the number of parts required, purchase time can be reduced. By improving the molding process and labor skill, management can reduce the demands for molding time, inspection, and grinding. Thus, reporting value- and non-value-added

EXHIBIT 12-3	Value- and Non-Value-Added Cost Report for the Year Ended December 31, 2006		
Activity	**Value-Added Costs**	**Non-Value-Added Costs**	**Actual Costs**
Purchasing	$400,000	$ 60,000	$460,000
Molding	360,000	48,000	408,000
Inspecting	0	90,000	90,000
Grinding	0	30,000	30,000
Total	$760,000	$228,000	$988,000

costs at a point in time may trigger actions to manage activities more effectively. Once they see the amount of waste, managers may be induced to search for ways to improve activities and bring about cost reductions. Reporting these costs may also help managers improve planning, budgeting, and pricing decisions. For example, a manager might consider it possible to lower a selling price to meet a competitor's price if that manager can see the potential for reducing non-value-added costs to absorb the effect of the price reduction.

Trend Reporting of Non-Value-Added Costs

As managers take actions to improve activities, do the cost reductions follow as expected? One way to answer this question is to compare the costs for each activity over time. The goal is activity improvement as measured by cost reduction. We should see a decline in non-value-added costs from one period to the next—provided the activity improvement initiatives are effective. Assume, for example, that at the beginning of 2007, the production and molding process was redesigned and the employees in molding were trained in a new work technique. The objective of the initiatives was to improve activity performance. How effective were these decisions? Did cost reductions occur as expected? Exhibit 12-4 provides a cost report that compares the *non-value-added* costs of 2007 with those that occurred in 2006. The 2007 costs are assumed but would be computed the same way as shown for 2006. We assume that SQ is the same for both years.

The trend report reveals that more than half of the non-value-added costs have been eliminated. There is still ample room for improvement, but activity improvement so far has been successful. Reporting non-value-added costs, however, not only reveals reduction but also indicates where the reduction occurred. It provides managers with

EXHIBIT 12-4	Trend Report: Non-Value-Added Costs		
	Non-Value-Added Costs		
Activity	**2006**	**2007**	**Change**
Purchasing	$ 60,000	$ 20,000	$ 40,000
Molding	48,000	35,000	13,000
Inspecting	90,000	30,000	60,000
Grinding	30,000	15,000	15,000
Total	$228,000	$100,000	$128,000

information on how much potential for cost reduction remains, assuming that the value-added standards remain the same. Value-added standards, however, like other standards, are not cast in stone. New technology, new designs, and other innovations can change the nature of activities performed. As new ways for improvement surface, value-added standards can change. Managers should not become content but should continually seek higher levels of efficiency.

Drivers and Behavioral Effects

Activity output measures are needed to compute and track non-value-added costs. Reducing a non-value-added activity should produce a reduction in the demand for the activity and, therefore, a reduction in the activity output measures. If a team's performance is affected by its ability to reduce non-value-added costs, then the selection of activity drivers (as output measures) and the way the drivers are used can affect behavior. For example, if the output measure for setup costs is chosen as setup time, an incentive is created for workers to reduce setup time. Since the value-added standard for setup costs calls for their complete elimination, then the incentive to drive setup time to zero is compatible with the company's objectives, and the induced behavior is beneficial.

Suppose, however, that the objective is to reduce the number of unique parts a company processes, thus reducing the demand for activities such as purchasing and incoming inspection. If the costs of these activities are assigned to products based on the number of parts, the incentive created is to reduce the number of parts in a product. Yet, if too many parts are eliminated, the functionality of the product may be reduced to a point where its marketability is adversely affected. Identifying the value-added standard number of parts for each product through the use of functional analysis can discourage this type of behavior.[2] Designers can then be encouraged to reduce the non-value-added costs by designing to reach the value-added standard number of parts. The standard has provided a concrete objective and defined the kind of behavior that the incentive allows.

The Role of Kaizen Standards

Kaizen costing is concerned with reducing the costs of *existing* products and processes. In operational terms, this translates into reducing non-value-added costs. Controlling this cost reduction process is accomplished through the repetitive use of two major subcycles: (1) the kaizen or continuous improvement cycle and (2) the maintenance cycle. The kaizen subcycle is defined by a Plan-Do-Check-Act sequence. If a company is emphasizing the reduction of non-value-added costs, the amount of improvement planned for the coming period (month, quarter, etc.) is set (the *Plan* step). A **kaizen standard** reflects the planned improvement for the upcoming period. The planned improvement is assumed to be attainable, and kaizen standards are a type of currently attainable standard. Actions are taken to implement the planned improvements (the *Do* step). Next, actual results (e.g., costs) are compared with the kaizen standard to provide a measure of the level of improvement attained (the *Check* step). Setting this new level as a minimum standard for future performance locks in the realized improvements and simultaneously initiates the maintenance cycle and a search for additional improvement opportunities (the *Act* step). The maintenance cycle follows a traditional Establish-Do-Check-Act sequence. A standard is set based on prior improvements (locking in these improvements). Next, actions are taken (the *Do* step) and the results checked to ensure that performance conforms to this new level (the *Check* step). If not, then corrective actions are taken to restore performance (the *Act* step). The kaizen cost reduction process is summarized in Exhibit 12-5.

---

2. Functional analysis compares the price customers are willing to pay for a particular product function with the cost of providing that function.

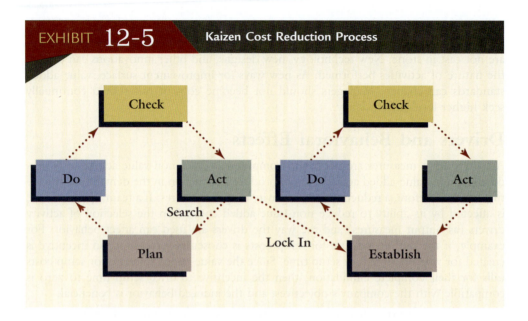

EXHIBIT 12-5   **Kaizen Cost Reduction Process**

For example, assume that an automotive parts division engages in a setup activity for the subassemblies that it produces. The value-added standard for this activity calls for zero setup hours with a cost of $0 per batch of subassemblies. Assume that in the prior year, the company used eight hours to set up each batch at a cost of $18 per hour. The actual setup cost per batch was $144 ($18 × 8 hrs.). This was also the non-value-added cost. For the coming quarter, the company is planning on implementing a new setup method developed by its industrial engineers that is expected to reduce setup time by 50 percent. Thus, the planned cost reduction is $72 per batch. The kaizen standard per batch is now $72: defined as four hours per setup with a standard cost of $18 per hour, which is equal to the actual prior-year cost less the targeted reduction ($144 − $72). Now, suppose that the actual cost achieved after implementing the new production process is $72. The actual improvements expected did materialize, and the new minimum standard is $72 per batch, locking in the improvements. Until further improvements are achieved, setup costs should be no more than $72 per setup. For subsequent periods, additional improvements would be sought and a new kaizen standard defined. The ultimate objective is to reduce setup time and cost to zero through a series of kaizen improvements.

In some cases, companies have formalized the process of revising standards. For example, **Shionogi Pharmaceuticals** first assesses whether the improvements are attributable to kaizen activities or to random fluctuations. If kaizen activities are the source, Shionogi then evaluates the *sustainability* of the kaizen improvements. Improvements are locked in through revision of standards only if the improvements are judged to be sustainable.[3]

Benchmarking

Benchmarking is complimentary to kaizen costing and activity-based management, and it can be used as a search mechanism to identify opportunities for improvement. **Benchmarking** uses best practices found within and outside the organization as the standard for evaluating and improving activity performance. The objective of benchmarking is to become the best at performing activities and processes (thus, benchmarking represents an important activity management methodology). The approach certainly seems

---

3. Robin Cooper, *When Lean Enterprises Collide* (Boston: Harvard Business School Press, 1995).

to have considerable merit. A study of 111 benchmarking companies revealed benchmarking returns ranging from $1.4 million to $189.4 million.[4]

Internal Benchmarking

Benchmarking against internal operations is called *internal benchmarking*. Within an organization, different units (for example, different plant sites) that perform the same activities are compared. The unit with the best performance for a given activity sets the standard. Other units then have a target to meet or exceed. Furthermore, the best-practices unit can share information with other units on how it has achieved its superior results. Internal benchmarking has several advantages. First, a significant amount of information is often readily available that can be shared throughout the organization. Second, immediate cost reductions are often realized. Third, the best internal standards that spread throughout the organization become the benchmark for comparison against external benchmarking partners. This last advantage also suggests the major disadvantage of internal benchmarking. Specifically, the best internal performance may fall short of what others are doing, particularly direct competitors.

There are numerous examples of the benefits of internal benchmarking.[5] **Thomson Corporation** collected and broadcast best practices through internal benchmarking throughout the company and saved $200 million in one year. **Chevron** saved $150 million by transferring energy use management techniques throughout the company. **Public Service Enterprise Group** used internal benchmarking to improve the process for ripping up a street, repairing a line, backfilling the hole, and repaving the area. The improvement dropped costs from an average of $2,200 to just $200 per incident.

External Benchmarking

Benchmarking that involves comparison with others outside the organization is called *external benchmarking*. The three types of external benchmarking are competitive benchmarking, functional benchmarking, and generic benchmarking. Competitive benchmarking is a comparison of activity performance with direct competitors. The main problem with competitive benchmarking is that it is very difficult to obtain information beyond that found in the public domain. At times, however, it is possible. **The Ritz-Carlton**, for example, dramatically improved its housekeeping process by studying the best practices of a competitor.[6] Functional benchmarking is a comparison with firms that are in the same industry but do not compete in the same markets. For example, a Japanese communications firm might be able to compare its customer service process with that of **AT&T**. Generic benchmarking studies the best practices of noncompetitors outside a firm's industry. Certain activities and processes are common to all organizations. If superior external best practices can be identified, then they can be used as standards to motivate internal improvements. For example, **Verizon** improved its field service process by studying the field service process of an elevator company.[7]

Activity Flexible Budgeting

The ability to identify changes in activity costs as activity output changes allows managers to more carefully plan and monitor activity improvements. **Activity flexible budgeting** is the prediction of what activity costs will be as activity output changes. Variance analysis within an activity framework makes it possible to improve traditional budgetary performance reporting. It also enhances the ability to manage activities.

---

4. *Benchmarking: Leveraging Best-Practices Strategies*, an APQC white paper (see knowledge management content), accessed October 6, 2004 at http://www.APQC.org/portal/apqc/ksn.

5. Frank Jossi, "Take a Peek Inside," *HRMagazine* (June 2002): 46–52.

6. Robert C. Camp, *Business Process Benchmarking* (Milwaukee, WI: ASQC Quality Press, 1995): 273.

7. Ibid.

In a functional-based approach, budgeted costs for the actual level of activity are obtained by assuming that a single unit-based driver (units of product or direct labor hours) drives all costs. A cost formula is developed for each cost item as a function of units produced or direct labor hours. Exhibit 12-6 presents a functional-based flexible budget based on direct labor hours. If, however, costs vary with respect to more than one driver and the drivers are not highly correlated with direct labor hours, then the predicted costs can be misleading.

EXHIBIT 12-6			Flexible Budget: Direct Labor Hours	
	Cost Formula		**Direct Labor Hours**	
	Fixed	**Variable**	**10,000**	**20,000**
Direct materials	—	$10	$100,000	$200,000
Direct labor	—	8	80,000	160,000
Maintenance	$ 20,000	3	50,000	80,000
Machining	15,000	1	25,000	35,000
Inspections	120,000	—	120,000	120,000
Setups	50,000	—	50,000	50,000
Purchasing	220,000	—	220,000	220,000
Total	$425,000	$22	$645,000	$865,000

The solution, of course, is to build flexible budget formulas for more than one driver. Cost estimation procedures (high-low method, the method of least squares, and so on) can be used to estimate and validate the cost formulas for each activity. In principle, the variable cost component for each activity should correspond to resources acquired as needed (flexible resources), and the fixed cost component should correspond to resources acquired in advance of usage (committed resources). This multiple-formula approach allows managers to predict more accurately what costs should be for different levels of activity usage, as measured by the activity output measure. These costs can then be compared with the actual costs to help assess budgetary performance. Exhibit 12-7 illustrates an activity flexible budget. Notice that the budgeted amounts for direct materials and direct labor are the same as those reported in Exhibit 12-6; they use the same activity output measure. The budgeted amounts for the other items differ significantly from the traditional amounts because the activity output measures differ.

Assume that the first activity level for each driver in Exhibit 12-7 corresponds to the actual activity usage levels. Exhibit 12-8 compares the budgeted costs for the actual activity usage levels with the actual costs. One item is on target, and the other six items are mixed. The net outcome is a favorable variance of $21,500.

The performance report in Exhibit 12-8 compares total budgeted costs for the actual level of activity with the total actual costs for each activity. It is also possible to compare the actual fixed activity costs with the budgeted fixed activity costs, and the actual variable activity costs with the budgeted variable costs. For example, assume that the actual fixed inspection costs are $82,000 (due to a midyear salary adjustment, reflecting a more favorable union agreement than anticipated) and that the actual variable inspection costs are $43,500. The variable and fixed budget variances for the inspection activity are computed on page 562.

EXHIBIT 12-7   Activity Flexible Budget

DRIVER: DIRECT LABOR HOURS

	Formula		Level of Activity	
	Fixed	Variable	10,000	20,000
Direct materials	$—	$10	$100,000	$200,000
Direct labor	—	8	80,000	160,000
Subtotal	$—	$18	$180,000	$360,000

DRIVER: MACHINE HOURS

	Fixed	Variable	8,000	16,000
Maintenance	$20,000	$5.50	$64,000	$108,000
Machining	15,000	2.00	31,000	47,000
Subtotal	$35,000	$7.50	$95,000	$155,000

DRIVER: NUMBER OF SETUPS

	Fixed	Variable	25	30
Inspections	$80,000	$2,100	$132,500	$143,000
Setups	—	1,800	45,000	54,000
Subtotal	$80,000	$3,900	$177,500	$197,000

DRIVER: NUMBER OF ORDERS

	Fixed	Variable	15,000	25,000
Purchasing	$211,000	$1	$226,000	$236,000
Total			$678,500	$948,000

EXHIBIT 12-8   Activity-Based Performance Report*

	Actual Costs	Budgeted Costs	Budget Variance
Direct materials	$101,000	$100,000	$ 1,000 U
Direct labor	80,000	80,000	—
Maintenance	55,000	64,000	9,000 F
Machining	29,000	31,000	2,000 F
Inspections	125,500	132,500	7,000 F
Setups	46,500	45,000	1,500 U
Purchasing	220,000	226,000	6,000 F
Total	$657,000	$678,500	$21,500 F

*Actual levels of drivers: 10,000 direct labor hours, 8,000 machine hours, 25 setups, and 15,000 orders.

Activity	Actual Cost	Budgeted Cost 25 Setups Level	Variance
Inspection:			
Fixed	$ 82,000	$ 80,000	$2,000 U
Variable	43,500	52,500	9,000 F
Total	$125,500	$132,500	$7,000 F

Breaking each variance into fixed and variable components provides more insight into the source of the variation in planned and actual expenditures. Activity budgets also provide valuable information about capacity usage.

Activity Capacity Management

Activity capacity is the number of times an activity can be performed. Activity drivers measure activity capacity. For example, consider inspecting finished goods as the activity. A sample from each batch is taken to determine the batch's overall quality. The demand for the inspection activity determines the amount of activity capacity that is required. For instance, suppose that the number of batches inspected measures activity output. Now, suppose that 60 batches are scheduled to be produced. Then, the required capacity is 60 batches. Finally, assume that a single inspector can inspect 20 batches per year. Thus, three inspectors must be hired to provide the necessary capacity. If each inspector is paid a salary of $40,000, the budgeted cost of the activity capacity is $120,000. This is the cost of the resources (labor) acquired in advance of usage. The budgeted activity rate is $2,000 per batch ($120,000/60).

Several questions relate to activity capacity and its cost. First, what *should* the activity capacity be? The answer to this question provides the ability to measure the amount of improvement possible. Second, how much of the capacity acquired was actually used? The answer to this question signals a nonproductive cost and, at the same time, an opportunity for capacity reduction and cost savings.

Capacity Variances

Exhibit 12-9 illustrates the calculation of two capacity variances: the *activity volume variance* and the *unused capacity variance*. The **activity volume variance** is the difference between the actual activity level acquired (practical capacity, AQ) and the value-added standard quantity of activity that should be used (SQ). Assuming that inspection is a non-

---

EXHIBIT 12-9   **Activity Capacity Variances**

AQ = Activity capacity acquired (practical capacity)
SQ = Activity capacity used
AU = Actual usage of the activity
SP = Fixed activity rate

$SP \times SQ$	$SP \times AQ$	$SP \times AU$
$2,000 \times 0$	$2,000 \times 60$	$2,000 \times 40$
$0	$120,000	$80,000

	Volume Variance		Unused Capacity Variance	
	$120,000 U		$40,000 F	

value-added activity, $SQ = 0$ is the value-added standard. The volume variance in this framework has a useful economic interpretation: it is the non-value-added cost of the inspection activity. It measures the amount of improvement that is possible through analysis and management of activities ($120,000, in this example). However, since the supply of the activity in question (inspections) must be acquired in blocks (one inspector at a time), it is also important to measure the current demand for the activity (actual usage).

When supply exceeds demand by a large enough quantity, management can take action to reduce the quantity of the activity provided. Thus, the **unused capacity variance**, the difference between activity availability (AQ) and activity usage (AU), is important information that should be provided to management. The goal is to reduce the demand for the activity until such time as the unused capacity variance equals the volume variance. Why? Because the volume variance is a non-value-added cost and the unused activity variance measures the progress made in reducing this non-value-added cost. The calculation of the unused capacity variance is also illustrated in Exhibit 12-9. Notice that the unused capacity is 20 batches valued at $40,000. Assume that this unused capacity exists because management has been engaged in a quality-improvement program that has reduced the need to inspect certain batches of products. This difference between the supply of the inspection resources and their usage should impact future spending plans (reduction of a non-value-added activity is labeled as favorable).

For example, we know that the supply of inspection resources is greater than its usage. Furthermore, because of the quality-improvement program, we can expect this difference to persist and even become greater (with the ultimate goal of reducing the cost of inspection activity to zero). Management now must be willing to exploit the unused capacity it has created. Essentially, activity availability can be reduced; thus, the spending on inspection can be decreased. A manager can use several options to achieve this outcome. Since the inspection demand has been reduced by 20 batches, the company needs only two full-time inspectors. The extra inspector could be permanently reassigned to an activity where resources are in short supply. If reassignment is not feasible, the company should lay off the extra inspector.

This example illustrates an important feature of activity capacity management. Activity improvement can create unused capacity, but managers must be willing and able to make the tough decisions to reduce resource spending on the redundant resources to gain the potential profit increase. Profits can be increased by reducing resource spending or by transferring the resources to other activities that will generate more revenues.

Implementing Activity-Based Management

Activity-based management (ABM) is a more comprehensive system than an ABC system. ABM adds a process view to the cost view of ABC. ABM encompasses ABC and uses it as a major source of information. ABM can be viewed as an information system that has the broad objectives of (1) improving decision making by providing accurate cost information and (2) reducing costs by encouraging and supporting continuous improvement efforts. The first objective is the domain of ABC, while the second objective belongs to process value analysis. The second objective requires more detailed data than ABC's objective of improving the accuracy of costing assignments. If a company intends to use both ABC and PVA, then its approach to implementation must be carefully conceived. For example, if ABC creates aggregate cost pools based on homogeneity, much of the detailed activity information may not be needed. Yet, for PVA, this detail must be retained. Clearly, how to implement an ABM system is a major consideration. Exhibit 12-10 provides a representation of an ABM implementation model.

Discussion of the ABM Implementation Model

The model in Exhibit 12-10 shows that the overall objective of ABM is to improve a firm's profitability, an objective achieved by identifying and selecting opportunities for

EXHIBIT 12-10 ABM Implementation Model

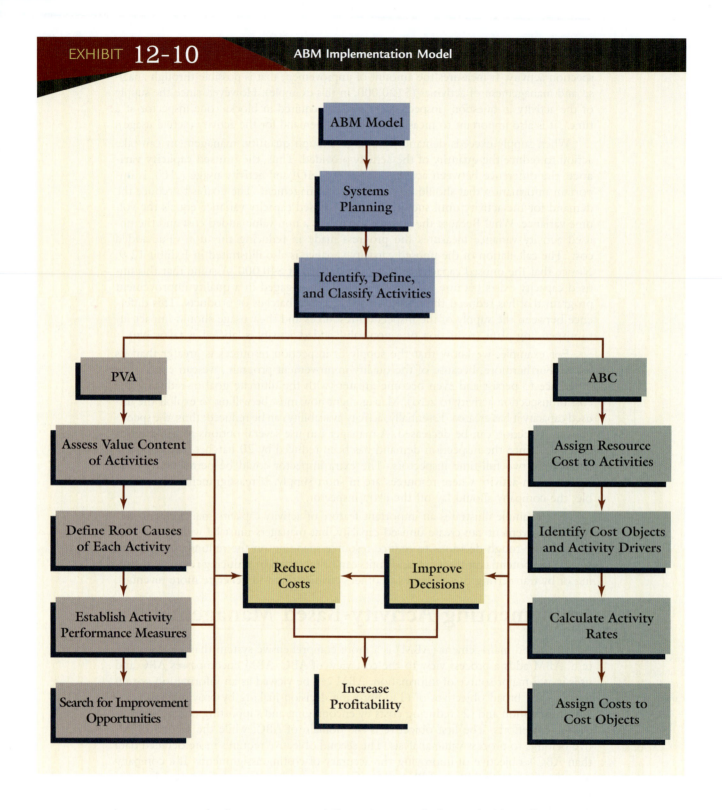

improvement and using more accurate information to make better decisions. Root cause analysis, for example, reveals opportunities for improvement. By identifying non-value-added costs, priorities can be established based on the initiatives that offer the most cost reduction. Furthermore, the potential cost reduction itself is measured by ABC calculations.

Exhibit 12-10 also reveals that 10 steps define an ABM implementation: two common steps and four that are associated with either ABC or PVA. The PVA steps have been discussed extensively in this chapter, whereas the ABC steps were discussed in Chapter 4. The two common steps are (1) systems planning and (2) activity identification, definition, and classification.

Systems Planning

Systems planning provides the justification for implementing ABM and addresses the following issues:

1. The purpose and objectives of the ABM system
2. The organization's current and desired competitive position
3. The organization's business processes and product mix
4. The timeline, assigned responsibilities, and resources required for implementation
5. The ability of the organization to implement, learn, and use new information

To obtain buy-in by operating personnel, the objectives of an ABM system must be carefully identified and related to the firm's desired competitive position, business processes, and product mix. The broad objectives have already been mentioned (improving accuracy and continuous improvement); however, it is also necessary to develop specific desired outcomes associated with each of these two objectives. For example, one specific outcome is that of changing the product mix based on more accurate costs (with the expectation that profits will increase). Another specific outcome is that of improving the firm's competitive position by increasing process efficiency through elimination of non-value-added activities. Planning also entails establishing a timeline for the implementation project, assigning specific responsibilities to individuals or teams, and developing a detailed budget. Although all five issues listed are important, the information usage issue deserves special attention. Successful implementation is strongly dependent on the organization's ability to learn how to use the new information provided by ABM. Users must be convinced that this new information can solve specific problems. They also need to be trained to use activity-based costing information to produce better decisions, and they need to understand how ABM drives and supports continuous improvement.

Activity Identification, Definition, and Classification

Identifying, defining, and classifying activities requires more attention for ABM than for ABC. The activity dictionary should include a detailed listing of the tasks that define each activity. Knowing the tasks that define an activity can be very helpful for improving the efficiency of value-added activities. Classification of activities also allows ABM to connect with other continuous improvement initiatives such as JIT, total quality management, and total environmental quality cost management. For example, identifying quality-related and environmental activities enables management to focus attention on the non-value-added activities of the quality and environmental categories. ABC also provides a more complete understanding of the effect that quality and environmental costs have on products, processes, and customers. It is important to realize that successful implementation requires time and patience. This is especially true when it comes to using the new information provided by an ABM system. For example, one survey revealed that it takes an average of 3.1 years for nonaccounting personnel to grow accustomed to using ABC information.[8]

Why ABM Implementations Fail

ABM can fail as a system for a variety of reasons. One of the major reasons is the lack of support of higher-level management. Not only must this support be obtained before undertaking an implementation project, but it must also be maintained. Loss of support can occur if the implementation takes too long or the expected results do not

---

8. Kip. R. Krumwiede, "ABC: Why It's Tried and How It Succeeds," *Management Accounting* (April 1998): 32–38.

materialize. Results may not occur as expected because operating and sales managers do not have the expertise to use the new activity information. Thus, significant efforts to train and educate need to be undertaken. Advantages of the new data need to be spelled out carefully, and managers must be taught how these data can be used to increase efficiency and productivity. Resistance to change should be expected; it is not unusual for managers to receive the new cost information with skepticism. Showing how this information can enable them to be better managers should help to overcome this resistance. Involving nonfinancial managers in the planning and implementation stages may also reduce resistance and secure the required support.

Failure to integrate the new system is another major reason for an ABM system breakdown. The probability of success is increased if the ABM system is not in competition with other improvement programs or the official accounting system. It is important to communicate the concept that ABM complements and enhances other improvement programs. Moreover, it is important that ABM be integrated to the point that activity costing outcomes are not in direct competition with the traditional accounting numbers. Managers may be tempted to continue using the traditional accounting numbers in lieu of the new data.

Financial-Based versus Activity-Based Responsibility Accounting

OBJECTIVE 5

Explain how activity-based management is a form of responsibility accounting, and tell how it differs from financial-based responsibility accounting.

Responsibility accounting is a fundamental tool of managerial control and is defined by four essential elements: (1) assigning responsibility, (2) establishing performance measures or benchmarks, (3) evaluating performance, and (4) assigning rewards. The objective of responsibility accounting is to influence behavior in such a way that individual and organizational initiatives are aligned to achieve a common goal or goals. Exhibit 12-11 illustrates the responsibility accounting model.

A particular responsibility accounting system is defined by how the four elements in Exhibit 12-11 are defined. Three types of responsibility accounting systems have evolved over time: *financial-based*, *activity-based*, and *strategic-based*. All three are found in practice today. Essentially, firms choose the responsibility accounting system that is

EXHIBIT 12-11   The Responsibility Accounting Model

Responsibility is defined.

↓

Performance measures are established.

↓

Performance is measured.

↓

Rewards are provided based on performance.

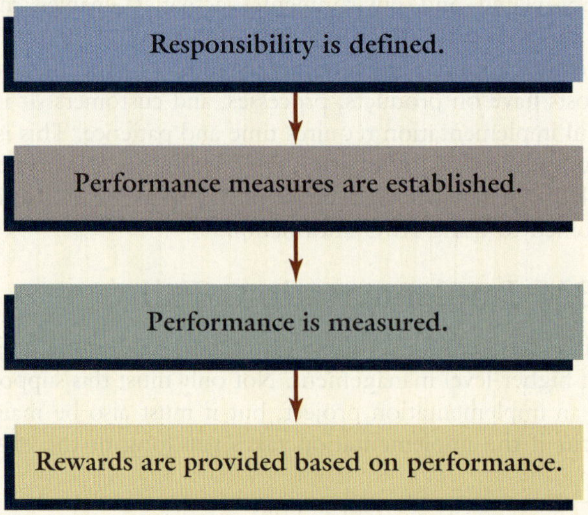

compatible with the requirements and economics of their particular operating environment. Firms that operate in a stable environment with standardized products and processes and low competitive pressures will likely find the less complex, financial-based responsibility accounting systems to be quite adequate. As organizational complexity increases and the competitive environment becomes much more dynamic, activity-based and strategic-based systems are likely to be more suitable. Strategic-based responsibility accounting systems are discussed in Chapter 13.

The responsibility accounting system for a stable environment is referred to as *financial-based responsibility accounting*. A **financial-based responsibility accounting system** assigns responsibility to organizational units and expresses performance measures in financial terms. It emphasizes a financial perspective. *Activity-based responsibility accounting*, on the other hand, is the responsibility accounting system developed for those firms operating in continuous improvement environments. **Activity-based responsibility accounting** assigns responsibility to processes and uses both financial and nonfinancial measures of performance, thus emphasizing both financial and process perspectives. A comparison of each of the four elements of the responsibility accounting model for each responsibility system reveals the key differences between the two approaches.

Assigning Responsibility

Exhibit 12-12 lists the differences in responsibility assignments between the two systems. Financial-based responsibility accounting focuses on *functional* organizational units and individuals. First, a responsibility center is identified. This center is typically an organizational unit such as a plant, department, or production line. Whatever the functional unit is, responsibility is assigned to the individual in charge. Responsibility is defined in financial terms (for example, costs). Emphasis is on achieving optimal financial results at the local level (i.e., organizational unit level). Exhibit 12-12 reveals that in an activity- or process-based responsibility system, the focal point changes from units and individuals to processes and teams. Systemwide optimization is the emphasis. Also, financial responsibility continues to be vital. The reasons for the change in focus are simple. In a continuous improvement environment, the financial perspective translates into continuously *enhancing revenues*, *reducing costs*, and *improving asset utilization*. Creating this continuous growth and improvement requires an organization to constantly improve its capabilities of delivering value to customers and shareholders. A process perspective is chosen instead of an organizational-unit perspective because processes are the *sources* of value for customers and shareholders and because they are the key to achieving an organization's financial objectives. The customer can be internal or external to the organization. Procurement, new product development, manufacturing, and customer service are examples of processes.

Since processes are the way things are done, changing the way things are done means changing processes. Three methods can change the way things are done: *process*

EXHIBIT 12-12	Responsibility Assignments Compared
Financial-Based Responsibility	**Activity-Based Responsibility**
1. Organizational units	1. Processes
2. Local operating efficiency	2. Systemwide efficiency
3. Individual accountability	3. Team accountability
4. Financial outcomes	4. Financial outcomes

improvement, *process innovation*, and *process creation*. **Process improvement** refers to incremental and constant increases in the efficiency of an existing process. For example, **Medtronic Xomed**, a manufacturer of surgical products (for eyes, ears and nose specialists), improved their processes by providing written instructions telling workers the best way to do their jobs. Over a three-year period, the company reduced rework by 57%, scrap by 85%, and experienced a 38% reduction in the cost of its shipped products.[9] Activity-based management is particularly useful for bringing about process improvements. Processes are made up of activities that are linked by a common objective. Listing these activities and classifying them as value-added or non-value-added immediately suggests a way to make the process better: eliminate the non-value-added activities.

Process innovation (business reengineering) refers to the performance of a process in a radically new way with the objective of achieving dramatic improvements in response time, quality, and efficiency. **IBM Credit**, for example, radically redesigned its credit approval process and reduced its time for preparing a quote from seven days to one; similarly, **Federal-Mogul**, a parts manufacturer, used process innovation to reduce development time for part prototypes from 20 weeks to 20 days.[10] **Process creation** refers to the installation of an entirely new process with the objective of meeting customer and financial objectives. **Chemical Bank**, for example, identified three *new* internal processes: understanding customer segments, developing new products, and cross-selling the product line.[11] These new internal processes were viewed as critical by the bank's management for improving the customer and profit mix and creating an enabled organization. It should be mentioned that process creation does not mean that the process has to be *original* to the organization. It means that it is *new* to the organization. For example, developing new products is a process common to many organizations but evidently was new to Chemical Bank.

Many processes cut across functional boundaries. This facilitates an integrated approach that emphasizes the firm's value-chain activities. It also means that cross-functional skills are needed for effective process management. Teams are the natural outcome of this process management requirement. Teams also improve the quality of work life by fostering friendships and a sense of belonging. Process improvement, innovation, and creation require significant group activity (and support) and cannot be carried out effectively by individuals. **General Electric**, **Xerox**, **Martin Marietta**, and **Aetna Life Insurance** have all begun to use teams as their basic work unit.[12]

Establishing Performance Measures

Once responsibility is defined, performance measures must be identified and standards set to serve as benchmarks for performance measurement. Exhibit 12-13 provides a comparison of the two systems' approach to the task of defining performance measures. According to Exhibit 12-13, budgeting and standard costing are the cornerstones of the benchmark activity for a financial-based system. This, of course, implies that performance measures are objective and financial in nature. Furthermore, they tend to support the status quo and are relatively stable over time. Exhibit 12-13 reveals some striking differences for firms operating in a continuous improvement environment. First, performance measures are process-oriented and, thus, must be concerned with process attributes such as process time, quality, and efficiency. Second, performance measurement standards are structured to support change. Therefore, standards are dynamic in nature. They change to reflect new conditions and new goals and to help maintain any

9. William Leventon, "Manufacturers Get Lean to Trim Waste," Medical Device & Diagnostic Industry, September, 2004.: Online journal, http://www.devicelink.com/mddi/archive/04/09/contents.html.

10. Thomas H. Davenport, *Process Innovation* (Boston: Harvard Business School Press, 1993): 2.

11. Norman Klein and Robert Kaplan, *Chemical Bank: Implementing the Balanced Scorecard* (Harvard Business School, Case 125–210, 1995): 5–6.

12. Davenport, *Process Innovation*, 97.

EXHIBIT 12-13   **Performance Measures Compared**

Financial-Based Measures	Activity-Based Measures
1. Organizational unit budgets	1. Process-oriented standards
2. Standard costing	2. Value-added standards
3. Static standards	3. Dynamic standards
4. Currently attainable standards	4. Optimal standards

---

progress that has been realized. For example, standards can be set that reflect some desired level of improvement for a process. Once the desired level is achieved, the standard is changed to encourage an additional increment of improvement. In an environment where constant improvement is sought, standards cannot be static. Third, optimal standards assume a vital role. They set the ultimate achievement target and, thus, identify the potential for improvement. Finally, standards should reflect the value added by individual activities and processes. Identifying a value-added standard for each activity is much more ambitious than the traditional financial responsibility system. It expands control to include the entire organization.

Evaluating Performance

Exhibit 12-14 compares performance evaluation under financial- and activity-based responsibility accounting systems. In a financial-based framework, performance is measured by comparing actual outcomes with budgeted outcomes. In principle, individuals are held accountable only for those items over which they have control. Financial performance, as measured by the ability to meet or beat a stable financial standard, is strongly emphasized. In the activity-based framework, performance is concerned with more than just the financial perspective. The process perspective adds time, quality, and efficiency as critical dimensions of performance. Decreasing the time a process takes to deliver its output to customers is viewed as a vital objective. Thus, nonfinancial, process-oriented measures such as cycle-time and on-time deliveries become important. Performance is evaluated by gauging whether these measures are improving over time. The same is true for measures relating to quality and efficiency. Improving a process should translate into better financial results. Hence, measures of cost reductions achieved, trends in cost, and cost per unit of output are all useful indicators of whether a process has improved. Progress toward achieving optimal standards and interim standards needs to be measured. The objective is to provide low-cost, high-quality products, delivered on a timely basis.

EXHIBIT 12-14   **Performance Evaluation Compared**

Financial-Based Performance Evaluation	Activity-Based Performance Evaluation
1. Financial efficiency	1. Time reductions
2. Controllable costs	2. Quality improvements
3. Actual versus standard	3. Cost reductions
4. Financial measures	4. Trend measurement

Assigning Rewards

In both systems, individuals are rewarded or penalized according to the policies and discretion of higher management. As Exhibit 12-15 shows, many of the same financial instruments (e.g., salary increases, bonuses, profit sharing, and promotions) are used to provide rewards for good performance. Of course, the nature of the incentive structure differs in each system. For example, the reward system in a financial-based responsibility accounting system is designed to encourage individuals to achieve or beat budgetary standards. Furthermore, for the activity-based responsibility system, rewarding individuals is more complicated than it is in a functional-based setting. Individuals simultaneously have accountability for team and individual performance. Since process-related improvements are mostly achieved through team efforts, group-based rewards are more suitable than individual rewards. In one company (a producer of electronic components), for example, optimal standards have been set for unit costs, on-time delivery, quality, inventory turns, scrap, and cycle time.[13] Bonuses are awarded to the team whenever performance is maintained on all measures and improves on at least one measure. Notice the multidimensional nature of this measurement and reward system. Another difference concerns the notion of gainsharing versus profit sharing. Profit sharing is a global incentive designed to encourage employees to contribute to the overall financial well-being of the organization. Gainsharing is more specific. Employees are allowed to share in gains related to specific improvement projects. Gainsharing helps obtain the necessary buy-in for specific improvement projects inherent to activity-based management.

EXHIBIT 12-15	Rewards Compared
Financial-Based Rewards	**Activity-Based Rewards**
1. Financial performance basis	1. Multidimensional performance basis
2. Individual rewards	2. Group rewards
3. Salary increases	3. Salary increases
4. Promotions	4. Promotions
5. Bonuses and profit sharing	5. Bonuses, profit sharing, and gainsharing

13. C. J. McNair, "Responsibility Accounting and Controllability Networks," *Handbook of Cost Management* (Boston: Warren Gorham Lamont, 1993): E41–E43.

SUMMARY

Activity-based management encompasses both activity-based costing and process value analysis. Activity-based costing is concerned with accurate assignment of costs to cost objects and is an important source of information for managing activities. ABC, however, is not concerned with the issue or presence of waste in activities. Identifying waste and its causes and eliminating it fall within the domain of process value analysis.

Process value analysis emphasizes activity management with the intent of maximizing systemwide performance. It consists of three elements: driver analysis, activity analysis, and performance measurement. Driver analysis is also referred to as root cause analysis. It seeks to identify why activities are performed. Activity analysis identifies all activities and the resources they consume and classifies activities as value-added or non-value-added. Performance measurement is concerned with how well activities are performed.

Reporting value- and non-value-added costs is an integral part of a sound activity-based management system. Tracking trends in these costs over time is an effective control measure. Once management determines the source of non-value-added costs, a focused program of continuous improvement can be implemented. Kaizen costing is a well-accepted approach for reducing costs by eliminating waste. Activity flexible budgeting and activity capacity management offer additional control capabilities. Activity flexible budgeting differs from the traditional approach by using more than unit-level drivers to predict what costs will be at different levels of activity output.

Implementing an activity-based management system requires careful planning and execution. The objectives of the system must be identified and explained. The benefits of the system and the anticipated effects should also be noted. A key issue is assessing and managing the ability of the organization to implement, learn, and use the new activity information. Strong support from higher management is also critical.

A firm can adopt one of three responsibility accounting systems. Two are discussed in this chapter: financial-based responsibility accounting and activity-based responsibility accounting. Financial-based responsibility accounting focuses on organizational units such as departments and plants; uses financial outcome measures, static standards, and benchmarks to evaluate performance; and emphasizes status quo and organizational stability. Activity-based responsibility accounting focuses on processes, uses both operational and financial measures, employs dynamic standards, and emphasizes and supports continuous improvement.

REVIEW PROBLEMS AND SOLUTIONS

1 FINANCIAL-BASED RESPONSIBILITY ACCOUNTING VERSUS ACTIVITY-BASED RESPONSIBILITY ACCOUNTING

The labor standard for a company is two hours per unit produced, which includes setup time. At the beginning of the last quarter, 20,000 units had been produced and 44,000 hours used. The production manager was concerned about the prospect of reporting an unfavorable labor efficiency variance at the end of the year. Any unfavorable variance over 9 to 10 percent of the standard usually meant a negative performance rating. Bonuses were adversely affected by negative ratings. Accordingly, for the last quarter, the production manager decided to reduce the number of setups and use longer production runs. He knew that his production workers usually were within 5 percent of the standard. The real problem was with setup times. By reducing the setups, the actual hours used would be within 7 to 8 percent of the standard hours allowed.

Required:

1. Explain why the behavior of the production manager is unacceptable for a continuous improvement environment.
2. Explain how an activity-based responsibility accounting approach would discourage the kind of behavior described.

SOLUTION

1. In a continuous improvement environment, efforts are made to reduce inventories and eliminate non-value-added costs. The production manager is focusing on meeting the labor usage standard and is ignoring the impact on inventories that longer production runs may have.

2. Activity-based responsibility accounting focuses on activities and activity performance. For the setup activity, the value-added standard would be zero setup

time and zero setup costs. Thus, avoiding setups would neither save labor time nor affect the labor variance. Of course, labor variances themselves would not be computed—at least not at the operational level.

2 ACTIVITY VOLUME VARIANCE, UNUSED ACTIVITY CAPACITY, VALUE- AND NON-VALUE-ADDED COST REPORTS, KAIZEN STANDARDS

Pollard Manufacturing has developed value-added standards for its activities including material usage, purchasing, and inspecting. The value-added output levels for each of the activities, their actual levels achieved, and the standard prices are as follows:

Activity	Activity Driver	SQ	AQ	SP
Using lumber	Board feet	24,000	30,000	$10
Purchasing	Purchase orders	800	1,000	50
Inspecting	Inspection hours	0	4,000	12

Assume that material usage and purchasing costs correspond to flexible resources (acquired as needed) and that inspection uses resources that are acquired in blocks or steps of 2,000 hours. The actual prices paid for the inputs equal the standard prices.

Required:

1. Assume that continuous improvement efforts reduce the demand for inspection by 30 percent during the year (actual activity usage drops by 30 percent). Calculate the volume and unused capacity variances for the inspection activity. Explain their meaning. Also, explain why there is no volume or unused capacity variance for the other two activities.
2. Prepare a cost report that details value- and non-value-added costs.
3. Suppose that the company wants to reduce all non-value-added costs by 30 percent in the coming year. Prepare kaizen standards that can be used to evaluate the company's progress toward this goal. How much will these measures save in resource spending?

SOLUTION

1.

$SP \times SQ$	$SP \times AQ$	$SP \times AU$
12×0	$12 \times 4,000$	$12 \times 2,800$
$0	$48,000	$33,600

Volume Variance	Unused Capacity Variance
$48,000 U	$14,400 F

The activity volume variance is the non-value-added cost. The unused capacity variance measures the cost of the unused activity capacity. The other two activities have no volume variance or capacity variance because they use only flexible resources. No activity capacity is acquired in advance of usage; thus, there cannot be an unused capacity variance or a volume variance.

2.

	Costs		
	Value-Added	Non-Value-Added	Total
Using lumber	$240,000	$ 60,000	$300,000
Purchasing	40,000	10,000	50,000
Inspecting	0	48,000	48,000
Total	$280,000	$118,000	$398,000

3.

	Kaizen Standards	
	Quantity	*Cost*
Using lumber	28,200	$282,000
Purchasing	940	47,000
Inspecting	2,800	33,600

If the standards are met, then the savings are as follows:

$$\text{Using lumber: } \$10 \times 1,800 = \$18,000$$
$$\text{Purchasing: } \$50 \times 60 \quad = \quad \underline{3,000}$$
$$\text{Savings} \qquad\qquad\qquad \underline{\$21,000}$$

There is no reduction in resource spending for inspecting because it must be purchased in increments of 2,000 and only 1,200 hours were saved—another 800 hours must be reduced before any reduction in resource spending is possible. The unused capacity variance must reach $24,000 before resource spending can be reduced.

KEY TERMS

Activity analysis 550

Activity capacity 562

Activity elimination 553

Activity flexible budgeting 559

Activity output measure 550

Activity reduction 553

Activity selection 553

Activity sharing 553

Activity volume variance 562

Activity-based management (ABM) 549

Activity-based responsibility accounting 567

Benchmarking 558

Continuous improvement 548

Driver analysis 550

Financial measures 554

Financial-based responsibility accounting system 567

Kaizen costing 553

Kaizen standard 557

Non-value-added activities 551

Non-value-added costs 552

Process creation 568

Process improvement 568

Process innovation (business reengineering) 568

Process value analysis (PVA) 550

Responsibility accounting 566

Unused capacity variance 563

Value-added activities 551

Value-added costs 551

Value-added standard 554

QUESTIONS FOR WRITING AND DISCUSSION

1. What are the two dimensions of the activity-based management model? How do they differ?
2. What is driver analysis? What role does it play in process value analysis?
3. What is activity analysis? Why is this approach compatible with the goal of continuous improvement?
4. What are value-added activities? Value-added costs?
5. What are non-value-added activities? Non-value-added costs? Give an example of each.

6. Identify and define four different ways to manage activities so that costs can be reduced.
7. What is a kaizen standard? Describe the kaizen and maintenance subcycles.
8. Explain how benchmarking can be used to improve activity performance.
9. Explain how activity flexible budgeting differs from functional-based flexible budgeting.
10. In implementing an ABM system, what are some of the planning considerations?
11. Explain why a detailed task description is needed for ABM and not for ABC.
12. What are some of the reasons that ABM implementation may lose the support of higher management?
13. Explain how lack of integration of an ABM system may cause its failure.
14. Describe a financial-based responsibility accounting system.
15. Describe an activity-based responsibility accounting system. How does it differ from financial-based responsibility accounting?

EXERCISES

12-1   ABC VERSUS ABM

LO1, LO2   Timesaver, Inc., produces deluxe and regular microwaves. Recently, Timesaver has been losing market share with its regular microwaves because of competitors offering a product with the same quality and features but at a lower price. A careful market study revealed that if Timesaver could reduce its regular model price by $10 per unit, it would regain its former share of the market. Management, however, is convinced that any price reduction must be accompanied by a cost reduction of $10 so that per-unit profitability is not affected. Earlene Day has indicated that poor overhead costing assignments may be distorting management's view of each product's cost and, therefore, the ability to know how to set selling prices. Earlene has identified the following overhead activities: machining, testing, and rework. The three activities, their costs, and practical capacities are as follows:

Activity	Cost	Practical Capacity
Machining	$1,800,000	150,000 machine hours
Testing	1,200,000	40,000 testing hours
Rework	600,000	20,000 rework hours

The consumption patterns of the two products are as follows:

	Regular	Deluxe
Units	100,000	10,000
Machine hours	50,000	10,000
Testing hours	20,000	20,000
Rework hours	5,000	15,000

Timesaver assigns overhead costs to the two products using a plantwide rate based on machine hours.

Required:

1. Calculate the unit overhead cost of the regular microwave product using machine hours to assign overhead costs. Now, repeat the calculation using ABC to assign overhead costs. Did improving the accuracy of cost assignments solve Timesaver's competitive problem? What did it reveal?

2. Now, assume that *in addition* to improving the accuracy of cost assignments, Earlene observes that defective supplier components are the root cause of both the testing and rework activities. Suppose further that Timesaver has found a new supplier that provides higher-quality components such that testing and rework costs are reduced by 50 percent. Now, calculate the cost of each product (assuming that testing and rework time are also reduced by 50 percent) using ABC. The relative consumption patterns also remain the same. Comment on the difference between ABC and ABM.

12-2   ROOT CAUSE (DRIVER ANALYSIS)

LO2   For the following two activities, ask a series of "why" questions (with your answers) that reveal the root cause. Once the root cause is identified, use a "how" question to reveal how the activity can be improved (with your answer).

Activity 1: Daily cleaning of a puddle of oil near production machinery.
Activity 2: Providing customers with sales allowances.

12-3   NON-VALUE-ADDED ACTIVITIES: NON-VALUE-ADDED COST

LO2   Honley Company has 20 clerks that work in its accounts payable department. A study revealed the following activities and the relative time demanded by each activity:

Activities	*Percentage of Clerical Time*
Comparing purchase orders and receiving orders and invoices	15%
Resolving discrepancies among the three documents	70
Preparing checks for suppliers	10
Making journal entries and mailing checks	5

The average salary of a clerk is $30,000.

Required:

Classify the four activities as value-added or non-value-added, and calculate the clerical cost of each activity. For non-value-added activities, indicate why they are non-value-added.

12-4   ROOT CAUSE (DRIVER) ANALYSIS

LO2   Refer to **Exercise 12-3**.

Required:

Suppose that clerical error—either Honley's or the supplier's—is the common root cause of the non-value-added activities. For each non-value-added activity, ask a series of "why" questions that identify clerical error as the activity's root cause.

12-5   PROCESS IMPROVEMENT/INNOVATION

LO2, LO5   Refer to **Exercise 12-3**. Suppose that clerical error is the common root cause of the non-value-added activities. Paying bills is a subprocess that belongs to the procurement process. The procurement process is made up of three subprocesses: purchasing, receiving, and paying bills.

Required:

1. What is the definition of a process? Identify the common objective for the procurement process. Repeat for each subprocess.
2. Now, suppose that Honley decides to attack the root cause of the non-value-added activities of the bill-paying process by improving the skills of its purchasing and receiving clerks. As a result, the number of discrepancies found drops by 30 percent. Discuss the potential effect this initiative might have on the bill-paying process. Does this initiative represent process improvement or process innovation? Explain.

12-6 PROCESS IMPROVEMENT/INNOVATION

LO2, LO5   Refer to **Exercise 12-5**. Suppose that Honley attacks the root cause of the non-value-added activities by establishing a totally different approach to procurement called electronic data interchange (EDI). EDI gives suppliers access to Honley's online database that reveals Honley's production schedule. By knowing Honley's production schedule, suppliers can deliver the parts and supplies needed just in time for their use. When the parts are shipped, an electronic message is sent from the supplier to Honley that the shipment is en route. When the order arrives, a bar code is scanned with an electronic wand initiating payment for the goods. EDI involves no paper—no purchase orders—no receiving orders—and no invoices.

Required:

Discuss the potential effects of this solution on Honley's bill-paying process. Is this process innovation or process improvement? Explain.

12-7 VALUE- AND NON-VALUE-ADDED COSTS, UNUSED CAPACITY

LO2, LO3   For Situations 1 through 6, provide the following information:

a. An estimate of the non-value-added cost caused by each activity.
b. The root causes of the activity cost (such as plant layout, process design, and product design).
c. The appropriate cost reduction measure: activity elimination, activity reduction, activity sharing, or activity selection.

1. It takes 45 minutes and six pounds of material to produce a product using a traditional manufacturing process. A process reengineering study provided a new manufacturing process design (using existing technology) that would take 15 minutes and four pounds of material. The cost per labor hour is $12, and the cost per pound of material is $8.
2. With its original design, a product requires 15 hours of setup time. Redesigning the product could reduce the setup time to an absolute minimum of 30 minutes. The cost per hour of setup time is $200.
3. A product currently requires eight moves. By redesigning the manufacturing layout, the number of moves can be reduced from eight to zero. The cost per move is $10.
4. Inspection time for a plant is 8,000 hours per year. The cost of inspection consists of salaries of four inspectors, totaling $120,000. Inspection also uses supplies costing $2 per inspection hour. A supplier evaluation program, product redesign, and process redesign reduced the need for inspection by creating a zero-defect environment.
5. Each unit of a product requires five components. The average number of components is 5.3 due to component failure, requiring rework and extra components.

By developing relations with the right suppliers and increasing the quality of the purchased component, the average number of components can be reduced to five components per unit. The cost per component is $600.

6. A plant produces 100 different electronic products. Each product requires an average of eight components that are purchased externally. The components are different for each part. By redesigning the products, it is possible to produce the 100 products so that they all have four components in common. This will reduce the demand for purchasing, receiving, and paying bills. Estimated savings from the reduced demand are $900,000 per year.

12-8 CALCULATION OF VALUE- AND NON-VALUE-ADDED COSTS, ACTIVITY VOLUME AND UNUSED CAPACITY VARIANCES

LO2, LO3, LO4

Calculo produces a variety of pocket PCs. Due to competitive pressures, the company is implementing an activity-based management (ABM) system with the objective of reducing costs. ABM focuses attention on processes and activities. Inspecting incoming goods was among the processes (activities) that were carefully studied. The study revealed that the number of inspection hours was a good driver for inspecting goods. During the last year, the company incurred fixed inspection costs of $400,000 (salaries of 10 employees). The fixed costs provide a capacity of 20,000 hours (2,000 per employee at practical capacity). Management decided that inspecting incoming goods is a non-value-added activity. The number of actual inspection hours used in the most recent period was 18,000.

Required:

1. Calculate the volume and unused capacity variances for inspecting. Explain what each variance means.
2. Prepare a report that presents value-added, non-value-added, and actual costs for inspecting. Explain why highlighting the non-value-added costs is important.
3. Explain why inspecting should be viewed as a non-value-added activity. In providing your explanation, consider the following counterargument: "Inspecting incoming goods adds value because it reduces the demand for other unnecessary activities such as rework, reordering, and warranty work."
4. Assume that management is able to reduce the demand for the inspecting activity so that the actual hours needed drop from 18,000 to 9,000. What actions should now be taken regarding activity capacity management?

12-9 COST REPORT, VALUE-ADDED AND NON-VALUE-ADDED COSTS

LO2, LO3

Zurcher Company has developed value-added standards for four activities: purchasing parts, receiving parts, moving parts, and setting up equipment. The activities, the activity drivers, the standard and actual quantities, and the price standards for 2006 are as follows:

Activities	Activity Driver	SQ	AQ	SP
Purchasing parts	Purchase orders	1,000	1,400	$150
Receiving parts	Receiving orders	2,000	3,000	100
Moving parts	Number of moves	0	1,000	200
Setting up equipment	Setup hours	0	4,000	60

The actual prices paid per unit of each activity driver were equal to the standard prices.

Required:

1. Prepare a cost report that lists the value-added, non-value-added, and actual costs for each activity.
2. Which activities are non-value-added? Explain why. Also, explain why value-added activities can have non-value-added costs.

12-10   TREND REPORT, NON-VALUE-ADDED COSTS

LO2, LO3   Refer to **Exercise 12-9**. Suppose that for 2007, Zurcher Company has chosen suppliers that provide higher-quality parts and redesigned its plant layout to reduce material movement. Additionally, Zurcher implemented a new setup procedure and provided training for its purchasing agents. As a consequence, less setup time is required and fewer purchasing mistakes are made. At the end of 2007, the following information is provided:

Activities	Activity Driver	SQ	AQ	SP
Purchasing parts	Purchase orders	1,000	1,200	$150
Receiving parts	Receiving orders	2,000	2,400	100
Moving parts	Number of moves	0	400	200
Setting up equipment	Setup hours	0	1,000	60

Required:

1. Prepare a report that compares the non-value-added costs for 2007 with those of 2006.
2. What is the role of activity reduction for non-value-added activities? For value-added activities?
3. Comment on the value of a trend report.

12-11   IMPLEMENTATION OF ACTIVITY-BASED MANAGEMENT

LO4   Jane Erickson, manager of an electronics division, was not pleased with the results that had recently been reported concerning the division's activity-based management implementation project. For one thing, the project had taken eight months longer than projected and had exceeded the budget by nearly 35 percent. But even more vexatious was the fact that after all was said and done, about three-fourths of the plants were reporting that the activity-based product costs were not much different for most of the products than those of the old costing system. Plant managers were indicating that they were continuing to use the old costs as they were easier to compute and understand. Yet, at the same time, they were complaining that they were having a hard time meeting the bids of competitors. Reliable sources were also revealing that the division's product costs were higher than many competitors'. This outcome perplexed plant managers because their control system still continued to report favorable materials and labor efficiency variances. They complained that ABM had failed to produce any significant improvement in cost performance.

Jane decided to tour several of the plants and talk with the plant managers. After the tour, she realized that her managers did not understand the concept of non-value-added costs nor did they have a good grasp of the concept of kaizen costing. No efforts were being made to carefully consider the activity information that had been produced. One typical plant manager threw up his hands and said: "This is too much data. Why should I care about all this detail? I do not see how this can help me improve my plant's performance. They tell me that inspection is not a necessary activity and does not add value. I simply can't believe that inspecting isn't value-added and necessary. If we did not inspect, we would be making and sending more bad products to customers."

Required:

Explain why Jane's division is having problems with its ABM implementation.

12-12   FINANCIAL-BASED VERSUS ACTIVITY-BASED RESPONSIBILITY ACCOUNTING

LO5   For each of the following situations, two scenarios are described, labeled A and B. Choose which scenario is descriptive of a setting corresponding to activity-based responsibility accounting and which is descriptive of financial-based responsibility accounting. Provide a brief commentary on the differences between the two systems for each situation, addressing the possible advantages of the activity-based view over the financial-based view.

Situation 1

A: The purchasing manager, receiving manager, and accounts payable manager are given joint responsibility for procurement. The charges given to the group of managers are to reduce costs of acquiring materials, decrease the time required to obtain materials from outside suppliers, and reduce the number of purchasing mistakes (e.g., wrong type of materials or the wrong quantities ordered).

B: The plant manager commended the manager of the grinding department for increasing his department's machine utilization rates—and doing so without exceeding the department's budget. The plant manager then asked other department managers to make an effort to obtain similar efficiency improvements.

Situation 2

A: Delivery mistakes had been reduced by 70 percent, saving over $40,000 per year. Furthermore, delivery time to customers had been cut by two days. According to company policy, the team responsible for the savings was given a bonus equal to 25 percent of the savings attributable to improving delivery quality. Company policy also provided a salary increase of 1 percent for every day saved in delivery time.

B: Bill Johnson, manager of the product development department, was pleased with his department's performance on the last quarter's projects. They had managed to complete all projects under budget, virtually assuring Bill of a fat bonus, just in time to help with this year's Christmas purchases.

Situation 3

A: "Harvey, don't worry about the fact that your department is producing at only 70 percent capacity. Increasing your output would simply pile up inventory in front of the next production department. That would be costly for the organization as a whole. Sometimes, one department must reduce its performance so that the performance of the entire organization can improve."

B: "Susan, I am concerned about the fact that your department's performance measures have really dropped over the past quarter. Labor usage variances are unfavorable, and I also see that your machine utilization rates are down. Now, I know you are not a bottleneck department, but I get a lot of flack when my managers' efficiency ratings drop."

Situation 4

A: Colby was muttering to himself. He had just received last quarter's budgetary performance report. Once again, he had managed to spend more than budgeted for both materials and labor. The real question now was how to improve his performance for the next quarter.

B: Great! Cycle time had been reduced and, at the same time, the number of defective products had been cut by 35 percent. Cutting the number of defects reduced production costs by more than planned. Trends were favorable for all three performance measures.

Situation 5

A: Cambry was furious. An across-the-board budget cut! "How can they expect me to provide the computer services required on less money? Management is convinced that costs are out of control, but I would like to know where—at least in my department!"

B: After a careful study of the accounts payable department, it was discovered that 80 percent of an accounts payable clerk's time was spent resolving discrepancies between the purchase order, receiving document, and the supplier's invoice. Other activities such as recording and preparing checks consumed only 20 percent of a clerk's time. A redesign of the procurement process eliminated virtually all discrepancies and produced significant cost savings.

Situation 6

A: Five years ago, the management of Breeann Products commissioned an outside engineering consulting firm to conduct a time-and-motion study so that labor efficiency standards could be developed and used in production. These labor efficiency standards are still in use today and are viewed by management as an important indicator of productive efficiency.

B: Janet was quite satisfied with this quarter's labor performance. When compared with the same quarter of last year, labor productivity had increased by 23 percent. Most of the increase was due to a new assembly approach suggested by production line workers. She was also pleased to see that materials productivity had increased. The increase in materials productivity was attributed to reducing scrap because of improved quality.

Situation 7

A: "The system converts materials into products, not people at work stations. Therefore, process efficiency is more important than labor efficiency—but we also must pay particular attention to those who use the products we produce, whether inside or outside the firm."

B: "I was quite happy to see a revenue increase of 15 percent over last year, especially when the budget called for a 10 percent increase. However, after reading the recent copy of our trade journal, I now wonder whether we are doing so well. I found out that the market expanded by 30 percent, and our leading competitor increased its sales by 40 percent."

PROBLEMS

12-13   ABM Implementation, Activity Analysis, Activity Drivers, Driver Analysis, Behavioral Effects

LO1, LO2, LO4   Joseph Fox, controller of Thorpe Company, has been in charge of a project to install an activity-based cost management system. This new system is designed to support the company's efforts to become more competitive. For the past six weeks, he and the project committee members have been identifying and defining activities, associating workers with activities, and assessing the time and resources consumed by individual activities. Now, he and the project committee are focusing on three additional implementation issues: (1) identifying activity drivers, (2) assessing value content, and (3) identifying cost drivers (root causes). Joseph has assigned a committee member the responsibilities of assessing the value content of five activities, choosing a suitable activity driver for each activity, and identifying the possible root causes of the activities. Following are the five activities with possible activity drivers:

Activity	Possible Activity Drivers
Setting up equipment	Setup time, number of setups
Performing warranty work	Warranty hours, number of defective units
Welding subassemblies	Welding hours, subassemblies welded
Moving materials	Number of moves, distance moved
Inspecting components	Hours of inspection, number of defective components

The committee member ran a regression analysis for each potential activity driver, using the method of least squares to estimate the variable and fixed cost components. In all five cases, costs were highly correlated with the potential drivers. Thus, all drivers appeared to be good candidates for assigning costs to products. The company plans to reward production managers for reducing product costs.

Required:

1. What is the difference between an activity driver and a cost driver? In answering the question, describe the purpose of each type of driver.
2. For each activity, assess the value content and classify each activity as value-added or non-value-added (justify the classification). Identify some possible root causes of each activity, and describe how this knowledge can be used to improve activity performance. For purposes of discussion, assume that the value-added activities are not performed with perfect efficiency.
3. Describe the behavior that each activity driver will encourage, and evaluate the suitability of that behavior for the company's objective of becoming more competitive.

12-14   ABM, KAIZEN COSTING

LO2, LO3, LO5   Daspart, Inc. supplies carburetors for a large automobile manufacturing company. The auto company has recently requested that Daspart decrease its delivery time. Daspart made a commitment to reduce the lead time for delivery from eight days to two days. To help achieve this goal, engineering and production workers had made the commitment to reduce time for the setup activity (other activities such as moving materials and rework were also being examined simultaneously). Current setup times were 12 hours. Setup cost was $300 per setup hour. For the first quarter, engineering developed a new process design that it believed would reduce the setup time from 12 hours to eight hours. After implementing the design, the actual setup time dropped from 12 hours to nine hours. In the second quarter, production workers suggested a new setup procedure. Engineering gave the suggestion a positive evaluation, and they projected that the new approach would save an additional five hours of setup time. Setup labor was trained to perform the new setup procedures. The actual reduction in setup time based on the suggested changes was six hours.

Required:

1. What kaizen setup standard would be used at the beginning of each quarter?
2. Describe the kaizen subcycle using the two quarters of data provided by Daspart.
3. Describe the maintenance subcycle using the two quarters of data provided by Daspart.
4. How much non-value-added cost was eliminated by the end of two quarters? Discuss the role of kaizen costing in activity-based management.
5. Explain why kaizen costing is compatible with activity-based responsibility accounting while standard costing is compatible with financial-based responsibility accounting.

12-15   ACTIVITY FLEXIBLE BUDGETING, PERFORMANCE REPORT, VOLUME VARIANCE

LO3   Innovator, Inc., wants to develop an activity flexible budget for the activity of moving materials. Innovator uses eight forklifts to move materials from receiving to stores. The forklifts are also used to move materials from stores to the production area. The forklifts are obtained through an operating lease that costs $12,000 per year per forklift. Innovator employs 25 forklift operators who receive an average salary of $45,000 per year, including benefits. Each move requires the use of a crate. The crates are used to store the parts and are emptied only when used in production. Crates are disposed of after one cycle (two moves), where a cycle is defined as a move from receiving to stores to production. Each crate costs $1.20. Fuel for a forklift costs $1.80 per gallon. A gallon of gas is used every 20 moves. Forklifts can make three moves per hour and are available for 280 days per year, 24 hours per day (the remaining time is downtime for various reasons). Each operator works 40 hours per week and 50 weeks per year.

Required:

1. Prepare a flexible budget for the activity of moving materials, using the number of cycles as the activity driver.
2. Calculate the activity capacity for moving materials. Suppose Innovator works 90 percent of activity capacity and incurs the following costs:

Salaries	$1,170,000
Leases	96,000
Crates	91,200
Fuel	14,450

   Prepare the budget for the 90 percent level and then prepare a performance report for the moving materials activity.
3. Calculate and interpret the volume variance for moving materials.
4. Suppose that a redesign of the plant layout reduces the demand for moving materials to one-third of the original capacity. What would be the budget formula for this new activity level? What is the budgeted cost for this new activity level? Has activity performance improved? How does this activity performance evaluation differ from that described in Requirement 2? Explain.

12-16   ACTIVITY-BASED MANAGEMENT, NON-VALUE-ADDED COSTS, TARGET COSTS, KAIZEN COSTING

LO2, LO3   Jerry Goff, president of Harmony Electronics, was concerned about the end-of-the-year marketing report that she had just received. According to Emily Hagood, marketing manager, a price decrease for the coming year was again needed to maintain the company's annual sales volume of integrated circuit boards (CBs). This would make a bad situation worse. The current selling price of $18 per unit was producing a $2-per-unit profit—half the customary $4-per-unit profit. Foreign competitors keep reducing their prices. To match the latest reduction would reduce the price from $18 to $14. This would put the price below the cost to produce and sell it. How could the foreign firms sell for such a low price? Determined to find out if there were problems with the company's operations, Jerry decided to hire Jan Booth, a well-known consultant who specializes in methods of continuous improvement. Jan indicated that she felt that an activity-based management system needed to be implemented. After three weeks, Jan had identified the following activities and costs:

Batch-level activities:	
Setting up equipment	$ 125,000
Materials handling	180,000
Inspecting products	122,000
Product-sustaining activities:	
Engineering support	120,000
Handling customer complaints	100,000
Filling warranties	170,000
Storing goods	80,000
Expediting goods	75,000
Unit-level activities:	
Using materials	500,000
Using power	48,000
Manual insertion labor[a]	250,000
Other direct labor	150,000
Total costs	$1,920,000[b]

[a]Diodes, resistors, and integrated circuits are inserted manually into the circuit board.
[b]This total cost produces a unit cost of $16 for last year's sales volume.

Jan indicated that some preliminary activity analysis shows that per-unit costs can be reduced by at least $7. Since Emily had indicated that the market share (sales volume) for the boards could be increased by 50 percent if the price could be reduced to $12, Jerry became quite excited.

Required:

1. What is activity-based management? What connection does it have to continuous improvement?
2. Identify as many non-value-added costs as possible. Compute the cost savings per unit that would be realized if these costs were eliminated. Was Jan correct in her preliminary cost reduction assessment? Discuss actions that the company can take to reduce or eliminate the non-value-added activities.
3. Compute the target cost required to maintain current market share, while earning a profit of $4 per unit. Now, compute the target cost required to expand sales by 50 percent. How much cost reduction would be required to achieve each target?
4. Assume that Jan suggested that kaizen costing be used to help reduce costs. The first suggested kaizen initiative is described by the following: switching to automated insertion would save $60,000 of engineering support and $90,000 of direct labor. Now, what is the total potential cost reduction per unit available? With these additional reductions, can Harmony achieve the target cost to maintain current sales? To increase it by 50 percent? What form of activity analysis is this kaizen initiative: reduction, sharing, elimination, or selection?
5. Calculate income based on current sales, prices, and costs. Now, calculate the income using a $14 price and a $12 price, assuming that the maximum cost reduction possible is achieved (including Requirement 4's kaizen reduction). What price should be selected?

12-17   VALUE-ADDED AND KAIZEN STANDARDS, NON-VALUE-ADDED COSTS, VOLUME VARIANCE, UNUSED CAPACITY

LO3   Tom Young, vice president of Dunn Company (a producer of plastic products), has been supervising the implementation of an activity-based cost management system. One of Tom's objectives is to improve process efficiency by improving the activities that define the processes. To illustrate the potential of the new system to the president, Tom has decided to focus on two processes: production and customer service.

Within each process, one activity will be selected for improvement: molding for production and sustaining engineering for customer service. (Sustaining engineers are responsible for redesigning products based on customer needs and feedback.) Value-added standards are identified for each activity. For molding, the value-added standard calls for nine pounds per mold. (Although the products differ in shape and function, their size, as measured by weight, is uniform.) The value-added standard is based on the elimination of all waste due to defective molds (materials is by far the major cost for the molding activity). The standard price for molding is $15 per pound. For sustaining engineering, the standard is 60 percent of current practical activity capacity. This standard is based on the fact that about 40 percent of the complaints have to do with design features that could have been avoided or anticipated by the company.

Current practical capacity (at the end of 2006) is defined by the following requirements: 18,000 engineering hours for each product group that has been on the market or in development for five years or less, and 7,200 hours per product group of more than five years. Four product groups have less than five years' experience, and 10 product groups have more. There are 72 engineers, each paid a salary of $70,000. Each engineer can provide 2,000 hours of service per year. There are no other significant costs for the engineering activity.

For 2006, actual pounds used for molding were 25 percent above the level called for by the value-added standard; engineering usage was 138,000 hours. There were 240,000 units of output produced. Tom and the operational managers have selected some improvement measures that promise to reduce non-value-added activity usage by 30 percent in 2007. Selected actual results achieved for 2007 are as follows:

Units produced	240,000
Pounds of material	2,600,000
Engineering hours	126,200

The actual prices paid per pound and per engineering hour are identical to the standard or budgeted prices.

Required:

1. For 2006, calculate the non-value-added usage and costs for molding and sustaining engineering. Also, calculate the cost of unused capacity for the engineering activity.
2. Using the targeted reduction, establish kaizen standards for molding and engineering (for 2007).
3. Using the kaizen standards prepared in Requirement 2, compute the 2007 usage variances, expressed in both physical and financial measures, for molding and engineering. (For engineering, explain why it is necessary to compare actual resource usage with the kaizen standard.) Comment on the company's ability to achieve its targeted reductions. In particular, discuss what measures the company must take to capture any realized reductions in resource usage.

12-18 BENCHMARKING AND NON-VALUE-ADDED COSTS, TARGET COSTING

LO2, LO3

Karebien, Inc., has two plants that manufacture a line of hospital beds. One is located in St. Louis and the other in Oklahoma City. Each plant is set up as a profit center. During the past year, both plants sold the regular model for $810. Sales volume averages 20,000 units per year in each plant. Recently, the St. Louis plant reduced the price of the regular model to $720. Discussion with the St. Louis manager revealed that the price reduction was possible because the plant had reduced its manufacturing and selling costs by reducing what was called "non-value-added costs." The St. Louis plant's manufacturing and selling costs for the regular model were $630 per unit. The St. Louis manager offered to loan the Oklahoma City plant his cost accounting manager to help it achieve similar results. The Oklahoma City plant manager readily agreed, knowing that his plant must keep pace—not only with the St. Louis plant but also with competitors. A local competitor had also reduced its price on a similar model, and Oklahoma City's marketing manager had indicated that the price must be matched or sales would drop dramatically. In fact, the marketing manager suggested that if the price were dropped to $702 by the end of the year, the plant could expand its share of the market by 20 percent. The plant manager agreed but insisted that the current profit per unit must be maintained. He also wants to know if the plant can at least match the $630-per-unit cost of the St. Louis plant and if the plant can achieve the cost reduction using the approach of the St. Louis plant.

The plant controller and the St. Louis cost accounting manager have assembled the following data for the most recent year. The actual cost of inputs, their value-added (ideal) quantity levels, and the actual quantity levels are provided (for production of 20,000 units). Assume there is no difference between actual prices of activity units and standard prices.

	SQ	AQ	Actual Cost
Materials (lbs.)	427,500	450,000	$ 9,450,000
Labor (hrs.)	102,600	108,000	1,350,000
Setups (hrs.)	—	7,200	540,000
Materials handling (moves)	—	18,000	1,260,000
Warranties (no. repaired)	—	18,000	1,800,000
Total			$14,400,000

Required:

1. Calculate the target cost for expanding the Oklahoma City market share by 20 percent, assuming that the per-unit profitability is maintained as requested by the plant manager.
2. Calculate the non-value-added cost per unit. Assuming that non-value-added costs can be reduced to zero, can the Oklahoma City plant match the St. Louis plant's per-unit cost? Can the target cost for expanding market share be achieved? What actions would you take if you were the plant manager?
3. Describe the role benchmarking played in the effort of the Oklahoma City plant to protect and improve its competitive position.

12-19   FINANCIAL VERSUS ACTIVITY FLEXIBLE BUDGETING

LO2, LO3, LO5   Kelly Gray, production manager, was upset with the latest performance report, which indicated that she was $100,000 over budget. Given the efforts that she and her workers had made, she was confident that they had met or beat the budget. Now, she was not only upset but also genuinely puzzled over the results. Three items—direct labor, power, and setups—were over budget. The actual costs for these three items follow:

Actual Costs	
Direct labor	$210,000
Power	135,000
Setups	140,000
Total	$485,000

Kelly knew that her operation had produced more units than originally had been budgeted, so more power and labor had naturally been used. She also knew that the uncertainty in scheduling had led to more setups than planned. When she pointed this out to John Huang, the controller, he assured her that the budgeted costs had been adjusted for the increase in productive activity. Curious, Kelly questioned John about the methods used to make the adjustment.

JOHN: If the actual level of activity differs from the original planned level, we adjust the budget by using budget formulas—formulas that allow us to predict what the costs will be for different levels of activity.

KELLY: The approach sounds reasonable. However, I'm sure something is wrong here. Tell me exactly how you adjusted the costs of labor, power, and setups.

JOHN: First, we obtain formulas for the individual items in the budget by using the method of least squares. We assume that cost variations can be explained by variations in productive activity where activity is measured by direct labor hours. Here is a list of the cost formulas for the three items you mentioned. The variable X is the number of direct labor hours:

$$\text{Labor cost} = \$10X$$
$$\text{Power cost} = \$5,000 + \$4X$$
$$\text{Setup cost} = \$100,000$$

KELLY: I think I see the problem. Power costs don't have a lot to do with direct labor hours. They have more to do with machine hours. As production increases, machine hours increase more rapidly than direct labor hours. Also, . . .

JOHN: You know, you have a point. The coefficient of determination for power cost is only about 50 percent. That leaves a lot of unexplained cost variation. The coefficient for labor, however, is much better—it explains about 96 percent of the cost variation. Setup costs, of course, are fixed.

KELLY: Well, as I was about to say, setup costs also have very little to do with direct labor hours. And I might add that they certainly are not fixed—at least not all of them. We had to do more setups than our original plan called for because of the scheduling changes. And we have to pay our people when they work extra hours. It seems as if we are always paying overtime. I wonder if we simply do not have enough people for the setup activity. Supplies are used for each setup, and these are not cheap. Did you build these extra costs of increased setup activity into your budget?

JOHN: No, we assumed that setup costs were fixed. I see now that some of them could vary as the number of setups increases. Kelly, let me see if I can develop some cost formulas based on better explanatory variables. I'll get back with you in a few days.

Assume that after a few days' work, John developed the following cost formulas, all with a coefficient of determination greater than 90 percent:

$$\text{Labor cost} = \$10X, \text{ where } X = \text{Direct labor hours}$$
$$\text{Power cost} = \$68,000 + 0.9Y, \text{ where } Y = \text{Machine hours}$$
$$\text{Setup cost} = \$98,000 + \$400Z, \text{ where } Z = \text{Number of setups}$$

The actual measures of each of the activity drivers are as follows:

Direct labor hours	20,000
Machine hours	90,000
Number of setups	110

Required:

1. Prepare a performance report for direct labor, power, and setups using the direct-labor-based formulas.

2. Prepare a performance report for direct labor, power, and setups using the multiple cost driver formulas that John developed.
3. Of the two approaches, which provides the most accurate picture of Kelly's performance? Why?
4. After reviewing the approach to performance measurement, a consultant remarked that non-value-added cost trend reports would be a much better performance measurement approach than comparing actual costs with budgeted costs—even if activity flexible budgets were used. Do you agree or disagree? Explain.

12-20 ACTIVITY FLEXIBLE BUDGETING, NON-VALUE-ADDED COSTS

LO2, LO3, LO5   Douglas Davis, controller for Marston, Inc., prepared the following budget for manufacturing costs at two different levels of activity for 2007:

	Level of Activity	
Driver: Direct Labor Hours	*50,000*	*100,000*
Direct materials	$ 300,000	$ 600,000
Direct labor	200,000	400,000
Depreciation (plant)	100,000	100,000
Subtotal	$ 600,000	$1,100,000
Driver: Machine Hours	*200,000*	*300,000*
Maintaining equipment	$ 360,000	$ 510,000
Machining	112,000	162,000
Subtotal	$ 472,000	$ 672,000
Driver: Material Moves	*20,000*	*40,000*
Moving materials	$ 165,000	$ 290,000
Driver: Number of Batches Inspected	*100*	*200*
Inspecting products	$ 125,000	$ 225,000
Total	$1,362,000	$2,287,000

During 2007, Marston worked a total of 80,000 direct labor hours, used 250,000 machine hours, made 32,000 moves, and performed 120 batch inspections. The following actual costs were incurred:

Direct materials	$440,000
Direct labor	355,000
Depreciation	100,000
Maintaining equipment	425,000
Machining	142,000
Moving materials	232,500
Inspecting products	160,000

Marston applies overhead using rates based on direct labor hours, machine hours, number of moves, and number of batches. The second level of activity (the right column in the preceding table) is the practical level of activity (the available activity for resources acquired in advance of usage) and is used to compute predetermined overhead pool rates.

Required:

1. Prepare a performance report for Marston's manufacturing costs in 2007.
2. Assume that one of the products produced by Marston is budgeted to use 10,000 direct labor hours, 15,000 machine hours, and 500 moves and will be

produced in five batches. A total of 10,000 units will be produced during the year. Calculate the budgeted unit manufacturing cost.

3. One of Marston's managers said the following: "Budgeting at the activity level makes a lot of sense. It really helps us manage costs better. But the previous budget really needs to provide more detailed information. For example, I know that the moving materials activity involves the use of forklifts and operators, and this information is lost when only the total cost of the activity for various levels of output is reported. We have four forklifts, each capable of providing 10,000 moves per year. We lease these forklifts for five years, at $10,000 per year. Furthermore, for our two shifts, we need up to eight operators if we run all four forklifts. Each operator is paid a salary of $30,000 per year. Also, I know that fuel costs about $0.25 per move."

   Assuming that these are the only three items, expand the detail of the flexible budget for moving materials to reveal the cost of these three resource items for 20,000 moves and 40,000 moves, respectively. Based on these comments, explain how this additional information can help Marston better manage its costs. (Especially consider how activity-based budgeting may provide useful information for non-value-added activities.)

12-21   COLLABORATIVE LEARNING EXERCISE

LO5   Howard Johnson, plant manager, was given the charge to produce 120,000 bolts used in the manufacture of small twin engine aircraft. Directed by his divisional manager to give the bolt production priority over other jobs, he had two weeks to produce the units. Meeting the delivery date was crucial for renewal of a major contract with a large airplane manufacturer. Each bolt requires 20 minutes of direct labor and five ounces of metal. After producing a batch of bolts, each bolt is subjected to a stress test. Those that pass are placed in a carton, which is stamped "Inspected by inspector no. ____" (the inspector's identification number is inserted). Defective units are discarded, having no salvage value. Because of the nature of the process, rework is not possible.

At the end of the first week, the plant had produced 60,000 acceptable units and used 24,000 direct labor hours, 4,000 hours more than the standard allowed. Furthermore, a total of 65,000 bolts had been produced and 5,000 had been rejected, creating an unfavorable materials usage variance of 25,000 ounces. Howard knew that a performance report would be prepared when the 120,000 bolts were completed. This report would compare the labor and materials used with that allowed. Any variance in excess of 5 percent of standard would be investigated. Howard expected the same or worse performance for the coming week and was worried about a poor performance rating for himself. Accordingly, at the beginning of the second week, Howard moved his inspectors to the production line (all inspectors had production experience). However, for reporting purposes, the production hours provided by inspectors would not be counted as part of direct labor. They would still appear as a separate budget item on the performance report. Additionally, Howard instructed the inspectors to pack the completed bolts in the cartons and stamp them as inspected. One inspector objected; Howard reassigned the inspector temporarily to materials handling and gave an inspection stamp with a fabricated identification number to a line worker who was willing to stamp the cartons of bolts as inspected.

Required:

Form groups of six and divide these groups into three categories: A, B, and C. Groups of Category A will solve Requirement 1, groups of Category B will solve Requirement 2, and groups of Category C will solve Requirement 3. After preparing an answer to each requirement, new groups will be formed made up of two members from A, two members from B, and two members from C. Members of A will share their answer to Requirement 1 with the other group members, followed by B members sharing their answer with other group members, and finally, C members will share their answer with the other group members. (*Note:* The structure may be adapted to class size—the critical idea is to have three types of groups who solve each part and then come together to share with each other the answers to the other requirements.)

1. Explain why Howard stopped inspections on the bolts and reassigned inspectors to production and materials handling. Discuss the ethical ramifications of this decision.
2. What features in the financial-based responsibility accounting system provided the incentive(s) for Howard to take the actions described? Would an activity-based responsibility accounting system have provided incentives that discourage this kind of behavior? Explain.
3. What likely effect would Howard's actions have on the quality of the bolts? Was the decision justified by the need to obtain renewal of the contract, particularly if the plant returns to a normal inspection routine after the rush order is completed? Do you have any suggestions about the quality approach taken by this company? Explain why activity-based responsibility accounting might play a useful role in this setting.

12-22 CYBER RESEARCH CASE

LO1, LO2, LO3 The objective of benchmarking is to improve performance by identifying, understanding, and adopting outstanding best practices from others. If this process is carried out inside the organization, then it is called internal benchmarking. It is not uncommon for one facility within an organization to have better practices than another. Unfortunately, it is unusual for these better practices to naturally spread throughout the organization. The American Productivity & Quality Center (APQC) has conducted a study to understand what prevents the transfer of practices within a company. It also has made some recommendations concerning internal benchmarking.

Required:

Access http://www.apqc.org and/or other Internet resources to see if you can answer the following:

1. Why is internal benchmarking an attractive option for an organization?
2. Why do companies want to engage in internal benchmarking?
3. What are some of the organizational obstacles relating to internal benchmarking?
4. Identify some recommendations that will make internal transfers of best practices more effective.
5. Internal benchmarking is a prominent example of what is called knowledge management or knowledge sharing. Use the APQC site and other Internet resources to define knowledge management (or knowledge sharing). Now, go to KnowledgeLeader and Internal Audit and Risk Management Community (http://www. knowledgeleader.com), and describe its external knowledge sharing service. (Alternatively, you may also wish to access and describe Ernst & Young's knowledge sharing service called "Ernie.")

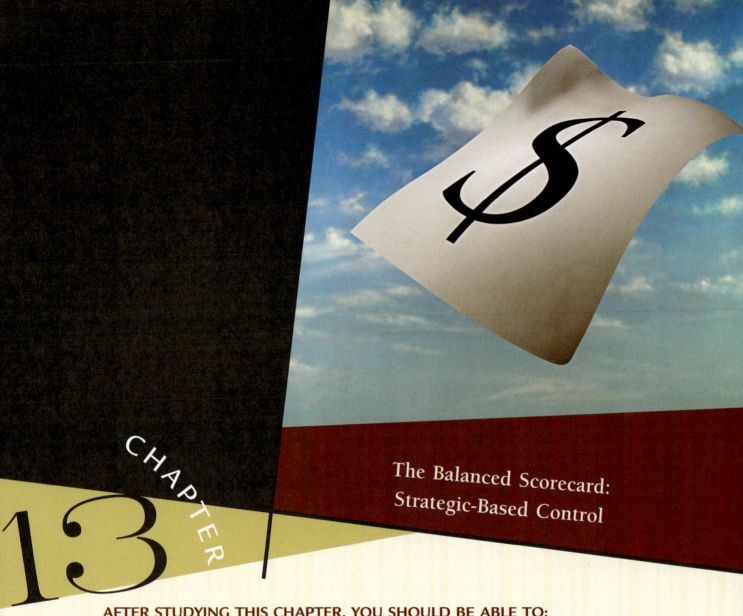

The Balanced Scorecard: Strategic-Based Control

AFTER STUDYING THIS CHAPTER, YOU SHOULD BE ABLE TO:

1. Compare and contrast activity-based and strategic-based responsibility accounting systems.

2. Discuss the basic features of the Balanced Score-card.

3. Explain how the Balanced Scorecard links measures to strategy.

4. Describe how an organization can achieve strategic alignment.

Many firms operate in an environment where change is rapid. Products and processes are constantly being redesigned and improved, and stiff national and international competitors are always present. The competitive environment demands that firms offer customized products and services to diverse customer segments. This, in turn, means that firms must find cost efficient ways of producing high-variety, low-volume products. This usually means that more attention is paid to linkages between the firm and its suppliers and customers with the goal of improving cost, quality, and response times for all parties in the value chain. Furthermore, for many industries, product life cycles are shrinking, placing greater demands on the need for innovation. Thus, organizations operating in a dynamic, rapidly changing environment are finding that adaptation and change are essential to survival. In Chapter 4, we learned that activity-based management describes the fundamental economics that drive a firm and thus allows managers to have a better understanding of the causes of cost. In turn, understanding the root causes of costs enables managers to more effectively improve performance by continuously improving processes.

Activity-based management also produced a new form of responsibility accounting, one that better fit environments that demand continuous improvement because of keen competitive conditions and dynamic change. Recall that the responsibility accounting model is defined by four essential elements: (1) assigning responsibility, (2) establishing performance measures or benchmarks, (3) evaluating performance, and (4) assigning rewards. The traditional or financial-based responsibility accounting model emphasizes financial performance of organizational units and evaluates and rewards performance using static financial-oriented standards (e.g., budgets and standard costing). While this model is useful for firms operating in a stable environment that wish to emphasize maintaining the status quo, it is certainly not suitable for firms operating in a dynamic environment that requires continuous improvement. For this reason, activity-based responsibility accounting was developed. (Chapter 12 detailed the differences between the two models.) However, while the activity-based responsibility accounting model was a significant improvement, it soon became apparent that it suffered from some limitations. This then led to the development of *strategic-based responsibility accounting*, the topic of this chapter.

Activity-Based versus Strategic-Based Responsibility Accounting

OBJECTIVE 1

Compare and contrast activity-based and strategic-based responsibility accounting systems.

Activity-based responsibility accounting represents a significant change in how responsibility is assigned, measured, and evaluated. Effectively, the activity-based system added a process perspective to the financial perspective of the functional-based responsibility accounting system. Processes represent how things are done within an organization; therefore, any effort to improve organizational performance had to involve improving processes. It also altered the financial perspective by changing the point of view from that of cost control to maintain the status quo to that of cost reduction by continuous learning and change. Thus, responsibility accounting changed from a one-dimensional system to a two-dimensional system, and from a control system to a *performance management system*. Although these changes were dramatic and in the right direction, it was soon discovered that the new approach also had some limitations. The most significant shortcoming was the fact that the continuous improvement efforts were often fragmented, and they failed to connect with an organization's overall mission and strategy. Lacking was a navigational system, and the result was undirected and rudderless continuous improvement. Consequently, at times, the expected competitive successes did not materialize.

What was needed was *directed continuous improvement*. Providing direction meant that managers needed to carefully specify a mission and strategy for their organization and identify the objectives, performance measures, and initiatives necessary to accomplish this overall mission and strategy. In other words, a *strategic-based responsibility accounting system* was the next step in the evolution of responsibility accounting. A **strategic-based responsibility accounting system (strategic-based performance management system)** translates the strategy of an organization into operational objectives and measures. A strategic performance management system can assume different forms, the most common being that of the Balanced Scorecard. The **Balanced Scorecard** is a strategic-based performance management system that typically identifies objectives and measures for four different perspectives: the financial perspective, the customer perspective, the process perspective, and the learning and growth perspective.[1]

---

1. Robert S. Kaplan and David P. Norton, *The Balanced Scorecard* (Boston: Harvard Business School Press, 1996).

The Balanced Scorecard converts a company's strategy into executable actions that are deployed throughout the organization. The Balanced Scorecard approach has spread rapidly in the United States. One study estimated that about 40 percent of the *Fortune 1000* companies had implemented the Balanced Scorecard by the end of 2000.[2] Because of its widespread use and popularity, we will focus our discussion of performance management on the Balanced Scorecard. A general overview of the Balanced Scorecard will first be provided by comparing the specific responsibility elements of activity-based responsibility accounting with those of the Balanced Scorecard. In the remainder of the chapter, more specific details of the Balanced Scorecard will be provided.

Assigning Responsibility

Exhibit 13-1 reveals that the strategic-based responsibility accounting system adds direction to improvement efforts by tying responsibility to the firm's strategy. It also maintains the process and financial perspectives of the activity-based approach but adds a customer and a learning and growth (infrastructure) perspective, increasing the number of responsibility dimensions to four. Although more perspectives could be added, these four perspectives are essential for creating a competitive advantage and allowing managers to articulate and communicate the organization's mission and strategy. Only perspectives that serve as a potential source for a competitive advantage should be included (e.g., an environmental perspective). This leaves open the possibility of expanding the number of perspectives. Notice that the two additional perspectives consider the interests of customers and employees, interests that were not fully considered by the activity-based responsibility system. Another difference is that the Balanced Scorecard diffuses responsibility for the perspectives throughout the entire organization. Ideally, all individuals in the organization should understand the organization's strategy and know how their specific responsibilities support achievement of the strategy. The key to this diffusion is proper and careful definition of performance measures.

EXHIBIT 13-1	Responsibility Assignments Compared
Activity-Based Responsibility	**Strategic-Based Responsibility**
1. No tie to strategy	1. Linked to strategy
2. Systemwide efficiency	2. Systemwide efficiency
3. Team accountability	3. Team accountability
4. Financial perspective	4. Financial perspective
5. Process perspective	5. Process perspective
	6. Customer perspective
	7. Learning and growth perspective

Establishing Performance Measures

Exhibit 13-2 reveals that the strategic-based approach carries over the financial and process-oriented standards of the activity-based system, including the concepts of value-added and dynamic standards. None of the advances developed in an activity approach are thrown out, but the strategic-based approach adds some important refinements. In a strategic-based responsibility accounting system, performance measures must be integrated so that they are mutually consistent and reinforcing. In effect, performance mea-

2. Tom Sullivan, "Scorecard Eases Businesses' Balancing Act," *InfoWorld 2001* (January 8, 2001).

sures should be designed so that they are derived from and communicate an organization's strategy and objectives. By translating the organization's strategy into objectives and measures that can be understood, communicated, and acted upon, it is possible to more completely align individual and organizational goals and initiatives. Thus, the measures must be balanced and linked to the organization's strategy.

EXHIBIT 13-2	Performance Measures Compared
Activity-Based Measures	**Strategic-Based Measures**
1. Process-oriented and financial standards	1. Standards for all four perspectives
2. Value-added standards	2. Used to communicate strategy
3. Dynamic standards	3. Used to help align objectives
4. Optimal standards	4. Linked to strategy and objectives
	5. Balanced measures

For a firm to have balanced measures, it means that the measures selected are balanced between *lag measures* and *lead measures*, between *objective measures* and *subjective measures*, between *financial measures* and *nonfinancial measures*, and between *external measures* and *internal measures*. **Lag measures** are outcome measures, measures of results from past efforts (e.g., customer profitability). **Lead measures (performance drivers)** are factors that drive future performance (e.g., hours of employee training). **Objective measures** are those that can be readily quantified and verified (e.g., market share), whereas **subjective measures** are less quantifiable and more judgmental in nature (e.g., employee capabilities). **Financial measures** are those expressed in monetary terms, whereas **nonfinancial measures** use nonmonetary units (e.g., cost per unit and number of dissatisfied customers). **External measures** are those that relate to *customers* versus *shareholders* (e.g., customer satisfaction and return on investment). **Internal measures** are those measures that relate to the *processes* and *capabilities* that create value for customers and shareholders (e.g., process efficiency and employee satisfaction).

A strategic performance management system uses many different kinds of measures because of the need to build a closer link to strategy. In the traditional, financial-based responsibility model, performance measures are almost always financial and, therefore, almost always lag measures. Financial and lag measures are not sufficient to link with strategy. Many strategic objectives are nonfinancial in nature and require the use of nonfinancial measures to promote and measure progress. For example, increasing customer loyalty may be a key strategic objective that will lead to increased revenues and profits. Yet, how is customer loyalty measured? The number of repeat orders is a good possible measure, and it is a nonfinancial measure. And what are some of the drivers of customer loyalty? Increasing product quality? Increasing on-time deliveries? Or both? And how are these critical success factors measured? Percentage of defective units and percentage of on-time deliveries are good possibilities. Clearly, to express the desired linkages among strategic objectives, nonfinancial measures are needed.

The concept of lead measures is also critical. A lead measure, by definition, is one that has a causal linkage with the strategy. For example, if the number of defective units decreases, will customer loyalty actually increase? If the number of repeat orders increases, will revenues and profits actually increase? Assuming a causal relationship exists, when in reality it does not, can be quite costly. For example, **Xerox** assumed that increasing customer satisfaction would lead to increased financial performance. It then spent millions on surveying and measuring customer satisfaction only to discover that increasing customer satisfaction did not increase financial performance. As it turned out, a customer loyalty measure was the correct lead measure for improving financial performance.[3]

Finally, it should be noted that to communicate an organization's strategy through the language of measurement requires both scope and flexibility. Scope implies that both internal and external measures are needed. Flexibility requires subjective and objective measurement as well as nonfinancial measures. In effect, a Balanced Scorecard expresses the complete story of a company's strategy through an integrated set of financial and nonfinancial measures that are both predictive and historical and which may be measured subjectively or objectively.

Performance Measurement and Evaluation

In an activity-based responsibility system, performance measures are process oriented. Thus, performance evaluation focuses on improvement of process characteristics, such as time, quality, and efficiency. Financial consequences of improving processes are also measured, usually by cost reductions achieved. Therefore, a financial perspective is included. A strategic performance management system expands these evaluations to include the customer and learning and growth perspectives as well as a more comprehensive financial view. The organization must also deal with performance evaluation of things, such as customer satisfaction, customer retention, employee capabilities, and revenue growth from new customers and new products. However, the difference is more profound than simply expanding the number and type of measures being evaluated. Exhibit 13-3 summarizes the comparison of performance evaluation for the activity- and strategic-based approaches.

EXHIBIT 13-3	Performance Evaluation Compared: ABC versus Strategic-Based
Activity-Based Performance Evaluation	**Strategic-Based Performance Evaluation**
1. Time reductions	1. Time reductions
2. Quality improvements	2. Quality improvements
3. Cost reductions	3. Cost reductions
4. Trend measurements	4. Trend measurements
	5. Expanded set of metrics
	6. Stretch targets for all four perspectives

Performance evaluation in a Balanced Scorecard framework is deeply concerned with the effectiveness and viability of the organization's strategy. Furthermore, the Balanced Scorecard approach is used to drive organizational change, and much of this change emphasis is expressed through performance evaluation. This is communicated by establishing *stretch* targets for the individual performance measures of the various perspectives. Stretch targets are targets that are set at levels that, if achieved, will transform the organization within a period of three to five years. Performance for a given period is evaluated by comparing the actual values of the various measures with the targeted values. Two key features make stretch targets feasible: (1) the measures are linked by causal relationships and (2) because of the linkages, the targets are not set in isola-

---

3. Christopher Ittner and David Larcker, "Coming Up Short on Nonfinancial Performance Measurement," *Harvard Business Review,* November 2003, 88–95.

tion but rather through a consensus of all those in the organization. Exhibit 13-4 reveals that the reward systems of the two systems are strikingly similar and differ only on the number of dimensions being evaluated.

EXHIBIT **13-4**	Rewards Compared
Activity-Based Rewards	**Strategic-Based Rewards**
1. Performance evaluated on two or more dimensions	1. Performance evaluated on four or more dimensions
2. Group rewards	2. Group rewards
3. Salary increases	3. Salary increases
4. Promotions	4. Promotions
5. Bonuses, profit sharing, and gainsharing	5. Bonuses, profit sharing, and gainsharing

Assigning Rewards

For any performance management system to be successful, the reward system must be linked to the performance measures. The activity- and strategic-based systems both use the same financial instruments to provide compensation to those who achieve targeted performance goals. A key difference for both systems from the traditional control system is the fact that rewards are based on much more than financial measures. In the case of the Balanced Scorecard, four dimensions of performance must be considered instead of the two in an activity-based performance system. It is very unlikely that an organization can secure the needed support for a Balanced Scorecard of measures unless compensation is tied to the scorecard measures. Both systems must also face the thorny problem of team-based rewards.

OBJECTIVE **2**

Discuss the basic features of the Balanced Scorecard.

Basic Concepts of the Balanced Scorecard

The Balanced Scorecard permits an organization to create a strategic focus by *translating* an organization's strategy into operational objectives and performance measures for four different perspectives: the financial perspective, the customer perspective, the internal business process perspective, and the learning and growth (infrastructure) perspective. The Balanced Scorecard is an effective way of implementing and managing a company's strategy. A number of companies attribute their recent financial success to this strategic performance management system.

Strategy Translation

Strategy, according to the creators of the Balanced Scorecard framework, is defined as:[4]

> *choosing the market and customer segments the business unit intends to serve, identifying the critical internal and business processes that the unit must excel at to deliver the value propositions to customers in the targeted market segments, and selecting the individual and organizational capabilities required for the internal, customer, and financial objectives.*

Strategy, then, is identifying and defining management's desired relationships among the four perspectives. *Strategy translation*, on the other hand, means specifying objectives,

---

4. Kaplan and Norton, *The Balanced Scorecard*, 37.

measures, targets, and initiatives for each perspective. The strategy translation process is illustrated in Exhibit 13-5. Consider, for example, a company that wishes to pursue a revenue growth strategy. For the financial perspective, the company may specify an *objective* of growing revenues by introducing new products. The *performance measure* may be the percentage of revenues from the sale of new products. The *target* or *standard* for the coming year for the measure may be 20 percent. (That is, twenty percent of the total revenues for the coming year must be from the sale of new products.) The *initiative* describes *how* this is to be accomplished. The "how," of course, involves the other three perspectives. The customer segments, internal processes, and individual and organizational capabilities that will permit the realization of the revenue growth objective must now be identified. This illustrates the fact that the financial objectives serve as the focus for the objectives, measures, and initiatives of the other three perspectives. It also illustrates the need to carefully define the relationships among the four perspectives so that strategy becomes visible and operational. However, before examining how these causal relationships define and operationalize the strategy, we first need a better understanding of the four perspectives, their objectives, and their measures.

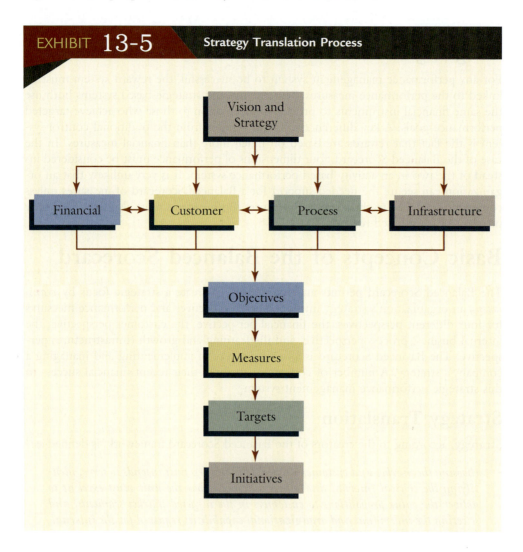

EXHIBIT 13-5   Strategy Translation Process

The Financial Perspective, Objectives, and Measures

The **financial perspective** establishes the long- and short-term financial performance objectives expected from the organization's strategy and simultaneously describes the economic consequences of actions taken in the other three perspectives. This implies that the objectives and measures of the other perspectives should be chosen so that they cause or bring about the desired financial outcomes. The financial perspective has three strategic themes: revenue growth, cost reduction, and asset utilization. These themes serve as the building blocks for the development of specific operational objectives and measures. Of course, the three themes are constrained by the need for managers to manage risk.

Revenue Growth

Increasing revenues can be achieved in a variety of ways, and the potential strategic objectives reflect these possibilities. Among these possibilities are the following objectives: increase the number of new products, create new applications for existing products, develop new customers and markets, and adopt a new pricing strategy. Once operational objectives are known, performance measures can be designed. Possible measures for the preceding list of objectives (in the order given) are percentage of revenue from new products, percentage of revenue from new applications, percentage of revenues from new customers and market segments, and profitability by product or customer.

Cost Reduction

Reducing the cost per unit of product, per customer, or per distribution channel are examples of cost reduction objectives. The appropriate measures are obvious: the cost per unit of the particular cost object. Trends in these measures will tell whether or not the costs are being reduced. For these objectives, the accuracy of cost assignments is especially important. Activity-based costing can play an essential measurement role, especially for selling and administrative costs—costs not usually assigned to cost objects like customers and distribution channels.

Asset Utilization

Improving asset utilization is the principal objective. Financial measures such as return on investment and economic value added are used. Since return on investment and economic value-added measures were discussed in detail in Chapter 10, they will not be discussed here. The objectives and measures for the financial perspective are summarized in Exhibit 13-6.

Risk Management

Managing the risk associated with the adopted strategy is another critical strategic theme—one that is common to the three strategic financial themes already discussed.

EXHIBIT 13-6	Summary of Objectives and Measures: Financial Perspective
Objectives	**Measures**
Revenue Growth:	
Increase the number of new products	Percentage of revenues from new products
Create new applications	Percentage of revenues from new applications
Develop new customers and markets	Percentage of revenues from new sources
Adopt a new pricing strategy	Product and customer profitability
Cost Reduction:	
Reduce unit product cost	Unit product cost
Reduce unit customer cost	Unit customer cost
Reduce distribution channel cost	Cost per distribution channel
Asset Utilization:	
Improve asset utilization	Return on investment
	Economic value added

Diversification of customer types, product lines, and suppliers are common means of lowering risk. Sourcing materials from only one supplier may lower costs, but it may also jeopardize the firm's throughput if something happens to the supplier (e.g., a labor strike). Similarly, revenues may be increased by relying on one very large customer—but what happens if the customer decides to buy elsewhere? Thus, any strategic initiative must be balanced with careful consideration of the risk involved.

Customer Perspective, Objectives, and Measures

The customer perspective defines the customer and market segments in which the business unit will compete and describes the way that value is created for customers. The customer perspective is the source of the revenue component for the financial objectives. Failure to deliver the right kinds of products and services to the targeted customers means revenue will not be generated.

Core Objectives and Measures

Once the customers and segments are defined, then *core objectives* and *measures* are developed. Core objectives and measures are those that are common across all organizations. There are five key core objectives: increase market share, increase customer retention, increase customer acquisition, increase customer satisfaction, and increase customer profitability. Possible core measures for these objectives, respectively, are market share (percentage of the market), percentage growth of business from existing customers and percentage of repeating customers, number of new customers, ratings from customer satisfaction surveys, and individual and segment profitability. Activity-based costing is a key tool in assessing customer profitability (see Chapter 11). Notice that customer profitability is the only financial measure among the core measures. This measure, however, is critical because it emphasizes the importance of the *right* kind of customers. What good is it to have customers if they are not profitable? The obvious answer spells out the difference between being customer focused and customer obsessed.

Customer Value

In addition to the core measures and objectives, measures are needed that drive the creation of *customer value* and, thus, drive the core outcomes. For example, increasing customer value builds customer loyalty (increases retention) and increases customer satisfaction. Customer value is the difference between realization and sacrifice, where realization is what the customer receives and sacrifice is what is given up. Realization includes such attributes as product functionality (features), product quality, reliability of delivery, delivery response time, image, and reputation. Sacrifice includes attributes such as product price, time required to learn to use the product, operating cost, maintenance cost, and disposal cost. The costs incurred by the customer *after* purchase are called post-purchase costs.

The attributes associated with realization and sacrifice provide the basis for the objectives and measures that will lead to improving the core outcomes. The objectives for the sacrifice side of the value equation are the simplest: decrease price and decrease post-purchase costs. Selling price and post-purchase costs are important measures of value creation. Decreasing these costs decreases customer sacrifice, and, thus, increases customer value. Increasing customer value should impact favorably on most of the core objectives. Similar favorable effects can be obtained by increasing realization. Realization objectives, for example, would include the following: improve product functionality, improve product quality, increase delivery reliability, and improve product image and reputation. Possible measures for these objectives include, respectively, feature satisfaction ratings, percentage of returns, on-time delivery percentage, and product recognition rating. Of these objectives and measures, delivery reliability will be used to illustrate how measures can affect managerial behavior, indicating the need to be careful in the choice and use of performance measures.

Delivery reliability means that output is delivered on time. On-time delivery is a commonly used operational measure of reliability. To measure on-time delivery, a firm sets delivery dates and then finds on-time delivery performance by dividing the orders delivered on time by the total number of orders delivered. The goal, of course, is to achieve a ratio of 100 percent. However, this measure used by itself may produce undesirable behavioral consequences.[5] Specifically, plant managers were giving priority to filling orders not yet late over orders that were already late. The performance measure was encouraging managers to have one very late shipment rather than several moderately late shipments! A chart measuring the age of late deliveries could help mitigate this problem. Exhibit 13-7 summarizes the objectives and measures for the customer perspective.

EXHIBIT 13-7	Summary of Objectives and Measures: Customer Perspective
Objectives	**Measures**
Core:	
Increase market share	Market share (percentage of market)
Increase customer retention	Percentage growth, existing customers
	Percentage of repeating customers
Increase customer acquisition	Number of new customers
Increase customer satisfaction	Ratings from customer surveys
Increase customer profitability	Customer profitability
Performance Value:	
Decrease price	Price
Decrease post-purchase costs	Post-purchase costs
Improve product functionality	Ratings from customer surveys
Improve product quality	Percentage of returns
Increase delivery reliability	On-time delivery percentage
	Aging schedule
Improve product image and reputation	Ratings from customer surveys

Process Perspective, Objectives, and Measures

The **internal business process perspective** describes the internal processes needed to provide value for customers and owners. Processes are the means by which strategies are executed. Thus, the process perspective entails the identification of the critical processes needed that affect customer and shareholder satisfaction. To provide the framework needed for this perspective, a *process value chain* is defined. The **process value chain** is made up of three processes: the *innovation process*, the *operations process*, and the *postsales process*.[6] The **innovation process** anticipates the emerging and potential needs of customers and creates new products and services to satisfy those needs. It represents what is called the *long-wave* of value creation. The **operations process** produces and delivers *existing* products and services to customers. It begins with a customer order and ends with the delivery of the product or service. It is the *short-wave* of value creation. The **postsales service process** provides critical and responsive services to customers after the product or service has been delivered.

---

5. Joseph Fisher, "Nonfinancial Performance Measures," *Journal of Cost Management* (Spring 1992): 31–38.
6. Kaplan and Norton, *The Balanced Scorecard*, 96.

Innovation Process: Objectives and Measures

Objectives for the innovation process include the following: increase the number of new products, increase percentage of revenue from proprietary products, and decrease the time to develop new products. Associated measures are actual new products developed versus planned products, percentage of total revenues from new products, percentage of revenues from proprietary products, and development cycle time (time to market).

Operations Process: Objectives and Measures

Three operations process objectives are almost always mentioned and emphasized: increase process quality, increase process efficiency, and decrease process time. Examples of process quality measures are quality costs, output yields (good output/good input), and percentage of defective units (good output/total output). Quality costing and control are discussed extensively in Chapter 14. Measures of process efficiency are concerned mainly with process cost and process productivity. Measuring and tracking process costs are facilitated by activity-based costing and process value analysis. These issues were explored in depth in the activity-based management chapter (Chapter 12). Productivity measurement is explored in Chapter 15. Common process time measures are cycle time, velocity, and manufacturing cycle effectiveness (MCE).

Cycle Time and Velocity

The time it takes a company to respond to a customer order is referred to as *responsiveness*. *Cycle time* and *velocity* are two operational measures of responsiveness. **Cycle time (manufacturing)** is the length of time it takes to produce a unit of output from the time materials are received (starting point of the cycle) until the good is delivered to finished goods inventory (finishing point of the cycle).[7] Thus, cycle time is the time required to produce a product (time/units produced). **Velocity** is the number of units of output that can be produced in a given period of time (units produced/time). Although cycle time has been defined for the operations process, it is defined in a similar way for innovation and postsales service processes. For example, how long does it take to create a new product and introduce it to the market? Or, how long does it take to resolve a customer complaint (from start to finish)?

Incentives can be used to encourage operational managers to reduce manufacturing cycle time or to increase velocity, thus improving delivery performance. A natural way to accomplish this objective is to tie product costs to cycle time and reward operational managers for reducing product costs. For example, in a JIT firm, cell conversion costs can be assigned to products on the basis of the time that it takes a product to move through the cell. Using the theoretical productive time available for a period (in minutes), a value-added standard cost per minute can be computed.

$$\text{Standard cost per minute} = \text{Cell conversion costs/Minutes available}$$

To obtain the conversion cost per unit, this standard cost per minute is multiplied by the actual cycle time used to produce the units during the period. By comparing the unit cost computed using the actual cycle time with the unit cost possible using the theoretical or optimal cycle time, a manager can assess the potential for improvement. Note that the more time it takes a product to move through the cell, the greater the unit product cost. With incentives to reduce product cost, this approach to product costing encourages operational managers and cell workers to find ways to decrease cycle time or increase velocity.

---

7. Other definitions of cycles are possible, e.g., a cycle's starting point could begin when the customer order is received and the finishing point when the goods are delivered to the customer. For a JIT firm, delivery to the customer is a reasonable finishing point. Another possibility for the finishing point is when the customer receives the goods. Cycle time measures the time elapsed from start to finish, regardless of how the starting and finishing points are defined.

An example will illustrate these concepts. Assume that a company has the following data for one of its manufacturing cells:

> Theoretical velocity: 40 units per hour
> Productive minutes available (per year): 1,200,000
> Annual conversion costs: $4,800,000
> Actual velocity: 30 units per hour

The actual and theoretical conversion costs per unit are shown in Exhibit 13-8. Notice from Exhibit 13-8 that the per-unit conversion cost can be reduced from $8 to $6 by decreasing cycle time from two minutes per unit to one and one-half minutes per unit (or increasing velocity from 30 units per hour to 40 units per hour). At the same time, the objective of improving delivery performance is achieved.

EXHIBIT 13-8   Conversion Cost Computations

Actual Conversion Cost per Unit

Standard cost per minute	= $4,800,000/1,200,000
	= $4 per minute
Actual cycle time	= 60 minutes/30 units
	= 2.0 minutes per unit
Actual conversion cost	= $4 × 2
	= $8 per unit

Theoretical Conversion Cost per Unit

Theoretical cycle time	= 60 minutes/40 units
	= 1.5 minutes per unit
Ideal conversion cost	= $4 × 1.5
	= $6 per unit

Manufacturing Cycle Efficiency (MCE)

Another time-based operational measure calculates manufacturing cycle efficiency (MCE) as follows:

> MCE = Processing time/(Processing time + Move time + Inspection time
> + Waiting time + Other non-value-added time)

where processing time is the time it takes to convert materials into a finished good. The other activities and their times are viewed as wasteful, and the goal is to reduce those times to zero. If this is accomplished, the value of MCE would be 1.0. As MCE improves (moves toward 1.0), cycle time decreases. Furthermore, since the only way MCE can improve is by decreasing waste, cost reduction must also follow.

To illustrate MCE, let's use the data from Exhibit 13-8. The actual cycle time is 2.0 minutes, and the theoretical cycle time is 1.5 minutes. Thus, the time wasted is 0.50 minute (2.0 − 1.5), and MCE is computed as follows:

$$MCE = 2.0/2.5$$
$$= 0.80$$

Actually, this is a fairly efficient process, as measured by MCE. Many manufacturing companies have MCEs less than 0.05.[8]

---

8. Kaplan and Norton, *The Balanced Scorecard*, 117.

Postsales Service Process: Objectives and Measures

Increasing quality, increasing efficiency, and decreasing process time are also objectives that apply to the postsales service process. Service quality, for example, can be measured by first-pass yields where first-pass yields are defined as the percentage of customer requests resolved with a single service call. Efficiency can be measured by cost trends and productivity measures. Process time can be measured by cycle time where the starting point of the cycle is defined as the receipt of a customer request and the finishing point is when the customer's problem is solved. The objectives and measures for the process perspective are summarized in Exhibit 13-9.

EXHIBIT 13-9	Summary of Objectives and Measures: Process Perspective
Objectives	**Measures**
Innovation:	
Increase the number of new products	Number of new products/total products; R&D expenses
Increase proprietary products	Percentage revenue from proprietary products Number of patents pending
Decrease product development cycle time	Time to market (from start to finish)
Operations:	
Increase process quality	Quality costs Output yields Percentage of defective units
Increase process efficiency	Unit cost trends Output/input(s)
Decrease process time	Cycle time and velocity MCE
Postsales Service:	
Increase service quality	First-pass yields
Increase service efficiency	Cost trends Output/input(s)
Decrease service time	Cycle time

Learning and Growth Perspective

The learning and growth (infrastructure) perspective defines the capabilities that an organization needs to create long-term growth and improvement. This last perspective is concerned with three major *enabling factors*: employee capabilities, information systems capabilities, and employee attitudes (motivation, empowerment, and alignment). These factors enable processes to be executed efficiently. The learning and growth perspective is the source of the capabilities that enable the accomplishment of the other three perspectives' objectives. This perspective has three major objectives: increase employee capabilities; increase motivation, empowerment, and alignment; and increase information systems capabilities.

Employee Capabilities

Three core *outcome* measurements for employee capabilities are employee satisfaction ratings, employee turnover percentages, and employee productivity (e.g., revenue per employee). Examples of lead measures or performance drivers for employee capabilities include hours of training and strategic job coverage ratios (percentage of critical job requirements filled). As new processes are created, new skills are often demanded. Training and hiring are sources of these new skills. Furthermore, the percentage of the employees needed in certain key areas with the requisite skills signals the capability of the organization to meet the objectives of the other three perspectives.

Motivation, Empowerment, and Alignment

Employees must not only have the necessary skills but they must also have the freedom, motivation, and initiative to use those skills effectively. The number of suggestions per employee and the number of suggestions implemented per employee are possible measures of motivation and empowerment. Suggestions per employee provide a measure of the degree of employee involvement, whereas suggestions implemented per employee signal the quality of the employee participation. The second measure also signals to employees whether or not their suggestions are being taken seriously.

COST MANAGEMENT   Technology in Action

Tele Danmark (TDC), Denmark's leading telecommunications service provider, implemented the Balanced Scorecard using five perspectives: financial, customer (market), innovation, human resources, and business processes. To provide incentives for managers, it has linked managers' pay to outcomes. The Balanced Scorecard is based on an SAS Data Warehouse, which makes it possible to obtain, organize, and store the company's data relating to the Balanced Scorecard. According to management, the Balanced Scorecard system could not be effectively managed without an information technology (IT) solution. The Balanced Scorecard with IT support has enabled TDC to have an effective management system that supports management's vision and provides the ability to target critical focus areas.

The IT capability allows the company to analyze deviations by scrutinizing the data to see exactly where the problem is. IT also allows the company to link to a variety of data sources (such as SAP, project management systems, production systems, etc.). Using IT facilitates the implementation and use of the Balanced Scorecard because it integrates, analyzes, and distributes information across the company. (The company is divided into a series of business sectors that are subdivided further into divisions, and each strategic business unit has its own Balanced Scorecard.) Intranet capability is a particularly useful way of communicating and monitoring strategic objectives and associated measures.

Source: Taken from the Web site, http://www.sas.com/success/tdc.html as of September 18, 2004.

Information Systems Capabilities

Increasing information system capabilities means providing more accurate and timely information to employees so that they can improve processes and effectively execute new processes. Measures should be concerned with the *strategic information availability*. For example, possible measures include percentage of processes with real-time feedback capabilities and percentage of customer-facing employees with online access to customer and product information. Exhibit 13-10, on the following page, summarizes the objectives and measures for the learning and growth perspective.

OBJECTIVE 3

Explain how the Balanced Scorecard links measures to strategy.

Linking Measures to Strategy

The Balanced Scorecard is a collection of critical performance measures that have some special properties. First, the performance measures are derived from a company's vision, strategy, and objectives. To link measures to a strategy, they must be derived from strategy. Second, performance measures should be chosen so that they are *balanced* between outcome and lead measures. Outcome measures such as profitability, return on investment, and market share tend to be generic and, therefore, common to most strategies and organizations. Performance drivers make things happen; consequently, lead measures

EXHIBIT 13-10	Summary of Objectives and Measures: Learning and Growth Perspective

Objectives	Measures
Increase employee capabilities	Employee satisfaction ratings
	Employee turnover percentages
	Employee productivity (revenue/employee)
	Hours of training
	Strategic job coverage ratio (percentage of critical job requirements filled)
Increase motivation and alignment	Suggestions per employee
	Suggestions implemented per employee
Increase information systems capabilities	Percentage of processes with real-time feedback capabilities
	Percentage of customer-facing employees with online access to customer and product information

are indicators of how the outcomes are going to be realized. Lead measures usually distinguish one strategy from another. Thus, lead measures are often unique to a strategy and because of this uniqueness support the objective of linking measures to strategy. Third, all scorecard measures should be linked by cause-and-effect relationships.

The Concept of a Testable Strategy

This last requirement—that of linking through the use of cause-and-effect relationships—is the most important requirement. Cause-and-effect relationships are the means by which lead and lag measures are integrated and simultaneously serve as the mechanism for expressing and revealing the firm's strategy. Outcome measures are important because they reveal whether the strategy is being implemented successfully with the desired economic consequences. Lead measures supposedly cause the outcome. For example, if the number of defective products is decreased (a lead measure), does this result in a greater market share (an outcome measure)? Does a greater market share (acting now as a lead measure), in turn, result in more revenues and profits (lag measures)? These questions reveal the vital role of cause-and-effect relationships in expressing an operational model of a strategy—a strategy that can be expressed in a testable format. In fact, a **testable strategy** can be defined as a set of linked objectives aimed at an overall goal. The testability of the strategy is achieved by restating the strategy into a set of cause-and-effect hypotheses that are expressed by a sequence of if-then statements.[9] Consider, for example, the following value-growth strategy expressed as a sequence of if-then statements:

> *If employee skills are upgraded and if the manufacturing process is redesigned, then manufacturing cycle time will be decreased; if cycle time decreases, then delivery reliability will improve and process costs will decrease; if delivery reliability improves, then customer retention will increase; if customer retention increases, then market share will increase; if market share increases, then sales will increase; if sales increase and costs decrease, then profits will increase; if profits increase, then shareholder value will increase.*

---

9. Kaplan and Norton, *The Balanced Scorecard*, 149. (Kaplan and Norton describe the sequence of if-then statements only as a strategy. Calling it a testable strategy distinguishes it from the earlier, more general definition offered.)

The *strategy map* of Exhibit 13-11 illustrates the value-growth strategy, as described by this sequence of if-then statements. This exhibit reveals at least four interesting features. First, each of the four perspectives is represented by strategic objectives linked through the cause-and-effect relationships hypothesized.

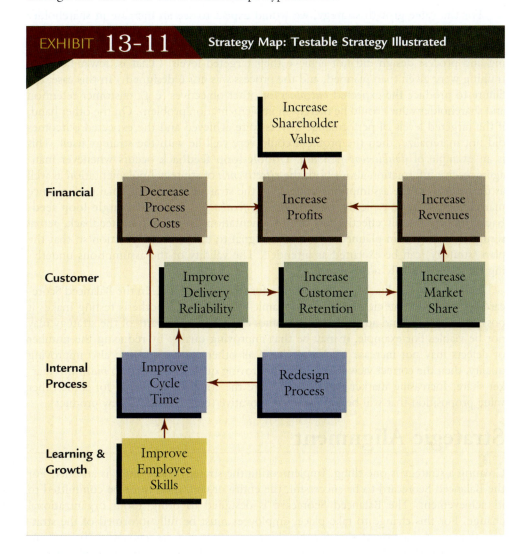

EXHIBIT 13-11   Strategy Map: Testable Strategy Illustrated

Second, notice that process improvement and employee skills are jointly hypothesized to cause an improvement in process cycle time. This emphasizes the fact that an outcome can be caused by more than one performance driver. Third, it is also possible that a lead indicator can cause more than one outcome. Notice that decreasing cycle time causes both an improvement in delivery reliability (affecting the customer perspective) and a decrease in process costs (affecting the financial perspective). Fourth, a performance measure can serve both as a lag indicator and a lead indicator. For example, under the influence of employee skills and process redesign, cycle time serves as a lag indicator. But changes in cycle time affect process costs and delivery performance, thus serving as a lead indicator.

Strategic Feedback

Perhaps the most important message associated with the cause-and-effect structure is that the viability of the strategy is testable. Strategic feedback is available that allows managers to test the reasonableness of the strategy. For example, the strategic objectives portrayed in Exhibit 13-11 have associated measures: Hours of training, process redesign (either the process was redesigned or it wasn't), cycle time, percentage of on-time deliveries, number of repeat orders, market share, revenues, cost, profits, and shareholder value are all observable measures. Thus, the claimed relationships can be checked to see if the strategy produces the expected results.

For the value-growth strategy, we would expect to see an increase in shareholder value. If not, it could be due to one of two causes: (1) implementation problems or (2) an invalid strategy. First, it is possible that *key performance indicators* such as training and process design did not achieve their targeted levels. (That is, fewer hours of training were given than planned, and the process was not redesigned.) In this case, the failure to produce the expected *outcomes* for other objectives (e.g., customer retention and shareholder value) could be merely an implementation problem. On the other hand, if the targeted levels of performance drivers were achieved and the expected outcomes did not materialize, then the problem could very well lie with the strategy itself. This is an example of *double-loop feedback*. **Double-loop feedback** occurs whenever managers receive information about both the *effectiveness* of strategy implementation as well as the *validity* of the assumptions underlying the strategy. In a traditional performance management system, typically, only *single-loop feedback* is provided. **Single-loop feedback** emphasizes only effectiveness of implementation. In single-loop feedback, actual results deviating from planned results are a signal to take corrective action so that the plan (strategy) can be executed as intended. The validity of the assumptions underlying the plan is usually not questioned.

Double-loop feedback is the foundation for strategic learning. In the Balanced Scorecard framework, strategic planning is dynamic—not static. Hypothesis testing makes it possible to change and adapt once it becomes clear that some parts of the strategy may not be viable. For example, it may be that improving quality by reducing the number of defects may not increase market share. If all other competitors are also improving quality, then the correct view may be that improving quality is needed to *maintain* market share. Increasing market share may require the company to search for some other value proposition that will be unique and innovative (e.g., offering a new product).

Strategic Alignment

OBJECTIVE 4

Describe how an organization can achieve strategic alignment.

Creating a strategy is one thing. Implementing the strategy successfully is another. For the Balanced Scorecard to be successful, the entire organization must be committed to its achievement. The Balanced Scorecard is designed to bring about organizational change. For this change to take place, employees must be fully informed of the strategy; they must share ownership for the objectives, measures, targets, and initiatives; incentives must be structured to support the strategy; and resources must be allocated to support the strategy.

Communicating the Strategy

The scorecard objectives and measures, once developed, become the means for articulating and communicating the strategy of the organization to its employees and managers. The objectives and measures also serve the purpose of aligning individual objectives and actions with organizational objectives and initiatives. Videos, newsletters, brochures, and the company's computer network are examples of media that can be used to inform employees of the strategy, objectives, and measures associated with the Balanced Scorecard. How much specific detail to communicate is certainly a relevant question. Communicating too much detail may create a potential problem with competitors. The Balanced Scorecard is a very explicit representation of the company's targeted markets and the means required for obtaining gains in these markets. This can be very sensitive information; the more employees who are aware of it, the more likely it may end up in the hands of competitors. Yet, it is important that employees have a sufficient understanding of what is happening so that they will accept and agree to the strategic efforts of the organization. Articulation of the Balanced Scorecard should be clear enough that individuals can see the linkage between what they do and the organization's long-term objectives. Seeing this linkage increases the likelihood that personal goals and actions are congruent with organizational goals.

Targets and Incentives

Once objectives and measures have been defined and communicated, performance expectations must be established. Performance expectations are communicated by setting targeted values for the measures associated with each objective. Managers are held accountable for the assigned responsibility by comparing the actual values of the measures with the targeted values. Finally, compensation is linked to achievement of the scorecard objectives. It is vital that the reward system be tied to all the scorecard objectives and not just to traditional financial measures. Failure to change the compensation system will encourage managers to continue their focus on short-term financial performance with little reason to pay attention to the strategic objectives of the scorecard.

Exhibit 13-12 provides an example of targets using the objectives and measures for the example illustrated in Exhibit 13-11. The relative importance management has assigned to each perspective and objective is revealed by weights expressed as percentages. Targets are set for both the long-term and the short-term (e.g., a 3- to 5-year horizon and a 1-year horizon) and should be backed up with initiatives that can be undertaken to achieve them. For example, is it really possible to increase share prices by 50 percent over a 3-year span? And how much increase will be targeted for the coming year? The increase is dependent on increasing revenues by 30 percent and decreasing costs by 20 percent. These changes are, in turn, dependent on other events in other perspectives. Can cycle time be reduced to two days (say, from a current level of five days)?

EXHIBIT 13-12   **Targets and Weighting Scheme Illustrated**

Perspectives	Objectives	Measures	Targets
Financial (25%)	Increase shareholder value (25%)	Share price	50% increase
	Increase profits (25%)	Profits	100%
	Increase revenues (25%)	Revenues	30% increase
	Decrease process costs (25%)	Costs	20% decrease
Customer (25%)	Increase market share (20%)	Market share	25%
	Increase customer retention (30%)	Repeat orders	70%
	Improve delivery reliability (50%)	On-time percentage	100%
Internal Process (25%)	Improve cycle time (60%)	Cycle time	2 days
	Redesign process (40%)	Yes or No	Yes
Learning & Growth (25%)	Improve employee skills (100%)	Hours of training	30 hours per employee

---

How to structure incentive compensation with multiple dimensions is a challenging task. Typically, weights that reflect the relative importance of the perspectives are used to determine the percentage of the bonus pool that will be assigned to each perspective. Thus, from Exhibit 13-12, we see that for this example each perspective would be assigned 25 percent of the total bonus pool. But within each category, there are usually multiple objectives and multiple measures. For example, within the customer category, there are three performance measures. How much of the 25 percent bonus pool should be assigned to each measure? Again, weights that reflect the relative importance of each objective within its category are used to make this determination. Exhibit 13-12, for example, reveals that management has decided to assign 50 percent of the customer category bonus to the on-time delivery objective, 30 percent to the customer retention objective, and 20 percent to the market share objective. Thus, of the original bonus pool, 12.5 percent is assigned to the delivery objective (0.50×0.25).

Distributing potential bonus money to the various perspectives and measures is one thing, but payment of incentive compensation is dependent on *performance*. The actual values of the measures are compared to the targeted values for a given time period. Compensation is then paid, based on the percentage achievement of each objective. However, there is one major qualification for the Balanced Scorecard framework. To ensure that proper (balanced) attention is given to all measures, no incentive compensation is paid unless each strategic measure exceeds a prespecified minimum threshold value.[10]

Firms adopting the Balanced Scorecard seem to realize the necessity of connecting their reward system to the objectives and measures of the new performance management system. A Mercer study in 1999 found that 88 percent of the responsding companies reported that linking the reward system to the Balanced Scorecard was effective.[11] **Mobil**, for example, reported that they would not have had the same focus on the scorecard if there was not a link to compensation.[12] The CEO of **Cigna Property and Casualty** observed that linking compensation to the new measurement system was key to gaining acceptance of the new measurement approach.[13] In another survey by the Hay Group, it was found that 13 of 15 firms studied linked compensation to the Scorecard. Specifically, about 25 to 33 percent of the total compensation is affected by the Balanced Scorecard, with about 40 percent focused on the financial perspective and 20 percent assigned to each of the three remaining perspectives.[14]

Resource Allocation

Achieving strategic targets such as those envisioned in Exhibit 13-12 requires that resources be allocated to the corresponding strategic initiatives. This requires two major changes. First, an organization must decide how much of the strategic targets will be achieved for the coming year. Second, the operational budgetary process must be structured to provide the resources necessary for achievement of these short-time advances along the strategic path. If these changes are not incorporated, then it is difficult to imagine that the strategy will truly become actionable.

---

10. Ibid., 219–220.
11. Mercer, William and Company, 1999. Rewarding Employees: Balanced Scorecard Fax-Back Survey Results, May 20. London U.K.
12. Robert S. Kaplan and David P. Norton, "Transforming the Balanced Scorecard from Performance Measurement to Strategic Management: Part II," *Accounting Horizons*, June 2001, 147–160.
13. Ibid.
14. Todd Manas, "Making the Balanced Scorecard Approach Payoff," *ACA Journal*, Second Quarter, 1999, Volume 8, Number 2.

SUMMARY

Activity-based responsibility accounting focuses on processes, uses both operational and financial measures, employs dynamic standards, and emphasizes and supports continuous improvement. Strategic-based responsibility accounting expands the number of responsibility dimensions from two to four. Customer and learning and growth perspectives are added. Furthermore, the performance measures become an integrated set of measures, linked to an organization's mission and strategy. Functional-based responsibility accounting works best for organizations operating in stable environments, and activity- and strategic-based responsibility accounting systems work best for firms operating in dynamic environments.

The Balanced Scorecard is a strategic performance management system that translates the vision and strategy of an organization into operational objectives and measures. Objectives and measures are developed for each of four perspectives: the financial perspective, the customer perspective, the process perspective, and the learning and growth perspective. The objectives and measures of the four perspectives are linked by a series of cause-and-effect hypotheses. This produces a testable strategy that provides strategic feedback to managers. The Balanced Scorecard is compatible with activity-based responsibility accounting because it focuses on processes and requires the use of activity-based information to implement many of its objectives and measures. Alignment with the strategy expressed by the Balanced Scorecard is achieved by communication, incentives, and allocation of resources to support the strategic initiatives.

REVIEW PROBLEMS AND SOLUTIONS

1   PERSPECTIVES, MEASURES, AND STRATEGIC OBJECTIVES

The following measures belong to one of four perspectives: financial, customer, process, or learning and growth.

a.   Revenues from new products
b.   On-time delivery percentage
c.   Economic value added
d.   Employee satisfaction
e.   Cycle time
f.   First-pass yields
g.   Strategic job coverage ratio
h.   Number of new customers
i.   Unit product cost
j.   Customer profitability

Required:

Classify each measure by perspective, and suggest a possible strategic objective that might be associated with the measure.

Perspective	Objective
a. Financial	Increase number of new products
b. Customer	Increase delivery reliability
c. Financial	Improve asset utilization
d. Learning & Growth	Increase motivation and alignment
e. Process	Decrease process time
f. Process	Increase service quality
g. Learning & Growth	Increase employee capabilities
h. Customer	Increase customer acquisition
i. Financial	Decrease product cost
j. Customer	Increase customer profitability

2   CYCLE TIME AND VELOCITY, MCE

Currently, a company can produce 60 units per hour of a particular product. During this hour, move time and wait time take 30 minutes, while actual processing time is 30 minutes.

Required:

1. Calculate the current MCE.
2. Calculate the current cycle time.
3. Suppose that move time and wait time are reduced by 50 percent. What is the new velocity? The new cycle time? The new MCE?

SOLUTION

1. MCE = Process time/(Process time + Move time + Wait time)
   = 30 minutes/60 minutes
   = 0.50

2. Cycle time = 1/Velocity = 1/60 hr., or 1 minute

3. The time now required to produce 60 units is 45 minutes (30 minutes process time + move and wait time of 15 minutes). Thus, velocity = 60/(3/4 hr.) = 80 units per hour; cycle time = 1/80 hr., or 0.75 minute. Finally, MCE = 30/(30 + 15) = 0.67.

KEY TERMS

QUESTIONS FOR WRITING AND DISCUSSION

1. Describe a strategic-based responsibility accounting system. How does it differ from activity-based responsibility accounting?
2. What is a Balanced Scorecard?
3. What is meant by balanced measures?
4. What is a lag measure? A lead measure?
5. What is the difference between an objective measure and a subjective measure?
6. What are stretch targets? What is their strategic purpose?
7. How does the reward system for a strategic-based system differ from the traditional approach?
8. What are the three strategic themes of the financial perspective?
9. Identify the five core objectives of the customer perspective.
10. Explain what is meant by the long-wave and the short-wave of value creation.

11. Define the three processes of the process value chain.
12. Identify three objectives of the learning and growth perspective.
13. What is a testable strategy?
14. What is meant by double-loop feedback?
15. Identify and explain three methods for achieving strategic alignment.

EXERCISES

13-1 ACTIVITY-BASED RESPONSIBILITY ACCOUNTING VERSUS STRATEGIC-BASED RESPONSIBILITY ACCOUNTING

LO1 The following comment was made by the CEO of a company that recently implemented the Balanced Scorecard: "Responsibility in a strategic-based performance management system differs on the three D's: Direction, Dimension, and Diffusion."

Required:

Explain how this comment describes differences in responsibility between an activity-based and a strategic-based performance management system.

13-2 ACTIVITY-BASED RESPONSIBILITY ACCOUNTING VERSUS STRATEGIC-BASED RESPONSIBILITY ACCOUNTING

LO1 "A Balanced Scorecard expresses the complete story of a company's strategy through an integrated set of financial and nonfinancial measures that are both predictive and historical and which may be measured subjectively or objectively."

Required:

1. Using the above statement about scorecard measures, explain how scorecard measurement differs from that of an activity-based management system.
2. Explain what is meant by historical and predictive measures. Why are both types important for describing a company's strategy?

13-3 ACTIVITY-BASED RESPONSIBILITY ACCOUNTING VERSUS STRATEGIC-BASED RESPONSIBILITY ACCOUNTING

LO1, LO3 The Balanced Scorecard is an approach that has the objective of driving change. Performance evaluation is an integral part of this effort. Performance evaluation within the Balanced Scorecard framework is also concerned with the effectiveness and viability of the organization's strategy.

Required:

1. Describe how the Balanced Scorecard is used to drive organizational change.
2. Explain how performance evaluation is used to assess the effectiveness and viability of an organization's strategy.

13-4 BALANCED SCORECARD, PERSPECTIVES, CLASSIFICATION OF PERFORMANCE MEASURES

LO1, LO2 Consider the following list of scorecard measures:

a. Ratings from customer surveys
b. Cycle time to resolve customer complaints

c. Unit customer cost
d. Return on investment
e. Employee satisfaction ratings
f. Percentage of defective units
g. Post-purchase costs
h. Time to market (from start to finish)
i. Suggestions implemented per employee
j. Customer profitability
k. Percentage of revenues from new products
l. MCE

Required:

Classify each measure according to the following: perspective, financial or nonfinancial, subjective or objective, and external or internal. When the perspective is process, identify which type of process: innovation, operations, or postsales service.

13-5 CYCLE TIME AND CONVERSION COST PER UNIT

LO2   The theoretical cycle time for a product is 48 minutes per unit. The budgeted conversion costs for the manufacturing cell dedicated to the product are $4,320,000 per year. The total labor minutes available are 960,000. During the year, the cell was able to produce 0.60 unit of the product per hour. Suppose also that production incentives exist to minimize unit product costs.

Required:

1. Compute the theoretical conversion cost per unit.
2. Compute the applied conversion cost per minute (the amount of conversion cost actually assigned to the product).
3. Discuss how this approach to assigning conversion cost can improve delivery time performance. Explain how conversion cost acts as a performance driver for on-time deliveries.

13-6 CYCLE TIME AND VELOCITY, MCE

LO2   A manufacturing plant has the theoretical capability to produce 54,000 printers per quarter but currently produces 20,250 units. The conversion cost per quarter is $2,430,000. There are 13,500 production hours available within the plant per quarter. In addition to the processing minutes per unit used, the production of printers uses nine minutes of move time, six minutes of wait time, and 10 minutes of rework time. (All work is done by cell workers.)

Required:

1. Compute the theoretical and actual velocities (per hour) and the theoretical and actual cycle times (minutes per unit produced).
2. Compute the ideal and actual amounts of conversion cost assigned per printer.
3. Calculate MCE. How does MCE relate to the conversion cost per printer?

13-7 MCE, EXPRESSION OF A TESTABLE STRATEGY, DOUBLE-LOOP FEEDBACK

LO2, LO3   Refer to **Exercise 13-6.** Assume that the company identifies poor plant layout as the root cause of wait time and move time.

Required:

1. Express an improvement strategy as a series of if-then statements that will reduce the conversion cost per printer.
2. Assume that you set an MCE target of 60 percent, based on the improvement strategy described in Requirement 1. What is the expected conversion cost per unit? Explain how you can use these targets to test the viability of your quality improvement strategy.

13-8 BALANCED SCORECARD, LEAD AND LAG VARIABLES, DOUBLE-LOOP FEEDBACK

LO1, LO2, LO3

The following if-then statements were taken from a Balanced Scorecard:

a. If employee productivity increases, then process efficiency will increase.
b. If process efficiency increases, then product price can be decreased.

Required:

1. Identify the lead and lag variables, and explain your reasoning.
2. Discuss the implications of Requirement 1 for the financial and learning and growth perspectives.
3. Using the first if-then statement, explain the concept of double-loop feedback.

13-9 TESTABLE STRATEGY, STRATEGY MAP

LO3

Consider the following quality improvement strategy as expressed by a series of if-then statements:

- If design engineers receive quality training, then they can redesign products to reduce the number of defective units.
- If the number of defective units is reduced, then customer satisfaction will increase.
- If customer satisfaction increases, then market share will increase.
- If market share increases, then sales will increase.
- If sales increase, then profits will increase.

Required:

1. Prepare a strategy map that shows the cause-and-effect relationships of the quality improvement strategy (see Exhibit 13-11 for an illustrative example).
2. Explain how the quality improvement strategy can be tested.

13-10 BALANCED SCORECARD, STRATEGY TRANSLATION, STRATEGY MAP, DOUBLE-LOOP FEEDBACK

LO2, LO3

Bannister Company, an electronics firm, buys circuit boards and manually inserts various electronic devices into the printed circuit board. Bannister sells its products to original equipment manufacturers. Profits for the last two years have been less than expected. Mandy Confer, owner of Bannister, was convinced that her firm needed to adopt a revenue growth and cost reduction strategy to increase overall profits.

After a careful review of her firm's condition, Mandy realized that the main obstacle for increasing revenues and reducing costs was the high defect rate of her products (a 6 percent reject rate). She was certain that revenues would grow if the defect rate was reduced dramatically. Costs would also decline as there would be fewer rejects and less rework. By decreasing the defect rate, customer satisfaction would increase, causing, in turn, an increase in market share. Mandy also felt that the following actions were needed to help ensure the success of the revenue growth and cost reduction strategy:

a. Improve the soldering capabilities by sending employees to an outside course.
b. Redesign the insertion process to eliminate some of the common mistakes.
c. Improve the procurement process by selecting suppliers that provide higher-quality circuit boards.

Required:

1. State the revenue growth and cost reduction strategy using a series of cause-and-effect relationships expressed as if-then statements.
2. Illustrate the strategy using a strategy map.
3. Explain how the revenue growth strategy can be tested. In your explanation, discuss the role of lead and lag measures, targets, and double-loop feedback.

13-11   BALANCED SCORECARD, STRATEGIC ALIGNMENT

LO4   Refer to **Exercise 13-10**. Suppose that Mandy communicates the following weights to her CEO:

Perspective: Financial, 40%; Customer, 20%; Process, 20%; Learning & growth, 20%

Financial objectives: Profits, 50%; Revenues, 25%; Costs, 25%

Customer objectives: Customer satisfaction, 60%; Market share, 40%

Process objectives: Defects decrease, 40%; Supplier selection, 30%; Redesign process, 30%

Learning & growth objective: Training, 100%

Mandy next sets up a bonus pool of $100,000 and indicates that the weighting scheme just described will be used to determine the amount of potential bonus for each perspective and each objective.

Required:

1. Calculate the potential bonus for each perspective and objective.
2. Describe how Mandy might award actual bonuses so that her managers will be encouraged to implement the Balanced Scorecard.
3. What are some other ways that Mandy can use to encourage alignment with the company's strategic objectives (other than incentive compensation)?

PROBLEMS

13-12   ACTIVITY-BASED RESPONSIBILITY ACCOUNTING VERSUS STRATEGIC-BASED RESPONSIBILITY ACCOUNTING

LO1   Carson Wellington, president of Mallory Plastics, was considering a report sent to him by Emily Sorensen, vice president of operations. The report was a summary of the progress made by an activity-based management system that was implemented three years ago. Significant progress had indeed been realized. At the conclusion of the report, Emily urged Carson to consider the adoption of the Balanced Scorecard as a logical next step in the company's efforts to establish itself as a leader in its industry. Emily clearly was impressed by the Balanced Scorecard and intrigued by the possibility that the change would enhance the overall competitiveness of Mallory. She requested a meeting of the executive committee to explain the similarities and differences between the two approaches. Carson agreed to schedule the meeting but asked Emily to prepare a memo in advance, listing the most important similarities and differences between the two approaches to responsibility accounting.

Required:

Prepare the memo requested by Carson.

13-13   SCORECARD MEASURES, STRATEGY TRANSLATION

LO2, LO3

Spreadsheet

At the end of 2005, Activo Company implemented a low-cost strategy to improve its competitive position. Its objective was to become the low-cost producer in its industry. A Balanced Scorecard was developed to guide the company toward this objective. To lower costs, Activo undertook a number of improvement activities such as JIT production, total quality management, and activity-based management. Now, after two years of operation, the president of Activo wants some assessment of the achievements. To help provide this assessment, the following information on one product has been gathered:

	2005	2007
Theoretical annual capacity*	124,800	124,800
Actual production**	104,000	117,000
Market size (in units sold)	650,000	650,000
Production hours available (20 workers)	52,000	52,000
Very satisfied customers	41,600	70,200
Actual cost per unit	$162.50	$130
Days of inventory	7.8	3.9
Number of defective units	6,500	2,600
Total worker suggestions	52	156
Hours of training	130	520
Selling price per unit	$195	$195
Number of new customers	2,600	13,000

*Amount that could be produced given the available production hours; everything produced is sold.

**Amount that was produced given the available production hours.

Required:

1. Compute the following measures for 2005 and 2007:
    a. Actual velocity and cycle time
    b. Percentage of total revenue from new customers (assume one unit per customer)
    c. Percentage of very satisfied customers (assume each customer purchases one unit)
    d. Market share
    e. Percentage change in actual product cost (for 2007 only)
    f. Percentage change in days of inventory (for 2007 only)
    g. Defective units as a percentage of total units produced
    h. Total hours of training
    i. Suggestions per production worker
    j. Total revenue
    k. Number of new customers
2. For the measures listed in Requirement 1, list likely strategic objectives, classified according to the four Balance Scorecard perspectives. Assume there is one measure per objective.

13-14   IF-THEN STATEMENTS, STRATEGY MAP

LO2, LO3   Refer to the data in **Problem 13-13**.

1. Express Activo's strategy as a series of if-then statements. What does this tell you about Balanced Scorecard measures?

2. Prepare a strategy map that illustrates the relationships among the likely strategic objectives.

13-15 STRATEGIC OBJECTIVES, SCORECARD MEASURES, STRATEGY MAP

LO2, LO3   The following strategic objectives have been derived from a strategy that seeks to improve asset utilization by more careful development and use of its human assets and internal processes:

a. Increase revenue from new products.
b. Increase implementation of employee suggestions.
c. Decrease operating expenses.
d. Decrease cycle time for the development of new products.
e. Decrease rework.
f. Increase employee morale.
g. Increase customer satisfaction.
h. Increase access of key employees to customer and product information.
i. Increase customer acquisition.
j. Increase return on investment (ROI).
k. Increase employee productivity.
l. Decrease the collection period for accounts receivable.
m. Increase employee skills.

The heart of the strategy is developing the company's human resources. Management is convinced that empowering employees will lead to an increase in economic returns. Studies have shown that there is a positive relationship between employee morale and customer satisfaction. Furthermore, the more satisfied customers pay their bills more quickly. It was hypothesized that as employees became more involved and more productive their morale would improve. Thus, the strategy incorporated key objectives that would lead to an increase in productivity and involvement.

Required:

1. Classify the objectives by perspective, and suggest a measure for each objective.
2. Prepare a strategy map that illustrates the likely causal relationships among the strategic objectives.

13-16 CYCLE TIME, CONVERSION COST PER UNIT, MCE

LO2   A manufacturing cell has the theoretical capability to produce 150,000 subassemblies per quarter. The conversion cost per quarter is $1,500,000. There are 50,000 production hours available within the cell per quarter.

Required:

1. Compute the theoretical velocity (per hour) and the theoretical cycle time (minutes per unit produced).
2. Compute the ideal amount of conversion cost that will be assigned per subassembly.
3. Suppose the actual time required to produce a subassembly is 30 minutes. Compute the amount of conversion cost actually assigned to each unit produced. What happens to product cost if the time to produce a unit is decreased to 25 minutes? How can a firm encourage managers to reduce cycle time? Finally, discuss how this approach to assigning conversion cost can improve delivery time.

4. Calculate MCE. How much non-value-added time is being used? How much is it costing per unit?
5. Cycle time, velocity, MCE, conversion cost per unit (theoretical conversion rate $\times$ actual conversion time), and non-value-added costs are all measures of performance for the cell process. Discuss the incentives provided by these measures.

13-17   MCE, Testable Strategy, Strategy Map

LO2, LO3 Auflegger, Inc., manufactures a product that experiences the following activities (and times):

	Hours
Processing (two departments)	42.0
Inspecting	2.8
Rework	7.0
Moving (three moves)	11.2
Waiting (for the second process)	33.6
Storage (before delivery to customer)	43.4

Required:

1. Compute the MCE for this product.
2. A study lists the following root causes of the inefficiencies: poor quality components from suppliers, lack of skilled workers, and plant layout. Suggest a possible cost reduction strategy, expressed as a series of if-then statements, that will reduce MCE and lower costs Finally, prepare a strategy map that illustrates the causal paths. In preparing the map, use only three perspectives: learning and growth, process, and financial.
3. Is MCE a lag or a lead measure? If and when MCE acts as a lag measure, what lead measures would affect it?

13-18   Cycle Time, Velocity, Product Costing

LO2 Wilton Company has a JIT system in place. Each manufacturing cell is dedicated to the production of a single product or major subassembly. One cell, dedicated to the production of snowmobiles, has four operations: machining, finishing, assembly, and qualifying (testing). The machining process is automated, using computers. In this process, the model's frame and engine are constructed. In finishing, the frame is sandblasted, buffed, and painted. In assembly, the frame and engine are assembled. Finally, each model is tested to ensure operational capability.

For the coming year, the snowmobile cell has the following budgeted costs and cell time (both at theoretical capacity):

Budgeted conversion costs	$7,750,000
Budgeted materials	$9,300,000
Cell time	12,400 hours
Theoretical output	9,300 models

During the year, the following actual results were obtained:

Actual conversion costs	$7,750,000
Actual materials	$8,060,000
Actual cell time	12,400 hours
Actual output	7,750 models

Required:

1. Compute the velocity (number of models per hour) that the cell can theoretically achieve. Now, compute the theoretical cycle time (number of hours or minutes per model) that it takes to produce one model.
2. Compute the actual velocity and the actual cycle time.
3. Compute MCE. Comment on the efficiency of the operation.
4. Compute the budgeted conversion cost per minute. Using this rate, compute the conversion cost per model if theoretical output is achieved. Using this measure, compute the conversion cost per model for actual output. Does this product costing approach provide an incentive for the cell manager to reduce cycle time? Explain.

13-19   BALANCED SCORECARD, NON-VALUE-ADDED ACTIVITIES, STRATEGY TRANSLATION, KAIZEN COSTING

LO1, LO2, LO3, LO4   At the beginning of the last quarter of 2005, Youngston, Inc., a consumer products firm, hired Maria Carrillo to take over one of its divisions. The division manufactured small home appliances and was struggling to survive in a very competitive market. Maria immediately requested a projected income statement for 2005. In response, the controller provided the following statement:

Sales	$25,000,000
Variable expenses	20,000,000
Contribution margin	$ 5,000,000
Fixed expenses	6,000,000
Projected loss	$(1,000,000)

After some investigation, Maria soon realized that the products being produced had a serious problem with quality. She once again requested a special study by the controller's office to supply a report on the level of quality costs. By the middle of November, Maria received the following report from the controller:

Inspection costs, finished product	$ 400,000
Rework costs	2,000,000
Scrapped units	600,000
Warranty costs	3,000,000
Sales returns (quality-related)	1,000,000
Customer complaint department	500,000
Total estimated quality costs	$7,500,000

Maria was surprised at the level of quality costs. They represented 30 percent of sales, certainly excessive. She knew that the division had to produce high-quality products to survive. The number of defective units produced needed to be reduced dramatically. Thus, Maria decided to pursue a quality-driven turnaround strategy. Revenue growth and cost reduction could both be achieved if quality could be improved. By growing revenues and decreasing costs, profitability could be increased.

After meeting with the managers of production, marketing, purchasing, and human resources, Maria made the following decisions, effective immediately (end of November 2005):

a. More will be invested in employee training. Workers will be trained to detect quality problems and empowered to make improvements. Workers will be allowed a bonus of 10 percent of any cost savings produced by their suggested improvements.

b. Two design engineers will be hired immediately, with expectations of hiring one or two more within a year. These engineers will be in charge of redesigning processes and products with the objective of improving quality. They will also be given the responsibility of working with selected suppliers to help improve the quality of their products and processes. Design engineers were considered a strategic necessity.

c. Implement a new process: evaluation and selection of suppliers. This new process has the objective of selecting a group of suppliers that are willing and capable of providing nondefective components.

d. Effective immediately, the division will begin inspecting purchased components. According to production, many of the quality problems are caused by defective components purchased from outside suppliers. Incoming inspection is viewed as a transitional activity. Once the division has developed a group of suppliers capable of delivering nondefective components, this activity will be eliminated.

e. Within three years, the goal is to produce products with a defect rate less than 0.10 percent. By reducing the defect rate to this level, marketing is confident that market share will increase by at least 50 percent (as a consequence of increased customer satisfaction). Products with better quality will help establish an improved product image and reputation, allowing the division to capture new customers and increase market share.

f. Accounting will be given the charge to install a quality information reporting system. Daily reports on operational quality data (e.g., percentage of defective units), weekly updates of trend graphs (posted throughout the division), and quarterly cost reports are the types of information required.

g. To help direct the improvements in quality activities, kaizen costing is to be implemented. For example, for the year 2005, a kaizen standard of 6 percent of the selling price per unit was set for rework costs, a 25 percent reduction from the current actual cost.

To ensure that the quality improvements were directed and translated into concrete financial outcomes, Maria also began to implement a Balanced Scorecard for the division. By the end of 2006, progress was being made. Sales had increased to $26,000,000, and the kaizen improvements were meeting or beating expectations. For example, rework costs had dropped to $1,500,000.

At the end of 2007, two years after the turnaround quality strategy was implemented, Maria received the following quality cost report:

Quality training	$ 500,000
Supplier evaluation	230,000
Incoming inspection costs	400,000
Inspection costs, finished product	300,000
Rework costs	1,000,000
Scrapped units	200,000
Warranty costs	750,000
Sales returns (quality-related)	435,000
Customer complaint department	325,000
Total estimated quality costs	$4,140,000

Maria also received an income statement for 2007:

Sales	$30,000,000
Variable expenses	22,000,000
Contribution margin	$ 8,000,000
Fixed expenses	5,800,000
Income from operations	$ 2,200,000

Maria was pleased with the outcomes. Revenues had grown, and costs had been reduced by at least as much as she had projected for the 2-year period. Growth next year should be even greater as she was beginning to observe a favorable effect from the higher-quality products. Also, further quality cost reductions should materialize as incoming inspections were showing much higher-quality purchased components.

Required:

1. Identify the strategic objectives, classified by Balanced Scorecard perspective. Next, suggest measures for each objective.
2. Using the results from Requirement 1, describe Maria's strategy using a series of if-then statements. Next, prepare a strategy map.
3. Explain how you would evaluate the success of the quality-driven turnaround strategy. What additional information would you like to have for this evaluation?
4. Explain why Maria felt that the Balanced Scorecard would increase the likelihood that the turnaround strategy would actually produce good financial outcomes.
5. Advise Maria on how to encourage her employees to align their actions and behavior with the turnaround strategy.

13-20   COLLABORATIVE LEARNING EXERCISE

**LO1, LO2,
LO3, LO4**

Form groups of three to five. Divide the groups into four sets: A, B, C, and D.

Required:

Use Chapters 12 and 13 to do the following:

1. Group A will compare responsibility under a traditional financial responsibility structure with responsibility under a strategic performance management system.
2. Group B will analyze the differences in performance measures under traditional financial responsibility structures and those under strategic responsibility accounting systems.
3. Group C will compare and contrast performance evaluation of a traditional financial responsibility accounting system with that of a strategic responsibility accounting system.
4. Group D will compare and contrast the reward systems of the traditional responsibility system with that of a strategic responsibility accounting system.
5. One group of each type will report the results of their analyses to the class as a whole.

13-21   CYBER RESEARCH CASE

**LO1, LO2,
LO3, LO4**

Search the Internet to find a complete description of a company that has implemented the Balanced Scorecard. Possible sources include the following: The Balanced Scorecard Collaborative (http://www.bscol.com), SAP (http://www.sap.com/sem), and http://www.bettermanagement.com. Once you have a company located, answer the following questions:

1. What is/are the strategy or strategies of the company?
2. What perspectives were used?
3. What are the strategic objectives?
4. What are the measures?
5. Did the company present a strategy map?
6. Were there any problems identified in implementation? If so, what were the problems?
7. What were the results? Did the Balanced Scorecard make a difference?

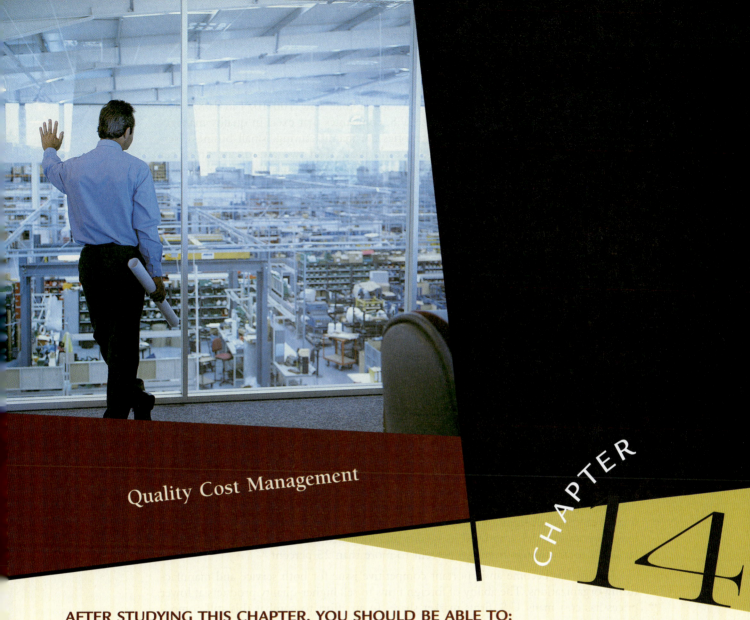

Quality Cost Management

AFTER STUDYING THIS CHAPTER, YOU SHOULD BE ABLE TO:

1. Define quality, describe the four types of quality costs, and discuss the approaches used for quality cost measurement.

2. Prepare a quality cost report, and explain its use.

3. Explain why quality cost information is needed and how it is used.

4. Describe and prepare three different types of quality performance reports.

There are numerous quality-related activities, all of which consume resources that determine the level of quality costs incurred by a firm. Inspecting or testing parts, for example, is an appraisal activity that has the objective of detecting bad products. Detecting bad products and correcting them before they are sent to customers is usually less expensive than letting them be acquired by customers. The objective of quality cost management is to find ways to minimize total quality costs.

Competitive forces are requiring firms to pay increasing attention to quality. Customers are demanding higher-quality products and services. Improving quality may actually be the key to survival for many firms. Improving process quality and the quality of products and services is a fundamental strategic objective that is part of any well-designed Balanced Scorecard. If quality is improved, then customer satisfaction increases; if customer satisfaction increases, then market share will increase; and if market share increases, then revenues will increase; moreover, if quality improves, then operating costs will also decrease. Thus, improving quality can increase market share and sales, while simultaneously decreasing costs. The overall effect enhances a firm's financial and competitive position.

One indication of the importance of quality in the United States is the creation of the Malcolm Baldrige National Quality Award (Public Law 100-107) in 1987. The Baldrige award was created to recognize U.S. companies that excel in quality management and achievement. The award categories are manufacturing, small business, service, educational, and health entities. Since no more than two awards are given per category, it is difficult to win and highly sought after. The first awards were given in 1988. Winners of the Baldrige award in 2003 included **Medrad, Inc., Boeing Aerospace Support, Caterpillar Financial Services Corporation**, and **Baptist Hospital, Inc.** Winners in earlier years included **Dana Corporation's Spicer Driveshaft Division, Karlee Company, Operations Management International Inc., Los Alamos National Bank, Texas Nameplate Company, Inc.**, and **Boeing Aircraft and Tanker Programs**.[1]

Improving quality can increase firm value because it increases a firm's profitability. Improving quality can increase profitability in at least two ways: (1) by increasing customer demand and (2) by decreasing the costs of providing goods and services.

Costs of Quality

OBJECTIVE *1*

Define quality, describe the four types of quality costs, and discuss the approaches used for quality cost measurement.

Over the past 20 years, American industry has made significant strides in improving quality. Even so, much remains to be done. The costs of quality can be substantial and a source of significant savings. Wane Kost, president of **Philip Crosby Associates II**, maintains that the costs of quality (the "price of nonconformance") for manufacturing organizations fall between 20 to 25 percent of sales for manufacturing firms and 30 to 40 percent of sales for service organizations.[2] Yet, quality experts indicate that the optimal quality level should be about 2 to 4 percent of sales. This difference between actual and optimal figures represents a veritable gold mine of opportunity. Improving quality can produce significant improvements in profitability. Caterpillar Financial Services Corporation U.S. improved its quality and increased its contributions to Caterpillar Inc.'s total earnings from 5.6 percent to more than 25 percent.[3]

Quality has become an important competitive issue for both service and manufacturing organizations. The ability of foreign firms to sell higher-quality products at lower prices has cost many U.S. firms market share. In an effort to combat this stiff competition, U.S. firms have increasingly paid more attention to quality and productivity, especially given the potential to reduce costs and improve product quality simultaneously. In general, evidence exists that most American manufacturing industries have boosted quality. **General Motors**, for example, was ranked fourth in a vehicle dependability study on quality (behind **Toyota, American Honda Motor Co., Inc.**, and **Porsche Cars North America**).[4] Other American companies are following suit and are striving to meet consumer quality expectations.

As companies implement quality improvement programs, a need arises to monitor and report on the progress of these programs. Managers need to know what quality costs are and how they are changing over time. Reporting and measuring quality performance is absolutely essential to the success of an ongoing quality improvement program. A fundamental prerequisite for this reporting is measuring the costs of quality. But to measure those costs, an operational definition of quality is needed.

---

1. As reported at http://www.nist.gov/ as of September 18, 2004.

2. Stephanie Fellenstein, "Taking Control of Quality Costs," an online article at http://www.eaglegroupusa.com/pubart/qim1298.htm, as of September 18, 2004.

3. "Quality Conversation with James S. Beard," *Quality Digest*, accessed at http://www.qualitydigest.com as of September 25, 2004.

4. Larry Adams, "Top 100 in Quality," *Quality Magazine*, accessed at http://www.qualitymag.com as of September 1, 2004.

The Meaning of Quality

Quality is often referred to as the "degree or grade of excellence"; thus, it is a relative measure of goodness. Defining quality as goodness is so general that it offers no operational content. Adopting a customer focus provides operational content. Operationally, a **quality product or service** is one that meets or exceeds customer expectations. Customer expectations relate to attributes such as product performance, reliability, durability, and fitness for use. A quality specification is the specific level of performance planned for a given quality attribute. Customers expect a quality product or service to perform according to specifications. **Quality of conformance** is a measure of how a product meets its specifications.

Conformance is strongly emphasized because it is the key to meeting customer expectations. In fact, most quality experts believe that "quality is conformance" is the best operational definition of quality. There is some logic to this position. Product specifications should explicitly consider such things as reliability, durability, fitness for use, and performance. Implicitly, a conforming product is reliable, durable, fit for use, and performs well. The product should be produced as specified by the design; specifications should be met. Conformance is the basis for defining what is meant by a nonconforming, or *defective*, product.

A **defective product** is one that does not conform to specifications. **Zero defects** means that all products conform to specifications. But what is meant by "conforming to specifications"? Traditional conformance defines an acceptable range of values for each specification or quality characteristic. A target value is defined, and upper and lower limits are set that describe acceptable product variation for a given quality characteristic. Any unit that falls within the limits is deemed nondefective. For example, the targeted specification for a machined part may be a drilled hole that is two inches in diameter, and any part that is within 1/32 inch of the target is acceptable. On the other hand, the *robust quality view* of conformance emphasizes exactness of conformance. **Robustness** means exact conformance to the target value (no tolerance allowed). There is no range in which variation is acceptable. A nondefective machine part in the robust setting would be one that has a drilled hole that measures exactly two inches. Since evidence exists that product variation can be costly, the robust quality definition of conformance is superior to the traditional definition.

An example of the difference between the traditional approach and the robust quality approach can be found in two plants of the **Sony Corporation**. Both the Tokyo and the San Diego plants produce color television sets. One important feature of a color television set is color density. Sony sets a target value for color density as well as an upper specification limit and a lower specification limit. Any set with color density falling outside the specification limits is considered defective. Does that mean any set falling within the specification limits is acceptable? The viewpoint differs between the two plants. The San Diego plant emphasized zero defects in the traditional sense. In evaluating the quality of the color density of television sets, any television falling within the specification limits was deemed acceptable and shipped to customers. Sony of Tokyo, working with a robust quality viewpoint, strove to hit the target value for color density. Exhibit 14-1, on the following page, illustrates the distribution of color density of television sets shipped from the two plants.

When Sony evaluated customer satisfaction, it found that customers preferred the reduced variation of televisions produced at the Tokyo plant. These customers reported greater satisfaction and filed fewer warranty claims.[5]

---

5. Harold P. Roth and Thomas L. Albright, "What Are the Costs of Variability?" *Management Accounting* (June 1994): 51–55; and Genichi Taguchi and Don Clausing, "Robust Quality," *Harvard Business Review* (January–February 1990): 65–75.

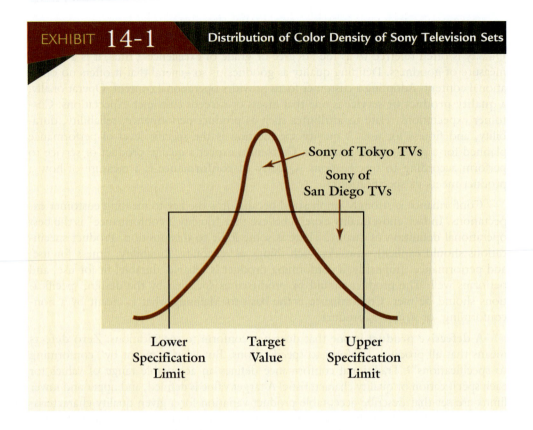

EXHIBIT 14-1   **Distribution of Color Density of Sony Television Sets**

Sony of Tokyo TVs

Sony of San Diego TVs

| Lower Specification Limit | Target Value | Upper Specification Limit |

Defining Quality Costs

Quality-linked activities are those activities performed because poor quality may or does exist. The costs of performing these activities are referred to as costs of quality. Thus, **costs of quality** are the costs that exist because poor quality may or does exist. This definition implies that quality costs are associated with two subcategories of quality-related activities: *control activities* and *failure activities*. **Control activities** are performed by an organization to prevent or detect poor quality (because poor quality may exist). Thus, control activities are made up of prevention and appraisal activities. **Control costs** are the costs of performing control activities. **Failure activities** are performed by an organization or its customers in response to poor quality (poor quality does exist). If the response to poor quality occurs before delivery of a bad (nonconforming, unreliable, not durable, and so on) product to a customer, the activities are classified as internal failure activities; otherwise, they are classified as external failure activities. **Failure costs** are the costs incurred by an organization because failure activities are performed. Notice that the definitions of failure activities and failure costs imply that customer response to poor quality can impose costs on an organization. The definitions of quality-related activities also imply four categories of quality costs: (1) prevention costs, (2) appraisal costs, (3) internal failure costs, and (4) external failure costs.

Prevention costs are incurred to prevent poor quality in the products or services being produced. As prevention costs increase, we would expect the costs of failure to decrease. Examples of prevention costs are quality engineering, quality training programs, quality planning, quality reporting, supplier evaluation and selection, quality audits, quality circles, field trials, and design reviews.

Appraisal costs are incurred to determine whether products and services are conforming to their requirements or customer needs. Examples include inspecting and testing materials, packaging inspection, supervising appraisal activities, product acceptance, process acceptance, measurement (inspection and test) equipment, and outside endorsements. Two of these terms require further explanation.

Product acceptance involves sampling from batches of finished goods to determine whether they meet an acceptable quality level; if so, the goods are accepted. *Process acceptance* involves sampling goods while in process to see if the process is in control and producing nondefective goods; if not, the process is shut down until corrective action can be taken. The main objective of the appraisal function is to prevent nonconforming goods from being shipped to customers.

Internal failure costs are incurred because products and services do not conform to specifications or customer needs. This nonconformance is detected prior to being shipped or delivered to outside parties. These are the failures detected by appraisal activities. Examples of internal failure costs are scrap, rework, downtime (due to defects), reinspection, retesting, and design changes. These costs disappear if no defects exist.

External failure costs are incurred because products and services fail to conform to requirements or satisfy customer needs after being delivered to customers. Of all the costs of quality, this category can be the most devastating. Costs of recalls, for example, can run into the hundreds of millions. Other examples include lost sales because of poor product performance, returns and allowances because of poor quality, warranties, repair, product liability, customer dissatisfaction, lost market share, and complaint adjustment. External failure costs, like internal failure costs, disappear if no defects exist.

Exhibit 14-2 summarizes the four quality cost categories and lists specific examples of costs. Each of the costs could have been expressed as the cost of quality-related activities such as the cost of certifying vendors, inspecting incoming materials, adjusting complaints, etc.

Quality Cost Measurement

Quality costs can also be classified as *observable* or *hidden*. **Observable quality costs** are those that are available from an organization's accounting records. **Hidden quality**

EXHIBIT 14-2   **Examples of Quality Costs by Category**

Prevention Costs	Appraisal (Detection) Costs
Quality engineering	Inspection of materials
Quality training	Packaging inspection
Recruiting	Product acceptance
Quality audits	Process acceptance
Design reviews	Field testing
Quality circles	Continuing supplier verification
Marketing research	
Prototype inspection	
Vendor certification	

Internal Failure Costs	External Failure Costs
Scrap	Lost sales (performance-related)
Rework	Returns/allowances
Downtime (defect-related)	Warranties
Reinspection	Discounts due to defects
Retesting	Product liability
Design changes	Complaint adjustment
Repairs	Recalls
	Ill will

costs are opportunity costs resulting from poor quality. (Opportunity costs are not usually recognized in accounting records.) Consider, for example, all the examples of quality costs listed in Exhibit 14-2. With the exception of lost sales, customer dissatisfaction, and lost market share, all the quality costs are observable and should be available from the accounting records. Note also that the hidden costs are all in the external failure category. These hidden quality costs can be significant and should be estimated. Although estimating hidden quality costs is not easy, three methods have been suggested: (1) the multiplier method, (2) the market research method, and (3) the Taguchi quality loss function.

The Multiplier Method

The multiplier method assumes that the total failure cost is simply some multiple of measured failure costs:

Total external failure cost = k(Measured external failure costs)

where k is the multiplier effect. The value of k is based on experience. For example, **Westinghouse Electric** reports a value of k between 3 and 4.[6] Thus, if the measured external failure costs are $3 million, the actual external failure costs are between $9 million and $12 million. Including hidden costs in assessing the amount of external failure costs allows management to more accurately determine the level of resource spending for prevention and appraisal activities. Specifically, with an increase in failure costs, we would expect management to increase its investment in control costs.

The Market Research Method

Formal market research methods are used to assess the effect of poor quality on sales and market share. Customer surveys and interviews with members of a company's sales force can provide significant insights into the magnitude of a company's hidden costs. Market research results can be used to project future profit losses attributable to poor quality.

The Taguchi Quality Loss Function

The traditional zero defects definition assumes that hidden quality costs exist only for units that fall outside the upper and lower specification limits. The **Taguchi loss function** assumes that any variation from the target value of a quality characteristic causes hidden quality costs. Furthermore, the hidden quality costs increase quadratically as the actual value deviates from the target value. The Taguchi quality loss function, illustrated in Exhibit 14-3, can be described by the following equation:

$$L(y) = k(y - T)^2 \qquad (17.1)$$

where

k = A proportionality constant dependent upon the organization's external failure cost structure
y = Actual value of quality characteristic
T = Target value of quality characteristic
L = Quality loss

Exhibit 14-3 demonstrates that the quality cost is zero at the target value and increases symmetrically, at an increasing rate, as the actual value varies from the target value. Assume, for example, that a company produces watches and the quality characteristic is accuracy (as measured by how much time is gained or lost in three months). Assume k = $2 and T = 0 minutes. Exhibit 14-4 illustrates the computation of the

---

6. T. L. Albright and P. R. Roth, "The Measurement of Quality Costs: An Alternative Paradigm," *Accounting Horizons* (June 1992): 15–27.

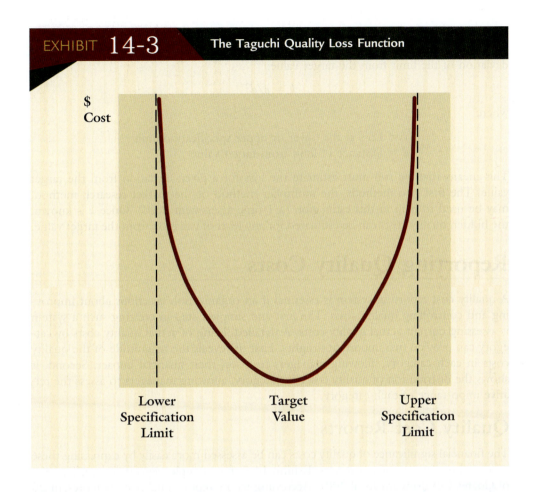

EXHIBIT 14-3   The Taguchi Quality Loss Function

$ Cost

Lower Specification Limit

Target Value

Upper Specification Limit

EXHIBIT 14-4   Quality Loss Computation Illustrated

Unit No.	Time Gained (Lost) (y)	y − T	(y − T)²	k(y − T)²
1	−1	−1	1	$ 2.00
2	2	2	4	8.00
3	4	4	16	32.00
4	−3	−3	9	18.00
			30	$60.00
Units			÷ 4	÷ 4
Average			7.5	$15.00

quality loss for four units. Notice that the cost quadruples when the deviation from target doubles (Units 2 and 3). Notice also that the average deviation squared and the average loss per unit can be computed. These averages can be used to compute the total expected hidden quality costs for a product. If, for example, the total units produced are 5,000 and the average squared deviation is 7.5, then the expected cost per unit is $15 (7.5 × $2) and the total expected loss for the 5,000 units would be $75,000 ($15 × 5,000).

To apply the Taguchi loss function, k must be estimated. The value for k is computed by dividing the estimated cost at one of the specification limits by the squared deviation of the limit from the target value:

$$k = c/d^2$$

where

c = Loss at the lower or upper specification limit
d = Distance of limit from target value

This means that we still must estimate the loss for a given deviation from the target value. The first two methods, the multiplier method or the market research method, may be used to help in this estimation (a 1-time assessment need). Once k is known, the hidden quality costs can be estimated for any level of variation from the target value.

Reporting Quality Costs

OBJECTIVE 2

Prepare a quality cost report, and explain its use.

A quality cost reporting system is essential if an organization is serious about improving and controlling quality costs. The first and simplest step in creating such a system is assessing current actual quality costs. A detailed listing of actual quality costs by category can provide two important insights. First, it reveals the magnitude of the quality costs in each category, allowing managers to assess their financial impact. Second, it shows the distribution of quality costs by category, allowing managers to assess the relative importance of each category.

Quality Cost Reports

The financial significance of quality costs can be assessed more easily by expressing these costs as a percentage of actual sales. Exhibit 14-5, for example, reports the quality costs of Goates Company for fiscal 2007. According to the report, quality costs represent 20 percent of sales. Given the rule of thumb that quality costs should be no more than 2 to 4 percent, Goates has ample opportunity to improve profits by decreasing quality costs. Understand, however, that reduction in costs should come through improvement of quality. Reduction of quality costs without any effort to improve quality could prove to be a disastrous strategy.

Additional insight concerning the relative distribution of quality costs can be realized by constructing charts that show the relative amount of costs in each category. Exhibit 14-6 provides a bar graph and pie chart that show each category's percentage contribution to total quality costs. The graphs reveal that failure costs are approximately 82 percent of the total quality costs, suggesting that Goates has ample opportunity to improve quality and lower total quality costs. But by how much? What is the optimal relative distribution of quality costs?

Distribution of Quality Costs: The Acceptable Quality View

One view of optimal quality cost distribution is the *acceptable quality view*. Although this view is no longer widely accepted, it serves as a useful point of reference for understanding the current views on how quality costs should be distributed. According to the acceptable quality view, there is an optimal tradeoff between failure and control costs. As control costs increase, failure costs should decrease. As long as the decrease in failure costs is greater than the corresponding increase in control costs, a company should continue increasing its efforts to prevent or detect nonconforming units. Eventually, a point is reached at which any additional increase in this effort costs more than the corresponding reduction in failure costs. This point represents the minimum level of total quality costs. It is the optimal balance between control costs and failure costs

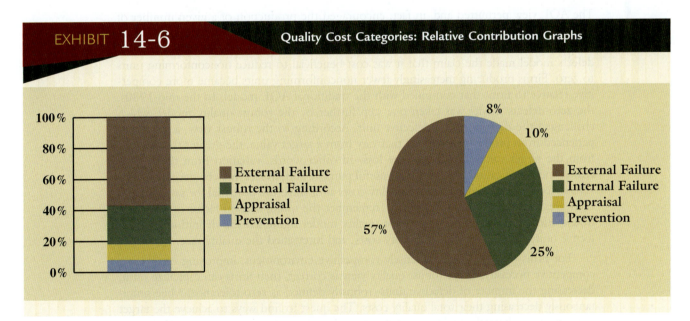

EXHIBIT 14-5   Quality Cost Report

Goates Company
Quality Cost Report
For the Year Ended June 30, 2007

	Quality Costs		Percentage of Sales[a]
Prevention costs:			
Quality training	$ 10,000		
Reliability engineering	65,000	$ 75,000	1.50%
Appraisal costs:			
Materials inspection	$ 5,000		
Product acceptance	20,000		
Process acceptance	75,000	100,000	2.00
Internal failure costs:			
Scrap	$150,000		
Rework	100,000	250,000	5.00
External failure costs:			
Customer complaints	$150,000		
Warranty	250,000		
Returns and allowances	175,000	575,000	11.50
Total quality costs		$1,000,000	20.00%[b]

[a]Actual sales of $5,000,000.
[b]$1,000,000/$5,000,000 = 20 percent.

EXHIBIT 14-6   Quality Cost Categories: Relative Contribution Graphs

and defines what is known as the **acceptable quality level (AQL)**. This theoretical relationship is illustrated in Exhibit 14-7 on the following page. The graph reveals that total quality costs decrease as quality improves up to a point. After that, no further improvement is possible. Thus, AQL identifies an optimal level of defective units. Note that this level does not correspond to that of zero defects.

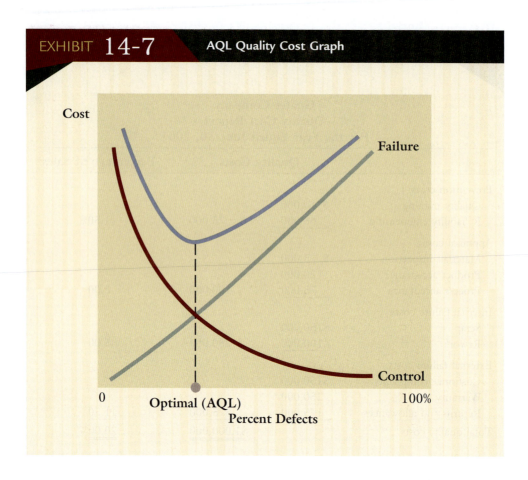

EXHIBIT 14-7   AQL Quality Cost Graph

Distribution of Quality Costs: Zero-Defects View

The AQL view permitted and, in fact, encouraged the production of a given number of defective units. This model prevailed in the quality control world until the late 1970s, when the AQL model was challenged by the zero-defects model. Essentially, the zero-defects model made the claim that it was cost-beneficial to reduce nonconforming units to zero. Firms producing increasingly fewer nonconforming units became more competitive relative to firms that continued with the traditional AQL model. In the mid-1980s, the zero-defects model was taken one step further by the robust quality model, which challenged the definition of a defective unit. According to the robust view, a loss is experienced from producing products that vary from a target value; the greater the distance from the target value, the greater the loss. In other words, variation from the ideal is costly, and specification limits serve no useful purpose and, in fact, may be deceptive. The zero-defects model understates the quality costs and, thus, the potential for savings from even greater efforts to improve quality (remember the multiplication factor of **Westinghouse Electric**). Therefore, the robust quality model tightened the definition of a defective unit, refined our view of quality costs, and intensified the quality race.

For firms operating in an intensely competitive environment, improving quality is a competitive necessity. If the robust quality view is correct, then firms can capitalize on it, decreasing the number of defective units (robustly defined as zero tolerance) while simultaneously decreasing their total quality costs. The quest to find ways to achieve the target value creates a dynamic quality world as opposed to the static quality world of AQL.

Robust Quality View and Quality Cost Distribution

Exhibit 14-8 shows a quality cost function consistent with the robust quality view. Essentially, what happens is that as firms increase their prevention and appraisal costs and reduce their failure costs, they discover that they can then cut back on their prevention

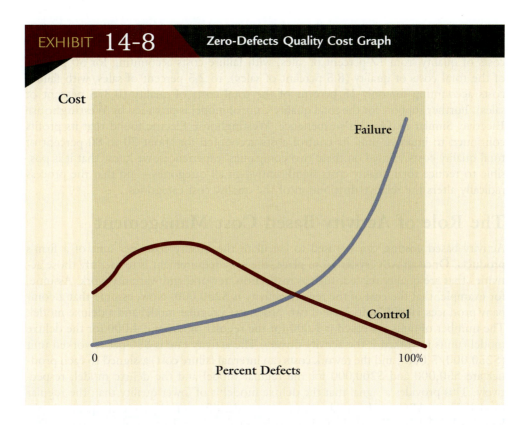

EXHIBIT 14-8   **Zero-Defects Quality Cost Graph**

and appraisal costs. What initially appears to be a trade-off turns out to be a permanent reduction in costs for all quality cost categories. There are some key differences. First, control costs do not increase without limit as a robust zero-defect state is approached. Second, control costs may increase and then decrease as the robust state is approached. Third, failure costs can be driven to zero.

Suppose, for example, that a firm has decided to improve the quality of its products by reengineering its manufacturing processes. The objective is to identify ways of producing products that have less chance of being defective. As the firm works to implement this program, additional costs may be incurred (for example, special studies, consulting fees, and hiring of additional process design engineers, etc.). Initially, other prevention and appraisal costs may continue at their current levels. However, once the program is fully implemented and evidence is surfacing that the failure costs are being reduced (for example, less rework, fewer customer complaints, and fewer repairs), then the company may decide to cut back on inspections of product, customer complaint departments, and so on. The net effect is a reduction in all quality cost categories. And quality has increased!

This example is consistent with the strategy to reduce quality costs recommended by the American Society for Quality Control:[7]

> *The strategy for reducing quality costs is quite simple: (1) take direct attack on failure costs in an attempt to drive them to zero; (2) invest in the "right" prevention activities to bring about improvement; (3) reduce appraisal costs according to results achieved; and, (4) continuously evaluate and redirect prevention efforts to gain further improvement. This strategy is based on the premise that:*

- *For each failure there is a* root cause.
- *Causes are* preventable.
- *Prevention is always* cheaper.

---

7. Jack Campanella, ed., *Principles of Quality Costs* (Milwaukee: ASQC Quality Press, 1990): 12.

This ability to reduce total quality costs dramatically in all categories is borne out by real-world experiences. **Tennant**, for example, over an 8-year period, reduced its costs of quality from 17 percent of sales, with failure costs accounting for 50 percent of the total costs of quality (8.5 percent of sales), to 2.5 percent of sales, with failure costs accounting for only 15 percent of the total costs of quality (0.375 percent of sales). Further support for the total quality control model is provided by **Westinghouse Electric**. Similar to Tennant's experience, Westinghouse Electric found that its profits continued to improve until its control costs accounted for about 70 to 80 percent of total quality costs.[8] Based on these two companies' experiences, we know that it is possible to reduce total quality costs significantly—in all categories—and that the process radically alters the relative distribution of the quality cost categories.

The Role of Activity-Based Cost Management

Activity-based costing can be used to calculate the quality costs per unit of a firm's products. Once an ABC system is in place, the only requirement is to identify those activities that are quality related, such as inspection, rework, and warranty work. Assume, for example, that the cost of the rework activity is $250,000. Now, assume that a company produces 10,000 units each of two products: a regular model and a deluxe model. The number of units reworked is 1,000 for the regular model and 4,000 for the deluxe model (units reworked is the activity driver). The activity rate is $50 per reworked unit ($250,000/5,000), and the rework costs (an internal failure cost) assigned to each product are $50,000 and $200,000 for the regular model and the deluxe model, respectively. This provides a signal that the deluxe model is of lower quality than the regular model. Thus, ABC can be used as a means to identify cost objects with quality problems, such as low-quality products, low-quality processes, and low-quality suppliers. This can then allow more focused management of quality costs.

Activity-based management is also useful. ABM classifies activities as value-added and non-value-added and keeps only those that add value. This principle can be applied to quality-related activities. Appraisal and failure activities and their associated costs are non-value-added and should be eliminated (eventually). Prevention activities—performed efficiently—can be classified as value-added and should be retained. **Grede Foundries, Inc.**, of Milwaukee, the world's largest foundry company, has been tracking all four categories of quality costs for more than 15 years. However, it does not report prevention costs as part of its final cost-of-quality figures because it does not want its managers to reduce quality costs by cutting prevention activities. It feels strongly that spending money on prevention activities pays off. For example, it has found that a 1 percent reduction in scrap reduces external defects by about 5 percent.[9]

Root causes (cost drivers) can also be identified, especially for failure activities, and used to help managers understand what is causing the costs of the activities. This information can then be used to select ways of reducing quality costs to the level demonstrated in Exhibit 14-8. In effect, activity-based management supports the robust zero-defect view of quality costs. There is no optimal trade-off between control and failure costs; the latter are non-value-added costs and should be reduced to zero. Some control activities are non-value-added and should be eliminated. Other control activities are value-added but may be performed inefficiently, and the costs caused by the inefficiency are non-value-added. Thus, costs for these categories may also be reduced to lower levels.

---

8. These factual observations are based on those reported by Carr and Tyson, "Planning Quality Cost Expenditures," *Management Accounting* (August 1995).

9. Nancy Chase, "Accounting for Quality: Counting Costs, Reaping Returns," *Quality*. Vol. 37, Issue 10 (October 1998): 38–42.

OBJECTIVE **3**

Explain why quality cost information is needed and how it is used.

Quality Cost Information and Decision Making

Reporting quality costs can improve managerial planning, control, and decision making. For example, if a company wants to implement a process reengineering program to improve the quality of its products, it will need to assess the following: current quality costs by item and by category, the additional costs associated with the program, and the projected savings by item and by category. *When* the costs and savings will occur must also be projected. Then, a capital budgeting analysis can be done to determine the merits of the proposed program. If the outcome is favorable and the program is initiated, then it becomes important to monitor the program through performance reporting.

Using quality cost information to implement and monitor the effectiveness of quality programs is only one use of a quality cost system. Other important uses can also be identified. Quality cost information is an important input to management decision making. It is also important to outside parties as they assess the quality of the company, through programs such as ISO 9000.

Decision Making Contexts

Managers need quality cost information in a number of decision-making contexts. Two of these contexts are strategic pricing and cost-volume-profit analysis.

Strategic Pricing

Consider AMD, Inc., which produces electronic measurement devices. Market share for the company's low-level electronic measurement instruments had been steadily dropping. Linda Werther, marketing manager, identified price as the major problem. She knew that Japanese firms produced and sold the low-level instruments for less than AMD could. If AMD reduced its price to that of the competition, the new price would be below cost. Yet, if something were not done, the Japanese firms would continue to expand their market share. One possibility was simply to drop the low-level line and concentrate on instruments in the medium- and high-level categories. Linda knew, however, that this was a short-term solution, since soon the same Japanese firms would be competing at the higher levels. A brief income statement for the low-level instruments is as follows:

Revenues (1,000,000 @ $20)	$20,000,000
Cost of goods sold	(15,000,000)
Operating expenses	(3,000,000)
Product-line income	$ 2,000,000

Linda strongly believed that a 15 percent price decrease would restore the instrument line's market share and profitability to its former levels. One possibility was the implementation of total quality management. Her first action was to request information on the quality costs for the lower-level instruments. AMD's controller, Eugene Sadler, admitted that the costs were not tracked separately. For example, the cost of scrap was buried in the work-in-process inventory account. He did promise, however, to estimate some of the costs. Data from his report for the low-level instruments are as follows:

Quality costs (estimated):	
Inspection of materials	$ 200,000
Scrap	800,000
Rejects	500,000
Rework	400,000
Product inspection	300,000
Warranty work	1,000,000
Total estimate	$3,200,000

Upon receiving the report, Linda, Eugene, and Art Smith, manager of the quality control department, met to determine possible ways of reducing quality costs for the low-level line. Art was confident that the quality costs could be reduced by 50 percent within 18 months. He had already begun planning the implementation of a new quality program. Linda calculated that a 50 percent reduction in the quality costs associated with the low-level instruments would reduce costs by about $1.60 per unit ($1,600,000/1,000,000)—which would make up slightly more than half of the $3 reduction in selling price that would be needed (the reduction is 15 percent of $20). Based on this outcome, Linda decided to implement the price reduction in three phases: a $1 reduction immediately, a $1 reduction in six months, and the final reduction of $1 in 12 months. This phased reduction would likely prevent any further erosion of market share and would start increasing market share sometime in the second phase. By phasing in the price reductions, the quality control department would have time to reduce costs so that any big losses could be avoided.

The AMD, Inc., example illustrates that both quality cost information and the implementation of a total quality control program contributed to a significant strategic decision. It also illustrates that improving quality was not a panacea. The reductions were not as large as needed to bear the full price reduction. Other productivity gains will be needed to ensure the long-range viability of the product line. Implementing JIT manufacturing, for example, might reduce inventories and decrease costs of materials handling and maintenance.

Cost-Volume-Profit Analysis and Strategic Design Decisions

Traditionally, cost-volume-profit analysis relies on the analysis of fixed and variable costs in conjunction with cost. Terry Foster, the marketing manager, and Sharon Fox, the design engineer, discovered shortcomings in the traditional analysis when they proposed a new product. They had been certain that a proposal for the new product was going to be approved. Instead, they received the following report from the controller's office.

Report: New Product Analysis, Project 675

Projected sales potential: 44,000 units
Production capacity: 45,000 units
Unit selling price: $60
Unit variable costs: $40
Fixed costs:

Product development	$ 500,000
Manufacturing	200,000
Selling	300,000
Total	$1,000,000

Projected break-even: 50,000 units
Decision: Reject
Reason(s): The break-even point is greater than the production capacity as well as the projected sales volume.

In an effort to discover just why the cost figures came out so poorly for a project that both individuals felt strongly would be profitable, the two met with Bob Brown, the assistant controller. The following conversation took place.

SHARON: Bob, I would like to know why there is a $3-per-unit scrap cost. Can you explain it?

BOB: Sure. It's based on the scrap cost that we track for existing, similar products.

SHARON: Well, I think you have overlooked the new design features of this new product. Its design virtually eliminates any waste—especially when you consider that the product will be made on a numerically controlled machine.

TERRY: Also, this $2-per-unit charge for repair work should be eliminated. The new design that Sharon is proposing solves the failure problems we have had with related products. It also means that the $100,000 of fixed costs associated with the Repair Center can be eliminated.

BOB: Sharon, how certain are you that this new design will eliminate some of these quality problems?

SHARON: I'm absolutely positive. The early prototypes did exactly as we expected. The results of those tests are included in the proposal.

BOB: Right. Reducing the variable cost by $5 per unit and the fixed costs by $100,000 produces a break-even point of 36,000 units. These changes alone make the project viable. I'll change the report to reflect a positive recommendation.

The above scenario illustrates the importance of further classifying quality costs by behavior. Although only unit-based behavior is assumed, activity-based classification is also possible and could enhance the decision usefulness of quality costs. The scenario also reinforces the importance of identifying and reporting quality costs separately. The new product was designed to reduce its quality costs, and only by knowing the quality costs assigned could Sharon and Terry have discovered the error in the break-even analysis. Finally, notice the effect total quality management has on design decisions. By being aware of the quality costs and their causes, the new product's design was structured to avoid many of the existing quality problems.

Certifying Quality through ISO 9000

Just as a company assesses the quality of its suppliers, that same company may supply other companies that require vendor certification of quality. A relatively new program called ISO 9000 has evolved in response to the need for a standardized set of procedures for supplier quality verification.

ISO (pronounced ICE-OH) 9000 is a standard of quality measurement. Developed by the International Organization for Standardization in Geneva, Switzerland, it is a series of five international quality standards. These standards center on the concept of documentation and control of nonconformance and change. ISO 9000 has been a success in Europe, and U.S. companies doing business in Europe were the first to board the ISO 9000 bandwagon, simply because it is a requirement of doing business. Companies that attain ISO 9000 certification have been audited by an independent test company, which certifies that the company meets certain quality standards. These standards do not apply to the production of a particular product or service. Instead, they apply to the way in which a company ensures quality, for example, by testing products, training employees, keeping records, and fixing defects.

It is important to note that ISO 9000 does not certify either the quality of the product itself or the commitment of the company to continuous improvement. In fact, ISO 9000 is a vocabulary and a set of five standards. These are given in Exhibit 14-9.[10] As a result, companies that require ISO 9000 certification (like **Motorola** or **GE**) do not stop auditing their suppliers. Requiring ISO 9000 certification is just a first step.

EXHIBIT 14-9   **ISO 9000 Standards**

ISO 8402: Quality—Vocabulary
ISO 9000: Quality management and quality assurance standards—Guidelines for selection and use
ISO 9001: Quality systems—Model for quality assurance in design/development, production, installation, and servicing
ISO 9002: Quality systems—Model for quality assurance in production and installation
ISO 9003: Quality systems—Model for quality assurance in final inspection and test
ISO 9004: Quality management and quality system elements—Guidelines

---

On the plus side, many companies have found that the process of applying for ISO 9000 certification, while lengthy and expensive (it can take many months and cost $1,000,000 or more for larger companies), yields important benefits in terms of self-knowledge and improved financial performance. For example, **Haworth Furniture**, a maker of office furniture, posts placards with words and pictures at work stations throughout its five factories to show employees exactly what should be done. These placards help to ensure that all workers are following company policies consistently, a hallmark of conformance quality. Similarly, **Allen-Bradley**'s Twinsburg plant has improved quality and productivity significantly by replacing a system of paper manuals with an electronic mail system. Now, when engineering changes are made, the system purges the old instructions and inserts the new ones. Workers no longer tape personal directions to their work stations—directions which were quickly out of date.

ISO 9000 is not a quality system. It is a first step in supplier certification. However, companies are finding it hard to resist paying for an independent audit of their quality processes. By 1998, 21,482 ISO 9000 certifications had been awarded in the United

---

10. These steps are listed in A. Faye Borthick and Harold P. Roth, "Will Europeans Buy Your Company's Products?" *Management Accounting* (July 1992): 28–32. This article is an excellent introduction to ISO 9000 certification and includes a useful listing of quality definitions.

States; worldwide, over 500,000 certifications have been issued.[11] ISO 9000 standards have been adopted by 90 countries. Many large companies, including **DuPont**, **GE**, **Eastman Kodak**, and **British Telecom**, are urging their suppliers to obtain certificates.

OBJECTIVE 4

Describe and prepare three different types of quality performance reports.

Controlling Quality Costs

Good quality cost management requires that quality costs be reported and controlled (control having a cost reduction emphasis). Control enables managers to compare actual outcomes with standard outcomes to gauge performance and take any necessary corrective actions. Quality cost performance reports have two essential elements: actual outcomes and standard or expected outcomes. Deviations of actual outcomes from the expected outcomes are used to evaluate managerial performance and provide signals concerning possible problems.

Performance reports are essential to quality improvement programs. A report like the one shown in Exhibit 14-5 (see page 629) forces managers to identify the various costs that should appear in a performance report, to identify the current quality performance level of the organization, and to begin thinking about the level of quality performance that should be achieved. Identifying the quality standard is a key element in a quality performance report. The standard should emphasize cost reduction opportunities.

Choosing the Quality Standard

The Traditional Approach

In the traditional approach, the appropriate quality standard is an acceptable quality level (AQL). An AQL is simply an admission that a certain number of defective products will be produced and sold. For example, the AQL may be set at 3 percent. In this case, any lot of products (or production run) that has no more than 3 percent defective units will be shipped to customers. Typically, the AQL reflects the current operating status, not what is possible if a firm has an excellent quality program. As the basis for a quality standard, AQL has the same problems as historical experience does for materials and labor usage standards: it may perpetuate past operating mistakes.

Unfortunately, AQL has additional problems. Setting a 3 percent AQL is a commitment to deliver defective products to customers. Out of every 1 million units sold, 30,000 will yield dissatisfied customers. Why plan to make a certain number of defective units? Why not plan instead to make the product according to its specifications? Is there not a matter of integrity involved here? How many customers would accept a product if they knew that it was defective? How many people would consult a surgeon if they knew that the surgeon planned to botch three of every 100 operations?

The Total Quality Approach

These questions reflect a new attitude toward quality. A more sensible standard is to produce products as they are intended to be. This standard will be referred to as the robust *zero-defects standard*. It reflects a philosophy of total quality control and calls for products and services to be produced and delivered that meet the targeted value. Thus, when we say zero defects, we are referring to defective units in the robust sense. Recall that the need for total quality control is inherent in a JIT manufacturing approach. Thus, the movement toward total quality control is being sustained by the firms adopting JIT. JIT, however, is not a prerequisite for moving toward total quality control. This approach can stand by itself.

Admittedly, the total quality standard is one that may not be completely attainable; however, evidence exists that it can be closely approximated. Defects are caused either

---

11. Charles J. Corbett, Maria J. Montes, David A. Kirsch, and Maria Jose Alvarez-Gil, "Does ISO Certification Pay?" *Special Reports*, at www.iso.org/iso/fr/iso9000-14000/articles/specialreports.html, accessed December 16, 2004.

by lack of knowledge or by lack of attention. Lack of knowledge can be corrected by proper training and lack of attention by effective leadership. Note also that total quality control implies the ultimate elimination of failure costs. Those who believe that no defects should be permitted will continue to search for new ways to improve quality costs.

Some may wonder whether adherence to the ideal is a realistic standard. Consider the following anecdote. An American firm placed an order for a particular component with a Japanese firm. In the order, the American firm specified that 1,000 components should be delivered with an AQL of 5 percent defects. When the order arrived, it came in two boxes—one large and one small. A note explained that the large box contained 950 good components and the small one held the 50 defective components; the note also asked why the firm wanted 50 defective parts (implying the capability of delivering no defective parts).

Consider another case. A firm engaged in a significant volume of business through mailings. On average, fifteen percent of the mailings were sent to the wrong address. Returned merchandise, late payments, and lost sales all resulted from this error rate. In one case, a tax payment was sent to the wrong address. By the time the payment arrived, it was late, causing a penalty of $300,000. Why not spend the resources (surely less than $300,000) to get the mailing list right and have no errors? Is a mailing list that is 100 percent accurate really impossible to achieve? Why not do it right the first time?

Quantifying the Quality Standard

Quality can be measured by its costs; as the costs of quality decrease, higher quality results—at least up to a point. Even if the standard of zero defects is achieved, a company must still have prevention and appraisal costs. A company with a well-run quality management program can get by with quality costs of about 2.5 percent of sales. (If zero defects are achieved, this cost is for prevention and appraisal.) This 2.5 percent standard is accepted by many quality control experts and many firms that are adopting aggressive quality improvement programs.

The 2.5 percent standard is for total costs of quality. Costs of individual quality factors, such as quality training or materials inspection, will be less. Each organization must determine the appropriate standard for each individual factor. Budgets can be used to set spending for each standard so that the total budgeted cost meets the 2.5 percent goal.

Physical Standards

For line managers and operating personnel, physical measures of quality—such as number of defects per unit, the percentage of external failures, billing errors, contract errors, and other physical measures—may be more meaningful. For physical measures, the quality standard is zero defects or errors. The objective is to get everyone to do it right the first time.

Use of Interim Standards

For most firms, the standard of zero defects is a long-range goal. The ability to achieve this standard is strongly tied to supplier quality. For most companies, materials and services purchased from outside parties make up a significant part of a product's cost. For example, more than 65 percent of the product cost for **Tennant Company** was from materials and parts purchased from more than 500 different suppliers. To achieve the desired quality level, Tennant had to launch a major campaign to involve its suppliers in similar quality improvement programs. Developing the relationships and securing the needed cooperation from suppliers takes time—in fact, it takes years. Similarly, getting people within the company itself to understand the need for quality improvement and to have confidence in the program can take several years.

Because improving quality to the zero-defects level can take years, yearly quality improvement standards should be developed so that managers can use performance reports to assess the progress made on an interim basis. These **interim quality standards** express quality goals for the year. Progress should be reported to managers and employees in order to gain the confidence needed to achieve the ultimate standard of zero defects. Even though reaching the zero-defects level is a long-range project, management should expect significant progress on a yearly basis. For example, Tennant cut its quality costs from 17 percent of sales to 8 percent of sales over a period of six years—an average reduction of more than 1 percent per year. Furthermore, once the 2.5 percent goal is reached, efforts must be expended continuously to maintain it. Performance reports, at this stage, assume a strict control role.

Types of Quality Performance Reports

Quality performance reports measure the progress realized by an organization's quality improvement program. Three types of progress can be measured and reported:

1. Progress with respect to a current-period standard or goal (an interim standard report)
2. The progress trend since the inception of the quality improvement program (a multiple-period trend report)
3. Progress with respect to the long-range standard or goal (a long-range report)

Interim Standard Report

The organization must establish an interim quality standard each year and make plans to achieve this targeted level. Since quality costs are a measure of quality, the targeted level can be expressed in dollars budgeted for each category of quality costs and for each cost item within the category. At the end of the period, the **interim quality performance report** compares the actual quality costs for the period with the budgeted costs. This report measures the progress achieved within the period relative to the planned level of progress for that period. Exhibit 14-10 illustrates such a report.

The interim report reveals the within-period quality improvement relative to specific objectives as reflected by the budgeted figures. For AMD, the overall performance is close to what was planned: total actual quality costs differ by $29,000 from total budgeted quality costs and the actual costs, a mere 0.36 percent as a percentage of sales.

Multiple-Period Trend Report

The report in Exhibit 14-10 provides management with information concerning the within-period progress measured relative to specific goals. Also useful is a picture of how the quality improvement program has been doing since its inception. Is the multiple-period trend—the overall change in quality costs—moving in the right direction? Are significant quality gains being made each period? Answers to these questions can be given by providing a chart or graph that tracks the change in quality from the beginning of the program to the present. Such a graph is called a **multiple-period quality trend report**. By plotting quality costs as a percentage of sales against time, the overall trend in the quality program can be assessed. The first year plotted is the year prior to the implementation of the quality improvement program. Assume that AMD, Inc., has experienced the following:

	Quality Costs	*Actual Sales*	*Costs as a Percentage of Sales*
2003	$1,000,000	$5,000,000	20.0%
2004	990,000	5,500,000	18.0
2005	900,000	6,000,000	15.0
2006	868,000	6,200,000	14.0
2007	800,000	8,000,000	10.0

Letting 2003 be Year 1, 2004 be Year 2, and so on, Exhibit 14-11, on page 641, shows a bar graph that reveals the trend in quality cost as a percentage of sales. Periods of time are plotted on the horizontal axis and percentages on the vertical.

EXHIBIT 14-10   Interim Quality Performance Report

AMD, Inc.
Interim Standard Performance Report: Quality Costs
For the Year Ended June 30, 2007

	Actual Costs	Budgeted Costs	Variance
Prevention costs:			
Quality training	$ 80,000	$ 80,000	$ 0
Reliability engineering	160,000	160,000	0
Total prevention costs	$240,000	$240,000	$ 0
Appraisal costs:			
Materials inspection	$ 75,000	$ 83,000	$ 8,000 F
Product acceptance	40,000	40,000	0
Process acceptance	65,000	55,000	10,000 U
Total appraisal costs	$180,000	$178,000	$ 2,000 U
Internal failure costs:			
Scrap	$ 50,000	$ 44,000	$ 6,000 U
Rework	100,000	96,500	3,500 U
Total internal failure costs	$150,000	$140,500	$ 9,500 U
External failure costs:			
Customer complaints	$ 65,000	$ 65,000	$ 0
Warranty	78,000	68,500	9,500 U
Repair	87,000	79,000	8,000 U
Total external failure costs	$230,000	$212,500	$17,500 U
Total quality costs	$800,000	$771,000	$29,000 U
Percentage of actual sales of $8,000,000	10.0%	9.64%	0.36% U

The graph reveals that there has been a steady downward trend in quality costs expressed as a percentage of sales. The graph also reveals that there is still ample room for improvement toward the long-run target percentage.

Additional insight can be provided by analyzing the trend for each individual quality category. Assume that each category is expressed as a percentage of sales for the same period of time.

	Prevention	*Appraisal*	*Internal Failure*	*External Failure*
2003	2.0%	2.0%	6.0%	10.0%
2004	3.0	2.4	4.0	8.6
2005	3.0	3.0	3.0	6.0
2006	4.0	3.0	2.5	4.5
2007	4.1	2.4	2.0	1.5

The graph showing the trend for each category (as a percentage of sales) is displayed in Exhibit 14-12. From Exhibit 14-12, we can see that AMD has had dramatic success in reducing external and internal failures. More money is being spent on prevention (the amount has doubled as a percentage). Appraisal costs have increased and then decreased.

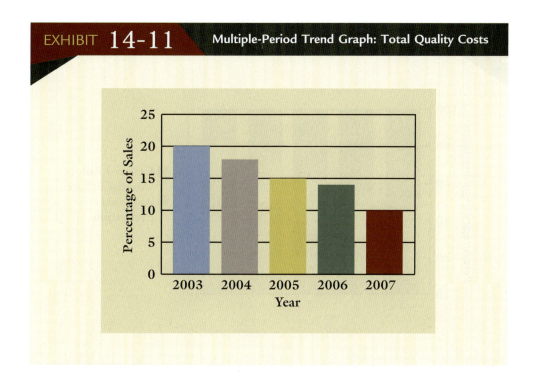

EXHIBIT 14-11   Multiple-Period Trend Graph: Total Quality Costs

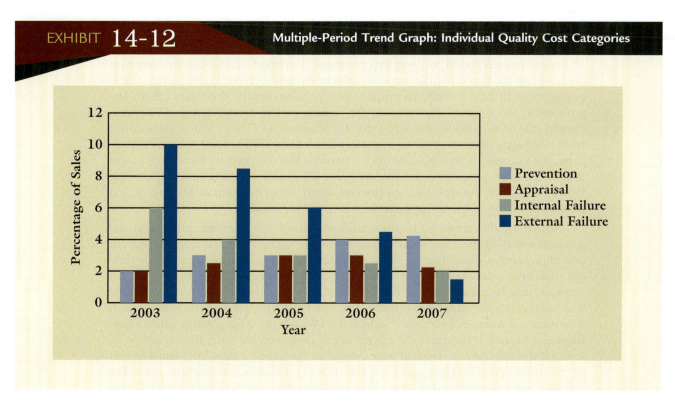

EXHIBIT 14-12   Multiple-Period Trend Graph: Individual Quality Cost Categories

Additional insight can be obtained by examining the trend in the relative distribution of quality costs. Exhibit 14-13 provides a graph showing this feature. Note also that the relative distribution of costs has changed. In 2003, failure costs were 80 percent of the total quality costs (16%/20%). In 2007, they are 35 percent of the total (3.5%/10%). Note also that control costs have increased from 20% (4%/20%) to 65% (6.5%/10%). Combining the two, we see evidence that the mix of quality costs is the key to cost reduction. Increasing prevention costs causes non-value-added quality costs to decrease.

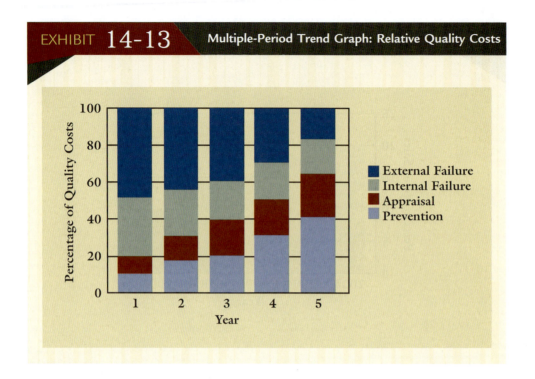

EXHIBIT 14-13   Multiple-Period Trend Graph: Relative Quality Costs

Long-Range Report

At the end of each period, a report that compares the period's actual quality costs with the costs that the firm eventually hopes to achieve should be prepared. This report forces management to keep the ultimate quality goal in mind, reveals the room left for improvement, and facilitates planning for the coming period. Under a zero-defects philosophy, the costs of failure should be virtually nonexistent. (They are non-value-added costs.) Reducing the costs of failure increases a firm's competitive ability. **Tennant Company**, for example, is now able to offer warranties that last two to four times longer than those of its competitors because of improved quality resulting in lower external failure rates. Thus, not only have quality costs been reduced by almost 50 percent, but because of improved quality, sales performance has increased.

Remember that achieving higher quality will not totally eliminate prevention and appraisal costs. (In fact, increased emphasis on zero defects may actually increase the cost of prevention, depending on the type and level of prevention activities initially present.) Generally, we would expect appraisal costs to decrease. Product acceptance, for example, may be phased out entirely as product quality increases; however, increased emphasis on process acceptance is likely. The firm must have assurance that the process is operating in a zero-defects mode. Exhibit 14-14 illustrates a **long-range quality performance report**. It compares the current actual costs with the costs that would be allowed if the zero-defects standard were being met (assuming a sales level equal to that of the current period). The target costs are, if chosen properly, value-added costs. The variances are non-value-added costs. Thus, the long-range performance report is simply a variation of the value- and non-value-added cost report.

The report emphasizes the fact that the company is still spending too much money on quality—too much money for not doing things right the first time. As quality improves, savings can be realized by having fewer workers correcting the mistakes made initially. Rework costs, for example, will disappear when there is no more rework, warranty costs will stop when there are no failures in the field, and so on.

By spending less money on defects, a company can use the money to expand and to employ additional people to support this expansion. Increased quality may naturally

EXHIBIT 14-14	Long-Range Quality Performance Report

AMD, Inc. Long-Range Quality Performance Report For the Year Ended June 30, 2007	Actual Costs	Target Costs*	Variance
Prevention costs:			
Fixed:			
Quality training	$ 80,000	$ 50,000	$ 30,000 U
Reliability engineering	160,000	100,000	60,000 U
Total prevention costs	$240,000	$150,000	$ 90,000 U
Appraisal costs:			
Variable:			
Materials inspection	$ 75,000	$ 5,000	$ 70,000 U
Product acceptance	40,000	0	40,000 U
Process acceptance	65,000	20,000	45,000 U
Total appraisal costs	$180,000	$ 25,000	$155,000 U
Internal failure costs:			
Variable:			
Scrap	$ 50,000	$ 0	$ 50,000 U
Rework	100,000	0	100,000 U
Total internal failure costs	$150,000	$ 0	$150,000 U
External failure costs:			
Fixed:			
Customer complaints	$ 65,000	$ 0	$ 65,000 U
Variable:			
Warranty	78,000	0	78,000 U
Repair	87,000	0	87,000 U
Total external failure costs	$230,000	$ 0	$230,000 U
Total quality costs	$800,000	$175,000	$625,000 U
Percentage of actual sales	10%	2.2%	7.81% U

*Based on actual current sales of $8,000,000. These costs are value-added costs.

cause expansion by increasing the competitive position of a firm. By having fewer problems with existing products, a firm can focus more attention on growth. Thus, although improved quality may mean fewer jobs in some areas, it also means that additional jobs will be created through expanded business activity. In fact, more jobs will probably be added than are lost.

Incentives for Quality Improvement

Most organizations provide both monetary and nonmonetary recognition for significant contributions to quality improvement. Of the two types of incentives, many quality experts believe that the nonmonetary are more useful.

Nonmonetary Incentives As with budgets, participation helps employees internalize quality improvement goals as their own. One approach used by many companies in their efforts to involve employees is the use of error cause identification forms. **Error cause identification** is a program in which employees describe problems that interfere with their ability to do the job right the first time. The error-cause-removal approach is one of the 14 steps in Philip Crosby's quality improvement program.[12] To ensure the success of the program, each employee submitting an entry should receive a note of appreciation from management. Additional recognition should be given to those who submit particularly beneficial information.

Other nonfinancial awards can also be given to recognize employees for their efforts. One restaurant, for example, gives monthly awards to food servers who have made no errors when punching diners' orders into the kitchen printout computer. Servers who make the most errors see their names posted on an error list (no punishment, just names). The error rate plummeted, saving the restaurant thousands of dollars a month in wasted food.[13] The important thing is not the award itself but the public recognition of outstanding achievement. By publicly recognizing significant quality contributions, management underscores its commitment to quality improvement. Also, the individuals and groups so recognized feel the benefits of that recognition, which include pride, job satisfaction, and a further commitment to quality.

Monetary Incentives Gainsharing provides cash incentives for a company's entire workforce that are keyed to quality or productivity gains. For example, suppose a company has a target of reducing the number of defective units by 10 percent during the next quarter for a particular plant. If the goal is achieved, the company estimates that $1,000,000 will be saved (through avoiding such things as reworks and warranty repairs). Gainsharing provides an incentive by offering a bonus to the employees equal to a percentage of the cost savings. At **Tennant Company**, for example, employees who submitted adopted proposals for quality changes receive 20 percent of the first year's savings realized from these submissions.

Ford Motor Company has proposed overhauling its compensation program for its top 5,000 executives, implementing a new compensation program that replaces profit-driven bonus structures with performance-based measures such as overall product quality. The size of the bonus pool can grow or shrink depending on how well productivity and quality targets are met. **Sun Microsystems** provides another example.[14] Bonuses are tied to customer loyalty and customer quality indices. Sun Microsystems has found that such quality measures as late deliveries and software defects have declined steadily, while the customer loyalty measures have increased. Pay-for-performance plans allowing employees to share in the benefits seem to create additional interest and commitment. Gainsharing plans are entirely complementary, and perhaps even essential, to an integrated measurement system such as the Balanced Scorecard.

---

12. Phillip Crosby, *Quality Is Free* (New York: New American Library, 1980).
13. Leonard L. Berry and A. Parasuramna, *Marketing Services: Competing Through Quality* (New York: The Free Press, Macmillan, 1991).
14. Both examples are taken from the following source: Melissa Larson, "Betting Your Bonus on Quality." *Quality*. Vol. 37, Issue 5 (May 1998): 30.

SUMMARY

To understand quality costs, it is first necessary to understand what is meant by quality. Quality means goodness, but its operational meaning is more relevant. Operationally, a quality product is one that meets customer expectations. Customer expectations are closely connected with conformance to specifications. Quality of conformance, thus, is concerned with meeting the specifications claimed by the product.

Two philosophical approaches to quality were described. The zero-defects approach allows variation from a target within certain specification limits. The robust quality approach stresses reduction of variation, noting that any variation entails hidden quality costs. The Taguchi quality loss function illustrates the hidden quality costs associated with the robustness philosophy.

Quality costs are those costs that are incurred because products may fail or actually fail to meet design specifications (and are, therefore, associated with quality of conformance). There are four categories of quality costs: prevention, appraisal, internal failure, and external failure. Prevention costs are those incurred to prevent poor quality. Appraisal costs are those incurred to detect poor quality. Internal failure costs are those incurred because products fail to conform to requirements, and this lack of conformity is discovered before an external sale. External failure costs are those incurred because products fail to conform to requirements after an external sale is made.

A quality cost report is prepared by listing costs for each item within each of the four major quality cost categories (see Exhibit 14-2 on page 625). Two views concern the optimal distribution of quality costs: the AQL view and the zero-defects view. The AQL view holds that there is a trade-off between costs of failure and prevention and appraisal costs. This trade-off produces an optimal level of performance called the acceptable quality level (the level at which the number of defects allowed minimizes total quality costs). The zero-defects view, on the other hand, espouses total quality control. Total quality control maintains that the conflict between failure and appraisal and prevention costs is more conjecture than real. The actual optimal level of defects is the zero-defects level; companies should be striving to achieve this level of quality. Although quality costs do not vanish at this level, they are much lower than the optimal envisioned by the now outmoded AQL view.

Quality cost information is needed to help managers control quality performance and to serve as input for decision making. It can be used to evaluate the overall performance of quality improvement programs. It can also be used to help improve a variety of managerial decisions, for example, strategic pricing and cost-volume-profit analysis. Perhaps the most important observation is that quality cost information is fundamental in a company's pursuit of continual improvement. Quality is one of the major competitive dimensions for world-class competitors. Many companies now have their dedication to quality certified by an external reporting firm under, for example, ISO 9000 specifications.

Three quality performance reports are mentioned in the chapter: (1) the interim report, (2) the multiple-period trend report, and (3) the long-range report. The interim report is used to evaluate the firm's ability to meet its budgeted quality costs. Managers use the report to compare the actual quality costs with those that were targeted for the period. The multiple-period trend report is a trend graph for several years. The graph allows managers to assess the direction and magnitude of change since the inception of a total quality program. Finally, the long-range report compares actual costs with the ideal level.

REVIEW PROBLEM AND SOLUTION

QUALITY COST CLASSIFICATION, QUALITY IMPROVEMENT, AND PROFITABILITY

At the beginning of the year, Kare Company initiated a quality improvement program. Considerable effort was expended to reduce the number of defective units produced. By the end of the year, reports from the production manager revealed that scrap and rework had both decreased. The president of the company was pleased to hear of the success but wanted some assessment of the financial impact of the improvements. To make this assessment, the following financial data were collected for the current and preceding years:

	Preceding Year (2006)	Current Year (2007)
Sales	$10,000,000	$10,000,000
Scrap	400,000	300,000
Rework	600,000	400,000
Product inspection	100,000	125,000
Product warranty	800,000	600,000
Quality training	40,000	80,000
Materials inspection	60,000	40,000

Required:

1. Classify the costs as prevention, appraisal, internal failure, or external failure.
2. Compute quality cost as a percentage of sales for each of the two years. By how much has profit increased because of quality improvements? Assuming that quality costs can be reduced to 2.5 percent of sales, how much additional profit is available through quality improvements (assume that sales revenues will remain the same)?

SOLUTION

1. Prevention costs: Quality training
   Appraisal costs: Product inspection and materials inspection
   Internal failure costs: Scrap and rework
   External failure costs: Warranty

2. *Preceding year*—Total quality costs: $2,000,000; percentage of sales: 20 percent ($2,000,000/$10,000,000). *Current year*—Total quality costs: $1,545,000; percentage of sales: 15.45 percent ($1,545,000/$10,000,000). Profit has increased by $455,000. If quality costs drop to 2.5 percent of sales, another $1,295,000 of profit improvement is possible ($1,545,000 − $250,000).

KEY TERMS

QUESTIONS FOR WRITING AND DISCUSSION

1. What is the difference between quality of design and quality of conformance?
2. Why are quality costs the costs of doing things wrong?
3. What is the difference between the zero-defects philosophy and the robust quality philosophy?
4. Describe the Taguchi quality loss function, and relate it to robust quality.
5. Identify and discuss the four kinds of quality costs.
6. Explain why external failure costs can be more devastating to a firm than internal failure costs.
7. Many quality experts maintain that quality is free. Do you agree or disagree? Why or why not?
8. What is the purpose of interim quality standards?
9. Describe the three types of quality performance reporting. How can managers use each report to help evaluate their quality improvement programs?
10. Discuss the different kinds of incentives that can be used to motivate employees to become involved in quality improvement programs. Explain gainsharing.
11. If a firm's annual sales are $200 million, what percentage of sales should be spent on quality costs? Suppose that the firm is spending 18 percent of sales on quality costs. What is the potential savings from quality improvement?
12. Explain why it is important for a manager to assess the relative distribution of quality costs among the four categories.
13. Discuss the benefits of quality cost reports that simply list the quality costs for each category.
14. Explain why the accounting department should be responsible for producing quality cost reports.
15. What is ISO 9000? Why do so many companies want this certification?

EXERCISES

14-1   QUALITY DEFINITION AND QUALITY COSTS

LO1   Rachel Boyce, president of a company that manufactures electronic components, has a number of questions concerning quality and quality costs. She has heard a few things about quality and has asked you to respond to the following:

Required:

1. What does it mean to have a quality product or service? Explain how product quality and conformance are related.
2. Yesterday, my quality manager told me that we need to redefine what we mean by a defective product. He said that conforming to specifications ignores the cost of product variability and that further reduction of product variability is a veritable gold mine—just waiting to be mined. What did he mean?

14-2   QUALITY DEFINITION AND QUALITY COSTS

LO1   Quality attributes such as performance and aesthetics are important to customers. Performance refers to how consistently and how well a product functions. Aesthetics is concerned with the appearance of tangible products as well as the appearance of the facilities, equipment, personnel, and communication materials associated with services.

Required:

1. Do you agree that aesthetics is an important quality dimension for services? Use dental services as the framework for providing your response.
2. For services, performance can be more carefully defined by expanding its definition to include responsiveness, assurance, and empathy. Describe what you think is meant by these three characteristics as applied to service quality.

14-3 TAGUCHI LOSS FUNCTION

LO1 Gray Company estimates its hidden external failure costs using the Taguchi loss function. Gray produces plastic sheets that vary in thickness and grade. For one of its large-volume products, it was determined that $k = \$20,000$ and $T = 0.20$ inches in diameter. A sample of four units produced the following values:

Unit No.	Actual Diameter (y)
1	0.23
2	0.22
3	0.18
4	0.19

Required:

1. Calculate the average loss per unit.
2. Assuming that 30,000 units were produced, what is the total hidden cost?
3. Assume that the multiplier for Gray's hidden external failure costs is five. What are the measured external costs? Explain the difference between measured costs and hidden costs.

14-4 QUALITY COST CLASSIFICATION

LO1 Classify the following quality costs as prevention costs, appraisal costs, internal failure costs, or external failure costs:

Spreadsheet

1. Inspection of reworked units
2. Inspecting and testing a newly developed product (not yet being sold)
3. Retesting a reworked product
4. Repairing a computer still under warranty
5. Discount allowed to customers because products failed to meet customer specifications
6. Goods returned because they failed to meet specifications
7. The cost of evaluating and certifying suppliers
8. Stopping work to correct process malfunction (discovered using statistical process control procedures)
9. Testing products in the field
10. Discarding products that cannot be reworked
11. Lost sales because of recalled products
12. Inspection of incoming materials
13. Redesigning a product to eliminate the need to use an outside component with a high defect rate
14. Purchase order changes
15. Replacing a defective product
16. Inspecting and testing prototypes
17. Repairing products in the field
18. Correcting a design error discovered during product development
19. Engineering resources used to help selected suppliers improve their product quality
20. Packaging inspection

21. Processing and responding to consumer complaints
22. Training production line workers in new quality procedures
23. Sampling a batch of goods to determine if the batch has an acceptable defect rate

14-5 ACTIVITY-BASED QUALITY COSTING

LO1, LO2 Maxwell Company produces two different carburetors and is concerned about their quality. The company has identified the following quality activities and costs associated with the two products:

	Carburetor A	Carburetor B
Units produced	170,000	340,000
Warranty work (units)	1,700	850
Scrapped units (number)	3,400	850
Inspection (hours)	3,400	1,700
Quality training (hours)	85	85

Activities:	
Performing warranty work	$204,000
Scrapping units	153,000
Inspecting	76,500
Quality training	42,500

Required:

1. Calculate the quality cost per unit for each product, and break this unit cost into quality cost categories. Which of the two seems to have the lowest quality?
2. How might a manager use the unit quality cost information?

14-6 QUALITY COST REPORT

LO2 Benton Company reported sales of $8,100,000 in 2007. At the end of the year, the following quality costs were reported:

Design review	$405,000
Recalls	135,000
Reinspection	67,500
Materials inspection	54,000
Quality training	135,000
Process acceptance	67,500
Scrap	47,250
Lost sales	270,000
Product inspection	40,500
Returned goods	128,250

Required:

1. Prepare a quality cost report.
2. Prepare a graph (pie chart or bar graph) that shows the relative distribution of quality costs, and comment on the distribution.

14-7 QUALITY IMPROVEMENT AND PROFITABILITY

LO2, LO3 Reading Company reported the following sales and quality costs for the past four years. Assume that all quality costs are variable and that all changes in the quality cost ratios are due to a quality improvement program.

Year	Sales Revenues	Quality Costs as a Percent of Revenues
1	$10,000,000	21%
2	11,000,000	18
3	11,000,000	14
4	12,000,000	10

Required:

1. Compute the quality costs for all four years. By how much did net income increase from Year 1 to Year 2 because of quality improvements? From Year 2 to Year 3? From Year 3 to Year 4?
2. The management of Reading Company believes it is possible to reduce quality costs to 2.5 percent of sales. Assuming sales will continue at the Year 4 level, calculate the additional profit potential facing Reading. Is the expectation of improving quality and reducing costs to 2.5 percent of sales realistic? Explain.
3. Assume that Reading produces one type of product, which is sold on a bid basis. In Years 1 and 2, the average bid was $200. In Year 1, total variable costs were $125 per unit. In Year 3, competition forced the bid to drop to $190. Compute the total contribution margin in Year 3 assuming the same quality costs as in Year 1. Now, compute the total contribution margin in Year 3 using the actual quality costs for Year 3. What is the increase in profitability resulting from the quality improvements made from Year 1 to Year 3?

14-8 QUALITY COSTS: PROFIT IMPROVEMENT AND DISTRIBUTION ACROSS CATEGORIES, GAINSHARING

LO2, LO3, LO4   Pawnee Company had sales of $30,000,000 in 2003. In 2007, sales had increased to $37,500,000. A quality improvement program was implemented at the beginning of 2003. Overall conformance quality was targeted for improvement. The quality costs for 2003 and 2007 follow. Assume any changes in quality costs are attributable to improvements in quality.

	2003	2007
Internal failure costs	$2,250,000	$112,500
External failure costs	3,000,000	75,000
Appraisal costs	1,350,000	281,250
Prevention costs	900,000	468,750
Total quality costs	$7,500,000	$937,500

Required:

1. Compute the quality cost-to-sales ratio for each year. Is this type of improvement possible?
2. Calculate the relative distribution of costs by category for 2003. What do you think of the way costs are distributed? (A pie chart or bar graph may be of some help.) How do you think they will be distributed as the company approaches a zero-defects state?
3. Calculate the relative distribution of costs by category for 2007. What do you think of the level and distribution of quality costs? (A pie chart or bar graph may be of some help.) Do you think further reductions are possible?
4. The quality manager for Pawnee indicated that the external failure costs reported are only the measured costs. He argued that the 2007 external costs were much higher than those reported and that additional investment ought to be made in control costs. Discuss the validity of his viewpoint.

5. Suppose that the manager of Pawnee received a bonus equal to 10 percent of the quality cost savings each year. Do you think that gainsharing is a good or a bad idea? Discuss the risks of gainsharing.

14-9 TRADE-OFFS AMONG QUALITY COST CATEGORIES, TOTAL QUALITY CONTROL, GAINSHARING

LO2, LO4 Javier Company has sales of $8 million and quality costs of $1,600,000. The company is embarking on a major quality improvement program. During the next three years, Javier intends to attack failure costs by increasing its appraisal and prevention costs. The "right" prevention activities will be selected, and appraisal costs will be reduced according to the results achieved. For the coming year, management is considering six specific activities: quality training, process control, product inspection, supplier evaluation, prototype testing, and redesign of two major products. To encourage managers to focus on reducing non-value-added quality costs and select the right activities, a bonus pool is established relating to reduction of quality costs. The bonus pool is equal to 10 percent of the total reduction in quality costs.

Current quality costs and the costs of these six activities are given in the following table. Each activity is added sequentially so that its effect on the cost categories can be assessed. For example, after quality training is added, the control costs increase to $320,000, and the failure costs drop to $1,040,000. Even though the activities are presented sequentially, they are totally independent of each other. Thus, only beneficial activities need be selected.

	Control Costs	Failure Costs
Current quality costs	$ 160,000	$1,440,000
Quality training	320,000	1,040,000
Process control	520,000	720,000
Product inspection	600,000	656,000
Supplier evaluation	720,000	200,000
Prototype testing	960,000	120,000
Engineering redesign	1,000,000	40,000

Required:

1. Identify the control activities that should be implemented, and calculate the total quality costs associated with this selection. Assume that an activity is selected only if it increases the bonus pool.
2. Given the activities selected in Requirement 1, calculate the following:
    a. The reduction in total quality costs
    b. The percentage distribution for control and failure costs
    c. The amount for this year's bonus pool
3. Suppose that a quality engineer complained about the gainsharing incentive system. Basically, he argued that the bonus should be based only on reductions of failure and appraisal costs. In this way, investment in prevention activities would be encouraged, and eventually, failure and appraisal costs would be eliminated. After eliminating the non-value-added costs, focus could then be placed on the level of prevention costs. If this approach were adopted, what activities would be selected? Do you agree or disagree with this approach? Explain.

14-10 TREND, LONG-RANGE PERFORMANCE REPORT

LO4 In 2006, Tru-Delite Frozen Desserts, Inc., instituted a quality improvement program. At the end of 2007, the management of the corporation requested a report to show the amount saved by the measures taken during the year. The actual sales and quality costs for 2006 and 2007 are as follows:

	2006	2007
Sales	$600,000	$600,000
Scrap	15,000	15,000
Rework	20,000	10,000
Training program	5,000	6,000
Consumer complaints	10,000	5,000
Lost sales, incorrect labeling	8,000	—
Test labor	12,000	8,000
Inspection labor	25,000	24,000
Supplier evaluation	15,000	13,000

Tru-Delite's management believes that quality costs can be reduced to 2.5 percent of sales within the next five years. At the end of 2012, Tru-Delite's sales are projected to grow to $750,000. The projected relative distribution of quality costs at the end of 2012 is as follows:

Scrap	15%
Training program	20
Supplier evaluation	25
Test labor	25
Inspection labor	15
Total quality costs	100%

Required:

1. Profits increased by what amount due to quality improvements made in 2007?
2. Prepare a long-range performance report that compares the quality costs incurred at the end of 2007 with the quality cost structure expected at the end of 2012.
3. Are the targeted costs in the year 2012 all value-added costs? How would you interpret the variances if the targeted costs are value-added costs?
4. What would be the profit increase in 2012 if the 2.5 percent performance standard is met in that year?

14-11 MULTIPLE-YEAR TREND REPORTS

LO4 The controller of Willson Company has computed quality costs as a percentage of sales for the past five years (2004 was the first year the company implemented a quality-improvement program). This information is as follows:

	Prevention	*Appraisal*	*Internal Failure*	*External Failure*	*Total*
2003	2%	3%	8.0%	12%	25.0%
2004	3	4	7.0	10	24.0
2005	4	5	5.5	6	20.5
2006	5	4	3.0	5	17.0
2007	6	3	1.0	2	12.0

Required:

1. Prepare a trend graph for total quality costs. Comment on what the graph has to say about the success of the quality improvement program.
2. Prepare a graph that shows the trend for each quality cost category. What does the graph have to say about the success of the quality improvement program? Does this graph supply more insight than the total cost trend graph does?

3. Prepare a graph that compares the trend in relative quality costs. What does this graph tell you?

PROBLEMS

14-12 QUALITY COST REPORT, TAGUCHI LOSS FUNCTION

LO1, LO2 Marlene Briggs, president of Shorts Company, was concerned with the trend in sales and profitability. The company had been losing customers at an alarming rate. Furthermore, the company was barely breaking even. Investigation revealed that poor quality was at the root of the problem. At the end of 2007, Marlene decided to begin a quality improvement program. As a first step, she identified the following costs in the accounting records as quality related:

	2007
Sales (400,000 units @ $100)	$40,000,000
Reinspection	1,200,000
Downtime (due to defects)	1,600,000
Vendor certification	480,000
Consumer complaints	800,000
Warranty	1,600,000
Test labor	1,200,000
Inspection labor	1,000,000
Design reviews	120,000

Required:

1. Prepare a quality cost report by quality cost category.
2. Calculate the relative distribution percentages for each quality cost category. Comment on the distribution.
3. Using the Taguchi loss function, an average loss per unit is computed to be $15 per unit. What are the hidden costs of external failure? How does this affect the relative distribution?
4. Shorts's quality manager decided not to bother with the hidden costs. What do you think was his reasoning? Any efforts to reduce measured external failure costs will also reduce the hidden costs. Do you agree or disagree? Explain.

14-13 TAGUCHI LOSS FUNCTION

LO2 Timpanogas Company manufactures a component for small portable DVD players (designed for use on automobile trips). Weight and durability of the component are the two most important quality characteristics for the DVD manufacturers. With respect to the weight dimension, the component has a target value of 240 grams. Specification limits are 240 grams, plus or minus 10 grams. Products produced at the lower specification limit of 230 grams lose $40. A sample of five units produced the following weight measures:

Unit No.	*Measured Weight*
1	250
2	260
3	270
4	220
5	225

During the first quarter, 100,000 units were produced.

Required:

1. Calculate the loss for each unit. Calculate the average loss for the sample of five.
2. Using the average loss, calculate the hidden quality costs for the first quarter.
3. Durability is another important quality characteristic. The target value is 18,000 hours of operation before failure. The lower specification limit set by engineering and marketing is 17,000 hours. They agreed that there should be no upper specification limit. They also noted that there is a $750 loss at the lower specification limit. Explain why there would be no upper specification limit. Use the lower limit and the *left half* of the Taguchi quadratic loss function to estimate the loss for components with the following lives: 4,500 hours, 9,000 hours, and 13,500 hours. What does this reveal about the importance of durability?

14-14   QUALITY COSTS, PRICING DECISIONS, MARKET SHARE

LO3   Gaston Company manufactures furniture. One of its product lines is an economy-line kitchen table. During the last year, Gaston produced and sold 100,000 units for $100 per unit. Sales of the table are on a bid basis, but Gaston has always been able to win sufficient bids using the $100 price. This year, however, Gaston was losing more than its share of bids. Concerned, Larry Franklin, owner and president of the company, called a meeting of his executive committee (Megan Johnson, marketing manager; Fred Davis, quality manager; Kevin Jones, production manager; and Helen Jackson, controller).

LARRY: I don't understand why we're losing bids. Megan, do you have an explanation?

MEGAN: Yes, as a matter of fact. Two competitors have lowered their price to $92 per unit. That's too big a difference for most of our buyers to ignore. If we want to keep selling our 100,000 units per year, we will need to lower our price to $92. Otherwise, our sales will drop to about 20,000 to 25,000 per year.

HELEN: The unit contribution margin on the table is $10. Lowering the price to $92 will cost us $8 per unit. Based on a sales volume of 100,000, we'd make $200,000 in contribution margin. If we keep the price at $100, our contribution margin would be $200,000 to $250,000. If we have to lose, let's just take the lower market share. It's better than lowering our prices.

MEGAN: Perhaps. But the same thing could happen to some of our other product lines. My sources tell me that these two companies are on the tail-end of a major quality improvement program—one that allows them significant savings. We need to rethink our whole competitive strategy—at least if we want to stay in business. Ideally, we should match the price reduction and work to reduce the costs to recapture the lost contribution margin.

FRED: I think I have something to offer. We are about to embark on a new quality improvement program of our own. I have brought the following estimates of the current quality costs for this economy line. As you can see, these costs run about 16 percent of current sales. That's excessive, and we believe that they can be reduced to about 4 percent of sales over time.

Scrap	$ 700,000
Rework	300,000
Rejects (sold as seconds to discount houses)	250,000
Returns (due to poor workmanship)	350,000
	$1,600,000

LARRY: This sounds good. Fred, how long will it take for you to achieve this reduction?

FRED: All these costs vary with sales level, so I'll express their reduction rate in those terms. Our best guess is that we can reduce these costs by about 1 percent of sales per quarter. So it should take about 12 quarters, or three years, to achieve the full benefit. Keep in mind that this is with an improvement in quality.

MEGAN: This offers us some hope. If we meet the price immediately, we can maintain our market share. Furthermore, if we can ever reach the point of reducing the price below the $92 level, then we can increase our market share. I estimate that we can increase sales by about 10,000 units for every $1 of price reduction beyond the $92 level. Kevin, how much extra capacity for this line do we have?

KEVIN: We can handle an extra 30,000 or 40,000 tables per year.

Required:

1. Assume that Gaston immediately reduces the bid price to $92. How long will it be before the unit contribution margin is restored to $10, assuming that quality costs are reduced as expected and that sales are maintained at 100,000 units per year (25,000 per quarter)?
2. Assume that Gaston holds the price at $92 until the 4 percent target is achieved. At this new level of quality costs, should the price be reduced? If so, by how much should the price be reduced, and what is the increase in contribution margin? Assume that price can be reduced only in $1 increments.
3. Assume that Gaston immediately reduces the price to $92 and begins the quality improvement program. Now, suppose that Gaston does not wait until the end of the 3-year period before reducing prices. Instead, prices will be reduced when profitable to do so. Assume that prices can be reduced only by $1 increments. Identify when the first future price change should occur (if any).
4. Discuss the differences in viewpoints concerning the decision to decrease prices and the short-run contribution margin analysis done by Helen, the controller. Did quality cost information play an important role in the strategic decision making illustrated by the problem?

14-15 CLASSIFICATION OF QUALITY COSTS

LO1 Classify the following quality costs as prevention, appraisal, internal failure, or external failure. Also, label each cost as variable or fixed with respect to sales volume.

1. Quality engineering
2. Scrap
3. Product recalls
4. Returns and allowances because of quality problems
5. Sales data re-entered because of keying errors
6. Supervision of in-process inspection
7. Quality circles
8. Component inspection and testing
9. Quality training
10. Reinspection of reworked product
11. Product liability
12. Internal audit assessing the effectiveness of quality system
13. Disposal of defective product
14. Downtime attributable to quality problems
15. Quality reporting
16. Proofreading
17. Correction of typing errors
18. In-process inspection
19. Process controls
20. Pilot studies

14-16   QUALITY COST SUMMARY

LO2

Wayne Johnson, president of Banshee Company, recently returned from a conference on quality and productivity. At the conference, he was told that many American firms have quality costs totaling 20 to 30 percent of sales. He, however, was skeptical about this statistic. But even if the quality gurus were right, he was sure that his company's quality costs were much lower—probably less than 5 percent. On the other hand, if he was wrong, he would be passing up an opportunity to improve profits significantly and simultaneously strengthen his competitive position. The possibility was at least worth exploring. He knew that his company produced most of the information needed for quality cost reporting—but there never was a need to bother with any formal quality data gathering and analysis.

This conference, however, had convinced him that a firm's profitability can increase significantly by improving quality—provided the potential for improvement exists. Thus, before committing the company to a quality improvement program, Wayne requested a preliminary estimate of the total quality costs currently being incurred. He also indicated that the costs should be classified into four categories: prevention, appraisal, internal failure, or external failure. He has asked you to prepare a summary of quality costs and to compare the total costs to sales and profits. To assist you in this task, the following information has been prepared from the past year, 2007:

a. Sales revenue, $15,000,000; net income, $1,500,000.
b. During the year, customers returned 90,000 units needing repair. Repair cost averages $1 per unit.
c. Four inspectors are employed, each earning an annual salary of $60,000. These four inspectors are involved only with final inspection (product acceptance).
d. Total scrap is 150,000 units. Of this total, sixty percent is quality related. The cost of scrap is about $5 per unit.
e. Each year, approximately 750,000 units are rejected in final inspection. Of these units, eighty percent can be recovered through rework. The cost of rework is $0.75 per unit.
f. A customer cancelled an order that would have increased profits by $150,000. The customer's reason for cancellation was poor product performance.
g. The company employs three full-time employees in its complaint department. Each earns $40,500 a year.
h. The company gave sales allowances totaling $45,000 due to substandard products being sent to the customer.
i. The company requires all new employees to take its 3-hour quality training program. The estimated annual cost of the program is $30,000.

Required:

1. Prepare a simple quality cost report classifying costs by category.
2. Compute the quality cost-sales ratio. Also, compare the total quality costs with total profits. Should Wayne be concerned with the level of quality costs?
3. Prepare a pie chart for the quality costs. Discuss the distribution of quality costs among the four categories. Are they properly distributed? Explain.
4. Discuss how the company can improve its overall quality and at the same time reduce total quality costs.
5. By how much will profits increase if quality costs are reduced to 2.5 percent of sales?

14-17   QUALITY COST REPORT, INTERIM PERFORMANCE REPORT

LO1, LO2,
LO4

Recently, Ulrich Company received a report from an external consulting group on its quality costs. The consultants reported that the company's quality costs total about 21

Spreadsheet

percent of its sales revenues. Somewhat shocked by the magnitude of the costs, Rob Rustin, president of Ulrich Company, decided to launch a major quality-improvement program. For the coming year, management decided to reduce quality costs to 17 percent of sales revenues. Although the amount of reduction was ambitious, most company officials believed that the goal could be realized. To improve the monitoring of the quality-improvement program, Rob directed Pamela Golding, the controller, to prepare quarterly performance reports comparing budgeted and actual quality costs. Budgeted costs and sales for the first two months of the year are as follows:

	January	*February*
Sales	$500,000	$600,000
Quality costs:		
Warranty	$15,000	$ 18,000
Scrap	10,000	12,000
Incoming materials inspection	2,500	2,500
Product acceptance	13,000	15,000
Quality planning	2,000	2,000
Field inspection	12,000	14,000
Retesting	6,000	7,200
Allowances	7,500	9,000
New product review	500	500
Rework	9,000	10,800
Complaint adjustment	2,500	2,500
Downtime (defective parts)	5,000	6,000
Quality training	1,000	1,000
Total budgeted costs	$86,000	$100,500
Quality costs-sales ratio	17.2%	16.75%

The following actual sales and actual quality costs were reported for January:

Sales	$550,000
Quality costs:	
Warranty	17,500
Scrap	12,500
Incoming materials inspection	2,500
Product acceptance	14,000
Quality planning	2,500
Field inspection	14,000
Retesting	7,000
Allowances	8,500
New product review	700
Rework	11,000
Complaint adjustment	2,500
Downtime (defective parts)	5,500
Quality training	1,000

Required:

1. Reorganize the quarterly budgets so that quality costs are grouped in one of four categories: appraisal, prevention, internal failure, or external failure. (Essentially, prepare a budgeted cost of quality report.) Also, identify each cost as variable or fixed. (Assume that no costs are mixed.)
2. Prepare a performance report for January that compares actual costs with budgeted costs. Comment on the company's progress in improving quality and reducing its quality costs.

14-18 QUALITY COST PERFORMANCE REPORTING: ONE-YEAR TREND, LONG-RANGE ANALYSIS

LO4 In 2007, Major Company initiated a full-scale, quality improvement program. At the end of the year, Jack Aldredge, the president, noted with some satisfaction that the defects per unit of product had dropped significantly compared to the prior year. He was also pleased that relationships with suppliers had improved and defective materials had declined. The new quality training program was also well accepted by employees. Of most interest to the president, however, was the impact of the quality improvements on profitability. To help assess the dollar impact of the quality improvements, the actual sales and the actual quality costs for 2006 and 2007 are as follows by quality category:

	2006	*2007*
Sales	$8,000,000	$10,000,000
Appraisal costs:		
Packaging inspection	320,000	300,000
Product acceptance	40,000	28,000
Prevention costs:		
Quality circles	4,000	40,000
Design reviews	2,000	20,000
Quality improvement projects	2,000	100,000
Internal failure costs:		
Scrap	280,000	240,000
Rework	360,000	320,000
Yield losses	160,000	100,000
Retesting	200,000	160,000
External failure costs:		
Returned materials	160,000	160,000
Allowances	120,000	140,000
Warranty	400,000	440,000

All prevention costs are fixed (by discretion). Assume all other quality costs are unit-level variable.

Required:

1. Compute the relative distribution of quality costs for each year. Do you believe that the company is moving in the right direction in terms of the balance among the quality cost categories? Explain.
2. Prepare a 1-year trend performance report for 2007 (compare the actual costs of 2007 with those of 2006, adjusted for differences in sales volume). How much have profits increased because of the quality improvements made by Major Company?
3. Estimate the additional improvement in profits if Major Company ultimately reduces its quality costs to 2.5 percent of sales revenues (assume sales of $25 million).

14-19 DISTRIBUTION OF QUALITY COSTS

LO2 Paper Products Division produces paper diapers, napkins, and paper towels. The divisional manager has decided that quality costs can be minimized by distributing quality costs evenly among the four quality categories and reducing them to no more than 5 percent of sales. He has just received the following quality cost report:

Paper Products Division
Quality Cost Report
For the Year Ended December 31, 2007

	Diapers	Napkins	Paper Towels	Total
Prevention costs:				
Quality training	$ 3,000	$ 2,500	$ 2,000	$ 7,500
Quality engineering	3,500	1,000	2,500	7,000
Quality audits	—	500	1,000	1,500
Quality reporting	2,500	2,000	1,000	5,500
Total prevention costs	$ 9,000	$ 6,000	$ 6,500	$ 21,500
Appraisal costs:				
Inspection, materials	$ 2,000	$ 3,000	$ 3,000	$ 8,000
Process acceptance	4,000	2,800	1,200	8,000
Product acceptance	2,000	1,200	2,300	5,500
Total appraisal costs	$ 8,000	$ 7,000	$ 6,500	$ 21,500
Internal failure costs:				
Scrap	$10,000	$ 3,000	$ 2,500	$ 15,500
Disposal costs	7,000	2,000	1,500	10,500
Downtime	1,000	1,500	2,500	5,000
Total internal failure costs	$18,000	$ 6,500	$ 6,500	$ 31,000
External failure costs:				
Allowances	$10,000	$ 3,000	$ 2,750	$ 15,750
Customer complaints	4,000	1,500	3,750	9,250
Product liability	1,000	—	—	1,000
Total external failure costs	$15,000	$ 4,500	$ 6,500	$ 26,000
Total quality costs	$50,000	$24,000	$26,000	$100,000

Assume that all prevention costs are fixed and that the remaining quality costs are variable (unit-level).

Required:

1. Assume that the sales revenue for the year totaled $2 million, with sales for each product as follows: diapers, $1 million; napkins, $600,000; paper towels, $400,000. Evaluate the distribution of costs for the division as a whole and for each product line. What recommendations do you have for the divisional manager?

2. Now, assume that total sales are $1 million and have this breakdown: diapers, $500,000; napkins, $300,000; paper towels, $200,000. Evaluate the distribution of costs for the division as a whole and for each product line in this case. Do you think it is possible to reduce the quality costs to 5 percent of sales for each product line and for the division as a whole and, simultaneously, achieve an equal distribution of the quality costs? What recommendations do you have?

3. Assume total sales of $1 million with this breakdown: diapers, $500,000; napkins, $180,000; paper towels, $320,000. Evaluate the distribution of quality costs. What recommendations do you have for the divisional manager?

4. Discuss the value of having quality costs reported by segment.

14-20   TREND ANALYSIS, QUALITY COSTS

LO4   In 2003, Milton Thayne, president of Carbondale Electronics, received a report indicating that quality costs were 31 percent of sales. Faced with increasing pressures from imported goods, Milton resolved to take measures to improve the overall quality of the company's products. After hiring a consultant in 2004, the company began an aggressive program of total quality control. At the end of 2007, Milton requested an analysis of the progress the company had made in reducing and controlling quality costs. The accounting department assembled the following data:

	Sales	Prevention	Appraisal	Internal Failure	External Failure
2003	$500,000	$ 5,000	$10,000	$80,000	$60,000
2004	600,000	25,000	15,000	60,000	50,000
2005	700,000	35,000	30,000	35,000	25,000
2006	600,000	40,000	15,000	25,000	20,000
2007	500,000	50,000	5,000	12,000	8,000

Required:

1. Compute the quality costs as a percentage of sales by category and in total for each year.
2. Prepare a multiple-year trend graph for quality costs, both by total costs and by category. Using the graph, assess the progress made in reducing and controlling quality costs. Does the graph provide evidence that quality has improved? Explain.
3. Using the 2003 quality cost relationships (assume all costs are variable), calculate the quality costs that would have prevailed in 2006. By how much did profits increase in 2006 because of the quality improvement program? Repeat for 2007.

14-21   CASE ON QUALITY COST PERFORMANCE REPORTS

LO4   Iona Company, a large printing company, is in its fourth year of a 5-year, quality improvement program. The program began in 2003 with an internal study that revealed the quality costs being incurred. In that year, a 5-year plan was developed to lower quality costs to 10 percent of sales by the end of 2007. Sales and quality costs for each year are as follows:

	Sales Revenues	Quality Costs
2003	$10,000,000	$2,000,000
2004	10,000,000	1,800,000
2005	11,000,000	1,815,000
2006	12,000,000	1,680,000
2007*	12,000,000	1,320,000

*Budgeted figures.

Quality costs by category are expressed as a percentage of sales as follows:

	Prevention	Appraisal	Internal Failure	External Failure
2003	1.0%	3.0%	7.0%	9.0%
2004	2.0	4.0	6.0	6.0
2005	2.5	4.0	5.0	5.0
2006	3.0	3.5	4.5	3.0
2007	3.5	3.5	2.0	2.0

The detail of the 2007 budget for quality costs is also provided.

Prevention costs:	
Quality planning	$ 150,000
Quality training	20,000
Quality improvement (special project)	80,000
Quality reporting	10,000
Appraisal costs:	
Proofreading	500,000
Other inspection	50,000
Failure costs:	
Correction of typos	150,000
Rework (because of customer complaints)	75,000
Plate revisions	55,000
Press downtime	100,000
Waste (because of poor work)	130,000
Total quality costs	$1,320,000

All prevention costs are fixed; all other quality costs are variable.

During 2007, the company had $12 million in sales. Actual quality costs for 2006 and 2007 are as follows:

	2007	2006
Quality planning	$150,000	$140,000
Quality training	20,000	20,000
Special project	100,000	120,000
Quality reporting	12,000	12,000
Proofreading	520,000	580,000
Other inspection	60,000	80,000
Correction of typos	165,000	200,000
Rework	76,000	131,000
Plate revisions	58,000	83,000
Press downtime	102,000	123,000
Waste	136,000	191,000

Required:

1. Prepare an interim quality cost performance report for 2007 that compares actual quality costs with budgeted quality costs. Comment on the firm's ability to achieve its quality goals for the year.
2. Prepare a 1-period quality performance report for 2007 that compares the actual quality costs of 2006 with the actual costs of 2007. How much did profits change because of improved quality?
3. Prepare a graph that shows the trend in total quality costs as a percentage of sales since the inception of the quality improvement program.
4. Prepare a graph that shows the trend for all four quality cost categories for 2003 through 2007. How does this graph help management know that the reduction in total quality costs is attributable to quality improvements?
5. Assume that the company is preparing a second 5-year plan to reduce quality costs to 2.5 percent of sales. Prepare a long-range quality cost performance report assuming sales of $15 million at the end of five years. Assume that the final planned relative distribution of quality costs is as follows: proofreading, 50 percent; other inspection, 13 percent; quality training, 30 percent; and quality reporting, 7 percent.

14-22   COLLABORATIVE LEARNING EXERCISE

LO1, LO3   Lindell Manufacturing embarked on an ambitious quality program that is centered around continual improvement. This improvement is operationalized by declining quality costs from year to year. Lindell rewards plant managers, production supervisors, and workers with bonuses ranging from $100 to $1,000 if their factory meets its annual quality cost goals.

Len Smith, manager of Lindell's Boise plant, felt obligated to do everything he could to provide this increase to his employees. Accordingly, he has decided to take the following actions during the last quarter of the year to meet the plant's budgeted quality cost targets:

a.   Decrease inspections of the process and final product by 50 percent and transfer inspectors temporarily to quality training programs. Len believes this move will increase the inspectors' awareness of the importance of quality; also, decreasing inspection will produce significantly less downtime and less rework. By increasing the output and decreasing the costs of internal failure, the plant can meet the budgeted reductions for internal failure costs. Also, by showing an increase in the costs of quality training, the budgeted level for prevention costs can be met.

b.   Delay replacing and repairing defective products until the beginning of the following year. While this may increase customer dissatisfaction somewhat, Len believes that most customers expect some inconvenience. Besides, the policy of promptly dealing with dissatisfied customers could be reinstated in three months. In the meantime, the action would significantly reduce the costs of external failure, allowing the plant to meet its budgeted target.

c.   Cancel scheduled worker visits to customers' plants. This program, which has been very well received by customers, enables Lindell workers to see just how the machinery they make is used by the customer and also gives them first-hand information on any remaining problems with the machinery. Workers who went on previous customer site visits came back enthusiastic and committed to Lindell's quality program. Lindell's quality program staff believes that these visits will reduce defects during the following year.

Required:

Form groups of four. Each group will review the answers to the following requirements. In each group, select one member that will rotate to another group. The rotating member has the responsibility of comparing and contrasting the solution of his or her group with that of the group being visited.

1.   Evaluate Len's ethical behavior. In this evaluation, consider his concern for his employees. Was he justified in taking the actions described? If not, what should he have done?

2.   Assume that the company views Len's behavior as undesirable. What can the company do to discourage it?

3.   Assume that Len is a CMA and a member of the IMA. Refer to the ethical code for management accountants in Chapter 1. Were any of these ethical standards violated?

14-23   CYBER RESEARCH CASE

LO1, LO3   The ISO 9000 series and QS 9000 have had a significant impact in industrial practice. Web sites that provide a good starting point for information about these quality standards include http://www.isoeasy.org, http://www.aiag.org, and http://www.findarticles.com. The last address allows you to search for articles that deal with ISO 9000 and QS 9000. Using these sources and others you might locate on the Internet, answer the following questions:

1. What is the International Standards Organization?
2. What standards make up the ISO 9000 family?
3. Describe the revised ISO 9000 standards.
4. What are the differences between ISO 9000 and QS 9000? Be specific.
5. What is the average cost to register and maintain QS 9000? What is the average benefit?
6. Describe the experience of one company that has implemented QS 9000. Include in your description some of the quality improvements that were the result of QS 9000 registration.

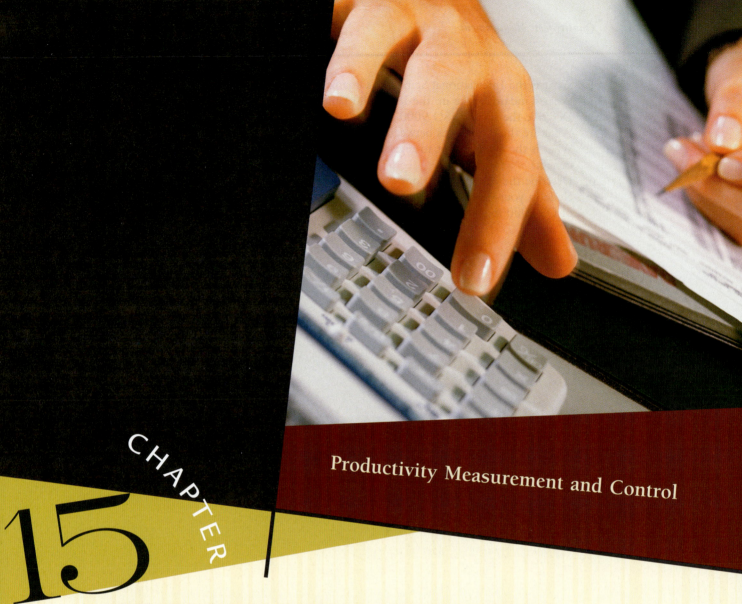

15

Productivity Measurement and Control

AFTER STUDYING THIS CHAPTER, YOU SHOULD BE ABLE TO:

1. Explain the meaning of productive efficiency, and describe the difference between technical and allocative efficiency.

2. Define partial productivity measurement, and list its advantages and disadvantages.

3. Explain what total productivity measurement is, and name its advantages.

4. Discuss the role of productivity measurement in assessing activity improvement.

Technology often leads to increases in labor productivity. Laptops, for example, may allow workers to solve problems on the spot and reduce the amount of lost production time. Producing more with the same or less inputs often promises significant increases in profitability.

Continuous improvement implies that efficiency is increasing over time. In fact, to be competitive, organizations must increase efficiency. An organization must be as good or better than its competitors at taking materials, labor, machines, power, and other inputs and turning out high-quality goods and services. A company can create a competitive advantage by using fewer inputs to produce a given output or by producing more output for a given set of inputs. Management needs to assess the potential and actual effectiveness of decisions that are geared to improve efficiency. Management also needs to monitor and control efficiency changes. Efficiency measures satisfy these performance and control objectives. In previous chapters, various approaches to measuring efficiency have been presented. For example, we have presented and discussed such measurement approaches as value-added and non-value-added cost reports, trends in cost, and activity flexible budgeting. In this chapter, we will explore efficiency measures that are concerned with the relationship of inputs and outputs, referred to as *productivity measures.*

Productive Efficiency

OBJECTIVE 1

Explain the meaning of productive efficiency, and describe the difference between technical and allocative efficiency.

Productivity is concerned with producing output efficiently, and it specifically addresses the relationship of output and the inputs used to produce the output. Usually, different combinations or mixes of inputs can be used to produce a given level of output. **Total productive efficiency** is the point at which two conditions are satisfied: (1) for any mix of inputs that will produce a given output, no more of any one input is used than necessary to produce the output and (2) given the mixes that satisfy the first condition, the least costly mix is chosen. The first condition is driven by technical relationships and, therefore, is referred to as **technical efficiency**. Viewing activities as inputs, the first condition requires the elimination of all non-value-added activities and requires that value-added activities be performed with the minimal quantities needed to produce the given output. The second condition is driven by relative input price relationships and, therefore, is referred to as **allocative efficiency**. Input prices determine the *relative proportions* of each input that should be used. Deviation from these fixed proportions creates allocative inefficiency.

Productivity improvement programs involve moving toward a state of total productive efficiency. Technical improvements in productivity can be achieved by using fewer inputs to produce the same output, by producing more output using the same inputs, or by producing more output with relatively fewer inputs. For example, in 2002, the Lansing C Michigan plant of **General Motors** (GM) used 20.11 hours per vehicle (Pontiac Grand Am and Oldsmobile Alero); in 2003, the Lansing C Michigan plant used 1864 hours per vehicle. Thus, labor productivity increased by 7.3 percent.[1] Exhibit 15-1, on the following page, illustrates the three ways to achieve an improvement in technical efficiency. The output is vehicles, and the inputs are labor (number of workers) and capital (dollars invested in automated equipment). Notice that the relative proportions of the inputs are held constant so that all productivity improvement is attributable to improving technical efficiency. Productivity improvement can also be achieved by trading off more costly inputs for less costly inputs. Exhibit 15-2, on page 667, illustrates the possibility of improving productivity by increasing allocative efficiency. Although improving technical efficiency is what most people think of when improving productivity is mentioned, allocative efficiency can offer significant opportunities for increasing overall economic efficiency. Choosing the right combination of inputs can be as critical as choosing the right quantity of inputs. Notice in Exhibit 15-2 that input Combination I produces the same output as input Combination II but that the cost is $5,000,000 less. Total measures of productivity are usually a combination of changes in technical and allocative efficiency.

Partial Productivity Measurement

OBJECTIVE 2

Define partial productivity measurement, and list its advantages and disadvantages.

Productivity measurement is simply a quantitative assessment of productivity changes. The objective is to assess whether productive efficiency has increased or decreased. Productivity measurement can be actual or prospective. Actual productivity measurement allows managers to assess, monitor, and control changes. Prospective measurement is forward-looking, and it serves as input for strategic decision making. Specifically, prospective measurement allows managers to compare relative benefits of different input combinations, choosing the inputs and input mix that provide the greatest benefit. Productivity measures can be developed for each input separately or for all inputs jointly. Measuring productivity for one input at a time is called **partial productivity measurement**.

1. Harbour Report (2203 and 2003), http://www.autointell.com, accessed Nov. 4, 2004.

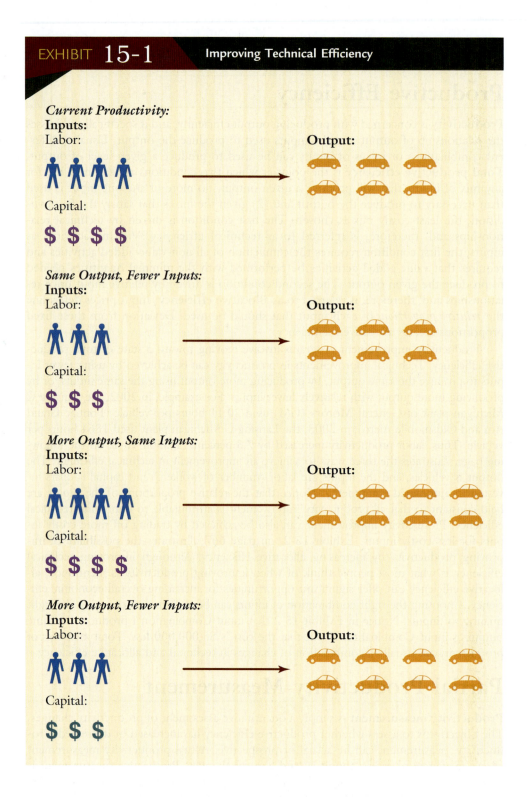

EXHIBIT 15-1   **Improving Technical Efficiency**

Current Productivity:
Inputs:
Labor:

Capital:

Same Output, Fewer Inputs:
Inputs:
Labor:

Capital:

More Output, Same Inputs:
Inputs:
Labor:

Capital:

More Output, Fewer Inputs:
Inputs:
Labor:

Capital:

Output:

Output:

Output:

Output:

Partial Productivity Measurement Defined

Productivity of a single input is typically measured by calculating the ratio of the output to the input as follows:

$$\text{Productivity ratio} = \text{Output/Input}$$

Because the productivity of only one input is being measured, the measure is called a *partial productivity measure*. If both output and input are measured in physical quan-

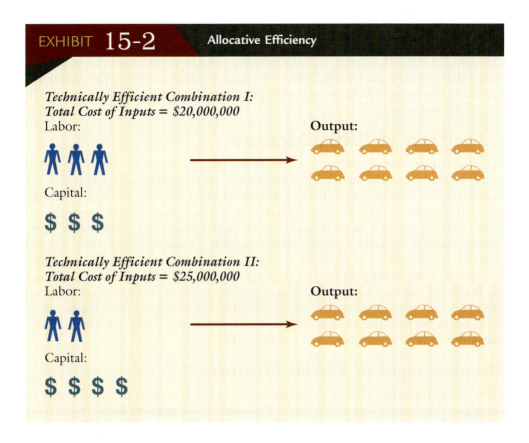

EXHIBIT **15-2**	Allocative Efficiency

Technically Efficient Combination I:
Total Cost of Inputs = $20,000,000
Labor:

Output:

Capital:

Technically Efficient Combination II:
Total Cost of Inputs = $25,000,000
Labor:

Output:

Capital:

tities, then we have an **operational productivity measure**. If output or input is expressed in dollars, then we have a **financial productivity measure**.

Assume, for example, that in 2006, Nevada Company produced 240,000 frames for snowmobiles and used 60,000 hours of labor. The labor productivity ratio is four frames per hour (240,000/60,000). This is an operational measure, since the units are expressed in physical terms. If the selling price of each frame is $30 and the cost of labor is $15 per hour, then output and input can be expressed in dollars. The labor productivity ratio, expressed in financial terms, is $8 of revenue per dollar of labor cost ($7,200,000/$900,000).

Partial Measures and Measuring Changes in Productive Efficiency

The labor productivity ratio of four frames per hour measures the 2006 productivity experience of Nevada. By itself, the ratio conveys little information about productive efficiency or whether the company has improving or declining productivity. It is possible, however, to make a statement about increasing or decreasing productivity efficiency by measuring *changes* in productivity. To do so, the actual current productivity measure is compared with the productivity measure of a prior period. This prior period is referred to as the **base period** and serves to set the benchmark or standard for measuring changes in productive efficiency. The prior period can be any period desired. It could, for example, be the preceding year, the preceding week, or even the period during which the last batch of products was produced. For strategic evaluations, the base period is usually chosen as an earlier year. For operational control, the base period tends to be close to the current period—such as the preceding batch of products or the preceding week.

To illustrate, assume that 2006 is the base period and that the labor productivity standard, therefore, is four frames per hour. Further assume that late in 2006, Nevada decided to try a new procedure for producing and assembling the frames with the expectation that the new procedure would use less labor. In 2007, 250,000 frames were produced, using 50,000 hours of labor. The labor productivity ratio for 2007 is five frames per hour (250,000/50,000). The *change* in productivity is a one-unit-per-hour *increase* in productivity (from four units per hour in 2006 to five units per hour in 2007). The change is a significant improvement in labor productivity and provides evidence supporting the efficacy of the new process.

Advantages of Partial Measures

Partial measures allow managers to focus on the use of a particular input. Operating partial measures have the advantage of being easily interpreted by everyone within the organization. Consequently, partial operational measures are easy to use for assessing productivity performance of operating personnel. Laborers, for instance, can relate to units produced per hour or units produced per pound of material. Thus, partial operational measures provide feedback that operating personnel can relate to and understand—measures that deal with the specific inputs over which they have control. The ability of operating personnel to understand and relate to the measures increases the likelihood that the measures will be accepted. Furthermore, for operational control, the standards for performance are often very short run in nature. For example, standards can be the productivity ratios of prior batches of goods. Using this standard, productivity trends within the year itself can be tracked.

Disadvantages of Partial Measures

Partial measures, used in isolation, can be misleading. A decline in the productivity of one input may be necessary to increase the productivity of another. Such a trade-off is desirable if overall costs decline, but the effect would be missed by using either partial measure. For example, changing a process so that direct laborers take less time to assemble a product may increase scrap and waste while leaving total output unchanged. Labor productivity has increased, but productive use of materials has declined. If the increase in the cost of waste and scrap outweighs the savings of the decreased labor, then overall productivity has declined.

Two important conclusions can be drawn from this example. First, the possible existence of trade-offs mandates a total measure of productivity for assessing the merits of productivity decisions. Only by looking at the total productivity effect of all inputs can managers accurately draw any conclusions about overall productivity performance. Second, because of the possibility of trade-offs, a total measure of productivity must assess the aggregate financial consequences and, therefore, should be a financial measure.

Total Productivity Measurement

Measuring productivity for all inputs at once is called **total productivity measurement**. In practice, it may not be necessary to measure the effect of all inputs. Many firms measure the productivity of only those factors that are thought to be relevant indicators of organizational performance and success. Thus, in practical terms, total productivity measurement can be defined as focusing on a limited number of inputs, which, in total, indicates organizational success. In either case, total productivity measurement requires the development of a multifactor measurement approach. A common multifactor approach suggested in the productivity literature (but rarely found in practice) is the use of aggregate productivity indices. Aggregate indices are complex and difficult to interpret and have not been generally accepted. Two approaches that have gained some acceptance are *profile measurement* and *profit-linked productivity measurement*.

OBJECTIVE 3

Explain what total productivity measurement is, and name its advantages.

Profile Productivity Measurement

Producing a product involves numerous critical inputs such as labor, materials, capital, and energy. **Profile measurement** provides a series or vector of separate and distinct partial operational measures. Profiles can be compared over time to provide information about productivity changes. To illustrate the profile approach, we will use only two inputs: labor and materials. Let's return to the Nevada Company example. As before, Nevada implements a new production and assembly process in 2007. Only now, let's assume that the new process affects both labor and materials. Initially, let's look at the case for which the productivity of both inputs moves in the same direction. The following data for 2006 and 2007 are available:

	2006	*2007*
Number of frames produced	240,000	250,000
Labor hours used	60,000	50,000
Materials used (lbs.)	1,200,000	1,150,000

Exhibit 15-3 provides productivity ratio profiles for each year. The 2006 profile is (4, 0.200), and the 2007 profile is (5, 0.217). Comparing profiles for the two years, we can see that productivity increased for both labor and materials (from 4 to 5 for labor and from 0.200 to 0.217 for materials). The profile comparison provides enough information for a manager to conclude that the new assembly process has definitely improved overall productivity. The *value* of this improvement, however, is not revealed by the ratios.

EXHIBIT **15-3**	Productivity Measurement: Profile Analysis, No Trade-Offs	
Partial Operational Productivity Ratios	**2006 Profile[a]**	**2007 Profile[b]**
Labor productivity ratio	4.000	5.000
Material productivity ratio	0.200	0.217

[a]Labor: 240,000/60,000; Materials: 240,000/1,200,000.
[b]Labor: 250,000/50,000; Materials: 250,000/1,150,000.

As just shown, profile analysis can provide managers with useful insights about changes in productivity. However, comparing productivity profiles will not always reveal the nature of the overall change in productive efficiency. In some cases, profile analysis will not provide any clear indication of whether a productivity change is good or bad. To illustrate, let's revise the Nevada Company data to allow for trade-offs among the two inputs. Assume that all the data are the same except for materials used in 2007. Let the materials used in 2007 be 1,300,000 pounds. Using this revised number, the productivity profiles for 2006 and 2007 are presented in Exhibit 15-4. The productivity profile for 2006 is still (4, 0.200), but the profile for 2007 has changed to (5, 0.192). Comparing productivity profiles now provides a mixed signal. Productivity for labor has increased from 4 to 5, but productivity for materials has decreased from 0.200 to 0.192. The new process has caused a trade-off in the productivity for the two measures. Furthermore, while a profile analysis reveals that the trade-off exists, it does not reveal whether the trade-off is good or bad. If the economic effect of the productivity changes is positive, then the trade-off is good; otherwise, it must be viewed as bad.

EXHIBIT 15-4	Productivity Measurement: Profile Analysis with Trade-Offs	
Partial Operational Productivity Ratios	**2006 Profile[a]**	**2007 Profile[b]**
Labor productivity ratio	4.000	5.000
Material productivity ratio	0.200	0.192

[a]Labor: 240,000/60,000; Materials: 240,000/1,200,000.
[b]Labor: 250,000/50,000; Materials: 250,000/1,300,000.

Valuing the trade-offs would allow us to assess the economic effect of the decision to change the assembly process. Furthermore, by valuing the productivity change, we obtain a total measure of productivity.

Profit-Linked Productivity Measurement

Assessing the effects of productivity changes on current profits is one way to value productivity changes. Profits change from the base period to the current period. Some of that profit change is attributable to productivity changes. Measuring the amount of profit change attributable to productivity change is defined as **profit-linked productivity measurement**.

Assessing the effect of productivity changes on current-period profits will help managers understand the economic importance of productivity changes. Linking productivity changes to profits is described by the following rule:

> **Profit-Linkage Rule.** *For the current period, calculate the cost of the inputs that would have been used in the absence of any productivity change and compare this cost with the cost of the inputs actually used. The difference in costs is the amount by which profits changed because of productivity changes.*

To apply the linkage rule, the inputs that would have been used for the current period in the absence of a productivity change must be calculated. Let *PQ* represent this productivity-neutral quantity of input. To determine the productivity-neutral quantity for a particular input, divide the current-period output by the input's base-period productivity ratio:

$$PQ = \text{Current-period output/Base-period productivity ratio}$$

To illustrate the application of the profit-linked rule, let's return to the Nevada example with input trade-offs. We must add some cost information to the data. The expanded Nevada data set is as follows:

	2006	2007
Number of frames produced	240,000	250,000
Labor hours used	60,000	50,000
Materials used (lbs.)	1,200,000	1,300,000
Unit selling price (frames)	$30	$30
Wages per labor hour	$15	$15
Cost per pound of material	$3	$3.50

Current output (2007) is 250,000 frames. From Exhibit 15-4, we know that the base-period productivity ratios are 4 and 0.200 for labor and materials, respectively. Using this information, the productivity-neutral quantity for each input is computed as follows:

$$PQ \text{ (labor)} = 250,000/4 = 62,500 \text{ hrs.}$$
$$PQ \text{ (materials)} = 250,000/0.200 = 1,250,000 \text{ lbs.}$$

For our example, PQ gives labor and material inputs that *would have been used* in 2007, assuming no productivity change. What the cost would have been for these productivity-neutral quantities in 2007 is computed by multiplying each individual input quantity (PQ) by its current price (P) and adding:[2]

Cost of labor: $PQ \times P = 62,500 \times \$15 =$		$ 937,500
Cost of materials: $PQ \times P = 1,250,000 \times \$3.50 =$		4,375,000
Total PQ cost		$5,312,500

The actual cost of inputs is obtained by multiplying the actual quantity (AQ) by current input price (P) for each input and adding:

Cost of labor: $AQ \times P = 50,000 \times \$15 =$		$ 750,000
Cost of materials: $AQ \times P = 1,300,000 \times \$3.50 =$		4,550,000
Total current cost		$5,300,000

Finally, the productivity effect on profits is computed by subtracting the total current cost from the total PQ cost as follows:

$$\text{Profit-linked effect} = \text{Total } PQ \text{ cost} - \text{Total current cost}$$
$$= \$5,312,500 - \$5,300,000$$
$$= \$12,500 \text{ increase in profits}$$

The calculation of the profit-linked effect is summarized in Exhibit 15-5 on the following page.

The summary in Exhibit 15-5 reveals that the net effect of the process change was favorable. Profits increased by $12,500 because of the productivity changes. Notice also that profit-linked productivity effects can be assigned to individual inputs. The increase in labor productivity creates a $187,500 increase in profits; however, the drop in materials productivity caused a $175,000 decrease in profits. Most of the profit decrease came from an increase in materials usage—apparently, waste, scrap, and spoiled units are much greater with the new process. Thus, the profit-linked measure provides partial measurement effects as well as a total measurement effect. The total profit-linked productivity measure is the sum of the individual partial measures. This property makes the profit-linked measure ideal for assessing trade-offs. A much clearer picture of the effects of the changes in productivity emerges. Unless waste and scrap can be brought under better control, the company ought to return to the old assembly process. Of

---

2. Base-period input prices are frequently used to value productivity changes. However, it has been shown that current input prices provide more accurate profit-linked productivity measurement. See Hansen, Mowen, and Hammer, "Profit-Linked Productivity Measurement," *Journal of Management Accounting Research* (Fall 1992): 79–98.

	(1)	(2)	(3)	(4)	(2) − (4)
Input	**PQ***	**PQ × P**	**AQ**	**AQ × P**	**(PQ × P) − (AQ × P)**
Labor	62,500	$ 937,500	50,000	$ 750,000	$ 187,500
Materials	1,250,000	4,375,000	1,300,000	4,550,000	(175,000)
		$5,312,500		$5,300,000	$ 12,500

EXHIBIT 15-5   Profit-Linked Productivity Measurement

*Labor: 250,000/4; Materials: 250,000/0.200.

course, it is possible that the learning effects of the new process are not yet fully captured and further improvements in labor productivity might be observed. As labor becomes more proficient at the new process, it is possible that the materials usage could also decrease.

Price-Recovery Component

The profit-linked measure computes the amount of profit change from the base period to the current period attributable to productivity changes. Generally, this will not be equal to the total profit change between the two periods. The difference between the total profit change and the profit-linked productivity change is called the **price-recovery component**. This component is the change in revenue less a change in the cost of inputs, *assuming no productivity changes.* It, therefore, measures the ability of revenue changes to cover changes in the cost of inputs, assuming no productivity change.

To calculate the price-recovery component, we first need to compute the change in profits for each period. This computation is as follows:

	2006	2007	Difference
Revenues	$7,200,000	$7,500,000	$ 300,000
Cost of inputs	4,500,000	5,300,000	(800,000)
Profit	$2,700,000	$2,200,000	$(500,000)

$$\text{Price-recovery} = \text{Profit change} - \text{Profit-linked productivity change}$$
$$= (\$500,000) - \$12,500$$
$$= (\$512,500)$$

The increase in revenues would not have been sufficient to recover the increase in the cost of the inputs. The increase in productivity provided some relief for the price-recovery problem. Increases in productivity can be used to offset price-recovery losses.

Measuring Changes in Activity and Process Efficiency

An activity-based responsibility accounting system focuses on improving the efficiency of processes and activities. As we have just seen, it is possible to measure the value of changes in productive efficiency by analyzing changes in input and output relationships over time. Although the analysis was done for products produced and sold, the same concepts can be applied to any type of output. Activities, for example, consume inputs such as labor, materials, and energy, and they produce an output such as hours of in-

OBJECTIVE 4

Discuss the role of productivity measurement in assessing activity improvement.

spection or number of setups. Thus, it is possible to measure changes in activity productive efficiency. Measuring changes in activity efficiency can be an important part of an activity-based management system. **Activity productivity analysis** is an approach that directly measures changes in activity productivity. Similarly, a process produces an output, and it is also possible to measure process productivity. In fact, since processes are collections of activities with a common goal, activity productivity changes must affect process productivity. **Process productivity analysis** measures changes in process productivity.

Activity Productivity Analysis

An activity can be viewed as an entity that transforms inputs into an output. The inputs are the resources consumed by an activity. Recall that resources are the economic elements that allow an activity to be performed. Thus, in effect, resources are the inputs or factors of production that are used by an activity to create its output. These inputs or resources are identical in concept to the factors used to produce a product: materials, labor, capital, energy, etc. Accordingly, the key to activity productivity analysis is defining activity output and an appropriate activity output measure. Once the output measure is identified, then both profile and profit-linked productivity analyses are possible. Exhibit 15-6 illustrates the activity model that provides the conceptual foundation for activity productivity analysis.

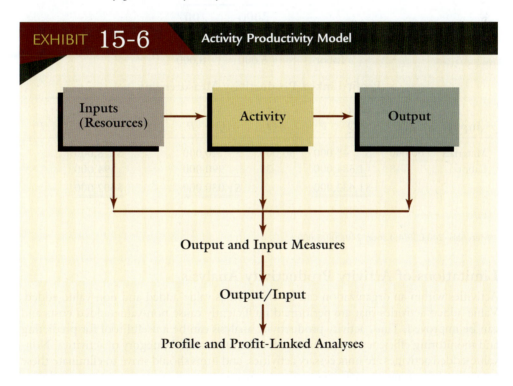

EXHIBIT 15-6   **Activity Productivity Model**

Inputs (Resources) → Activity → Output

Output and Input Measures

Output/Input

Profile and Profit-Linked Analyses

An Illustrative Example

To illustrate activity productivity analysis, we will focus on a single activity. Suppose that the activity is purchasing. The output of purchasing is a purchase order, and the number of purchase orders is a possible output measure. For simplicity, assume that labor and materials (forms, postage stamps, and envelopes) are the only resources consumed by the activity. At the end of 2006, the purchasing activity had been streamlined by redesigning the purchase order, reducing the number of suppliers, and reducing the number of distinct parts that needed to be ordered. Activity data for purchasing for 2006 and 2007 follow. The 2007 data reflect the effect of the activity improvements.

	2006	2007
Number of purchase orders	200,000	240,000
Materials used (lbs.)	50,000	50,000
Labor used (number of workers)	40	30
Cost per pound of material	$1	$0.80
Cost (salary) per worker	$30,000	$33,000

Exhibit 15-7 presents the profile and profit-linked analyses for the purchasing activity. Profile analysis reveals that productivity improved for both partial input measures. The value of these productivity improvements is $602,000—with the majority of the value being created by an increase in purchasing labor productivity. Thus, changes in activity productivity can be assessed or predicted using the same methodology available for assessing manufacturing productivity.

EXHIBIT 15-7   **Activity Productivity Analysis Illustrated**

Profile Analysis

	2006	2007
Materials	4	4.8
Labor	5,000	8,000

Profit-Linked Productivity Measurement

Input	(1) PQ*	(2) PQ × P	(3) AQ	(4) AQ × P	(2) − (4) (PQ × P) − AQ × P)
Materials	60,000	$ 48,000	50,000	$ 40,000	$ 8,000
Labor	48	1,584,000	30	990,000	594,000
		$1,632,000		$1,030,000	$602,000

*Materials: 240,000/4; Labor: 240,000/5,000.

Limitations of Activity Productivity Analysis

Activities within an organization can be classified as value-added and non-value-added. Value-added activities that are performed inefficiently cause non-value-added costs and can be improved. Thus, activity productivity analysis can be a useful tool for predicting and monitoring efficiency improvements for the value-added category of activities. Non-value-added activities are unnecessary activities, and firms should strive to eliminate these activities. Increasing the efficiency of an unnecessary activity does not make a lot of sense. In fact, it is possible that productivity ratios taken over time might signal a decrease in non-value-added activity productivity, and yet the underlying change may very well be consistent with the objective of reducing and eliminating the non-value-added activity. For example, suppose that the output of materials handling is measured by number of moves and that labor is the only significant activity input. Suppose that efforts are made to reduce the user demands for materials handling. In 2006, 50,000 moves were made using 10 workers, producing a productivity ratio of 5,000 moves per worker. In 2007, the demand for materials movement decreased to 22,000 moves and five workers because of the improvement efforts, producing a productivity ratio of 4,400 moves per worker. Comparing ratios indicates that activity productivity has decreased. Yet, the actions taken have produced results that are fully consistent with reducing and eliminating the materials handling activity. Thus, it seems reasonable to exercise caution in the use of interpretation of activity productivity analysis for non-value-added activities. One possibility is to limit non-value-added productivity analysis to changes in actual activity costs, where decreases are viewed as favorable and increases as unfavorable. A third possibility is to consider non-value-added productivity analysis only within the context of process productivity changes.

Process Productivity Analysis

Processes are defined by activities with a common goal. The common goal is usually defined as the output produced by the process. A process's output consumes the activities of the process, which, in turn, consume resources (labor, materials, etc.). This suggests that process productivity changes are defined by two components: (1) changes in the efficiency of activities consuming resources and (2) changes in the efficiency of the process output's consumption of activities. The process for measuring the resource efficiency component has already been discussed and can be reviewed by examining Exhibit 15-6. The second component treats *activity outputs* as inputs and evaluates productivity by relating activities to the output produced by the process. A partial measure of productivity is computed for each activity that belongs to the process. These partial measures are used for profile and profit-linked analyses. Exhibit 15-8 summarizes and illustrates the productivity model for the second process component (activity output efficiency). Notice that the input for the productivity calculation of this process component is simply the activity output measure, and the output is the product of the process. The *cost* per unit of input (i.e., activity output in this case) is the *activity rate derived from* PQ *and current prices.*[3] Process output must also be defined and measured. Each organization has a variety of processes such as product development, procurement, manufacturing, sales, order fulfillment, and customer service. Each process has one or more outputs. Manufacturing, for example, may produce two or more products. In this case, products are the output of manufacturing. Where a process has multiple output measures,

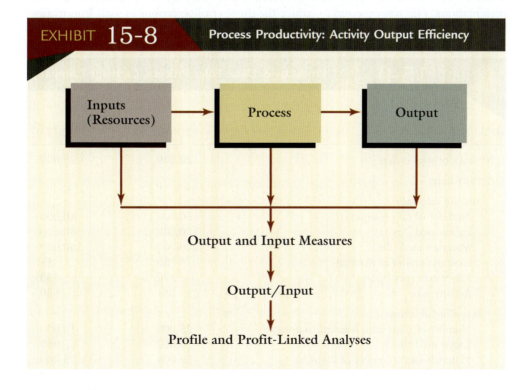

EXHIBIT 15-8   **Process Productivity: Activity Output Efficiency**

Inputs (Resources) → Process → Output

Output and Input Measures

Output/Input

Profile and Profit-Linked Analyses

---

3. The cost assigned to an activity to calculate the activity rate is based on Q and current input prices. A rate based on AQ and current prices will not capture the savings from reducing demand for activity output.

productivity analysis is carried out for each type of output. Inputs are measured by computing the demands that each product (output) makes on each activity.

Process Productivity Model

Total process productivity change is simply the sum of the two components: Resource efficiency + Activity output efficiency. This approach has the advantage of allowing both value-added and non-value-added activities to be considered simultaneously. The sum of the two components should reveal the correct effect of changes in both types of activities. Also, it is possible to evaluate the effect on process productivity resulting from trade-offs among activities that make up the process. Process improvement or innovation means finding new ways—often, radically new ways—of producing the process's output. This is accomplished by using activity selection, activity reduction, activity elimination, and activity sharing. The effect is to change the mix and quantity of activities that define the process. Process productivity analysis offers a way to measure the proposed and actual *economic* effects of process improvement or innovation.

An Illustrative Example

Process productivity analysis can be applied to any process within the firm: product development, sales, order fulfillment, customer service, manufacturing, etc. The sales process, for example, is defined by activities such as locating prospects, qualifying prospects, making sales calls (approaching the customer), preparing sales presentations, handling objections, closing the sale, and following up. The output of the sales process is a sales order. Consider the sales process of Carthage Company and two of its activities: making sales calls and handling objections. Of the two activities, making sales calls is value-added, and handling objections is non-value-added. At the end of 2006, Carthage initiated some process changes that were designed to improve sales efficiency. Carthage initiated actions to improve the customer locating and qualifying activities, believing that this would improve the efficiency of sales calls and reduce the number of objections from potential customers. Sales personnel were also provided more training to improve their sales presentations. This was expected to reduce the number of objections as well. Information relating to the sales process, its output, and the two activities is presented in Exhibit 15-9

EXHIBIT 15-9	Productivity Data: Sales Process, Carthage Company	
	2006	**2007**
Number of sales orders	20,000	25,000
Activity data:		
Making sales calls		
Number of calls (output)	50,000	40,000
Labor used (hrs.)	100,000	80,000
Materials used (lbs.)	200,000	200,000
Cost per pound of material	$6	$5
Labor cost (per hour)	$30	$30
Activity rate	$84	$80
Handling objections		
Number of objections handled (output)	25,000	10,000
Labor used (hrs.)	30,000	15,000
Materials used (number of samples)	25,000	5,000
Cost per sample	$40	$40
Labor cost per hour	$30	$30
Activity rate	$76	$76

for the years 2006 and 2007. For simplicity, the analysis is confined to only two activities.

Resource inputs, their prices, and activity output are needed for analyzing resource efficiency. On the other hand, activity output, activity rates, and process output are needed for analyzing activity output efficiency. Exhibit 15-9 provides the needed data for both analyses. Using data from Exhibit 15-9, Exhibit 15-10 provides the productivity analysis for the resource efficiency component, and Exhibit 15-11, Panel A, (on the following page) provides the productivity analysis for the activity output efficiency component. The total process productivity effect (the sum of the two components) is shown in Panel B of Exhibit 15-11.

Panel B of Exhibit 15-11 shows that overall process productivity increased dramatically, causing an increase in profits totaling $3,326,440. This increase is mostly

---

EXHIBIT 15-10   **Resource Efficiency Component (Activity Productivity)**

A. Making Sales Calls

Profile Analysis

	2006	2007
Labor	0.50	0.50
Materials	0.25	0.20

Profit-Linked Productivity Measurement

Input	(1) PQ^*	(2) $PQ \times P$	(3) AQ	(4) $AQ \times P$	(2) − (4) $(PQ \times P) - (AQ \times P)$
Labor	80,000	$2,400,000	80,000	$2,400,000	$ 0
Materials	160,000	800,000	200,000	1,000,000	(200,000)
		$3,200,000		$3,400,000	$(200,000)

*Labor: 40,000/0.50; Materials: 40,000/0.25.

B. Handling Objections

Profile Analysis

	2006	2007
Labor	0.83	0.67
Materials	1.00	2.00

Profit-Linked Productivity Measurement

Input	(1) PQ^*	(2) $PQ \times P$	(3) AQ	(4) $AQ \times P$	(2) − (4) $(PQ \times P) - (AQ \times P)$
Labor	12,048	$361,440	15,000	$450,000	$ (88,560)
Materials	10,000	400,000	5,000	200,000	200,000
		$761,440		$650,000	$111,440

*Labor: 10,000/0.83; Materials: 10,000/1.0.

EXHIBIT 15-11   Activity Output Efficiency and Total Process Productivity

A. Activity Output Efficiency

Profile Analysis		
	2006	**2007**
Making sales calls[a]	0.400	0.625
Handling objections[b]	0.800	2.500

[a] 20,000/50,000; 25,000/40,000.
[b] 20,000/25,000; 25,000/10,000.

	Profit-Linked Productivity Measurement				
Input	**(1)** PQ^*	**(2)** $PQ \times P$	**(3)** AQ	**(4)** $AQ \times P$	**(2) − (4)** $(PQ \times P) − (AQ \times P)$
Calls	62,500	$5,000,000	40,000	$3,200,000	$1,800,000
Objections	31,250	2,375,000	10,000	760,000	1,615,000
		$7,375,000		$3,960,000	$3,415,000

*25,000/0.4; 25,000/0.8.
Note: P is the activity rate for 2007.

B. Total Process Productivity

		Source
Resource usage component:		
Making calls	$ (200,000)	Exhibit 15-10
Handling objections	111,440	Exhibit 15-10
Activity output component	3,415,000	Panel A, Exhibit 15-11
Total process productivity change	$3,326,440	

---

attributable to the fact that demand has dropped sharply for activity output. For example, profile analysis reveals that the orders per complaint have increased from 0.800 to 2.500 (Exhibit 15-11, Panel A), a significant increase in productivity. Similarly, the orders per sales call have increased from 0.400 to 0.625. However, of the two activities, only one contributed to increasing process efficiency by increasing activity resource efficiency. In fact, the net activity resource efficiency was negative (see Exhibit 15-10).

Service Productivity

The process productivity model is easily adapted to service organizations. All organizations have processes. These processes can be identified, activities and output can be defined, and productivity measurement can occur. **IBM Credit**, for example, is a service organization that offers financing for the computers, software, and services that **IBM Corporation** sells.[4] Within IBM Credit, one of the major processes is its quote preparation process. The quote preparation process is defined by the following activities: logging the request, assessing

---

4. A more complete discussion of the IBM Credit example can be found in the following two sources: Michael Hammer and James Champy, *Reengineering the Corporation* (New York: HarperBusiness, 1993): 36–39; and Thomas H. Davenport, *Process Innovation* (Boston: Harvard Business School Press, 1993): 2, 32–33, and 158.

creditworthiness, modifying loan covenants, pricing, and preparing and delivering a quote letter. Since the activities were located in separate departments, the process also included a movement activity—an activity that required the transfer of each activity's output from one location to another. Essentially, the customer's credit application was transferred from department to department, a transfer occurring only after a particular department had finished its activity (e.g., the credit department transfers the application to the business practices department after it has assessed creditworthiness). The process's output can be defined as financing approval and can be measured by the number of quotes. Before any effort at process improvement, it took about six days to prepare a quote. IBM Credit redesigned the process by eliminating the non-value-added movement activity. It accomplished this by having one person process the entire application from beginning to end. This had two outcomes. First, the time required to process an application was reduced from six days to a few hours. Second, the labor productivity ratio was dramatically improved. The number of workers remained about the same, and yet the number of quotes being processed increased 100 times. This means, for example, that if the partial labor productivity ratio was 10 before the improvement, it is now 1,000!

Activities and Process Productivity Measurement

Since activity output is a process input, reducing non-value-added activities should normally show up as a process productivity improvement. Why? Reducing non-value-added activities means finding ways to produce the same or higher process output with less non-value-added activity output. Thus, the output/input ratios will show an increase in process productivity (through the activity output efficiency component). The objective is to produce process output without any non-value-added activity input. Reducing and eliminating non-value-added activities means improving the technical efficiency of processes. Therefore, it is important to identify all non-value-added activity inputs for a process. This means that we must exercise caution in identifying and defining the activities that are used by the process being evaluated.

Quality and Productivity

Improving quality may improve productivity, and vice versa. For example, consider rework, an internal failure activity. If rework is reduced by producing fewer defective units, then less labor and fewer materials are used to produce the same output. Reducing the number of defective units improves quality; reducing the amount of inputs used improves productivity.

Since most quality improvements reduce the amount of resources used to produce and sell an organization's output, most quality improvements will improve productivity. Thus, quality improvements will generally be reflected in productivity measures. However, there are other ways to improve productivity other than through quality improvement. A firm may produce a good with little or no defects but still have an inefficient process.

For example, consider a good that passes through two 5-minute processes. (Assume the good is produced free of defects.) One unit, then, requires 10 minutes to pass through both processes. Currently, units are produced in batches of 1,200. Process 1 produces 1,200 units. Then, the batch is conveyed by forklift to another location, where the units pass through Process 2. Thus, for each process, a total of 6,000 minutes, or 100 hours, is needed to produce a batch. The 1,200 finished units, then, require a total of 200 hours (100 hours for each process) plus conveyance time (assume that to be 15 minutes).

By redesigning the manufacturing process, efficiency can be improved. Suppose that the second process is located close enough to the first process so that as soon as a unit is completed by the first process, it is passed to the second process. In this way, the first and second processes can be working at the same time. The second process no longer has to wait for the production of 1,200 units plus conveyance time before it can begin operation. The total time to produce 1,200 units now is 6,000 minutes plus the waiting time for the first unit (five minutes). Thus, production of 1,200 units has been reduced from 200 hours and 15 minutes to 100 hours and five minutes. More output can be produced with fewer inputs. The moving and waiting activities are non-value-added inputs that have been virtually eliminated, thereby improving process productivity.

SUMMARY

Productivity deals with how efficiently inputs are used to produce the output. Partial measures of productivity evaluate the efficient use of single inputs. Total measures of productivity assess efficiency for all inputs. Profit-linked productivity effects are calculated by using the linkage rule. Essentially, the profit effect is computed by taking the difference between the cost of the inputs that would have been used without any productivity change and the cost of the actual inputs used. Because of the possibility of input trade-offs, it is essential to value productivity changes. Only in this way can the effect of productivity changes be properly assessed. Productivity analysis can be used to assess activity performance. Two approaches can be used to assess activity efficiency: activity productivity analysis and process productivity analysis. Activity productivity analysis is primarily used for assessing changes in the efficiency of value-added activities. Process productivity analysis can be used to assess productivity of processes and of both value- and non-value-added activities that define the process.

REVIEW PROBLEM AND SOLUTION

PRODUCTIVITY

At the end of 2006, Homer Company implemented a new labor process and redesigned its product with the expectation that input usage efficiency would increase. Now, at the end of 2007, the president of the company wants an assessment of the changes in the company's productivity. The data needed for the assessment are as follows:

	2006	2007
Output	10,000	12,000
Output prices	$20	$20
Materials (lbs.)	8,000	8,400
Materials unit price	$6	$8
Labor (hrs.)	5,000	4,800
Labor rate per hour	$10	$10
Power (kwh)	2,000	3,000
Price per kwh	$2	$3

Required:

1. Compute the partial operational measures for each input for both 2006 and 2007. What can be said about productivity improvement?
2. Prepare a partial income statement for each year, and calculate the total change in profits.
3. Calculate the profit-linked productivity measure for 2007. What can be said about the productivity program?
4. Calculate the price-recovery component. What does this tell you?

SOLUTION

1. Partial measures:

	2006	2007
Materials	10,000/8,000 = 1.25	12,000/8,400 = 1.43
Labor	10,000/5,000 = 2.00	12,000/4,800 = 2.50
Power	10,000/2,000 = 5.00	12,000/3,000 = 4.00

Profile analysis indicates that productive efficiency has increased for materials and labor and decreased for power. The outcome is mixed, and no statement about overall productivity improvement can be made without valuing the trade-off.

2. Income statements:

	2006	2007
Sales	$200,000	$240,000
Cost of inputs	102,000	124,200
Gross profit	$ 98,000	$115,800

Total change in profits: $115,800 − $98,000 = $17,800 increase

3. Profit-linked measurement:

Input	(1) PQ*	(2) PQ × P	(3) AQ	(4) AQ × P	(2) − (4) (PQ × P) − (AQ × P)
Materials	9,600	$ 76,800	8,400	$ 67,200	$ 9,600
Labor	6,000	60,000	4,800	48,000	12,000
Power	2,400	7,200	3,000	9,000	(1,800)
		$144,000		$124,200	$19,800

*Materials: 12,000/1.25; Labor: 12,000/2; Power: 12,000/5.

The value of the increases in efficiency for materials and labor more than offsets the increased usage of power. Thus, the productivity improvement program should be labeled successful.

4. Price recovery:

Price-recovery component = Total profit change − Profit-linked productivity change

Price-recovery component = $17,800 − $19,800

= ($2,000)

This says that without the productivity improvement, profits would have declined by $2,000. The $40,000 increase in revenues would not have offset the increase in the cost of inputs. From the solution to Requirement 3, the cost of inputs without a productivity increase would have been $144,000 (column 2). The increase in the input cost without productivity would have been $144,000 − $102,000 = $42,000. This is $2,000 more than the increase in revenues. Only because of the productivity increase did the firm show an increase in profitability.

KEY TERMS

QUESTIONS FOR WRITING AND DISCUSSION

1. Define *total productive efficiency.*
2. Explain the difference between technical and allocative efficiency.
3. What is productivity measurement?
4. Explain the difference between partial and total measures of productivity.
5. What is an operational productivity measure? A financial measure?
6. Discuss the advantages and disadvantages of partial measures of productivity.
7. What is the purpose of a base period?
8. What is profile measurement and analysis? What are the limitations of this approach?
9. What is profit-linked productivity measurement and analysis?
10. Explain why profit-linked productivity measurement is important.
11. What is the price-recovery component?
12. What is activity productivity analysis, and what are its limitations?
13. What is process productivity analysis?
14. Can productivity improvements be achieved without improving quality? Explain.
15. Why is it important for managers to be concerned with both productivity and quality?

EXERCISES

15-1   TECHNICAL AND PRICE EFFICIENCY

LO1   Listed below are several possible input combinations for producing 5,000 units of a pocket PC. Two of the input combinations are technically efficient.

	Materials	*Labor*	*Energy*
Unit input prices	$150	$125	$50
Input combinations:			
A	250	480	1,800
B	275	450	1,350
C	230	475	1,425
D	375	500	1,500

Required:

1. Identify the technically efficient input combinations. Explain your choices.
2. Which of the two technically efficient input combinations should be used? Explain.

15-2   PRODUCTIVITY MEASUREMENT, TECHNICAL AND ALLOCATIVE EFFICIENCY, PARTIAL MEASURES

LO1, LO2   Gambiano Company produces hand-crafted pottery that uses two inputs, materials and labor. During the past quarter, 20,000 units were produced, requiring 80,000 pounds of material and 40,000 hours of labor. An engineering efficiency study commissioned by the local university revealed that Gambiano can produce the same 20,000 units of output using either of the following two combinations of inputs:

	Materials	Labor
Combinations:		
F1	60,000	30,000
F2	66,000	28,000

The cost of materials is $8 per pound; the cost of labor is $12 per hour.

Required:

1. Compute the output-input ratio for each input of Combination F1. Does this represent a productivity improvement over the current use of inputs? What is the total dollar value of the improvement? Classify this as a technical or an allocative efficiency improvement.
2. Compute the output-input ratio for each input of Combination F2. Does this represent a productivity improvement over the current use of inputs? Now, compare these ratios to those of Combination F1. What has happened?
3. Compute the cost of producing 20,000 units of output using Combination F1. Compare this cost to the cost using Combination F2. Does moving from Combination F1 to Combination F2 represent a productivity improvement? Explain.

15-3   INTERPERIOD MEASUREMENT OF PRODUCTIVITY, PROFILES

LO2   Helena Company needs to increase its profits and so has embarked on a program to increase its overall productivity. After one year of operation, Kent Olson, manager of the Columbus plant, reported the following results for the base period and its most recent year of operations:

	2006	2007
Output	307,200	360,000
Power (quantity used)	38,400	18,000
Materials (quantity used)	76,800	81,000

Required:

Compute the productivity profiles for each year. Did productivity improve? Explain.

15-4   INTERPERIOD MEASUREMENT OF PRODUCTIVITY, PROFIT-LINKED MEASUREMENT

LO3   Refer to **Exercise 15-3**. Suppose the following input prices are provided for each year:

Spreadsheet

	2006	2007
Unit price (power)	$ 2	$ 3
Unit price (materials)	16	15
Unit selling price	6	8

Required:

1. Compute the profit-linked productivity measure. By how much did profits increase due to productivity?
2. Calculate the price-recovery component for 2007. Explain its meaning.

15-5 ACTIVITY PRODUCTIVITY, NON-VALUE-ADDED ACTIVITY

LO4

Rework, a non-value-added activity, is part of Jorgensen Manufacturing's assembly process. Testing often revealed that one or more components (almost always sourced from outside suppliers) had failed. At the end of 2006, Jorgensen initiated efforts designed to buy higher-quality components. Consequently, the demand for the rework activity was expected to decrease. The following data pertain to the reordering activity for the years 2006 and 2007:

	2006	2007
Units assembled	300,000	300,000
Units reworked	7,500	3,600
Rework components (number)	15,000	7,200
Rework labor hours	12,000	6,000
Labor cost per hour	$12	$15
Cost per component	$20	$20
Activity rate	$59	$64

Required:

1. Identify the output measure for the rework activity.
2. Calculate the productivity profile and the profit-linked measure for the rework activity. Is reducing the demand for a non-value-added activity the correct decision? Does this benefit show up in the productivity measure? Explain.

15-6 PROCESS PRODUCTIVITY, NON-VALUE-ADDED ACTIVITY

LO4 Refer to **Exercise 15-5**.

Required:

1. Identify the output measure for the assembly process. Calculate the productivity profile and profit-linked measure of the assembly process where the output of the rework activity is viewed as a process input. Does this indicate anything about the value of reducing demand for a non-value-added activity?
2. Calculate the total process productivity change. What does this indicate about the actions taken regarding the non-value-added activity?

15-7 PRODUCTIVITY MEASUREMENT: TRADE-OFFS, PROFILE AND PROFIT-LINKED ANALYSES

LO2, LO3

Bradshaw Company has recently installed a computer-aided manufacturing system. The decision to automate was made so that material waste could be reduced. Better quality and a reduction of labor inputs were also expected. After one year of operation, management wants to see if the expected productivity improvements have materialized. The president is particularly interested in knowing whether the trade-off between capital, labor, and materials was favorable. Data concerning output, labor, materials, and capital are provided for the year before implementation and the year after.

	Year Before	Year After
Output	100,000	120,000
Input quantities:		
Materials (lbs.)	25,000	20,000
Labor (hours)	5,000	2,000
Capital (dollars)	$10,000	$300,000
Input prices:		
Materials	$5	$5
Labor	$10	$10
Capital	10%	10%

Required:

1. Prepare a productivity profile for each year. Evaluate the productivity changes.
2. Calculate the change in profits attributable to the change in productivity of the three inputs. Assuming that these are the only three inputs, evaluate the decision to automate.

15-8 PROSPECTIVE PRODUCTIVITY MEASUREMENT, TECHNICAL AND ALLOCATIVE EFFICIENCY, PROFILE AND PROFIT-LINKED ANALYSES

LO1, LO2, LO3   The manager of Blakely Company was reviewing two competing projects for the molding department. The projects represented different methods of preparing the molds for one of the company's more popular product lines. One project changed the way molds were poured and promised a savings in material usage. The second project redesigned the process so that labor was used more efficiently. The fiscal year was coming to a close, and the manager wanted to make a decision concerning the proposed process changes so that they could be used, if beneficial, during the coming year. The process changes would affect the department's input usage. For the year just ended, the accounting department provided the following information about the inputs used to produce 100,000 units of output:

	Quantity	Unit Prices
Materials	200,000 lbs.	$ 8
Labor	80,000 hrs.	10
Energy	40,000 kwh	2

Each project offers a different process design from the one currently being used. Neither project would cost anything to implement. Expected input usage for producing 120,000 units (the expected output for the coming year) for each project is as follows:

	Project I	Project II
Materials	200,000 lbs.	220,000 lbs.
Labor	80,000 hrs.	60,000 hrs.
Energy	40,000 kwh	40,000 kwh

Input prices are expected to remain the same for the coming year.

Required:

1. Prepare a productivity profile analysis for the most recently completed year and each project. Does either proposal improve technical efficiency? Explain. Can you make a recommendation about either project using only the physical measures?

2. Calculate the profit-linked productivity measure for each proposal. Which proposal offers the best outcome for the company? How does this relate to the concept of price efficiency? Explain.

15-9 BASICS OF PRODUCTIVITY MEASUREMENT

LO1, LO2, LO3

Spreadsheet

Holbrook Company gathered the following data for the past two years:

	Base Year	Current Year
Output	900,000	1,080,000
Output prices	$15	$15
Input quantities:		
Materials (lbs.)	1,200,000	720,000
Labor (hrs.)	300,000	540,000
Input prices:		
Materials	$5	$6
Labor	$8	$8

Required:

1. Prepare a productivity profile for each year.
2. Prepare partial income statements for each year. Calculate the total change in income.
3. Calculate the change in profits attributable to productivity changes.
4. Calculate the price-recovery component. Explain its meaning.

15-10 ACTIVITY PRODUCTIVITY

LO3, LO4

In an effort to become more competitive, Hardy Company has embarked on a program to reduce and eliminate its non-value-added activities and to improve the efficiency of its value-added activities. The activity of paying bills has been classified as value-added and in need of improvement. The major inputs for the activity are clerks, personal computers (PCs), and supplies. Activity output is defined as "paid bills" and is measured by the number of checks issued. The materials handling activity, on the other hand, is classified as a non-value-added activity and is targeted for reduction and possible elimination (at least as a significant activity). The major inputs for materials movement (the output) are labor, forklifts, and supplies. Over a 2-year period, Hardy has made some changes in the way each activity is performed. For example, Hardy has redesigned its plant layout to reduce the demand for materials movement. Process innovation also dramatically changed the way that bills were paid. Data are provided for the two activities for a base year and the most recent year completed. The year just completed was the second year of Hardy's improvement program.

Activity	Base Year	Most Recent Year
Paying bills:		
Output	300,000	320,000
Inputs:		
Clerks (no.)	15	5
PCs (no.)	15	5
Supplies (lbs.)	150,000	40,000
Moving materials:		
Output	20,000	5,000
Inputs:		
Labor (hrs.)	10,000	3,000
Forklifts (no.)	5	2
Supplies (lbs.)	4,000	2,000

Required:

1. Prepare productivity profiles for both activities. Comment on the usefulness of these profiles for assessing improvement in activity performance.
2. Given the following most recent year's input prices for the paying bills activity, calculate the activity's profit-linked measure:

Clerks	$25,000 per person
PCs	$5,000 per system
Supplies	$1 per pound

PROBLEMS

15-11   PROCESS AND ACTIVITY PRODUCTIVITY

LO3, LO4   In 2006, Maravilla Auto's Motor Division hired a consulting firm to help identify and define the processes used within the division. Megan Dorr, the divisional manager, also asked the consulting firm to make recommendations concerning the reengineering of the processes to improve overall efficiency. Six major processes were defined. The consulting firm prepared six documents—one for each process. The following memo from Bill Gray, the consulting partner in charge, summarizes the major points for the procurement process. (The procurement process is one of the six major processes.)

MEMO

To: Megan Dorr, Divisional Manager
From: Bill Gray, Partner, Jackson Consulting
Subject: Procurement Process
Date: April 15, 2006

The procurement process consists of three major activities: purchasing, receiving, and paying bills. Currently, the procurement process begins with the purchasing department sending a purchase order to a supplier. When the order is received from the supplier, the receiving department fills out a receiving document and sends it to accounts payable. Accounts payable also receives an invoice from the supplier (through the mail). Clerks in accounts payable compare the three documents and issue a check if all three match. At times, there are discrepancies, and accounts payable clerks are responsible for resolving these discrepancies before payment is made. Resolution of discrepancies may take weeks and often consumes considerable clerical resources. This resolution activity is non-value-added, and a process redesign can eliminate it and save significant resources. We estimate that about 80 percent of clerical time is spent dealing with these discrepancies.

We recommend that payment authorization be changed from accounts payable to receiving. This change requires the acquisition of several terminals that will be used to access purchase information in the company's database. It also requires new software that will permit the following: (1) When the goods arrive from a supplier, the receiving clerk will check to see if the shipment is supported with an outstanding purchase order; (2) If there is a corresponding purchase order indicating the type and quantity of goods received, then the clerk can signal acceptance using the keyboard, and the computer will issue a check at the appropriate time for payment; (3) If there is no supporting documentation or if the type and quantity of goods received differ from the purchase order, then the goods are simply shipped back to the supplier.

After reviewing the memo, Megan Dorr set in motion the necessary actions to implement the consultant's recommendations. The terminals were purchased, and the required supporting software was developed. Since suppliers often shipped partial orders, the software was modified to allow for this possibility. Now, two years later, Megan wants an analysis of the productivity gains or losses that have resulted from the process changes that have been implemented. Output for the procurement process is defined as the number of units purchased and paid for (of all types). Data for 2006 and 2008 for the procurement process and its activities are as follows:

Process Output, Activity Demands, and Input Prices

	2006	2008
Units purchased and paid for	3,000,000	3,600,000
Purchase orders	100,000	120,000
Receiving orders	150,000	180,000
Bills paid	150,000	180,000
Input prices:		
Supplies (per lb.)	$1.80	$2
Clerks (salary per person)	$30,000	$40,000
Capital (interest rate)	10%	10%

Activity Information

	Purchasing	Receiving	Paying Bills
2006:			
Supplies (lbs.)	50,000	40,000	75,000
Clerks (no.)	25	50	100
Capital (dollars)	$1,000,000	$800,000	$500,000
2008:			
Supplies (lbs.)	60,000	30,000	5,000
Clerks (no.)	25	50	10
Capital (dollars)	$1,200,000	$3,000,000	$1,000,000
Activity rates	$12.00	$14.40	$28.00

Required:

1. Compute the profit-linked measure of productivity for each of the three activities. This is the first component of procurement process productivity analysis.
2. Calculate the profit-linked measure for the activity output efficiency component of process productivity analysis.
3. Now, add the two profit-linked measures of Requirements 1 and 2. Explain the meaning of this measure. Was the company successful in increasing the productivity of the procurement process?

15-12 PRODUCTIVITY AND QUALITY, PROSPECTIVE ANALYSIS

LO2, LO3   Walnut Company is considering the acquisition of a computerized manufacturing system. The new system has a built-in quality function that increases the control over product specifications. An alarm sounds whenever the product falls outside the programmed specifications. An operator can then make some adjustments on the spot to restore the desired product quality. The system is expected to decrease the number of units scrapped because of poor quality. The system is also expected to decrease the amount of labor inputs needed. The production manager is pushing for the acquisition because he believes that productivity will be greatly enhanced—particularly when it comes to labor and material inputs. Output and input data follow. The data for the computerized system are projections.

	Current System	Computerized System
Output (units)	20,000	20,000
Output selling price	$40	$40
Input quantities:		
Materials	80,000	70,000
Labor	40,000	30,000
Capital (dollars)	$40,000	$200,000
Energy	20,000	50,000
Input prices:		
Materials	$4.00	$4.00
Labor	$9.00	$9.00
Capital (percent)	10.00%	10.00%
Energy	$2.00	$2.50

Required:

1. Compute the partial operational ratios for materials and labor under each alternative. Is the production manager right in thinking that materials and labor productivity increase with the automated system?
2. Compute the productivity profiles for each system. Does the computerized system improve productivity?
3. Determine the amount by which profits will change if the computerized system is adopted. Are the trade-offs among the inputs favorable? Comment on the system's ability to improve productivity.

15-13 PRODUCTIVITY MEASUREMENT, BASICS

LO3   Fowler Company produces handcrafted leather purses. Virtually all of the manufacturing cost consists of materials and labor. Over the past several years, profits have been declining because the cost of the two major inputs has been increasing. Wilma Fowler, the president of the company, has indicated that the price of the purses cannot be increased; thus, the only way to improve or at least stabilize profits is to increase overall productivity. At the beginning of 2007, Wilma implemented a new cutting and assembly process that promised less materials waste and a faster production time. At the end of 2007, Wilma wants to know how much profits have changed from the prior year because of the new process. In order to provide this information to Wilma, the controller of the company gathered the following data:

	2006	2007
Unit selling price	$16	$16
Purses produced and sold	18,000	24,000
Materials used	36,000	40,000
Labor used	9,000	10,000
Unit price of materials	$4	$4.50
Unit price of labor	$9	$10

Required:

1. Compute the productivity profile for each year. Comment on the effectiveness of the new production process.
2. Compute the increase in profits attributable to increased productivity.
3. Calculate the price-recovery component, and comment on its meaning.

15-14 PRODUCTIVITY MEASUREMENT, TECHNICAL AND PRICE EFFICIENCY

LO1, LO3   In 2006, Fleming Chemicals used the following input combination to produce 55,000 gallons of an industrial solvent:

Materials	33,000 lbs.
Labor	66,000 hrs.

In 2007, Fleming again planned to produce 55,000 gallons of solvent and was considering two different changes in process, both of which would be able to produce the desired output. The following input combinations are associated with each process change:

	Change I	Change II
Materials	38,500 lbs.	27,500 lbs.
Labor	44,000 hrs.	55,000 hrs.

The following combination is optimal for an output of 55,000 units. However, this optimal input combination is unknown to Fleming.

Materials	22,000 lbs.
Labor	44,000 hrs.

The cost of materials is $60 per pound, and the cost of labor is $15 per hour. These input prices hold for 2006 and 2007.

Required:

1. Compute the productivity profiles for each of the following:
    a.   The actual inputs used in 2006
    b.   The inputs for each proposed 2007 process change
    c.   The optimal input combination
    Will productivity increase in 2007, regardless of which change is used? Which process change would you recommend based on the prospective productivity profiles?
2. Compute the cost of 2006's productive inefficiency relative to the optimal input combination. Repeat for 2007 proposed input changes. Will productivity improve from 2006 to 2007 for each process change? If so, by how much? Explain. Include in your explanation a discussion of changes in technical and allocative efficiency.
3. Since the optimal input combination is not known by Fleming, suggest a way to measure productivity improvement. Use this method to measure the productivity improvement achieved from 2006 to 2007. How does this measure compare with the productivity improvement measure computed using the optimal input combination?

15-15 PROCESS PRODUCTIVITY MEASUREMENT: SECOND COMPONENT (ACTIVITY OUTPUT EFFICIENCY)

LO3, LO4   Wright Manufacturing has recently studied its order-filling process and initiated some changes that were expected to improve its efficiency. The changes involved such things as redesign of the plant layout, redesign of documents, keyboard training, and improvement in automated system controls. The changes were expected to improve process productivity over a period of several years. The order-filling process is defined by the following three activities: handling goods, entering data, and detecting errors. The output measure for the process is the number of orders filled. The handling activity's output (movement of goods) is measured by yards traveled; the entering data activity's output is measured by data entry time; and the output of detecting errors is measured by the number of documents inspected (compares document data with input record). Data for the year prior to the changes and for two years following the changes are as follows:

	2005	2006	2007
Output measures:			
Number of orders filled	150,000	165,000	200,000
Yards traveled	1,500,000	825,000	400,000
Data entry time (hrs.)	50,000	41,250	40,000
Documents inspected	150,000	82,500	50,000
Activity rates:			
Handling goods (per yard)	$1	$1	$1.25
Entering data (per hour)	$7	$7	$8.00
Detecting errors (per document)	$2	$2	$2.00

Required:

1. Calculate the productivity profiles for all three years. What can you say about productivity improvement for this process? Comment on the value of multiyear comparisons of productivity profiles.
2. Calculate the profit-linked measures for 2006 and 2007, using 2005 as the base year for 2006 and using 2006 as the base year for 2007. Is there any value to changing base years? Explain.

15-16 PRODUCTIVITY MEASUREMENT, PRICE RECOVERY

LO2, LO3 The Small Motors Division of Polson Company has recently engaged in a vigorous effort to reduce manufacturing costs by increasing productivity (through process innovation). Over the past several years, price competition has become very intense, and recent events called for another significant price decrease. Without the price decrease, the marketing manager estimates that the division's market share would drop by 30 percent. The marketing manager estimates that a price decrease of $5.00 per unit is needed in 2007 to maintain market share. (Since the market is expanding, maintaining the market share means an increase in units sold.) The small motors sold for $70 each in 2006. However, the divisional manager indicated that the revenues lost by the price decrease must be offset by increased cost efficiency. Any further deterioration in profits could threaten the division's continued existence. Thus, in 2007, processes were reengineered in an effort to improve productivity. At the end of 2007, the divisional manager wanted an assessment of the effects of the process changes. To assess the changes in productive efficiency, the following data were gathered:

	2006	2007
Output	50,000	60,000
Input quantities:		
Materials	50,000	40,000
Labor	200,000	100,000
Capital	$2,000,000	$5,000,000
Energy	50,000	150,000
Input prices:		
Materials	$8	$10
Labor	$10	$12
Capital	15%	10%
Energy	$2	$2

Required:

1. Calculate the productivity profile for each year. Can you say that productivity has improved? Explain.
2. Calculate the total profit change from 2006 to 2007. How much of this change is attributable to productivity? To price recovery?
3. Calculate the cost per unit for 2006 and 2007. Was the division able to decrease its per-unit cost by at least $5.00? Comment on the relationship of competitive advantage and productive efficiency.

15-17 QUALITY AND PRODUCTIVITY, INTERACTION, USE OF OPERATIONAL MEASURES

LO3   Andy Confer, production-line manager, had arranged a visit with Will Keating, plant manager. He had some questions about the new operational measures that were being used.

ANDY: Will, my questions are more to satisfy my curiosity than anything else. At the beginning of the year, we began some new procedures that require us to work toward increasing our output per pound of material and decreasing our output per labor hour. As instructed, I've been tracking these operational measures for each batch we've produced so far this year. Here's a copy of a trend report for the first five batches of the year. Each batch had 10,000 units in it.

Batches	Material Usage	Ratio	Labor Usage	Ratio
1	4,000 lbs.	2.50	2,000 hrs.	5.00
2	3,900	2.56	2,020	4.95
3	3,750	2.67	2,150	4.65
4	3,700	2.70	2,200	4.55
5	3,600	2.78	2,250	4.44

WILL: Andy, this report is very encouraging. The trend is exactly what we hoped for. I'll bet we meet our goal of getting the batch productivity measures. Let's see, those goals were 3.00 units per pound for materials and 4.00 units per hour for labor. Last year's figures were 2.50 for materials and 5.00 for labor. Things are looking good. I guess tying bonuses and raises to improving these productivity stats was a good idea.

ANDY: Maybe so—but I don't understand why you want to make these trade-offs between materials and labor. Materials cost only $5 per pound, and labor costs $10 per hour. It seems as if you're simply increasing the cost of making this product.

WILL: Actually, it may seem that way, but it's not so. There are other factors to consider. You know we've been talking quality improvement. Well, the new procedures you are implementing are producing products that conform to the product's specification. More labor time is needed to achieve this, and as we take more time, we do waste fewer materials. But the real benefit is the reduction in our external failure costs. Every defect in a batch of 10,000 units costs us $1,000—warranty work, lost sales, a customer service department, and so on. If we can reach the material and labor productivity goals, our defects will drop from 20 per batch to five per batch.

Required:

1. Discuss the advantages of using only operational measures of productivity for controlling shop-level activities.
2. Assume that the batch productivity statistics are met by the end of the year. Calculate the change in a batch's profits from the beginning of the year to the end that is attributable to changes in materials and labor productivity.

3. Now, assume that three inputs are to be evaluated: materials, labor, and quality. Quality is measured by the number of defects per batch. Calculate the change in a batch's profits from the beginning of the year to the end that is attributable to changes in productivity of all three inputs. Do you agree that quality is an input? Explain.

15-18   COLLABORATIVE LEARNING EXERCISE

LO1, LO2, LO3

Kathy Shorts, president of Carbon Industrial Cleaners, had just concluded a meeting with two of her plant managers. She had told each of them that one of their high-volume industrial cleaners was going to have a 50 percent increase in demand—next year—over this year's output (which is expected to be 50,000 barrels). A major foreign source of the material had been shut down because of a trade embargo. It would be years before the source would be available again. The result was twofold. First, the price of the material input was expected to quadruple. Second, many of the less efficient competitors would leave the business, creating more demand and higher output prices—in fact, output prices would double.

In discussing the situation with her plant managers, she reminded them that the automated process now allowed them to increase the productivity of the material. By using more machine hours, evaporation could be decreased significantly. (This was a recent development and would be operational by the beginning of the new fiscal year.) There were, however, only two other feasible settings beyond the current setting. The current usage of inputs for the 50,000-barrel output (current setting) and the input usage for the other two settings follow. The input usage for the remaining two settings is for an output of 75,000 barrels. Inputs are measured in barrels for the material and in machine hours for the equipment.

	Current	*Setting A*	*Setting B*
Input quantities:			
Materials	125,000	75,000	150,000
Equipment	30,000	75,000	37,500

The current prices for this year's inputs are $3 per barrel for materials and $12 per machine hour for the equipment. The materials price will change for next year as explained, but the $12 rate for machine hours will remain the same. The chemical is currently selling for $20 per barrel. Based on separate productivity analyses, one plant manager chose Setting A and the other chose Setting B.

The manager who chose Setting B justified his decision by noting that it was the only setting that clearly signaled an increase in both partial measures of productivity. The other manager agreed that Setting B was an improvement but that Setting A was even better.

Required:

Work the following requirements before coming to class. Next, form groups of three to four, and compare and contrast the answers within the group. Finally, form modified groups by exchanging one member of your group with a member of another group. The modified groups will compare and contrast each group's answers to the requirements.

1. Prepare productivity profiles for the current year and for the two settings. Which of the two settings signals an increase in productivity for both inputs?
2. Calculate the profits that will be realized under each setting *for the coming year.* Which setting provides the greatest profit increase?
3. Calculate the profit change for each setting attributable to productivity changes. Which setting offers the greatest productivity improvement? By how much? Explain why this happened.

15-19 CYBER RESEARCH CASE

LO2, LO4 Productivity concepts apply to service settings as well as manufacturing. For example, in the health care industry, increasing productivity is a possible means to control rising medical costs. It is also a means of increasing retention.

Required:

1. Go to http://www.findarticles.com, and search for articles on productivity using "Productivity Accounting" as the search phrase (or you can try your own search phrase relating to productivity). Find three articles that relate to productivity of services, where at least one is in the health care industry. Read these articles, and provide a brief summary of their content. Now, answer the following questions:
   a. Did any of the articles mention partial productivity measures?
   b. If so, were the measures operational or financial?
   c. Was there any mention of total productivity measurement? If not, speculate on the reasons why.
   d. What was the purpose of productivity measurement?
2. Now, do a search at the FindArticles site using "Productivity Plus Award." Answer the following questions:
   a. What is the purpose of the award?
   b. Describe two companies that have received the award, and provide a brief summary of why they received it.

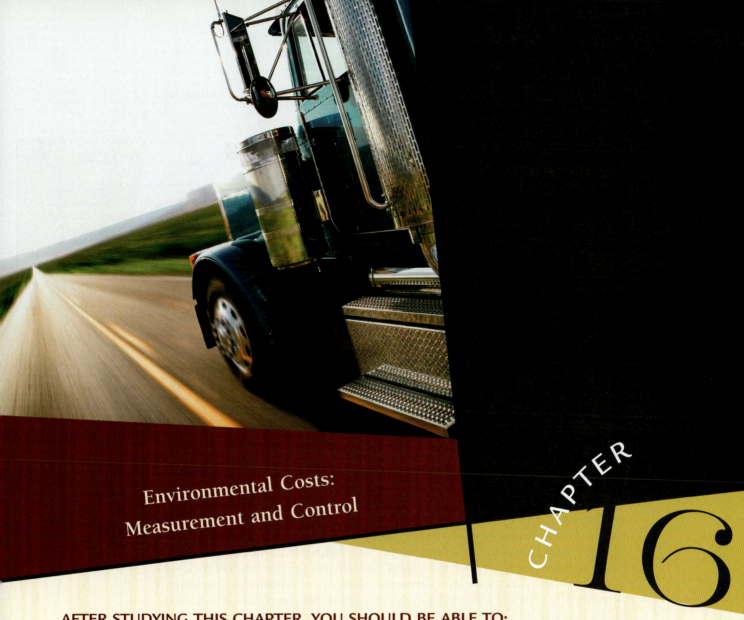

CHAPTER 16

Environmental Costs: Measurement and Control

AFTER STUDYING THIS CHAPTER, YOU SHOULD BE ABLE TO:

1. Explain how environmental costs can be measured and reduced.

2. Discuss environmental costs, and show how they are assigned to products and processes.

3. Describe the life-cycle cost assessment model.

4. Compare and contrast activity-based and strategic-based environmental control.

Historically, firms have often released contaminants into the atmosphere and water without bearing the full cost of such activities. Many people believe that polluters should bear the full cost of any environmental damage caused by production of goods and services (the polluter pays principle). By bearing the full cost (it is argued), firms may then seek more ecoefficient production methods. Interestingly, some initial experiences suggest that it may be possible to improve environmental quality without reducing useful goods and services while simultaneously increasing profits.

Responsible environmental management is an important focus for many companies. In fact, many companies spend hundreds of millions of dollars each year on environmental activities. Yet, environmental decisions are often made with little support from the cost management information system. Often, environmental decisions are made simply to comply with environmental regulation. In other words, a reactive approach, rather than a proactive approach to environmental cost management seems to be the norm. A proactive approach, however, is more promising if evidence exists that environmental damage can be prevented while simultaneously reducing costs. Proactive environmental decisions require information about environmental costs and benefits—information that has not existed as a separate and well-defined category.

Defining, Measuring, and Controlling Environmental Costs

The emergence of a proactive approach means that management of environmental costs is becoming a matter of high priority and intense interest. Several reasons can be offered for this increased interest, but two in particular stand out. First, in many countries, environmental regulations have increased significantly. Often, the regulatory laws carry enormous fines or penalties; thus, strong incentives for compliance exist. Furthermore, the costs for compliance can be significant. Selecting the least costly way of compliance becomes a major objective. To satisfy this objective, compliance costs must be measured and their fundamental causes identified. Second, regulators and companies are beginning to realize that it may be more cost effective to prevent pollution rather than to clean it up. The approach to environmental regulation seems to be shifting from a command-and-control approach to a market-driven approach.[1] This new market-driven approach means that successful treatment of environmental concerns is now a significant competitive issue. Corporations are discovering that meeting sound business objectives and resolving environmental concerns are not mutually exclusive. To understand this critical observation, it is important to examine a concept known as *ecoefficiency*.

The Ecoefficiency Paradigm

Ecoefficiency is defined as the ability to produce competitively priced goods and services that satisfy customer needs while *simultaneously* reducing negative environmental impacts, resource consumption, and costs. Ecoefficiency means producing more goods and services using less materials, energy, water, and land, while, at the same time, minimizing air emissions, water discharges, waste disposal, and the dispersion of toxic substances. However, perhaps the most important claim of the ecoefficiency paradigm is that preventing pollution and avoiding waste is economically beneficial—that it is possible to do more with less. Moreover, it is complementary to and supportive of *sustainable development*. **Sustainable development** is defined as development that meets the needs of the present without compromising the ability of future generations to meet their own needs. Although absolute sustainability may not be attainable, progress toward its achievement certainly seems to have some merit.

Ecoefficiency implies a positive relationship between environmental and economic performance. Exhibit 16-1 illustrates the objectives, opportunities, and outcomes that define the relationships envisioned by ecoefficiency.[2] Four broad objectives are revealed: (1) reduce the consumption of resources, (2) reduce the environmental impact, (3) increase product value, and (4) reduce environmental liability. Reducing the consumption of resources entails such things as reducing the use of energy, materials, water, and land. It also includes increasing product durability and enhancing product recyclability. Reducing environmental impact is primarily concerned with minimizing releases of pollutants into the environment and encouraging the sustainable use of renewable resources. Increasing product value means that products are produced that provide the functionality that customers need but with fewer materials and less resources. It also means that products are

---

1. David Shields, Beth Beloff, and Miriam Heller, "Environmental Cost Accounting for Chemical and Oil Companies: A Benchmarking Study," an online Environmental Protection Agency (EPA) article at http://www.epa.gov/opptintr/acctg/ as of October 19, 2004.

2. The objectives and opportunities are those identified by the World Business Council for Sustainable Development (WBCSD). See the WBCSD paper, "Ecoefficency: Creating More Value with Less Impact," online at http://www.wbcsd.ch as of October 20, 2004.

produced without degrading the environment, and their use and disposal are environmentally friendly. The fourth objective, reducing environmental liability, requires that a company identify and efficiently manage the risks and opportunities relating to the environment. Achievement of the objectives requires a firm to seek opportunities to improve ecoefficiency, which brings us to the second level of Exhibit 16-1.

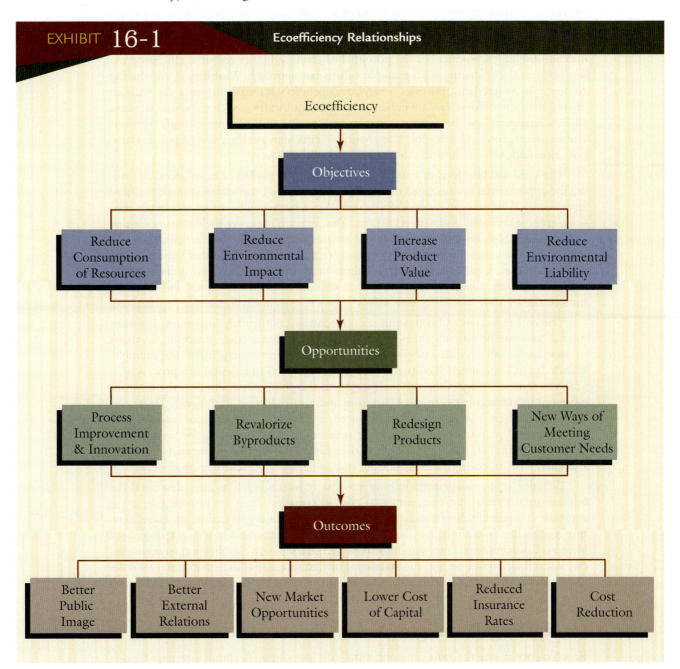

EXHIBIT 16-1   **Ecoefficiency Relationships**

Ecoefficiency

Objectives

Reduce Consumption of Resources

Reduce Environmental Impact

Increase Product Value

Reduce Environmental Liability

Opportunities

Process Improvement & Innovation

Revalorize Byproducts

Redesign Products

New Ways of Meeting Customer Needs

Outcomes

Better Public Image

Better External Relations

New Market Opportunities

Lower Cost of Capital

Reduced Insurance Rates

Cost Reduction

Process improvement and innovation are familiar methods for increasing efficiency. In this case, however, the objective is to increase ecoefficiency, which means that process changes must focus simultaneously on reducing costs and improving environmental performance. Process improvement is most useful for improving relative environmental performance, but process reengineering is probably more suitable for major advances in ecoefficiency. Revalorizing by-products describes the search for ways to convert waste materials into useful products or useful inputs for other companies' products. **Lura Group**, for example, converted the sludge from its wastewater treatment facility into commercial compost.[3] Product design is another key method for improving ecoefficiency. Products can be redesigned so that they use fewer materials, a smaller variety of materials, and less toxic materials and are easier to take apart for recycling while simultaneously providing a high degree of functionality for users. **Volkswagen**'s Lupo 3L TDI passenger car, for example, is designed to facilitate the segregation of materials in the dismantling and recycling processes.[4] Finally, ecoefficiency can be improved by finding different and better ways of satisfying customer needs. This may entail redefining markets and reshaping supply and demand. For example, providing a service instead of selling a product has the potential of creating higher resource efficiency and less pollution. Car sharing is an example of this last approach. **Mobility**, a car-sharing company in Switzerland, provides a service to people who want to use a car without buying their own. These cars are parked at convenient locations such as railway stations. Clients arrange to use the cars for a prearranged period of time. Interestingly, this service has changed travel behavior. Car-sharing clients increase their use of public transportation and, thus, reduce the need for cars and fuel.[5]

The third and final level of Exhibit 16-1 illustrates the payoffs of ecoefficiency. Pursuing the opportunities just discussed can produce a number of beneficial outcomes. Reduced environmental impacts can create social benefits like a better public image and better relations in the community and with regulators. This, in turn, improves the company's image and enhances its ability to sell products and services. Efforts to improve ecoefficiency also may increase revenues by creating new markets (e.g., creating outputs that were formerly classified as useless residues). Ecoefficient firms tend to reduce their environmental risks and, consequently, capture external benefits such as a lower cost of capital and lower insurance rates. Finally, cost reductions follow improvements in environmental performance.

The cost reduction and competitiveness incentive is particularly important. Environmental costs can be a significant percentage of total operating costs; interestingly, many of these costs can be reduced or eliminated through effective management. For example, knowledge of environmental costs and their causes may lead to redesign of a process that, as a consequence, reduces the materials used and the pollutants emitted to the environment (an interaction between the innovation and cost reduction incentives). Thus, current and future environmental costs are reduced, and the firm becomes more competitive. For example, **bpi.industrial**, a supplier of heavy duty polythene sacks for animal feed, chemicals, and other industries, has saved over £700,000 per year in materials, solvents, and energy by improving process controls and switching to solvent-free processes.[6]

Effective cost management leading to cost reduction such as that described for bpi.industrial means that environmental cost information must be provided to management. To provide this financial information, it is necessary to define, measure, classify, and assign environmental costs to processes, products, and other cost objects of interest. Environmental costs should be reported as a separate classification so managers can assess their impact on firm profitability. Furthermore, assigning environmental costs to products and processes reveals the sources of these costs and helps identify their fundamental causes so that they can be controlled.

Competing Paradigms

Ecoefficiency is not the only environmental cost paradigm. A competing paradigm is that of *compliance management*. **Compliance management** is simply the practice of achieving the minimal environmental performance required by regulations—and to do so as cheaply as possible. No effort is made to go beyond this minimal environmental

---

3. WBCSB paper, "Ecoefficiency: Creating More Value with Less Impact."
4. Ibid.
5. Ibid.
6. "CS 274, *Process Changes at Plastics Company Saves Costs and Waste*," *Envirowise*, at http://www.envirowise.gov.uk/envirowisev3.nsf/key/CROD4W6H6D as of October 22, 2004.

performance because the belief held is that improving environmental performance and improving economic performance are incompatible objectives. This view is driven by the concept that pollution, a negative output, could be reduced only by using resources that could have been used to produce good output. Thus, improving environmental performance is virtually always a costly activity for a firm.

A second competing paradigm is that of *guided ecoefficiency*. Guided ecoefficiency maintains that pollution is a form of economic inefficiency and that properly designed environmental regulations will stimulate innovation such that environmental performance and economic efficiency will simultaneously improve. Under this view, the type of regulation required is that which specifies the required level of improvement in environmental performance *without specifying how this improvement is to be achieved*. According to this view, regulatory intervention is required because managers have bounded rationality and if left to themselves will not voluntarily undertake actions to improve environmental performance. Regulation signals to managers that economic inefficiencies are present and that, through innovation, cost savings can be realized with attendant improvement in environmental performance.[7]

Environmental Costs Defined

Before environmental cost information can be provided to management, environmental costs must be defined. Various possibilities exist; however, an appealing approach is to adopt a definition consistent with a total environmental quality model. In the total environmental quality model, the ideal state is that of zero damage to the environment (analogous to the zero-defects state of total quality management). Damage is defined as either direct degradation of the environment such as the emission of solid, liquid, or gaseous residues into the environment (e.g., water contamination and air pollution) or indirect degradation such as *unnecessary* usage of materials and energy. Accordingly, environmental costs can be referred to as *environmental quality costs*. In a similar sense to quality costs, environmental costs are costs that are incurred because poor environmental quality exists or *may* exist. Thus, environmental costs are associated with the creation, detection, remediation, and prevention of environmental degradation. With this definition, environmental costs can be classified into four categories: prevention costs, detection costs, internal failure costs, and external failure costs. External failure costs, in turn, can be subdivided into realized and unrealized categories.

Environmental prevention costs are the costs of activities carried out to prevent the production of contaminants and/or waste that could cause damage to the environment. Pollution prevention activities are often referred to as "P2" activities. Examples of prevention activities include evaluating and selecting suppliers, evaluating and selecting equipment to control pollution, designing processes and products to reduce or eliminate contaminants, training employees, studying environmental impacts, auditing environmental risks, undertaking environmental research, developing environmental management systems, recycling products, and obtaining ISO 14001 certification.[8]

Environmental detection costs are the costs of activities executed to determine if products, processes, and other activities within the firm are in compliance with appropriate environmental standards. The environmental standards and procedures that a firm seeks to follow are defined in three ways: (1) regulatory laws of governments, (2) voluntary standards (ISO 14000) developed by the International Standards Organization, and (3) environmental policies developed by management. Examples of

---

7. Michael Porter and Class van der Linde, "Toward a New Conception of the Environmental Competitiveness Relationship, *Journal of Economic Perspective* 9(4) (1995): 97–118.

8. ISO 14001 certification is obtained when an organization installs an environmental management system that satisfies specific, privately set international standards. These standards are concerned with environmental *management* procedures and do not directly indicate acceptable levels of environmental performance. The certification, therefore, functions primarily as a signal that a firm is interested and willing to improve its environmental performance.

detection activities are auditing environmental activities, inspecting products and processes (for environmental compliance), developing environmental performance measures, carrying out contamination tests, verifying supplier environmental performance, and measuring levels of contamination.

Environmental internal failure costs are costs of activities performed because contaminants and waste have been produced but not discharged into the environment. Thus, internal failure costs are incurred to eliminate and manage contaminants or waste once produced. Internal failure activities have one of two goals: (1) to ensure that the contaminants and waste produced are not released to the environment or (2) to reduce the level of contaminants released to an amount that complies with environmental standards. Examples of internal failure activities include operating equipment to minimize or eliminate pollution, treating and disposing of toxic materials, maintaining pollution equipment, licensing facilities for producing contaminants, and recycling scrap.

Environmental external failure costs are the costs of activities performed *after* discharging contaminants and waste into the environment. **Realized external failure costs** are those incurred and paid for by the firm. **Unrealized external failure (societal) costs** are caused by the firm but are incurred and paid for by parties outside the firm. Societal costs can be further classified as (1) those resulting from environmental degradation and (2) those associated with an adverse impact on the property or welfare of individuals. In either case, the costs are borne by others and not by the firm even though the firm causes them. Of the four environmental cost categories, the external failure category is the most devastating. For example, the General Accounting Office estimated $259 million in cleanup costs of hazardous materials at six military installations.[9] Furthermore, during fiscal year 2003, more companies spent $2.9 billion in cleanup activities resulting from enforcement actions of the federal government.[10] Examples of realized external failure activities are cleaning up a polluted lake, cleaning up oil spills, cleaning up contaminated soil, using materials and energy inefficiently, settling personal injury claims from environmentally unsound practices, settling property damage claims, restoring land to its natural state, and losing sales from a bad environmental reputation. Examples of societal costs include receiving medical care because of polluted air (individual welfare), losing a lake for recreational use because of contamination (degradation), losing employment because of contamination (individual welfare), and damaging ecosystems from solid waste disposal (degradation).

Exhibit 16-2 summarizes the four environmental cost categories and lists specific activities for each category. Within the external failure cost category, societal costs are labeled with an "S." The costs for which the firm is financially responsible are called **private costs**. All costs without the S label are private costs.

Environmental Cost Report

Environmental cost reporting is essential if an organization is serious about improving its environmental performance and controlling environmental costs. A good first step is a report that details the environmental costs by category. Reporting environmental costs by category reveals two important outcomes: (1) the impact of environmental costs on firm profitability and (2) the relative amounts expended in each category. Exhibit 16-3, on page 702, provides an example of a simple environmental cost report.

The report in Exhibit 16-3 highlights the importance of the environmental costs by expressing them as a percentage of total operating costs. In this report, environmental costs are 30 percent of total operating costs, seemingly a significant amount. From a practical point of view, environmental costs will receive managerial attention

---

9. GAO-02-117, "Environmental Liabilities: Cleanup Costs from Certain DOD Operations Are Not Being Reported," December 2001.
10. Bruce Geiselman, "Polluters Pay Billions in Cleanup Costs," *Business Insurance*, Vol. 38, Issue 1 (January 2004): 21.

EXHIBIT 16-2   Classification of Environmental Costs by Activity

Prevention Activities

Evaluating and selecting suppliers
Evaluating and selecting pollution
  control equipment
Designing processes
Designing products
Carrying out environmental studies
Auditing environmental risks
Developing environmental management
  systems
Recycling products
Obtaining ISO 14001 certification

Detection Activities

Auditing environmental activities
Inspecting products and processes
Developing environmental performance
  measures
Testing for contamination
Verifying supplier environmental
  performance
Measuring contamination levels

Internal Failure Activities

Operating pollution control equipment
Treating and disposing of toxic waste
Maintaining pollution equipment
Licensing facilities for producing
  contaminants
Recycling scrap

External Failure Activities

Cleaning up a polluted lake
Cleaning up oil spills
Cleaning up contaminated soil
Settling personal injury claims
  (environmentally related)
Restoring land to natural state
Losing sales due to poor environmental
  reputation
Using materials and energy inefficiently
Receiving medical care due to polluted
  air (S)
Losing employment because of
  contamination (S)
Losing a lake for recreational use (S)
Damaging ecosystems from solid waste
  disposal (S)

Note: "S" = societal costs.

only if they represent a significant amount. Considerable evidence now exists concerning this issue. Companies like **GM**, **Commonwealth Edison**, and **Andersen Corporation** have saved millions of dollars by reducing or eliminating significant environmental impacts associated with their supply chains.[11] Other companies like **Xerox Europe**, **Ipiranga Group**, and **UPM-Kymmene** have produced significant savings while simultaneously improving environmental performance and operating efficiency.[12] It appears that reducing environmental costs by improving environmental performance can significantly increase a firm's profitability.

The cost report also provides information relating to the relative distribution of the environmental costs. A relative distribution of environmental costs is shown in Exhibit 16-4 on page 703. Of the total environmental costs, only 20 percent are from the prevention and detection categories. Thus, eighty percent of the environmental costs are failure costs—costs that exist because of poor environmental performance. This distribution emphasizes the need to increase P2 activities. Like the quality costing model, the underlying concept is that increasing prevention activities will drive down the costs of failure activities in a way that is cost-beneficial.

---

11. EPA, *The Lean and Green Supply Chain: A Practical Guide for Materials Managers to Reduce Costs and Improve Financial Performance*, EPA 742-R-00-001, January 2000.
12. See the case studies described at http://www.wbcsd.ch as of October 2004.

EXHIBIT **16-3**   **Environmental Cost Report**

Verde Corporation
Environmental Cost Report
For the Year Ended December 31, 2007

	Environmental Costs		Percentage of Operating Costs*
Prevention costs:			
Training employees	$ 180,000		
Designing products	540,000		
Selecting equipment	120,000	$ 840,000	2.80%
Detection costs:			
Inspecting processes	$ 720,000		
Developing measures	240,000	960,000	3.20
Internal failure costs:			
Operating pollution equipment	$1,200,000		
Maintaining pollution equipment	600,000	1,800,000	6.00
External failure costs:			
Cleaning up lake	$2,700,000		
Restoring land	1,500,000		
Property damage claim	1,200,000	5,400,000	18.00
Totals		$9,000,000	30.00%

*Total operating costs are $30,000,000.

Environmental Cost Reduction

Investing more in prevention (P2) and detection activities can bring about a significant reduction in environmental failure costs. For example, **Texas Petrochemicals Corporation** modified its existing on-site electrical generating system with the objective of reducing the consumption of energy, water, and chemicals. These objectives were all achieved and produced savings of $2.3 million annually, with a capital investment of $650,000 to bring about the modifications. Thus, the payback was just a little over three months.[13] In the organic chemical industrial sector, studies concerned with efforts to prevent toxic waste have shown that for every dollar spent on prevention activities, $3.49 was saved from environmental failure activities (per year).[14]

Environmental costs appear to behave in much the same way as quality costs. The lowest environmental costs are attainable at the *zero-damage point* much like the zero-defects point of the total quality cost model. Thus, an ecoefficient solution would focus on prevention with the usual justification that *prevention is cheaper than the cure.* Analogous to the total quality management model, zero damage is the lowest cost point for environmental costs.

13. From "The Virtual Tour of Regulations and P2 Information (case studies)," at http://www.chemalliance. org/Handbook/plant/index.htm as of October 23, 2004.

14. Michael E. Porter and Claus van der Linde, "Green and Competitive: Ending the Stalemate," *Harvard Business Review* (September–October 1995): 120–134.

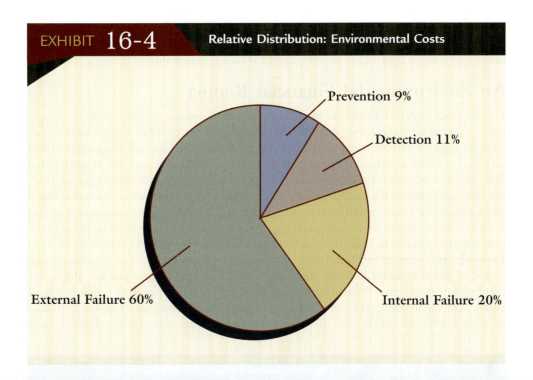

EXHIBIT 16-4   **Relative Distribution: Environmental Costs**

- Prevention 9%
- Detection 11%
- Internal Failure 20%
- External Failure 60%

COST MANAGEMENT   Technology in Action

E-commerce has produced a rather interesting means of promoting and facilitating recycling. **Throwplace.com** is what one might call the "Internet's landfill alternative." Throwplace.com provides a site where surplus inventory and outdated equipment can be listed—without cost—for donation to charities, nonprofit institutions, and businesses for reuse. Items can be placed into one of three categories: Charity, Business, or Up-For-Grabs. In the Charity category, charities and nonprofit businesses can make requests for listings and are required to provide receipts to donors. In the Business category, businesses and individuals claim the listed items for reuse or recycling. The Up-For-Grabs category provides items such as bottle caps, corkscrews, and egg crates—items that can be of interest to those doing art projects or looking for unusual items to collect.

The tax write-off for listed items often produces more benefit to retailers than having the items tie up valuable shelf space. Furthermore, the site provides a means for businesses involved in recycling and refurbishing to locate equipment that can be refurbished and resold or used as a source of parts. Throwplace.com is also a forum where collectors and recyclers can place ads for specific items. The motto for Throwplace.com is "Take what you need, and Throw what you don't." The site claims to be a place where "the public and sustainable business communities interact, raising awareness of our world-wide need to reuse and recycle consumables."

Source: Throwplace.com, "The Internet's Landfill Alternative," September 21, 2004.

Evidence exists that zero degradation is the low cost point for many types of contaminating activities. For example, **Texas Eastman**, a producer of resins, produced a waste by-product that was being sent to landfills at the rate of 500,000 pounds per year. A system was installed to rework the waste material back into the production process and refine it into an acceptable product.[15] The cost of the system was $435,000, the 500,000 pounds of waste were totally eliminated, and the savings were $395,000 per year (from sale of the recovered product and reduced disposal fees). The payback of the new system was just a little over a year. It is interesting to point out that the decision to invest in the zero-waste system was economically sound and was not a charitable act on the part of

15. From "The Virtual Tour of Regulations and P2 Information (case studies)," at http://www.chemalliance.org/Handbook/plant/index.htm as of October 23, 2004.

Texas Eastman. Even without regulatory mandates, the investment in the new system was justified. As more firms become aware of ecoefficient possibilities, the demand for command and control approaches to environmental management should decrease.

An Environmental Financial Report

Ecoefficiency suggests a possible modification to environmental cost reporting. Specifically, in addition to reporting environmental costs, why not report *environmental benefits?* In a given period, there are three types of benefits: additional revenues, current savings, and cost avoidance (ongoing savings). Additional revenues are revenues that flow into the organization due to environmental actions such as recycling paper, finding new applications for nonhazardous waste (e.g., using wood scraps to make wood chess pieces and boards), and increased sales due to an enhanced environmental image. Cost avoidance refers to ongoing savings of costs that had been paid in prior years. Current savings refer to reductions in environmental costs achieved in the current year. By comparing benefits produced with environmental costs incurred in a given period, a type of environmental financial statement is produced. Managers can use this statement to assess progress (benefits produced) and potential for progress (environmental costs). The environmental financial statement could also form part of an environmental progress report that is provided to shareholders on an annual basis. Exhibit 16-5

EXHIBIT 16-5	Environmental Financial Statement

Verde Corporation
Environmental Financial Statement
For the Year Ended December 31, 2007

Environmental benefits:	
Income sources:	
Recycling income	$ 600,000
Revenues from waste-derived products	150,000
Ongoing savings:	
Cost reductions, contaminants	900,000
Cost reductions, hazardous waste disposal	1,200,000
Current savings:	
Energy conservation cost savings	300,000
Packaging cost reductions	450,000
Total environmental benefits	$3,600,000
Environmental costs:	
Prevention costs:	
Designing processes for the environment	$ 640,000
Supplier evaluation and selection	200,000
Detection costs:	
Testing for contamination	560,000
Measuring contamination levels	400,000
Internal failure costs:	
Waste treatment, transport, and disposal	1,500,000
Operating pollution control equipment	300,000
External failure costs:	
Inefficient materials usage	1,400,000
Cleaning up soil	4,000,000
Total environmental costs	$9,000,000

provides an example of an environmental financial statement. The benefits reported reveal good progress, but the costs are still two and one-half times the benefits, indicating that more improvements are clearly needed.

Environmental Costing

OBJECTIVE 2

Discuss environmental costs, and show how they are assigned to products and processes.

Both products and processes are sources of environmental costs. Processes that *produce* products can create solid, liquid, and gaseous residues that are subsequently introduced into the environment. These residues have the potential of degrading the environment. Residues, then, are the causes of both internal and external environmental failure costs (e.g., investing in equipment to prevent the introduction of the residues into the environment and cleaning up residues after they are allowed into the environment). Production processes are not the only source of environmental costs. Packaging is also a source. For example, in the United States, thirty percent of all municipal solid waste is packaging material.[16]

Products themselves can be the source of environmental costs. After selling a product, its use and disposal by the customer can produce environmental degradation. These are examples of *environmental post-purchase costs*. Most of the time environmental post-purchase costs are borne by society and not by the company and, thus, are societal costs. On occasion, however, environmental post-purchase costs are converted into realized external costs.

Environmental Product Costs

The environmental costs of processes that produce, market, and deliver products and the environmental post-purchase costs caused by the use and disposal of the products are examples of *environmental product costs*. **Full environmental costing** is the assignment of all environmental costs, both private and societal, to products. **Full private costing** is the assignment of only private costs to individual products. Private costing, then, would assign the environmental costs to products caused by the internal processes of the organization. Private costing is probably a good starting point for many firms. Private costs can be assigned using data created *inside* the firm. Full costs require gathering of data that are produced outside the firm from third parties. As the firm gains experience with environmental costing, it may be well advised to expand product cost assignments and implement an approach called *life-cycle cost assessment*, which is discussed later in the chapter.

Assigning environmental costs to products can produce valuable managerial information. For example, it may reveal that a particular product is responsible for much more toxic waste than other products. This information may lead to an alternative design for the product or its associated processes that is more efficient and environmentally friendly. It could also reveal that with the environmental costs correctly assigned, the product is not profitable. This could mean something as simple as dropping the product to achieve significant improvement in environmental performance and economic efficiency. Many opportunities for improvement may exist, but knowledge of the environmental product costs is the key. Moreover, environmental costs must be assigned accurately.

Unit-Based Environmental Cost Assignments

In most cost accounting systems, environmental costs are hidden within overhead. Using the environmental cost definitions and classification framework just developed, environmental costs must first be separated into an environmental cost pool. Once separated into their own pool, unit-based costing would assign these costs to individual products using unit-level drivers such as direct labor hours and machine hours. This approach may

---

16. T. E. Graedel and B. R. Allenby, *Industrial Ecology* (Englewood Cliffs, NJ: Prentice Hall, 1995): 243.

work well for a homogeneous product setting; however, in a multiple-product firm, with product diversity, a unit-based assignment can produce cost distortions.

Suppose, for example, that a company produces two products: window and door parts. There are 200,000 parts of each type produced, and each part requires *one-fourth* of a machine hour. Assume that machine hours will be used to assign environmental costs to products. In producing the parts, methylene chloride emissions occur. To produce these emissions, a special government permit must be purchased that costs $600,000. The permit must be renewed every three years. Thus, the permit cost is $200,000 per year. The permit authorizes a certain level of methylene chloride emissions. If emissions exceed the allowed level, a fine is imposed. One unannounced inspection occurs each quarter. The firm averages $100,000 per year in fines. Thus, the annual cost of methylene chloride emissions is $300,000 ($200,000 + $100,000). The environmental cost per machine hour is $3 ($300,000/100,000 machine hours). Use of this rate produces an environmental cost per unit of $0.75 for each product ($3 × 1/4 machine hour).

The accuracy of the assignment is critical. For example, what if the window parts are responsible for all or most of the emissions? If window parts are responsible for all of the emissions, then the environmental cost should be $1.50 per unit for this product and $0 per unit for door parts. In this case, the window parts were undercosted, and the door parts were overcosted. This possibility is not imaginary. Something very similar happened with **Spectrum Glass**, a producer of specialty glass. In producing its glass products, cadmium emissions occurred. It discovered that only one product, "Ruby Red," was responsible for all its cadmium emissions.[17] Yet, its cost accounting system was assigning a portion of this cost to every product produced.

Activity-Based Environmental Cost Assignments

The emergence of activity-based costing facilitates environmental costing. Tracing the environmental costs to the products responsible for the environmental costs is a fundamental requirement of a sound environmental accounting system. Assigning costs using causal relationships is needed. This approach, of course, is exactly what ABC does.

The Methylene Chloride Example Revisited

Emitting methylene chloride is the environmental activity (in this case, an external failure activity). The cost of the activity is the cost of the fine and the permit fees: $300,000. Assume now that the quantity of emissions is the activity output measure. Let that quantity be 60,000 units. The activity rate is $5.00 per unit ($300,000/60,000 units). If window parts produce 60,000 units of emissions and door parts produce zero units, then the cost assignments are as they should be: $300,000 to window parts ($5.00 × 60,000) and $0 to door parts. This ABC assignment produces a unit environmental cost of $1.50 for window parts ($300,000/200,000) and $0 for door parts.

The costs assigned in this example are all private costs. Societal costs are also possible. If they occur and can be estimated, then a fuller costing approach can be used. For example, suppose that methylene chloride emissions cause $300,000 per year in medical expenses for those who live in the community affected by the emissions. In this case, the cost per unit for window parts would double.

Example with Multiple Activities

The methylene chloride example had only one activity. In reality, there will be multiple environmental activities. Each activity will be assigned costs, and activity rates will be computed. These rates will then be used to assign environmental costs to products based on usage of the activity. Exhibit 16-6 shows the assignment of environmental costs to two products (two different types of industrial solvents) when there are a variety of activities. This cost assignment allows managers to see the relative environmental economic

---

17. Daniel Baker, "Environmental Accounting's Conflicts and Dilemmas," *Management Accounting* (October 1996): 46–48.

impact of the two products. To the extent that environmental costs reflect environmental damage, the unit environmental cost can also act as an index or measure of product cleanliness. The "dirtier" products can then be the focus of efforts to improve environmental performance and economic efficiency. Exhibit 16-6 reveals, for example, that Solvent IIY has more environmental problems than Solvent IX. Solvent IIY's environmental costs total $760,000 ($7.60 × 100,000) and are 19 percent of the total manufacturing costs. Furthermore, its environmental failure costs are $700,000 ($7.00 × 100,000), representing 92 percent of the total environmental costs. Solvent IX portrays a much better picture. Its environmental costs total $156,000, which is 8 percent of the total manufacturing costs ($156,000/$1,960,000), and the failure costs ($0.46 × 100,000) are 29.5 percent of the total environmental costs ($46,000/$156,000). It is evident that Solvent IIY offers the most potential for environmental and economic improvement.

EXHIBIT 16-6	ABC Environmental Costing	
Activities	**Solvent IX**	**Solvent IIY**
Prevention and Detection Activities:		
Evaluate and select suppliers	$ 0.40	$ 0.10
Design processes (to reduce pollution)	0.20	0.20
Inspect processes (for pollution problems)	0.50	0.30
Subtotal	$ 1.10	$ 0.60
Failure Activities:		
Capture and treat chlorofluorocarbons	$ 0.10	$ 2.00
Maintain environmental equipment	0.00	1.00
Toxic waste disposal	0.20	3.50
Excessive material usage	0.16	0.50
Subtotal	$ 0.46	$ 7.00
Environmental cost per unit	$ 1.56	$ 7.60
Other (nonenvironmental) manufacturing costs per unit	18.04	32.40
Total unit cost	$19.60	$40.00
Units produced	100,000	100,000

Life-Cycle Cost Assessment

OBJECTIVE 3

Describe the life-cycle cost assessment model.

The environmental product costs may reveal a need to improve a company's *product stewardship*. **Product stewardship** is the practice of designing, manufacturing, maintaining, and recycling products to minimize adverse environmental impacts. *Life-cycle assessment* is the means for improving product stewardship. **Life-cycle assessment** identifies the environmental consequences of a product through its entire life cycle and then searches for opportunities to obtain environmental improvements. **Life-cycle cost assessment** assigns costs and benefits to the environmental consequences and improvements.

Product Life Cycle

The EPA has identified four stages in the life cycle of a product: resource extraction, product manufacture, product use, and recycling and disposal.[18] Another possible stage, not explicitly considered by the EPA guidelines, is that of product packaging. Product

---

18. *Life-Cycle Assessment: Inventory Guidelines and Principles*, EPA/600/R-92/245 (February 1993).

life cycle, including packaging, is illustrated in Exhibit 16-7. As illustrated, the different life-cycle stages can be under the control of someone other than the producer of the product. Note that the source of materials for the product can come through extraction (raw materials) or from recycling. If all or some of the product's components cannot be recycled, then disposal is required, and waste management becomes an issue.

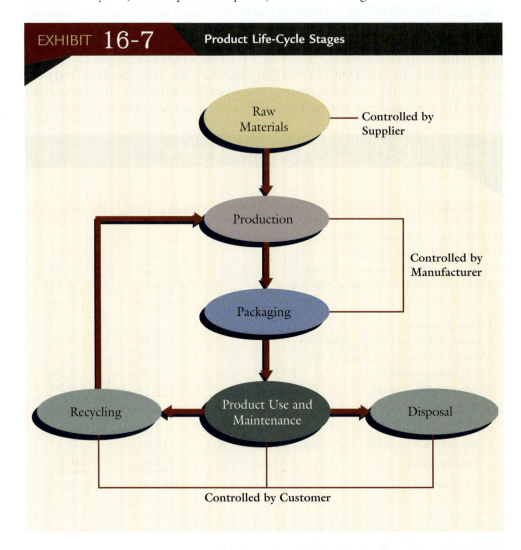

EXHIBIT 16-7   **Product Life-Cycle Stages**

The life-cycle viewpoint adopted combines supplier, manufacturer, and customer viewpoints. Thus, both internal and external linkages are considered important in assessing environmental consequences of different products, product designs, and process designs. If the cost accounting system is going to play a role in life-cycle assessment, then the most obvious system is assessing and assigning the environmental costs caused by the producer in each of the life-cycle stages. Managers will then be able to compare the economic effects of competing designs. However, before discussing cost assessment, a more detailed understanding of life-cycle analysis is needed.

Assessment Stages

Life-cycle assessment is defined by three formal stages: (1) inventory analysis, (2) impact analysis, and (3) improvement analysis.[19] **Inventory analysis** specifies the types and quantities of materials and energy inputs needed and the resulting environmental releases in

---

19. Graedel and Allenby, *Industrial Ecology*, 108–121.

the form of solid, liquid, and gaseous residues. Inventory analysis spans the product's life cycle. Impact analysis assesses the environmental effects of competing designs and provides a relative ranking of those effects. Improvement analysis has the objective of reducing the environmental impacts revealed by the inventory and impact steps.

Inventory Analysis

To illustrate inventory analysis, consider single-use, hot-drink cups for fast-food restaurants. A producer can choose to make the cups using either paper or polystyrene foam. Each stage in the cup's life cycle produces certain key questions:

- What are the materials required for each type of cup?
- What are the energy requirements to produce each product?
- What kinds of effluents and emissions are produced by each?
- What is the recycle potential?
- What are the resources required for ultimate disposal?

Answering these questions defines inventory analysis. Exhibit 16-8 provides answers for the questions based on data reported in a study by Martin Hocking.[20]

EXHIBIT 16-8   Inventory Analysis

	Paper Cup	Polyfoam Cup
Material usage per cup:		
Wood and bark (g)	33.0	0.0
Petroleum (g)	4.1	3.2
Finished weight (g)	10.0	11.5
Utilities per Mg of material:		
Steam (kg)	9,000–12,000	5,000
Power (GJ)	3.5	0.4–0.6
Cooling water (m³)	50	154
Water effluent per Mg of material:		
Volume (m³)	50–190	0.5–2.0
Suspended solids (kg)	35–600	trace
BOD(kg)	30–500	0.07
Organochlorides (kg)	5–70	0
Metal salts (kg)	1–20	20
Air emissions per Mg of material:		
Chlorine (kg)	0.5	0
Sulfides (kg)	2.0	0
Particulates (kg)	5–15	0.1
Pentane (kg)	0	35–50
Recycle potential:		
Primary user	Possible	Easy
After use	Low	High
Ultimate disposal:		
Heat recovery (Mj/kg)	20	40
Mass to landfill (g)	10.1	11.5
Biodegradable	Yes	No

---

20. M. B. Hocking , "Paper versus Polystyrene: A Complex Choice," *Science*, 251 (1991): 504–505.

Impact Analysis

Impact analysis next assesses the meaning of the values provided by the inventory analysis step. For example, one advantage of paper cups is that paper is made from a renewable resource (wood and chips), whereas the polyfoam cup relies on petroleum, a nonrenewable resource. More careful examination, however, reveals that paper cups actually use more petroleum than polyfoam cups! The reason? To convert wood chips to pulp to paper cups uses energy. Effluents and emissions produced during the products' life cycles are also listed in Exhibit 16-8. Interestingly, the only significant environmental release for polyfoam cups is pentane, a blowing agent. On the other hand, production of paper cups requires extensive use of inorganic chemicals and large amounts of water effluents. Furthermore, recycling seems to favor polyfoam cups. However, ultimate disposal, at least in landfills, tends to favor paper cups because of their biodegradability. Yet, this advantage is called into question by recent studies indicating that biodegradable materials in anaerobic landfills remain *undegraded* over relatively long periods of time.[21] From the viewpoint of a variety of environmental impacts, perhaps polyfoam cups are better than paper cups!

Cost Assessment

Up to this point, the analysis has used only nonfinancial measures and qualitative factors. The hot-drink cup example, however, does offer the opportunity to introduce costs and discuss their value in life-cycle assessment. Life-cycle cost assessment is determining the financial consequences of the environmental impacts identified in the inventory and improvement steps of life-cycle assessment. Assessing environmental costs for the inventory stage can facilitate impact analysis. In the paper cup versus polyfoam cup example, the comparisons of operational data were fairly clean in the sense that one product's environmental impacts were almost always less than the other product's. But even here, some questions can be raised. For example, what is the cost of producing pentane emissions compared to the cost of water effluents and particulates? What are the economic benefits from recycling polyfoam cups? The advantage of assigning costs is that the total environmental costs provide an index that can be used for ranking the competing alternatives. How are costs assigned?

    The answer to the cost assignment question has already been given. Materials costs are assigned through direct tracing. We can identify the amount of materials consumed per unit and then multiply by the price paid for the materials. Energy costs and the costs of producing environmental releases are assigned through driver tracing. Thus, for existing products (or processes, if they are the cost object), we simply identify the associated environmental activities and their costs, calculate an activity rate, and assign those costs to the respective products. If some of the energy consumption and environmental releases are associated with the use of the product after purchase, then a full environmental costing analysis requires their inclusion. It is also possible to assign only private costs. Recycling and disposal are separate but important issues. Many of the costs here are societal costs, and their measurement becomes more difficult. Taking only a private costing approach is also possible for recycling and disposal.

    For example, assume that the following environmental costs per unit have been determined for the two cups:

	Paper Cups	*Polyfoam Cups*
Material usage	$ 0.010	$ 0.004
Utilities	0.012	0.003
Contaminant-related resources	0.008	0.005
Total private costs	$ 0.030	$ 0.012
Recycling benefits (societal)	(0.001)	(0.004)
Environmental cost per unit	$ 0.029	$ 0.008

---

21. Graedel and Allenby, *Industrial Ecology*, 149.

The unit life-cycle costs provide a summary measure of the relative environmental impacts of the two products and serve to support the qualitative interpretations of the operational and subjective environmental data found in Exhibit 16-8.

These observations are borne out by actual experience. **Chrysler Corporation**, for example, used life-cycle cost management analysis to choose a mercury-free switch over a mercury switch for an underhood convenience lighting package. Before considering the associated environmental costs, the mercury switch had a $0.12 price advantage over the mercury-free switch. However, after factoring in environmental costs stemming from such sources as recyclability, end-of-cycle disposal costs, tooling costs (to manufacture labels), labeling requirements, insurance premiums, environmental training, personal protective equipment, and emissions, the cost advantage shifted to the mercury-free switch (producing a $0.12 advantage over the mercury switch—a $0.24 turnaround).[22]

Improvement Analysis

Assessing the environmental impacts in operational and financial terms sets the stage for the final step, that of searching for ways to reduce the environmental impacts of the alternatives being considered or analyzed. It is this step that connects with the control system of an organization. Improving the environmental performance of existing products and processes is the overall objective of an environmental control system.

OBJECTIVE 4

Compare and contrast activity-based and strategic-based environmental control.

Strategic-Based Environmental Responsibility Accounting

The overall goal of improving environmental performance suggests that a continuous improvement framework for environmental control would be the most appropriate. In fact, an environmental perspective is a possible fifth perspective for the Balanced Scorecard framework that we discussed in Chapter 13. The creators of the Balanced Scorecard mention a specific instance where a company added an environmental perspective to their Balanced Scorecard.[23] If one accepts the ecoefficiency paradigm, then an environmental perspective is legitimate because improving environmental performance can be the source of a competitive advantage (the criterion for a perspective to be included). A strategic-based environmental management system provides an operational framework for improving environmental performance. For example, linking the environmental perspective to the process perspective is critical for improving environmental performance. Knowledge of root causes for environmental activities is fundamental to any process design changes needed to improve environmental performance. Thus, the Balanced Scorecard framework supplies objectives and measures that are integrated to achieve the overall goal of improving environmental performance.

Environmental Perspective

We can identify at least five core objectives for the environmental perspective: (1) minimize the use of raw or virgin materials; (2) minimize the use of hazardous materials; (3) minimize energy requirements for production and use of the product; (4) minimize the release of solid, liquid, and gaseous residues; and (5) maximize opportunities to recycle.

Two environmental themes are associated with materials and energy (the first three core objectives). First, no more energy and materials should be used than absolutely

---

22. *Environmental Accounting Data Base*, Case Studies, http://www.emawebsite.org as of October 15, 2004.
23. Robert S. Kaplan and David P. Norton, *The Balanced Scorecard* (Boston: Harvard Business School, 1996): 35.

necessary (conservation issue). Second, means should be sought to eliminate the use of materials and energy that damage the environment (hazardous substance issue). Performance measures should reflect these two themes. Thus, possible measures would be total and per-unit quantities of the different types of materials and energy (e.g., pounds of toxic chemicals used), productivity measures (output/materials, output/ energy), and hazardous materials (energy) costs expressed as a percentage of total materials cost.

The fourth core objective can be realized in one of two ways: (1) using technology and methods to prevent the release of residues, *once produced*, and (2) *avoiding* production of the residues by identifying fundamental causes and redesigning products and processes to eliminate the causes. Of the two methods, the second is preferred. The first method is analogous to obtaining product quality by inspection and rework (*inspecting in quality*). Experience with quality management has revealed that this approach is much more costly than *doing it right the first time*. This same outcome is likely to be true for the control of residues once produced. It makes more sense to avoid residues than to contain them once produced. Performance measures for this objective include pounds of toxic waste produced, cubic meters of effluents, tons of greenhouse gases produced, and percentage reduction of packaging materials.

The fifth objective emphasizes conservation of nonrenewable resources by their reuse. Recycling reduces the demand for extraction of additional raw materials. It also reduces environmental degradation by reducing the waste disposal requirements placed on end-users. Measures include pounds of materials recycled, number of different materials (the fewer, the better), number of different components (the fewer, the better for recycling), percentage of units remanufactured, and energy produced from incineration. Exhibit 16-9 summarizes the objectives and measures for the environmental perspective.

EXHIBIT 16-9   Objectives and Measures: Environmental Perspective

Objectives	Measures
Minimize hazardous materials	Types and quantities (total and per-unit) Percentage of total materials cost Productivity measures (output/input)
Minimize raw or virgin materials	Types and quantities (total and per-unit) Productivity measures (output/input)
Minimize energy requirements	Types and quantities (total and per-unit) Productivity measures (output/input)
Minimize release of residues	Pounds of toxic waste produced Cubic meters of effluents Tons of greenhouse gases produced Percentage reduction of packaging materials
Maximize opportunities to recycle	Pounds of materials recycled Number of different components Percentage of units remanufactured Energy produced from incineration

The Role of Activity Management

Analysis of environmental activities is critical for a sound environmental control system. Of course, as we already know, identifying environmental activities and assessing their costs are prerequisites for activity-based environmental costing. Knowing the environmental costs and what products and processes are causing them is absolutely essential as a first step for control. Next, environmental activities must be classified as value-added and non-value-added.

Non-value-added activities are those that are not necessary if the firm were operating in an optimal environmentally efficient state. Interestingly, Porter and van der Linde claim that environmental pollution is equivalent to economic inefficiency.[24] If production of contaminants is equivalent to economic efficiency as they claim, then all failure activities must be labeled non-value-added. Adopting an ecoefficiency paradigm implies that activities will always exist that can simultaneously prevent environmental degradation and produce a state of economic efficiency better than the current state. Failure activities, of course, are not the only non-value-added activities. Many detection activities, such as inspection, are non-value-added as well.

Non-value-added environmental costs are the costs of non-value-added activities. These costs represent the benefits that can be captured by improving environmental performance. The key to capturing these benefits is identifying root causes for non-value-added activities and then redesigning products and processes to minimize and ultimately eliminate these non-value-added activities.

Design for the Environment

This special design approach aimed at minimizing non-value-added activities is called *design for the environment*. It touches products, processes, materials, energy, and recycling. In other words, the entire product life cycle and its effects on the environment must be considered. Manufacturing processes, for example, are the direct sources of many solid, liquid, and gaseous residues. Many of these residues end up being released into the environment. Often, redesign of a process can eliminate the production of such residues. Product designs can also reduce environmental degradation. **Eastman Kodak**, for example, has designed its expendable cameras to facilitate recycling.[25] The expendable cameras have components that are color-coded. These components can be separated and used to build new cameras. Approximately 86 percent of each new camera is made of recycled materials. It is estimated that five million units have been recycled since the introduction of this product, totaling about 700,000 pounds of materials.

Financial Measures

Environmental improvements ought to produce significant and beneficial financial consequences. This means that the firm has achieved a favorable trade-off among failure activities and prevention activities. If ecoefficient decisions are being made, then total environmental costs should diminish as environmental performance improves. Thus, environmental cost trends are an important performance measure. One possibility is preparing a non-value-added environmental cost report for the current period and comparing these costs with the non-value-added costs of the prior period. An example of such a report is shown in Exhibit 16-10 on the following page. Some care should be taken in how costs and trends are measured. Cost reductions should be attributable to environmental

24. Michael E. Porter and Claus van der Linde, "Green and Competitive: Ending the Stalemate," *Harvard Business Review* (September–October 1995): 120–134.
25. Joseph Fiskel, "Competitive Excellence through Environmental Excellence," *Corporate Environmental Strategy* (Summer 1997): 55–61.

EXHIBIT 16-10   Non-Value-Added Cost Trends: Environmental Costs

Non-Value-Added Environmental Activity	Year	
	2006	2007
Inspecting processes	$ 720,000	$ 600,000
Operating pollution equipment	1,200,000	1,050,000
Maintaining pollution equipment	600,000	600,000
Cleaning up water pollution	2,700,000	2,100,000
Property damage claim	1,200,000	900,000
Totals	$6,420,000	$5,250,000

improvements and not simply to discharging some environmental liability. Thus, external failure costs should reflect the average annual obligations resulting from current environmental efficiency. Therefore, the cost of cleaning up water pollution in 2006 is the expected annual cost, assuming current environmental performance remains the same. The $2,700,000 cleanup cost, for example, could be the annual amount that must be set aside to make available total funds necessary to execute cleanup efforts five years from now. As actions are taken to improve environmental performance, this may

EXHIBIT 16-11   Environmental Cost Trend Graph

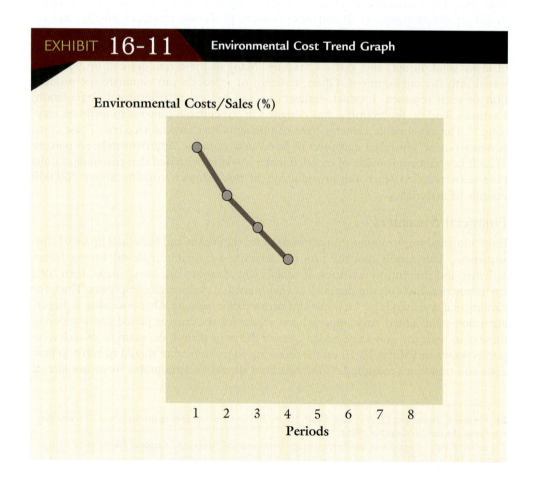

Environmental Costs/Sales (%)

Periods

mean that the amount of future cleanup will diminish, thus reducing the annual fund amount to $2,100,000. The $600,000 trend improvement, then, is attributable to improved environmental performance.

Another possibility is computing total environmental costs as a percentage of sales and tracking this value over several periods. Exhibit 16-11 illustrates such a trend graph. This graph is of particular interest because it tracks all environmental costs, not just non-value-added environmental costs. If ecoefficient decisions are being made, we should observe a reduction in *total* environmental costs. This implies that there is a favorable trade-off between investments in environmentally related prevention activities and reduction of environmental failure costs. The trend should be downward as ecoefficient investments are made.

Other graphical illustrations for specific areas can also be used to show progress. For example, a bar graph can be used to show the total amount of a pollutant emitted on a year-by-year basis. A downward trend would be a favorable indication. Pie charts can be useful as well. For example, a pie chart could visually display hazardous waste management by category: percentage of waste incinerated, percentage of waste treated, percentage of waste recycled/reclaimed, percentage of waste landfilled, and percentage of waste deep well injected. Exhibit 16-12 illustrates a bar graph analysis of CFC (chlorofluorocarbon) releases over a 4-year period, and Exhibit 16-13, on the following page, shows a pie chart for hazardous waste management.

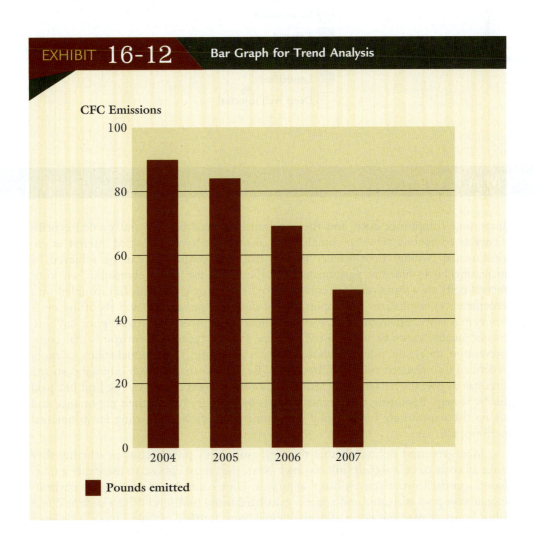

EXHIBIT **16-12**   Bar Graph for Trend Analysis

CFC Emissions

Pounds emitted

EXHIBIT **16-13**   Hazardous Waste Management Pie Chart

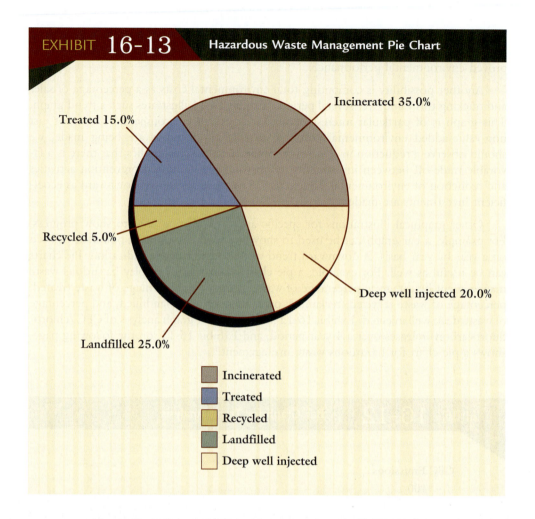

- Incinerated 35.0%
- Treated 15.0%
- Recycled 5.0%
- Deep well injected 20.0%
- Landfilled 25.0%

- Incinerated
- Treated
- Recycled
- Landfilled
- Deep well injected

SUMMARY

Increasing compliance costs and the emergence of ecoefficiency and guided ecoefficiency as competing views to compliance management have intensified interest in environmental costing. Ecoefficiency implies that cost reductions can be achieved by increasing environmental performance. Furthermore, for many companies, environmental costs are a significant percentage of total operating costs. This fact, coupled with ecoefficiency, emphasizes the importance of defining, measuring, and reporting environmental costs. Environmental costs are those costs incurred because poor environmental quality exists or may exist. There are four categories of environmental costs: prevention, detection, internal failure, and external failure. The external failure category is divided into realized and unrealized costs. Realized costs are those external costs the firm has to pay; unrealized or societal costs are those costs caused by the firm but paid for by society. Reporting environmental costs by category reveals their importance and shows the opportunity for reducing environmental costs by improving environmental performance.

Managers must decide whether they will assign only private costs or whether they want all costs to be assigned (full costing). Next, they must choose to use either a unit-based approach or an activity-based approach. Under unit-based costing, an environmental cost pool is created and a rate is calculated using unit-level drivers such as direct labor hours or machine hours. Environmental costs are then assigned to each product based on their usage of direct labor hours or machine hours. This approach is probably satisfactory for those firms with little product diversity. For firms with product diversity, activity-based assignments are likely to be superior. ABC would assign costs to environmental activities and then calculate activity rates. These rates are then used to assign environmental costs to products.

Life-cycle cost assessment is a fundamental part of life-cycle assessment. Life-cycle cost assessment assigns costs to the environmental impacts of competing product designs. These costs are a function of the materials used, the energy consumed, and the environmental releases resulting from the manufacture of a product. Thus, before assessing these cost assignments, it is first necessary to do an inventory analysis that details materials, energy, and environmental releases. This analysis is carried out over the life cycle of the product itself. Once completed, the financial and operational impacts can be assessed and steps taken to improve environmental performance.

Controlling environmental costs relies on a strategic-based responsibility accounting system. This system has two important features: a strategic component and an operational component. The strategic component uses the Balanced Scorecard framework. The adaptation for environmental control is the addition of a fifth perspective: the environmental perspective. The environmental perspective has five objectives relating to materials and energy usage, production and release of environmental residues, and recycling. Operational measures such as pounds of hazardous materials and pounds of recycled materials are developed for each objective. Activity-based management provides the operational system that produces environmental improvements. Non-value-added environmental activities and their root causes are identified. Design for the environment approaches are then used to eliminate these non-value-added activities. Ecoefficient improvements should produce favorable financial consequences that can be measured using trends in non-value-added environmental costs and total environmental costs.

REVIEW PROBLEMS AND SOLUTIONS

1 ENVIRONMENTAL COSTS

At the beginning of 2007, Greener Company initiated a program to improve its environmental performance. Efforts were made to reduce the production and emission of contaminating gaseous, solid, and liquid residues. By the end of the year, in an executive meeting, the environmental manager indicated that the company had made significant improvement in its environmental performance, reducing the emission of contaminating residues of all types. The president of the company was pleased with the reported success but wanted an assessment of the financial consequences of the environmental improvements. To satisfy this request, the following financial data were collected for 2006 and 2007 (all changes in cost are a product of environmental improvements):

	2006	2007
Sales	$60,000,000	$60,000,000
Evaluating and selecting suppliers	0	1,800,000
Treating and disposing of toxic materials	3,600,000	2,400,000
Inspecting processes (environmental objective)	600,000	900,000
Land restoration (annual fund contribution)	4,800,000	3,600,000
Maintaining pollution equipment	1,200,000	900,000
Testing for contaminants	450,000	300,000

Required:

1. Classify the costs as prevention, detection, internal failure, or external failure.
2. Prepare an environmental cost report for the most recent year, where costs are expressed as a percentage of sales (instead of operating costs).

SOLUTION

1. Prevention costs: Evaluating and selecting suppliers; Detection costs: Testing for contaminants and inspecting processes; Internal failure costs: Maintaining pollution equipment and treating and disposing of toxic materials; External failure costs: Land restoration.

2.

Greener Company
Environmental Cost Report
For the Year Ended December 31, 2007

	Environmental Costs	Percentage of Sales
Prevention costs:		
Evaluating and selecting suppliers	$1,800,000	3.00%
Detection costs:		
Testing for contaminants	$ 300,000	
Inspecting processes	900,000	
Total detection costs	$1,200,000	2.00
Internal failure costs:		
Maintaining pollution equipment	$ 900,000	
Treating and disposing of toxic materials	2,400,000	
Total internal failure costs	$3,300,000	5.50
External failure costs:		
Land restoration	$3,600,000	6.00
Total environmental costs	$9,900,000	16.50%

2   ASSIGNING ENVIRONMENTAL COSTS, LIFE-CYCLE COST ASSESSMENT, ENVIRONMENTAL COST CONTROL

Searle Company produces two types of fertilizers: Rapidfeed and Timefeed. Searle has recently received significant criticism from environmental groups, local residents, and the federal government concerning its environmental performance. John Taylor, president of Searle, wants to know how the company's environmental activities affect the cost of each product. He believes that the main source of the environmental problems lies with Rapidfeed, but he would like some evidence to support (or refute) this belief. The controller has assembled the following data to help answer this question:

	Rapidfeed	Timefeed
Pounds of fertilizer produced	3,000,000	6,000,000
Engineering hours (process design)	4,500	13,500
Pounds of solid residues treated	90,000	30,000
Inspection hours (environmental)	30,000	15,000
Cleanup hours (local lake)	24,000	6,000

Additionally, the following environmental activity costs were reported:

Designing process	$ 450,000
Treating residues	1,800,000
Inspecting processes	360,000
Cleaning up lake	600,000

Required:

1. Calculate the environmental cost per pound of fertilizer for each product.
2. Based on the calculations in Requirement 1, which product appears to be the most environmentally harmful?
3. Would life-cycle cost assessment provide stronger evidence for the environmental suitability of each product? Explain.
4. Explain how a strategic-based responsibility accounting system can be used to help improve Searle's performance.

SOLUTION

1. First, calculate activity rates:

Designing process	$450,000/18,000 = $25 per engineering hour
Treating residues	$1,800,000/120,000 = $15 per pound of residue
Inspecting processes	$360,000/45,000 = $8 per inspection hour
Cleaning up lake	$600,000/30,000 = $20 per cleanup hour

Second, use rates to assign environmental costs and calculate unit environmental costs:

Rapidfeed

$25 × 4,500	$ 112,500
$15 × 90,000	1,350,000
$8 × 30,000	240,000
$20 × 24,000	480,000
Total	$ 2,182,500
	÷ 3,000,000
Unit cost	$ 0.7275

Timefeed

$25 × 13,500	$ 337,500
$15 × 30,000	450,000
$8 × 15,000	120,000
$20 × 6,000	120,000
Total	$ 1,027,500
	÷ 6,000,000
Unit cost	$ 0.17125

2. As measured by the environmental cost per unit, Rapidfeed appears to be the product causing the most environmental damage, confirming the president's beliefs.

3. Life-cycle assessment has three steps: inventory analysis, impact analysis, and improvement analysis. Of the three steps, the first two are concerned with identifying the materials and energy requirements, environmental releases, and the environmental effects of competing process and product designs (over the life cycle of the products). Thus, a life-cycle assessment provides a more comprehensive analysis of environmental effects than the environmental cost per unit (unless the cost per unit is a life-cycle environmental cost per unit).

4. The environmental perspective can improve environmental performance by translating an environmental improvement strategy into operational objectives, measures, targets, and initiatives. For example, consider the five core environmental objectives. These objectives, if followed, will reduce the amounts of materials and energy used (including hazardous materials) and will also reduce residues

released. Furthermore, the environmental perspective is tied to the other four perspectives of the Balanced Scorecard. Thus, it is explicitly recognized that improving environmental performance means that capabilities, processes, customers, and financial consequences must be considered.

KEY TERMS

Compliance management **698**

Ecoefficiency **696**

Environmental costs **699**

Environmental detection costs **699**

Environmental external failure costs **700**

Environmental internal failure costs **700**

Environmental prevention costs **699**

Full environmental costing **705**

Full private costing **705**

Guided ecoefficiency **699**

Impact analysis **709**

Improvement analysis **709**

Inventory analysis **708**

Life-cycle assessment **707**

Life-cycle cost assessment **707**

Private costs **700**

Product stewardship **707**

Realized external failure costs **700**

Sustainable development **696**

Unrealized external failure (societal) costs **700**

QUESTIONS FOR WRITING AND DISCUSSION

1. What is ecoefficiency?
2. What are the four objectives associated with ecoefficiency?
3. Describe the four opportunities for improving ecoefficiency.
4. What is an environmental cost?
5. What are the four categories of environmental costs? Define each category.
6. What is the difference between a realized external failure cost (environmental) and an unrealized external failure (societal) cost?
7. What does full environmental costing mean? Full private costing?
8. What information is communicated by the unit environmental cost of a product?
9. What is life-cycle assessment?
10. How can life-cycle costing improve life-cycle analysis?
11. What is the justification for adding an environmental perspective to the Balanced Scorecard?
12. What are the five core objectives of the environmental perspective?
13. Do you agree that all environmental failure activities are non-value-added activities? Explain.
14. What is the meaning of design for the environment? What is its role in activity-based management of environmental activities?
15. Describe the possible value of financial measures of environmental performance. Give several examples.

EXERCISES

16-1   ECOEFFICIENCY

LO1   For years, companies dealt with pollution problems through compliance management (ensuring that a company follows environmental laws and regulations as cheaply as possible). No effort was made to improve environmental performance beyond the minimal performance that satisfied environmental regulations (improving environmental performance and increasing economic efficiency were viewed as incompatible objectives). Recently, two alternative views of managing environmental cost have been proposed: (1) ecoefficiency and (2) guided ecoefficiency.

Required:

1. Explain why ecoefficiency may be a better view of the world than that espoused by compliance management. Discuss factors that may support this view.
2. Some believe that even if the ecoefficient view is true, regulatory intervention still may be needed. The type of intervention, however, must be carefully designed. Explain what is meant by properly designed regulation, and identify the key assumptions that must hold for the guided ecoefficiency view to be valid.

16-2   ECOEFFICIENCY AND SUSTAINABLE DEVELOPMENT

LO1   Achieving sustainable development will likely require the cooperation of communities, governments, and businesses. The World Business Council for Sustainable Development (WBCSD) claims that ecoefficiency is "the business contribution to sustainable development."

Required:

1. What is sustainable development?
2. Explain why the WBCSD's claim about ecoefficiency may be true.
3. WBSCD has recently noted (http://www.wbcsd.ch): "the good news is that ecoefficiency is working in the companies that try it. The troubling news is that it is not being tried on a large enough scale, even though it makes good business sense." Why do you think the ecoefficiency paradigm is not as widely accepted as it perhaps ought to be? What would you suggest to increase the number of companies involved in ecoefficient projects?

16-3   ECOEFFICIENCY: OBJECTIVES AND OPPORTUNITIES

LO1   Consider the following ecoefficient actions:

a. Improve the performance of a steam system used to generate electricity, reducing the use of energy and water.
b. Install a system that converts a waste product into a salable product.
c. Replaced solvent-based additives in a detergent blend with plant-extracted essential oils (reducing health and safety concerns).
d. Encoding plastic components to enable easier identification for disassembly and recycling.
e. Installation of a closed-loop water treatment plant to prevent the discharge of wastewater into a local river.
f. Redesigning a process reduces toxic releases and decreases energy consumption.
g. Converting sludge from a wastewater treatment facility into commercial compost.
h. Substitution of lower-cost, water-based solvents for flammable, toxic solvents.

Required:

Refer to Exhibit 16-1 (on page 697). Identify the objectives and opportunities associated with each of the actions listed above.

16-4   CLASSIFICATION OF ENVIRONMENTAL COSTS

LO1   Classify the following environmental activities as prevention costs, detection costs, internal failure costs, or external failure costs. For external failure costs, classify the costs as societal or private. Also, label those activities that are compatible with sustainable development (SD).

1. A company takes actions to reduce the amount of material in its packages.
2. After the activated carbon's useful life, a soft-drink producer returns this material used for purifying water for its beverages to the supplier. The supplier reactivates the carbon for a second use in nonfood applications. As a consequence, many tons of material are prevented from entering landfills.
3. An evaporator system is installed to treat wastewater and collect usable solids for other uses.
4. The inks used to print snack packages (for chips) contain heavy metals.
5. Processes are inspected to ensure compliance with environmental standards.
6. Delivery boxes are used five times and then recycled. This prevents 112 million pounds of cardboard from entering landfills and saves two million trees per year.
7. Scrubber equipment is installed to ensure that air emissions are less than the level permitted by law.
8. Local residents are incurring medical costs from illnesses caused by air pollution from automobile exhaust pollution.
9. As part of implementing an environmental perspective for the Balanced Scorecard, environmental performance measures are developed.
10. Because of liquid and solid residues being discharged into a local lake, the lake is no longer fit for swimming, fishing, and other recreational activities.
11. To reduce energy consumption, magnetic ballasts are replaced with electronic ballasts, and more efficient light bulbs and lighting sensors are installed. As a result, 2.3 million kilowatt-hours of electricity are saved per year.
12. Due to a legal settlement, a chemicals company must spend $20,000,000 to clean up contaminated soil.
13. A soft-drink company uses the following practice: In all bottling plants, packages damaged during filling are collected and recycled (glass, plastic, and aluminum).
14. Products are inspected to ensure that the gaseous emissions produced during operation follow legal and company guidelines.
15. The cost of operating pollution control equipment.
16. An internal audit is conducted to verify that environmental policies are being followed.

16-5   ENVIRONMENTAL COST REPORT

LO1   At the end of 2007, Hender Chemicals began to implement an environmental quality management program. As a first step, it identified the following costs in its accounting records as environmentally related for the year just ended:

	2007
Settling personal injury claims	$1,200,000
Treating and disposing of toxic waste	4,800,000
Cleanup of chemically contaminated soil	1,800,000
Inspecting products and processes	600,000
Operating pollution control equipment	840,000
Licensing facilities for producing contaminants	360,000
Evaluating and selecting suppliers	120,000
Developing performance measures	60,000
Recycling products	75,000

Required:

1. Prepare an environmental cost report by category. Assume that total operating costs are $60,000,000.

2. Use a pie chart to illustrate the relative distribution percentages for each environmental cost category. Comment on what this distribution communicates to a manager.

16-6 REPORTING SOCIAL COSTS

LO1 Refer to **Exercise 16-5**. Suppose that the newly hired environmental manager examines the report and makes the following comment: "This report understates the total environmental costs. It fails to consider the costs we are imposing on the local community. For example, we have polluted the river and lake so much that swimming and fishing are no longer possible. I have heard rumblings from the local citizens, and I'll bet that we will be facing a big cleanup bill in a few years."

Subsequent to the comment, environmental engineering estimated that cleanup costs for the river and lake will cost $3,000,000, assuming the cleanup efforts are required within five years. To pay for the cleanup, annual contributions of $525,000 will be invested with the expectation that the fund will grow to $3,000,000 by the end of the fifth year. Assume also that the loss of recreational opportunities is costing the local community $1,200,000 per year.

Required:

1. How would this information alter the report in **Exercise 16-5**?
2. Current financial reporting standards require that contingent liabilities be disclosed if certain conditions are met. Thus, it is possible that Hender may need to disclose the $3,000,000 cleanup liability. Yet, the opportunity cost for the recreational opportunities need not be disclosed to outside parties. Should Hender voluntarily disclose this cost? Is it likely that it would?

16-7 ENVIRONMENTAL COST ASSIGNMENT

LO2 Coyle Pharmaceuticals produces two organic chemicals (Org AB, and Org XY) used in the production of two of its most wide-selling anti-cancer drugs. The controller and environmental manager have identified the following environmental activities and costs associated with the two products:

	Org AB	*Org XY*
Pounds produced	7,500,000	18,750,000
Packaging materials (pounds)	2,250,000	1,125,000
Energy usage (kilowatt-hours)	750,000	375,000
Toxic releases (pounds into air)	1,875,000	375,000
Pollution control (machine hours)	300,000	75,000
Costs of activities:		
Using packaging materials	$3,375,000	
Using energy	900,000	
Releasing toxins (fines)	450,000	
Operating pollution control equipment	1,050,000	

Required:

1. Calculate the environmental cost per pound for each product. Which of the two products appears to cause the most degradation to the environment?
2. In which environmental category would you classify excessive use of materials and energy?

(continued)

3. Suppose that the toxin releases cause health problems for those who live near the chemical plant. The costs, due to missed work and medical treatments, are estimated at $2,025,000 per year. How would assignment of these costs change the unit cost? Should they be assigned?

16-8 ENVIRONMENTAL COSTING, ECOEFFICIENCY, AND COMPETITIVE ADVANTAGE

LO1, LO2

Refer to the data in **Exercise 16-7**. Suppose that Coyle's manager decides to launch an environmental performance improvement program. First, efforts were made to reduce the amount of packaging. The demand for packaging materials was reduced by 10 percent. Second, a way was found to reuse the packaging materials. Usage of packaging materials changed from one time to two times. Both changes together saved $1,856,250 in packaging costs. Third, the manufacturing processes were redesigned to produce a reduced environmental load. The new processes were able to reduce emissions by 50 percent and private emission costs by 75 percent. The new processes also reduced the demand for energy by one-third. Energy costs were also reduced by the same amount. There was no change in the demand or cost of operating pollution control equipment.

The cost of implementing the changes was $753,750 (salaries of $450,000 for hiring six environmental engineers and $303,750 for treating the packaging materials so they can be reused). Engineering hours used for each process are 11,250 for the Org AB process and 3,750 for the Org XY process.

Required:

1. Calculate the new cost per pound for each product. Assume that the environmental reductions for each product are in the same proportions as the total reductions.
2. Calculate the net savings produced by the environmental changes for each product, in total, and on a per-unit basis. Does this support the concept of ecoefficiency?
3. Classify the activities as prevention, detection, internal failure, or external failure.
4. Describe how the environmental improvements can contribute to improving the firm's competitive position.

16-9 LIFE-CYCLE COST ASSESSMENT

LO3

Jackman Cleanser Division produces surfactants, ingredients used in producing laundry detergents. (Surfactants are the components that help release soil from clothing.) It is possible to make different types of surfactants, depending on the nature of the material input. One possibility, for example, is to use petrochemical stock as the primary material input. Another possibility is the use of beef tallow as the primary material input. The primary input plus other inputs and energy sources are used to produce the surfactants. An inventory analysis produces the following for the production of surfactants:

	Petrochemical	Tallow
Materials (kg per 1,000 kg of surfactant)	900	850
Water usage (kg per 1,000 kg of surfactants used)	50	500
Energy usage (kilowatt-hours per 1,000 kg of surfactants):		
For production of materials	55	30
Transportation	10	20
Processing (production of surfactants)	60	60

(continued)

	Petrochemical	Tallow
Residues (emissions per 1,000 kg of surfactants):		
Particulates (air contaminant)	2	12
Hydrocarbons (air contaminant)	40	30
Dissolved solids (liquid contaminant)	6	4
Land contamination (solid residue)	80	160

The greater water usage for tallow relates to the requirement that water must be used to produce feed for beef. The cost per kilogram of petrochemical stock is $0.40. The cost per kilogram of tallow is $0.60. Water costs $0.50 per kilogram, and energy is $1.20 per kilowatt-hour. When air contaminants exceed five per 1,000 kilograms, pollution control equipment must be purchased and installed. The cost of acquiring and operating this equipment is $500 per five units of contaminants. Liquid contaminants are more trouble. If dumped into local streams over the life cycle, the costs are estimated to be $120 per unit of liquid contaminant. If a water treatment system is used, the cost is $60 per unit of contaminant. Finally, soil cleanup is estimated at $20 per unit of solid residue.

Required:

1. Assess the relative environmental impacts of the two approaches to producing surfactants using only operational environmental measures. Which of the two approaches would you recommend? Justify your choice.
2. Use the cost information and calculate an environmental impact cost per 1,000 kg of surfactants. Which of the two approaches would you now recommend? Does the life-cycle cost approach have limitations? Explain.
3. Which parts of the life cycle described by the inventory analysis are controlled by the supplier? By the producer? What part of the inventory analysis is missing?

16-10   LIFE-CYCLE ASSESSMENT: PACKAGING AND PRODUCT USE, IMPACT ANALYSIS

LO3   Burnham Munchies, Inc., is an international producer of potato chips. At the end of 2006, Mandy Pohlson, president of Burnham, appointed a task force to focus on the packaging and product use segments of its product's life cycle. Since customers consumed the contents of the package (if not consumed, the contents are biodegradable), the main concern was on the ability to conserve, recycle, and dispose of packaging materials. A new packaging proposal was being considered. A partial inventory analysis of the current packaging and the new packaging is as follows:

	Current	New
Delivery boxes:		
Recycle potential	Low	High
Times used before disposal	1	5
Paper bags:		
Average package weight (ounces)	2	1.5
Ink with heavy metals	Yes	No
Ultimate disposal:		
Safe for incineration	No	Yes

Upon seeing the inventory analysis, Mandy was pleased to see the apparent environmental benefits of the new packaging. However, she wanted a more detailed analysis of the impact of the new packaging. In response to this request, environmental engineering and cost accounting provided the following estimates:

Annual packages produced and sold	200,000,000
Current demand for delivery boxes	300,000,000 pounds
Recycle forecast	90% of delivery boxes used
Cost per ounce (package)	$0.02
Cost per pound (delivery boxes)	$0.60

The company's environmental engineers also indicated that in Europe and Japan about 75 percent of the packaging will participate in waste-to-energy combustion programs for the generation of steam or electricity. In the United States, only about 25 percent of the packaging will participate in such programs. Environmental engineering also noted that saving 300 pounds of paperboard is equivalent to saving one tree.

Required:

1. Calculate the total pounds of delivery boxes saved because of the new packaging. How much does this save in dollars? How many trees are saved because of recycling and reduction in demand for boxes? Because of recycling, how many pounds of cardboard are diverted from landfills?
2. Calculate the total pounds of materials saved by reducing packaging (bag) weight. What are the dollar savings? Now, assume that a design engineer has indicated that by reducing the packaging seal from the industry standard one-half inch to one-fourth inch, an additional 5 percent reduction in bag packaging can be achieved. How many pounds of materials are saved? Dollars saved?
3. Explain why the ultimate disposal qualities of packaging are important environmental considerations.
4. Why emphasize saving a material that comes from a renewable resource (trees)?

16-11 ENVIRONMENTAL PERFORMANCE MEASURES AND CORE OBJECTIVES

LO4   Identify the *core environmental objective* associated with each of the following measures:

a. Tons of greenhouse gas emissions
b. Tons of hazardous waste delivered for off-site management
c. Pounds of plastic recycled
d. British thermal units (BTUs)
e. Cars produced/pounds of steel used
f. Percentage of vehicles powered by propane gas
g. Percentage of recycled paper used (green purchasing)
h. Pounds of toxic chemical releases
i. Hazardous waste cost/Total materials cost
j. Pounds of nonhazardous waste/Pounds of materials issued
k. Percentage reduction in packaging materials
l. Pounds of organic chemicals in effluents sent to local river
m. Percentage of nonhazardous waste recycled

PROBLEMS

16-12 COST CLASSIFICATION, ENVIRONMENTAL RESPONSIBILITY ACCOUNTING

LO1, LO4   At the beginning of 2004, Limon Company, an international telecommunications company, embarked on an environmental improvement program. The company set a goal to have all its facilities ISO 14001 registered by 2007. (There are 30 facilities world-wide.) It also adopted the Balanced Scorecard with an environmental perspective added as a fifth perspective. To communicate the environmental progress made, management decided to issue, on a voluntary basis, an annual environmental progress report. Internally, the accounting department issued monthly progress reports and developed a number of measures that could be reported even more frequently to assess progress. Limon also asked an international CPA firm to prepare an auditor's report that would comment on the reasonableness and fairness of Limon's approach to assessing and measuring environmental performance.

At the end of 2007, the controller had gathered data that would be used in preparing the environmental progress report. A sample of the data collected is as follows:

Year	Number of ISO 14001 Registrations	Energy Consumption (BTUs)[a]	Greenhouse Gases[b]
2004	3	3,000	40,000
2005	9	2,950	39,000
2006	15	2,900	38,000
2007	24	2,850	36,000

[a]In billions (measures electricity, natural gas, and heating oil usage).
[b]In tons.

Required:

1. What is the justification for adding an environmental perspective to the Balanced Scorecard?
2. Limon Company decided to do the following: obtain ISO 14001 registration, prepare an annual environmental progress report, prepare internal environmental progress reports, and request an audit of the external report. How do these decisions fit within the Balanced Scorecard framework? To what environmental cost categories do these activities belong?
3. Using the data, prepare a bar graph for each of the three environmental variables provided (registrations, energy, and greenhouse gases). Comment on the progress made on these three dimensions. To which core objectives do each of the three measures relate?

16-13 ENVIRONMENTAL RESPONSIBILITY ACCOUNTING, COST TRENDS

LO4   Refer to **Problem 16-12**. As part of its environmental cost reporting system, Limon tracks its total environmental costs. Consider the following cost and sales data:

Year	Total Environmental Costs	Sales Revenue
2004	$30,000,000	$250,000,000
2005	25,000,000	250,000,000
2006	22,000,000	275,000,000
2007	19,250,000	275,000,000

Required:

1. Prepare a bar graph for environmental costs expressed as a percentage of sales. Assuming that environmental performance has improved, explain why environmental costs have decreased.

(continued)

2. Normalize energy consumption by expressing it as a percentage of sales. Now, prepare a bar graph for energy. Comment on the progress made in reducing energy consumption. How does this compare with the conclusion that would be reached using a nonnormalized measure of progress? Which is the best approach? Explain.

16-14 COST CLASSIFICATION, ECOEFFICIENCY, STRATEGIC ENVIRONMENTAL OBJECTIVES

LO1, LO2, LO4

The following items are listed in an environmental financial statement (issued as part of an environmental progress report):

Environmental benefits (savings, income, and cost avoidance):
- Ozone-depleting substances cost reductions
- Hazardous waste disposal cost reductions
- Hazardous waste material cost reductions
- Nonhazardous waste disposal cost reductions
- Nonhazardous waste material cost reductions
- Recycling income
- Energy conservation cost savings
- Packaging cost reductions

Environmental costs:
- Corporate-level administrative costs
- Auditor fees
- Environmental engineering
- Facility professionals and programs
- Packaging professionals and programs for packaging reductions
- Pollution controls: Operations and maintenance
- Pollution controls: Depreciation
- Attorney fees for cleanup claims, notices of violations (NOVs)
- Settlements of government claims
- Waste disposal
- Environmental taxes for packaging
- Remediation/Cleanup: On-site
- Remediation/Cleanup: Off-site

Required:
1. Classify each item in the statement as prevention, detection, internal failure, or external failure. In classifying the items listed in the environmental benefits category, first classify the underlying cost item (e.g., the cost of hazardous waste disposal). Next, think of how you would classify the cost of the activities that led to the cost reduction. That is, how would you classify the macro activity: *reducing hazardous waste cost disposal*?
2. For each item in the environmental benefits category, indicate a possible measure or measures (i.e., pounds, tons, kilowatt-hours, etc.) and the core strategic environmental objective that would be associated with the measure. Is it possible that a measure may be associated with more than one objective? Explain.
3. Assuming ecoefficiency, what relationship over time would you expect to observe between the environmental benefits category and the environmental cost category?

16-15 ENVIRONMENTAL FINANCIAL REPORTING, ECOEFFICIENCY, IMPROVING ENVIRONMENTAL PERFORMANCE

LO1, LO2, LO4

Refer to **Problem 16-14**. In the environmental benefits section of the report, three types of benefits are listed: income, savings, and cost avoidance. Now, consider the following data for selected items for a 4-year period:

Year	Engineering Design Costs	Cost of Ozone-Depleting Substances
2004	$ 180,000	$3,240,000
2005	1,440,000	2,160,000
2006	720,000	1,440,000
2007	90,000	360,000

The engineering design costs were incurred to redesign the production processes and products. Redesign of the product allowed the substitution of a material that produced less ozone-depleting substances. Modifications in the design of the processes also accomplished the same objective. Because of the improvements, the company was able to reduce the demand for pollution control equipment (with its attendant depreciation and operating costs) and avoid fines and litigation costs. All of the savings generated in a given year represent costs avoided for future years. The engineering costs are investments in design projects. Once the results of the project are realized, design costs can be reduced to lower levels. However, since some ongoing design activity is required for maintaining the system and improving it as needed, the environmental engineering cost will not be reduced lower than the $90,000 reported in 2007.

Required:

1. Prepare a partial environmental financial statement, divided into benefit and cost sections for 2005, 2006, and 2007.
2. Evaluate and explain the outcomes. Does this result support or challenge ecoefficiency? Explain.

16-16   ENVIRONMENTAL FINANCIAL REPORT

LO1   The following environmental cost reports for 2005, 2006, and 2007 are for the Communications Products Division of Kartel, a telecommunications company. In 2005, Kartel committed itself to a continuous environmental improvement program, which was implemented throughout the company.

Environmental Activity	2005	2006	2007
Disposing hazardous waste	$200,000	$150,000	$ 50,000
Measuring contaminant releases	10,000	100,000	70,000
Releasing air contaminants	500,000	400,000	250,000
Producing scrap (nonhazardous)	175,000	150,000	125,000
Operating pollution equipment	260,000	200,000	130,000
Designing processes and products	50,000	300,000	100,000
Using energy	180,000	162,000	144,000
Training employees (environmental)	10,000	20,000	40,000
Remediation (cleanup)	400,000	300,000	190,000
Inspecting processes	0	100,000	80,000

At the beginning of 2007, Kartel began a new program of recycling nonhazardous scrap. The effort produced recycling income totaling $25,000. The marketing vice president and the environmental manager estimated that sales revenue had increased by $200,000 per year since 2005 because of an improved public image relative to environmental performance. The company's finance department also estimated that Kartel saved $80,000 in 2007 because of reduced finance and insurance costs, all attributable to improved environmental performance. All reductions in environmental costs from 2005 to 2007 are attributable to improvement efforts. Furthermore, any reductions represent ongoing savings.

Required:

1. Prepare an environmental financial statement for 2007 (for the Products Division). In the cost section, classify environmental costs by category (prevention, detection, etc.).
2. Evaluate the changes in environmental performance.

16-17 ASSIGNMENT OF ENVIRONMENTAL COSTS

LO2 Refer to **Problem 16-16**. In 2005, Jack Carter, president of Kartel, requested that environmental costs be assigned to the two major products produced by the company. He felt that knowledge of the environmental product costs would help guide the design decisions that would be necessary to improve environmental performance. The products represent two different models of a cellular phone (Model XA2 and Model KZ3). The models use different processes and materials. To assign the costs, the following data were gathered for 2005:

Activity	Model XA2	Model KZ3
Disposing hazardous waste (tons)	20	180
Measuring contaminant releases (transactions)	1,000	4,000
Releasing air contaminants (tons)	25	225
Producing scrap (pounds of scrap)	25,000	25,000
Operating pollution equipment (hours)	120,000	400,000
Designing processes and products (hours)	1,500	500
Using energy (BTUs)	600,000	1,200,000
Training employees (hours)	50	50
Remediation (labor hours)	5,000	15,000

During 2005, Kartel's division produced 200,000 units of Model XA2 and 300,000 units of Model KZ3.

Required:

1. Using the activity data, calculate the environmental cost per unit for each model. How will this information be useful?
2. Upon examining the cost data produced in Requirement 1, an environmental engineer made the following suggestions: (1) substitute a new plastic for a material that appeared to be the source of much of the hazardous waste (the new material actually cost less than the contaminating material it would replace) and (2) redesign the processes to reduce the amount of air contaminants produced.

    As a result of the first suggestion, by 2007, the amount of hazardous waste produced had diminished to 50 tons, 10 tons for Model XA2 and 40 tons for Model KZ3. The second suggestion reduced the contaminants released by 50 percent by 2007 (15 tons for Model XA2 and 110 tons for Model KZ3). The need for pollution equipment also diminished, and the hours required for operating this equipment for Model XA2 and Model KZ3 were reduced to 60,000 and 200,000, respectively. Calculate the unit cost reductions for the two models associated with the actions and outcomes described (assume the same production as in 2005). Do you think the efforts to reduce the environmental cost per unit were economically justified? Explain.

16-18 LIFE-CYCLE ASSESSMENT

LO3 Thomas Manufacturing produces automobile components used in automobile assembly. One of its divisions manufactures automotive front-end pieces. The division is currently considering two different designs: one using galvanized steel and the other using

Spreadsheet

a polymer composite. Both products are considered equally durable. The main issue being considered is the environmental effects of the designs. To help in this assessment, an inventory analysis and associated cost information for the two designs are as follows:

	Polymer	Galvanized Steel
Materials:		
Virgin materials (pounds)	8	14
Reused production scrap (pounds)	1	6
Energy:		
During production (kilowatts/pound)	15	10
During product use (pounds of petroleum used per year per unit)	66	110
Contaminants:		
Gaseous residues (pounds per unit)	0.4	0.2
Solid residues (pounds per unit)	0.6	2.0
Recycle potential:		
Incineration (pounds)	7.0	—
Quantity to landfill (pounds)	1.0	0.5
Recycled (pounds)	—	8.5
Financial information:		
Cost per pound of materials	$ 30.00	$ 15.00
Cost per kilowatt-hour 0.50	0.50	0.50
Cost per pound of petroleum	0.70	0.70
Cost per pound of gaseous residue	100.00	100.00
Cost per pound of solid residue	40.00	50.00
Incineration benefits per unit	2.00	—
Recycle benefits per unit	—	20.00

Required:

1. Using the operational measures, assess the environmental impact of each design. What other information would be useful?
2. Using the financial information, calculate an environmental life-cycle cost per unit. Discuss the strengths and weaknesses of this information.
3. Explain why a manager might wish to include product use and disposal information in the assessment of environmental performance. After all, these costs are not incurred by the company. For example, the petroleum consumption per year is a cost incurred by the end user.
4. Based on all the information, what recommendation would you make?

16-19   ENVIRONMENTAL RESPONSIBILITY ACCOUNTING, BALANCED SCORECARD

LO4   Carol Thayn, president of Milton, Inc., a consumer products firm, has decided to follow an environmental improvement strategy. The goal is to increase profits by increasing revenues and decreasing environmental costs. Carol is convinced that revenues could be increased if she could improve the company's environmental image. Customers have been demanding cleaner products, and her marketing manager had indicated that producing "greener" products would definitely lead to an increase in market share. Furthermore, Carol had recently returned from an environmental management seminar where she had learned about ecoefficiency. She now believes that costs could be reduced while simultaneously improving environmental performance. She has two objectives in mind: Reduce packaging and reduce production and release of contaminating residues. Carol has decided on the following actions to achieve the desired improvements:

1. Hire two environmental engineers to provide the capabilities needed to improve environmental performance. One engineer would be responsible for a new packaging design and reduction process. The other would be given responsibility to redesign products and processes with the objective of reducing the production of residues. Carol expected the actions to reduce packaging costs and pollution control costs.
2. All employees would be sent to several training seminars to learn about environmental management. They would then be empowered to make improvements in environmental performance (e.g., ways to reduce contaminants and packaging materials).
3. Once the processes and products were redesigned, she would participate in a third-party environmental certification program so that customers would be assured that the environmental improvements were valid.

Required:

1. Explain why adding an environmental perspective to the Balanced Scorecard is considered to be legitimate.
2. Express the environmental improvement strategy as a series of cause-and-effect relationships expressed as if-then statements.
3. Illustrate the strategy using a causal flow diagram with one important modification: add an environmental perspective (the flow diagram should then illustrate five perspectives). Place the environmental perspective in between the customer and process perspectives.

16-20   COLLABORATIVE LEARNING EXERCISE

LO1, LO4 During the past four years, Monticello Company has made significant efforts to improve its environmental performance. Two of the strategic objectives that have received considerable attention are those of minimizing hazardous materials and minimizing release of liquid residues. Actually, two objectives are associated with hazardous waste. First, the company wants to reduce the amount produced. Second, the company wants to shift the ways of dealing with hazardous waste from landfill and deep well injections to such methods as incineration, treatment, and recycling. Lori Anders, president of Monticello, also required the accounting department to track and report on environmental progress. Internal and external environmental progress reports are prepared. The following data pertain to the two strategic objectives that have been emphasized.

Hazardous waste objective (measure is in tons):

Year	Incinerated	Treated	Recycled	Landfilled	Injection	Total
2004	2,000	2,000	1,000	35,000	10,000	50,000
2005	4,000	2,000	2,000	30,000	10,000	48,000
2006	8,000	3,000	3,000	25,000	7,000	46,000
2007	15,000	3,000	3,500	15,000	3,500	40,000

Liquid residue objective:

Year	Tons of Sulfates
2004	100
2005	92
2006	81
2007	73

The cost of landfilling hazardous waste is $50 per ton; injection is $60 per ton; incineration is $70 per ton; treatment is $100 per ton; and recycling produces a benefit of $10 per ton. Recycling, however, can be done only for a certain type of hazardous waste and only with a 70 percent successful yield. Treatment is also limited to certain types of waste. Fines, pollution control equipment, and expected cleanup costs are $4,000 per ton for the liquid residues.

Required:

Form groups of three to five members, where the total number of groups is at least four. Assign the letters A through D to each group. Groups with the A designation will solve Requirement 1, B will solve Requirement 2, C will solve Requirement 3, and D will solve Requirement 4. The groups will then share their answers with the other groups.

1. Prepare a bar graph for hazardous waste that shows trends. Comment on the progress revealed.
2. Prepare a pie chart for hazardous waste for the years 2004 and 2007. Comment on the progress in reducing reliance on landfills and injections.
3. Prepare a bar graph for the liquid residue.
4. Calculate the environmental cost for hazardous waste and liquid residue in 2004 and 2007. Comment on environmental progress as measured by the financial outcomes. Is it possible that the savings are understated? Explain.

16-21 CYBER RESEARCH CASE

LO1, LO2,
LO3, LO4

Many companies are now preparing corporate sustainability reports. Many such reports are found at http://www.sustainability-reports.com. Other reports can be found at the Web sites of individual companies. For example, **Baxter** and **3M** voluntarily prepare and publish reports on health, safety, and the environment. In 2000, Baxter expanded its environmental reporting to include a report on sustainability reporting. 3M has indicated that it intends to change its environmental reporting to better reflect the three elements of sustainability: environmental effects, economic effects, and social effects. To this end, 3M gathered data throughout 2001 and issued its first report on sustainability performance in 2003. You can find the reports for these two companies at http://www.3m.com and http://www.baxter.com. Find the environmental reports of three companies, where at least one is a U.S. company. Examine the environmental reports of these three companies, including their reports on sustainability performance. Answer the following questions for each firm.

1. How much has been saved due to environmental actions? Which firm has saved the most?
2. Describe each firm's packaging reduction efforts and the resulting savings. (Savings can be expressed in nonfinancial terms.)
3. Describe each firm's recycling activities—both for their own products as well as the materials they receive from suppliers.
4. What kinds of environmental performance measures are being used by each firm? Can you relate these to the core strategic objectives discussed in the chapter?
5. Evaluate the sustainability performance of each firm. Which do you think is closer to the concept of sustainable development?
6. What reasons do they offer for providing environmental information?
7. How do the environmental reports compare? Which report did you like best? Why?

DECISION MAKING

PART 4

http://hansen.swlearning.com

AFTER STUDYING THIS CHAPTER, YOU SHOULD BE ABLE TO:

1. Determine the number of units that must be sold to break even or to earn a targeted profit.

2. Calculate the amount of revenue required to break even or to earn a targeted profit.

3. Apply cost-volume-profit analysis in a multiple-product setting.

4. Prepare a profit-volume graph and a cost-volume-profit graph, and explain the meaning of each.

5. Explain the impact of risk, uncertainty, and changing variables on cost-volume-profit analysis.

6. Discuss the impact of activity-based costing on cost-volume-profit analysis.

Cost-volume-profit analysis (CVP analysis) is a powerful tool for planning and decision making. Because CVP analysis emphasizes the interrelationships of costs, quantity sold, and price, it brings together all of the financial information of the firm. CVP analysis can be a valuable tool in identifying the extent and magnitude of the economic trouble a company is facing and helping pinpoint the necessary solution. For example, **General Motors**' European division faced losses in the early 2000s. To approach break even, the division acted to reduce production capacity by 15 percent and to slash the number of dealers from 870 to 470.[1] These moves decreased fixed costs and set the stage for projected break even by 2004. At the same time, GM worked to increase the profitability of its North American division by boosting sales rev-

---

1. "GM Europe Chases Elusive Break-Even," *Detroit Free Press News Services*, http://www.auto.com/industry/gme5_20030305.htm as of March 5, 2003.

enues through the introduction of rebates and discounts on new cars and the rollout of new GM products.[2] CVP analysis can address many issues, such as the number of units that must be sold to break even, the impact a given reduction in fixed costs can have on the break-even point, and the impact an increase in price can have on profit. Additionally, CVP analysis allows managers to conduct sensitivity analyses by examining the impact of various price or cost levels on profit.

While this chapter deals with the mechanics and terminology of CVP analysis, your objective in studying CVP analysis is more than to learn the mechanics. You should keep in mind that CVP analysis is an integral part of financial planning and decision making. Every accountant and manager should be thoroughly conversant in its concepts.

The Break-Even Point in Units

OBJECTIVE 1

Determine the number of units that must be sold to break even or to earn a targeted profit.

Since we are interested in how revenues, expenses, and profits behave as volume changes, it is natural to begin by finding the firm's break-even point in units sold. Two frequently used approaches to finding the break-even point in units are the operating income approach and the contribution margin approach. We will first discuss these two approaches to find the **break-even point** (the point of zero profit) and then see how each can be expanded to determine the number of units that must be sold to earn a targeted profit.

The firm's initial decision in implementing a units-sold approach to CVP analysis is the determination of just what a unit is. For manufacturing firms, the answer is obvious. **Procter & Gamble** may define a unit as a bar of Ivory soap. Service firms face a more difficult choice. **Southwest Airlines** may define a unit as a passenger mile or a one-way trip. **Disney**'s Animal Kingdom counts the number of visitor-days. The **Jacksonville Naval Supply Center**, which provides naval, industrial, and general supplies to U.S. Navy ships stationed in northeastern Florida and the Caribbean, defines "productive units" to measure the activities involved in delivering services. In this way, more complicated services are assigned more productive units than are less complicated services, thereby standardizing service efforts.[3]

A second decision centers on the separation of costs into fixed and variable components. CVP analysis focuses on the factors that effect a change in the components of profit. Because we are looking at CVP analysis in terms of units sold, we need to determine the fixed and variable components of cost and revenue with respect to units. (This assumption will be relaxed when we incorporate activity-based costing into CVP analysis.) It is important to realize that we are focusing on the firm as a whole. Therefore, the costs we are talking about are all costs of the company: manufacturing, marketing, and administrative. Thus, when we say variable costs, we mean all costs that increase as more units are sold, including direct materials, direct labor, variable overhead, and variable selling and administrative costs. Similarly, fixed costs include fixed overhead and fixed selling and administrative expenses.

Operating Income Approach

The operating income approach focuses on the income statement as a useful tool in organizing the firm's costs into fixed and variable categories. The income statement can be expressed as a narrative equation:

Operating income = Sales revenues − Variable expenses − Fixed expenses

Note that we are using the term **operating income** to denote income or profit *before* income taxes. Operating income includes only revenues and expenses from the

---

2. Jeffrey McCracken, "GM Expects Sales, Net to Show Gains," *Detroit Free Press*, http://www.freep.com/money/autonews/gm9_20040109.htm as of January 9, 2004.

3. David J. Harr, "How Activity Accounting Works in Government," *Management Accounting* (September 1990): 36–40.

firm's normal operations. We will use the term **net income** to mean operating income minus income taxes.

Once we have a measure of units sold, we can expand the operating income equation by expressing sales revenue and variable expenses in terms of unit dollar amounts and number of units. Specifically, sales revenue is expressed as the unit selling price times the number of units sold, and total variable costs are the unit variable cost times the number of units sold. With these expressions, the operating income statement becomes:

$$\text{Operating income} = (\text{Price} \times \text{Number of units}) - (\text{Variable cost per unit} \times \text{Number of units}) - \text{Total fixed costs}$$

Suppose you were asked how many units must be sold in order to break even, or earn a zero profit. You could answer that question by setting operating income equal to zero and then solving the operating income equation for the number of units.

Let's use the following example to solve for the break-even point in units. Assume that More-Power Company manufactures a variety of power tools. The Topeka plant is devoted to the production of sanders. For the coming year, the controller has prepared the following projected income statement:

Sales (72,500 units @ $40)	$2,900,000
Less: Variable expenses	1,740,000
Contribution margin	$1,160,000
Less: Fixed expenses	800,000
Operating income	$ 360,000

We see that for More-Power Company, the price is $40 per unit, and the variable cost is $24 ($1,740,000/72,500 units). Fixed costs are $800,000. At the break-even point, then, the operating income equation would take the following form:

$$0 = (\$40 \times \text{Units}) - (\$24 \times \text{Units}) - \$800,000$$
$$0 = (\$16 \times \text{Units}) - \$800,000$$
$$\$16 \times \text{Units} = \$800,000$$
$$\text{Units} = 50,000$$

Therefore, More-Power must sell 50,000 sanders just to cover all fixed and variable expenses. A good way to check this answer is to formulate an income statement based on 50,000 units sold.

Sales (50,000 units @ $40)	$2,000,000
Less: Variable expenses	1,200,000
Contribution margin	$ 800,000
Less: Fixed expenses	800,000
Operating income	$ 0

Indeed, selling 50,000 units does yield a zero profit.

An important advantage of the operating income approach is that all further CVP equations are derived from the variable-costing income statement. As a result, you can solve any CVP problem by using this approach.

Contribution Margin Approach

A refinement of the operating income approach is the contribution margin approach. In effect, we are simply recognizing that at break-even, the total contribution margin equals the fixed expenses. The **contribution margin** is sales revenue minus total variable costs. If we substitute the unit contribution margin for price minus unit variable cost in the operating income equation and solve for the number of units, we obtain the following break-even expression:

$$\text{Number of units} = \text{Fixed costs}/\text{Unit contribution margin}$$

Using More-Power Company as an example, we can see that the contribution margin per unit can be computed in one of two ways. One way is to divide the total contribution margin by the units sold for a result of $16 per unit ($1,160,000/72,500). A second way is to compute price minus variable cost per unit. Doing so yields the same result, $16 per unit ($40 − $24). Now, we can use the contribution margin approach to calculate the break-even number of units.

$$\begin{aligned}
\text{Number of units} &= \$800,000/(\$40 - \$24) \\
&= \$800,000/\$16 \text{ per unit} \\
&= 50,000 \text{ units}
\end{aligned}$$

Of course, the answer is identical to that computed using the operating income approach.

Profit Targets

While the break-even point is useful information, most firms would like to earn operating income greater than zero. CVP analysis gives us a way to determine how many units must be sold to earn a particular targeted income. Targeted operating income can be expressed as a dollar amount (e.g., $20,000) or as a percentage of sales revenue (e.g., 15 percent of revenue). Both the operating income approach and the contribution margin approach can be easily adjusted to allow for targeted income.

Targeted Income as a Dollar Amount

Assume that More-Power Company wants to earn operating income of $424,000. How many sanders must be sold to achieve this result? Using the operating income approach, we form the following equation:

$$\begin{aligned}
\$424,000 &= (\$40 \times \text{Units}) - (\$24 \times \text{Units}) - \$800,000 \\
\$1,224,000 &= \$16 \times \text{Units} \\
\text{Units} &= 76,500
\end{aligned}$$

Using the contribution margin approach, we simply *add* targeted profit of $424,000 to the fixed costs and solve for the number of units.

$$\begin{aligned}
\text{Units} &= (\$800,000 + \$424,000)/(\$40 - \$24) \\
&= \$1,224,000/\$16 \\
&= 76,500
\end{aligned}$$

More-Power must sell 76,500 sanders to earn a before-tax profit of $424,000. The following income statement verifies this outcome:

Sales (76,500 units @ $40)	$3,060,000
Less: Variable expenses	1,836,000
Contribution margin	$1,224,000
Less: Fixed expenses	800,000
Income before income taxes	$ 424,000

Another way to check this number of units is to use the break-even point. As was just shown, More-Power must sell 76,500 sanders, or 26,500 more than the break-even volume of 50,000 units, to earn a profit of $424,000. The contribution margin per sander is $16. Multiplying $16 by the 26,500 sanders *above* break-even produces the profit of $424,000 ($16 × 26,500). This outcome demonstrates that contribution margin per unit for each unit above break-even is equivalent to profit per unit. Since the break-even point had already been computed, the number of sanders to be sold to yield a $424,000 operating income could have been calculated by dividing the unit contribution margin into the target profit and adding the resulting amount to the break-even volume.

In general, assuming that fixed costs remain the same, the impact on a firm's profits resulting from a change in the number of units sold can be assessed by multiplying the unit contribution margin by the change in units sold. For example, if 80,000 sanders instead of 76,500 are sold, how much *more* profit will be earned? The change in units sold is an increase of 3,500 sanders, and the unit contribution margin is $16. Thus, profits will increase by $56,000 ($16 × 3,500).

Targeted Income as a Percent of Sales Revenue

Assume that More-Power Company wants to know the number of sanders that must be sold in order to earn a profit equal to 15 percent of sales revenue. Sales revenue is selling price multiplied by the quantity sold. Thus, the targeted operating income is 15 percent of selling price times quantity. Using the operating income approach (which is simpler in this case), we obtain the following:

$$0.15(\$40)(\text{Units}) = (\$40 \times \text{Units}) - (\$24 \times \text{Units}) - \$800,000$$
$$\$6 \times \text{Units} = (\$40 \times \text{Units}) - (\$24 \times \text{Units}) - \$800,000$$
$$\$6 \times \text{Units} = (\$16 \times \text{Units}) - \$800,000$$
$$\$10 \times \text{Units} = \$800,000$$
$$\text{Units} = 80,000$$

Does a volume of 80,000 sanders achieve a profit equal to 15 percent of sales revenue? For 80,000 sanders, the total revenue is $3.2 million ($40 × 80,000). The profit can be computed without preparing a formal income statement. Remember that above break-even, the contribution margin per unit is the profit per unit. The break-even volume is 50,000 sanders. If 80,000 sanders are sold, then 30,000 (80,000 − 50,000) sanders above the break-even point are sold. The before-tax profit, therefore, is $480,000 ($16 × 30,000), which is 15 percent of sales ($480,000/$3,200,000).

After-Tax Profit Targets

When calculating the break-even point, income taxes play no role. This is because the taxes paid on zero income are zero. However, when the company needs to know how many units to sell to earn a particular net income, some additional consideration is needed. Recall that net income is operating income after income taxes and that our targeted income figure was expressed in before-tax terms. As a result, when the income target is expressed as net income, we must add back the income taxes to get operating income. Therefore, to use either approach, the after-tax profit target must first be converted to a before-tax profit target.

In general, taxes are computed as a percentage of income. The after-tax profit is computed by subtracting the tax from the operating income (or before-tax profit).

$$\begin{aligned} \text{Net income} &= \text{Operating income} - \text{Income taxes} \\ &= \text{Operating income} - (\text{Tax rate} \times \text{Operating income}) \\ &= \text{Operating income}(1 - \text{Tax rate}) \end{aligned}$$

or

$$\text{Operating income} = \text{Net income}/(1 - \text{Tax rate})$$

Thus, to convert the after-tax profit to before-tax profit, simply divide the after-tax profit by the quantity (1 − Tax rate).

Suppose that More-Power Company wants to achieve net income of $487,500 and its income tax rate is 35 percent. To convert the after-tax profit target into a before-tax profit target, complete the following steps:

$$\$487,500 = \text{Operating income} - 0.35(\text{Operating income})$$
$$\$487,500 = 0.65(\text{Operating income})$$
$$\$750,000 = \text{Operating income}$$

In other words, with an income tax rate of 35 percent, More-Power Company must earn $750,000 before income taxes to have $487,500 after income taxes.[4] With this conversion, we can now calculate the number of units that must be sold.

$$\text{Units} = (\$800,000 + \$750,000)/\$16$$
$$= \$1,550,000/\$16$$
$$= 96,875$$

Let's check this answer by preparing an income statement based on sales of 96,875 sanders.

Sales (96,875 @ $40)	$3,875,000
Less: Variable expenses	2,325,000
Contribution margin	$1,550,000
Less: Fixed expenses	800,000
Income before income taxes	$ 750,000
Less: Income taxes (35% tax rate)	262,500
Net income	$ 487,500

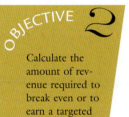

OBJECTIVE 2

Calculate the amount of revenue required to break even or to earn a targeted profit.

Break-Even Point in Sales Dollars

In some cases when using CVP analysis, managers may prefer to use sales revenue as the measure of sales activity instead of units sold. A units-sold measure can be converted to a sales-revenue measure simply by multiplying the unit sales price by the units sold. For example, the break-even point for More-Power Company was computed to be 50,000 sanders. Since the selling price for each sander is $40, the break-even volume in sales revenue is $2,000,000 ($40 × 50,000). Any answer expressed in units sold can be easily converted to one expressed in sales revenue, but the answer can be computed more directly by developing a separate formula for the sales-revenue case. In this case, the important variable is sales dollars, so both the revenue and the variable costs must be expressed in dollars instead of units. Since sales revenue is always expressed in dollars, measuring that variable is no problem. Let's look more closely at variable costs and see how they can be expressed in terms of sales dollars.

To calculate the break-even point in sales dollars, variable costs are defined as a percentage of sales rather than as an amount per unit sold. Exhibit 17-1 illustrates the division of sales revenue into variable cost and contribution margin. In this exhibit, price is $10, and variable cost is $6. Of course, the remainder is contribution margin of $4 ($10 − $6). Focusing on 10 units sold, total variable costs are $60 ($6 × 10 units sold). Alternatively, since each unit sold earns $10 of revenue, we would say that for every $10 of revenue earned, $6 of variable costs are incurred, or, equivalently, that 60 percent of each dollar of revenue earned is attributable to variable cost ($6/$10). Thus, focusing on sales revenue, we would expect total variable costs of $60 for revenues of $100 (0.60 × $100).

In expressing variable cost in terms of sales dollars, we computed the **variable cost ratio**. It is simply the proportion of each sales dollar that must be used to cover variable costs. The variable cost ratio can be computed by using either total data or unit data. Of course, the percentage of sales dollars remaining after variable costs are covered is the contribution margin ratio. The **contribution margin ratio** is the proportion of each sales dollar available to cover fixed costs and provide for profit. In Exhibit 17-1, if the variable cost ratio is 60 percent of sales, then the contribution margin must be the remaining 40 percent of sales. It makes sense that the complement of the variable cost ratio is the contribution margin ratio. After all, the proportion

---

4. To practice the after-tax to before-tax conversion, calculate how much before-tax income More-Power would need to have $487,500 in after-tax income if the tax rate were 40 percent. [Answer: $812,500]

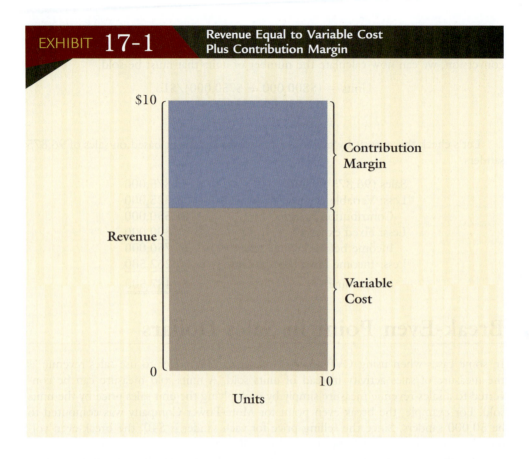

EXHIBIT 17-1   Revenue Equal to Variable Cost Plus Contribution Margin

of the sales dollars left after variable costs are covered should be the contribution margin component.

Just as the variable cost ratio can be computed using total or unit figures, the contribution margin ratio (40 percent in our exhibit) can also be computed in these two ways. That is, one can divide the total contribution margin by total sales ($40/$100), or one can use unit contribution margin divided by price ($4/$10). Naturally, if the variable cost ratio is known, it can be subtracted from one to yield the contribution margin ratio ($1 - 0.60 = 0.40$).

Where do fixed costs fit into this? Since the contribution margin is revenue remaining after variable costs are covered, it must be the revenue available to cover fixed costs and contribute to profit. Exhibit 17-2 uses the same price and variable cost data from Exhibit 17-1 to show the impact of fixed costs on profit. Panel A of Exhibit 17-2 shows the amount of fixed costs equal to the contribution margin. Of course, profit is zero. (The company is at break-even.) Panel B shows fixed costs less than the contribution margin. In this case, the company earns a profit. Finally, Panel C shows fixed costs greater than the contribution margin. Here, the company faces an operating loss.

Now, let's turn to a couple of examples based on More-Power Company to illustrate the **sales-revenue approach**. Restated below is More-Power Company's variable-costing income statement for 72,500 sanders.

	Dollars	Percent of Sales
Sales	$2,900,000	100%
Less: Variable costs	1,740,000	60
Contribution margin	$1,160,000	40%
Less: Fixed costs	800,000	
Operating income	$ 360,000	

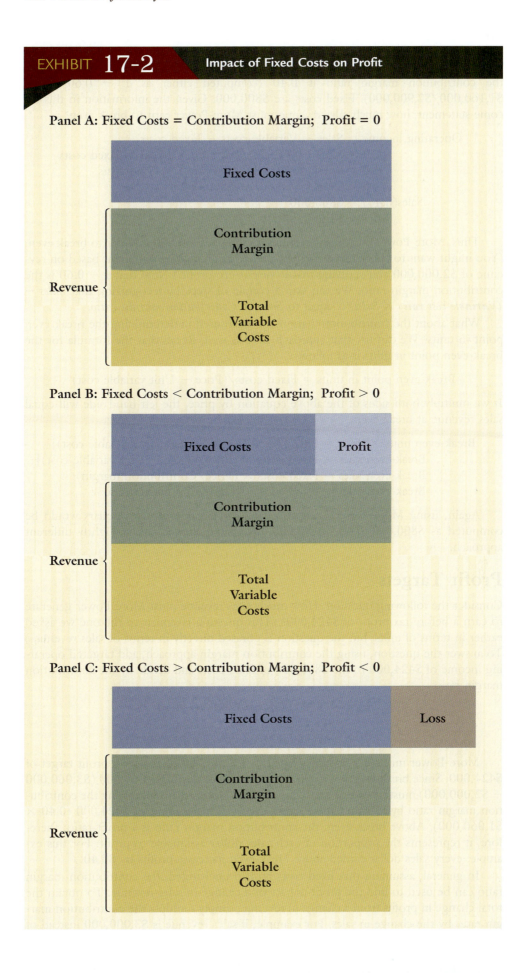

EXHIBIT 17-2   Impact of Fixed Costs on Profit

Notice that sales revenue, variable costs, and contribution margin have been expressed in the form of percent of sales. The variable cost ratio is 0.60 ($1,740,000/$2,900,000); the contribution margin ratio is 0.40 (computed either as 1 − 0.60 or as $1,160,000/$2,900,000). Fixed costs are $800,000. Given the information in this income statement, how much sales revenue must More-Power earn to break even?

$$\text{Operating income} = \text{Sales} - \text{Variable costs} - \text{Fixed costs}$$
$$0 = \text{Sales} - (\text{Variable cost ratio} \times \text{Sales}) - \text{Fixed costs}$$
$$0 = \text{Sales}(1 - \text{Variable cost ratio}) - \text{Fixed costs}$$
$$0 = \text{Sales}(1 - 0.60) - \$800,000$$
$$\text{Sales}(0.40) = \$800,000$$
$$\text{Sales} = \$2,000,000$$

Thus, More-Power must earn revenues totaling $2,000,000 in order to break even. (You might want to check this answer by preparing an income statement based on revenue of $2,000,000 and verifying that it yields zero profit.) Note that 1 − 0.60 is the contribution margin ratio. We can skip a couple of steps by recognizing that *Sales − (Variable cost ratio × Sales)* is equal to *Sales × Contribution margin ratio*.

What about the contribution margin approach used in determining the break-even point in units? We can use that approach here as well. Recall that the formula for the break-even point in units is as follows:

$$\text{Break-even point in units} = \text{Fixed costs}/(\text{Price} - \text{Unit variable cost})$$

If we multiply both sides of the above equation by price, the left-hand side will equal sales revenue at break-even.

$$\text{Break-even units} \times \text{Price} = \text{Price}[\text{Fixed costs}/(\text{Price} - \text{Unit variable cost})]$$
$$\text{Break-even sales} = \text{Fixed costs} \times [\text{Price}/(\text{Price} - \text{Unit variable cost})]$$
$$\text{Break-even sales} = \text{Fixed costs} \times (\text{Price}/\text{Contribution margin})$$
$$\text{Break-even sales} = \text{Fixed costs}/\text{Contribution margin ratio}$$

Again, using More-Power Company data, the break-even sales dollars would be computed as $800,000/0.40, or $2,000,000. Same answer, just a slightly different approach.

Profit Targets

Consider the following question: How much sales revenue must More-Power generate to earn a before-tax profit of $424,000? (This question is similar to the one we asked earlier in terms of units, but the question is phrased directly in terms of sales revenue.) To answer the question, using the contribution margin approach, add targeted operating income of $424,000 to the $800,000 of fixed costs and divide by the contribution margin ratio.

$$\text{Sales} = (\$800,000 + \$424,000)/0.40$$
$$= \$1,224,000/0.40$$
$$= \$3,060,000$$

More-Power must earn revenues equal to $3,060,000 to achieve a profit target of $424,000. Since break-even is $2,000,000, additional sales of $1,060,000 ($3,060,000 − $2,000,000) must be earned above break-even. Notice that multiplying the contribution margin ratio by revenues above break-even yields the profit of $424,000 (0.40 × $1,060,000). Above break-even, the contribution margin ratio is a profit ratio; therefore, it represents the proportion of each sales dollar assignable to profit. For this example, every sales dollar earned above break-even increases profits by $0.40.

In general, assuming that fixed costs remain unchanged, the contribution margin ratio can be used to find the profit impact of a change in sales revenue. To obtain the total change in profits from a change in revenue, simply multiply the contribution margin ratio by the change in sales. For example, if sales revenue is $3,000,000 instead of

$3,060,000, how will the expected profits be affected? A decrease in sales revenue of $60,000 will cause a decrease in profits of $24,000 (0.40 × $60,000).

Comparison of the Two Approaches

For a single-product setting, converting the break-even point in units answer to a sales-revenue answer is simply a matter of multiplying the unit sales price by the units sold. Then why bother with a separate formula for the sales-revenue approach? For a single-product setting, neither approach has any real advantage over the other. Both offer much the same level of conceptual and computational difficulty.

However, in a multiple-product setting, CVP analysis is more complex, and the sales-revenue approach is significantly easier. This approach maintains essentially the same computational requirements found in the single-product setting, whereas the units-sold approach becomes more difficult. Even though the conceptual complexity of CVP analysis does increase with multiple products, the operation is reasonably straightforward.

OBJECTIVE 3

Apply cost-volume-profit analysis in a multiple-product setting.

Multiple-Product Analysis

More-Power Company has decided to offer two models of sanders: a regular sander to sell for $40 and a mini-sander, with an assortment of drill-like tips that will fit into tight corners and grooves, to sell for $60. The marketing department is convinced that 75,000 regular sanders and 30,000 mini-sanders can be sold during the coming year. The controller has prepared the following projected income statement based on the sales forecast:

	Regular Sander	Mini-Sander	Total
Sales	$3,000,000	$1,800,000	$4,800,000
Less: Variable expenses	1,800,000	900,000	2,700,000
Contribution margin	$1,200,000	$ 900,000	$2,100,000
Less: Direct fixed expenses	250,000	450,000	700,000
Product margin	$ 950,000	$ 450,000	$1,400,000
Less: Common fixed expenses			600,000
Operating income			$ 800,000

Note that the controller has separated direct fixed expenses from common fixed expenses. The **direct fixed expenses** are those fixed costs which can be traced to each segment and would be avoided if the segment did not exist. The **common fixed expenses** are the fixed costs that are not traceable to the segments and that would remain even if one of the segments was eliminated.

Break-Even Point in Units

The owner of More-Power is somewhat apprehensive about adding a new product line and wants to know how many of each model must be sold to break even. If you were given the responsibility to answer this question, how would you respond?

One possible response is to use the equation we developed earlier in which fixed costs were divided by the contribution margin. This equation presents some immediate problems, however. It was developed for a single-product analysis. For two products, there are two unit contribution margins. The regular sander has a contribution margin per unit of $16 ($40 − $24), and the mini-sander has one of $30 ($60 − $30).[5]

---

5. The variable cost per unit is derived from the income statement. For the mini-sander, total variable costs are $900,000 based on sales of 30,000 units. This yields a per-unit variable cost of $30 ($900,000/30,000). A similar computation produces the per-unit variable cost for the regular sander.

One possible solution is to apply the analysis separately to each product line. It is possible to obtain individual break-even points when income is defined as product margin. Break-even for the regular sander is as follows:

Regular sander break-even units
= Fixed costs/(Price − Unit variable cost)
= $250,000/$16
= 15,625 units

Break-even for the mini-sander can be computed as well.

Mini-sander break-even units
= Fixed costs/(Price − Unit variable cost)
= $450,000/$30
= 15,000 units

Thus, 15,625 regular sanders and 15,000 mini-sanders must be sold to achieve a break-even product margin. But a break-even product margin covers only direct fixed costs; the common fixed costs remain to be covered. Selling these numbers of sanders would result in a loss equal to the common fixed costs. No break-even point for the firm as a whole has yet been identified. Somehow, the common fixed costs must be factored into the analysis.

Allocating the common fixed costs to each product line before computing a break-even point may resolve this difficulty. The problem with this approach is that allocation of the common fixed costs is arbitrary. Thus, no meaningful break-even volume is readily apparent.

Another possible solution is to convert the multiple-product problem into a single-product problem. If this can be done, then all of the single-product CVP methodology can be applied directly. The key to this conversion is to identify the expected sales mix, in units, of the products being marketed.

Sales Mix

Sales mix is the relative combination of products being sold by a firm. Sales mix can be measured in units sold or in proportion of revenue. For example, if More-Power plans on selling 75,000 regular sanders and 30,000 mini-sanders, then the sales mix in units is 75,000:30,000. Usually, the sales mix is reduced to the smallest possible whole numbers. Thus, the relative mix 75,000:30,000 can be reduced to 75:30 and further to 5:2. That is, for every five regular sanders sold, two mini-sanders are sold.

Alternatively, the sales mix can be represented by the percent of total revenue contributed by each product. In that case, the regular sander revenue is $3,000,000 ($40 × 75,000), and the mini-sander revenue is $1,800,000 ($60 × 30,000). The regular sander accounts for 62.5 percent of total revenue, and the mini-sander accounts for the remaining 37.5 percent. It may seem as though the two sales mixes are different. The sales mix in units is 5:2; that is, of every five sanders sold, about 71 percent are regular sanders and about 29 percent are mini-sanders. However, the revenue-based sales mix is 62.5 percent for the regular sanders. There is really no difference. The sales mix in revenue takes the sales mix in units and weights it by price. Therefore, even though the underlying proportion of sanders sold remains 5:2, the lower priced regular sanders are weighted less heavily when price is factored in. In the remaining discussion, we will use the sales mix expressed in units.

A number of different sales mixes can be used to define the break-even volume. For example, a sales mix of 2:1 will define a break-even point of 41,935 regular sanders and 20,968 mini-sanders. The total contribution margin produced by this mix is $1,300,000 [($16 × 41,935) + ($30 × 20,968)]. Similarly, if 28,261 regular sanders and 28,261 mini-sanders are sold (corresponding to a 1:1 sales mix), the total contribution margin is also $1,300,000[6] [($16 × 28,261) + ($30 × 28,261)]. Since total

---

6. Actually, the contribution margin is $1,300,006 due to rounding.

fixed costs are $1,300,000, both sales mixes define break-even points. Fortunately, every sales mix need not be considered. Can More-Power really expect a sales mix of 2:1 or 1:1? For every two regular sanders sold, does More-Power expect to sell a mini-sander? Or for every regular sander, can More-Power really sell one mini-sander?

According to More-Power's marketing study, a sales mix of 5:2 can be expected. This is the ratio that should be used; the others can be ignored. The sales mix that is expected to prevail should be used for CVP analysis.

Sales Mix and CVP Analysis

Defining a particular sales mix allows us to convert a multiple-product problem to a single-product CVP format. Since More-Power expects to sell five regular sanders for every two mini-sanders, it can define the single product it sells as a package containing five regular sanders and two mini-sanders. By defining the product as a package, the multiple-product problem is converted into a single-product one. To use the break-even-point-in-units approach, the package selling price and variable cost per package must be known. To compute these package values, the sales mix, the individual product prices, and the individual variable costs are needed. Given the individual product data found on the projected income statement, the package values can be computed as follows:

Product	Price	Unit Variable Cost	Unit Contribution Margin	Sales Mix	Package Unit Contribution Margin
Regular sander	$40	$24	$16	5	$ 80[a]
Mini-sander	60	30	30	2	60[b]
Package total					$140

[a]Found by multiplying the number of units in the package (5) by the unit contribution margin ($16).
[b]Found by multiplying the number of units in the package (2) by the unit contribution margin ($30).

Given the package contribution margin, the single-product CVP equation can be used to determine the number of packages that need to be sold to break even. From More-Power's projected income statement, we know that the total fixed costs for the company are $1,300,000. Thus, the break-even point is computed as follows:

$$\text{Break-even point} = \text{Fixed cost/Package contribution margin}$$
$$= \$1,300,000/\$140$$
$$= 9,285.71 \text{ packages}$$

More-Power must sell 46,429 regular sanders (5 × 9,285.71) and 18,571 mini-sanders (2 × 9,285.71) to break even. (Notice that the packages are not rounded off to a whole number. This is because the number of packages is not an end in itself. The decimal amount may be important when it is multiplied by the sales mix. However, it is important to round the number of sanders to whole units, since no one will buy a fraction of a sander.) An income statement verifying this solution is presented in Exhibit 17-3 on the following page.

For a given sales mix, CVP analysis can be used as if the firm were selling a single product. However, actions that change the prices of individual products can affect the sales mix because consumers may buy relatively more or less of the product. Accordingly, pricing decisions may involve a new sales mix and must reflect this possibility. Keep in mind that a new sales mix will affect the units of each product that need to be sold in order to achieve a desired profit target. If the sales mix for the coming period is uncertain, it may be necessary to look at several different mixes. In this way, a manager can gain some insight into the possible outcomes facing the firm.

The complexity of the break-even-point-in-units approach increases dramatically as the number of products increases. Imagine performing this analysis for a firm with

EXHIBIT 17-3	Income Statement: Break-Even Solution		
	Regular Sander	**Mini-Sander**	**Total**
Sales	$1,857,160	$1,114,260	$2,971,420
Less: Variable expenses	1,114,296	557,130	1,671,426
Contribution margin	$ 742,864	$ 557,130	$1,299,994
Less: Direct fixed expenses	250,000	450,000	700,000
Product margin	$ 492,864	$ 107,130	$ 599,994
Less: Common fixed expenses			600,000
Operating income*			$ (6)

*Operating income is not exactly equal to zero due to rounding.

several hundred products. This observation seems more overwhelming than it actually is. Computers can easily handle a problem with so much data. Furthermore, many firms simplify the problem by analyzing product groups rather than individual products. Another way to handle the increased complexity is to switch from the units-sold to the sales-revenue approach. This approach can accomplish a multiple-product CVP analysis using only the summary data found in an organization's income statement. The computational requirements are much simpler.

Sales Dollars Approach

To illustrate the break-even point in sales dollars, the same examples will be used. However, the only information needed is the projected income statement for More-Power Company as a whole.

Sales	$4,800,000
Less: Variable costs	2,700,000
Contribution margin	$2,100,000
Less: Fixed costs	1,300,000
Operating income	$ 800,000

Notice that this income statement corresponds to the total column of the more detailed income statement examined previously. The projected income statement rests on the assumption that 75,000 regular sanders and 30,000 mini-sanders will be sold (a 5:2 sales mix). The break-even point in sales revenue also rests on the expected sales mix. (As with the units-sold approach, a different sales mix will produce different results.)

With the income statement, the usual CVP questions can be addressed. For example, how much sales revenue must be earned to break even? To answer this question, we divide the total fixed costs of $1,300,000 by the contribution margin ratio of 0.4375 ($2,100,000/$4,800,000).

Break-even sales = Fixed costs/Contribution margin ratio
= $1,300,000/0.4375
= $2,971,429

The break-even point in sales dollars implicitly uses the assumed sales mix but avoids the requirement of building a package contribution margin. No knowledge of individual product data is needed. The computational effort is similar to that used in the single-product setting. Moreover, the answer is still expressed in sales revenue. Unlike the break-even point in units, the answer to CVP questions using sales dollars is still expressed in a single summary measure. The sales-revenue approach, however, does sacrifice information concerning individual product performance.

OBJECTIVE 4

Prepare a profit-volume graph and a cost-volume-profit graph, and explain the meaning of each.

Graphical Representation of CVP Relationships

Visual portrayals may further our understanding of CVP relationships. A graphical representation can help managers see the difference between variable cost and revenue. It may also help managers understand quickly what impact an increase or decrease in sales will have on the break-even point. Two basic graphs, the profit-volume graph and the cost-volume-profit graph, are presented here.

The Profit-Volume Graph

A **profit-volume graph** visually portrays the relationship between profits and sales volume. The profit-volume graph is the graph of the operating income equation [Operating income = (Price × Units) − (Unit variable cost × Units) − Fixed costs]. In this graph, operating income (profit) is the dependent variable, and units is the independent variable. Usually, values of the independent variable are measured along the horizontal axis and values of the dependent variable along the vertical axis.

To make this discussion more concrete, a simple set of data will be used. Assume that Tyson Company produces a single product with the following cost and price data:

Total fixed costs	$100
Variable cost per unit	5
Selling price per unit	10

Using these data, operating income can be expressed as follows:

$$\text{Operating income} = (\$10 \times \text{Units}) - (\$5 \times \text{Units}) - \$100$$
$$= (\$5 \times \text{Units}) - \$100$$

We can graph this relationship by plotting units along the horizontal axis and operating income (or loss) along the vertical axis. Two points are needed to graph a linear equation. While any two points will do, the two points often chosen are those that correspond to zero sales volume and zero profits. When units sold are zero, Tyson experiences an operating loss of $100 (or a profit of −$100). The point corresponding to zero sales volume, therefore, is (0, −$100). In other words, when no sales take place, the company suffers a loss equal to its total fixed costs. When operating income is zero, the units sold are equal to 20. The point corresponding to zero profits (break-even) is (20, $0). These two points, plotted in Exhibit 17-4 on the following page, define the profit graph shown in the same figure.

The graph in Exhibit 17-4 can be used to assess Tyson's profit (or loss) at any level of sales activity. For example, the profit associated with the sale of 40 units can be read from the graph by (1) drawing a vertical line from the horizontal axis to the profit line and (2) drawing a horizontal line from the profit line to the vertical axis. As illustrated in Exhibit 17-4, the profit associated with sales of 40 units is $100. The profit-volume graph, while easy to interpret, fails to reveal how costs change as sales volume changes. An alternative approach to graphing can provide this detail.

The Cost-Volume-Profit Graph

The **cost-volume-profit graph** depicts the relationships among cost, volume, and profits. To obtain the more detailed relationships, it is necessary to graph two separate lines:

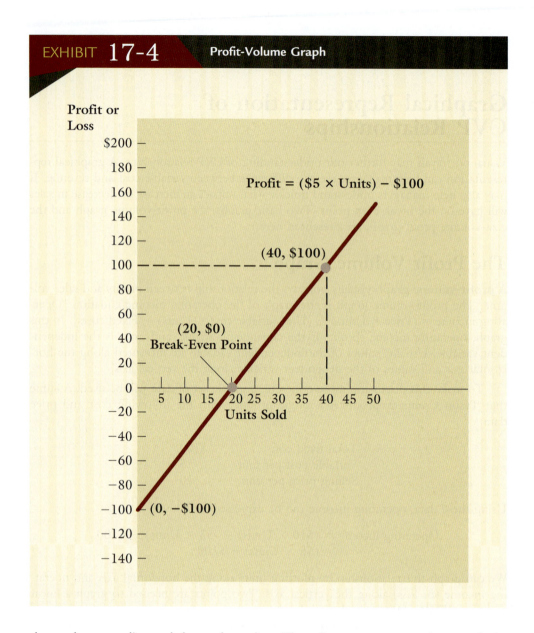

EXHIBIT 17-4   **Profit-Volume Graph**

Profit or Loss

Profit = ($5 × Units) − $100

(40, $100)

(20, $0)
Break-Even Point

Units Sold

(0, −$100)

the total revenue line and the total cost line. These lines are represented, respectively, by the following two equations:

$$\text{Revenue} = \text{Price} \times \text{Units}$$
$$\text{Total cost} = (\text{Unit variable cost} \times \text{Units}) + \text{Fixed costs}$$

Using the Tyson Company example, the revenue and cost equations are as follows:

$$\text{Revenue} = \$10 \times \text{Units}$$
$$\text{Total cost} = (\$5 \times \text{Units}) + \$100$$

To portray both equations in the same graph, the vertical axis is measured in dollars and the horizontal axis in units sold.

Two points are needed to graph each equation. We will use the same x-coordinates used for the profit-volume graph. For the revenue equation, setting number of units equal to zero results in revenue of $0; setting number of units equal to 20 results in revenue of $200. Therefore, the two points for the revenue equation are (0, $0) and (20, $200). For the cost equation, units sold of zero and units sold equal to 20 produce the points (0, $100) and (20, $200). The graphs of both equations appear in Exhibit 17-5.

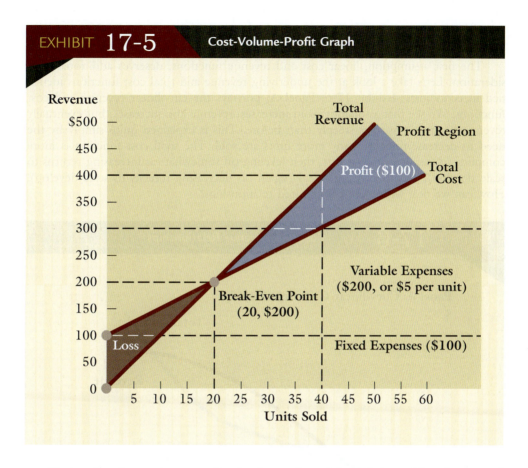

EXHIBIT 17-5   **Cost-Volume-Profit Graph**

Notice that the total revenue line begins at the origin and rises with a slope equal to the selling price per unit (a slope of 10). The total cost line intercepts the vertical axis at a point equal to total fixed costs and rises with a slope equal to the variable cost per unit (a slope of 5). When the total revenue line lies below the total cost line, a loss region is defined. Similarly, when the total revenue line lies above the total cost line, a profit region is defined. The point where the total revenue line and the total cost line intersect is the break-even point. To break even, Tyson Company must sell 20 units and thus receive $200 in total revenues.

Now, let's compare the information available from the CVP graph to that available from the profit-volume graph. To do so, consider the sale of 40 units. Recall that the profit-volume graph revealed that selling 40 units produced profits of $100. Examine Exhibit 17-5 again. The CVP graph also shows profits of $100, but it reveals more than that. The CVP graph discloses that total revenues of $400 and total costs of $300 are associated with the sale of 40 units. Furthermore, the total costs can be broken down into fixed costs of $100 and variable costs of $200. The CVP graph provides revenue and cost information not provided by the profit-volume graph. Unlike the profit-volume graph, some computation is needed to determine the profit associated with a given sales volume. Nonetheless, because of the greater information content, managers are likely to find the CVP graph a more useful tool.

Assumptions of Cost-Volume-Profit Analysis

The profit-volume and cost-volume-profit graphs just illustrated rely on some important assumptions. Some of these assumptions are as follows:

1. The analysis assumes a linear revenue function and a linear cost function.
2. The analysis assumes that price, total fixed costs, and unit variable costs can be accurately identified and remain constant over the relevant range.
3. The analysis assumes that what is produced is sold.

4. For multiple-product analysis, the sales mix is assumed to be known.
5. The selling prices and costs are assumed to be known with certainty.

The first assumption, linear cost and revenue functions, deserves additional consideration. Let's take a look at the underlying revenue and total cost functions identified in economics. Exhibit 17-6, Panel A, portrays the curvilinear revenue and cost functions. We see that as quantity sold increases, revenue also increases, but eventually revenue begins to rise less steeply than before. This is explained quite simply by the need to decrease price as many more units are sold. The total cost function is more complicated, rising steeply at first, then leveling off somewhat (as increasing returns to scale develop), and then rising steeply again (as decreasing returns to scale develop). How can we deal with these complicated relationships?

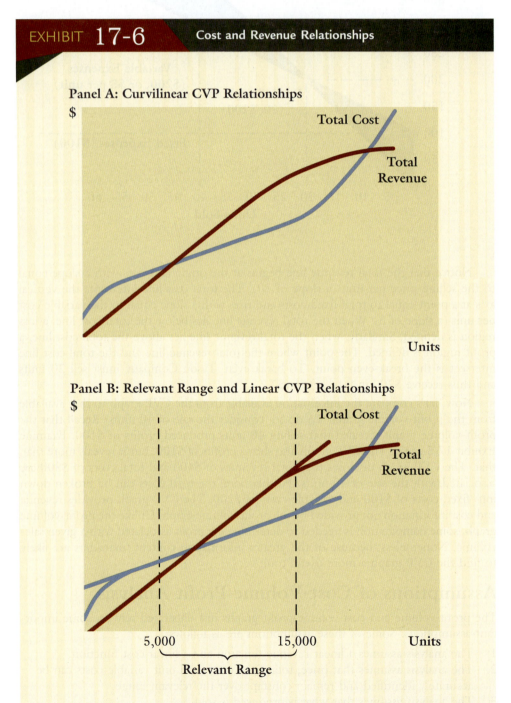

EXHIBIT 17-6   **Cost and Revenue Relationships**

Panel A: Curvilinear CVP Relationships

$

Total Cost

Total
Revenue

Units

Panel B: Relevant Range and Linear CVP Relationships

$

Total Cost

Total
Revenue

5,000   15,000   Units

Relevant Range

Relevant Range

Fortunately, we do not need to consider all possible ranges of production and sales for a firm. Remember that CVP analysis is a short-run decision-making tool. (We know that it is short run in orientation because some costs are fixed.) It is only necessary for us to determine the current operating range, or **relevant range**, for which the linear cost and revenue relationships are valid. Exhibit 17-6, Panel B, illustrates a relevant range from 5,000 to 15,000 units. Note that the cost and revenue relationships are roughly linear in this range, allowing us to use our linear CVP equations. Of course, if the relevant range changes, different fixed and variable costs and different prices must be used.

The second assumption is linked to the definition of relevant range. Once a relevant range has been identified, then the cost and price relationships are assumed to be known and constant.

Production Equal to Sales

The third assumption is that what is produced is sold. There is no change in inventory over the period. The fact that inventory has no impact on break-even analysis makes sense. Break-even analysis is a short-run decision-making technique, so we are looking to cover all costs of a particular period of time. Inventory embodies costs of a previous period and is not considered.

Constant Sales Mix

The fourth assumption is a constant sales mix. In single-product analysis, the sales mix is obviously constant—100 percent of sales is applied to one product. Multiple-product break-even analysis requires a constant sales mix. However, it is virtually impossible to predict the sales mix with certainty. Typically, this constraint is handled in practice through sensitivity analysis. By using the capabilities of spreadsheet analysis, the sensitivity of variables to a variety of sales mixes can be readily assessed.

Prices and Costs Known with Certainty

Finally, the fifth assumption is that prices and costs are known. In actuality, firms seldom know variable costs and fixed costs with certainty. A change in one variable usually affects the value of others. Often, there is a probability distribution with which to contend. Furthermore, there are formal ways of explicitly building uncertainty into the CVP model. Exploration of these issues is introduced in the next section.

Explain the impact of risk, uncertainty, and changing variables on cost-volume-profit analysis.

Changes in the CVP Variables

Because firms operate in a dynamic world, they must be aware of changes in prices, variable costs, and fixed costs. They must also account for the effects of risk and uncertainty. We will take a look at the effects on the break-even point of changes in price, unit variable cost, and fixed costs. We will also look at ways managers can handle risk and uncertainty within the CVP framework.

Let's return to the More-Power Company example before the mini-sander was introduced. (That is, only the regular sander is produced.) Suppose that the Sales Department recently conducted a market study that revealed three different alternatives.

> **Alternative 1:** If advertising expenditures increase by $48,000, sales will increase from 72,500 units to 75,000 units.
>
> **Alternative 2:** A price decrease from $40 per sander to $38 per sander would increase sales from 72,500 units to 80,000 units.
>
> **Alternative 3:** Decreasing prices to $38 and increasing advertising expenditures by $48,000 will increase sales from 72,500 units to 90,000 units.

Should More-Power maintain its current price and advertising policies, or should it select one of the three alternatives described by the marketing study?

Consider the first alternative. What is the effect on profits if advertising costs increase by $48,000 and sales increase by 2,500 units? This question can be answered without using the equations but by employing the contribution margin per unit. We know that the unit contribution margin is $16. Since units sold increase by 2,500, the incremental increase in total contribution margin is $40,000 ($16 × 2,500 units). However, since fixed costs increase by $48,000, profits will actually decrease by $8,000 ($48,000 − $40,000). Exhibit 17-7 summarizes the effects of the first alternative. Notice that we need to look only at the incremental increase in total contribution margin and fixed expenses to compute the increase in total profits.

EXHIBIT 17-7 — Summary of the Effects of the First Alternative

	Before the Increased Advertising	With the Increased Advertising
Units sold	72,500	75,000
Unit contribution margin	× $16	× $16
Total contribution margin	$1,160,000	$1,200,000
Less: Fixed expenses	800,000	848,000
Profit	$ 360,000	$ 352,000

	Difference in Profit
Change in sales volume	2,500
Unit contribution margin	× $16
Change in contribution margin	$40,000
Less: Increase in fixed expenses	48,000
Decrease in profit	$(8,000)

For the second alternative, fixed expenses do not increase. Thus, it is possible to answer the question by looking only at the effect on total contribution margin. For the current price of $40, the contribution margin per unit is $16. If 72,500 units are sold, the total contribution margin is $1,160,000 ($16 × 72,500). If the price is dropped to $38, then the contribution margin drops to $14 per unit ($38 − $24). If 80,000 units are sold at the new price, then the new total contribution margin is $1,120,000 ($14 × 80,000). Dropping the price results in a profit decline of $40,000 ($1,160,000 − $1,120,000). The effects of the second alternative are summarized in Exhibit 17-8.

The third alternative calls for a decrease in the unit selling price and an increase in advertising costs. Like the first alternative, the profit impact can be assessed by looking at the incremental effects on contribution margin and fixed expenses. The incremental profit change can be found by (1) computing the incremental change in total contribution margin, (2) computing the incremental change in fixed expenses, and (3) adding the two results.

As shown, the current total contribution margin (for 72,500 units sold) is $1,160,000. Since the new unit contribution margin is $14, the new total contribution margin is $1,260,000 ($14 × 90,000 units). Thus, the incremental increase in total contribution margin is $100,000 ($1,260,000 − $1,160,000). However, to achieve this incremental increase in contribution margin, an incremental increase of $48,000 in fixed costs is needed. The net effect is an incremental increase in profits of $52,000. The effects of the third alternative are summarized in Exhibit 17-9.

EXHIBIT 17-8 **Summary of the Effects of the Second Alternative**

	Before the Proposed Price Increase	With the Proposed Price Increase
Units sold	72,500	80,000
Unit contribution margin	× $16	× $14
Total contribution margin	$1,160,000	$1,120,000
Less: Fixed expenses	800,000	800,000
Profit	$ 360,000	$ 320,000

	Difference in Profit
Change in contribution margin ($1,160,000 − $1,120,000)	$(40,000)
Less: Change in fixed expenses	—
Decrease in profit	$(40,000)

EXHIBIT 17-9 **Summary of the Effects of the Third Alternative**

	Before the Proposed Price and Advertising Change	With the Proposed Price Decrease and Advertising Increase
Units sold	72,500	90,000
Unit contribution margin	× $16	× $14
Total contribution margin	$1,160,000	$1,260,000
Less: Fixed expenses	800,000	848,000
Profit	$ 360,000	$ 412,000

	Difference in Profit
Change in contribution margin ($1,260,000 − $1,160,000)	$100,000
Less: Change in fixed expenses ($848,000 − $800,000)	48,000
Increase in profit	$ 52,000

Of the three alternatives identified by the marketing study, the only one that promises a benefit is the third. It increases total profits by $52,000. Both the first and second alternatives actually decrease profits.

These examples are all based on a units-sold approach. However, we could just as easily have applied a sales-revenue approach. The answers would be the same.

Introducing Risk and Uncertainty

An important assumption of CVP analysis is that prices and costs are known with certainty. This is seldom the case. Risk and uncertainty are a part of business decision making and must be dealt with in some manner. Formally, risk differs from uncertainty in that with risk, the probability distributions of the variables are known. With uncertainty, the probability distributions are not known. For our purposes, however, the terms will be used interchangeably.

How do managers deal with risk and uncertainty? A variety of methods may be used. First, of course, management must realize the uncertain nature of future prices, costs, and quantities. Next, managers move from consideration of a break-even point to what might be called a break-even band. In other words, given the uncertain nature of the data, perhaps a firm might break even when 1,800 to 2,000 units are sold—instead of the point estimate of 1,900 units. Further, managers may engage in sensitivity or what-if analyses. In this regard, a computer spreadsheet is helpful, as managers set up the break-even (or targeted profit) relationships and then check to see the impact that varying costs and prices have on quantity sold. Two concepts useful to management are *margin of safety* and *operating leverage*. Both of these may be considered measures of risk. Each requires knowledge of fixed and variable costs.

Margin of Safety

The **margin of safety** is the units sold or expected to be sold or the revenue earned or expected to be earned above the break-even volume. For example, if the break-even volume for a company is 200 units and the company is currently selling 500 units, the margin of safety is 300 units (500 − 200). The margin of safety can be expressed in sales revenue as well. If the break-even volume is $200,000 and current revenues are $350,000, then the margin of safety is $150,000.

The margin of safety can be viewed as a crude measure of risk. There are always events, unknown when plans are made, that can lower sales below the original expected level. If a firm's margin of safety is large given the expected sales for the coming year, the risk of suffering losses should sales take a downward turn is less than if the margin of safety is small. Managers who face a low margin of safety may wish to consider actions to increase sales or decrease costs. For example, **Walt Disney Company** faced lower theme park earnings in the last quarter of 2004 due to the unprecedented number of hurricanes that hit Florida during August. Disney's CFO explained that "near-term local attendance could be impacted as people put their lives together" after the disasters. He also noted that the company would focus on "increasing occupancy at theme park hotels, per capita spending by visitors to the theme parks, and managing costs." The objective is to reach an operating margin of at least 20 percent over the next three to four years.[7] A more robust operating margin at all theme parks would cushion Disney in the event of unforeseen events.

Operating Leverage

In physics, a lever is a simple machine used to multiply force. Basically, the lever magnifies the amount of effort applied to create a greater effect. The larger the load moved by a given amount of effort, the greater the mechanical advantage. In financial terms, operating leverage is concerned with the relative mix of fixed costs and variable costs in an organization. It is sometimes possible to trade off fixed costs for variable costs. As variable costs decrease, the unit contribution margin increases, making the contribution of each unit sold that much greater. In such a case, the effect of fluctuations in sales on profitability increases. Thus, firms that have lowered variable costs by increasing the proportion of fixed costs will benefit with greater increases in profits as sales increase than will firms with a lower proportion of fixed costs. Fixed costs are being used as leverage to increase profits. Unfortunately, it is also true that firms with a higher operating leverage will also experience greater reductions in profits as sales decrease. Therefore, **operating leverage** is the use of fixed costs to extract higher percentage changes in profits as sales activity changes.

---

7. Dwight Oestricher, "Disney CFO Staggs Sees Theme Park 1Q Hurt by Storms," *The Wall Street Journal* (September 30, 2004): B1 and B2.

The greater the degree of operating leverage, the more that changes in sales activity will affect profits. Because of this phenomenon, the mix of costs that an organization chooses can have a considerable influence on its operating risk and profit level.

The **degree of operating leverage** can be measured for a given level of sales by taking the ratio of contribution margin to profit, as follows:

$$\text{Degree of operating leverage} = \text{Contribution margin/Profit}$$

If fixed costs are used to lower variable costs such that contribution margin increases and profit decreases, then the degree of operating leverage increases—signaling an increase in risk.

To illustrate the utility of these concepts, consider a firm that is planning to add a new product line. In adding the line, the firm can choose to rely heavily on automation or on labor. If the firm chooses to emphasize automation rather than labor, fixed costs will be higher, and unit variable costs will be lower. Relevant data for a sales level of 10,000 units follow:

	Automated System	Manual System
Sales	$1,000,000	$1,000,000
Less: Variable expenses	500,000	800,000
Contribution margin	$ 500,000	$ 200,000
Less: Fixed expenses	375,000	100,000
Operating income	$ 125,000	$ 100,000
Unit selling price	$100	$100
Unit variable cost	50	80
Unit contribution margin	50	20

The degree of operating leverage for the automated system is 4.0 ($500,000/$125,000).

The degree of operating leverage for the manual system is 2.0 ($200,000/$100,000). What happens to profit in each system if sales increase by 40 percent? We can generate the following income statements to see.

	Automated System	Manual System
Sales	$1,400,000	$1,400,000
Less: Variable expenses	700,000	1,120,000
Contribution margin	$ 700,000	$ 280,000
Less: Fixed expenses	375,000	100,000
Operating income	$ 325,000	$ 180,000

Profits for the automated system would increase by $200,000 ($325,000 − $125,000) for a 160 percent increase. In the manual system, profits increase by only $80,000 ($180,000 − $100,000), for an 80 percent increase. The automated system has a greater percentage increase because it has a higher degree of operating leverage.

In choosing between the two systems, the effect of operating leverage is a valuable piece of information. As the 40 percent increase in sales illustrates, this effect can bring a significant benefit to the firm. However, the effect is a two-edged sword. As sales decrease, the automated system will also show much higher percentage profit decreases. Moreover, the increased operating leverage is available under the automated system because of the presence of increased fixed costs. The break-even point for the automated system is 7,500 units ($375,000/$50), whereas the break-even point for the manual system is 5,000 units ($100,000/$20). Thus, the automated system has greater operating risk. The increased risk, of course, provides a potentially higher profit level (as long as units sold exceed 9,167).[8]

In choosing between the automated and manual systems, the manager must assess the likelihood that sales will exceed 9,167 units. If, after careful study, there is a strong belief that sales will easily exceed this level, the choice is obvious: the automated system. On the other hand, if sales are unlikely to exceed 9,167 units, the manual system is preferable. Exhibit 17-10 summarizes the relative difference between the manual and automated systems in terms of some of the CVP concepts.

EXHIBIT 17-10	Differences between Manual and Automated Systems	
	Manual System	**Automated System**
Price	Same	Same
Variable costs	Relatively higher	Relatively lower
Fixed costs	Relatively lower	Relatively higher
Contribution margin	Relatively lower	Relatively higher
Break-even point	Relatively lower	Relatively higher
Margin of safety	Relatively higher	Relatively lower
Degree of operating leverage	Relatively lower	Relatively higher
Down-side risk	Relatively lower	Relatively higher
Up-side potential	Relatively lower	Relatively higher

COST MANAGEMENT   Technology in Action

A partnership between supply chain optimization software and the Web can help companies understand and manage the dynamic relationships among costs, prices, and volume. **Manugistics Group** is a global provider of supply chain optimization and e-commerce solutions. Its clients, including **Amazon.com**, **Boeing**, **Ford**, **Harley-Davidson**, and **Levi Strauss & Company**, use Manugistics's software to manage supply chain complexity.

Recently, Manugistics teamed up with **PricewaterhouseCoopers** to deliver fully integrated solutions to the pharmaceutical industry. Previously, the pharmaceutical industry focused on drug discovery and marketing. However, the ability to respond swiftly to market opportunities—through focused manufacturing and distribution—can do much to enhance a company's profitability. For example, a manufacturer that could respond rapidly to a flu epidemic could realize a return from the perishable flu vaccine. This use of supply chain software leads to an earlier break-even on new drugs.

Talus Solutions, a company that recently combined with Manugistics, developed dynamic pricing and revenue optimization (PRO) software. PRO works on the revenue side of cost-volume-profit models by optimizing prices for products and services that companies sell. The software uses advanced statistical techniques powered by the immense volume and variety of data made available by the Internet to examine a number of variables, including product availability, shifting demand, competitor pricing, production costs, inventory, market share objectives, and customer buying behavior. It then forecasts the response of different customer market segments to prices of products throughout their life cycles. **Tickets.com** is an example of a company that uses PRO to respond quickly to changes in demand for a perishable product—live entertainment. A particular number of seats are available for an event, and once the event is over, the product ceases to exist. The PRO software analyzes consumer behavior to construct a case-specific pricing structure. This enables Tickets.com to set ticket prices on the basis of customer demand, rather than on the basis of a preset price. The objectives are to fill the venue to capacity and to maximize the revenue for each event.

Source: Taken from the Web site, http://www.Tickets.com.

---

8. This benchmark is computed by equating the profit equations of the two systems and solving for X:
$50X - \$375,000 = \$20X - \$100,000$ so $X = 9,167$.

Sensitivity Analysis and CVP

The pervasiveness of personal computers and spreadsheets has made cost analysis within reach of most managers. An important tool is sensitivity analysis, a what-if technique that examines the impact of changes in underlying assumptions on an answer. It is relatively simple to input data on prices, variable costs, fixed costs, and sales mix and set up formulas to calculate break-even points and expected profits. Then, the data can be varied as desired to see what impact changes have on the expected profit.

In the example given previously for operating leverage, a company analyzed the impact on profit of using an automated versus a manual system. The computations were essentially done by hand, and too much variation was cumbersome. Using the power of a computer, it would be an easy matter to change the sales price in $1 increments between $75 and $125, with related assumptions about quantity sold. At the same time, variable and fixed costs could be adjusted. For example, suppose that the automated system has fixed costs of $375,000, but that those costs could easily range up to twice as much in the first year and come back down in the second and third years as bugs are worked out of the system and workers learn to use it. Again, the spreadsheet can effortlessly handle the many computations.

Finally, we must note that the spreadsheet, while wonderful for cranking out numerical answers, cannot do the most difficult job in CVP analysis. That job is determining the data to be entered in the first place. The accountant must be familiar with the cost and price distributions of the firm, as well as with the impact of changing economic conditions on these variables. The fact that variables are seldom known with certainty is no excuse for ignoring the impact of uncertainty on CVP analysis. Fortunately, sensitivity analysis can also give managers a feel for the degree to which a poorly forecast variable will affect an answer. That is also an advantage.

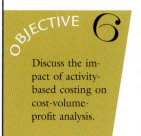

OBJECTIVE 6

Discuss the impact of activity-based costing on cost-volume-profit analysis.

CVP Analysis and Activity-Based Costing

Conventional CVP analysis assumes that all costs of the firm can be divided into two categories: those that vary with sales volume (variable costs) and those that do not (fixed costs). Furthermore, costs are assumed to be a linear function of sales volume.

In an activity-based costing system, costs are divided into unit- and non-unit-based categories. Activity-based costing admits that some costs vary with units produced and some costs do not. However, while activity-based costing acknowledges that non-unit-based costs are fixed with respect to production volume changes, it also argues that many non-unit-based costs vary with respect to other cost drivers.

The use of activity-based costing does not mean that CVP analysis is less useful. In fact, it becomes more useful, since it provides more accurate insights concerning cost behavior. These insights produce better decisions. CVP analysis within an activity-based framework, however, must be modified. To illustrate, assume that a company's costs can be explained by three variables: a unit-level cost driver, units sold; a batch-level cost driver, number of setups; and a product-level cost driver, engineering hours. The ABC cost equation can then be expressed as follows:

Total cost = Fixed costs + (Unit variable cost × Number of units) + (Setup cost × Number of setups) + (Engineering cost × Number of engineering hours)

Operating income, as before, is total revenue minus total cost. This is expressed as follows:

Operating income = Total revenue − [Fixed costs + (Unit variable cost × Number of units) + (Setup cost × Number of setups) + (Engineering cost × Number of engineering hours)]

Let's use the contribution margin approach to calculate the break-even point in units. At break-even, operating income is zero, and the number of units that must be sold to achieve break-even is as follows.

Break-even units = [Fixed costs + (Setup cost × Number of setups) + (Engineering cost × Number of engineering hours)]/(Price − Unit variable cost)

A comparison of the ABC break-even point with the conventional break-even point reveals two significant differences. First, the fixed costs differ. Some costs previously identified as being fixed may actually vary with non-unit cost drivers, in this case setups and engineering hours. Second, the numerator of the ABC break-even equation has two non-unit-variable cost terms: one for batch-related activities and one for product-sustaining activities.

Example Comparing Conventional and ABC Analysis

To make the previous discussion more concrete, a comparison of conventional cost-volume-profit analysis with activity-based costing is useful. Let's assume that a company wants to compute the units that must be sold to earn a before-tax profit of $20,000. The analysis is based on the following data:

Data about Variables

Cost Driver	Unit Variable Cost	Level of Cost Driver
Units sold	$ 10	—
Setups	1,000	20
Engineering hours	30	1,000

Other data:
Total fixed costs (conventional)	$100,000
Total fixed costs (ABC)	50,000
Unit selling price	20

The units that must be sold to earn a before-tax profit of $20,000 are computed as follows:

$$\text{Units} = (\text{Targeted income} + \text{Fixed costs})/(\text{Price} - \text{Unit variable cost})$$
$$= (\$20,000 + \$100,000)/(\$20 - \$10)$$
$$= \$120,000/\$10$$
$$= 12,000$$

Using the ABC equation, the units that must be sold to earn an operating income of $20,000 are computed as follows:

$$\text{Units} = (\$20,000 + \$50,000 + \$20,000 + \$30,000)/(\$20 - \$10)$$
$$= \$120,000/\$10$$
$$= 12,000$$

The number of units that must be sold is identical under both approaches. The reason is simple. The total fixed cost pool under conventional costing consists of non-unit-based variable costs plus costs that are fixed regardless of the cost driver. ABC breaks out the non-unit-based variable costs. These costs are associated with certain levels of each cost driver. For the batch-level cost driver, the level is 20 setups; for the product-level variable, the level is 1,000 engineering hours. As long as the levels of activity for the non-unit-based cost drivers remain the same, then the results for the conventional and ABC computations will also be the same. But these levels can change, and because of this, the information provided by the two approaches can be significantly different. The ABC equation for CVP analysis is a richer representation of the underlying cost behavior and can provide important strategic insights. To see this, let's use the same data provided previously and look at a different application.

Strategic Implications: Conventional CVP Analysis versus ABC Analysis

Suppose that after the conventional CVP analysis, marketing indicates that selling 12,000 units is not possible. In fact, only 10,000 units can be sold. The president of the company then directs the product design engineers to find a way to reduce the cost of making the product. The engineers also have been told that the conventional cost equation, with fixed costs of $100,000 and a unit variable cost of $10, holds. The variable cost of $10 per unit consists of the following: direct labor, $4; direct materials, $5; and variable overhead, $1. To comply with the request to reduce the break-even point, engineering produces a new design that requires less labor. The new design reduces the direct labor cost by $2 per unit. The design would not affect direct materials or variable overhead. Thus, the new variable cost is $8 per unit, and the break-even point is calculated as follows:

$$\text{Units} = \text{Fixed costs}/(\text{Price} - \text{Unit variable cost})$$
$$= \$100{,}000/(\$20 - \$8)$$
$$= 8{,}333$$

The projected income if 10,000 units are sold is computed as follows:

Sales ($20 × 10,000)	$200,000
Less: Variable expenses ($8 × 10,000)	80,000
Contribution margin	$120,000
Less: Fixed expenses	100,000
Operating income	$ 20,000

Excited, the president approves the new design. A year later, the president discovers that the expected increase in income did not materialize. In fact, a loss is realized. Why? The answer is provided by an ABC approach to CVP analysis.

The original ABC cost relationship for the example is as follows:

$$\text{Total cost} = \$50{,}000 + (\$10 \times \text{Units}) + (\$1{,}000 \times \text{Setups})$$
$$+ (\$30 \times \text{Engineering hours})$$

Suppose that the new design requires a more complex setup, increasing the cost per setup from $1,000 to $1,600. Also, suppose that the new design, because of increased technical content, requires a 40 percent increase in engineering support (from 1,000 hours to 1,400 hours). The new cost equation, including the reduction in unit-level variable costs, is as follows:

$$\text{Total cost} = \$50{,}000 + (\$8 \times \text{Units}) + (\$1{,}600 \times \text{Setups})$$
$$+ (\$30 \times \text{Engineering hours})$$

The break-even point, setting operating income equal to zero and using the ABC equation, is calculated as follows (assume that 20 setups are still performed):

$$\text{Units} = [\$50{,}000 + (\$1{,}600 \times 20) + (\$30 \times 1{,}400)]/(\$20 - \$8)$$
$$= \$124{,}000/\$12$$
$$= 10{,}333$$

And the income for 10,000 units is (recall that a maximum of 10,000 can be sold) as follows:

Sales ($20 × 10,000)		$200,000
Less: Unit-based variable expenses ($8 × 10,000)		80,000
Contribution margin		$120,000
Less non-unit-based variable expenses:		
Setups ($1,600 × 20)	$32,000	
Engineering support ($30 × 1,400)	42,000	74,000
Traceable margin		$ 46,000
Less: Fixed expenses		50,000
Operating income (loss)		$ (4,000)

How could the engineers have been off by so much? Didn't they know that the new design would increase setup cost and engineering support? Yes and no. They were probably aware of the increases in these two variables, but the conventional cost equation diverted attention from figuring just how much impact changes in those variables would have. The information conveyed to the engineers by the conventional equation gave the impression that any reduction in labor cost—not affecting direct materials or variable overhead—would reduce total costs, since changes in the level of labor activity would not affect the fixed costs. The ABC equation, however, indicates that a reduction in labor input that adversely affects setup activity or engineering support might be undesirable. By providing more insight, better design decisions can be made. Providing ABC cost information to the design engineers would probably have led them down a different path—a path that would have been more advantageous to the company.

CVP Analysis and JIT

If a firm has adopted JIT, the variable cost per unit sold is reduced, and fixed costs are increased. Direct labor, for example, is now viewed as fixed instead of variable. Direct materials, on the other hand, is still a unit-based variable cost. In fact, the emphasis on total quality and long-term purchasing makes the assumption even more true that direct materials cost is strictly proportional to units produced (because waste, scrap, and quantity discounts are eliminated). Other unit-based variable costs such as power and sales commissions also persist. Additionally, the batch-level variable is gone (in JIT, the batch is one unit). Thus, the cost equation for JIT can be expressed as follows:

Total cost = Fixed costs + (Unit variable cost × Units) + (Engineering cost
                × Number of engineering hours)

Since its application is a special case of the ABC equation, no example will be given.

SUMMARY

Cost-volume-profit analysis focuses on prices, revenues, volume, costs, profits, and sales mix. It can be used to determine the sales volume or revenue necessary to break even or achieve a targeted profit. Changes in the fixed and variable cost patterns affect the profitability of a firm. The firm can use CVP analysis to see just how a particular change in price or cost would affect the break-even point.

In a single-product setting, the break-even point can be computed in units or sales dollars. Two approaches were detailed: the operating income approach and the contribution margin approach.

Multiple-product analysis requires that an assumption be made concerning the expected sales mix. Given a particular sales mix, a multiple-product problem can be converted into a single-product analysis. However, it should be remembered that the answers change as the sales mix changes. If the sales mix changes in a multiple-product firm, the break-even point will also change. In general, increases in the sales of high contribution margin products will decrease the break-even point, while increases in the sales of low contribution margin products will increase the break-even point.

CVP is based on several assumptions that must be considered in applying it to business problems. The analysis assumes linear revenue and cost functions, no finished goods ending inventories, and a constant sales mix. CVP analysis also assumes that selling prices and fixed and variable costs are known with certainty. These assumptions form the basis for simple graphical analysis using the profit-volume graph and the cost-volume-profit graph.

Measures of risk and uncertainty, such as the margin of safety and operating leverage, can be used to give managers more insight into CVP answers. Sensitivity analysis gives still more insight into the effect of changes in underlying variables on CVP relationships.

CVP can be used with activity-based costing, but the analysis must be modified. In effect, under ABC, a type of sensitivity analysis is used. Fixed costs are separated from a variety of costs that vary with particular activity drivers. At this stage, it is easiest to organize variable costs as unit-level, batch-level, or product-level. Then, the impact of decisions on batches and products can be examined within the CVP framework.

The subject of cost-volume-profit analysis naturally lends itself to the use of numerous equations. Some of the more common equations used in this chapter are summarized in Exhibit 17-11.

EXHIBIT 17-11   Summary of Important Equations

1. Operating income = (Price × Number of units) − (Variable cost per unit × Number of units) − Total fixed costs
2. Break-even point in units = Fixed costs/(Price − Unit variable cost)
3. Revenue = Price × Units
4. Break-even point in sales dollars = Fixed costs/Contribution margin ratio
   or   = Fixed costs/(1 − Variable cost ratio)
5. Variable cost ratio = Total variable cost/Sales
   or   = Unit variable cost/Price
6. Contribution margin ratio = Contribution margin/Sales
   or   = (Price − Unit variable cost)/Price
7. Margin of safety = Sales − Break-even sales
8. Degree of operating leverage = Contribution margin/Profit
9. Percentage change in profits = Degree of operating leverage × Percentage change in sales
10. After-tax income = Operating income − (Tax rate × Operating income)
11. Income taxes = Tax rate × Operating income
12. Before-tax profit = After-tax profit/(1 − Tax rate)
13. ABC total cost = Fixed costs + (Unit variable cost × Number of units) + (Batch-level cost × Batch driver) + (Product-level cost × Product driver)
14. ABC break-even units = [Fixed costs + (Batch-level cost × Batch driver) + (Product-level cost × Product driver)]/(Price − Unit variable cost)

REVIEW PROBLEMS AND SOLUTIONS

1   BREAK-EVEN POINT, TARGETED PROFIT, MARGIN OF SAFETY

Cutlass Company's projected profit for the coming year is as follows:

	Total	*Per Unit*
Sales	$200,000	$20
Less: Variable expenses	120,000	12
Contribution margin	$ 80,000	$ 8
Less: Fixed expenses	64,000	
Operating income	$ 16,000	

Required:

1. Compute the break-even point in units.
2. How many units must be sold to earn a profit of $30,000?
3. Compute the contribution margin ratio. Using that ratio, compute the additional profit that Cutlass would earn if sales were $25,000 more than expected.
4. Suppose Cutlass would like to earn operating income equal to 20 percent of sales revenue. How many units must be sold for this goal to be realized? Prepare an income statement to prove your answer.
5. For the projected level of sales, compute the margin of safety.

SOLUTION

1. The break-even point is as follows:

$$\text{Units} = \text{Fixed costs}/(\text{Price} - \text{Unit variable cost})$$
$$= \$64,000/(\$20 - \$12)$$
$$= \$64,000/\$8$$
$$= 8,000$$

2. The number of units that must be sold to earn a profit of $30,000 is as follows:

$$\text{Units} = (\$64,000 + \$30,000)/\$8$$
$$= \$94,000/\$8$$
$$= 11,750$$

3. The contribution margin ratio is $8/$20 = 0.40. With additional sales of $25,000, the additional profit would be 0.40 × $25,000 = $10,000.

4. To find the number of units sold for a profit equal to 20 percent of sales, let target income equal (0.20)(Price × Units) and solve for units.

$$\text{Operating income} = (\text{Price} \times \text{Units}) - (\text{Unit variable cost} \times \text{Units}) - \text{Fixed costs}$$
$$(0.2)(\$20)\text{Units} = (\$20 \times \text{Units}) - (\$12 \times \text{Units}) - \$64,000$$
$$\$4 \times \text{Units} = \$64,000$$
$$\text{Units} = 16,000$$

The income statement is as follows:

Sales (16,000 × $20)	$320,000
Less: Variable expenses (16,000 × $12)	192,000
Contribution margin	$128,000
Less: Fixed expenses	64,000
Operating income	$ 64,000

Operating income/Sales = $64,000/$320,000 = 0.20, or 20%

5. The margin of safety is 10,000 − 8,000 = 2,000 units, or $40,000 in sales revenues.

2 CVP with Activity-Based Costing

Dory Manufacturing Company produces T-shirts that are screen-printed with the logos of various sports teams. Each shirt is priced at $10. Costs are as follows:

Cost Driver	Unit Variable Cost	Level of Cost Driver
Units sold	$ 5	—
Setups	450	80
Engineering hours	20	500

Other data:	
Total fixed costs (conventional)	$96,000
Total fixed costs (ABC)	50,000

Required:

1. Compute the break-even point in units using conventional analysis.
2. Compute the break-even point in units using activity-based analysis.
3. Suppose that Dory could reduce the setup cost by $150 per setup and could reduce the number of engineering hours needed to 425. How many units must be sold to break even in this case?

SOLUTION

1. Break-even units = Fixed costs/(Price − Unit variable cost)
   = $96,000/($10 − $5)
   = 19,200 units

2. Break-even units = [Fixed costs + (Setups × Setup cost) + (Engineering hours × Engineering cost)]/(Price − Unit variable cost)
   = [$50,000 + ($450 × 80) + ($20 × 500)]/($10 − $5)
   = 19,200 units

3. Break-even units = [$50,000 + ($300 × 80) + ($20 × 425)]/($10 − $5)
   = $82,500/$5
   = 16,500 units

KEY TERMS

Break-even point 737

Common fixed expenses 745

Contribution margin 738

Contribution margin ratio 741

Cost-volume-profit graph 749

Degree of operating leverage 757

Direct fixed expenses 745

Margin of safety 756

Net income 738

Operating income 737

Operating leverage 756

Profit-volume graph 749

Relevant range 753

Sales mix 746

Sales-revenue approach 742

Sensitivity analysis 759

Variable cost ratio 741

QUESTIONS FOR WRITING AND DISCUSSION

1. Explain how CVP analysis can be used for managerial planning.
2. Describe the difference between the units-sold approach to CVP analysis and the sales-revenue approach.
3. Define the term *break-even point*.
4. Explain why contribution margin per unit becomes profit per unit above the break-even point.
5. A restaurant owner who had yet to earn a monthly profit said, "The busier we are, the more we lose." What do you think is happening in terms of contribution margin?
6. What is the variable cost ratio? The contribution margin ratio? How are the two ratios related?
7. If the contribution margin increases from 30 to 35 percent of sales, what will happen to the break-even point, and why will this occur?
8. Suppose a firm with a contribution margin ratio of 0.3 increased its advertising expenses by $10,000 and found that sales increased by $30,000. Was it a good decision to increase advertising expenses? Why is this simple problem an important one for business people to understand?

9. Define the term *sales mix*, and give an example to support your definition.
10. Explain how CVP analysis developed for single products can be used in a multiple-product setting.
11. Why might a multiple-product firm choose to calculate just overall break-even revenue rather than the break-even quantity by product?
12. How do income taxes affect the break-even point and CVP analysis?
13. Explain how a change in sales mix can change a company's break-even point.
14. Define the term *margin of safety*. Explain what is meant by the term *operating leverage*. What impact does an increase in the margin of safety have on risk? What impact does an increase in leverage have on risk?
15. Why does the activity-based costing approach to CVP analysis offer more insight than the conventional approach does?

EXERCISES

17-1 BREAK-EVEN IN UNITS

LO1

Mello-Tote Company manufactures nylon arm-band carriers for use with popular portable MP3 devices. Variable costs are $18 per arm-band carrier, the price is $28, and fixed costs are $43,000.

Required:

1. What is the contribution margin for one arm-band carrier?
2. How many arm-band carriers must Mello-Tote Company sell to break even?
3. If Mello-Tote Company sells 6,000 arm-band carriers, what is the operating income?

17-2 BREAK-EVEN IN UNITS

LO1

Olmos Company manufactures room-sized air purifiers. Fixed costs amount to $1,386,000 per year. Variable costs per air purifier are $98, and the average price per air purifier is $120.

Required:

1. How many air purifiers must Olmos Company sell to break even?
2. If Olmos Company sells 85,000 air purifiers in a year, what is the operating income?
3. If Olmos Company's variable costs decrease to $70 per air purifier while the price and fixed costs remain unchanged, what is the new break-even point?

17-3 BREAK-EVEN IN UNITS, TARGET INCOME

LO1

Glass-Works, Inc., makes and sells a variety of cut glass vases. Fixed costs are $216,000 per year. The average price for a cut glass vase is $24, and the average variable cost is $16 per item.

Required:

1. How many vases must be sold to break even?
2. If Glass-Works wants to earn $130,000 in profit, how many vases must be sold? Prepare a variable-costing income statement to verify your answer.

17-4 BREAK-EVEN FOR A SERVICE FIRM

LO1   Leota Mohrman owns and operates The Hassle-Free Hothouse (THH), which provides live plants and flower arrangements to professional offices. Leota has fixed costs of $2,380 per month for office/greenhouse rent, advertising, and a delivery van. Variable costs for the plants, fertilizer, pots, and other supplies average $25 per job. THH charges $60 per month for the average job.

Required:
1. How many jobs must THH average each month to break even?
2. What is the operating income for THH in a month with 65 jobs? With 100 jobs?
3. Suppose that THH decides to increase the price to $75 per job. What is the new break-even point in number of jobs per month?

17-5 BREAK-EVEN IN SALES DOLLARS

LO2, LO5

Green Bay Motors, Inc., employs 20 sales personnel to market its line of luxury automobiles. The average car sells for $65,000, and a 6 percent commission is paid to the salesperson. Green Bay Motors is considering a change to the commission arrangement where the company would pay each salesperson a salary of $1,500 per month plus a commission of 2 percent of the sales made by that salesperson. What is the amount of total monthly car sales at which Green Bay Motors would be indifferent as to which plan to select? *(CMA adapted)*

17-6 BREAK-EVEN IN SALES DOLLARS, MARGIN OF SAFETY

LO2, LO5   StarSports, Inc., represents professional athletes and movie and television stars. The agency had revenue of $10,780,000 last year, with total variable costs of $5,066,600 and fixed costs of $2,194,200.

Required:
1. What is the contribution margin ratio for StarSports based on last year's data? What is the break-even point in sales revenue?
2. What was the margin of safety for StarSports last year?
3. One of StarSports's agents proposed that the firm begin cultivating high school sports stars around the nation. This proposal is expected to increase revenue by $150,000 per year, with increased fixed costs of $140,000. Is this proposal a good idea? Explain.

17-7 BREAK-EVEN IN UNITS, AFTER-TAX
TARGET INCOME, CVP ASSUMPTIONS

LO1, LO4, LO5

Almo Company manufactures and sells adjustable canopies that attach to motor homes and trailers. The market covers both new unit purchases as well as replacement canopies. Almo developed its 2007 business plan based on the assumption that canopies would sell at a price of $400 each. The variable costs for each canopy were projected at $200, and the annual fixed costs were budgeted at $100,000. Almo's after-tax profit objective was $240,000; the company's effective tax rate is 40 percent.

While Almo's sales usually rise during the second quarter, the May financial statements reported that sales were not meeting expectations. For the first five months of the year, only 350 units had been sold at the established price, with variable costs as planned, and it was clear that the 2007 after-tax profit projection would not be reached unless some actions were taken. Almo's president assigned a management committee to analyze the situation and develop several alternative courses of action. The following mutually exclusive alternatives, labeled A, B, and C, were presented to the president.

A. Reduce the sales price by $40. The sales organization forecasts that with the significantly reduced sales price, 2,700 units can be sold during the remainder of the year. Total fixed and variable unit costs will stay as budgeted.

B. Lower the variable costs per unit by $25 through the use of less expensive materials and slightly modified manufacturing techniques. The sales price will also be reduced by $30, and sales of 2,200 units for the remainder of the year are forecast.

C. Cut fixed costs by $10,000, and lower the sales price by 5 percent. Variable costs per unit will be unchanged. Sales of 2,000 units are expected for the remainder of the year.

Required:

1. Determine the number of units that Almo Company must sell in order to break even assuming no changes are made to the selling price and cost structure.
2. Determine the number of units that Almo Company must sell in order to achieve its after-tax profit objective.
3. Determine which one of the alternatives Almo Company should select to achieve its annual after-tax profit objective. Be sure to support your selection with appropriate calculations.
4. The precision and reliability of CVP analysis are limited by several underlying assumptions. Identify at least four of these assumptions. *(CMA adapted)*

17-8   CVP, BEFORE- AND AFTER-TAX TARGETED INCOME

LO1   Head-Gear Company produces helmets for bicycle racing. Currently, Head-Gear charges a price of $30 per helmet. Variable costs are $20.40 per helmet, and fixed costs are $38,680. The tax rate is 25 percent. Last year, 13,400 helmets were sold.

Required:

1. What is Head-Gear's net income for last year?
2. What is Head-Gear's break-even revenue?
3. Suppose Head-Gear wants to earn before-tax operating income of $153,320. How many units must be sold?
4. Suppose Head-Gear wants to earn after-tax net income of $150,000. How many units must be sold? (Round to the nearest unit.)

17-9   BREAK-EVEN IN SALES DOLLARS, CHANGES IN VARIABLES

LO2, LO5   Lauterbach Corporation manufactures skateboards and is in the process of preparing next year's budget. The pro forma income statement for the current year is as follows:

CMA

Sales		$1,500,000
Cost of sales:		
Direct materials	$250,000	
Direct labor	150,000	
Variable overhead	80,000	
Fixed overhead	100,000	580,000
Gross profit		$ 920,000
Selling and administrative expenses:		
Variable	$300,000	
Fixed	250,000	550,000
Operating income		$ 370,000

Required:

1. What is the break-even point (rounded to the nearest dollar) for Lauterbach Corporation for the current year?
2. For the coming year, the management of Lauterbach Corporation anticipates a 10 percent increase in variable costs and a $45,000 increase in fixed expenses. What is the break-even point in dollars for next year? *(CMA adapted)*

17-10 ASSUMPTIONS AND USE OF VARIABLES

LO1, LO5   Choose the *best* answer for each of the following multiple-choice questions.

1. Cost-volume-profit analysis includes some simplifying assumptions. Which of the following is **not** one of these assumptions?
   a. Cost and revenues are predictable.
   b. Cost and revenues are linear over the relevant range.
   c. Changes in beginning and ending inventory levels are insignificant in amount.
   d. Sales mix changes are irrelevant.

2. The term *relevant range*, as used in cost accounting, means the range
   a. over which costs may fluctuate.
   b. over which cost relationships are valid.
   c. of probable production.
   d. over which production has occurred in the past ten years.

3. How would the following be used in calculating the number of units that must be sold to earn a targeted operating income?

	Price per Unit	Targeted Operating Income
a.	Denominator	Numerator
b.	Numerator	Numerator
c.	Not used	Denominator
d.	Numerator	Denominator

4. Information concerning Korian Corporation's product is as follows:

Sales	$300,000
Variable costs	240,000
Fixed costs	40,000

   Assuming that Korian increased sales of the product by 20 percent, what should the operating income be?
   a. $20,000
   b. $24,000
   c. $32,000
   d. $80,000

5. The following data apply to McNally Company for last year:

Total variable costs per unit	$3.50
Contribution margin/Sales	30%
Break-even sales (present volume)	$1,000,000

   McNally wants to sell an additional 50,000 units at the same selling price and contribution margin. By how much can fixed costs increase to generate additional profit equal to 10 percent of the sales value of the additional 50,000 units to be sold?
   a. $50,000
   b. $57,500
   c. $67,500
   d. $125,000

6. Bryan Company's break-even point is 8,500 units. Variable cost per unit is $140, and total fixed costs are $297,500 per year. What price does Bryan charge?
   a. $140
   b. $35
   c. $175
   d. cannot be determined from the above data

17-11   CONTRIBUTION MARGIN, CVP, NET INCOME, MARGIN OF SAFETY

LO1, LO5   Chromatics, Inc., produces novelty nail polishes. Each bottle sells for $3.60. Variable unit costs are as follows:

Acrylic base	$0.75
Pigments	0.38
Other ingredients	0.35
Bottle, packing material	1.15
Selling commission	0.25

Fixed overhead costs are $12,000 per year. Fixed selling and administrative costs are $6,720 per year. Chromatics sold 35,000 bottles last year.

Required:

1. What is the contribution margin per unit for a bottle of nail polish? What is the contribution margin ratio?
2. How many bottles must be sold to break even? What is the break-even sales revenue?
3. What was Chromatics's operating income last year?
4. What was the margin of safety?
5. Suppose that Chromatics, Inc., raises the price to $4.00 per bottle, but anticipated sales will drop to 30,400 bottles. What will the new break-even point in units be? Should Chromatics raise the price? Explain.

17-12   OPERATING LEVERAGE

LO5   Income statements for two different companies in the same industry are as follows:

	Trimax, Inc.	Quintex, Inc.
Sales	$500,000	$500,000
Less: Variable costs	250,000	100,000
Contribution margin	$250,000	$400,000
Less: Fixed costs	200,000	350,000
Operating income	$ 50,000	$ 50,000

Required:

1. Compute the degree of operating leverage for each company.
2. Compute the break-even point for each company. Explain why the break-even point for Quintex, Inc., is higher.
3. Suppose that both companies experience a 50 percent increase in revenues. Compute the percentage change in profits for each company. Explain why the percentage increase in Quintex's profits is so much greater than that of Trimax.

17-13 CVP ANALYSIS WITH MULTIPLE PRODUCTS

LO3

Reingold Company produces wireless phones. One model is the miniphone—a basic model that is very small and slim. The miniphone fits into a shirt pocket. Another model, the netphone, has a larger display and is Internet-ready. For the coming year, Reingold expects to sell 200,000 miniphones and 600,000 netphones. A segmented income statement for the two products is as follows:

	Miniphone	Netphone	Total
Sales	$5,000,000	$36,000,000	$41,000,000
Less: Variable costs	2,400,000	30,000,000	32,400,000
Contribution margin	$2,600,000	$ 6,000,000	$ 8,600,000
Less: Direct fixed costs	1,200,000	960,000	2,160,000
Segment margin	$1,400,000	$ 5,040,000	$ 6,440,000
Less: Common fixed costs			1,280,000
Operating income			$ 5,160,000

Required:

1. Compute the number of miniphones and netphones that must be sold to break even.
2. Using information only from the total column of the income statement, compute the sales revenue that must be generated for the company to break even.

17-14 AFTER-TAX TARGET INCOME, PROFIT ANALYSIS

LO1, LO5

Siberian Ski Company recently expanded its manufacturing capacity, which will allow it to produce up to 15,000 pairs of cross-country skis of the mountaineering model or the touring model. The sales department assures management that it can sell between 9,000 and 13,000 pairs of either product this year. Because the models are very similar, Siberian Ski will produce only one of the two models.

The following information was compiled by the accounting department:

Per-Unit (Pair) Data		
	Mountaineering	Touring
Selling price	$88.00	$80.00
Variable costs	52.80	52.80

Fixed costs will total $369,600 if the mountaineering model is produced but will be only $316,800 if the touring model is produced. Siberian Ski is subject to a 40 percent income tax rate.

Required:

1. If Siberian Ski Company desires an after-tax net income of $24,000, how many pairs of touring model skis will the company have to sell?
2. Suppose that Siberian Ski Company decided to produce only one model of skis. What is the total sales revenue at which Siberian Ski Company would make the same profit or loss regardless of the ski model it decided to produce?
3. If the sales department could guarantee the annual sale of 12,000 pairs of either model, which model would the company produce, and why? *(CMA adapted)*

PROBLEMS

17-15   BREAK-EVEN IN UNITS

LO1

CMA

Don Masters and two of his colleagues are considering opening a law office in a large metropolitan area that would make inexpensive legal services available to those who could not otherwise afford these services. The intent is to provide easy access for their clients by having the office open 360 days per year, 16 hours each day from 7:00 A.M. to 11:00 P.M. The office would be staffed by a lawyer, paralegal, legal secretary, and clerk-receptionist for each of the two 8-hour shifts.

In order to determine the feasibility of the project, Don hired a marketing consultant to assist with market projections. The results of this study show that if the firm spends $500,000 on advertising the first year, the number of new clients expected each day would have the following probability distribution.

Number of New Clients per Day	Probability
20	0.10
30	0.30
55	0.40
85	0.20

Don and his associates believe these numbers are reasonable and are prepared to spend the $500,000 on advertising. Other pertinent information about the operation of the office is as follows.

The only charge to each new client would be $30 for the initial consultation. All cases that warranted further legal work would be accepted on a contingency basis with the firm earning 30 percent of any favorable settlements or judgments. Don estimates that 20 percent of new client consultations will result in favorable settlements or judgments averaging $2,000 each. Repeat clients are not expected during the first year of operations.

The hourly wages of the staff are projected to be $25 for the lawyer, $20 for the paralegal, $15 for the legal secretary, and $10 for the clerk-receptionist. Fringe benefit expenses will be 40 percent of the wages paid. A total of 400 hours of overtime is expected for the year; this will be divided equally between the legal secretary and the clerk-receptionist positions. Overtime will be paid at one and one-half times the regular wage, and the fringe benefit expense will apply to the full wages.

Don has located 6,000 square feet of suitable office space, which rents for $28 per square foot annually. Associated expenses will be $22,000 for property insurance and $32,000 for utilities.

It will be necessary for the group to purchase malpractice insurance, which is expected to cost $180,000 annually.

The initial investment in office equipment will be $60,000; this equipment has an estimated useful life of four years.

The cost of office supplies has been estimated to be $4 per expected new client consultation.

Required:

1. Determine how many new clients must visit the law office being considered by Don Masters and his colleagues in order for the venture to break even during its first year of operations.
2. Using the information provided by the marketing consultant, determine if it is feasible for the law office to achieve break-even operations. *(CMA adapted)*

17-16   USING A COMPUTER SPREADSHEET TO SOLVE MULTIPLE-PRODUCT BREAK-EVEN, VARYING SALES MIX

LO2   The following projected income statement for More-Power Company is repeated for your convenience. Recall that the projection is based on sales of 75,000 regular sanders and 30,000 mini-sanders.

	Regular Sander	Mini-Sander	Total
Sales	$3,000,000	$1,800,000	$4,800,000
Less: Variable expenses	1,800,000	900,000	2,700,000
Contribution margin	$1,200,000	$ 900,000	$2,100,000
Less: Direct fixed expenses	250,000	450,000	700,000
Product margin	$ 950,000	$ 450,000	$1,400,000
Less: Common fixed expenses			600,000
Operating income			$ 800,000

Required:

1. Set up the given income statement on a spreadsheet (e.g., Excel™). Then, substitute the following sales mixes, and calculate operating income. Be sure to print the results for each sales mix (a through d).

	Regular Sander	Mini-Sander
a.	75,000	37,500
b.	60,000	60,000
c.	30,000	90,000
d.	30,000	60,000

2. Calculate the break-even units for each product for each of the preceding sales mixes.

17-17   CONTRIBUTION MARGIN, UNIT AMOUNTS

LO1   Consider the following information on four independent companies.

	A	B	C	D
Sales	$10,000	$?	$?	$9,000
Less: Variable costs	8,000	11,700	9,750	?
Contribution margin	$ 2,000	$ 3,900	$?	$?
Less: Fixed costs	?	5,000	?	750
Operating income	$ 1,000	$?	$ 400	$2,850
Units sold	?	1,300	125	90
Price/Unit	$5	$?	$130	$?
Variable cost/Unit	$?	$9	$?	$?
Contribution margin/Unit	$?	$3	$?	$?
Contribution margin ratio	?	?	40%	?
Break-even in units	?	?	?	?

Required:

Calculate the correct amount for each question mark.

17-18 BREAK-EVEN IN SALES DOLLARS, VARIABLE-COSTING RATIO, CONTRIBUTION MARGIN RATIO, MARGIN OF SAFETY

LO2, LO5   Gossimer, Inc., is a manufacturer of exercise equipment. The budgeted income statement for the coming year is as follows.

Sales	$900,000
Less: Variable expenses	342,000
Contribution margin	$558,000
Less: Fixed expenses	363,537
Income before taxes	$194,463
Less: Income taxes	77,785
Net income	$116,678

Required:

1. What is Gossimer's variable cost ratio? Its contribution margin ratio?
2. Suppose Gossimer's actual revenues are $150,000 greater than budgeted. By how much will before-tax profits increase? Give the answer without preparing a new income statement.
3. How much sales revenue must Gossimer earn in order to break even? What is the expected margin of safety? (Round your answers to the nearest dollar.)
4. How much sales revenue must Gossimer generate to earn a before-tax profit of $200,000? An after-tax profit of $120,000? Prepare a contribution margin income statement to verify the accuracy of your last answer.

17-19 CHANGES IN BREAK-EVEN POINTS WITH CHANGES IN UNIT PRICES

LO5   Belmont produces and sells plastic storage containers. Last year, Belmont sold 125,000 units. The income statement for Belmont, Inc., for last year is as follows:

Sales	$625,000
Less: Variable expenses	343,750
Contribution margin	$281,250
Less: Fixed expenses	180,000
Operating income	$101,250

Required:

1. Compute the break-even point in units and in revenues. Compute the margin of safety for last year.
2. Suppose that the selling price increases by 10 percent. Will the break-even point increase or decrease? Recompute it.
3. Suppose that the variable cost per unit increases by $0.35. Will the break-even point increase or decrease? Recompute it.
4. Can you predict whether the break-even point increases or decreases if both the selling price and the unit variable cost increase? Recompute the break-even point incorporating both of the changes in Requirements 1 and 2.
5. Assume that total fixed costs increase by $50,000. (Assume no other changes from the original data.) Will the break-even point increase or decrease? Recompute it.

17-20 Break-Even, After-Tax Target Income, Margin of Safety, Operating Leverage

LO1, LO2, LO5

Coastal Carolina Company produces a single product. The projected income statement for the coming year, based on sales of 100,000 units, is as follows:

Sales	$2,000,000
Less: Variable costs	1,100,000
Contribution margin	$ 900,000
Less: Fixed costs	765,000
Operating income	$ 135,000

Required:

1. Compute the unit contribution margin and the units that must be sold to break even. Suppose that 30,000 units are sold above the break-even point. What is the profit?
2. Compute the contribution margin ratio and the break-even point in dollars. Suppose that revenues are $200,000 greater than expected. What would the total profit be?
3. Compute the margin of safety.
4. Compute the operating leverage. Compute the new profit level if sales are 20 percent higher than expected.
5. How many units must be sold to earn a profit equal to 10 percent of sales?
6. Assume the income tax rate is 40 percent. How many units must be sold to earn an after-tax profit of $180,000?

17-21 Basic CVP Concepts

LO1, LO5

Devonly Company produces a variety of products. One division makes gas grills for outdoor cooking. The division's projected income statement for the coming year is as follows:

Sales (120,000 units)	$7,500,000
Less: Variable expenses	3,450,000
Contribution margin	$4,050,000
Less: Fixed expenses	3,375,000
Operating income	$ 675,000

Required:

1. Compute the contribution margin per unit, and calculate the break-even point in units. Repeat, using the contribution margin ratio.
2. The divisional manager has decided to increase the advertising budget by $100,000 and cut the average selling price to $58. These actions will increase sales revenues by $1 million. Will the division be made better off?
3. Suppose sales revenues exceed the estimated amount on the income statement by $540,000. Without preparing a new income statement, determine by how much profits are underestimated.
4. How many units must be sold to earn an after-tax profit of $1.254 million? Assume a tax rate of 34 percent.
5. Compute the margin of safety in dollars based on the given income statement.
6. Compute the operating leverage based on the given income statement. If sales revenues are 20 percent greater than expected, what is the percentage increase in profits?

17-22 CVP Analysis: Sales-Revenue Approach, Pricing, After-Tax Target Income

LO2, LO5   Kline Consulting is a service organization that specializes in the design, installation, and servicing of mechanical, hydraulic, and pneumatic systems. For example, some manufacturing firms, with machinery that cannot be turned off for servicing, need some type of system to lubricate the machinery during use. To deal with this type of problem for a client, Kline designed a central lubricating system that pumps lubricants intermittently to bearings and other moving parts.

The operating results for the firm for the previous year are as follows:

Sales	$802,429
Less: Variable expenses	430,000
Contribution margin	$372,429
Less: Fixed expenses	154,750
Operating income	$217,679

In the coming year, Kline expects variable costs to increase by 5 percent and fixed costs by 4 percent.

Required:

1. What is the contribution margin ratio for the previous year?
2. Compute Kline's break-even point for the previous year in dollars.
3. Suppose that Kline would like to see a 6 percent increase in operating income in the coming year. What percent (on average) must Kline raise its bids to cover the expected cost increases and obtain the desired operating income? Assume that Kline expects the same mix and volume of services in both years.
4. In the coming year, how much revenue must be earned for Kline to earn an after-tax profit of $175,000? Assume a tax rate of 34 percent.

17-23 Multiple Products, Break-Even Analysis, Operating Leverage, Segmented Income Statements

LO3, LO5   Ironjay, Inc., produces two types of weight-training equipment: the jay-flex (a weight machine that allows the user to perform a number of different exercises) and a set of free weights. Ironjay sells the jay-flex to sporting goods stores for $200. The free weights sell for $75 per set. The projected income statement for the coming year follows:

Sales	$600,000
Less: Variable expenses	390,000
Contribution margin	$210,000
Less: Fixed expenses	157,500
Operating income	$ 52,500

The owner of Ironjay estimates that 40 percent of the sales revenues will be produced by sales of the jay-flex, with the remaining 60 percent by free weights. The jay-flex is also responsible for 40 percent of the variable expenses. Of the fixed expenses, one-third are common to both products, and one-half are directly traceable to the jay-flex line.

Required:

1. Compute the sales revenue that must be earned for Ironjay to break even.
2. Compute the number of jay-flex machines and free weight sets that must be sold for Ironjay to break even.

3. Compute the degree of operating leverage for Ironjay. Now, assume that the actual revenues will be 40 percent higher than the projected revenues. By what percentage will profits increase with this change in sales volume?
4. Ironjay is considering adding a new product—the jay-rider. The jay-rider is a cross between a rowing machine and a stationary bicycle (like the Nordic rider™). For the first year, Ironjay estimates that the jay-rider will cannibalize 600 units of sales from the jay-flex. Sales of free weight sets will remain unchanged. The jay-rider will sell for $180 and have variable costs of $140. The increase in fixed costs to support manufacture of this product is $5,700. Compute the number of jay-flex machines, free weight sets, and jay-riders that must be sold for Ironjay to break even. For the coming year, is the addition of the jay-rider a good idea? Why or why not? Why might Ironjay choose to add the jay-rider anyway?

17-24   BREAK-EVEN IN UNITS AND SALES DOLLARS, MARGIN OF SAFETY

LO1, LO2, LO5

Drake Company produces a single product. Last year's income statement is as follows:

Sales (20,000 units)	$1,218,000
Less: Variable costs	812,000
Contribution margin	$ 406,000
Less: Fixed costs	300,000
Operating income	$ 106,000

Required:

1. Compute the break-even point in units and sales dollars.
2. What was the margin of safety for Drake Company last year?
3. Suppose that Drake Company is considering an investment in new technology that will increase fixed costs by $250,000 per year, but will lower variable costs to 45 percent of sales. Units sold will remain unchanged. Prepare a budgeted income statement assuming Drake makes this investment. What is the new break-even point in units, assuming the investment is made?

17-25   CVP ANALYSIS, IMPACT OF ACTIVITY-BASED COSTING

LO6

Salem Electronics currently produces two products: a programmable calculator and a tape recorder. A recent marketing study indicated that consumers would react favorably to a radio with the Salem brand name. Owner Kenneth Booth was interested in the possibility. Before any commitment was made, however, Kenneth wanted to know what the incremental fixed costs would be and how many radios must be sold to cover these costs.

In response, Betty Johnson, the marketing manager, gathered data for the current products to help in projecting overhead costs for the new product. The overhead costs follow. (The high and low production volumes as measured by direct labor hours were used to assess cost behavior.)

	Fixed	Variable
Materials handling	$ —	$18,000
Power	—	22,000
Engineering	100,000	—
Machine costs	30,000*	80,000
Inspection	40,000	—
Setups	60,000	—

*All depreciation.

The following activity data were also gathered:

	Calculators	Recorders
Units produced	20,000	20,000
Direct labor hours	10,000	20,000
Machine hours	10,000	10,000
Material moves	120	120
Kilowatt-hours	1,000	1,000
Engineering hours	4,000	1,000
Hours of inspection	700	1,400
Number of setups	20	40

Betty was told that a plantwide overhead rate was used to assign overhead costs based on direct labor hours. She was also informed by engineering that if 20,000 radios were produced and sold (her projection based on her marketing study), they would have the same activity data as the recorders (use the same direct labor hours, machine hours, setups, and so on).

Engineering also provided the following additional estimates for the proposed product line:

Prime costs per unit	$ 18
Depreciation on new equipment	18,000

Upon receiving these estimates, Betty did some quick calculations and became quite excited. With a selling price of $26 and just $18,000 of additional fixed costs, only 4,500 units had to be sold to break even. Since Betty was confident that 20,000 units could be sold, she was prepared to strongly recommend the new product line.

Required:

1. Reproduce Betty's break-even calculation using conventional cost assignments. How much additional profit would be expected under this scenario, assuming that 20,000 radios are sold?
2. Use an activity-based costing approach, and calculate the break-even point and the incremental profit that would be earned on sales of 20,000 units.
3. Explain why the CVP analysis done in Requirement 2 is more accurate than the analysis done in Requirement 1. What recommendation would you make?

17-26   ABC AND CVP ANALYSIS: MULTIPLE PRODUCTS

LO3, LO6   Good Scent, Inc., produces two colognes: Rose and Violet. Of the two, Rose is more popular. Data concerning the two products follow:

	Rose	Violet
Expected sales (in cases)	50,000	10,000
Selling price per case	$100	$80
Direct labor hours	36,000	6,000
Machine hours	10,000	3,000
Receiving orders	50	25
Packing orders	100	50
Material cost per case	$50	$43
Direct labor cost per case	$10	$7

The company uses a conventional costing system and assigns overhead costs to products using direct labor hours. Annual overhead costs follow. They are classified as fixed or variable with respect to direct labor hours.

	Fixed	Variable
Direct labor benefits	$ —	$200,000
Machine costs	200,000*	262,000
Receiving department	225,000	—
Packing department	125,000	—
Total costs	$550,000	$462,000

*All depreciation.

Required:

1. Using the conventional approach, compute the number of cases of Rose and the number of cases of Violet that must be sold for the company to break even.
2. Using an activity-based approach, compute the number of cases of each product that must be sold for the company to break even.

17-27 COLLABORATIVE LEARNING EXERCISE

PART I: ABC AND CVP ANALYSIS, USE OF REGRESSION

LO6 Sorrentino Company, which has been in business for one year, manufactures specialty Italian pastas. The pasta products start in the mixing department, where durum flour, eggs, and water are mixed to form dough. The dough is kneaded, rolled flat, and cut into fettucine or lasagna noodles, then dried and packaged.

Paul Gilchrist, controller for Sorrentino Company, is concerned because the company has yet to make a profit. Sales were slow in the first quarter but really picked up by the end of the year. Over the course of the year, 726,800 boxes were sold. Paul is interested in determining how many boxes must be sold to break even. He has begun to determine relevant fixed and variable costs and has accumulated the following per-unit data:

Price	$0.90
Direct materials	0.35
Direct labor	0.25

He has had more difficulty separating overhead into fixed and variable components. In examining overhead-related activities, Paul has noticed that machine hours appear to be closely correlated with units in that 100 boxes of pasta can be produced per machine hour. Setups are an important batch-level activity. Paul has accumulated the following information on overhead costs, number of setups, and machine hours for the past 12 months:

	Overhead	Number of Setups	Machine Hours
January	$5,700	18	595
February	4,500	6	560
March	4,890	12	575
April	5,500	15	615
May	6,200	20	650
June	5,000	10	610
July	5,532	16	630
August	5,409	12	625
September	5,300	11	650
October	5,000	12	550
November	5,350	14	593
December	5,470	14	615

Selling and administrative expenses, all fixed, amounted to $180,000 last year.

Required:

Form a group of three to four students. The group will work this exercise together, then designate one member of the group to present the results to the class.

1. Separate overhead into fixed and variable components using ordinary least squares (regression) analysis. Run three regressions, using the following independent variables: (a) number of setups, (b) number of machine hours, and (c) a multiple regression using both number of setups and machine hours. Which regression equation is best? Why?
2. Using the results from the multiple regression equation (from Requirement 1), calculate the number of boxes of pasta which must be sold to break even.

PART II: MULTIPLE-PRODUCT CVP ANALYSIS, ABC

LO3, LO5, LO6   (This problem is an extension of Part I of **Problem 17-27**.) Sorrentino Company has decided to expand into the production of sauces to top its pastas. Sauces are also started in the mixing department, using the same equipment. The sauces are mixed, cooked, and packaged into plastic containers. One jar of sauce is priced at $2 and requires $0.75 of direct materials and $0.50 of direct labor. Fifty jars of sauce can be produced per machine hour. The setup is identical to the setup for pasta and should cost the same amount. The production manager believes that with careful scheduling, he can keep the total number of setups (for both pasta and sauce) to the same number as used last year. The marketing director believes Sorrentino Company can sell two boxes of pasta for every one jar of sauce.

Required:

Maintain the same group that was formed in Part I. One to two members of your group should work Requirement 1, and the remaining members will work Requirement 2. The group will come together to discuss Requirement 3.

1. Using the data from **Problem 17-27**, Part I and the results of the multiple regression equation, calculate the break-even number of boxes of pasta and jars of sauce.
2. Suppose that the production manager is wrong and that the number of setups doubles. Calculate the new break-even number of boxes of pasta and jars of sauce.
3. Comment on the effect of uncertainty in the sales mix and in cost estimates and on risk for Sorrentino Company.

17-28 CYBER RESEARCH CASE

LO1   Find five companies with home pages on the Internet. Be sure that there is at least one company from each of the following categories: manufacturing, service, and wholesale-retail. Determine how each of the companies would define its product(s) for the purposes of cost-volume-profit analysis. Write a brief description of each company and your assessment of its product/service structure. Give your rationale for choosing the type(s) of product or service.

CHAPTER 18

Activity Resource Usage Model and Tactical Decision Making

AFTER STUDYING THIS CHAPTER, YOU SHOULD BE ABLE TO:

1. Describe the tactical decision-making model.
2. Define the concept of relevant costs and revenues.
3. Explain how the activity resource usage model is used in assessing relevancy.
4. Apply the tactical decision-making concepts in a variety of business situations.

Tom and Ray Magliozzi (also known as Click and Clack, the Tappet Brothers) have a weekly radio show and newspaper column advising readers on their automotive problems. Frequently, Tom and Ray use tactical decision making to suggest possible repairs. For example, in October 2004, a reader asked what to do about his wife's 1991 Ford escort. The car needed its air filter replaced every six weeks due to oil buildup in the box that holds the filter. No mechanic had been able to solve the problem. Tom and Ray zoomed in the answer. They diagnosed the problem as "blowby"—a situation that occurs when combustion gases leak from inside the cylinders into the crankcase. The gas and pressure overwhelm the crankcase ventilation system, and oil is blown back into the air-filter housing, which ruins the air filter. Now, how can the problem of blowby be solved? Tom and Ray suggested two solutions. First, replace the engine. This will solve the underlying problem. However, it will cost about $1,500. Second, just keep replacing the air filter every six weeks. They figured that, at $10 per replacement, the reader could have a new air filter installed every six weeks for the next 17 years. The point, of course, is that placing a new engine in a 1991 car was almost surely a waste of money—the rest of the car would give out long before the new engine wore out.[1]

One of the major roles of the cost management information system is supplying cost and revenue data that are useful in tactical decision making. How cost and revenue data can be used to make tactical decisions is the focus of this chapter. To make sound decisions, the user of the cost information must be able to decide what is relevant to the decision and what is not relevant.

Tactical Decision Making

OBJECTIVE **1**

Describe the tactical decision-making model.

Tactical decision making consists of choosing among alternatives with an immediate or limited end in view. Accepting a special order for less than the normal selling price to utilize idle capacity and increase this year's profits is an example. The immediate objective is to exploit idle productive capacity so that short-run profits can be increased. Thus, some tactical decisions tend to be *short run* in nature; however, it should be emphasized that short-run decisions often have long-run consequences. Consider a second example. Suppose that a company is considering the possibility of producing a component instead of buying it from suppliers. The immediate objective may be to lower the cost of making the main product. Yet, this tactical decision may be a small part of the overall strategy of establishing a cost leadership position for the firm. Thus, tactical decisions are often *small-scale actions* that serve a larger purpose. Recall that the overall objective of strategic decision making is to select among alternative strategies so that a long-term competitive advantage is established. Tactical decision making should support this overall objective, even if the immediate objective is short run (accepting a 1-time order to increase profits) or small scale (making instead of buying a component). Thus, *sound* tactical decision making means that the decisions made achieve not only the limited objective but also serve a larger purpose. In fact, no tactical decision should be made that does not serve the overall strategic goals of an organization.

The Tactical Decision-Making Process

With this very important qualification, it is possible to outline the tactical decision-making process. The five steps describing the process are as follows:

1. Recognize and define the problem.
2. Identify alternatives as possible solutions to the problem, and eliminate alternatives that are not feasible.
3. Identify the predicted costs and benefits associated with each feasible alternative. Eliminate the costs and benefits that are not relevant to the decision.
4. Compare the *relevant* costs and benefits for each alternative, and relate each alternative to the overall strategic goals of the firm and other important qualitative factors.
5. Select the alternative with the greatest benefit which also supports the organization's strategic objectives.

Step 1: Defining the Problem

To illustrate the steps of the process, consider an apple producer. Each year, approximately 25 percent of the apples harvested are small and odd-shaped. These apples cannot be sold in the normal distribution channels and have simply been dumped in the orchards for fertilizer. This approach seems costly, and the owner is not satisfied with it. What to do with these apples is the problem facing the apple producer.

---

1. *Car Talk,* http://www.cartalk.com/content/columns/latest.html as of October 2004.

Step 2: Identifying Feasible Alternatives

Several alternatives are being considered:

1. Sell the apples to pig farmers.
2. Bag the apples (5-pound bags) and sell them to local supermarkets as seconds.
3. Rent a local canning facility and convert the apples to applesauce.
4. Rent a local canning facility and convert the apples to pie filling.
5. Continue with the current dumping practice.

Of the five alternatives, Alternative 1 was eliminated because there were not enough local pig farmers interested in the apples; Alternative 5 represented the status quo and was eliminated at the request of the owner; Alternative 4 was also eliminated because the local canning facility would need a major capital investment to buy fittings that would convert the equipment to pie-filling capability. The apple producer did not have the ability to raise the capital needed. However, the local facility's equipment could be used (without conversion) for producing applesauce. Thus, Alternative 3 was a possibility. Furthermore, since local supermarkets agreed to buy 5-pound bags of irregular apples and bagging could be done at the warehouse, this option was also a possibility. Thus, two alternatives were deemed feasible.

Step 3: Predicting Costs and Benefits and Eliminating Irrelevant Costs

Suppose that the apple producer predicts that labor and materials (bags and ties) for the bagging option would cost $0.05 per pound. The 5-pound bags of apples could be sold for $1.30 per bag to the local supermarkets. Making applesauce would cost $0.40 per pound for rent, labor, apples, cans, and other materials (rent is charged on a per-pound processed basis). It takes six pounds of apples to produce five, 16-ounce cans of applesauce. Each 16-ounce can will sell for $0.78. The apple producer decides that the cost of growing and harvesting the apples is not relevant to choosing between the bagging alternative and the applesauce alternative.

Step 4: Comparing Relevant Costs and Relating to Strategic Goals

The bagging alternative costs $0.25 to produce a 5-pound bag ($0.05 × 5 pounds), and the revenue is $1.30 per bag, or $0.26 per pound. Thus, the net benefit is $0.21 per pound ($0.26 − $0.05). For the applesauce alternative, six pounds of apples produce five 16-ounce cans of applesauce. The revenue for five cans is $3.90 (5 × $0.78), which converts to $0.65 per pound ($3.90/6). Thus, the net benefit is $0.25 per pound ($0.65 − $0.40). Of the two alternatives, the applesauce option offers $0.04 more per pound than the bagging option. The applesauce alternative, from the viewpoint of the apple producer, requires a forward integration strategy. The apple producer currently is not involved in producing any apple consumer products. Moreover, the apple producer is reluctant to move into applesauce production. The producer has absolutely no experience in this part of the industrial value chain and knows little about the channels of distribution for applesauce. An outside expert would need to be hired. Finally, the rental opportunity is a year-to-year issue. In the long term, a major capital commitment would be needed. Bagging the small apples, on the other hand, is a product differentiation strategy that allows the producer to operate within familiar territory.

Step 5: Selecting the Best Alternative

Since the apple producer is reluctant to follow a forward integration strategy, the bagging alternative should be chosen. This alternative maintains the current position in the industrial value chain and strengthens the producer's competitive position by following a differentiation strategy for the small, odd-shaped apples.

Summary of Decision-Making Process

The five steps define a simple decision model. A decision model is a set of procedures that, if followed, will lead to a decision. Exhibit 18-1, on the following page, summarizes and illustrates the steps for the decision model that describe the tactical decision-making process.

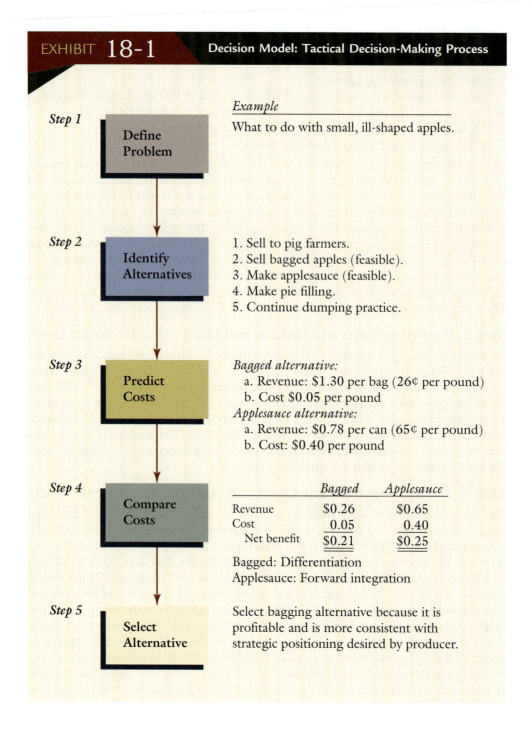

EXHIBIT 18-1   Decision Model: Tactical Decision-Making Process

Example

Step 1 — Define Problem
What to do with small, ill-shaped apples.

Step 2 — Identify Alternatives
1. Sell to pig farmers.
2. Sell bagged apples (feasible).
3. Make applesauce (feasible).
4. Make pie filling.
5. Continue dumping practice.

Step 3 — Predict Costs
Bagged alternative:
   a. Revenue: $1.30 per bag (26¢ per pound)
   b. Cost $0.05 per pound
Applesauce alternative:
   a. Revenue: $0.78 per can (65¢ per pound)
   b. Cost: $0.40 per pound

Step 4 — Compare Costs

	Bagged	Applesauce
Revenue	$0.26	$0.65
Cost	0.05	0.40
Net benefit	$0.21	$0.25

Bagged: Differentiation
Applesauce: Forward integration

Step 5 — Select Alternative
Select bagging alternative because it is profitable and is more consistent with strategic positioning desired by producer.

Steps three and four define *tactical cost analysis.* Tactical cost analysis is the use of relevant cost data to identify the alternative that provides the greatest benefit to the organization. Thus, tactical cost analysis includes predicting costs, identifying relevant costs, and comparing relevant costs.

Tactical cost analysis, however, is only part of the overall decision process. Qualitative factors also must be considered.

Qualitative Factors

While cost analysis plays a key role in tactical decision making, it does have its limitations. Relevant cost information is not all the information a manager should consider. Other information, often qualitative in nature, is needed to make an informed decision.

For example, the relationship of the alternatives being considered to the organization's strategic objectives is essentially a qualitative assessment.

Other qualitative factors are also important. For example, emergency rooms may decide to use surgical glue rather than sutures to close a child's wound. The cost of the gluing kit is roughly the same as the cost of a suture kit. However, gluing does not require an anesthetic (i.e., a shot of Novocain), it is faster and less painful for the patient, and it dries to a cool blue color—a real plus for hip elementary-age children. Parents have been known to shop for an emergency room that uses surgical glue for just these qualitative reasons.[2] The lesson here is that cost analysis can and should be viewed as only one input for the final decision.

How should qualitative factors be handled in the decision-making process? First of all, they must be identified. Secondly, the decision maker should try to quantify them. Often, qualitative factors are simply more difficult to quantify, but not impossible. For example, possible unreliability of the outside supplier might be quantified as the probable number of days late multiplied by the labor cost of downtime in the plant. Finally, truly qualitative factors, such as the impact of late orders on customer relations, must be taken into consideration in the final step of the decision-making model—the selection of the alternative with the greatest overall benefit.

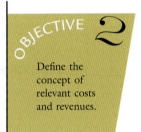

OBJECTIVE 2

Define the concept of relevant costs and revenues.

Relevant Costs and Revenues

A significant input in choosing among the alternatives is cost. All other things being equal, the alternative with the lower cost should be chosen. In choosing between the two alternatives, only the costs and revenues relevant to the decision should be considered. Identifying and comparing relevant costs and revenues is the heart of the tactical decision model illustrated in Exhibit 18-1. Thus, it is essential to know what is meant by relevant costs and revenues. **Relevant costs (revenues)** are future costs (revenues) that differ across alternatives. The definition is the same for costs or revenues; thus, to keep things simple, our discussion will focus on relevant costs, with the understanding that the same principles also apply to revenues. All decisions relate to the future; accordingly, only future costs can be relevant to decisions. However, to be relevant, a cost must not only be a future cost, but it also must differ from one alternative to another. If a future cost is the same for more than one alternative, it has no effect on the decision. Such a cost is an *irrelevant* cost. The ability to identify relevant and irrelevant costs is an important decision-making skill.

Relevant Costs Illustrated

To illustrate the concept of relevant costs, consider Avicom, Inc., a company that makes jet engines for commercial aircraft. A supplier has approached the company and offered to sell one component, nacelles (enclosures for jet engines), for what appears to be an attractive price. The company is now faced with a make-or-buy decision. Assume that the cost of direct materials used to produce the nacelles is $270,000 per year (based on normal volume). Should this cost be a factor in the decision? Is the direct materials cost a future cost that differs across the two alternatives? It is certainly a future cost. To produce the component for another year requires materials which must be purchased. But does the direct materials cost differ across the two alternatives? If the component is purchased from an external supplier, no internal production is needed. The need to purchase materials for producing the nacelles can be eliminated, reducing the materials cost to zero. Since the cost of direct materials differs across alternatives ($270,000 for the make alternative and $0 for the buy alternative), it is a relevant cost.

---

2. Tara Parker-Pope, "Surgical Glue Removes Much Pain and Time from Closing Wounds," *The Wall Street Journal* (December 28, 1998): B1.

Implicit in this analysis is the use of a past cost to estimate a future cost. For example, assume that the most recent cost of materials to support production of the nacelles was $260,000. Adjusting this past cost for anticipated price increases produced the projected cost of $270,000. Thus, although past costs are never relevant, they are often used as the basis for predicting what future costs will be.

Irrelevant Cost Illustrated

Avicom uses machinery to manufacture nacelles. This machinery was purchased five years ago and is being depreciated at an annual rate of $50,000. Is this $50,000 a relevant cost? In other words, is depreciation a future cost that differs across the two alternatives?

Past Costs

Depreciation, in this case, represents an allocation of a cost already incurred. (The cost is being allocated to time periods.) It is a **sunk cost**, an allocation of a past cost. Thus, regardless of which alternative is chosen, the acquisition cost of the machinery cannot be avoided. It is the same across both alternatives. Although we allocate this sunk cost to future periods and call that allocation *depreciation*, none of the original cost is avoidable. Sunk costs are past costs. They are always the same across alternatives and are therefore always irrelevant. Thus, the acquisition cost of the machinery and its associated depreciation should not be a factor in the make-or-buy decision.

Future Costs

Assume that the cost to heat and cool the plant—$40,000 per year—is allocated to different production departments, including the department that produces nacelles, which receives $4,000 of the cost. Is this $4,000 cost relevant to the make-or-buy decision facing Avicom?

The cost of providing plant utilities is a future cost, since it must be paid in future years. But does the cost differ across the make-and-buy alternatives? It is unlikely that the cost of heating and cooling the plant will change whether nacelles are produced or not. Thus, the cost is the same across both alternatives. The amount of the utility payment allocated to the remaining departments may change if production of nacelles is stopped, but the level of the total payment is unaffected by the decision. It is therefore an irrelevant cost.

Relevant Costs and Benefits in International Trade

Relevant costs and benefits are useful in decision making in the international trade arena. For example, a company may import materials for use in production. While this transaction may look identical to the purchase of materials from domestic suppliers, U.S. tariffs add complexity and cost. A **tariff** is a tax on imports levied by the federal government. Any cost associated with the purchase of materials, such as freight-in or a tariff, is a materials cost. Companies search for ways to reduce tariffs. They may restrict the amount of imported materials, alter the materials by adding U.S. resources (to increase the domestic content and gain a more favorable tariff status), or utilize foreign trade zones.

Foreign Trade Zones

The U.S. government has set up **foreign trade zones (FTZs)**, or areas that are physically on U.S. soil but considered to be outside U.S. commerce. Companies in FTZs can engage in warehousing and/or manufacturing. If the items leave the FTZ bound for non-U.S. destinations, then no tariff is due. If they leave the zone for U.S. destinations, then the tariff is due. Because foreign trade zones must be located near a customs port of entry, they are often located near seaports or airports. San Antonio, New

Orleans, and Oklahoma City are examples of cities with foreign trade zones. Goods imported into a foreign trade zone are duty-free until they leave the zone. This has important implications for manufacturing firms that import materials. Some U.S. companies set up manufacturing plants within the foreign trade zones. Since tariffs are not paid until the imported materials leave the zone, as part of a finished product, the company can postpone payment of duty and the associated loss of working capital. Additionally, the company does not pay duty on defective materials or inventory that has not yet been included in finished products.

An example may help to illustrate the potential cost advantages. Suppose that Roadrunner, Inc., operates a petrochemical plant located in a foreign trade zone. The plant imports volatile materials (i.e., chemicals that experience substantial evaporation loss during processing) for use in production. Wilycoyote, Inc., operates an identical plant just outside the foreign trade zone. Consider the impact on duty and related expenditures for the two plants for the purchase of $400,000 of crude oil imported from Venezuela. Both Roadrunner and Wilycoyote use the oil in chemical production. Each purchases the oil about three months before use in production, and the finished chemicals remain in inventory about five months before sale and shipment to the customer. About 30 percent of the oil is lost through evaporation during production. Duty is assessed at 6 percent of cost. Each company faces a 12 percent carrying cost.

Wilycoyote pays duty, at the point of purchase, of $24,000 (0.06 × $400,000). In addition, Wilycoyote has carrying cost associated with the duty payment of 12 percent per year times the portion of the year that the oil is in materials or finished goods inventory. In this case, the months in inventory equal 8 (3 + 5). Total duty-related carrying cost is $1,920 (0.12 × 8/12 × $24,000). Together, duty and duty-related carrying cost totals $25,920. Roadrunner, on the other hand, pays duty at the time of sale because it is in a foreign trade zone. Imported goods do not incur duty until (unless) they are moved out of the zone. Since 70 percent of the original imported oil remains in the final product, duty equals $16,800 (0.7 × $400,000 × 0.06). No carrying cost is associated with the duty. The duty-related costs for the two companies are summarized as follows:

	Roadrunner	*Wilycoyote*
Duty paid at purchase	$ 0	$24,000
Carrying cost of duty	0	1,920
Duty paid at sale	16,800	0
Total duty and duty-related cost	$16,800	$25,920

Clearly, Roadrunner has saved $9,120 ($25,920 − $16,800) on just one purchase of imported materials by locating in the foreign trade zone.

In the above example, the underlying business decision involves whether or not to locate in a foreign trade zone. Relevant costs include the cost of duty and the carrying cost of duty for plants located inside and outside the zone. Additional potential for cost reduction inside the zone occurs when goods that do not meet U.S. health, safety, and pollution control regulations are subject to fine. Noncomplying foreign goods can be imported into foreign trade zones and modified to comply with the law without being subject to the fine. Another example of the efficient use of foreign trade zones is the assembly of high-tariff component parts into a lower-tariff finished product. In this case, the addition of domestic labor raises the domestic content of the finished product and makes the embedded foreign parts eligible for more favorable tariff treatment.[3]

---

3. These examples are taken from James E. Groff and John P. McCray, "Foreign-Trade Zones: Opportunity for Strategic Development in the Southwest," *Journal of Business Strategies* (Spring 1992): 14–26.

A qualitative factor is that logistics may be streamlined by using foreign trade zones, leading to quicker and more efficient clearance of customs.

Relevancy, Cost Behavior, and the Activity Resource Usage Model

OBJECTIVE 3

Explain how the activity resource usage model is used in assessing relevancy.

Understanding cost behavior is basic in determining relevancy. When costs were primarily unit-based, a simple distinction between fixed and variable costs could be made. Now, however, the ABC model has us focusing on unit-level, batch-level, product-level, and facility-level costs. The first three are variable, but with respect to different types of activity drivers. The activity resource usage model can help us sort out the behavior of various activity costs and assess their relevance.

The activity resource usage model has two resource categories: (1) flexible resources and (2) committed resources. Recall from Chapter 3 that flexible resources are those that are acquired as used and needed. Committed resources are acquired in advance of usage. These categories and their usefulness in relevant costing are described in the following sections.

Flexible Resources

Resource spending is the cost of acquiring activity capacity. The amount paid for the supply of an activity is the activity cost. For flexible resources, the activity resources demanded (used) equal the resources supplied. Thus, for this resource category, *if the demand for an activity changes across alternatives*, then resource spending will change and the cost of the activity is relevant to the decision. For example, electricity supplied internally uses fuel for the generator. Fuel is a flexible resource. Now, consider the following two alternatives: (1) accept a special, 1-time order and (2) reject the special order. If accepting the order increases the demand for kilowatt-hours (power's activity driver), then the cost of power will differ across alternatives by the increase in fuel consumption (assuming fuel is the only resource acquired as needed). Therefore, power cost is relevant to the decision.

Committed Resources

Committed resources are acquired in advance of usage through implicit contracting, and they are usually acquired in lumpy amounts. Consider an organization's salaried and hourly employees. The implicit understanding is that the organization will maintain employment levels even though there may be temporary downturns in the amount of an activity used. This means that an activity may have unused capacity available. Thus, an increase in demand for an activity across alternatives may not mean that the activity cost will increase (because all the increased demand is absorbed by the unused activity capacity). For example, assume a company has five manufacturing engineers who supply a capacity of 10,000 engineering hours (2,000 hours each). The cost of this activity capacity is $250,000, or $25 per hour. Suppose that this year the company expects to use only 9,000 engineering hours for its normal business. This means that the engineering activity has 1,000 hours of unused capacity. In deciding to reject or accept a special order that requires 500 engineering hours, the cost of engineering would be irrelevant. The order can be filled using unused engineering capacity, and the resource spending is the same for each alternative ($250,000 will be spent whether or not the order is accepted).

However, *if a change in demand across activities produces a change in resource supply*, then the activity cost will change and be relevant to the decision. A change in resource supply means a change in resource spending and consequently a change in activity cost. A change in resource spending can occur in one of two ways: (1) the demand for the resource exceeds the supply (increases resource spending) and (2) the demand for the resource drops permanently and supply exceeds demand enough so that activity capacity can be reduced (decreases resource spending).

To illustrate the first change, consider once again the engineering activity and the special order decision. Suppose that the special order requires 1,500 engineering hours. This exceeds the resource supply. To meet the demand, the organization would need to hire a sixth engineer or perhaps use a consulting engineer. Either way, resource spending increases if the order is accepted; thus, the cost of engineering is now a relevant cost.

To illustrate the second type of change, suppose that the company's manager is considering purchasing a component used for production instead of making it in-house. Assume the same facts about engineering capacity: 10,000 hours available and 9,000 used. If the component is purchased, then the demand for engineering hours will drop from 9,000 to 7,000. This is a permanent reduction because engineering support will no longer be needed for manufacturing the component. Unused capacity is now 3,000 hours, 2,000 permanent and 1,000 temporary. Furthermore, since engineering capacity is acquired in chunks of 2,000, this means that the company can reduce activity capacity and resource spending by laying off one engineer or reassigning the engineer to another plant where the services are in demand. Either way, the resource supply is reduced to 8,000 hours. If an engineer's salary is $50,000, then engineering cost would differ by $50,000 across the make-or-buy alternatives. This cost is then relevant to the decision. However, if the demand for the engineering activity drops by less than 2,000 hours, the increase in unused capacity is not enough to reduce resource supply and resource spending; in this case, the cost of the engineering activity would not be relevant.

Often, committed resources are acquired in advance for multiple periods—before the resource demands are known. Leasing or buying a building are examples. Buying multiperiod activity capacity is often done by paying cash up front. In this case, an annual expense may be recognized, but no additional resource spending is needed. Up-front resource spending is a sunk cost and thus never relevant. Periodic resource spending, such as leasing, is essentially independent of resource usage. Even if a permanent reduction of activity usage is experienced, it is difficult to reduce resource spending because of formal contractual commitments.

For example, assume a company leases a plant for $100,000 per year for 10 years. The plant is capable of producing 20,000 units of a product—the level expected when the plant was leased. After five years, suppose that the demand for the product drops and the plant needs to produce only 15,000 units each year. The lease payment of $100,000 still must be paid each year even though production activity has decreased. Now, suppose that demand increases beyond the 20,000-unit capability. In this case, the company may consider acquiring or leasing an additional plant. Here, resource spending could change across alternatives. The decision, however, to acquire long-term activity capacity is not in the realm of tactical decision making. This is not a short-term or small-scale decision. Decisions involving multiperiod capabilities are called capital investment decisions and are covered in Chapter 20. Thus, for the multiperiod resource category, changes in activity demands across alternatives rarely affect resource spending and are therefore not usually relevant for tactical decision making. When resource spending does change, it means assessing the prospect of a multiperiod commitment, which is properly treated using capital investment decision models. Exhibit 18-2, on the following page, summarizes the activity resource usage model's role in assessing relevancy.

EXHIBIT 18-2	Resource Demand and Supply

Category	Relationships	Relevancy
Flexible	Supply = Demand	
	a. Demand changes	a. Relevant
	b. Demand constant	b. Not relevant
Committed	Supply − Demand = Unused capacity	
	a. Demand increase < Unused capacity	a. Not relevant
	b. Demand increase > Unused capacity	b. Relevant
	c. Demand decrease (permanent)	
	1. Activity capacity reduced	1. Relevant
	2. Activity capacity unchanged	2. Not relevant

Illustrative Examples of Tactical Decision Making

OBJECTIVE 4

Apply the tactical decision-making concepts in a variety of business situations.

The activity resource usage model and the concept of relevancy are valuable tools in making tactical decisions. It is important to see how they are used to solve a variety of problems. Applications include decisions to make or buy a component, to keep or drop a segment or product line, to accept or reject a special order at less than the usual price, and to process a joint product further or sell it at the split-off point. Of course, this is not an exhaustive list. However, the same decision-making principles can be applied to other settings. Once you see how they are used, it is relatively easy to apply them in any appropriate setting. In illustrating the applications, we assume that the first two steps of the tactical decision-making model (see Exhibit 18-1) have already been done. Thus, the emphasis is on tactical cost analysis.

Make-or-Buy Decisions

Organizations are often faced with a **make-or-buy decision**—a decision of whether to make or to buy components or services used in making a product or providing a service. For example, a physician can buy laboratory tests from external suppliers (hospitals or for-profit laboratories), or these lab tests can be done internally. Similarly, a PC computer manufacturer can make its own disk drives, or they can be bought from external suppliers.

Outsourcing of technical and professional jobs is becoming an important make-or-buy issue. **Outsourcing** is the payment by a company for a business function that was formerly done in-house. For example, some domestic companies outsource their legal needs to outside law firms rather than hiring corporate attorneys. Outsourcing refers to the move of a business function to another company, either inside or outside the United States. In the 1990s, for example, a number of companies set up design and call center operations in non-U.S. locations. **Texas Instruments (TI)** set up an engineering facility in Bangalore, India. The availability of underemployed college graduates in India meant the combination of low wage rates and high productivity. However, the underdeveloped Indian infrastructure required considerable capital investment. TI installed its own electrical generators and satellite dishes, some hauled in by oxcart, to operate efficiently. Then, the company's engineers in Dallas and in Miho, Japan, designed parts of a memory chip and forwarded their work via computers and satellites to engineers at Bangalore for completion.

Of course, qualitative considerations also play into the outsourcing decision. Time is a valuable resource, and many companies have found that a global presence leads to time and quality enhancement. For example, software companies have found that locating call centers in Ireland and the United States increases the number of hours of available customer service each day. A customer in New York who needs an answer to a question may not get help from a California-based call center but will get help from a Dublin-based center. On the negative side, the political ramifications of outsourcing, with its overtones of "exporting jobs," have led companies to weigh the decision more carefully.

Make-or-buy decisions are not short run in nature but fall into the small-scale tactical decision category. For example, the decision to make or buy may be motivated by cost leadership and/or differentiation strategies. Making instead of buying or buying instead of making may be one way of reducing the cost of producing the main product. Alternatively, choosing to make or buy may be a way of increasing the quality of the component and thus increasing the overall quality of the final product (differentiating on the basis of quality).

Cost Analysis: Activity-Based Cost Management System

To illustrate the cost analysis for a make-or-buy problem, assume that Talmage Company produces a mechanical part used in one of its engines. (Talmage produces engines for snowblowers.) An outside supplier has offered to sell a part (Part 34B) for $4.75. The company normally produces 100,000 units of the part each year. The activities associated with producing the part and other useful information are listed in Exhibit 18-3. The cost formulas that use units as the activity driver refer to units of Part 34B. The remaining activity cost formulas are more general and reflect all demands made on the activity. All activity capacities are annual capacity measures. The cost of providing space includes annual plant depreciation, property taxes, and annual maintenance. This cost is allocated to the products based on the square feet of space occupied by the product's production equipment. The variable component of each activity represents the cost of flexible resources. The fixed cost component represents the cost of committed resources. Whenever there is a fixed component, the activity capacity refers to the capacity acquired by spending in advance of usage. Units of purchase indicate how many units of the activity (as measured by its driver) must be acquired at a time (if more than

---

EXHIBIT 18-3   Activity and Cost Information

Activity	Cost Driver	Cost Formula	Activity Capacity	Expected Activity Usage	Part 34B Activity Usage	Units of Purchase
Using materials	Units	$Y = \$0.50X$	As needed	100,000	100,000	1
Using direct labor	Units	$Y = \$2X$	As needed	100,000	100,000	1
Providing supervision	Number of lines	$Y = \$300,000$	15	15	3	3
Moving materials	Number of moves	$Y = \$250,000 + \$0.60X$	250,000	240,000	40,000	25,000
Providing power	Machine hours	$Y = \$3X$	As needed	30,000	30,000	1
Inspecting products	Inspection hours	$Y = \$280,000 + \$1.50X$	16,000	14,000	2,000	2,000
Setting up equipment	Setup hours	$Y = \$600,000$	60,000	58,000	6,000	2,000
Providing space	Square feet	$Y = \$1,000,000$	50,000	50,000	5,000	50,000
Equipment depreciation	Units	$Y = \$0.50X$	120,000	100,000	100,000	15,000

one, it is called a "lumpy" amount). For committed resources, the cost of acquiring the lumpy amount is obtained by dividing the activity fixed cost by activity capacity and then multiplying this amount by the units of purchase. For example, the cost of acquiring three units of supervision is $60,000 [($300,000/15) \times 3]$.

From the perspective of tactical cost analysis, whether or not Talmage should continue making Part 34B or buy it from an external supplier depends on how much *resource spending* can be reduced because of the ability to reduce resource usage (by buying instead of making). If Talmage buys Part 34B instead of making it, *resource usage* decreases for each of the nine activities (by the amount indicated in the Part 34B Activity Usage column). Thus, for activities associated with committed resources—providing space and equipment depreciation—spending will not change, and so the cost is not relevant (see Exhibit 18-2). For activities associated with flexible resources, activity demand changes, and so the cost of these resources is relevant to the decision (see Exhibit 18-2). These activities include using materials, using direct labor, providing power, and the variable components of moving materials and inspecting products. The change in resource spending is simply the cost per unit of driver multiplied by the variable rate in the cost formula. For example, for materials, resource spending decreases by $50,000 if Part 34B is purchased rather than made ($0.50 \times 100,000$). The variable cost of moving materials, on the other hand, decreases by $24,000 ($0.60 \times 40,000$ moves). The changes in costs for the five activities with variable components (resources acquired as needed) are as follows:

Activity	Make[a]	Buy[b]	Differential Cost[c]
Using materials	$ 50,000	$ 0	$ 50,000
Using direct labor	200,000	0	200,000
Moving materials	144,000	120,000	24,000
Providing power	90,000	0	90,000
Inspecting products	21,000	18,000	3,000

[a]Variable rate $\times$ Expected activity usage.
[b]Variable rate $\times$ (Expected usage $-$ Part 34B usage).
[c]Make activity cost $-$ Buy activity cost.

Some committed resources are more difficult to analyze. These include providing supervision, moving materials, inspecting products, and setting up equipment.

For the make-or-buy decision, all four activities experience a permanent decrease in activity demand. The issue is whether or not activity capacity can be reduced so that resource spending can be reduced (see Exhibit 18-2). Assume that any current unused capacity (Capacity $-$ Expected usage) is temporary. The permanent demand decrease is measured only by the drop in Part 34B activity usage. Resource spending can be reduced if activity capacity can be decreased because of the permanent drop in resource usage. For example, providing supervision must be purchased in units of three. The decrease in demand for this activity by dropping Part 34B is three units. Thus, the cost of providing supervision is relevant because resource spending on supervision can be decreased by $60,000 [($300,000/15) \times 3]$. The analysis for moving materials provides additional insight. If Part 34B is no longer made, the demand for this activity will decrease by 40,000 units. However, since capacity for moving materials is purchased in units of 25,000, activity capacity can only be decreased by 25,000 units. The reduction in resource spending is $25,000 [($250,000/250,000) \times 25,000]$. The cost is relevant, but the difference in cost between the two alternatives is less than the reduction of the cost of resource usage because of the lumpy nature of the resource. Similar analyses can be done for the inspections and setup activities. The changes in activity cost for short-term resources acquired in advance are as follows:

Activity	Make[a]	Buy[b]	Differential Cost[c]
Providing supervision	$300,000	$240,000	$60,000
Moving materials	250,000	225,000	25,000
Inspecting products	280,000	245,000	35,000
Setting up equipment	600,000	540,000	60,000

[a]Fixed activity cost.
[b](Fixed cost/Activity capacity) × Reduction in activity capacity.
[c]Make activity cost − Buy activity cost.

To complete the cost analysis, we need only information concerning the activity costs that are added *because* of buying rather than making. The most obvious is the acquisition cost of the part itself. For simplicity, let's assume that the procurement activities (purchasing, receiving, and paying suppliers) have sufficient unused capacity to absorb any increase in demand from acquiring Part 34B. With this assumption, the elements of the make-or-buy analysis are now complete. The cost analysis is summarized in Exhibit 18-4. The costs for each activity resource category are aggregated so that we have a total picture of the effects of making versus buying. The tactical cost analysis supports the buy alternative. This alternative provides a $72,000 benefit over the make alternative. Based on 100,000 units, buying is cheaper by $0.72 per unit ($72,000/100,000). All things being equal, Talmage should buy Part 34B instead of making it.

EXHIBIT 18-4   **ABC Make-or-Buy Analysis: Talmage Company**

Activity	Make	Buy	Differential Cost
Using materials	$ 50,000	$ 0	$ 50,000
Using direct labor	200,000	0	200,000
Providing supervision	300,000	240,000	60,000
Moving materials	394,000	345,000	49,000
Providing power	90,000	0	90,000
Inspecting products	301,000	263,000	38,000
Setting up equipment	600,000	540,000	60,000
Acquiring Part 34B	0	475,000	(475,000)
Totals	$1,935,000	$1,863,000	$ 72,000

Cost Analysis: Functional-Based Cost Management System

A functional-based cost management system would not supply detailed information about non-unit-level activities and costs; it would provide only unit-level activity data. Non-unit-level costs are all assumed to be fixed with respect to changes in production volume. A typical functional-based analysis would identify the costs of materials, labor, power, and supervision of Part 34B as relevant. (Supervision of Part 34B would be viewed as a direct fixed cost and would disappear if production of Part 34B stops; therefore, it is relevant.) All other costs would be classified as irrelevant because they would not change as production volume changes. A summary of the functional-based make-or-buy analysis is provided in Exhibit 18-5 on the following page. This analysis supports the make alternative, indicating a $75,000 benefit to making over buying. This analysis is more limited because it has less access to activity information. The use of a more limited information set may lead to erroneous decisions.

EXHIBIT 18-5	Functional-Based Make-or-Buy Analysis: Talmage Company		
Activity	**Make**	**Buy**	**Differential Cost**
Using materials	$ 50,000	$ 0	$ 50,000
Using direct labor	200,000	0	200,000
Providing supervision	300,000	240,000	60,000
Providing power	90,000	0	90,000
Acquiring Part 34B	0	475,000	(475,000)
Totals	$640,000	$715,000	$ (75,000)

Keep-or-Drop Decisions

Often, a manager needs to determine whether a segment, such as a product line, should be kept or dropped. **General Motors**, for example, decided to drop the Oldsmobile line. A **keep-or-drop decision** uses relevant cost analysis to determine whether a segment of a business should be kept or dropped. In a functional-based cost management system, segmented income statements, using unit-based fixed or variable costs, improve the ability to make keep-or-drop decisions. Similarly, by increasing traceability, segmented reporting using ABC classifications and the resource usage model offers a significant improvement in information content over the unit-based, variable-costing segmented report. JIT manufacturing offers even more capabilities. By localizing many costs (e.g., maintenance, materials handling, and inspection) that were formerly common to a variety of products and by changing the behavior of some costs (e.g., direct labor), the number of directly attributable costs has been increased. Decisions to drop or keep a segment are facilitated by the increased number of directly attributable costs in a JIT environment.

Keep-or-Drop: Functional-Based Analysis

The logic underlying a functional-based keep-or-drop analysis is fairly straightforward. Revenues and costs that belong to a segment are identified. Directly attributable revenues, unit-based variable costs, and directly attributable fixed costs are defined as costs that belong to the segment. If the segment is dropped, then only the traceable revenues and costs should vanish; thus, the traceable revenues and costs are relevant to the decision. Furthermore, the traceable income (loss) determines whether a segment should be dropped or kept. If the segment income is positive, then the segment is kept; if negative, then the decision is to drop the segment (this assumes that the segment income is expected to persist over time). Exhibit 18-6 shows a functional-based segmented income statement, where products are defined as segments. More detail is provided on the statement than usual so that the effects of moving to an activity-based statement can be illustrated more clearly. The statement indicates that both seat covers and floor mats are providing positive product margins. It is unlikely, based on the information here, that the company would drop either product line. Yet, overall profitability for the company is not impressive—barely above the break-even point. An important issue—in fact, a critical issue in segmented analysis—is the ability to trace costs to individual segments. Improved traceability is offered by ABC classifications.

Keep-or-Drop: ABC Analysis

Exhibit 18-7, on page 796, presents an activity-based segmented statement. The same example used for functional-based segmented reporting is used so that both keep-or-drop decisions can be compared. For the ABC approach, machine depreciation is traced to each segment using machine hours to measure usage (units-of-production

EXHIBIT 18-6	Functional-Based Segmented Income Statement		
	Seat Covers	**Floor Mats**	**Total**
Sales	$ 950,000	$1,680,000	$2,630,000
Less variable costs:			
Direct materials	(300,000)	(400,000)	(700,000)
Direct labor	(210,000)	(210,000)	(420,000)
Maintenance	(90,000)	(90,000)	(180,000)
Power	(35,000)	(25,000)	(60,000)
Commissions	(30,000)	(40,000)	(70,000)
Contribution margin	$ 285,000	$ 915,000	$1,200,000
Less direct fixed costs:			
Advertising	(30,000)	(20,000)	(50,000)
Supervision	(50,000)	(50,000)	(100,000)
Product margin	$ 205,000	$ 845,000	$1,050,000
Less common fixed expenses:			
Depreciation—machinery			(100,000)
Depreciation—plant			(160,000)
Inspecting products			(200,000)
Customer service			(150,000)
General administration			(180,000)
Materials handling			(140,000)
Sales administration			(80,000)
Operating income			$ 40,000

depreciation method). Two batch-level costs—inspecting products and materials handling—are assigned to products using batch-level drivers (number of batches and moves). Assume that cost analysts have determined that these two batch-level activities have both flexible and committed resources. Flexible resources are labeled as a non-unit variable expense. The cost of committed resources is treated as a fixed expense and, where possible, is divided into two categories: *traceable fixed expenses*, representing the cost of fixed resource usage traced to each segment using activity drivers, and *unused activity expenses*, treated as a common fixed expense. Notice that the cost of facility-level activities is not traced to the two products. Two product-level costs—customer service and sales administration—are also assigned to products using the number of complaints and number of sales orders. Resources associated with these two activities are all committed resources, and the resources used by each product are labeled as traceable fixed expenses. It could also be argued that advertising and supervision are product-level activities (the cost of these activities increases as the number of products increases). There is no need, however, to use an activity driver to trace advertising or supervision costs to each product line. Advertising and supervision costs are traceable to each product using direct tracing and are labeled as direct fixed costs.

The ABC segmented statement provides a much different view of product profitability than does the functional-based segmented statement. First, we see that the company is paying for resources that are not being used, totaling $90,000. Second, seat covers are unprofitable and are causing a significant drain on company resources. Thus, the ABC segmented income statement reveals three possible ways of increasing income: (1) reducing resource spending by exploiting the current unused activity capacities, (2) eliminating the unprofitable product line, and (3) a combination of (1) and (2).

EXHIBIT 18-7	ABC Segmented Income Statement		
	Seat Covers	**Floor Mats**	**Total**
Sales	$ 950,000	$1,680,000	$2,630,000
Less unit-level variable expenses:			
Direct materials	(300,000)	(400,000)	(700,000)
Direct labor	(210,000)	(210,000)	(420,000)
Maintenance	(90,000)	(90,000)	(180,000)
Power	(35,000)	(25,000)	(60,000)
Commissions	(30,000)	(40,000)	(70,000)
Contribution margin	$ 285,000	$ 915,000	$1,200,000
Less traceable expenses:			
Advertising, direct fixed	(30,000)	(20,000)	(50,000)
Supervision, direct fixed	(50,000)	(50,000)	(100,000)
Machine depreciation, traceable fixed	(50,000)	(50,000)	(100,000)
Inspecting products, non-unit variable	(20,000)	(10,000)	(30,000)
Inspecting products, traceable fixed	(80,000)	(50,000)	(130,000)
Materials handling, non-unit variable	(10,000)	(14,000)	(24,000)
Materials handling, traceable fixed	(70,000)	(26,000)	(96,000)
Customer service, traceable fixed	(45,000)	(75,000)	(120,000)
Sales administration, traceable fixed	(50,000)	(30,000)	(80,000)
Product margin	$(120,000)	$ 590,000	$ 470,000
Less common expenses:			
Unused activity:			
Inspecting products			(40,000)
Materials handling			(20,000)
Customer service			(30,000)
Facility-level:			
Plant depreciation			(160,000)
General administration			(180,000)
Operating income			$ 40,000

Of the three ways of increasing income, the last two consider the possibility of dropping the seat cover line. Before making a decision about keeping or dropping the unprofitable line, the manager needs to know how much resource spending will change. First, all unit and non-unit variable expenses will vanish if the line is dropped, as will direct fixed expenses. Notice, however, that machine depreciation—even though unitized—is not relevant to the decision. (Depreciation is an allocation of a sunk cost.) Dropping the unprofitable line increases the cost of unused resources from $90,000 to $325,000. (The total increases by the sum of the seat cover's traceable fixed expenses, excluding machine depreciation, since it's not relevant.) If seat covers are dropped, the demand for inspecting products, customer service, materials handling, and sales administration will decrease. Thus, the key to completing the keep-or-drop analysis is assessing how much of the cost of unused capacity for these activities can be eliminated. Exhibit 18-8 indicates the activity capacity, unused activity (before dropping), seat cover activity usage, and units of purchase for each of the four activities with potentially relevant traceable fixed expenses. The unused activity (before dropping) for inspecting and customer service is viewed as permanent—a result of a quality improvement program implemented last year. Unused activity for the materials handling activity is temporary.

Convenience stores constantly balance the need to offer a wide selection of products with the need to streamline offerings so that they can fit into the small-store format. In the past, the stores determined which products to stock based on each one's profitability. Profit was calculated as the difference between wholesale and retail prices. While this sounds reasonable, it completely ignores the additional costs associated with carrying and stocking each product line. In early 2001, the American Wholesale Marketers Association and the National Association of Convenience Stores presented the results of a study of new software designed to "assess each item's profitability by factoring in the operating, labor, inventory, and overhead costs of each item." In the past, the cost of handling a product was not considered when determining per-product costs. However, handling costs are a significant part of the total cost structure.

One owner of a chain of convenience stores tested the software and learned that every auto fuse and bulb sold resulted in a loss of 50 cents. He surveyed customers and found that they were willing to pay a higher price. As a result, he raised the price by one dollar. This achieved two goals. The bulbs and fuses now make money, and customers still appreciate the opportunity to pop into the convenience store for suddenly needed products. The same chain determined that three kinds of laundry detergent were two, too many. It pared its offering to one brand and displayed it more prominently. Sales increased by 20 percent, while costs fell because the sole brand could be ordered by the case.

Source: Ann Zimmerman, "Convenience Stores Create Software to Boost Profitability and Cut Costs," *The Wall Street Journal Interactive Edition* (February 15, 2001).

EXHIBIT 18-8   Activity Information: Keep-or-Drop Analysis

Activity	Activity Driver	Activity Capacity	Unused Activity	Seat Cover Activity Usage	Units of Purchase
Inspecting products	No. of batches	170	40	45	85
Materials handling	No. of moves	2,320	400	1,400	350
Customer service	No. of complaints	300	60	90	60
Sales administration	No. of sales orders	500	0	150	500

Using the information in Exhibit 18-8, the keep-or-drop analysis can be completed. The full analysis is presented in Exhibit 18-9 on the following page. Dropping the product saves the company $45,000 per year. Part of the benefit comes from adding enough to already existing unused capacity so that activity capacity can be reduced, causing a reduction in resource spending. The inspecting products activity illustrates this possibility. The activity could be done by two salaried inspectors, who can each inspect 85 batches per year. Adding 45 more batches of unused activity to the existing unused activity then makes it possible to lay off one inspector.

Special-Order Decisions

Price discrimination laws require that firms sell identical products at the same price to competing customers in the same market. These restrictions do not apply to competitive bids or to noncompeting customers. Bid prices can vary to customers in the same market, and firms often have the opportunity to consider 1-time special orders from potential customers in markets not ordinarily served. **Special-order decisions** focus on whether a specially priced order should be accepted or rejected. Special-order decisions are examples of tactical decisions with a short-term focus. Increasing short-term profits is the limited objective represented by this type of decision. Care should be taken so

EXHIBIT 18-9	ABC Keep-or-Drop Analysis	
	Keep Alternative	**Drop Alternative**
Contribution margin	$285,000	$ 0
Advertising, direct fixed	(50,000)	0
Supervision, direct fixed	(30,000)	0
Inspecting products,[a] non-unit variable	(20,000)	0
Inspecting products, traceable fixed	(80,000)	0
Inspecting products, unused capacity	(40,000)	0
Materials handling,[b] non-unit variable	(10,000)	0
Materials handling, traceable fixed	(70,000)	0
Customer service,[c] traceable fixed	(45,000)	(15,000)
Total	$ (60,000)	$(15,000)

[a]Dropping seat covers will increase the unused capacity from 40 batches to 85 batches. Since activity capacity is purchased in units of 85, this allows the resource spending to be reduced by the traceable fixed expenses plus the cost of unused capacity.

[b]Dropping seat covers will increase the unused capacity from 400 moves to 1,800 moves; however, only 1,400 of the unused capacity is permanent (corresponding to the seat cover's activity usage). Since more capacity must be purchased in units of 350, capacity can be reduced by exactly 1,400 moves, saving all the traceable fixed activity expenses.

[c]Since capacity is purchased in blocks of 60, the existing unused capacity can be reduced by this amount regardless of whether the product is dropped or kept and is therefore not relevant. If the product is dropped, the effect is to create 90 more units of unused capacity. Of these 90 units, 60 units of capacity can be eliminated, reducing the cost of resource spending by $30,000 {[($45,000 + $75,000 + $30,000)/300] × 60}.

that acceptance of special orders does not jeopardize normal distribution channels or adversely affect other strategic elements. With this qualification, it should be noted that special orders often can be attractive, especially when the firm is operating below its maximum productive capacity and when other activities have sufficient unused capacity to absorb any incremental demands the order may make. For this situation, the company can focus its analysis on resources acquired as needed—because this will be the source of any increase in resource spending attributable to the order. Relevance is established by assessing where activity demand increases.

Suppose, for example, that Polarcreme, Inc., an ice-cream company, is operating at 80 percent of its productive capacity. Assume a similar condition exists for non-unit-level activities. The company has a capacity of 20 million half-gallon units. The company expects to produce 8 million units each of regular and premium ice cream. The total costs associated with producing and selling 8 million units of premium ice cream are given in Exhibit 18-10.

An ice-cream distributor from a geographic region not normally served by the company has offered to buy 2 million units of premium ice cream at $1.75 per unit, provided its own label can be attached to the product. The distributor has also agreed to pay the transportation costs. Since the distributor approached the company directly, there is no sales commission. The company estimates that the special order will increase the purchase orders by 10,000, receiving orders by 20,000, and setups by 13. Furthermore, although the order increases the demand for these and other activities, existing unused activity capacity is sufficient to absorb the increased demand. Should the company accept this order or reject it?

The offer of $1.75 is well below the normal selling price of $2.50; in fact, it is even below the total unit cost. Nonetheless, accepting the order may be profitable for the

	Total[a]	Unit Cost
EXHIBIT 18-10 Data for Polarcreme, Inc.: Premium Ice Cream		
Unit-level variable costs:		
Dairy ingredients	$ 5,600	$0.70
Sugar	800	0.10
Flavoring	1,200	0.15
Direct labor	2,000	0.25
Packaging	1,600	0.20
Commissions	160	0.02
Distribution	240	0.03
Other	400	0.05
Total unit-level costs	$12,000	$1.50
Non-unit-level variable costs:		
Purchasing ($8 × 40,000 purchase orders)	$ 320	$0.04
Receiving ($6 × 80,000 receiving orders)	480	0.06
Setting up ($8,000 × 50 setups)	400	0.05
Total non-unit-level costs	$ 1,200	$0.15
Fixed activity costs:		
Total fixed costs[b]	$ 1,600	$0.20
Total costs	$14,800	$1.85
Wholesale selling price	$20,000	$2.50

[a]All costs expressed in thousands.
[b]The total cost of providing capacity for all activities within the firm assigned to premium.

company. The company does have idle capacity, and the order will not displace other units being produced to sell at the normal price. Additionally, many of the costs are not relevant; spending for resources acquired in advance of usage will not change regardless of whether the order is accepted or rejected.

If the order is accepted, a benefit of $1.75 per unit will be realized that otherwise would be unavailable. However, all of the unit-level variable costs except for distribution ($0.03) and commissions ($0.02) will be incurred, producing a cost of $1.45 per unit. Furthermore, the non-unit-level variable costs will also be incurred, producing a total incremental cost of $304,000, or $0.152 per unit (for an order of 2 million units). Therefore, the company will see a net benefit of $0.148 ($1.75 − $1.602). Thus, Polarcreme's profits would increase by $296,000 ($0.148 × 2,000,000). The relevant cost analysis is summarized in Exhibit 18-11 on the following page.

Decisions to Sell or Process Further

Joint products have common processes and costs of production up to a split-off point. At that point, they become distinguishable. For example, certain minerals such as copper and gold may both be found in a given ore. The ore must be mined, crushed, and treated before the copper and gold are separated. The point of separation is called the **split-off point**. The costs of mining, crushing, and treatment are common to both products.

Often, joint products are sold at the split-off point. But sometimes, it is more profitable to process a joint product further, beyond the split-off point, prior to selling it.

	EXHIBIT 18-11 Special-Order Cost Analysis: Polarcreme, Inc.		
	Accept	**Reject**	**Differential Effect**
Revenues	$ 3,500,000	$0	$ 3,500,000
Dairy ingredients	(1,400,000)	0	(1,400,000)
Sugar	(200,000)	0	(200,000)
Flavorings	(300,000)	0	(300,000)
Direct labor	(500,000)	0	(500,000)
Packaging	(400,000)	0	(400,000)
Other	(100,000)	0	(100,000)
Purchasing	(80,000)	0	(80,000)
Receiving	(120,000)	0	(120,000)
Setting up	(104,000)	0	(104,000)
Total	$ 296,000	$0	$ 296,000

Determining whether to **sell or process further** is an important decision that a manager must make.

To illustrate, consider Delrio Corporation. Delrio is an agricultural corporation that produces and sells fresh produce and canned food products. The San Juan Division of Delrio specializes in tomato products. San Juan has a large tomato farm that produces all the tomatoes used in its products. The farm is divided into manageable plots. Each plot produces approximately 1,500 pounds of tomatoes; this defines a load. Each plot must be cultivated, fertilized, sprayed, watered, and harvested. When the tomatoes have ripened, they are harvested. The tomatoes are then transported to a warehouse, where they are washed and sorted. The approximate cost of all these activities is $200 per load.

Tomatoes are sorted into two grades (A and B). Grade A tomatoes are larger and better shaped than Grade B. Grade A tomatoes are sold to large supermarkets. Grade B tomatoes are sent to the canning plant where they are processed into catsup, tomato sauce, and tomato paste. Each load produces about 1,000 pounds of Grade A tomatoes and 500 pounds of Grade B tomatoes. Recently, the manager of the canning plant requested that the Grade A tomatoes be used for a Delrio hot sauce. Studies have indicated that the Grade A tomatoes provided a better flavor and consistency for the sauce than did Grade B tomatoes. Furthermore, Grade B tomatoes are fully utilized for other products.

The hot sauce production would require using all of the Grade A output (from the San Juan farm). Grade A tomatoes are sold to large supermarkets for $0.40 per pound. In deciding whether to sell Grade A tomatoes at split-off or to process them further and sell the hot sauce, the common costs of cultivating, spraying, watering, and so on, are not relevant. Delrio must pay the $200 per load for these activities regardless of whether it sells the Grade A tomatoes at split-off or processes them further. However, the revenues earned at split-off are likely to differ from the revenues that would be received if the Grade A were sold as hot sauce. Therefore, revenues are a relevant item.

The relevance of processing costs depends on the nature of the resource demands. Clearly, the demand for resources acquired as needed will increase, and these costs are relevant (for such things as labor, peppers, water, bottles, and spices). For resources acquired in advance of usage, the increase in resource spending will depend on how much existing activity capacity must be increased. For example, the receiving activity may increase in capacity to handle the increased volume of tomatoes. The increased resource spending for receiving would be a relevant processing cost. However, it may be that the inspecting activity has sufficient permanent unused capacity to deal with the inspection requirements for the sauce. If so, then the cost of inspection would not be relevant. (The cost of inspection resources is the same whether or not the hot sauce is produced.)

Assume that the hot sauce sells for $1.50 per bottle. Also assume that the additional processing costs, including only resources acquired as needed and increases in activity capacity, amount to $1,000. Thus, the total revenues at split-off for Grade A tomatoes are $400 ($0.40 × 1,000 pounds). If the Grade A tomatoes are processed into hot sauce (one pound of tomatoes equals one bottle of hot sauce), the total revenues are $1,500 ($1.50 × 1,000 bottles). The incremental revenues from processing further are $1,100 per half ton of Grade A tomatoes ($1,500 − $400). Since revenues increase by $1,100 and processing costs by $1,000, the net benefit of processing the Grade A tomatoes is $100 per half ton. The analysis is summarized as follows:

	Sell	Process Further	Differential Amount to Process Further
Revenues	$400	$1,500	$1,100
Processing cost	—	1,000	1,000
Total	$400	$ 500	$ 100

Relevant Costing and Ethical Behavior

Relevant costs are used in making tactical decisions—decisions that have an immediate view or limited objective in mind. In making these decisions, however, decision makers should always keep the decisions within an ethical framework. Reaching objectives is important, but how you get there is perhaps even more important. Unfortunately, many managers have the opposite view. Part of the reason for the problem is the extreme pressure to perform that many managers feel. Often, the individual who is not a top performer may be laid off or demoted. Under such conditions, the temptation is often great to engage in questionable behavior.

For example, the price of cashmere decreased greatly during the 1990s. The lower price of cashmere fiber meant that sweaters and coats became much more affordable, and imports from China and Hong Kong more than doubled. Unfortunately, the cashmere content of the clothing was uneven, and, on occasion, misrepresented to the eventual seller. In the fall of 2000, **Lands' End** found that one of its blazers, advertised as a blend of lambswool and 30 percent cashmere, tested in the range of 10 to 30 percent cashmere. The company advised its operators to tell prospective purchasers of the variability and to offer $20 off the price to those who still wanted the jackets. Other sellers chose to take the "low road" and continued to advertise and sell their variable mix fiber sweaters and blazers at the higher percentage of cashmere.

There can be endless debates about what is right and what is wrong. As pointed out in Chapter 1, ethical standards have been developed to provide guidance for individuals. Additionally, many companies are hiring full-time ethics officers. Often, these officers set up hot lines so that employees can call and register complaints or ask about the propriety of certain actions. However, as pointed out in an article in *Fortune*: "The old advice is still the best: Don't do anything on the job you wouldn't want your mother to read about with her morning coffee."[4]

---

4. Kenneth Labich, "The New Crisis in Business Ethics," *Fortune* (April 20, 1992): 172.

SUMMARY

Tactical decision making consists of choosing among alternatives with an immediate or limited end in view. Tactical decisions can be short term or small scale in nature but must be made so that larger strategic objectives are served. Tactical decision making follows a 5-step process. The heart of the process is called tactical cost analysis. Tactical cost analysis includes identifying predicted costs and benefits associated with alternatives, eliminating those that are not relevant, and comparing the relevant costs and benefits. All other things being equal, the alternative with the greatest net benefit should be chosen.

An essential element of tactical cost analysis is identifying relevant costs and benefits. Costs and revenues are relevant provided they pertain to the future and differ across the alternatives being considered. All past costs are sunk and never relevant. The role of past costs in tactical decision making is predictive. Past costs can be used to estimate future costs.

Cost behavior is fundamental to understanding relevancy. The activity resource usage model is a useful tool for determining relevancy. Resources can be classified as flexible resources and committed resources. Flexible resources are acquired as needed; committed resources are acquired in advance of usage. The cost of flexible resources is relevant provided that demand changes across alternatives. The cost of committed resources is relevant provided that the demand changes across alternatives lead to a change in activity capacity. Changes in activity capacity cause resource spending to change.

Examples of tactical decisions include make-or-buy choices, keep-or-drop decisions, special-order decisions, and sell-or-process-further decisions. Special-order decisions are examples of tactical decisions with a short-term orientation. The other three are examples of small-scale tactical decisions.

REVIEW PROBLEM AND SOLUTION

ACTIVITY RESOURCE USAGE MODEL, STRATEGIC ELEMENTS, AND RELEVANT COSTING

Perkins Company has idle capacity. Recently, Perkins received an offer to sell 2,000 units of one of its products to a new customer in a geographic region not normally serviced. The offering price is $10 per unit. The product normally sells for $14. The activity-based accounting system provides the following information:

| | | | | Activity Rate[b] | |
	Cost Driver	Unused Capacity	Quantity Demanded[a]	Fixed	Variable
Direct materials	Units	0	2,000	—	$3.00
Direct labor	Direct labor hours	0	400	—	7.00
Setups	Setup hours	0	25	$50.00	8.00
Machining	Machine hours	6,000	4,000	4.00	1.00

[a]This represents only the amount of resources demanded by the special order being considered.
[b]Fixed activity rate is the price that must be paid per unit of activity capacity. The variable activity rate is the price per unit of resource for resources acquired as needed.

Although the fixed activity rate for setups is $50 per hour, any expansion of this resource must be acquired in blocks. The unit of purchase for setups is 100 hours of setup servicing. Thus, any expansion of setup activity must be done 100 hours at a time. The price per hour is the fixed activity rate.

Required:

1. Compute the change in income for Perkins Company if the order is accepted. Comment on whether or not the order should be accepted. (In particular, discuss the strategic issues.)
2. Suppose that the setup activity had 50 hours of unused capacity. How does this affect the analysis?

SOLUTION

1. The relevant costs are those that change if the order is accepted. These costs would consist of the variable activity costs (flexible resources) plus any cost of acquiring additional activity capacity (committed resources). The income will change by the following amount:

Revenues ($10 × 2,000 units)	$20,000
Less increase in resource spending:	
Direct materials ($3 × 2,000 units)	(6,000)
Direct labor ($7 × 400 direct labor hours)	(2,800)
Setups [($50 × 100 hours) + ($8 × 25 hours)]	(5,200)
Machining ($1 × 4,000 machine hours)	(4,000)
Income change	$ 2,000

Special orders should be examined carefully before acceptance. This order offers an increase in income of $2,000, but it does require expansion of the setup activity capacity. If this expansion is short run in nature, then it may be worth it. If it entails a long-term commitment, then the company would be exchanging a 1-year benefit of $2,000 for an annual commitment of $5,000. In this case, the order should be rejected. Even if the commitment is short term, other strategic factors need to be considered. Will this order affect any regular sales? Is the company looking for a permanent solution to its idle capacity, or are special orders becoming a habit (a response pattern that may eventually prove disastrous)? Will acceptance adversely affect the company's normal distribution channels? Acceptance of the order should be consistent with the company's strategic position.

2. If 50 hours of excess setup capacity exist, then the setup activity can absorb the special order's activity demands with no additional resource spending required for additional capacity. Thus, the profitability of the special order would be increased by $5,000 (the increase in resource spending that would have been required). Total income would increase by $7,000 if the order is accepted.

KEY TERMS

QUESTIONS FOR WRITING AND DISCUSSION

1. What is tactical decision making?
2. "Tactical decisions are often small-scale decisions that serve a larger purpose." Explain what this means.
3. What is tactical cost analysis? What steps in the tactical decision model correspond to tactical cost analysis?
4. Describe a tactical decision you personally have had to make. Apply the tactical decision-making model to your decision. How did it turn out? (*Hint:* You could discuss buying a car, choosing a college, buying a puppy, etc.)
5. What is a relevant cost? Explain why depreciation on an existing asset is always irrelevant.
6. Give an example of a future cost that is not relevant.
7. Relevant costs always determine which alternative should be chosen. Do you agree or disagree? Explain.
8. Can direct materials ever be irrelevant in a make-or-buy decision? Explain. Give an example of a fixed cost that is relevant.
9. What role do past costs play in tactical cost analysis?
10. When will flexible resources be relevant to a decision?
11. When will the cost of committed resources be relevant to a decision?
12. What are the main differences between a functional-based and an activity-based make-or-buy analysis?
13. Explain why activity-based segmented reporting provides more insight concerning keep-or-drop decisions.
14. Should joint costs be considered in a sell-or-process-further decision? Explain.
15. Why would a firm ever offer a price on a product that is below its full cost?

EXERCISES

18-1 IDENTIFYING PROBLEMS AND ALTERNATIVES, RELEVANT COSTS

LO1, LO2 Norton Products, Inc., manufactures potentiometers. (A potentiometer is a device that adjusts electrical resistance.) Currently, all parts necessary for the assembly of products are produced internally. Norton has a single plant located in Wichita, Kansas. The facilities for the manufacture of potentiometers are leased, with five years remaining on the lease. All equipment is owned by the company. Because of increases in demand, production has been expanded significantly over the five years of operation, straining the capacity of the leased facilities. Currently, the company needs more warehousing and office space, as well as more space for the production of plastic moldings. The current output of these moldings, used to make potentiometers, needs to be expanded to accommodate the increased demand for the main product.

Leo Tidwell, owner and president of Norton Products, has asked his vice president of marketing, John Tidwell, and his vice president of finance, Linda Thayn, to meet and discuss the problem of limited capacity. This is the second meeting the three have had concerning the problem. In the first meeting, Leo rejected Linda's proposal to build the company's own plant. He believed it was too risky to invest the capital necessary to build a plant at this stage of the company's development. The combination of leasing a larger facility and subleasing the current plant was also considered but was rejected; subleasing would be difficult, if not impossible. At the end of the first meeting, Leo asked John to explore the possibility of leasing another facility comparable to the current one. He also assigned Linda the task of identifying other possible solutions. As the second meeting began, Leo asked John to give a report on the leasing alternative.

JOHN: After some careful research, I'm afraid that the idea of leasing an additional plant is not a very good one. Although we have some space problems, our current level of production doesn't justify another plant. In fact, I expect it will be at least five years before we need to be concerned about expanding into another facility like the one we have now. My market studies reveal a modest growth in sales over the next five years. All this growth can be absorbed by our current production capacity. The large increases in demand that we experienced the past five years are not likely to be repeated. Leasing another plant would be an overkill solution.

LEO: Even modest growth will aggravate our current space problems. As you both know, we are already operating three production shifts. But, John, you are right—except for plastic moldings, we could expand production, particularly during the graveyard shift. Linda, I hope that you have been successful in identifying some other possible solutions. Some fairly quick action is needed.

LINDA: Fortunately, I believe that I have two feasible alternatives. One is to rent an additional building to be used for warehousing. By transferring our warehousing needs to the new building, we will free up internal space for offices and for expanding the production of plastic moldings. I have located a building within two miles of our plant that we could use. It has the capacity to handle our current needs and the modest growth that John mentioned. The second alternative may be even more attractive. We currently produce all the parts that we use to manufacture potentiometers, including shafts and bushings. In the last several months, the market has been flooded with these two parts. Prices have tumbled as a result. It might be better to buy shafts and bushings instead of making them. If we stop internal production of shafts and bushings, this would free up the space we need. Well, Leo, what do you think? Are these alternatives feasible? Or should I continue my search for additional solutions?

LEO: I like both alternatives. In fact, they are exactly the types of solutions we need to consider. All we have to do now is choose the one best for our company.

Required:
1. Define the problem facing Norton Products.
2. Identify all the alternatives that were considered by Norton Products. Which ones were classified as not feasible? Why? Now identify the feasible alternatives.
3. For the feasible alternatives, what are some potential costs and benefits associated with each alternative? Of the costs that you have identified, which do you think are relevant to the decision?

18-2 RESOURCE SUPPLY AND USAGE, SPECIAL ORDER, RELEVANCY

LO2, LO3, LO4 Chasteen, Inc., has four salaried clerks to process purchase orders. Each clerk is paid a salary of $27,400 and is capable of processing as many as 8,000 purchase orders per year. Each clerk uses a PC and laser printer in processing orders. Time available on each PC system is sufficient to process 8,000 orders per year. The depreciation on each PC system is $1,800 per year. In addition to the salaries, Chasteen spends $20,800 for forms, postage, and other supplies (assuming 32,000 purchase orders are processed). During the year, 29,320 orders were processed.

Required:
1. Classify the resources associated with purchasing as flexible or committed.
2. Compute the total activity availability, and break this into activity usage and unused activity.

3. Calculate the total cost of resources supplied (activity cost), and break this into the cost of activity used and the cost of unused activity.
4. (a) Suppose that a large special order will cause an additional 1,000 purchase orders. What purchasing costs are relevant? By how much will purchasing costs increase if the order is accepted? (b) Suppose that the special order causes 4,500 additional purchase orders. How will your answer to part (a) change?

18-3 DETERMINING RELEVANT COSTS

LO2 Six months ago, Kelly O'Connor purchased a fire-engine red, used LeBaron convertible for $10,000. Kelly was looking forward to the feel of the sun on her shoulders and the wind whipping through her hair as she zipped along the highways of life. Unfortunately, the wind turned her hair into straw, and she didn't do much zipping along since the car spent so much of its time in the shop. So far, she has spent $1,200 on repairs, and she's afraid there is no end in sight. In fact, Kelly anticipates the following costs of restoration:

Rebuilt engine	$ 700
New paint job	800
Tires	360
New interior	500
Miscellaneous maintenance	340
Total	$2,700

On a visit to a used car dealer, Kelly found a 4-year-old Toyota RAV4 in excellent condition for $10,000—Kelly thinks she might really be more the sport-utility type anyway. Kelly checked the blue book values and found that she can sell the LeBaron for only $3,600. If she buys the RAV4, she will pay cash but would need to sell the LeBaron.

Required:

1. In trying to decide whether to restore the LeBaron or buy the RAV4, Kelly is distressed because she has already spent $11,200 on the LeBaron. The investment seems too much to give up. How would you react to her concern?
2. List all costs that are relevant to Kelly's decision. What advice would you give her?

18-4 SPECIAL-ORDER DECISION, FUNCTIONAL-BASED ANALYSIS, QUALITATIVE ASPECTS

LO4 Boujoaudes, Inc., manufactures croquet sets. A national sporting goods chain recently submitted a special order for 4,000 croquet sets. Boujoaudes was not operating at capacity and could use the extra business. Unfortunately, the order's offering price of $21 per croquet set was below the cost to produce the sets. The controller was opposed to taking a loss on the deal. However, the personnel manager argued in favor of accepting the order even though a loss would be incurred; it would avoid the problem of layoffs and would help maintain the community image of the company. The full cost to produce a croquet set is as follows:

Direct materials	$ 7.90
Direct labor	5.40
Variable overhead	4.75
Fixed overhead	3.10
Total	$21.15

No variable selling or administrative expenses would be associated with the order. Non-unit-level activity costs are a small percentage of total costs and are therefore not considered.

Required:

1. Assume that the company would accept the order only if it increased total profits. Should the company accept or reject the order? Provide supporting computations.
2. Consider the personnel manager's concerns. Discuss the merits of accepting the order even if it decreases total profits.

18-5 MAKE-OR-BUY, FUNCTIONAL-BASED ANALYSIS

LO2, LO4

Watanabe Company is currently manufacturing Part NIM-06, producing 15,000 units annually. The part is used in the production of several products made by Watanabe. The cost per unit for NIM-06 is as follows:

Direct materials	$70.00
Direct labor	20.00
Variable overhead	3.00
Fixed overhead	1.50
Total	$94.50

Of the total fixed overhead assigned to NIM-06, $12,000 is direct fixed overhead (the annual lease cost of machinery used to manufacture Part NIM-06), and the remainder is common fixed overhead. An outside supplier has offered to sell the part to Watanabe for $94. There is no alternative use for the facilities currently used to produce the part. No significant non-unit-based overhead costs are incurred.

Required:

1. Should Watanabe Company make or buy Part NIM-06?
2. What is the maximum amount per unit that Watanabe would be willing to pay to an outside supplier?

18-6 MAKE-OR-BUY, FUNCTIONAL-BASED AND ABC ANALYSIS

LO3, LO4

Golf-2-Go, Inc., a manufacturer of motorized carts for golfers, has just received an offer from a supplier to provide 2,000 units of a component used in its main product. The component is a wheel assembly that is currently produced internally. The supplier has offered to sell the wheel assembly for $115 per unit. Golf-2-Go is currently using a functional, unit-based costing system that assigns overhead to jobs on the basis of direct labor hours. The estimated functional-based full cost of producing the wheel assembly is as follows:

Direct materials	$70
Direct labor	30
Variable overhead	10
Fixed overhead	50

Prior to making a decision, the company's CEO commissioned a special study to see whether there would be any decrease in the fixed overhead costs. The results of the study revealed the following:

2 setups—$1,800 each (The setups would be avoided, and total spending could be reduced by $1,800 per setup.)

One half-time inspector is needed. The company already uses part-time inspectors hired through a temporary employment agency. The yearly cost of the part-time inspectors for the wheel assembly operation is $12,300 and could be totally avoided if the part were purchased.

Engineering work: 615 hours, $20/hr. (Although the work decreases by 615 hours, the engineer assigned to the wheel assembly line also spends time on other products, and there would be no reduction in his salary.)

200 fewer material moves at $40 per move

Required:

1. Ignore the special study, and determine whether the wheel assembly should be produced internally or purchased from the supplier.
2. Now, using the special study data, repeat the analysis.
3. Discuss the qualitative factors that would affect the decision, including strategic implications.
4. After reviewing the special study, the controller made the following remark: "This study ignores the additional activity demands that purchasing would cause. For example, although the demand for inspecting the part on the production floor decreases, will we not have a need to inspect the incoming parts in the receiving area? Will we actually save any inspection costs?" Is the controller right? Would this problem be avoided if Golf-2-Go had an activity-based costing system in place?

18-7   RESOURCE USAGE MODEL, SPECIAL ORDER

LO3, LO4   Nesbitt, Inc., manufactures display cases for retail stores. Good-4-U Foods, Inc., is a grocery chain that decided to expand into video rental and needs display cases. Good-4-U Foods offered to purchase 14,000 display cases for $35 each. Normally, this type of case sells for $45, but Nesbitt is operating at 80 percent of capacity and wants to make the special order work. Nesbitt's controller looked into the cost of the display cases using the following information from the activity-based accounting system:

	Activity Driver	Unused Capacity	Quantity[a] Demanded	Activity Rate[b] Fixed	Activity Rate[b] Variable
Direct materials	Display cases	0	14,000	—	$20
Direct labor	Direct labor hours	0	10,500	—	15
Setups	Setup hours	60	80	$175	5
Inspection	Inspection hours	800	400	10	1
Machining	Machine hours	6,000	7,000	20	3

[a]This represents only the amount of resources demanded by the special order being considered.
[b]This is expected activity cost divided by activity capacity.

Expansion of activity capacity for setups, inspection, and machining must be done in steps. For setups, each step provides an additional 25 hours of setup activity and is priced at the fixed activity rate. For inspection, activity capacity is expanded by 2,000 hours per year, and the cost is $20,000 per year (the salary for an additional inspector). Machine capacity can be leased for a year at a rate of $20 per machine hour. Machine capacity must be acquired, however, in steps of 2,500 machine hours.

Required:

1. Compute the change in income for Nesbitt, Inc., if the order is accepted.
2. Suppose that the machining activity has 7,500 hours of unused capacity. How is the analysis affected?
3. Suppose that the setup activity has 80 hours of unused capacity and that the machining activity has 6,500 hours of unused capacity. How is the analysis affected?

18-8   KEEP-OR-DROP: FUNCTIONAL-BASED VERSUS ACTIVITY-BASED ANALYSIS

LO3, LO4   Lincoln, Inc., produces two types of peanut butter: Smooth and Crunchy. Of the two, Smooth is the more popular. Data concerning the two products follow:

	Smooth	Crunchy	Unused Capacity[a]	Units of Purchase[b]
Expected sales (in cases)	50,000	10,000	—	—
Selling price per case	$100	$80	—	—
Direct labor hours	40,000	10,000	—	As needed
Machine hours	10,000	2,500	—	2,500
Receiving orders	500	250	250	500
Packing orders	1,000	500	500	250
Material cost per case	$50	$48	—	—
Direct labor cost per case	$10	$8	—	—
Advertising costs	$200,000	$60,000	—	—

[a]Practical capacity less expected usage (all unused capacity is permanent).
[b]In some cases, activity capacity must be purchased in steps (whole units). These steps are provided as necessary. The cost per step is the fixed activity rate multiplied by the step units. The fixed activity rate is the expected fixed activity costs divided by practical activity capacity.

Annual overhead costs are as follows. These costs are classified as fixed or variable with respect to the appropriate activity driver.

Activity	Fixed[a]	Variable[b]
Direct labor benefits	$ 0	$200,000
Machine	200,000	250,000
Receiving	200,000	22,500
Packing	100,000	45,000
Total costs	$500,000	$517,500

[a]Costs associated with practical activity capacity. The machine fixed costs are all depreciation.
[b]These costs are for the actual levels of the cost driver.

Required:

1. Prepare functional- and activity-based segmented income statements. In the functional-based system, a unit-level overhead rate is used, based on direct labor hours.
2. Using a functional-based approach, determine whether the Crunchy peanut butter product line should be kept or dropped.
3. Repeat the keep-or-drop analysis using an ABC approach.

18-9 SELL OR PROCESS FURTHER, BASIC ANALYSIS

LO2, LO4   Diehlman, Inc., is a pork processor. Its plants, located in the Midwest, produce several products from a common process: sirloin roasts, chops, spare ribs, and the residual. The roasts, chops, and spare ribs are packaged, branded, and sold to supermarkets. The residual consists of organ meats and leftover pieces that are sold to sausage and hotdog processors. The joint costs for a typical week are as follows:

Direct materials	$73,000
Direct labor	26,000
Overhead	39,000

The revenues from each product are as follows: sirloin roasts, $50,000; chops, $70,000; spare ribs, $33,000; and residual, $15,000.

Diehlman's management has learned that certain organ meats are a prized delicacy in Asia. They are considering separating those from the residual and selling them abroad for $50,000. This would bring the value of the residual down to $8,500. In addition, the organ meats would need to be packaged and then air freighted to Asia. Further processing cost per week is estimated to be $30,000 (the cost of renting additional packaging equipment, purchasing materials, and hiring additional direct labor). Transportation cost would be $7,500 per week. Finally, resource spending would need to be expanded for other activities as well (purchasing, receiving, and internal shipping). The increase in resource spending for these activities is estimated to be $2,175 per week.

Required:

1. What is the gross profit earned by the original mix of products for one week?
2. Should the company separate the organ meats for shipment overseas or continue to sell them at split-off? What is the effect of the decision on weekly gross profit?

18-10   FOREIGN TRADE ZONES

LO2   Elmondo, Inc., is considering opening a new warehouse to serve the Southwest region. Jefferson Moore, controller for Elmondo, has been reading about the advantages of foreign trade zones. He wonders if locating in one would be of benefit to his company, which imports about 90 percent of its merchandise (e.g., chess sets from the Philippines, jewelry from Thailand, pottery from Mexico, etc.). Jefferson estimates that the new warehouse will store imported merchandise costing about $3,450,000 per year. Inventory shrinkage at the warehouse (due to breakage and mishandling) is about 4 percent of the total. The average tariff rate on these imports is 20 percent.

Required:

1. If Elmondo locates the warehouse in a foreign trade zone, how much will be saved in tariffs? Why?
2. Suppose that, on average, the merchandise stays in an Elmondo warehouse for seven months before shipment to retailers. Carrying cost for Elmondo is 12 percent per year. If Elmondo locates the warehouse in a foreign trade zone, how much will be saved in carrying costs? What will the total tariff-related savings be?

PROBLEMS

18-11   KEEP-OR-DROP FOR SERVICE FIRM, COMPLEMENTARY EFFECTS, FUNCTIONAL-BASED ANALYSIS

LO2, LO4   Serene Assurance Company provides both automobile and life insurance. The projected income statements for the two products are as follows:

	Automobile Insurance	*Life Insurance*
Sales	$4,200,000	$12,000,000
Less: Variable expenses	3,830,000	9,600,000
Contribution margin	$ 370,000	$ 2,400,000
Less: Direct fixed expenses	400,000	500,000
Segment margin	$ (30,000)	$ 1,900,000
Less: Common fixed expenses (allocated)	100,000	200,000
Operating income (loss)	$ (130,000)	$ 1,700,000

The president of the company is considering dropping the automobile insurance. However, some policyholders prefer having their auto and life insurance with the same company, so if automobile insurance is dropped, sales of life insurance will drop by 15 percent. No significant non-unit-level activity costs are incurred.

Required:

1. If Serene Assurance Company drops automobile insurance, by how much will income increase or decrease? Provide supporting computations.
2. Assume that increasing the advertising budget by $50,000 will increase sales of automobile insurance by 10 percent and life insurance by 3 percent. Prepare a segmented income statement that reflects the effect of increased advertising. Should advertising be increased?

18-12 SPECIAL ORDER, FUNCTIONAL-BASED ANALYSIS

LO2, LO4

CMA

Lancaster Company manufactures two types of hair conditioners, Creemy and Shiney, out of a joint process. The joint (common) costs incurred are $840,000 for a standard production run that generates 360,000 gallons of Creemy and 240,000 gallons of Shiney. Additional processing costs beyond the split-off point are $2.80 per gallon for Creemy and $1.80 per gallon for Shiney. Creemy sells for $4.80 per gallon, while Shiney sells for $7.80 per gallon.

Comida Buena, a supermarket chain, has asked Lancaster to supply it with 480,000 gallons of Shiney at a price of $7.30 per gallon. Comida Buena plans to have the conditioner bottled in 16-ounce bottles with its own Comida Buena label.

If Lancaster accepts the order, it will save $0.10 per gallon in packaging of Shiney. There is sufficient excess capacity for the order. However, the market for Creemy is saturated, and any additional sales of Creemy would take place at a price of $3.20 per gallon. Assume that no significant non-unit-level activity costs are incurred.

Required:

1. What is the profit normally earned on one production run of Creemy and Shiney?
2. Should Lancaster accept the special order? Explain. *(CMA adapted)*

18-13 RESOURCE USAGE, SPECIAL ORDER

LO3, LO4

Perry Medical Center (PMC) has five medical technicians who are responsible for conducting sonogram testing. Each technician is paid a salary of $36,000 and is capable of processing 1,000 tests per year. The sonogram equipment is one year old and was purchased for $150,000. It is expected to last five years. The equipment's capacity is 25,000 tests over its life. Depreciation is computed on a straight-line basis, with no salvage value expected. The reading of the sonogram is verified by an outside physician whose fee is $10 per test. The technician's report with the outside physician's note of verification is sent to the referring physician. In addition to the salaries and equipment, PMC spends $10,000 for forms, paper, power, and other supplies needed to operate the equipment (assuming 5,000 tests are processed). When PMC purchased the equipment, it fully expected to perform 5,000 tests per year. In fact, during its first year of operation, 5,000 tests were run. However, a larger hospital has established a clinic in Perry and will siphon off some of PMC's business. During the coming years, PMC is expected to run only 4,200 sonogram tests yearly. PMC has been charging $65 for the test—enough to cover the direct costs of the test plus an assignment of general overhead (e.g., depreciation on the hospital building, lighting and heating, and janitorial services).

At the beginning of the second year, an HMO from a neighboring community approached PMC and offered to send its clients to PMC for sonogram testing provided that the charge per test would be $35. The HMO estimates that it can provide about

500 patients per year. The HMO has indicated that the arrangement is temporary—for one year only. The HMO expects to have its own testing capabilities within one year.

Required:

1. Classify the resources associated with the sonogram activity into one of the following: (1) committed resources or (2) flexible resources.
2. Calculate the activity rate for the sonogram testing activity. Break the activity rate into fixed and variable components. Now, classify each activity resource as relevant or irrelevant with respect to the following alternatives: (1) accept the HMO offer and (2) reject the HMO offer. Explain your reasoning.
3. Assume that PMC will accept the HMO offer if it reduces the hospital's operating costs. Should the HMO offer be accepted?
4. Harry Birdwell, PMC's hospital controller, argued against accepting the HMO's offer. Instead, he argued that the hospital should be increasing the charge per test rather than accepting business that doesn't even cover full costs. He also was concerned about local physician reaction if word got out that the HMO was receiving tests for $35. Discuss the merits of Harry's position. Include in your discussion an assessment of the price increase that would be needed if the objective is to maintain total revenues from sonogram testing experienced in the first year of operation.
5. Elaine Day, PMC's administrator, has been informed that one of the sonogram technicians is leaving for an opportunity at a larger hospital. She has met with the other technicians, and they have agreed to increase their hours to pick up the slack so that PMC won't need to hire another technician. By working a couple hours extra every week, each remaining technician can perform 1,050 tests per year. They agreed to do this for an increase in salary of $2,000 per year. How does this outcome affect the analysis of the HMO offer?
6. Assuming that PMC wants to bring in the same revenues earned in the sonogram activity's first year less the reduction in resource spending attributable to using only four technicians, how much must PMC charge for a sonogram test?

18-14 ACTIVITY-BASED RESOURCE USAGE MODEL, MAKE-OR-BUY

LO3, LO4   Brandy Dees recently bought Nievo Enterprises, a company that manufactures ice skates. Brandy decided to assume management responsibilities for the company and appointed herself president shortly after the purchase was completed. When she bought the company, Brandy's investigation revealed that with the exception of the blades, all parts of the skates are produced internally. The investigation also revealed that Nievo once produced the blades internally and still owned the equipment. The equipment was in good condition and was stored in a local warehouse. Nievo's former owner had decided three years earlier to purchase the blades from external suppliers.

Brandy Dees is seriously considering making the blades instead of buying them from external suppliers. The blades are purchased in sets of two and cost $8 per set. Currently, 100,000 sets of blades are purchased annually.

Skates are produced in batches, according to shoe size. Production equipment must be reconfigured for each batch. The blades could be produced using an available area within the plant. Prime costs will average $5.00 per set. There is enough equipment to set up three lines of production, each capable of producing 80,000 sets of blades. A supervisor would need to be hired for each line. Each supervisor would be paid a salary of $40,000. Additionally, it would cost $1.50 per machine hour for power, oil, and other operating expenses. Since three types of blades would be produced, additional demands would be made on the setup activity. Other overhead activities affected include purchasing, inspection, and materials handling. The company's ABC system provides the following information about the current status of the overhead activities that would be affected. (The lumpy quantity indicates how much capacity must be purchased should any expansion of activity supply be needed—the units of purchase. The purchase cost per unit is the fixed activity rate. The variable rate is the cost per unit of resources acquired as needed for each activity.)

Activity	Cost Driver	Current Activity Capacity	Activity Usage	Lumpy Quantity	Fixed Activity Rate	Variable Activity Rate
Setups	Number of setups	1,000	800	100	$200	$500
Purchasing	Number of orders	50,000	47,000	5,000	10	0.50
Inspecting	Inspection hours	20,000	18,000	2,000	15	none
Materials handling	Number of moves	9,000	8,700	500	30	1.50

The demands that *production* of blades places on the overhead activities are as follows:

Activity	Resource Demands
Machining	50,000 machine hours
Setups	250 setups
Purchasing	4,000 purchase orders (associated with materials)
Inspection	1,500 inspection hours
Materials handling	650 moves

If the blades are made, the purchase of the blades from outside suppliers will cease. Therefore, purchase orders will decrease by 6,500 (the number associated with their purchase). Similarly, the moves for the handling of incoming blades will decrease by 400. Any unused activity capacity is viewed as permanent.

Required:

1. Should Nievo make or buy the blades?
2. Explain how the ABC resource usage model helped in the analysis. Also, comment on how a conventional approach would have differed.

18-15 SEGMENTED INCOME STATEMENTS, KEEP-OR-DROP DECISION, SPECIAL-ORDER DECISION, JIT AND ACTIVITY-BASED COSTING, STRATEGIC CONSIDERATIONS

LO3, LO4 Emery Company, a manufacturer of motors for washing machines, has installed a JIT purchasing and manufacturing system. After several years of operation, Emery has succeeded in reducing inventories to insignificant levels. During the coming year, Emery expects to produce 200,000 motors: 150,000 of the Regular Model and 50,000 of the Heavy Duty Model. The motors are produced in manufacturing cells. The expected output represents 80 percent of the capacity for the Regular Model cell and 100 percent of capacity for the Heavy Duty Model cell. (This capacity includes time for cell workers to perform maintenance and materials handling.) The selling price for the Regular Model is $60; for the Heavy Duty Model, $70.

The relevant data for next year's expected production are as follows:

	Regular Cell	Heavy Duty Cell
Direct materials	$3,500,000	$1,000,000
Labor*	$900,000	$315,000
Power	$250,000	$100,000
Depreciation	$800,000	$300,000
Number of runs	100	100
Number of cell workers	20	5
Square footage	20,000	10,000

*Responsible for production, maintenance, and materials handling.

The following overhead costs are common to each cell:

Plant depreciation	$900,000
Production scheduling	300,000
Cafeteria	100,000
Personnel	150,000

These costs are assigned to the cells using cost drivers selected from the cell activity data given above.

In addition to the overhead costs, the company expects the following nonmanufacturing costs:

Commissions (2% of sales)	$250,000
Advertising:	
Regular Model	400,000
Heavy Duty Model	200,000
Administration (all fixed)	500,000

Keith Golding, president of Emery Company, is concerned about the profit performance of each model. He wants to know the effect on the company's profitability if the Heavy Duty Model is dropped. At the same time this request was made, the company was approached by a customer in a market not normally served by the company. This customer offered to buy 30,000 units of the Regular Model at $30 per unit. The order was requested on a direct contact basis, and no commissions will be paid. Keith was inclined to reject the offer, since it was half the model's normal selling price. However, before making the decision, he wanted to know the effect of accepting the offer on the company's profits.

To help decide on the two issues, the following additional data have been made available:

Activity	Cost Driver	Supply	Usage	Lumpy Quantity*	Fixed Rate
Scheduling	Runs	250	200	25	$1,200
Cafeteria	Cell workers	45	25	15	1,800
Personnel	Cell workers	40	25	20	3,750

*Lumpy quantity is the amount of resource that would be acquired (saved) if the *capacity* of the activity is expanded (reduced); the fixed rate is the per-unit price of the resource (which, however, can only be purchased in the lumpy amounts indicated).

Of the three activities, the cafeteria activity is the only one with a variable activity rate. This rate is $760 per cell worker.

Required:

1. Prepare an ABC segmented income statement for Emery Company using products as segments. Can the unused activity be exploited to increase overall profits? Explain.

2. By how much will profits be affected if the Heavy Duty Model is dropped?
3. Prepare an analysis that shows what the effect on company profitability will be if the special order is accepted. Was the president correct in his feelings concerning the special order?
4. Now, assume that the models are regularly sold to companies that produce medium- to high-quality washing machines. The special-order customer will use the motors in a low-end washing machine and plans to advertise the fact that the low-end washing machine can be purchased at a lower price with the same quality as a so-called higher-quality brand. Given this information and the results of Requirement 2, should the order be accepted? Explain.

18-16   MAKE-OR-BUY, FUNCTIONAL-BASED ANALYSIS, QUALITATIVE CONSIDERATIONS

LO2, LO4   Gray Dentistry Services is part of an HMO that operates in a large metropolitan area. Currently, Gray has its own dental laboratory to produce porcelain and gold crowns. The unit costs to produce the crowns are as follows:

	Porcelain	*Gold*
Direct materials	$ 60	$ 90
Direct labor	20	20
Variable overhead	5	5
Fixed overhead	22	22
Total	$107	$137

Fixed overhead is detailed as follows:

Salary (supervisor)	$30,000
Depreciation	5,000
Rent (lab facility)	20,000

Overhead is applied on the basis of direct labor hours. The rates above were computed using 5,500 direct labor hours. No significant non-unit-level overhead costs are incurred.

A local dental laboratory has offered to supply Gray all the crowns it needs. Its price is $100 for porcelain crowns and $132 for gold crowns; however, the offer is conditional on supplying both types of crowns—it will not supply just one type for the price indicated. If the offer is accepted, the equipment used by Gray's laboratory would be scrapped (it is old and has no market value), and the lab facility would be closed. Gray uses 1,500 porcelain crowns and 1,000 gold crowns per year.

Required:

1. Should Gray continue to make its own crowns, or should they be purchased from the external supplier? What is the dollar effect of purchasing?
2. What qualitative factors should Gray consider in making this decision?
3. Suppose that the lab facility is owned rather than rented and that the $20,000 is depreciation rather than rent. What effect does this have on the analysis in Requirement 1?
4. Refer to the original data. Assume that the volume of crowns is 3,000 porcelain and 2,000 gold. Should Gray make or buy the crowns? Explain the outcome.

18-17   SELL OR PROCESS FURTHER

LO4   Chemco Corporation buys three chemicals that are processed to produce two popular ingredients for liquid cough syrups. The three chemicals are in liquid form. The purchased chemicals are blended for two to three hours and then heated for 15 minutes.

The results of the process are two separate ingredients, Suppressant AB2 and Suppressant AB3. For every 2,200 gallons of chemicals used, 1,000 gallons of each suppressant are produced. The suppressants are sold to companies that process them into their final form. The selling prices are $25 per gallon for AB2 and $12 per gallon for AB3. The costs to produce 1,000 gallons of each chemical are as follows:

Chemicals	$11,000
Direct labor	9,000
Catalyst	3,600
Overhead	7,000

The suppressants are bottled in 5-gallon plastic containers and shipped. The cost of each container is $1.65. The costs of shipping are $0.20 per container.

Chemco Corporation could process Suppressant AB2 further by mixing it with inert powders and flavoring to form cough tablets. The tablets can be sold directly to retail drug stores as a generic brand. If this route is taken, the revenue received per case of tablets would be $8.50, with 10 cases produced by every gallon of Suppressant AB2. The costs of processing into tablets total $5.00 per gallon of AB2. Packaging costs $4.86 per case. Shipping costs $0.40 per case.

Required:

1. Should Chemco sell Suppressant AB2 at split-off, or should AB2 be processed and sold as tablets?
2. If Chemco normally sells 360,000 gallons of AB2 per year, what will be the difference in profits if AB2 is processed further?

18-18   PLANT SHUTDOWN OR CONTINUE OPERATIONS, QUALITATIVE CONSIDERATIONS, FUNCTIONAL-BASED ANALYSIS

LO2, LO4

CMA

GianAuto Corporation manufactures automobiles, vans, and trucks. Among the various GianAuto plants around the United States is the Denver cover plant, where vinyl covers and upholstery fabric are sewn. These are used to cover interior seating and other surfaces of GianAuto products.

Pam Vosilo is the plant manager for the Denver cover plant—the first GianAuto plant in the region. As other area plants were opened, Pam, in recognition of her management ability, was given the responsibility to manage them. Pam functions as a regional manager, although the budget for her and her staff is charged to the Denver plant.

Pam has just received a report indicating that GianAuto could purchase the entire annual output of the Denver cover plant from outside suppliers for $30 million. Pam was astonished at the low outside price, because the budget for the Denver plant's operating costs was set at $52 million. Pam believes that the Denver plant will have to close down operations in order to realize the $22 million in annual cost savings.

The budget (in thousands) for the Denver plant's operating costs for the coming year follows:

Materials		$12,000
Labor:		
Direct	$13,000	
Supervision	3,000	
Indirect plant	4,000	20,000

(continued)

Overhead:

Depreciation—Equipment	$ 5,000	
Depreciation—Building	3,000	
Pension expense	4,000	
Plant manager and staff	2,000	
Corporate allocation	6,000	20,000
Total budgeted costs		$52,000

Additional facts regarding the plant's operations are as follows:

Due to the Denver plant's commitment to use high-quality fabrics in all of its products, the purchasing department was instructed to place blanket orders with major suppliers to ensure the receipt of sufficient materials for the coming year. If these orders are cancelled as a consequence of the plant closing, termination charges would amount to 15 percent of the cost of direct materials.

Approximately 700 plant employees will lose their jobs if the plant is closed. This includes all direct laborers and supervisors as well as the plumbers, electricians, and other skilled workers classified as indirect plant workers. Some would be able to find new jobs, but many others would have difficulty. All employees would have difficulty matching the Denver plant's base pay of $9.40 per hour, the highest in the area. A clause in the Denver plant's contract with the union may help some employees; the company must provide employment assistance to its former employees for 12 months after a plant closing. The estimated cost to administer this service would be $1 million for the year.

Some employees would probably elect early retirement because the company has an excellent pension plan. In fact, $3 million of next year's pension expense would continue whether or not the plant is open.

Pam and her staff would not be affected by the closing of the Denver plant. They would still be responsible for administering three other area plants.

Equipment depreciation for the plant is considered to be a variable cost and the units-of-production method is used to depreciate equipment; the Denver plant is the only GianAuto plant to use this depreciation method. However, it uses the customary straight-line method to depreciate its building.

Required:

1. Prepare a quantitative analysis to help in deciding whether or not to close the Denver plant. Explain how you would treat the nonrecurring relevant costs.
2. Consider the analysis in Requirement 1, and add to it the qualitative factors that you believe are important to the decision. What is your decision? Would you close the plant? Explain. (*CMA adapted*)

18-19   MAKE-OR-BUY, FUNCTIONAL-BASED ANALYSIS

LO1, LO2, LO4   Morrill Company produces two different types of gauges: a density gauge and a thickness gauge. The segmented income statement for a typical quarter follows.

Spreadsheet

	Density Gauge	Thickness Gauge	Total
Sales	$150,000	$80,000	$230,000
Less: Variable expenses	80,000	46,000	126,000
Contribution margin	$ 70,000	$34,000	$104,000
Less: Direct fixed expenses*	20,000	38,000	58,000
Segment margin	$ 50,000	$ (4,000)	$ 46,000
Less: Common fixed expenses			30,000
Operating income			$ 16,000

*Includes depreciation.

The density gauge uses a subassembly that is purchased from an external supplier for $25 per unit. Each quarter, 2,000 subassemblies are purchased. All units produced are sold, and there are no ending inventories of subassemblies. Morrill is considering making the subassembly rather than buying it. Unit-level variable manufacturing costs are as follows:

Direct materials	$2
Direct labor	3
Variable overhead	2

No significant non-unit-level costs are incurred.

Morrill is considering two alternatives to supply the productive capacity for the subassembly.

a. Lease the needed space and equipment at a cost of $27,000 per quarter for the space and $10,000 per quarter for a supervisor. There are no other fixed expenses.
b. Drop the thickness gauge. The equipment could be adapted with virtually no cost and the existing space utilized to produce the subassembly. The direct fixed expenses, including supervision, would be $38,000, $8,000 of which is depreciation on equipment. If the thickness gauge is dropped, sales of the density gauge will not be affected.

Required:

1. Should Morrill Company make or buy the subassembly? If it makes the subassembly, which alternative should be chosen? Explain and provide supporting computations.
2. Suppose that dropping the thickness gauge will decrease sales of the density gauge by 10 percent. What effect does this have on the decision?
3. Assume that dropping the thickness gauge decreases sales of the density gauge by 10 percent and that 2,800 subassemblies are required per quarter. As before, assume that there are no ending inventories of subassemblies and that all units produced are sold. Assume also that the per-unit sales price and variable costs are the same as in Requirement 1. Include the leasing alternative in your consideration. Now, what is the correct decision?

18-20   EXPORTING, MAQUILADORAS, FOREIGN TRADE ZONES

LO2   Paladin Company manufactures plain-paper fax machines in a small factory in Minnesota. Sales have increased by 50 percent in each of the past three years, as Paladin has expanded its market from the United States to Canada and Mexico. As a result, the Minnesota factory is at capacity. Beryl Adams, president of Paladin, has examined the situation and developed the following alternatives.

a. Add a permanent second shift at the plant. However, the semi-skilled workers who assemble the fax machines are in short supply, and the wage rate of $15 per hour would probably have to be increased across the board to $18 per hour in order to attract sufficient workers from out of town. The total wage increase (including fringe benefits) would amount to $125,000. The heavier use of plant facilities would lead to increased plant maintenance and small tool cost.
b. Open a new plant and locate it in Mexico. Wages (including fringe benefits) would average $3.50 per hour. Investment in plant and equipment would amount to $300,000.
c. Open a new plant and locate it in a foreign trade zone, possibly in Dallas. Wages would be somewhat lower than in Minnesota, but higher than in Mexico. The advantages of postponing tariff payments on imported parts could amount to $50,000 per year.

Required:

Advise Beryl of the advantages and disadvantages of each alternative.

18-21   MANAGERIAL DECISION CASE: CENTRALIZE VERSUS DECENTRALIZE

LO2, LO4   Central University, a Midwestern university with approximately 17,400 students, was in the middle of a budget crisis. For the third consecutive year, state appropriations for higher education remained essentially unchanged. (The university is currently in its 2006–2007 academic year.) Yet, utilities, Social Security benefits, insurance, and other operating expenses have increased. Moreover, the faculty were becoming restless, and some members had begun to leave for other, higher-paying opportunities.

The president and the academic vice president had announced their intention to eliminate some academic programs and to reduce others. The savings that result would be used to cover the increase in operating expenses and to allow raises for the remaining faculty. Needless to say, the possible dismissal of tenured faculty aroused a great deal of concern throughout the university.

With this background, the president and academic vice president called a meeting of all department heads and deans to discuss the budget for the coming year. As the budget was presented, the academic vice president noted that continuing education, a separate, centralized unit, had accumulated a deficit of $504,000 over the past several years, which must be eliminated during the coming fiscal year. The vice president noted that allocating the deficit equally among the seven colleges would create a hardship on some of the colleges, wiping out all of their operating budgets except for salaries.

After some discussion of alternative ways to allocate the deficit, the head of the accounting department suggested an alternative solution: decentralize continuing education, allowing each college to assume responsibility for its own continuing education programs. In this way, the overhead of a centralized continuing education could be avoided.

The academic vice president responded that the suggestion would be considered, but it was received with little enthusiasm. The vice president observed that continuing education was now generating more revenues than costs—and that the trend was favorable.

A week later, at a meeting of the Deans' Council, the vice president reviewed the role of continuing education. He pointed out that only the dean of continuing education held tenure. If continuing education were decentralized, her salary ($50,000) would continue. However, she would return to her academic department, and the university would save $20,000 of instructional wages, since fewer adjunct faculty would be needed in her department. All other employees in the unit were classified as staff. Continuing education had responsibility for all noncredit offerings. Additionally, it had nominal responsibility for credit courses offered in the evening on campus and for credit courses offered off campus. However, all scheduling and staffing of these evening and off-campus courses were done by the heads of the academic departments. The head of each department had to approve the courses offered and the staffing. According to the vice president, advertising is one of the main contributions of the continuing education department to the evening and off-campus programs. He estimated that $30,000 per year is being spent.

After reviewing this information, the vice president made available the following information pertaining to the department's performance for the past several years (the 2006–2007 data were projections). He once again defended keeping a centralized department, emphasizing the favorable trend revealed by the accounting data. (All numbers are expressed in thousands.)

	2003–2004	*2004–2005*	*2005–2006*	*2006–2007*
Tuition revenues:				
Off-campus	$ 300	$ 400	$ 400	$ 410
Evening	—	525	907	1,000
Noncredit	135	305	338	375
Total	$ 435	$1,230	$1,645	$1,785
Operating costs:				
Administration	$ 132	$ 160	$ 112	$ 112
Off-campus:				
Direct[b]	230	270	270	260
Indirect	350	410	525	440
Evening	—[a]	220	420	525
Noncredit	135	305	338	375
Total	$ 847	$1,365	$1,665	$1,712
Income (loss)	$(412)	$ (135)	$ (20)	$ 73

[a]In 2003–2004, the department had no responsibility for evening courses. Beginning in 2004–2005, it was given the responsibility to pay for any costs of instruction incurred when adjunct faculty were hired to teach evening courses. Tuition revenues earned by evening courses also began to be assigned to the department at the same time.

[b]Instructional wages.

The dean of the College of Business was unimpressed by the favorable trend identified by the academic vice president. The dean maintained that decentralization still would be in the best interests of the university. He argued that although decentralization would not fully solve the deficit, it would provide a sizable contribution each year to the operating budgets for each of the seven colleges.

The academic vice president disagreed vehemently. He was convinced that continuing education was now earning its own way and would continue to produce additional resources for the university.

Required:

You have been asked by the president of Central University to assess which alternative, centralization or decentralization, is in the best interest of the school. The president is willing to decentralize provided that significant savings can be produced and the mission of the continuing education department will still be carried out. Prepare a memo to the president that details your analysis and reasoning and recommends one of the two alternatives. Provide both qualitative and quantitative reasoning in the memo.

18-22 COLLABORATIVE LEARNING EXERCISE

LO4 Rick Morgan sat at his desk mulling over an important decision. As plant manager for the Salina factory, he was under pressure to reduce costs and improve productivity. He had been approached several weeks before by Lauren Gosnell, the purchasing manager, who told him that a major supplier had offered to supply the plant with Component A56 at a delivered cost that was less than the factory's full cost to manufacture the component. Rick was well aware that good deals are sometimes not as good as they sound. So, he had asked Lauren and James Terrant, the plant controller, to prepare full cost analyses of the offer. The results lay on his desk.

Lauren's report was brief and to the point. The factory used 50,000 units of Part A56 each year. The full manufacturing cost was $45 each; the proposed price from the supplier was $39 each. This would result in a $300,000 per year cost savings. Lauren was wholeheartedly in favor of outsourcing this component.

James's report was also brief. He detailed the direct materials, direct labor, and overhead assigned to Part A56. His analysis supported Lauren's assertion that the full cost of the component was $45 each. James also recommended outsourcing.

While both reports were in favor of outside purchase, Rick was troubled. He wondered if there were hidden costs of outsourcing. He also wondered about the internal costs—and what would happen to the employees who worked on the A56 line. Were there any costs associated with the layoffs that had not been considered? Rick picked up the phone and called his former business professor, Kate Buchanan, and asked her to meet him for lunch the next day.

RICK: Kate, you've had a chance to read these two reports. Tell me, does it seem that anything is missing? Is this as great a deal as it sounds?"

KATE: Well, on the surface, Rick, it certainly looks good. But you may be right—there are some missing factors. For one thing, the outsourcing of this component will lead to the idling of one of your production lines. What are you planning to do with the excess capacity? Are there some costs hidden in overhead that will continue even though you aren't making the part anymore?

RICK: What do you mean by hidden?

KATE: I mean that some costs are flexible, but others are committed. Basically, flexible costs disappear immediately when you stop making a part—like direct materials. If you don't make A56, then you don't need to buy the sheet metal and solder. However, other costs are committed. For example, you use welding equipment on that line, what will happen to it? Right now, depreciation on the equipment is included in the overhead assigned to A56. When you stop making the part, will you still have the welding equipment? If so, the depreciation will still be there, but will be spread over other items you manufacture. I think you are right to consider the impact of the layoff, too. We often think of direct labor as being a variable or flexible cost. But any worker laid off will file for unemployment insurance. Your rates on all your remaining workers will skyrocket and will stay high for the next three years. And that is assuming no further layoffs. Plus, there's more.

RICK: More? How so?

KATE: Remember activity-based costing from our accounting class? Your plant clearly uses a functional-based approach to assigning overhead. If it used activity-based costing, you might find out that purchasing and receiving costs will go up if the supplier's offer is accepted. Of course, there could also be a decrease in that the materials used now would no longer be purchased, received, and stored.

RICK: Wow, Kate, how am I going to get all the information I need? I'm afraid I can't just ask James. He's been here forever. I tried to get him to look into ABC a year or so ago. He won't—says it's a fad that isn't worth the trouble. And Lauren is really enthusiastic about this possibility. I won't be getting an objective assessment from her. Would you like to take this on as a project? I'll pay your consulting rate.

KATE: (shaking her head) I sympathize, Rick. Unfortunately, it looks as if you might have to start making some tough decisions—starting with the Accounting Department. If James can't do an appropriate analysis of this one opportunity, he won't be able to meet your needs for information in the future. I think you need more than a one-time analysis. You need ongoing managerial accounting help. I can recommend a couple of recent accounting grads. One in particular has over 10 years of experience in industry and an outstanding academic record in our graduate program. He's intelligent, flexible, and energetic.

RICK: You may be right. Could you e-mail me his name and phone number when you get back to the office? I'd like to consider this. Meanwhile, let's grab a second cup of coffee and you can bring me up to speed on this flexible versus committed costing idea.

Required:

Form groups of three to five students to discuss the following questions. Choose one representative from your group to present the group's answers to the class.

1. Suggest some costing features that a controller should consider in evaluating the outsourcing opportunity. How would you go about getting the appropriate information?
2. Why do you think Lauren is so enthusiastic about the outsourcing opportunity? Could there be any reason(s) other than cost savings? Did James violate any of the ethical standards described in Chapter 1?
3. Rick is clearly considering a change in the controller. Do you think he should fire James? Where should Rick's loyalties lie?

18-23   CYBER RESEARCH CASE

LO1, LO2   For years, companies have been announcing outsourcing decisions and plant closings. Check the recent business news (e.g., http://www.wsj.com or http://www.businessweek.com) for this type of announcement. Go to the company's Web site for information on the decision. Write a brief (1- to 2-page) description of the decision, and speculate on what types of costing information might have led to it.

Pricing and Profitability Analysis

AFTER STUDYING THIS CHAPTER, YOU SHOULD BE ABLE TO:

1. Discuss basic pricing concepts.
2. Calculate a markup on cost and a target cost.
3. Discuss the impact of the legal system and ethics on pricing.
4. Explain why firms measure profit, and calculate measures of profit using absorption and variable costing.
5. Determine the profitability of segments.

6. Compute the sales price, price volume, contribution margin, contribution margin volume, sales mix, market share, and market size variances.
7. Discuss the variations in price, cost, and profit over the product life cycle.
8. Describe some of the limitations of profit measurement.

Henry Ford once said, "A business that does not make a profit for the buyer of a commodity, as well as for the seller, is not a good business. Buyer and seller must both be wealthier in some way as a result of a transaction, else the balance is broken."[1] Henry Ford's comment reminds us that the relationship between buyer and seller is an exchange relationship. Both expect to profit from it. But what is profit? How do we measure it? Since profit is the difference between revenues and costs, we must examine both parts of the expression. Price and revenue will be discussed first. Then, we will look at profit—the interplay of price and cost.

1. Henry Ford, *Today and Tomorrow* (Portland, OR: Productivity Press, 1926, reprinted in 1988).

Basic Pricing Concepts

One of the more difficult decisions faced by a company is pricing. The accountant is frequently the primary resource the firm turns to when financial data are needed, whether that information relates to cost or to price. As a consequence, accountants must be familiar with sources of revenue data as well as the economic and marketing concepts needed to interpret those data.

Demand and Supply

In general, customers want high-quality goods and services at a low price. Although customer demand is studied in detail in marketing classes, accountants need to be cognizant of demand, especially as demand interacts with supply.

All else being equal, customers will buy more at lower prices and less at higher prices. Producers, on the other hand, are willing (and able) to supply more at higher prices than they can at lower prices. The market-clearing or equilibrium price is located at the intersection of the supply and demand curves. It is the price for which the amount that producers are willing to supply just equals the amount that consumers demand. Note that if firms charge a price that is higher than the market-clearing price, demand falls short of supply. Producers see inventories piling up as consumers buy other goods. If the price is lower than the market-clearing price, everything that is produced is bought. Shortages and backlogs occur. This is a signal to increase production and/or to raise prices.

Factors other than price that influence demand include consumer income, quality of goods offered for sale, availability of substitutes, demand for complementary goods, whether the good is a necessity or a luxury, and so on. However, the basic demand-supply relationship remains, and producers know that raising prices almost inevitably results in less sold. Price elasticity and market structure are two factors that influence the degree of freedom companies have to adjust price.

Price Elasticity of Demand

Since price affects quantity sold, producers want to know just how much a price change will change quantity demanded. In general, **elastic demand** for a good means that a price increase (decrease) of a certain percent lowers (raises) the quantity demanded by more than that percentage. The opposite holds for **inelastic demand**, which occurs when a price change of a certain percent is associated with a quantity change of less than that percent. To apply elasticity concepts, we must analyze the characteristics of goods and services that are more or less elastic.

Goods that are price elastic tend to have many substitutes, are not necessities, and take a relatively large amount of consumer income. The demand for movie tickets, restaurant meals, and automobiles is relatively elastic.

Price-inelastic goods have few substitutes, are necessities, or constitute a relatively small percentage of consumer income. Prescription drugs, electricity, and local telephone service are examples of price-inelastic goods.

Ideally, a company could charge different prices to different customers according to their individual demands for the product. In practice, it is difficult to determine each customer's demand. In addition, it can be very expensive to implement differential pricing. Most retail stores in the United States, for example, mark the price on each item, and no negotiation is permitted. This results in the same price being charged to all customers regardless of their incomes or need for the good. The advantage is that relatively lower personnel costs are incurred; sales clerks need not haggle with each customer.

In other industries, the pricing policy is based on excess capacity and differing elasticities of demand; a higher price is charged to the core market and lower prices to secondary markets. In order for this to work, there must be no arbitrage. **Arbitrage** occurs when the customers who purchase the good at the lower price are able to resell it to other customers.

For example, airlines define their core market as business travelers. These travelers have inelastic demand for air travel. They need the flexibility to purchase tickets at the last minute, to change reservations, and to fly during the work week. Vacationers, on the other hand, have relatively elastic demand for air travel. A low price is the main attraction. If the airlines could fill their planes with full-fare business travelers, they would. However, there are not enough business travelers to completely fill the planes. In addition, the marginal cost of filling an empty seat on a plane is very low. This explains the airlines' convoluted pricing schemes. Full fares are charged for tickets purchased at the time of need and for travel during the work week. Lower prices are charged for tickets purchased seven to 21 days in advance that include a Saturday night stayover—a condition few business travelers can (or want to) meet. Of course, elasticity of demand is just one factor that influences price. Another important determinant of price is market structure.

Market Structure and Price

Market structure affects price, as well as the costs necessary to support that price. In general, there are four types of market structure: perfect competition, monopolistic competition, oligopoly, and monopoly. These markets differ according to the number of buyers and sellers, the degree of uniqueness of the product, and the relative ease of entry by firms into and out of the market (i.e., barriers to entry).

The **perfectly competitive market** has many buyers and sellers—no one of which is large enough to influence the market—a homogeneous product, and easy entry into and exit from the industry. Firms in a perfectly competitive market cannot charge a higher price than the market price because no one would buy their product, and they will not set a lower price because they can sell all they can produce at the market price.

At the opposite extreme is a monopoly. In a **monopoly**, barriers to entry are so high that there is only one firm in the market. As a result, the product is unique. This setting allows the monopolistic firm to be a price setter. However, just because the monopolist sets the price does not mean it can force consumers to buy. It does mean that a somewhat higher price (with concomitantly lower quantity sold) can be set than would be set in a competitive market. Some monopolies have legally enforced barriers to entry (e.g., the **United States Post Office**). Other firms are monopolies because of patent protection, specialized knowledge, or exceptionally high-cost production equipment. Pharmaceutical companies have a monopoly on new drugs due to patent protection. When the patent expires, generic drug companies can produce it, and the price of the drug plummets.

Monopolistic competition has characteristics of both monopoly and perfect competition, but it is much closer to the competitive situation. Basically, there are many sellers and buyers, but the products are differentiated on some basis. Restaurants are good examples of monopolistic competitors. Each restaurant serves food but attempts to differentiate itself in some way—ethnic style of food, closeness to work or schools, availability of a party room, gourmet versus casual atmosphere, and so on. The end result is to slightly raise prices above the perfectly competitive price, as customers agree to pay a little more for the unique feature that appeals to them.

An **oligopoly** is characterized by a few sellers. Typically, barriers to entry are high, and they are usually cost related. For example, the cereal industry is dominated by **Kellogg's**, **General Mills**, and **Quaker Oats**. The reason is not the high cost of manufacturing corn flakes. Instead, the huge selling expenditures (e.g., advertising and shelf space fees) of the big three effectively prevent smaller companies from entering the market. The oligopolist has some market power to set price, but it constantly must be aware of its competitors' actions. Often, there is a price leader, which sets a price that the others follow. The price leader may raise prices and see if the others follow suit. If they do not, the first firm, no longer a leader, typically reduces price immediately.

The various types of market structure and their characteristics are summarized in Exhibit 19-1. Companies need to be aware of the market structure in which they operate in order to understand their pricing options. Note that these market structures also have implications for the supply or cost side. The firm in the perfectly competitive industry has lower marketing costs (advertising, positioning, discounting, coupons) than the firm in the monopolistically competitive industry, which must constantly reinforce the consumer's perception that it has a unique product. The monopolist need not incur high costs to remind consumers of its unique product. However, it typically incurs expenses while protecting its monopoly position, often through legal fees and lobbying (included in administrative expenses).

EXHIBIT 19-1   Characteristics of the Four Basic Types of Market Structure

Market Structure Type	Number of Firms in Industry	Barriers to Entry	Uniqueness of Product	Expenses Related to Structure Type
Perfect competition	Many	Very low	Not unique	No special expenses
Monopolistic competition	Many	Low	Some unique features	Advertising, coupons, costs of differentiation
Oligopoly	Few	High	Fairly unique	Costs of differentiation, advertising, rebates, coupons
Monopoly	One	Very high	Very unique	Legal and lobbying expenditures

Pricing Policies

OBJECTIVE 2

Calculate a markup on cost and a target cost.

Companies use various strategies to set price. Since cost is an important determinant of supply and known to the producer, many companies base price on cost. Still other companies use a target-costing strategy, or strategies based on the initial conditions in the market.

Cost-Based Pricing

Demand is one side of the pricing equation; supply is the other side. Since revenue must cover cost for the firm to make a profit, many companies start with cost to determine price. That is, they calculate product cost and add the desired profit. The mechanics of this approach are straightforward. Usually, there is some cost base and a markup. The **markup** is a percentage applied to base cost; it includes desired profit and any costs not included in the base cost. Companies that bid for jobs routinely base bid price on cost.

Consider AudioPro Company, owned and operated by Chris Brown, which sells and installs audio equipment in homes, cars, and trucks. Costs of the components and other direct materials are easy to trace. Direct labor cost is similarly easy to trace to each job. Assemblers receive, on average, $12 per hour. Last year, AudioPro Company incurred $73,500 of direct labor cost. Overhead, consisting of utilities, small tools, building space, and so on, amounted to $49,000. AudioPro's income statement for last year is as follows:

Revenues		$350,350
Cost of goods sold:		
Direct materials	$122,500	
Direct labor	73,500	
Overhead	49,000	245,000
Gross profit		$105,350
Selling and administrative expenses		25,000
Operating income		$ 80,350

Suppose that Chris wants to earn about the same amount of profit on each job as was earned last year. She could calculate a markup on cost of goods sold by summing selling and administrative expenses and operating income and dividing by cost of goods sold.

$$\text{Markup on COGS} = (\text{Selling and administrative expenses} + \text{Operating income})/\text{COGS}$$
$$= (\$25,000 + \$80,350)/\$245,000$$
$$= 0.43$$

The markup on cost of goods sold is 43 percent. Notice that the 43 percent markup covers both profit and selling and administrative cost. The markup is not pure profit.

The markup can be calculated using a variety of bases. Clearly, for AudioPro Company, the cost of purchased materials is the largest component. Last year, direct materials were greater than any of the other costs or profit.

$$\text{Markup on direct materials} = (\text{Direct labor} + \text{Overhead} + \text{Selling and administrative expenses} + \text{Operating income})/\text{Direct materials}$$
$$= (\$73,500 + \$49,000 + \$25,000 + \$80,350)/\$122,500$$
$$= 1.86$$

A markup percentage of 186 percent of direct materials cost would also yield the same amount of profit, assuming the level of operations and other expenses remained stable. The choice of base and markup percentage generally rests on convenience. If Chris finds that the labor varies in rough proportion to the cost of materials (e.g., more expensive components take more time to set up) and that the cost of materials is easier to track than the cost of goods sold, then materials might be the better base.

To see how the markup can be used in pricing, suppose that Chris wants to expand her company's product line to include automobile alarm systems and electronic remote car door openers. She estimates the following costs for the sale and installation of one electronic remote car door opener.

Direct materials (components and two remote controls)	$ 40.00
Direct labor (2.5 hours × $12)	30.00
Overhead (65% of direct labor cost)	19.50
Estimated cost of one job	$ 89.50
Plus: 43% markup on COGS	38.49
Bid price	$127.99

Thus, AudioPro's initial price is about $128. Note that this is just the first pass at a price. Chris can adjust the price based on her knowledge of competition for this type of job and other factors. The markup is a guideline, not an absolute rule.

If AudioPro Company actually sets this price, is it guaranteed to make a profit? No, not at all. If very few jobs are won, the entire markup will go toward selling and administrative expenses, the costs not explicitly included in the pricing calculations.

Markup pricing is often used by retail stores, and their typical markup is 100 percent of cost. Thus, if a sweater is purchased by Graham Department Store for $24, the retail price marked is $48 [$24 + (1.00)($24)]. Of course, the 100 percent markup is not pure profit; it goes toward the salaries of the clerks, payment for space and equipment (cash registers, etc.), utilities, advertising, and so on. A major advantage of markup pricing is that standard markups are easy to apply. Consider the difficulty of setting a price for every piece of merchandise in a store. For example, **Pottery Barn** stocks a wide variety of goods, from glassware and pottery to furniture and textiles. Pricing each item by assessing its supply and demand characteristics would be far too time consuming. It is much simpler to apply a uniform markup to cost and then adjust prices as needed if less is demanded than anticipated.

Target Costing and Pricing

Most American companies, and nearly all European firms, set the price of a new product as the sum of the costs and the desired profit. The rationale is that the company must earn sufficient revenues to cover all costs and yield a profit. Peter Drucker writes, "This is true but irrelevant: Customers do not see it as their job to ensure manufacturers a profit. The only sound way to price is to start out with what the market is willing to pay."[2]

Target costing is a method of determining the cost of a product or service based on the price (target price) that customers are willing to pay. The marketing department determines what characteristics and price for a product are most acceptable to consumers. Then, it is the job of the company's engineers to design and develop the product such that cost and profit can be covered by that price. Japanese firms have been doing this for years; American companies are beginning to use target costing.

Retail stores employ target costing when they look for goods that can be priced at a particular level to appeal to customers. For example, many department stores work with clothing companies to develop house labels. The house label goods are typically good quality items that cost less and are priced lower than comparable name brand items. The house label gives the store flexibility. The store is not in the business of manufacturing sweaters, but it can find a source to deliver sweaters of particular quality for the cost that will allow the store to achieve a target price and profit.

Let's return to the AudioPro Company example. Suppose Chris finds that other aftermarket audio installers price the remote car door opener at $110. Should she drop her plans to expand into this product line? No, not if she can tailor her price to the market price. Recall that the original price called for $40 of direct materials and $30 of direct labor. Perhaps Chris could offer one remote device instead of two, saving $5 in cost. In addition, she might be able to shave one half hour off the direct labor, once the workers are trained and able to work more efficiently. This would result in $6 of savings. Prime cost would be $59 ($40 − $5 + $30 − $6) instead of the original $70.

Recall that AudioPro Company applies overhead at the rate of 65 percent of direct labor cost. However, Chris must think carefully about this job. Perhaps somewhat less overhead will be incurred because purchasing is reduced. (Only one reliable supplier is needed, and the tools and facilities can be shared with the audio installation.) Perhaps overhead for this job will amount to $12 (50 percent of direct labor). That would make the cost of one job $71 ($35 + $24 + $12).

Now, if the standard markup of 43 percent is applied, the price would be $101.53, well within the other firms' price of $110. As you can see, target costing is an iterative process. Chris will go through the cycle until she either achieves the target cost or determines that she cannot. Note, however, that target costing has given Chris a chance to develop a profitable market; a chance she might not have had if the original cost-based price had been set.

Target costing involves much more upfront work than cost-based pricing. However, additional work must be done if the cost-based price turns out to be higher than

---

2. Peter Drucker, "The Five Deadly Business Sins," *The Wall Street Journal* (October 21, 1993): A22.

what customers will accept. Then, the arduous task of bringing costs into line to support a lower price, or the opportunity cost of missing the market altogether, begins.

Other Pricing Policies

Target costing is also effectively used in conjunction with marketing decisions to engage in price skimming or penetration pricing. **Penetration pricing** is the pricing of a new product at a low initial price, perhaps even lower than cost, to build market share quickly. This is useful when the product or service is new and customers have great uncertainty as to its value. We must distinguish penetration pricing from predatory pricing. The important difference is the intent. The penetration price is not meant to destroy competition. Accountants, lawyers, and other professionals with new practices often use penetration pricing to establish a customer base.

Price skimming means that a higher price is charged when a product or service is first introduced. In essence, the company skims the cream off the market. It is used most effectively when the product is new, a small group of consumers values it, and the company enjoys a monopolistic advantage. Companies that engage in price skimming are hoping to recoup the expenses of research and development through high initial pricing. A cost consideration is that, in the start-up phase of production, economies of scale and learning effects have not occurred. For example, in the late 1960s, **Hewlett-Packard** produced hand-held calculators. These were truly novel and very expensive. Priced at over $400, only scientists and engineers, who used the calculators in their work, felt the need for this product. As the market for hand-held calculators grew and technology improved, economies of scale kicked in, and the cost and price dropped dramatically. By the 1980s, tiny solar calculators were given away as enticements to new subscribers of magazines.

Closely related to skimming is price gouging. **Price gouging** is said to occur when firms with market power price products "too high." How high is too high? Surely, cost is a consideration. Any time price just covers cost, gouging does not occur. This is why many firms go to considerable trouble to explain their cost structure and point out costs that consumers may not realize exist. Pharmaceutical companies, for example, emphasize the research and development costs associated with new drugs. When a high price is not clearly supported by cost, buyers take offense.

OBJECTIVE 3

Discuss the impact of the legal system and ethics on pricing.

The Legal System and Pricing

While demand and supply are important determinants of price, government also has an important impact on pricing. Over time, many laws have been passed regulating the level and way in which firms can set prices. The basic principle behind much pricing regulation is that competition is good and should be encouraged. Therefore, collusion by companies to set prices and the deliberate attempt to drive competitors out of business are prohibited.

Predatory Pricing

Predatory pricing is the practice of setting prices below cost for the purpose of injuring competitors and eliminating competition. It is important to note that pricing below cost is not necessarily predatory pricing. Companies frequently price an item below cost, by running weekly specials in a grocery store, or practicing penetration pricing, for example. State laws on predatory pricing create a patchwork of legal definitions. Twenty-two states have laws against predatory pricing, each differing somewhat in definition and rules.

For example, three Conway, Arkansas, drugstores filed suit against **Wal-Mart**.[3] The druggists contended that Wal-Mart engaged in predatory pricing by selling more than

---

3. Wal-Mart lost the suit in October 1993 but won on appeal.

100 products below cost. One difficulty is showing exactly what cost is. Wal-Mart has low overhead and phenomenal buying power. Suppliers are regularly required to shave prices to win Wal-Mart's business. Smaller concerns cannot win such price breaks. Thus, the fact that Wal-Mart prices products below competitors' costs does not necessarily mean that those products are priced below Wal-Mart's cost. (Although in this case, the CEO of Wal-Mart did concede that Wal-Mart on occasion prices products below its own cost.) More importantly, if predatory pricing is truly taking place, the below-cost price must be for the purpose of driving out competitors, a difficult point to prove. In general, states follow federal law in predatory pricing cases, and federal law makes it difficult to prove predatory pricing, since price competition is so highly valued.

Predatory pricing on the international market is called **dumping**, which occurs when companies sell below cost in other countries, and domestic industry is injured. For years, U.S. steel manufacturers have accused Japanese, Russian, and Brazilian companies of dumping. Companies found guilty of dumping products in the United States are subject to trade restrictions and stiff tariffs—which act to increase the price of the good. The defense against a charge of dumping is demonstrating that the price is indeed above or equal to costs, or that domestic industry is unhurt.[4]

Price Discrimination

The Robinson-Patman Act was passed in 1936 as a means of outlawing price discrimination.[5] **Price discrimination** refers to the charging of different prices to different customers for essentially the same product. A key feature of the Robinson-Patman Act is that only manufacturers or suppliers are covered by the act; services and intangibles are not included.

Importantly, the Robinson-Patman Act does allow price discrimination under certain specified conditions: (1) if the competitive situation demands it and (2) if costs (including costs of manufacture, sale, or delivery) can justify the lower price. Clearly, this second condition is important for the accountant, as a lower price offered to one customer must be justified by identifiable cost savings. Additionally, the amount of the discount must be at least equaled by the amount of cost saved.

What about quantity discounts—are they permissible under Robinson-Patman? Consider the quantity discounts offered by **Morton Salt** during the 1940s. Morton offered substantial discounts to purchasers of a carload or more of product. The Supreme Court, in a 1948 decision, found that Morton Salt had violated the Robinson-Patman Act because so few buyers qualified for the quantity discount; at the time, only five large chain stores had purchases high enough to qualify for the lowest price. While the discounts were available to all purchasers, the Court noted that for all practical purposes, small wholesalers and retail grocers could not qualify for the discounts. A key point here is that so few purchasers were eligible for the discount that competition was lessened. So while the act states that quantity discounts can be given, they must not appreciably lessen competition.

Freight is considered part of price for purposes of the Robinson-Patman Act. If a company requires the customer to pay freight charges, then there is no problem. However, price discrimination may occur if the price charged includes delivery. Suppose the firm charges a uniform delivery price. Then, customers located next to the firm pay the same price as customers located 1,000 miles away. Because the cost of delivering to nearby customers is much less than delivering to distant customers, the nearby customers are paying "phantom freight."

---

4. Chris Adams, "Steelmakers Complain About Foreign Steel; They Also Import It," *The Wall Street Journal* (March 22, 1999): A1 and A8.

5. This section relies on two sources. William A. Rutter, *Anti-Trust*, 3rd ed. (Gardena, CA: Gilbert Law Summaries, 1972): 57–64; and William A. Baldwin, *Market Power, Competition, and Antitrust Policy* (Homewood, IL: Richard D. Irwin, Inc., 1987): 430–435.

The burden of proof for firms accused of violating the Robinson-Patman Act is on the firms. The cost justification argument must be buttressed by substantial cost data. Proving a cost justification is an absolute defense; however, the expense of preparing evidence and the FTC's restrictive interpretations of the defense have made it a seldom used choice in the past. Now, the availability of large databases, the development of activity-based costing, and powerful computing make it a more palatable alternative. Still, problems remain. Cost allocations make such determinations particularly thorny. In justifying quantity discounts to larger companies, a company might keep track of sales calls, differences in time and labor required to make small and large deliveries, and so on.

In computing a cost differential, the company must create classes of customers based on the average costs of selling to those customers and then charge all customers in each group a cost-justifiable price.

Let's look at Cobalt, Inc., which manufactures vitamin supplements. The manufacturing costs average $163 per case (a case contains 100 bottles of vitamins). Cobalt, Inc., sold 250,000 cases last year to the following three classes of customer:

Customer	Price per Case	Cases Sold
Large drug store chain	$200	125,000
Small local pharmacies	232	100,000
Individual health clubs	250	25,000

Clearly, there is price discrimination, but is it justifiable? To answer that question, we need more information about the customer classes.

The large drug store chain requires Cobalt to put the chain's label on each bottle. This special labeling costs about $0.03 per bottle. The chain orders through electronic data interchange (EDI), which costs Cobalt about $50,000 annually in operating expenses and depreciation. Cobalt pays all shipping costs, which amounted to $1.5 million last year.

The small local pharmacies order in smaller lots, which requires special picking and packing in the Cobalt factory. This special handling adds $20 to the cost of each case sold. Sales commissions to the independent jobbers who sell Cobalt products to the pharmacies average 10 percent of sales. Bad debts expense is not high and amounts to 1 percent of sales.

Individual health clubs purchase vitamins in lots even smaller than those of the local pharmacies. The special picking and packaging costs average $30 per case. There are no sales commissions for the health clubs. Instead, Cobalt advertises in health club management magazines and accepts orders by phone. In addition, Cobalt has created point-of-sale posters and displays for the clubs. These marketing costs amount to $100,000 per year. Bad debts expense is a serious problem with the health clubs, as they frequently go out of business or change ownership. Bad debts expense for this class of customer averages 10 percent.

Now, it is possible to analyze the cost of each customer class. Exhibit 19-2, on the following page, shows the costs associated with each customer class. It is easy to see that there are significant cost differences in serving the three classes. Cobalt realizes 10.8 percent profit on the cost of sales to the chain store [($200 − $178.40)/$200]. The pharmacies provide about 10.1 percent profit [($232 − $208.52)/$232]. The health club related profit percentage is 11.2 percent [($250 − $222)/$250]. Even though the highest price ($250) is 25 percent above the lowest price ($200), profits vary within a narrow 1 percent range. The cost differences among the three classes of customer appear to explain the price differences.

Ethics

Just as a company can practice unethical behavior in applying costs, it can mislead in pricing. A good example is the practice of some airlines of providing "automatic upgrades."

EXHIBIT 19-2   **Analysis of Cobalt, Inc., Customer Class Costs**

Chain store:

Manufacturing cost per case	$163.00
Special labeling cost ($0.03 × 100)	3.00
EDI ($50,000/125,000 cases)	0.40
Shipping ($1,500,000/125,000 cases)	12.00
Total cost per case	$178.40

Small pharmacies:

Manufacturing cost per case	$163.00
Special handling per case	20.00
Sales commission ($232 × 0.10)	23.20
Bad debts expense ($232 × 0.01)	2.32
Total cost per case	$208.52

Health clubs:

Manufacturing cost per case	$163.00
Special handling per case	30.00
Selling expense ($100,000/25,000 cases)	4.00
Bad debts expense ($250 × 0.10)	25.00
Total cost per case	$222.00

For example, from San Francisco to Washington, **Continental Airlines** had two unrestricted, 1-way coach prices—$409 and $703. The higher price resulted in an automatic upgrade to first class, while the receipt showed "coach fare." Why would the customer want such a ticket? Easy, because the customer's company reimburses only coach fares.[6]

Measuring Profit

Profit is a measure of the difference between what a firm puts into making and selling a product or service and what it receives. It is the degree to which the firm becomes wealthier on account of engaging in transactions. The desire of firms to measure the increase in wealth has led to numerous definitions of profit. Some are used for external reporting and some for internal reporting.

Reasons for Measuring Profit

Clearly, firms are interested in measuring profit. In fact, firms are classified according to whether or not profit is the primary objective—they are either for-profit or not-for-profit entities. Profits are measured for a number of reasons. These include determining the viability of the firm, measuring managerial performance, determining whether or not a firm adheres to government regulations, and signaling the market about the opportunities for others to earn a profit.

Owners of a company want to know if the company is viable in both the short term and the long term. Work gives meaning to life. Staying in business is not only a means

OBJECTIVE 4

Explain why firms measure profit and calculate measures of profit using absorption and variable costing.

---

6. Scott McCartney, "Why Ticket Says Coach but Seat Is Up Front," *The Wall Street Journal* (September 29, 1995): B1.

to an end but an end in itself. *The Money Game*, by Adam Smith,[7] contains an interesting passage in which he puzzles through John Maynard Keynes's reference to the stock market as a game. Smith writes:

> *Game? Game? Why did the Master say game? He could have said business, or profession, or occupation or what have you. What is a game? It is "sport, play, frolic or fun;" "a scheme or art employed in the pursuit of an object or purpose;" "a contest, conducted according to set rules, for amusement, recreation, or winning a stake." Does that sound like Owning a Share of American Industry? Participating in the Long-Term Growth of the American Economy? No, but it sounds like the stock market.*

That not only sounds like the stock market, it also sounds like many businesses. Steve Jobs started **Apple Computer** in a garage. Years later, a multimillionaire, he was eased out of Apple management—and immediately started **Next**. Later, he returned to Apple and is heavily involved in **Pixar**. Sam Walton stayed involved with **Wal-Mart** until his death, as did John D. Rockefeller with **Standard Oil**. Playing the game is important, and profit is a way of keeping score. Players must maintain positive profits to stay in the game. Enough losses and you're out.

Profit can be used to measure managerial performance. In this sense, profit indicates efficiency in the use of resources, because the costs are kept below the benefits. Assessing performance is complicated, but profit, because it is measured in dollars, simplifies scorekeeping. Top management is usually evaluated on the basis of profit and/or return on investment. Both measures require benefits to exceed costs.

Regulated firms must keep profits within certain limits. The profitability of a regulated monopoly is monitored to ensure that the public is served by this structure and that prices do not escalate to the level of an unregulated monopoly. Note that price alone is not set—instead, the price must be set to ensure a "reasonable rate of return," and it is tied to the costs incurred by the regulated firm. Examples of companies subject to regulation are utilities, local telephone companies, and cable television companies. These companies enjoy monopoly status, and they pay for the privilege through adherence to regulations.

Profit is also of interest to those outside a company because it is a signal of the opportunities available. A highly profitable firm signals the market that others might also benefit from entry. Low profits do not entice competition. For this reason, companies may deliberately avoid high short-term profits. For example, in the 1940s, **DuPont** marketed nylon to manufacturers of women's hosiery and lingerie at a price that was only 60 percent of what could have been charged—despite the fact that nylon was patented and there was virtually no competition. As a result, competition was delayed for five to six years, and the overall market for nylon expanded dramatically into unanticipated areas, such as its use in automobile tires.[8]

It should also be noted that even though a not-for-profit entity has no profit, it still is engaged in an exchange relationship and must assess its performance and long-term viability. While data on charities expands (some watchdog groups, such as the **National Charities Information Bureau** in New York, even have Internet Web sites and will take complaints online), the usability of the data leaves something to be desired. Corporate donors, in particular, want better measures of how well a charity fulfills its mission. The reason, of course, is that not-for-profit entities use and must account for resources. Supplies, postage, telephones, and office space all require money.

---

7. Actually, Adam Smith is a pseudonym for George J. W. Goodman. But you can probably find *The Money Game* (New York: Vintage Books, 1976) under Adam Smith. The book is a very readable exploration of investing and investors. The passage cited here can be found on page 16.
8. Drucker, *op. cit.*

Employees do not necessarily make less than a market wage. They simply have no claim to any residual. As a result, many of the concepts covered in this chapter have relevance to not-for-profit entities. The **Girl Scouts of America**, for example, expect to profit from cookie sales, although they may not refer to the money made above cost as profit. Not-for-profit firms are still interested in the relationship between revenues and expenses, or inflows and outflows.

Absorption-Costing Approach to Measuring Profit

Absorption costing, or full costing, is required for external financial reporting. According to GAAP, profit is a long-run concept and depends on the difference between revenues and expenses. Over the long run, of course, all costs are variable. Therefore, fixed costs are treated as if they were variable by assigning some to each unit of production. Absorption costing assigns all manufacturing costs, direct materials, direct labor, variable overhead, and a share of fixed overhead to each unit of product. In this way, each unit of product absorbs some of the fixed manufacturing overhead in addition to the variable costs incurred to manufacture it. When a unit of product is finished, it takes these costs into inventory with it. When it is sold, these manufacturing costs are shown on the income statement as cost of goods sold. It is absorption costing that is used to calculate three measures of profit: gross profit, operating income, and net income.

Preparing the Absorption-Costing Income Statement

Lasersave, Inc., a company that recycles used toner cartridges for laser printers, began operations in August and manufactured 1,000 cartridges during the month with the following costs:

Direct materials	$ 5,000
Direct labor	15,000
Variable overhead	3,000
Fixed overhead	20,000
Total manufacturing cost	$43,000

During August, 1,000 cartridges were sold at a price of $60. Variable marketing cost was $1.25 per unit, and fixed marketing and administrative expenses were $12,000. The unit product cost of each toner cartridge is $43 ($43,000/1,000 units). This amount includes direct materials ($5), direct labor ($15), variable overhead ($3), and fixed overhead ($20). Notice that the fixed overhead is treated as if it were variable. That is, the total amount is divided by production and applied to each unit. Thus, the cost of goods sold for August is $43,000 ($43 × 1,000 units sold). Exhibit 19-3 illustrates the absorption-costing income statement for Lasersave for the month of August.

EXHIBIT **19-3**	Absorption-Costing Income Statement for Lasersave, Inc., for August	

		Percent of Sales
Sales	$ 60,000	100.00%
Less: Cost of goods sold	43,000	71.67
Gross profit	$ 17,000	28.33%
Less: Variable marketing expenses	(1,250)	(2.08)
Fixed marketing and administrative expenses	(12,000)	(20.00)
Operating income	$ 3,750	6.25%

The income statement shown in Exhibit 19-3 is the familiar full costing income statement used for external reporting. Recall that the difference between revenue and cost of goods sold is gross profit (or gross margin). This is not equal to operating income, because the marketing and administrative expenses remain to be covered. At one time, gross profit was a fairly useful measure of profitability. Marketing and administrative expenses were relatively stable and could be adjusted fairly easily. In today's economic environment, that is less true. Government regulations affect businesses in sometimes unforeseen ways. Environmental cleanup and modification of facilities to comply with the Americans with Disabilities Act are just two examples of regulations that increase nonmanufacturing expenses. Additionally, research and development, also an expense subtracted from gross profit to yield operating income, is increasingly important. Now, gross profit is less useful and cannot be used as a sole measure of the long-run health of the firm.

Exhibit 19-3 also shows the "Percent of Sales" column which is often associated with the absorption-costing income statement. Notice that Lasersave, Inc., earned a gross profit of just over 28 percent of sales and that operating income was 6.25 percent of sales. Is this good or bad performance? It depends on the typical experience for the industry. If most firms in the industry earned a gross margin of 35 percent of sales, Lasersave would be considered below average, and it might look for opportunities to decrease cost of goods sold or to increase revenue.

What about absorption-costing operating income? Is it a reasonable measure of performance? Problems exist with this measure, too. First, managers can remove some current-period costs from the income statement by producing for inventory. Second, the absorption-costing format is not useful for decision making.

Disadvantages of Absorption Costing

In general, a company manufactures a product in order to sell it. In fact, that was the case for Lasersave for the month of August when every unit produced was sold. But what happens when the company produces for inventory? Suppose that in September, Lasersave produces 1,250 units but sells only 1,000. The price, variable cost per unit, and total fixed costs remain the same. Will September operating income equal August operating income? Exhibit 19-4 shows the income statement for September.

EXHIBIT 19-4	Absorption-Costing Income Statement for Lasersave, Inc., for September

Sales	$ 60,000
Less: Cost of goods sold*	39,000
Gross profit	$ 21,000
Less:	
Variable marketing expenses	(1,250)
Fixed marketing and administrative expenses.	(12,000)
Operating income	$ 7,750

*Direct materials ($5 × 1,250)	$ 6,250
Direct labor ($15 × 1,250)	18,750
Variable overhead ($3 × 1,250)	3,750
Fixed overhead	20,000
Total manufacturing overhead	$48,750
Add: Beginning inventory	0
Less: Ending inventory	(9,750)
Cost of goods sold	$39,000

Operating income in September is $7,750 versus operating income for August of $3,750. The same number of units was sold, at the same price, and the same costs. What happened? The culprit is treating fixed manufacturing overhead as if it were variable. In August, 1,000 units were produced, and each one absorbed $20 ($20,000/1,000) of fixed overhead. In September, however, the same total fixed manufacturing overhead of $20,000 was spread out over 1,250 units, so each unit absorbed only $16 ($20,000/1,250). The 250 units that went into ending inventory took with them all of their variable costs of production of $5,750 ($23 × 250) plus $4,000 (250 × $16) of fixed manufacturing overhead from September. That $4,000 of inventoried fixed manufacturing overhead is precisely equal to the $4,000 difference in operating incomes.

Clearly, the absorption-costing income statement gives the wrong message in September. It seems to say that September performance was better than August performance, when the sales performance was identical and, arguably, production was off by 250 units. (Even if the company wanted to produce for inventory, it is misleading to increase income for the period as a result.)

Of course, the whole purpose of manipulating income by producing for inventory is to increase profit above what it would have been without the extra production. Managers who are evaluated on the basis of operating income know that they can temporarily improve profitability by increasing production. They may do this to ensure year-end bonuses or promotions. As a result, the usefulness of operating or net income as a measure of profitability is weakened. Companies that use absorption-costing income as a measure of profitability may institute rules regarding production. For example, a manufacturer of floor care products insists that the factory produce only the amounts called for in the master budget. While this will not erase the impact of changes in inventory on operating income, it does mean that the factory manager cannot deliberately manipulate production to increase income.

The second disadvantage of absorption costing is that it is not a useful format for decision making. Suppose that Lasersave was considering accepting a special order for 100 toner cartridges at $38. Should the company accept? If we focus on the absorption-costing income statement, who can tell? In August, the manufacturing cost per unit was $43. In September, it was $39. Neither figure included the marketing cost. The treatment of fixed overhead as a unit-level variable cost has made it difficult to see just what the incremental cost is.

Variable-Costing Approach to Measuring Profit

An approach to measuring profitability that avoids the problems inherent in making fixed overhead a variable cost is variable costing. **Variable costing** (sometimes called direct costing) assigns only unit-level variable manufacturing costs to the product; these costs include direct materials, direct labor, and variable overhead. Fixed overhead is treated as a period cost and is not inventoried with the other product costs. Instead, it is expensed in the period incurred.

The result of treating fixed manufacturing overhead as a period expense is to reduce the factory costs that are inventoriable. Under variable costing, only direct materials, direct labor, and variable overhead are inventoried. (Remember that marketing and administrative expenses are never inventoried—whether variable or fixed.) Therefore, the inventoriable variable product cost for Lasersave is $23 ($5 direct materials + $15 direct labor + $3 variable overhead).

The variable-costing income statement is set up a little differently from the absorption-costing income statement. Exhibit 19-5 gives Lasersave's variable-costing income statements for August and September. Notice that all unit-level variable costs (including variable manufacturing and variable marketing expenses) are summed and subtracted from sales to yield contribution margin. Then, all fixed expenses for the period, whether they are incurred by the factory or by marketing and administration, are subtracted to yield operating income.

	For the Month of August	For the Month of September
EXHIBIT 19-5	Variable-Costing Income Statements for Lasersave, Inc.	
Sales	$ 60,000	$ 60,000
Less: Variable expenses*	24,250	24,250
Contribution margin	$ 35,750	$ 35,750
Less:		
Fixed manufacturing overhead	(20,000)	(20,000)
Fixed marketing and administrative expenses	(12,000)	(12,000)
Operating income	$ 3,750	$ 3,750

*Direct materials	$ 5,000
Direct labor	15,000
Variable overhead	3,000
Total variable manufacturing expenses	$23,000
Add: Variable marketing expenses	1,250
Total variable expenses	$24,250

Notice that the August and September income statements for Lasersave are identical. This seems right. Each month had identical sales and costs. While September production was higher, that will show up as an increase in inventory on the balance sheet. As we can see, variable-costing operating income cannot be manipulated through overproduction, since fixed manufacturing overhead is not carried into inventory.

Let's take a closer look at each month. In August, production exactly equaled sales. In this case, none of the period's costs go into inventory, and absorption-costing operating income is equal to variable-costing income. In September, inventory increased, and absorption-costing operating income is higher than variable-costing operating income. The difference, $4,000 ($7,750 − $3,750), is just equal to the fixed overhead per unit multiplied by the increase in inventory ($16 × 250 units).

What happens when inventory decreases? Again, there is an effect on operating income under absorption costing but not under variable costing. Let's take Lasersave into the month of October, when production is 1,250 units (just like September), but 1,300 units are sold. Exhibit 19-6, on the following page, gives the comparative income statements for both absorption and variable costing.

In this case, when inventory decreases (or production is less than sales), variable-costing operating income is greater than absorption-costing operating income. The difference of $800 ($14,475 − $13,675) is equal to the 50 units that, under absorption costing, came from inventory with $16 of the previous month's fixed manufacturing overhead attached. Exhibit 19-7, on the following page, summarizes the impact of changes in inventory on operating income under absorption costing and variable costing.

To summarize, when inventories change from the beginning to the end of the period, the two costing approaches will give different operating incomes. The reason for this is that absorption costing assigns fixed manufacturing overhead to units produced. If those units are sold, the fixed overhead appears on the income statement under cost of goods sold. If the units are not sold, the fixed overhead goes into inventory. Under variable costing, however, all fixed overhead for the period is expensed. As a result, absorption costing allows managers to manipulate operating income by producing for inventory.

	Absorption Costing			Variable Costing
Sales	$ 78,000	Sales		$ 78,000
Less: Cost of goods sold*	50,700	Less: Variable expenses		31,525
Gross profit	$ 27,300	Contribution margin		$ 46,475
Less:		Less:		
Variable marketing expenses	(1,625)	Fixed manufacturing overhead		(20,000)
Fixed marketing and administrative expenses	(12,000)	Fixed marketing and administrative expenses		(12,000)
Operating income	$ 13,675	Operating income		$ 14,475

EXHIBIT 19-6 Comparative Income Statements for Lasersave, Inc., for the Month of October

*1,300 × $39 = $50,700.

EXHIBIT 19-7 Changes in Inventory under Absorption and Variable Costing

If	Then
1. Production > Sales	Absorption-costing income > Variable-costing income
2. Production < Sales	Absorption-costing income < Variable-costing income
3. Production = Sales	Absorption-costing income = Variable-costing income

The variable-costing income statement has an advantage in addition to providing better signals regarding performance. It also provides more useful information for management decision making. Look again at Exhibit 19-6. How much additional profit can be made on the sale of one more toner cartridge? The absorption-costing income statement indicates that $21 ($27,300/1,300) is the per-unit gross profit. However, that figure includes some fixed overhead, and fixed overhead will not change if another unit is produced and sold. The variable-costing income statement gives more useful information. Additional contribution margin of the extra unit is $35.75 ($46,475/1,300). The key insight of variable costing is that fixed expenses do not change as units produced and sold change. Therefore, while the variable-costing income statement cannot be used for external reporting, it is a valuable tool for some management decisions.

The measures of profit discussed in this section all applied to the company. Additional factors must be considered in using any income statement for internal reporting and performance evaluation. Neither operating income nor net income (operating income less income taxes) are completely sufficient for profitability analysis. In other words, the questions that firms most want answered cannot be answered with an analysis of net income alone. One reason for the insufficiency of net income is aggregation of data. Aggregation refers to the summing of components of profit into more general categories. The fine detail necessary to determine the existence of problems and to take corrective action is missing from the income statement. For example, the income statement may indicate low revenue, but it does not indicate why it is low. Is quantity sold down? Has price decreased? Are some products experiencing increased sales while others have experienced decreased sales? More analysis is needed to answer these questions and others.

Profitability of Segments

Companies frequently want to know the profitability of a segment of the business. That segment could be a product, division, sales territory, or customer group. Determining the profit attributable to subdivisions of the company is harder than determining over-all profit because of the need to allocate expenses. Accurate tracing of costs to each segment is difficult. Still, the importance of segmental profit to management decision making can make the exercise worthwhile.

Profit by Product Line

It is easy to understand why a firm would like to know whether or not a particular product is profitable. A product that consistently loses money and has no potential to become profitable could be dropped. This would free up resources for a product with higher potential. On the other hand, a profitable product may merit additional time and attention.

Movie studios now use sophisticated software to predict the popularity of films based on the popularity of similar films in particular neighborhoods. For example, Fox can target a teen flick like "Drive Me Crazy" to screens located near suburban malls, rather than blanketing movie theaters across the country. The more limited release saves $3,000 in film-duplication cost per copy, allowing the movie to post a reasonable profit.[9]

Product-line profitability would be easy to compute if all costs and revenues were easily traceable to each product. This is seldom the case. Therefore, companies must first determine how profit will be computed. Three possibilities (in order of increasing accuracy) are absorption costing, variable costing, and activity-based costing. Each allocates cost to a product line in a different way and will give a different result. The company's need for accuracy determines which is used.

Let's examine Alden Company, which manufactures two products: basic fax machines and multi-function fax machines. The basic fax machine has telephone and fax capability. This type of machine is less expensive and easier to produce. The multi-function fax machine is the high-end machine. It is a combination of 2-line telephone, fax, computer printer, and copier. The multi-function fax machine uses more advanced technology and is more difficult to produce. Data on each product follow:

	Basic	*Multi-Function*
Number of units	20,000	10,000
Direct labor hours	40,000	15,000
Price	$200	$350
Prime cost per unit	$55	$95
Overhead per unit*	$30	$22.50

*Annual overhead is $825,000, and overhead is applied on the basis of direct labor hours.

Marketing expenses, all variable, amount to 10 percent of sales. Administrative expenses of $2 million, all fixed, are allocated to the products in accordance with revenue. Absorption-costing income by product line is shown in Exhibit 19-8 on the following page.

Clearly, the multi-function fax machine is more profitable. But what does this tell us? Can we conclude that each basic fax machine sold adds $41.65 ($833,000/20,000 units) to profit? Does each multi-function fax machine sold add $104.20 ($1,042,000/10,000) to profit? No, Alden Company has intermingled variable and fixed costs and has allocated administrative expenses on the basis of revenue, when there is no reason to believe that

9. Ronald Grover, "Fox's New Star: The Internet," *Business Week E. Biz* (November 1, 1999): 42–46.

EXHIBIT 19-8

Alden Company Absorption-Costing Income Statement (In thousands of dollars)	Basic	Multi-Function	Total
Sales	$ 4,000	$3,500	$ 7,500
Less: Cost of goods sold	1,700	1,175	2,875
Gross profit	$ 2,300	$2,325	$ 4,625
Less:			
Marketing expenses	(400)	(350)	(750)
Administrative expenses	(1,067)	(933)	(2,000)
Operating income	$ 833	$1,042	$ 1,875

revenue drives administrative expenses. Additionally, overhead has been assigned to the products on a per-unit basis, but we do not know just what it includes. Is $22.50 an accurate representation of the overhead resources required to produce one multi-function fax machine? If not, a different costing system might be used.

Using Variable Costing to Measure Segment Profit

Alden Company could use variable costing and segregate direct fixed and common fixed expenses as well. To apply variable costing to Alden Company, we need additional information on fixed and variable costs of overhead.

	Variable	Fixed
Overhead:		
Setups		$ 40,000
Maintenance		120,000
Supplies	$ 80,000	
Power	280,000	
Machine depreciation		250,000
Other factory costs		55,000
Total	$360,000	$465,000

Recall that overhead is applied on the basis of direct labor hours. Therefore, the variable overhead assigned to basic fax machines is $261,818 [$360,000 × (40,000/55,000)]. The variable overhead assigned to multi-function fax machines is $98,182 [$360,000 × (15,000/55,000)]. Now, we can prepare a segmented income statement as shown in Exhibit 19-9.

While absorption-based operating income equals variable-costing operating income in this case (because all units produced were sold), the variable-costing income statement provides more useful information. Now, we can see how much more profit is made if another fax machine is sold. An additional basic fax machine adds $111.90 ($2,238,000/20,000) to profit. An additional multi-function fax machine adds $210.20 ($2,102,000/10,000) to profit. The key insight of variable costing is that fixed expenses do not change as units produced and sold change. Therefore, while the variable-costing income statement cannot be used for external reporting, it is a valuable tool for some management decisions. One problem remains with the variable-costing approach. The fixed costs were not assigned to either product. Is this appropriate? If all fixed costs

EXHIBIT **19-9**

Alden Company
Variable-Costing Income Statement
(In thousands of dollars)

	Basic	Multi-Function	Total
Sales	$ 4,000	$ 3,500	$ 7,500
Less:			
Variable cost of goods sold	(1,362)	(1,048)	(2,410)
Sales commissions	(400)	(350)	(750)
Contribution margin	$ 2,238	$ 2,102	$ 4,340
Less:			
Fixed overhead			(465)
Administrative expenses			(2,000)
Operating income			$ 1,875

must be incurred despite which products are produced, the answer is yes. However, often a cost is fixed with respect to units produced but is variable according to another activity driver. In this case, activity-based costing yields more accurate cost information.

Using Activity-Based Costing to Measure Segment Profit

An activity-based costing approach, with its insight into unit-level, batch-level, product-level, and facility-level costs, may give management a more accurate feel for profits attributable to different product lines. Let's revisit Alden Company and look for additional information on the drivers for each overhead cost. Exhibit 19-10 contains

EXHIBIT **19-10**   Overhead Activities and Drivers

Overhead Cost Category	Cost Driver	Total Cost
Setups	Number of setups	$ 40,000
Maintenance	Maintenance hours	120,000
Supplies	Direct labor hours	80,000
Power	Machine hours	280,000
Machine depreciation	Machine hours	250,000
Other factory costs	(None)	55,000
		$825,000

	Usage of Cost Drivers by Product	
	Basic	Multi-Function
Number of setups	10	30
Maintenance hours	2,000	8,000
Direct labor hours	40,000	15,000
Machine hours	10,000	90,000

this information along with cost driver usage by product. Note that there is no activity driver for other factory costs, since these are facility-level costs and will remain no matter which product is manufactured.

Now, we can recast the product-line income statement using the activity-based costing information. This is done in Exhibit 19-11. The value of the activity-based costing income statement is that it reminds management that costs cannot be simply separated into fixed and variable components on the basis of units alone. Alden Company can see that the multi-function fax machines add overhead cost in the form of more setups and more usage of power and machinery. Importantly, management can now concentrate on reducing the use of drivers that directly add cost. Previously, overhead was applied on the basis of direct labor hours. This misleads management into thinking that the reduction of direct labor hours will result in decreased overhead. However, an activity-based approach shows the complexity of the manufacturing operation and reminds managers that a decrease in power costs can only be achieved with a decrease in machine usage (perhaps by the use of more efficient machinery). Similarly, a decrease in setup cost can only come about through the streamlining or elimination of setup activity. Reducing activities reduces actual costs and leads to increased profits.

EXHIBIT 19-11

Alden Company
Activity-Based Costing Income Statement
(In thousands of dollars)

	Basic	Multi-Function	Total
Sales	$ 4,000	$3,500	$ 7,500
Less:			
Prime costs	(1,100)	(950)	(2,050)
Setups	(10)	(30)	(40)
Maintenance	(24)	(96)	(120)
Supplies	(58)	(22)	(80)
Power	(28)	(252)	(280)
Machine depreciation	(25)	(225)	(250)
Sales commissions	(400)	(350)	(750)
Contribution margin	$ 2,355	$1,575	$ 3,930
Less:			
Other fixed overhead			(55)
Administrative expenses			(2,000)
Operating income			$ 1,875

It should be pointed out that a pure activity-based costing approach is not acceptable for external financial reporting. This is because firms using a pure ABC system would treat facility-level costs as period expenses. They are certainly not attached to units produced. However, GAAP require that units produced absorb some of this overhead. As a result, ABC is used internally for management decision making.

Once management believes the cost data are adequate and the initial profit computation is completed, they will want to ask further questions. These might relate to what the managers will do with the profitability information. A very high profit might signal that the multi-function fax machine is overpriced—leaving the door open for competitors. A low or even negative product profit may signal the need to start looking for a replacement—one with higher potential. Declining profit, coupled with the knowledge that customers dislike curled faxes, may lead management to discontinue the basic fax machine even with the positive profit it shows. This would free up resources for production of the next generation of fax machines. Alternatively, a low-profit product may be kept if customers appreciate dealing with a company that offers a full line of products. Management requires data on profitability to aid in sales mix decisions.

Divisional Profit

Just as companies want to know the relative profitability of different products, they may want to assess the relative profitability of different divisions of the company. Divisional profit is often used in evaluating the performance of managers. Failure to earn a profit can lead to the division's closing. For example, **General Motors** decided to drop the Oldsmobile line due to its continued unprofitability.

Divisional profit may be calculated using any of three approaches described in the preceding section. Usually, the absorption-based approach is used, and a share of corporate expense is allocated to each division to remind them that all expenses of the company must be covered. Suppose that Polyglyph, Inc., is a conglomerate with four divisions: Alpha, Beta, Gamma, and Delta. Corporate expenses of $10 million are allocated to each division on the basis of sales. The divisional income statements are as follows:

	Alpha	*Beta*	*Gamma*	*Delta*	*Total*
Sales	$ 90	$ 60	$ 30	$120	$300
Cost of goods sold	35	20	11	98	164
Gross profit	$ 55	$ 40	$ 19	$ 22	$136
Division expenses	(20)	(10)	(15)	(20)	(65)
Corporate expenses	(3)	(2)	(1)	(4)	(10)
Operating income (loss)	$ 32	$ 28	$ 3	$ (2)	$ 61

How might Polyglyph view these results? Clearly, Delta has an operating loss. Corporate would raise questions about Delta's continuing viability. If Delta has good potential for an improved profit picture, for example, it might be afforded additional time to turn a profit. Delta's divisional expenses are relatively high. Perhaps this is due to an ambitious research and development program. If payoffs from this program can be anticipated, corporate management will be much less concerned than if the divisional expenses do not have potential. Corporate management will also be concerned with trends over time and the immediate and long-term prospects for each division. Even a seemingly profitable division, like Alpha, may need attention if it is in a declining industry or if it uses significantly more resources than indicated by the corporate expense allocation. Additional material on divisional profitability and responsibility accounting is covered in Chapter 10.

Customer Profitability

While customers are clearly important to profit, some are more profitable than others. Companies that assess the profitability of various customer groups can more accurately target their markets and increase profits. The first step in determining customer profitability is to identify the customer. The second step is to determine which customers add value to the company.

The identification of a company's customer may seem obvious. Grocery stores and automobile repair shops can easily identify their customers, and they may even know them by name. However, sometimes the company is part of a complex chain of customer relationships. For example, **Aetna, Inc.**, is the largest U.S. health insurer. Its customer base includes companies that buy health insurance, the employees who use it, and the doctors and hospitals that provide health services. Each group is a customer group with particular needs. If one group is unserved and goes elsewhere, the other groups are affected.[10]

Originating and Keeping Customers

Once customer groups have been identified, the second step is to determine which customer groups are the most profitable, work to keep the existing customers in those groups, and add more of them. Sometimes, the company may need to add an initially unprofitable customer group and increase efficiency to make the group profitable.

It is generally more costly to win a customer than to keep a customer. Originating a customer may require advertising, sales calls, the drafting of proposals, and the generation of prospective customers lists. All of these activities are costly. Keeping existing customers happy also requires effort. For example, many stores provide free gift wrapping—a service to the customer who has already made a purchase. Firms must have profitability data to understand the profit contribution of customer relationships and to match the costs of increased service with the benefits. Many companies are now taking a customer life-cycle approach by recognizing that a loyal customer will yield significant revenue over the years. For example, the lifetime revenue stream of a pizza eater can be $8,000. For more expensive products, like a Cadillac, the amount approaches $332,000.[11]

Finally, some customers are so unprofitable that they should not be kept. **Rice Lake Products, Inc.**, manufactures movable owl and geese decoys. The company sold to both specialty stores and to **Wal-Mart**. However, the Wal-Mart sales, at $19 each, infuriated the specialty stores that charged $20. Even worse from Rice Lake Products' point of view was the fact that the profit on a Wal-Mart sale averaged just $0.50 while the profit on a specialty store sale amounted to $4. The reason for the difference was that Wal-Mart required special packaging and promotion and returned product that did not sell. The company chose to concentrate on sales to specialty stores.[12]

Example of Customer Profitability Analysis in a Service Company

BZW Securities, the investment arm of **Barclays Bank** in the United Kingdom, developed an ABC model of service profitability.[13] BZW executes trades for clients and also trades on its own account. Thus, it has two sources of profit: net commissions on customer trades and gains (or losses) on its own trades. Like many securities firms, BZW had difficulty tracing revenues and costs to particular trades. As a result, managers could not determine whether certain customers were profitable. For example, customers of BZW can call brokers at the firm to obtain market research, trading advice, trading services, and so on. The cost to BZW of providing each service differs. However, clients are not charged on the basis of which services they use, or even how much of the service they use. Clients are charged only commissions on stocks bought and sold. In general, a commission of 0.2 percent is charged on the price of each trade, so if a customer buys £50,000 of stock, the commission is £100 (£50,000 × 0.002). It is easy to see that a customer who requires significant market advice yet trades only £10,000 may be less profitable than a customer who requires the same amount of market advice but trades £100,000. To remedy this problem, BZW created an activity-based model to track revenues and costs to each trading transaction.

---

10. Barbara Martinez, "In Bid to Help Bottom Line, Aetna Tries to Improve Bedside Manner," *The Wall Street Journal* (February 23, 2001): 1.

11. James L. Heskett, Thomas O. Jones, Gary W. Loveman, W. Earl Sasser, Jr., and Leonard A. Schlesinger, "Putting the Service-Profit Chain to Work," *Harvard Business Review* (March/April 1994): 164–174.

12. Christie Brown, "A Great Way to Retire," *Forbes* (October 9, 1995): 96–97.

13. Information in this section was taken from Nicolas Stuchfield and Bruce W. Weber, "Modeling the Profitability of Customer Relationships: Development and Impact of Barclays de Zoete Wedd's BEATRICE," *Journal of Management Information Systems*, 9, No. 2 (Fall 1992): 53–76.

When **Fleet Financial Group** merged with **BankBoston**, it found that it needed more sophisticated measures of customer profitability. Previously, Fleet used a software package called Integrated Profit Management System (IPMS) to determine product and organizational profitability. Developed by **PMG Systems, Inc.**, IPMS allowed the company to "capture costs related to different types of transactions, such as teller salaries, courier fees, operational processes, and technology . . . let[ting] managers compare expenses related to customers making branch deposits versus those of customers making mail or automated teller machine deposits."

Fleet's new system, also provided by PMG Systems, Inc., is the Customer Profitability Management System (CPMS). IPMS measures the profitability of business processes and products, whereas CPMS measures the profitability of the bank's 20 million customers. For example, the software has indicated that customers who use branches cost more than those using ATMs or the telephone.

CPMS was introduced in 1997 in the **Canadian Imperial Bank of Commerce**. According to the bank's vice president of customer marketing, Rick Miller, Canadian Imperial has found that CPMS "fundamentally changed our business processes." Previously, "Canadian Imperial segmented customers by the amount of funds they held. Now the bank also analyzes the actual transactions customers conduct, by channel, to calculate the cost of serving each one." The bank has found significant differences in the profitability of customers holding the same amount of assets. This information has been used to conduct more precisely targeted marketing campaigns and to develop strategies based on customers' profit potential. Customers with current high profitability can be identified and given personal attention. Low-profit customers with low potential for future profit are encouraged to use less costly channels such as the ATM or telephone.

Source: Adriana Senior, "Fleet Picks PMG Software to Track Customer Costs," *American Banker* (August 3, 1999, Vol. 164, i147): 13.

After all the data on customer trades, costs, and revenues were collected, BZW segmented customers into four classes. The first class consists of customers with adequate profit levels and the potential for increased trading volume. Customers in this class are targeted for additional contact by BZW's senior people. The second class is composed of customers who are profitable at their current mix of services but unlikely to respond to attempts to upgrade. The current mix of services is maintained for these clients. The third class of customers includes those customers whose revenues do not fully cover costs but whose marginal revenue does contribute to fixed overhead and who do have the potential for upgrade. Discussions with these clients may lead to upgraded volume or to a reduction in the services least valued by the clients. In other words, BZW attempts to increase the profitability of this class through frank discussion and decision making. For example, less profitable clients are encouraged to use electronic order entry, an alternative that requires less telephone time with BZW's staff. A further alternative for BZW is to change the mix of services provided to a client by altering the seniority of its staff.

The fourth class is definitely unprofitable and has little potential to improve. BZW has a number of alternatives regarding unprofitable customers. It can try to increase trading volume with that customer, offer fewer services, or increase the commission charged.

Prior to the development of the activity-based costing model, BZW could calculate only the total revenue (commissions) associated with each customer. Individual customer profitability was impossible to calculate, since costs could not be traced to each customer. BZW's management could not assess the effectiveness of its expenditures and service efforts. Now, it can assess not only the profitability of each client but also the reasons why.

Overall Profit

The computation of segmental profit is clearly useful in many management decisions. However, the allocation problems inherent in computing profit on divisions, segments, and product lines may mean that overall profit is most useful in some contexts. It is certainly easiest to compute, and it does have meaning. If the overall profit is consistently positive, the company remains in business, even if one or more segments is losing money. For example, High Flight is a company that engages in three services: flight training, short-haul flight services (basically a courier service for regional banks), and airplane leasing. High Flight had real difficulty determining the profitability of each service. The same planes were used for each, so the allocation of airplane depreciation to the three services would seem reasonable. But the owner of High Flight realized that such an allocation would divert attention from the underlying question: Should all three services be offered? Some costs were easily traceable to each segment, e.g., fuel costs and pilot services. Other costs were difficult to allocate; plane depreciation and hangar rent are examples. Ultimately, High Flight performed a modified profitability analysis of each service and determined that flight training was probably a money loser. What did management decide? They kept all three because they realized that pilots preferred to rent planes from the place where they received flight training. Thus, the linkage between flight training and airplane rental meant that the company had to retain both or neither.

Analysis of Profit-Related Variances

OBJECTIVE **6**

Compute the sales price, price volume, contribution margin, contribution margin volume, sales mix, market share, and market size variances.

Managers frequently want to compare actual profit earned with expected profit. This leads naturally to variance analysis, in which actual and budgeted amounts are compared. Profit variances center on the difference between budgeted and actual prices, volumes, and contribution margin.

Sales Price and Price Volume Variances

Actual revenue may differ from expected revenue because actual price differs from expected price or because quantity sold differs from expected quantity sold, or both. The **sales price variance** is the difference between actual price and expected price multiplied by the actual quantity or volume sold. In equation form, it is the following:

Sales price variance = (Actual price − Expected price) × Quantity sold

The **price volume variance** is the difference between actual volume sold and expected volume sold multiplied by the expected price. It can be expressed in the following equation:

Price volume variance = (Actual volume − Expected volume) × Expected price

As is the case with all variances, the sales price and price volume variances are labeled favorable if the variance increases profit above the amount expected. They are labeled unfavorable if the variance decreases profit below the amount expected.

Suppose that Armour Company distributes produce. In May, Armour Company expects to sell 20,000 pounds of produce at an average price of $0.20 per pound. Actual results are 23,000 pounds sold at an average price of $0.19 per pound. The sales price variance is $230 unfavorable [($0.20 − $0.19) × 23,000]. Note that the sales price variance is unfavorable because the actual price of $0.19 per pound is less than the expected price of $0.20. The price volume variance is $600 favorable [(23,000 − 20,000) × $0.20]. The price volume variance is favorable because a higher quantity was sold than expected, acting to raise revenue.

The sum of the sales price and price volume variances is the **total (overall) sales variance**. Of course, this is simply the difference between actual and expected revenue. Breaking the overall sales variance into price and volume components gives managers a better feel for why actual revenue may differ from budgeted revenue.

It is important to note that these variances just begin to alert managers to problems in pricing and sales. As is the case with all variances, significant variances are investigated to discover the underlying reasons for the difference between expected and actual results. In the case of an unfavorable sales price variance, the reason may be the giving of unanticipated price discounts, perhaps to meet competitors' prices. The sales price and price volume variances interact. For example, an unfavorable sales price variance may be paired with a favorable price volume variance because the lower price raised quantity sold.

Contribution Margin Variance

The **contribution margin variance** is simply the difference between actual and budgeted contribution margin.

> Contribution margin variance = Actual contribution margin − Budgeted contribution margin

This variance is favorable if the actual contribution margin earned is higher than the budgeted amount.

Consider Birdwell, Inc., which produces two types of bird feeders. The regular type is a simple plastic and wood model, which can be hung from a tree branch. The deluxe model is a larger, stand-alone model, which includes a post and a round squirrel shield to prevent squirrels from eating the bird seed. Budgeted and actual data for the two models are shown in Exhibit 19-12.

| EXHIBIT 19-12 | Data for Birdwell, Inc. |

	Budgeted Amounts		
	Regular Model	Deluxe Model	Total
Sales:			
($10 × 1,500)	$15,000		
($50 × 500)		$25,000	$40,000
Variable expenses	9,000	17,500	26,500
Contribution margin	$ 6,000	$ 7,500	$13,500

	Actual Amounts		
	Regular Model	Deluxe Model	Total
Sales:			
($10 × 1,250)	$12,500		
($50 × 625)		$31,250	$43,750
Variable expenses	7,500	21,875	29,375
Contribution margin	$ 5,000	$ 9,375	$14,375

The contribution margin variance for Birdwell, Inc., is $875 favorable ($14,375 − $13,500). This variance can be broken down into a volume variance and a sales mix variance.

Contribution Margin Volume Variance

The **contribution margin volume variance** is the difference between the actual quantity sold and the budgeted quantity sold multiplied by the budgeted average unit contribution margin. Note the difference between the contribution margin volume variance and the price volume variance. Both look at the difference between actual and budgeted volume sold. However, the price volume variance multiplies that difference by sales price, while the contribution margin volume variance multiplies that difference by contribution margin. Therefore, the contribution margin volume variance gives management information about gained or lost profit due to changes in the quantity of sales.

> Contribution margin volume variance = (Actual quantity sold − Budgeted quantity sold) × Budgeted average unit contribution margin

The budgeted average unit contribution margin is the total budgeted contribution margin divided by the budgeted total number of units of all products to be sold.

In the Birdwell example, the total volume budgeted is 2,000 units (1,500 regular and 500 deluxe). The actual units sold amounted to 1,875 (1,250 regular and 625 deluxe). The budgeted average unit contribution margin is $6.75 ($13,500/2,000). Therefore, the contribution margin volume variance is $843.75 unfavorable [(2,000 − 1,875) × $6.75].

The unfavorable contribution margin volume variance is clearly the result of selling fewer units, in total, than budgeted. Still, we can see that Birdwell, Inc., actually had a higher contribution margin than expected. The shift in the sales mix explains why.

Sales Mix Variance

The sales mix represents the proportion of total sales yielded by each product. A company which produces only one product obviously has a sales mix of 100 percent for that product. All units sold will be that product, and there is no effect of changing sales mix on profit. Multiproduct firms, however, do experience shifting in their sales mix. If relatively more of the high-profit product is sold, profit will be higher than expected. If the sales mix shifts toward the low-profit product, profit will be lower than expected. We can define the **sales mix variance** as the sum of the change in units for each product multiplied by the difference between the budgeted contribution margin and the budgeted average unit contribution margin.

> Sales mix
> variance = [(P1 actual units − P1 budgeted units) × (P1 budgeted unit contribution margin − Budgeted average unit contribution margin)] + [(P2 actual units − P2 budgeted units) × (P2 budgeted unit contribution margin − Budgeted average unit contribution margin)]

The preceding sales mix variance equation is for two products. If three products were produced, we would simply keep adding the change in units times the change in contribution margin for every additional product.

Again consider Birdwell, Inc., data from Exhibit 19-12. The budgeted data show a sales mix of 1,500 regular models and 500 deluxe models. This reduces to a 3:1 sales ratio (1,500:500 is equivalent to 3:1). However, the actual data show that 1,250 regular and 625 deluxe models were sold. This is a ratio of 2:1.

The sales mix variance for Birdwell is computed as follows:

> Birdwell sales mix variance = [(1,250 − 1,500) × ($4.00 − $6.75)]
> + [(625 − 500) × ($15.00 − $6.75)]
> = $1,718.75 Favorable

Now, we can see that the favorable sales mix variance of $1,718.75, combined with the unfavorable contribution margin volume variance of $843.75, explains the overall favorable contribution margin variance of $875.

Market Share and Market Size Variances

Managers not only want to look inward at contribution margin through the volume and sales mix variances, but they also want to look outward to see how their company is doing compared with the rest of their industry. **Market share** gives the proportion of industry sales accounted for by a company. **Market size** is the total revenue for the industry. Clearly, both market size and market share have an impact on a company's profits.

The **market share variance** is the difference between the actual market share percentage and the budgeted market share percentage multiplied by actual industry sales in units times budgeted average unit contribution margin. The **market size variance** is the difference between actual and budgeted industry sales in units multiplied by the budgeted market share percentage times the budgeted average unit contribution margin.

Market share variance = [(Actual market share percentage − Budgeted market
$\qquad$ share percentage) × (Actual industry sales in units)] ×
$\qquad$ (Budgeted average unit contribution margin)

Market size variance = [(Actual industry sales in units − Budgeted industry
$\qquad$ sales in units) × (Budgeted market share percentage)] ×
$\qquad$ (Budgeted average unit contribution margin)

Suppose that the budgeted unit sales for the bird feeder industry were 20,000 (of all model types), and actual unit sales for the industry were 23,000. Then, the Birdwell budgeted market share is 10 percent (2,000/20,000). Birdwell's actual market share is 8.152 percent (1,875/23,000). The market share variance for Birdwell is $2,869 unfavorable [(0.08152 − 0.10) × 23,000 × $6.75]. In other words, Birdwell's reduction in market share from 10 percent to 8.152 percent cost the company $2,869 in contribution margin.

The impact of changing market size on Birdwell's profits can be assessed through the market size variance. It is $2,025 favorable [(23,000 − 20,000) × 0.10 × $6.75]. This means that the company's contribution margin would have increased by this amount had the actual market share percentage equaled the budgeted market share percentage. Unfortunately for Birdwell, the market share percentage slipped. Still, Birdwell is better off due to increasing market size, since a market share of 8.2 percent would yield even smaller profits from a smaller market.

While the contribution margin variances and the market share and market size variances yield important insights into profitability, companies may want to analyze profit further. The next section examines another dimension of profitability by looking at profit over the product life cycle.

OBJECTIVE 7

Discuss the variations in price, cost, and profit over the product life cycle.

The Product Life Cycle

Many products have a predictable profit or product life cycle. Using the marketing viewpoint, the **product life cycle** describes the profit history of the product according to four stages: introduction, growth, maturity, and decline. In the introductory phase, profits are low for two reasons. First, revenues are low as the product gains market acceptance. Second, investment and learning may be high, leading to higher expenses. The growth stage is characterized by increasing market acceptance and sales, as well as economies of scale, which bring down expenses. The product breaks even, and profit rises. In the maturity phase, profits stabilize. The product has found its market, and revenues are relatively stable. Investment is down, and all learning effects in production are realized, leading to stable costs. Finally, in the decline phase, the product reaches the end of its cycle, and revenues and profits decline. Costs may still be low, but not enough to slip in below sales. Exhibit 19-13, on the following page, illustrates the interaction of profit and the product life cycle with its four stages.

The product life cycle helps marketers understand the different competitive pressures on a product in each stage. Thus, it is important for planning purposes. The regularities in manufacturing, costs, and profit make the product life cycle just as important in cost management. Each stage of the product life cycle demonstrates a fairly predictable impact on various types of costs. Exhibit 19-14, on the following page, summarizes these effects.

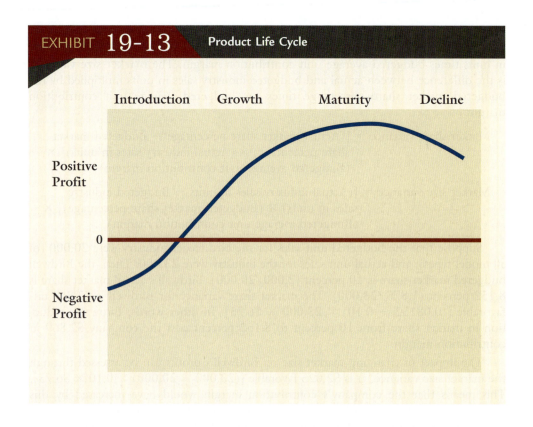

EXHIBIT **19-13**   Product Life Cycle

	Introduction	Growth	Maturity	Decline
Product	Basic design, few models	Some improvements, expanding product line	Proliferation of product lines, extensive differentiation	Minimal changes, reduced number of product lines
Learning effects	High costs, much learning, but little payoff	Still strong, learning begins to reduce costs	Stable production, little to no learning	No learning, labor as efficient as it can be
Setups	Few, but new and unfamiliar	More, as new models are introduced	Many, as product differentiation occurs	Fewer, as only best selling lines are produced
Purchasing	May be high as new materials and suppliers are sought	Lower, reliable suppliers found, few material changes	May be high depending on line changes	Fewer suppliers and orders as existing inventories are liquidated
Marketing expense	Low selling and distribution costs to small number of target markets	Increased advertising and distribution	Supportive advertising, increased trade discounts, high distribution cost	Minimal advertising, distribution, and promotion

EXHIBIT **19-14**   Impact of the Product Life Cycle on Cost Management

How long is the product life cycle? That depends on the product and the environment that the product faces. Television took years to reach maturity, partially due to its introduction during World War II, when necessary technical assets were diverted to the war effort. Video games typically reach maturity very quickly—in a matter of months. Fad products, such as Sourballs, may zip through the product life cycle in a matter of weeks.

Knowledge of the product life cycle is important for cost management. We can easily see the impact of the four stages on marketing and the growth and decline of sales. Less obvious is the impact on the cost side. Manufacturing must be aware of the impact of newness on costs. Any time a new product is introduced, there are learning effects. In other words, as a company makes more of the product, the employees become better at making it. Purchasing locates and becomes familiar with suppliers of the needed materials. Manufacturing learns to set up more quickly and efficiently the equipment for a new batch. The industrial engineers are able to "work the bugs out" of the process. The whole production process smoothes out and becomes faster and more efficient—and less expensive. However, that is not the whole story. As we can see in Exhibit 19-14, the maturity phase is marked by extensive product differentiation as line extensions proliferate. **Mattel**'s Barbie is over 50 years old—but we're not just talking basic Barbie anymore. Barbie has changed. Her arms and legs are bendable, and her hair is any number of lengths and colors. She has a dizzying array of outfits and accessories. Each version requires different materials and setups. In addition, Barbie and ex-boyfriend Ken have lots of friends—each with different production requirements. According to Mattel, every second, three Barbie dolls are sold somewhere in the world. With each decade's new cohort of little girls, Barbie, Cali (California Barbie), and new boyfriend Blaine may be in the maturity phase for quite some time to come.[14]

The product life cycle has implications for activity-based costing. Recall that ABC categories are unit level, batch level, product level, and facility level. Unit-level costs are highest in the introduction phase, as new materials are sought in small order quantities. In addition, direct labor is higher per unit as labor learns how to manufacture the new item. Unit-level costs begin to fall in the growth phase as learning takes effect and quantity discounts on materials may occur. Similarly, the maturity phase should lead to stable unit-level costs. The decline phase, with fewer units produced, does not enjoy quantity discounts, but unit costs may remain low due to the liquidation of existing inventories and the avoidance of increasing prices.

Batch-level costs follow a similar pattern. Purchasing, receiving, setups, and inspection are high in the introductory phase due to unfamiliarity. In the growth phase, batch-level costs should decrease as the positive impact of learning occurs. Workers are better able to execute setups, for example. In the maturity phase, batch-level costs may increase as product differentiation occurs. Setup number and complexity increase, purchasing orders rise, and inspection costs may increase. Finally, in the decline stage, batch-level costs again fall as product lines are streamlined to just a few best-selling lines and batches decrease in number and complexity.

Product-level costs are highest in the introductory phase and generally fall throughout the rest of the life cycle—with possible spikes upward for new models in the maturity phase. An example is engineering change orders, which occur most frequently when the product is started into production. Facility-level costs may or may not be affected unless the product calls for a new facility or equipment—then they are highest in the introductory phase. Exhibit 19-15, on the following page, depicts the general direction of costs in the ABC categories throughout the product life cycle.

---

14. "It's Splitsville for Barbie and Ken: Couple 'will remain friends,' says Mattel," http://www.cnn.com/2004/US/02/12/offbeat.barbie.breakup.ap/ as of February 12, 2004.

	EXHIBIT 19-15		**Product Life-Cycle Costs in the ABC Categories**	

	Product Life-Cycle Phase			
ABC Category	**Introduction**	**Growth**	**Maturity**	**Decline**
Unit-level costs	High	Lower	Low to stable	Low
Batch-level costs	High	Lower	Higher	Low
Product-level costs	High	Lower	Low to stable	Low
Facility-level costs	High	Low	Low	Low

Limitations of Profit Measurement

OBJECTIVE 8

Describe some of the limitations of profit measurement.

Most people think the entire purpose of business is to make a profit. But profit is no more the purpose of business than eating is the purpose of living. Both are essential, but neither is the point of the exercise. Business survives because it continually creates a better world for itself.[15]

As the above quotation suggests, profit measurement is important, and accountants can genuinely help a business by measuring profit levels. Still, there is more to life and business than monetary profit measurement. In this section, we look at the limitations of profit measurement.

One limitation to profitability analysis is its focus on past, not future, performance. The economic environment is unpredictable, and consistent profitability—brought about by great management, productive employees, and a high-quality product—does not guarantee success when economic conditions change. At that point, shifts in strategy may prove crucial. For example, the shift from payment for costs incurred to payment by diagnosis code has changed life considerably in the health care industry. Previously, insurance companies and the federal government paid doctors and hospitals for all costs incurred. Clearly, cost cutting was not important. Now, the emphasis on efficiency and cost control has had a significant impact on all participants in the medical field. **Johnson & Johnson**, for example, worked hard to change the rate of reimbursement for stents used in angioplasty. The J&J stent was technically superior to others on the market and cost more. However, Medicare paid hospitals the same amount no matter which stent was used. J&J was able to show, using data on 200,000 Medicare patients, that patients using the J&J stent were able to avoid a second and third angioplasty. Stent reimbursement increased.[16] The point is that companies must remain flexible and be aware of changing business conditions.

The savvy cost manager is aware of economic and environmental trends outside the company. These can determine the success of management plans. They also help provide a reference point for management in determining whether profits are good or bad. A small increase in profit during a recession may signal outstanding performance. The same increase during economic expansion raises doubts about management's ability.

Another limitation is profit's emphasis on quantifiable measures. Henry Ford said that both buyer and seller must be wealthier in some form as a result of a transaction.

---

15. Thomas Petzinger, Jr., "For Barbara Vasaris, Part of the Profit Is Helping Kids Learn," *The Wall Street Journal* (June 12, 1998): B1.

16. Ron Winslow, "Johnson & Johnson Misses Beat with Device for Cardiac Surgery," *The Wall Street Journal* (September 18, 1998): A1.

But must wealth always be measured in money? Some aspects of profit are, no doubt, qualitative. Start-up companies may be thrilled to have made it past the 1-year mark. The confidence that comes with being able to successfully start and continue a business is part of their wealth. Many companies give back a portion of their profits to their communities; this, too, is a form of wealth.

The quote from the beginning of this section was taken from an article on **The Anderson Group**, a small network installation firm in Akron, Ohio. The Anderson Group's founder, Barbara Vasaris, hires generalists who are committed to service. One technician who had left for a higher-paying job with another company returned because "[he] felt as though [he] no longer made a difference in people's lives."[17] The Anderson Group deliberately takes low-return jobs with school districts, deciding that overall profit, not per-job profit, is most important.

Finally, we must remember that profit has a strong impact on people's behavior. Predictably, individuals prefer profit to loss. Their jobs, promotions, and bonuses may depend on the annual profit, and this dependence can affect their behavior in expected and unexpected ways. As accountants, it is important to realize that profit measurement can lead to different incentives for individuals to work harder and to act ethically.

People's desire to avoid losses and their inclination to take a short-run perspective can affect the potential for unethical conduct. Unethical conduct can take any number of forms, but basically it comes down to lying. Companies may try to pass off inferior work or materials as high-quality work—worthy of a higher price. Companies may keep two sets of books—for the purpose of cheating on income and inventory taxes. They may overstate the value of inventory in order to understate the cost of goods sold and thereby overstate net income.

Companies that value numerical profit above all else should not be surprised if employees act accordingly and do what is in their power to increase the numbers. Not only does this overreliance on numerical profit lead to unethical behavior, but it also provides incentives to ignore the less measurable outcomes which might benefit the company. Workers basically look for companies to "put their money where their mouth is." If raises, promotions, and bonuses are awarded only on the basis of profit, employees will work to increase profits. Even if the company says other factors are important (e.g., good corporate citizenship, innovation, and high-quality products), this will be seen as mere lip service.

The ever-present salience of monthly, quarterly, and annual profit and loss statements may cause companies to emphasize short-run results. Too much emphasis on short-run optimization can lead to ethical problems. A solution is to focus on the long run. Companies that take a long-run orientation know that they cannot cheat customers and expect to retain their business. Eventually, shoddy materials and workmanship will be realized by the customer. The customer will go elsewhere, and regaining trust once lost is an agonizingly slow process. As a result, ethical people and companies often emphasize the long run as the best basis for behavior.

---

17. Petzinger, *op. cit.*

SUMMARY

Many considerations factor into the determination of price. Economic considerations include customer demand, price elasticity of demand, and market structure. In general, customers buy less at a high price than they do at a low price. Price elasticity of demand may vary from elastic to inelastic. When demand is inelastic, a price change has relatively little effect on quantity demand. The opposite holds for elastic demand. Market structure affects the firm's degree of freedom to change price.

Most American firms use cost-based pricing. First, cost is determined, and then, a desired profit is added to calculate price. This strategy does not take demand into account until late in the process, when the resulting price is considered in reference to demand and competition. The target cost-based pricing strategy, on the other hand, begins with price, then works backward to calculate a cost which will allow the firm to achieve a desired profit. This strategy is proving to be more successful.

The legal system, to an extent, supports competition. As a result, certain business practices are outlawed. Predatory pricing and certain types of price discrimination are illegal. Fairness and ethical conduct prevent the exploitation of market power in certain instances. Price gouging and dumping are considered to be unfair.

Various measures of profit have been suggested. Absorption-costing income measurement is required for external financial reporting. Variable costing and ABC give better signals regarding performance and incremental costs.

Profitability analysis can be accomplished for individual segments. These segments include product lines, divisions, and customer groups. Each analysis adds to management understanding.

Profit-related variances are computed to analyze the changes in profit from one time period to another. The sales price and price volume variances are used to analyze changes in revenue by decomposing revenue into price and quantity sold. The contribution margin variances and market share and size variances are also used to analyze changes in profit.

The product life cycle has an important impact on price. Price cannot be determined from the stage of the life cycle alone, but when used in conjunction with other influences, pricing strategies emerge.

Limitations of profit include focus on past performance, uncertain economic conditions, and the difficulty of capturing all important factors in financial measures. Successful firms measure far more than accounting profit. They are aware of their impact on the community and on their employees. Ethical behavior is fostered by appropriate emphasis on profit.

REVIEW PROBLEMS AND SOLUTIONS

1   PRICING

Melcher Company produces and sells small household appliances. A few years ago, it designed and developed a new hand-held mixer, named the "Mixalot." The Mixalot can be used to mix milkshakes and light batter. With the mincer attachment, it can mince up to a cup of vegetables or fruits. The Mixalot was very different from the standard table model Melcher mixer. Because of this, over $250,000 was spent on design and development. Another $50,000 was spent on consumer focus groups, in which prototypes of the Mixalot were kitchen tested by consumers. It was in those groups that safety problems surfaced. For example, one of the testers sliced his hand. This necessitated adding a plastic guard around the blade. Molding and attaching the blade would add $1.50 to prime costs of the Mixalot, which had originally been estimated to cost $3.50 to produce. Information regarding the first five years of operations is as follows:

	Year 1	Year 2	Year 3	Year 4	Year 5
Unit sales	25,000	150,000	400,000	400,000	135,000
Price	$15	$20	$20	$18	$15
Prime cost	$125,000	$600,000	$1,640,000	$1,640,000	$526,500
Setup cost	$5,000	$9,600	$80,000	$80,000	$12,000
Purchase of special equipment	$65,000	—	—	—	—
Expediting	—	$15,000	$40,000	$35,000	—
Rework	$12,500	$45,000	$60,000	$60,000	$6,750
Other overhead	$50,000	$300,000	$800,000	$800,000	$270,000
Warranty repair	$6,250	$7,500	$10,000	$10,000	$3,375
Commissions (5%)	$18,750	$150,000	$400,000	$360,000	$101,250
Advertising	$250,000	$150,000	$100,000	$100,000	$25,000

During the first year, Melcher's prime costs included the safety guard. The special equipment was for molding and attaching the guard. It had a life of five years with no salvage value.

Required:

1. What is the cost of goods sold per unit for the Mixalot in each of the five years?
2. What marketing expenses were associated with the Mixalot in each of the five years? Calculate them on a per-unit basis.
3. Calculate operating income for the Mixalot in each of the five years. Then, compare all costs to revenues for the Mixalot over the entire product life cycle. Was the Mixalot profitable?
4. Discuss the pricing strategy of Melcher Company for the Mixalot, initially and over the product life cycle.

SOLUTION

1.

	Year 1	Year 2	Year 3	Year 4	Year 5
Prime cost	$125,000	$600,000	$1,640,000	$1,640,000	$526,500
Setup cost	5,000	9,600	80,000	80,000	12,000
Depreciation on special equipment	13,000	13,000	13,000	13,000	13,000
Expediting	—	15,000	40,000	35,000	—
Rework	12,500	45,000	60,000	60,000	6,750
Other overhead	50,000	300,000	800,000	800,000	270,000
Total COGS	$205,500	$982,600	$2,633,000	$2,628,000	$828,250
Divided by units	÷ 25,000	÷150,000	÷ 400,000	÷ 400,000	÷135,000
Unit COGS	$ 8.22	$ 6.55	$ 6.58	$ 6.57	$ 6.14

2.

	Year 1	Year 2	Year 3	Year 4	Year 5
Warranty repair	$ 6,250	$ 7,500	$ 10,000	$ 10,000	$ 3,375
Commissions (5%)	18,750	150,000	400,000	360,000	101,250
Advertising	250,000	150,000	100,000	100,000	25,000
Total marketing expenses	$275,000	$ 307,500	$ 510,000	$ 470,000	$ 129,625
Divided by units	÷ 25,000	÷150,000	÷400,000	÷400,000	÷135,000
Unit marketing expense	$ 11.00	$ 2.05	$ 1.28	$ 1.18	$ 0.96

3.

	Year 1	Year 2	Year 3	Year 4	Year 5
Sales	$ 375,000	$3,000,000	$8,000,000	$7,200,000	$2,025,000
Less: COGS	205,500	982,600	2,633,000	2,628,000	828,250
Gross profit	$ 169,500	$2,017,400	$5,367,000	$4,572,000	$1,196,750
Less: Marketing expenses	275,000	307,500	510,000	470,000	129,625
Operating income (loss)	$(105,500)	$1,709,900	$4,857,000	$4,102,000	$1,067,125

Five-year operating income	$11,630,525
Less: Design and development expenses	300,000
Excess of revenue over all costs	$11,330,525

Yes, the Mixalot was profitable over the 5-year cycle, even after the design and development expenses were subtracted. Note that these expenses do not appear on the operating income statement required for external reporting.

4. The initial price set for the Mixalot was $15. This is the lowest price of those charged during the 5-year period. It appears that Melcher Company was using a penetration pricing strategy for the Mixalot. This makes sense given that the Mixalot was not a radically new product, i.e., there were other appliances on the market that could do what the Mixalot could do. There were blenders to mix milkshakes, knives and chopping boards to cut up vegetables, and food processors to mix and chop. Melcher Company needed to get the Mixalot out into actual kitchens to build demand. Notice, too, the large marketing expenditures in the first year to create awareness. This also helps to support price increases down the line. Finally, by the fifth year, the Mixalot is in the declining stage of the product life cycle. Probably other companies have begun producing competing products, and the number of new Mixalots demanded has declined.

2 ABSORPTION AND VARIABLE COSTING, SEGMENTED INCOME STATEMENTS

Acme Novelty Company produces coin purses and key chains. Selected data for the past year are as follows:

	Coin Purse	Key Chain
Production (units)	100,000	200,000
Sales (units)	90,000	210,000
Selling price	$5.50	$4.50
Direct labor hours	50,000	80,000
Manufacturing costs:		
Direct materials	$ 75,000	$100,000
Direct labor	250,000	400,000
Variable overhead	20,000	24,000
Fixed overhead	50,000	80,000
Nonmanufacturing costs:		
Variable selling	30,000	60,000
Direct fixed selling	35,000	40,000
Common fixed selling*	25,000	25,000

*Common fixed selling cost totals $50,000 and is divided equally between the two products.

Budgeted fixed overhead for the year, $130,000, equaled the actual fixed overhead. Fixed overhead is assigned to products using a plantwide rate based on expected direct labor hours, which were 130,000. The company had 10,000 key chains in inventory at the beginning of the year. These key chains had the same unit cost as the key chains produced during the year.

Required:

1. Compute the unit cost for the coin purses and key chains using the variable-costing method. Compute the unit cost using absorption costing.
2. Prepare an income statement using absorption costing.
3. Prepare an income statement using variable costing.
4. Explain the reason for any difference between absorption- and variable-costing operating incomes.
5. Prepare a segmented income statement using products as segments.

SOLUTION

1. Unit cost for the coin purse is as follows:

Direct materials ($75,000/100,000)	$0.75
Direct labor ($250,000/100,000)	2.50
Variable overhead ($20,000/100,000)	0.20
Variable cost per unit	$3.45
Fixed overhead [(50,000 × $1.00)/100,000]	0.50
Absorption cost per unit	$3.95

The unit cost for the key chain is as follows:

Direct materials ($100,000/200,000)	$0.50
Direct labor ($400,000/200,000)	2.00
Variable overhead ($24,000/200,000)	0.12
Variable cost per unit	$2.62
Fixed overhead [(80,000 × $1.00)/200,000]	0.40
Absorption cost per unit	$3.02

Notice that the only difference between the two unit costs is the assignment of the fixed overhead cost. Notice also that the fixed overhead unit cost is assigned using the predetermined fixed overhead rate ($130,000/130,000 direct labor hours = $1 per direct labor hour). For example, the coin purses used 50,000 direct labor hours and so receive $1 × 50,000, or $50,000, of fixed overhead. This total, when divided by the units produced, gives the $0.50 per-unit fixed overhead cost. Finally, observe that variable nonmanufacturing costs are not part of the unit cost under variable costing. For both approaches, only manufacturing costs are used to compute the unit costs.

2. The income statement under absorption costing is as follows:

Sales [($5.50 × 90,000) + ($4.50 × 210,000)]	$1,440,000
Less: Cost of goods sold [($3.95 × 90,000) + ($3.02 × 210,000)]	989,700
Gross margin	$ 450,300
Less: Selling expenses*	215,000
Operating income	$ 235,300

*The sum of selling expenses for both products.

3. The income statement under variable costing is as follows:

Sales [($5.50 × 90,000) + ($4.50 × 210,000)]	$1,440,000
Less variable expenses:	
Variable cost of goods sold	
[($3.45 × 90,000) + ($2.62 × 210,000)]	(860,700)
Variable selling expenses	(90,000)
Contribution margin	$ 489,300
Less fixed expenses:	
Fixed overhead	(130,000)
Fixed selling	(125,000)
Operating income	$ 234,300

4. Variable-costing income is $1,000 less ($235,300 − $234,300) than absorption-costing income. This difference can be explained by the net change of fixed overhead found in inventory under absorption costing.

Coin purses:	
Units produced	100,000
Units sold	90,000
Increase in inventory	10,000
Unit fixed overhead	× $0.50
Increase in fixed overhead	$ 5,000

Key chains:	
Units produced	200,000
Units sold	210,000
Decrease in inventory	(10,000)
Unit fixed overhead	× $0.40
Decrease in fixed overhead	$ (4,000)

The net change is a $1,000 ($5,000 − $4,000) increase in fixed overhead in inventories. Thus, under absorption costing, there is a net flow of $1,000 of the current period's fixed overhead into inventory. Since variable costing recognized all of the current period's fixed overhead as an expense, variable-costing income should be $1,000 lower than absorption-costing income, as it is.

5. Segmented income statement:

	Coin Purses	Key Chains	Total
Sales	$ 495,000	$ 945,000	$1,440,000
Less variable expenses:			
Variable cost of goods sold	(310,500)	(550,200)	(860,700)
Variable selling expenses	(30,000)	(60,000)	(90,000)
Contribution margin	$ 154,500	$ 334,800	$ 489,300
Less direct fixed expenses:			
Fixed overhead	(50,000)	(80,000)	(130,000)
Direct selling expenses	(35,000)	(40,000)	(75,000)
Product margin	$ 69,500	$ 214,800	$ 284,300
Less common fixed expenses:			
Common selling expenses			(50,000)
Operating income			$ 234,300

KEY TERMS

QUESTIONS FOR WRITING AND DISCUSSION

1. Define *elastic demand*. Define *inelastic demand*. Give an example of a product with relatively elastic demand and an example of a product with relatively inelastic demand. (Give examples not given in the text.)
2. What are the features of a perfectly competitive market? Give two examples of competitive markets. How could a firm in such a market move to a less competitive market?
3. How do you calculate the markup on cost of goods sold? Is the markup pure profit? Explain.
4. How does target costing differ from traditional costing? How does a target cost relate to price?
5. What is the difference between penetration pricing and price skimming?
6. Why do gas stations in the middle of town typically charge a little less for gasoline than do gas stations located on interstate highway turnoffs?
7. What is price discrimination? Is it legal?
8. Why do firms measure profit? Why do regulated firms care about the level of profit?
9. What is a segment, and why would a company want to measure profits of segments?
10. Suppose that Alpha Company has four product lines, three of which are profitable and one (let's call it "Loser") which generally incurs a loss. Give several reasons why Alpha Company may choose not to drop the Loser product line.
11. How does absorption costing differ from variable costing? When will absorption-costing operating income exceed variable-costing operating income?
12. What are some advantages and disadvantages of using net income as a measure of profitability?
13. Why do some firms measure customer profitability? In what situation(s) would a firm not want to measure customer profitability?
14. What variances do managers use in trying to understand the difference between actual and planned revenue?
15. Describe the product life cycle. How do unit-level costs behave in relation to the product life cycle? Batch-level costs? Product-level costs? Facility-level costs?

EXERCISES

19-1   ELASTICITY OF DEMAND AND MARKET STRUCTURE

LO1   Janet Gordon and Phil Hopkins graduated several years ago with M.S. degrees in accounting and set up a full-service accounting firm. Janet and Phil have many small business clients and have noticed some pricing trends while compiling annual financial statements. The following data are for five of the pizza parlors which are Janet and Phil's clients:

	Quantity Sold	Average Price
Mamma Mia's	18,000	$10.00
Happy Time Pizza	21,000	7.90
Keg and Pie Pizza	22,000	8.00
Fast Freddy's Pizza	30,000	7.00
Pizza-pizza	24,000	7.50

Required:

1. Is the demand for pizza relatively more elastic or inelastic?
2. What type of market structure characterizes the pizza industry? How do you suppose that Mamma Mia's can charge so much more per pizza than Fast Freddy's does?

19-2   DEMAND CURVE AND CHARACTERISTICS OF MARKET STRUCTURE

LO1   Amy Chang wants to start a business supplying florists with field-grown flowers. She has located an appropriate acreage and believes she can grow daisies, asters, chrysanthemums, carnations, and other assorted types during a 9-month growing period. By growing the flowers in a field as opposed to a greenhouse, Amy expects to save a considerable amount on herbicide and pesticide. She is considering passing the savings along to her customers by charging $1.25 per standard bunch versus the prevailing price of $1.50 per standard bunch.

Amy has turned to her neighbor, Bob Winters, for help. Bob is an accountant in town who is familiar with general business conditions. Bob gathered the following information for Amy.

a. There are 50 growers within a 1-hour drive of Amy's acreage.
b. In general, there is little variability in price. Flowers are treated as commodities, and one aster is considered to be pretty much like any other aster.
c. There are numerous florists in the city, and the amount that Amy would supply could be easily absorbed by the florists at the prevailing price.

Required:

1. What type of market structure characterizes the flower-growing industry in Amy's region? Explain.
2. Given your answer to Requirement 1, what price should Amy charge per standard bunch? Why?

19-3   BASICS OF DEMAND, LIFE-CYCLE PRICING

LO1, LO2   Foster Hancock is an accountant just ready to open an accounting firm in his hometown. He has heard that established accountants in town charge $65 per hour. That sounds good to Foster. In fact, he believes that he should be able to charge $75 an hour given his high GPA and the fact that he is up to date on current accounting issues.

Required:

Should Foster charge $75 per hour? What would you advise him to do?

19-4 MARKUP ON COST, COST-BASED PRICING

LO2 Walker Construction acts as the general contractor on building projects ranging from $500,000 to $5 million. Each job requires a bid that includes Walker's direct costs and subcontractor costs as well as an amount referred to as "overhead and profit." Walker's bidding policy is to estimate the direct materials cost, direct labor cost, and subcontractors' costs. These are totaled, and a markup is applied to cover overhead and profit. In the coming year, the company believes it will be the successful bidder on 10 jobs with the following total revenues and costs:

Revenue		$23,580,000
Direct materials	$6,500,000	
Direct labor	4,316,000	
Subcontractors	8,834,000	19,650,000
Overhead and profit		$ 3,930,000

Required:

1. Given the preceding information, what is the markup percentage on total direct costs?
2. Suppose Walker is asked to bid on a job with estimated direct costs of $980,000. What is the bid? If the customer complains that the profit seems pretty high, how might Walker counter that accusation?

19-5 MARKUP ON COST

LO2 Many different businesses employ markup on cost to arrive at a price. For each of the following situations, explain what the markup covers and why it is the amount that it is.

a. Department stores have a markup of 100 percent of purchase cost.
b. Jewelry stores charge anywhere from 100 percent to 300 percent of the cost of the jewelry. (The 300 percent markup is referred to as "keystone.")
c. Johnson Construction Company charges 12 percent on direct materials, direct labor, and subcontracting costs.
d. Hamilton Auto Repair charges customers for direct materials and direct labor. Customers are charged $45 per direct labor hour worked on their job; however, the employees actually cost Hamilton $15 per hour.

19-6 ABSORPTION AND VARIABLE COSTING WITH OVER- AND UNDERAPPLIED OVERHEAD

LO4 Abruzzi, Inc., has just completed its first year of operations. The unit costs on a normal costing basis are as follows:

Manufacturing costs (per unit):	
Direct materials (2 lbs. @ $3.50)	$ 7.00
Direct labor (0.5 hr. @ $16)	8.00
Variable overhead (0.5 hr. @ $6)	3.00
Fixed overhead (0.5 hr. @ $9)	4.50
Total	$22.50

(continued)

Selling and administrative costs:

Variable	$3 per unit
Fixed	$123,000

During the year, the company had the following activity:

Units produced	24,000
Units sold	21,300
Unit selling price	$35
Direct labor hours worked	12,000

Actual fixed overhead was $12,000 less than budgeted fixed overhead. Budgeted variable overhead was $5,000 less than the actual variable overhead. The company used an expected actual activity level of 24,000 direct labor hours to compute the predetermined overhead rates. Any overhead variances are closed to Cost of Goods Sold.

Required:

1. Compute the unit cost using:
   a. Absorption costing
   b. Variable costing
2. Prepare an absorption-costing income statement.
3. Prepare a variable-costing income statement.
4. Reconcile the difference between the two income statements.

19-7 VARIABLE COSTING, ABSORPTION COSTING

LO4 During its first year of operations, Snobegon, Inc., (located in Lake Snobegon, Minnesota) produced 30,000 plastic snow scoops. Snow scoops are oversized shovel-type scoops that are used to push snow away. Unit sales were 29,000 scoops. Fixed overhead was applied at $0.75 per unit produced. Fixed overhead was underapplied by $3,000. This fixed overhead variance was closed to Cost of Goods Sold. There was no variable overhead variance. The results of the year's operations are as follows (on an absorption-costing basis):

Sales (29,000 units @ $18)	$522,000
Less: Cost of goods sold	304,600
Gross margin	$217,400
Less: Selling and administrative expenses (all fixed)	190,000
Operating income	$ 27,400

Required:

1. Give the cost of the firm's ending inventory under absorption costing. What is the cost of the ending inventory under variable costing?
2. Prepare a variable-costing income statement. Reconcile the difference between the two income figures.

19-8 COST-BASED PRICING, TARGET PRICING

LO2 Carina Franks operates a catering company in Austin, Texas. Carina provides food and servers for parties. She also rents tables, chairs, dinnerware, glassware, and linens. Estefan and Maria Montero have contacted Carina about plans for their soon-to-be 15-year-old daughter's Quineanera (a festive party thrown by Hispanic parents to celebrate their daughters' fifteenth birthdays). The Monteros would like a catered affair on the lawn of a rural church. They have requested an open bar, a sit-down dinner for 350 people, a large tent, and a dance floor. Of course, they expect Carina to supply serving staff, tables with linens, dinnerware, and glassware. They will handle the flowers, decorations, and hiring the band on their own. Carina put together this bid:

Food (350 × $25)	$ 8,750
Beverages (350 × $15)	5,250
Servers (6 × 4 hours × $10)	240
Bartenders (2 × 4 hours × $10)	80
Clean-up staff (3 × 3 hours × $10)	90
Rental of:	
Dance floor	300
Linens	80
Tables	200
Dinnerware	120
Glassware	150
Total	$15,260

Required:

1. Explain where costs for Carina's services and profit are calculated in the preceding bid.
2. Suppose that the Monteros blanch when they see the preceding bid. One of them suggests that they had hoped to spend no more than $10,000 or so on the party. How could Carina work with the Monteros to achieve a target cost of that amount?
3. Estefan Montero protests the cost of dance floor rental. He says, "I've seen those for rent at U-Rent-It for $75." How would you respond to this remark if you were Carina? (*Hint*: You want this job so telling him "Go ahead and do it yourself, Cheapskate!" is not an option.)

19-9 COST-BASED PRICING

LO2

Marcus Fibers, Inc., specializes in the manufacture of synthetic fibers that the company uses in many products such as blankets, coats, and uniforms for police and firefighters. Marcus has been in business since 1975 and has been profitable every year since 1983. The company uses a standard cost system and applies overhead on the basis of direct labor hours.

Marcus has recently received a request to bid on the manufacture of 800,000 blankets scheduled for delivery to several military bases. The bid must be stated at full cost per unit plus a return on full cost of no more than 9 percent after income taxes. Full cost has been defined as including all variable costs of manufacturing the product, a reasonable amount of fixed overhead, and reasonable incremental administrative costs associated with the manufacture and sale of the product. The contractor has indicated that bids in excess of $25 per blanket are not likely to be considered.

In order to prepare the bid for the 800,000 blankets, Andrea Lightner, cost accountant, has gathered the following information about the costs associated with the production of the blankets.

Direct materials	$1.50 per pound of fibers
Direct labor	$7.00 per hour
Direct machine costs[a]	$10.00 per blanket
Variable overhead	$3.00 per direct labor hour
Fixed overhead	$8.00 per direct labor hour
Incremental administrative costs	$2,500 per 1,000 blankets
Special fee[b]	$0.50 per blanket
Materials usage	6 pounds per blanket
Production rate	4 blankets per direct labor hour
Effective tax rate	40%

[a]Direct machine costs consist of items such as special lubricants, replacement of needles used in stitching, and maintenance costs. These costs are not included in the normal overhead rates.

[b]Marcus recently developed a new blanket fiber at a cost of $750,000. In an effort to recover this cost, Marcus has instituted a policy of adding a $0.50 fee to the cost of each blanket using the new fiber. To date, the company has recovered $125,000. Lightner knows that this fee does not fit within the definition of full cost, as it is not a cost of manufacturing the product.

Required:

1. Calculate the minimum price per blanket that Marcus Fibers could bid without reducing the company's operating income.
2. Using the full-cost criteria and the maximum allowable return specified, calculate Marcus Fibers's bid price per blanket.
3. Without prejudice to your answer to Requirement 2, assume that the price per blanket that Marcus Fibers calculated using the cost-plus criteria specified is greater than the maximum bid of $25 per blanket allowed. Discuss the factors that Marcus Fibers should consider before deciding whether or not to submit a bid at the maximum acceptable price of $25 per blanket. *(CMA adapted)*

19-10   LIFE-CYCLE PRICING, SALES PRICE AND PRICE VOLUME VARIANCES

LO6, LO7   Data for Lorraine Company are as follows:

Budgeted price $14.30
Actual price $13.00
Budgeted quantity   1,450
Actual quantity sold   1,400

Required:

1. Calculate the sales price variance.
2. Calculate the price volume variance.
3. Suppose that the product is at the end of the maturity stage of the product life cycle. What information do these two variances provide to Lorraine's managers?

19-11   PRICING STRATEGY, SALES VARIANCES

LO1, LO6   Howerton, Inc., manufactures and sells three products: K, M, and P. In January, Howerton, Inc., budgeted sales of the following:

	Budgeted Volume	Budgeted Price
Product K	110,000	$50
Product M	165,000	20
Product P	20,000	20

At the end of the year, actual sales for Product K and Product M were $5,600,000 and $3,270,000, respectively. The actual price charged for each was equal to the budgeted price. Product P, however, had revenues of $600,000. While total revenue was higher than expected, the actual price of $10 represented a last-minute revision from budget to increase consumer acceptance of the product.

Required:

1. Calculate the sales price and price volume variances for each of the three products based on the original budget.
2. Suppose that Product P is a new product just introduced during the year. What pricing strategy is Howerton, Inc., following for this product?

19-12   PRICE DISCRIMINATION AND THE ROBINSON-PATMAN ACT

LO3   For each of the following situations, determine whether or not price discrimination has occurred and whether the Robinson-Patman Act has been violated.

a. Albion Shoes manufactures and sells shoes to retail outlets. A popular women's flat sells for $15 to all customers, FOB shipping from Albion's factory in Menomenee Falls.

b. Dr. Sidney Ferris, an orthopedic surgeon, charges $1,500 for arthroscopic knee surgery to privately insured patients. He charges a greatly reduced rate to other patients.

c. Castle Cosmetics charges a single price for each of its products to all customers, even though Castle can document that it costs up to three times as much to sell and distribute to certain small boutiques.

d. Paxton, Inc., manufactures toothpaste and mouthwash. Paxton charges a higher price to individual drugstores than to large chains because smaller stores do not have the same purchasing power as larger chains.

PROBLEMS

19-13   PRICE DISCRIMINATION

LO3 Bernese, Inc., manufactures and distributes a variety of health products, including velcro-fastened wrist stabilizers for people with carpal tunnel syndrome. Annual production of wrist stabilizers averages 200,000 units. A large chain store purchases about 40 percent of Bernese's production. Several thousand independent retail drugstores and medical supply stores purchase the other 60 percent. Bernese incurs the following costs of production per box:

Direct materials	$2.20
Direct labor	1.05
Overhead	0.75
Total	$4.00

Bernese has one salesperson assigned to the chain store account at a cost of $65,600 per year. Delivery is made in 1,000 unit batches about three times a month at a delivery cost of $600 per batch. Four salespeople service the remaining accounts. They call on the stores and incur salary and mileage expenses of approximately $39,900 each. Delivery costs vary from store to store, averaging $0.45 per unit.

Bernese charges the chain store $6.25 per box and the independent stores $6.50 per box.

Required:

Is Bernese's pricing policy supported by cost differences in serving the two different classes of customer? Support your answer with relevant calculations.

19-14   UNIT COSTS, INVENTORY VALUATION, VARIABLE AND ABSORPTION COSTING

LO4 Moyer Company produced 80,000 units during its first year of operations and sold 76,000 at $9 per unit. The company chose practical activity—at 80,000 units—to compute its predetermined overhead rate. Manufacturing costs are as follows:

Direct materials	$240,000
Direct labor	88,000
Expected and actual variable overhead	72,000
Expected and actual fixed overhead	36,000

Required:

1. Calculate the unit cost and the cost of finished goods inventory under absorption costing.

2. Calculate the unit cost and the cost of finished goods inventory under variable costing.
3. What is the dollar amount that would be used to report the cost of finished goods inventory to external parties. Why?

19-15 INCOME STATEMENTS, VARIABLE AND ABSORPTION COSTING

LO4   The following information pertains to Caesar, Inc., for last year:

Beginning inventory, units	—
Units produced	60,000
Units sold	57,400
Variable costs per unit:	
Direct materials	$9.00
Direct labor	$6.50
Variable overhead	$3.60
Variable selling expenses	$3.00
Fixed costs per year:	
Fixed overhead	$234,000
Fixed selling and administrative expenses	$236,000

There are no work-in-process inventories. Normal activity is 60,000 units. Expected and actual overhead costs are the same.

Required:

1. How many units are in ending inventory?
2. Without preparing an income statement, indicate what the difference will be between variable-costing income and absorption-costing income.
3. Assume the selling price per unit is $32. Prepare an income statement using:
   a. Variable costing
   b. Absorption costing

19-16 INCOME STATEMENTS AND FIRM PERFORMANCE: VARIABLE AND ABSORPTION COSTING

LO4   Zimmer Company had the following operating data for its first two years of operations:

Variable costs per unit:	
Direct materials	$ 5.00
Direct labor	3.00
Variable overhead	1.50
Fixed costs per year:	
Overhead	90,000
Selling and administrative	17,200

Zimmer produced 30,000 units in the first year and sold 25,000. In the second year, it produced 25,000 units and sold 30,000 units. The selling price per unit each year was $15. Zimmer uses an actual costing system for product costing.

Required:

1. Prepare income statements for both years using absorption costing. Has firm performance, as measured by income, improved or declined from Year 1 to Year 2?
2. Prepare income statements for both years using variable costing. Has firm performance, as measured by income, improved or declined from Year 1 to Year 2?
3. Which method do you think most accurately measures firm performance? Why?

19-17   ABSORPTION- AND VARIABLE-COSTING INCOME STATEMENTS

LO4

CMA

Portland Optics, Inc., specializes in manufacturing lenses for large telescopes and cameras used in space exploration. As the specifications for the lenses are determined by the customer and vary considerably, the company uses a job-order costing system. Manufacturing overhead is applied to jobs on the basis of direct labor hours, utilizing the absorption- or full-costing method. Portland's predetermined overhead rates for 2006 and 2007 were based on the following estimates:

	2006	2007
Direct labor hours	32,500	44,000
Direct labor cost	$325,000	$462,000
Fixed manufacturing overhead	$130,000	$176,000
Variable manufacturing overhead	$162,500	$198,000

Jim Bradford, Portland's controller, would like to use variable (direct) costing for internal reporting purposes as he believes statements prepared using variable costing are more appropriate for making product decisions. In order to explain the benefits of variable costing to the other members of Portland's management team, Jim plans to convert the company's income statement from absorption costing to variable costing. He has gathered the following information for this purpose, along with a copy of Portland's 2006–2007 comparative income statement.

Portland Optics, Inc.
Comparative Income Statement
For the Years 2006–2007

	2006	2007
Net sales	$1,140,000	$1,520,000
Cost of goods sold:		
Finished goods at January 1	$ 16,000	$ 25,000
Cost of goods manufactured	720,000	976,000
Total available	$ 736,000	$1,001,000
Less: Finished goods at December 31	25,000	14,000
Unadjusted cost of goods sold	$ 711,000	$ 987,000
Overhead adjustment	12,000	7,000
Cost of goods sold	$ 723,000	$ 994,000
Gross profit	$ 417,000	$ 526,000
Selling expenses	(150,000)	(190,000)
Administrative expenses	(160,000)	(187,000)
Operating income	$ 107,000	$ 149,000

Portland's actual manufacturing data for the two years are as follows:

	2006	2007
Direct labor hours	30,000	42,000
Direct labor cost	$300,000	$435,000
Direct materials used	$140,000	$210,000
Fixed manufacturing overhead	$132,000	$175,000

The company's actual inventory balances were as follows:

	December 31, 2005	December 31, 2006	December 31, 2007
Direct materials	$32,000	$36,000	$18,000
Work in process:			
Costs	$44,000	$34,000	$60,000
Direct labor hours	1,800	1,400	2,500
Finished goods:			
Costs	$16,000	$25,000	$14,000
Direct labor hours	700	1,080	550

For both years, all administrative expenses were fixed, while a portion of the selling expenses resulting from an 8 percent commission on net sales was variable. Portland reports any over- or underapplied overhead as an adjustment to the cost of goods sold.

Required:

1. For the year ended December 31, 2007, prepare the revised income statement for Portland Optics, Inc., utilizing the variable-costing method. Be sure to include the contribution margin on the revised income statement.
2. Describe two advantages of using variable costing rather than absorption costing.

(CMA adapted)

19-18   CONTRIBUTION MARGIN VARIANCE, CONTRIBUTION MARGIN VOLUME VARIANCE, SALES MIX VARIANCE

LO6

Spreadsheet

Kingston Company provides management services for apartments and rental units. In general, Kingston packages its services into two groups: basic and complete. The basic package includes advertising vacant units, showing potential renters through them, and collecting monthly rent and remitting it to the owner. The complete package adds maintenance of units and bookkeeping to the basic package. Packages are priced on a per-rental unit basis. Actual results from last year are as follows:

	Basic	Complete
Sales (rental units)	700	300
Selling price	$120	$260
Variable expenses	$70	$180

Kingston had budgeted the following amounts:

	Basic	Complete
Sales (units)	715	285
Selling price	$110	$275
Variable expenses	$70	$200

Required:

1. Calculate the contribution margin variance.
2. Calculate the contribution margin volume variance. (Round calculations to three decimal places.)
3. Calculate the sales mix variance. (Round calculations to three decimal places.)

19-19 CONTRIBUTION MARGIN VARIANCE, CONTRIBUTION MARGIN VOLUME VARIANCE, MARKET SHARE VARIANCE, MARKET SIZE VARIANCE

LO6

CMA

Patel, Inc., produces and sells gel-filled ice packs. Patel's performance report for April follows:

	Actual	*Budgeted*
Units sold	50,000	40,000
Sales	$350,000	$290,000
Variable costs	225,000	190,000
Contribution margin	$125,000	$100,000
Market size (in units)	1,000,000	1,000,000

Required:

1. Calculate the contribution margin variance and the contribution margin volume variance.
2. Calculate the market share variance and the market size variance. *(CMA adapted)*

19-20 SEGMENTED INCOME STATEMENTS, ANALYSIS OF PROPOSALS TO IMPROVE PROFITS

LO4, LO5

Spreadsheet

Shannon, Inc., has two divisions. One produces and sells paper party supplies (napkins, paper plates, invitations); the other produces and sells cookware. A segmented income statement for the most recent quarter is as follows:

	Party Supplies Division	*Cookware Division*	*Total*
Sales	$500,000	$750,000	$1,250,000
Less: Variable expenses	425,000	460,000	885,000
Contribution margin	$ 75,000	$290,000	$ 365,000
Less: Direct fixed expenses	85,000	110,000	195,000
Segment margin	$(10,000)	$180,000	$ 170,000
Less: Common fixed expenses			130,000
Operating income			$ 40,000

On seeing the quarterly statement, Madge Shannon, president of Shannon, Inc., was distressed and discussed her disappointment with Bob Ferguson, the company's vice president of finance.

MADGE: The Party Supplies Division is killing us. It's not even covering its own fixed costs. I'm beginning to believe that we should shut down that division. This is the seventh consecutive quarter it has failed to provide a positive segment margin. I was certain that Paula Kelly could turn it around. But this is her third quarter, and she hasn't done much better than the previous divisional manager.

BOB: Well, before you get too excited about the situation, perhaps you should evaluate Paula's most recent proposals. She wants to spend $10,000 per quarter for the right to use familiar cartoon figures on a new series of invitations, plates, and napkins and at the same time increase the advertising budget by $25,000 per quarter to let the public know about them. According to her marketing people, sales should increase by 10 percent if the right advertising is done—and done quickly. In addition, Paula wants to lease some new production machinery that will increase the rate of production, lower labor costs, and result in less waste of materials. Paula claims that variable costs will be reduced by 30 percent. The cost of the lease is $95,000 per quarter.

Upon hearing this news, Madge calmed considerably, and, in fact, was somewhat pleased. After all, she was the one who had selected Paula and had a great deal of confidence in Paula's judgment and abilities.

Required:

1. Assuming that Paula's proposals are sound, should Madge Shannon be pleased with the prospects for the Party Supplies Division? Prepare a segmented income statement for the next quarter that reflects the implementation of Paula's proposals. Assume that the Cookware Division's sales increase by 5 percent for the next quarter and that the same cost relationships hold.
2. Suppose that everything materializes as Paula projected except for the 10 percent increase in sales—no change in sales revenues took place. Are the proposals still sound? What if the variable costs are reduced by 40 percent instead of 30 percent with no change in sales?

19-21   IMPACT OF INVENTORY CHANGES ON ABSORPTION-COSTING INCOME, DIVISIONAL PROFITABILITY

LO4, LO5   Dana Baird was manager of a new Medical Supplies Division. She had just finished her second year and had been visiting with the company's vice president of operations. In the first year, the operating income for the division had shown a substantial increase over the prior year. Her second year saw an even greater increase. The vice president was extremely pleased and promised Dana a $5,000 bonus if the division showed a similar increase in profits for the upcoming year. Dana was elated. She was completely confident that the goal could be met. Sales contracts were already well ahead of last year's performance, and she knew that there would be no increases in costs.

At the end of the third year, Dana received the following data regarding operations for the first three years:

	Year 1	Year 2	Year 3
Production	10,000	11,000	9,000
Sales (in units)	8,000	10,000	12,000
Unit selling price	$10	$10	$10
Unit costs:			
Fixed overhead*	$2.90	$3.00	$3.00
Variable overhead	$1.00	$1.00	$1.00
Direct materials	$1.90	$2.00	$2.00
Direct labor	$1.00	$1.00	$1.00
Variable selling	$0.40	$0.50	$0.50
Actual fixed overhead	$29,000	$30,000	$30,000
Other fixed costs	$9,000	$10,000	$10,000

*The predetermined fixed overhead rate is based on expected actual units of production and expected fixed overhead. Expected production each year was 10,000 units. Any under- or overapplied fixed overhead is closed to Cost of Goods Sold.

Yearly Income Statements

	Year 1	Year 2	Year 3
Sales revenue	$80,000	$100,000	$120,000
Less: Cost of goods sold*	54,400	67,000	86,600
Gross margin	$25,600	$ 33,000	$ 33,400
Less: Selling and administrative expenses	12,200	15,000	16,000
Operating income	$13,400	$ 18,000	$ 17,400

*Assumes a LIFO inventory flow.

Upon examining the operating data, Dana was pleased. Sales had increased by 20 percent over the previous year, and costs had remained stable. However, when she saw the yearly income statements, she was dismayed and perplexed. Instead of seeing a significant increase in income for the third year, she saw a small decrease. Surely, the accounting department had made an error.

Required:

1. Explain to Dana why she lost her $5,000 bonus.
2. Prepare variable-costing income statements for each of the three years. Reconcile the differences between the absorption-costing and variable-costing incomes.
3. If you were the vice president of Dana's company, which income statement (variable-costing or absorption-costing) would you prefer to use for evaluating Dana's performance? Why?

19-22 ETHICAL ISSUES, ABSORPTION COSTING, PERFORMANCE MEASUREMENT

LO3, LO4, LO8   Bill Fremont, division controller and CMA, was upset by a recent memo he received from the divisional manager, Steve Preston. Bill was scheduled to present the division's financial performance at headquarters in one week. In the memo, Steve had given Bill some instructions for this upcoming report. In particular, Bill had been told to emphasize the significant improvement in the division's profits over last year. Bill, however, didn't believe that there was any real underlying improvement in the division's performance and was reluctant to say otherwise. He knew that the increase in profits was because of Steve's conscious decision to produce for inventory.

In an earlier meeting, Steve had convinced his plant managers to produce more than they knew they could sell. He argued that by deferring some of this period's fixed costs, reported profits would jump. He pointed out two significant benefits. First, by increasing profits, the division could exceed the minimum level needed so that all the managers would qualify for the annual bonus. Second, by meeting the budgeted profit level, the division would be better able to compete for much-needed capital. Bill objected but had been overruled. The most persuasive counterargument was that the increase in inventory could be liquidated in the coming year as the economy improved. Bill, however, considered this event unlikely. From past experience, he knew that it would take at least two years of improved market demand before the productive capacity of the division was exceeded.

Required:

1. Discuss the behavior of Steve Preston, the divisional manager. Was the decision to produce for inventory an ethical one?
2. What should Bill Fremont do? Should he comply with the directive to emphasize the increase in profits? If not, what options does he have?

3. Chapter 1 listed ethical standards for management accountants. Identify any standards that apply in this situation.

19-23 SEGMENTED INCOME STATEMENTS, ADDING AND DROPPING PRODUCT LINES

LO5 Louise Bordner has just been appointed manager of Palmroy's Glass Products Division. She has two years to make the division profitable. If the division is still showing a loss after two years, it will be eliminated, and Louise will be reassigned as an assistant divisional manager in another division. The divisional income statement for the most recent year is as follows:

Sales	$5,350,000
Less: Variable expenses	4,750,000
Contribution margin	$ 600,000
Less: Direct fixed expenses	750,000
Divisional margin	$ (150,000)
Less: Common fixed expenses (allocated)	200,000
Divisional profit (loss)	$ (350,000)

Upon arriving at the division, Louise requested the following data on the division's three products:

	Product A	Product B	Product C
Sales (units)	10,000	20,000	15,000
Unit selling price	$150.00	$140.00	$70.00
Unit variable cost	$100.00	$110.00	$103.33
Direct fixed costs	$100,000.00	$500,000.00	$150,000.00

She also gathered data on a proposed new product (Product D). If this product is added, it would displace one of the current products; the quantity that could be produced and sold would equal the quantity sold of the product it displaces, although demand limits the maximum quantity that could be sold to 20,000 units. Because of specialized production equipment, it is not possible for the new product to displace part of the production of a second product. The information on Product D is as follows:

Unit selling price	$ 70
Unit variable cost	30
Direct fixed costs	640,000

Required:

1. Prepare segmented income statements for Products A, B, and C.
2. Determine the products that Louise should produce for the coming year. Prepare segmented income statements that prove your combination is the best for the division. By how much will profits improve given the combination that you selected? (*Hint:* Your combination may include one, two, or three products.)

19-24 OPERATING INCOME FOR SEGMENTS

LO5 Jerrell, Inc., manufactures and sells automotive tools through three divisions: Southwest, Midwest, and Northeast. Each division is evaluated as a profit center. Data for each division for last year are as follows (in thousands of dollars):

	Southwest	Midwest	Northeast
Sales	$2,300	$1,100	$3,500
Cost of goods sold	1,380	840	2,100
Selling and administrative expenses	300	180	620

Jerrell, Inc., had corporate administrative expenses equal to $250,000; these were not allocated to the divisions.

Required:

1. Prepare a segmented income statement for Jerrell, Inc., for last year.
2. Comment on the performance of each of the divisions.

19-25   PRODUCT PROFITABILITY

LO5, LO7   Porter Insurance Company has three lines of insurance: automobile, property, and life. The life insurance segment has been losing money for the past five quarters, and Leah Harper, Porter's controller, has done an analysis of that segment. She has discovered that the commission paid to the agent for the first year the policy is in place is 55 percent of the first-year premium. The second-year commission is 20 percent, and all succeeding years a commission equal to 5 percent of premiums is paid. No salaries are paid to agents; however, Porter does advertise on television and in magazines. Last year, the advertising expense was $500,000. The loss rate (payout on claims) averages 50 percent. Administrative expenses equal $450,000 per year. Revenue last year was $10,000,000 (premiums). The percentage of policies of various lengths is as follows:

First year in force	65%
Second year	25
More than two years in force	10

Experience has shown that if a policy remains in effect for more than two years, it is rarely cancelled.

Leah is considering two alternative plans to turn this segment around. Plan 1 requires spending $250,000 on improved customer claim service in hopes that the percentage of policies in effect will take on the following distribution:

First year in force	50%
Second year	15
More than two years in force	35

Total premiums would remain constant at $10,000,000, and there are no other changes in fixed or variable cost behavior.

Plan 2 involves dropping the independent agent and commission system and having potential policyholders phone in requests for coverage. Leah estimates that revenue would drop to $7,000,000. Commissions would be zero, but administrative expenses would rise by $1,200,000, and advertising (including direct mail solicitation) would increase by $1,000,000.

Required:

1. Prepare a variable-costing income statement for last year for the life insurance segment of Porter Insurance Company.
2. What impact would Plan 1 have on income?
3. What impact would Plan 2 have on income?

19-26   CUSTOMER PROFITABILITY, LIFE-CYCLE REVENUE

LO5, LO7   Refer to the original data in **Problem 19-25**. Fred Morton has just purchased a life insurance policy from Porter with premiums equal to $1,500 per year.

Required:

1. Assume Fred holds the policy for one year and then drops it. What is his contribution to Porter's operating income?
2. Assuming Fred holds the policy for three years, what is his contribution to Porter's operating income in the second and third years? Over a 3-year period? What implications does this hold for Porter's efforts to retain policyholders?

19-27   CUSTOMER PROFITABILITY

LO4   Olin Company manufactures and distributes carpentry tools. Production of the tools is in the mature portion of the product life cycle. Olin has a salesforce of 20. Salespeople are paid a commission of 7 percent of sales, plus expenses of $35 per day for days spent on the road away from home, plus $0.30 per mile. They deliver products in addition to making the sales, and each salesperson is required to own a truck suitable for making deliveries.

For the coming quarter, Olin estimates the following:

Sales	$1,300,000
Cost of goods sold	450,000

On average, a salesperson travels 6,000 miles per quarter and spends 38 days on the road. The fixed marketing and administrative expenses total $400,000 per quarter.

Required:

1. Prepare an income statement for Olin Company for the next quarter.
2. Suppose that a large hardware chain, MegaHardware, Inc., wants Olin Company to produce its new SuperTool line. This would require Olin Company to sell 80 percent of total output to the chain. The tools will be imprinted with the SuperTool brand, requiring Olin to purchase new equipment, use somewhat different materials, and reconfigure the production line. Olin's industrial engineers estimate that cost of goods sold for the SuperTool line would increase by 15 percent. No sales commission would be incurred, and MegaHardware would link Olin to its EDI system. This would require an annual cost of $100,000 on the part of Olin. MegaHardware would pay shipping. As a result, the salesforce would shrink by 80 percent. Should Olin accept MegaHardware's offer? Support your answer with appropriate calculations.

19-28   SEGMENTED REPORTING AND VARIANCES

LO5, LO6

CMA

Pittsburgh-Walsh Company (PWC) is a manufacturing company whose product line consists of lighting fixtures and electronic timing devices. The Lighting Fixtures Division assembles units for the upscale and mid-range markets. The Electronic Timing Devices Division manufactures instrument panels that allow electronic systems to be activated and deactivated at scheduled times for both efficiency and safety purposes. Both divisions operate out of the same manufacturing facilities and share production equipment.

PWC's budget for the year ending December 31, 2007, follows and was prepared on a business segment basis under the following guidelines:

a. Variable expenses are directly assigned to the incurring division.
b. Fixed overhead expenses are directly assigned to the incurring division.

c. The production plan is for 8,000 upscale fixtures, 22,000 mid-range fixtures, and 20,000 electronic timing devices. Production equals sales.

PWC established a bonus plan for division management that required meeting the budget's planned operating income by product line, with a bonus increment if the division exceeds the planned product-line operating income by 10 percent or more.

PWC Budget
For the Year Ending December 31, 2007
(in thousands of dollars)

| | Lighting Fixtures | | Electronic | |
	Upscale	Mid-Range	Timing Devices	Total
Sales	$1,440	$ 770	$ 800	$ 3,010
Variable expenses:				
Cost of goods sold	(720)	(439)	(320)	(1,479)
Selling and administrative	(170)	(60)	(60)	(290)
Contribution margin	$ 550	$ 271	$ 420	$ 1,241
Fixed overhead expenses	140	80	80	300
Segment margin	$ 410	$ 191	$ 340	$ 941

Shortly before the year began, the CEO, Jack Parkow, suffered a heart attack and retired. After reviewing the 2007 budget, the new CEO, Joe Kelly, decided to close the lighting fixtures mid-range product line by the end of the first quarter and use the available production capacity to grow the remaining two product lines. The marketing staff advised that electronic timing devices could grow by 40 percent with increased direct sales support. Increases above that level and increasing sales of upscale lighting fixtures would require expanded advertising expenditures to increase consumer awareness of PWC as an electronics and upscale lighting fixtures company. Joe approved the increased sales support and advertising expenditures to achieve the revised plan. Joe advised the divisions that for bonus purposes the original product-line operating income objectives must be met, but he did allow the Lighting Fixtures Division to combine the operating income objectives for both product lines for bonus purposes.

Prior to the close of the fiscal year, the division controllers were furnished with preliminary actual data for review and adjustment, as appropriate. These preliminary year-end data reflect the revised units of production amounting to 12,000 upscale fixtures, 4,000 mid-range fixtures, and 30,000 electronic timing devices and are presented as follows:

PWC Preliminary Actuals
For the Year Ending December 31, 2007
(In thousands of dollars)

| | Lighting Fixtures | | Electronic | |
	Upscale	Mid-Range	Timing Devices	Total
Sales	$ 2,160	$140	$1,200	$ 3,500
Variable expenses:				
Cost of goods sold	(1,080)	(80)	(480)	(1,640)
Selling and administrative	(260)	(11)	(96)	(367)
Contribution margin	$ 820	$ 49	$ 624	$ 1,493
Fixed overhead expenses	140	14	80	234
Segment margin	$ 680	$ 35	$ 544	$ 1,259

The controller of the Lighting Fixtures Division, anticipating a similar bonus plan for 2008, is contemplating deferring some revenues to the next year on the pretext that the sales are not yet final and accruing in the current year expenditures that will be applicable to the first quarter of 2008. The corporation would meet its annual plan, and the division would exceed the 10 percent incremental bonus plateau in 2007 despite the deferred revenues and accrued expenses contemplated.

Required:

1. Outline the benefits that an organization realizes from segment reporting. Evaluate segment reporting on a variable-costing basis versus an absorption-costing basis.
2. Calculate the contribution margin, contribution margin volume, and sales mix variances.
3. Explain why the variances occurred. *(CMA adapted)*

19-29   COLLABORATIVE LEARNING EXERCISE

LO7   Shangri-La Videos is marketing a new line of wellness-oriented videotapes. These videotapes emphasize proper nutrition, low-impact exercise, and stress reduction techniques. Shangri-La's marketing director (and president), Sherry Benson, believes that a comprehensive marketing campaign to introduce the videotapes will be necessary. Sherry has estimated the following marketing costs:

Commission	3% of undiscounted price
Marketing testing	$7,000 per city
Rebates:	
Fixed cost to print the certificates	$625
Variable cost to redeem each certificate	$7.50
Advertising:	
Quarter 1	$25,000
Quarter 2	$50,000
Quarters 3 through 7	$20,000 per quarter
Quarter 8	none

The market testing will occur during the first quarter. Sherry believes that conducting tests in three cities will be sufficient to gather feedback regarding the video.

Sherry estimates that the total cost of writing the script and producing the master for the videotape will come to $55,000. The cost of copying a new videotape from the master, packaging, and shrink-wrapping it will be $3 per tape. The videotape market is fickle and competitive. Sherry believes that the wellness tape can be sold for eight quarters at the most. Her estimates of unit sales for each quarter are as follows:

Quarter	Unit Sales
1	5,000
2	15,000
3	27,000
4	30,000
5	30,000
6	30,000
7	15,000
8	2,000

In Quarters 1 through 7, the videotape will be priced at $20. In Quarter 8, the price will decrease to $10, and no commission will be paid. In Quarter 1, the rebate certificate will be attached. Customers who buy the videotape and mail in the certificate (with original cash register receipt) will receive $5 by return mail. Past experience indicates that only 25 percent of the customers eligible for the rebate will take advantage of it. (The remaining 75 percent who do not claim the rebate are referred to as "slippage." Companies count on a hefty amount of slippage when offering a generous rebate program.)

Required:

Form groups of three or four. Each group will work this exercise. Be prepared to share with the class the group's discussion of Requirements 1 and 3.

1. Tell which phase of the product life cycle for the wellness videotape applies to each quarter.
2. Prepare income statements for each of the eight quarters. (You may round all amounts to the nearest $1,000.) Is the videotape profitable in each quarter? Overall?
3. List the stages of the product life cycle, and find two products not mentioned in the text that fit into each stage.

19-30   CYBER RESEARCH CASE

LO7   View the Web site for **SAP** at http://www.mysap.com to see how the company helps other companies improve profitability. Write a brief paper on the companies featured on the SAP site, and tell how the software company's product can improve profits.

20

Capital Investment

AFTER STUDYING THIS CHAPTER, YOU SHOULD BE ABLE TO:

1. Describe the difference between independent and mutually exclusive capital investment decisions.

2. Explain the roles of the payback period and accounting rate of return in capital investment decisions.

3. Calculate the net present value (NPV) for independent projects.

4. Compute the internal rate of return (IRR) for independent projects.

5. Tell why NPV is better than IRR for choosing among mutually exclusive projects.

6. Convert gross cash flows to after-tax cash flows.

7. Describe capital investment for advanced technology and environmental impact settings.

Organizations are often faced with the opportunity (or need) to invest in assets or projects that represent long-term commitments. New production systems, new plants, new equipment, and new product development are examples of assets and projects that fit this category. Usually, many alternatives are available. For example, **Federal Express** has chosen to make a capital investment in airplanes, sorting equipment, and distribution facilities. The FedEx hub in Memphis represents a significant outlay of funds (capital outlay). Sound capital investment decision making of this type requires the estimation of a project's cash flows. How cash flows can be used to evaluate the merits of a proposed project is the focus of this chapter. We will study four financial models that are useful in capital investment analysis: the payback period, the accounting rate of return, net present value, and the internal rate of return.

OBJECTIVE   *1*

Describe the difference between independent and mutually exclusive capital investment decisions.

Capital Investment Decisions

Capital investment decisions are concerned with the process of planning, setting goals and priorities, arranging financing, and using certain criteria to select long-term assets. Because capital investment decisions place large amounts of resources at risk for long periods of time and simultaneously affect the future development of the firm, they are among the most important decisions managers make. Every organization has limited resources, which should be used to maintain or enhance its long-run profitability. Poor capital investment decisions can be costly. For example, a study of capital expenditure decisions made by deregulated utility plants revealed that 25 to 30 percent of the capital projects were unnecessary.[1] One example offered by the study is a $17 million investment to rebuild a low-pressure turbine; yet, the turbine that was rebuilt posed no danger nor was it having any negative impact on operations. Perhaps these unnecessary capital investment decisions explain why production costs increased by 20 percent in spite of the fact that each plant averaged between $2 and $3 million in new capital investments. Normally, the expectation is that capital investments will enhance profitability—not reduce it.

The process of making capital investment decisions is often referred to as **capital budgeting**. Two types of capital budgeting projects will be considered. **Independent projects** are projects that, if accepted or rejected, do not affect the cash flows of other projects. Suppose that the managers of the marketing and research and development departments jointly propose the addition of a new product line where each would entail significant outlays of working capital and equipment. Acceptance or rejection of one product line does not require the acceptance or rejection of the other product line. Thus, the investment decisions for the product lines are independent of each other.

The second type of capital budgeting project requires a firm to choose among competing alternatives that provide the same basic service. Acceptance of one option precludes the acceptance of another. Thus, **mutually exclusive projects** are those projects that, if accepted, preclude the acceptance of all other competing projects. For example, when **Monsanto**'s Fiber Division decided to automate its Pensacola, Florida, plant, it was faced with the choice of continuing with its existing manual production operation or replacing it with an automated system. In all likelihood, part of the company's deliberation concerned different types of automated systems. If three different automated systems were being considered, this would produce four alternatives—the current system plus the three potential new systems. Once one system is chosen, the other three are excluded; they are mutually exclusive.

Notice that one of the competing alternatives in the example is that of maintaining the status quo (the manual system). This emphasizes the fact that new investments replacing existing investments must prove to be economically superior. Of course, at times, replacement of the old system is mandatory and not discretionary if the firm wishes to remain in business (e.g., equipment in the old system may be worn out; thus, the old system is not a viable alternative). In such a situation, going out of business could be a viable alternative, especially if none of the new investment alternatives is profitable.

Capital investment decisions often are concerned with investments in long-term capital assets. With the exception of land, these assets depreciate over their lives, and the original investment is used up as the assets are employed. In general terms, a sound capital investment will earn back its original capital outlay over its life and, at the same time, provide a reasonable return on the original investment. Therefore, one task of a manager is to decide whether or not a capital investment will earn back its original outlay and provide a reasonable return. By making this assessment, a manager can decide

---

1. Holt Bradswahw, "Merchant Costs: Reckless Abandonment," *Public Utilities Fortnightly* (April 2004): 30–34.

on the acceptability of independent projects and compare competing projects on the basis of their economic merits. But what is meant by reasonable return? It is generally agreed that any new project must cover the *opportunity cost* of the funds invested. For example, if a company takes money from a money market fund that is earning 6 percent and invests it in a new project, then the project must provide at least a 6 percent return (the return that could have been earned had the money been left in the money market fund). Of course, in reality, funds for investment often come from different sources—each representing a different opportunity cost. The return that must be earned is a blend of the opportunity costs of the different sources. Thus, if a company uses two sources of funds, one with an opportunity cost of 4 percent and the other with an opportunity cost of 6 percent, then the return that must be earned is somewhere between 4 and 6 percent, depending on the relative amounts used from each source. Furthermore, it is usually assumed that managers should select projects that promise to maximize the wealth of the owners of the firm.

COST MANAGEMENT   Technology in Action

In health care, IT systems represent 2 to 3 percent of the annual operating budget and consume between 15 and 30 percent of the capital budget. Thus, purchasing a new information system or upgrading existing technology can have a significant effect on the operating margin of a hospital. IT capital budget requests tend to come with a variety of objectives. Some projects are designed to improve services and others to improve care quality or revenue or even to satisfy some level of regulatory compliance. Numerous examples of these different project types are available. For example, at **Brigham and Women's Hospital**, an investment in an in-patient order entry system led to a 55 percent reduction in medication errors. At **Massachusetts General Hospital**, investment in a picture archival and communication system reduced the time spent for interpreting radiology images from 72 hours to one hour. Other investments target increasing quality by reducing patient wait time, increasing physician access to patient information, improving treatment outcomes, and reducing errors in treatment. IT capital investments can also provide new products (and thus new sources of revenues), such as Web access to clinical guidelines and consumer-oriented medical textbooks.

Source: John Glaser, "Analyzing Information Technology Value," *Healthcare Financial Management* (March 2003): 98–102.

To make a capital investment decision, a manager must estimate the quantity and timing of cash flows, assess the risk of the investment, and consider the impact of the project on the firm's profits. One of the most difficult tasks is to estimate the cash flows. Projections must be made years into the future, and forecasting is far from a perfect science. Obviously, as the accuracy of cash flow forecasts increases, the reliability of the decision improves. In making projections, managers must identify and quantify the benefits associated with the proposed project(s). For example, an automated cash deposit system can produce the following benefits (relative to a manual system): bank charge reductions, productivity gains, forms cost reduction, greater data integrity, lower training costs, and savings in time required to audit and do bank/cash reconciliations. The dollar value of these benefits must be assessed. Although forecasting future cash flows is a critical part of the capital investment process, forecasting methods will not be considered here. Consequently, cash flows are assumed to be known; the focus will be on making capital investment decisions *given* these cash flows.

Managers must set goals and priorities for capital investments. They also must identify some basic criteria for the acceptance or rejection of proposed investments. In this chapter, we will study four basic methods to guide managers in accepting or rejecting potential investments. The methods include both nondiscounting and discounting decision approaches. (Two methods are discussed for each approach.) The discounting methods are applied to investment decisions involving both independent and mutually exclusive projects.

Explain the roles of the payback period and accounting rate of return in capital investment decisions.

Payback and Accounting Rate of Return: Nondiscounting Methods

Models used for making capital investment decisions fall into two major categories: *nondiscounting models* and *discounting models*. **Nondiscounting models** ignore the time value of money, whereas **discounting models** explicitly consider it. Although many accounting theorists disparage the nondiscounting models because they ignore the time value of money, many firms continue to use them in making capital investment decisions. However, the use of discounting models has increased over the years, and few firms use only one model—indeed, firms seem to use both types of models. This suggests that both categories supply useful information to managers as they struggle to make capital investment decisions.

Payback Period

One type of nondiscounting model is the *payback period*. The **payback period** is the time required for a firm to recover its original investment. For example, assume that a dentist invests in a new grinder costing $160,000. The cash flow (cash inflows less cash outflows) generated by the equipment is $80,000 per year. Thus, the payback period is two years ($160,000/$80,000). When the cash flows of a project are assumed to be even, the following formula can be used to compute the project's payback period:

Payback period = Original investment/Annual cash flow

If, however, the cash flows are uneven, the payback period is computed by adding the annual cash flows until such time as the original investment is recovered. If a fraction of a year is needed, it is assumed that cash flows occur evenly within each year. For example, suppose that a laundromat requires an investment of $200,000 and has a life of five years with the following expected annual cash flows: $60,000, $80,000, $100,000, $120,000, and $140,000. The payback period for the project is 2.6 years, computed as follows: $60,000 (1 year) + $80,000 (1 year) + $60,000 (0.6 year). In the third year, when only $60,000 is needed and $100,000 is available, the amount of time required to earn the $60,000 is found by dividing the amount needed by the annual cash flow ($60,000/$100,000). Exhibit 20-1 summarizes this analysis.

One way to use the payback period is to set a maximum payback period for all projects and to reject any project that exceeds this level. Why would a firm use the payback period in this way? Some analysts suggest that the payback period can be used as a

EXHIBIT 20-1	Payback Analysis	
Year	**Unrecovered Investment (Beginning of Year)**	**Annual Cash Flow**
1	$200,000	$ 60,000
2	140,000	80,000
3	60,000*	100,000
4	—	120,000
5	—	140,000

*At the beginning of Year 3, $60,000 is needed to recover the investment. Since a net cash inflow of $100,000 is expected, only 0.6 year ($60,000/$100,000) is needed to recover the $60,000. Thus, the payback period is 2.6 years (2 + 0.6).

rough measure of risk, with the notion that the longer it takes for a project to pay for itself, the riskier it is. Also, firms with riskier cash flows could require a shorter payback period than normal. Additionally, firms with liquidity problems would be more interested in projects with quick paybacks. Another critical concern is obsolescence. In some industries, the risk of obsolescence is high; firms within these industries would be interested in recovering funds rapidly.

Another reason, less beneficial to the firm, may also be at work. Many managers in a position to make capital investment decisions may choose investments with quick payback periods out of self-interest. If a manager's performance is measured using such short-run criteria as annual operating income, he or she may choose projects with quick paybacks to show improved operating income as quickly as possible. Consider that division managers often are responsible for making capital investment decisions and are evaluated on divisional profit. The tenure of divisional managers, however, is typically short—three to five years would be average. Consequently, the incentive is for such managers to shy away from investments that promise healthy long-run returns but relatively meager returns in the short run. These problems can be eliminated by corporate budgeting policies and a budget review committee.

The payback period can be used to choose among competing alternatives. Under this approach, the investment with the shortest payback period is preferred over investments with longer payback periods. However, this use of the payback period is less defensible because this measure suffers from two major deficiencies: (1) it ignores the performance of the investments beyond the payback period and (2) it ignores the time value of money.

These two significant deficiencies are easily illustrated. Assume that a tire manufacturing firm is considering two different types of automated conveyor systems—Autocon and Maticmuv. Each system requires an initial outlay of $600,000, has a 5-year life, and displays the following annual cash flows:

Investment	Year 1	Year 2	Year 3	Year 4	Year 5
Autocon	$360,000	$240,000	$200,000	$200,000	$200,000
Maticmuv	160,000	440,000	100,000	100,000	100,000

Both investments have payback periods of two years. If a manager uses the payback period to choose among competing investments, then the two investments would be equally desirable. In reality, however, the Autocon system should be preferred over the Maticmuv system for two reasons. First, the Autocon system provides a much larger dollar return for the years beyond the payback period ($600,000 versus $300,000). Second, the Autocon system returns $360,000 in the first year, while Maticmuv returns only $160,000. The extra $200,000 that the Autocon system provides in the first year could be put to productive use, such as investing it in another project. It is better to have a dollar now than a dollar one year from now because the dollar on hand can be invested to provide a return one year from now.

In summary, the payback period provides managers with information that can be used as follows:

1. To help control the risks associated with the uncertainty of future cash flows.
2. To help minimize the impact of an investment on a firm's liquidity problems.
3. To help control the risk of obsolescence.
4. To help control the effect of the investment on performance measures.

However, the method suffers significant deficiencies: it ignores a project's total profitability and the time value of money. While the computation of the payback period may be useful to a manager, to rely on it solely for a capital investment decision would be foolish.

Accounting Rate of Return

The **accounting rate of return (ARR)** is the second commonly used nondiscounting model. The accounting rate of return measures the return on a project in terms of income, as opposed to using a project's cash flow. It is computed by the following formula:

Accounting rate of return = Average income/Original investment

or

Accounting rate of return = Average income/Average investment

Income is not equivalent to cash flows because of accruals and deferrals used in its computation. The average income of a project is obtained by adding the income for each year of the project and then dividing this total by the number of years. Average income for a project can be approximated by subtracting average depreciation from average cash flow. Assuming that all revenues earned in a period are collected and that depreciation is the only noncash expense, the approximation is exact.

Investment can be defined as the original investment or as the average investment. Letting I equal original investment, S equal salvage value, and assuming that the investment is uniformly consumed, average investment is defined as follows:

Average investment = $(I + S)/2$

To illustrate the computation of the accounting rate of return, assume that an investment requires an initial outlay of $300,000. The life of the investment is five years with the following cash flows: $90,000, $90,000, $120,000, $90,000, and $150,000. Assume that the asset has no salvage value after the five years and that all revenues earned within a year are collected in that year. The total cash flow for the five years is $540,000, making the average cash flow $108,000 ($540,000/5). Average depreciation is $60,000 ($300,000/5). The average income is the difference between these two figures: $48,000 ($108,000 − $60,000). Using the average income and original investment, the accounting rate of return is 16 percent ($48,000/$300,000). If average investment were used instead of original investment, then the accounting rate of return would be 32 percent ($48,000/$150,000).

Unlike the payback period, the accounting rate of return does consider a project's profitability; like the payback period, it ignores the time value of money. Ignoring the time value of money is a critical deficiency and can lead a manager to choose investments that do not maximize profits. Unfortunately, incentive plans may actually encourage the use of the accounting rate of return. Bonuses to managers are often based on accounting income or return on assets. Thus, managers may have a personal interest in seeing that any new investment contributes significantly to income. A manager seeking to maximize personal income will select investments that return the highest income per dollar invested.

It is because the payback period and the accounting rate of return ignore the time value of money that they are referred to as *nondiscounting models*. Discounting models use **discounted cash flows**, which are future cash flows expressed in terms of their present value. The use of discounting models requires an understanding of the present value concepts. Present value concepts are reviewed in Appendix A at the end of this chapter. You should review these concepts and make sure that you understand them before studying capital investment discount models. Present value tables (Exhibits 20B-1 and 20B-2) are presented in Appendix B at the end of this chapter. These tables are referred to and used throughout the rest of the chapter.

OBJECTIVE 3
Calculate the net present value (NPV) for independent projects.

The Net Present Value Method

Net present value (NPV) is one of two discounting models that explicitly consider the time value of money and, therefore, incorporate the concept of discounting cash inflows and outflows. The other discounting model is the *internal rate of return* (IRR). The net present value method will be discussed first; the internal rate of return method is discussed in the following section.

The Meaning of NPV

Net present value is the difference in the present value of the cash inflows and outflows associated with a project:

$$NPV = [\Sigma \; CF_t/(1 + i)^t] - I \qquad\qquad (20.1)$$
$$= [\Sigma \; (CF_t)(df_t)] - I$$
$$= P - I$$

where

I = The present value of the project's cost (usually the initial outlay)
CF_t = The cash inflow to be received in period t, with $t = 1, \ldots , n$
i = The required rate of return
n = The useful life of the project
t = The time period
P = The present value of the project's future cash inflows
$df_t = 1/(1 + i)^t$, the discount factor

Net present value measures the profitability of an investment. If the NPV is positive, it measures the increase in wealth. For a firm, this means that the size of a positive NPV measures the increase in the value of the firm resulting from an investment. To use the NPV method, a required rate of return must be defined. The **required rate of return** is the minimum acceptable rate of return. It is also referred to as the *discount rate* or the *hurdle rate* and should correspond to the *cost of capital* (but often does not as firms frequently choose discount rates greater than the cost of capital).

If the net present value is positive, it signals that (1) the initial investment has been recovered, (2) the required rate of return has been recovered, and (3) a return in excess of (1) and (2) has been received. Thus, if NPV is greater than zero, then the investment is profitable and therefore acceptable. It also conveys the message that the value of the firm should increase because more than the cost of capital is being earned. If NPV equals zero, then the decision maker will find acceptance or rejection of the investment equal. Finally, if NPV is less than zero, then the investment should be rejected. In this case, it is earning less than the required rate of return.

Weighted Average Cost of Capital

The cost of capital is a blend of the costs of capital from *all* sources. It is a weighted average of the costs from the various sources, where the weight is defined by the *relative* amount from each source. Assume, for example, that a new firm has two sources of capital: (1) $500,000 from a loan with an after-tax cost of 8 percent and (2) $500,000 raised from issuing stock to shareholders that expect a return of 12 percent. In other words, each source contributes 50 percent ($500,000/$1,000,000) to the total capital raised. The relative weights, then, are 0.5 for the loan and 0.5 for the capital stock. The *weighted cost of capital* is computed as follows:

Source	Amount of Capital	Percentage Cost	Dollar Cost
Loan	$ 500,000	8%	$ 40,000
Stock	500,000	12	60,000
	$1,000,000	10*	$100,000

*The weighted average can be computed in two ways: as $100,000/$1,000,000 or as $(0.5 \times 0.08) + (0.5 \times 0.12)$.

An Example Illustrating Weighted Average Cost of Capital

Polson Company has developed new cell phones that are less costly to produce than those of competitors. The marketing manager is excited about the new product's prospects after completing a detailed market study that revealed expected annual revenues of $750,000. The cell phone has a projected product life cycle of five years. Equipment to produce the cell phone would cost $800,000. After five years, that equipment can be sold for $100,000. In addition to the equipment expenditure, working capital is expected to increase by $100,000 because of increases in inventories and receivables. The firm expects to recover the investment in working capital at the end of the project's life. Annual cash operating expenses are estimated at $450,000. Assuming that the required rate of return is 12 percent, should the company manufacture the new cell phone?

To answer the question, two steps must be taken: (1) the cash flow for each year must be identified, and (2) the NPV must be computed using the cash flow from step 1. The solution to the problem is given in Exhibit 20-2 on the following page. Notice that step 2 offers two approaches for computing NPV. Step 2A computes NPV by using discount factors from Exhibit 20B-1. Step 2B simplifies the computation by using a single discount factor from Exhibit 20B-2 for the even cash flow occurring in Years 1–4. Polson should manufacture the cell phone because the NPV is greater than zero.

OBJECTIVE 4

Compute the internal rate of return (IRR) for independent projects.

Internal Rate of Return

The **internal rate of return (IRR)** is defined as the interest rate that sets the present value of a project's cash inflows equal to the present value of the project's cost. In other words, it is the interest rate that sets the project's NPV at zero. The following equation can be used to determine a project's IRR:

$$I = \Sigma\ CF_t/(1 + i)^t \tag{20.2}$$

where

$$t = 1,\ \ldots\ ,\ n$$

The right-hand side of Equation 20.2 is the present value of future cash flows, and the left-hand side is the investment. I, CF_t, and t are known. Thus, the IRR (the interest rate, i, in the equation) can be found using trial and error. Once the IRR for a project is computed, it is compared with the firm's required rate of return. If the IRR is greater than the required rate, the project is deemed acceptable; if the IRR is equal to the required rate of return, acceptance or rejection of the investment is equal; and if the IRR is less than the required rate of return, the project is rejected.

The internal rate of return is the most widely used of the capital investment techniques. One reason for its popularity may be that it is a rate of return, a concept that managers are comfortable in using. Another possibility is that managers may believe (in most cases, incorrectly) that the IRR is the true or actual compounded rate of return being earned by the initial investment. Whatever the reasons for its popularity, a basic understanding of the IRR is necessary.

Example with Uniform Cash Flows

To illustrate the computation of the IRR with even cash flows, assume that an engineering firm has the opportunity to invest $240,000 in a new computer-aided design system that will produce net cash inflows of $99,900 at the end of each year for the next three years. The IRR is the interest rate that equates the present value of the three equal receipts of $99,900 to the investment of $240,000. Since the series of cash flows is uniform, a single discount factor from Exhibit 20B-2 can be used to compute the

| EXHIBIT 20-2 | Cash Flow and NPV Analysis |

Step 1. Cash Flow Identification

Year	Item	Cash Flow
0	Equipment	$(800,000)
	Working capital	(100,000)
	Total	$(900,000)
1–4	Revenues	$ 750,000
	Operating expenses	(450,000)
	Total	$ 300,000
5	Revenues	$ 750,000
	Operating expenses	(450,000)
	Salvage	100,000
	Recovery of working capital	100,000
	Total	$ 500,000

Step 2A. NPV Analysis

Year	Cash Flow[a]	Discount Factor[b]	Present Value
0	$(900,000)	1.000	$(900,000)
1	300,000	0.893	267,900
2	300,000	0.797	239,100
3	300,000	0.712	213,600
4	300,000	0.636	190,800
5	500,000	0.567	283,500
Net present value			$ 294,900

Step 2B. NPV Analysis

Year	Cash Flow	Discount Factor	Present Value
0	$(900,000)	1.000	$(900,000)
1–4	300,000	3.037	911,100
5	500,000	0.567	283,500
Net present value			$ 294,600[c]

[a]From step 1.
[b]From Exhibit 20B-1.
[c]Differs from computation in step 2A because of rounding.

present value of the annuity. Letting *df* be this discount factor and *CF* be the annual cash flow, Equation 20.2 assumes the following form:

$$I = CF(df)$$

Solving for *df*, we obtain:

$$df = I/CF$$
$$= \text{Investment/Annual cash flow}$$

Once the discount factor is computed, go to Exhibit 20B-2, find the row corresponding to the life of the project, and move across that row until the computed discount factor is found. The interest rate corresponding to this discount factor is the IRR.

For example, the discount factor for the firm's investment is 2.402 ($240,000/ $99,900). Since the life of the investment is three years, we must find the third row in Exhibit 20B-2 and move across this row until we encounter 2.402. The interest rate corresponding to 2.402 is 12 percent, which is the IRR.

Exhibit 20B-2 does not provide discount factors for every possible interest rate. To illustrate, assume that the annual cash inflows expected by the engineering firm are $102,000 instead of $99,900. The new discount factor is 2.353 ($240,000/$102,000). Going once again to the third row in Exhibit 20B-2, we find that the discount factor—and thus the IRR—lies between 12 and 14 percent. It is possible to approximate the IRR by interpolation; however, for our purposes, we will simply identify the range for the IRR as indicated by the table values.

IRR and Uneven Cash Flows

If the cash flows are not uniform, then Equation 20.2 must be used. For a multiple-period setting, Equation 20.2 can be solved by trial and error or by using a business calculator or a software package like Excel®. To illustrate solution by trial and error, assume that a $50,000 investment in an inventory management system produces labor savings of $30,000 and $36,000 for each of two years. The IRR is the interest rate that sets the present value of these two cash inflows equal to $50,000:

$$P = [\$30,000/(1 + i)] + [\$36,000/(1 + i)^2]$$
$$= \$50,000$$

To solve the above equation by trial and error, start by selecting a possible value for i. Given this first guess, the present value of the future cash flows is computed and then compared to the initial investment. If the present value is greater than the initial investment, the interest rate is too low; if the present value is less than the initial investment, the interest rate is too high. The next guess is adjusted accordingly.

Assume the first guess is 18 percent. Using i equal to 0.18, Exhibit 20B-1 yields the following discount factors: 0.847 and 0.718. These discount factors produce the following present value for the two cash inflows:

$$P = (0.847 \times \$30,000) + (0.718 \times \$36,000)$$
$$= \$51,258$$

Since P is greater than $50,000, the interest rate selected is too low. A higher guess is needed. If the next guess is 20 percent, we obtain the following:

$$P = (0.833 \times \$30,000) + (0.694 \times \$36,000)$$
$$= \$49,974$$

Since this value is reasonably close to $50,000, we can say that the IRR is 20 percent. (The IRR is, in fact, exactly 20 percent; the present value is slightly less than the investment due to rounding of the discount factors found in Exhibit 20B-1.)

OBJECTIVE 5

Tell why NPV is better than IRR for choosing among mutually exclusive projects.

NPV versus IRR: Mutually Exclusive Projects

Up to this point, we have focused on independent projects. Many capital investment decisions deal with mutually exclusive projects. How NPV analysis and IRR are used to choose among competing projects is an intriguing question. An even more interesting question to consider is whether NPV and IRR differ in their ability to help managers make wealth-maximizing decisions in the presence of competing alternatives. For example, we already know that the nondiscounting models can produce erroneous choices because they ignore the time value of money. Because of this deficiency, the discounting models are judged to be superior. Similarly, it can be shown that the NPV model is generally preferred to the IRR model when choosing among mutually exclusive alternatives.

NPV Compared with IRR

NPV and IRR both yield the same decision for independent projects. For example, if the NPV is greater than zero, then the IRR is also greater than the required rate of return; both models signal the correct decision. However, for competing projects, the two methods can produce different results. Intuitively, we believe that, for mutually exclusive projects, the project with the highest NPV or the highest IRR should be chosen. Since it is possible for the two methods to produce different rankings of mutually exclusive projects, the method that consistently reveals the wealth-maximizing project should be preferred. As will be shown, the NPV method is that model.

NPV differs from IRR in two major ways. First, NPV assumes that each cash inflow received is reinvested at the required rate of return, whereas the IRR method assumes that each cash inflow is reinvested at the computed IRR. Second, the NPV method measures profitability in absolute terms, whereas the IRR method measures it in relative terms. Because NPV is measured in absolute terms, it is affected by the size of the investment, whereas IRR is size independent. For example, an investment of $100,000 that produces a cash flow one year from now of $121,000 has the same IRR (21 percent) as an investment of $10,000 that produces a cash flow one year from now of $12,100. Note, however, that the NPV is $10,000 for the first investment and $1,000 for the second. Since absolute measures often produce different rankings than relative measures, it shouldn't be too surprising that NPV and IRR can, on occasion, produce different signals regarding the attractiveness of projects. When a conflict does occur between the two methods, NPV produces the correct signal, as can be shown by a simple example.

Assume that a manager is faced with the prospect of choosing between two mutually exclusive investments whose cash flows, timing, NPV, and IRR are given in Exhibit 20-3. (A required rate of return of 8 percent is assumed for NPV computation.) Both projects have the same life, require the same initial outlay, have positive NPVs, and have IRRs greater than the required rate of return. However, Project A has a higher NPV, whereas Project B has a higher IRR. The NPV and IRR give conflicting signals regarding which project should be chosen.

EXHIBIT 20-3	NPV and IRR: Conflicting Signals	
Year	**Project A**	**Project B**
0	$(1,000,000)	$(1,000,000)
1	—	686,342
2	1,440,000	686,342
IRR	20%	24%
NPV	$234,080	$223,748

The preferred project can be identified by modifying the cash flows of one project so that the cash flows of both can be compared year by year. The modification, which appears in Exhibit 20-4, was achieved by carrying the Year 1 cash flow of Project B forward to Year 2. This can be done by assuming that the Year 1 cash flow of $686,342 is invested to earn the required rate of return. Under this assumption, the future value

EXHIBIT **20-4**	Modified Comparison of Projects A and B	

| | Projects | |
Year	A	Modified B
0	$(1,000,000)	$(1,000,000)
1	—	—
2	1,440,000	1,427,591*

*1.08($686,342) + $686,342.

of $686,342 is equal to $741,249 (1.08 × $686,342). When $741,249 is added to the $686,342 received at the end of Year 2, the cash flow expected for Project B is $1,427,591.

As can be seen from Exhibit 20-4, Project A is preferable to Project B. It has the same outlay initially and a greater cash inflow in Year 2. (The difference is $12,409.) Since the NPV approach originally chose Project A over Project B, it provided the correct signal for wealth maximization.

Some may object to this analysis, arguing that Project B should be preferred, since it does provide a cash inflow of $686,342 at the end of Year 1, which can be reinvested at a much more attractive rate than the firm's required rate of return. The response is that if such an investment does exist, the firm should still invest in Project A, borrow $686,342 at the cost of capital, and invest that money in the attractive opportunity. Then, at the end of Year 2, the firm should repay the money borrowed plus the interest by using the combined proceeds of Project A and the other investment. For example, assume that the other investment promises a return of 20 percent. The modified cash inflows for Projects A and B are shown in Exhibit 20-5 (assuming that the additional investment at the end of Year 1 is made under either alternative). Notice that Project A is still preferable to Project B—and by the same $12,409.

EXHIBIT **20-5**	Modified Cash Flows with Additional Opportunity	

| | Projects | |
Year	A	Modified B
0	$(1,000,000)	$(1,000,000)
1	—	—
2	1,522,361[a]	1,509,952[b]

[a]$1,440,000 + [(1.20 × $686,342) − (1.08 × $686,342)]. This last term is what is needed to repay the capital and its cost at the end of Year 2.
[b]$686,342 + (1.20 × $686,342).

NPV provides the correct signal for choosing among mutually exclusive investments. At the same time, it measures the impact competing projects have on the value of the firm. Choosing the project with the largest NPV is consistent with maximizing the wealth of shareholders. On the other hand, IRR does not consistently result in choices that maximize wealth. IRR, as a *relative* measure of profitability, has the virtue of measuring accurately the rate of return of funds that remain internally invested. However, maximizing IRR will not necessarily maximize the wealth of firm owners because it cannot, by nature, consider the absolute dollar contributions of projects. In the final analysis, what counts are the total dollars earned—the absolute profits—not the relative profits. Accordingly, NPV, not IRR, should be used for choosing among competing, mutually exclusive projects, or competing projects when capital funds are limited.

An independent project is acceptable if its NPV is positive. For mutually exclusive projects, the project with the largest NPV is chosen. Selecting the best project from several competing projects involves three steps: (1) assessing the cash flow pattern for each project, (2) computing the NPV for each project, and (3) identifying the project with the greatest NPV. To illustrate NPV analysis for competing projects, an example is provided.

Example: Mutually Exclusive Projects

Milagro Travel Agency is setting up an office in Milwaukee and is trying to select a computer system. Two different systems are being considered: the Standard T2 System and the Custom Travel System. (The systems are offered by competitors and include equipment and software.) The Custom Travel System is more elaborate than the Standard T2 System and requires a larger investment and greater annual operating costs; however, it will also generate greater annual revenues. The projected annual revenues, annual costs, capital outlays, and project life for each system (in after-tax cash flows) are as follows:

	Standard T2	*Custom Travel*
Annual revenues	$240,000	$300,000
Annual operating costs	120,000	160,000
System investment	360,000	420,000
Project life	5 years	5 years

Assume that the cost of capital for the company is 12 percent.

The Standard T2 System requires an initial outlay of $360,000 and has a net annual cash inflow of $120,000 (revenues of $240,000 minus costs of $120,000). The Custom Travel System, with an initial outlay of $420,000, has a net annual cash inflow of $140,000 ($300,000 − $160,000). With this information, the cash flow pattern for each project can be described and the NPV and IRR computed. These are shown in Exhibit 20-6. Based on NPV analysis, the Custom Travel System is more profitable; it has the larger NPV. Accordingly, the company should select the Custom Travel System.

Interestingly, both systems have identical internal rates of return. As Exhibit 20-6 illustrates, both systems have a discount factor of 3.0. From Exhibit 20B-2, it is easily seen that a discount factor of 3.0 and a life of five years yields an IRR of approximately 20 percent. Although both projects have an IRR of 20 percent, the firm should not consider the two systems equally desirable. The analysis above has just shown that the Custom Travel System produces a larger NPV and therefore will increase the value of the firm more than the Standard T2 System. The Custom Travel System should be chosen.

Computing After-Tax Cash Flows

Determining the cash flow pattern for each project being considered is a critical step in capital investment analysis. In fact, the computation of cash flows may be the most critical step in the capital investment process. Erroneous estimates may result in erroneous decisions, regardless of the sophistication of the decision models being used. Two steps are needed to compute cash flows: (1) forecasting revenues, expenses, and capital outlays and (2) adjusting these gross cash flows for inflation and tax effects. Of the two steps, the more challenging is the first. Forecasting cash flows is technically demand-

OBJECTIVE **6**

Convert gross cash flows to after-tax cash flows.

EXHIBIT 20-6	Cash Flow Pattern, NPV and IRR Analysis: Standard T2 versus Custom Travel

Cash Flow Pattern

Year	Standard T2	Custom Travel
0	$(360,000)	$(420,000)
1	120,000	140,000
2	120,000	140,000
3	120,000	140,000
4	120,000	140,000
5	120,000	140,000

Standard T2: NPV Analysis

Year	Cash Flow	Discount Factor[a]	Present Value
0	$(360,000)	1.000	$(360,000)
1–5	120,000	3.605	432,600
Net present value			$ 72,600
IRR			≈20%

IRR Analysis[b]

Discount factor = Initial investment/Annual cash flow
= $360,000/$120,000
= 3.0

Custom Travel System: NPV Analysis

Year	Cash Flow	Discount Factor[a]	Present Value
0	$(420,000)	1.000	$(420,000)
1–5	140,000	3.605	504,700
Net present value			$ 84,700
IRR			≈20%

IRR Analysis[b]

Discount factor = Initial investment/Annual cash flow
= $420,000/$140,000
= 3.0

[a]From Exhibit 20B-2.
[b]From Exhibit 20B-2, *df* = 3.0 implies that IRR ≈20%.

ing, and its methodology is typically studied in management science and statistics courses. It is important to understand that estimating future cash flows involves considerable judgment on the part of managers. Once gross cash flows are estimated, they should be adjusted for significant inflationary effects. Finally, straightforward applications of tax law can then be used to compute the after-tax cash flows. At this level of study, we assume that gross cash forecasts are available and focus on adjusting forecasted cash flows to improve their accuracy and utility in capital expenditure analysis.

Inflationary Adjustments

In the United States, inflation has been relatively modest, and the need to adjust cash flows may not be as critical. For firms that operate in the international environment, however, the effect on capital investment decisions can be dramatic because inflation can be very high in certain countries. Many Latin American countries like Peru and Venezuela, for example, have experienced double-digit inflation rates for years. Thus, it is important to know how to adjust the capital budgeting models for inflationary effects—particularly given the fact that many U.S. firms make capital investment decisions within many different national environments.

In an inflationary environment, financial markets react by increasing the cost of capital to reflect inflation. Thus, the cost of capital is composed of two elements:

1. The real rate
2. The inflationary element (Investors demand a premium to compensate for the loss in general purchasing power of the dollar or local currency.)

Since the required rate of return (which should be the cost of capital) used in capital investment analysis reflects an inflationary component at the time NPV analysis is performed, inflation must also be considered in predicting the operating cash flows. If the operating cash flows are not adjusted to account for inflation, an erroneous decision may result. In adjusting predicted cash flows, specific price change indexes should be used if possible. If that is not possible, a general price index can be used.

Note, however, that the cash inflows due to the tax effects of depreciation need *not* be adjusted for inflation as long as the national tax law requires that depreciation be based on the *original* dollar investment. In this case, depreciation deductions should not be increased for inflation.

To illustrate, assume that a subsidiary of a U.S. firm operating in Venezuela is considering a project that requires an investment of 10,000,000 bolivares and is expected to produce annual cash inflows of 5,800,000 bolivares for the coming two years. The required rate of return is 20 percent, which includes an inflationary component. The general inflation rate in Venezuela is expected to average 15 percent for the next two years. Net present value analysis with and without the adjustment of predicted cash flows for inflation is given in Exhibit 20-7. (*Note:* All cash flows in Exhibit 20-7 are given in bolivares, expressed as "Bs".) As the analysis shows, *not* adjusting predicted cash flows for inflation leads to a decision to reject the project, whereas adjusting for inflation leads to a decision to accept it. Thus, failure to adjust the predicted cash flows for inflationary effects can lead to an incorrect conclusion.

Conversion of Gross Cash Flows to After-Tax Cash Flows

Assuming that inflation-adjusted gross cash flows are predicted with the desired degree of accuracy, the analyst must adjust these cash flows for taxes. To analyze tax effects, cash flows are usually broken into three categories: (1) the initial cash outflows needed to acquire the assets of the project, (2) the cash flows produced over the life of the project (operating cash flows), and (3) the cash flows from the final disposal of the project. Cash outflows and cash inflows adjusted for tax effects are called *net* cash outflows and inflows. Net cash flows include provisions for revenues, operating expenses, depreciation, and relevant tax implications. They are the proper inputs for capital investment decisions.

After-Tax Cash Flows: Year 0

The net cash outflow in Year 0 (the initial out-of-pocket outlay) is simply the difference between the initial cost of the project and any cash inflows directly associated with

EXHIBIT 20-7	The Effects of Inflation on Capital Investment

	Without Inflationary Adjustment		
Year	**Cash Flow**	**Discount Factor[a]**	**Present Value**
0	Bs(10,000,000)	1.000	Bs(10,000,000)
1–2	5,800,000	1.528	8,862,400
NPV			Bs (1,137,600)

	With Inflationary Adjustment		
Year	**Cash Flow[b]**	**Discount Factor[c]**	**Present Value**
0	Bs(10,000,000)	1.000	Bs(10,000,000)
1	6,670,000	0.833	5,556,110
2	7,670,500	0.694	5,323,327
NPV			Bs 879,437

[a]From Exhibit 20B-2.
[b]6,670,000 bolivares = 1.15 × 5,800,000 bolivares (adjustment for one year of inflation)
7,670,500 bolivares = 1.15 × 1.15 × 5,800,000 bolivares (adjustment for two years of inflation).
[c]From Exhibit 20B-1.

it. The gross cost of the project includes such things as the cost of land, the cost of equipment (including transportation and installation), taxes on gains from the sale of assets, and increases in working capital. Cash inflows occurring at the time of acquisition include tax savings from the sale of assets, cash from the sale of assets, and other tax benefits such as tax credits.

Under current tax law, all costs relating to the acquisition of assets other than land must be capitalized and written off over the useful life of the assets. (The write-off is achieved through depreciation.) Depreciation is deducted from revenues in computing taxable income during each year of the asset's life; however, at the point of acquisition, no depreciation expense is computed. Thus, depreciation is not relevant at Year 0. The principal tax implications at the point of acquisition are related to recognition of gains and losses on the sale of existing assets and to the recognition of any investment tax credits.

Gains on the sale of assets produce additional taxes and, accordingly, reduce the cash proceeds received from the sale of old assets. Losses, on the other hand, are non-cash expenses that reduce taxable income, producing tax savings. Consequently, the cash proceeds from the sale of an old asset are increased by the amount of the tax savings.

Adjusting cash inflows and outflows for tax effects requires knowledge of current corporate tax rates. Currently, most corporations face a federal tax rate of 35 percent. State corporate tax rates vary by state. For purposes of analysis, we will assume that 40 percent is the combined rate for state and federal taxes.

Let us look at an example. Currently, Lewis Company uses two types of manufacturing equipment (M1 and M2) to produce one of its products. It is now possible to replace these two machines with a flexible manufacturing system. Management wants to know the net investment needed to acquire the flexible system. If the system is acquired, the old equipment will be sold.

Disposition of Old Machines

	Book Value	Sale Price
M1	$ 600,000	$ 780,000
M2	1,500,000	1,200,000

Acquisition of Flexible System

Purchase cost	$7,500,000
Freight	60,000
Installation	600,000
Additional working capital	540,000
Total	$8,700,000

The net investment can be determined by computing the net proceeds from the sale of the old machines and subtracting those proceeds from the cost of the new system. The net proceeds are determined by computing the tax consequences of the sale and adjusting the gross receipts accordingly.

The tax consequences can be assessed by subtracting the book value from the selling price. If the difference is positive, the firm has experienced a gain and will owe taxes. Money received from the sale will be reduced by the amount of taxes owed. On the other hand, if the difference is negative, a loss is experienced—a noncash loss. However, this noncash loss does have cash implications. It can be deducted from revenues and, as a consequence, can shield revenues from being taxed; accordingly, taxes will be saved. Thus, a loss produces a cash inflow equal to the taxes saved.

To illustrate, consider the tax effects of selling M1 and M2 as illustrated in Exhibit 20-8.

EXHIBIT 20-8   Tax Effects of the Sale of M1 and M2

Asset	Gain(Loss)
M1[a]	$ 180,000
M2[b]	(300,000)
Net gain (loss)	$(120,000)
Tax rate	× 0.40
Tax savings	$ 48,000

[a]Sale price minus book value is $780,000 − $600,000.
[b]Sale price minus book value is $1,200,000 − $1,500,000.

By selling the two machines, the company receives the following net proceeds:

Sale price, M1	$ 780,000
Sale price, M2	1,200,000
Tax savings	48,000
Net proceeds	$2,028,000

Given these net proceeds, the net investment can be computed as follows:

Total cost of flexible system	$8,700,000
Less: Net proceeds of old machines	2,028,000
Net investment (cash outflow)	$6,672,000

After-Tax Operating Cash Flows: Life of the Project

In addition to determining the initial out-of-pocket outlay, managers must also estimate the annual after-tax operating cash flows expected over the life of the project. If the project generates revenue, the principal source of cash flows is from operations. Operating cash inflows can be assessed from the project's income statement. The annual after-tax cash flows are the sum of the project's after-tax profits and its noncash expenses. In terms of a simple formula, this computation can be represented as follows:

$$\text{After-tax cash flow} = \text{After-tax net income} + \text{Noncash expenses}$$
$$CF = NI + NC$$

The most prominent examples of noncash expenses are depreciation and losses. At first glance, it may seem odd that after-tax cash flows are computed using noncash expenses. Noncash expenses are not cash flows, but they do generate cash flows by reducing taxes. By shielding revenues from taxation, actual cash savings are created. The use of the income statement to determine after-tax cash flows is illustrated in the following example. The example is also used to show how noncash expenses can increase cash inflows by saving taxes.

Assume that a company plans to make a new product that requires new equipment costing $1,600,000. The new product is expected to increase the firm's annual revenues by $1,200,000. Materials, labor, and other cash operating expenses will be $500,000 per year. The equipment has a life of four years and will be depreciated on a straight-line basis. The machine is not expected to have any salvage value at the end of four years. The income statement for the project is as follows:

Revenues	$1,200,000
Less: Cash operating expenses	(500,000)
Depreciation	(400,000)
Income before income taxes	$ 300,000
Less: Income taxes (@ 40%)	120,000
Net income	$ 180,000

Cash flow from the income statement is computed as follows:

$$CF = NI + NC$$
$$= \$180,000 + \$400,000$$
$$= \$580,000$$

The income approach to determine operating cash flows can be decomposed to assess the after-tax, cash flow effects of each individual category on the income statement. The decomposition approach calculates the operating cash flows by computing the after-tax cash flows for each item of the income statement as follows:

$$CF = [(1 - \text{Tax rate}) \times \text{Revenues}] - [(1 - \text{Tax rate}) \times \text{Cash expenses}] + (\text{Tax rate} \times \text{Noncash expenses})$$

The first term, $[(1 - \text{Tax rate}) \times \text{Revenues}]$, gives the after-tax cash inflows from cash revenues. For our example, the cash revenue is projected to be $1,200,000. The firm, therefore, can expect to keep $720,000 of the revenues received: $(1 - \text{Tax rate}) \times \text{Revenues} = 0.60 \times \$1,200,000 = \$720,000$. The after-tax revenue is the actual amount of after-tax cash available from the sales activity of the firm.

The second term, [(1 − Tax rate) × Cash expenses], is the after-tax cash outflows from cash operating expenses. Because cash expenses can be deducted from revenues to arrive at taxable income, the effect is to shield revenues from taxation. The consequence of this shielding is to save taxes and to reduce the actual cash outflow associated with a given expenditure. In our example, the firm has cash operating expenses of $500,000. The actual cash outflow is not $500,000 but $300,000 (0.60 × $500,000). The cash outlay for operating expenses is reduced by $200,000 because of tax savings. To see this, assume that operating expense is the only expense and that the firm has revenues of $1,200,000. If operating expense is *not* tax deductible, then the tax owed is $480,000 (0.40 × $1,200,000). If the operating expense is deductible for tax purposes, then the taxable income is $700,000 ($1,200,000 − $500,000), and the tax owed is $280,000 (0.40 × $700,000). Because the deductibility of operating expense saves $200,000 in taxes, the actual outlay for that expenditure is reduced by $200,000.

The third term, (Tax rate × Noncash expenses), is the cash inflow from the tax savings produced by the noncash expenses. Noncash expenses, such as depreciation, also shield revenues from taxation. The depreciation *shields* $400,000 of revenues from being taxed and, thus, saves $160,000 (0.40 × $400,000) in taxes.

The sum of the three items is as follows:

After-tax revenues	$ 720,000
After-tax cash expenses	(300,000)
Depreciation tax shield	160,000
Operating cash flow	$ 580,000

The decomposition approach yields the same outcome as the income approach. For convenience, the three decomposition terms are summarized in Exhibit 20-9.

EXHIBIT 20-9   Computation of Operating Cash Flows: Decomposition Terms

After-tax cash revenues (cash inflow) = (1 − Tax rate) × Revenues
After-tax cash expenses (cash outflow) = (1 − Tax rate) × Cash expenses
Tax savings, noncash expenses (cash inflow) = Tax rate × Noncash expenses

---

One feature of decomposition is the ability to compute after-tax cash flows in a spreadsheet format. This format highlights the cash flow effects of individual items and facilitates the use of spreadsheet software packages. The spreadsheet format is achieved by creating four columns, one for each of the three cash flow categories and one for the total after-tax cash flow, which is the sum of the first three. This format is illustrated in Exhibit 20-10 for our example. Recall that cash revenues were $1,200,000 per year for four years, annual cash expenses were $500,000, and annual depreciation was $400,000.

A second feature of decomposition is the ability to compute the after-tax cash effects on an item-by-item basis. For example, suppose that a firm is considering a project and is uncertain as to which method of depreciation should be used. By computing the tax savings produced under each depreciation method, a firm can quickly assess which method is most desirable.

For tax purposes, all depreciable business assets other than real estate are referred to as *personal property*, which is classified into one of six classes. Each class specifies the life of the assets that must be used for figuring depreciation. This life must be used even if the actual expected life is different from the class life; the class lives are set for

EXHIBIT 20-10	Illustration of the Spreadsheet Format		

Year	$(1 - t)R^a$	$-(1 - t)C^b$	tNC^c	CF
1	$720,000	$(300,000)	$160,000	$580,000
2	720,000	(300,000)	160,000	580,000
3	720,000	(300,000)	160,000	580,000
4	720,000	(300,000)	160,000	580,000

[a] R = Revenues; t = tax rate; $(1 - t)R = (1 - 0.40)\$1,200,000 = \$720,000$.
[b] C = Cash expenses; $-(1 - t)C = -(1 - 0.40)\$500,000 = (\$300,000)$.
[c] NC = Noncash expenses; $tNC = 0.40(\$400,000) = \$160,000$.

purposes of recognizing depreciation and usually will be shorter than the actual life. Most equipment, machinery, and office furniture are classified as **7-year assets**. Light trucks, automobiles, and computer equipment are classified as **5-year assets**. Most small tools are classified as **3-year assets**. Because the majority of personal property can be put into one of these categories, we will restrict our attention to them.

The taxpayer can use either the straight-line method or the **modified accelerated cost recovery system (MACRS)** to compute annual depreciation. Current law defines MACRS as the double-declining-balance method.[2] In computing depreciation, no consideration of salvage value is required. However, under either method, a **half-year convention** applies.[3] This convention assumes that a newly acquired asset is in service for one-half of its first taxable year of service, regardless of the date that use of the asset actually began. When the asset reaches the end of its life, the other half year of depreciation can be claimed in the following year. If an asset is disposed of before the end of its class life, the half-year convention allows half the depreciation for that year.

For example, assume that an automobile is purchased on March 1, 2006. The automobile costs $30,000, and the firm elects the straight-line method. Automobiles are 5-year assets (for tax purposes). The annual depreciation is $6,000 for a 5-year period ($30,000/5). However, using the half-year convention, the firm can deduct only $3,000 for 2006, half of the straight-line amount (0.5 × $6,000). The remaining half is deducted in the sixth year (or the year of disposal, if earlier). Deductions are as follows:

Year	Depreciation Deduction
2006	$3,000 (half-year amount)
2007	6,000
2008	6,000
2009	6,000
2010	6,000
2011	3,000 (half-year amount)

Assume that the asset is disposed of in April 2008. In this case, only $3,000 of depreciation can be claimed for 2008 (early disposal rule).

If the double-declining-balance method is selected, the amount of depreciation claimed in the first year is twice that of the straight-line method. Under this method,

2. The tax law also allows the 150-percent-declining-balance method; however, we will focus only on the straight-line method and the double-declining version of MACRS.
3. The tax law requires a mid-quarter convention if more than 40 percent of personal property is placed in service during the last three months of the year. We will not illustrate this scenario.

the amount of depreciation claimed becomes progressively smaller until eventually it is exceeded by that claimed under the straight-line method. When this happens, the straight-line method is used to finish depreciating the asset. Exhibit 20-11 provides a table of depreciation rates for the double-declining-balance method for assets belonging to the 3-year, 5-year, and 7-year classes. The rates shown in this table incorporate the half-year convention and therefore are the MACRS depreciation rates.

EXHIBIT 20-11   **MACRS Depreciation Rates**

Year	Three-Year Assets	Five-Year Assets	Seven-Year Assets
1	33.33%	20.00%	14.29%
2	44.45	32.00	24.49
3	14.81	19.20	17.49
4	7.41	11.52	12.49
5		11.52	8.93
6		5.76	8.92
7		—	8.93
8		—	4.46

Both the straight-line and double-declining-balance methods yield the same total amount of depreciation over the life of the asset. Both methods also produce the same total tax savings (assuming the same tax rate over the life of the asset). However, since the depreciation claimed in the early years of a project is greater using the double-declining-balance method, the tax savings are also greater during those years. Considering the time value of money, it is preferable to have the tax savings earlier than later. Thus, firms should prefer the MACRS method of depreciation to the straight-line method. This conclusion is illustrated by the following example.

A firm is considering the purchase of computer equipment for $60,000. The tax guidelines require that the cost of the equipment be depreciated over five years. However, tax guidelines also permit the depreciation to be computed using either the straight-line or double-declining-balance method. Of course, the firm should choose the double-declining-balance method because it brings the greater benefit.

From decomposition, we know that the cash inflows caused by shielding can be computed by multiplying the tax rate by the amount depreciated ($t \times NC$). The cash flows produced by each depreciation method and its present value, assuming a discount rate of 10 percent, are given in Exhibit 20-12. As you will see, the present value of the tax savings from using MACRS is greater than the present value realized using straight-line depreciation.

After-Tax Cash Flows: Final Disposal

At the end of the life of the project, there are two major sources of cash: (1) release of working capital and (2) preparation, removal, and sale of the equipment (salvage value effects). Any working capital committed to a project is released at this point. The release of working capital is a cash inflow with no tax consequences. Thus, if $180,000 of additional working capital is needed at the beginning of a project, this $180,000 will be a cash inflow at the end of the project's life. Disposing of an asset associated with a project also has cash consequences. At times, an asset may have a market value at the end of its life. The selling price less the cost of removal and cleanup produces a gross cash inflow. For example, if an asset has a selling price of $120,000 and if its removal and cleanup costs are $30,000, then the gross cash inflow is $90,000. The tax

EXHIBIT 20-12 — Value of Accelerated Methods Illustrated

Straight-Line Method

Year	Depreciation	Tax Rate	Tax Savings	Discount Factor	Present Value
1	$ 6,000	0.40	$2,400.00	0.909	$ 2,181.60
2	12,000	0.40	4,800.00	0.826	3,964.80
3	12,000	0.40	4,800.00	0.751	3,604.80
4	12,000	0.40	4,800.00	0.683	3,278.40
5	12,000	0.40	4,800.00	0.621	2,980.80
6	6,000	0.40	2,400.00	0.564	1,353.60
Net present value					$17,364.00

MACRS Method

Year	Depreciation*	Tax Rate	Tax Savings	Discount Factor	Present Value
1	$12,000	0.40	$4,800.00	0.909	$ 4,363.20
2	19,200	0.40	7,680.00	0.826	6,343.68
3	11,520	0.40	4,608.00	0.751	3,460.61
4	6,912	0.40	2,764.80	0.683	1,888.36
5	6,912	0.40	2,764.80	0.621	1,716.94
6	3,456	0.40	1,382.40	0.564	779.67
Net present value					$18,552.46

*Computed by multiplying the 5-year rates in Exhibit 20-11 by $60,000. For example, depreciation for Year 1 is 0.20 × $60,000.

effects of the transaction must also be assessed. If, for example, the book value of the asset is $15,000, then the firm must recognize a $75,000 *gain* on the sale of the asset ($90,000 − $15,000). If the tax rate is 40 percent, then the cash inflow from disposition is reduced by $30,000 ($75,000 × 0.40). Therefore, the expected cash inflow at the end of the project's life is $60,000 ($90,000 − $30,000).

OBJECTIVE 7

Describe capital investment for advanced technology and environmental impact settings.

Capital Investment: Advanced Technology and Environmental Considerations

In today's manufacturing environment, long-term investments in advanced technology and in pollution prevention (P2) technology can be the sources of a significant competitive advantage. Investing in advanced manufacturing technology such as robotics and computer-integrated manufacturing can improve quality, increase flexibility and reliability, and decrease lead times. As a consequence, customer satisfaction will likely increase, which will then produce an increase in market share. Likewise, pollution prevention (P2) opportunities are now beginning to attract the attention of management. P2 takes a proactive approach that targets the causes of pollution rather than the consequences. It often calls for the redesign of complex products and processes and investment in new technologies. The potential for a competitive advantage stems from the possibility that a firm can eliminate the pollutants at their source and, thus, avoid the need for treating or disposing of these pollutants later on. This will then reduce environmental costs. The argument is that the reduction in environmental costs will produce positive net present values. **Irving Pulp and Paper**, a pulp mill, invested in technologies that resulted in the reuse and reduction of water and also reduced the amount of energy and materials used in the pulp making process. Its on-site surface water discharges were reduced by over 80 percent, preventing a number of chemicals from entering the aquatic ecosystem. The savings from investing in mill modernization and pollution prevention technologies are estimated to be $8 to $10 million per year.[4]

Although discounted cash flow analysis (using net present value and internal rate of return) remains preeminent in capital investment decisions involving advanced technology or P2 opportunities, more attention must be paid to the inputs used in discounted cash flow models. How investment is defined, how operating cash flows are estimated, how salvage value is treated, and how the discount rate is chosen are all different in nature from the traditional approach.[5]

How Investment Differs

Investment in automated manufacturing processes is much more complex than investment in the standard manufacturing equipment of the past. For standard equipment, the direct costs of acquisition represent virtually the entire investment. For automated manufacturing, the direct costs can represent as little as 50 or 60 percent of the total investment; software, engineering, training, and implementation are a significant percentage of the total costs. Thus, great care must be exercised to assess the actual cost of an automated system. It is easy to overlook the peripheral costs, which can be substantial. For example, U.S. bankers and insurance companies have found that their substantial investment in computer technology is only now starting to pay off. The reason is that there were very large investments to be made in training. Until the companies had experience with the technology, they were unable to adequately use its power and improve productivity. Similar comments can be made about P2 investments. P2 investments may involve radical new technology, and indirect costs can be substantial as well.

How Estimates of Operating Cash Flows Differ

Estimates of operating cash flows from investments in standard equipment have typically relied on directly identifiable tangible benefits, such as direct savings from labor, power, and scrap. Similarly, environmental investments in end-of-pipe emissions control have relied on the direct environmental cost savings, e.g., reductions in the costs of waste management and regulatory compliance. In reality, many environmental costs are hidden within other costs. Some are buried in overhead, e.g., the portion of maintenance cost attributable to maintaining equipment associated with end-of-pipe emissions control. **Quebecor Printing Mount Morris, Inc.**, found that a project to improve a wastewater treatment system was more cost effective when indirect environmental costs were fully considered.[6] On the other hand, **Monsanto**'s Fibers Division used direct labor savings as the main justification for automating its Pensacola, Florida, plant.[7]

4. *Pollution Prevention Canadian Success Stories*, http://www.ec.gc.ca/pp/en/storyoutput.cfm?storyid=112, as of October 26, 2004.

5. See the following sources: Robert A. Howell and Stephen R. Soucy, "Capital Investment in the New Manufacturing Environment," *Management Accounting* (November 1987): 26–32; Callie Berliner and James A. Brimson, eds., *Cost Management for Today's Advanced Manufacturing* (Boston: Harvard Business School Press, 1988); Thomas Klammer, "Improving Investment Decisions," *Management Accounting* (July 1993): 35–43; David Sinason, "A Dynamic Model for Present Value Analysis," *Journal of Cost Management* (Spring 1991): 40–45; and James Boyd, "Searching for Profit in Pollution Prevention: Case Studies in the Corporate Evaluation of Environmental Opportunities," April 1998, EPA 742-R-98-005.

6. Tellus Institute, "Strengthening Corporate Commitment to Pollution Prevention in Illinois: Concepts & Case Studies of Total Cost Assessment," http://www.emawebsite.org/library_detail.asp?record=214, as of October 25, 2004.

7. Raymond C. Cole and H. Lee Hales, "How Monsanto Justified Automation," *Management Accounting* (January 1992): 39–43.

Intangible benefits and indirect savings were ignored as they often are in traditional capital investment analyses; however, the intangible and indirect benefits can be material and critical to the viability of the project. Greater quality, more reliability, reduced lead time, improved customer satisfaction, and an enhanced ability to maintain market share are all important intangible benefits of an advanced manufacturing system. Reduction of labor in support areas such as production scheduling and stores are indirect benefits. More effort is needed to measure these intangible and indirect benefits in order to assess more accurately the potential value of investments. Monsanto discovered, for example, that the new automated system in its Pensacola plant produced large savings in terms of reduced waste, lower inventories, increased quality, and reduced indirect labor. Productivity increased by 50 percent. What if the direct labor savings had not been sufficient to justify the investment? Consider the lost returns that Monsanto would have experienced by what could have been a faulty decision. Monsanto's experience also illustrates the importance of a *postaudit*. A **postaudit** is a follow-up analysis of a capital project once it is implemented. It compares the actual benefits and costs with the estimated benefits and costs. For Monsanto, the postaudit revealed the importance of intangible and indirect benefits. In future investment decisions, these factors are more likely to be considered.

An Example: Investing in Advanced Technology

An example can be used to illustrate the importance of considering intangible and indirect benefits. Consider a company that is evaluating a potential investment in a flexible manufacturing system (FMS). The choice facing the company is to continue producing with its traditional equipment, expected to last 10 years, or to switch to the new system, which is also expected to have a useful life of 10 years. The company's discount rate is 12 percent. The data pertaining to the investment are presented in Exhibit 20-13 on the following page. Using these data, the net present value of the proposed system can be computed as follows:

Present value ($4,000,000 × 5.65*)	$22,600,000
Less: Investment	18,000,000
Net present value	$ 4,600,000

*Discount factor for an interest rate of 12 percent and a life of 10 years (see Exhibit 20B-2).

The net present value is positive and large in magnitude, and it clearly signals the acceptability of the FMS. This outcome is strongly dependent, however, on explicit recognition of both intangible and indirect benefits. If those benefits are eliminated, then the direct savings total $2.2 million, and the NPV is negative.

Present value ($2,200,000 × 5.65)	$12,430,000
Less: Investment	18,000,000
Net present value	$(5,570,000)

The rise of activity-based costing has made identifying indirect benefits easier with the use of activity drivers. Once they are identified, they can be included in the analysis if they are material.

Examination of Exhibit 20-13 reveals the importance of intangible benefits. One of the most important intangible benefits is maintaining or improving a firm's competitive position. A key question that needs to be asked is what will happen to the cash flows of the firm if the investment is *not* made. That is, if the company chooses to forgo an investment in technologically advanced equipment, will it be able to continue to compete with other firms on the basis of quality, delivery, and cost? (The question becomes especially relevant if competitors choose to invest in advanced equipment.) If the competitive position deteriorates, the company's current cash flows will decrease.

EXHIBIT 20-13	Investment Data: Direct, Intangible, and Indirect Benefits	
	FMS	**Status Quo**
Investment (current outlay):		
Direct costs	$10,000,000	$ 0
Software, engineering	8,000,000	—
Total current outlay	$18,000,000	$ 0
Net after-tax cash flow	$ 5,000,000	$1,000,000
Less: After-tax cash flow for status quo	1,000,000	n/a
Incremental benefit	$ 4,000,000	n/a
Incremental Benefit Explained		
Direct benefits:		
Direct labor	$1,500,000	
Scrap reduction	500,000	
Setups	200,000	$2,200,000
Intangible benefits: Quality savings		
Rework	$ 200,000	
Warranties	400,000	
Maintenance of competitive position	1,000,000	1,600,000
Indirect benefits:		
Production scheduling	$ 110,000	
Payroll	90,000	200,000
Total		$4,000,000

If cash flows decrease if the investment is not made, this decrease should show up as an incremental benefit for the advanced technology. In Exhibit 20-13, the company estimates this competitive benefit as $1,000,000. Estimating this benefit requires some serious strategic planning and analysis, but its effect can be critical. If this benefit had been ignored or overlooked, then the net present value would have been negative, and the investment alternative rejected. This calculation is as follows:

Present value ($3,000,000 × 5.65)	$16,950,000
Less: Investment	18,000,000
Net present value	$(1,050,000)

Salvage Value

Terminal or salvage value has often been ignored in investment decisions. The usual reason offered is the difficulty in estimating it. Because of this uncertainty, the effect of salvage value has often been ignored or heavily discounted. This approach may be unwise, however, because salvage value could make the difference between investing or not investing. Given the highly competitive environment, companies cannot afford to make incorrect decisions. A much better approach to deal with uncertainty is to use sensitivity analysis. **Sensitivity analysis** changes the assumptions on which the capital investment analysis relies and assesses the effect on the cash flow pattern. Sensitivity analysis is often referred to as **what-if analysis**. For example, this approach is used to address such questions as *what* is the effect on the decision to invest in a project *if* the cash receipts are 5 percent less than projected? 5 percent more? Although sensitivity analysis is computationally demanding if done manually, it can be done rapidly and easily using computers and software packages such as Lotus® and Excel®. In fact, these packages can also be used to carry out the NPV and IRR computations that have been illustrated manually throughout the chapter. They have built-in NPV and IRR functions that greatly facilitate the computational requirements.

To illustrate the potential effect of terminal value, assume that the after-tax annual operating cash flow of the project shown in Exhibit 20-13 is $3.1 million instead of $4 million. The net present value without salvage value is as follows:

Present value ($3,100,000 × 5.65)	$17,515,000
Less: Investment	18,000,000
Net present value	$ (485,000)

Without the terminal value, the project would be rejected. The net present value with salvage value of $2 million, however, is a positive result, meaning that the investment should be made.

Present value ($3,100,000 × 5.65)	$ 17,515,000
Present value ($2,000,000 × 0.322*)	644,000
Less: Investment	(18,000,000)
Net present value	$ 159,000

*Discount factor, 12 percent and 10 years (Exhibit 20B-1).

But what if the salvage value is less than expected? Suppose that the worst possible outcome is a salvage value of $1,600,000? What is the effect on the decision? The NPV can be recomputed under this new scenario.

Present value ($3,100,000 × 5.65)	$ 17,515,000
Present value ($1,600,000 × 0.322)	515,200
Less: Investment	(18,000,000)
Net present value	$ 30,200

Thus, under a pessimistic scenario, the NPV is still positive. This illustrates how sensitivity analysis can be used to deal with the uncertainty surrounding salvage value. It can also be used for other cash flow variables.

Discount Rates

Being overly conservative with discount rates can prove even more damaging. In theory, if future cash flows are known with certainty, the correct discount rate is a firm's cost of capital. In practice, future cash flows are uncertain, and managers often choose a discount rate higher than the cost of capital to deal with that uncertainty. If the rate chosen is excessively high, it will bias the selection process toward short-term investments.

To illustrate the effect of an excessive discount rate, consider the project in Exhibit 20-13 once again. Assume that the correct discount rate is 12 percent but that the firm uses 18 percent. The net present value using an 18 percent discount rate is calculated as follows:

Present value ($4,000,000 × 4.494*)	$17,976,000
Less: Investment	18,000,000
Net present value	$ (24,000)

*Discount rate for 18 percent and 10 years (Exhibit 20B-2).

The project would be rejected. With a higher discount rate, the discount factor decreases in magnitude much more rapidly than the discount factor for a lower rate. (Compare the discount factor for 12 percent, 5.65, with the factor for 18 percent, 4.494.) The effect of a higher discount factor is to place more weight on earlier cash flows and less weight on later cash flows, which favors short-term over long-term investments. This outcome makes it more difficult for automated manufacturing systems to appear as viable projects, since the cash returns required to justify the investment are received over a longer period of time. The same problem exists with P2 projects.[8]

---

8. Michael Porter, for example, contends that firms use excessively high hurdle rates to evaluate environmental projects. See Michael E. Porter, "Green and Competitive: Ending the Stalemate," *Harvard Business Review* (September–October 1995): 120–134.

SUMMARY

Capital investment decisions are concerned with the acquisition of long-term assets and usually involve a significant outlay of funds. The two types of capital investment projects are independent and mutually exclusive. Independent projects are projects that, if accepted or rejected, do not affect the cash flows of other projects. Mutually exclusive projects are those projects that, if accepted, preclude the acceptance of all other competing projects.

Managers make capital investment decisions by using formal models to decide whether to accept or reject proposed projects. These decision models are classified as nondiscounting or discounting, depending on whether they address the question of the time value of money. The two nondiscounting models are the payback period and the accounting rate of return.

The payback period is the time required for a firm to recover its initial investment. For even cash flows, it is calculated by dividing the investment by the annual cash flow. For uneven cash flows, the cash flows are summed until the investment is recovered. If only a fraction of a year is needed, the cash flow is estimated by assuming that the cash flows occur evenly within each year. The payback period ignores the time value of money and the profitability of projects because it does not consider the cash inflows available beyond the payback period. However, it does supply some useful information. The payback period is useful in assessing and controlling risk, minimizing the impact of an investment on a firm's liquidity, and controlling the risk of obsolescence.

The accounting rate of return is computed by dividing the average income expected from an investment by either the original or average investment. Unlike the payback period, it does consider the profitability of a project; however, it ignores the time value of money. The accounting rate of return may be useful to managers to screen new investments to ensure that certain accounting ratios are not adversely affected (specifically, accounting ratios that may be monitored to ensure compliance with debt covenants).

NPV is the difference between the present value of future cash flows and the initial investment outlay. To use the model, a required rate of return must be identified (usually, the cost of capital). The NPV method uses the required rate of return to compute the present value of a project's cash inflows and outflows. If the present value of the inflows is greater than the present value of the outflows, the net present value is greater than zero, and the project is profitable. If the NPV is less than zero, the project is not profitable and should be rejected.

The IRR is computed by finding the interest rate that equates the present value of a project's cash inflows with the present value of its cash outflows. If the IRR is greater than the required rate of return (cost of capital), the project is acceptable. If the IRR is less than the required rate of return, the project should be rejected.

In evaluating mutually exclusive or competing projects, managers have a choice of using NPV or IRR. When choosing among competing projects, the NPV model correctly identifies the best investment alternative. IRR, at times, may choose an inferior project. Thus, since NPV always provides the correct signal, it should be used.

Accurate and reliable cash flow forecasts are absolutely critical for capital budgeting analyses. Managers should assume responsibility for the accuracy of cash flow projections. All cash flows in a capital investment analysis should be after-tax cash flows. There are two different, but equivalent, ways to compute after-tax cash flows: the income method and the decomposition method. Although depreciation is not a cash flow, it does have cash flow implications because tax laws allow depreciation to be deducted in computing taxable income. Straight-line and double-declining-balance depreciation both produce the same total depreciation deductions over the life of the depreciated asset. Because the latter method accelerates depreciation, however, it would be preferred.

Capital investment in advanced technology and P2 projects is affected by the way in which inputs are determined. Much greater attention must be paid to the investment outlays because peripheral items can require substantial resources. Furthermore, in assessing benefits, intangible items such as product quality, environmental quality, and maintaining competitive position can be deciding factors. Choice of the required rate of return is also critical. The tendency of firms to use hurdle rates that are much greater than the cost of capital should be discontinued. Also, since the salvage value of an automated system can be considerable, it should be estimated and included in the analysis.

Appendix A: Present Value Concepts

An important feature of money is that it can be invested and can earn interest. A dollar today is not the same as a dollar tomorrow. This fundamental principle is the backbone of discounting methods. Discounting methods rely on the relationships between current and future dollars. Thus, to use discounting methods, we must understand these relationships.

Future Value

Suppose a bank advertises a 4 percent annual interest rate. If a customer invests $100, he or she would receive, after one year, the original $100 plus $4 interest [$100 + (0.04 ? $100) = (1 + 0.04) × $100 = 1.04 × $100 = $104]. This result can be expressed by the following equation, where F is the future amount, P is the initial or current outlay, and i is the interest rate:

$$F = P(1 + i) \qquad\qquad (20A.1)$$

For the example, $F = \$100 \times (1 + 0.04) = \$100 \times 1.04 = \$104$.

Now suppose that the same bank offers a 5 percent rate if the customer leaves the original deposit, plus any interest, on deposit for a total of two years. How much will the customer receive at the end of two years? Again, assume that a customer invests $100. Using Equation 20A.1, the customer will earn $105 at the end of Year 1 [$F = \$100 \times (1 + 0.05) = \$100 \times 1.05 = \$105$]. If this amount is left in the account for a second year, Equation 20A.1 is used again with P now assumed to be $105. At the end of the second year, then, the total is $110.25 [$F = \$105 \times (1 + 0.05) = \$105 \times 1.05 = \$110.25$]. In the second year, interest is earned on both the original deposit and the interest earned in the first year. The earning of interest on interest is referred to as **compounding of interest**. The value that will accumulate by the end of an investment's life, assuming a specified compound return, is the **future value**. The future value of the $100 deposit in the second example is $110.25.

A more direct way to compute the future value is possible. Since the first application of Equation 20A.1 can be expressed as $F = \$105 = \$100 \times 1.05$, the second application can be expressed as $F = \$105 \times 1.05 = \$100 \times 1.05 \times 1.05 = \$100(1.05)^2 = P(1 + i)^2$. This suggests the following formula for computing amounts for n periods into the future:

$$F = P(1 + i)^n \qquad (20A.2)$$

Present Value

Often, a manager needs to compute not the future value but the amount that must be invested *now* in order to earn some given future value. The amount that must be invested now to produce the future value is known as the **present value** of the future amount. For example, how much must be invested now in order to earn $363 two years from now, assuming that the interest rate is 10 percent? Or, put another way, what is the present value of $363 to be received two years from now?

In this example, the future value, the years, and the interest rate are all known; we want to know the current outlay that will produce that future amount. In Equation 20A.2, the variable representing the current outlay (the present value of F) is P. Thus, to compute the present value of a future outlay, all we need to do is solve Equation 20A.2 for P:

$$P = F/(1 + i)^n \qquad (20A.3)$$

Using Equation 20A.3, we can compute the present value of $363:

$$\begin{aligned} P &= \$363/(1 + 0.1)^2 \\ &= \$363/1.21 \\ &= \$300 \end{aligned}$$

The present value, $300, is what the future amount of $363 is worth *today*. All other things being equal, having $300 today is the same as having $363 two years from now. Put another way, if a firm requires a 10 percent rate of return, the most the firm would be willing to pay today is $300 for any investment that yields $363 two years from now.

The process of computing the present value of future cash flows is often referred to as **discounting**; thus, we say that we have discounted the future value of $363 to its present value of $300. The interest rate used to discount the future cash flow is the **discount rate**.

The expression $1/(1 + i)^n$ in Equation 20A.3 is the **discount factor**. By letting the discount factor, called *df*, equal $1/(1 + i)^n$, Equation 20A.3 can be expressed as $P = F(df)$. To simplify the computation of present value, a table of discount factors is given for various combinations of i and n (see Exhibit 20B-1 in Appendix B). For example, the discount factor for $i = 10$ percent and $n = 2$ is 0.826 (simply go to the 10 percent column of the table and move down to the second row). With the discount factor, the present value of $363 is computed as follows:

$$\begin{aligned} P &= F(df) \\ &= \$363 \times 0.826 \\ &= \$300 \text{ (rounded)} \end{aligned}$$

Present Value of an Uneven Series of Cash Flows

Exhibit 20B-1 can be used to compute the present value of any future cash flow or series of future cash flows. A series of future cash flows is called an **annuity**. The present value of an annuity is found by computing the present value of each future cash flow and then summing these values. For example, suppose that an investment is expected to produce the following annual cash flows: $110, $121, and $133.10. Assuming a discount rate of 10 percent, the present value of this series of cash flows is computed in Exhibit 20A-1 on the following page.

Present Value of a Uniform Series of Cash Flows

If the series of cash flows is even, the computation of the annuity's present value is simplified. Assume, for example, that an investment is expected to return $100 per year for three years. Using Exhibit 20B-1 and assuming a discount rate of 10 percent, the present value of the annuity is computed in Exhibit 20A-2 on the following page.

As with the uneven series of cash flows, the present value in Exhibit 20A-2 was computed by calculating the present value of each cash flow separately and then summing them. However, in the case of an annuity displaying uniform cash flows, the computations can be reduced from three to one as described in the note to the exhibit. The sum of the individual discount factors can be thought of as a discount factor for an annuity of uniform cash flows. A table of discount factors that can be used for an annuity of uniform cash flows is available in Exhibit 20B-2 in Appendix B.

EXHIBIT 20A-1	Present Value of an Uneven Series of Cash Flows		
Year	**Cash Receipt**	**Discount Factor**	**Present Value***
1	$110.00	0.909	$100.00
2	121.00	0.826	100.00
3	133.10	0.751	100.00
			$300.00

*Rounded.

EXHIBIT 20A-2	Present Value of a Uniform Series of Cash Flows		
Year	**Cash Receipt**	**Discount Factor**	**Present Value**
1	$100	0.909	$ 90.90
2	100	0.826	82.60
3	100	0.751	75.10
		2.486	$248.60

Note: The annual cash flow of $100 can be multiplied by the sum of the discount factors (2.486) to obtain the present value of the uniform series ($248.60).

Appendix B: Present Value Tables

EXHIBIT 20B-1

Present Value of $1*

Periods	2%	4%	6%	8%	10%	12%	14%	16%	18%	20%	22%	24%	26%	28%	30%	32%	40%
1	0.980	0.962	0.943	0.926	0.909	0.893	0.877	0.862	0.847	0.833	0.820	0.806	0.794	0.781	0.769	0.758	0.714
2	0.961	0.925	0.890	0.857	0.826	0.797	0.769	0.743	0.718	0.694	0.672	0.650	0.630	0.610	0.592	0.574	0.510
3	0.942	0.889	0.840	0.794	0.751	0.712	0.675	0.641	0.609	0.579	0.551	0.524	0.500	0.477	0.455	0.435	0.364
4	0.924	0.855	0.792	0.735	0.683	0.636	0.592	0.552	0.516	0.482	0.451	0.423	0.397	0.373	0.350	0.329	0.260
5	0.906	0.822	0.747	0.681	0.621	0.567	0.519	0.476	0.437	0.402	0.370	0.341	0.315	0.291	0.269	0.250	0.186
6	0.888	0.790	0.705	0.636	0.564	0.507	0.456	0.410	0.370	0.335	0.303	0.275	0.250	0.227	0.207	0.189	0.133
7	0.871	0.760	0.665	0.583	0.513	0.452	0.400	0.354	0.314	0.279	0.249	0.222	0.198	0.178	0.159	0.143	0.095
8	0.853	0.731	0.627	0.540	0.467	0.404	0.351	0.305	0.266	0.233	0.204	0.179	0.157	0.139	0.123	0.108	0.068
9	0.837	0.703	0.592	0.500	0.424	0.361	0.308	0.263	0.225	0.194	0.167	0.144	0.125	0.108	0.094	0.082	0.048
10	0.820	0.676	0.558	0.463	0.386	0.322	0.270	0.227	0.191	0.162	0.137	0.116	0.099	0.085	0.073	0.062	0.035
11	0.804	0.650	0.527	0.429	0.350	0.287	0.237	0.195	0.162	0.135	0.112	0.094	0.079	0.066	0.056	0.046	0.025
12	0.788	0.625	0.497	0.397	0.319	0.257	0.208	0.168	0.137	0.112	0.092	0.076	0.062	0.052	0.043	0.036	0.018
13	0.773	0.601	0.469	0.368	0.290	0.229	0.182	0.145	0.116	0.093	0.075	0.061	0.050	0.040	0.033	0.027	0.013
14	0.758	0.577	0.442	0.340	0.263	0.205	0.160	0.125	0.099	0.078	0.062	0.049	0.039	0.032	0.025	0.021	0.009
15	0.743	0.555	0.417	0.315	0.239	0.183	0.140	0.108	0.084	0.065	0.051	0.040	0.031	0.025	0.020	0.016	0.006
16	0.728	0.534	0.394	0.292	0.218	0.163	0.123	0.093	0.071	0.054	0.042	0.032	0.025	0.019	0.015	0.012	0.005
17	0.714	0.513	0.371	0.270	0.198	0.146	0.108	0.080	0.060	0.045	0.034	0.026	0.020	0.015	0.012	0.009	0.003
18	0.700	0.494	0.350	0.250	0.180	0.130	0.095	0.069	0.051	0.038	0.028	0.021	0.016	0.012	0.009	0.007	0.002
19	0.686	0.475	0.331	0.232	0.164	0.116	0.083	0.060	0.043	0.031	0.023	0.017	0.012	0.009	0.007	0.005	0.002
20	0.673	0.456	0.312	0.215	0.149	0.104	0.073	0.051	0.037	0.026	0.019	0.014	0.010	0.007	0.005	0.004	0.001
21	0.660	0.439	0.294	0.199	0.135	0.093	0.064	0.044	0.031	0.022	0.015	0.011	0.008	0.006	0.004	0.003	0.001
22	0.647	0.422	0.278	0.184	0.123	0.083	0.056	0.038	0.026	0.018	0.013	0.009	0.006	0.004	0.003	0.002	0.001
23	0.634	0.406	0.262	0.170	0.112	0.074	0.049	0.033	0.022	0.015	0.010	0.007	0.005	0.003	0.002	0.002	0.000
24	0.622	0.390	0.247	0.158	0.102	0.066	0.043	0.028	0.019	0.013	0.008	0.006	0.004	0.003	0.002	0.001	0.000
25	0.610	0.375	0.233	0.146	0.092	0.059	0.038	0.024	0.016	0.010	0.007	0.005	0.003	0.002	0.001	0.001	0.000
26	0.598	0.361	0.220	0.135	0.084	0.053	0.033	0.021	0.014	0.009	0.006	0.004	0.002	0.002	0.001	0.001	0.000
27	0.586	0.347	0.207	0.125	0.076	0.047	0.029	0.018	0.011	0.007	0.005	0.003	0.002	0.001	0.001	0.001	0.000
28	0.574	0.333	0.196	0.116	0.069	0.042	0.026	0.016	0.010	0.006	0.004	0.002	0.002	0.001	0.001	0.001	0.000
29	0.563	0.321	0.185	0.107	0.063	0.037	0.022	0.014	0.008	0.005	0.003	0.002	0.001	0.001	0.000	0.000	0.000
30	0.552	0.308	0.174	0.099	0.057	0.033	0.020	0.012	0.007	0.004	0.003	0.002	0.001	0.001	0.001	0.000	0.000

*$P_n = A/(1 + i)^n$.

EXHIBIT 20B-2   Present Value of an Annuity of $1 in Arrears*

Periods	2%	4%	6%	8%	10%	12%	14%	16%	18%	20%	22%	24%	26%	28%	30%	32%	40%
1	0.980	0.962	0.943	0.926	0.909	0.893	0.877	0.862	0.847	0.833	0.820	0.806	0.794	0.781	0.769	0.758	0.714
2	1.942	1.866	1.833	1.783	1.736	1.690	1.647	1.605	1.566	1.528	1.492	1.457	1.424	1.392	1.361	1.331	1.224
3	2.884	2.775	2.673	2.577	2.487	2.402	2.322	2.246	2.174	2.106	2.042	1.981	1.923	1.868	1.816	1.766	1.589
4	3.808	3.630	3.465	3.312	3.170	3.037	2.914	2.798	2.690	2.589	2.494	2.404	2.320	2.241	2.166	2.096	1.849
5	4.713	4.452	4.212	3.993	3.791	3.605	3.433	3.274	3.127	2.991	2.864	2.745	2.635	2.532	2.436	2.345	2.035
6	5.601	5.242	4.917	4.623	4.355	4.111	3.889	3.685	3.498	3.326	3.167	3.020	2.885	2.759	2.643	2.534	2.168
7	6.472	6.002	5.582	5.206	4.868	4.564	4.288	4.039	3.812	3.605	3.416	3.242	3.083	2.937	2.802	2.677	2.263
8	7.325	6.733	6.210	5.747	5.335	4.968	4.639	4.344	4.078	3.837	3.619	3.421	3.241	3.076	2.925	2.786	2.331
9	8.162	7.435	6.802	6.247	5.759	5.328	4.946	4.607	4.303	4.031	3.786	3.566	3.366	3.184	3.019	2.868	2.379
10	8.983	8.111	7.360	6.710	6.145	5.650	5.216	4.833	4.494	4.192	3.923	3.682	3.465	3.269	3.092	2.930	2.414
11	9.787	8.760	7.887	7.139	6.495	5.938	5.453	5.029	4.656	4.327	4.035	3.776	3.543	3.335	3.147	2.978	2.438
12	10.575	9.385	8.384	7.536	6.814	6.194	5.660	5.197	4.793	4.439	4.127	3.851	3.606	3.387	3.190	3.013	2.456
13	11.348	9.986	8.853	7.904	7.103	6.424	5.842	5.342	4.910	4.533	4.203	3.912	3.656	3.427	3.223	3.040	2.469
14	12.106	10.563	9.295	8.244	7.367	6.628	6.002	5.468	5.008	4.611	4.265	3.962	3.695	3.459	3.249	3.061	2.478
15	12.849	11.118	9.712	8.559	7.606	6.811	6.142	5.575	5.092	4.675	4.315	4.001	3.726	3.483	3.268	3.076	2.484
16	13.578	11.652	10.106	8.851	7.824	6.974	6.265	5.668	5.162	4.730	4.357	4.033	3.751	3.503	3.283	3.088	2.489
17	14.292	12.166	10.477	9.122	8.022	7.120	6.373	5.749	5.222	4.775	4.391	4.059	3.771	3.518	3.295	3.097	2.492
18	14.992	12.659	10.828	9.372	8.201	7.250	6.467	5.818	5.273	4.812	4.419	4.080	3.786	3.529	3.304	3.104	2.494
19	15.678	13.134	11.158	9.604	8.365	7.366	6.550	5.877	5.316	4.843	4.442	4.097	3.799	3.539	3.311	3.109	2.496
20	16.351	13.590	11.470	9.818	8.514	7.469	6.623	5.929	5.353	4.870	4.460	4.110	3.808	3.546	3.316	3.113	2.497
21	17.011	14.029	11.764	10.017	8.649	7.562	6.687	5.973	5.384	4.891	4.476	4.121	3.816	3.551	3.320	3.116	2.498
22	17.658	14.451	12.042	10.201	8.772	7.645	6.743	6.011	5.410	4.909	4.488	4.130	3.822	3.556	3.323	3.118	2.498
23	18.292	14.857	12.303	10.371	8.883	7.718	6.792	6.044	5.432	4.925	4.499	4.137	3.827	3.559	3.325	3.120	2.499
24	18.914	15.247	12.550	10.529	8.985	7.784	6.835	6.073	5.451	4.937	4.507	4.143	3.831	3.562	3.327	3.121	2.499
25	19.523	15.622	12.783	10.675	9.077	7.843	6.873	6.097	5.467	4.948	4.514	4.147	3.834	3.564	3.329	3.122	2.499
26	20.121	15.983	13.003	10.810	9.161	7.896	6.906	6.118	5.480	4.956	4.520	4.151	3.837	3.566	3.330	3.123	2.500
27	20.707	16.330	13.211	10.935	9.237	7.943	6.935	6.136	5.492	4.964	4.524	4.154	3.839	3.567	3.331	3.123	2.500
28	21.281	16.663	13.406	11.051	9.307	7.984	6.961	6.152	5.502	4.970	4.528	4.157	3.840	3.568	3.331	3.124	2.500
29	21.844	16.984	13.591	11.158	9.370	8.022	6.983	6.166	5.510	4.975	4.531	4.159	3.841	3.569	3.332	3.124	2.500
30	22.396	17.292	13.765	11.258	9.427	8.055	7.003	6.177	5.517	4.979	4.534	4.160	3.842	3.569	3.332	3.124	2.500

$$^{*}P_n = (1/i)[1 - 1/(1 + i)^n].$$

REVIEW PROBLEMS AND SOLUTIONS

1 BASICS OF CAPITAL INVESTMENT (IGNORE INCOME TAXES FOR THIS EXERCISE.)

Kenn Day, manager of Day Laboratory, is investigating the possibility of acquiring some new test equipment. To acquire the equipment requires an initial outlay of $300,000. To raise the capital, Kenn will sell stock valued at $200,000 (the stock pays dividends of $24,000 per year) and borrow $100,000. The loan for $100,000 would carry an interest rate of 6 percent. Kenn figures that his weighted cost of capital is 10 percent [(2/3 × 0.12) + (1/3 × 0.06)]. This weighted cost of capital is the rate he will use for capital investment decisions.

Kenn estimates that the new test equipment will produce a cash inflow of $50,000 per year. Kenn expects the equipment to last for 20 years.

Required:

1. Compute the payback period.
2. Assuming that depreciation is $14,000 per year, compute the accounting rate of return (on total investment).
3. Compute the NPV of the investment.
4. Compute the IRR of the investment.
5. Should Kenn buy the equipment? Explain.

1. The payback period is $300,000/$50,000, or six years.

2. The accounting rate of return is ($50,000 − $14,000)/$300,000, or 12 percent.

3. From Exhibit 20B-2, the discount factor for an annuity with *i* at 10 percent and *n* at 20 years is 8.514. Thus, the NPV is [(8.514 × $50,000) − $300,000], or $125,700.

4. The discount factor associated with the IRR is 6.00 ($300,000/$50,000). From Exhibit 20B-2, the IRR is between 14 and 16 percent (using the row corresponding to period 20).

5. Since the NPV is positive and the IRR is greater than Kenn's cost of capital, the test equipment is a sound investment. This assumes, of course, that the cash flow projections are accurate.

2 CAPITAL INVESTMENT WITH COMPETING PROJECTS (WITH TAX EFFECTS)

Weins Postal Service (WPS) has decided to acquire a new delivery truck. The choice has been narrowed to two models. The following information has been gathered for each model:

	Custom	*Deluxe*
Acquisition cost	$20,000	$25,000
Annual operating costs	$3,500	$2,000
Depreciation method	MACRS	MACRS
Expected salvage value	$5,000	$8,000

WPS's cost of capital is 14 percent. The company plans to use the truck for five years and then sell it for its salvage value. Assume the combined state and federal tax rate is 40 percent.

Required:

1. Compute the after-tax operating cash flows for each model.
2. Compute the NPV for each model, and make a recommendation.

1. For light trucks, MACRS guidelines allow a 5-year life. Using the rates from Exhibit 20-11 on page 898, depreciation is calculated for each model.

Year	Custom	Deluxe
1	$ 4,000	$ 5,000
2	6,400	8,000
3	3,840	4,800
4	2,304	2,880
5	1,152*	1,440*
Total	$17,696	$22,120

*Only half the depreciation is allowed in the year of disposal.

The after-tax operating cash flows are computed using the spreadsheet format.

Custom

Year	$(1 - t)R$	$-(1 - t)C$	tNC	Other	CF
1	n/a	$(2,100)	$1,600		$ (500)
2	n/a	(2,100)	2,560		460
3	n/a	(2,100)	1,536		(564)
4	n/a	(2,100)	922		(1,178)
5	$1,618[a]	(2,100)	461	$2,304[b]	2,283

[a]Salvage value ($5,000) − Book value ($20,000 − $17,696 = $2,304) = $2,696; 0.60 × $2,696 = $1,618
[b]Recovery of capital = Book value = $2,304. Capital recovered is not taxed—only the gain on sale. Footnote (a) illustrates how the gain is treated.

Deluxe

Year	$(1 - t)R$	$-(1 - t)C$	tNC	Other	CF
1	n/a	$(1,200)	$2,000		$ 800
2	n/a	(1,200)	3,200		2,000
3	n/a	(1,200)	1,920		720
4	n/a	(1,200)	1,152		(48)
5	$3,072[a]	(1,200)	576	$2,880[b]	5,328

[a]Salvage value ($8,000) − Book value ($25,000 − $22,120 = $2,880) = $5,120; 0.60 × $5,120 = $3,072.
[b]Recovery of capital = Book value = $2,880. Capital recovered is not taxed—only the gain on sale of the asset. Footnote (a) illustrates how the gain is treated. The nontaxable item requires an additional column for the spreadsheet analysis.

2. NPV computation—Custom:

Year	Cash Flow	Discount Factor	Present Value
0	$(20,000)	1.000	$(20,000)
1	(500)	0.877	(439)
2	460	0.769	354
3	(564)	0.675	(381)
4	(1,178)	0.592	(697)
5	2,283	0.519	1,185
Net present value			$(19,978)

NPV computation—Deluxe:

Year	Cash Flow	Discount Factor	Present Value
0	$(25,000)	1.000	$(25,000)
1	800	0.877	702
2	2,000	0.769	1,538
3	720	0.675	486
4	(48)	0.592	(28)
5	5,328	0.519	2,765
Net present value			$(19,537)

The Deluxe model should be chosen, since it has the larger NPV, indicating that it is the least costly of the two cars. Note also that the net present values are negative and that we are choosing the least costly investment.

KEY TERMS

QUESTIONS FOR WRITING AND DISCUSSION

1. Explain the difference between independent projects and mutually exclusive projects.
2. Explain why the timing and quantity of cash flows are important in capital investment decisions.
3. The time value of money is ignored by the payback period and the accounting rate of return. Explain why this is a major deficiency in these two models.
4. What is the payback period? Name and discuss three possible reasons that the payback period is used to help make capital investment decisions.
5. What is the accounting rate of return?
6. What is the cost of capital? What role does it play in capital investment decisions?
7. The IRR is the true or actual rate of return being earned by the project. Do you agree or disagree? Discuss.
8. Explain how the NPV is used to determine whether a project should be accepted or rejected.
9. Explain why NPV is generally preferred over IRR when choosing among competing or mutually exclusive projects. Why would managers continue to use IRR to choose among mutually exclusive projects?
10. Why is it important to have accurate projections of cash flows for potential capital investments?
11. What are the principal tax implications that should be considered in Year 0?
12. Explain why the MACRS method of recognizing depreciation is better than the straight-line method.
13. Explain the important factors to consider for capital investment decisions relating to advanced technology and P2 opportunities.
14. Explain what a postaudit is and how it can provide useful input for future capital investment decisions—especially those involving advanced technology.
15. Explain what sensitivity analysis is. How can it help in capital budgeting decisions?

EXERCISES

20-1 PAYBACK AND ARR

LO2 Each of the following scenarios is independent. All cash flows are after-tax cash flows.

Required:

1. Don Blackburn has purchased a tractor for $62,500. He expects to receive a net cash flow of $15,625 per year from the investment. What is the payback period for Don?
2. Bill Johnson invested $600,000 in a laundromat. The facility has a 10-year life expectancy with no expected salvage value. The laundromat will produce a net cash flow of $180,000 per year. What is the accounting rate of return? Use original investment for the computation.
3. Kathleen Shorts has purchased a business building for $700,000. She expects to receive the following cash flows over a 10-year period:

Year 1: $87,500
Year 2: $122,500
Years 3–10: $175,000

What is the payback period for Kathleen? What is the accounting rate of return (using average investment and assuming straight-line depreciation over the 10 years)?

20-2   FUTURE VALUE, PRESENT VALUE

Appendix   The following cases are each independent of the others.

Required:

1. Sam Lilliam places $5,000 in a savings account that pays 3 percent. Suppose Sam leaves the original deposit plus any interest in the account for two years. How much will Sam have in savings after two years?
2. Suppose that the parents of a 12-year-old son want to have $80,000 in a fund six years from now to provide support for his college education. How much must they invest now to have the desired amount if the investment can earn 4 percent? 6 percent? 8 percent?
3. Killian Manufacturing is asking $500,000 for automated equipment, which is expected to last six years and will generate equal annual net cash inflows (because of reductions in labor costs, material waste, and so on). What is the minimum cash inflow that must be realized each year to justify the acquisition? The cost of capital is 8 percent.

20-3   NPV AND IRR

LO1, LO3, LO4   Each of the following scenarios is independent. All cash flows are after-tax cash flows.

Required:

1. Jackman Corporation is considering the purchase of a computer-aided manufacturing system. The cash benefits will be $1,000,000 per year. The system costs $6,000,000 and will last eight years. Compute the NPV assuming a discount rate of 10 percent. Should the company buy the new system?
2. Lehi Henderson has just invested $1,350,000 in a restaurant specializing in Italian food. He expects to receive $217,350 per year for the next eight years. His cost of capital is 5.5 percent. Compute the internal rate of return. Did Lehi make a good decision?

20-4   BASIC CONCEPTS

LO1, LO2, LO3, LO4   Roberts Company is considering an investment in equipment that is capable of producing electronic parts twice as fast as existing technology. The outlay required is $2,340,000. The equipment is expected to last five years and will have no salvage value. The expected cash flows associated with the project are as follows:

Year	Cash Revenues	Cash Expenses
1	$3,042,000	$2,340,000
2	3,042,000	2,340,000
3	3,042,000	2,340,000
4	3,042,000	2,340,000
5	3,042,000	2,340,000

Required:

1. Compute the project's payback period.
2. Compute the project's accounting rate of return on:
    a. Initial investment
    b. Average investment
3. Compute the project's net present value, assuming a required rate of return of 10 percent.
4. Compute the project's internal rate of return.

20-5 NPV

LO1, LO3   A hospital is considering the possibility of two new purchases: new X-ray equipment and new biopsy equipment. Each project would require an investment of $750,000. The expected life for each is five years with no expected salvage value. The net cash inflows associated with the two independent projects are as follows:

Year	X-Ray Equipment	Sonogram Equipment
1	$375,000	$ 75,000
2	150,000	75,000
3	300,000	525,000
4	150,000	600,000
5	75,000	675,000

Required:

Compute the net present value of each project, assuming a required rate of 12 percent.

20-6 PAYBACK, ACCOUNTING RATE OF RETURN

LO1, LO2   Refer to **Exercise 20-5**.

1. Compute the payback period for each project. Assume that the manager of the hospital accepts only projects with a payback period of three years or less. Offer some reasons why this may be a rational strategy even though the NPV computed in **Exercise 20-5** may indicate otherwise.
2. Compute the accounting rate of return for each project using average investment.

20-7 NPV: BASIC CONCEPTS

LO3   Escucha Hearing Clinic is considering an investment that requires an outlay of $370,000 and promises a net cash inflow one year from now of $450,000. Assume the cost of capital is 12 percent.

Required:

1. Break the $450,000 future cash inflow into three components:
    a. The return of the original investment
    b. The cost of capital
    c. The profit earned on the investment
    Now, compute the present value of the profit earned on the investment.
2. Compute the NPV of the investment. Compare this with the present value of the profit computed in Requirement 1. What does this tell you about the meaning of NPV?

20-8 SOLVING FOR UNKNOWNS

LO3, LO4   Consider each of the following independent cases.

Required:

1. Hal's Stunt Company is investing $120,000 in a project that will yield a uniform series of cash inflows over the next four years. If the internal rate of return is 14 percent, how much cash inflow per year can be expected?
2. Warner Medical Clinic has decided to invest in some new blood diagnostic equipment. The equipment will have a 3-year life and will produce a uniform series of cash savings. The net present value of the equipment is $1,750, using a

discount rate of 8 percent. The internal rate of return is 12 percent. Determine the investment and the amount of cash savings realized each year.

3. A new lathe costing $60,096 will produce savings of $12,000 per year. How many years must the lathe last if an IRR of 18 percent is realized?

4. The NPV of a new product (a new brand of candy) is $6,075. The product has a life of four years and produces the following cash flows:

Year 1	$15,000
Year 2	20,000
Year 3	30,000
Year 4	?

The cost of the project is three times the cash flow produced in Year 4. The discount rate is 10 percent. Find the cost of the project and the cash flow for Year 4.

20-9   ADVANCED TECHNOLOGY, PAYBACK, NPV, IRR, SENSITIVITY ANALYSIS

LO2, LO3, LO4, LO5, LO7

Gina Ripley, president of Dearing Company, is considering the purchase of a computer-aided manufacturing system. The annual net cash benefits/savings associated with the system are described as follows:

Decreased waste	$300,000
Increased quality	400,000
Decrease in operating costs	600,000
Increase in on-time deliveries	200,000

The system will cost $9,000,000 and last 10 years. The company's cost of capital is 12 percent.

Required:

1. Calculate the payback period for the system. Assume that the company has a policy of only accepting projects with a payback of five years or less. Would the system be acquired?

2. Calculate the NPV and IRR for the project. Should the system be purchased—even if it does not meet the payback criterion?

3. The project manager reviewed the projected cash flows and pointed out that two items had been missed. First, the system would have a salvage value, net of any tax effects, of $1,000,000 at the end of 10 years. Second, the increased quality and delivery performance would allow the company to increase its market share by 20 percent. This would produce an additional annual net benefit of $300,000. Recalculate the payback period, NPV, and IRR given this new information. (For the IRR computation, initially ignore salvage value.) Does the decision change? Suppose that the salvage value is only half what is projected. Does this make a difference in the outcome? Does salvage value have any real bearing on the company's decision?

20-10   NPV VERSUS IRR

LO5   Covington Pharmacies has decided to automate its insurance claims process. Two networked computer systems are being considered. The systems have an expected life of two years. The net cash flows associated with the systems are as follows. The cash benefits represent the savings created by switching from a manual to an automated system.

Year	System I	System II
0	$(120,000)	$(120,000)
1	—	76,628
2	162,708	76,628

The company's cost of capital is 10 percent.

Required:

1. Compute the NPV and the IRR for each investment.
2. Show that the project with the larger NPV is the correct choice for the company.

20-11 COMPUTATION OF AFTER-TAX CASH FLOWS

LO6 Masamora Company is considering two independent projects. One project involves a new product line, and the other involves the acquisition of forklifts for the materials handling department. The projected annual operating revenues and expenses are as follows:

Project I (investment in a new product)

Revenues	$ 90,000
Cash expenses	(45,000)
Depreciation	(15,000)
Income before income taxes	$ 30,000
Income taxes	(12,000)
Net income	$ 18,000

Project II (acquisition of two forklifts)

Cash expenses	$30,000
Depreciation	30,000

Required:

Compute the after-tax cash flows of each project. The tax rate is 40 percent and includes federal and state assessments.

20-12 MACRS, NPV

LO3, LO6 Lilly Company is planning to buy a set of special tools for its grinding operation. The cost of the tools is $18,000. The tools have a 3-year life and qualify for the use of the 3-year MACRS. The tax rate is 40 percent; the cost of capital is 12 percent.

Spreadsheet

Required:

1. Calculate the present value of the tax depreciation shield, assuming that straight-line depreciation with a half-year life is used.
2. Calculate the present value of the tax depreciation shield, assuming that MACRS is used.
3. What is the benefit to the company of using MACRS?

20-13 INFLATION

LO3, LO6 Excalibur Company is planning on introducing a new product that will have a 2-year life. Producing the product requires an initial outlay of $20,000; it will generate after-tax cash inflows of $11,000 and $12,000 in the two years. The company's cost of capital is 12 percent. During the coming two years, inflation is expected to average 5 percent. The cash flows have not been adjusted for inflation. The cost of capital, however, reflects an inflationary component.

Required:

1. Compute the NPV using the unadjusted cash flows.
2. Compute the NPV using cash flows adjusted for inflationary effects.

20-14 VARIOUS CASH FLOW COMPUTATIONS

LO6   Solve each of the following independent cases:

1. A printing company has decided to purchase a new printing press. Its old press will be sold for $10,000. (It has a book value of $25,000.) The new press will cost $50,000. Assuming that the tax rate is 40 percent, compute the net after-tax cash outflow.

2. The maintenance department is purchasing new diagnostic equipment costing $30,000. Additional cash expenses of $2,000 per year are required to operate the equipment. MACRS depreciation will be used (5-year property qualification). Assuming a tax rate of 40 percent, prepare a schedule of after-tax cash flows for the first four years.

3. The projected income for a project during its first year of operation is as follows:

Cash revenues	$120,000
Less: Cash expenses	(50,000)
Depreciation	(20,000)
Income before income taxes	$ 50,000
Less: Income taxes	20,000
Net income	$ 30,000

Compute the following:

a. After-tax cash flow
b. After-tax cash flow from revenues
c. After-tax cash expenses
d. Cash inflow from the shielding effect of depreciation

PROBLEMS

20-15 POLLUTION PREVENTION, P2 INVESTMENT

LO2, LO3,   Lewis Company produces jewelry that requires electroplating with gold, silver, and other
LO4, LO5,   valuable metals. Electroplating uses large amounts of water and chemicals, producing
LO6, LO7   wastewater with a number of toxic residuals. Currently, Lewis uses settlement tanks to remove waste; unfortunately, the approach is inefficient, and much of the toxic residue is left in the water that is discharged into a local river. The amount of toxic discharge exceeds the legal, allowable amounts, and the company is faced with substantial, ongoing environmental fines. The environmental violations are also drawing unfavorable public reaction, and sales are being affected. A lawsuit is also impending, which could prove to be quite costly.

Management is now considering the installation of a zero-discharge, closed-loop system to treat the wastewater. The proposed closed-loop system would not only purify the wastewater, but it would also produce cleaner water than that currently being used, increasing plating quality. The closed-loop system would produce only four pounds of sludge, and the sludge would be virtually pure metal, with significant market value. The system requires an investment of $420,000 and will cost $30,000 in increased annual operation plus an annual purchase of $5,000 of filtration medium. However, management projects the following savings:

Water usage	$ 45,000
Chemical usage	28,000
Sludge disposal	60,000
Recovered metal sales	30,000
Sampling of discharge	80,000
Total	$243,000

The equipment qualifies as a 7-year MACRS asset. Management has decided to use straight-line depreciation for tax purposes, using the required half-year convention. The tax rate is 40 percent. The projected life of the system is 10 years. The hurdle rate is 16 percent for all capital budgeting projects, although the company's cost of capital is 12 percent.

Required:

1. Based on the financial data provided, prepare a schedule of expected cash flows.
2. What is the payback period?
3. Calculate the NPV of the closed-loop system. Should the company invest in the system?
4. The calculation in Requirement 3 ignored several factors that could affect the project's viability: savings from avoiding the annual fines, positive effect on sales due to favorable environmental publicity, increased plating quality from the new system, and the avoidance of the lawsuit. Can these factors be quantified? If so, should they have been included in the analysis? Suppose, for example, that the annual fines being incurred are $50,000, the sales effect is $40,000 per year, the quality effect is not estimable, and that cancellation of the lawsuit because of the new system would avoid an expected settlement at the end of Year 3 (including legal fees) of $200,000. Assuming these are all after-tax amounts, what effect would their inclusion have on the payback period? On the NPV?

20-16 DISCOUNT RATES, QUALITY, MARKET SHARE, CONTEMPORARY MANUFACTURING ENVIRONMENT

LO3, LO5, LO7   Sweeney Manufacturing has a plant where the equipment is essentially worn out. The equipment must be replaced, and Sweeney is considering two competing investment alternatives. The first alternative would replace the worn-out equipment with traditional production equipment; the second alternative uses contemporary technology and has computer-aided design and manufacturing capabilities. The investment and after-tax operating cash flows for each alternative are as follows:

Year	Traditional Equipment	Contemporary Technology
0	$(1,000,000)	$(4,000,000)
1	600,000	200,000
2	400,000	400,000
3	200,000	600,000
4	200,000	800,000
5	200,000	800,000
6	200,000	800,000

(continued)

Year	Traditional Equipment	Contemporary Technology
7	200,000	1,000,000
8	200,000	2,000,000
9	200,000	2,000,000
10	200,000	2,000,000

The company uses a discount rate of 18 percent for all of its investments. The company's cost of capital is 14 percent.

Required:

1. Calculate the net present value for each investment using a discount rate of 18 percent.
2. Calculate the net present value for each investment using a discount rate of 14 percent.
3. Which rate should the company use to compute the net present value? Explain.
4. Now, assume that if the traditional equipment is purchased, the competitive position of the firm will deteriorate because of lower quality (relative to competitors who did automate). Marketing estimates that the loss in market share will decrease the projected net cash inflows by 50 percent for Years 3–10. Recalculate the NPV of the traditional equipment given this outcome. What is the decision now? Discuss the importance of assessing the effect of intangible and indirect benefits.

20-17   COMPETING P2 INVESTMENTS

LO3, LO5, LO6, LO7

Spreadsheet

Ron Booth, the CEO for Sunders Manufacturing, was wondering which of two pollution control systems he should choose. The firm's current production process produces a gaseous and a liquid residue. A recent state law mandated that emissions of these residues be reduced to levels considerably below current performance. Failure to reduce the emissions would invoke stiff fines and possible closure of the operating plant. Fortunately, the new law provided a transition period, and Ron had used the time wisely. His engineers had developed two separate proposals. The first proposal involved the acquisition of scrubbers for gaseous emissions and a treatment facility to remove the liquid residues. The second proposal was more radical. It entailed the redesign of the manufacturing process and the acquisition of new production equipment to support this new design. The new process would solve the environmental problem by avoiding the production of residues.

Although the equipment for each proposal normally would qualify as 7-year property, the state managed to obtain an agreement with the federal government to allow any pollution abatement equipment to qualify as 5-year property. State tax law follows federal guidelines. Both proposals qualify for the 5-year property benefit.

Ron's vice president of marketing has projected an increase in revenues because of favorable environmental performance publicity. This increase is the result of selling more of Sunders's products to environmentally conscious customers. However, because the second approach is "greener," the vice president believes that the revenue increase will be greater. Cost and other data relating to the two proposals are as follows:

	Scrubbers and Treatment	Process Redesign
Initial outlay	$50,000,000	$100,000,000
Incremental revenues	10,000,000	30,000,000
Incremental cash expenses	24,000,000	10,000,000

The expected life for each investment's equipment is six years. The expected salvage value is $2,000,000 for scrubbers and treatment equipment and $3,000,000 for process redesign equipment. The combined federal and state tax rate is 40 percent. The cost of capital is 10 percent.

Required:

1. Compute the NPV of each proposal and make a recommendation to Ron Booth.
2. The environmental manager observes that the scrubbers and treatment facility enable the company to just meet state emission standards. She feels that the standards will likely increase within three years. If so, this would entail a modification at the end of three years costing an additional $8,000,000. Also, she is concerned that continued liquid residue releases—even those meeting state standards—could push a local lake into a hazardous state by the end of three years. If so, this could prompt political action requiring the company to clean up the lake. Cleanup costs would range between $40,000,000 and $60,000,000. Analyze and discuss the effect this new information has on the two alternatives. If you have read the chapter on environmental cost management, describe how the concept of ecoefficiency applies to this setting.

20-18 PAYBACK, NPV, MANAGERIAL INCENTIVES, ETHICAL BEHAVIOR

LO1, LO2, LO3

Spreadsheet

Kent Tessman, manager of a Dairy Products Division , was pleased with his division's performance over the past three years. Each year, divisional profits had increased, and he had earned a sizable bonus. (Bonuses are a linear function of the division's reported income.) He had also received considerable attention from higher management. A vice president had told him in confidence that if his performance over the next three years matched his first three, he would be promoted to higher management.

Determined to fulfill these expectations, Kent made sure that he personally reviewed every capital budget request. He wanted to be certain that any funds invested would provide good, solid returns. (The division's cost of capital is 10 percent.) At the moment, he is reviewing two independent requests. Proposal A involves automating a manufacturing operation that is currently labor intensive. Proposal B centers on developing and marketing a new ice cream product. Proposal A requires an initial outlay of $250,000, and Proposal B requires $312,500. Both projects could be funded, given the status of the division's capital budget. Both have an expected life of six years and have the following projected after-tax cash flows:

Year	Proposal A	Proposal B
1	$150,000	$ (37,500)
2	125,000	(25,000)
3	75,000	(12,500)
4	37,500	212,500
5	25,000	275,000
6	12,500	337,500

After careful consideration of each investment, Kent approved funding of Proposal A and rejected Proposal B.

Required:

1. Compute the NPV for each proposal.
2. Compute the payback period for each proposal.
3. According to your analysis, which proposal(s) should be accepted? Explain.

4. Explain why Kent accepted only Proposal A. Considering the possible reasons for rejection, would you judge his behavior to be ethical? Explain.

20-19   BASIC IRR ANALYSIS

LO1, LO4   Ireland Company is considering installing a new IT system. The cost of the new system is estimated to be $750,000, but it would produce after-tax savings of $150,000 per year in labor costs. The estimated life of the new system is 10 years, with no salvage value expected. Intrigued by the possibility of saving $150,000 per year and having a more reliable information system, the president of Ireland has asked for an analysis of the project's economic viability. All capital projects are required to earn at least the firm's cost of capital, which is 12 percent.

Required:

1. Calculate the project's internal rate of return. Should the company acquire the new IT system?
2. Suppose that savings are less than claimed. Calculate the minimum annual cash savings that must be realized for the project to earn a rate equal to the firm's cost of capital. Comment on the safety margin that exists, if any.
3. Suppose that the life of the IT system is overestimated by two years. Repeat Requirements 1 and 2 under this assumption. Comment on the usefulness of this information.

20-20   REPLACEMENT DECISION, COMPUTING AFTER-TAX CASH FLOWS, BASIC NPV ANALYSIS

LO1, LO3,   Okmulgee Hospital (a large metropolitan for-profit hospital) is considering replacing
LO5, LO6   its MRI equipment with a new model manufactured by a different company. The old MRI equipment was acquired three years ago, has a remaining life of five years, and will have a salvage value of $100,000. The book value is $2,000,000. Straight-line depreciation with a half-year convention is being used for tax purposes. The cash operating costs of the existing MRI equipment total $1,000,000 per year.

The new MRI equipment has an initial cost of $5,000,000 and will have cash operating costs of $500,000 per year. The new MRI will have a life of five years and a salvage value of $1,000,000 at the end of the fifth year. MACRS depreciation will be used for tax purposes. If the new MRI equipment is purchased, the old one will be sold for $500,000. The company needs to decide whether to keep the old MRI equipment or buy the new one. The cost of capital is 12 percent. The combined federal and state tax rate is 40 percent.

Required:

Compute the NPV of each alternative. Should the company keep the old MRI equipment or buy the new one?

20-21   INFLATION AND CAPITAL BUDGETING

LO3, LO5,   Leo Thayn, manager of the Electronics Manufacturing Division, has been pushing head-
LO6   quarters to grant approval for the installation of a new computer-aided design system. Finally, in the last executive meeting, Leo was told that if he could show the new system would increase the firm's value, then it would be approved. Leo has collected the following information:

	Old System	CAD System
Initial investment	—	$1,250,000
Annual operating costs	$300,000	$95,000
Annual depreciation	$100,000	MACRS
Effective tax rate*	34%	34%
Cost of capital	12%	12%
Expected life	10 years	10 years
Salvage value	none	none

*The division is located in a state that provided a tax incentive package that lowers the tax rate from the usual average of 40 percent to 34 percent. This incentive package was granted for a 15-year period. Ten years of benefits remain.

With the exception of the cost of capital, the preceding information ignores the rate of inflation, which has been 4 percent per year and is expected to continue at this level for the next decade.

Required:

1. Compute the NPV for each system.
2. Compute the NPV for each system, adjusting the future cash flows for the rate of inflation.
3. Comment on the importance of adjusting cash flows for inflationary effects.

20-22   CAPITAL INVESTMENT, DISCOUNT RATES, INTANGIBLE AND INDIRECT BENEFITS, TIME HORIZON, CONTEMPORARY MANUFACTURING ENVIRONMENT

LO3, LO6, LO7

Mallette Manufacturing, Inc., produces washing machines, dryers, and dishwashers. Because of increasing competition, Mallette is considering investing in an automated manufacturing system. Since competition is most keen for dishwashers, the production process for this line has been selected for initial evaluation. The automated system for the dishwasher line would replace an existing system (purchased one year ago for $6 million). Although the existing system will be fully depreciated in nine years, it is expected to last another 10 years. The automated system would also have a useful life of 10 years.

The existing system is capable of producing 100,000 dishwashers per year. Sales and production data using the existing system are provided by the accounting department:

Sales per year (units)	100,000
Selling price	$300
Costs per unit:	
Direct materials	80
Direct labor	90
Volume-related overhead	20
Direct fixed overhead	40*

*All cash expenses with the exception of depreciation, which is $6 per unit. The existing equipment is being depreciated using straight-line with no salvage value considered.

The automated system will cost $34 million to purchase, plus an estimated $20 million in software and implementation. (Assume that all investment outlays occur at the beginning of the first year.) If the automated equipment is purchased, the old equipment can be sold for $3 million.

The automated system will require fewer parts for production and will produce with less waste. Because of this, the direct material cost per unit will be reduced by 25 percent. Automation will also require fewer support activities, and as a consequence, volume-related overhead will be reduced by $4 per unit and direct fixed overhead (other than depreciation) by $17 per unit. Direct labor is reduced by 60 percent. Assume, for simplicity, that the new investment will be depreciated on a pure straight-line basis for tax purposes with no salvage value. Ignore the half-life convention.

The firm's cost of capital is 12 percent, but management chooses to use 20 percent as the required rate of return for evaluation of investments. The combined federal and state tax rate is 40 percent.

Required:

1. Compute the net present value for the old system and the automated system. Which system would the company choose?
2. Repeat the net present value analysis of Requirement 1, using 12 percent as the discount rate.
3. Upon seeing the projected sales for the old system, the marketing manager commented: "Sales of 100,000 units per year cannot be maintained in the current competitive environment for more than one year unless we buy the automated system. The automated system will allow us to compete on the basis of quality and lead time. If we keep the old system, our sales will drop by 10,000 units per year." Repeat the net present value analysis, using this new information and a 12 percent discount rate.
4. An industrial engineer for Mallette noticed that salvage value for the automated equipment had not been included in the analysis. He estimated that the equipment could be sold for $4 million at the end of 10 years. He also estimated that the equipment of the old system would have no salvage value at the end of 10 years. Repeat the net present value analysis using this information, the information in Requirement 3, and a 12 percent discount rate.
5. Given the outcomes of the previous four requirements, comment on the importance of providing accurate inputs for assessing investments in automated manufacturing systems.

20-23   NPV, MAKE OR BUY, MACRS, BASIC ANALYSIS

LO3, LO6

Jonfran Company manufactures three different models of paper shredders including the waste container, which serves as the base. While the shredder heads are different for all three models, the waste container is the same. The number of waste containers that Jonfran will need during the next five years is estimated as follows:

2007	50,000
2008	50,000
2009	52,000
2010	55,000
2011	55,000

The equipment used to manufacture the waste container must be replaced because it is broken and cannot be repaired. The new equipment would have a purchase price of $945,000 with terms of 2/10, n/30; the company's policy is to take all purchase discounts. The freight on the equipment would be $11,000, and installation costs would total $22,900. The equipment would be purchased in December 2006 and placed into service on January 1, 2007. It would have a 5-year economic life and would be treated as 3-year property under MACRS. This equipment is expected to have a salvage value of $12,000 at the end of its economic life in 2007. The new equipment would be more efficient than the old equipment, resulting in a 25 percent reduction in both direct material and variable overhead. The savings in direct material would result in an additional 1-time decrease in working capital requirements of $2,500, resulting from a reduction in direct material inventories. This working capital reduction would be recognized at the time of equipment acquisition.

The old equipment is fully depreciated and is not included in the fixed overhead. The old equipment from the plant can be sold for a salvage amount of $1,500. Rather than replace the equipment, one of Jonfran's production managers has suggested that the waste containers be purchased. One supplier has quoted a price of $27 per container. This price is $8 less than Jonfran's current manufacturing cost, which is as follows:

Direct materials		$10
Direct labor		8
Variable overhead		6
Fixed overhead:		
Supervision	$2	
Facilities	5	
General	4	11
Total unit cost		$35

Jonfran uses a plantwide fixed overhead rate in its operations. If the waste containers are purchased outside, the salary and benefits of one supervisor, included in fixed overhead at $45,000, would be eliminated. There would be no other changes in the other cash and noncash items included in fixed overhead except depreciation on the new equipment.

Jonfran is subject to a 40 percent tax rate. Management assumes that all cash flows occur at the end of the year and uses a 12 percent after-tax discount rate.

Required:

1. Prepare a schedule of cash flows for the make alternative. Calculate the NPV of the make alternative.
2. Prepare a schedule of cash flows for the buy alternative. Calculate the NPV of the buy alternative.
3. Which should Jonfran do—make or buy the containers? What qualitative factors should be considered? *(CMA adapted)*

20-24 STRUCTURED PROBLEM SOLVING, CASH FLOWS, NPV, CHOICE OF DISCOUNT RATE, ADVANCED MANUFACTURING ENVIRONMENT

LO3, LO6, LO7

Brindon Thayn, president and owner of Orangeville Metal Works, has just returned from a trip to Europe. While there, he toured several plants that use robotic manufacturing. Seeing the efficiency and success of these companies, Brindon became convinced that robotic manufacturing is essential for Orangeville to maintain its competitive position.

Based on this conviction, Brindon requested an analysis detailing the costs and benefits of robotic manufacturing for the materials handling and merchandising equipment group. This group of products consists of such items as cooler shelving, stocking carts, and bakery racks. The products are sold directly to supermarkets.

A committee, consisting of the controller, the marketing manager, and the production manager, was given the responsibility to prepare the analysis. As a starting point, the controller provided the following information on expected revenues and expenses for the existing manual system:

		Percentage of Sales
Sales	$400,000	100%
Less: Variable expenses[a]	228,000	57
Contribution margin	$172,000	43
Less: Fixed expenses[b]	92,000	23
Income before income taxes	$ 80,000	20

[a]Variable cost detail (as a percentage of sales):

Direct materials	16%
Direct labor	20
Variable overhead	9
Variable selling	12

[b]$20,000 is depreciation; the rest is cash expenses.

Given the current competitive environment, the marketing manager thought that the preceding level of profitability would not likely change for the next decade.

After some investigation into various robotic equipment, the committee settled on an Aide 900 system, a robot that has the capability to weld stainless steel or aluminum. It is capable of being programmed to adjust the path, angle, and speed of the torch. The production manager was excited about the robotic system because it would eliminate the need to hire welders. This was an attractive possibility because the market for welders seemed perpetually tight. By reducing the dependence on welders, better production scheduling and fewer late deliveries would result. Moreover, the robot's production rate is four times that of a person.

It was also discovered that robotic welding is superior in quality to manual welding. As a consequence, some of the costs of poor quality could be reduced. By providing better-quality products and avoiding late deliveries, the marketing manager was convinced that the company would have such a competitive edge that it would increase sales by 50 percent for the affected product group by the end of the fourth year. The marketing manager provided the following projections for the next 10 years, the useful life of the robotic equipment:

	Year 1	*Year 2*	*Year 3*	*Years 4–10*
Sales	$400,000	$450,000	$500,000	$600,000

Currently, the company employs four welders, who work 40 hours per week and 50 weeks per year at an average wage of $10 per hour. If the robot is acquired, it will need one operator, who will be paid $10 per hour. Because of improved quality, the robotic system will also reduce the cost of direct materials by 25 percent, the cost of variable overhead by 33.33 percent, and variable selling expenses by 10 percent. All of these reductions will take place immediately after the robotic system is in place and operating. Fixed costs will be increased by the depreciation associated with the robot. The robot will be depreciated using MACRS. (The manual system uses straight-line depreciation without a half-year convention and has a current book value of $200,000.) If the robotic system is acquired, the old system will be sold for $40,000.

The robotic system requires the following initial investment:

Purchase price	$380,000
Installation	70,000
Training	30,000
Engineering	40,000

At the end of 10 years, the robot will have a salvage value of $20,000. Assume that the company's cost of capital is 12 percent. The tax rate is 40 percent.

Required:

1. Prepare a schedule of after-tax cash flows for the manual and robotic systems.
2. Using the schedule of cash flows computed in Requirement 1, compute the NPV for each system. Should the company invest in the robotic system?
3. In practice, many financial officers tend to use a higher discount rate than is justified by the firm's cost of capital. For example, a firm may use a discount rate of 20 percent when its cost of capital is or could be 12 percent. Offer some reasons for this practice. Assume that the annual after-tax cash benefit of adopting the robotic system is $80,000 per year more than the manual system. The initial outlay for the robotic system is $340,000. Compute the NPV using 12 percent and 20 percent. Would the robotic system be acquired if 20 percent is used? Could this conservative approach have a negative impact on a firm's ability to stay competitive?

20-25 COLLABORATIVE LEARNING EXERCISE

LO2, LO3, LO4

Peter Hennings, manager of the Cosmetics Division, had asked Laura Gibson, divisional controller and CMA, to meet with him regarding a recent analysis of a capital budgeting proposal. Peter was disappointed that the proposal had not met the company's minimum guidelines. Specifically, the company requires that all proposals show a positive net present value, have an IRR that exceeds the cost of capital (which is 11 percent), and have a payback period of less than five years. Funding for any new proposal had to be approved by company headquarters. Typically, proposals are approved if they meet the minimum guidelines and if the division's allocated share of the capital budget is not exhausted. The following conversation took place at their meeting:

PETER: Laura, I asked you to meet with me to discuss Proposal 678. Reviewing your analysis, I see that the NPV is negative and that the IRR is 9 percent. The payback is 5.5 years. In my opinion, the automated materials handling system in this proposal is an absolute must for this division. I feel that the consulting firm has underestimated the cash savings.

LAURA: I did some checking on my own because of your feelings about the matter. I called a friend who is an expert in the area and asked him to review the report on the system. After a careful review, he agreed with the report—in fact, he indicated that the savings were probably on the optimistic side.

PETER: Well, I don't agree. I know this business better than any of these so-called consulting experts. I think that the cash savings are significantly better than indicated.

LAURA: Why don't you explain this to headquarters? Perhaps they will allow an exception this time and fund the project.

PETER: No, that's unlikely. They're pretty strict when it comes to those guidelines, especially with the report from an outside consulting firm. I have a better idea, but I need your help. So far, you're the only one besides me who has seen the outside report. I think it is flawed. I would like to modify it so that it reflects my knowledge of the potential of the new system. Then, you can take the revised figures and prepare a new analysis for submission to headquarters. You need to tell me how much I need to revise the cash savings so that the project is viable. Although I am confident that the savings are significantly underestimated, I would prefer to revise them so that the minimum guidelines are slightly exceeded. Believe me, I will ensure that the project exceeds expectations once it's online.

Required:

Individually, read the ethical problem, and formulate answers to the following questions. Form groups of three or four. Each group member should write on a slip of paper the word TALK. This piece of paper is the Talking Chip. The Talking Chip is the ticket that allows a group member to speak. Group discussion begins with a volunteer. Discussion begins with Requirement 1 and moves to the next requirement only after all members have contributed to the discussion. After making his/her contribution, this person places the Talking Chip down in full view of the other members. Another person then contributes and subsequently places the Talking Chip down in full view. This continues until all members have contributed. Once all members have contributed, the chips can be retrieved and a second round of discussion can begin.

1. Evaluate the conduct of Peter Hennings. Are his suggestions unethical?
2. Suppose you were in Laura's position. What should you do?
3. Refer to the IMA code in Chapter 1. If Laura complies with Peter's request to modify the capital budgeting analysis, are any of the Standards of Ethical Conduct for Management Accountants violated? Which ones, if any?
4. Suppose that Laura tells Peter she will consider his request. She then meets with Jay Dixon, Peter's superior, and describes Peter's request. Upon hearing of the incident, Jay chuckles and says that he pulled a couple of stunts like that when he was a divisional manager. He tells Laura not to worry about it—to go ahead and support Peter—and assures her that he will keep her visit confidential. Given this development, what should Laura do?

20-26   CYBER RESEARCH CASE

ENVIRONMENTAL ISSUES, CAPITAL BUDGETING

LO1, LO2, LO3, LO4, LO7   Capital budgeting for environmental projects offers an interesting area for additional study. The Environmental Protection Agency has partnered with Tellus Institute to further its ongoing interest in environmental cost management. All of the information relating to the U.S. EPA environmental accounting project is now incorporated in the Environmental Management Accounting International Web site (http://www.emawebsite.org). This new Web site deals with such topics as environmental cost definitions, decisions using environmental costs, and capital budgeting. The focus of the Web site is the use of environmental accounting as a management accounting tool of internal business decisions. Using this Web site and other sources that you can locate, answer the following questions:

1. What evidence exists that firms use the payback period for screening and evaluating environmental projects? If payback is used, can you find the most common hurdle rate that firms use to justify environmental projects?
2. Are NPV and IRR used for environmental project approval? Can you find out what the hurdle rate is for IRR? Do you think this hurdle rate is the cost of capital? If not, then discuss why a different required rate is used.
3. Do you think the approval thresholds for environmental projects tend to be higher, lower, or the same when compared to nonenvironmental projects? See if you can find any evidence to support your viewpoint. Why might the approval thresholds differ from nonenvironmental projects?
4. See if you can find a discussion on how capital budgeting for environmental projects may differ from that of conventional projects. List these differences.

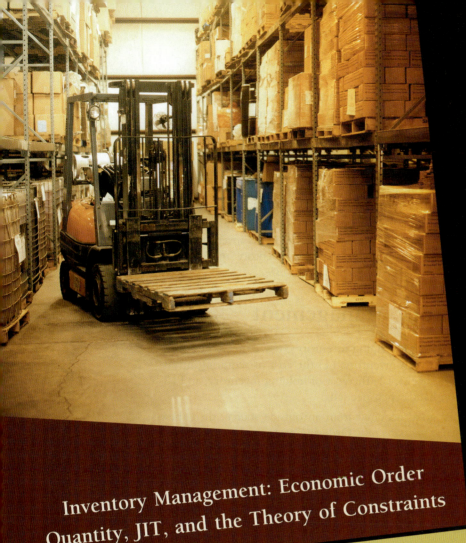

Inventory Management: Economic Order Quantity, JIT, and the Theory of Constraints

AFTER STUDYING THIS CHAPTER, YOU SHOULD BE ABLE TO:

1. Describe the just-in-case inventory management model.

2. Discuss just-in-time (JIT) inventory management.

3. Explain the basic concepts of constrained optimization.

4. Define the theory of constraints, and tell how it can be used to manage inventory.

Excessive amounts of inventory can prove to be very costly. There are many ways to manage inventory costs, including the EOQ model, JIT, and the theory of constraints. All three methods offer ways of reducing inventory costs. The best approach usually depends on the nature of the organization as well as the nature of the inventory itself.

Inventory represents a significant investment of capital for most companies. Inventory ties up money that could be used more productively elsewhere. Thus, effective inventory management offers the potential for significant cost savings. Furthermore, quality, product engineering, prices, overtime, excess capacity, ability to respond to customers (due-date performance), lead times, and overall profitability are all affected by inventory levels. For example, **Bal Seal Engineering** used the theory of constraints to reduce inventory by 50 percent and double profits.[1]

---

1. Taken from the Web site, http://www.goldratt.com, as of January 19, 2001.

Describing how inventory policy can be used to reduce costs and help organizations strengthen their competitive position is the main purpose of this chapter. First, we review **just-in-case inventory management**—a traditional inventory model based on anticipated demand. Learning the basics of this model and its underlying conceptual foundation will help us understand where it can still be appropriately applied. Understanding just-in-case inventory management also provides the necessary background for grasping the advantages of inventory management methods that are used in the contemporary manufacturing environment. These methods include JIT and the theory of constraints. To fully appreciate the theory of constraints, a brief introduction to constrained optimization (linear programming) is also needed. Although the focus of this chapter is inventory management, the theory of constraints is much more than an inventory management technique, and so we also explore what is called *constraint accounting*.

Just-in-Case Inventory Management

Inventory management is concerned with managing inventory costs. Three types of inventory costs can be readily identified with inventory: (1) the cost of acquiring inventory (other than the cost of the good itself), (2) the cost of holding inventory, and (3) the cost of not having inventory on hand when needed.

OBJECTIVE **1**

Describe the just-in-case inventory management model.

If the inventory is a material or good acquired from an outside source, then these inventory-acquisition costs are known as *ordering costs*. **Ordering costs** are the costs of placing and receiving an order. Examples include the costs of processing an order (clerical costs and documents), insurance for shipment, and unloading costs. If the material or good is produced internally, then the acquisition costs are called *setup costs*. **Setup costs** are the costs of preparing equipment and facilities so they can be used to produce a particular product or component. Examples are wages of idled production workers, the cost of idled production facilities (lost income), and the costs of test runs (labor, materials, and overhead). Ordering costs and setup costs are similar in nature—both represent costs that must be incurred to acquire inventory. They differ only in the nature of the prerequisite activity (filling out and placing an order versus configuring equipment and facilities). Thus, in the discussion that follows, any reference to ordering costs can be viewed as a reference to setup costs.

Carrying costs are the costs of holding inventory. Examples include insurance, inventory taxes, obsolescence, the opportunity cost of funds tied up in inventory, handling costs, and storage space.

If demand is not known with certainty, a third category of inventory costs—called *stock-out costs*—exists. **Stock-out costs** are the costs of not having a product available when demanded by a customer. Examples are lost sales (both current and future), the costs of expediting (increased transportation charges, overtime, and so on), and the costs of interrupted production.

Justifying Inventory

Effective inventory management requires that inventory-related costs be minimized. Minimizing carrying costs favors ordering or producing in small lot sizes, whereas minimizing ordering costs favors large, infrequent orders (minimization of setup costs favors long, infrequent production runs). The need to balance these two sets of costs so that the *total* cost of carrying and ordering can be minimized is one reason organizations choose to carry inventory.

Demand uncertainty is a second major reason for holding inventory. If the demand for materials or products is greater than expected, inventory can serve as a buffer, giving organizations the ability to meet delivery dates (thus keeping customers satisfied). Although balancing conflicting costs and dealing with uncertainty are the two most frequently cited reasons for carrying inventories, other reasons exist.

Inventories of parts and materials are often viewed as necessary because of supply uncertainties. That is, inventory buffers of parts and materials are needed to keep production flowing in case of late deliveries or no deliveries. (Strikes, bad weather, and bankruptcy are examples of uncertain events that can cause an interruption in supply.) Unreliable production processes may also create a demand for producing extra inventory. For example, a company may decide to produce more units than needed to meet demand because the production process usually yields a large number of nonconforming units. Similarly, buffers of inventories may be required to continue supplying customers or processes with goods even if a process goes down because of a failed machine. Finally, organizations may acquire larger inventories than normal to take advantage of quantity discounts or to avoid anticipated price increases. Exhibit 21-1 summarizes the reasons typically offered for carrying inventory. It is important to realize that these reasons are given to *justify* carrying inventories. A host of other reasons can be offered that *encourage* the carrying of inventories. For example, performance measures such as measures of machine and labor efficiency may promote the buildup of inventories.

EXHIBIT 21-1   Traditional Reasons for Carrying Inventory

1. To balance ordering or setup costs and carrying costs
2. Demand uncertainty
3. Machine failure
4. Defective parts
5. Unavailable parts
6. Late delivery of parts
7. Unreliable production processes
8. To take advantage of discounts
9. To hedge against future price increases

Economic Order Quantity: A Model for Balancing Acquisition and Carrying Costs

Of the nine reasons for holding inventory listed in Exhibit 21-1, the first reason is directly concerned with the trade-off between acquisition and carrying costs. Most of the other reasons are concerned directly or indirectly with stock-out costs, with the exception of the last two (which are concerned with managing the cost of the good itself). Initially, we will assume away the stock-out cost problem and focus only on the objective of balancing acquisition costs with carrying costs. To develop an inventory policy that deals with the trade-offs between these two costs, two basic questions must be addressed:

1. How much should be ordered (or produced) to minimize inventory costs?
2. When should the order be placed (or the setup done)?

The first question needs to be addressed before the second can be answered.

Minimizing Total Ordering and Carrying Costs

Assuming that demand is known, the total ordering (or setup) and carrying cost can be described by the following equation:

$$TC = PD/Q + CQ/2 \tag{21.1}$$
$$= \text{Ordering (or setup) cost} + \text{Carrying cost}$$

where

TC = The total ordering (or setup) and carrying cost
 P = The cost of placing and receiving an order (or the cost of setting up a production run)
 Q = The number of units ordered each time an order is placed (or the lot size for production)
 D = The known annual demand
 C = The cost of carrying one unit of stock for one year

The cost of carrying inventory can be computed for any organization that carries inventories, although the inventory cost model using setup costs and lot size as inputs pertains only to manufacturers. To illustrate Equation 21.1, consider Mantener Corporation, a service organization that does warranty work for a major producer of video recorders. Assume that the following values apply for a part used in the repair of the video recorders (the part is purchased from external suppliers):

$$D = 25{,}000 \text{ units}$$
$$Q = 500 \text{ units}$$
$$P = \$40 \text{ per order}$$
$$C = \$2 \text{ per unit}$$

The number of orders per year is D/Q, which is 50 (25,000/500). Multiplying the number of orders per year by the cost of placing and receiving an order ($D/Q \times P$) yields the total ordering cost of $2,000 (50 × $40).

Carrying cost for the year is $CQ/2$, which is simply the average inventory on hand ($Q/2$) multiplied by the carrying cost per unit (C). (Assuming average inventory to be $Q/2$ is equivalent to assuming that inventory is consumed uniformly.) For our example, the average inventory is 250 (500/2) and the carrying cost for the year is $500 ($2 × 250). Applying Equation 21.1, the total cost is $2,500 ($2,000 + $500). An order quantity of 500 with a total cost of $2,500, however, may not be the best choice. Some other order quantity may produce a lower total cost. The objective is to find the order quantity that minimizes the total cost, known as the **economic order quantity (EOQ)**. The EOQ model is an example of a *just-in-case* or *push inventory system*. In a push system, the acquisition of inventory is initiated in *anticipation* of future demand—not in reaction to present demand. Fundamental to the analysis is the assessment of D, the future demand.

Calculating EOQ

The decision variable for Equation 21.1 is the order quantity (or lot size). We seek the quantity that minimizes the total cost expressed by Equation 21.1. This quantity is the economic order quantity and is derived by taking the first derivative of Equation 21.1 with respect to Q and solving for Q:[2]

$$Q = EOQ = \sqrt{(2DP/C)} \qquad (21.2)$$

The data of the preceding example are used to illustrate the calculation of EOQ using Equation 21.2:

$$EOQ = \sqrt{(2 \times 25{,}000 \times \$40)/\$2}$$
$$= \sqrt{1{,}000{,}000}$$
$$= 1{,}000$$

Substituting 1,000 as the value of Q in Equation 21.1 yields a total cost of $2,000. The number of orders placed would be 25 (25,000/1,000); thus, the total ordering cost is $1,000 (25 × $40). The average inventory is 500 (1,000/2), with a total carrying cost

---

2. $d(TC)/dQ = C/2 - DP/Q^2 = 0$; thus, $Q^2 = 2DP/C$ and $Q = \sqrt{2DP/Cw}$.

of $1,000 (500 × $2). Notice that the carrying cost equals the ordering cost. This is always true for the simple EOQ model described by Equation 21.2. Also, notice that an order quantity of 1,000 is less costly than an order quantity of 500 ($2,000 versus $2,500).

When to Order or Produce

Not only must we know how much to order (or produce) but we also must know when to place an order (or to set up for production). Avoiding stock-out costs is a key element in determining when to place an order. The **reorder point** is the point in time when a new order should be placed (or setup started). It is a function of the EOQ, the lead time, and the rate at which inventory is depleted. **Lead time** is the time required to receive the economic order quantity once an order is placed or a setup is initiated.

To avoid stock-out costs and to minimize carrying costs, an order should be placed so that it arrives just as the last item in inventory is used. Knowing the rate of usage and lead time allows us to compute the reorder point that accomplishes these objectives:

$$\text{Reorder point} = \text{Rate of usage} \times \text{Lead time} \qquad (21.3)$$

To illustrate Equation 21.3, we will continue to use the video recorder example. Assume that the repair activity uses 100 parts per day and that the lead time is four days. If so, an order should be placed when the inventory level of the VCR part drops to 400 units (100 × 4). Exhibit 21-2 provides a graphical illustration. Note that the inventory is depleted just as the order arrives and that the quantity on hand jumps back up to the EOQ level.

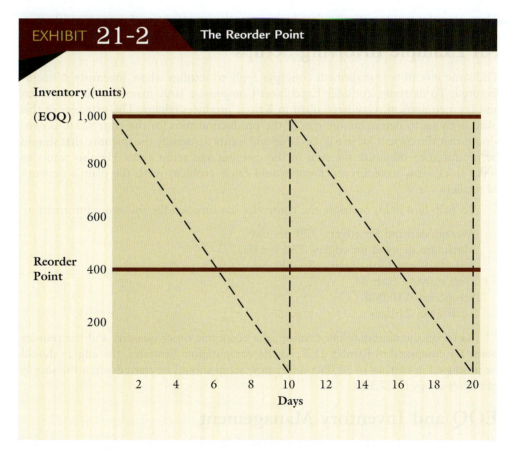

EXHIBIT 21-2   The Reorder Point

Demand Uncertainty and Reordering

If the demand for the part or product is not known with certainty, the possibility of stock-out exists. For example, if the VCR part was used at a rate of 120 parts a day instead of 100, the firm would use 400 parts after three and one-third days. Since the new order would not arrive until the end of the fourth day, repair activity requiring this part would be idled for two-thirds of a day. To avoid this problem, organizations often choose to carry safety stock. **Safety stock** is extra inventory carried to serve as insurance against fluctuations in demand. Safety stock is computed by multiplying the lead time by the difference between the maximum rate of usage and the average rate of usage. For example, if the maximum usage of the VCR part is 120 units per day, the average usage is 100 units per day, and the lead time is four days, then the safety stock is computed as follows:

Maximum usage	120
Average usage	(100)
Difference	20
Lead time	$\times$ 4
Safety stock	80

With the presence of safety stock, the reorder point is computed as follows:

$$\text{Reorder point} = (\text{Average rate of usage} \times \text{Lead time}) + \text{Safety stock} \quad (21.4)$$

For the repair service example, the reorder point with safety stock is computed as follows:

$$\text{Reorder point} = (100 \times 4) + 80$$
$$= 480 \text{ units}$$

Thus, an order is automatically placed whenever the inventory level drops to 480 units.

An Example Involving Setups

The same inventory management concepts apply to settings where inventory is manufactured. To illustrate, consider Expedition Company, a large manufacturer of garden and lawn equipment. One large plant in Kansas produces edgers. The manager of this plant is trying to determine the size of the production runs for the edgers. He is convinced that the current lot size is too large and wants to identify the quantity that should be produced to minimize the sum of the carrying and setup costs. He also wants to avoid stock-outs, since any stock-out would cause problems with the plant's network of retailers.

To help him in his decision, the controller has supplied the following information:

Average demand for edgers: 720 per day
Maximum demand for edgers: 780 per day
Annual demand for edgers: 180,000
Unit carrying cost: $4
Setup cost: $10,000
Lead time: 22 days

Based on the preceding information, the economic order quantity and the reorder point are computed in Exhibit 21-3. As the computation illustrates, the edgers should be produced in batches of 30,000, and a new setup should be started when the supply of edgers drops to 17,160.

EOQ and Inventory Management

The traditional approach to managing inventory has been referred to as a *just-in-case system*.[3] In some settings, a just-in-case inventory system is entirely appropriate. For ex-

---

3. Eliyahi M. Goldratt and Robert E. Fox, *The Race* (Croton-on-Hudson, NY: North River Press, 1986).

EXHIBIT 21-3   EOQ and Reorder Point Illustrated

$$EOQ = \sqrt{2DP/C}$$
$$= \sqrt{(2 \times 180{,}000 \times \$10{,}000)/\$4}$$
$$= \sqrt{900{,}000{,}000}$$
$$= 30{,}000 \text{ edgers}$$

Safety stock:

Maximum usage	780
Average usage	(720)
Difference	60
Lead time	× 22
Safety stock	1,320

$$\text{Reorder point} = (\text{Average usage} \times \text{Lead time}) + \text{Safety stock}$$
$$= (720 \times 22) + 1{,}320$$
$$= 17{,}160 \text{ edgers}$$

ample, hospitals need inventories of medicines, drugs, and other critical supplies on hand at all times so that life-threatening situations can be handled. Using an economic order quantity coupled with safety stock would seem eminently sensible in such an environment. Relying on a critical drug to arrive just in time to save a heart attack victim is simply not practical. Furthermore, many smaller retail stores, manufacturers, and services may not have the buying power to command alternative inventory management systems such as just-in-time purchasing.

As the edger example illustrates (Exhibit 21-3), the EOQ model is very useful in identifying the optimal trade-off between inventory carrying costs and setup costs. It also is useful in helping to deal with uncertainty by using safety stock. The historical importance of the EOQ model in many American industries can be better appreciated by understanding the nature of the traditional manufacturing environment. This environment has been characterized by the mass production of a few standardized products that typically have a very high setup cost. The production of the edgers fits this pattern. The high setup cost encouraged a large batch size: 30,000 units. The annual demand of 180,000 units can be satisfied using only six batches. Thus, production runs for these firms tended to be quite long. Furthermore, diversity was viewed as being costly and was avoided. Producing variations of the product can be quite expensive, especially since additional, special features would usually demand even more expensive and frequent setups—the reason for the standardized products.

OBJECTIVE 2

Discuss just-in-time (JIT) inventory management.

JIT Inventory Management

The manufacturing environment for many of these traditional, large-batch, high-setup-cost firms has changed dramatically in the past 10 to 20 years. For one thing, the competitive markets are no longer defined by national boundaries. Advances in transportation and communication have contributed significantly to the creation of global competition. Advances in technology have contributed to shorter life cycles for products, and product diversity has increased. Foreign firms offering higher-quality, lower-cost products with *specialized features* have created tremendous pressures for our domestic large-batch, high-setup-cost firms to increase both quality and product diversity while simultaneously reducing total costs. These competitive pressures have led many firms to abandon the EOQ model in favor of a JIT approach. JIT has two strategic objectives: to increase profits and to improve a firm's competitive position. These two objectives are achieved by controlling costs (enabling better price competition and increased profits), improving delivery performance, and improving quality. JIT offers increased cost efficiency and simultaneously has the flexibility to respond to customer demands for better quality and more variety. Quality, flexibility, and cost efficiency are foundational principles for world-class competition.

Just-in-time inventory management represents the continual pursuit of productivity through the elimination of waste. *Non-value-added* activities are a major source of waste. From Chapter 12, we know that non-value-added activities are either unnecessary or necessary, but inefficient and improvable. Necessary activities are essential to the business and/or are of value to customers. Eliminating non-value-added activities is a major thrust of JIT, but it is also a basic objective of any company following the path of continuous improvement—regardless of whether or not JIT is being used.

Clearly, JIT is much more than an inventory management system. Inventories, however, are particularly viewed as representing waste. They tie up resources such as cash, space, and labor. They also conceal inefficiencies in production and increase the complexity of a firm's information system. Thus, even though JIT focuses on more than inventory management, control of inventory is an important ancillary benefit. In this chapter, the inventory dimension of JIT is emphasized. In Chapter 11, other benefits and features of JIT were described. Chapter 12, in particular, focused on nonvalue-added activity analysis.

A Pull System

JIT is a manufacturing approach that maintains that goods should be pulled through the system by present demand rather than pushed through the system on a fixed schedule based on anticipated demand. Many fast-food restaurants, like **Burger King**, use a pull system to control their finished goods inventory. When a customer orders a hamburger, it is taken from the rack. When the number of hamburgers gets too low, the cooks make new hamburgers. Customer demand pulls the materials through the system. This same principle is used in manufacturing settings. Each operation produces only what is necessary to satisfy the demand of the succeeding operation. The material or subassembly arrives just in time for production to occur so that demand can be met.

One effect of JIT is to reduce inventories to very low levels. The pursuit of insignificant levels of inventories is vital to the success of JIT. This idea of pursuing insignificant inventories, however, necessarily challenges the traditional reasons for holding inventories (see Exhibit 21-1). These reasons are no longer viewed as valid.

According to the traditional view, inventories solve some underlying problem related to each of the reasons listed in Exhibit 21-1. For example, the problem of resolving the conflict between ordering or setup costs and carrying costs is solved by selecting an inventory level that minimizes the sum of these costs. If demand is greater than expected or if production is reduced by breakdowns and production inefficiencies, then inventories serve as buffers, providing customers with products that otherwise might not have been available. Similarly, inventories can prevent stock-outs caused by late delivery of material, defective parts, and failures of machines used to produce subassemblies. Finally, inventories are often the solution to the problem of buying the best materials for the least cost through the use of quantity discounts.

JIT refuses to use inventories as the solution to these problems. In fact, the JIT approach can be seen as substituting information for inventories. Companies must track materials and finished goods more carefully. To do that, the logistics industry has gone high-tech. **Schneider National Company**, a logistics firm, uses satellite tracking to tell a customer just where a particular shipment is and when it will be delivered. In an example of partnering, Schneider engineers assisted client **PPG Industries** by showing its Pennsylvania plant employees how to use the shipping and receiving facilities more efficiently.[4]

---

4. Jon Bigness, "In Today's Economy There Is Big Money to Be Made in Logistics," *The Wall Street Journal* (September 6, 1995): A1 and A9.

JIT inventory management offers alternative solutions that do not require high inventories.

Setup and Carrying Costs: The JIT Approach

JIT takes a radically different approach to minimizing total carrying and setup costs. The traditional approach accepts the existence of setup costs and then finds the order quantity that best balances the two categories of costs. JIT, on the other hand, does not accept setup costs (or ordering costs) as a given; rather, JIT attempts to drive these costs to zero. If setup costs and ordering costs become insignificant, the only remaining cost to minimize is carrying cost, which is accomplished by reducing inventories to very low levels. This approach explains the push for zero inventories in a JIT system.

Long-Term Contracts, Continuous Replenishment, and Electronic Data Interchange

Ordering costs are reduced by developing close relationships with suppliers. Negotiating long-term contracts for the supply of outside materials will obviously reduce the number of orders and the associated ordering costs. Retailers have found a way to reduce ordering costs by adopting an arrangement known as *continuous replenishment.* **Continuous replenishment** means a manufacturer assumes the inventory management function for the retailer. The manufacturer tells the retailer when and how much stock to reorder. The retailer reviews the recommendation and approves the order if it makes sense. **Wal-Mart** and **Procter & Gamble**, for example, use this arrangement.[5] The arrangement has reduced inventories for Wal-Mart and has also reduced stock-out problems. Additionally, Wal-Mart often sells Procter & Gamble's goods before it has to pay for them. Procter & Gamble, on the other hand, has become a preferred supplier, has more and better shelf space, and also has less demand uncertainty. The ability to project demand more accurately allows Procter & Gamble to produce and deliver continuously in smaller lots—a goal of JIT manufacturing. Similar arrangements can be made between manufacturers and suppliers.

The process of continuous replenishment is facilitated by *electronic data interchange.* **Electronic data interchange (EDI)** allows suppliers access to a buyer's online database. By knowing the buyer's production schedule (in the case of a manufacturer), the supplier can deliver the needed parts where they are needed just in time for their use. EDI involves no paper—no purchase orders or invoices. The supplier uses the production schedule, which is in the database, to determine its own production and delivery schedules. When the parts are shipped, an electronic message is sent from the supplier to the buyer that a shipment is en route. When the parts arrive, a bar code is scanned with an electronic wand, and this initiates payment for the goods. Clearly, EDI requires a close working arrangement between the supplier and the buyer—they almost operate as one company rather than two separate companies.

Reducing Setup Times

Reducing setup times requires a company to search for new, more efficient ways to accomplish setup. Fortunately, experience has indicated that dramatic reductions in setup times can be achieved. A classic example is that of **Harley-Davidson**. Upon adopting a JIT system, Harley-Davidson reduced setup time by more than 75 percent on the machines evaluated.[6] In some cases, Harley-Davidson was able to reduce the setup times from hours to minutes. Other companies have experienced similar results. Generally, setup times can be reduced by at least 75 percent.

5. Michael Hammer and James Champy, *Reengineering the Corporation* (New York: Harper Business, 1993).
6. Gene Schwind, "Man Arrives Just in Time to Save Harley-Davidson," *Material Handling Engineering* (August 1984): 28–35.

Due-Date Performance: The JIT Solution

Due-date performance is a measure of a firm's ability to respond to customer needs. In the past, finished goods inventories have been used to ensure that a firm is able to meet a requested delivery date. JIT solves the problem of due-date performance not by building inventory but by dramatically reducing lead times. Shorter lead times increase a firm's ability to meet requested delivery dates and to respond quickly to the demands of the market. Thus, the firm's competitiveness is improved. JIT cuts lead times by reducing setup times, improving quality, and using cellular manufacturing.

Manufacturing cells reduce travel distance between machines and inventory; they can also have a dramatic effect on lead time. For example, in a traditional manufacturing system, one company took two months to manufacture a valve. By grouping the lathes and drills used to make the valves into U-shaped cells, the lead time was reduced to two or three days. A chain saw manufacturer was able to reduce travel distance from 2,620 feet to 173 feet and lead times from 21 days to three. Because of the reduced lead time and plans for even further reduction, the company will be filling orders directly from the factory rather than from finished goods warehouses.[7] These reductions in lead time are not unique—most companies experience at least a 90 percent reduction in lead times when they implement JIT.[8]

Manufacturers are not the only companies using a JIT approach to improve time to market. **Benetton** calls itself an apparel services company, not a retailer. Operating one giant distribution center in Castrette, Italy, Benetton uses robots to send the latest fashions to any of its company stores in 120 countries within 12 days.

Avoidance of Shutdown and Process Reliability: The JIT Approach

Most shutdowns occur for one of three reasons: machine failure, defective material or subassembly, and unavailability of a material or subassembly. Holding inventories is one solution to all three problems.

Those espousing the JIT approach claim that inventories do not solve the problems but cover up or hide them. JIT proponents use the analogy of rocks in a lake. The rocks represent the three problems, and the water represents inventories. If the lake is deep (inventories are high), then the rocks are never exposed, and managers can pretend they do not exist. By reducing inventories to zero, the rocks are exposed and can no longer be ignored. JIT solves the three problems by emphasizing total preventive maintenance and total quality control in addition to building the right kind of relationship with suppliers.

Total Preventive Maintenance

Zero machine failures is the goal of **total preventive maintenance**. By paying more attention to preventive maintenance, most machine breakdowns can be avoided. This objective is easier to attain in a JIT environment because of the interdisciplinary labor philosophy. It is fairly common for a cell worker to be trained in maintenance of the machines he or she operates. Because of the pull-through nature of JIT, cell workers may have idle manufacturing time. Some of this time, then, can be used productively by having the cell workers involved in preventive maintenance.

Total Quality Control

The problem of defective parts is solved by striving for zero defects. Because JIT manufacturing does not rely on inventories to replace defective parts or materials, the emphasis on quality for both internally produced and externally purchased materials

---

7. Jack Bailes and Ilene K. Kleinsorge, "Cutting Waste with JIT," *Management Accounting* (May 1992): 28–32.
8. William J. Stoddard and Nolan W. Rhea, "Just-in-Time Manufacturing: The Relentless Pursuit of Productivity," *Material Handling Engineering* (March 1985): 70–76.

increases significantly. The outcome is impressive: the number of rejected parts tends to fall by 75–90 percent. Decreasing defective parts also diminishes the justification for inventories based on unreliable processes.

The Kanban System

To ensure that parts or materials are available when needed, a system called the **Kanban system** is employed. This is an information system that controls production through the use of markers or cards. The Kanban system is responsible for ensuring that the necessary products (or parts) are produced (or acquired) in the necessary quantities at the necessary time. It is the heart of the JIT inventory management system.

A Kanban system uses cards or markers, which are plastic, cardboard, or metal plates measuring four inches by eight inches. The Kanban is usually placed in a vinyl sack and attached to the part or a container holding the needed parts.

A basic Kanban system uses three cards: a *withdrawal Kanban*, a *production Kanban*, and a *vendor Kanban*. The first two control the movement of work among the manufacturing processes, while the third controls movement of parts between the processes and outside suppliers. A **withdrawal Kanban** specifies the quantity that a subsequent process should withdraw from the preceding process. A **production Kanban** specifies the quantity that the preceding process should produce. **Vendor Kanbans** are used to notify suppliers to deliver more parts; they also specify when the parts are needed. The three Kanbans are illustrated in Exhibits 21-4, 21-5, and 21-6 (on the following page), respectively.

How Kanban cards are used to control the work flow can be illustrated with a simple example. Assume that two processes are needed to manufacture a product. The first process (CB Assembly) builds and tests printed circuit boards (using a U-shaped manufacturing

---

EXHIBIT 21-4   **Withdrawal Kanban**

Item No.	15670T07	Preceding Process
Item Name	**Circuit Board**	**CB Assembly**
Computer Type	**TR6547 PC**	
Box Capacity	8	Subsequent Process
Box Type	C	**Final Assembly**

EXHIBIT 21-5   **Production Kanban**

Item No.	15670T07	Preceding Process
Item Name	**Circuit Board**	**CB Assembly**
Computer Type	**TR6547 PC**	
Box Capacity	8	
Box Type	C	

EXHIBIT 21-6   Vendor Kanban

Item No.	15670T07	Name of Receiving Company
Item Name	**Computer Casting**	**Electro PC**
Box Capacity	**8**	Receiving Gate
Box Type	**A**	75
Time to Deliver	**8:30 A.M., 12:30 P.M., 2:30 P.M.**	
Name of Supplier	**Gerry Supply**	

cell). The second process (Final Assembly) puts eight circuit boards into a subassembly purchased from an outside supplier. The final product is a personal computer.

Exhibit 21-7 provides the plant layout corresponding to the manufacture of the personal computers. Refer to the exhibit as the steps involved in using Kanbans are outlined.

EXHIBIT 21-7   The Kanban Process

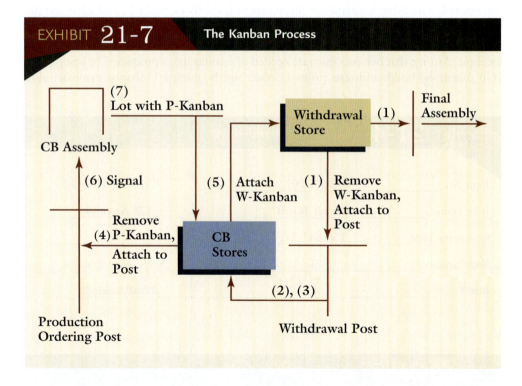

Consider first the movement of work between the two processing areas. Assume that eight circuit boards are placed in a container and that one such container is located in the CB stores area. Attached to this container is a production Kanban (P-Kanban). A second container with eight circuit boards is located near the Final Assembly line (the withdrawal store) with a withdrawal Kanban (W-Kanban). Now assume that the production schedule calls for the immediate assembly of a computer.

The Kanban setups can be described as follows:

1. A worker from the Final Assembly line goes to the withdrawal store, removes the eight circuit boards, and places them into production. The worker also removes the withdrawal Kanban and places it on the withdrawal post.

2. The withdrawal Kanban on the post signals that the Final Assembly unit needs an additional eight circuit boards.
3. A worker from Final Assembly (or a material handler called a *carrier*) removes the withdrawal Kanban from the post and carries it to CB stores.
4. At the CB stores area, the carrier removes the production Kanban from the container of eight circuit boards and places it on the production ordering post.
5. The carrier next attaches the withdrawal Kanban to the container of parts and carries the container back to the Final Assembly area. Assembly of the next computer can begin.
6. The production Kanban on the production ordering post signals the workers of CB Assembly to begin producing another lot of circuit boards. The production Kanban is removed and accompanies the units as they are produced.
7. When the lot of eight circuit boards is completed, the units are placed in a container in the CB stores area with the production Kanban attached. The cycle is then repeated.

The use of Kanbans ensures that the subsequent process (Final Assembly) withdraws the circuit boards from the preceding process (CB Assembly) in the necessary quantity at the appropriate time. The Kanban system also controls the preceding process by allowing it to produce only the quantities withdrawn by the subsequent process. In this way, inventories are kept at a minimum, and the components arrive just in time to be used.

Essentially, the same steps are followed for a purchased subassembly. The only difference is the use of a vendor Kanban in place of a production Kanban. A vendor Kanban on a vendor post signals to the supplier that another order is needed. As with the circuit boards, the subassemblies must be delivered just in time for use. A JIT purchasing system requires the supplier to deliver small quantities on a frequent basis. These deliveries could be weekly, daily, or even several times a day. This calls for a close working relationship with suppliers. Long-term contractual agreements tend to ensure supply of materials.

Discounts and Price Increases: JIT Purchasing versus Holding Inventories

Traditionally, inventories are carried so that a firm can take advantage of quantity discounts and hedge against future price increases of the items purchased. The objective is to lower the cost of inventory. JIT achieves the same objective without carrying inventories. The JIT solution is to negotiate long-term contracts with a few chosen suppliers located as close to the production facility as possible and to establish more extensive supplier involvement. Suppliers are not selected on the basis of price alone. Performance—the quality of the component and the ability to deliver as needed—and commitment to JIT purchasing are vital considerations. Other benefits of long-term contracts exist. They stipulate prices and acceptable quality levels. Long-term contracts also reduce dramatically the number of orders placed, which helps to drive down the ordering cost. Another effect of JIT purchasing is to lower the cost of purchased parts by 5 to 20 percent.[9]

JIT's Limitations

JIT is not simply an approach that can be purchased and plugged in with immediate results. Its implementation should be more of an evolutionary process than a revolutionary process. Patience is needed. JIT is often referred to as a program of simplification—yet, this does not imply that it is simple or easy to implement. Time is required, for example, to build sound relationships with suppliers. Insisting on immediate changes in

---

9. Ibid.

COST MANAGEMENT   Technology in Action

Mercedes-Benz U.S. International (MBUSI) produces an M-Class SUV in its Tuscaloosa, Alabama, plant. The plant produces a variety of models, including V6, V8, 4-cylinder, and left- and right-hand versions. The plant uses a JIT purchasing and manufacturing system to build the SUVs. The plant uses radio frequency identification (RFID) tags to ensure that materials are delivered on time to the production line. An RFID tag is placed on the vehicle at the beginning of production. When the vehicle reaches a certain stage of production, a broadcast is sent to one of six sequence suppliers. The supplier builds the needed part and delivers it to the point in the production line just as it is needed. The RFID technology is also used to communicate to the suppliers whether the Tuscaloosa plant is running fast, slow, or normal, thus helping them with their daily production planning. In other words, RFID tags serve as an automated version of the vendor Kanbans.

Source: Ken Krizner, "Daffron, Andy—Interviews," *Frontline Solutions*, Vol. 1, Issue 9 (August 2000): 9.

delivery times and quality may not be realistic and may cause difficult confrontations between a company and its suppliers. Partnership, not coercion, should be the basis of supplier relationships. To achieve the benefits that are associated with JIT purchasing, a company may be tempted to redefine unilaterally its supplier relationships. Unilaterally redefining supplier relationships by extracting concessions and dictating terms may create supplier resentment and actually cause suppliers to retaliate. In the long run, suppliers may seek new markets, find ways to charge higher prices (than would exist with a preferred supplier arrangement), or seek regulatory relief. These actions may destroy many of the JIT benefits extracted by the impatient company.

Workers also may be affected by JIT. Studies have shown that sharp reductions in inventory buffers may cause a regimented work flow and high levels of stress among production workers. Some have suggested a deliberate pace of inventory reduction to allow workers to develop a sense of autonomy and to encourage their participation in broader improvement efforts. Forced and dramatic reductions in inventories may indeed reveal problems—but it may cause more problems: lost sales and stressed workers. If the workers perceive JIT as a way of simply squeezing more out of them, then JIT efforts may be doomed. Perhaps a better strategy for JIT implementation is one where inventory reductions follow the process improvements that JIT offers. Implementing JIT is not easy; it requires careful and thorough planning and preparation. Companies should expect some struggle and frustration.

The most glaring deficiency of JIT is the absence of inventory to buffer production interruptions. Current sales are constantly being threatened by an unexpected interruption in production. In fact, if a problem occurs, JIT's approach consists of trying to find and solve the problem before any further production activity occurs. Retailers who use JIT tactics also face the possibility of shortages. JIT retailers order what they need now—not what they expect to sell—because the idea is to flow goods through the channel as late as possible, hence keeping inventories low and decreasing the need for markdowns. If demand increases well beyond the retailer's supply of inventory, the retailer may be unable to make order adjustments quickly enough to avoid irked customers and lost sales. For example, a dockworkers' strike at U.S. west coast docks during the fall of 2002 had a strong impact on the Christmas shopping season. Many retailers were affected as products ordered for delivery during the fall were locked up at the docks. **Toys "R" Us** saw shortages of "Hello Kitty" merchandise result in significant lost sales. Manufacturers also face problems with shortages. For example, **NUMMI** (the U.S.-based joint venture between GM and Toyota) had to shut down its Fremont, California, manufacturing plant due to shortages of imported engines and transmissions. Yet, in spite of the downside, many retailers and manufacturers seem to be strongly committed to JIT. Apparently, losing sales on occasion is less costly than carrying high levels of inventory.

Even so, we must recognize that a sale lost today is a sale lost forever. Installing a JIT system so that it operates with very little interruption is not a short-run project. Thus, losing sales is a real cost of installing a JIT system. An alternative, and perhaps complementary approach, is the theory of constraints (TOC). In principle, TOC can be used in conjunction with JIT manufacturing. After all, JIT manufacturing environments also have constraints. Furthermore, the TOC approach has the very appealing quality of protecting current sales while also striving to increase future sales by increasing quality, lowering response time, and decreasing operating costs. However, before we introduce and discuss the theory of constraints, we need to provide a brief introduction to constrained optimization theory.

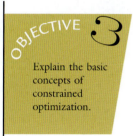

OBJECTIVE 3

Explain the basic concepts of constrained optimization.

Basic Concepts of Constrained Optimization

Manufacturing and service organizations must choose the mix of products that they will produce and sell. Decisions about product mix can have a significant impact on an organization's profitability. Each mix represents an alternative that carries with it an associated profit level. A manager should choose the alternative that maximizes total profits. The usual approach is to assume that only unit-based variable costs are relevant to the product mix decision. Thus, assuming that non-unit-level costs are the same for different mixes of products, a manager needs to choose the mix alternative that maximizes total contribution margin.

If a firm possesses unlimited resources and the demand for each product being considered is unlimited, then the product mix decision is simple—produce an infinite number of each product. Unfortunately, every firm faces limited resources and limited demand for each product. These limitations are called constraints. External constraints are limiting factors imposed on the firm from external sources (such as market demand). Internal constraints are limiting factors found within the firm (such as machine or labor time availability). Although resources and demands may be limited, certain mixes may not meet all the demand or use all of the resources available to be used. Constraints whose limited resources are not fully used by a product mix are loose constraints. If, on the other hand, a product mix uses all of the limited resources of a constraint, then the constraint is a binding constraint.

Constrained optimization is choosing the optimal mix given the constraints faced by the firm. Assume, for example, that Schaller Company produces two types of machine parts: X and Y, with unit contribution margins of $300 and $600, respectively. Assuming that Schaller can sell all that is produced, some may argue that only Part Y should be produced and sold because it has the larger contribution margin. However, this solution is not necessarily the best. The selection of the optimal mix can be significantly affected by the relationships of the constrained resources to the individual products. These relationships affect the quantity of each product that can be produced and, consequently, the total contribution margin that can be earned. This point is most vividly illustrated with one binding internal resource constraint.

One Binding Internal Constraint

Assume that each part must be drilled by a special machine. The firm owns three machines that together provide 120 drilling hours per week. Part X requires one hour of drilling, and Part Y requires three hours of drilling. Assuming no other binding constraints, what is the optimal mix of parts? Since each unit of Part X requires one hour of drilling, 120 units of Part X can be produced per week (120/1). At $300 per unit, Schaller can earn a total contribution margin of $36,000 per week. On the other hand, Part Y requires three hours of drilling per unit; therefore, forty (120/3) parts can be produced. At $600 per unit, the total contribution margin is $24,000 per week. Producing only Part X yields a higher profit level than producing only Part Y—even though the unit contribution margin for Part Y is twice the amount of Part X.

The contribution margin per unit of each product is not the critical concern. The contribution margin per unit of *scarce resource* is the deciding factor. The product yielding the highest contribution margin per drilling hour should be selected. Part X earns $300 per machine hour ($300/1), while Part Y earns only $200 per machine hour ($600/3). Thus, the optimal mix is 120 units of Part X and none of Part Y, producing a total contribution margin of $36,000 per week.

Internal Binding Constraint and External Binding Constraint

The contribution margin per unit of scarce resource can also be used to identify the optimal product mix when a binding external constraint exists. For example, assume the same internal constraint of 120 drilling hours, but also assume that Schaller can sell at most 60 units of Part X and 100 units of Part Y. The internal constraint allows Schaller to produce 120 units of Part X, but this is no longer a feasible choice because only 60 units of X can be sold. Thus, we now have a binding external constraint—one that affects the earlier decision to produce and sell only Part X. Since the contribution per unit of scarce resource (machine hour) is $300 for Part X and $200 for Part Y, it still makes sense to produce as much of Part X as possible before producing any of Part Y. Schaller should first produce 60 units of Part X, using 60 machine hours. This leaves 60 machine hours, allowing the production of 20 units of Part Y. The optimal mix is now 60 units of Part X and 20 units of Part Y, producing a total contribution margin of $30,000 per week [($300 × 60) + ($600 × 20)].

Multiple Internal Binding Constraints

It is possible for an organization to have more than one binding constraint. All organizations face multiple constraints: limitations of materials, limitations of labor inputs, limited machine hours, and so on. The solution of the product mix problem in the presence of multiple internal binding constraints is considerably more complicated and requires the use of a specialized mathematical technique known as *linear programming*.

Linear Programming

Linear programming is a method that searches among possible solutions until it finds the optimal solution. The theory of linear programming permits many solutions to be ignored. In fact, all but a finite number of solutions are eliminated by the theory, with the search then limited to the resulting finite set.

To illustrate how linear programming can be used to identify the optimal mix with multiple internally constrained resources, we will continue to use the Schaller Company example. However, the example will be expanded to include a wider variety of constraints. In addition to the constraints already identified, two more internal constraints will be added. Assume that the two parts (X and Y) are produced in three sequential processes: grinding, drilling, and polishing. The grinding process uses two machines that provide a total of 80 grinding hours per week. Each part requires one hour of grinding. The polishing process is labor intensive. This process provides 90 labor hours per week. Part X uses two hours per unit, and Part Y uses one hour per unit. Information on Schaller's constraints is summarized in Exhibit 21-8. As before, the objective is to maximize Schaller's total contribution margin subject to the constraints faced by Schaller.

The objective of maximizing total contribution margin can be expressed mathematically. Let X be the number of units produced and sold of Part X, and let Y stand for Part Y. Since the unit contribution margins are $300 and $600 for X and Y, respectively, the total contribution margin (Z) can be expressed as follows:

$$Z = \$300X + \$600Y \qquad (21.5)$$

Equation 21.5 is called the **objective function**, the function to be optimized.

		Part X Resource Usage: per Unit	Part Y Resource Usage: per Unit
Resource Name	**Resource Available**		
Grinding	80 grinding hours	One hour	One hour
Drilling	120 drilling hours	One hour	Three hours
Polishing	90 labor hours	Two hours	One hour
Market demand: Part X	60 units	One unit	Zero units
Market demand: Part Y	100 units	Zero units	One unit

EXHIBIT 21-8   Constraint Data: Schaller Company

Schaller also has five constraints. Using the information in Exhibit 21-8, the constraints are expressed mathematically as follows:

Internal constraints:

$$X + Y \leq 80 \tag{21.6}$$
$$X + 3Y \leq 120 \tag{21.7}$$
$$2X + Y \leq 90 \tag{21.8}$$

External constraints:

$$X \leq 60 \tag{21.9}$$
$$Y \leq 100 \tag{21.10}$$

Schaller's problem is to select the number of units of X and Y that maximize total contribution margin subject to the constraints in Equations 21.6–21.10. This problem can be expressed in the following way, which is the standard formulation for a linear programming problem (often referred to as a *linear programming model*):

$$\text{Max } Z = \$300X + \$600Y$$

subject to

$$X + Y \leq 80$$
$$X + 3Y \leq 120$$
$$2X + Y \leq 90$$
$$X \leq 60$$
$$Y \leq 100$$
$$X \geq 0$$
$$Y \geq 0$$

The last two constraints are called *nonnegativity constraints* and simply reflect the reality that negative quantities of a product cannot be produced. All constraints, taken together, are referred to as the **constraint set**.

A **feasible solution** is a solution that satisfies the constraints in the linear programming model. The collection of all feasible solutions is called the **feasible set of solutions**. For example, producing and selling one unit of Part X and one unit of Part Y would be a feasible solution and a member of the feasible set. This product mix clearly satisfies all constraints. But the mix would earn only $900 per week. However, many feasible solutions offer higher profits (for example, producing two of each part). The objective is to identify the best. The best feasible solution—the one that maximizes the total contribution margin—is called the **optimal solution**.

Graphical Solution

When there are only two products, the optimal solution can be identified by graphing. Since solving the problem by graphing provides considerable insight into the way linear programming problems are solved, the Schaller problem will be solved in this way. Four steps are followed in solving the problem graphically.

1. Graph each constraint.
2. Identify the feasible set of solutions.
3. Identify all corner-point values in the feasible set.
4. Select the corner point that yields the largest value for the objective function.

The graph of each constraint for the Schaller example is shown in Exhibit 21-9. The nonnegativity constraints put the graph in the first quadrant. The other constraints are graphed by assuming that equality holds. Since each constraint is a linear equation, the graph is obtained by identifying two points on the line, plotting those points, and connecting them.

EXHIBIT **21-9**   **Graphical Solution**

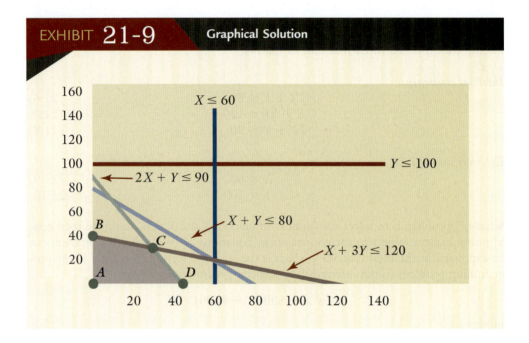

A feasible area for each constraint (except for the nonnegativity constraints) is determined by everything that lies below (or to the left of) the resulting line. The *feasible set* or *region* is the intersection of each constraint's feasible area. The feasible set is shown by the figure *ABCD* in the exhibit; it includes the boundary of the figure. Notice that only two of the five constraints qualify as candidates for binding constraints: the drilling and polishing constraints.

There are four corner points: *A*, *B*, *C*, and *D*. Their values, obtained directly from the graph, are (0, 0) for *A*, (0, 40) for *B*, (30, 30) for *C*, and (45, 0) for *D*. The impact of these values on the objective function is as follows (expressed in thousands):

Corner Point	*X-Value*	*Y-Value*	*Z* = *$300X* + *$600Y*
A	0	0	$ 0
B	0	40	24,000
C	30	30	27,000*
D	45	0	13,500

*Optimal solution.

The optimal solution calls for producing and selling 30 units of Part X per week and 30 units of Part Y per week. No other feasible solution will produce a larger contribution margin. It has been shown in the literature on linear programming that the optimal solution will always be one of the corner points. Thus, once the graph is drawn and the corner points are identified, finding the solution is simply a matter of computing the value of each corner point and selecting the one with the greatest value.

Graphical solutions are not practical with more than two or three products. Fortunately, an algorithm called the **simplex method** can be used to solve larger linear programming problems. This algorithm has been coded and is available for use on computers to solve these larger problems.

The linear programming model is an important tool for making product mix decisions. Although the linear programming model produces an optimal product mix decision, its real managerial value—particularly in today's business environment—may be more related to the kinds of inputs that must be generated for the model to be used. Unit-level prices and unit-level variable costs must be assessed. Furthermore, applying the model forces management to identify internal and external constraints. Internal constraints relate to how products consume resources; thus, resource usage relationships must be identified. Once the constrained relationships are known to management, they can be used by management to identify ways of improving a firm's performance in a variety of ways, including inventory management.

OBJECTIVE 4

Define the theory of constraints, and tell how it can be used to manage inventory.

Theory of Constraints

The goal of the **theory of constraints** is to make money now and in the future by managing constraints. The theory of constraints (TOC) recognizes that the performance of any organization (system) is limited by its constraints. In operational terms, every system has at least one constraint that limits its output. The theory of constraints develops a specific approach to manage constraints to support the objective of continuous improvement. TOC, however, focuses on the *system-level* effects of continuous improvement. Each company (i.e., system) is compared to a chain. Every chain has a weakest link that may limit the performance of the chain as a whole. The weakest link is the system's constraint and is the key to improving overall organizational performance. Why? Ignoring the weakest link and improving any other link costs money and will not improve system performance. On the other hand, by strengthening the weakest link, system performance can be improved. At some point, however, strengthening the weakest link shifts the focus to a different link that has now become the weakest. This next-weakest link is now the key system constraint, and it must be strengthened so that overall system performance can be improved. Thus, TOC can be thought of as a systems approach to continuous improvement.

Operational Measures

Given that the goal is to make money, TOC argues that the next crucial step is to identify operational measures that encourage achievement of the goal. TOC focuses on three operational measures of systems performance: *throughput, inventory,* and *operating expenses.* **Throughput** is the rate at which an organization generates money through sales.[10] Operationally, throughput is the *rate* at which *contribution dollars* come into the organization. Thus, we have the following operational definition:

$$\text{Throughput} = (\text{Sales revenue} - \text{Unit-level variable expenses})/\text{Time} \qquad (21.11)$$

Typically, the unit-level variable costs acknowledged are materials and power. Direct labor is viewed as a fixed unit-level expense and is not usually included in the definition.

---

10. This follows the definition of Eliyahi Goldratt and Robert Fox in *The Race*. Other definitions and basic concepts of the theory of constraints are also based upon the developments of Goldratt and Fox.

With this understanding, throughput corresponds to contribution margin. It is also important to note that it is a global measure and not a local measure. Finally, throughput is a rate. It is the contribution earned per unit of time (per day, per month, etc.).

Inventory is all the money the organization spends in turning materials into throughput. In operational terms, inventory is money invested in anything that it intends to sell and, thus, expands the traditional definition to include assets such as facilities, equipment (which are eventually sold at the end of their useful lives), fixtures, and computers. In the TOC world, inventory is the money spent on items that do not have to be immediately expensed. Thus, inventory represents the money tied up inside the organization.

Operating expenses are defined as all the money the organization spends in turning inventories into throughput and, therefore, represent all other money that an organization spends. This includes direct labor and all operating and maintenance expenses. Thus, throughput is a measure of money coming into an organization, inventory measures the money tied up within the system, and operating expenses represent money leaving the system. Based on these three measures, the objectives of management can be expressed as increasing throughput, minimizing inventory, and decreasing operating expenses.

By increasing throughput, minimizing inventory, and decreasing operating expenses, the following three traditional financial measures of performance will be affected favorably: net income and return on investment will increase and cash flow will improve. Of the three TOC factors, throughput is viewed as being the most important for improving financial performance, followed by inventory, and then by operating expenses. The rationale for this order is straightforward. Operating expenses and inventories can be reduced at most to zero (inventory, though, being the larger amount), while there is virtually no upper limit on throughput. Increasing throughput and decreasing operating expenses have always been emphasized as key elements in improving the three financial measures of performance; the role of minimizing inventory, however, in achieving these improvements has been traditionally regarded as less important than reducing operating expenses.

The theory of constraints, like JIT, assigns inventory management a much more prominent role than does the traditional just-in-case viewpoint. TOC recognizes that lowering inventory decreases carrying costs and, thus, decreases operating expenses and improves net income. TOC, however, argues that lowering inventory helps produce a competitive edge by having better products, lower prices, and faster response to customer needs.

Higher-Quality Products

Better products mean higher quality. It also means that the company is able to improve products and quickly provide these improved products to the market. The relationship between low inventories and quality has been described in the JIT section. Essentially, low inventories allow defects to be detected more quickly and the cause of the problem assessed.

Improving products is also a key competitive element. New or improved products need to reach the market quickly—before competitors can provide similar features. This goal is facilitated with low inventories. Low inventories allow new product changes to be introduced more quickly because the company has fewer old products (in stock or in process) that would need to be scrapped or sold before the new product is introduced.

Lower Prices

High inventories mean more productive capacity is needed, leading to a greater investment in equipment and space. Since lead time and high work-in-process inventories are usually correlated, high inventories may often be the cause of overtime. Overtime, of course, increases operating expenses and lowers profitability. Lower inventories reduce carrying costs, per-unit investment costs, and other operating expenses such as overtime and special shipping charges. By lowering investment and operating costs, the unit margin of each product is increased, providing more flexibility in pricing decisions.

Improved Delivery Performance

Delivering goods on time and producing goods with shorter lead times than the market dictates are important competitive tools. Delivering goods on time is related to a firm's ability to forecast the time required to produce and deliver goods. If a firm has higher inventories than its competitors, then the firm's production lead time is higher than the industry's forecast horizon. High inventories may obscure the actual time required to produce and fill an order. Lower inventories allow actual lead times to be more carefully observed, and more accurate delivery dates can be provided. Shortening lead times is also crucial. Shortening lead times is equivalent to lowering work-in-process inventories. A company carrying 10 days of work-in-process inventories has an average production lead time of 10 days. If the company can reduce lead time from 10 to five days, then the company should now be carrying only five days of work-in-process inventories. As lead times are reduced, it is also possible to reduce finished goods inventories. For example, if the lead time for a product is 10 days and the market requires delivery on demand, then the firms must carry, on average, 10 days of finished goods inventory (plus some safety stock to cover demand uncertainty). Suppose that the firm is able to reduce lead time to five days. In this case, finished goods inventory should also be reduced to five days. Thus, the level of inventories signals the organization's ability to respond. High levels relative to those of competitors translate into a competitive disadvantage. TOC, therefore, emphasizes reduction of inventories by reducing lead times.

Five-Step Method for Improving Performance

The theory of constraints uses five steps to achieve its goal of improving organizational performance:

1. Identify an organization's constraints.
2. Exploit the binding constraints.
3. Subordinate everything else to the decisions made in step 2.
4. Elevate the organization's binding constraints.
5. Repeat the process as a new constraint emerges to limit output.

Step 1: Identify an Organization's Constraints

Step 1 is identical in concept to the process described for linear programming. Internal and external constraints are identified. The optimal product mix is identified as the mix that maximizes throughput subject to all the organization's constraints. The optimal mix reveals how much of each constrained resource is used and which of the organization's constraints are binding.

Step 2: Exploit the Binding Constraints

One way to make the best use of any binding constraints is to ensure that the optimal product mix is produced. Making the best use of binding constraints, however, is more extensive than simply ensuring production of the optimal mix. This step is the heart of TOC's philosophy of short-run constraint management and is directly related to TOC's goal of reducing inventories and improving performance.

Most organizations have only a few binding resource constraints. The major binding constraint is defined as the **drummer**. Assume, for example, that there is only one internal binding constraint. By default, this constraint becomes the drummer. The drummer constraint's production rate sets the production rate for the entire plant. Downstream processes fed by the drummer constraint are naturally forced to follow its rate of production. Scheduling for downstream processes is easy. Once a part is finished at the drummer process, the next process begins its operation. Similarly, each subsequent operation begins when the prior operation is finished. Upstream processes that feed the drummer constraint are *scheduled* to produce at the same rate as the drummer constraint. Scheduling at the drummer rate prevents the production of excessive upstream work-in-process inventories.

For upstream scheduling, TOC uses two additional features in managing constraints to lower inventory levels and improve organizational performance: *buffers* and *ropes*. First, an inventory buffer is established in front of the major binding constraint. The inventory buffer is referred to as the *time buffer*. A **time buffer** is the inventory needed to keep the constrained resource busy for a specified time interval. The purpose of a time buffer is to protect the throughput of the organization from any disruption that can be overcome within the specified time interval. For example, if it takes one day to overcome most interruptions that occur upstream from the drummer constraint, then a 2-day buffer should be sufficient to protect throughput from any interruptions. Thus, in scheduling, the operation immediately preceding the drummer constraint should produce the parts needed by the drummer resource two days in advance of their planned usage. Any other preceding operations are scheduled backwards in time to produce so that their parts arrive just in time for subsequent operations.

Ropes are actions taken to tie the rate at which material is released into the plant (at the first operation) to the production rate of the constrained resource. The objective of a rope is to ensure that the work-in-process inventory will not exceed the level needed for the time buffer. Thus, the drummer rate is used to limit the rate of material release and effectively controls the rate at which the first operation produces. The rate of the first operation then controls the rates of subsequent operations. The TOC inventory system is often called the **drum-buffer-rope (DBR) system**. Exhibit 21-10 illustrates the DBR structure for a general setting.

The Schaller Company example used to illustrate constrained optimization also can be used to provide a specific illustration of the DBR system. Recall that there are three sequential processes: grinding, drilling, and polishing. Each of these processes has a limited amount of resources. Demand for each type of machine part produced is also limited. However, from Exhibit 21-9 we know that the only binding constraints are the drilling and polishing constraints. We also know that the optimal mix consists of 30 units of Part X and 30 units of Part Y (per week). This is the most that the drilling and polishing processes can handle. Since the drilling process feeds the polishing process, we can define the drilling constraint as the drummer for the plant. Assume that the demand for each part is uniformly spread out over the week. This means that the production rate should be six per day of each part (for a 5-day work week). A 2-day time buffer would require 24 completed parts from the grinding process: 12 for Part X and 12 for Part Y. To ensure that the time buffer does not increase at a rate greater than six per day for each part, materials should be released to the grinding process such that only six of each part can be produced each day. (This is the rope—tying the release of materials to the production rate of the drummer constraint.) Exhibit 21-11, on page 952, summarizes the specific DBR details for the Schaller Company.

Step 3: Subordinate Everything Else to the Decisions Made in Step 2

The drummer constraint essentially sets the capacity for the entire plant. All remaining departments should be subordinated to the needs of the drummer constraint. This principle requires many companies to change the way they view things. For example, the use of efficiency measures at the departmental level may no longer be appropriate. Consider the Schaller Company once again. Encouraging maximum productive efficiency for the grinding department would produce excess work-in-process inventories. The capacity of the grinding department is 80 units per week. Assuming the 2-day buffer is in place, the grinding department would add 20 units per week to the buffer in front of the drilling department. Over a period of a year, the potential exists for building very large work-in-process inventories (1,000 units of the two parts would be added to the buffer over a 50-week period).

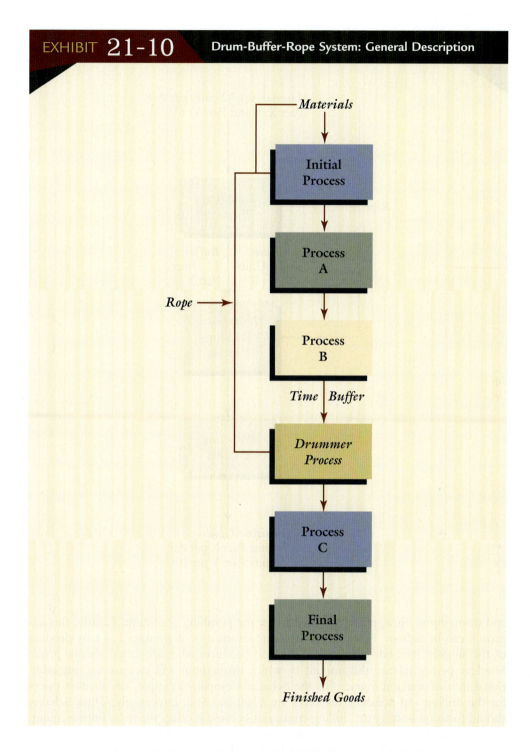

EXHIBIT 21-10   Drum-Buffer-Rope System: General Description

Step 4: Elevate the Organization's Binding Constraint(s)

Once actions have been taken to make the best possible use of the existing constraints, the next step is to embark on a program of continuous improvement by reducing the limitations that the binding constraints have on the organization's performance. However, if there is more than one binding constraint, which one should be elevated? For example, in the Schaller Company setting, there are two binding constraints: the drilling constraint and the polishing constraint. In this case, the guideline is to increase the resource of the constraint that produces the greatest increase in throughput. To determine the most profitable effort, assume that one additional unit of resource is available for drilling (other resources are held constant), and then calculate the new optimal mix

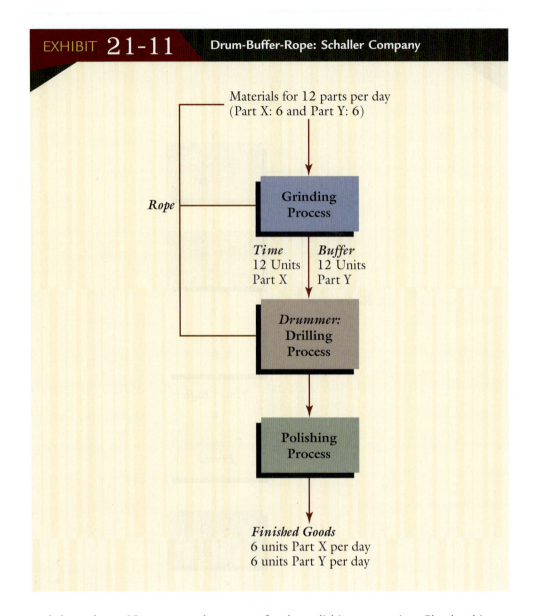

EXHIBIT 21-11   **Drum-Buffer-Rope: Schaller Company**

Materials for 12 parts per day
(Part X: 6 and Part Y: 6)

Rope

Grinding Process

Time	*Buffer*
12 Units	12 Units
Part X	Part Y

Drummer: **Drilling Process**

Polishing Process

Finished Goods
6 units Part X per day
6 units Part Y per day

and throughput. Now, repeat the process for the polishing constraint. Clearly, this approach can be tedious. Fortunately, the same information is produced as a by-product of the simplex method. The simplex method produces what are called *shadow prices*. Shadow prices indicate the amount by which throughput will increase for one additional unit of scarce resource. For the Schaller Company example, the shadow prices for the drilling and polishing resources are $180 and $60, respectively. Thus, Schaller should focus on busting the drilling constraint because it offers the most improvement.

Suppose, for example, that Schaller Company adds a half shift for the drilling department, increasing the drilling hours from 120 to 180 per week. Throughput will now be $37,800, an increase of $10,800 ($180 × 60 additional hours). Furthermore, as you can check, the optimal mix is now 18 units of Part X and 54 units of Part Y. Is the half shift worth it? This question is answered by comparing the cost of adding the half shift with the increased throughput. If the cost is labor—say overtime at $50 per hour (for all employees)—then the incremental cost is $3,000, and the decision to add the half shift is a good one.

Step 5: Repeat Process: Does a New Constraint Limit Throughput?

Eventually, the drilling resource constraint will be elevated to a point where the constraint is no longer binding. Suppose, for example, that the company adds a full shift for the drilling operation, increasing the resource availability to 240 hours. The new constraint set is shown in Exhibit 21-12. Notice that the drilling constraint no longer affects the optimal mix decision. The grinding and polishing resource constraints are possible candidates for the new drummer constraint. Once the drummer constraint is identified, then the TOC process is repeated (step 5). The objective is to continually improve performance by managing constraints. Do not allow inertia to cause a new constraint. Focus now on the next-weakest link.

EXHIBIT 21-12   **New Constraint Set: Schaller Company**

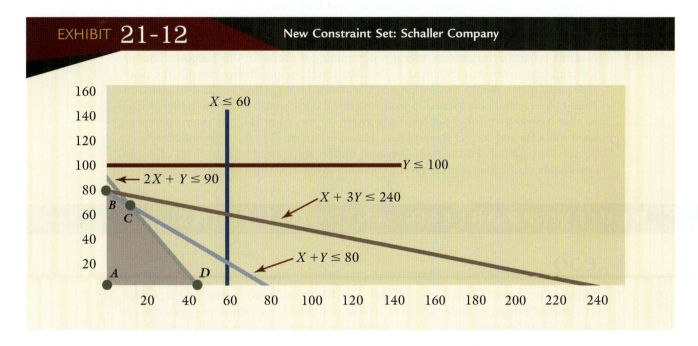

System Improvement

The five steps just described can produce significant improvements in systems performance. **Rockland Manufacturing**, a producer of attachments for heavy construction equipment, made more profit in the two years following TOC implementation than in the previous 10 years.[11] Rockland increased throughput, reduced work-in-process inventories, and achieved virtually a 100 percent on-time shipment rate. Similarly, **Boeing**'s Printed Circuit Board Center, after three years of TOC, managed to reduce lead time by 75 percent, increase throughput by over 100 percent, and achieve significant improvement in on-time delivery of its products.[12]

---

11. As described in "Success Stories," online at http://www.goldratt.com/success.htm, as of April 7, 1999.
12. Ibid.

SUMMARY

Three approaches to managing inventory were discussed: just-in-case, JIT, and theory of constraints. The traditional approach uses inventories to manage the trade-offs between ordering (setup) costs and carrying costs. The optimal trade-off defines the economic order quantity. Other reasons for inventories are also offered: due-date performance, avoiding shutdowns (protecting throughput), hedging against future price increases, and taking advantage of discounts. JIT and TOC, on the other hand, argue that inventories are costly and are used to cover up fundamental problems that need to be corrected so that the organization can become more competitive.

JIT uses long-term contracts, continuous replenishment, and EDI to reduce (eliminate) ordering costs. Engineering efforts are made to reduce setup times drastically. Once ordering costs and setup costs are reduced to minimal levels, then it is possible to reduce carrying costs by reducing inventory levels. JIT carries small buffers in front of each operation and uses a Kanban system to regulate production. Production is tied to market demand. If an interruption occurs, throughput tends to be lost because of the small buffers. Yet, future throughput tends to increase because efforts are made to improve such things as quality, productivity, and lead time.

TOC identifies an organization's constraints and exploits them so that throughput is maximized and inventories and operating costs are minimized. Identifying the optimal mix is part of this process. Linear programming is useful for this purpose. The major binding constraint is identified and is used to set the productive rate for the plant. Release of materials into the first process (operation) is regulated by the drummer constraint. A time buffer is located in front of critical constraints. This time buffer is sized so that it protects throughput from any interruptions. As in JIT, the interruptions are used to locate and correct the problem. However, unlike JIT, the time buffer serves to protect throughput. Furthermore, because buffers are located only in front of critical constraints, TOC may actually produce smaller inventories than JIT.

REVIEW PROBLEMS AND SOLUTIONS

1   EOQ

Verijon, Inc., uses 15,000 pounds of plastic each year in its production of plastic cups. The cost of placing an order is $10. The cost of holding one pound of plastic for one year is $0.30. Verijon uses an average of 60 pounds of plastic per day. It takes five days to place and receive an order.

Required:

1. Calculate the EOQ.
2. Calculate the annual ordering and carrying costs for the EOQ.
3. What is the reorder point?

SOLUTION

1. $\begin{aligned} \text{EOQ} &= \sqrt{2DP/C} \\ &= \sqrt{(2 \times 15{,}000 \times \$10)/\$0.30} \\ &= \sqrt{1{,}000{,}000} \\ &= 1{,}000 \end{aligned}$

2. Ordering cost $= (D/Q)P = (15{,}000/1{,}000)\$10 = \$150$
   Carrying cost $= (Q/2)C = (1{,}000/2)\$0.30 = \$150$

3. ROP $= 60 \times 5 = 300$ pounds (whenever inventory drops to this level, an order should be placed).

2   JIT, DRUM-BUFFER-ROPE SYSTEM

Both just-in-case and JIT inventory management systems have drummers—factors that determine the production rate of the plant. For a just-in-case system, the drummer is the excess capacity of the first operation. For JIT, the drummer is market demand.

Required:

1. Explain why the drummer of a just-in-case system is identified as excess demand of the first operation.
2. Explain how market demand drives the JIT production system.

3. Explain how a drummer constraint is used in the TOC approach to inventory management.

4. What are the advantages and disadvantages of the three types of drummers?

SOLUTION

1. In a traditional inventory system, local efficiency measures encourage the manager of the first operation to keep the department's workers busy. Thus, materials are released to satisfy this objective. This practice is justified because the inventory may be needed just in case demand is greater than expected, or just in case the first operation has downtime, etc.

2. In a JIT system, when the final operation delivers its goods to a customer, a backward rippling effect triggers the release of materials into the factory. First, the last process removes the buffer inventory from the withdrawal store, and this leads to a P-Kanban being placed on the production post of the preceding operation. This operation then begins production, withdrawing parts it needs from its withdrawal store, leading to a P-Kanban being placed on the production post of its preceding operation. This process repeats itself—all the way back to the first operation.

3. A drummer constraint sets the production rate of the factory to match its own production rate. This is automatically true for succeeding operations. For preceding operations, the rate is controlled by tying the drummer constraint's rate of production to that of the first operation. A time buffer is also set in front of the drummer constraint to protect throughput in the event of interruptions.

4. The excess capacity drummer typically will build excess inventories. This serves to protect current throughput. However, it ties up a lot of capital and tends to cover up problems such as poor quality, bad delivery performance, and inefficient production. Because it is costly and covers up certain critical productive problems, the just-in-case approach may be a threat to future throughput by damaging a firm's competitive position. JIT reduces inventories dramatically—using only small buffers in front of each operation as a means to regulate production flow and signal when production should occur. JIT has the significant advantage of uncovering problems and eventually correcting them. However, discovering problems usually means that current throughput will be lost while problems are being corrected. Future throughput tends to be protected because the firm is taking actions to improve its operations. TOC uses time buffers in front of the critical constraints. These buffers are large enough to keep the critical constraints operating while other operations may be down. Once the problem is corrected, the other resource constraints usually have sufficient excess capacity to catch up. Thus, current throughput is protected. Furthermore, future throughput is protected because TOC uses the same approach as JIT—namely, that of uncovering and correcting problems. TOC can be viewed as an improvement on JIT methods—correcting the lost throughput problem while maintaining the other JIT features.

KEY TERMS

QUESTIONS FOR WRITING AND DISCUSSION

1. What are ordering costs? What are setup costs? What are carrying costs? Provide examples of each type of cost.
2. Explain why, in the traditional view of inventory, carrying costs increase as ordering costs decrease.
3. Discuss the traditional reasons for carrying inventory.
4. What are stock-out costs?
5. Explain how safety stock is used to deal with demand uncertainty.
6. What is the economic order quantity?
7. What approach does JIT take to minimize total inventory costs?
8. One reason for inventory is to prevent shutdowns. How does the JIT approach to inventory management deal with this potential problem?
9. Explain how the Kanban system helps reduce inventories.
10. Explain how long-term contractual relationships with suppliers can reduce the acquisition cost of materials.
11. What is a constraint? An internal constraint? An external constraint?
12. Explain the procedures for graphically solving a linear programming problem. What solution method is used when the problem includes more than two or three products?
13. Define and discuss the three measures of organizational performance used by the theory of constraints.
14. Explain how lowering inventory produces better products, lower prices, and better responsiveness to customer needs.
15. What are the five steps that TOC uses to improve organizational performance?

EXERCISES

21-1 ORDERING AND CARRYING COSTS

LO1 Corsair, Inc., uses 40,000 plastic housing units each year in its production of paper shredders. The cost of placing an order is $40. The cost of holding one unit of inventory for one year is $5. Currently, Corsair places eight orders of 5,000 plastic housing units per year.

Required:

1. Compute the annual ordering cost.
2. Compute the annual carrying cost.
3. Compute the cost of Corsair's current inventory policy. Is this the minimum cost? Why or why not?

21-2 ECONOMIC ORDER QUANTITY

LO1   Refer to the data in **Exercise 21-1.**

Required:

1. Compute the economic order quantity.
2. Compute the ordering and carrying costs for the EOQ.
3. How much money does using the EOQ policy save the company over the policy of purchasing 5,000 plastic housing units per order?

21-3 ECONOMIC ORDER QUANTITY

LO1   Ulmer Company uses 312,500 pounds of sucrose each year. The cost of placing an order is $30, and the carrying cost for one pound of sucrose is $0.75.

Required:

1. Compute the economic order quantity for sucrose.
2. Compute the carrying and ordering costs for the EOQ.

21-4 REORDER POINT

LO1   Swann Company manufactures sleeping bags. A heavy-duty zipper is one part the company orders from an outside supplier. Information pertaining to the zipper is as follows:

Economic order quantity	4,200 units
Average daily usage	200 units
Maximum daily usage	240 units
Lead time	3 days

Required:

1. What is the reorder point assuming no safety stock is carried?
2. What is the reorder point assuming that safety stock is carried?

21-5 EOQ WITH SETUP COSTS

LO1   Pawnee Manufacturing produces casings for stereo sets: large and small. In order to produce the different casings, equipment must be set up. Each setup configuration corresponds to a particular type of casing. The setup cost per production run—for either casing—is $6,000. The cost of carrying small casings in inventory is $2 per casing per year. The cost of carrying large casings is $6 per year. To satisfy demand, the company produces 150,000 small casings and 50,000 large casings per year.

Required:

1. Compute the number of small casings that should be produced per setup to minimize total setup and carrying costs for this product.
2. Compute the total setup and carrying costs associated with the economic order quantity for the small casings.

21-6   EOQ with Setup Costs

LO1   Refer to **Exercise 21-5**.

Required:

1. Compute the number of large casings that should be produced per setup to minimize total setup and carrying costs for this product.
2. Compute the total setup and carrying costs associated with the economic order quantity for the large casings.

21-7   Reorder Point

LO1   Refer to **Exercise 21-5**. Assume the economic lot size for small casings is 30,000 and that of the large casings is 10,000. Pawnee Manufacturing sells an average of 590 small casings per workday and an average of 200 large casings per workday. It takes Pawnee three days to set up the equipment for small or large casings. Once set up, it takes 20 workdays to produce a batch of small casings and 20 days for large casings. There are 250 workdays available per year.

Required:

1. What is the reorder point for small casings? Large casings?
2. Using the economic order batch size, is it possible for Pawnee to produce the amount that can be sold of each casing? Does scheduling have a role here? Explain. Is this a push- or pull-through system approach to inventory management? Explain.

21-8   Safety Stock

LO1   Noble Manufacturing produces a component used in its production of clothes dryers. The time to set up and produce a batch of the components is two days. The average daily usage is 320 components, and the maximum daily usage is 375 components.

Required:

Compute the reorder point assuming that safety stock is carried by Noble Manufacturing. How much safety stock is carried by Noble?

21-9   Kanban System, EDI

LO2   Hales Company produces a product that requires two processes. In the first process, a subassembly is produced (subassembly A). In the second process, this subassembly and a subassembly purchased from outside the company (subassembly B) are assembled to produce the final product. For simplicity, assume that the assembly of one final unit takes the same time as the production of subassembly A. Subassembly A is placed in a container and sent to an area called the subassembly stores (SB stores) area. A production Kanban is attached to this container. A second container, also with one subassembly, is located near the assembly line (called the withdrawal store). This container has attached to it a withdrawal Kanban.

Required:

1. Explain how withdrawal and production Kanban cards are used to control the work flow between the two processes. How does this approach minimize inventories?

2. Explain how vendor Kanban cards can be used to control the flow of the purchased subassembly. What implications does this have for supplier relationships? What role, if any, do continuous replenishment and EDI play in this process?

21-10   JIT Limitations

LO2   Many companies have viewed JIT as a panacea—a knight in shining armor which promises rescue from sluggish profits, poor quality, and productive inefficiency. It is often lauded for its beneficial effects on employee morale and self-esteem. Yet, JIT may also cause a company to struggle and may produce a good deal of frustration. In some cases, JIT appears to deliver less than its reputation seems to call for.

Required:

Discuss some of the limitations and problems that companies may encounter when implementing a JIT system.

21-11   Product Mix Decision, Single Constraint

LO3   Behar Company makes three types of stainless steel frying pans. Each of the three types of pans requires the use of a special machine that has total operating capacity of 182,000 hours per year. Information on each of the three products is as follows:

Spreadsheet

	Basic	Standard	Deluxe
Selling price	$12.00	$17.00	$32.00
Unit variable cost	$7.00	$11.00	$12.00
Machine hours required	0.10	0.20	0.50

The marketing manager has determined that the company can sell all that it can produce of each of the three products.

Required:

1. How many of each product should be sold to maximize total contribution margin? What is the total contribution margin for this product mix?
2. Suppose that Behar can sell no more than 300,000 units of each type at the prices indicated. What product mix would you recommend, and what would be the total contribution margin?

21-12   Drum-Buffer-Rope System

LO4   Duckstein, Inc., manufactures two types of aspirin: plain and buffered. It sells all it produces. Recently, Duckstein implemented a TOC approach for its Fort Smith plant. One binding constraint was identified, and the optimal product mix was determined. The diagram on the following page reflects the TOC outcome:

Required:

1. What is the daily production rate? Which process sets this rate?
2. How many days of buffer inventory is Duckstein carrying? How is this time buffer determined?
3. Explain what the letters A, B, and C in the exhibit represent. Discuss each of their roles in the TOC system.

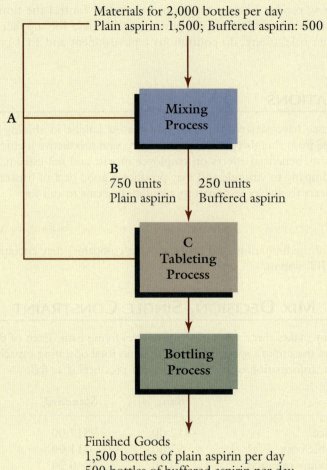

Materials for 2,000 bottles per day
Plain aspirin: 1,500; Buffered aspirin: 500

A

Mixing Process

B
750 units
Plain aspirin

250 units
Buffered aspirin

C Tableting Process

Bottling Process

Finished Goods
1,500 bottles of plain aspirin per day
500 bottles of buffered aspirin per day

PROBLEMS

21-13 EOQ, SAFETY STOCK, LEAD TIME, BATCH SIZE, AND JIT

LO1, LO2 Bateman Company produces helmets for drivers of motorcycles. Helmets are produced in batches according to model and size. Although the setup and production time vary for each model, the smallest lead time is six days. The most popular model, Model HA2, takes two days for setup, and the production rate is 750 units per day. The expected annual demand for the model is 36,000 units. Demand for the model, however, can reach 45,000 units. The cost of carrying one HA2 helmet is $3 per unit. The setup cost is $6,000. Bateman chooses its batch size based on the economic order quantity criterion. Expected annual demand is used to compute the EOQ.

Recently, Bateman has encountered some stiff competition—especially from foreign sources. Some of the foreign competitors have been able to produce and deliver the helmets to retailers in half the time it takes Bateman to produce. For example, a large retailer recently requested a delivery of 12,000 Model HA2 helmets with the stipulation that the helmets be delivered within seven working days. Bateman had 3,000 units of HA2 in stock. Bateman informed the potential customer that it could deliver 3,000 units immediately and the other 9,000 units in about 14 working days—with the possibility of interim partial orders being delivered. The customer declined the offer indicating that the total order had to be delivered within seven working days so that its stores could take advantage of some special local conditions. The customer expressed regret and indicated that it would accept the order from another competitor who could satisfy the time requirements.

Required:

1. Calculate the optimal batch size for Model HA2 using the EOQ model. Was Bateman's response to the customer right? Would it take the time indicated to produce the number of units wanted by the customer? Explain with supporting computations.

2. Upon learning of the lost order, the marketing manager grumbled about Bateman's inventory policy. "We lost the order because we didn't have sufficient inventory. We need to carry more units in inventory to deal with unexpected orders like these." Do you agree or disagree? How much additional inventory would have been needed to meet customer requirements? In the future, should Bateman carry more inventory? Can you think of other solutions?

3. Fenton Gray, the head of industrial engineering, reacted differently to the lost order. "Our problem is more complex than insufficient inventory. I know that our foreign competitors carry much less inventory than we do. What we need to do is decrease the lead time. I have been studying this problem, and my staff have found a way to reduce setup time for Model HA2 from two days to 1.5 hours. Using this new procedure, setup cost can be reduced to about $94. Also, by rearranging the plant layout for this product—creating what are called manufacturing cells—we can increase the production rate from 750 units per day to about 2,000 units per day. This is done simply by eliminating a lot of move time and waiting time—both non-value-added activities." Assume that the engineer's estimates are on target. Compute the new optimal batch size (using the EOQ formula). What is the new lead time? Given this new information, would Bateman have been able to meet the customer's time requirements? Assume that there are eight hours available in each workday.

4. Suppose that the setup time and cost are reduced to 0.5 hour and $10, respectively. What is the batch size now? As setup time approaches zero and the setup cost becomes negligible, what does this imply? Assume, for example, that it takes five minutes to set up, and costs are about $0.864 per setup.

21-14 PRODUCT MIX DECISIONS, MULTIPLE CONSTRAINTS

LO3 Cardin Company produces two types of gears: Model #12 and Model #15. Market conditions limit the number of each gear that can be sold. For Model #12, no more than 15,000 units can be sold, and for Model #15, no more than 40,000 units. Each gear must be notched by a special machine. Cardin owns eight machines that together provide 40,000 hours of machine time per year. Each unit of Model #12 requires two hours of machine time, and each unit of Model #15 requires one half hour of machine time. The unit contribution for Model #12 is $30 and for Model #15 is $15. Cardin wants to identify the product mix that will maximize total contribution margin.

Required:

1. Formulate Cardin's problem as a linear programming model.
2. Solve the linear programming model in Requirement 1.
3. Identify which constraints are binding and which are loose. Also, identify the constraints as internal or external.

21-15 PRODUCT MIX DECISION, SINGLE AND MULTIPLE CONSTRAINTS

LO3   Taylor Company produces two industrial cleansers that use the same liquid chemical input: Pocolimpio and Maslimpio. Pocolimpio uses two quarts of the chemical for every unit produced, and Maslimpio uses five quarts. Currently, Taylor has 6,000 quarts of the material in inventory. All of the material is imported. For the coming year, Taylor plans to import 6,000 quarts to produce 1,000 units of Pocolimpio and 2,000 units of Maslimpio. The detail of each product's unit contribution margin is as follows:

	Pocolimpio	*Maslimpio*
Selling price	$ 81	$139
Less variable expenses:		
Direct materials	(20)	(50)
Direct labor	(21)	(14)
Variable overhead	(10)	(15)
Contribution margin	$ 30	$ 60

Taylor Company has received word that the source of the material has been shut down by embargo. Consequently, the company will not be able to import the 6,000 quarts it planned to use in the coming year's production. There is no other source of the material.

Required:

1. Compute the total contribution margin that the company would earn if it could import the 6,000 quarts of the material.
2. Determine the optimal usage of the company's inventory of 6,000 quarts of the material. Compute the total contribution margin for the product mix that you recommend.
3. Assume that Pocolimpio uses three direct labor hours for every unit produced and that Maslimpio uses two hours. A total of 6,000 direct labor hours is available for the coming year.
   a. Formulate the linear programming problem faced by Taylor Company. To do so, you must derive mathematical expressions for the objective function and for the material and labor constraints.
   b. Solve the linear programming problem using the graphical approach.
   c. Compute the total contribution margin produced by the optimal mix.

21-16 PRODUCT MIX DECISION, SINGLE AND MULTIPLE CONSTRAINTS, BASICS OF LINEAR PROGRAMMING

LO3   Desayuno Products, Inc., produces cornflakes and branflakes. The manufacturing process is highly mechanized; both products are produced by the same machinery by using different settings. For the coming period, 200,000 machine hours are available. Management is trying to decide on the quantities of each product to produce. The following data are available:

Spreadsheet

	Cornflakes	*Branflakes*
Machine hours per unit	1.00	0.50
Unit selling price	$2.50	$3.00
Unit variable cost	$1.50	$2.25

Required:

1. Determine the units of each product that should be produced in order to maximize profits.

2. Because of market conditions, the company can sell no more than 150,000 packages of cornflakes and 300,000 boxes of branflakes. Do the following:
    a. Formulate the problem as a linear programming problem.
    b. Determine the optimal mix using a graph.
    c. Compute the maximum contribution margin given the optimal mix.

21-17 PRODUCT MIX DECISIONS

LO3

CMA

Calen Company manufactures and sells three products in a factory of three departments. Both labor and machine time are applied to the products as they pass through each department. The nature of the machine processing and of the labor skills required in each department is such that neither machines nor labor can be switched from one department to another.

Calen's management is attempting to plan its production schedule for the next several months. The planning is complicated by the fact that labor shortages exist in the community and some machines will be down several months for repairs.

Following is information regarding available machine and labor time by department and the machine hours and direct labor hours required per unit of product. These data should be valid for at least the next six months.

		Department		
Monthly Capacity		*1*	*2*	*3*
Labor hours available		3,700	4,500	2,750
Machine hours available		3,000	3,100	2,700
Product	**Input per Unit Produced**			
401	Labor hours	2	3	3
	Machine hours	1	1	2
402	Labor hours	1	2	—
	Machine hours	1	1	—
403	Labor hours	2	2	2
	Machine hours	2	2	1

Calen believes that the monthly demand for the next six months will be as follows:

Product	Units Sold
401	500
402	400
403	1,000

Inventory levels will not be increased or decreased during the next six months. The unit cost and price data for each product are as follows:

	Product		
	401	*402*	*403*
Unit costs:			
Direct material	$ 7	$ 13	$ 17
Direct labor	66	38	51
Variable overhead	27	20	25
Fixed overhead	15	10	32
Variable selling	3	2	4
Total unit cost	$118	$ 83	$129
Unit selling price	$196	$123	$167

Required:

1. Calculate the monthly requirement for machine hours and direct labor hours for producing Products 401, 402, and 403 to determine whether or not the factory can meet the monthly sales demand.
2. Determine the quantities of 401, 402, and 403 that should be produced monthly to maximize profits. Prepare a schedule that shows the contribution to profits of your product mix.
3. Assume that the machine hours available in department 3 are 1,500 instead of 2,700. Calculate the optimal monthly product mix using the graphing approach to linear programming. Prepare a schedule that shows the contribution to profits from this optimal mix. *(CMA adapted)*

21-18 IDENTIFYING AND EXPLOITING CONSTRAINTS, CONSTRAINT ELEVATION

LO4   Berry Company produces two different metal components used in medical equipment (Component X and Component Y). The company has three processes: molding, grinding, and finishing. In molding, molds are created, and molten metal is poured into the shell. Grinding removes the gates that allowed the molten metal to flow into the mold's cavities. In finishing, rough edges caused by the grinders are removed by small, hand-held pneumatic tools. In molding, the setup time is one hour. The other two processes have no setup time required. The demand for Component X is 300 units per day, and the demand for Component Y is 500 units per day. The minutes required per unit for each product are as follows:

	Minutes Required per Unit of Product		
Product	*Molding*	*Grinding*	*Finishing*
Component X	5	10	15
Component Y	10	15	20

The company operates one 8-hour shift. The molding process employs 12 workers (who each work eight hours). Two hours of their time, however, are used for setups (assuming both products are produced). The grinding process has sufficient equipment and workers to provide 200 grinding hours per shift.

The finishing department is labor intensive and employs 35 workers, who each work eight hours per day. The only significant unit-level variable costs are materials and power. For Component X, the variable cost per unit is $40, and for Component Y, it is $50. Selling prices for X and Y are $90 and $110, respectively. Berry's policy is to use two setups per day: an initial setup to produce all that is scheduled for Component X and a second setup (changeover) to produce all that is scheduled for Component Y. The amount scheduled does not necessarily correspond to each product's daily demand.

Required:

1. Calculate the time (in minutes) needed each day to meet the daily market demand for Component X and Component Y. What is the major internal constraint facing Berry Company?
2. Describe how Berry should exploit its major binding constraint. Specifically, identify the product mix that will maximize daily throughput.
3. Assume that manufacturing engineering has found a way to reduce the molding setup time from one hour to 10 minutes. Explain how this affects the product mix and daily throughput.

21-19   THEORY OF CONSTRAINTS, INTERNAL CONSTRAINTS

LO4   Pratt Company produces two replacement parts for a popular line of VCRs: Part A and Part B. Part A is made up of two components, one manufactured internally and one purchased from external suppliers. Part B is made up of three components, one manufactured internally and two purchased from suppliers. The company has two processes: fabrication and assembly. In fabrication, the internally produced components are made. Each component takes 20 minutes to produce. In assembly, it takes 30 minutes to assemble the components for Part A and 40 minutes to assemble the components for Part B. Pratt Company operates one shift per day. Each process employs 100 workers who each work eight hours per day.

Part A earns a unit contribution margin of $20, and Part B earns a unit contribution margin of $24 (calculated as the difference between revenue and the cost of materials and energy). Pratt can sell all that it produces of either part. There are no other constraints. Pratt can add a second shift of either process. Although a second shift would work eight hours, there is no mandate that it employ the same number of workers. The labor cost per hour for fabrication is $15, and the labor cost per hour for assembly is $12.

Required:

1. Identify the constraints facing Pratt, and graph them. How many binding constraints are possible? What is Pratt's optimal product mix? What daily contribution margin is produced by this mix?
2. What is the drummer constraint? How much excess capacity does the other constraint have? Assume that a 1.5-day buffer inventory is needed to deal with any production interruptions. Describe the drum-buffer-rope concept using the Pratt data to illustrate the process.
3. Explain why the use of local labor efficiency measures will not work in Pratt's TOC environment.
4. Suppose Pratt decides to elevate the binding constraint by adding a second shift of 50 workers (labor rates are the same as those of the first shift). Would elevation of Pratt's binding constraint improve its system performance? Explain with supporting computations.

21-20   TOC, INTERNAL AND EXTERNAL CONSTRAINTS

LO4   Bountiful Manufacturing produces two types of bike frames (Frame X and Frame Y). Frame X passes through four processes: cutting, welding, polishing, and painting. Frame Y uses three of the same processes: cutting, welding, and painting. Each of the four processes employs 10 workers who work eight hours each day. Frame X sells for $40 per unit, and Frame Y sells for $55 per unit. Materials is the only unit-level variable expense. The materials cost for Frame X is $20 per unit, and the materials cost for Frame Y is $25 per unit. Bountiful's accounting system has provided the following additional information about its operations and products:

Resource Name	Resource Available	Frame X Resource Usage per Unit	Frame Y Resource Usage per Unit
Cutting labor	4,800 minutes	15 minutes	10 minutes
Welding labor	4,800 minutes	15 minutes	30 minutes
Polishing labor	4,800 minutes	15 minutes	—
Painting labor	4,800 minutes	10 minutes	15 minutes
Market demand:			
Frame X	200 per day	One unit	—
Frame Y	100 per day	—	One unit

Bountiful's management has determined that any production interruptions can be corrected within two days.

Required:

1. Assuming that Bountiful can meet daily market demand, compute the potential daily profit. Now, compute the minutes needed for each process to meet the daily market demand. Can Bountiful meet daily market demand? If not, where is the bottleneck? Can you derive an optimal mix without using a graphical solution? If so, explain how.
2. Identify the objective function and the constraints. Then, graph the constraints facing Bountiful. Determine the optimal mix and the maximum daily contribution margin (throughput).
3. Explain how a drum-buffer-rope system would work for Bountiful.
4. Suppose that the engineering department has proposed a process design change that will increase the polishing time for Frame X from 15 to 23 minutes per unit and decrease the welding time from 15 minutes to 10 minutes per unit (for Frame X). The cost of process redesign would be $10,000. Evaluate this proposed change. What step in the TOC process does this proposal represent?

21-21 COLLABORATIVE LEARNING EXERCISE

LO1, LO2, LO4

The following reasons have been offered for holding inventories:

a. To balance ordering or setup costs and carrying costs
b. To satisfy customer demand (e.g., meet delivery dates)
c. To avoid shutting down manufacturing facilities because of:
    (1) Machine failure
    (2) Defective parts
    (3) Unavailable parts
d. Unreliable production processes
e. To take advantage of discounts
f. To hedge against future price increases

Required:

Form groups of three to five. Each of the groups will choose one of the letters, "a" through "f," corresponding to the above reasons for holding inventory. No group can choose a letter chosen by another group until all the letters are used. The letter selection process ends when each group has at least one letter. Each group will determine how the JIT approach responds to their designated reason(s) for holding inventory. The groups will then share their answers with the other groups.

21-22 CYBER RESEARCH CASE

LO4

Please answer each of the following:

1. Go to http://www.goldratt.com, and locate the list of cases detailing successful use of the theory of constraints. Pick three cases, and summarize the benefits each firm realized from implementing TOC.
2. Access the library at http://www.goldratt.com, and see if you can find any information on what TOC followers call the "Thinking Process." If not, then do a general Internet search to find the information. Once located, describe what is meant by the "Thinking Process."

A

ABC database the collected data sets that are organized and interrelated for use by an organization's activity-based costing information system.

absorption costing a costing method that assigns all manufacturing costs, including direct materials, direct labor, variable overhead, and a share of fixed overhead, to each unit of product.

absorption-costing income income computed by following a functional classification.

acceptable quality level (AQL) a predetermined level of defective products that a company permits to be sold.

accounting information system a system consisting of interrelated manual and computer parts that uses processes such as collecting, recording, summarizing, analyzing (using decision models), and managing data to provide output information to users.

accounting rate of return the rate of return obtained by dividing the average accounting net income by the original investment (or by average investment).

activity a basic unit of work performed within an organization. It also can be defined as an aggregation of actions within an organization useful to managers for purposes of planning, controlling, and decision making.

activity analysis the process of identifying, describing, and evaluating the activities an organization performs.

activity attributes financial and nonfinancial information items that provide descriptive labels for individual activities.

activity capacity the ability to perform activities or the number of times an activity can be performed.

activity dictionary lists the activities in an organization along with desired attributes.

activity drivers measure the demands that cost objects place on activities.

activity elimination the process of eliminating non-value-added activities.

activity flexible budgeting the prediction of what activity costs will be as activity output changes.

activity inputs resources consumed by an activity in producing its output. (They are the factors that enable the activity to be performed.)

activity inventory a listing of the activities performed within an organization.

activity output the result or product of an activity.

activity output measure assesses the number of times the activity is performed. It is the quantifiable measure of the output.

activity productivity analysis an approach that directly measures changes in activity productivity.

activity rate the average unit cost, obtained by dividing the resource expenditure by the activity's practical capacity.

activity reduction decreasing the time and resources required by an activity.

activity selection the process of choosing among sets of activities caused by competing strategies.

activity sharing increasing the efficiency of necessary activities by using economies of scale.

activity volume variance the cost difference of the actual activity capacity acquired and the capacity that should be used.

activity-based budgeting system budgeting the costs of resources at the activity level.

activity-based costing assigns costs to cost objects by first tracing costs to activities and then tracing costs to cost objects.

activity-based costing (ABC) system a cost accounting system that uses both unit and non-unit-based cost drivers to assign costs to cost objects by first tracing costs to activities and then tracing costs from activities to products.

activity-based management (ABM) an advanced control system that focuses management's attention on activities with the objective of improving the value received by the customer and the profit received by providing this value. It includes driver analysis, activity analysis, and performance evaluation and draws on activity-based costing as a major source of information.

activity-based responsibility accounting assigns responsibility to processes and uses both financial and nonfinancial measures of performance.

actual cost system a cost measurement system in which actual manufacturing costs are assigned to products.

adjusted cost of goods sold normal cost of goods sold adjusted to include overhead variance.

administrative costs all costs associated with the general administration of the organization that cannot be reasonably assigned to either marketing or production.

administrative expense budget a budget consisting of estimated expenditures for the overall organization and operation of the company.

advance pricing agreement (APAs) an agreement between the internal revenue service and a taxpayer on the acceptability of a transfer price. The agreement is private and is binding on both parties for a specified period of time.

aesthetics a quality attribute that is concerned with the appearance of tangible products (for example, style and beauty) as well as the appearance of the facilities, equipment, personnel, and communication materials associated with services.

allocation assignment of indirect costs to cost objects.

allocative efficiency the point at which given the mixes that satisfy the condition of technical efficiency, the least costly mix is chosen.

annuity a series of future cash flows.

applied overhead the overhead assigned to production using a predetermined overhead rate.

appraisal costs costs incurred to determine whether or not products and services are conforming to requirements.

arbitrage a situation when customers who purchase a good at a lower price are able to resell it to other customers.

assets unexpired costs.

B

backflush costing a simplified approach for cost flow accounting that uses trigger points to determine when manufacturing costs are assigned to key inventory and temporary accounts.

Balanced Scorecard a strategic-based performance management system that typically identifies objectives and measures for four different perspectives: the financial perspective, the customer perspective, the process perspective, and the learning and growth perspective.

base period a prior period used to set the benchmark for measuring productivity changes.

batch production processes a process that produces batches of different products that are identical in many ways but differ in others.

batch-level activities activities performed each time a batch is produced.

benchmarking uses best practices as the standard for evaluating activity performance.

bill of activities specifies the product, product quantity, activity, and amount of each activity expected to be consumed by each product.

binding constraint constraints whose limited resources are fully used by a product mix.

break-even point the point where total sales revenue equals total costs, i.e., the point of zero profits.

budget a plan of action expressed in financial terms.

budget committee a committee responsible for setting budgetary policies and goals, reviewing and approving the budget, and resolving any differences that may arise in the budgetary process.

budget director the individual responsible for coordinating and directing the overall budgeting process.

budgetary slack the process of padding the budget by overestimating costs and underestimating revenues.

business ethics learning what is right or wrong in the work environment and choosing what is right.

by-product a secondary product recovered in the course of manufacturing a primary product during a joint process.

C

capital budgeting the process of making capital investment decisions.

capital expenditures budget a financial plan outlining the acquisition of long-term assets.

capital investment decisions decisions concerned with the process of planning, setting goals and priorities, arranging financing, and using certain criteria to select long-term assets.

carrying costs the costs of holding inventory.

cash budget a detailed plan that outlines all sources and uses of cash.

causal factors activities or variables that invoke service costs. Generally, it is desirable to use causal factors as the basis for allocating service costs.

centralized decision making a system in which decisions are made at the top level of an organization and local managers are given the charge to implement them.

Certified Internal Auditor (CIA) an accountant certified to possess the professional qualifications of an internal auditor.

Certified Management Accountant (CMA) an accountant who has satisfied the requirements to hold a certificate in management accounting.

Certified Public Accountant (CPA) an accountant certified to possess the professional qualifications of an external auditor.

coefficient of correlation the square root of the coefficient of determination, which is used to express not only the degree of correlation between two variables but also the direction of the relationship.

coefficient of determination the percentage of total variability in a dependent variable (e.g., cost) that is explained by an independent variable (e.g., activity level). It assumes a value of between 0 and 1.

committed fixed expenses costs incurred for the acquisition of long-term activity capacity, usually as the result of strategic planning.

committed resources acquired as used and needed, these are a strictly variable cost. The quantity supplied equals quantity demanded, so there is no excess capacity.

common cost the cost of a resource used in the output of two or more services or products.

common fixed expenses fixed costs that are not traceable to the segments and that would remain even if one of the segments were eliminated.

comparable uncontrolled price method the transfer price most preferred by the Internal Revenue Service under Section 482. The comparable uncontrolled price is essentially equal to the market price.

competitive advantage creating better customer value for the same or lower cost than can competitors or equivalent value for lower cost than can competitors.

compliance management the practice of achieving the minimal environmental performance required by regulations, and to do as cheaply as possible.

compounding of interest paying interest on interest.

concatenated keys two or more keys that uniquely identify a record.

confidence interval prediction interval that provides a range of values for the actual cost with a prespecified degree of confidence.

constant gross margin percentage method a joint cost allocation method that maintains the same gross margin percentage for each product.

constrained optimization choosing the optimal mix given the constraints faced by the firm.

constraint set the collection of all constraints that pertain to a particular optimization problem.

constraints a mathematical expression that expresses a resource limitation.

consumable life the length of time that a product serves the needs of a customer.

consumption ratio the proportion of an overhead activity consumed by a product.

continuous improvement the relentless pursuit of improvement in the delivery of value to customers; searching for ways to increase overall efficiency by reducing waste, improving quality, and reducing costs.

continuous (or rolling) budget a moving twelve-month budget with a future month added as the current month expires.

continuous replenishment when a manufacturer assumes the inventory management function for the retailer.

contribution margin the difference between revenue and all variable expenses.

contribution margin ratio contribution margin divided by sales revenue. It is the proportion of each sales dollar available to cover fixed costs and provide for profit.

contribution margin variance the difference between actual and budgeted contribution margin.

contribution margin volume variance the difference between the actual quantity sold and the budgeted quantity sold multiplied by the budgeted average unit contribution margin.

control the process of setting standards, receiving feedback on actual performance, and taking corrective action whenever actual performance deviates significantly from planned performance.

control activities activities performed by an organization to prevent or detect poor quality (because poor quality may exist).

control costs costs incurred from performing control activities.

control limits the maximum allowable deviation from a standard.

controllable costs costs that managers have the power to influence.

controller the chief accountant of an organization.

controlling the monitoring of a plan through the use of feedback to ensure that the plan is being implemented as expected.

conversion cost the sum of direct labor cost and overhead cost.

core objectives and measures those objectives and measures common to most organizations.

cost the cash or cash equivalent value sacrificed for goods and services that are expected to bring a current or future benefit to the organization.

cost accounting a subsystem of cost management that is concerned with determining the cost of products, services, projects, activities, and other objects that may be of interest to managers.

cost accounting information system a cost management subsystem designed to assign costs to individual products and services and other objects as specified by management.

cost accumulation the recognition and recording of costs.

cost assignment the process of associating manufacturing costs with the units produced.

cost behavior the way in which a cost changes in relation to changes in activity usage.

cost center a responsibility center in which a manager is responsible for cost.

cost leadership strategy providing the same or better value to customers at a lower cost than offered by competitors.

cost management identifies, collects, measures, classifies, and reports information that is useful to managers in costing (determining what something costs), planning, controlling, and decision making.

cost management information system an accounting information subsystem that is primarily concerned with producing outputs for internal users using inputs and processes needed to satisfy management objectives.

cost measurement the process of assigning dollar values to cost items.

cost object any item such as products, departments, projects, activities, and so on, for which costs are measured and assigned.

cost of goods manufactured the total cost of goods completed during the current period.

cost of goods sold the cost of direct materials, direct labor, and overhead attached to the units sold.

cost reconciliation determining whether the costs assigned to units

transferred out and to units in ending work in process are equal to the costs in beginning work in process plus the manufacturing costs incurred in the current period.

cost-plus method a transfer price acceptable to the Internal Revenue Service under Section 482. The cost-plus method is simply a cost-based transfer price.

cost-volume-profit graph a graph that depicts the relationships among costs, volume, and profits. It consists of a total revenue line and a total cost line.

costs of quality costs incurred because poor quality may exist or because poor quality does exist.

cumulative average-time learning curve model the model stating that the cumulative average time per unit decreases by a constant percentage, or learning rate, each time the cumulative quantity of units produced doubles.

currency appreciation the state of a country's currency becoming stronger and being able to purchase more units of another country's currency.

currency depreciation the state of a country's currency becoming weaker and being able to purchase fewer units of another country's currency.

currency risk management a company's management of its transaction, economic, and translation exposure due to exchange rate fluctuations.

currently attainable standard a standard that reflects an efficient operating state; it is rigorous but achievable.

customer perspective a Balanced Scorecard viewpoint that defines the customer and market segments in which the business will compete.

customer value the difference between what a customer receives (customer realization) and what the customer gives up (customer sacrifice).

cycle time the length of time required to produce one unit of a product.

D

data set a grouping of logically related data.

decentralization the granting of decision-making freedom to lower operating levels.

decentralized decision making a system in which decisions are made and implemented by lower-level managers.

decision making the process of choosing among competing alternatives.

decision model a set of procedures that, if followed, will lead to a decision.

decision package a description of services, with associated costs, that a decision unit can or would like to offer.

decline stage the stage in a product's life cycle when the product loses market acceptance and sales begin to decrease.

defective product a product or service that does not conform to specifications.

degree of operating leverage a measure of the sensitivity of profit changes to changes in sales volume. It measures the percentage change in profits resulting from a percentage change in sales.

dependent variable a variable whose value depends on the value of another variable. For example, Y in the cost formula $Y = F + VX$ depends on the value of X.

deviation the difference between the cost predicted by a cost formula and the actual cost. It measures the distance of a data point from the cost line.

differentiation strategy an approach that strives to increase customer value by increasing what the customer receives.

direct costs costs that can be easily and accurately traced to a cost object.

direct fixed expenses fixed costs that can be traced to each segment and would be avoided if the segment did not exist.

direct labor labor that is traceable to the goods or services being produced.

direct labor budget a budget showing the total direct labor hours needed and the associated cost for the number of units in the production budget.

direct labor efficiency variance the difference between the actual direct labor hours used and the standard direct labor hours allowed multiplied by the standard hourly wage rate.

direct labor rate variance the difference between the actual hourly rate paid and the standard hourly rate multiplied by the actual hours worked.

direct materials those materials that are traceable to the good or service being produced.

direct materials price variance the difference between the actual price paid per unit of materials and the standard price allowed per unit multiplied by the actual quantity of materials purchased.

direct materials purchases budget a budget that outlines the expected usage of materials production and purchases of the direct materials required.

direct materials usage variance the difference between the direct materials actually used and the direct materials allowed for the actual output multiplied by the standard price.

direct method a method that allocates service costs directly to producing departments. This method ignores any interactions that may exist among service departments.

direct tracing the process of identifying costs that are specifically or physically associated with a cost object.

discount factor the factor used to convert a future cash flow to its present value.

discount rate the rate of return used to compute the present value of future cash flows.

discounted cash flows future cash flows expressed in present value terms.

discounting the act of finding the present value of future cash flows.

discounting models any capital investment model that explicitly considers the time value of money in identifying criteria for accepting or rejecting proposed projects.

discretionary fixed expenses costs incurred for the acquisition of short-term capacity or services, usually as the result of yearly planning.

double-loop feedback information about both the effectiveness of strategy implementation and the validity of assumptions underlying the strategy.

driver analysis the effort expended to identify those factors that are the root causes of activity costs.

driver tracing the use of drivers to assign costs to cost objects.

drivers factors that cause changes in resource usage, activity usage, costs, and revenues.

drum-buffer-rope (DBR) system the TOC inventory management system that relies on the drum beat of the major constrained resource, time buffers, and ropes to determine inventory levels.

drummer the major binding constraint.

dumping predatory pricing on the international market.

durability the length of time a product functions in its intended manner.

duration drivers measure the demands in terms of the time it takes to perform an activity, such as hours of hygienic care and monitoring hours.

dysfunctional behavior individual behavior that conflicts with the goals of the organization.

E

ecoefficiency a view of environmental management maintaining that organizations can produce more useful goods and services while *simultaneously* reducing negative environmental impacts, resource consumption, and costs.

economic order quantity (EOQ) the amount that should be ordered (or produced) to minimize the total ordering (or setup) and carrying costs.

economic risk the possibility that a firm's present value of future cash flows can be affected by exchange fluctuations.

economic value added (EVA) the after-tax operating profit minus the total annual cost of capital.

effectiveness the manager's performance of the right activities. Measures might focus on value-added versus non-value-added activities.

efficiency the performance of activities. May be measured by the number of units produced per hour or by the cost of those units.

efficiency variance *see* usage variance.

elastic demand when a price increase (decrease) of a certain percent lowers (raises) the quantity demanded by more than that percentage.

electronic commerce (e-commerce) any form of business that is executed using information and communications technology.

electronic data interchange (EDI) an inventory management method that allows suppliers access to a buyer's on-line data base.

ending finished goods inventory budget a budget that describes planned ending inventory of finished goods in units and dollars.

enterprise resource planning (ERP) software software that has the objective of providing an integrated system capability—a system that can run all the operations of a company and provide access to real-time data from the various functional areas of a company.

entities objects about which data are produced and gathered.

environmental costs costs that are incurred because poor environmental quality exists or may exist.

environmental detection costs costs incurred to detect poor environmental performance.

environmental external failure costs costs incurred after contaminants are introduced into the environment.

environmental internal failure costs costs incurred after contaminants are produced but before they are introduced into the environment.

environmental prevention costs costs incurred to prevent damage to the environment.

equivalent units of output the whole units that could have been produced in a period given the amount of manufacturing inputs used.

error cause identification a program in which employees describe problems that prevent them from doing their jobs right the first time.

error costs the costs associated with making poor decisions based on inaccurate product costs (or bad cost information).

ethical behavior behavior that results in choices/actions that are right, proper, and just.

exchange gain a gain on the exchange of one currency for another due to appreciation in the home currency.

exchange loss a loss on the exchange of one currency for another due to depreciation in the home currency.

exchange rates the rate at which a foreign currency can be exchanged for the domestic currency.

executional activities activities that define the processes of an organization.

expected activity level the level of production activity expected for the coming period.

expected global consumption ratio the proportion of the total activity costs consumed by a given product or cost object.

expenses expired costs.

external constraints limiting factors imposed on the firm from external sources.

external failure costs costs incurred because products fail to conform to requirements after being sold to outside parties.

external linkages the relationship of a firm's activities within its segment of the value chain with those activities of its suppliers and customers.

external measures measures that relate to customer and shareholder objectives.

F

facility-level activities activities that sustain a factory's general manufacturing processes.

failure activities activities performed by an organization or its customers in response to poor quality.

failure costs the costs incurred by an organization because failure activities are performed.

favorable (F) variance a variance produced whenever the actual amounts are less than the budgeted or standard allowances.

feasible set of solutions the collection of all feasible solutions.

feasible solution a product mix that satisfies all constraints.

feature costing assigns costs to activities and products or services based on the product's or service's features.

features (quality of design) characteristics of a product that differentiate functionally similar products.

feedback information that can be used to evaluate or correct steps being taken to implement a plan.

FIFO costing method a unit-costing method that excludes prior-period work and costs in computing current-period unit work and costs.

financial accounting the branch of the accounting system that is concerned with the preparation of financial reports for users external to the organization.

financial accounting information system an accounting information subsystem that is primarily concerned with producing outputs for external users and uses well-specified economic events as inputs and processes that meet certain rules and conventions.

financial budgets that portion of the master budget that includes the cash budget, the budgeted balance sheet, the budgeted statement of cash flows, and the capital budget.

financial measures measures expressed in dollar terms.

financial perspective a Balanced Scorecard viewpoint that describes the financial consequences of actions taken in the other three perspectives.

financial productivity measure a productivity measure in which in-

puts and outputs are expressed in dollars.

fitness for use the suitability of the product for carrying out its advertised functions.

five-year assets assets with an expected life for depreciation purposes of five years; light trucks, automobiles, and computer equipment fall into this category.

fixed costs costs that in total are constant within the relevant range as the level of the cost driver varies.

fixed overhead spending variance the difference between actual fixed overhead and applied fixed overhead.

fixed overhead volume variance the difference between budgeted fixed overhead and applied fixed overhead; it is a measure of capacity utilization.

flexible budget a budget that can specify costs for a range of activity.

flexible budget variances the difference between actual costs and expected costs given by a flexible budget.

flexible resources acquired as used and needed, these are a strictly variable cost. The quantity supplied equals quantity demanded, so there is no excess capacity.

focusing strategy selecting or emphasizing a market or customer segment in which to compete.

foreign trade zones (FTZs) areas physically on U.S. soil but considered to be outside U.S. commerce. Goods imported into a foreign trade zone are duty-free until they leave the zone.

forward contract an agreement that requires the buyer to exchange a specified amount of a currency at a specified rate (the forward rate) on a specified future date.

full environmental costing the assignment of all environmental costs, both private and societal, to products.

full private costing the assignment of only private costs to individual products.

full-costing income *see* absorption-costing income.

functional-based cost system a cost accounting system that uses only unit-based activity drivers to assign costs to cost objects.

functional-based operation control system a system that assigns costs to organizational units and then holds the organizational unit manager responsible for controlling the assigned costs.

functional-based responsibility accounting system assigns responsibility to organizational units and expresses performance measures in financial terms.

future value the value that will accumulate by the end of an investment's life if the investment earns a specified compounded return.

G

gainsharing providing cash incentives for a company's entire workforce that are keyed to quality or productivity gains.

goal congruence the alignment of a manager's personal goals with those of the organization.

goodness of fit the degree of association between Y and X (cost and activity). It is measured by how much of the total variability in Y is explained by X.

growth stage the stage in a product's life cycle when sales increase at an increasing rate.

guided ecoefficiency a competing environmental cost paradigm to ecoefficiency that sees pollution as a form of economic inefficiency and views properly designed environmental regulations as a way to stimulate innovation such that environmental performance and economic efficiency will simultaneously improve.

H

half-year convention a convention that assumes a newly acquired asset is in service for one-half of its first taxable year of service, regardless of the date that use of it actually began.

hedging one way of ensuring against gains and losses on foreign currency exchange.

heterogeneity refers to the greater chances for variation in the performance of services than in the production of products.

hidden quality costs opportunity costs resulting from poor quality.

high-low method a method for fitting a line to a set of data points using the high and low points in the data set. For a cost formula, the high and low points represent the high and low activity levels. It is used to break out the fixed and variable components of a mixed cost.

homogeneous cost pool a collection of overhead costs associated with activities that have the same process, have the same level, and can use the same activity driver to assign costs to products.

Hoshin Kanri a competing strategic-based performance management system that is widely used in Japan; known as *directed* planning.

hypothesis test of cost parameters a statistical assessment of a cost formula's reliability that indicates whether the parameters are different from zero.

hypothetical sales value an approximation of the sales value of a joint product at split-off. It is found by subtracting all separable (or further) processing costs from the eventual market value.

I

ideal standards standards that reflect perfect operating conditions.

impact analysis a life cycle assessment step where the environmental impacts of different product (or process) designs are compared and evaluated.

improvement analysis a life cycle assessment step where efforts are made to reduce the environmental impacts revealed by the inventory and impact steps.

incentives the positive or negative measures taken by an organization to induce a manager to exert effort toward achieving the organization's goals.

incremental (or baseline) budgeting the practice of taking the prior year's budget and adjusting it upward or downward to determine next year's budget.

incremental unit-time learning curve model decreases by a constant percentage each time the cumulative quantity of units produced doubles.

independent projects projects that, if accepted or rejected, will not affect the cash flows of another project.

independent variable a variable whose value does not depend on the value of another variable. For example, in the cost formula $Y = F + VX$, the variable X is an independent variable.

indirect costs costs that cannot be traced to a cost object.

industrial value chain the linked set of value-creating activities from basic raw materials to end-use customers.

inelastic demand when a price increase (decrease) of a certain percent is associated with a quantity decrease (increase) of less than that percent.

innovation process a process that anticipates the emerging and potential needs of customers and creates new products and services to satisfy those needs.

input tradeoff efficiency the least-cost, technically efficient mix of inputs.

inseparability an attribute of services that means that production and consumption are inseparable.

intangibility refers to the nonphysical nature of services as opposed to products.

intercept parameter the fixed cost, representing the point where the cost formula intercepts the vertical axis. In the cost formula $Y = F + VX$, F is the intercept parameter.

interim quality performance report a comparison of current actual quality costs with short-term budgeted quality targets.

interim quality standards a standard based on short-run quality goals.

internal business process perspective a Balanced Scorecard viewpoint that describes the internal processes needed to provide value for customers and owners.

internal constraints limiting factors found within the firm.

internal failure costs costs incurred because products and services fail to conform to requirements where lack of conformity is discovered prior to external sale.

internal linkages relationships among activities within a firm's value chain.

internal measures measures that relate to the processes and capabilities that create value for customers and shareholders.

internal rate of return the rate of return that equates the present value of a project's cash inflows with the present value of its cash outflows (i.e., it sets the NPV equal to zero). Also, the rate of return being earned on funds that remain internally invested in a project.

introduction stage a product life cycle stage characterized by preproduction and startup activities, where the focus is on obtaining a foothold in the market.

inventory the money an organization spends in turning raw materials into throughput.

inventory analysis a life cycle assessment step where the quantities and types of materials, energy, and environmental releases are described.

investment center a responsibility center in which a manager is responsible for revenues, costs, and investments.

J

job-order cost sheet a document or record used to accumulate manufacturing costs for a job.

job-order costing system a cost accumulation method that accumulates manufacturing costs by job.

joint products two or more products, each having relatively substantial value, that are produced simultaneously by the same process up to a "split-off" point.

joint venture a type of partnership in which investors co-own the enterprise.

just-in-case inventory management a traditional inventory model based on anticipated demand.

just-in-time inventory management the continual pursuit of productivity through the elimination of waste.

just-in-time (JIT) manufacturing a demand-pull system that strives to produce a product only when it is needed and only in the quantities demanded by customers.

just-in-time (JIT) purchasing a system that requires suppliers to deliver parts and materials just in time to be used in production.

K

kaizen costing efforts to reduce the costs of existing products and processes.

kaizen standard an interim standard that reflects the planned improvement for a coming period.

Kanban system an information system that controls production on a demand-pull basis through the use of cards or markers.

keep-or-drop decision a relevant costing analysis that focuses on keeping or dropping a segment of a business.

L

lag measures outcome measures or measures of results from past efforts.

lead measures (performance drivers) factors that drive future performance.

lead time for purchasing, the time to receive an order after it is placed. For manufacturing, the time to produce a product from start to finish.

learning and growth (infrastructure) perspective a Balanced Scorecard viewpoint that defines the capabilities that an organization needs to create long-term growth and improvement.

learning curve an important type of nonlinear cost curve that shows how the labor hours worked per unit decrease as the volume produced increases.

learning rate expressed as a percent, it gives the percentage of time needed to make the next unit, based on the time it took to make the previous unit.

life-cycle assessment identifying the environmental consequences of a product through its entire life cycle and then searching for opportunities to obtain environmental improvements.

life-cycle cost assessment assigning costs and benefits to environmental consequences and improvements.

life-cycle cost management actions taken that cause a product to be designed, developed, produced, marketed, distributed, operated, maintained, serviced, and disposed of so that life cycle profits are maximized.

life-cycle costs all costs associated with the product for its entire life cycle.

line position a position in an organization filled by an individual who is directly responsible for carrying out the organization's basic objectives.

linear programming a method that searches among possible solutions until it finds the optimal solution.

long run period of time for which all costs are variable, i.e., there are no fixed costs.

long-range quality performance report a performance report that compares current actual quality costs with long-range targeted quality costs (usually in the 2%–3% range).

loose constraints constraints whose limited resources are not fully used by a product mix.

loss a cost that expires without producing any revenue benefit; a negative profit.

M

make-or-buy decision a decision that focuses on whether a component (service) should be made (provided) internally or purchased externally.

management accounting a cost management subsystem that is concerned with how cost information and other financial and nonfinancial information should be used for planning, controlling, and decision making.

manufacturing cells a plant layout containing machines grouped in families, usually in a semicircle.

maquiladoras manufacturing plants located in Mexico that process imported materials and reexport them to the United States.

margin the ratio of net operating income to sales.

margin of safety the units sold or expected to be sold or sales revenue earned or expected to be earned above the break-even volume.

market share the proportion of industry sales accounted for by a company.

market share variance the difference between the actual market share percentage and the budgeted market share percentage multiplied by actual industry sales in units times budgeted average unit contribution margin.

market size the total revenue for the industry.

market size variance the difference between actual and budgeted industry sales in units multiplied by the budgeted market share percentage times the budgeted average unit contribution margin.

marketing expense budget a budget that outlines planned expenditures for selling and distribution activities.

marketing (selling) costs those costs necessary to market and distribute a product or service.

markup a percentage applied to base cost for the purpose of calculating price; the markup includes desired profit and any costs not included in the base.

master budget the collection of all area and activity budgets representing a firm's comprehensive plan of action.

materials requisition form a document used to identify the cost of raw materials assigned to each job.

maturity stage the stage in a product's life cycle when sales increase at a decreasing rate.

maximum transfer price the transfer price that will make the buying division no worse off if an input is acquired internally.

measurement costs the costs associated with the measurements required by a cost management system.

method of least squares a statistical method to find a line that best fits a set of data. It is used to break out the fixed and variable components of a mixed cost.

minimum transfer price the transfer price that will make the selling division no worse off if the intermediate product is sold internally.

mix variance the difference in the standard cost of the mix of actual material inputs and the standard cost of the material input mix that should have been used.

mixed costs costs that have both a fixed and a variable component.

modified accelerated cost recovery system (MACRS) a method of computing annual depreciation; defined as double-declining-balance method.

monopolistic competition a market that is close to the competitive market. There are many sellers and buyers, low barriers to entry, but the products are differentiated on some basis.

monopoly a market in which barriers to entry are so high that there is only one firm selling a unique product.

multinational corporation (MNC) a corporation for which a significant amount of business is done in more than one country.

multiple regression the use of least-squares analysis to determine the parameters in a linear equation involving two or more explanatory variables.

multiple-period quality trend report a graph that plots quality costs (as a percentage of sales) against time.

mutually exclusive projects projects that, if accepted, preclude the acceptance of competing projects.

myopic behavior managerial actions that improve budgetary performance in the short run at the expense of the long-run welfare of the organization.

N

net income operating income less taxes, interest expense, and research and development expense.

net present value the difference between the present value of a project's cash inflows and the present value of its cash outflows.

net realizable value method a method of allocating joint production costs to the joint products based on their proportionate share of eventual revenue less further processing costs.

noncost methods methods that make no attempt to cost the by-product or its inventory, but instead make some credit either to income or to main product.

nondiscounting models capital investment models that identify criteria for accepting or rejecting projects without considering the time value of money.

nonfinancial measures measures expressed in nonmonetary units.

noninventoriable (period) costs costs expensed in the period in which they are incurred.

nonproduction costs those costs associated with the functions of selling and administration.

non-unit-based drivers factors, other than the number of units produced, that measure the demands that cost objects place on activities.

non-unit-level drivers explain the changes in cost as factors other than units change.

non-value-added activities activities either unnecessary or necessary but inefficient and improvable.

non-value-added costs costs that are caused either by non-value-added activities or the inefficient performance of value-added activities.

normal activity level the average activity level that a firm experiences over more than one fiscal period.

normal cost of goods sold the cost of goods sold figure obtained when the per-unit normal cost is used.

normal costing system a cost measurement system in which the actual costs of direct materials and direct labor are assigned to production and a predetermined rate is used to assign overhead costs to production.

O

objective function the function to be optimized, usually a profit function; thus, optimization usually means maximizing profits.

objective measures measures that can be readily quantified and verified.

observable quality costs those quality costs that are available from an organization's accounting records.

oligopoly a market structure characterized by a few sellers and high barriers to entry.

operating assets those assets used to generate operating income, consisting usually of cash, inventories, receivables, property, plant, and equipment.

operating budgets budgets associated with the income-producing activities of an organization.

operating expenses the money an organization spends in turning inventories into throughput.

operating income revenues minus expenses from the firm's normal operations. Income taxes are excluded.

operating leverage the use of fixed costs to extract higher percentage changes in profits as sales activity changes. Leverage is achieved by increasing fixed costs while lowering variable costs.

operation costing a costing system that uses job-order costing to assign materials costs and process costing to assign conversion costs.

operational activities day-to-day activities performed as a result of the structure and processes selected by an organization.

operational control information system a cost management subsystem designed to provide accurate and timely feedback concerning the performance of managers and others relative to their planning and control of activities.

operational cost drivers those factors that drive the cost of operational activities.

operational productivity measure measures that are expressed in physical terms.

operations process a process that produces and delivers existing products and services to customers.

opportunity cost approach a transfer pricing system that identifies the minimum price that a selling division would be willing to accept and the maximum price that a buying division would be willing to pay.

optimal solution the feasible solution that produces the best value for the objective function (the largest value if seeking to maximize the objective function; the minimum otherwise).

ordering costs the costs of placing and receiving an order.

organizational cost drivers structural and procedural factors that determine the long-term cost structure of an organization.

outsourcing the payment by a company for a business function that was formerly done in-house.

overapplied overhead the overhead variance resulting when applied overhead is greater than the actual overhead cost incurred.

overhead all production costs other than direct materials and direct labor.

overhead budget a budget that reveals the planned expenditures for all indirect manufacturing items.

overhead variance the difference between the actual overhead and the applied overhead.

P

partial productivity measurement a ratio that measures productive efficiency for one input.

participative budgeting an approach to budgeting that allows managers who will be held accountable for budgetary performance to participate in the budget's development.

payback period the time required for a project to return its investment.

penetration pricing the pricing of a new product at a low initial price, perhaps even lower than cost, to build market share quickly.

perfectly competitive market a market (or industry) characterized by many buyers and sellers—no one of which is large enough to influence the market—a homogeneous product, and easy entry into and exit from the industry.

performance refers to how consistently and well a product functions.

performance reports accounting reports that provide feedback to managers by comparing planned outcomes with actual outcomes.

period costs costs such as marketing and administrative costs that are expensed in the period in which they are incurred.

perishability an attribute of services that means that they cannot be inventoried but must be consumed when performed.

perquisites a type of fringe benefit over and above salary which is received by managers.

physical flow schedule a schedule that accounts for all units flowing through a department during a period.

physical units method a method of allocating joint production costs based on each product's share of total units.

planning setting objectives and identifying methods to achieve those objectives.

pool rate the overhead costs for a homogeneous cost pool divided by the practical capacity of the activity driver associated with the pool.

postaudit a follow-up analysis of an investment decision.

post-purchase costs the costs of using, maintaining, and disposing of a product incurred by the customer after purchasing a product.

postsales service process a process that provides critical and responsive service to customers after the product or service has been delivered.

practical activity level the output a firm can achieve if it is operating efficiently.

practical capacity the efficient level of activity performance.

predatory pricing the practice of setting prices below cost for the purpose of injuring competitors and eliminating competition.

predetermined overhead rate estimated overhead divided by the estimated level of production activity. It is used to assign overhead to production.

present value the current value of a future cash flow. It represents the amount that must be invested now if the future cash flow is to be received assuming compounding at a given rate of interest.

prevention costs costs incurred to prevent defects in products or services being produced.

price discrimination charging different prices to different customers for essentially the same commodity.

price gouging when firms with market power (i.e., little or no competition) price products "too high."

price skimming a pricing strategy in which a higher price is charged at the beginning of a product's life cycle, then lowered at later phases of the life cycle.

price standards the price that should be paid per unit of input.

price (rate) variance the difference between standard price and actual price multiplied by the actual quantity of inputs used.

price volume variance the difference between actual volume sold and expected volume sold multiplied by the expected price.

price-recovery component the difference between the total profit change and the profit-linked productivity change.

primary activity an activity that is consumed by a product or customer (i.e., a final cost object).

primary key the attribute that uniquely identifies each row of data in a table.

prime cost the sum of direct materials cost and direct labor cost.

private costs environmental costs that an organization has to pay.

process a series of activities (operations) that are linked to perform a specific objective.

process-costing principle the period's unit cost is computed by dividing the costs of the period by the output of the period.

process creation installing an entirely new process to meet customer and financial objectives.

process improvement incremental and constant increases in the efficiency of an existing process.

process innovation (business reengineering) the performance of a process in a radically new way with the objective of achieving dramatic improvements in response time, cost, quality, and other important competitive factors.

process productivity analysis an approach that measures activity productivity by treating activities as inputs to a process and relating the input to the process's output.

process value analysis an analysis that defines activity-based responsibility accounting, focuses on accountability for activities rather than costs, and emphasizes the maximization of systemwide performance instead of individual performance.

process value chain the innovation, operations, and postsales service processes.

producing departments a unit within an organization responsible for producing the products or services that are sold to customers.

product cost a cost assignment method that satisfies a well-specified managerial objective.

product diversity the situation present when products consume overhead in different proportions.

product life cycle the time a product exists—from conception to abandonment; the profit history of the product according to four stages: introduction, growth, maturity, and decline.

product stewardship the practice of designing, manufacturing, maintaining, and recycling products to minimize adverse environmental impacts.

product-level activities activities performed that enable the various products of a company to be produced.

production budget a budget that shows how many units must be produced to meet sales needs and satisfy ending inventory requirements.

production (or product) costs those costs associated with the manufacture of goods or the provision of services.

production Kanban a card or marker that specifies the quantity the preceding process should produce.

production report a report that summarizes the manufacturing activity for a department during a period and discloses physical flow, equivalent units, total costs to account for, unit cost computation, and costs assigned to goods transferred out and to units in ending work in process.

productivity producing output efficiently, using the least quantity of inputs possible.

productivity measurement assessment of productivity changes.

profile measurement a series or vector of separate and distinct partial operational measures.

profit center a responsibility center in which a manager is responsible for both revenues and costs.

profit-linkage rule for the current period, calculate the cost of the inputs that would have been used in the absence of any productivity change and compare this cost with the cost of the inputs actually used. The difference in costs is the amount by which profits changed because of productivity changes.

profit-linked productivity measurement an assessment of the amount of profit change—from the base period to the current period—attributable to productivity changes.

profit-volume graph a graphical portrayal of the relationship between profits and sales activity.

pseudoparticipation a budgetary system in which top management solicits inputs from lower-level managers and then ignores those inputs. Thus, in reality, budgets are dictated from above.

Q

quality of conformance conforming to the design requirements of the product.

quality product or service a product which meets or exceeds customer expectations.

quantity standards the quantity of input allowed per unit of output.

R

rate variance *see* price variance.

realized external failure costs the environmental costs caused by environmental degradation and paid for by the responsible organization.

reciprocal method a method that simultaneously allocates service costs to all user departments. It gives full consideration to interactions among service departments.

relational structure a data structure that uses a table to represent the overall logical view within a data base.

relative value unit (RVU) a homogeneous work unit that measures the relative amount of time required to perform a procedure.

relevant costs (revenues) future costs (revenues) that differ across alternatives.

relevant range the range over which an assumed cost relationship is valid for the normal operations of a firm.

reliability the probability that the product or service will perform its intended function for a specified length of time.

reorder point the point in time at which a new order (or setup) should be initiated.

replacement cost method the cost of by-products utilized within the plant are valued at the opportunity cost of purchasing or replacing the products in question.

required rate of return the minimum rate of return that a project must earn in order to be acceptable. Usually corresponds to the cost of capital.

resale price method a transfer price acceptable to the Internal Revenue Service under Section 482. The resale price method computes a transfer price equal to the sales price received by the reseller less an appropriate markup.

research and development expense budget a budget that outlines planned expenditures for research and development.

residual income the difference between operating income and the minimum required dollar return on a company's operating assets.

resource drivers factors that measure the demands placed on resources by activities and are used to assign the cost of resources to activities.

responsibility accounting a system that measures the results of each responsibility center and compares those results with some measure of expected or budgeted outcome.

responsibility center a segment of the business whose manager is accountable for specified sets of activities.

return on investment (ROI) the ratio of operating income to average operating assets.

revenue center a responsibility center in which a manager is responsible only for sales.

revenue-producing life the time a product generates revenue for a company.

robustness exact conformance to the target value (no tolerance allowed).

ropes actions taken to tie the rate at which raw material is released into the plant (at the first operation) to the production rate of the constrained resource.

S

safety stock extra inventory carried to serve as insurance against fluctuations in demand.

sales budget a budget that describes expected sales in units and dollars for the coming period.

sales mix the relative combination of products (or services) being sold by an organization.

sales mix variance the sum of the change in units for each product multiplied by the difference between the budgeted contribution margin and the budgeted average unit contribution margin.

sales price variance the difference between actual price and expected price multiplied by the actual quantity or volume sold.

sales-revenue approach an approach to CVP analysis that uses sales revenue to measure sales activity. Variable costs and contribution margin are expressed as percentages of sales revenue.

sales-to-production-ratio method allocates joint costs in accordance with a weighting factor that compares percentage of sales with percentage of production.

sales-value-at-split-off method a method of allocating joint production costs based on each product's share of revenue realized at the split-off point.

scattergraph a plot of (X, Y) data points. For cost analysis, X is activity usage and Y is the associated cost at that activity level.

scatterplot method a method to fit a line to a set of data using two points that are selected by judgment. It is used to break out the fixed and variable components of a mixed cost.

secondary activity an activity that is consumed by intermediate cost objects such as materials and primary activities.

sell or process further relevant costing analysis that focuses on whether or not a product should be processed beyond the split-off point.

sensitivity analysis a "what if" technique that examines altering certain key variables to assess the effect on the original outcome.

separable costs costs that are easily traced to individual products.

sequential (or step) method a method that allocates service costs to user departments in a sequential manner. It gives partial consideration to interactions among service departments.

serviceability the ease of maintaining and/or repairing a product.

services a task or activity performed for a customer or an activity performed by a customer using an organization's products or facilities.

setup costs the costs of preparing equipment and facilities so that they can be used for production.

seven-year assets assets with an expected life for depreciation purposes of seven years; equipment, machinery, and office furniture fall into this category.

shadow price the amount by which throughput will increase for one additional unit of scarce resource.

short run period of time in which at least one cost is fixed.

simplex method an algorithm that identifies the optimal solution for a linear programming problem.

single-loop feedback information about the effectiveness of strategy implementation.

slope parameter the variable cost per unit of activity usage, represented by V in the cost formula $Y = F + VX$.

source document a document that describes a transaction and is used to keep track of costs as they occur.

special-order decisions decisions that focus on whether a specially priced order should be accepted or rejected.

split-off point the point at which the joint products become separate and identifiable.

spot rate the exchange rate of one currency for another for immediate delivery.

staff position a position in an organization filled by an individual who provides support for the line function; thus, a staff person is only indirectly involved with the basic objectives of an organization.

standard bill of materials a listing of the type and quantity of materials allowed for a given level of output.

standard cost per unit the per-unit cost that should be achieved given materials, labor, and overhead standards.

standard cost sheet a listing of the standard costs and standard quantities of direct materials, direct labor, and overhead that should apply to a single product.

standard hours allowed the direct labor hours that should have been used to produce the actual output (Unit labor standard × Actual output).

standard quantity of materials allowed the quantity of materials that should have been used to produce the actual output (Unit materials standard × Actual output).

static budget a budget for a particular level of activity.

step-cost function a cost function in which cost is defined for ranges of activity usage rather than point values. The function has the property of displaying constant cost over a range of activity usage and then changing to a different cost level as a new range of activity usage is encountered.

step-fixed costs a step-cost function in which cost remains constant over wide ranges of activity usage.

step-variable costs a step-cost function in which cost remains constant over relatively narrow ranges of activity.

stock option the right to purchase a certain amount of stock at a fixed price.

stock-out costs the costs of insufficient inventory.

strategic cost management the use of cost data to develop and identify superior strategies that will produce a sustainable competitive advantage.

strategic decision making choosing among alternative strategies with the goal of selecting a strategy or strategies that provide a company with reasonable assurance of long-term growth and survival.

strategic positioning the process of selecting the optimal mix of cost leadership, differentiation, and focusing strategies.

strategic-based responsibility accounting system (strategic-based performance management system) a responsibility accounting system that translates an orga-

nization's mission and strategy into operational objectives and measures for four different perspectives: the financial perspective, the customer perspective, the process perspective, and the learning and growth (infrastructure) perspective.

strategy choosing the market and customer segments, identifying critical internal business processes at which the firm must excel to increase customer value, and selecting the individual and organizational capabilities required to achieve the firm's internal, customer, and financial objectives.

stretch targets targets that are set at levels that, if achieved, will transform the organization within a period of three to five years.

structural activities activities that determine the underlying economic structure of the organization.

subjective measures measures that are nonquantifiable whose values are judgmental in nature.

sunk cost a past cost—a cost already incurred.

supplies materials necessary for production but that do not become part of the finished product or are not used in providing a service.

supply chain management the management of products and services from the acquisition of raw materials through manufacturing, warehousing, distribution, wholesaling, and retailing.

support departments a unit within an organization that provides essential support services for producing departments.

sustainable development development that meets the needs of the present without compromising the ability of future generations to meet their own needs.

system a set of interrelated parts that performs one or more processes to accomplish specific objectives.

T

tactical cost analysis the use of relevant cost data to identify the alternative that provides the greatest benefit to the organization.

tactical decision making choosing among alternatives with only an immediate or limited end in view.

Taguchi loss function a function that assumes any variation from the target value of a quality characteristic causes hidden quality costs.

tangible products goods produced by converting raw materials through the use of labor and capital inputs such as plant, land, and machinery.

target cost the difference between the sales price needed to achieve a projected market share and the desired per-unit profit.

target costing a method of determining the cost of a product or service based on the price that customers are willing to pay. Also referred to as price-driven costing.

tariff the tax on imports levied by the federal government.

technical efficiency point at which for any mix of inputs that will produce a given output, no more of any one input is used than is absolutely necessary.

testable strategy set of linked objectives aimed at an overall goal that can be restated into a sequence of cause-and-effect hypotheses.

theoretical activity level the maximum output possible for a firm under perfect operating conditions.

theory of constraints method used to continuously improve manufacturing activities and nonmanufacturing activities.

three-year assets assets with an expected life for depreciation purposes of three years; most small tools fall into this category.

throughput the rate at which an organization generates money through sales.

time buffer the inventory needed to keep the constrained resource busy for a specified time interval.

time ticket a document used to identify the cost of direct labor for a job.

total budget variance the difference between the actual cost of an input and its planned cost.

total (overall) sales variance the sum of the sales price and sales volume variances.

total preventive maintenance a program of preventive maintenance that has zero machine failures as its standard.

total product the complete range of tangible and intangible benefits a customer receives from a product.

total productive efficiency the point at which technical and price efficiency are achieved.

total productivity measurement an assessment of productive efficiency for all inputs combined.

total quality control an approach to managing quality that demands the production of defect-free products.

total quality management a philosophy that requires managers to strive to create an environment that will enable workers to manufacture perfect (zero-defects) products.

traceability the ability to assign a cost directly to a cost object in an economically feasible way using a causal relationship.

transaction drivers measure the number of times an activity is performed, such as the number of treatments and the number of requests.

transaction risk the possibility that future cash transactions will be affected by changing exchange rates.

transfer prices the price charged for goods transferred from one division to another.

transfer pricing problem the problem of finding a transfer pricing system that simultaneously satisfies the three objectives of accurate performance evaluation, goal congruence, and autonomy.

transferred-in cost the cost of goods transferred in from a prior process.

translation (or accounting) risk the degree to which a firm's financial statements are exposed to exchange rate fluctuation.

treasurer the financial officer responsible for the management of cash and investment capital.

turnover the ratio of sales to average operating assets.

U

underapplied overhead the overhead variance resulting when the actual overhead cost incurred is greater than the applied overhead.

unfavorable (U) variance a variance produced whenever the actual input amounts are greater than the budgeted or standard allowances.

unit standard cost the product of these two standards: Standard price × Standard quantity (SP × SQ).

unit-based drivers factors that measure the demands placed on unit-level activities by products.

unit-level activities activities that are performed each time a unit is produced.

unit-level drivers explain changes in cost as units produced change.

unrealized external failure (societal) costs environmental costs caused by an organization but paid for by society.

unused capacity the difference between the acquired activity capacity and the actual activity usage.

unused capacity variance the difference between acquired capacity (practical capacity) and actual capacity.

usage (efficiency) variance the difference between standard quantities and actual quantities multiplied by standard price.

V

value chain the set of activities required to design, develop, produce, market, distribute, and service a product (the product can be a service).

value-added activities activities that are necessary to achieve corporate objectives and remain in business.

value-added costs costs caused by value-added activities.

value-added standard the optimal output level for an activity.

value-chain analysis identifying and exploiting internal and external linkages with the objective of strengthening a firm's strategic position.

variable budget *see* flexible budget.

variable cost ratio variable costs divided by sales revenue. It is the proportion of each sales dollar needed to cover variable costs.

variable costing a costing method that assigns only variable manufacturing costs to the product; these costs include direct materials, direct labor, and variable overhead. Fixed overhead is treated as a period cost and is expensed in the period incurred.

variable costs costs that in total vary in direct proportion to changes in a cost driver.

variable overhead efficiency variance the difference between the actual direct labor hours used and the standard hours allowed multiplied by the standard variable overhead rate.

variable overhead spending variance the difference between the actual variable overhead and the budgeted variable overhead based on actual hours used to produce the actual output.

velocity the number of units that can be produced in a given period of time (e.g., output per hour).

vendor Kanban a card or marker that signals to a supplier the quantity of materials that need to be delivered and the time of delivery.

W

weight factor a value used to assign weights to various joint products in accordance with their relative size, difficulty to produce, etc.

weighted average cost of capital the proportionate share of each method of financing is multiplied by its percentage cost and summed.

weighted average costing method a unit-costing method that merges prior-period work and costs with current-period work and costs.

what-if analysis *see* sensitivity analysis.

withdrawal Kanban a marker or card that specifies the quantity that a subsequent process should withdraw from a preceding process.

work in process consists of all partially completed units found in production at a given point in time.

work orders used to collect production costs for product batches and to initiate production.

work-in-process inventory file the collection of all job cost sheets.

Y

yield variance the difference in the standard material cost of the standard yield and the standard material cost of the actual yield.

Z

zero defects a quality performance standard that requires all products and services to be produced and delivered according to specifications.

zero-base budgeting a method of budgeting in which the prior year's budgeted level is not taken for granted. Existing operations are analyzed, and continuance of the activity or operation must be justified on the basis of its need or usefulness to the organization.

Glossary

A

3M, 99, 733

A

ABC Technologies, 177
ABT, 357
Aetna Life Insurance, Inc., 568, 843
Allen-Bradley, 636
Amazon.com, 44, 758
American Express, 367
American Honda Motor Co., 622
American Productivity & Quality Center (APQC), 589
Andersen Corporation, 701
Anderson Group, 853
Apple Computer, 461, 833
Arm & Hammer, 505
Armstrong World Industries, Inc., 434
Armstrong-Laing, 177
AT&T, 510, 559
Avnet, Inc., 501

B

Baan, 66
Bal Seal Engineering, 929
BankBoston, 845
Baptist Hospital, Inc., 622
Barclays Bank, 501, 844
Bassett Furniture Industries, Inc., 186
Bausch & Lomb, 449
Baxter, 733
BellSouth, 501
Black & Decker, 510
Boeing, 120, 758
Boeing Aerospace Support (AS), 9, 622
Boeing Aircraft and Tanker Programs, 622
Borg-Warner, 510
bpi.industrial, 698
Briggs and Stratton, 443
Brigham and Women's Hospital, 880
British Telecom, 637
Burger King, 936
BZW Securities, 844, 845

C

C&C Group, 436
CAI, 66
Canadian Imperial Bank of Commerce, 845
Caterpillar Financial Services Corporation, 622
CDNow, 44

Chandler Engineering, 329
Chemical Bank, 568
Chevron, 559
Chrysler Corporation, 40, 510, 711
Cigna Property and Casualty, 608
Cisco, 458
Citicorp, 449
Coca-Cola Company, 5, 330, 441
Colorado Rockies, 338
Commonwealth Edison, 701
Conoco, 327
ConocoPhillips, 489
Continental Airlines, 832
CSX Corporation, 447

D

DaimlerChrysler, 4
Dana Corporation's Spicer Driveshaft Division, 622
Deloitte & Touche LLP, 16
Delta Air Lines, 40
Dow Chemical, 285
DuPont, 637, 833

E

Eastman Kodak, 358, 447, 637, 713
Elgin Sweeper Company, 99
Environmental Protection Agency, 928
Ernst & Young, 589
Exxon-Mobil, 489

F

Federal Express, 8, 356, 878
Federal-Mogul, 568
Fiat Auto Argentina, 230
First Union Corporation, 501
Fleet Financial Group, 845
Ford Motor Company, 296, 501, 510, 644, 758, 781
Frito-Lay, Inc., 434

G

General Accounting Office, 700
General Electric, 356, 434, 441, 449, 510, 568, 636, 637
General Mills, 434, 825
General Motors (GM), 40, 183, 510, 622, 665, 701, 736, 843, 942
Georgia, state of, 345
Gerber Products, 447
Gillette, 449
Girl Scouts of America, 834

Goldratt, 966
Grede Foundries, Inc., 632

H

Harley-Davidson, 510, 758, 937
Haworth Furniture, 636
Hershey Foods, 447
Hewlett-Packard, 9, 285, 447, 510, 829
Home Depot, 444
Honeywell, 497

I

IBM Corporation, 285, 327, 678
IBM Credit, 568, 678, 679
Indigo, Ltd., 185
Intel, 356, 441, 510
International Paper, 669
International Standards Organization, 662–663
Ipiranga Group, 701
Irving Pulp and Paper, 900

J

Jacksonville Naval Supply Center, 737
JD Edwards, 11, 66, 151, 177, 186
John Deere, 510
Johnson & Johnson, 99, 852

K

Kaiser Permanente, 225
Karlee Company, 622
Kellogg, 825
KFC, 434
Kraft, 189

L

Land's End, 45, 801
Levi Strauss & Company, 758
Lexus, 183
Loctite Corporation, 433
Los Alamos National Bank, 622
Lura Group, 697

M

Manugistics Group, 758
Mars, Inc., 5
Martin Marietta, 568
Massachusetts General Hospital, 880
MasterCard, 367
Mattel, 851
McDonald's, 184, 449